Cases and Text on
PROPERTY

ASPEN CASEBOOK SERIES

Cases and Text on
PROPERTY

Sixth Edition

Susan Fletcher French
Professor of Law Emerita
University of California at Los Angeles

Gerald Korngold
Professor of Law
New York Law School

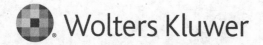 Wolters Kluwer

Published by Wolters Kluwer in New York.

Wolters Kluwer serves customers worldwide with CCH, Aspen Publishers, and Kluwer Law International products. (www.wolterskluwerlb.com)

To contact Customer Service, e-mail customer.service@wolterskluwer.com, call 1-800-234-1660, fax 1-800-901-9075, or mail correspondence to:

Wolters Kluwer
Attn: Order Department
PO Box 990
Frederick, MD 21705

Printed in the United States of America.

1 2 3 4 5 6 7 8 9 0

ISBN 978-1-4548-2500-5 (Casebound)

ISBN 978-1-4548-4820-2 (Loose Leaf)

Library of Congress Cataloging-in-Publication Data

French, Susan F., 1943- author.
   Cases and text on property / Susan Fletcher French, Professor of Law Emerita University of California at Los Angeles; Gerald Korngold, Professor of Law New York Law School.— Sixth edition.
      pages cm. — (Aspen casebook series)
   Includes bibliographical references and index.
   ISBN 978-1-4548-2500-5 (alk. paper)
   1. Property—United States. I. Korngold, Gerald, author. II. Title.
   KF560.C33 2015
   346.7304—dc23
                              2014040031

About Wolters Kluwer Law & Business

Wolters Kluwer Law & Business is a leading global provider of intelligent information and digital solutions for legal and business professionals in key specialty areas, and respected educational resources for professors and law students. Wolters Kluwer Law & Business connects legal and business professionals as well as those in the education market with timely, specialized authoritative content and information-enabled solutions to support success through productivity, accuracy and mobility.

Serving customers worldwide, Wolters Kluwer Law & Business products include those under the Aspen Publishers, CCH, Kluwer Law International, Loislaw, ftwilliam.com and MediRegs family of products.

CCH products have been a trusted resource since 1913, and are highly regarded resources for legal, securities, antitrust and trade regulation, government contracting, banking, pension, payroll, employment and labor, and healthcare reimbursement and compliance professionals.

Aspen Publishers products provide essential information to attorneys, business professionals and law students. Written by preeminent authorities, the product line offers analytical and practical information in a range of specialty practice areas from securities law and intellectual property to mergers and acquisitions and pension/benefits. Aspen's trusted legal education resources provide professors and students with high-quality, up-to-date and effective resources for successful instruction and study in all areas of the law.

Kluwer Law International products provide the global business community with reliable international legal information in English. Legal practitioners, corporate counsel and business executives around the world rely on Kluwer Law journals, looseleafs, books, and electronic products for comprehensive information in many areas of international legal practice.

Loislaw is a comprehensive online legal research product providing legal content to law firm practitioners of various specializations. Loislaw provides attorneys with the ability to quickly and efficiently find the necessary legal information they need, when and where they need it, by facilitating access to primary law as well as state-specific law, records, forms and treatises.

ftwilliam.com offers employee benefits professionals the highest quality plan documents (retirement, welfare and non-qualified) and government forms (5500/PBGC, 1099 and IRS) software at highly competitive prices.

MediRegs products provide integrated health care compliance content and software solutions for professionals in healthcare, higher education and life sciences, including professionals in accounting, law and consulting.

Wolters Kluwer Law & Business, a division of Wolters Kluwer, is headquartered in New York. Wolters Kluwer is a market-leading global information services company focused on professionals.

ABOUT THE AUTHORS

Susan F. French, Reporter for the *Restatement, Third, of Property, Servitudes,* taught Property, Wills and Trusts, Land Use, and Community Association Law at the University of California, Davis from 1975 until 1988 and at the University of California, Los Angeles School of Law, from 1989 through 2014. She served as an Adviser to Professor Casner on the *Restatement, Second, Donative Transfers,* and as an Adviser to the *Restatement, Third, of Property, Donative Transfers.* Her publications include articles on powers of appointment, class gifts, lapse and survival problems, and perpetuities, in addition to works on servitudes and common interest communities. She is co-author (with Wayne S. Hyatt) of the casebook *Community Association Law* (2d Ed. 2008). She also publishes a biennial edition of *A California Companion for the Course in Wills, Trusts & Estates.*

Gerald Korngold is Professor of Law at New York Law School. After private practice in the area of real estate law, he entered law teaching and focuses on the fields of property, real estate transactions, conservation law and policy, and international real estate transactions. Professor Korngold has published books and articles on real estate transactions, commercial lending, landlord and tenant, estates and future interests, servitudes and covenants, conservation easements, homeowner associations, and real property taxation. He is an elected member of the American Law Institute and the American College of Real Estate Lawyers. Professor Korngold served as an Adviser to the *Restatement, Third, of Property, Servitudes,* and is a Visiting Fellow at the Lincoln Institute of Land Policy in Cambridge, Massachusetts.

The original authors of this casebook were A. James Casner and W. Barton Leach, who published the first edition in 1951.

A. James Casner(1907-1990) began his teaching career at the University of Illinois, joined the Harvard Law School faculty in 1938 as a visiting lecturer, and became a regular faculty member in 1940. In 1930, Professor Casner began a long association with the American Law Institute, working with Richard Powell, the Reporter for the first Restatement of Property. Casner became associate reporter for chapter 23 of that Restatement (gifts to heirs and the like), and went on to serve as adviser and reporter for many projects. He was the Reporter for the Restatement, Second, of Property, Landlord Tenant, and Donative Transfers. Professor Casner was the general editor of the American Law of Property (1952-54).

Professor Casner pioneered the use of revocable intervivos trusts to avoid the expense, delay, and publicity of probate. It became the centerpiece of his treatise on estate planning, first published as a single volume in 1953, and expanded to six volumes by the fifth edition published in 1984. By the time of his death, the revocable intervivos trust had become a standard tool of estate planners throughout the United States.

W. Barton Leach (1900-1971) clerked for Justice Oliver Wendell Holmes and then taught at the Harvard Law School from 1929 until his retirement in 1969. He was a Special Reporter for the chapters on powers of appointment and the statute of limitations in the first Restatement of Property and contributed the chapters on powers and the common law rule against perpetuities in the American Law of Property (published 1952). Perhaps his best known pieces are the classic *Perpetuities in a Nutshell,* 51 Harv. L. Rev. 638 (1938) and *Perpetuities: The Nutshell Revisited,* 78 Harv. L. Rev. 973 (1965). Leach was a great teacher, a great wit, and a talented musician who played the accordion. He was a tireless campaigner for law reform, and almost single-handedly advanced the wait and see doctrine that ultimately prevailed, under Professor Casner's leadership, in the Restatement, Second, of Property, Donative Transfers.

Professors Leach and Casner both served in the Air Force during World War II. They returned to law teaching after the war and decided to pool their resources and develop a new basic property casebook. A temporary edition was published in 1947 and the first standard edition in 1951. *Cases and Text on Property* has been a leading casebook ever since.

For my husband, Tom Rowe,
my daughter Sarah,
and my grandchildren Ellie and Dylan
—SFF

For
My father of blessed memory,
David,
Ethan, Ellie, Gabriel and Benjamin,
Margaret and Matt,
and, especially, Alice
—G.K.

SUMMARY OF CONTENTS

PART I

INTRODUCTION TO PROPERTY: BASIC IDEAS, LEGAL PROTECTIONS, ACQUISITION BY CAPTURE, CONQUEST, ADVERSE POSSESSION, AND CREATIVE ACTIVITY   1

PART II

OWNERSHIP INTERESTS IN PROPERTY   295

PART III

VOLUNTARY TRANSFERS OF PROPERTY   503

PART IV

LAND USE PLANNING AND REGULATION   667

TABLE OF CONTENTS

CHAPTER 2

ACQUIRING PROPERTY: CAPTURE, FINDS, BAILMENT, AND SALVAGE   71

PART II
OWNERSHIP INTERESTS IN PROPERTY

CHAPTER 5

POSSESSORY ESTATES AND FUTURE INTERESTS   297

CHAPTER 6

LANDLORD-TENANT   351

CHAPTER 7

CONCURRENT ESTATES AND MARITAL PROPERTY 471

PART III
VOLUNTARY TRANSFERS OF POWER

CHAPTER 8

LIFETIME GIFTS THAT ARE NOT IN TRUST   505

CHAPTER 9

THE MODERN REAL ESTATE TRANSACTION   533

PART IV
LAND USE PLANNING AND REGULATION

CHAPTER 11

NUISANCE   669

CHAPTER 12

SERVITUDES AND COMMON INTEREST COMMUNITIES   685

CHAPTER 13

THE TAKINGS CLAUSE   811

PREFACE

First published in 1951 by Harvard Professors A. James Casner and W. Barton Leach, *Cases and Text on Property* established the contours of the modern Property course, integrating into one casebook material previously taught in separate courses including personal property, estates in land, future interests, conveyancing, and landlord and tenant. Through subsequent editions, the book has evolved to reflect continuing changes in property law and the society it serves. The increasing importance of intellectual property, common interest communities, and constitutional limits on the ability of government to acquire and regulate property, as well as other changes, are reflected in the materials included in this sixth edition.

This edition also responds to changes in the first year curriculum that have cut the number of hours devoted to Property and increased student options to pursue, or opt out of, studying land transactions, zoning, marital property, and trusts and wills. We have cut back from 1,370 pages in the fifth edition to 944 in this sixth edition. Chapters on medieval land law and zoning have been cut entirely and coverage of marital property is limited to a note that covers the differences between community and common law property regimes, the question whether professional degrees, celebrity status, and frozen ova, sperm, and embryos are marital property subject to division on divorce, rights of the surviving spouse on death of the first spouse, and pre-marital agreements. We have also replaced a number of principal cases with notes and have ruthlessly edited those that remain.

Major changes in this edition include beginning with a new chapter that introduces basic terminology and ideas about property and three causes of action that vindicate rights to possess, use and enjoy property: trespass, nuisance, and conversion. We have added exciting new cases on intellectual property: Keller v. Electronic Arts, Inc. (right of publicity), American Broadcasting Cos. Inc. v. Aereo Inc. (copyright), Toyota Motor Sales, USA, Inc. v. Tobari, Inc. (nominative fair use of trademarks). We have also added the latest cases from the U.S. Supreme Court on patentable subject matter: Bilski v. Kappos, Association for Molecular Pathology v. Myriad Genetics, Inc., and Alice Corporation Pty. Ltd. v. CLS Bank International. Bowman v. Monsanto on infringing use of patented seeds rounds out Chapter 4.

In other changes, nuisance coverage is split between Chapter 1, which covers nasty neighbor disputes, and Chapter 11, which covers conflicting land use cases. New cases on landlord tenant law are Providence Land Services LLC v. Jones (lease with no end date), Miller v. David Grace, Inc. (landlord tort liability), Elk Creek Management Co. v. Gilbert (retaliatory eviction), and Austin Hill Country Realty, Inc. v. Palisades Plaza (landlord's duty to mitigate). Chapter 7 adds new cases on tenancy in common, an increasingly important way of holding title: Estate of Hughes v. Patton (ouster), and Leg Investments v. Boxler (effect of right of first refusal on ability to partition). Two new cases have been added to Chapter 9 on real estate transactions: Genovese Drug Stores, Inc. v. Conn. Packing Co. (chain of title), and Commonwealth Electric Co. v. MacCardell (Torrens system).

Finally, Chapter 13 now combines eminent domain and regulatory takings. Several older cases have been removed to make way for Kelo v. City of New London, Stop the Beach Renourishment, Inc. v. Florida Dep't of Environmental Protection, Arkansas Game and Fish Commission v. United States, Lingle v. Chevron U.S.A., and Koontz v. St. Johns River Water Management District.

Despite the cuts, which make this book well suited for a four-unit course, it can also be readily adapted for a five- or six-unit course. Most of the fifth edition cases that have been cut will be available on our website along with supplemental materials.

Professors Casner and Leach ended their Preface to the second edition of this book, in 1969, by saying: "*We wonder why all of our colleagues are not fighting to get a chance to teach the first-year property course. We can only surmise that they want to live more sheltered lives. We do not envy them.*" We, too, would not trade places with our colleagues. Property is a fascinating and ever-evolving subject.

- Property law engages some of the most important and contentious topics of our time including allocation, use, and conservation of natural resources; protection of and access to the fruits of intellectual and creative activity; land use regulation; condemning land for private industry; privatizing local government through common-interest communities; improving substandard housing; and eliminating discrimination in housing.
- Property law involves some of the most immediate and personal of human interactions such as buying a house or renting an apartment; fighting with neighbors over noise, smells, pets, water, and boundaries; protecting property against trespassers; making gifts; providing for the family on death; dividing property on divorce.
- Property law draws the attention of some of the most interesting legal thinkers of our time, as it has in prior generations. The literature is rich.

The materials in this book are designed to expose students to the broad sweep of property law and to allow them to gain the basic knowledge critical to understanding property issues and relationships. They engage students in searching analysis of the policy choices that face judges and legislatures, and help them move along the road to becoming lawyers and scholars. The materials have been selected not only for their ability to teach law, lawyering, and legal analysis, and to highlight significant policy issues, but also with an eye to the human dramas and real-life consequences that make studying Property so interesting, as well as so important. The style and presentation are designed to be user-friendly with informative notes, examples, and charts. Questions and problems throughout the book focus attention in the soundness of rulings, examine the underlying policy issues, and encourage students to think beyond the decided cases.

To improve readability of the materials, we have sometimes omitted citations, corrected apparent typographical and spelling errors and broken up or combined paragraphs in opinions without noting the intervention. Footnotes by the court or a quoted author retain their original numbers; footnotes we have added are numbered consecutively throughout a chapter. Textual omissions are indicated by ellipses.

Susan F. French
Gerald Korngold

November, 2014

ACKNOWLEDGMENTS

American Bar Association, Model Rules of Professional Conduct, 2014 Edition. Copyright © 2014 by the American Bar Association. Reprinted with permission. Copies of ABA Model Rules of Professional Conduct, 2014 Edition are available from Service Center, American Bar Association, 321 North Clark Street, Chicago, IL 60654, 1-800-285-2221. This information or any portion thereof may not be copied or disseminated in any form or by any means or stored in an electronic database or retrieval system without the express written consent of the American Bar Association.

American Bar Association, Residential Real Estate Transaction: The Lawyer's Proper Role-Services-Compensation, 14 Real Property, Probate & Trust Journal, 581-607. Reprinted with permission. © Copyright 1979 by the American Bar Association. This information or any or portion thereof may not be copied or disseminated in any form or by any means or stored in an electronic database or retrieval system without the express written consent of the American Bar Association.

American Land Title Association, ALTA Owner's Policy (10/17/92). Reprinted by permission.

American Law Institute, Restatement (Second) of Property-Landlord Tenant, Vol. 1 (1977). Copyright © 1977 by the American Law Institute. Reprinted by permission.

American Law Institute, Restatement (Second) of Torts (1979). Copyright © 1979 by the American Law Institute. Reprinted by permission.

American Law Institute, Restatement (Third) of Property, Servitudes (2000). Copyright © 2000 by the American Law Institute. Reprinted by permission.

Berger, Curtis, Home is Where the Heart Is: A Brief Reply to Professor Epstein, 54 Brooklyn Law Review (1989). Copyright © 1989 Curtis Berger. Reprinted by permission of Brooklyn Law Review.

Braunstein, Michael, Structural Change and Inter-Professional Competitive Advantage: An Example Drawn from Real Estate Conveyancing, 62 Missouri L. Rev. 241, 278-279 (1977). Reprinted by permission.

Continuing Education of the Bar—California, Table of Consanguinity and Chart of Relationships, reproduced from California Decedent Estate Practice, Second Edition, Vol. 1, copyright © 2014 by the Regents of the University of California, with permission.

Downs, Anthony, Residential Rent Controls: an Evaluation, The Urban Land Institute (1988). Reprinted by permission from the publisher ULI — The Urban Land Institute, 1025 Thomas Jefferson St., NW, Washington, D.C. 20007-5201.

Echeverria, John D. and Thekla Hansen-Young, The Track Record on Takings Legislation: Lessons from Democracy's Laboratories 28 Stan. Envtl. L.J. 439, 441-46 (2009).

Epstein, Richard, Rent Control and the Theory of Efficient Regulation, 54 Brooklyn Law Review (1988). Copyright © Richard Epstein. Reprinted by permission of Brooklyn Law Review.

Gerchick, Randy G., No Easy Way Out: Making the Summary Eviction Process a Fairer and More Effective Alternative to Landlord Self-Help, 41 UCLA L. Rev. 759 (1994). Copyright © 1994, Randy G. Gerchick, reprinted by permission.

Glendon, Mary Ann, The Transformation of American Landlord-Tenant Law, 23 Boston College L. Rev (1982). Copyright © 1982, Mary Ann Glendon. Reprinted by permission.

Helmholz, R.H., Wrongful Possession of Chattels: Hornbook Law and Case Law, 80 Northwestern U. Law Rev. 1221-1224 (1986). Copyright © 1986 Northwestern University School of Law, Law Review, reprinted by permission.

Houck, Oliver A., Unfinished Stories II, 75 U. Colo. L. Rev. 331 (2004). Reprinted with permission of the University of Colorado Law Review.

Kades, Eric, The Dark Side of Efficiency: Johnson v. M'Intosh and the Expropriation of Indian Lands, 148 U. Penn. L. Rev. (2000). Reprinted by permission of the author.

Kennedy, Duncan, The Effect of the Warranty of Habitability on Low Income Housing: "Milking" and Class Violence, 15 Fla. St. U.L. Rev. 485 (1987). Copyright © 1987 Florida State University Law Review. Reprinted by permission.

McCarthy, J. Thomas, The Human Persona as Commercial Property, 19 Columbia VLA Journal of the Law and Arts (1995). Reprinted by permission of the author.

Meyers, Charles J., The Covenant of Habitability and the American Law Institute, 27 Stanford L. Rev. (1975). Reprinted by permission.

National Conference of Commissioners on Uniform State Laws, Uniform Residential Landlord and Tenant Act, 7B Uniform Laws Annotated (1985). Copyright © 1985 by the Uniform Law Commission. Reprinted by permission.

National Conference of Commissioners on Uniform State Laws, Uniform Statutory Rule Against Perpetuities. Copyright © 1990 by the Uniform Law Commission. Reprinted by permission.

Rabin, Edward, The Revolution in Residential Landlord-Tenant Law: Causes and Consequences, 69 Cornell L. Rev. 517, 562 (1984). Copyright © 1984 by Cornell Law Review. Reprinted by permission.

Radin, Margaret Jane, Residential Rent Control, 15 Phil. & Pub. Aff. 350, 359-62 (1986). Copyright © 1986 by John Wiley and Sons Inc. Reprinted by permission.

Rose, Carol M., Canons of Property Talk, or Blackstone's Anxiety, 108 Yale L.J. 601 (1998). Reprinted by permission of The Yale Law Journal Company and

Fred B. Rothman & Company from The Yale Law Journal, Vol. 108, pages 601-632.

Rose, Carol M., "Servitudes, Security, and Assent: Some Comments on Professors French and Reichman," V55: 6 Southern California Law Review, 1403-1414 (1982). Reprinted with the permission of the Southern California Law Review.

Somin, Ilya, The Judicial Reaction to Kelo, 4 Alb. Gov't L. Rev. 1, 2-3 (2011). Reprinted with the permission of the Albany Government Law Review.

Stevens, Justice John Paul (Ret.), Kelo, Popularity, and Substantive Due Process 63 Ala. L. Rev. 941 (2012).

Thompson, Jr., Barton H., Judicial Takings 76 Va. L. Rev. 1449, 1451-52 (1990). Used by permission of Virginia Law Review.

Underkuffler, Laura S., Judicial Takings: A Medley of Misconceptions 61 Syracuse L. Rev. 203, 206-08 (2011). Reprinted with permission of the author.

P A R T I

INTRODUCTION TO PROPERTY: BASIC IDEAS, LEGAL PROTECTIONS, ACQUISITION BY CAPTURE, CONQUEST, ADVERSE POSSESSION, AND CREATIVE ACTIVITY

To achieve proper self-development — to be a person — an individual needs some control over resources in the external environment. The necessary assurances of control take the form of property rights.

Margaret Jane Radin, *Property and Personhood,*
34 Stan. L. Rev. 957 (1982)

[I]n a state in which private property does not exist, citizens are dependent on the good will of government officials . . . . Whatever they have is a privilege and not a right. . . . Any challenge to the state may be stifled or driven underground by virtue of the fact that serious challenges could result in the withdrawal of the goods that give people basic security.

Cass R. Sunstein, *On Property and Constitutionalism,*
14 Cardozo L. Rev. 907, 915 (1993)

Property plays a fundamental role in our society, providing us with the material things we need to sustain life and a base from which we can participate in civic life. For most of us it does much more. We use our clothes, cars, and personal possessions to differentiate ourselves from one another; we use our property to shelter and nurture our families; and we use our wealth to support causes we want to support. Protection of our property is vital to our sense of security and is a core function of our legal system. But property law does not just protect pre-existing entitlements. It mediates disputes among those with too little property and those who have "too much," sometimes forcing reallocations for private or public good. It also resolves disputes among public-minded folks who claim that owners of historic sites and buildings, wetlands, wildlife habitat, rain forests, and the like should be regulated to protect public interests and the owners who want to stay in control of "their" property. Other disputes involve community claims of rights to regulate development in the interests of planning to meet community objectives for safety, traffic control, amenities, and fiscal support,

1

and more contentiously, claims of the government to take private property for economic development. Property lies at the core of our society. Throughout history disputes over property have been some of the most contentious and they remain so today.

In the first four chapters of this book we introduce you to four very fundamental aspects of this critical subject: (1) the basic causes of action available to protect interests in property; (2) acquiring property by capture, finds, and salvage; (3) acquiring property by conquest, adverse possession, and prescription; and (4) protecting property acquired by creative activity (herein of intellectual property).

To illustrate the very broad range of property law, we have included cases ranging from land to human body parts, with stops for wild animals, oil and gas, water, cash, sunken treasure, stolen art, human cannonball performances, celebrity personas, copyrights, trademarks, and patents. We also introduce you to a variety of perspectives on the role of property—particularly private property.

CHAPTER 1

Introduction to Property:
Basic Ideas and Causes of Action

There is nothing which so generally strikes the imagination, and engages the affections of mankind, as the right of property; or that sole and despotic dominion which one man claims and exercises over the external things of the world, in total exclusion of the right of any other individual in the universe. . . .

William Blackstone, *Commentaries* (1766)

. . . [P]roperty is the foundation stone of economic well-being. . . . The essential gist of a property regime is to let people take the payoffs from their work and investment, and at the same time to identify owners so that everyone can trade instead of fighting. Trade encourages specialization and even greater gains from investment and exchange. This virtuous spiral of work, investment, and trade makes everyone better off in the standard property rationale.

Carol Rose, *The Moral Subject of Property,*
48 Wm. & Mary L. Rev. 1897, 1905 (2006)

The concept of property holds two special places at the heart of American law. As the basis of our economic system, private property law can be viewed as the set of rules we use to resolve conflicts among individuals concerning control over tangible and intangible resources. . . . [T]hey help define the interests I can ask courts to protect and the entitlements with which I may enter the world of commercial exchange. . . . Property law . . . performs a second, equally vital role. Not only can one citizen invoke property claims to enlist the state in a struggle against another, but each citizen can call upon property law to protect herself against actions of the government. . . .

Jeremy Paul, *The Hidden Structure of Takings Law,*
64 S. Cal. L. Rev. 1393, 1409 (1991)

. . . [T]he essence of private property is always the right to exclude others. . . . If . . . somebody else wants to use the food, the house, the land, or the plow which the law calls mine, he has to get my consent. To the extent that these things are necessary to the life of my neighbor, the law thus confers on me a power, limited but real, to make him do what I want. . . . The money needed for purchasing things must for the vast majority be acquired by hard labor and disagreeable service to those to whom the law has accorded dominion over the things necessary for subsistence. . . . [T]he recognition of private property as a form of sovereignty is not itself an argument against it. Some form of government we must always have. . . . While, however, government is

3

*a necessity, not all forms of it are of equal value. At any rate it is necessary to apply
to the law of property all those considerations of social ethics and enlightened public
policy which ought to be brought to the discussion of any just form of government.*

Morris R. Cohen, *Property and Sovereignty*,
13 Cornell L.Q. 8-12, 14-30 (1927)

A.   TERMINOLOGY AND IDEAS

1.   *Terminology*

Here is some important terminology that we use when talking about property
and property law:

The word *property* refers to things that are or can be owned by people and
other entities like governments and corporations that have the power to own
things. Things that can be owned may be *tangible*, like land, cars, and computers, or *intangible* like bank accounts, patents, and copyrights. Land and things
attached to the land are classified as *real property*; all other property is classified
as *personal property*. Items of tangible personal property are often called *chattels*, a
word related to the word *cattle*. Another category of personal property is *intellectual property*, which includes patents, copyrights, and trademarks.

Property law governs the acquisition of property, the interests that can be created in property, and the rights and powers of the owners of interests in property. It also determines how and whether interests in property can be transferred, resolves conflicts over ownership, and determines the relative rights of
people and other entities that own interests in particular items of property. The
rights of a property owner with respect to others who have no legally recognized interest in that property are *in rem* rights—said to be "good against the
world," they arise out of possession and ownership. *In rem* rights contrast with
in personam rights—rights good against particular people that often arise out of
contracts among them.

The most common legal remedies available to someone whose property rights
have been violated are *damages* and *injunctions*. Damages are monetary awards;
injunctions are orders directing a party to do or refrain from doing something.
Compensatory damages are designed to redress the harm done; *punitive damages*
are designed to punish reprehensible conduct and deter others from similar
actions. Other legal remedies that may be available are *declaratory judgments* or
quiet title decrees that determine entitlements to property, and orders that someone dispossessed of property be restored to possession, usually by action of the
sheriff or other public official.

2.   *Ideas*

Here are a few of the ideas that you will find running through the cases and
commentary on property law. This list is by no means complete, but will give you
some things to think about as you begin your studies.

Ownership of property carries with it the right to determine how and whether the property will be used. Although subject to governmental regulations like zoning, licensing, safety requirements, and prohibitions against discrimination, the owner in an economic system based on private property decides how much to invest in the property, who can benefit from it, and how and when to dispose of it. Allowing private owners to make these basic determinations is generally cheaper and more productive than a system in which they are made by the government.

Protecting property owners from theft and expropriation encourages them to invest in making their property productive. An effective legal system of protection reduces the amount an owner needs to expend on self-help protection measures, like fences, dogs, or private armies.

Relatively simple, standardized packages of property entitlements and clear rules governing transfer promote productivity by facilitating trade and investment. Trade leads to economic productivity by allowing resources to move to those who value them the most.

Property owners should be free to use their property as they like, but should not be allowed to impose substantial costs on others (externalities), or should be required to internalize the cost of their externalities.

Rules that are easy to understand and comport with common moral understandings lead to high levels of voluntary compliance and low legal costs.

Clear rules, sometimes called bright-line rules, may be inexpensive to comply with and enforce, but may lead to unjust results because they fail to take into account the nuances of human relationships and situational differences.

Rules that can be applied only after extensive fact-finding or that require balancing a variety of considerations may produce just results, but may be costly to comply with and expensive to enforce.

B. LEGAL PROTECTIONS FOR PROPERTY: ACTIONS FOR TRESPASS, CONVERSION, AND NUISANCE

Three of the oldest—and still important—legal actions available to protect the rights of people in possession of property are the actions of trespass, nuisance, and conversion. Generally speaking, trespass and conversion protect the **right to exclude** others; nuisance protects the **right to use and enjoy** the property. In the case of land, the right to exclude is the right to decide who can enter the land and what they can do there; the right to use and enjoyment is the **right to be free from unreasonable interference**. Trespass cases usually present straightforward questions: Did the defendant enter plaintiff's land without permission and without a privilege to do so? Nuisance cases often present more complicated questions: Was defendant's activity unreasonable? Did it cause substantial harm to the plaintiff's use and enjoyment? Would a normal possessor have sustained similar harm? Is defendant's activity so useful that it should not be enjoined? Trespass cases leave little discretion to judges and juries; nuisance cases leave more discretion because so many variables are involved in a determination of reasonableness. Similar, but more limited, protections, including conversion, are available for personal property.

1.   Protecting the Land Holder's Right to Exclude: Trespass

JACQUE v. STEENBERG HOMES, INC.
Supreme Court of Wisconsin
563 N.W.2d 154 (Wis. 1997)

BABLITCH, J. . . . The relevant facts follow. Plaintiffs, Lois and Harvey Jacque, are an elderly couple, now retired from farming, who own roughly 170 acres near Wilke's Lake in the town of Schleswig. The defendant, Steenberg Homes, Inc. (Steenberg), is in the business of selling mobile homes. In the fall of 1993, a neighbor of the Jacques purchased a mobile home from Steenberg. Delivery of the mobile home was included in the sales price.

Steenberg determined that the easiest route to deliver the mobile home was across the Jacques' land . . . because the only alternative was a private road which was covered in up to seven feet of snow and contained a sharp curve which would require sets of "rollers" to be used when maneuvering the home around the curve. Steenberg asked the Jacques on several separate occasions whether it could move the home across the Jacques' farm field. The Jacques refused. The Jacques were sensitive about allowing others on their land because they had lost property valued at over $10,000 to other neighbors in an adverse possession action in the mid-1980s. Despite repeated refusals from the Jacques, Steenberg decided to sell the mobile home, which was to be used as a summer cottage, and delivered it on February 15, 1994.

On the morning of delivery, Mr. Jacque observed the mobile home parked on the corner of the town road adjacent to his property. He decided to find out where the movers planned to take the home. The movers, who were Steenberg employees, showed Mr. Jacque the path they planned to take with the mobile home to reach the neighbor's lot. The path cut across the Jacques' land. Mr. Jacque informed the movers that it was the Jacques' land they were planning to cross and that Steenberg did not have permission to cross their land. He told them that Steenberg had been refused permission to cross the Jacques' land.

One of Steenberg's employees called the assistant manager, who then came out to the Jacques' home. In the meantime, the Jacques called and asked some of their neighbors and the town chairman to come over immediately. Once everyone was present, the Jacques showed the assistant manager an aerial map and plat book of the township to prove their ownership of the land, and reiterated their demand that the home not be moved across their land.

At that point, the assistant manager asked Mr. Jacque how much money it would take to get permission. Mr. Jacque responded that it was not a question of money; the Jacques just did not want Steenberg to cross their land. Mr. Jacque testified that he told Steenberg to "[F]ollow the road, that is what the road is for." Steenberg employees left the meeting without permission to cross the land.

At trial, one of Steenberg's employees testified that, upon coming out of the Jacques' home, the assistant manager stated: "I don't give a _____ what

[Mr. Jacque] said, just get the home in there any way you can." The other Steenberg employee confirmed this testimony and further testified that the assistant manager told him to park the company truck in such a way that no one could get down the town road to see the route the employees were taking with the home. The assistant manager denied giving these instructions, and Steenberg argued that the road was blocked for safety reasons.

The employees, after beginning down the private road, ultimately used a "bobcat" to cut a path through the Jacques' snow-covered field and hauled the home across the Jacques' land to the neighbor's lot. One employee testified that after returning to the office and informing the assistant manager that they had gone across the field, the assistant manager reacted by giggling and laughing. The other employee confirmed this testimony. The assistant manager disputed this testimony.

When a neighbor informed the Jacques that Steenberg had, in fact, moved the mobile home across the Jacques' land, Mr. Jacque called the Manitowoc County Sheriff's Department. After interviewing the parties and observing the scene, an officer from the sheriff's department issued a $30 citation to Steenberg's assistant manager.

The Jacques commenced an intentional tort action . . . seeking compensatory and punitive damages from Steenberg. The case was tried before a jury on December 1, 1994. At the completion of the Jacques' case, Steenberg moved for a directed verdict. . . . For purposes of the motion, Steenberg admitted to an intentional trespass to land, but asked the circuit court to find that the Jacques were not entitled to compensatory damages or punitive damages based on insufficiency of the evidence. The circuit court denied Steenberg's motion and the questions of punitive and compensatory damages were submitted to the jury. The jury awarded the Jacques $1 nominal damages and $100,000 punitive damages. Steenberg filed post-verdict motions claiming that the punitive damage award must be set aside because Wisconsin law did not allow a punitive damage award unless the jury also awarded compensatory damages. Alternatively, Steenberg asked the circuit court to remit the punitive damage award. The circuit court granted Steenberg's motion to set aside the award. Consequently, it did not reach Steenberg's motion for remittitur.[1]

This case presents three issues: (1) whether an award of nominal damages for intentional trespass to land may support a punitive damage award and, if so; (2) whether the law should apply to Steenberg or should only be applied prospectively and, if we apply the law to Steenberg; (3) whether the $100,000 in punitive damages awarded by the jury is excessive. . . .

Steenberg argues that, as a matter of law, punitive damages could not be awarded by the jury because punitive damages must be supported by an award of compensatory damages and here the jury awarded only nominal and punitive damages. The Jacques contend that the rationale supporting the compensatory damage award requirement is inapposite when the wrongful act is an intentional trespass to land. We agree with the Jacques. . . .

The general rule was stated in Barnard v. Cohen, 162 N.W. 480 (Wis. 1917), where the question presented was: "In an action for libel, can there be a recovery of punitory damages if only nominal compensatory damages are found?"

---

1. An order reducing the amount of the jury award—EDS.

With the bare assertion that authority and better reason supported its conclusion, the *Barnard* court said no. *Barnard* continues to state the general rule of punitive damages in Wisconsin. The rationale for the compensatory damage requirement is that if the individual cannot show actual harm, he or she has but a nominal interest, hence, society has little interest in having the unlawful, but otherwise harmless, conduct deterred, therefore, punitive damages are inappropriate.

However, whether nominal damages can support a punitive damage award in the case of an intentional trespass to land has never been squarely addressed by this court. Nonetheless, Wisconsin law is not without reference to this situation. In 1854 the court established punitive damages, allowing the assessment of "damages as a punishment to the defendant for the purpose of making an example." McWilliams v. Bragg, 3 Wis. 424 (1854).[3] The *McWilliams* court related the facts and an illustrative tale from the English case of Merest v. Harvey, 128 Eng. Rep. 761 (C.P. 1814), to explain the rationale underlying punitive damages.

In *Merest*, a landowner was shooting birds in his field when he was approached by the local magistrate who wanted to hunt with him. Although the landowner refused, the magistrate proceeded to hunt. When the landowner continued to object, the magistrate threatened to have him jailed and dared him to file suit. Although little actual harm had been caused, the English court upheld damages of 500 pounds, explaining "in a case where a man disregards every principle which actuates the conduct of gentlemen, what is to restrain him except large damages?"

To explain the need for punitive damages, even where actual harm is slight, *McWilliams* related the hypothetical tale from *Merest* of an intentional trespasser:

> Suppose a gentleman has a paved walk in his paddock, before his window, and that a man intrudes and walks up and down before the window of his house, and looks in while the owner is at dinner, is the trespasser permitted to say "here is a halfpenny for you which is the full extent of the mischief I have done." Would that be a compensation? I cannot say that it would be. . . .

Thus, in the case establishing punitive damages in this state, this court recognized that in certain situations of trespass, the actual harm is not in the damage done to the land, which may be minimal, but in the loss of the individual's right to exclude others from his or her property and, the court implied that this right may be punished by a large damage award despite the lack of measurable harm. . . .

Because the Jacques did not receive a compensatory damage award, Steenberg contends that the punitive damage award must be set aside. The Jacques argue that both the individual and society have significant interests in deterring intentional trespass to land, regardless of the lack of measurable harm that results. We agree with the Jacques. An examination of the individual interests invaded by an intentional trespass to land, and society's interests in preventing intentional

---

3.   Because *McWilliams* was an action of trespass for assault and battery, we cite it not for its precedential value, but for its reasoning.

trespass to land, leads us to the conclusion that the *Barnard* rule should not apply when the tort supporting the award is intentional trespass to land.

We turn first to the individual landowner's interest in protecting his or her land from trespass. The United States Supreme Court has recognized that the private landowner's right to exclude others from his or her land is "one of the most essential sticks in the bundle of rights that are commonly characterized as property." Dolan v. City of Tigard, 512 U.S. 374 (1994) . . . . This court has long recognized "[e]very person['s] constitutional right to the exclusive enjoyment of his own property for any purpose which does not invade the rights of another person." Diana Shooting Club v. Lamoreux, 89 N.W. 880 (Wis. 1902) (holding that the victim of an intentional trespass should have been allowed to take judgment for nominal damages and costs). Thus, both this court and the Supreme Court recognize the individual's legal right to exclude others from private property.

Yet a right is hollow if the legal system provides insufficient means to protect it. Felix Cohen offers the following analysis summarizing the relationship between the individual and the state regarding property rights:

> [T]hat is property to which the following label can be attached:
>
> To the world:
>
> Keep off X unless you have my permission, which I may grant or withhold.
>
> Signed: Private Citizen
>
> Endorsed: The State

Felix S. Cohen, *Dialogue on Private Property*, IX Rutgers Law Review 357 (1954). Harvey and Lois Jacque have the right to tell Steenberg Homes and any other trespasser, "No, you cannot cross our land." But that right has no practical meaning unless protected by the State. And, as this court recognized as early as 1854, a "halfpenny" award does not constitute state protection.

The nature of the nominal damage award in an intentional trespass to land case further supports an exception to *Barnard*. . . . The action for intentional trespass to land is directed at vindication of the legal right. W. Page Keeton, *Prosser and Keeton on Torts*, § 13 (5th ed. 1984). . . . The law recognizes actual harm in every trespass to land whether or not compensatory damages are awarded. Thus, in the case of intentional trespass to land, the nominal damage award represents the recognition that, although immeasurable in mere dollars, actual harm has occurred.

The potential for harm resulting from intentional trespass also supports an exception to *Barnard*. A series of intentional trespasses, as the Jacques had the misfortune to discover in an unrelated action, can threaten the individual's very ownership of the land. The conduct of an intentional trespasser, if repeated, might ripen into prescription or adverse possession and, as a consequence, the individual landowner can lose his or her property rights to the trespasser.

Society has an interest in punishing and deterring intentional trespassers beyond that of protecting the interests of the individual landowner. Society has an interest in preserving the integrity of the legal system. Private landowners should feel confident that wrongdoers who trespass upon their land will be appropriately punished. When landowners have confidence in the legal system, they are less likely to resort to "self-help" remedies. In *McWilliams*, the court recognized the importance of " 'prevent[ing] the practice of dueling, [by permitting] juries [ ] to punish insult by exemplary damages.' " Although dueling is rarely a modern form of self-help, one can easily imagine a frustrated landowner taking the law into his or her own hands when faced with a brazen trespasser, like Steenberg, who refuses to heed no trespass warnings.

People expect wrongdoers to be appropriately punished. Punitive damages have the effect of bringing to punishment types of conduct that, though oppressive and hurtful to the individual, almost invariably go unpunished by the public prosecutor. The $30 forfeiture was certainly not an appropriate punishment for Steenberg's egregious trespass in the eyes of the Jacques. It was more akin to *Merest*'s "halfpenny." If punitive damages are not allowed in a situation like this, what punishment will prohibit the intentional trespass to land? Moreover, what is to stop Steenberg Homes from concluding, in the future, that delivering its mobile homes via an intentional trespass and paying the resulting Class B forfeiture, is not more profitable than obeying the law? . . .

. . . [T]he *Barnard* rule sends the wrong message to Steenberg Homes and any others who contemplate trespassing on the land of another. It implicitly tells them that they are free to go where they please, regardless of the landowner's wishes. . . . We conclude that both the private landowner and society have much more than a nominal interest in excluding others from private land. . . . Consequently, the *Barnard* rationale will not support a refusal to allow punitive damages when the tort involved is an intentional trespass to land. . . . [A]ssuming that the other requirements for punitive damages have been met, we hold that nominal damages may support a punitive damage award in an action for intentional trespass to land.

Our holding is supported by respected legal commentary. The *Restatement (Second) of Torts* supports the proposition that an award of nominal damages will support an award of punitive damages in a trespass to land action:

> The fact that the actor knows that his entry is without the consent of the possessor and without any other privilege to do so, while not necessary to make him liable, may affect the amount of damages recoverable against him, by showing such a complete disregard of the possessor's legally protected interest in the exclusive possession of his land as to justify the imposition of punitive in addition to nominal damages for even a harmless trespass, or in addition to compensatory damages for one which is harmful. *Restatement (Second) of Torts* § 163 cmt. *e* (1979). . . .

Prosser also finds the compensatory damages prerequisite unsupportable . . . *Prosser and Keeton on the Law of Torts* § 2, at 14 (5th ed. 1984). A minority of other jurisdictions follow this approach. *See*, Annotation, *Sufficiency of Showing of Actual Damages to Support Award of Punitive Damages — Modern Cases*, 40 A.L.R. 4th 11, 36 (1985). . . .

Steenberg argues that because it relied on the well-established *Barnard* rule at trial, and our holding today recognizes an exception to the *Barnard* rule, today's holding should not apply to this case. . . .

At times, inequities will occur when a court departs from precedent and announces a new rule of law. In an effort to avoid inequity on these rare occasions, the court has recognized exceptions to the Blackstonian Doctrine and used the device of prospective overruling, . . . to limit the effect of a newly announced rule when retroactive application would be inequitable. . . .

Retroactivity is usually justified as a reward for the litigant who has persevered in attacking an unsound rule. To refuse to apply the new rule here would deprive the Jacques of any benefit from their effort and expense in challenging the old rule which we now declare erroneous. That, we conclude, would be the greater injustice. Accordingly, we hold that the exception to *Barnard* that we recognize today shall be applied to Steenberg. . . .

Finally, we consider whether the jury's $100,000 punitive damages award to the Jacques is [clearly] excessive. . . . We conclude that it is not. Accordingly, we do not order remittitur. The punitive award neither shocks our conscience, nor takes our breath away. On the contrary, it is the brazen conduct of Steenberg Homes that we find shocking, not the $100,000 punitive damages award.

. . . Accordingly, we reverse and remand to the circuit court for reinstatement of the punitive damages award.

Notes and Questions

1. Note the court's use of precedent in this case. How did it justify refusing to apply the *Barnard* rule? What use did it make of *McWilliams v. Bragg*? How did it use the *Restatement (Second) of Torts*?

2. The court begins its opinion by setting forth the "relevant facts." Of what relevance are the facts that the Jacques are an elderly couple, now retired from farming? That they own roughly 170 acres? That the mobile home was to be used as a summer cottage? If you had represented the Jacques on appeal, would you have included those facts in your brief or your arguments?

3. Wouldn't everybody have been better off if the Jacques had sold Steenberg the right to cross their land to install the mobile home? Despite the Jacques's apparent belief that they risked permanent loss of property rights, they could safely have granted Steenberg a "license" for that limited purpose, as you will learn when we reach the subjects of adverse possession and prescription.

4. According to the "Coase Theorem,"[1] the legal allocation of entitlements (here, to the Jacques) should not prevent an efficient outcome (defined as everybody is better off) because, at least in the absence of transaction costs, the parties will bargain their way to an efficient result. Did misinformation keep the parties from reaching an efficient result here?

Carol Rose, a modern property theorist, suggests that more is needed than just low transaction costs (few people, good information, clear entitlements) for bargains to take place. Trading partners must also have some reason to trust each other. In her words, "There is a kind of mystery of 'niceness' and trust at the center of economic transactions." *See Canons of Property Talk, or Blackstone's Anxiety,* 108 Yale L.J. 601 (1998). Did lack of trust or niceness produce the legal dispute in *Jacque v. Steenberg*?

5. As the court notes, the Supreme Court of the United States has characterized the right to exclude as "one of the most essential sticks in the bundle of

---

1.   Ronald Coase, who was awarded the Nobel Prize for economic science in 1991, developed this theory in *The Problem of Social Cost,* 3 J.L. & Econ. 1 (1960).

rights[2] that are commonly characterized as property." Why is the right to exclude so important? Other rights associated with property ownership that have been identified as sticks in the bundle are the rights to use or not use, sell, destroy, and to give away during life and at death.

Although most lawyers today use the bundle of sticks metaphor in talking about property, it has come under increasing scrutiny. One criticism is that it can be used to justify increasing governmental restrictions on property rights without crossing the constitutional barrier against taking "property" for public use without compensation. For example, if only one or two of the sticks in the bundle are removed, the owner may still have the "property."

Functions of the Right to Exclude

Trespass law reflects and enforces our common understanding that private property belongs to the owner, who has the right to decide who can enter the property and what it can be used for. The duty not to enter or appropriate property of others is so widely understood and respected that it is not just a legal duty, but also a moral duty, the duty not to steal. In one respect, trespass law is very crude—anyone who crosses the boundary into private property without permission, with very few exceptions, is liable, whether or not any actual damage results. No inquiry need be made into the relative values of the activities of the trespasser and the owner. The owner need not justify decisions as to how the property is to be used or not used. If the boundaries are clear, there is seldom any need to litigate the question whether a trespass has occurred. In addition to giving the owner relatively free rein to decide how the property will be used, the simple trespass rules make it easy for everyone else to understand what their duty is—keep off unless you have permission. The right to exclude, based in ownership or possession, not agreement, is an *in rem* right.

The functions of the right to exclude are extensively examined by Professors Merrill and Smith in a series of articles, including Thomas W. Merrill, *Property and the Right to Exclude*, 77 Neb. L. Rev. 730 (1998), and Henry E. Smith, *Exclusion Versus Governance: Two Strategies for Delineating Property Rights*, 31 J. Legal Stud. 453 (2002). Two interesting articles exploring the relationship between property and morality are Carol M. Rose, *The Moral Subject of Property*, 48 Wm. & Mary L. Rev. 1897 (2007), and Thomas W. Merrill & Henry E. Smith, *The Morality of Property*, 48 Wm. & Mary L. Rev. 1849 (2006).

Limitations on the Right to Exclude

There are a number of well-recognized exceptions to the right to exclude as well as others that are more contested. In cases of emergency or necessity, a person may enter the land of another without liability for trespass. Retrieving a child,

2. Use of a bundle of sticks as a metaphor for property has been traced back to an 1888 book on eminent domain. It came into increasingly common use after publication of the first Restatement of Property in 1936. *See* Michael A. Heller, *The Boundaries of Private Property*, 108 Yale L.J. 1163, 1192 n.150 (1999).

pet, or other chattel that has wandered onto the land of another can ordinarily be accomplished without committing trespass. However, there may be liability for damage actually done, as where a boat tied up to a private dock during a storm damages the dock; in that case, there is liability for the damage but not for technical trespass. The landowner who refuses entry to one in an emergency situation may be liable for the damage that ensues. In *Protectus Alpha Navigation Co. v. North Pacific Grain Growers, Inc.*, 767 F.2d 1379 (9th Cir. 1985), for example, a dockowner that cast off a burning ship, which prevented firefighters from extinguishing the fire, was held liable for damages, including punitive damages. Another case in which there is a privilege to enter the land of another is where the landowner has wrongfully and forcibly taken a chattel belonging to someone else. The person from whom it was taken may enter the land and retake the chattel, so long as he is in "fresh pursuit."

Encroachments by one person's building onto the land of another are generally actionable as trespass, but the landowner is not always entitled to a remedy. In *Brownstone Condominium Ass'n v. Geller*, 415 N.E.2d 20 (Ill. App. Ct. 1980), a high-rise condominium association sued Geller, the owner of the single-family home next door, to compel removal of nine five-inch bolts that attached a board supporting a screened-in area at the back of the house to the outer garage wall of the condominium building. Less than three inches of the bolts entered the brick wall. The north wall of the condominium building sits on the property line between the two parties. In a previous suit Geller had sought unsuccessfully to enjoin the condominium association from using temporary scaffolding on the north wall that protruded into his airspace. In this case, the court affirmed denial of a preliminary injunction requiring removal of the bolts, adopting the reasoning of the trial court, an excerpt of which follows:

> To cloak this dispute with the important mantle of a preliminary mandatory injunction would be to elevate pettiness to a level that it does not merit. . . . To enter the serious and important writ of injunction on these facts would be to invite ridicule, would gravely deprecate the importance of that extraordinary writ, and would . . . be an invitation to others to try the same. . . . I entertain absolutely no illusions of grandeur about what I should be doing here on the bench. I do not believe that I was ordained to sit only on the most important and earth shaking matters. Like all other judges, I'm accustomed to hearing matters of no public importance — but all of those matters do have a common thread of being brought to protect a real, and not an imagined or contrived injury. Such is not the case here. This, to my view, is a spite case. . . . The mere fact there is a trespass does not warrant any affirmative action by the Court. The close quarters of an urban society demand flexibility when we encounter an intrusion on our personal bubble. . . . The limitations on the judicial system make it obvious that each of these transgressions cannot be litigated. There was a time when the economics of a case would militate against its being filed, but where, as here, a large condominium association chooses to pool its resources and file nonsense, then I believe the Court must resist . . . .

Other limits on the right to exclude, like that articulated in the following case, are less well established.

STATE v. SHACK

Supreme Court of New Jersey
277 A.2d 369 (1971)

WEINTRAUB, C.J. Defendants entered upon private property to aid migrant farmworkers employed and housed there. Having refused to depart upon the demand of the owner, defendants were charged with violating N.J.S.A. 2A:170-31 which provides that "(a)ny person who trespasses on any lands . . . after being forbidden so to trespass by the owner . . . is a disorderly person and shall be punished by a fine of not more than $50." Defendants were convicted in the Municipal Court . . . and again on appeal in the County Court . . . on a trial de novo. . . .

Before us, no one seeks to sustain these convictions. The complaints were prosecuted in the Municipal Court and in the County Court by counsel engaged by the complaining landowner, Tedesco. However Tedesco did not respond to this appeal, and the county prosecutor, while defending abstractly the constitutionality of the trespass statute, expressly disclaimed any position as to whether the statute reached the activity of these defendants.

Complainant, Tedesco, a farmer, employs migrant workers for his seasonal needs. As part of their compensation, these workers are housed at a camp on his property.

Defendant Tejeras is a field worker for SCOPE, a nonprofit corporation funded by the Office of Economic Opportunity pursuant to an act of Congress. The role of SCOPE includes providing for the "health services of the migrant farm worker." Defendant Shack is a staff attorney with Camden Regional Legal Services, Inc., known as "CRLS," also a nonprofit corporation funded by the Office of Economic Opportunity pursuant to an act of Congress. The mission of CRLS includes legal advice and representation for these workers.

Differences had developed between Tedesco and these defendants prior to the events which led to the trespass charges now before us. Hence when defendant Tejeras wanted to go upon Tedesco's farm to find a migrant worker who needed medical aid for the removal of 28 sutures, he called upon defendant Shack for his help with respect to the legalities involved. Shack, too, had a mission to perform on Tedesco's farm; he wanted to discuss a legal problem with another migrant worker there employed and housed. Defendants arranged to go to the farm together. Shack carried literature to inform the migrant farmworkers of the assistance available to them under federal statutes . . . .

Defendants entered upon Tedesco's property and as they neared the camp site where the farmworkers were housed, they were confronted by Tedesco who inquired of their purpose. Tejeras and Shack stated their missions. In response, Tedesco offered to find the injured worker, and as to the worker who needed legal advice, Tedesco also offered to locate the man but insisted that the consultation would have to take place in Tedesco's office and in his presence. Defendants declined, saying they had the right to see the men in the privacy of their living quarters and without Tedesco's supervision. Tedesco thereupon summoned a State Trooper who, however, refused to remove defendants except upon Tedesco's written complaint. Tedesco then executed the formal complaints charging violations of the trespass statute.

I.

The constitutionality of the trespass statute, as applied here, is challenged on several scores. It is urged that the First Amendment rights of the defendants and of the migrant farmworkers were thereby offended. Reliance is placed on Marsh v. Alabama, 326 U.S. 501 (1946), where it was held that free speech was assured by the First Amendment in a company-owned town which was open to the public generally and was indistinguishable from any other town except for the fact that the title to the property was vested in a private corporation. Hence a Jehovah's Witness who distributed literature on a sidewalk within the town could not be held as a trespasser. . . . [That case rests] upon the fact that the property was in fact opened to the general public. There may be some migrant camps with the attributes of the company town in *Marsh* and of course they would come within its holding. But there is nothing of that character in the case before us. . . .

Defendants also maintain that the application of the trespass statute to them is barred by the Supremacy Clause of the United States Constitution, Art. VI, cl. 2, . . . on the premise that the application of the trespass statute would defeat the purpose of the federal statutes, under which SCOPE and CRLS are funded. . . . The brief of the United States, Amicus Curiae, supports that approach. Here defendants rely upon cases construing the National Labor Relations Act, . . . and holding that an employer may in some circumstances be guilty of an unfair labor practice . . . if the employer denies union organizers an opportunity to communicate with his employees at some suitable place upon the employer's premises. . . . The brief of New Jersey State Office of Legal Services, Amicus Curiae, asserts the workers' Sixth Amendment right to counsel in criminal matters is involved and suggests also that a right to counsel in civil matters is a "penumbra" right emanating from the whole Bill of Rights . . . or is a privilege of national citizenship protected by the privileges and immunities clause of the Fourteenth Amendment, or is a right "retained by the people" under the Ninth Amendment . . . .

These constitutional claims are not established by any definitive holding. We think it unnecessary to explore their validity. . . . [W]e are satisfied that under our State law the ownership of real property does not include the right to bar access to governmental services available to migrant workers and hence there was no trespass within the meaning of the penal statute. The policy considerations which underlie that conclusion may be much the same as those which would be weighed with respect to one or more of the constitutional challenges, but a decision in nonconstitutional terms is more satisfactory, because the interests of migrant workers are more expansively served in that way than they would be if they had no more freedom than these constitutional concepts could be found to mandate, if indeed they apply at all.

II.

Property rights serve human values. They are recognized to that end, and are limited by it. Title to real property cannot include dominion over the destiny of persons the owner permits to come upon the premises. Their well-being must remain the paramount concern of a system of law. Indeed the needs of the occupants may be so imperative and their strength so weak, that the law will deny the occupants the power to contract away what is deemed essential to their health, welfare, or dignity.

Here we are concerned with a highly disadvantaged segment of our society. . . . The migrant farmworkers are a community within but apart from the local scene. They are rootless and isolated. Although the need for their labors is evident, they are unorganized and without economic or political power. It is their plight alone that summoned government to their aid. . . . Congress provided . . . [in] the Economic Opportunity Act of 1964 . . . for "assistance for migrant and other seasonally employed farmworkers and their families." . . . Section 2862(b)(1) provides for funding of programs "to meet the immediate needs of migrant and seasonal farmworkers and their families, such as day care for children, education, health services, improved housing and sanitation (including the provision and maintenance of emergency and temporary housing and sanitation facilities), legal advice and representation, and consumer training and counseling." . . . SCOPE is engaged in a program funded under this section, and CRLS also pursues the objectives of this section although . . . it is funded under § 2809(a)(3), which is not limited in its concern to the migrant and other seasonally employed farmworkers and seeks "to further the cause of justice among persons living in poverty by mobilizing the assistance of lawyers and legal institutions and by providing legal advice, legal representation, counseling, education, and other appropriate services."

These ends would not be gained if the intended beneficiaries could be insulated from efforts to reach them. It is in this framework that we must decide whether the camp operator's rights in his lands may stand between the migrant workers and those who would aid them. The key to that aid is communication. Since the migrant workers are outside the mainstream of the communities in which they are housed and are unaware of their rights and opportunities and of the services available to them, they can be reached only by positive efforts tailored to that end. The Report of the Governor's Task Force on Migrant Farm Labor (1968) noted that "One of the major problems related to seasonal farm labor is the lack of adequate direct information with regard to the availability of public services," and that "there is a dire need to provide the workers with basic educational and informational material in a language and style that can be readily understood by the migrant." The report stressed the problem of access and deplored the notion that property rights may stand as a barrier, saying "In our judgment, 'no trespass' signs represent the last dying remnants of paternalistic behavior."

A man's right in his real property of course is not absolute. It was a maxim of the common law that one should so use his property as not to injure the rights of others. . . . "Sic Utere Tuo ut Alienum Non Laedas." Although hardly a precise solvent of actual controversies, the maxim does express the inevitable proposition that rights are relative and there must be an accommodation when they meet. Hence it has long been true that necessity, private or public, may justify entry upon the lands of another. . . .

The subject is not static. As pointed out in 5 Powell, *Real Property* (Rohan 1970) § 745, while society will protect the owner in his permissible interests in land, yet

. . . (s)uch an owner must expect to find the absoluteness of his property rights curtailed by the organs of society, for the promotion of the best interests of others for whom these organs also operate as protective agencies. The necessity for such curtailments is greater in a modern industrialized and urbanized society than it was in the relatively simple American society of fifty, 100, or 200 years ago. The current balance between individualism and dominance of the social interest depends not only upon political and social ideologies, but also upon the physical and social facts of the time and place under discussion.

Professor Powell added in § 746:

As one looks back along the historic road traversed by the law of land in England and in America, one sees a change from the viewpoint that he who owns may do as he pleases with what he owns, to a position which hesitatingly embodies an ingredient of stewardship; which grudgingly, but steadily, broadens the recognized scope of social interests in the utilization of things. . . .

To one seeing history through the glasses of religion, these changes may seem to evidence increasing embodiments of the golden rule. To one thinking in terms of political and economic ideologies, they are likely to be labeled evidences of "social enlightenment," or of "creeping socialism" or even of "communistic infiltration," according to the individual's assumed definitions and retained or acquired prejudices. With slight attention to words or labels, time marches on toward new adjustments between individualism and the social interests.

The process involves not only the accommodation between the right of the owner and the interests of the general public in his use of this property, but involves also an accommodation between the right of the owner and the right of individuals who are parties with him in consensual transactions relating to the use of the property. Accordingly substantial alterations have been made as between a landlord and his tenant. *See* Reste Realty Corp. v. Cooper, 251 A.2d 268 (N.J. 1969). . . .

The argument in this case understandably included the question whether the migrant worker should be deemed to be a tenant and thus entitled to the tenant's right to receive visitors, or whether his residence on the employer's property should be deemed to be merely incidental and in aid of his employment, and hence to involve no possessory interest in the realty. . . . We see no profit in trying to decide upon a conventional category and then forcing the present subject into it. . . . The quest is for a fair adjustment of the competing needs of the parties, in the light of the realities of the relationship between the migrant worker and the operator of the housing facility.

Thus approaching the case, we find it unthinkable that the farmer-employer can assert a right to isolate the migrant worker in any respect significant for the worker's well-being. The farmer, of course, is entitled to pursue his farming activities without interference, and this defendants readily concede. But we see no legitimate need for a right in the farmer to deny the worker the opportunity for aid available from federal, State, or local services, or from recognized charitable groups seeking to assist him. Hence representatives of these agencies and organizations may enter upon the premises to seek out the worker at his living quarters. So, too, the migrant worker must be allowed to receive visitors there of his own choice, so long as there is no behavior hurtful to others, and members of the press may not be denied reasonable access to workers who do not object to seeing them.

It is not our purpose to open the employer's premises to the general public if in fact the employer himself has not done so. We do not say, for example, that solicitors or peddlers of all kinds may enter on their own; we may assume for the present that the employer may regulate their entry or bar them, at least if the employer's purpose is not to gain a commercial advantage for himself or if the regulation does not deprive the migrant worker of practical access to things he needs.

And we are mindful of the employer's interest in his own and in his employees' security. Hence he may reasonably require a visitor to identify himself, and also to state his general purpose if the migrant worker has not already informed him that the visitor is expected. But the employer may not deny the worker his privacy or interfere with his opportunity to live with dignity and to enjoy associations customary among our citizens. These rights are too fundamental to be denied on the basis of an interest in real property and too fragile to be left to the unequal bargaining strength of the parties.

It follows that defendants here invaded no possessory right of the farmer-employer. Their conduct was therefore beyond the reach of the trespass statute. The judgments are accordingly reversed and the matters remanded to the County Court with directions to enter judgments of acquittal.

Notes and Questions

1. If Tedesco wants to protect his right to exclude anyone except his employees and his invitees from his farm, is there any way he can legally do that? Would it make sense for him to arrange for housing off his premises or to stop providing housing altogether? Is the court's holding limited to situations where the workers are housed on the premises? Should it be?

2. Compare the policy concerns weighed by the court in *State v. Shack* with those in *Jacque v. Steenberg*. How much weight did the court give to Tedesco's interest in controlling access to his land, "one of the most essential sticks in the bundle" according to the *Jacque* court? How much to society's interest in preserving the integrity of the legal system? What countervailing interests persuaded the court to move away from the clear boundary-crossing line usually applied in trespass actions?

3. In *Hinman v. Pacific Air Lines Transport Corp.*, 84 F.2d 755 (9th Cir. 1936), the court refused to apply the ancient doctrine that ownership of land extends from the top of the sky to the center of the earth, known as the "ad coelum" doctrine, to allow a landowner to enjoin or obtain damages for trespass by airplanes flying over the land without proof of actual damage to the land.

> The air, like the sea, is by its nature incapable of private ownership, except in so far as one may actually use it. . . . When it is said that man owns, or may own, to the heavens, that merely means that no one can acquire a right to the space above him that will limit him in whatever use he can make of it as a part of his enjoyment of the land. To this extent his title to the air is paramount. No other person can acquire any title or exclusive right to any space above him. . . . It would be, and is, utterly impracticable and would lead to endless confusion, if the law should uphold attempts of landowners to stake out, or assert claims to definite, unused spaces in the air in order to protect some contemplated future use of it. . . . We cannot shut our eyes to the practical result of legal recognition of the asserted claims of appellants herein, for it leads to a legal implication to the effect that any use of airspace

above the surface owner of land, without his consent would be a trespass either by the operator of an airplane or a radio operator. We will not foist any such chimerical concept of property rights upon the jurisprudence of this country. . . .

The case differs from the usual case of enjoining a trespass. Ordinarily, if a trespass is committed upon land, the plaintiff is entitled to at least nominal damages without proving or alleging any actual damage. In the instant case, traversing the airspace above appellants' land is not, of itself, a trespass at all, but it is a lawful act unless it is done under circumstances which will cause injury to appellants' possession.

4. The extent of the right to exclude is the subject of both litigation and legislation. Civil rights statutes severely limit the ability of landowners to refuse to rent or sell to people on the basis of their race, religion, sex, and a variety of other grounds, as you will see in Chapter 10. Public accommodations statutes similarly limit the ability of business establishments open to the public to discriminate against would-be patrons. In *Uston v. Resorts International Hotel, Inc.*, 445 A.2d 370 (N.J. 1982), the New Jersey Supreme Court held that a casino had no right to exclude a card-counting blackjack player (card counting significantly increases the player's chances of beating the house). Constitutionally protected free speech rights may limit the rights of shopping centers to exclude people who want to gather signatures on political petitions. *See Robins v. Pruneyard Shopping Center*, 592 P.2d 341 (Cal. 1979); *Pruneyard Shopping Center v. Robins*, 447 U.S. 74 (1980). Private universities, too, may be required to allow the distribution of political literature on campus. *See State v. Schmid*, 423 A.2d 615 (N.J. 1980); *Commonwealth v. Tate*, 432 A.2d 1382 (Pa. 1981).

5. There is considerable disagreement among contemporary legal theorists on the extent of the right to exclude, ranging from Richard A. Epstein to Joseph W. Singer. Epstein argues for a nearly absolute right to exclude on the basis that absolute rights establish the basis for market transactions, and that, so long as there are a sufficient number of buyers and sellers, market forces will check abuse. *See Rights and "Rights Talk"* (Book Review), 105 Harv. L. Rev. 1106 (1992); *Property and Necessity*, 13 Harv. J.L. & Pub. Pol'y 2 (1990). Singer, by contrast, argues that a landowner's rights should not include the right to exclude persons who have developed reliance interests in continued access to the property because of relationships with the landowner. In his view, property rights must be redistributed from owners to nonowners to protect those who are vulnerable. *See The Reliance Interest in Property*, 40 Stan. L. Rev. 611 (1988).

Note, however, that the disagreements are not about the existence of a right to exclude — both the court in *State v. Shack* and Professor Singer recognize that the property owner has the right to exclude strangers who have no legitimate reasons to be on the property. No one argues that land, other than limited amounts of "public land," should be open to all. Do you see why? For a far-ranging analysis of land arrangements across history and cultures, see Robert C. Ellickson, *Property in Land*, 102 Yale L.J. 1315 (1993). Ellickson finds that every society produces some combination of property controlled by an individual or household with property that is shared and controlled by somewhat larger groups, property shared by an entire community, and property that is open to all (open-access property).

Blackstone and the Right to Exclude

Sir William Blackstone (1723-1780), the first Professor of English Law at an English university (Oxford, 1758-1766), may be the best known English or American writer on the law. His four-volume *Commentaries on the Laws of England*, published between 1765 and 1769, was the first accessible general treatment of English law and met with immediate success. In 1771, an edition was printed in the American colonies, and reissued nearly every two years thereafter, making it the most available book on the law. Blackstone was particularly influential in the post-revolutionary period in the United States, not only because it was one of the few available relatively comprehensive compilations of law in English, but because it could be cited without violating statutory bans on citation of King's and Queen's Bench cases. Frontier lawyers are said to have carried a copy in their saddlebags.[4]

We began this book with Blackstone's widely quoted description of property as "that sole and despotic dominion which one man claims and exercises over the external things of the world, in total exclusion of the right of any other individual in the universe." Although few modern American scholars actually read much of Blackstone, the idea that property is a right of absolute dominion and exclusion continues to intrigue and provoke people who think about property.

CANONS OF PROPERTY TALK, OR BLACKSTONE'S ANXIETY
Carol M. Rose, 108 Yale L.J. 601, 603-06 (1998)

When Blackstone described property as exclusive dominion, he may have had little idea of the resonance his words would have for later writers on property. Indeed, the notion of property as exclusive dominion—a notion to which I will refer as the Exclusivity Axiom—is far from self-evident, and it was even less self-evident when Blackstone wrote these lines. The axiom put aside the earlier medieval traditions in which property ownership had been hemmed in by intricate webs of military and other obligations; it ignored the family ties encapsulated in such devices as the entailed fee; and it ignored as well the general neighborly responsibilities of riparian and nuisance law. Blackstone himself was thoroughly aware of these pervasive and serious qualifications of exclusive dominion. Indeed, he discussed them at great length, particularly with respect to the feudal system and its later permutations. Moreover . . . Blackstone asserted that the law properly recognizes claims by the destitute to some minimal assistance from those who are more prosperous. This position links Blackstone to a traditional view tying property to social and political obligation—a view that clearly creates some tension with the idea of property as absolute or exclusive dominion. Hence it might be best to conclude that for Blackstone, the Exclusivity Axiom was in a sense a trope, a rhetorical figure describing an extreme or ideal type rather than reality.

---

4. Two works assessing Blackstone's impact in the United States are Albert W. Alschuler, *Rediscovering Blackstone*, 145 U. Pa. L. Rev. 1 (1996), and Dennis R. Nolan, *Sir William Blackstone and the New American Republic: A Study of Intellectual Impact*, 51 N.Y.U. L. Rev. 731 (1976).

Taken as a trope, however, the Exclusivity Axiom is powerfully suggestive. A right to exclude would not necessarily mean that property owners *do* exclude others; it would mean only that they can decide whether to exclude or not. This decisionmaking authority is what makes property a central libertarian value: The property owner has a small domain of complete mastery, complete self-direction, and complete protection from the whims of others. This authority is also what makes property so important in utilitarian thinking. The right to exclude means that an owner is solely responsible for the fate of her assets. Thus, whether she chooses to hold, share, or trade those assets, she has good reason to make her decisions prudently. In identifying property with the right to exclude, then, Blackstone struck a central nerve in modern discussion of property, and meditations, transmutations, and fulminations on the theme of exclusivity continue to run through modern cases and commentaries.

2.   *Protecting the Use and Enjoyment of Land: Private Nuisance*

Nuisances can be either public or private, or both. Private nuisances are activities that interfere with use and enjoyment of particular land or other property. Public nuisances are activities that interfere with rights of the public, like blocking roads, disturbing neighborhoods with gang or drug activities, polluting waterways, and the like. Suits to abate public nuisances are brought by public authorities. If a public nuisance inflicts special harm on private property, suit may be brought both by a public authority and the owner of the private property. Typical private nuisance cases involve spite fights between neighbors and incompatible uses of land. We look at spite cases in this chapter, but postpone incompatible land use cases until Chapter 11.

RATTIGAN v. WILE

Supreme Judicial Court of Massachusetts
841 N.E.2d 680 (2006)

COWIN, J. We conclude in this appeal that activities on one's property that create or maintain unreasonable aesthetic conditions for neighbors are actionable as a private nuisance. . . . The judge properly awarded damages and issued an injunction, although we modify both slightly. . . .

This matter involves two adjacent, prime oceanfront parcels located . . . [in] an affluent residential section of the city of Beverly. Both properties directly abut a sandy beach and enjoy commanding views of the water. One plot is owned by the plaintiffs, John Rattigan and Jeffrey Horvitz,[4] while the other is owned by the defendant, Evan Wile. The property owned by the plaintiffs is commonly known as Edgewater and contains a luxurious residence, pool, and manicured grounds. The parcel owned by the defendant consists of approximately 2.9 acres of undeveloped land. The defendant's only land access is by right of way to West Street over land owned by the plaintiffs.

---

4.   Rattigan, as trustee for the Edgewater House Trust, is the title owner of the property, which he holds for the benefit of Jeffrey Horvitz, who resides there with his family.

The plaintiffs purchased Edgewater at foreclosure auction in 1991. The next year the adjoining vacant property was also sold at foreclosure auction. The defendant outbid Horvitz for the parcel, and purchased with plans to build a home. Herewith began the problems.

Rattigan subsequently brought actions on behalf of the Edgewater House Trust in the Land Court in or around 1992, seeking determinations that the defendant did not enjoy a right of way through Edgewater and that the defendant's land was not buildable under Beverly zoning bylaws. These suits were ultimately unsuccessful and the defendant apparently regarded them, and other supplications to city officials that met with mixed success, as a form of "harassment." After Rattigan and Horvitz filed a successful challenge to the defendant's building permit, the defendant embarked on a campaign of retaliation in August, 1999.

Between August, 1999, and July, 2003, the defendant placed a number of unusual objects at the edge of his lot, immediately adjacent to the boundary with the Edgewater property. The judge found that although the defendant, who is a building contractor, was undoubtedly aware that final resolution of the dispute concerning his building permit was hardly imminent, he dumped construction debris along the boundary line with Edgewater — broken concrete blocks, used pipe, and rusted metal components including a crane bucket. Later, the defendant brought onto the boundary a "gigantic, red, metal ocean container . . . use[d] to ship freight."

When Horvitz added barriers to shield those on his property from viewing the objects, first a few shrubs and then a six foot trellis fence (the maximum he believed he could build), the defendant "moved the construction debris inexplicably" so that the materials continued to be prominently in view. For example, after Horvitz erected the fence, the defendant responded "almost immediately" by moving "the largest pieces of the debris," including the crane bucket, to the top of the red container so that they would remain visible. On a portion of the boundary of his property not protected by visual barriers, the defendant placed the detached bed of a pick-up truck that at one point held a large truck tire, and an unusual "wire frame or rack" from which hung a yellow detergent bottle and several plastic figures including a duck, a goose, and an owl. . . .

[S]oon after Horvitz built a section of fence to shield swimmers at Edgewater's pool from apparent catcalls by individuals on the defendant's lot, the defendant responded by moving to his side of the fence "a trailer, like an office trailer . . . on a construction site," and elevating it on cinder blocks "so that the top windows loomed above the trellis fence." In 2001 and 2002, the defendant placed several portable toilets near the pool, so close that a person could not walk between the toilets and the Edgewater fence. The toilets generated an offensive odor that wafted over the pool. In the summer of 2002, the defendant placed a fifteen foot white and yellow striped tent also within a few feet of the Edgewater pool area, "obliterating any view and light from that direction." The city quickly ordered removal of the tent.

The judge found that there was no "logical explanation" for the defendant's failure to locate elsewhere many of the objects that appeared along Edgewater's boundary, except to "annoy, harass or otherwise create an offensive, harmful condition." The defendant's parcel was "a huge lot with multiple" locations where these items could have been placed. . . .

Activity on the lot was also disconcerting. On occasions in the summers of 2001 and 2002, the defendant invited 150 to 200 people from a local youth center to a beach party. The defendant himself did not attend. The judge concluded that the invitation was "not born of a desire to be a charitable citizen in Beverly but, rather, was part of the campaign that was being waged against the Horvitzes to create a difficult and destructive neighborhood." The defendant intended the outing to be a recurring event but it was discontinued by the city because it was "disturbing the peace."

Between 1999 and 2002, the defendant, who is a licensed commercial helicopter pilot, used his property as a heliport. . . . On "more than one" of the many helicopter touchdowns and liftoffs, the helicopter's blades propelled small debris onto the Edgewater property; on one occasion, debris struck Horvitz's stepson, and on another, debris struck Horvitz's youngest daughter. By order of the Superior Court prior to trial, the defendant ceased landing on the plot but continued overflights to "check the property."

The plaintiffs filed this action on February 14, 2001, and in July, 2001, following a hearing, obtained a preliminary injunction that enjoined the defendant from, among other things, flying his helicopter near Edgewater and "committing . . . acts . . . intended to harass . . . Horvitz, his family, his employees or his guests." Prior to trial, the defendant was twice adjudged to be in contempt of the injunction . . . .

On July 29, 2003, after a jury-waived trial, a judge of the Superior Court found that the defendant had created an actionable nuisance, and determined that the plaintiffs could recover for costs of abatement and temporary diminishment of the value of Edgewater. The judge credited testimony of an expert appraiser that the potential rental value of Edgewater for the thirteen weeks of the summer rental season declined from $8,000 per week to $2,000 per week as a result of the conditions that were caused by the defendant's activities. The judge awarded damages for each week of the summer rental seasons of 1999, 2000, 2001, 2002, and 2003, an aggregate of sixty-five weeks, totaling $390,000. In addition, the judge awarded damages of $19,200 for costs incurred installing the trellis fence. With interest, total recovery amounted to $532,035.05. The judge also issued a broad injunction, which she read from the bench:

> "The defendant shall be permanently enjoined from doing anything or knowingly causing and/or permitting any activity to take place on or about his property that harasses plaintiff [Horvitz], his family or guests, or to commit, cause or permit any acts of harassment against plaintiff [Horvitz] or his family or guests. Harassment shall include any act that has the effect of causing substantial worry or annoyance or causing substantial offense to plaintiff [Horvitz], his family or other persons using and/or occupying the plaintiff's property. And this shall include the placement of objects, such as the tent, construction debris, [and] the trailer. This shall include not permitting large gatherings of children, people Mr. Wile doesn't even know . . . .
>
> "The defendant shall within ten days clear any and all objects from, other than currently growing plant material, an area not less than twenty feet from all boundaries of the plaintiff's property. Further, there shall remain, other than currently growing plant material, nothing taller than six feet within an area of not less than forty feet from all boundaries of the plaintiff's property. The defendant shall thereafter allow nothing to be placed on [the] defendant's property which violates the provision in this paragraph unless and until such time as [the] defendant obtains

a valid building permit for any proposed structure on the defendant's land and which permit is no longer able to be subject to challenge or appeal or until he obtains authorization from a court of competent jurisdiction."[12]

The defendant appealed and we transferred the case to this court on our own motion.

Nuisance. We accept the trial judge's findings of fact absent clear error, but whether the plaintiffs met their burden on the claim of private nuisance is a question of law. . . .

Our cases impose a heavy burden on the plaintiffs in such an action. The law of nuisance "does not concern itself with trifles, or seek to remedy all the petty annoyances of everyday life in a civilized community." W.L. Prosser & W.P. Keeton, *Torts* § 88 (5th ed. 1984). See, e.g., Wade v. Miller, 188 Mass. 6 (1905) ("Although the odor arising from the hen houses and yard, which at times was accompanied by the characteristic cry made by their occupants, may have been unpleasant," there was no actionable nuisance).

> "Life in organized society and especially in populous communities involves an unavoidable clash of individual interests. Practically all human activities unless carried on in a wilderness interfere to some extent with others . . . . Liability for damages is imposed [only] in those cases in which the harm or risk to one is greater than he ought to be required to bear under the circumstances, at least without compensation."

Restatement (Second) of Torts § 822 comment *g* (1979). For this action to succeed, the plaintiffs must have shown that the defendant caused "a substantial and unreasonable interference with the use and enjoyment of the property" of the plaintiff.[13] . . . The injury or annoyance must have substantially interfered "with the ordinary comfort . . . of human existence," or have been substantially detrimental to the "reasonable use or value of the property." . . .

The general rule is that a trier of fact may find an intentional invasion of another's interest in the use and enjoyment of land to be unreasonable if the "gravity of the harm" caused thereby "outweighs the utility" of the actor's conduct.[14] Restatement (Second) of Torts § 826(a). . . . Where an actor's "sole purpose" "is to annoy and harm his neighbor," the law recognizes no utility. Restatement (Second) of Torts § 829(a) & comment *c*. . . . Such an action is unreasonable. Every landowner "is bound to use his own property in such a manner as not to injure the property of another, or the reasonable and proper enjoyment of it." Wesson v. Washburn Iron Co., 95 Mass. 95 (1866).

A trier of fact may also find a landowner's conduct to be unreasonable if the harm to a neighbor is substantial and "it would be practicable for the actor

---

12. Subsequent to the injunction, the defendant was again adjudged in contempt, and assessed a fine and attorney's fees. Resolution of another subsequent complaint of contempt is not reflected in the record.

13. The requirement that the interference with the use of land be "unreasonable" and "substantial" helps to distinguish nuisance from trespass, which may be actionable regardless of whether the conduct is reasonable or the harm measurable. . . . Restatement (Second) of Torts § 821D comment *d* (1979).

14. This rule applies to intentional conduct. The judge found that the defendant's conduct was intentional, and the defendant does not argue otherwise.

to avoid the harm in whole or part without undue hardship." Restatement (Second) of Torts § 830 [comments *c* and *i*]:

> "The question is not whether the activity itself is an improper, unsuitable or illegal thing to do in the place where it is being carried on, but whether the actor is carrying it on in a careful manner or at a proper time. The problem is whether the actor could effectively and profitably achieve his main objective in such a way that the harm to others would be substantially reduced or eliminated." . . . "The one whose conduct causes the invasion may be able to reduce or eliminate the harm without undue hardship, and if so, he is the one to do the avoiding."

In this case, the judge found that the defendant's placement of items near the plaintiffs' property was intended to harass his neighbors and that the helicopter landings were made in disregard of public safety. Even if the defendant had persuaded the judge that there was a mixed purpose to his actions, she also found with respect to many of the activities that the defendant's goals could have been accomplished without undue hardship in a manner that substantially reduced or eliminated the impact on Edgewater—for example, by utilizing areas of the expansive undeveloped lot not immediately adjacent to the plaintiffs' property.[15] It is obviously worthy of weight in the fact-finding calculus that this campaign was apparently waged in retaliation for the plaintiffs' recourse to legal process in the underlying dispute.

The question whether the defendant's activities interfered with and substantially harmed the plaintiffs' use and enjoyment of Edgewater, to the extent that a tort remedy is available, is a closer one. The defendant concedes that placement of the portable toilets and use of the helicopter on his land were traditional, actionable invasions. . . . However, he claims that these invasions existed during only a portion of the extended period for which the judge granted nuisance damages. He argues that as to the remainder of the period, for which only visual conditions persisted, there was no substantial, continuing "invasion of another's interest in the private use and enjoyment of land." . . .

We interpret broadly one's right to use and enjoy his or her land. . . . "Nuisances at common law frequently arise from offensive sights, sounds or smells." General Outdoor Advertising Co. v. Department of Pub. Works, 289 Mass. 149 (1935). An actor need not "directly damage the land or prevent its use in order to constitute a nuisance." . . . The landowner's interest "comprehends the pleasure, comfort and enjoyment that a person normally derives from the occupancy of land." Restatement (Second) of Torts, at § 821D comment *b*. This interest is informed by "[t]he location, character and habits of the particular community." *Id.* at § 821F comment *e.* . . . "[C]ontinuance or recurrence of the interference" will also factor in the determination. Restatement (Second) of Torts, at § 821F comment *g.* See Stodder v. Rosen Talking Mach. Co., 241 Mass. 245 (1922), *S.C.,* 247 Mass. 60 (1923) (talking machine's "continuous and monotonous playing of piece after piece" "substantially all day," on most days, actionable).

---

15.   It is the timing of the defendant's activities and the absence of any legitimate purpose that render the present case quite unlike the ordinary dispute in which the aesthetic or value preferences of neighbors merely differ. See Restatement (Second) of Torts, at § 828(a) (factoring social value of conduct).

"If normal persons living in the community would regard the invasion in question as definitely offensive, seriously annoying or intolerable, then the invasion [suffices]. If normal persons in that locality would not be substantially annoyed or disturbed by the situation, then the invasion is not [actionable], even though the idiosyncracies of the particular plaintiff may make it unendurable to him." Restatement (Second) of Torts, at § 821F comment *d.* These are all issues of fact, . . . and it is often difficult for a trier of fact to determine whether an invasion is sufficiently substantial that an action in nuisance may succeed. See W.L. Prosser & W.F. Keeton, *Torts,* at § 88 . . . .

In the present case, the trial judge found that the community was residential and implicitly intolerant of the activities in which the defendant engaged. These findings were supported by expert opinion to the effect that one who might otherwise have rented Edgewater, if it had been offered for rent, would probably have declined to do so in light of the defendant's activities. The evidence also showed that the defendant's interferences continued for several years. Damages were ascertainable. See W.L. Prosser & W.P. Keeton, *Torts,* at § 88 ("Probably a good working rule would be that the annoyance cannot amount to unreasonable interference until it results in a depreciation in the market or rental value of the land"). . . . The judge's findings were not clearly erroneous.

Courts in other jurisdictions have reached similar conclusions. For example, in Statler v. Catalano, 167 Ill. App. 3d 397 . . . (1988), the court affirmed nuisance damages on evidence that the defendants accumulated garbage for five years on the edge of their property nearest that of the plaintiffs, to annoy the latter, and occasionally shot bullets through the plaintiffs' windows; strategically positioned shooting trophies to taunt the plaintiffs; and intentionally reduced the level of a shared body of water. Likewise, in Mark v. State Dep't of Fish & Wildlife, 158 Or. App. 355 (1999), *S.C.,* 191 Or. App. 563 (2004), the court concluded that a finding of nuisance was permissible from evidence of "uncontrolled and intrusive" human nudity at the defendants' wildlife area, occurring in a location immediately around the plaintiffs' property. The court determined that a finding of nuisance would have been permissible even in the absence of evidence of a sexual component to the activity (which was a nuisance at common law), although this too was shown. See Kirkwood v. Finegan, 95 Mich. 543 (1893) ("character and style" of fence made clear it was constructed in spite and thus actionable in nuisance); Lee's Summit v. Browning, 722 S.W.2d 114 (Mo. Ct. App. 1986) (. . . automobile salvage yard was nuisance in part because salvage material was visible from street); Yeager v. Traylor, 306 Pa. 530 (1932) (proposed parking garage abutting residences of "expensive character" was nuisance that could be abated, in part, by use of screen to hide its "unsightly appearance"); Foley v. Harris, 223 Va. 20 (1982) (sight of collection of several "junked . . . old, battered" automobiles actionable in nuisance); Martin v. Williams, 141 W. Va. 595 (1956) (used car lot in residential neighborhood actionable in nuisance based, in part, on unsightliness).

Other courts forbid actions in nuisance that are based solely on unsightly conditions. . . . These courts distinguish cases where "more" than visually offensive conditions were present. . . . However, the modern trend is toward recognition that aesthetic considerations may legitimately generate public and private concern. . . . This court long ago decided that aesthetic considerations, standing alone, could support limitations on the use of land. . . . Other courts have determined that the common law of nuisance permits suit on such incorporeal, value-based interferences as, among other things, disagreeable odors, obnoxious sounds, unreasonable illumination, disadvantageous blocking of light and air, and even undesired social influences from brothels, saloons, and gambling parlors. See Nagle, *Moral Nuisances*, 50 Emory L.J. 265 (2001); Coletta, *The Case for Aesthetic Nuisance: Rethinking Traditional Judicial Attitudes*, 48 Ohio St. L.J. 141 (1987). The invasion here was a composite of unpleasant odors, sounds, and visual conditions, and on this record the plaintiff established that the defendant's actions constituted a nuisance.

Damages. The defendant also advances several arguments with respect to the basis and magnitude of the damage award. He contends that diminution of rental value was an inappropriate measure of damages because the plaintiff never attempted to rent Edgewater. We disagree.

"The general rule for measuring property damage is diminution in market value." . . . "[W]here damage to real property is not permanent, the measure of recovery is the reasonable expense of repairing the injury plus the intervening loss of rental value for the period reasonably needed to repair the injury." . . . Diminution in rental value is an injury for which the occupant of the property at the time of the interference may recover. . . .

The judge also awarded $19,200, representing the cost of the trellis fence built by Horvitz as a barrier. The defendant argues that because the fence did not succeed in eliminating the defendant's interference with Edgewater, recovery of its cost was improper. However, the appropriate inquiry is whether, in the circumstances, the cost incurred for the fence was a reasonable response to the defendant's behavior. . . . That is not measured by whether the fence actually succeeded in its purpose, particularly when the defendant took action to thwart it.

The defendant also objects to the award of damages for those periods during which there was no evidence of nuisance and for those periods during which the judge deemed the interference insignificant. Damages were assessed for all thirteen weeks of the summer rental season of 1999, although the defendant began his campaign of harassment only in August of that year. In addition, the judge issued her findings of fact and rulings of law on July 29, 2003, and the defendant was ordered to remove the offending objects within ten days, but damages were nonetheless awarded for all of August, 2003. The plaintiff does not expressly contend otherwise. Thus, we are satisfied that the period for which damages are awarded should be reduced from sixty-five weeks to fifty-three weeks . . . . Thus, the rental value portion of the damage award should be reduced correspondingly from $390,000 to $318,000.

Finally, the defendant argues that the magnitude of the damage award was "unprecedented" and did not take into account the fact that many of his offensive activities were sporadic and did not continue during the entire period for which damages were awarded. . . . Nevertheless, we are satisfied that the award was supported at trial by duly qualified expert opinion . . . and flowed from evidence of a single, hostile, continuous, four-year campaign of interference with the use and enjoyment of the plaintiffs' valuable real estate. There was no error. . . .

Injunction. Given the defendant's creativity in persisting with his campaign of nuisance, the expansive nature of the injunction issued by the trial judge was understandable. The judge handled a difficult case well. Nevertheless, the defendant argues, and we agree, that the breadth of the injunction and the emphasis on the subjective effects of the defendant's actions raise concern that it may chill wholly legitimate uses of the almost three acre property. For example, the injunction prohibited any act that would cause "substantial worry" to the plaintiffs, but given the history between the parties, it appears likely that even the most reasonable of the defendant's actions might cause the plaintiffs consternation. Thus, we make minor amendments so that the injunction provides as follows.

> The defendant is permanently enjoined from unreasonably interfering with the use and enjoyment of the plaintiffs' property. Without limiting the scope of the foregoing prohibition, the defendant shall not leave unattended any objects more than six feet in height within forty feet of the plaintiffs' boundary line, such as tents, portable toilets, construction and industrial materials, trailers, and warning signs, except reasonable vegetation. The defendant shall not operate, or cause to be operated, a helicopter on his property or within the zone of interest above the property.[18] So long as the above provisions are not violated, the defendant shall not be enjoined from hosting gatherings on his property that he personally attends. This injunction is not intended to impede the defendant's ability to build on the property at issue; if he obtains lawful authority to build, he may seek modification of this injunction in the Superior Court.

Conclusion. . . . [J]udgment for the plaintiff is to be entered in the amount of $337,200 ($318,000 in diminished rental value and the $19,200 cost of the fence) plus interest. The injunction is modified as set forth above.

Notes and Questions

1. This litigation did not end the troubles between Wile and the Horvitzes. In *Horvitz v. Wile*, 956 N.E.2d 788 (Mass. Ct. App. 2011), the court affirmed a contempt award of $9,000 damages and $14,000 in attorneys' fees against Wile.

2. Injunctions are equitable remedies, which may be withheld if the party wronged has not acted equitably. In *Cline v. Berg*, 639 S.E.2d 231 (Va. 2007), for example, the court reversed an order enjoining removal of a 32-foot high, 200-foot long fence that interfered with the neighbor's use and enjoyment because the neighbor lacked clean hands. The fence was built because the neighbor installed surveillance cameras, motion sensors, and flood lights that intermittently lit up and tracked movements of people on defendants' property.

3. Trees planted for the purpose of annoying the neighbors may be enjoined as private nuisances. *See, e.g., Peters v. O'Leary*, 30 A.3d 825 (Me. 2011).

---

18.   See United States v. Causby, 328 U.S. 256 (1946) (regular operation of military aircraft eighty-three feet above private land implicated landowner interests); Burnham v. Beverly Airways, Inc., 311 Mass. 628 (1942) (operation of aircraft below normal limit of "navigable air space" may implicate landowner rights). . . .

WERNKE v. HALAS
Court of Appeals of Indiana
600 N.E.2d 117 (1992)

BAKER, Judge. America's wise and thoughtful poet laureate, Robert Frost, once wrote that "good fences make good neighbors." Lamentably, not everyone has read Frost.

In this private nuisance action, defendant-appellant Wernke challenges the trial court's grant of summary judgment in favor of . . . plaintiff-appellees John and Karen Halas, [and] . . . appeals the trial court's subsequent award of compensatory damages, punitive damages, and attorney fees . . . .

The facts taken in the light most favorable to . . . Wernke, reveal he and the Halases are next door neighbors, with abutting side yards. The Peacock family owns the other lot abutting Wernke's property. In 1990, after a period of mounting neighborhood tension over the fate of a tree growing astride the common Wernke-Halas-Peacock boundary . . . Wernke built a privacy fence facing the Halas property. The fence is constructed of vertically placed boards . . . no more than six feet tall. On the side . . . facing the Halases, Wernke placed some vinyl strips and a license plate over some of the cracks between the boards. He also attached a section of orange plastic construction fencing to the Halas side of the fence. The orange fencing ran almost the length of the board fence and was approximately five feet tall.

Wernke placed support posts sunken in concrete at regular intervals along the fence line. One day, as Wernke's work on the fence was progressing, vandals scrawled "Fuck J.H.," "Fuck R.P.," and "D. Head" into the wet concrete of a support post. No part of the concrete, the post, or the fence as a whole encroached upon any . . . neighbors' property.

Prior to Wernke's erection of the fence, the Peacocks nailed a toilet seat to a tree facing Wernke's yard. The Peacocks removed the seat after several months, and Wernke, in a display of equal taste, set up his own toilet seat, mounting the seat and its lid on a piece of plywood placed atop a post overlooking his neighbors' land. A brown spot, alleged by the Halases to represent human excrement, was painted on the plywood within the ring inscribed by the seat. Like the fence, the toilet rested entirely on Wernke's property.

The Halases filed suit . . . . On the advice of his attorney, Wernke removed the license plate from the fence, and the toilet and graffiti prior to the hearing on the Halases' motion for summary judgment. After the . . . hearing, the judge found as a matter of law that the toilet, the graffiti, and the fence constituted a nuisance. He therefore ordered the orange fencing and the vinyl strips removed, and Wernke complied.

Several weeks after summary judgment was entered, the court held a damages hearing. The Halases were awarded $5,600 for the loss in the rental value of their property during the period the graffiti, the toilet and the objectionable portions of the fence were visible, $2,400 for the discomfort and annoyance they suffered, $5,000 in punitive damages, and $3,937.50 in attorney fees. . . .

In Indiana, nuisances are defined by statute. IND. CODE 34-1-52-1 provides:

Whatever is injurious to health, or indecent, or offensive to the senses, or an obstruction to the free use of property, so as essentially to interfere with the comfortable enjoyment of life or property, is a nuisance, and the subject of an action.

"There is perhaps no more impenetrable jungle in the entire law than that which surrounds the word ' nuisance'." W. Prosser and W. Keeton, *Prosser and Keeton on Torts*, § 86 (5th ed. 1989). Our statutory language is therefore necessarily broad, but the general tenets of nuisance law are clear.

Nuisances may be either public or private. A public nuisance is one which affects an entire neighborhood or community, while a private nuisance affects only a single person or a determinate number of people. . . . The essence of a private nuisance is the use of property to the detriment of the use and enjoyment of another's property. . . .

Both public and private nuisances are further subdivided into nuisances *per se*, or nuisances at law, and nuisances *per accidens*, or nuisances in fact. "A nuisance *per se*, as the term implies, is that which is a nuisance in itself, and which, therefore, cannot be so conducted or maintained as to be lawfully carried on or permitted to exist." . . . Thus, for example, a house of prostitution and an obstruction that encroaches on the right-of-way of a public highway are nuisances *per se*. . . . On the other hand, an otherwise lawful use may become a nuisance *per accidens* by virtue of the circumstances surrounding the use. . . .

. . . [T]he determination that something is a nuisance *per se* is a question of law for the court, . . . and the determination "whether that which is not in itself a nuisance is a nuisance in fact" is a question for the jury or the judge as trier of fact. . . . The latter determination is to be made by the trier of fact in light of all the surrounding facts and circumstances. . . . The dispositive question "is whether the thing complained of produces such a condition as in the judgment of reasonable persons is naturally productive of actual physical discomfort to persons of ordinary sensibility, tastes, and habits." Wendt v. Kerkhof, 594 N.E.2d 795 (Ind. App. 1992).

The Fence[3]

In Indiana, at common law, a landowner had no nuisance claim against an adjacent landowner for erection of a fence that did not encroach on the landowner's property. Giller v. West, 69 N.E. 548 (Ind. 1904). The rule applied regardless of the adjacent landowner's motive in erecting the fence and regardless of the ugliness of the fence. . . .

Five years after *Giller*, in 1909, the legislature modified the common law. IND. CODE 32-10-10-1 provides "[a]ny fence or other structure in the nature of a fence unnecessarily exceeding six feet (6') in height, maliciously erected or maintained for the purpose of annoying the owners or occupants of adjoining property, shall be deemed a nuisance." . . .

Although these statutes provide a landowner aggrieved by an alleged spite fence with the full range of nuisance actions and remedies, they are in derogation of the common law, and must therefore be strictly construed. . . . Because the legislature framed the statute to exclude fences six feet in height or less from its ambit, . . . the common law rule of *Giller* still controls in cases involving those fences.

---

3. Although all the items the Halases complained of have been abated, we refer to them in the present tense for clarity.

The fence here, as the parties agree, is no more than six feet tall. Therefore, regardless of how unsightly the fence may be . . . it cannot be a nuisance. . . . Indeed . . . Wernke is entitled to judgment as a matter of law.

The Toilet

In Indiana, a plaintiff who has proved a *per accidens* nuisance may recover aesthetic damages. . . . These are damages for the "annoyance, discomfort, and inconvenience" caused by the nuisance. . . . It does not follow, however, that a use or structure may constitute a nuisance merely on the basis of displeasing aesthetics.

On the contrary, it is well-settled throughout this country that, standing alone, unsightliness, or lack of aesthetic virtue, does not constitute a private nuisance. . . .[6] Instead, aesthetics are the province of restrictive covenants, . . . and this is as it should be.

Aesthetic values are inherently subjective; if landowners in a given neighborhood or development wish to contract among themselves for the appearance of their homes, the courts stand ready, within well-settled limits, to provide enforcement. It would require a great leap of logic, however, to say that courts themselves should be the arbiters of proper aesthetics and good taste, and it is a leap we are unwilling to make. As the Colorado Supreme Court eloquently stated, "[i]n our populous society, the courts cannot be available to enjoin an activity solely because it causes some aesthetic discomfort or annoyance. Given our myriad and disparate tastes, life styles, mores, and attitudes, the availability of a judicial remedy for such complaints would cause inexorable confusion." Green v. Castle Concrete Co., 181 Colo. 309 (1973).

In the present case, the evidence concerning the toilet seat is undisputed. . . . Wernke claimed the entire contraption was a bird house, and indeed, three small boxes with holes suitable for birds surround the frame. It may be the ugliest bird house in Indiana, or it may merely be a toilet seat on a post. The distinction is irrelevant, however; Wernke's tasteless decoration is merely an aesthetic annoyance, and we are not engaged in the incommodious task of judging aesthetics. . . . [B]ecause the evidence is undisputed, Wernke, not the Halases, is entitled to judgment as a matter of law.

The Graffiti

Like the toilet, the graffiti is unattractive and vulgar. Nonetheless, it is not a nuisance. The law, especially in nuisance cases, when rights to the free use of property are concerned, does not deal in trifles, and "mere annoyance or inconvenience will not support an action for a nuisance . . . ." The inscriptions

---

6.   If unsightliness is coupled with additional harms, however, such as pollution or a physical invasion, a private nuisance may be established. . . . [Citations omitted.] Moreover, even without additional harms, a large amount of refuse, such as that associated with junkyards and salvage operations, may so essentially interfere with the comfortable enjoyment of life and property that it constitutes a nuisance. . . .

. . . are engraved in areas of concrete, no more than two feet in diameter, which surround the ground level bases of two of Wernke's fenceposts . . . are located at least several inches over the property line onto Wernke's property *beyond* the Halases' own chain link fence, and the letters comprising the inscriptions are only three to four inches tall. . . . [I]t is not the appearance of the graffiti, but rather knowledge of its presence, that causes annoyance. . . . [T]he Halases can no more claim nuisance because they know Wernke has offensive inscriptions in his yard than they could if they knew Wernke had an offensive color scheme in his bathroom.

Moreover, freedom of expression is at issue here, and although the language is offensive and vulgar, it is a "bedrock principle underlying the First Amendment that the government may not prohibit the expression of an idea simply because society finds the idea itself offensive or disagreeable." . . . The trial court erred in granting summary judgment on this issue. . . .

CONCLUSION

The trial court erred in granting summary judgment to the Halases for all three alleged nuisances. Because there is no genuine issue of material fact, . . . summary judgment is ordered for Wernke. The award of attorney fees . . . [is] also reversed.

Notes and Questions

1. *Bansbach v. Harbin*, 728 S.E.2d 533 (W. Va. 2012), held that defendants' creation of a junkyard to interfere with the view from plaintiffs' property, posting of offensive signs visible from the road referring to plaintiff wife as "nosey bitch" and directing visitors to beep three times for entry, twice on exit, and yelling profanities and insults when driving by plaintiff's home, did not create a private nuisance or provide grounds for issuance of an injunction, holding that "this type of conduct . . . is simply not what nuisance laws are aimed at remedying."

2. Spite fences are more likely to be successfully challenged than other aesthetic offenses, perhaps because the decision whether a fence is put up for spite is often easier to make than a decision whether something is sufficiently ugly that it should be enjoined, or whether the activity has sufficient expressive character that it may claim protection as speech. In *DeCecco v. Beach*, 381 A.2d 543 (Conn. 1977), the court ordered removal of the part of a 10-foot high stockade style fence that blocked plaintiff's view of a river based on evidence that defendant acted maliciously with desire to injure the plaintiff. Similarly, in *Apple Hill Farms Development, LLP v. Price*, 816 N.W.2d 914 (Wis. Ct. App. 2012), plaintiff was awarded $148,000 in damages for defendant's failure to face an exposed 32-foot long, 12-foot high bare concrete wall. The contractor who built the wall testified that defendant told him not to put brick facing on the wall because he wanted it to be ugly to devalue plaintiff's property.

3. As in Indiana, spite fences are often prohibited by statute, but the existence of the statute, as in *Wernke*, may preclude treating fences that don't meet the statutory criteria as private nuisances. In *Schaefer v. Dehauski*, 898 N.Y.S.2d 750 (App. Div. 2010), the court held that a fence less than 10 feet high was not a nuisance even though it blocked the plaintiff's view to the river and was erected maliciously; only fences that come within New York's spite fence statute can be enjoined as nuisances. Motivation is irrelevant for fences that do not come within the statute. What do these cases suggest about the relative utility of statutes as opposed to judicial decisions in making law?

3.   Protecting Personal Property: Trespass and Conversion

PLOTNIK v. MEIHAUS
California Court of Appeal
146 Cal. Rptr. 3d 585 (2012)

RYLAARSDAM, Acting P.J. Plaintiffs David and Joyce Plotnik sued their neighbor, defendant John Meihaus, Jr. . . . In part, plaintiffs sought recovery for the emotional distress they suffered when Meihaus injured their dog. The superior court entered a judgment on jury verdicts that awarded . . . emotional distress damages resulting from the dog's injury. . . .

FACTS AND PROCEDURAL BACKGROUND

Plaintiffs and their two children moved into a home in Laguna Niguel in 2003. The rear portion of the property slopes upward, abutting the Meihaus's lot. At the time, a three-foot high fence on the property line separated the two parcels.

Plaintiffs claimed that, shortly after moving into their home, they began to have problems with the Meihaus family. Plaintiffs built a six-foot fence along the parcels' common boundary. In response, Meihaus . . . sued plaintiffs and the community association. That lawsuit was resolved in 2007 by a written settlement. In it, plaintiffs agreed to relocate the rear fence, moving it three feet back from the common boundary. The new fence has a gate that allows plaintiffs access to the portion of their property on the opposite side of the fence. . . .

At trial, plaintiffs presented evidence of several incidents that occurred between the parties after the settlement. Plaintiffs testified they found yard clippings and trash on their side of the rear fence. They documented some of this activity by taking photographs and saving some of the debris. David Plotnik testified the flower clippings were similar to plants he saw in the Meihaus's backyard.

David Plotnik and his daughter testified that on several occasions when driving through the neighborhood, they saw Meihaus jogging. As they passed him, Meihaus often raised a fist and extended his middle finger at them. According to David Plotnik the "entire family witnessed [this gesture] probably 15 [to] 20 times." Meihaus testified he did not recall these incidents. . . . [Descriptions of several other incidents are omitted—EDS.]

Things came to a head on April 9, 2009. David Plotnik testified that, around noon, he went to the backyard and began photographing yard clippings. Romeo, the family's 12- to 15-pound, 12-inch tall miniature pinscher was with him. He denied Romeo was barking or growling. Plotnik heard loud banging against the opposite side of the rear fence. When he opened the gate, Romeo ran into the Meihaus's backyard. Losing sight of Romeo, Plotnik assumed the dog ran to the front of their residence. He returned to his lot and began walking along the adjacent public street. At that point, he heard Romeo barking and then squeal. He hurried home, arriving in time to see Romeo rolling down the slope through the open gate and hit a tree.

Plotnik went through the gate and saw Meihaus holding a bat, returning to his house. He confronted Meihaus, yelling " 'Why did you hit our dog?' " Plotnik testified Meihaus raised the bat to waist level, came within two feet of him, yelling, " 'You need to be more courteous and get your dog to stop barking.' " Plotnik then accused Meihaus of damaging the side yard fence and throwing debris over the rear fence, all of which Meihaus denied. Claiming Romeo was agitated and kept barking and growling at him, Meihaus testified he obtained a bat from the garage and used it to "guide" Romeo back to the Plotnik's yard. He denied striking the dog.

After this exchange, Plotnik returned to his residence to check on Romeo. The dog had difficulty walking. The family took him to a veterinarian. Eventually, Romeo needed surgery to repair his right rear leg. The surgery cost $2,600 and Joyce Plotnik paid another $209.53 for a stroller to help Romeo get around after the surgery. At trial, the veterinarian opined Romeo's leg injury resulted from a traumatic event. . . .

. . . [T]he jury found Meihaus intentionally harmed Romeo. It awarded David Plotnik damages of $2,600 for economic loss and $20,000 for emotional distress. In addition, the jury awarded Joyce Plotnik economic damages of $209.53 and emotional distress damages of $30,000. . . .

DISCUSSION . . .

4. *The Attack on Romeo*

Plaintiffs sought damages from Meihaus on causes of action for trespass to personal property and negligence arising from his injuring Romeo by striking the dog with a bat. On the trespass count, the jury awarded plaintiffs both economic damages for Romeo's surgery and postoperative care, plus damages for the emotional distress each plaintiff suffered as a result of the incident. On the negligence count the jury awarded additional emotional distress damages to plaintiffs. [Discussion of negligence claim omitted — EDS.]

Meihaus first contends he is not liable because he lawfully exercised his right of self-defense in response to Romeo's threat to bite him. The issues of whether Meihaus truly felt threatened by plaintiffs' 15-pound, 12-inch tall dog and actually struck Romeo with the bat presented factual questions for the jury to decide. Contrary to Meihaus's assertion, the relevant facts were not uncontested. . . . We must accept the jury's implied findings on these matters. . . .

Meihaus does not dispute the amount of the expenses plaintiffs incurred for Romeo's surgery and care after being injured. Consequently, we affirm the jury's economic damage awards on the trespass cause of action.

The primary issue here is whether plaintiffs can recover under the trespass to personal property cause of action for the emotional distress they suffered resulting from Meihaus's injuring Romeo by striking him with a bat. Generally, "[f]or the breach of an obligation not arising from contract, the measure of damages, except where otherwise expressly provided by . . . [statute], is the amount which will compensate for all the detriment proximately caused thereby, whether it could have been anticipated or not."

. . . Meihaus argues "California [has] rejected the concept that an animal owner may recover emotional distress damages due to injuries his animal received at the hands of a[nother] . . . ." We disagree.

"Under California law, trespass to chattels 'lies where an intentional interference with the possession of personal property *has proximately* caused injury.' . . . "Where the conduct complained of does not amount to a substantial interference with possession or the right thereto, but consists of intermeddling with or use of or damages to the personal property, the owner has a cause of action for trespass . . . ." . . . [S]ee Jamgotchian v. Slender (2009) 170 Cal. App. 4th 1384 [owner of horse injured in race could sue track steward for trespass when steward rejected request to scratch horse from race and prevented animal's removal from track grounds].)

Dogs are considered personal property. . . . Generally, trespass to personal property allows one to "recover only the actual damages suffered by reason of the impairment of the property or the loss of its use. . . . In Kimes v. Grosser (2011) 195 Cal. App. 4th 1556, the court held a pet owner could recover "the [reasonable and necessary] costs of care of the pet attributable to the injury" caused by another.

. . . [N]o case cited by Meihaus prohibits the recovery of damages for emotional distress. . . . We believe good cause exists to allow the recovery of damages for emotional distress under the circumstances of this case. In the early case of Johnson v. McConnell (Cal. 1889) 22 P. 219, the court noted "while it has been said that [dogs] have nearly always been held 'to be entitled to less regard and protection than more harmless domestic animals,' it is equally true that there are no other domestic animals to which the owner or his family can become more strongly attached, or the loss of which will be more keenly felt." Additionally, one can be held liable for punitive damages if he or she willfully or through gross negligence wrongfully injures an animal. (Civ.Code, § 3340.) Intentionally maiming, mutilating, torturing, or wounding an animal also constitutes a crime. (Pen.Code, § 597.)

Trespass to personal property often arises in circumstances where a defendant's interference with another's property falls short of that required for a conversion cause of action. Thus, cases have described this tort as "the 'little brother of conversion[.]'" . . . In Gonzales v. Personal Storage, Inc. (1997) 56 Cal. App. 4th 464, the court recognized "the limits imposed with respect to recovery for emotional distress caused by a defendant's negligence do not apply when distress is the result of a defendant's commission of the distinct torts of trespass, nuisance or conversion" and held "damages for emotional distress growing out of a defendant's conversion of personal property are recoverable"; see also Schroeder v. Auto Driveaway Co. (Cal. 1974) 523 P.2d 662 ["compensation for pain, suffering, and emotional distress" allowed in action for breach of contract, fraud, and conversion resulting from loss and destruction of goods while in transit]. Cases involving actions for trespass to real property and nuisance have also recognized a party may recover emotional distress damages. (Acadia, California, Ltd. v. Herbert (Cal. 1960) 353 P.2d 294 ["regardless of whether the occupant of land has sustained physical injury, he may recover damages for the discomfort and annoyance of himself and the members of his family and for mental suffering occasioned by fear for the safety of himself and his family when such discomfort or suffering has been proximately caused by a trespass or a nuisance"] . . . .

Furthermore, cases in other states have recognized a pet owner may recover for mental suffering caused by another's wrongful acts resulting in the pet's injury or death. (Womack v. Von Rardon (Wash. Ct. App. 2006) 135 P.3d 542 [cat set on fire; "malicious injury to a pet can support a claim for, and be considered a factor in measuring a person's emotional distress damages"]; La Porte v. Associated Independents, Inc. (Fla.1964) 163 So. 2d 267 [garbage collector hurled can at tethered dog, killing it; "the affection of a master for his dog is a very real thing and . . . the malicious destruction of the pet provides an element of damage for which the owner should recover, irrespective of the value of the animal"]; Brown v. Crocker (La. App. 1962) 139 So. 2d 779 [affirming recovery of damages "for shock and mental anguish experienced" for "death of . . . mare" and "loss of [stillborn] colt" "as a result of shooting"]; see also Annot., Recovery of Damages for Emotional Distress Due to Treatment of Pets and Animals (2001) 91 A.L.R.5th 545.)

Consequently, while we reverse the damages awarded plaintiffs on their negligence claim, we uphold both the economic and emotional distress damages plaintiffs recovered for trespass to personal property arising from Meihaus's act of intentionally striking Romeo with a bat.

Notes and Questions

1. What is the justification for allowing damages for emotional distress for a trespass to personal property? Is it similar to or different from the justification for allowing punitive damages in *Jacque v. Steenberg Homes*?

2. After the Plotniks replaced the original three-foot fence with a six-foot fence, Meihaus sued them and the community association. A community association is often created to enforce the covenants (which may be called CC&R's) that govern land use and impose obligations to support commonly owned facilities within a real estate development like tennis courts and swimming pools. Covenants and community associations are covered in Chapter 12.

INTEL CORPORATION v. HAMIDI

Supreme Court of California
71 P.3d 296 (2003)

WERDEGAR, J.[5] . . . [Kourosh Kenneth Hamidi, a former Intel engineer, together with others, formed an organization named Former and Current Employees of Intel (FACE-Intel) to disseminate information and views critical

_____

5.   The majority's discussion of free speech issues and most of the concurring and two dissenting opinions have been omitted. The fact statement in the bracketed portion combines portions of the first two sections of the majority opinion. — EDS.

of Intel's employment and personnel policies and practices. FACE-Intel maintained a website. . . . Over a 21-month period, Hamidi, on behalf of FACE-Intel, sent six mass e-mails to as many as 35,000 employee addresses on Intel's electronic mail system. The messages criticized Intel's employment practices, warned employees of the dangers those practices posed to their careers, suggested employees consider moving to other companies, solicited employees' participation in FACE-Intel, and urged employees to inform themselves further by visiting FACE-Intel's website. The messages stated that recipients could, by notifying the sender of their wishes, be removed from FACE-Intel's mailing list. Hamidi did not subsequently send messages to anyone who requested removal. There was no evidence Hamidi breached Intel's computer security in order to obtain the recipient addresses for his messages and internal company memoranda show that management concluded no security breach had occurred. Hamidi stated he created the recipient address list using an Intel directory on a floppy disk anonymously sent to him. Intel attempted to block the messages, but was only partly successful because Hamidi used different sending computers to evade the blocks. When Intel demanded in writing that Hamidi and FACE-Intel stop sending e-mails to Intel's computer system, Hamidi asserted the organization had a right to communicate with willing Intel employees and, thereafter, sent a new mass mailing.]

Intel sued Hamidi and FACE-Intel pleading causes of action for trespass to chattels and nuisance, and seeking both actual damages and an injunction against further e-mail messages. Intel later voluntarily dismissed its nuisance claim and waived its demand for damages. The trial court entered default against FACE-Intel upon that organization's failure to answer. The court then granted Intel's motion for summary judgment, permanently enjoining Hamidi, FACE-Intel, and their agents "from sending unsolicited e-mail to addresses on Intel's computer systems." Hamidi appealed; FACE-Intel did not.

The Court of Appeal, with one justice dissenting, affirmed the grant of injunctive relief. The majority took the view that the use of or intermeddling with another's personal property is actionable as a trespass to chattels without proof of any actual injury to the personal property; even if Intel could not show any damages resulting from Hamidi's sending of messages, "it showed he was disrupting its business by using its property and therefore is entitled to injunctive relief based on a theory of trespass to chattels." The dissenting justice warned that the majority's application of the trespass to chattels tort to "unsolicited electronic mail that causes no harm to the private computer system that receives it" would "expand the tort of trespass to chattel in untold ways and to unanticipated circumstances."

We granted Hamidi's petition for review. . . .

[W]e conclude that under California law the tort does not encompass, and should not be extended to encompass, an electronic communication that neither damages the recipient computer system nor impairs its functioning. Such an electronic communication does not constitute an actionable trespass to personal property, *i.e.*, the computer system, because it does not interfere with the possessor's use or possession of, or any other legally protected interest in, the personal property itself. . . . The consequential economic damage Intel claims to have suffered, *i.e.*, loss of productivity caused by employees reading and reacting to Hamidi's messages and company efforts to block the messages, is not an injury to the company's interest in its computers—which worked as intended and were unharmed by the communications—any more than the personal distress caused by reading an unpleasant letter would be an injury to the recipient's mailbox, or the loss of privacy caused by an intrusive telephone call would be an injury to the recipient's telephone equipment.

Our conclusion does not rest on any special immunity for communications by electronic mail; we do not hold that messages transmitted through the Internet are exempt from the ordinary rules of tort liability. To the contrary, e-mail, like other forms of communication, may in some circumstances cause legally cognizable injury to the recipient or to third parties and may be actionable under various common law or statutory theories. Indeed, on facts somewhat similar to those here, a company or its employees might be able to plead causes of action for interference with prospective economic relations (*see* Guillory v. Godfrey (1955) 134 Cal. App. 2d 628 . . . [defendant berated customers and prospective customers of plaintiffs' cafe with disparaging and racist comments]), interference with contract (*see* Blender v. Superior Court (1942) 55 Cal. App. 2d 24 . . . [defendant made false statements about plaintiff to his employer, resulting in plaintiff's discharge]) or intentional infliction of emotional distress (*see* Kiseskey v. Carpenters' Trust for So. California (1983) 144 Cal. App. 3d 222 . . . [agents of defendant union threatened life, health, and family of employer if he did not sign agreement with union].) And, of course, as with any other means of publication, third party subjects of e-mail communications may under appropriate facts make claims for defamation, publication of private facts, or other speech-based torts. (*See, e.g.,* Southridge Capital Management v. Lowry (S.D.N.Y. 2002) 188 F. Supp. 2d 388 . . . [allegedly false statements in e-mail sent to several of plaintiff's clients support actions for defamation and interference with contract].) Intel's claim fails not because e-mail transmitted through the Internet enjoys unique immunity, but because the trespass to chattels tort—unlike the causes of action just mentioned—may not, in California, be proved without evidence of an injury to the plaintiff's personal property or legal interest therein.

Nor does our holding affect the legal remedies of Internet service providers (ISP's) against senders of unsolicited commercial bulk e-mail (UCE), also known as "spam." . . . A series of federal district court decisions, beginning with CompuServe, Inc. v. Cyber Promotions, Inc. (S.D. Ohio 1997) 962 F. Supp. 1015, has approved the use of trespass to chattels as a theory of spammers' liability to ISP's, based upon evidence that the vast quantities of mail sent by spammers both overburdened the ISP's own computers and made the entire computer system harder to use for recipients, the ISP's customers. . . . In those cases . . . the underlying complaint was that the extraordinary *quantity* of UCE impaired the computer system's functioning. In the present case, the claimed injury is located in the disruption or distraction caused to recipients by the *contents* of the e-mail messages, an injury entirely separate from, and not directly affecting, the possession or value of personal property. . . .

I. CURRENT CALIFORNIA TORT LAW

Dubbed by Prosser the "little brother of conversion," the tort of trespass to chattels allows recovery for interferences with possession of personal property "not sufficiently important to be classed as conversion, and so to compel the defendant to pay the full value of the thing with which he has interfered." (Prosser & Keeton, Torts (5th ed.1984) § 14 . . . .)

Though not amounting to conversion, the defendant's interference must, to be actionable, have caused some injury to the chattel or to the plaintiff's rights in it. Under California law, trespass to chattels "lies where an intentional interference with the possession of personal property *has proximately caused injury.*" (Thrifty-Tel, Inc. v. Bezenek (1996) 46 Cal. App. 4th 1559 . . . italics added.) In cases of interference with possession of personal property not amounting to conversion, "the owner has a cause of action for trespass or case, *and may recover only the actual damages suffered by reason of the impairment of the property or the loss of its use.*" (Zaslow v. Kroenert, [(1946) 29 Cal. 2d 541], italics added). . . . In modern American law generally, "[t]respass remains as an occasional remedy for minor interferences, *resulting in some damage,* but not sufficiently serious or sufficiently important to amount to the greater tort" of conversion. . . .

The Restatement, too, makes clear that some actual injury must have occurred in order for a trespass to chattels to be actionable. Under section 218 of the Restatement Second of Torts, dispossession alone, without further damages, is actionable . . . , but other forms of interference require some additional harm to the personal property or the possessor's interests in it. . . . "The interest of a possessor of a chattel in its inviolability, unlike the similar interest of a possessor of land, is not given legal protection by an action for nominal damages for harmless intermeddlings with the chattel. In order that an actor who interferes with another's chattel may be liable, his conduct must affect some other and more important interest of the possessor. *Therefore, one who intentionally intermeddles with another's chattel is subject to liability only if his intermeddling is harmful to the possessor's materially valuable interest in the physical condition, quality, or value of the chattel, or if the possessor is deprived of the use of the chattel for a substantial time, or some other legally protected interest of the possessor is affected* . . . . Sufficient legal protection of the possessor's interest in the mere inviolability of his chattel is afforded by his privilege to use reasonable force to protect his possession against even harmless interference." . . .

> "Where the defendant merely interferes without doing any harm — as where, for example, he merely lays hands upon the plaintiff's horse, or sits in his car — there has been a division of opinion among the writers, and a surprising dearth of authority. *By analogy to trespass to land there might be a technical tort in such a case* . . . . *Such scanty authority as there is, however, has considered that the dignitary interest in the inviolability of chattels, unlike that as to land, is not sufficiently important to require any greater defense than the privilege of using reasonable force when necessary to protect them. Accordingly it has been held that nominal damages will not be awarded, and that in the absence of any actual damage the action will not lie.*" (Prosser § 14). . . .

The dispositive issue in this case, therefore, is whether the undisputed facts demonstrate Hamidi's actions caused or threatened to cause damage to Intel's computer system, or injury to its rights in that personal property, such as to entitle Intel to judgment as a matter of law. . . . Intel presented no evidence its system was slowed or otherwise impaired by the burden of delivering Hamidi's electronic messages. . . . [N]o evidence suggested that in sending messages through Intel's Internet connections and internal computer system Hamidi used the system in any manner in which it was not intended to function or impaired the system in any way. Nor does the evidence show the request of any employee to be removed from FACE-Intel's mailing list was not honored. . . .

Relying on a line of decisions, most from federal district courts, applying the tort of trespass to chattels to various types of unwanted electronic contact between computers, Intel contends that, while its computers were not damaged by receiving Hamidi's messages, its interest in the "physical condition, quality or value" (Rest. 2d Torts, §218, com. *e* . . .) of the computers was harmed. We disagree. The cited line of decisions does not persuade us that the mere sending of electronic communications that assertedly cause injury only because of their contents constitutes an actionable trespass to a computer system through which the messages are transmitted. Rather, the decisions finding electronic contact to be a trespass to computer systems have generally involved some actual or threatened interference with the computers' functioning. . . .

In each of . . . [the] spamming cases, the plaintiff showed, or was prepared to show, some interference with the efficient functioning of its computer system. In *CompuServe* [962 F. Supp. 1015], the plaintiff ISP's mail equipment monitor stated that mass UCE mailings, especially from nonexistent addresses such as those used by the defendant, placed "a tremendous burden" on the ISP's equipment, using "disk space and drain[ing] the processing power," making those resources unavailable to serve subscribers. . . . Similarly, in *Hotmail* . . . [1998 WL 388389] the court found the evidence supported a finding that the defendant's mailings "fill[ed] up Hotmail's computer storage space and threaten[ed] to damage Hotmail's ability to service its legitimate customers." . . .

Though Hamidi sent thousands of copies of the same message on six occasions over 21 months, that number is minuscule compared to the amounts of mail sent by commercial operations. . . . The functional burden on Intel's computers, or the cost in time to individual recipients, of receiving Hamidi's occasional advocacy messages cannot be compared to the burdens and costs caused ISP's and their customers by the ever-rising deluge of commercial e-mail. . . .

In addition to impairment of system functionality, *CompuServe* and its progeny also refer to the ISP's loss of business reputation and customer goodwill, resulting from the inconvenience and cost that spam causes to its members, as harm to the ISP's legally protected interests in its personal property. . . . Intel argues that its own interest in employee productivity, assertedly disrupted by Hamidi's messages, is a comparable protected interest in its computer system. We disagree.

Whether the economic injuries identified in *CompuServe* were properly considered injuries to the ISP's possessory interest in its personal property—the type of property interest the tort is primarily intended to protect— . . . has been questioned. . . . [*See*] Quilter, *The Continuing Expansion of Cyberspace Trespass to Chattels*, [2002] 17 Berkeley Tech. L.J. 421 at pp. 429-430 . . . [and] Burk, *The Trouble with Trespass* (2000) 4 J. Small & Emerging Bus. L. 27, 35 ["[T]his move cuts trespass to chattels free from its moorings of dispossession or the equivalent, allowing the court free reign [*sic*] to hunt for 'impairment.'"] But even if the loss of goodwill identified in *CompuServe* were the type of injury that would give rise to a trespass to chattels claim under California law, Intel's position would not follow, for Intel's claimed injury has even less connection to its personal property than did CompuServe's.

CompuServe's customers were annoyed because the system was inundated with unsolicited commercial messages, making its use for personal communication more difficult and costly. . . . Their complaint, which allegedly led some to cancel their CompuServe service, was about *the functioning of CompuServe's electronic mail service.* Intel's workers, in contrast, were allegedly distracted from their work . . . because of assertions and opinions the messages conveyed. Intel's complaint is thus about *the contents of the messages* rather than the functioning of the company's e-mail system. Even accepting *CompuServe's* . . . rationale, . . . Intel's position represents a further extension of the . . . tort, fictionally recharacterizing the allegedly injurious effect of a communication's *contents* on recipients as an impairment to the device which transmitted the message.

This theory of "impairment by content" (Burk, . . . *supra* . . .) threatens to stretch trespass law to cover injuries far afield from the harms to possession the tort evolved to protect. Intel's theory would expand the tort of trespass to chattels to cover virtually any unconsented-to communication that, solely because of its content, is unwelcome to the recipient or intermediate transmitter. . . . As the dissenting justice below explained " . . . [I]f a chattel's receipt of an electronic communication constitutes a trespass to that chattel, then not only are unsolicited telephone calls and faxes trespasses to chattel, but unwelcome radio waves and television signals also constitute a trespass to chattel every time the viewer inadvertently sees or hears the unwanted program." We agree. While unwelcome communications, electronic or otherwise, can cause a variety of injuries to economic relations, reputation and emotions, those interests are protected by other branches of tort law; in order to address them, we need not create a fiction of injury to the communication system. . . .

Intel connected its e-mail system to the Internet and permitted its employees to make use of this connection both for business and, to a reasonable extent, for their own purposes. In doing so, the company necessarily contemplated the employees' receipt of unsolicited as well as solicited communications from other companies and individuals. That some communications would, because of their contents, be unwelcome to Intel management was virtually inevitable. Hamidi did nothing but use the e-mail system for its intended purpose—to communicate with employees. . . . [His] occasional transmissions cannot reasonably be viewed as impairing the quality or value of Intel's computer system. . . .

II.   PROPOSED EXTENSION OF CALIFORNIA TORT LAW

We next consider whether California common law should be *extended* to cover, as a trespass to chattels, an otherwise harmless electronic communication whose contents are objectionable. . . . The property rule proposed is a rigid one, under which the sender of an electronic message would be strictly liable to the owner of equipment through which the communication passes . . . for any consequential injury flowing from the *contents* of the communication. . . .

Writing on behalf of several industry groups appearing as amici curiae, Professor Richard A. Epstein . . . urges us to excuse the required showing of injury to personal property in cases of unauthorized electronic contact between computers, "extending the rules of trespass to real property to all interactive Web sites and servers." . . . In effect, Professor Epstein suggests that a company's server should be its castle, upon which any unauthorized intrusion, however harmless, is a trespass.

Epstein's argument derives, in part, from the familiar metaphor of the Internet as a physical space, reflected in much of the language that has been used to describe it: "cyberspace," "the information superhighway," e-mail "addresses," and the like. Of course, the Internet is also frequently called simply the "Net," a term, Hamidi points out, "evoking a fisherman's chattel." A major component of the Internet is the World Wide "Web," a descriptive term suggesting neither personal nor real property, and "cyberspace" itself has come to be known by the oxymoronic phrase "virtual reality," which would suggest that any real property "located" in "cyberspace" must be "virtually real" property. Metaphor is a two-edged sword.

Indeed, the metaphorical application of real property rules would not, by itself, transform a physically harmless electronic intrusion on a computer server into a trespass. That is because, under California law, intangible intrusions on land, including electromagnetic transmissions, are not actionable as trespasses (though they may be as nuisances) unless they cause physical damage to the real property. (San Diego Gas & Electric Co. v. Superior Court (1996) 13 Cal.4th 893. . . .) Since Intel does not claim Hamidi's electronically transmitted messages physically damaged its servers, it could not prove a trespass to land even were we to treat the computers as a type of real property. Some further extension of the conceit would be required, under which the electronic signals Hamidi sent would be recast as tangible intruders, perhaps as tiny messengers rushing through the "hallways" of Intel's computers and bursting out of employees' computers to read them Hamidi's missives. But such fictions promise more confusion than clarity in the law. (*See* eBay [v. Bidder's Edge, Inc., 100 F. Supp. 2d 1058 (N.D. Cal. 2000)] . . . [rejecting eBay's argument that the defendant's automated data searches "should be thought of as equivalent to sending in an army of 100,000 robots a day to check the prices in a competitor's store"].)

The plain fact is that computers, even those making up the Internet, are — like such older communications equipment as telephones and fax machines — personal property, not realty. Professor Epstein observes that "[a]lthough servers may be moved in real space, they cannot be moved in cyberspace," because an Internet server must, to be useful, be accessible at a known address. But the same is true of the telephone: to be useful for incoming communication, the telephone must remain constantly linked to the same number (or, when the number is changed, the system must include some forwarding or notification capability, a qualification that also applies to computer addresses). Does this suggest that an unwelcome message delivered through a telephone or fax machine should be viewed as a trespass to a type of real property? We think not . . . .

More substantively, Professor Epstein argues that a rule of computer server inviolability will, through the formation or extension of a market in computer-to-computer access, create "the right social result." In most circumstances, he predicts, companies with computers on the Internet will continue to authorize transmission of information through e-mail, Web site searching, and page linking because they benefit by that open access. When a Web site owner does deny access to a particular sending, searching, or linking computer, a system of "simple one-on-one negotiations" will arise to provide the necessary individual licenses.

Other scholars are less optimistic about such a complete propertization of the Internet. Professor Mark Lemley . . . , writing on behalf of an amici curiae group of professors of intellectual property and computer law, observes that under a property rule of server inviolability, "each of the hundreds of millions of [Internet] users must get permission in advance from anyone with whom they want to communicate and anyone who owns a server through which their message may travel." The consequence for e-mail could be a substantial reduction in the freedom of electronic communication, as the owner of each computer through which an electronic message passes could impose its own limitations on message content or source. As Professor Dan Hunter . . . asks rhetorically: "Does this mean that one must read the 'Terms of Acceptable Email Usage' of every email system that one emails in the course of an ordinary day? If the University of Pennsylvania had a policy that sending a joke by email would be an unauthorized use of their system, then under the logic of [the lower court decision in this case], you would commit 'trespass' if you emailed me a . . . cartoon." (Hunter, *Cyberspace as Place, and the Tragedy of the Digital Anticommons* (2003) 91 Cal. L. Rev. 439, 508-509.)

Web site linking, Professor Lemley further observes, "would exist at the sufferance of the linked-to party, because a Web user who followed a 'disapproved' link would be trespassing on the plaintiff's server, just as sending an e-mail is trespass under the [lower] court's theory." Another writer warns that "[c]yber-trespass theory will curtail the free flow of price and product information on the Internet by allowing website owners to tightly control who and what may enter and make use of the information housed on its Internet site." (Chang, *Bidding on Trespass: eBay, Inc. v. Bidder's Edge, Inc. and the Abuse of Trespass Theory in Cyberspace Law* (2001) 29 AIPLA Q.J. 445, 459.) A leading scholar of Internet law and policy, Professor Lawrence Lessig . . . , has criticized Professor Epstein's theory of the computer server as quasi-real property, . . . on the ground that it ignores the costs to society in the loss of network benefits: ". . . It is this general feature of the Net that makes the Net so valuable to users and a source of great innovation. And to the extent that individual sites begin to impose their own rules of exclusion, the value of the network as a network declines. If machines must negotiate before entering any individual site, then the costs of using the network climb." (Lessig, *The Future of Ideas: The Fate of the Commons in a Connected World* (2001) p. 171; *see also* Hunter, . . . *supra,* . . . at p. 512 ["If we continue to mark out anticommons claims in cyberspace, not only will we preclude better, more innovative uses of cyberspace resources, but we will lose sight of what might be possible"].)

We discuss this debate among the amici curiae and academic writers only to note its existence and contours, not to attempt its resolution. Creating an absolute property right to exclude undesired communications from one's e-mail and Web servers might help force spammers to internalize the costs they impose on ISP's and their customers. But such a property rule might also create substantial new costs, to e-mail and e-commerce users and to society generally, in lost ease and openness of communication and in lost network benefits. In light of the unresolved controversy, we would be acting rashly to adopt a rule treating computer servers as real property for purposes of trespass law.

The Legislature has already adopted detailed regulations governing UCE. (Bus. & Prof. Code, §§ 17538.4, 17538.45 . . . .) It may see fit in the future also to regulate noncommercial e-mail, such as that sent by Hamidi, or other kinds of unwanted contact between computers on the Internet . . . . But we are not persuaded that these perceived problems call at present for judicial creation of a rigid property rule of computer server inviolability. . . .

The judgment of the Court of Appeal is reversed.

[Concurring opinion by KENNARD, J. and dissenting opinion by BROWN, J. omitted.]

Dissenting Opinion by MOSK, J.* . . . The majority fail to distinguish open communication in the public "commons" of the Internet from unauthorized intermeddling on a private, proprietary intranet. Hamidi is not communicating in the equivalent of a town square or of an unsolicited "junk" mailing through the United States Postal Service. His action, in crossing from the public Internet into a private intranet, is more like intruding into a private office mailroom, commandeering the mail cart, and dropping off unwanted broadsides on 30,000 desks. . . . [T]he majority leave Intel, which has exercised all reasonable self-help efforts, with no recourse unless he causes a malfunction or systems "crash." Hamidi's repeated intrusions . . . constituted a misappropriation of Intel's private computer system contrary to its intended use and against Intel's wishes. . . .

. . . Intel . . . should be entitled to control use [of its computer system] by outsiders and to seek injunctive relief when self-help fails. . . . Although other causes of action may under certain circumstances also apply to Hamidi's conduct, the remedy based on trespass to chattels is the most efficient and appropriate. It simply requires Hamidi to stop the unauthorized use of property without regard to the content of the transmissions. Unlike trespass to chattels, the other potential causes of action suggested by the majority and Hamidi would require an evaluation of the transmissions' content and, in the case of a nuisance action, for example, would involve questions of degree and value judgments based on competing interests.

. . . I believe that existing legal principles are adequate to support Intel's request for injunctive relief. But even if the injunction in this case amounts to an extension of the traditional tort of trespass to chattels, this is one of those cases in which, as Justice Cardozo suggested, "[t]he creative element in the judicial process finds its opportunity and power" in the development of the law. (Cardozo, *Nature of the Judicial Process* (1921) p. 165.)[5]

The law has evolved to meet economic, social, and scientific changes in society. . . . The age of computer technology and cyberspace poses new challenges to legal principles. . . . The court must now grapple with proprietary interests, privacy, and expression arising out of computer-related disputes. . . . Additionally, this is a case in which equitable relief is sought. . . . "[E]quitable relief is *flexible and expanding*, and the theory that 'for every wrong there is a remedy' [Civ.Code, § 3523] may be invoked by equity courts to justify the invention of new methods of relief for new types of wrongs." (11 Witkin, Summary of Cal. Law, Equity, § 3.) That the Legislature has dealt with some aspects of commercial unsolicited bulk email . . . should not inhibit the application of common law tort principles to deal with e-mail transgressions not covered by the legislation. . . .

By making more concrete damages a requirement for a remedy, the majority has rendered speech interests dependent on the impact of the e-mails. The sender will never know when or if the mass e-mails sent by him (and perhaps

---

* Associate Justice, Court of Appeal . . . assigned by the Chief Justice . . . .

5. "It is revolting to have no better reason for a rule of law than that so it was laid down in the time of Henry IV." (Holmes, *The Path of the Law* (1897) 10 Harv. L. Rev. 457, 469.)

others) will use up too much space or cause a crash in the recipient system, so as to fulfill the majority's requirement of damages. Thus, the sender is exposed to the risk of liability because of the possibility of damages. If, as the majority suggest, such a risk will deter "ease and openness of communication" . . . the majority's formulation does not eliminate such deterrence. Under the majority's position, the lost freedom of communication still exists. In addition, a business could never reliably invest in a private network that can only be kept private by constant vigilance and inventiveness, or by simply shutting off the Internet, thus limiting rather than expanding the flow of information.[6] . . . I believe the best approach is to clearly delineate private from public networks and identify as a trespass to chattels the kind of intermeddling involved here.

Notes and Questions

1. This case, like many in this book, has been extensively edited to allow greater coverage than would otherwise be possible. The Westlaw version, for example, runs to 36 pages. Unfortunately, that means that substantial portions of the arguments have been left out. We have tried to leave enough to allow you to capture the important points, but if you are curious about what else the judges said, or suspect that the case would make more sense if you read the entire opinion, you can find the case online or in the library. Shortly after the case was decided, the New York Times published a lengthy story about Hamidi's personal saga and the role of a second-year law student in mobilizing support for his case, Jill Andresky Fraser, *Fighting for the Right to Communicate*, N.Y. Times, July 13, 2003, Sec. 3; p. 1.

2. Neither the majority nor the dissenting opinions disagree with the Restatement's position that actual harm is not necessary for trespass to land, but is a necessary element of the cause of action for trespass to chattels. Do you agree that the law should treat them differently? What are the relevant differences between land and tangible personal property?

3. What would be the advantages of extending the tort of trespass to chattels to cover the situation in *Hamidi*? What would be the drawbacks?

4. The majority opinion cites Dan Hunter's view that "[i]f we continue to mark out anticommons claims in cyberspace, not only will we preclude better, more innovative uses of cyberspace resources, but we will lose sight of what might be possible," expressed in his article *Cyberspace as Place, and the Tragedy of the Digital Anticommons*, 91 Cal. L. Rev. 439 (2003). *Anticommons* is a term coined by Professor Frank Michelman in the 1980s to describe a property regime in which every member of the public has the right to exclude others so that no one can enter or use the property without the consent of all. Professor Michael Heller refined and developed the concept of anticommons property in *The Tragedy of the Anticommons: Property in the Transition from Marx to Markets*, 111 Harv. L. Rev. 621 (1998). His definition of an anticommons is property in which "multiple owners are each endowed with the right to exclude others from a scarce resource, and

---

6. Thus, the majority's approach creates the perverse incentive for companies to invest less in computer capacity in order to protect its property. In the view of the majority, Hamidi's massive e-mails would be actionable only if Intel had insufficient server or storage capacity to manage them.

no one has an effective privilege of use." Heller's insights have provided inspiration for others like Hunter, who are exploring the nature and consequences of the property regimes we establish for various kinds of resources.

5. The majority takes the position that this is a problem for the legislature; the Mosk dissent says this is a job for the court. What advantages does the legislative process provide? The judicial process?

6. In 2003, the federal CAN-SPAM Act (Controlling the Assault of Non-Solicited Pornography and Marketing Act of 2003) was adopted, 15 U.S.C. §§ 7701-7713. The Act preempts state regulation of e-mail use to send commercial messages "except to the extent . . . [it] prohibits falsity or deception" in the message or the information attached to it. The Act specifically states that it does not preempt use of state trespass, contract, or tort law that is not specific to electronic mail. 15 U.S.C. § 7707(b). For more information about spam laws, both state and federal, see http://www.spamlaws.com/us.shtml, which concludes that the federal statute has not been effective.

7. The Computer Fraud and Abuse Act, 18 U.S.C.A. § 1030, an anti-hacking statute, provides criminal penalties for intentionally accessing computers without authorization under various circumstances. Someone who is damaged by violation of the Act may bring a civil action for compensatory damages and injunctive relief. In *EF Cultural Travel BV v. Explorica, Inc.*, 274 F.3d 577 (1st Cir. 2001), the statute was successfully used against use of "scraper" software to gather prices from a competitor tour company's website so that its prices could be systematically undercut. Even if an employee is authorized to access the employer's computer system, the employee may violate the Stored Communications Act, 18 U.S.C.A. § 2701, by accessing the boss's e-mail account. *See Penrose Computer Marketgroup, Inc. v. Camin*, 682 F. Supp. 2d 202 (N.D.N.Y. 2010).

8. Metaphors play a critical and pervasive role in legal analysis and discourse, helping in understanding abstract concepts and new technologies, but they may also be dangerous because they focus our attention on certain aspects of the concept or technology and often obscure or marginalize the importance of others. As Justice Benjamin Cardozo once said, "Metaphors in law are to be narrowly watched, for starting as devices to liberate thought, they end often by enslaving it," *Berkey v. Third Ave. Ry. Co.*, 244 N.Y. 84, 94 (1926). Metaphors used to describe the internet have drawn a considerable amount of attention from scholars and courts. Two pieces you might find interesting are Jonathan H. Blavin & I. Glenn Cohen, *Gore, Gibson, and Goldsmith: The Evolution of Internet Metaphors in Law and Commentary*, 16 Harv. J.L. & Tech. 265 (2002), which summarizes contemporary scholarship on metaphors and their use in law, as well as tracing their evolution in legal thinking about the internet, and Alfred C. Yen, *Western Frontier or Feudal Society?: Metaphors and Perceptions of Cyberspace*, 17 Berkeley Tech. L.J. 1207 (2002).

KREMEN v. COHEN

United States Court of Appeals, Ninth Circuit
337 F.3d 1024 (2003)

KOZINSKI, Circuit Judge. . . . "Sex on the Internet?," they all said. "*That'll* never make any money." But computer-geek-turned-entrepreneur Gary Kremen knew an opportunity when he saw it. The year was 1994; domain names were free for the asking, and it would be several years yet before Henry Blodget and hordes of eager NASDAQ day traders would turn the Internet into the Dutch tulip craze of our times. With a quick e-mail to the domain name registrar Network Solutions, Kremen became the proud owner of sex.com. He registered the name to his business, Online Classifieds, and listed himself as the contact.

Con man Stephen Cohen, meanwhile, was doing time for impersonating a bankruptcy lawyer. He, too, saw the potential of the domain name. Kremen had gotten it first, but that was only a minor impediment for a man of Cohen's boundless resource and bounded integrity. Once out of prison, he sent Network Solutions what purported to be a letter he had received from Online Classifieds. It claimed the company had been "forced to dismiss Mr. Kremen," but "never got around to changing our administrative contact with the internet registration [sic] and now our Board of directors has decided to *abandon* the domain name sex.com." Why was this unusual letter being sent via Cohen rather than to Network Solutions directly? It explained:

> Because we do not have a direct connection to the internet, we request that you notify the internet registration on our behalf, to delete our domain name sex. com. Further, we have no objections to your use of the domain name sex.com and this letter shall serve as our authorization to the internet registration to transfer sex.com to your corporation.[2]

Despite the letter's transparent claim that a company called "*Online* Classifieds" had no Internet connection, Network Solutions made no effort to contact Kremen. Instead, it accepted the letter at face value and transferred the domain name to Cohen. When Kremen contacted Network Solutions some time later, he was told it was too late to undo the transfer. Cohen went on to turn sex.com into a lucrative online porn empire.

And so began Kremen's quest to recover the domain name that was rightfully his. He sued Cohen and several affiliated companies in federal court, seeking return of the domain name and disgorgement of Cohen's profits. The district court found that the letter was indeed a forgery and ordered the domain name returned to Kremen. It also told Cohen to hand over his profits, invoking the constructive trust doctrine and California's "unfair competition" statute . . . . It awarded $40 million in compensatory damages and another $25 million in punitive damages.

Kremen, unfortunately, has not had much luck collecting his judgment. The district court froze Cohen's assets, but Cohen ignored the order and wired large sums of money to offshore accounts. His real estate property, under the protection of a federal receiver, was stripped of all its fixtures—even cabinet doors and toilets—in violation of another order. The court commanded Cohen to appear and show cause why he shouldn't be held in contempt, but he ignored that order, too. The district judge finally took off the gloves—he declared Cohen a fugitive from justice, signed an arrest warrant and sent the U.S. Marshals after him.

---

2.   The letter was signed "Sharon Dimmick," purported president of Online Classifieds. Dimmick was actually Kremen's housemate at the time; Cohen later claimed she sold him the domain name for $1000. This story might have worked a little better if Cohen hadn't misspelled her signature.

Then things started getting *really* bizarre. Kremen put up a "wanted" poster on the sex.com site with a mug shot of Cohen, offering a $50,000 reward to anyone who brought him to justice. Cohen's lawyers responded with a motion to vacate the arrest warrant. They reported that Cohen was under house arrest in Mexico and that gunfights between Mexican authorities and would-be bounty hunters seeking Kremen's reward money posed a threat to human life. The district court rejected this story as "implausible" and denied the motion. Cohen, so far as the record shows, remains at large.

Given his limited success with the bounty hunter approach, it should come as no surprise that Kremen seeks to hold someone else responsible for his losses. That someone is Network Solutions, the exclusive domain name registrar at the time of Cohen's antics. Kremen sued it for mishandling his domain name, invoking four theories at issue here. He argues that he had an implied contract with Network Solutions, which it breached by giving the domain name to Cohen. He also claims the transfer violated Network Solutions's cooperative agreement with the National Science Foundation—the government contract that made Network Solutions the .com registrar. His third theory is that he has a property right in the domain name sex.com, and Network Solutions committed the tort of conversion by giving it away to Cohen. Finally, he argues that Network Solutions was a "bailee" of his domain name and seeks to hold it liable for "conversion by bailee."

The district court granted summary judgment in favor of Network Solutions on all claims. . . . It held that Kremen had no implied contract with Network Solutions because there was no consideration: Kremen had registered the domain name for free. It rejected the third-party contract claim on the ground that the cooperative agreement did not indicate a clear intent to grant enforceable contract rights to registrants.

The conversion claims fared no better. The court agreed that sex.com was Kremen's property. It concluded, though, that it was intangible property to which the tort of conversion does not apply. The conversion by bailee claim failed for the additional reason that Network Solutions was not a bailee. Kremen appeals. . . . [Portion of opinion agreeing with district court on contract claims omitted.—Eds.]

Conversion

Kremen's conversion claim is another matter. To establish that tort, a plaintiff must show "ownership or right to possession of property, wrongful disposition of the property right and damages." . . . The preliminary question, then, is whether registrants have property rights in their domain names. Network Solutions all but concedes that they do. This is no surprise, given its positions in prior litigation. *See* Network Solutions, Inc. v. Umbro Int'l, Inc., 529 S.E.2d 80 (Va. 2000). . . .

Property is a broad concept that includes "every intangible benefit and prerogative susceptible of possession or disposition." . . . We apply a three-part test to determine whether a property right exists: "First, there must be an interest capable of precise definition; second, it must be capable of exclusive possession or control; and third, the putative owner must have established a legitimate claim to exclusivity." G.S. Rasmussen & Assocs., Inc. v. Kalitta Flying Serv., Inc., 958 F.2d 896 (9th Cir. 1992). . . . Domain names satisfy each criterion. Like a share of corporate stock or a plot of land, a domain name is a well-defined interest. Someone who registers a domain name decides where on the Internet those who invoke that particular name — whether by typing it into their web browsers, by following a hyperlink, or by other means — are sent. Ownership is exclusive in that the registrant alone makes that decision. Moreover, like other forms of property, domain names are valued, bought and sold, often for millions of dollars . . . and they are now even subject to *in rem* jurisdiction, *see* 15 U.S.C. § 1125(d)(2).

Finally, registrants have a legitimate claim to exclusivity. Registering a domain name is like staking a claim to a plot of land at the title office. It informs others that the domain name is the registrant's and no one else's. Many registrants also invest substantial time and money to develop and promote websites that depend on their domain names. Ensuring that they reap the benefits of their investments reduces uncertainty and thus encourages investment in the first place, promoting the growth of the Internet overall. . . .

Kremen therefore had an intangible property right in his domain name, and a jury could find that Network Solutions "wrongful[ly] dispos[ed] of" that right to his detriment by handing the domain name over to Cohen. . . . The district court nevertheless rejected Kremen's conversion claim. It held that domain names, although a form of property, are intangibles not subject to conversion. This rationale derives from a distinction tort law once drew between tangible and intangible property: Conversion was originally a remedy for the wrongful taking of another's lost goods, so it applied only to tangible property. *See Prosser and Keeton on the Law of Torts* § 15 (W. Page Keeton ed., 5th ed.1984). Virtually every jurisdiction, however, has discarded this rigid limitation to some degree. Many courts ignore or expressly reject it. *See Kremen*, 325 F.3d at 1045-46 n.5 (Kozinski, J., dissenting) (citing cases); Astroworks, Inc. v. Astroexhibit, Inc., 257 F.Supp.2d 609, 618 (S.D.N.Y.2003) (holding that the plaintiff could maintain a claim for conversion of his website); Val D. Ricks, *The Conversion of Intangible Property: Bursting the Ancient Trover Bottle with New Wine*, 1991 B.Y.U. L. Rev. 1681, 1682. Others reject it for some intangibles but not others. The Restatement, for example, recommends the following test:

> (1) Where there is conversion of a document in which intangible rights are merged, the damages include the value of such rights.
> (2) One who effectively prevents the exercise of intangible rights of the kind customarily *merged in a document* is subject to a liability similar to that for conversion, even though the document is not itself converted.

Restatement (Second) of Torts § 242 (1965) (emphasis added). An intangible is "merged" in a document when, "by the appropriate rule of law, the right to the immediate possession of a chattel and the power to acquire such possession is *represented by* [the] document," or when "an intangible obligation [is] *represented by* [the] document, which is regarded as equivalent to the obligation." *Id*. cmt. *a* (emphasis added). The district court applied this test and found no evidence that Kremen's domain name was merged in a document.

The court assumed that California follows the Restatement on this issue. Our review, however, revealed that "there do not appear to be any California cases squarely addressing whether the 'merged with' requirement is a part of California law." *Kremen*, 325 F.3d at 1042. We invoked the California Supreme Court's certification procedure to offer it the opportunity to address the issue. . . . The Court declined . . . and the question now falls to us.

We conclude that California does not follow the Restatement's strict merger requirement. Indeed, the leading California Supreme Court case rejects the tangibility requirement altogether. In Payne v. Elliot, 54 Cal. 339 (1880), the Court considered whether shares in a corporation (as opposed to the share certificates themselves) could be converted. It held that they could, reasoning: "[T]he action no longer exists as it did at common law, but has been developed into a remedy for the conversion of *every species of personal property.*" (emphasis added). While *Payne*'s outcome might be reconcilable with the Restatement, its rationale certainly is not: It recognized conversion of shares, not because they are customarily represented by share certificates, but because they are a species of personal property and, perforce, protected.[7]

Notwithstanding *Payne*'s seemingly clear holding, the California Court of Appeal held in Olschewski v. Hudson, 87 Cal. App. 282 (1927), that a laundry route was not subject to conversion. It explained that *Payne*'s rationale was "too broad a statement as to the application of the doctrine of conversion." Rather than follow binding California Supreme Court precedent, the court retheorized *Payne* and held that corporate stock could be converted only because it was "represented by" a tangible document. . . .

Were *Olschewski* the only relevant case on the books, there might be a plausible argument that California follows the Restatement. But in Palm Springs-La Quinta Development Co. v. Kieberk Corp., 46 Cal.App.2d 234 (1941), the court of appeal allowed a conversion claim for intangible information in a customer list when some of the index cards on which the information was recorded were destroyed. The court allowed damages not just for the value of the cards, but for the value of the intangible information lost. . . . Section 242(1) of the Restatement, however, allows recovery for intangibles only if they are merged in the converted document. Customer information is not merged in a document in any meaningful sense. A Rolodex is not like a stock certificate that actually *represents* a property interest; it is only a means of recording information.

Palm Springs and *Olschewski* are reconcilable on their facts — the former involved conversion of the document itself while the latter did not. But this distinction can't be squared with the Restatement. The plaintiff in *Palm Springs* recovered damages for the value of his intangibles. But if those intangibles were merged in the index cards for purposes of section 242(1), the plaintiff . . . in *Olschewski* . . . should have recovered under section 242(2) — laundry routes surely are customarily written down *somewhere*. "Merged" can't mean one thing in one section and something else in the other.

California courts ignored the Restatement again in A & M Records, Inc. v. Heilman, 75 Cal. App.3d 554 (1977), which applied the tort to a defendant who

---

7. Intangible interests in *real* property, on the other hand, remain unprotected by conversion, presumably because trespass is an adequate remedy. *See* Goldschmidt v. Maier, 73 P. 984 (Cal.1903) (per curiam) ("[A] leasehold of real estate is not the subject of an action of trover."); Vuich v. Smith, 140 Cal.App. 453 (1934) (same). Some California cases also preserve the traditional exception for indefinite sums of money. *See* 5 Witkin *Torts* § 614.

sold bootlegged copies of musical recordings. The court held broadly that "such misappropriation and sale of the intangible property of another without authority from the owner is conversion." It gave no hint that its holding depended on whether the owner's intellectual property rights were merged in some document. One might imagine physical things with which the intangible was associated—for example, the medium on which the song was recorded. But an intangible intellectual property right in a song is not merged in a phonograph record in the sense that the record *represents* the composer's intellectual property right. The record is not like a certificate of ownership; it is only a medium for one instantiation of the artistic work.

Federal cases applying California law take an equally broad view. We have applied *A & M Records* to intellectual property rights in an audio broadcast, *see* Lone Ranger Television, Inc. v. Program Radio Corp., 740 F.2d 718 (9th Cir. 1984), and to a regulatory filing, *see G.S. Rasmussen*, 958 F.2d at 906-07. Like *A & M Records*, both decisions defy the Restatement's "merged in a document" test. An audio broadcast may be recorded on a tape and a regulatory submission may be typed on a piece of paper, but neither document *represents* the owner's intangible interest. . . .

Our own recent decision in Bancroft & Masters, Inc. v. Augusta National Inc., 223 F.3d 1082 (9th Cir. 2000), is especially relevant. That case involved a domain name—precisely the type of property at issue here. The primary question was personal jurisdiction, but a majority of the panel joined the judgment only on the understanding that the defendant had committed conversion of a domain name, which it characterized as "tortious conduct." . . .

Were it necessary to settle the issue once and for all, we would toe the line of *Payne* and hold that conversion is "a remedy for the conversion of every species of personal property." But we need not do so to resolve this case. Assuming *arguendo* that California retains some vestigial merger requirement, it is clearly minimal, and at most requires only *some* connection to a document or tangible object—not representation of the owner's intangible interest in the strict Restatement sense.

Kremen's domain name falls easily within this class of property. He argues that the relevant document is the Domain Name System, or "DNS"—the distributed electronic database that associates domain names like sex.com with particular computers connected to the Internet. We agree that the DNS is a document (or perhaps more accurately a collection of documents). That it is stored in electronic form rather than on ink and paper is immaterial. . . . It would be a curious jurisprudence that turned on the existence of a *paper* document rather than an electronic one. Torching a company's file room would then be conversion while hacking into its mainframe and deleting its data would not. That is not the law, at least not in California. . . .

Kremen's domain name is protected by California conversion law, even on the grudging reading we have given it. Exposing Network Solutions to liability when it gives away a registrant's domain name on the basis of a forged letter is no different from holding a corporation liable when it gives away someone's shares under the same circumstances. . . . We have not "creat[ed] new tort duties" in reaching this result. *Cf.* Moore v. Regents of the Univ. of Cal., 51 Cal. 3d 120 (1990). We have only applied settled principles of conversion law to what the parties and the district court all agree is a species of property.

. . . [T]here is nothing unfair about holding a company responsible for giving away someone else's property even if it was not at fault. Cohen is obviously the guilty party here, and the one who should in all fairness pay for his theft. But he's skipped the country, and his money is stashed in some offshore bank account. Unless Kremen's luck with his bounty hunters improves, Cohen is out of the picture. The question becomes whether Network Solutions should be open to liability for its decision to hand over Kremen's domain name. Negligent or not, it was Network Solutions that gave away Kremen's property. Kremen never did anything. It would not be unfair to hold Network Solutions responsible and force *it* to try to recoup its losses by chasing down Cohen. This, at any rate, is the logic of the common law, and we do not lightly discard it.

The district court was worried that "the threat of litigation threatens to stifle the registration system by requiring further regulations by [Network Solutions] and potential increases in fees." Given that Network Solutions's "regulations" evidently allowed it to hand over a registrant's domain name on the basis of a facially suspect letter without even contacting him, "further regulations" don't seem like such a bad idea. And the prospect of higher fees presents no issue here that it doesn't in any other context. A bank could lower its ATM fees if it didn't have to pay security guards, but we doubt most depositors would think that was a good idea.

The district court thought there were "methods better suited to regulate the vagaries of domain names" and left it "to the legislature to fashion an appropriate statutory scheme." The legislature, of course, is always free (within constitutional bounds) to refashion the system that courts come up with. But that doesn't mean we should throw up our hands and let private relations degenerate into a free-for-all in the meantime. We apply the common law until the legislature tells us otherwise. And the common law does not stand idle while people give away the property of others. . . .

Conversion by Bailee

. . . Kremen's "conversion by bailee" claim does not state a cause of action independent of his conversion claim. As we read California law, "conversion by bailee" is not a distinct tort, but merely the tort of conversion committed by one who is a bailee. . . .

Kremen had a viable claim for conversion. The judgment of the district court is reversed on this count, and the case is remanded for further proceedings. . . .

Notes and Questions

1. Kremen obtained a judgment for $40 million in compensatory and $21 million in punitive damages against Cohen under theories of constructive trust and unfair competition. A constructive trust may be imposed on the owner of wrongfully obtained property and requires the owner to convey it to the person who should be the rightful owner. Where the wrongful owner has generated profits from the property, the profits may be awarded to the person who should have been the owner. In a conversion action, the usual measure of damages is the value of the property at the time of the conversion. What would be the appropriate measure of damages against Network Solutions?

2. Is there any reason to limit the availability of conversion to actions involving tangible property and intangible property merged in a document, or is Judge Kozinski right that conversion should be available for all types of personal property?

Restatement (Second) of Torts § 222A (1965)

§ 222A What Constitutes Conversion

> **(1) Conversion is an intentional exercise of dominion or control over a chattel which so seriously interferes with the right of another to control it that the actor may justly be required to pay the other the full value of the chattel.**
>
> **(2) In determining the seriousness of the interference and the justice of requiring the actor to pay the full value, the following factors are important:**
>
>> **(a) the extent and duration of the actor's exercise of dominion or control;**
>>
>> **(b) the actor's intent to assert a right in fact inconsistent with the other's right of control;**
>>
>> **(c) the actor's good faith;**
>>
>> **(d) the extent and duration of the resulting interference with the other's right of control;**
>>
>> **(e) the harm done to the chattel;**
>>
>> **(f) the inconvenience and expense caused to the other.**

Comment:

a. The modern action for the tort called conversion is descended from the old common law action of trover. This action originated at an early date as a remedy against the finder of lost goods who refused to return them to the owner but instead "converted" them to his own use. Until comparatively recent times the fiction of losing and finding persisted in many jurisdictions in the pleading of the action.

Trover was soon extended to cases of dispossession, or of withholding possession by others than finders. The basis of the tort was considered to be an interference with possession of the chattel, or with the right to immediate possession. Trover became a more or less universal remedy applicable to cases in which the plaintiff had been deprived of his chattel, whether by a wrongful taking, a wrongful detention, some wrongful disposal, or other interference with it. It was not at all clearly distinguished from the action of trespass.

The modern law of conversion began with Fouldes v. Willoughby, 8 M. & W. 540, 151 Eng.Rep. 1153 (1841), where the court first drew a distinction between a mere trespass interfering with possession of a chattel, and a conversion, which must involve some exercise of the defendant's hostile dominion or control over it. From this there has developed the present rule, which regards conversion as an exercise of the defendant's dominion or control over the chattel, as distinguished from a mere interference with the chattel itself, or with the possession of it. Since any interference with the chattel is to some extent an exercise of "dominion," the difference between the two becomes almost entirely a matter of degree.

b. Extension beyond trover. Under the older common law, the tort of conversion was identified with the action of trover; and where trover would not lie, there could be no conversion. With the abolition of the forms of action under procedural codes, and their modification in those states which still retain common law pleading, the name "conversion" has been extended to include some interferences with chattels for which the action of trover would not lie. For example, "conversion" is used by many courts to describe an interference with the rights of one who is not in possession of the chattel, and who has no right to immediate possession, but has only a right of future possession. (See § 243.) Trover would not lie in such a case, but there was a common law action on the case which permitted recovery of the same damages. Other courts, while refusing to call such an interference conversion, say that there is an action "in the nature of conversion," which leads to the same result. Apart from the technicalities of pleading, it is obviously of little importance what the action is called. In this Restatement, "conversion" is used in this broader sense, and is not restricted to torts for which the action of trover would lie.

  c. Recovery of full value of chattel. The importance of the distinction between trespass to chattels and conversion, which has justified its survival long after the forms of action of trespass and trover have become obsolete, lies in the measure of damages. In trespass the plaintiff may recover for the diminished value of his chattel because of any damage to it, or for the damage to his interest in its possession or use. Usually, although not necessarily, such damages are less than the full value of the chattel itself. In conversion the measure of damages is the full value of the chattel, at the time and place of the tort. When the defendant satisfies the judgment in the action for conversion, title to the chattel passes to him, so that he is in effect required to buy it at a forced judicial sale. Conversion is therefore properly limited, and has been limited by the courts, to those serious, major, and important interferences with the right to control the chattel which justify requiring the defendant to pay its full value.

  d. No one factor is always predominant in determining the seriousness of the interference, or the justice of requiring the forced purchase at full value. Those listed in Subsection (2) are not intended to be exclusive. The question is nearly always one of degree, and no fixed line can be drawn. There is probably no type of conduct with respect to a chattel which is always and under all circumstances sufficiently important to amount to a conversion, since the interference with the right of the plaintiff may in each case be either trivial or serious. Not only the conduct of the defendant, but also its consequences, are to be taken into account. In each case the question to be asked is whether the actor has exercised such dominion and control over the chattel, and has so seriously interfered with the other's right to control it, that in justice he should be required to buy the chattel.

MOORE v. REGENTS OF THE UNIVERSITY OF CALIFORNIA

Supreme Court of California
51 Cal. 3d 120, 793 P.2d 479 (1990), cert. denied, 499 U.S. 936 (1991)

. . . PANELLI, J. . . . We granted review in this case to determine whether plaintiff has stated a cause of action against his physician and other defendants for using his cells in potentially lucrative medical research without his permission. Plaintiff alleges that his physician failed to disclose preexisting research and economic interests in the cells before obtaining consent to the medical procedures by which they were extracted. The superior court sustained all defendants' demurrers to the third amended complaint, and the Court of Appeal reversed. We hold that the complaint states a cause of action for breach of the physician's disclosure obligations, but not for conversion. . . .

FACTS

We briefly summarize the pertinent factual allegations of the 50-page complaint.

. . . The plaintiff is John Moore . . . . The five defendants are: (1) Dr. David W. Golde . . . , a physician who attended Moore at UCLA Medical Center; (2) the Regents of the University of California . . . ; (3) Shirley G. Quan, a researcher employed by the Regents; (4) Genetics Institute, Inc. . . . ; and (5) Sandoz Pharmaceuticals Corporation and related entities . . . .

Moore first visited UCLA Medical Center on October 5, 1976, shortly after he learned that he had hairy-cell leukemia. After hospitalizing Moore and "withdr[awing] extensive amounts of blood, bone marrow aspirate, and other bodily substances," Golde confirmed that diagnosis. At this time all defendants, including Golde, were aware that "certain blood products and blood components were of great value in a number of commercial and scientific efforts" and that access to a patient whose blood contained these substances would provide "competitive, commercial, and scientific advantages."

. . . Golde recommended that Moore's spleen be removed. Golde informed Moore "that he had reason to fear for his life, and that the proposed splenectomy operation . . . was necessary to slow down the progress of his disease." Based upon Golde's representations, Moore signed a written consent form authorizing the splenectomy.

Before the operation, Golde and Quan "formed the intent and made arrangements to obtain portions of [Moore's] spleen following its removal" and to take them to a separate research unit. Golde gave written instructions to this effect . . . . These research activities "were not intended to have . . . any relation to [Moore's] medical . . . care." However, neither Golde nor Quan informed Moore of their plans to conduct this research or requested his permission. Surgeons at UCLA Medical Center, whom the complaint does not name as defendants, removed Moore's spleen on October 20, 1976.

Moore returned to the UCLA Medical Center several times between November 1976 and September 1983 . . . at Golde's direction and based upon representations "that such visits were necessary and required for his health and well-being, and based upon the trust inherent in and by virtue of the physician-patient relationship." . . . On each of these visits Golde withdrew additional samples of "blood, blood serum, skin, bone marrow aspirate, and sperm." On each occasion Moore traveled to the UCLA Medical Center from his home in Seattle because he had been told that the procedures were to be performed only there and only under Golde's direction.

"In fact, [however,] throughout the period of time that [Moore] was under [Golde's] care and treatment, . . . the defendants were actively involved in a number of activities which they concealed from [Moore] . . . ." Specifically, defendants were conducting research on Moore's cells and planned to "benefit financially and competitively . . . [by exploiting the cells] and [their] exclusive access to [the cells] by virtue of [Golde's] ongoing physician-patient relationship. . . ."

Sometime before August 1979, Golde established a cell line from Moore's T-lymphocytes.[2] On January 30, 1981, the Regents applied for a patent on the

---

2. A T-lymphocyte is a type of white blood cell. T-lymphocytes produce lymphokines, or proteins that regulate the immune system. Some lymphokines have potential therapeutic value. If the genetic material responsible for producing a particular lymphokine can be identified, it can sometimes be used to manufacture large quantities of the lymphokine through the techniques of

cell line, listing Golde and Quan as inventors. "[B]y virtue of an established policy . . . , [the] Regents, Golde, and Quan would share in any royalties or profits . . . arising out of [the] patent." The patent issued on March 20, 1984, naming Golde and Quan as the inventors of the cell line and the Regents as the assignee of the patent.

The Regent's patent also covers various methods for using the cell line to produce lymphokines. Moore admits in his complaint that "the true clinical potential of each of the lymphokines . . . [is] difficult to predict, [but] . . . competing commercial firms in the relevant fields have published reports in biotechnology industry periodicals predicting a potential market of approximately $3.01 Billion Dollars by the year 1990 for a whole range of [such lymphokines] . . . ."

With the Regents' assistance, Golde negotiated agreements for commercial development of the cell line and products to be derived from it. Under an agreement with Genetics Institute, Golde "became a paid consultant" and "acquired the rights to 75,000 shares of common stock." Genetics Institute also agreed to pay Golde and the Regents "at least $330,000 over three years, including a pro-rata share of [Golde's] salary and fringe benefits, in exchange for . . . exclusive access to the materials and research performed" on the cell line and products derived from it. On June 4, 1982, Sandoz "was added to the agreement," and compensation payable to Golde and the Regents was increased by $110,000. "[T]hroughout this period, . . . Quan spent as much as 70 [percent] of her time working for [the] Regents on research" related to the cell line.

Based upon these allegations, Moore attempted to state 13 causes of action.[4] Each defendant demurred to each purported cause of action. The superior court, however, expressly considered the validity of only the first cause of action, conversion. Reasoning that the remaining causes of action incorporated the earlier, defective allegations, the superior court sustained a general demurrer to the entire complaint with leave to amend. In a subsequent proceeding, the superior court sustained Genetics Institute's and Sandoz's demurrers without leave to amend on the grounds that Moore had not stated a cause of action for conversion and that the complaint's allegations about the entities' secondary liability were too conclusory.

With one justice dissenting, the Court of Appeal reversed, holding that the complaint did state a cause of action for conversion. . . .

---

recombinant DNA. (*See generally,* U.S. Congress, Office of Technology Assessment, New Developments in Biotechnology: Ownership of Human Tissues and Cells (1987) at pp. 31-46 (hereafter OTA Report).)

While the genetic code for lymphokines does not vary from individual to individual, it can nevertheless be quite difficult to locate the gene responsible for a particular lymphokine. . . . Moore's T-lymphocytes were interesting to the defendants because they overproduced certain lymphokines, thus making the corresponding genetic material easier to identify. . . .

4. (1) "Conversion"; (2) "lack of informed consent"; (3) "breach of fiduciary duty"; (4) "fraud and deceit"; (5) "unjust enrichment"; (6) "quasi-contract"; (7) "bad faith breach of the implied covenant of good faith and fair dealing"; (8) "intentional infliction of emotional distress"; (9) "negligent misrepresentation"; (10) "intentional interference with prospective advantageous economic relationships"; (11) "slander of title"; (12) "accounting"; and (13) "declaratory relief."

DISCUSSION

A. Breach of Fiduciary Duty and Lack of Informed Consent

Moore repeatedly alleges that Golde failed to disclose the extent of his research and economic interests in Moore's cells[6] before obtaining consent to the medical procedures by which the cells were extracted. These allegations, in our view, state a cause of action against Golde for invading a legally protected interest of his patient. This cause of action can properly be characterized either as the breach of a fiduciary duty to disclose facts material to the patient's consent or, alternatively, as the performance of medical procedures without first having obtained the patient's informed consent. . . .

. . . [W]e hold that a physician who is seeking a patient's consent for a medical procedure must, in order to satisfy his fiduciary duty and to obtain the patient's informed consent, disclose personal interests unrelated to the patient's health, whether research or economic, that may affect his medical judgment.

B. Conversion

Moore also attempts to characterize the invasion of his rights as a conversion. . . . He theorizes that he continued to own his cells following their removal from his body, at least for the purpose of directing their use, and that he never consented to their use in potentially lucrative medical research. Thus, . . . defendants' unauthorized use of his cells constitutes a conversion. As a result of the alleged conversion, Moore claims a proprietary interest in each of the products that any of the defendants might ever create from his cells or the patented cell line.

No court, however, has ever in a reported decision imposed conversion liability for the use of human cells in medical research.[15] While that fact does not end our inquiry, it raises a flag of caution. In effect, what Moore is asking us to do is to impose a tort duty on scientists to investigate the consensual pedigree of each human cell sample used in research.[16] To impose such a duty, which would affect medical research of importance to all of society, implicates policy concerns far removed from the traditional, two-party ownership disputes in which the law of conversion arose.[17] Invoking a tort theory originally used to

---

6. In this opinion we use the inclusive term "cells" to describe all of the cells taken from Moore's body, including blood cells, bone marrow, spleen, etc.

15. The absence of such authority cannot simply be attributed to recent developments in technology. The first human tumor cell line, which still is widely used in research, was isolated in 1951. (OTA Rep., *supra* fn. *2*, at p. 34.)

16. Imposing liability for conversion is equivalent to the imposition of such a duty, since only through investigation would users of cells be able to avoid liability.

17. Conversion arose out of the common law action of trover. "We probably do not have the earliest examples of its use, but they were almost certainly cases in which the finder of lost goods did not return them, but used them himself, or disposed of them to someone else. . . . By 1554 the allegations of the complaint had become more or less standardized: that the plaintiff was possessed of certain goods, that he casually lost them, that the defendant found them, and that the defendant did not return them, but instead 'converted them to his own use.' From that phrase in the pleading came the name of the tort." (Prosser & Keeton, Torts (5th ed. 1984) § 15, p. 89.)

determine whether the loser or the finder of a horse had the better title, Moore claims ownership of the results of socially important medical research, including the genetic code for chemicals that regulate the functions of every human being's immune system.

. . . [W]hen the proposed application of a very general theory of liability in a new context raises important policy concerns, it is especially important to face those concerns and address them openly. . . . [W]e should be hesitant to "impose [new tort duties] when to do so would involve complex policy decisions," especially when such decisions are more appropriately the subject of legislative deliberation and resolution. . . . This certainly is not to say that the applicability of common law torts is limited to the historical or factual contexts of existing cases. But on occasions when we have opened or sanctioned new areas of tort liability, we "have noted that the 'wrongs and injuries involved were both comprehensible and assessable within the existing judicial framework.' . . ."

[W]e first consider whether the tort of conversion clearly gives Moore a cause of action under existing law. We do not believe it does. Because of the novelty of Moore's claim to own the biological materials at issue, to apply the theory of conversion in this context would frankly have to be recognized as an extension of the theory. Therefore, we consider next whether it is advisable to extend the tort to this context.

1. *Moore's Claim Under Existing Law*

. . . Since Moore clearly did not expect to retain possession of his cells following their removal, to sue for their conversion he must have retained an ownership interest in them. But there are several reasons to doubt that he did retain any such interest. First, no reported judicial decision supports Moore's claim, either directly or by close analogy. Second, California statutory law drastically limits any continuing interest of a patient in excised cells. Third, the subject matters of the Regents' patent—the patented cell line and the products derived from it—cannot be Moore's property.

Neither the Court of Appeal's opinion, the parties' briefs, nor our research discloses a case holding that a person retains a sufficient interest in excised cells to support a cause of action for conversion. We do not find this surprising, since the laws governing such things as human tissues, transplantable organs,[22] blood,[23]

---

22.   *See* the Uniform Anatomical Gift Act . . . . The act permits a competent adult to "give all or part of [his] body" for certain designated purposes, including "transplantation, therapy, medical or dental education, research, or advancement of medical or dental science." (Health & Saf. Code, §§ 7151, 7153.) The act does not, however, permit the donor to receive "valuable consideration" for the transfer. (Health *&* Saf. Code, § 7155.)

23.   *See* Health and Safety Code section 1601 *et seq.*, which regulates the procurement, processing, and distribution of human blood. . . . [S]ection 1606 declares that "[t]he procurement, processing, distribution, or use of whole blood, plasma, blood products, and blood derivatives for the purpose of injecting or transfusing the same . . . is declared to be, for all purposes whatsoever, the rendition of a service . . . and shall not be construed to be, and is declared not to be, a sale . . . for any purpose or purposes whatsoever."

fetuses,[24] pituitary glands,[25] corneal tissue,[26] and dead bodies[27] deal with human biological materials as objects *sui generis,* regulating their disposition to achieve policy goals rather than abandoning them to the general law of personal property. It is these specialized statutes, not the law of conversion, to which courts ordinarily should and do look for guidance on the disposition of human biological materials.

Lacking direct authority for importing the law of conversion into this context, Moore relies, as did the Court of Appeal, primarily on decisions addressing privacy rights. One line of cases involves unwanted publicity. . . . These opinions hold that every person has a proprietary interest in his own likeness and that unauthorized, business use of a likeness is redressible as a tort. But in neither opinion did the authoring court expressly base its holding on property law. . . .

Not only are the wrongful-publicity cases irrelevant to the issue of conversion, but the analogy to them seriously misconceives the nature of the genetic materials and research involved in this case. Moore . . . argues that "[i]f the courts have found a sufficient proprietary interest in one's persona, how could one not have a right in one's own genetic material, something far more profoundly the essence of one's human uniqueness than a name or a face?" However, as the defendants' patent makes clear . . . the goal and result of defendants' efforts has been to manufacture lymphokines. Lymphokines, unlike a name or a face, have the same molecular structure in every human being and the same, important functions in every human being's immune system. Moreover, the particular genetic material which is responsible for the natural production of lymphokines, and which defendants use to manufacture lymphokines in the laboratory, is also the same in every person; it is no more unique to Moore than the number of vertebrae in the spine or the chemical formula of hemoglobin.

Another privacy case offered by analogy to support Moore's claim establishes only that patients have a right to refuse medical treatment. (Bouvia v. Superior Court (1986) 179 Cal. App. 3d 1127.) In this context the court . . . wrote that " '[e]very human being of adult years and sound mind has a right to determine what shall be done with his own body . . . .' " . . . Relying on this language to support the proposition that a patient has a continuing right to control the use of excised cells, the Court of Appeal in this case concluded that "[a] patient must have the ultimate power to control what becomes of his or her tissues. To hold otherwise would open the door to a massive invasion of human privacy and dignity in the name of medical progress." Yet one may earnestly wish to protect

24.   *See* Health and Safety Code section 7054.3: "Notwithstanding any other provision of law, a recognizable dead human fetus of less than 20 weeks uterogestation not disposed of by interment shall be disposed of by incineration."

25.   *See* Government Code section 27491.46: "The coroner [following an autopsy] shall have the right to retain pituitary glands solely for transmission to a university, for use in research or the advancement of medical science" or "for use in manufacturing a hormone necessary for the physical growth of persons who are, or may become, hypopituitary dwarfs . . . ."

26.   *See* Government Code section 27491.47: "The coroner may, in the course of an autopsy [and subject to specified conditions], remove . . . corneal eye tissue from a body . . ." (*id.,* subd. (a)) for "transplant, therapeutic, or scientific purposes" (*id.,* subd. (a)(5)).

27.   *See* Health and Safety Code section 7000 *et seq.* While the code does not purport to grant property rights in dead bodies, it does give the surviving spouse, or other relatives, "[t]he right to control the disposition of the remains of a deceased person, unless other directions have been given by the decedent. . . ." (Health *&* Saf. Code, § 7100.)

privacy and dignity without accepting the extremely problematic conclusion that interference with those interests amounts to a conversion of personal property. Nor is it necessary to force the round pegs of "privacy" and "dignity" into the square hole of "property" in order to protect the patient, since the fiduciary-duty and informed-consent theories protect these interests directly by requiring full disclosure.

The next consideration . . . is California statutory law, which drastically limits a patient's control over excised cells. Pursuant to Health and Safety Code section 7054.4, "[n]otwithstanding any other provision of law, recognizable anatomical parts, human tissues, anatomical human remains, or infectious waste following conclusion of scientific use shall be disposed of by interment, incineration, or any other method determined by the state department [of health services] to protect the public health and safety." Clearly the Legislature did not specifically intend this statute to resolve the question whether a patient is entitled to compensation for the nonconsensual use of excised cells. A primary object of the statute is to ensure the safe handling of potentially hazardous biological waste materials.[33] Yet one cannot escape the conclusion that the statute's practical effect is to limit, drastically, a patient's control over excised cells. By restricting how excised cells may be used and requiring their eventual destruction, the statute eliminates so many of the rights ordinarily attached to property that one cannot simply assume that what is left amounts to "property" or "ownership" for purposes of conversion law.

It may be that some limited right to control the use of excised cells does survive the operation of this statute. There is, for example, no need to read the statute to permit "scientific use" contrary to the patient's expressed wish. A fully informed patient may always withhold consent to treatment by a physician whose research plans the patient does not approve. That right, however, . . . is protected by the fiduciary-duty and informed-consent theories.

Finally, the subject matter of the Regents' patent—the patented cell line and the products derived from it—cannot be Moore's property. . . . [T]he patented cell line is both factually and legally distinct from the cells taken from Moore's body.[35] Federal law permits the patenting of organisms that represent the product of "human ingenuity," but not naturally occurring organisms.

33.   The policy of keeping biological materials in safe hands has substantial relevance to this case. The catalog of the American Type Culture Collection, an organization that distributes cell lines to researchers, gives this warning about the cell line derived from Moore's T-lymphocytes: Because "[t]he cells . . . contain a replication competent genome of Human T Cell Leukemia Virus II (HTLV-II) [i.e., genetic material capable of reproducing the virus] . . . , they must be handled as potentially biohazardous material under P-II [level II] containment." . . .

35.   The distinction between primary cells (cells taken directly from the body) and patented cell lines is not purely a legal one. Cells change while being developed into a cell line and continue to change over time. . . . "[I]t is clear that most established cell lines . . . are not completely normal. Besides [an] enhanced growth potential relative to primary cells, they frequently have highly abnormal chromosome numbers. . . ." (2 Watson et al., Molecular Biology of the Gene, 4th ed. 1987) p. 967 . . . .

The cell line in this case, for example, after many replications began to generate defective and rearranged forms of the HTLV-II virus. A published research paper to which defendants contributed suggests that "the defective forms of virus were probably generated during the passage [or replication] of the cells rather than being present in the original tumour cells of the patient." Possibly because of these changes in the virus, the cell line has developed new abilities to grow in different media. (Chen, McLaughlin, Gasson, Clark & Golde, *Molecular Characterization of Genome of a Novel Human T-cell Leukaemia Virus*, Nature (Oct. 6, 1983) vol. 305, p. 505.)

(Diamond v. Chakrabarty (U.S. 1980)). Human cell lines are patentable because "[l]ong-term adaptation and growth of human tissues and cells in culture is difficult—often considered an art . . . ," and the probability of success is low. (OTA Rep., at p. 33.) It is this inventive effort that patent law rewards, not the discovery of naturally occurring raw materials. . . . Moore's allegations that he owns the cell line and the products derived from it are inconsistent with the patent, which constitutes an authoritative determination that the cell line is the product of invention.[37]

2. Should Conversion Liability Be Extended?

There are three reasons why it is inappropriate to impose liability for conversion based upon the allegations of Moore's complaint. First, a fair balancing of the relevant policy considerations counsels against extending the tort. Second, problems in this area are better suited to legislative resolution. Third, the tort of conversion is not necessary to protect patients' rights. . . .

Of the relevant policy considerations, two are of overriding importance. The first is protection of a competent patient's right to make autonomous medical decisions. . . . This policy weighs in favor of providing a remedy to patients when physicians act with undisclosed motives that may affect their professional judgment. The second important policy consideration is that we not threaten with disabling civil liability innocent parties who are engaged in socially useful activities, such as researchers who have no reason to believe that their use of a particular cell sample is, or may be, against a donor's wishes.

To reach an appropriate balance of these policy considerations is extremely important. In its report to Congress, the Office of Technology Assessment emphasized that "[u]ncertainty about how courts will resolve disputes between specimen sources and specimen users could be detrimental to both academic researchers and the infant biotechnology industry, particularly when the rights are asserted long after the specimen was obtained. The assertion of rights by sources would affect not only the researcher who obtained the original specimen, but perhaps other researchers as well.

"Biological materials are routinely distributed to other researchers for experimental purposes, and scientists who obtain cell lines or other specimen-derived products, such as gene clones, from the original researcher could also be sued under certain legal theories [such as conversion]. Furthermore, the uncertainty could affect product developments as well as research. Since inventions containing human tissues and cells may be patented and licensed for commercial use, companies are unlikely to invest heavily in developing, manufacturing, or marketing a product when uncertainty about clear title exists." (OTA Rep. at p. 27.)

Indeed, so significant is the potential obstacle to research stemming from uncertainty about legal title to biological materials that the Office of Technology

---

37. To avoid this conclusion, the dissent endorses a proposal to expand Congress's definition of "joint inventor" (35 U.S.C. § 116) to include the human source of biological materials used in research. (Dis. opn. of Mosk, J . . . .) Because exclusive power to effect change in the law of patents lies with Congress and the federal courts . . . the dissent's criticism of the law's present state has no legitimate bearing on our disposition of this case.

Assessment reached this striking conclusion: "[R]egardless of the merit of claims by the different interested parties, resolving the current uncertainty may be more important to the future of biotechnology than resolving it in any particular way."

We need not, however, make an arbitrary choice between liability and nonliability. . . . Liability based upon existing disclosure obligations, rather than an unprecedented extension of the conversion theory, protects patients' rights of privacy and autonomy without unnecessarily hindering research.

. . . [T]he threat of liability for conversion might help to enforce patients' rights . . . because physicians might be able to avoid liability by obtaining patients' consent . . . to any conceivable subsequent research use of excised cells. Unfortunately, . . . [s]ince conversion is a strict liability tort, it would impose liability on all those into whose hands the cells come, whether or not the particular defendant participated in, or knew of, the inadequate disclosures that violated the patient's right to make an informed decision. In contrast to the conversion theory, the fiduciary-duty and informed-consent theories protect the patient directly, without punishing innocent parties or creating disincentives to the conduct of socially beneficial research. . . .[42]

If the scientific users of human cells are to be held liable for failing to investigate the consensual pedigree of their raw materials, we believe the Legislature should make that decision. . . . Finally, there is no pressing need to impose a judicially created rule of strict liability, since enforcement of physicians' disclosure obligations will protect patients against the very type of harm with which Moore was threatened. . . .

DISPOSITION

. . . The case is remanded to the Court of Appeal, which shall direct the superior court to: (1) overrule Golde's demurrers to the causes of action for breach of fiduciary duty and lack of informed consent; (2) sustain, with leave to amend, the demurrers of the Regents, Quan, Sandoz, and Genetics Institute to the purported causes of action for breach of fiduciary duty and lack of informed consent; (3) sustain, without leave to amend, all defendants' demurrers to the purported cause of action for conversion; and (4) hear and determine all defendants' remaining demurrers.

LUCAS, C.J., EAGLESON, J., and KENNARD, J., concur.

ARABIAN, J., concurring. . . . I write separately to give voice to a concern that I believe informs much of that opinion but finds little or no expression therein. I speak of the moral issue. Plaintiff has asked us to recognize and enforce a right

---

42. To make conversion liability seem less of a threat to research, the dissent argues that researchers could avoid liability by using only cell lines accompanied by documentation of the source's consent. (Dis. opn. of Mosk, J.) But consent forms do not come with guaranties of validity. Moreover, it is sheer fantasy to hope that waivers might be obtained for the thousands of cell lines and tissue samples presently in cell repositories and, for that reason, already in wide use among researchers. The cell line derived from Moore's T-lymphocytes, for example, has been available since 1984 to any researcher from the American Type Culture Collection. Other cell lines have been in wide use since as early as 1951.

to sell one's own body tissue for profit. He entreats us to regard the human vessel—the single most venerated and protected subject in any civilized society—as equal with the basest commercial commodity. He urges us to commingle the sacred with the profane. He asks much.

My learned colleague, Justice Mosk, in an impressive if ultimately unpersuasive dissent, recognizes the moral dimension of the matter. "[O]ur society," he writes, "acknowledges a profound ethical imperative to respect the human body as the physical and temporal expression of the unique human persona." He concludes, however, that morality militates in favor of recognizing plaintiff's claim for conversion of his body tissue. Why? Essentially, he answers, because of these defendants' moral shortcomings, duplicity and greed. Let them be compelled, he argues, to disgorge a portion of their ill-gotten gains to the uninformed individual whose body was invaded and exploited and without whom such profits would not have been possible.

I share Justice Mosk's sense of outrage, but I cannot follow its path. His eloquent paean to the human spirit illuminates the problem, but not the solution. Does it uplift or degrade the "unique human persona" to treat human tissue as a fungible article of commerce? Would it advance or impede the human condition, spiritually or scientifically, by delivering the majestic force of the law behind plaintiff's claim? I do not know the answers to these troubling questions, nor am I willing—like Justice Mosk—to treat them simply as issues of "tort" law, susceptible of judicial resolution.

The ramifications of recognizing and enforcing a property interest in body tissues are not known, but are greatly feared—the effect on human dignity of a marketplace in human body parts, the impact on research and development of competitive bidding for such materials, and the exposure of researchers to potentially limitless and uncharted tort liability.

Whether, as plaintiff urges, his cells should be treated as property susceptible to conversion is not, in my view, ours to decide. The question implicates choices which not only reflect, but which ultimately define our essence. A mark of wisdom for us as expositors of the law is the recognition that we cannot cure every ill, mediate every dispute, resolve every conundrum. Sometimes, as Justice Brandeis said, "the most important thing we do, is not doing."[1]

Where then shall a complete resolution be found? Clearly the Legislature, as the majority opinion suggests, is the proper deliberative forum. Indeed, a legislative response creating a licensing scheme, which establishes a fixed rate of profit sharing between researcher and subject, has already been suggested.[6] . . . Such an arrangement would not only avoid the moral and philosophical objections to a free market operation in body tissue, but would also address stated concerns by eliminating the inherently coercive effect of a waiver system and by compensating donors regardless of temporal circumstances. . . .

BROUSSARD, J., concurring and dissenting. . . . With respect to the conversion cause of action, I dissent. . . .

---

1. Bickel, The Least Dangerous Branch (1962) page 71.
6. Mary Taylor Danforth, *Cells, Sales, and Royalties: The Patient's Right to a Portion of the Profits*, 6 Yale L. & Pol'y Rev. 179, 198-201 (1988).—EDS.

[T]he majority's stated concern that extension of conversion law into this area will hinder research] does not provide any justification for barring plaintiff from bringing a conversion action against a party who does not obtain organs or cells from a cell bank but who directly interferes with or misappropriates a patient's right to control the use of his organs or cells. . . . [T]he existence of a breach-of-fiduciary-duty cause of action does not provide a complete answer. . . . For example, if a patient donated his removed cells to a medical center, reserving the right to approve or disapprove the research projects for which the cells would be used, and if another medical center or a drug manufacturer stole the cells after removal and used them in an unauthorized manner for its own economic gain, no breach-of-fiduciary-duty cause of action would be available and a conversion action would be necessary to vindicate the patient's rights. . . . [E]ven if there were compelling policy reasons to limit the potential liability of innocent researchers who use cells obtained from an existing cell bank, those policy considerations would not justify the majority's broad abrogation of all conversion liability for the unauthorized use of body parts.

It is certainly arguable that, as a matter of policy or morality, it would be wiser . . . to require all valuable excised body parts to be deposited in a public repository which would make such materials freely available to all scientists for the betterment of society as a whole. The Legislature, if it wished, could create such a system, as it has done with respect to organs that are donated for transplantation. Justice Arabian's concurring opinion suggests that the majority's conclusion is informed by the precept that it is immoral to sell human body parts for profit. But the majority's rejection of plaintiff's conversion cause of action does not mean that body parts may not be bought or sold for research or commercial purposes or that no private individual or entity may benefit economically from the fortuitous value of plaintiff's diseased cells. Far from elevating these biological materials above the marketplace, the majority's holding simply bars plaintiff, the source of the cells, from obtaining the benefit of the cells' value, but permits defendants, who allegedly obtained the cells from plaintiff by improper means, to retain and exploit the full economic value of their ill-gotten gains free of their ordinary common law liability for conversion.

Mosk, J., dissenting. . . . [T]he concept of property is often said to refer to a "bundle of rights" that may be exercised with respect to that object—principally the rights to possess the property, to use the property, to exclude others from the property, and to dispose of the property by sale or by gift. . . . But the same bundle of rights does not attach to all forms of property. For a variety of policy reasons, the law limits or even forbids the exercise of certain rights over certain forms of property. For example, both law and contract may limit the right of an owner of real property to use his parcel as he sees fit.[6] Owners of various forms

---

6.   Zoning or nuisance laws, or covenants running with the land or equitable servitudes, or condominium declarations, may prohibit certain uses of the parcel or regulate the number, size, location, etc., of buildings an owner may erect on it. Even if rental of the property is a permitted use, rent control laws may limit the benefits of that use. Other uses may, on the contrary, be compelled: e.g., if the property is a lease to extract minerals, the lease may be forfeited by law or contract if the lessee does not exploit the resource. Historic preservation laws may prohibit an owner from demolishing a building on the property, or even from altering its appearance. And endangered species laws may limit an owner's right to develop the land from its natural state.

of personal property may likewise be subject to restriction on the time, place, and manner of their use.[7] Limitations on the disposition of real property, while less common, may also be imposed.[8] Finally, some types of personal property may be sold but not given away,[9] while others may be given away but not sold,[10] and still others may neither be given away nor sold.[11]

In each of the foregoing instances, the limitation or prohibition diminishes the bundle of rights that would otherwise attach to the property, yet what remains is still deemed in law to be a protectible property interest. . . . The same rule applies to Moore's interest in his own body tissue. . . . Above all, at the time of its excision he at least had the right to do with his own tissue whatever the defendants did with it: *i.e.*, he could have contracted with researchers and pharmaceutical companies to develop and exploit the vast commercial potential of his tissue and its products.

Notes and Questions

1. Is the court correct that recognizing a property right in *Moore* would significantly chill medical research? If the courts did recognize patients' property rights in their tissue and body parts, what do you think would happen? Legislation? Establishment of a national registry for theft and conversion claims? Amended hospital consent forms? Development of "certificates of provenance" for tissue samples?

2. If the court had been willing to recognize a property right in *Moore*, what would be the appropriate measure of damages? If Golde had used a stolen petri dish in the course of developing the Mo Cell line, would the owner of the petri dish be entitled to a share of the profits from the cell line? The usual measure of damages for conversion is the value of the property at the time of the conversion. When did the conversion alleged by Moore occur? How would you determine how much Moore's spleen was worth at that time? How could Moore claim a share of the profits earned by Golde's subsequent research activities and the patent obtained on the cell line?

3. The law of accession and improvers might provide analogies for thinking about the problem presented in *Moore*. Accession covers the case where one person uses property that belongs to another in making something else. For example, a woodworker chops down a tree on someone else's land and makes a piece of furniture out of it. Or an artist uses someone else's canvas to paint a picture.

---

7. Public health and safety laws restrict in various ways the manufacture, distribution, purchase, sale, and use of such property as food, drugs, cosmetics, tobacco, alcoholic beverages, firearms, flammable or explosive materials, and waste products. Other laws regulate the operation of private and commercial motor vehicles, aircraft, and vessels.

8. Provisions in a condominium declaration may give the homeowners association a right of first refusal over a proposed sale by a member. Provisions in a commercial lease may require the lessor's consent to an assignment of the lease.

9. A person contemplating bankruptcy may sell his property at its "reasonably equivalent value," but he may not make a gift of the same property. (*See* 11 U.S.C. § 548(a).)

10. A sportsman may give away wild fish or game that he has caught or killed pursuant to his license, but he may not sell it. (Fish *&* G. Code, §§ 3039, 7121.)

11. E.g., a license to practice a profession, or a prescription drug in the hands of the person for whom it is prescribed.

The law of improvers may come into play when someone, either deliberately or by mistake, builds a structure on someone else's land. Several questions arise here: Who owns the resulting product? Does the owner have to pay the other for the value of her contribution? Who is entitled to the amount by which the value of the new thing exceeds the value of the raw materials contributed by the parties? Resolution of these questions often involves the relative values of the parties' contributions and their good or bad faith. To learn more about accessions, see Barlow Burke, Personal Property in a Nutshell 359-69 (3d ed. 2003). To learn more about the law of improvers, see 41 Am. Jur. 2d *Improvements* § 3.

4. Once the tissue was removed from Moore, did it become property? A former immunologist at the National Institutes of Health was held liable for conversion of a cell line developed by a colleague after he introduced poison into the cell flasks. A federal district judge in Baltimore ordered him to pay $5,000. The cells, which mimicked the function of brain cells, allowed researchers to study the effect of various chemicals on the brain. N.Y. Times, Aug. 31, 1994.

5. We recognize that people can sell blood, hair, semen, or ova, and that they can give away a kidney or part of a liver during life, implicitly treating these things as property.[7] Do any of the opinions in *Moore* offer a defensible rationale for treating those items as property while refusing to recognize a property interest in Moore's spleen?

6. Justice Arabian's concurring opinion gives voice to the unease felt by many people at the thought of treating human body parts as property ("commodifying" them, to use a popular description). Professor Margaret Jane Radin has been a leading advocate for thinking about property in terms of "fungible" property, which is appropriately bought and sold, and condemned by the government for public use, and "personal" property, which cannot be taken away and replaced with money or other things without harm to the person's identity and existence,[8] as a way of allowing moral evaluation of legal rules. She has taken the position that even discussing a person's interests in the integrity of her body in market exchange terms poses threats to personhood. In her article, *Market Inalienability*, 100 Harv. L. Rev. 1849, 1885-87 (1987), she concludes:

> Market rhetoric, if adopted by everyone, and in many contexts would . . . transform the texture of the human world. This rhetoric leads us to view politics as just rent seeking, reproductive capacity as just a scarce good for which there is a high demand, and the repugnance of slavery as just a cost. . . . Market rhetoric, the rhetoric of alienability of all "goods," is also the rhetoric of alienation of ourselves from what we can be as persons. . . . Universal market rhetoric transforms our world of concrete persons, whose uniqueness and individuality is expressed in specific personal attributes, into a world of disembodied, fungible, attribute-less entities possessing a wealth of alienable, severable "objects." This rhetoric reduces the conception of a person to an abstract, fungible unit with no individuating characteristics.

7. What were the true facts of the Moore case? In an appeal from the grant of a demurrer, the court accepts as true the facts alleged in the complaint. In

---

7.   An Associated Press story carried in the L.A. Times on Oct. 24, 1999, at p. A16, reported that Ron Harris, a Malibu fashion photographer, planned to offer the eggs of eight models for sale in an online auction with bids starting at $15,000. According to the article, Harris says "his offer is a reflection of a society in which beauty can be purchased by the highest bidder."

8.   Margaret Jane Radin, *Property and Personhood*, 34 Stan. L. Rev. 957 (1982).

a talk given by Professor Hank Greely of Stanford University Law School, "The True Facts of the Strange Case of John Moore's Spleen," several interesting facts were revealed. Moore's parents lived in Los Angeles and his father was a doctor. His father identified Dr. Golde as one of the leading researchers in the field of hairy cell leukemia, and Moore stayed with his parents during his initial treatment and follow-up visits. Golde's ongoing research on the nature of cells that become malignant in hairy cell leukemia included trying to create cell lines from all his patients. The unusual character of Moore's cell line did not emerge until about six months after the surgery, and was probably due to changes that occurred after the cell line was created. In fact, the cell line never became valuable and the University allowed the patent to lapse in 1997.

Golde claimed that he did tell Moore that he would use him in his research and later about the patent, which led to the litigation. After remand, Moore settled for several hundred thousand dollars, which he considered a "token" amount, and continued his campaign for patients' rights. His leukemia remained in remission from the time his spleen was removed in 1976 until 1996. He died on October 1, 2001, at age 56.

8. Should researchers be willing, or even required, to share profits with people who make their research possible by donating their tissue? In an article in the New York Times on May 15, 2000, *Sharing of Profits Is Debated as the Value of Tissue Rises*, Gina Kolata relates several stories of people who contributed to scientific advances in AIDS and Canavan's disease, but were cut out of the profits. The parents of children with Canavan's disease who sought out researchers, raised funds to support the research, and helped researchers obtain blood, urine, and skin biopsy samples were appalled when Miami Children's Hospital Research Institute, where the research was done, obtained a patent and decided to charge a $12.50 royalty for each test. The parents had expected that the gene test would be placed in the public domain. As awareness of the value of tissue spreads, will people become less willing to participate as volunteers?

9. Tumor cells removed from Henrietta Lacks, who died in 1951, gave rise to the first cell line. The cells, known as HeLa cells, were subsequently used in more than 74,000 studies. Her family became aware of the cell line in 1973 when a scientist asked them for blood samples to study their genes. In 2013, scientists in Europe and the United States sequenced the HeLa genome without the consent of the family. After the family objected to publication, primarily on privacy grounds, the National Institutes of Health negotiated an agreement giving the family some say in how the data will be used. Carl Zimmer, *A Family Consents to a Medical Gift, 62 Years Later*, N.Y. Times, Aug. 7, 2013, http://www.nytimes.com/2013/08/08/science/after-decades-of-research-henrietta-lacks-family-is-asked-for-consent.html?_r=1&. The story of Henrietta Lacks is told by Rebecca Skloot in *The Immortal Life of Henrietta Lacks* (2010).

Meaning of "Property" Varies with Context

The majority in *Moore v. The Regents* held that John Moore did not have a property interest sufficient to support a conversion action in the spleen that had been surgically removed from his body. In *Newman v. Sathyavaglswaran*, 287 F.3d 786 (9th Cir. 2002), decided shortly after *Moore*, the court held that the parents of deceased children had a sufficient property interest in the corneas of their dead children to sustain an action under 42 U.S.C. § 1983 for deprivation of their property without due process of law. The corneas had been removed by the Los Angeles County Coroner's office pursuant to a state statute that authorized the coroner to remove corneal eye tissue from a body in the coroner's custody without any effort to notify and obtain the consent of the next of kin unless the coroner knew of an objection to the removal. The statute also provided that the coroner was not liable for the removal to any person who had not objected before the removal.

The court in *Newman* relied on California cases and statutes that give a person the right dispose of her corpse by will and in the absence of a will, give that right to the next of kin. The court noted that the substantive interest is created by state law, but whether the interest is a property interest protected by the Due Process Clause is a matter of federal constitutional law. Welfare benefits and public employees' interest in continued employment have been held protected by procedural due process requirements. *See Goldberg v. Kelly*, 397 U.S. 183 (1970); *Connell v. Higginbotham*, 403 U.S. 207 (1971).

Whether government benefits create property protected by the Fourteenth Amendment depends on the determinacy of the benefit. If a statute provides that everyone meeting the eligibility criteria is entitled to the benefit, an eligible person's right to the benefit is generally entitled to due process protection. However, if the statute leaves room for the exercise of discretion in selecting recipients, the benefit is less likely to receive protection. In *Washington Legal Clinic for the Homeless v. Barry*, 107 F.3d 32 (D.C. Cir. 1997), for example, a divided court held that the right to adequate shelter under the District of Columbia Right to Overnight Shelter Act was not a constitutionally protected property interest because the District did not have enough space to accommodate all persons seeking shelter and the statute did not specify how available spaces were to be allocated. Because the persons running the program were free to use their discretion in allocating spaces, applicants did not have a right to a hearing before others were given priority over them.

When the government takes property for public use, it is required to give just compensation to the owner. When someone claims a right to compensation, the threshold question is whether the government has taken property from the claimant. In *United States v. Willow River Power Co.*, 324 U.S. 499 (1945), the power company sued the United States for the damage done to its electric generation capacity when the government raised the water level of the St. Croix River three feet above ordinary high water. The higher water level, due to a dam built to aid navigation, did not result in the intrusion of water into the power company's land, but reduced the amount of drop from the water level at its plant on the Willow River to the St. Croix River, thus reducing its generation capacity. The three-foot reduction in its "power head" was valued at $25,000 for which the power company sought compensation. The Supreme Court held that no compensation was owed because what was taken was not property—the power company's interest in the preexisting highwater level of the St. Croix River was not a protected right.

Human Organs as Property

Even if human organs are treated as property, it is illegal to sell them in the United States, National Organ Transplant Act, 42 U.S.C. § 274(e). After the first successful human organ transplant in 1963, a great imbalance developed between the number of people in need of organs and the supply. The 2011 Annual Data Report of the Organ Procurement and Transplantation Network and the U.S. Scientific Registry of Transplant Recipients reported that 17,604 kidney transplants were performed in 2011, but 54,599 people were on the wait list as of December 31, 2011.[9]

One response to the shortage was the kind of "presumed consent" statute at issue in *Newman v. Sathyavaglswaran*, 287 F.3d 786 (9th Cir. 2002), which presumes there is consent to removal of organs for transplant unless the decedent or the next of kin has made known an objection. These have not been very successful—the California statute was amended to require actual consent in 1998. Another option that has been extensively explored in the literature is changing the law to allow markets for organs. A Westlaw search in the JLR database on February 17, 2014 for titles that included the words "organ and market" returned 18 law review articles ranging from Glenn Cohen, *Transplant Tourism: The Ethics and Regulation of International Markets for Organs*, 41 J.L. Med. & Ethics 269 (2013), to Lloyd R. Cohen, *Increasing the Supply of Transplant Organs: The Virtues of a Futures Market*, 58 Geo. Wash. L. Rev. 1 (1989).

In China, the major supply of organs for transplant has come from executed prisoners. The practice raised substantial moral and ethical concerns because the organs were taken without consent of the prisoner, or the prisoner's family, and the conviction and sentencing of prisoners often lacked meaningful due process protection.[10] In 2007, the government outlawed the sale of organs and in 2009 began a pilot project to encourage the donation of organs. However, high demand for transplants and very limited supply remains a significant problem. *See* Austin Ramzy, *No Quick Fixes for China's Overwhelmed Organ Transplant System*, N.Y. Times, Nov. 10, 2013.

Israel has been able to increase the number of donated organs by giving priority for transplants to people who themselves, or through their families, agree to organ donations. *See* Danielle Ofri, M.D., *In Israel, a New Approach to Organ Donation*, N.Y. Times, Feb. 16, 2012.

---

9. http://srtr.transplant.hrsa.gov/annual_reports/2011/pdf/2011_SRTR_ADR.pdf.

10. *See* the statement of Michael E. Parmly, Principal Deputy Assistant Secretary of State, Bureau of Democracy, Human Rights, and Labor, *Sale of Human Organs in China*, Hearing Before the Subcommittee on International Operations and Human Rights, House International Relations, Washington, DC, June 27, 2001, available at http://www.state.gov/g/drl/rls/rm/2001/3792.htm. *See also* three articles in the New York Times by Craig S. Smith, *Doctor Says He Took Transplant Organs from Executed Chinese Prisoners*, June 29, 2001, *Quandary in U.S. over Use of Organs of Chinese Inmates*, Nov. 11, 2001, and *China Resists Efforts to Make Donation of Organs Feasible*, Dec. 5, 2001.

CHAPTER 2

Acquiring Property: Capture, Finds, Bailments, and Salvage

Possession is eleven points in the law.

Colley Cibber, *Woman's Wit* (1696)

A. THE CAPTURE DOCTRINE

1. Wild Animals

We hear of those to whom a lawsuit is an agreeable relaxation, a gentle excitement. One of this class, when remonstrated with, retorted, that while one friend kept dogs, and another horses, he, as he had a right to do, kept a lawyer; and no one had a right to dispute his taste.

Isabella Beeton, *The Book of Household Management* (1861)

So many law students have begun their legal studies with *Pierson v. Post*, which follows, that it is almost unthinkable that an American-educated lawyer would be unfamiliar with the case. That's not the only reason to study it, however, as it introduces the "capture doctrine," which still plays an important role in the acquisition of property rights.

PIERSON v. POST
Supreme Court of Judicature of New York
3 Cai. R. 175 (N.Y. Sup. Ct. 1805)

This was an action of trespass on the case, commenced in a justice's court by the present defendant against the now plaintiff. The declaration stated that Post, being in possession of certain dogs and hounds under his command, did, "upon a certain wild and uninhabited, unpossessed and waste land, called the beach, find and start one of those noxious beasts called a fox," and whilst there hunting, chasing and pursuing the same with his dogs and hounds, and when

71

in view thereof, Pierson, well knowing the fox was so hunted and pursued, did, in the sight of Post, to prevent his catching the same, kill and carry it off. A verdict having been rendered for the plaintiff below, the defendant there sued out a *certiorari*, and now assigned for error, that the declaration and matters therein contained were not sufficient in law to maintain an action.[1]

TOMPKINS, J., delivered the opinion of the court. This cause comes before us on a return to a *certiorari* directed to one of the justices of Queens county. The question submitted by the counsel in this cause for our determination is, whether Lodowick Post, by the pursuit with his hounds in the manner alleged in his declaration, acquired such a right to, or property in the fox, as will sustain an action against Pierson for killing and taking him away?

issue.

The cause was argued with much ability by the counsel on both sides, and presents for our decision a novel and nice question. It is admitted that a fox is an animal *ferae naturae*, and that property in such animals is acquired by occupancy only. These admissions narrow the discussion to the simple question of what acts amount to occupancy, applied to acquiring right to wild animals?

If we have recourse to the ancient writers upon general principles of law, the judgment below is obviously erroneous. *Justinian's Institutes*, lib. 2, tit. I, sect. 13, and *Fleta*, lib. III, c. II, page 175, adopt the principle, that pursuit alone, vests no property or right in the huntsman; and that even pursuit accompanied with wounding, is equally ineffectual for that purpose, unless the animal be actually taken. The same principle is recognized by *Bracton*, lib. II, c. I, page 8.

Puffendorf, lib. IV, c. 6, sec. 2, § 10, defines occupancy of beasts *ferae naturae*, to be the actual corporal possession of them, and *Bynkershoek* is cited as coinciding in this definition. It is indeed with hesitation that *Puffendorf* affirms that a wild beast mortally wounded, or greatly maimed, cannot be fairly intercepted by another, whilst the pursuit of the person inflicting the wound continues. The foregoing authorities are decisive to show that mere pursuit gave Post no legal right to the fox, but that he became the property of Pierson, who intercepted and killed him.

Post has no property rights to the fox.

It therefore only remains to inquire whether there are any contrary principles, or authorities, to be found in other books, which ought to induce a different decision. Most of the cases which have occurred in England, relating to property in wild animals, have either been discussed and decided upon the principles of their positive statute regulations, or have arisen between the huntsman and the owner of the land upon which beasts *ferae naturae* have been apprehended; the former claiming them by title of occupancy, and the latter *ratione soli*. Little satisfactory aid can, therefore, be derived from the English reporters.

Barbeyrac, in his notes on *Puffendorf*, does not accede to the definition of occupancy by the latter, but, on the contrary, affirms that actual bodily seizure is

---

1.   When the defendant "sued out a *certiorari*," he petitioned the supreme court to issue a writ of certiorari ordering the trial court to certify its record and transmit it to the supreme court for review. The supreme court issued the writ, and then the trial court prepared a copy of the proceedings before it, certified that the copy was accurate, and sent it to the supreme court.

At the time of this case, the Supreme Court was not, and is not now, the highest court in New York. In 1805, the Court of Errors was the highest court; its presiding officer was the president of the state senate, and it comprised the senators, the Chancellor, and the judges of the Supreme Court. Since 1846, the Court of Appeals has been the highest court. All of its members are judges. The Supreme Court now comprises both trial courts (special term and trial term) and intermediate appellate courts, known as the Appellate Division of the Supreme Court. —EDS.

not, in all cases, necessary to constitute possession of wild animals. He does not, however, *describe* the acts which, according to his ideas, will amount to an appropriation of such animals to private use, so as to exclude the claims of all other persons, by title of occupancy, to the same animals; and he is far from averring that pursuit alone is sufficient for that purpose. To a certain extent, and as far as *Barbeyrac* appears to me to go, his objections to *Puffendorf's* definition of occupancy are reasonable and correct. That is to say, that actual bodily seizure is not indispensable to acquire right to, or possession of, wild beasts; but that, on the contrary, the mortal wounding of such beasts, by one not abandoning his pursuit, may, with the utmost propriety, be deemed possession of him; since thereby, the pursuer manifests an unequivocal intention of appropriating the animal to his individual use, has deprived him of his natural liberty, and brought him within his certain control.

[Margin note: DictA. When mortally wound can still be in pursuit ₃ have possession. (But not holding)]

So also, encompassing and securing such animals with nets and toils, or otherwise intercepting them, in such a manner as to deprive them of their natural liberty, and render escape impossible, may justly be deemed to give possession of them to those persons who, by their industry and labor, have used such means of apprehending them. . . . The case now under consideration is one of mere pursuit, and presents no circumstances or acts which can bring it within the definition of occupancy by *Puffendorf,* . . . or the ideas of *Barbeyrac* upon that subject. . . .

The case cited from 11 *Mod.* 74-130 [*Keeble v. Hickeringill*—EDS.], I think clearly distinguishable from the present; inasmuch as there the action was for maliciously hindering and disturbing the plaintiff in the exercise and enjoyment of a private franchise; and in the report of the same case, (3 *Salk.* 9) Holt, Ch.J., states, that the ducks were in the plaintiff's decoy pond, and *so in his possession,* from which it is obvious the court laid much stress in their opinion upon the plaintiff's possession of the ducks, *ratione soli.*

[Margin note: trespass. not allowed to hunt on land owner's property.]

We are the more readily inclined to confine possession or occupancy of beasts *ferae naturae,* within the limits prescribed by the learned authors above cited, for the sake of certainty, and preserving peace and order in society. If the first seeing, starting, or pursuing such animals, without having so wounded, circumvented, or ensnared them, so as to deprive them of their natural liberty, and subject them to the control of their pursuer, should afford the basis of actions against others for intercepting and killing them, it would prove a fertile source of quarrels and litigation.

However uncourteous or unkind the conduct of Pierson towards Post, in this instance, may have been, yet his act was productive of no injury or damage for which a legal remedy can be applied. We are of the opinion the judgment below was erroneous, and ought to be reversed.

[Margin note: Holding.]

LIVINGSTON, J. My opinion differs from that of the court. Of six objections taken to the proceedings below, all are abandoned except the third, which reduces the controversy to a single question.

[Margin note: Dissent.]

Whether a person who, with his own hounds, starts and hunts a fox on waste and uninhabited ground, and is on the point of seizing his prey, acquires such an interest in the animal, as to have a right of action against another, who in view of the huntsman and his dogs in full pursuit, and with knowledge of the chase, shall kill and carry him away?

[Margin note: Dissent's issue]

This is a knotty point, and should have been submitted to the arbitration of sportsmen, without poring over *Justinian, Fleta, Bracton, Puffendorf, Locke, Barbeyrac,* or *Blackstone,* all of whom have been cited; they would have had no difficulty in coming to a prompt and correct conclusion. In a court thus constituted, the skin and carcass of poor *reynard* would have been properly disposed of, and a precedent set, interfering with no usage or custom which the experience of ages has sanctioned, and which must be so well known to every votary of *Diana.* But the parties have referred the question to our judgment, and we must dispose of it as well as we can, from the partial lights we possess, leaving to a higher tribunal, the correction of any mistake which we may be so unfortunate as to make. By the pleadings it is admitted that the fox is a "wild and noxious beast." Both parties have regarded him, as the law of nations does a pirate, "*hostem, humani generis*"[2] and although "*de mortuis nil nisi bonum,*"[3] be a maxim of our profession, the memory of the deceased has not been spared. His depredations on farmers and on barn yards have not been forgotten; and to put him to death wherever found, is allowed to be meritorious, and of public benefit. Hence it follows, that our decision should have in view the greatest possible encouragement to the destruction of an animal, so cunning and ruthless in his career.

But who would keep a pack of hounds; or what gentleman, at the sound of the horn, and at peep of day, would mount his steed, and for hours together, "*sub jove frigido,*" or a vertical sun, pursue the windings of this wily quadruped, if, just as night came on, and his stratagems and strength were nearly exhausted, a saucy intruder, who had not shared in the honours or labours of the chase, were permitted to come in at the death, and bear away in triumph the object of pursuit? Whatever *Justinian* may have thought of the matter, it must be recollected that his code was compiled many hundred years ago, and it would be very hard indeed at the distance of so many centuries, not to have a right to establish a rule for ourselves. In his day, we read of no order of men who made it a business, in the language of the declaration of this cause, "with hounds and dogs to find, start, pursue, hunt, and chase," these animals, and that, too, without any other motive than the preservation of Roman poultry; if this diversion had been then in fashion, the lawyers who composed his institutes, would have taken care not to pass it by, without suitable encouragement. If any thing, therefore, in the digests or pandects shall appear to militate against the defendant in error, who, on this occasion, was the foxhunter, we have only to say *tempora mutantur,*[4] and if men themselves change with the times, why should not laws also undergo an alteration?

It may be expected, however, by the learned counsel, that more particular notice be taken of their authorities. I have examined them all, and feel great difficulty in determining, whether to acquire dominion over a thing, before in common, it be sufficient that we barely see it, or know where it is, or wish for it, or make a declaration of our will respecting it; or whether, in the case of wild beasts, setting a trap, or lying in wait, or starting, or pursuing, be enough; or if an actual wounding, or killing, or bodily tact and occupation be necessary.

2. "Enemy of humankind."—EDS.
3. "Don't speak ill of the dead."—EDS.
4. "Times change."—EDS.

Writers on general law, who have favoured us with their speculations on these points, differ on them all; but, great as is the diversity of sentiment among them, some conclusion must be adopted on the question immediately before us. After mature deliberation, I embrace that of *Barbeyrac*, as the most rational, and least liable to objection. If at liberty, we might imitate the courtesy of a certain emperor, who, to avoid giving offence to the advocates of any of these different doctrines, adopted a middle course, and by ingenious distinctions, rendered it difficult to say (as often happens after a fierce and angry contest) to whom the palm of victory belonged. He ordained, that if a beast be followed with *large dogs and hounds*, he shall belong to the hunter, not to the chance occupant; and in like manner, if he be killed or wounded with a lance or sword; but if chased with *beagles only*, then he passed to the captor, not to the first pursuer. If slain with a dart, a sling, or a bow, he fell to the hunter, if still in chase, and not to him who might afterwards find and seize him.

[handwritten margin note: hunter vs captor]

Now, as we are without any municipal regulations of our own, and the pursuit here, for aught that appears on the case, being with dogs and hounds of *imperial stature*, we are at liberty to adopt one of the provisions just cited, which comports also with the learned conclusion of Barbeyrac, that property in animals *ferae naturae* may be acquired without bodily touch or manucaption, provided the pursuer be within reach, or have a *reasonable* prospect (which certainly existed here) of taking, what he has *thus* discovered [with] an intention of converting to his own use.

When we reflect also that the interest of our husbandmen, the most useful of men in any community, will be advanced by the destruction of a beast so pernicious and incorrigible, we cannot greatly err, in saying that a pursuit like the present, through waste and unoccupied lands, and which must inevitably and speedily have terminated in corporal possession, or bodily *seisin*, confers such a right to the object of it, as to make any one a wrongdoer, who shall interfere and shoulder the spoil. The *justice's* judgment ought, therefore, in my opinion, to be affirmed.

Notes and Questions

1. *Justinian, Bracton, Puffendorf, Barbeyrac, and Fleta.* Justinian (born Petrus Sabbatius in 482) was a Roman emperor who ruled from 527-565. Committed to restoring the greatness of the Roman Empire, he appointed commissions to codify imperial constitutions from the time of Hadrian forward, which were published as the *Codex Justinianus* in 528, and to excerpt and codify the works of the classical jurists, which were published in the *Digest*, in 533. He also was responsible for creation of the *Institutes*, a textbook of Roman law intended primarily for students. The Institutes were enormously influential in the development of law in Europe after the Dark Ages.

Henry Bracton, a 13th century judge and scholar, compiled what was to be a comprehensive treatise on English law. The treatise, *On the Laws and Customs of England*, is available at http://bracton.law.cornell.edu/ bracton. *Fleta* is another English work about 40 years later than Bracton. The book takes its name from the Fleet prison where its unknown author was imprisoned. Puffendorf (1632-1694) and Barbeyrac (1674-1744) were European "civil law jurisconsults," legal scholars and commentators who were regularly cited by American lawyers both before and after the Revolution. *See* R.H. Helmholz, *Use of the Civil Law in Post-Revolutionary American Jurisprudence*, 66 Tul. L. Rev. 1649 (1992).

2. John Locke, the English philosopher (1632-1704) mentioned in Justice Livingston's dissent, is another historical figure whose work has figured prominently in the history of property law. In his Second Treatise of Government (1689) Locke espoused what has become known as the "labor" theory or the "labor-desert" theory of property.[5] Very briefly, the theory is that property is created by the labor exerted in removing things from the common state of nature and by the labor invested in cultivating and improving the land. Beginning with the proposition that "every man has a Property in his own Person," he reasons to the conclusion that the labor invested in removing something from the common state of nature makes it the property of the laborer. Is Pierson or Post more likely to have cited Locke in his argument to the court?

3. *Sources of law.* Why does the majority use these old commentaries as sources of law? Would it have been better to submit the case to "the arbitration of sportsmen" as Livingston suggested? Although it seems unlikely that the court could have brought in a panel of sportsmen to decide the case, it could have used the custom of sportsmen as the basis for developing a rule of law. Should it have done that? If the court is developing law that applies to farmers and others, as well as sportsmen, is it fair to use a rule created by sportsmen?

4. *Trespass on the case.* Note that this was an action in trespass on the case, defined in Black's Law Dictionary as follows: "At common law, an action to recover damages that are not the immediate result of a wrongful act but rather a later consequence. This action was the precursor to a variety of modern-day tort claims, including negligence, nuisance, and business torts."

5. All-or-nothing solutions like that reached by the court in this case are often encountered in the common law, but there are other ways of solving conflicts over resources. Because both Pierson and Post contributed to the capture of the fox, the court could have divided the fox between them or awarded the fox to one and compensation to the other for the value of his contribution. There are several ways the fox could have been divided. Pierson and Post could have been made joint owners with equal rights to the fox, or the fox could have been cut in pieces and divided between them, or sold and the proceeds divided. If there was no market for the fox, they could have submitted sealed bids to the court, and whoever submitted the higher bid would receive the fox and the other the money. Alternatively, the court could have awarded one of them the fox and the other the value of his investment or other contribution to the enterprise. Should the court have adopted one of these other approaches?

6. What was this case really about? The majority seems to think that what's at stake is certainty in the law and preserving peace and order. The dissent seems to think it's about exterminating varmints. The following excerpt seems to suggest that for the parties it was about something else:

> Jesse Pierson, son of Capt. David, . . . saw a fox run down an unused well near Peter's Pond, and killed and took the fox. Lodowick Post and a company with him

---

5. *See* Richard Schlatter, *Private Property: The History of an Idea* 154 (1951). For a modern theory of labor and desert as the basis of private property, see Stephen R. Munzer, A Theory of Property, ch. 10 (1990).

were in pursuit and chasing the fox, and saw Jesse with it and claimed it as theirs, while Jesse persisted in his claim. Capt. Pierson said his son Jesse should have the fox and Capt. Post said the same of his son Lodowick and hence the law suit contested and appealed to the highest court in the State. . . . This became the leading case often cited, because it established, and I think for the first time, by the court of last resort in the State, that to give an individual right in wild animals, the claimant must capture them. To the public the decision was worth its cost. To the parties who each expended over a thousand pounds, the fox cost very dear. J.T. Adams, *Memorials of Old Bridgehampton* 166 (1916, 1962).

good for public
expensive for parties.

7. What are the advantages of certainty in legal rules? Property rules range from "bright-line" clear rules, like first in time gets it all, to "mushy" rules that require sharing resources like water "reasonably" or that mandate "equitable" division of property on dissolution of marriage. How would you characterize the rule that Post wanted the court to adopt?

8. That this became "the leading case" is no doubt attributable in part to the reputation of the New York Supreme Court in 1805. Its Chief Justice was James Kent (1763-1847), who is best known as Chancellor Kent, the author of *Kent's Commentaries on American Law.* Kent, who studied law after graduating from Yale in 1781 and was admitted to the bar in 1785, was appointed the first professor of law at Columbia University in 1793. In 1798, he was named justice of the New York Supreme Court, and then in 1814, he was elevated to the position of chancellor of the New York Court of Chancery, the highest judicial officer in the state. He published his famous *Commentaries* after returning to Columbia in 1823.

KEBLE AGAINST HICKRINGILL

Queen's Bench
11 Mod. 74 (Easter Term, 1707)

The question was, Whether an action upon the case for shooting at, disturbing, and fearing wild ducks from a decoy-pond, without coming upon the plaintiff's soil, was such a damage as to support this action?

HOLT, Chief Justice, said he was not satisfied with this case. — It is agreed on all hands, that while the ducks are in the pond the plaintiff has a property, and the defendant was a wrong-doer to disturb him . . . . But suppose the defendant had shot in his own ground, if he had had occasion to shoot, it would have been one thing; but to shoot on purpose to damage the plaintiff is another thing, and a wrong . . . .

POWELL, Justice. Every one has a property of things ferae naturae ratione soli. A man may have a free warren in another man's soil, which he has rationae privilegii, and not soli, for one man may have a privilege in another man's freehold. A man may have such a property in hares, as if he put it up in his ground, and course and kill it in another man's ground, still the original property is in him, and the coursing is a continuance of this property. As this case is, the defendant has done an injury to the plaintiff's property; for by frightening them away you have destroyed his property.

Powys and Gould, Justices, to the same intent. A man may lawfully shoot in his own ground, as to kill venison, &tc. But not to destroy maliciously the property of another.

. . . Adjourned . . . until next Term.

KEEBLE v. HICKERINGILL

Queen's Bench
11 East 574, 103 Eng. Rep. 1127 (Trinity Term, 1707)

Action upon the case. Plaintiff declares that he was, 8th *November* in the second year of the queen [1704 — Eds.], lawfully possessed of a close of land called *Minott's Meadow,* . . . *a decoy pond,* to which divers wildfowl used to resort and come; and the plaintiff had at his own costs and charges prepared and procured divers decoy-ducks, nets, machines, and other engines for the decoying and taking of the wildfowl, and enjoyed the benefit in taking them; the defendant, knowing which, *and intending to damnify the plaintiff in his vivary,* and *to fright and drive away the wildfowl used to resort thither, and deprive him of his profit,* did, on the 8th of *November,* resort to the head of the said pond and vivary, and did discharge six guns laden with gunpowder, and with the noise and stink of the gunpowder did drive away the wildfowl then being in the pond; and on the 11th and 12th days of *Nov.* the defendant, *with design to damnify the plaintiff, and frighten away the wildfowl,* did place himself with a gun near the vivary, and there did discharge the said gun several times that was then charged with the gunpowder against the said decoy pond, whereby the wildfowl was frighted away, and did forsake the said pond. Upon not guilty pleaded, a verdict was found for the plaintiff and 20£ damages.

Holt, C.J. I am of the opinion that this action doth lie. It seems to be new in its instance, but is not new in the reason or principle of it. For, 1st, this using or making a decoy is lawful. 2dly, This employment of his ground to that use is profitable to the plaintiff, as is the skill and management of that employment. . . . Every man that hath a property may employ it for his pleasure and profit, as for alluring and procuring decoy ducks to come to his pond. To learn the trade of seducing other ducks to come there in order to be taken is not prohibited either by the law of the land or the moral law; but it is as lawful to use art to seduce them, to catch them, and destroy them for the use of mankind, as to kill and destroy wildfowl or tame cattle. Then when a man useth his art or his skill to take them to sell and dispose of for his profit, this is his trade; and he that hinders another in his trade or livelihood is liable to an action for so hindering him. . . .

[W]here a violent or malicious act is done to a man's occupation, profession, or way of getting a livelihood; there an action lies in all cases. But if a man doth him damage by using the same employment; as if Mr. Hickeringill had set up another decoy on his own ground near the plaintiff's, and that had spoiled the custom of the plaintiff, no action would lie because he had as much liberty to make and use a decoy as the plaintiff. This is like the case of 11 H. 4, 47. One schoolmaster sets up a new school to the damage of an ancient school, and thereby the scholars are allured from the old school to come to his new. (The action there was held not to lie.) But suppose Mr. Hickeringill should lie in the way with his guns, and fright the boys from going to school, and their parents would not let them to thither; sure that schoolmaster might have an action for the loss of his scholars. 29 E. 3, 18. A man hath a market, to which he hath toll for horses sold: a man is bringing his horse to market to sell: a stranger hinders and obstructs him from going thither to the market: an action lies because it imports damage. Action upon the case lies against one that shall by threats fright away his tenant at will. 9 H. 7, 8. 21 H. 6, 31. 9 H. 7, 7. 14 Ed. 4, 7 . . . .

There was an objection that did occur to me, though I do not remember it to be made at the bar; which is, that it is not mentioned in the declaration what number or nature of wildfowl were frighted away by the defendant's shooting. . . . Now considering the nature of the case, it is not possible to declare of the number that were frighted away; because the plaintiff had not possession of them to count them. Where a man brings trespass for taking his goods, he must declare of the quantity, because he, by having had the possession, may know what he had, and therefore must know what he lost. . . . The plaintiff in this case brings his action for the apparent injury done him in the use of that employment of his freehold, his art, and skill that he uses thereby. . . .

[O]f long time in the kingdom these artificial contrivances of decoy ponds and decoy ducks have been used for enticing into those ponds wildfowl, in order to be taken for the profit of the owner of the pond, who is at the expence of servants, engines, and other management, whereby the markets of the nation may be furnished; there is great reason to give encouragement thereunto; that the people who are so instrumental by their skill and industry so as to furnish the markets should reap the benefit and have their action. But, in short, that which is the true reason, is, that this action is not brought to recover damage for the loss of the fowl, but for the disturbance.

Notes and Questions

1. *Early English Reports.* Judicial opinions today are written out and officially published, but before the 19th century, reporting of English opinions was handled by private enterprise, working from a variety of sources. Some reporters were better than others, and some had better access to materials than others. Sometimes several reports of the same case were published. In *Keeble*, there were four: *Keeble v. Hickeringall*, Cas. T. Holt 14, 17, 19; *Keble v. Hickringill*, 11 Mod. 74, 11 Mod. 130; *Keeble v. Hickeringhall*, 3 Salk. 9; and *Keeble v. Hickeringill*, 11 East 574. The report in East, which claims that it is "taken from a copy of Lord C.J. Holt's own MS. in my possession," is thought to be the most accurate, but it was not published until 1815. If you need to work with older English cases, the best guide to the accuracy of the reports is Wallace, *The Reporters* (4th ed. 1882). Wallace was a reporter of decisions for the United States Supreme Court.

2. *The Year Books.* The citation of Y.B. 11 H. 4, 47 in the court's opinion refers to a case noted in the Year Book for the 11th year of the reign of King Henry IV (1410), page 47. In some reports, this reference is cut down to 11 H.4.47. The Year Books, which run from 1238 to 1535, contain anonymous notes of cases and are an important source of legal history.

3. Contrast the interests protected by the decisions in *Pierson* and *Keeble*. Note that the majority opinion in *Pierson* distinguished *Keeble* on the grounds that, there, the plaintiff had possession of the ducks *ratione soli.* (*Ratione soli* means on account of the soil, and expresses a legal conclusion that a person in possession of the land has "constructive" possession of things that are on or under the land even though they are not actually in his control.) If the East report of the case had been available in 1805, could Post's lawyer have made a stronger argument? If this case was brought as a modern private nuisance case, how would it come out?

4. *What about the fox?* In a provocative article, *Should Trees Have Standing?—Toward Legal Rights for Natural Objects,* 45 S. Cal. L. Rev. 450 (1972), Prof. Christopher Stone proposed that natural objects be given rights to seek legal redress. Like infants and incompetent people, he suggested, natural objects could be represented by guardians who could speak for them. The idea that animals should have legally protectable rights gained substantial momentum in the 1990s as the animal rights movement took hold in the legal world, and continues in the 21st century with the Nonhuman Rights Project. Founded by long-time professor and animal rights activist Steven Wise, the project's mission is "to change the common law status of at least some nonhuman animals from mere 'things,' which lack the capacity to possess any legal right, to 'persons,' who possess such fundamental rights as bodily integrity and bodily liberty, and those other legal rights to which evolving standards of morality, scientific discovery, and human experience entitle them." http://www.nonhumanrightsproject.org/. The project filed habeas corpus proceedings in December 2013 seeking freedom for four chimpanzees. Unsuccessful at the trial court level, the project will appeal.

Some readings you may find interesting are Steven M. Wise, *Legal Personhood and the Nonhuman Rights Project,* 17 Animal Law 1 (2010), Steven M. Wise, *Science and the Case for Animal Rights* (2002), Steven J. Bartlett, *Roots of Human Resistance to Animal Rights: Psychological and Conceptual Blocks,* 8 Animal L.J. 143 (2002), Laurence H. Tribe, *Ten Lessons Our Constitutional Experience Can Teach Us About the Puzzle of Animal Rights: The Work of Stephen M. Wise,* 7 Animal L.J. 1 (2001); Richard A. Posner, *Animal Rights Rattling the Cage: Toward Legal Rights for Animals by Steven M. Wise,* 110 Yale L.J. 527 (2000) (book review); Cass R. Sunstein, *Standing for Animals (With Notes on Animal Rights),* 47 UCLA L. Rev. 1333 (2000); Gary L. Francione, *Rain Without Thunder: The Ideology of the Animal Rights Movement* (1996); Josephine Donovan & Carol J. Adams, eds., *Beyond Animal Rights: A Feminist Caring Ethic for the Treatment of Animals* (1996); Gary L. Francione, *Animals, Property, and the Law* (1995).

5. *Hunter harassment statutes.* All but one or two states and the U.S. Congress have enacted statutes that prohibit obstructing or interfering with people engaged in the lawful taking of wildlife. *See, e.g.,* 16 U.S.C.A. § 5201 and Conn. Gen. Stat. Ann. § 53a-183a. These statutes, promoted by the U.S. Sportsmen's Alliance (formerly the Wildlife Legislative Fund of America), the National Rifle Association, and the Sportsmen's Caucus in the U.S. Congress, were widely thought to violate constitutional safeguards for free speech rights. But the statutes have generally been upheld on the grounds that they prohibit conduct, not speech, and protect important state interests in controlling animal populations, promoting safety by reducing contact between hunters and activists and between deer and cars, protecting property by limiting grazing, limiting transmission of rabies and Lyme disease, providing recreational opportunities, and producing revenue. *See, e.g., Connecticut v. Ball,* 796 A.2d 542 (Conn. 2002). Articles questioning the constitutionality of these statutes include Andrew N. Ireland Moore,

Comment, *Caging Animal Advocates' Political Freedoms: The Unconstitutionality of the Animal and Ecological Terrorism Act*, 11 Animal Law 255 (2005); Jaqueline Tresl, *Shoot First, Talk Later: Blowing Holes in Freedom of Speech*, 8 Animal Law 177 (2002); Katherine Hessler, *Where Do We Draw the Line Between Harassment and Free Speech? An Analysis of Hunter Harassment Law*, 3 Animal Law 129 (1997); Jeffery E. Sherr, *Does the Federal Crime Bill's Hunter Harassment Provision Violate the First Amendment or If an Animal Rights Protester Falls Down in the Woods and a Hunter Hears, Is It a Federal Crime?*, 11 J. Nat. Resources & Envtl. L. 119 (1995-1996); Aileen M. Ugalde, *The Right to Arm Bears: Activists' Protests Against Hunting*, 45 U. Miami L. Rev. 1109 (1991). For a general review of the cases, see Frank J. Wozniak, *Validity and Construction of Statutes Prohibiting Harassment of Hunters, Fishermen, or Trappers*, 17 A.L.R. 5th 837 (2005). The U.S. Sportsmen's Alliance says that it "protects and defends America's wildlife conservation programs and pursuits—hunting, fishing and trapping—which generate the money to pay for them," www.ussportsmen.org.

In *McCullen v. Coakley*, 134 S. Ct. 2518 (2014), the Supreme Court upheld a challenge to a Massachusetts statute that required a 35-foot buffer zone around the entrances, exits, and driveways of abortion clinics on the ground that it violated the free speech rights of plaintiffs who claimed they were not protesters, but wanted to engage in quiet counseling of women seeking abortions. The Court held that the statute was not narrowly tailored to serve a significant governmental interest. How might that decision affect the validity of hunter harassment laws?

First in Time, Trespassers, and Ratione Soli

Competing claims are often resolved by deciding who got there first. If there are 10 seats available and 20 people in line, the first 10 people get them. The same principle is frequently applied in law. If there are two legitimate claims and not enough to go around, the earlier claim often wins. In actions of trespass and conversion, for example, both plaintiff and defendant may have been possessors of the chattel, but the law protects the one who first had possession. Why do you suppose this is so? What are the alternatives are to deciding things on a first-come, first-served basis?

When a hunter kills or captures a wild animal on land that belongs to someone else without permission, the landowner may sue to gain either possession of the animal (replevin) or its value (conversion). In either case, the action is based on the theory that the landowner had prior possession of the animal. Operating within a first-in-time framework that counted possession as the critical factor, courts constructed a rationale for awarding the entitlement to the landowner rather than the trespassing hunter. Known as *ratione soli*, the rationale is that the landowner already had possession of the animal by virtue of possessing the land when the trespasser killed or captured the animal. Treating something as though it were something else (here, possession of the land as if it were possession of the animals on the land) is a useful technique in the common-law system, in which decisions are justified by categorizing situations so that they fit into a line of precedents developed from cases involving different situations. This technique is often heralded by use of the word "constructive."

A person with constructive possession is treated as if she has possession even though, in fact, she doesn't.

Why do you suppose the courts decided to prefer the landowner over the trespassing hunter? What instrumental ends does the *ratione soli* doctrine serve?

Although theoretically landowners had a right of action against trespassing hunters, early American attitudes led to statutes creating a presumption that landowners consented to hunting on their undeveloped, unenclosed lands unless they posted a "No Hunting" notice. In addition, judges sometimes refused to award damages for taking wildlife the landowner did not control.[6] For an extensive discussion of the common law of wild animals, see Barlow Burke, Personal Property in a Nutshell 1-44 (3d ed. 2003), and for discussion of posting statutes, see Mark R. Sigmon, *Hunting and Posting on Private Land in America*, 54 Duke L.J. 549 (2004). Increasing population and development of commercial hunting businesses have led to substantial decreases in the amount of private land open to the public for hunting. *See* Tom Simmons, *Highways, Hunters and Section Lines: Tensions Between Public Access and Private Rights*, 2 Great Plains Nat. Resources J. 240 (1997).

GHEN v. RICH

United States District Court, Massachusetts
8 Fed. 159 (D. Mass. 1881)

NELSON, D.J. This is a libel to recover the value of a fin-back whale. The libellant lives in Provincetown and the respondent in Wellfleet. The facts, as they appeared at the hearing, are as follows:

In the early spring months the easterly part of Massachusetts bay is frequented by the species of whale known as the fin-back whale. Fishermen from Provincetown pursue them in open boats from the shore, and shoot them with bomb-lances fired from guns made expressly for the purpose. When killed they sink at once to the bottom, but in the course of from one to three days they rise and float on the surface. Some of them are picked up by vessels and towed into Provincetown. Some float ashore at high water and are left stranded on the beach as the tide recedes. Others float out to sea and are never recovered. The person who happens to find them on the beach usually sends word to Provincetown, and the owner comes to the spot and removes the blubber. The finder usually receives a small salvage for his services. Try-works are established in Provincetown for trying out the oil. The business is of considerable extent, but, since it requires skill and experience, as well as some outlay of capital, and is attended with great exposure and hardship, few persons engage in it. The average yield of oil is about 20 barrels to a whale. It swims with great swiftness, and for that reason cannot be taken by the harpoon and line. Each boat's crew engaged in the business has its peculiar mark or device on its lances, and in this way it is known by whom a whale is killed.

---

6. *See, e.g.,* Beach v. Morgan, 41 A. 349 (N.H. 1893), where the court held a trespassing fisherman liable for $1.00 for the trespass to land but refused to award the landowner the value of the trout the fisherman had caught "for they are *ferae naturae*."

The usage on Cape Cod, for many years, has been that the person who kills a whale in the manner and under the circumstances described, owns it, and this right has never been disputed until this case. The libellant has been engaged in this business for ten years past. On the morning of April 9, 1880, in Massachusetts bay, near the end of Cape Cod, he shot and instantly killed with a bomb-lance the whale in question. It sunk immediately, and on the morning of the 12th was found stranded on the beach in Brewster, within the ebb and flow of the tide, by one Ellis, 17 Miles from the spot where it was killed. Instead of sending word to Provincetown, as is customary, Ellis advertised the whale for sale at auction, and sold it to the respondent, who shipped off the blubber and tried out the oil. The libellant heard of the finding of the whale on the morning of the 15th, and immediately sent one of his boat's crew to the place and claimed it. Neither the respondent nor Ellis knew the whale had been killed by the libellant, but they knew or might have known, if they had wished, that it had been shot and killed with a bomb-lance, by some person engaged in this species of business.

The libellant claims title to the whale under this usage. The respondent insists that this usage is invalid. It was decided . . . in Taber v. Jenny, 1 Sprague, 315, that when a whale has been killed, and is anchored and left with marks of appropriation, it is the property of the captors; and if it is afterwards found, still anchored, by another ship, there is no usage or principle of law by which the property of the original captors is diverted, even though the whale may have dragged from its anchorage. The learned judge says:

"When the whale had been killed and taken possession of by the boat of the Hillman, (the first taker,) it became the property of the owners of that ship, and all was done which was then practicable in order to secure it. They left it anchored, with unequivocal marks of appropriation."

In Bartlett v. Budd, 1 Low. 223, the facts were these: The first officer of the libellant's ship killed a whale in the Okhotsk sea, anchored it, attached a waif to the body, and then left it and went ashore at some distance for the night. The next morning the boats of the respondent's ship found the whale adrift, the anchor not holding, the cable coiled round the body, and no waif or irons attached to it. Judge Lowell held that, as the libellants had killed and taken actual possession of the whale, the ownership vested in them. In his opinion the learned judge says:

"A whale, being ferae naturae, does not become property until a firm possession has been established by the taker. But when such possession has become firm and complete, the right of property is clear, and has all the characteristics of property."

He doubted whether a usage set up but not proved by the respondents, that a whale found adrift in the ocean is the property of the finder, unless the first taker should appear and claim it before it is cut in, would be valid, and remarked that "there would be great difficulty in upholding a custom that should take the property of A. and give it to B., under so very short and uncertain a substitute for the statute of limitations, and one so open to fraud and deceit." Both the cases cited were decided without reference to usage, upon the ground that the property had been acquired by the first taker by actual possession and appropriation.

In Swift v. Gifford, 2 Low, 110, Judge Lowell decided that a custom among whalemen in the Arctic seas, that the iron holds the whale was reasonable and valid. In that case a boat's crew from the respondent's ship pursued and struck a whale in the Arctic ocean, and the harpoon and the line attached to it remained in the whale, but did not remain fast to the boat. A boat's crew from the libellant's ship continued the pursuit and captured the whale, and the master of the respondent's ship claimed it on the spot. It was held by the learned judge that the whale belonged to the respondents. It was said by Judge Sprague, in Bourne v. Ashley, an unprinted case referred to by Judge Lowell in Swift v. Gifford, that the usage for the first iron, whether attached to the boat or not, to hold the whale was fully established; and he added that, although local usages of a particular port ought not to be allowed to set aside the general maritime law, this objection did not apply to a custom which embraced an entire business, and had been concurred in for a long time by every one engaged in the trade.

In Swift v. Gifford, Judge Lowell also said:

"The rule of law invoked in this case is one of very limited application. The whale fishery is the only branch of industry of any importance in which it is likely to be much used, and if a usage is found to prevail generally in that business, it will not be open to the objection that it is likely to disturb the general understanding of mankind by the interposition of an arbitrary exception."

I see no reason why the usage proved in this case is not as reasonable as that sustained in the cases cited. Its application must necessarily be extremely limited, and can affect but a few persons. It has been recognized and acquiesced in for many years. It requires in the first taker the only act of appropriation that is possible in the nature of the case. Unless it is sustained, this branch of industry must necessarily cease, for no person would engage in it if the fruits of his labor could be appropriated by any chance finder. It gives reasonable salvage for securing or reporting the property. That the rule works well in practice is shown by the extent of the industry which has grown up under it, and the general acquiescence of a whole community interested to dispute it. It is by no means clear that without regard to usage the common law would not reach the same result. That seems to be the effect of the decisions in Taber v. Jenny and Bartlett v. Budd. If the fisherman does all that is possible to do to make the animal his own, that would seem to be sufficient. Such a rule might well be applied in the interest of trade, there being no usage or custom to the contrary. Holmes, Com. Law, 217. But be that as it may, I hold the usage to be valid, and that the property in the whale was in the libellant.

The rule of damages is the market value of the oil obtained from the whale, less the cost of trying it out and preparing it for the market, with interest on the amount so ascertained from the date of conversion. As the question is new and important, and the suit is contested on both sides, more for the purpose of having it settled than for the amount involved, I shall give no costs.

Decree for libellant for $71.05, without costs.

Notes and Questions

1. Libellant is the name used for the plaintiff in cases in admiralty, which are largely within the exclusive jurisdiction of the federal courts.

2. Note the court's use of custom as the source of law. Was it more appropriate to use custom in this case than in *Pierson v. Post*?

More About Wild Animals

As we have seen, a person can establish ownership of a wild animal by killing it and taking it into his or her possession. What happens if the animal is captured alive and later escapes? There is a surprising amount of litigation on this question involving animals from sea lions to parrots. Blackstone, quoted in *Mullett v. Bradley* (below), says: "These animals [*ferae naturae*] are no longer the property of a man than while they continue in his keeping or actual possession; but if at any time they regain their natural liberty, his property instantly ceases; unless they have *animus revertendi*,[7] which is only to be known by their usual custom of returning." Does this statement explain the following cases? If not, what other principles are at work? What factors should be taken into account in resolving these competing claims?

In *C.B. Wiley v. Baker*, 597 S.W.2d 3 (Tex. Civ. App. 1980), the owner of a game farm sued to recover the value of an elk that escaped, remained out of range of the farm owner's tranquilizing rifle, and was shot by the defendant a month later. The elk was not native to the area. The court held for the defendant. In *Mullett v. Bradley*, 53 N.Y.S. 781 (Sup. Ct. 1898), a sea lion captured by the plaintiff in the Pacific Ocean for a marine display escaped from a small island in the New York harbor. The defendant bought it from a fisherman who had found it a couple of weeks later about 70 miles from New York. Sea lions are not normally found in the Atlantic Ocean. The plaintiff learned that the defendant had the sea lion about a year later and sued for its value. The defendant won. In *E.A. Stephens & Co. v. Albers*, 256 P.2d 15 (Colo. 1927), a valuable nonnative silver fox escaped from the plaintiff's breeding ranch and was shot by a farmer who found it prowling around his chicken house. The farmer sold the pelt to the defendant, a fur-buying company. Although it was clear from the pelt that the fox had been shot (rather than poisoned or crushed as was usual with ranch-bred fox killed for their pelts), the pelt did have tattoos in the ears. The plaintiff won. In *Conti v. ASPCA*, 353 N.Y.S. 288 (Sup. Ct. 1974), Chester, a parrot used by the ASPCA (American Society for the Prevention of Cruelty to Animals) in educational exhibitions escaped. A few days later, the plaintiff befriended a parrot who had flown into his yard. When he called the ASPCA for advice on caring for the parrot, the ASPCA claimed it was theirs and took it back. The ASPCA won.

Governmental Regulation of Wild Animals and Fisheries and the Public Trust

Today extensive state and federal laws regulate rights to capture, use, and kill wild animals. *Geer v. Connecticut*, 161 U.S. 519 (1896), upheld a statute that

---

7.   This means a disposition to return. — EDS.

Connecticut owns all the wildlife

prohibited shipping certain game birds out of state, even though they had lawfully been killed in the state, on the ground that the state owned all the wildlife in the state and held it in trust for the benefit of the people. In *Hughes v. Oklahoma*, 441 U.S. 322, 335 (1979) (which overruled *Geer* on the interstate shipping point), the court explained the idea that a state owns the wildlife within its borders is a way of expressing "the importance to its people that a State have power to preserve and regulate the exploitation of an important resource."[8]

The statements in cases and statutes that the state "owns" wildlife have led some landowners to claim that the state is liable for damage done to their property or for forage consumed by wildlife. In *Clajon Production Corp. v. Petera*, 854 F. Supp. 843 (D. Wyo. 1994), a large landowner claimed that state game laws severely limiting hunting rights unconstitutionally "took" its right to exclusive hunting rights on its property, or, alternatively, that if the state's assertion of ownership of the wildlife was valid, the state "took" his property by allowing the animals to enter without his consent and by their consumption of forage.[9] The court rejected both claims, holding that even if the state's claim of ownership was "pure fantasy," it had ample power to limit hunting rights on private property. A similar result was reached in *Moerman v. California*, 21 Cal. Rptr. 2d 329 (Ct. App. 1993), where the plaintiff claimed that the state was liable for damage to his fences and forage done by endangered tule elk relocated by the state to part of their historic range. The court said, "[T]he tule elk are not instrumentalities of the state nor controlled by the state, and therefore, there has been no physical taking of [the plaintiff's] property."

Problem: Reasoning by Analogy

Broadcast Co. put a communications services satellite in orbit around the earth. Subsequently, Monitor Co. placed a natural resources-monitoring satellite in a different orbit. On a regular and predictable basis, the monitoring satellite passes through the space between Broadcast Co.'s satellite and its receiving stations on earth, disrupting transmissions. Monitor Co. refuses to compensate Broadcast Co. for its losses and insists that it cannot carry out its mission without interfering with Broadcast Co.'s transmissions. Broadcast Co. sues Monitor Co.[10] Assume that *Pierson v. Post*, *Keeble v. Hickeringill*, and *Ghen v. Rich* are the only judicial precedents available. What arguments should the lawyers for each party make? How should the case be decided?

---

8. The state's interest in preserving endangered species can be furthered by criminalizing sales of previously killed animals. *See* Andrus v. Allard, 444 U.S. 51 (1979).

9. Under the Fifth Amendment to the U.S. Constitution, made applicable to the states by the Fourteenth Amendment, government cannot take property for public use without paying just compensation.

10. This problem is adapted from one found in Robert D. Cooter & Thomas S. Ulen, *Law and Economics* (1988, 2d ed. 1996).

POPOV v. HAYASHI

Superior Court, San Francisco County, California
No. 400545, 2002 WL 31833731 (Dec. 18, 2002)

McCarthy, J. In 1927, Babe Ruth hit sixty home runs. That record stood for thirty four years until Roger Maris broke it in 1961 with sixty one home runs. Mark McGwire hit seventy in 1998. On October 7, 2001, at PacBell Park in San Francisco, Barry Bonds hit number seventy three. . . . With that in mind, many people who attended the game came prepared for the possibility that a record setting ball would be hit in their direction.[1] Among this group were plaintiff Alex Popov and defendant Patrick Hayashi. . . . Both men brought baseball gloves . . . . They, along with a number of others, positioned themselves in the arcade section of the ballpark . . . a standing room only area located near right field. It is in this general area that Barry Bonds hits the greatest number of home runs.[2] . . . Barry Bonds came to bat in the first inning. With nobody on base and a full count, Bonds swung at a slow knuckleball. He connected. The ball sailed over the right-field fence and into the arcade.

Josh Keppel, a cameraman . . . captured the event on videotape. . . . In addition to the Keppel tape, seventeen percipient witnesses[11] testified as to what they saw after the ball came into the stands. . . . The factual findings in this case are the result of an analysis of the testimony of all the witnesses as well as a detailed review of the Keppel tape. Those findings are as follows:

When the seventy-third home run ball went into the arcade, it landed in the upper portion of the webbing of a softball glove worn by Alex Popov. While the glove stopped the trajectory of the ball, it is not at all clear that the ball was secure. Popov had to reach for the ball and in doing so, may have lost his balance. Even as the ball was going into his glove, a crowd of people began to engulf Mr. Popov.[3] He was tackled and thrown to the ground while still in the process of attempting to complete the catch. Some people intentionally descended on him for the purpose of taking the ball away, while others were involuntarily forced to the ground by the momentum of the crowd. Eventually, Mr. Popov was buried face down on the ground under several layers of people. . . . Mr. Popov was grabbed, hit and kicked. People reached underneath him in the area of his glove. Neither the tape nor the testimony is sufficient to establish which individual members of the crowd were responsible for the assaults on Mr. Popov. The videotape clearly establishes that this was an out of control mob, engaged in violent, illegal behavior. . . .

Mr. Popov intended at all times to establish and maintain possession of the ball. At some point the ball left his glove and ended up on the ground. It is impossible to establish the exact point in time that this occurred or what caused it to occur. Mr. Hayashi was standing near Mr. Popov when the ball came into the stands. He, like Mr. Popov, was involuntarily forced to the ground. He

---

1.   It has been suggested that the ball might sell for something in excess of $1,000,000.
2.   The Giants' website contains a page which shows where each of Bonds' home runs landed in 2001. This page was introduced into evidence and is part of the record. It shows that most of the balls are clustered in the arcade area.
11.   A percipient witness testifies as to what she has seen, heard, or felt.—Eds.
3.   Ted Kobayashi, a defense expert, testified that there was insufficient reaction time for the crowd to descend on Mr. Popov. This opinion is completely unconvincing. . . .

committed no wrongful act. . . . While on the ground he saw the loose ball. He picked it up, rose to his feet and put it in his pocket. Although the crowd was still on top of Mr. Popov, security guards had begun the process of physically pulling people off. Some people resisted those efforts. . . . Mr. Hayashi kept the ball hidden. He asked Mr. Keppel to point the camera at him. At first, Mr. Keppel did not comply and Mr. Hayashi continued to hide the ball. Finally after someone else in the crowd asked Mr. Keppel to point the camera at Mr. Hayashi, Mr. Keppel complied. It was only at that point that Mr. Hayashi held the ball in the air for others to see. Someone made a motion for the ball and Mr. Hayashi put it back in his glove. It is clear that Mr. Hayashi was concerned that someone would take the ball away from him and that he was unwilling to show it until he was on videotape. . . .

Mr. Popov eventually got up from the ground. He made several statements while he was on the ground and shortly after he got up which are consistent with his claim that he had achieved some level of control over the ball and that he intended to keep it. . . . When he saw that Mr. Hayashi had the ball he expressed relief and grabbed for it. Mr. Hayashi pulled the ball away.[6] Security guards then took Mr. Hayashi to a secure area of the stadium.

. . . Neither the camera nor the percipient witnesses were able to establish whether Mr. Popov retained control of the ball as he descended into the crowd. Mr. Popov's testimony on this question is inconsistent on several important points, ambiguous on others and, on the whole, unconvincing. . . . Perhaps the most critical factual finding of all is one that cannot be made. We will never know if Mr. Popov would have been able to retain control of the ball had the crowd not interfered with his efforts to do so. Resolution of that question is the work of a psychic, not a judge.

Legal Analysis

Plaintiff has pled causes of actions for conversion, trespass to chattel, injunctive relief and constructive trust. Conversion is the wrongful exercise of dominion over the personal property of another. . . . Wrongful withholding of property can constitute actual interference even where the defendant lawfully acquired the property. If a person entitled to possession . . . demands its return, the unjustified refusal to give the property back is conversion. The act constituting conversion must be intentionally done. There is no requirement, however, that the defendant know that the property belongs to another or that the defendant intends to dispossess the true owner of its use and enjoyment. Wrongful purpose is not a component of conversion. The injured party may elect to seek either specific recovery of the property or monetary damages.

Trespass to chattel, in contrast, exists where personal property has been damaged or where the defendant has interfered with the plaintiff's use of the property. Actual dispossession is not an element of the tort. . . . Mr. Popov is

---

6. Defense counsel has attempted to characterize this encounter as one in which Mr. Popov congratulates Mr. Hayashi for getting the ball and offers him a high five. This is an argument that only a true advocate could embrace.

not claiming that Mr. Hayashi damaged the ball or that he interfered with Mr. Popov's use and enjoyment of the ball. He claims instead that Mr. Hayashi intentionally took it from him and refused to give it back. There is no trespass to chattel. If there was a wrong at all, it is conversion. . . . One who has neither title nor possession, nor any right to possession, cannot sue for conversion. The deciding question in this case then, is whether Mr. Popov achieved possession or the right to possession as he attempted to catch and hold on to the ball.

The parties have agreed . . . [that before] the ball was hit, it was possessed and owned by Major League Baseball. At the time it was hit it became intentionally abandoned property. The first person who came in possession of the ball became its new owner.[16] The parties fundamentally disagree about the definition of possession. . . . [T]o assist the court in resolving this disagreement, four distinguished law professors participated in a forum to discuss the legal definition of possession.[17] The professors also disagreed. The disagreement is understandable. Although the term possession appears repeatedly throughout the law, its definition varies depending on the context in which it is used. . . . Because each industry has different customs and practices, a single definition of possession cannot be applied to different industries without creating havoc.

This does not mean that there are no central principles governing the law of possession. . . . Professor Roger Bernhardt[20] has recognized that "[p]ossession requires both physical control over the item and an intent to control it or exclude others from it. But these generalizations function more as guidelines than as direct determinants of possession issues. Possession is a blurred question of law and fact." . . .

. . . Mr. Popov has clearly evidenced an intent to possess the baseball and has communicated that intent to the world.[23] The question is whether . . . his acts [were] sufficient to create a legally cognizable interest in the ball?

Mr. Hayashi argues that possession does not occur until the fan has complete control of the ball. Professor Brian Gray suggests the following definition[:] "A person who catches a baseball that enters the stands is its owner. A ball is caught if the person has achieved complete control of the ball at the point in time that the momentum of the ball and the momentum of the fan while attempting to catch the ball ceases. A baseball, which is dislodged by incidental contact with an inanimate object or another person, before momentum has ceased, is not possessed. Incidental contact with another person is contact that is not intended by the other person. The first person to pick up a loose ball and secure it becomes its possessor."[24]

---

16. *See generally, Past and Future: The Temporal Dimension in the Law of Property* (1986) 64:667 Washington U.L. Quarterly, Professor Richard A. Epstein . . . ; Irwin v. Phillips (1855) 5 Cal. 140; Potter v. Knowles (1855) 5 Cal. 87.

17. They are Professor Brian E. Gray, University of California, Hastings College of the Law; Professor Roger Bernhardt, Golden Gate University School of Law; Professor Paul Finkelman, The Chapman Distinguished Professor of Law, The University of Tulsa School of Law; and Professor Jan Stiglitz, California Western School of Law. The discussion was held during an official session of the court convened at The University of California, Hastings College of the Law. The session was attended by a number of students and professors including one first year property law class which used this case as [a] vehicle to understand the law of possession.

20. Professor Bernhardt is the author of the textbook Property, Cases and Statutes . . . as well as the co-author of Real Property in a Nutshell with Professor Ann M. Burkhart.

23. Literally.

24. This definition is hereinafter referred to as Gray's Rule.

π rejects
Δ's argument
b/c need
unequivocal
dominion
(rejected by
precident)

π suggest
possession
before uneq.
dominion.

Mr. Popov argues that this definition requires that a person seeking to establish possession . . . show unequivocal dominion and control, a standard rejected by several leading cases.[25] Instead, he offers the perspectives of Professor Bernhardt and Professor Paul Finkelman[26] who suggest that possession occurs when an individual intends to take control of a ball and manifests that intent by stopping the forward momentum of the ball whether or not complete control is achieved. Professors Finkelman and Bernhardt have correctly pointed out that some cases recognize possession even before absolute dominion and control is achieved. Those cases require the actor to be actively and ably engaged in efforts to establish complete control[27] . . . [which] must be significant and . . . reasonably calculated to result in unequivocal dominion and control . . . in the near future.[28]

This rule is applied in cases involving the hunting or fishing of wild animals[29] or the salvage of sunken vessels.[30] The hunting and fishing cases recognize that a mortally wounded animal may run for a distance before falling. The hunter acquires possession upon the act of wounding the animal not the eventual capture. Similarly, whalers acquire possession by landing a harpoon, not by subduing the animal.[31] In the salvage cases, an individual may take possession of a wreck by exerting as much control "as its nature and situation permit." Inadequate efforts, however, will not support a claim of possession. . . .

These rules are contextual in nature, . . . crafted in response to the unique nature of the conduct they seek to regulate, [and] influenced by the custom and practice of each industry. The reason that absolute dominion and control is not required to establish possession in the cases cited by Mr. Popov is that such a rule would be unworkable and unreasonable. . . . It is impossible to wrap one's arms around a whale, a fleeing fox or a sunken ship.

The opposite is true of a baseball hit into the stands of a stadium. Not only is it physically possible for a person to acquire unequivocal dominion and control of an abandoned baseball, but fans generally expect a claimant to have

25.   Pierson v. Post 3 Caines R. (N.Y. 1805), Young v. Hitchens 6 Q.B. 606 (1844); State v. Shaw (1902) 67 Ohio St. 157.

26.   Professor Finkelman is the author of the definitive law review article on the central issue in this case, *Fugitive Baseballs and Abandoned Property: Who Owns the Home Run Ball?;* Cardozo Law Review, May 2002, Paul Finkelman. . . .

27.   The degree of control necessary to establish possession varies from circumstance to circumstance. "The law . . . does not always require that one who discovers lost or abandoned property must actually have it in hand before he is vested with a legally protected interest. The law protects not only the title acquired by one who finds lost or abandoned property but also the right of the person who discovers such property, and is actively and ably engaged in reducing it to possession, to complete this process without interference from another. The courts have recognized that in order to acquire a legally cognizable interest in lost or abandoned property a finder need not always have manual possession of the thing. Rather, a finder may be protected by taking such constructive possession of the property as its nature and situation permit." Treasure Salvors Inc. v. The Unidentified Wrecked and Abandoned Sailing Vessel (1981) 640 F.2d 560, 571. . . .

28.   Brady v. S.S. African Queen 179 F.Supp. 321 (E.D.Va. 1960); Eads v. Brazelton (1861) 22 Ark. 499; Treasure Salvors Inc. *id.* at 571.

29.   Liesner v. Wanie (1914) 145 N.W. 374; Ghen v. Rich 8 F. 159 (D.Mass.1881); Pierson v. Post 3 Caines R. (N.Y. 1805); Young v. Hitchens 6 Q.B. 606 (1844); State v. Shaw (1902) 67 Ohio St. 157. . . .

30.   Indian River Recovery Company v. The China 645 F.Supp. 141, 144 (D.Del.1986); Treasure Salvors Inc. v. The Unidentified Wrecked and Abandoned Sailing Vessel (1981) 640 F.2d 560; Richard v. Pringle 293 F.Supp.981 (S.D.N.Y. 1968).

31.   Swift v. Gifford 23 F. Cas. 558 (D.Mass.1872).

accomplished as much. The custom and practice of the stands creates a reasonable expectation that a person will achieve full control of a ball before claiming possession. There is no reason for the legal rule to be inconsistent with that expectation. Therefore Gray's Rule is adopted as the definition of possession in this case. . . . Mr. Popov has not established by a preponderance of the evidence that he would have retained control of the ball after all momentum ceased and after any incidental contact with people or objects. Consequently, he did not achieve full possession.

That finding, however, does not resolve the case. The reason we do not know whether Mr. Popov would have retained control of the ball is . . . because he was attacked. His efforts to establish possession were interrupted by the collective assault of a band of wrongdoers.[34] A decision which ignored that fact would endorse the actions of the crowd by not repudiating them. Judicial rulings, particularly in cases that receive media attention, affect the way people conduct themselves. This case demands vindication of an important principle. We are a nation governed by law, not by brute force.

As a matter of fundamental fairness, Mr. Popov should have had the opportunity to try to complete his catch unimpeded by unlawful activity. . . . [T]he analysis cannot stop with the valid observation that Mr. Popov has not proved full possession.[36] The legal question presented at this point is whether an action for conversion can proceed where the plaintiff has failed to establish possession or title. It can. An action for conversion may be brought where the plaintiff has title, possession or the right to possession. . . .

Here Mr. Popov seeks, in effect, a declaratory judgment that he has either possession or the right to possession. In addition he seeks the remedies of injunctive relief and a constructive trust. These are all actions in equity. A court sitting in equity has the authority to fashion rules and remedies designed to achieve fundamental fairness.

Consistent with this principle, the court adopts the following rule. Where an actor undertakes significant but incomplete steps to achieve possession of a piece of abandoned personal property and the effort is interrupted by the unlawful acts of others, the actor has a legally cognizable pre-possessory interest in the property. That pre-possessory interest constitutes a qualified right to possession which can support a cause of action for conversion. . . . Mr. Popov [is vested] with a qualified right to possession . . . [that] enables him to advance a legitimate claim to the baseball based on a conversion theory. Moreover it addresses the harm done by the unlawful actions of the crowd. It does not, however, address the interests of Mr. Hayashi. . . .

Mr. Hayashi was not a wrongdoer. He was a victim of the same bandits that attacked Mr. Popov. The difference is that he was able to extract himself from their assault. . . . When he picked up [the loose ball] and put it in his pocket he attained unequivocal dominion and control.

---

34. Professor Gray has suggested that the way to deal with this problem is to demand that Mr. Popov sue the people who assaulted him. This suggestion is unworkable for a number of reasons. First, it was an attack by a large group of people. It is impossible to separate out the people who were acting unlawfully from the people who were involuntarily pulled into the mix. Second, . . . to prove damages related to the loss of the ball, Mr. Popov would have to prove that but for the actions of the crowd he would have achieved possession of the ball. . . . [T]his is impossible.

36. The court is indebted to Professor Jan Stiglitz of California Western School of Law for his valuable insights and suggestions on this issue.

If Mr. Popov had achieved complete possession before Mr. Hayashi got the ball, those actions would not have divested Mr. Popov of any rights, nor would they have created any rights to which Mr. Hayashi could lay claim. Mr. Popov, however, . . . [has] only a qualified pre-possessory interest in the ball, [which] . . . does not establish a full right to possession that is protected from a subsequent legitimate claim. . . . [W]hile Mr. Hayashi appears on the surface to have done everything necessary to claim full possession of the ball, the ball itself is encumbered by the qualified pre-possessory interest of Mr. Popov. At the time Mr. Hayashi came into possession of the ball, it had, in effect, a cloud on its title.

An award of the ball to Mr. Popov would be unfair to Mr. Hayashi. . . . An award of the ball to Mr. Hayashi would unfairly penalize Mr. Popov. . . . Both men have a superior claim to the ball as against all the world. Each man has a claim of equal dignity as to the other. We are, therefore, left with something of a dilemma.

Thankfully, there is a middle ground. The concept of equitable division was fully explored in a law review article authored by Professor R.H. Helmholz in the December 1983 edition of the Fordham Law Review.[38] Professor Helmholz addressed the problems associated with rules governing finders of lost and mislaid property. For . . . reasons not directly relevant to . . . this case, Helmholz suggested employing the equitable remedy of division to resolve competing claims between finders of lost or mislaid property and the owners of land on which the property was found. There is no reason . . . the same remedy cannot be applied in a case such as this, where issues of property, tort and equity intersect. The concept of equitable division has its roots in ancient Roman law. As Helmholz points out, it is useful in that it "provides an equitable way to resolve competing claims which are equally strong." Moreover, "[i]t comports with what one instinctively feels to be fair."

Although there is no California case directly on point, Arnold v. Producers Fruit Company (1900) 128 Cal. 637 provides some insight. There, a number of different prune growers contracted with Producer's Fruit Company to dry and market their product. Producers . . . mixed fruit from many different growers together in a single bin and much of the fruit rotted because it was improperly treated. When one of the plaintiffs offered proof that the fruit in general was rotten, Producers objected . . . that the plaintiff could not prove . . . the prunes he contributed to the mix were the same prunes that rotted. The court concluded that it did not matter. After the mixing was done, each grower had an undivided interest in the whole, in proportion to the amount of fruit each had originally contributed. The principle at work here is that where more than one party has a valid claim to a single piece of property, the court will recognize an undivided interest in the property in proportion to the strength of the claim.

Application of the principle of equitable division is illustrated in the case of Keron v. Cashman (1896) 33 A. 1055. In that case, five boys were walking home along a railroad track. . . . The youngest . . . came upon an old sock that was tied shut and contained something heavy. He picked it up and swung it. The oldest

---

38.   *Equitable Division and the Law of Finders* (1983) Fordham Law Review, Professor R.H. Helmholz, University of Chicago School of Law. This article built on a student comment published in 1939. *Lost, Mislaid and Abandoned Property* (1939) 8 Fordham Law Review 222.

boy took it away from him and beat the others with it. The sock passes from boy to boy. Each controlled it for a short time. At some point in the course of play, the sock broke open and out spilled $775. . . . None of the boys intended to take possession until it became apparent that the sock contained money. Each boy had physical control of the sock at some point before that discovery was made. Because none could present a superior claim of concurrent control and intent, the court held that each boy was entitled to an equal share of the money. . . .

Here, . . . both men intended to possess the ball at the time they were in physical contact with it. . . . [T]hey stand before the court in exactly the same legal position as did the five boys . . . and they are equally entitled to the ball. The court therefore declares that both plaintiff and defendant have an equal and undivided interest in the ball. Plaintiff's cause of action for conversion is sustained only as to his equal and undivided interest. . . . [T]o effectuate this ruling, the ball must be sold and the proceeds divided equally between the parties.

The parties are ordered to meet and confer forthwith before Judge Richard Kramer to come to an agreement as to how to implement this decision. If no decision is made by December 30, 2002, the parties are directed to appear before this court on that date at 9:00 A.M. The court retains jurisdiction to issue orders consistent with this decision. The ball is to remain in the custody of the court until further order.

Notes and Questions

1. Why did the court adopt the Gray definition of possession rather than the Bernhardt/Finkelstein definition? Was this an appropriate case for the use of custom?

2. *Wild animal analogy.* How did the parties use the wild animal cases in their arguments? Did the court accept or reject the suggested analogy between a wild animal and an abandoned baseball?

3. *Confusion doctrine.* When indistinguishable items of personal property belonging to different owners are mixed together so that it is not possible to determine which belongs to whom, the confusion doctrine dictates that each will receive a pro rata portion of the whole based on the amount contributed. If division of the whole is not possible, the contributors own the whole as tenants in common. How did the court use this doctrine, which was the basis for the result in *Arnold v. Producers Fruit Company*, in deciding this case? Do you see any relevant differences between the case of a unique item and fungible items such as prunes?

4. The ball was sold at an auction broadcast live on ESPN from the ESPNZone restaurant in Times Square on June 25, 2003. Although estimates of the sale price had gone as high as $2 million, bidding stopped after only 4 minutes at $450,000. The winning bidder was Todd McFarlane, a toy manufacturer and former comic book artist. He previously bought McGwire's ball for $3.2 million. Patrick Hayashi, 37, who had hoped to use his share to cover his expenses studying for a master's degree at San Diego State, estimated that his share would only cover his legal fees. Alex Popov, 38, owner of a health-food store in San Francisco, had planned to use some of the money to send his parents on a cruise and buy a Jack Russell puppy he would name Homer. *See* Ira Berkow, *Baseball:*

Bonds's Record Ball Is a Little Nest Egg, International Herald Tribune Online, Friday, June 27, 2003, www.iht.com; *Historic Bonds Ball Set to Be Auctioned Off*, NBC11.Com, May 28, 2003, www.nbc11.com.

2. *Oil and Gas*

ANDERSON v. BEECH AIRCRAFT CORPORATION

Supreme Court of Kansas
699 P.2d 1023 (Kan. 1985)

PRAGER, J. This is an action brought by the owners of a tract of land and the lessee under an oil and gas lease against Beech Aircraft Corporation to quiet title, to recover damages for slander of title and trespass, and for an accounting. The basic dispute is over the ownership of non-native gas injected by Beech Aircraft into an underground reservoir used by Beech for gas storage for many years and which gas the plaintiffs now seek to produce. Plaintiffs are Lowell L. Anderson and Aileen R. Anderson, the landowners, and Avanti Petroleum, Inc., the lessee under an oil and gas lease on the Anderson property.

This case is before the court on an interlocutory appeal . . . from an order of the district court which granted plaintiffs partial summary judgment on their quiet title claim and which held that the plaintiffs were entitled to produce any non-native gas injected for storage by Beech Aircraft which entered into plaintiffs' property.

[The undisputed facts are that Avanti Petroleum has drilled a well on the Anderson farm and is producing gas from the Stalnaker reservoir. Sometime in the past, native gas was produced from the Stalnaker reservoir, and after it was substantially depleted, Beech bought gas from interstate pipelines and injected it into the reservoir through wells on its property. Beech stored the gas for later use in its plant. The gas that Avanti is producing is the gas that Beech injected into the reservoir. The reservoir underlies the land of Beech and the adjoining Anderson farm. Beech does not hold a lease, license, or other permit for use of the part of the reservoir that underlies the Anderson farm. — EDS.]

. . . We turn now to consider the issue raised on this appeal which, simply stated, is as follows:

> Do the owners of land and of an oil and gas lease have the right to produce as their own non-native gas from their land, which gas has previously been purchased, injected, and stored in a common reservoir by another landowner having no license, permit, or lease covering the land from which the non-native gas is produced?

The trial court answered this question in the affirmative. . . .

The specific issue presented in this case is truly one of first impression in Kansas. As far as natural gas is concerned, Kansas has long recognized the law of capture, holding that natural gas in the ground is part of the real estate until it is actually produced and severed. At that point, it becomes personalty.

As underground reservoirs for natural gas have become more common, the issue of title to the stored gas has been presented to the courts. The issue of title was first addressed in Hammonds v. Central Kentucky Natural Gas Co., 75 S.W.2d

204 (Ky. 1934). In *Hammonds*, the gas company depleted an underground reservoir underlying approximately 15,000 acres and subsequently injected gas from distant wells into the reservoir for storage purposes. Della Hammonds owned 54 acres within the boundary of the reservoir which was never leased to the gas company. It was undisputed the reservoir lay under the Hammonds property. Della Hammonds sued the gas company for trespass and sought to recover damages for use and occupation of the reservoir underlying her property. The lower court held for the gas company and Hammonds appealed. The Kentucky Court of Appeals affirmed. But Hammonds won the victory in the long run. The Kentucky court initially discussed the doctrine of capture, declaring that "oil and gas are not the property of any one until reduced to actual possession by extraction, although by virtue of his proprietorship the owner of the surface, or his grantee of the severed mineral estate, has the exclusive right of seeking to acquire and of appropriating the oil and gas directly beneath." The court also recognized the nature of oil and gas as being fugitive and migratory, having the power and tendency to escape without the volition of its owner. The court analogized oil and gas to wild animals or animals *ferae naturae.* It noted that ownership in birds and wild animals becomes vested in the person capturing or reducing them to possession. However, when restored to their natural wild and free state, the dominion and individual proprietorship of any person over them is at an end and they resume their status as common property. The court also considered cases involving subterranean and percolating water where it has been held that, once the water is restored to the earth or to the running stream, a prior possessor's exclusive, individual title is lost. The court concluded in *Hammonds* that, if non-native injected gas wanders into the land of an adjoining landowner, the gas company is not liable for trespass as the gas company no longer owns the gas.

The *Hammonds* doctrine was recognized by a Pennsylvania trial court in Protz v. Peoples Natural Gas Co., 93 Pitts. Leg. J. 239, *aff'd*, 94 Pitts. Leg. J. 139 (1945). The plaintiffs in that case sought an injunction to prevent the installation of a proposed gas storage facility, part of which would underly their farm, on the basis that storage constituted a continuing trespass. Injunctive relief was denied. The court held by way of dictum that the presence of this gas would not constitute an invasion of the plaintiffs' property rights since the defendant had lost title to the gas. The court did note, however, that if the plaintiffs could prove that the storage project would endanger their safety and peaceful use of their land, then perhaps injunctive relief might be available. . . .

The nonownership theory which was adopted in *Hammonds* has been criticized by writers in the field. One writer argued that the theory expressed in the *Hammonds* decision is illogical and invalid for the reason that once man has reduced natural gas to possession, and processed and transported it to the storage area, the gas in no way resembles gas in its native state. Smith, *Rights and Liabilities on Subsurface Operations*, Southwestern Legal Foundation, Eighth Annual Institute on Oil and Gas Law and Taxation 1, 25-6 (1957). Several courts have refused to follow the rationale set forth in *Hammonds.* . . .

In addition to these court decisions, there have been statutes enacted in various states to regulate the underground storage of natural gas. These statutes vary widely in their provisions. . . .

With this background in mind, we turn now to the statutory scheme adopted in Kansas. . . . [In] 1951 . . . the legislature enacted K.S.A. 55-1201 *et seq.*, which regulates the underground storage of gas. . . . K.S.A. 55-1203 provides that any natural gas public utility may appropriate for its use for the underground storage of natural gas any subsurface stratum or formation in any land which the commission shall have found to be suitable and in the public interest for the underground storage of natural gas. K.S.A. 55-1204 provides that, as a condition precedent to the exercise of the right of eminent domain as to any property for the underground storage of natural gas, the natural gas public utility shall obtain from the state corporation commission a certificate setting out the findings of the commission (1) that the underground stratum or formation sought to be acquired is suitable for the underground storage of natural gas and that its use for such purposes is in the public interest; and (2) the amount of recoverable oil and native gas, if any, remaining therein. Section (b) of 55-1204 provides that the commission shall issue no such certificate until after public hearing is had on application and upon reasonable notice to interested parties.

. . . [I]t is clear that the expressed intention of the legislature is that the condemnation of property for the underground storage of natural gas is restricted to natural gas public utilities. Furthermore, it is clear that under the legislative scheme, before an underground gas storage area may be established, a certificate must be obtained from the Kansas Corporation Commission. . . .

In determining the issue presented in this case, this court has the obligation to consider more than the relative merits and demerits of the wild animal theory adopted in *Hammonds* . . . . We have concluded that, in order to carry out the legislative intent and to adopt a rule which will be fairest and most beneficial to the people of this state, in a factual situation such as is presented in this case, where the landowner, Beech Aircraft Corporation, is not a natural gas public utility and has attempted to create an underground storage reservoir under the property of an adjoining landowner without acquiring by contract the right to do so, the law of capture should be applied to any non-native gas which is purchased elsewhere and injected into the common pool for storage. We thus hold that Beech Aircraft lost its ownership of the stored gas after injecting it into the reservoir in this case.

In arriving at this conclusion, we have considered the undesirable consequences of the position which Beech Aircraft has asserted in this case. Beech Aircraft contends that it has the right to store gas under the land of an adjoining landowner without obtaining a permit, license, or rights afforded by condemnation, and without paying any rentals or other compensation. In our judgment, the adoption of such a rule would result in extensive litigation between adjoining property owners . . . . For example, if there is gas production near a storage reservoir on land without license for gas storage, there is bound to be litigation to determine how much of the gas being produced is native and how much is stored gas, what damages are owed to what adjacent landowner for the storage of unauthorized gas, and who is entitled to what share of the gas produced.

. . . In the event the legislature should determine that it would be in the best interests of the people of Kansas to adopt different legal principles to regulate the storage of gas, that is a matter for future legislative action.

The judgment of the district court is affirmed.

Notes and Questions

1. As the court noted, the gas company in the *Hammonds* case, discussed in *Anderson v. Beech Aircraft*, won the battle but lost the war. What alternative arguments might you have used if you had represented the gas company in *Hammonds*, or Beech Aircraft in this case?

2. After Beech Aircraft loses the case, what alternatives are open to it? If Beech tries to negotiate with the Andersons and Avanti, how likely are they to reach an agreement? They appear to be in a bilateral monopoly situation,[12] which often precludes coming to terms because each side will try to bargain "strategically" to get as much as possible of the gains that would become available by making a deal. If you represented the Andersons and Avanti, how would you figure out how much to ask for? And if you represented Beech? If they don't reach a deal, what is likely to happen?

3. Where are the equities here? Do the Andersons have a morally justifiable claim to Beech's gas, or are they simply taking advantage of a legal technicality to claim property bought and paid for by someone else? The Andersons' suit included claims for trespass and accounting. If the court had gone the other way on the quiet title claim, should it have awarded the Andersons anything? The same court that decided the *Hammonds* case applied the maxim *cujus est solum, ejus est usque ad coelum ad infernos*[13] in upholding an order that the owner of the mouth of the Great Onyx Cave allow surveyors to enter the cave to determine whether his cave tours were trespassing on property belonging to the neighbors, who had no access to the cave. *See Edwards v. Sims*, 24 S.W.2d 619 (Ky. 1929). After the surveyors determined that one-third of the exhibited cave was under the plaintiff's land, the court ordered defendant to account to the plaintiff's estate for one-third of the net profits even though defendant alone had explored and developed the cave. *See Edwards v. Lee's Administrator*, 96 S.W.2d 1028 (Ky. 1936). Is this a fair result? How far above and below the earth's surface should the right to exclude extend?

4. The Kentucky court cast considerable doubt on the continuing vitality of the *Hammonds* decision in *Texas American Energy Corp. v. Citizens Fidelity Bank & Trust Co.*, 736 S.W.2d 25, 28 (Ky. 1987). It held that "when previously extracted gas stored in underground reservoirs capable of being defined with certainty and the integrity of said reservoirs is capable of being maintained, title to such oil or gas is not lost and said minerals do not become subject to the rights of the owners of the surface above the storage fields." The court rejected the wild animal analogy, quoting from *Lone Star Gas Co. v. Murchison*, 353 S.W.2d 870, 879 (Tex. 1962): "Gas has no similarity to wild animals. Gas is an inanimate, diminishing non-reproductive substance lacking any will of its own, and instead of running wild and roaming at large as animals do, is subject to be moved solely by pressure or mechanical means. . . . [I]nstead of being turned loose in the woods as the fanciful fox or placed in the streams as the fictitious fish, gas, a privately owned commodity, has been stored for use . . . subject to . . . control and withdrawal at any time."

5. In *Pacific Gas & Electric Co. v. Zuckerman*, 234 Cal. Rptr. 630 (Ct. App. 1987), PG&E acquired storage rights to an exhausted gas reservoir and also entered into an oil and gas agreement with the landowner to operate a well on an adjacent parcel. The agreement required it to pay royalties on the gas extracted

---

12. A bilateral monopoly is a market with only one seller and only one buyer—a monopoly on each side.

13. Whoever owns the soil owns everything up to the sky and down to the depths, Black's Law Dictionary (7th ed. 1999), Appendix A.

from the well. After a few years, it discovered that gas injected into the storage reservoir was migrating to the adjacent well and it was paying royalties on its own gas. The court held that PG&E did not lose title to the stored gas and thus was not liable for royalties on it. The court concluded: "To be sure an owner who allows gas to escape to the property of another may be liable in trespass, nuisance, inverse condemnation, or on other applicable theories, but it still remains the owner of such gas."

The Capture Doctrine, Wild Animals, and Natural Gas

The label "capture doctrine" is used in two different senses. In one sense, it simply means that a person is allowed to acquire property rights in something by simply taking possession of it, or by "occupancy," to use the old terminology. Modernly, that right is often conditioned on obtaining a permit from the government and is often denied to trespassers. In another common usage, the term *capture doctrine* is used to describe an unlimited right to acquire property rights in a resource, as long as the resource can be obtained without trespassing on the land of another. When used in this sense, it may describe the right of a landowner to take all the wild animals that can be lured to his or her land (as in *Keeble*) or natural gas (as in *Beech Aircraft*) without regard to the effect on neighboring landowners. Similar rights have been recognized with respect to groundwater. When you use or encounter the term *capture*, be sure to identify the sense in which it is being used.

There are several alternatives to an unlimited right of capture. With respect to wild animals, most states limit the total catch of many animals, and there are a number of federal statutes that limit or prohibit taking animals such as migratory birds, marine mammals, and threatened and endangered species.[14] With respect to oil and gas, where preservation of a breeding stock is not the problem, different alternatives have been developed, ranging from simple prohibitions on wasteful uses to sophisticated systems of allocation and management.

The primary problem caused by application of an unlimited capture doctrine to oil and gas is that it encourages inefficient use of resources. Either one entity must obtain control of drilling rights on all the land overlying the reservoir, which gives each landowner an incentive to hold out for as high a price as possible, or each landowner will attempt to grab as much of the resource as possible to avoid losing it to the others. This leads to overinvestment in wells and drilling equipment, careless but speedy extractive processes, and premature exploitation of the resource. In response to these concerns, some courts have modified the capture doctrine by imposing some kind of "reasonable use" limit designed to prevent egregiously wasteful practices. Others have gone further and capped

---

14. Dean Lueck explores "the complex mix of legal, regulatory, and contractual rules that make up wildlife institutions" in the United States "by examining the structure of property rights to wildlife resources," in *Property Rights and the Economic Logic of Wildlife Institutions*, 35 Nat. Resources J. 625 (1995). He points out that while state governments regulate hunting and federal agencies protect endangered species, private landowners control much of the access to habitat. Whether landowners act to enhance wildlife habitat depends on the relative values of the wildlife and other uses that can be made of the land.

the amount each landowner may withdraw to a "fair share," which is usually calculated by the amount of oil or gas originally underlying his or her land. This is sometimes described as an "ownership in place" rule, which displaces the capture doctrine.

Legislative responses to the problems brought about by the unlimited capture doctrine include regulations that simply limit the number and spacing of wells that can be drilled and more sophisticated rules that establish "unitization" or "pooling" arrangements in which the reservoir is managed as a single unit for the benefit of all the overlying owners. If you are interested in more information about oil and gas law, you can get an overview from 38 Am. Jur. 2d *Gas and Oil* and a more in-depth treatment from Howard R. Williams & Charles J. Meyers, *Oil and Gas Law* (first published 1959, loose leaf with updates and revisions).

Notes and Questions

1. What are the relative advantages and disadvantages of the various resource management regimes described? What kind of information or technology is required to make them work? How much expense and difficulty is likely to be involved in administering them? Which are best suited for long-range conservation and management of natural resources?

2. How apt is the analogy between wild animals and natural gas? What differences do you see that might lead to different kinds of entitlements and regulatory regimes?

3. In every state, landowners are free to set up unitization or pooling arrangements for joint management of their interests in an oil or gas reservoir without state involvement, and often do so. If that is the case, what is the justification for statutory schemes that force unitization either at the request of one surface owner or at the request of some specified percentage of surface owners? What factors are likely to prevent all the surface owners from reaching agreement?

3. Water

American common law divides water into three categories: water in lakes and streams; diffused surface waters (runoff); and percolating groundwaters. Water in underground streams is treated the same as water in aboveground streams. Although advances in hydrogeology have proved these categories factually inaccurate, they persist in law. We begin our brief treatment of this very important subject with a look at groundwater, which first came onto the legal landscape in the mid-19th century when improvements in pumping and drilling technology allowed much increased water withdrawals to meet the demands for steam-powered engines and the widespread dewatering necessary for mining activities. As a result of this increased use of groundwater, land subsided and wells and springs dried up. Most courts responded to the inevitable lawsuits by adopting a bright-line "absolute dominion" rule, which came to be known as the "English rule." Like the unlimited capture doctrine adopted in early cases on oil and gas withdrawal, the absolute dominion rule allows landowners to pump without regard to the interests of their neighbors. When first faced with conflicts over rights to gas and oil, courts rejected the analogy to coal mining, which had well-developed rules, in favor of the wild animal analogy. In the area of groundwater, early courts rejected the analogy to streams and lakes, which were governed either by a rule of reasonable use or by the natural flow doctrine (except in the West where the prior appropriation doctrine was developed).

a.　Groundwater

CLINE v. AMERICAN AGGREGATES CORPORATION

Supreme Court of Ohio
474 N.E.2d 324 (1984)

Syllabus by the Court.
. . . American Aggregates Corporation, appellee herein, operates a sand, gravel, and stone quarrying operation in Jackson Township which is located in Franklin County. Since 1971 appellee has extracted limestone from its quarry. As part of the procedure utilized by appellee to extract limestone from its property, water must be pumped from the pits created by the quarrying operation.

Appellants herein are twenty-six landowners whose properties are also located in Jackson Township. Appellants commenced an action in the court of common pleas alleging that their entire domestic water needs are supplied by wells located on their properties. Appellants further alleged that their properties and appellee's property "overlie a well-defined semi-artesian aquifer composed of glacial outwash till resting upon a bed of limestone rock." Appellants claimed that appellee's pumping of its quarry pits unreasonably caused dewatering and pollution of appellants' wells.

The trial court granted appellee's motion for summary judgment on the basis that this state did not recognize a cause of action for appellants' injuries. The court of appeals affirmed, but suggested that the common law, as evidenced by *Frazier v. Brown* (1861), 12 Ohio St. 294, which did not recognize a cause of action on behalf of a landowner for damages resulting from a neighbor's use of underground percolating water, should be reexamined.

The cause is now before the court upon the allowance of a motion to certify the record.

JAMES P. CELEBREZZE, J. This court is today asked to reexamine the common law of Ohio as it is applied to ground water. The current standard recognizes no correlative rights with respect to ground water between adjoining landowners. This court last examined the issues encompassed in the present case in *Frazier v. Brown* . . . . In *Frazier* the "English rule" was applied to resolve any conflict involving percolating ground water.

This court stated in *Frazier*:

> . . . "[T]here are no correlative rights existing between the proprietors of adjoining lands, in reference to the use of the water in the earth, or percolating under its surface. Such water is to be regarded as part of the land itself, to be enjoyed absolutely by the proprietor within whose territory it is; and to it the law governing the use of running streams is inapplicable."

In support of the application of this absolute ownership doctrine the *Frazier* opinion further explained:

> . . . In the absence of express contract, and of positive authorized legislation, as between proprietors of adjoining lands, the law recognizes no correlative rights in respect to underground waters percolating, oozing or filtrating through the earth; and this mainly from considerations from public policy. 1. Because the existence, origin, movement and course of such waters, and the causes which govern and direct their movements, are so secret, occult and concealed, that an attempt to administer any set of legal rules in respect to them would be involved in hopeless uncertainty, and would be, therefore, practically impossible. 2. Because any such recognition of correlative rights, would interfere, to the material detriment of the common wealth, with drainage and agriculture, mining, the construction of highways and roadways, with sanitary regulations, building and the general progress of improvement in works of embellishment and utility.

Adherence to the English rule or absolute ownership doctrine has been the subject of criticism since its inception. Critics have remarked that the rule fails to acknowledge advances in the understanding of subsurface waters since the early 1800's. The "mysterious and occult" description of ground water flows does not describe or recognize the present state of scientific advancement.

One justification for the absolute ownership doctrine was predicated on the alleged protection it afforded to the property rights of landowners whose activities resulted in ground water diversion. Jurisdictions have, however, recognized the uncertainty and harshness associated with adherence to the doctrine. In Meeker v. East Orange (1909), 74 A. 379, the New Jersey Supreme Court explained . . . that:

> It is sometimes said that unless the English rule be adopted, landowners will be hampered in the development of their property because of the uncertainty that would thus be thrown about their rights. It seems to us that this reasoning is wholly faulty. If the English rule is to obtain, a man may discover upon his own land springs of great value for medicinal purpose or for use in special forms of manufacture, and may invest large sums of money upon their development; yet he is subject at any time to have the normal supply of such springs wholly cut off by a neighboring landowner, who may, with impunity, sink deeper wells and employ more powerful machinery, and thus wholly drain the sub-surface water from the land of the first discoverer.

Other American decisions have recognized that the advancement of scientific knowledge can insure the protection of a landowner's property rights in ground water to the same degree that the riparian doctrine protects the interests of land owners adjacent to a stream. . . . [Citations omitted. —Eds.]

The injustice of the English rule was best summed up by the California Supreme Court in Katz v. Walkinshaw (1903), 74 P. 766, where the court stated:

> Traced to its true foundation, the rule is simply this: that owing to the difficulties the courts will meet in securing persons from the infliction of great wrong and injustice by the diversion of percolating water, if any property right in such water is recognized, the task must be abandoned as impossible, and those who have valuable property acquired by and dependent on the use of such water must be left to their own resources to secure protection for their property from attacks of their

more powerful neighbors, and failing in this, must suffer irretrievable loss; that might is the only protection.

> The good old rule
> Sufficeth them, the simple plan,
> That they should take who have the power,
> And they should keep who can.

The field is open for exploitation to every man who covets the possessions of another or the water which sustains and preserves them, and he is at liberty to take that water if he has the means to do so, and no law will prevent or interfere with him, or preserve his victim from attack. The difficulties to be encountered must be insurmountable to justify the adoption or continuance of a rule which brings about such consequences.

Appellants suggest, and this court is persuaded, that the better standard to apply to ground water issues is found in the Restatement of the Law 2d, Torts, Section 858. Section 858 applies a reasonable use doctrine to underground water, as set forth below:

> (1) A proprietor of land or his grantee who withdraws ground water from the land and uses it for a beneficial purpose is not subject to liability for interference with the use of water by another, unless
>
> (a) the withdrawal of ground water unreasonably causes harm to a proprietor of neighboring land through lowering the water table or reducing artesian pressure,
>
> (b) the withdrawal of ground water exceeds the proprietor's reasonable share of the annual supply or total store of ground water, or
>
> (c) the withdrawal of the ground water has a direct and substantial effect upon a watercourse or lake and unreasonably causes harm to a person entitled to the use of its water.

Finding this reasonable use doctrine to be much more equitable in the resolution of ground water conflicts, this court overrules Frazier v. Brown and all its progeny and adopts Section 858 of the Restatement of the Law 2d, Torts, as the common law of Ohio. Therefore, the judgment of the court of appeals is reversed and the cause is remanded to the trial court for further proceedings.

HOLMES, J., concurring. While examining the law of percolating waters as a member of the Tenth Appellate District in Huelsmann v. State (1977), 56 Ohio App.2d 100, I stated that the modern day needs of our growing industrialized state may dictate a change in the law to provide for a greater conservation of one of our greatest natural resources. At that time, however, it was my view that the General Assembly should accept the challenge to reconstruct the law pertaining to water rights. Since our legislators have not acted, I agree with this court's adoption of Section 858 of the Restatement of the Law 2d, Torts.

. . . Until today, the traditional approach in Ohio was that the owner of the soil had absolute ownership in the percolating water beneath it. . . . This approach stemmed from the common-law principle set forth in the English case of Acton v. Blundell (Exch.1843), 12 M. & W. 324, 152 Eng. Rep. 1223. *See, also,* Note, *Establishing Liability for Damage Resulting from the Use of Underground Percolating*

Water: Smith-Southwest Industries v. Friendswood Development Company (1978), 15 Houston L. Rev. 454.

The Restatement standard preserves the general rule of nonliability, i.e., the privilege to use the water beneath one's land, and it also recognizes the exception when there is usually enough water for all users but one landowner removes an excess to the detriment of others. It is that owner who should bear the costs necessitated by a lowering of the water table.

The adopted rule will justly meet the changing needs of the users of water. What is a reasonable use of the water can be redetermined as surrounding circumstances change. The flexibility of the rule will allow for the utilization of water where it is most necessary.

The Restatement theory also provides security that one's source of ground water cannot be usurped by a neighbor. A damaged proprietor will be able to recover costs necessitated by the lowering of the water table. The solution is for the person causing the harm to supply the needs of the person harmed, and placing liability on the person causing the harm will encourage this result.

In addition, the rule promotes economic efficiency and encourages the reasonable use of water. Industries which utilize large amounts of underground waters will not be liable unless their use is unreasonable and creates a burden to neighboring landowners. Rural owners are also protected from commercial users who drastically lower the water table. A court's task will be to make whole the damaged property owner.

Finally, a primary goal of water law should be that the legal system conforms to hydrologic fact. Scientific knowledge in the field of hydrology has advanced in the past decade to the point that water tables and sources are more readily discoverable. This knowledge can establish the cause and effect relationship of the tapping of underground water to the existing water level. Thus, liability can now be fairly adjudicated with these advances which were sorely lacking when this court decided *Frazier* more than a century ago.

Notes and Questions

1. Since the 1920s, most American jurisdictions have abandoned the absolute dominion rule. By the end of the 20th century, only three states, Indiana, Maine, and Texas, clearly retained the rule, and in both Indiana and Texas, legislation had been enacted to regulate consumption in times of shortage. *See Waters and Water Rights* § 20.07 (Amy K. Kelley ed., 3d ed. 2014).

2. The Supreme Court of Maine rejected switching to reasonable use in *Maddocks v. Giles*, 728 A.2d 150 (Me. 1999), explaining:

> . . . First, we are not convinced that the absolute dominion rule is the wrong rule for Maine. We recognize that we are not bound by the doctrine of stare decisis when the underpinnings of the previous decisions are disproved and when the conditions of society have changed so that the prior law no longer fulfills a need and is counterproductive. . . . Although modern science has enlightened our knowledge of groundwater, this does not mean that the rule itself has interfered with water use or has caused the development of unwise water policy. The Maddockses did not present evidence or point to any studies showing that the absolute dominion rule has not functioned well in Maine. Furthermore, for over a century landowners

in Maine have relied on the absolute dominion rule. . . . In the absence of reliable information that the absolute dominion rule is counterproductive and a hindrance to achieving justice, we will not depart from our prior decisions.

Second, we are not persuaded that we, as opposed to the Legislature, should be weighing the heavy policy considerations involved in this issue, not the least of which is the reliance of land owners on the present property laws. The Legislature can study the ramifications of a change in policy; it can call upon experts to give their opinions as to the best water policy for Maine; and it can survey Maine's water needs. . . .

3. The Texas Supreme Court also refused to abandon the absolute dominion rule on the ground that such a change should be made by the legislature, saying "we are reluctant to make so drastic a change as abandoning our rule of capture and moving into the arena of water-use regulation by judicial fiat." *Sipriano v. Great Spring Waters of America*, 1 S.W.3d 75, 80 (Tex. 1999). By contrast, the concurring justice in *Cline*, the principal case, believed it proper for the court to act because the legislature had not acted. Who is right?

4. Courts unhappy with the absolute dominion rule developed two alternatives: the reasonable use rule, which originated in New Hampshire, and the correlative rights doctrine, which originated in California.[15] Although early cases tended to use the terms interchangeably, they eventually became quite different. Under the reasonable use rule, a landowner was not prevented from withdrawing groundwater for any reasonable use on the overlying land, even if damage to the neighbors resulted. In times of shortage, a landowner was not required to limit consumption for reasonable purposes (such as mining, agriculture, or the like) to leave water for others. The only limits imposed were that the landowner could not maliciously divert water, waste water, or divert the water away from the land overlying the aquifer. Under the correlative rights doctrine, by contrast, landowners have coequal rights in a common water basin and in times of shortage can take only their reasonable shares. Resolving conflicts under the correlative rights doctrine can be considerably more expensive than under the classic reasonable use doctrine because of the difficulty determining each landowner's reasonable share of the water source. How would you describe the Restatement rule the court adopted in *Cline*? How does it differ from the classic reasonable use rule?

5. The court in *Cline* remanded the case for application of the reasonable use rule of the Restatement. How should the court decide whether the harm caused by the water withdrawal is unreasonable? Should it weigh the value of the American Aggregates' quarrying business to the community against the value to the neighbors of the wells on their properties? Which of the various groundwater withdrawal rules provides the most secure basis for investments that depend on the availability of groundwater?

6. When American Aggregates started its quarry business, the law allowed it to draw down the water table without having to compensate the neighbors for any damage that might result. The damage was what is called an "externality"—a cost American Aggregates was not required to take into account in deciding

---

15.   Chapters 22 and 23 in Volume 3 of Waters and Watercourses (Robert E. Beck ed. 1991), respectively, cover the correlative rights doctrine and the reasonable use rule as they apply to groundwater. Chapter 21 covers the absolute dominion rule.

whether to go into business or in pricing its product. If it now has to compensate the neighbors, it has been forced to "internalize" the cost. Sometimes the existence of externalities is justified on the ground that it would be impractical or too expensive to internalize them. What are the likely costs involved in requiring a quarry operator to avoid unreasonable harm to the neighbors and what are the likely results of raising its costs?

7. Subsidence claims are treated differently from dry-well claims in some states, which impose a duty on landowners to maintain lateral support for adjacent properties. *See, e.g., City of Valparaiso v. Defler,* 694 N.E.2d 1177 (Ind. App. 1998), *transfer denied,* 714 N.E.2d 164 (Ind. 1999); *Gamer v. Town of Milton,* 195 N.E.2d 65 (Mass. 1964); A. Dan Tarlock, *Law of Water Rights and Resources* § 4:19 (1988 & Supp. 1989-2011). Others, whether applying the absolute dominion rule or the traditional reasonable use rule, hold quarry operators exempt from subsidence claims, at least if their dewatering operations are not negligent or malicious. *See, e.g., Finley v. Teeter Stone, Inc.,* 248 A.2d 106 (Md. 1968).

8. In *Edwards Aquifer Authority v. Day,* 369 S.W.3d 814 (Tex. 2010), the Texas Supreme Court held that surface owners own the groundwater underneath their lands (groundwater in place), the same as they own oil and gas in place, and that this is a property interest protected by the constitutional limitations on taking private property for public use without payment of just compensation. However, the ownership lasts only so long as the water remains underneath the land and is lost when the water moves away.

9. In *Spear T. Ranch, Inc. v. Knaub,* 691 N.W.2d 116 (Neb. 2005), the court adopted Restatement § 858 to govern liability of groundwater pumpers to surface water users with prior appropriation rights where the waters are hydrologically connected, holding that:

> A proprietor of land or his [or her] grantee who withdraws ground water from the land and uses it for a beneficial purpose is not subject to liability for interference with the use of water of another, unless . . . the withdrawal of the ground water has a direct and substantial effect upon a watercourse or lake and unreasonably causes harm to a person entitled to the use of its water.

Property Rules and Liability Rules

If a court decides that a groundwater pumper is liable to a neighbor for injury caused by drawing down the water table, it may grant relief to the plaintiff either by issuing an injunction or by awarding damages. If the court issues an injunction to protect the plaintiff's entitlement to a certain water level, we may say that it is protected by a *property rule.* If, instead, the court limits relief to an award of damages, we may say that the plaintiff is protected only by a *liability rule.* These terms were made famous by an article published in 1972, Guido Calabresi & A. Douglas Melamed, *Property Rules, Liability Rules and Inalienability: One View of the Cathedral,* 85 Harv. L. Rev. 1089. Protection by an injunction is described as a property rule because the plaintiff can decide whether and at what price she will sell defendant a right to diminish her entitlement. Limiting relief to damages, by contrast, allows the pumper to continue invading plaintiff's entitlement at a price determined by the court. There is considerable dispute over the propriety of recognizing a property right but then protecting it only by a liability rule.

b. Water in Lakes and Streams: Riparian Rights and Prior Appropriation

Restatement (Second) of Torts, Introductory Note on the Nature of Riparian Rights and Legal Theories for Determination of the Rights

Riparian rights—History. In the early English common law there was little litigation over the private use of water. Uses of water were limited mainly to withdrawals for domestic purposes and impoundments for running small grist mills. Many early cases were concerned with the effects of grants by landowners of privileges to operate mills, and many involved problems of prescription and ancient rights that had existed from time immemorial. Several cases contained language that could be construed as stating a rule of priority, that the first user had a better right than a later user, while some seemed to be based on the "golden rule," that one should not so use his property as to cause harm to others. Underlying all the cases, however, was the idea that there could be property rights to the use of running water that stemmed from the ownership of the land through which the stream flowed. Throughout the formative period there is evidence that the courts were searching for an appropriate legal standard that would permit the fullest beneficial use of the rivers and streams.

With the advent of the Industrial Revolution there came a marked increase in the use of water for powering machinery, and industrial wastes added a new dimension to pollution problems. In the resulting increase of litigation over water use the underlying principle was brought forth and clearly stated: each riparian proprietor has a right to use the stream as it passes his property, but no riparian proprietor has a right to use water to the injury of another. This developed into what has been called the natural flow theory, which required the stream to be left substantially unchanged except for minor effects of reasonable means of harnessing and using it as it passed.

As American industry grew it became obvious that many economically and socially desirable uses of water could not fit this pattern of leaving the streams substantially unchanged. A large mill required not merely a small dam to create a head of water but a reservoir for storage of water. The consumption of water increased as steam power freed the mills from the river banks, irrigation expanded and railroads and other industries multiplied. The idea of preserving the natural stream gave way to the need to alter it materially in order to enable the water to be put to these beneficial uses. The use, not the stream, came to be the thing protected by law, and injury to a reasonable use became the tort. In this fashion the common law of riparian rights split into two fundamentally different theories. One is the **natural flow theory** adopted by the English courts and still used to some extent in some American states. The other is the **reasonable use theory** more recently adopted by most American jurisdictions. . . .

The natural flow theory. Under this theory the primary or fundamental right of each riparian proprietor of a watercourse is to have the body of water flow as it was wont to flow in nature, qualified only by the privilege of each to make limited uses of the water.

The legal consequences of this theory are as follows:

(1) An unprivileged use of water that perceptibly depletes the volume of water on a riparian proprietor's land violates that proprietor's right to the natural condition of the water and is actionable by him, even though it interferes with no use that he is making and causes him no tangible harm.

(2) The cause of action arises at the time the unprivileged use is made and the period of prescription starts running from that time.

(3) If the unprivileged use is continuous, an injunction may properly be granted to prevent the acquisition of a prescriptive right.

(4) Riparian privileges are limited to use of the water on or in connection with a use of riparian land and consequently are not transferable apart from that land to nonriparians. A grant purporting to make a transfer does not pass privileges as against riparian proprietors; at most it bars the grantor from complaining of his grantee's nonriparian use.

In the early days of the Industrial Revolution when many mills and factories were powered by water, the doctrine served a very utilitarian purpose as it passed the water down from one mill dam to the next. In today's economy it is not utilitarian and prohibits many beneficial uses of water although those uses may be causing no one any harm and although the water would run to waste if not so used.

The reasonable use theory. Under the reasonable use theory the primary or fundamental right of each riparian proprietor on a watercourse or lake is to be free from unreasonable uses that cause harm to his own reasonable use of the water. Emphasis is placed on a full and beneficial use of the advantages of the stream or lake, and each riparian proprietor has a privilege to make a reasonable use of water for any purpose, provided that his use does not cause harm to the reasonable uses of others. Each riparian must make his use in a manner that will accommodate as many other uses as possible.

The legal consequences of this theory are as follows:

(1) There is, in its strictest application, no primary right in anyone to have the natural integrity of a stream or lake maintained for its own sake. The primary right of a riparian proprietor is to receive protection for his reasonable use of the stream or lake from an unreasonable use by another.

(2) A use of water by a riparian proprietor, whether for riparian or nonriparian purposes, is privileged if it does not cause harm to the existing reasonable use of another riparian proprietor.

(3) There is no cause of action against one who is making a use unless it causes harm or is otherwise unreasonable.

(4) One proprietor's use of all the water in a stream when others are making no use of it would be reasonable.

(5) The period of prescription does not start to run until a use is harmed by an unreasonable use.

(6) There are no categorical limitations on the purposes for which a use may be made.

(7) The riparian privileges of use, not being limited to use on or in connection with the use of riparian land, may include reasonable nonriparian uses, and may to that extent be transferred apart from the land to nonriparians.

The major advantage of this theory is that it tends to promote the beneficial use of water resources.

The reasonable use theory has won an almost complete victory in the American courts, although a considerable amount of natural flow language can still be found. Some cases do not require a clear distinction, since the natural flow theory allows many reasonable accommodations between users and the reasonable use theory sometimes results in holdings that the maintenance of a stream or lake in its natural condition is reasonable under particular circumstances. Even when the reasonable use rule is applied in its strictest form, the natural flow preference for "natural wants" is preserved in the form of a preference for domestic uses. Some courts have applied the reasonable use theory in cases between riparians and the natural flow theory in cases between a riparian and a nonriparian. In some western states the streams were regarded merely as sources for irrigating the arid land; and the courts applied the reasonable use theory to its ultimate extreme and permitted the streams to be dried up completely. In eastern states, however, where a stream is regarded as an amenity that may add value to land though it remains unused, courts that usually apply the reasonable use rule will sometimes use natural flow language to preserve a living stream, although what is preserved is the minimum flow required to protect its values, not the full natural flow.

The natural flow rule had a double aspect, in that it prohibited both substantial withdrawals and substantial pollution. When the American courts substituted the reasonable use rule, they used it also in both situations, although two quite different torts were thus lumped together. One was interference with the water supply needed by riparians for domestic, irrigation and manufacturing uses, for water power and storage, or for boating and fishing. The other was interference with the quality of water to the injury of riparian users. The distinction between the two types of cases was not often made explicit, and in both situations the courts purported to apply the same rule of reasonable use. This led to some pollution being authorized as a reasonable use. Many courts, however, found that expanding beneficial use was desirable but that increasing pollution was not, and came to apply the rule differently in the two types of cases. The distinction can be found in the results. In the water quality cases, reasonableness depends upon a balancing of the interests of the plaintiff and the defendant in each case, in a manner identical to the process used in cases of nuisance. Indeed, in many water pollution cases the courts employ the nuisance formula. In some cases, therefore, a defendant's pollution is held to be justified because the utility of the defendant's conduct outweighs the gravity of the harm imposed upon the plaintiffs. . . . This avoids sanctioning the pollution as the exercise of a property right. In the water quantity cases, the rule of reasonableness is applied quite differently. The plaintiff's use is required to be beneficial, suitable to the watercourse, and to have economic and social value. If these requirements are met and the defendant takes the substance of the water from the plaintiff and uses it himself, in most of the cases the decision is that the taking is unreasonable. . . . This gives the riparian who puts water to a beneficial use many of the advantages of an enforceable property right, while those advantages are denied the polluter. . . .

Prior Appropriation and Riparian Systems Compared

Eighteen western states use the prior appropriation doctrine, either alone or in conjunction with the riparian rights doctrine to allocate water rights. Under the riparian rights doctrine, water rights in rivers and lakes are allocated to landowners along the banks of the lake or river and water cannot generally be sold for use off the riparian land or out of the watershed. The prior appropriation doctrine, which originated in the gold mining camps in California, allocates water rights on a first-in-time basis to those who make beneficial uses of the water, without regard to their status as riparian landowners. Prior appropriation spread through the western states because it allowed miners and farmers to take and use water even though they owned no land abutting the water source. The riparian system, which had grown up in the East, where water was plentiful and the primary users were mills and power plants located on rivers, would have severely limited development in the arid West.

In prior appropriation systems, conflicts over water usage in times of shortage are resolved on the basis of first in time, rather than reasonable use. The "senior" appropriator is entitled to take her entire allotment (or so much of it as can be put to "beneficial" use) before a "junior" appropriator is entitled to anything. Water rights are much more clearly specified and stable under prior appropriation systems than they are in riparian systems. Although prior appropriation doctrine originated in the courts' recognition of custom among miners, it has become heavily regulated by statute. Priority today is generally determined on the basis of state-issued permits. Eight states, Arizona, Colorado, Idaho, Montana, Nevada, New Mexico, Utah, and Wyoming, followers of the "Colorado doctrine," have pure appropriation systems; 10 others, Alaska, California, Kansas, Nebraska, North Dakota, Oklahoma, Oregon, South Dakota, Texas, and Washington, have dual systems in which there may be holders of both riparian and appropriated rights in the same water source ("California doctrine").

Prior appropriation systems create some problems and opportunities that pure riparian systems do not. It can be more difficult to reduce the amount diverted from a water source to protect wildlife or enhance recreational opportunities and vistas because diversion rights are fixed. On the other hand, the fixed nature of water rights should make it easier to develop markets for water, which should lead to more efficient use of water. In the rapidly growing cities of the Southwest, there has been a lot of interest in buying water rights from farmers, who could be much more efficient in their use of water if they had sufficient incentive. Farmers, so far, have proved reluctant traders, perhaps because they fear becoming another Owens Valley—the valley turned into a desert by William Mulholland's shipment of vast quantities of water to Los Angeles after buying up the water rights in the early 20th century.[16]

Changes in the economy and increased appreciation for the environmental, recreational, and esthetic values of lakes and rivers, along with increasing population pressures, have led to changes and pressure for more changes in both riparian law and prior appropriation law. Increasing knowledge of hydrogeology suggests that groundwater, diffused surface water, and water in lakes and streams are all connected and the law should treat them as an integrated system. Climate change is creating even more significant challenges to the ways we manage our water resources. Water law is a dynamic subject that you can pursue further in a course on natural resource law and in *Waters and Water Rights* (Amy K. Kelley ed., 3d ed. 2014) and A. Dan Tarlock, *Water Rights and Resources* (1988 & Supp. 1989-2011). For a very interesting essay on the development of water rights as part of a larger story on the development of property rights generally, see Carol M. Rose, *Energy and Efficiency in the Realignment of Common Law Water Rights*, in *Property and Persuasion: Essays on the History, Theory, and Rhetoric of Property Ownership* 163 (1994).

---

16.   The movie *Chinatown* is built around this story.

c. Diffuse Surface Waters (Runoff)

The rules on a landowner's right to change drainage and runoff patterns have gone through an evolution similar to those on groundwater and waters in lakes and streams. Early cases adopted bright-line rules—either the "common enemy" doctrine under which landowners could divert water off their land without regard to consequences for the neighbors, or the "natural flow" doctrine under which landowners could not divert water from natural drainage patterns to the detriment of neighbors. Dissatisfaction with those bright-line rules has generally led to adoption of mushier "reasonableness" rules that require courts to weigh competing interests of the parties. As a result, much water litigation today is governed by principles that look very much like nuisance law.

B. FINDERS AND BAILEES

In this section, we take up questions dealing with acquiring property interests in things that currently belong, or previously belonged, to others without their consent, with the rights of possessors without title against wrongdoers, and with conflicts between people who find things and the owners of the places where the things were found.

As we have seen, you can acquire a property interest in a wild animal by capturing it, assuming you aren't breaking the law, but you may lose your interest if the animal escapes. What about other things? If you lose your laptop and someone else finds it, does he get to keep it? The answer is clearly no—at least if you can satisfactorily establish your ownership and the statute of limitations has not run on your cause of action. The brothers Kapiloff, who were philatelists, spotted an ad in a national catalog offering for sale stamps they owned and had thought they had in their possession. Ganter, who consigned the stamps to the auction house, had found the stamps in a dresser he bought for $30 in a used furniture store. He refused to give the stamps back to the Kapiloffs, claiming they were his on the ground of "finders keepers." The court in *Ganter v. Kapiloff*, 516 A.2d 611 (Md. Ct. Spec. App. 1986), awarded the stamps to the Kapiloffs, saying:

> The first reference that we have discovered to the adage about "finders keepers" appears in the writings of Plautus who penned in Trinummis 1. 63 (c.194 B.C.), "Habeas ut nanctus: He keeps that finds." In Charles Reade's *It is Never Too Late to Mend*, Ch. 65 (1856), the saying was reported as "Losers seekers, finders keepers." That expression has evolved into the more familiar "Finders keepers, losers weepers." Whatever its origin, the maxim is legally unsound.

As between the owner and the finder, the owner prevails, but that doesn't mean the finder has no rights.

1. Finders versus Wrongdoers

ARMORY v. DELAMIRIE

King's Bench
1 Str. 505 (1722)

The plaintiff being a chimney sweeper's boy found a jewel and carried it to the defendant's shop (who was a goldsmith) to know what it was, and delivered it into the hands of the apprentice, who under pretense of weighing it took out the stones, and calling to the master to let him know it came to three halfpence, the master offered the boy the money, who refused to take it, and insisted to have the thing again; whereupon the apprentice delivered him back the socket without the stones. And now in trover against the master these points were ruled:

1. That the finder of a jewel, though he does not by such finding acquire an absolute property or ownership, yet he has such a property as will enable him to keep it against all but the rightful owner, and consequently may maintain trover.
2. That the action well lay against the master, who gives a credit to his apprentice, and is answerable for his neglect.
3. As to the value of the jewel several of the trade were examined to prove what a jewel of the finest water that would fit the socket would be worth; and the Chief Justice (Pratt, C.J.) directed the jury that unless the defendant did produce the jewel and show it not to be of the finest water, they should presume the strongest against him and make the value of the best jewels the measure of their damages: which they accordingly did.

Notes and Questions

1. The court found that the sweeper's boy had a property interest sufficient to maintain an action of trover. How did he acquire that interest? How would you describe it (what are the characteristics of the property interest)? If another boy had spotted the jewel first, but Armory reached it and picked it up first, which boy would be entitled to it? Would they have to share it? Should they have to?

2. *Jus tertii.* Why wasn't Armory's lack of title to the jewel a good defense for the goldsmith? *Restatement (Second) of Torts § 895, Rights of Third Persons—Jus Tertii*, says:

(1) . . . [O]ne who is otherwise liable to another for harm to or interference with land or a chattel is not relieved of the liability because a third person has a legally protected interest in the land or chattel superior to that of the other.

What are the possible justifications for this rule? If Armory clearly had stolen the jewel, should the court have allowed the *jus tertii* defense? Comment *h* to Rest. § 895 states:

Subsection (1) is not intended to prevent a court from refusing, in a proper case, to lend its aid to a plaintiff who is clearly a wrongdoer, and particularly to one who is clearly a criminal.

3. *Trover and conversion; detinue and replevin.* Trover is an old common-law form of action that lay for recovery of damages for the conversion of personal property. Conversion is a wrongful act that essentially amounts to an appropriation of someone else's property. To maintain an action in trover, the plaintiff was required to prove either ownership or right to possession of the property at the time of the conversion. Two other forms of action, detinue and replevin, were available to the plaintiff who sought return of the property rather than damages. Originally, replevin was used if the property was taken unlawfully, while detinue was used if the defendant had acquired possession of the property lawfully but then refused to return it. To maintain either action, the plaintiff had to show an immediate right to possession of the property. Why do you suppose Armory brought the action in trover rather than detinue or replevin?

4. What does the court mean when it says that "the action well lay against the master, who gives a credit to his apprentice"? Why should the master be liable for wrongdoing by the apprentice?

5. *Burden of proof and measure of damages.* Ordinarily, the plaintiff is required to prove the amount of his damages in order to recover. Why does the court shift the burden to the goldsmith? What measure of damages was the jury directed to use?

The Supreme Court of the United States explains the principle:

The most elementary conceptions of justice and public policy require that the wrongdoer shall bear the risk of the uncertainty which his own wrong has created. That principle is an ancient one, Armory v. de Lamerie, 1 Strange 505 . . . . [I]n cases where a wrongdoer has incorporated the subject of a plaintiff's patent or trade-mark in a single product to which the defendant has contributed other elements of value or utility, and has derived profits from the sale of the product, this Court has sustained recovery of the full amount of defendant's profits where his own wrongful action has made it impossible for the plaintiff to show in what proportions he and the defendant have contributed to the profits. *Westinghouse Electric & Mfg. Co. v. Wagner Electric & Mfg. Co.*, 225 U.S. 604; *Bigelow v. RKO Radio Pictures,* 327 U.S. 251 (1946).

6. *Extent of finder's recovery.* Armory was awarded the full value of the jewel even though his interest was certainly worth less since it was subject to the right of the true owner to reclaim it. Is this a justifiable result?

7. *Rights of true owner.* If the owner of the jewel learns that de Lamerie had possession of her jewel and refused to return it to the finder, can she sue? If the jeweler refuses to give her the jewel or its value, the answer is yes — both the prior possessor and the owner have causes of action that they may pursue to judgment. However, satisfaction of a judgment in favor of either the prior possessor or the owner extinguishes both causes of action and bars recovery by the other. A settlement or release by either has the same effect. *See Restatement (Second) of Torts* § 895(2)(b). If Armory had accepted the jeweler's offer of three halfpence, would that prevent the true owner from recovering the actual value of the jewel from de Lamerie? Is there anything the owner could do to protect herself? Comment *g* to § 895 recognizes that the rule "may obviously involve potentialities of hardship . . . if the plaintiff mishandles the suit or he is not to be trusted with the proceeds. The court may therefore properly stay the action until the third person has been notified and afforded a reasonable time to intervene or to take other steps that may be necessary for his protection." But this doesn't help the owner who doesn't learn what has happened until after the finder has settled with the converter. Can you construct an argument that the Restatement rule should be applied only when the owner voluntarily gave possession of the chattel to the plaintiff?

8. The defendant in this case was Paul de Lamerie, a famous 18th century English silversmith whose extravagantly rococo work, which is held in both private and museum collections, commands very high prices at auction today. An inkwell he created for Sir Robert Walpole in 1729 sold at Sotheby's, New York, in April 1998 for $1,150,000. A 10-pound green turtle soup tureen, used at a dinner held for the King of Sweden in 1932 (which turned up at the back of a dining-room cupboard in Bordeaux after being "lost" for 50 years) was sold in 1997 at Christie's for £815,500. The Rugby World Cup is one of his creations. de Lamerie's name appears regularly in the press. You can see images of some of his work at the website of the Victoria & Albert Museum (London) at http://www.vam.ac.uk/content/articles/s/paul-de-lamerie-objects/.

2. Bailees versus Wrongdoers

A bailment is created when possession of a chattel is transferred from one person (the bailor) to another (the bailee) for a limited purpose. When you lend your car to a friend, or hand it over to a valet, or leave your camera at a shop to be repaired, you have created a bailment. If the bailee refuses to return your chattel, that's a conversion and, if you are successful in your conversion action, you force the bailee to buy it from you at its value at the time the conversion took place. Most bailments are "voluntary" in the sense that they are deliberately created by the bailor. However, bailments may also be created when people take chattels into their possession without the consent of the owner or possessor. These "involuntary" bailees include finders, towing companies that impound illegally parked cars, and others, like police, who seize personal property for various purposes.

A bailee has a duty to return the property to the bailor and has some level of responsibility for taking care of the bailed item, which may vary depending on the jurisdiction and whether the bailment primarily benefits the bailor or the bailee. In *Coggs v. Bernard*, 92 Eng. Rep. 107 (K.B. 1703), the court distinguished six different types of bailments for purposes of determining what level of care the bailee owed the bailor, but the modern trend has been to simplify the law by reducing the number of categories, or by eliminating them altogether and simply requiring the bailee to use the care an ordinary person would use under like circumstances. In *Hadfield v. Gilchrist*, 538 S.E.2d 268 (S.C. 2000), for example, the court concluded that when the towing company impounded the plaintiff's car, the resulting bailment was for their mutual benefit, and that the towing company owed the plaintiff a duty to use ordinary care to safeguard his car. Plaintiff was awarded $4,035 for vandalism damage that occurred in the defendant's storage yard.

When a chattel in the bailee's possession is wrongfully damaged, destroyed, or appropriated by a third party, the bailee may seek redress from the wrongdoer, but, as the next case shows, the basis for that rule remained in some doubt until the beginning of the 20th century.

THE WINKFIELD
Court of Appeal
[1902] P. 42, 1900-1903 All E.R. 346 (1901)

The case raised the question as to the rights of the Postmaster-General as bailee of letters and parcels in transit by post. . . . On April 5, 1900, a collision occurred in a fog off Table Bay, on the coast of Cape Colony, South Africa, between the Government transport Winkfield, . . . outward bound to the Cape with troops for service in South Africa, and the Union mail steam vessel Mexican from Cape Town, homeward bound to Southampton with mails, passengers, and cargo. The Winkfield was damaged and the Mexican sank, but not until all the passengers, crew, and some of the mails and luggage of the Mexican had been got on board the other vessel.

The owners . . . of the Mexican and . . . the Winkfield commenced cross-actions, which resulted in the owners of the Winkfield admitting liability for a moiety of the damage sustained by the Mexican, and, the owners of the Winkfield having commenced proceedings against the owners of the Mexican and all other persons having claims arising out of the collision, they . . . obtained the usual decree, under § 503 of the Merchant Shipping Act, 1894, limiting their liability . . . to £8 per ton, and paid into court (inclusive of interest) the sum of £32,514. . . . Against this fund claims . . . were filed in the Admiralty Registry . . . including a claim . . . by the Postmaster-General, on behalf of himself and the Postmasters-General of Cape Colony and Natal, . . . of £1706 . . . , the estimated value of the contents of letters and parcels in respect of which no claim had been made by . . . the senders or addressees, but which the Postmaster-General undertook to distribute amongst them, and . . . further undertook to indemnify the fund in court against any claims put forward by the actual owners. [This claim was refused by the registrar. — EDS.]

. . . [T]he President . . . upheld the decision of the registrar, on the . . . ground . . . that the Postmaster-General, as representing the Crown, was not under any liability to the parties interested in the lost letters and parcels . . . and, therefore, was precluded . . . from claiming for their value. . . .

The case was dealt with by all parties in the Court below as a claim by a bailee who was under no liability to his bailor for the loss in question, as to which it was admitted that the authority of Claridge v. South Staffordshire Tramway Co., [1 Q.B. 422 (1892)], was conclusive, and the President . . . dismissed the claim. The Postmaster-General now appeals.

COLLINS M.R. . . . It seems to me that the position, that possession is good against a wrongdoer and that the latter cannot set up the jus tertii unless he claims under it, is well established in our law, and really concludes this case against the respondents. . . . [T]he wrongdoer who is not defending under the title of the bailor is quite unconcerned with what the rights are between the bailor and bailee, and must treat the possessor as the owner of the goods for all purposes quite irrespective of the rights and obligations as between him and the bailor.

I think this position is well established in our law, though it may be that reasons for its existence have been given in some of the cases which are not quite satisfactory. . . . It cannot be denied that since the case of Armory v. Delamirie, not to mention earlier cases from the Year Books onward, a mere finder may recover against a wrongdoer the full value of the thing converted. That decision involves the principle that as between possessor and wrongdoer the presumption of law is, in the words of Lord Campbell in Jeffries v. Great Western Ry. Co. [5 E & B. 802, 805-806], "that the person who has possession has the property." In the same case he says: "I am of opinion that the law is that a person possessed of goods as his property has a good title as against every stranger, and that one who takes them from him, having no title in himself, is a wrongdoer, and cannot defend himself by shewing that there was title in some third person, for against a wrongdoer possession is title. . . ."

The ground of the decision in Claridge's Case was that the plaintiff . . . , being under no liability to his bailor, could recover no damages. . . . There is no doubt that the reason given in Heydon and Smith's Case [13 Rep. 69] — and itself drawn from the Year Books — has been repeated in many subsequent cases. The words are these: "Clearly, the bailee, or he who hath a special property, shall have a general action of trespass against a stranger, and shall recover all in damages because . . . he is chargeable over."

It is now well established that the bailee is accountable, as stated in the passage cited and repeated in many subsequent cases. But whether the obligation to account was a condition of his right to sue, or only an incident arising upon his recovery of damages, is a very different question, though it was easy to confound one view with the other.

Holmes C.J. in his admirable lectures on the Common Law, in the chapter devoted to bailments, traces the origin of the bailee's right to sue and recover the whole value of chattels converted, and arrives at the clear conclusion that the bailee's obligation to account arose from the fact that he was originally the only person who could sue, though afterwards by an extension, not perhaps quite logical, the right to sue was conceded to the bailor also. He says at p. 167: "At first the bailee was answerable to the owner because he was the only person who could sue; now it was said he could sue because he was answerable to the owner." And again at p. 170: "The inverted explanation of Beaumanoir[17] will be remembered, that the bailee could sue because he was answerable over, in place of the original rule that he was answerable over so strictly because only he could sue." This inversion, as he points out, is traceable through the Year Books, and has survived into modern times. . . . It may be that in early times the obligation of the bailee to the bailor was absolute, that is to say, he was an insurer. But long after the decision of Coggs v. Bernard [92 Eng. Rep. 107 (K.B. 1703)], which classified the obligations of bailees, the bailee has, nevertheless, been allowed to recover full damages against a wrongdoer, where the facts would have afforded a complete answer for him against his bailor. . . .

Therefore, as I said at the outset, and as I think I have now shewn by authority,[18] the root principle of the whole discussion is that, as against a wrongdoer, possession is title. The chattel that has been converted or damaged is deemed to be

---

17.   Philippe de Beaumanoir (1250-1296) wrote Coutumes du Beauvaisis (1283), one of the first compilations of customary law in medieval Europe. — EDS.

the chattel of the possessor and of no other, and therefore its loss or deterioration is his loss, and to him, if he demands it, it must be recouped. His obligation to account to the bailor is really not ad rem in the discussion. It only comes in after he has carried his legal position to its logical consequence against a wrongdoer, and serves to soothe a mind disconcerted by the notion that a person who is not himself the complete owner should be entitled to receive back the full value of the chattel converted or destroyed. There is no inconsistency between the two positions; the one is the complement of the other. As between bailee and stranger possession gives title — that is, not a limited interest, but absolute and complete ownership, and he is entitled to receive back a complete equivalent for the whole loss or deterioration of the thing itself. As between bailor and bailee the real interests of each must be inquired into, and, as the bailee has to account for the thing bailed, so he must account for that which has become its equivalent and now represents it. What he has received above his own interest he has received to the use of his bailor. The wrongdoer, having once paid full damages to the bailee, has an answer to any action by the bailor. . . .

. . . [T]herefore it seems to me that there is no such preponderance of convenience in favour of limiting the right of the bailee as to make it desirable, much less obligatory, upon us to modify the law as it rested upon the authorities antecedent to Claridge's Case. . . .

Notes and Questions

1. Is there greater justification for granting a voluntary bailee such as the Postmaster General full recovery for the value of the destroyed chattels than there is for granting it to a finder?

2. Lessees of chattels are covered by the same rules. In *Wallander v. Barnes*, 671 A.2d 962 (Md. 1996), the lessee of a Mercedes on a 36-month lease with option to purchase was held entitled to recover the full value of the car from a car dealer that wrongfully repossessed it. The court noted that the common law result was reinforced in that case because the lease placed the risk of loss on the lessee, requiring either replacement of the vehicle, or payment of the present value of the stream of unpaid rent plus the agreed value of the residual interest.

3. Finders versus Owners of the Locus in Quo[19]

HANNAH v. PEEL

King's Bench
1 K.B. 509 (1945)

On December 13, 1938, the freehold of Gwernhaylod House, Overton-on-Dee, Shropshire, was conveyed to the defendant, Major Hugh Edward Ethelston

---

18.   The court's discussion of the authorities, which included several American treatises and cases, is omitted. — EDS.

19.   Latin for "the place in which," this phrase is a useful shorthand for "the place in which the item was found."

Peel, who from that time to the end of 1940 never himself occupied the house, and it remained unoccupied until October 5, 1939, when it was requisitioned. In August, 1940, the plaintiff, Duncan Hannah, a lance corporal, serving in a battery of the Royal Artillery, was stationed at the house and on the 21st of that month, when in a bedroom, used as a sick-bay, he was adjusting the black-out curtains when his hand touched something on the top of a window frame, loose in a crevice, which he thought was a piece of dirt or plaster. The plaintiff grasped it and dropped it on the outside window ledge. On the following morning he saw that it was a brooch covered with cobwebs and dirt. Later, he took it with him when he went home on leave and his wife having told him it might be of value, at the end of October, 1940, he informed his commanding officer of his find and, on his advice, handed it over to the police, receiving a receipt for it.

In August, 1942, the owner not having been found the police handed the brooch to the defendant, who sold it in October, 1942, for £66, to Messrs. Spink & Son, Ltd., of London, who resold it the following month for £88. There was no evidence that the defendant had any knowledge of the existence of the brooch before it was found by the plaintiff. The defendant had offered the plaintiff a reward for the brooch, but the plaintiff refused to accept this and maintained throughout his right to the possession of the brooch as against all persons other than the owner, who was unknown. By a letter, dated October 5, 1942, the plaintiff's solicitors demanded the return of the brooch from the defendant, but it was not returned and on October 21, 1943, the plaintiff issued his writ claiming the return of the brooch, or its value, and damages for its detention. By his defense, the defendant claimed the brooch on the ground that he was the owner of Gwernhaylod House and in possession thereof.

BIRKETT, J. There is no issue of fact in this case between the parties. As to the issue in law, the rival claims of the parties can be stated in this way: the plaintiff says: "I claim the brooch as its finder and I have a good title against all the world, save only the true owner." The defendant says: "My claim is superior to yours inasmuch as I am the freeholder. The brooch was found on my property, although I was never in occupation, and my title, therefore, ousts yours and in the absence of the true owner I am entitled to the brooch or its value." Unhappily the law on this issue is in a very uncertain state and there is need of an authoritative decision of a higher court . . . .

The case of Bridges v. Hawkesworth, 21 L.J. (Q.B.) 75, 15 Jur. 1079 [1851], was . . . an appeal against a decision of the county court judge at Westminster. The facts appear to have been that in the year 1847 the plaintiff, who was a commercial traveller, called on a firm named Byfield & Hawkesworth on business, as he was in the habit of doing, and as he was leaving the shop he picked up a small parcel lying on the floor. He immediately showed it to the shopman, and opened it in his presence, when it was found to consist of a quantity of Bank of England notes, to the amount of £65. The defendant, who was a partner in the firm of Byfield & Hawkesworth, was then called, and the plaintiff told him he had found the notes, and asked the defendant to keep them until the owner appeared to claim them, and three years having elapsed since they were found, the plaintiff applied to the defendant to have the notes returned to him, and offered to pay the expenses of the advertisements and to give an indemnity. The defendant refused to deliver them up to the plaintiff, and an action was brought in the county court of Westminster in consequence of that refusal. The county court judge decided that the defendant, the shopkeeper, was entitled to the custody of the notes as against the plaintiff, and gave judgment for the defendant. Thereupon the appeal was brought which came before the court composed of Patteson, J. and Wightman, J. Patteson, J., said:

. . . The general right of the finder to any article which has been lost, as against all the world, except the true owner, was established in the case of Armory v. Delamirie, which has never been disputed. This right would clearly have accrued to the plaintiff had the notes been picked up by him outside the shop of the defendant and if he once had the right, the case finds that he did not intend, by delivering the notes to the defendant, to waive the title (if any) which he had to them, but they were handed to the defendant merely for the purpose of delivering them to the owner should he appear. . . . The case, therefore, resolves itself into the single point on which it appears that the learned judge decided it, namely, whether the circumstances of the notes being found inside the defendant's shop gives him, the defendant, the right to have them as against the plaintiff, who found them. . . . If the discovery had never been communicated to the defendant, could the real owner have had any cause of action against him because they were found in his house? Certainly not. The notes never were in the custody of the defendant, nor within the protection of his house, before they were found, as they would have been had they been intentionally deposited there; and the defendant has come under no responsibility, except from the communication made to him by the plaintiff, the finder, and the steps taken by way of advertisement. . . . We find, therefore, no circumstances in this case to take it out of the general rule of law, that the finder of a lost article is entitled to it as against all persons except the real owner, and we think that that rule must prevail, and that the learned judge was mistaken in holding that the place in which they were found makes any legal difference. . . .

With regard to South Staffordshire Water Co. v. Sharman, [1896] 2 Q.B. 44, the first two lines of the head note are: "The possessor is generally entitled, as against the finder, to chattels found on the land." I am not sure that this is accurate. The facts were that the defendant Sharman, while cleaning out, under the orders of the plaintiffs, the South Staffordshire Water Company, a pool of water on their land, found two rings embedded in the mud at the bottom of the pool. He declined to deliver them to the plaintiffs, but failed to discover the real owner. In an action brought by the company against Sharman in detinue it was held that the company were entitled to the rings. Lord Russell of Killowen, C.J., said, [1896] 2 Q.B. 46:

The principle on which this case must be decided, and the distinction which must be drawn between this case and that of Bridges v. Hawkesworth, is to be found in a passage in Pollock and Wright's "Essay on Possession in the Common Law," p. 41: "The possession of land carries with it in general, by our law, possession of everything which is attached to or under that land, and in the absence of a better title elsewhere, the right to possess it also. . . . And it makes no difference that the possessor is not aware of the thing's existence."

. . . It has been said that it [South Staffordshire Water Co. v. Sharman] establishes that if a man finds a thing as the servant or agent of another, he finds it not for himself, but for that other, and indeed that seems to afford a sufficient explanation of the case. The rings found at the bottom of the pool were not in the possession of the company, but it seems that though Sharman was the first to obtain possession of them, he obtained them for his employers and could claim no title for himself.

The only other case to which I need refer is Elwes v. Brigg Gas Co., 33 Ch. D. 562, in which land had been demised to a gas company for ninety-nine years with a reservation to the lessor of all mines and minerals. A prehistoric boat embedded in the soil was discovered by the lessees when they were digging to make a gasholder. It was held that the boat, whether regarded as a mineral, or as part of the soil in which it was embedded when discovered, or as a chattel, did not pass to the lessees by the demise, but was the property of the lessor though he was ignorant of its existence at the time of granting the lease. Chitty, J., said (33 Ch. D. 568):

> The first question in this case is whether the boat belonged to the plaintiff at the time of the granting of the lease. I hold that it did, whether it ought to be regarded as a mineral, or as part of the soil, or as a chattel. If it was a mineral or part of the soil, then it clearly belonged to the owners of the inheritance as part of the inheritance itself. But if it ought to be regarded as a chattel, I hold the property in the chattel was vested in the plaintiff . . . . The plaintiff, then, had a lawful possession, good against all the world, and therefore the property in the boat. In my opinion it makes no difference, in these circumstances, that the plaintiff was not aware of the existence of the boat.

. . . It is fairly clear from the authorities that a man possess everything which is attached to or under his land. Secondly, it would appear to be the law from the authorities I have cited, and particularly from Bridges v. Hawkesworth, that a man does not necessarily possess a thing which is lying unattached on the surface of his land even though the thing is not possessed by someone else. . . .

There is no doubt that in this case the brooch was lost in the ordinary meaning of that term, and I should imagine it had been lost for a very considerable time. But the moment the plaintiff discovered that the brooch might be of some value, he took the advice of his commanding officer and handed it to the police. His conduct was commendable and meritorious. The defendant was never physically in possession of these premises at any time. It is clear that the brooch was never his, in the ordinary acceptation of the term, in that he had the prior possession. He had no knowledge of it, until it was brought to his notice by the finder. A discussion of the merits does not seem to help, but it is clear on the facts that the brooch was "lost" in the ordinary meaning of that word; that it was "found" by the plaintiff in the ordinary meaning of that word, that its true owner has never been found, that the defendant was the owner of the premises and had his notice drawn to this matter by the plaintiff, who found the brooch. In those circumstances I propose to give judgment in this case for the plaintiff for £66.

Notes and Questions

1. What use did the court make of the precedents it discussed? Can you draw ideas from them that would have been useful in resolving the dispute between Major Peel and Lance Corporal Hannah? What ideas do you draw from this case that might be useful in resolving other finder-landowner disputes?

2. Suppose the person who owned and lived in the house before Major Peel bought it consulted you after learning that the brooch had been found. She had not known it was there, but would like the money. What advice would you give her? Assume that instead of a £66 brooch, the item found was a de Lamerie silver piece. Would that make a difference? Should it make a difference?

3. Could Major Peel's lawyer have used *The Winkfield* to cast doubt on the continued authority of *Bridges v. Hawkesworth*? Notice how Patteson, J., in *Bridges v. Hawksworth*, used the idea that the shop owner would not have been liable to the owner of the banknotes if the discovery had not been communicated to him as the basis for concluding that the banknotes should be awarded to the finder rather than the shop owner.

McAVOY v. MEDINA

Supreme Judicial Court of Massachusetts
93 Mass. 548 (1866)

Tort to recover a sum of money. . . . [T]he defendant was a barber, and the plaintiff, being a customer in the defendant's shop, saw and took up a pocket-book which was lying upon a table there, and said, "See what I have found." The defendant came to the table and asked where he found it. The plaintiff laid it back in the same place and said, "I found it right there." The defendant then took it and counted the money and the plaintiff told him to keep it, and if the owner should come to give [it] to him; and otherwise to advertise it; which the defendant promised to do. Subsequently the plaintiff made three demands for the money, and the defendant never claimed to hold the same till the last demand. It was agreed . . . that the owner had not been found. . . .

DEWEY, J. It seems to be the settled law that the finder of lost property has a valid claim to the same against all the world except the true owner, and generally that the place in which it is found creates no exception to this rule. Bridges v. Hawkesworth, 7 Engl. Law & Eq. R. 424.

But this property is not, under the circumstances, to be treated as lost . . . in that sense in which a finder has a valid claim to hold the same until called for by the true owner. This property was voluntarily placed upon a table in the defendant's shop by a customer . . . who accidentally left the same there. . . . The plaintiff also came there as a customer, and first saw the same and took it up from the table. The plaintiff did not by this acquire the right to take the property from the shop, but it was rather the duty of the defendant, when the fact became thus known to him, to use reasonable care for the safekeeping of the same until the owner should call for it. In . . . Bridges v. Hawkesworth the property . . . was found on the floor . . . and had not been placed there voluntarily by the owner. . . . The present case more resembles that of Lawrence v. The State, 1 Humph. (Tenn.) 228. . . . The court there take a distinction between the case of property thus placed by the owner and neglected to be removed, and property lost. It was there held that "to place a pocket-book upon a table and to forget to take it away is not to lose it, in the sense in which the authorities referred to speak of lost property."

We accept this as the better rule, and especially as one better adapted to secure the rights of the true owner.

Notes and Questions

1. How can you tell whether property is lost or mislaid? Was the brooch in *Hannah v. Peel* lost or mislaid? What function does this distinction serve?

2. Does the public or private character of the space where the object was found make a difference? The finder often, but not always, loses in cases where valuables are found in bank safe deposit box vaults, *see, e.g., Pyle v. Springfield Marine Bank,* 70 N.E.2d 257 (Ill. App. Ct. 1946); *Dennis v. Northwestern National Bank,* 81 N.W.2d 254 (Minn. 1957) (ordinary law of finders does not apply to safety deposit vault area). A few cases, however, have awarded temporary custody to the bank and eventual possession to the finder after the property has remained with the bank for a suitable period, *see, e.g., Pasat v. Old Orchard Bank & Trust Co.,* 378 N.E.2d 1264 (Ill. App. Ct. 1978) (to customer/finder); *Burnley v. First National Bank,* 87 Pa. D. & C. 433 (Pa. C.P. 1954) (bank employee/finder).

3. English cases decided after *Hannah v. Peel* have settled on a rule that awards the objects found in or attached to land to the owner of the *locus in quo.* Objects that are found on or unattached to the land go to the finder, unless the owner of the *locus in quo* exercises such manifest control over the locus as to indicate an intention to control the locus and anything found on it. *See Waverley Borough Council v. Fletcher,* [1996] Q.B. 334, 4 All E.R. 765 (medieval brooch buried nine inches below surface found using a metal detector in a public park awarded to park's owner); *Parker v. British Airways Board* [1982] Q.B. 1004, 1 All E.R. 834 (gold necklace found on floor of British Airways' international executive airport passenger lounge awarded to finder). Is this a useful distinction American courts and legislators should adopt?

BENJAMIN v. LINDNER AVIATION, INC.

Supreme Court of Iowa (en banc)
534 N.W.2d 400 (1995)

TERNUS, J. Appellant, Heath Benjamin, found over $18,000 in currency inside the wing of an airplane. At the time of this discovery, appellee, State Central Bank, owned the plane and it was being serviced by appellee, Lindner Aviation, Inc. All three parties claimed the money as against the true owner. After a bench trial, the district court held that the currency was mislaid property and belonged to the owner of the plane. The court awarded a finder's fee to Benjamin. Benjamin appealed and Lindner Aviation and State Central Bank cross-appealed. We reverse on the bank's cross-appeal and otherwise affirm the judgment of the district court. . . .

In April of 1992, State Central Bank became the owner of an airplane when the bank repossessed it from its prior owner who had defaulted on a loan. In August of that year, the bank took the plane to Lindner Aviation for a routine annual inspection. Benjamin worked for Lindner Aviation and did the inspection.

As part of the inspection, Benjamin removed panels from the underside of the wings. Although these panels were to be removed annually as part of the routine inspection, a couple of the screws holding the panel on the left wing were so rusty that Benjamin had to use a drill to remove them. Benjamin testified that the panel probably had not been removed for several years.

Inside the left wing Benjamin discovered two packets approximately four inches high and wrapped in aluminum foil. He removed the packets from the wing and took off the foil wrapping. Inside the foil was paper currency, tied in string and wrapped in handkerchiefs. The currency was predominately twenty-dollar bills with mint dates before the 1960s, primarily in the 1950s. The money smelled musty.

Benjamin took one packet to his jeep and then reported what he had found to his supervisor, offering to divide the money with him. However, the supervisor reported the discovery to the owner of Lindner Aviation, William Engle. Engle insisted that they contact the authorities and he called the Department of Criminal Investigation. The money was eventually turned over to the Keokuk police department.

Two days later, Benjamin filed an affidavit with the county auditor claiming that he was the finder of the currency under the provisions of Iowa Code chapter 644 (1991).[1] Lindner Aviation and the bank also filed claims to the money. The notices required by chapter 644 were published and posted. No one came forward within twelve months claiming to be the true owner of the money. *See id.* § 644.11 (if true owner does not claim property within twelve months, the right to the property vests in the finder).

Benjamin filed this declaratory judgment action against Lindner Aviation and the bank to establish his right to the property. The parties tried the case to the court. The district court held that chapter 644 applies only to "lost" property and the money here was mislaid property. The court awarded the money to the bank, holding that it was entitled to possession of the money to the exclusion of all but the true owner. The court also held that Benjamin was a "finder" within the meaning of chapter 644 and awarded him a ten percent finder's fee. *See id.* § 644.13 (a finder of lost property is entitled to ten percent of the value of the lost property as a reward).

Benjamin appealed. He claims that chapter 644 governs the disposition of all found property and any common law distinctions between various types of found property are no longer valid. He asserts alternatively that even under the common law classes of found property, he is entitled to the money he discovered. He claims that the trial court should have found that the property was treasure trove or was lost or abandoned rather than mislaid, thereby entitling the finder to the property.

The bank and Lindner Aviation cross-appealed. Lindner Aviation claims that if the money is mislaid property, it is entitled to the money as the owner of the premises on which the money was found . . . . It argues in the alternative that it is the finder, not Benjamin, because Benjamin discovered the money during his work for Lindner Aviation. The bank asserts in its cross-appeal that it owns the premises where the money was found—the airplane—and that no one is entitled to a finder's fee because chapter 644 does not apply to mislaid property. . . .

Whether the money found by Benjamin was treasure trove or was mislaid, abandoned or lost property is a fact question. Therefore, the trial court's finding that the money was mislaid is binding on us if supported by substantial evidence. . . .

1. Chapter 644 was renumbered . . . [in] the 1995 Iowa Code and is now found in chapter 556F.

Benjamin argues that chapter 644 governs the rights of finders of property and abrogates the common law distinctions between types of found property. As he points out, lost property statutes are intended "to encourage and facilitate the return of property to the true owner, and then to reward a finder for his honesty if the property remains unclaimed." . . . Willsmore v. Township of Oceola, 308 N.W.2d 796 (Mich. App. 1981) (lost goods act "provides protection to the finder, a reasonable method of uniting goods with their true owner, and a plan which benefits the people of the state through their local governments").[2] These goals, Benjamin argues, can best be achieved by applying such statutes to all types of found property.

The Michigan Court of Appeals had an additional reason in *Willsmore* to apply the Michigan statute to all classes of discovered property. The Michigan court noted that the common law distinctions between categories of found property were embraced in Michigan after the enactment of its lost property statute. Based on this fact, the Michigan court concluded that the legislature could not have intended to reflect in the term "lost property" distinctions not then in existence. However, the Michigan court did not address the fact that the common law distinctions were first developed in England, before the enactment of most states' lost property statutes.[3] *See* Goodard v. Winchell, 52 N.W. 1124 (Iowa 1892) (citing to English common law); Hurley v. City of Niagara Falls, 289 N.Y.S.2d 889 (App. Div. 1968) (stating that common law principles relating to lost property were established as early as 1722).[20]

Although a few courts have adopted an expansive view of lost property statutes, we think Iowa law is to the contrary. In 1937, we quoted and affirmed a trial court ruling that "the old law of treasure trove is not merged in the statutory law . . . of Iowa." Zornes v. Bowen, 274 N.W. 877 (Iowa 1937). . . . The relevant sections of . . . [the statute] are unchanged since our 1937 decision. As recently as 1991, we stated that "[t]he rights of finders of property vary according to the characterization of the property found." Ritz v. Selma United Methodist Church, 467 N.W.2d 266 (Iowa 1991). We went on to define and apply the common law classifications of found property in deciding the rights of the parties. As our prior cases show, we have continued to use the common law distinctions between classes of found property despite the legislature's enactment of chapter 644 and its predecessors.

The legislature has had many opportunities since our decision in *Zornes* to amend the statute so that it clearly applies to all types of found property.

---

2. The Michigan statute had two provisions lacking in the Iowa lost property statute. . . . [It] provided for registration of a find in a central location so that the true owner could locate the goods with ease. . . . It also required notice to potential true owners. Because Iowa's statute has no central registry and requires only posting and publication of notice, Iowa's law does not accomplish as well the goal of reuniting property with its true owner. Finally, under the Michigan statute, the local government obtains one-half the value of the goods. Iowa's law does not include this public benefit.

3. Iowa's lost property statute was adopted in 1851 at Iowa's constitutional convention. . . . It had earlier appeared in Revised Statutes of the Territory of Iowa ch. 158 (1843).

20. The cases cited do not support the court's assertion. Goodard v. Winchell cites no English cases and the only English case cited in *Hurley* is Armory v. Delamirie. McAvoy v. Medina, *supra*, an early American decision distinguishing lost and mislaid property, relied on an early Tennessee case that distinguished "left" property from "lost" property in determining that the defendant was guilty of larceny. Early New York cases cited in *Hurley*, which cite Coke, but no other English authority, also deal with cases of larceny. — EDS.

However, it has not done so. . . . Therefore, we presume . . . that the legislature approves of our application of chapter 644 to lost property only. . . . We note this position is consistent with that taken by most jurisdictions . . . .

Under the common law, there are four categories of found property: (1) abandoned property, (2) lost property, (3) mislaid property, and (4) treasure trove. The rights of a finder of property depend on how the found property is classified.

A. *Abandoned property*. Property is abandoned when the owner no longer wants to possess it. Abandonment is shown by proof that the owner intends to abandon the property and has voluntarily relinquished all right, title and interest in the property. Abandoned property belongs to the finder of the property against all others, including the former owner.

B. *Lost property.* "Property is lost when the owner unintentionally and involuntarily parts with its possession and does not know where it is." Stolen property found by someone who did not participate in the theft is lost property. . . .

C. *Mislaid property.* Mislaid property is voluntarily put in a certain place by the owner who then overlooks or forgets where the property is. It differs from lost property in that the owner voluntarily and intentionally places mislaid property in the location where it is eventually found by another. In contrast, property is not considered lost unless the owner parts with it involuntarily. *See* Hill v. Schrunk, 292 P.2d 141 (Or. 1956) (carefully concealed currency was mislaid property, not lost property).

The finder of mislaid property acquires no rights to the property. The right of possession of mislaid property belongs to the owner of the premises upon which the property is found, as against all persons other than the true owner.

D. *Treasure trove.* Treasure trove consists of coins or currency concealed by the owner. It includes an element of antiquity. To be classified as treasure trove, the property must have been hidden or concealed for such a length of time that the owner is probably dead or undiscoverable. . . . Treasure trove belongs to the finder as against all but the true owner. . . .

We think there was substantial evidence to find that the currency discovered by Benjamin was mislaid property. . . .

The place where Benjamin found the money and the manner in which it was hidden are . . . important here. The bills were carefully tied and wrapped and then concealed in a location that was accessible only by removing screws and a panel. These circumstances support an inference that the money was placed there intentionally. This inference supports the conclusion that the money was mislaid. Jackson v. Steinberg, 200 P.2d 376 (Or. 1948) (fact that $800 in currency was found concealed beneath the paper lining of a dresser indicates that money was intentionally concealed with intention of reclaiming it; therefore, property was mislaid, not lost); Schley v. Couch, 284 S.W.2d 333 (Tex. 1955) (. . . money found buried under garage floor was mislaid property as a matter of law because circumstances showed that money was placed there deliberately and court presumed that owner had either forgotten where he hid the money or had died before retrieving it).

The same facts that support the trial court's conclusion that the money was mislaid prevent us from ruling as a matter of law that the property was lost. . . . *See Sovern*, 20 P. at 105 (holding that coins found in a jar under a wooden floor of a barn were not lost property because the circumstances showed that the money was hidden there intentionally); *see* Farrare v. City of Pasco, 68 Wash. App. 459

(1993) (where currency was deliberately concealed, it cannot be characterized as lost property). Contrary to Benjamin's position the circumstances here do not support a conclusion that the money was placed in the wing of the airplane unintentionally. . . . [T]here was no evidence suggesting that the money was placed in the wing by someone other than the owner of the money and that its location was unknown to the owner.

We also reject Benjamin's assertion that as a matter of law this money was abandoned property. Both logic and common sense suggest that it is unlikely someone would voluntarily part with over $18,000 with the intention of terminating his ownership. The location where this money was found is much more consistent with the conclusion that the owner of the property was placing the money there for safekeeping. . . .

Finally, we also conclude that the trial court was not obligated to decide that this money was treasure trove. Based on the dates of the currency, the money was no older than thirty-five years. The mint dates, the musty odor and the rusty condition of a few of the panel screws indicate that the money may have been hidden for some time. However, there was no evidence of the age of the airplane or the date of its last inspection. These facts may have shown that the money was concealed for a much shorter period of time.

Moreover, it is also significant that the airplane had a well-documented ownership history. The record reveals that there were only two owners of the plane prior to the bank. One was the person from whom the bank repossessed the plane; the other was the original purchaser of the plane when it was manufactured. Nevertheless, there is no indication that Benjamin or any other party attempted to locate and notify the prior owners of the plane, which could very possibly have led to the identification of the true owner of the money. Under these circumstances, we cannot say as a matter of law that the money meets the antiquity requirement or that it is probable that the owner of the money is not discoverable. . . .

Because the money discovered by Benjamin was properly found to be mislaid property, it belongs to the owner of the premises where it was found. Mislaid property is entrusted to the owner of the premises where it is found rather than the finder of the property because it is assumed that the true owner may eventually recall where he has placed his property and return there to reclaim it.

We think that the premises where the money was found is the airplane, not Lindner Aviation's hangar where the airplane happened to be parked when the money was discovered. . . . If the true owner of the money attempts to locate it, he would initially look for the plane; it is unlikely he would begin his search by contacting businesses where the airplane might have been inspected. Therefore, we affirm the trial court's judgment that the bank, as the owner of the plane, has the right to possession of the property as against all but the true owner. . . .

Benjamin claims that if he is not entitled to the money, he should be paid a ten percent finder's fee under section 644.13. The problem with this claim is that only the finder of "lost goods, money, bank notes, and other things" is rewarded with a finder's fee under chapter 644. Because the property found by Benjamin was mislaid property, not lost property, section 644.13 does not apply . . . . The trial court erred in awarding Benjamin a finder's fee.

Affirmed in part; reversed in part. All justices concur except HARRIS, SNELL, and ANDREASEN, JJ., who dissent.

SNELL, J. . . . I respectfully dissent. The life of the law is logic, it has been said. *See* Davis v. Aiken, 111 Ga. App. 505 (1965) (quoting Sir Edward Coke[21]). If so, it should be applied here. . . .

After considering the four categories of found money, the majority decides that Benjamin found mislaid money. The result is that the bank gets all the money; Benjamin, the finder, gets nothing. Apart from the obvious unfairness in result, I believe this conclusion fails to come from logical analysis.

Mislaid property is property voluntarily put in a certain place by the owner who then overlooks or forgets where the property is. . . . I do not believe that the facts, logic, or common sense lead to a finding that this requirement is met. It is not likely or reasonable to suppose that a person would secrete $18,000 in an airplane wing and then forget where it was.

Cases cited by the majority contrasting "mislaid" property and "lost" property are appropriate for a comparison of these principles but do not foreclose other considerations. After finding the money, Benjamin proceeded to give written notice of finding the property as prescribed . . . [by statute]. [N]otices were posted on the courthouse door and in three other public places in the county. In addition, notice was published once each week for three consecutive weeks in a newspaper of general circulation in the county. Also, affidavits of publication were filed with the county auditor who then had them published as part of the board of supervisors' proceedings. After twelve months, if no person appears to claim and prove ownership of the property, the right to the property rests irrevocably in the finder. Iowa Code § 556F.11.

The purpose of this type of legal notice is to give people the opportunity to assert a claim if they have one. If no claim is made, the law presumes there is none or for whatever reason it is not asserted. Thus, a failure to make a claim after legal notice is given is a bar to a claim made thereafter.

Benjamin followed the law in giving legal notice of finding property. None of the parties dispute this. The suggestion that Benjamin should have initiated a further search for the true owner is not a requirement of the law, is therefore irrelevant, and in no way diminishes Benjamin's rights as finder.

The scenario unfolded in this case convinces me that the money found in the airplane wing was abandoned. The money had been there for years, possibly thirty. No owner had claimed it in that time. No claim was made by the owner after legally prescribed notice was given that it had been found. Thereafter, logic and the law support a finding that the owner has voluntarily relinquished all right, title, and interest in the property. Whether the money was abandoned due to its connection to illegal drug trafficking or is otherwise contraband property is a matter for speculation. . . . I would hold that Benjamin is legally entitled

---

21.   Sir Edward Coke was Queen Elizabeth I's savage prosecutor (Essex, Southampton, Raleigh, the Gunpowder Plot conspirators) and the first man to bear the title of Lord Chief Justice of England. His name is ordinarily pronounced "Cook" following the British practice. Coke is the most famous of the English reporters as well. His 13 volumes of reports of cases from 1572 to 1616 have such standing that they are usually referred to as the Reports (Rep. or Co. Rep.). They contain not only reports of cases, but also Coke's commentaries and statements as to historical background. In the thick of political battle from adolescence to the Grave, Coke's retort to James I, "Non sub homine sed sub Deo et lege" ranks among the great utterances in the history of liberty.

In contrast to Coke, Oliver Wendell Holmes, Jr., opened The Common Law (1881) by saying that "The life of the law has not been logic; it has been experience." You can find the book online at http://biotech.law.lsu.edu/Books/Holmes/claw03.htm. — EDS.

to the entire amount of money that he found in the airplane wing as the owner of abandoned property.

Notes and Questions

1. Whether property is lost, mislaid, or abandoned depends on what the owner was thinking—or not thinking—when she parted with the goods. Does it make sense to base the law on determining the one thing that can't possibly be known? *See* John V. Orth, *What's Wrong with the Law of Finders and How to Fix It*, 4 Green Bag 2d 391 (2001).

2. Do you think the Iowa court should have taken this opportunity to simplify the law of finders by interpreting the statute to cover all found property? How well does the court's ruling protect the interests of the owners of lost property? Will this decision affect the behavior of future finders?

3. Finder statutes typically cut off the interests of true owners who do not appear within a set period of time after notice. Is this fair? The current Michigan statute, for example, provides that property not claimed within six months shall be returned to the finder, Mich. Comp. Laws Ann. § 434.26. In *Willsmore v. Township of Oceola*, 308 N.W.2d 796, 803 (Mich. Ct. App. 1981), discussed in the principal case, the court said:

> Obviously there is a potential for a true owner to turn up in a year and a day to discover that his title had been cut off. However, a line must be drawn to establish clear title to goods at some point. . . . Public policy in favor of honesty by finders supports vesting clear title in them at some point. To do otherwise would cause practical problems of continuous bailment. . . . If a true owner were to present himself at a later date, even years after goods were found, the holder of the goods would have to give a good account.

4. Finder statutes typically award the found property to the finder if the true owner does not claim it within the allowed period. Is this a good idea? If someone came to your house for dinner and found a valuable ring in a corner, should she be able to keep it if the true owner did not appear within the statutory period?

5. *Rewards.* Why didn't the court allow Benjamin some sort of reward? The answer is that the common law has not yet developed a doctrine allowing a finder's fee or other reward if the owner shows up, or if the property is awarded to the owner of the *locus in quo*. The finder is entitled to reimbursement for expenses reasonably incurred in taking care of the found item under the law of bailments, but nothing more. Given its apparent concern for the owners of "mislaid" property, should the court have awarded the property to the bank only on condition that it pay an award to Benjamin?

6. Would this have been an appropriate case for application of the equitable division principle adopted by the court in *Popov v. Hayashi, supra*? The *Popov* court relied on R.H. Helmholz, *Equitable Division and the Law of Finders*, 52 Fordham L. Rev. 313 (1983), which argues that found property should be equitably divided between the finder and the owner of the *locus in quo* when the locus is neither truly open to the public nor truly private. What would be an equitable division of the $18,000 found in *Benjamin*?

7. If the person who put the $18,000 in the plane was a prior owner of the plane and later shows up to claim the money from the bank, will the bank have to turn over the money? *See Ritz v. Selma United Methodist Church*, 467 N.W.2d 266 (Iowa 1991) (daughter's heirs entitled to $25,000 buried in jars and tin cans in the yard by her father even though property was abandoned by her estate because of substantial unpaid taxes and church that found the money had bought the property at the tax foreclosure sale).

8. *Meteorites.* Peter Hoagland's family saw a meteorite fall onto the prairie south of their land on May 2, 1890. Peter dug it up (it had buried itself in the ground to a depth of three feet), took it home, and three days later sold it for $105 to defendant Winchell. Goodard, the owner of the land where the meteorite fell, sued Winchell in replevin and won. The court refused to apply finders law: "The subject of this controversy was never lost or abandoned. Whence it came is not known, but, under the natural law of its government, it became a part of this earth, and, we think, should be treated as such." *Goodard v. Winchell*, 52 N.W. 1124 (Iowa 1892).

9. *Property found by employees.* If Lindner Aircraft had been successful in its claim that it was the owner of the *locus in quo*, would Benjamin have been entitled to the money? Cases involving property found by employees and other agents go all over the place. If the employee's job description includes turning over items found on the job, the employer is usually entitled to them; the cases arise where the employment contract is silent. If there is any discernible thread to the opinions, it seems that women performing menial jobs usually lose, while other finders fare better. Contrast, for example, *Jackson v. Steinberg*, 200 P.2d 376 (Or. 1948) (hotel owner entitled to $800 found by maid in dresser drawer), with *Erickson v. Sinykin*, 26 N.W.2d 172 (Minn. 1947) (interior decorator entitled to $760 he found under rug in hotel room he was redecorating). In *Burnley v. First National Bank*, 87 Pa. D. & C. 433 (Pa. C.P. 1954), a bank employee who found money in a safe deposit box booth was held entitled to it when six years had passed without any claim by the true owner. In *Kalyvakis v. The T.S.S. Olympia*, 181 F. Supp. 32 (S.D.N.Y. 1960), a ship steward was held entitled to $3,000 he found on the floor of a public men's room on the ship.

WRONGFUL POSSESSION OF CHATTELS:
HORNBOOK LAW AND CASE LAW

R.H. Helmholz,
80 Nw. U. L. Rev. 1221, 1221-24 (1986)

It is hornbook law that possession of a chattel, even without claim of title, gives the possessor a superior right to the chattel against everyone but the true owner. The possessor has a "special" property interest in the chattel that only the chattel's owner, or someone claiming under him, can dispute. This special property interest exists even in the most extreme case: That in which the possessor has obtained the chattel by trespass, fraud, or theft. Even a wrongful possessor may reclaim the chattel from any nonowner who violates this possessory right. Such is the oft-stated rule of simple possession.

Support for this statement of the law is formidable. It boasts a strong leading case, *Anderson v. Gouldberg*, an 1892 Minnesota decision which held that a possessor of logs acquired by trespass had a right to them "against all the world except those having a better title." The court's decision rested on the logically unanswerable argument that if the law were to embrace any standard but that of simple possession, the consequence would be "an endless series of unlawful seizures and reprisals in every case where property had once passed out of the possession of the rightful owner."

In addition, the rule claims the weighty authority of Justice Holmes,[5] Dean Ames,[6] and Sir Frederick Pollock.[7] They described the rule as one firmly established at common law, and they stated that it clearly demonstrated the law's longstanding preference for purely objective standards. Holmes, in particular, used the rule to show the law's indifference toward moral considerations. He argued that since the wrongful possessor could obtain rights to a chattel equal to those enjoyed by a lawful possessor, the law took an objective view of externally verifiable facts. Holmes, therefore, could use the rule to support his vision of a law cleansed of morality.

Yet doubts persist. Despite Holmes' view, morality has been a strong force in American public life, and *Anderson* has turned out to be a peculiar leading case. Although routinely and usefully included in property casebooks, *Anderson* rarely has been cited in subsequent reported cases. No citations for it appear at all after 1950, and most of the earlier cases that cited *Anderson* with approval involved a possessor with rights in addition to that of simple possession. Moreover, scholars recently have criticized Holmes' description of the law as representing largely his own subjective preferences. . . .

This Article examines whether the rule of simple possession "fits the facts" of modern case law. The Article rests upon an examination of the cases decided since *Anderson* that have involved the legal rights of wrongful possessors of chattels as against persons who could make no claim of title. Although the cases are not abundant, their number is by no means negligible, and therefore allows a fair quantitative test of the rule. The problem of wrongful possession also arises in several quite different legal settings, allowing the rule to be examined qualitatively as well. Both types of examination show that the black letter rule of simple possession is incomplete and also suggest how easily absolute statements of the rule can become misleading. While later cases do not indicate that *Anderson* was wrongly decided, the case law since 1892 shows three ways in which its black letter rule has been overextended.

First, the paradigmatic situation of *Anderson* almost never has arisen in actual litigation. Virtually all the cases addressing the rights of simple possession have not been contests between two wrongdoers. The argument on which *Anderson* is based—that anything but a simple possession rule would lead to an endless series of seizures by persons having no right to the chattel, although logically sound, turns out not to address the problems most often raised in actual litigation. If there are thieves involved in successive seizures of stolen goods, few of them find their way into a court of law. When they do, the thieves are apt to be defendants to criminal charges, not plaintiffs seeking to vindicate possessory rights. Most cases have involved parties whose claims to property could be weighed against each other, without relying upon who had possession first. The possibility of "endless seizures" is a specter more theoretically frightening than real.

---

5. O.W. Holmes, The Common Law 190 (M. Howe ed. 1963). . . .
6. Ames, *The Disseisin of Chattels*, in Lectures on Legal History 172, 179 (1913).
7. F. Pollock & R. Wright, An Essay on Possession in the Common Law 91-93 (1888).

Second, the traditional statement of the rule of simple possession entirely omits one of the most important distinctions that emerges from the case law: That between rightful and wrongful possession. The omission of moral considerations is, of course, exactly what Holmes desired. But Holmes' view does not square with the facts of a large number of subsequent cases. Courts regularly have examined the legitimacy of possession of chattels, and have refused to accord possessory rights when they have found *mala fides* or misconduct on the part of the possessor. Sometimes this has involved balancing equities between two competing possessors, neither of whom has a claim to title. More often, however, it simply has involved closing the door on wrongdoers who are seeking to take advantage of their own wrongs.

Third, although the above might suggest that the rule of simple possession rarely appears in the case law, in fact the opposite is true. Judges use it with some frequency. They do not invoke it, however, to protect wrongfully acquired possession. On the contrary, courts invoke the rule when it can be used to buttress claims of rightful possession. In other words, courts have not employed the rule of simple possession to protect simple possession. Hornbook law could usefully be amended to take account of what the rule actually does.

Problem

Draft a new finders statute for Iowa that will simplify the law and safeguard the interests of the owners of lost goods while, at the same time, taking into account (1) the interests of owners or occupiers of the place where the goods are found; (2) the interests of employers of finders; and (3) the legitimate expectations of finders. For ideas on what such a statute might contain, see John V. Orth, *What's Wrong with the Law of Finders and How to Fix It*, 4 Green Bag 2d 391 (2001), and *Parker v. British Airways*, [1982] Q.B. 1004, 1 All E.R. 834.[22]

Treasure Trove

American courts are split on the disposition of treasure trove. The earlier cases tended to award it to the finder; more recent cases award it to the landowner. In *Corliss v. Wenner*, 34 P.3d 1100 (Idaho 2001), the court awarded four pounds of gold coins dating from 1857 to 1914 to the owner of the land, rather than to the person who found them while excavating for a driveway, saying:

> There is no reason for a special rule for gold and silver coins, bullion, or plate as opposed to other property. Insofar as personal property . . . buried or secreted on privately owned realty is concerned, the distinctions between treasure trove, lost property, and mislaid property are anachronistic and of little value. The principle point of such distinctions is the intent of the true owner which, absent some written declaration indicating such, is obscured in the mists of time and subject to a great deal of speculation.
>
> By holding that property classed as treasure trove . . . in other jurisdictions is classed in Idaho as . . . property embedded in the soil . . . possession will be awarded

---

22. United Kingdom decisions are available on Westlaw and Lexis.

to the owner of the soil. . . . Thus we craft a simple and reasonable solution to the problem, discourage trespass, and avoid the risk of speculating about the true owner's intent. . . . Additionally, the true owner, if any will have the opportunity to recover the property.

In Louisiana, which follows the Roman law model, the finder and the owner of the locus split the treasure equally under La. Civ. Code § 3420. For an excellent discussion of treasure trove, see Leanna Izuel, *Comment, Property Owners' Constructive Possession of Treasure Trove: Rethinking the Finders Keepers Rule*, 38 UCLA L. Rev. 1659 (1991).

Treasure trove is much more important in English and Scottish law because treasure trove belongs to the crown. The treasure trove doctrine originated in the old Germanic idea that all unowned things (including wild animals) belong to the King.[23] Introduced to England during Anglo-Saxon times, the idea was refined in medieval English law so that by Bracton's time (c. 1250) the doctrine had taken the basic shape it retained until adoption of the Treasure Act in 1996.[24] Treasure trove only applied to metal objects (eventually defined as containing at least 50 percent gold or silver) that had been buried with the intention of returning to recover them. Objects buried in graves, abandoned property, and lost property belonged either to the finder or to the owner of the *locus in quo*; they were not treasure trove belonging to the crown.

Over the succeeding centuries, the importance of treasure trove gradually shifted from providing a source of revenue for the crown to conserving Britain's archaeological heritage. In the latter half of the 19th century, the practice of paying a reward to the finder was instituted to encourage finders to report their finds, and the reward came to reflect the fair market value of the find, determined by appraisal. In practice, treasure trove law gave the British Museum an option to buy the find at its appraised value. As metal detectors became increasingly available in the latter half of the 20th century, the number of finds greatly increased. A 1995 survey estimated that in the neighborhood of 400,000 objects of archaeological importance were being found each year in England and Wales and that a scant 5 to 10 percent of them were reported to museums. The medieval law of treasure trove increasingly was perceived as inadequate. Its coverage was too limited,[25] and it led to expensive and ridiculous litigation as finders tried to prove that their objects had been lost or abandoned rather than deliberately

23. Roman law was quite different: Things found on unowned property belonged to the finder; things found on land owned by another were split between the landowner and the finder.

24. The following account is largely based on an abbreviated version of a paper by Roger Bland published in Art, Antiquity and Law I at 11-26 (Feb. 1, 1996), which appears at http://www.amnumsoc2.org/inc/treasur2.htm. Bland cites a 1995 survey by the Council for British Archaeology that estimates that several hundred thousand archaeological objects are found each year, primarily due to the widespread use of metal detectors, and only about 5 to 10 percent are reported to museums.

25. There were several problems with the law. It was too limited in that it did not cover nonmetallic objects of historic or cultural value; second, after 1982, it covered only objects of at least 50 percent gold and silver, leaving many hoards of ancient coins open to dispersal on the open market without proper study or documentation of the sites where they were found. Twelve of 21 Roman hoards discovered and reported in 1993 were not treasure trove, and several of these were broken up before records were made. Proving that the object had been buried with intention to recover it, instead of lost or abandoned, led to extensive and basically ridiculous litigation on a question that had nothing to do with the modern interest in preserving antiquities as part of the nation's cultural heritage. The failure to cover objects buried in graves also failed to meet modern historical and archaeological interests.

buried for later recovery. Another shortcoming of the old law was that it took no account of the interests of landowners on whose land the objects were found.

The Treasure Act of 1996 swept away all the old distinctions. It applies to all coins and other objects that are at least 300 years old. All finds likely to be treasure must be reported within two weeks to the coroner, who must make reasonable efforts to inform occupiers and landowners of finds on their lands. If items are found to be treasure, they are appraised by an independent group of appraisers and offered to British museums at the appraised value. If no museum wishes to buy them, the finder keeps them. If they are purchased, the reward usually goes to the finder and landowner equally. Rewards may be reduced or eliminated to penalize wrongdoing by either the finder or the landowner. The number of finds offered to museums has increased dramatically since adoption of the Act.[26]

The treasure trove doctrine has played a significantly less important role in the United States because no right of the government or the public to treasure is recognized. In the 1970s, however, greater interest in preservation of archaeological resources for public benefit resulted in passage of the Archeological Resources Protection Act of 1979, 16 U.S.C. §§ 470aa *et seq.*, which prohibits excavation or removal of archaeological resources that are at least 100 years old from federal public lands and Indian lands without a permit. State and local statutes and regulations may also protect archaeological resources found on state and privately owned lands.

C.   SUNKEN TREASURE AND SALVAGE LAW

Shipwrecks provide another source of great treasure and cultural artifacts, and here too, technological innovations have radically increased the numbers located in recent years. The body of law that covers shipwrecks, at least until recently, is admiralty law—law that developed separately from common law. In the United States, admiralty law is in the exclusive jurisdiction of the federal courts.

COLUMBUS-AMERICA DISCOVERY GROUP v. ATLANTIC MUTUAL INSURANCE CO.

United States Court of Appeals, Fourth Circuit
974 F.2d 450 (4th Cir. 1992)

[From the early 1970s Tommy Thompson (known as Harvey to his friends) was fascinated by the problem of recovering items from the deep ocean. After years of research and fundraising, he finally set to sea in 1986 to search for

---

26. Before 1997, 26 finds per year on average were treasure trove; in 2011, 970 finds were reported as treasure, 95 percent of which were found by amateur metal detector users. *See* Roger Bland, *Response: The English Treasure Act and Portable Antiquities Scheme,* http://inarch.ac.uk/journal/issue33/bland.cfm. Bland is the Keeper, Departments of Prehistory & Europe and Portable Antiquities Scheme at the British Museum.

the S.S. Central America, which sank in a hurricane on September 12, 1857, with more than a million dollars worth of California gold aboard. After a false start on another wreck in the summer of 1987, Thompson's group, known as the Columbus-America Discovery Group, located the wreck 160 miles off the coast of South Carolina in 8,000 feet of water on September 11, 1988, almost exactly 131 years after it sank. Using the Nemo, a 13,000-pound underwater robot Thompson designed and built to allow complete documentation of deep-water historical sites and recovery of artifacts without damage, the Columbus-America team recovered the treasure of the *Central America* in an operation that set wholly new standards for recovery and preservation of historic artifacts from the sea. The Nemo worked at pressures of 3,000 pounds per square inch to provide both video and still photographs of the site and recovered without damage artifacts ranging from a 1,000-pound anchor to small china cups, papers, and gold coins. Between 1985 and 1992, Thompson's group put in 411,295 hours of work and spent 487 days at sea. The costs of the recovery were close to $30 million by the end of 1992.

The Columbus-America group secured exclusive rights to salvage the *Central America* from the federal district court for the Eastern District of Virginia, which acted in the exercise of its admiralty jurisdiction. When the group publicly announced that it had found the treasure, 39 insurance companies claimed ownership of the treasure. Their claims are the subject of the opinion that follows.]

Russell, Donald, C.J. . . .

. . . [F]or the next several weeks newspapers around the country devoted much space to the disaster which befell the CENTRAL AMERICA. While people mourned the over four hundred persons who had . . . lost their lives, they also feared that the loss of such a large amount of specie would exacerbate the country's already serious financial situation.[27] The commercial shipments of gold had been insured, though, and the insurance underwriters began advertising in the newspapers that they would pay off their commitments upon the proper proofs being presented. Approximately one-third of the treasure had been underwritten by New York insurers while the rest was underwritten in London. Without doubt, most, if not all, of the claims were promptly paid off by the underwriters.

Under applicable law, then and now, once the underwriters paid the claims made upon them by the owners of the gold, the treasure became theirs. Thus, less than two weeks after the disaster, the underwriters began negotiating with the Boston Submarine Armor Company about possibly raising the ship and her cargo. Also, on June 28, 1858, two of the underwriters (Atlantic Mutual Insurance Company and Sun Mutual Insurance Company) contracted with Brutus de Villeroi, a Frenchman then living in Pennsylvania, to salvage the gold. The contract states that de Villeroi, "by means of his Invention of a Submarine boat" and at his own expense, would raise the treasure and receive a salvage award of seventy-five percent. At this time, though, no one was quite sure where the boat had gone down . . . . At first, some estimated the ship was in only twenty-eight fathoms of water (168 feet), when in fact it was over 8,000 feet below the surface. As would be expected, nothing came of the salvage attempts in the late 1850s . . . .

27. The panic of 1850.—Eds.

Beginning in the 1970s, a number of individuals and groups began discussing and planning the salvage of the CENTRAL AMERICA, as the decade before had seen a great advance in the technology necessary for deep sea salvage. . . . While the underwriters negotiated with several groups about the salvage, they did not enter into any salvage contracts nor did they relinquish any of their rights to the gold. . . .

On September 29, 1989 [after the announcement that the *Central America* had been found], many of the original underwriters of the gold, plus the Superintendent of Insurance of the State of New York for several insurance companies now defunct, filed claims with the district court asserting that they were the proper owners of the gold. . . .

The trial . . . lasted ten days and received much national attention. Over its course, many witnesses appeared and hundreds of exhibits were entered into evidence. . . . On August 14, 1990, the Court found for Columbus-America on all the issues. . . . [T]he district court held that the underwriters had abandoned the gold, and thus Columbus-America was its finder and sole owner. The Court based this finding of abandonment primarily on the supposed fact that the underwriters had intentionally destroyed any documentation they had once had concerning the case. . . . The underwriters . . . appeal.

Historically, courts have applied the maritime law of salvage when ships or their cargo have been recovered from the bottom of the sea . . . . Under this law, the original owners . . . retain their ownership interests in such property, although the salvors are entitled to a very liberal salvage award. . . . [S]ee 3A M. Norris, *Benedict on Admiralty: The Law of Salvage* (7th ed. rev. 1991).

A related legal doctrine is the common law of finds, which . . . [t]raditionally, . . . was applied only to maritime property which had never been owned by anybody, such as ambergris, whales, and fish. A relatively recent trend in the law, though, has seen the law of finds applied to long lost and abandoned shipwrecks.

Courts in admiralty favor applying salvage law rather than the law of finds. As has been succinctly stated by Judge Abraham D. Sofaer:

> The law of finds is disfavored in admiralty because of its aims, its assumptions, and its rules. The primary concern of the law of finds is title. The law of finds defines the circumstances under which a party may be said to have acquired title to ownerless property. Its application necessarily assumes that the property involved either was never owned or was abandoned. . . . To justify an award of title (albeit of one that is defeasible), the law of finds requires a finder to demonstrate not only the intent to acquire the property involved, but also possession of that property, that is, a high degree of control over it.
>
> These rules encourage certain types of conduct and discourage others. . . . If either intent or possession is found lacking, the would-be finder receives nothing; neither effort alone nor acquisition unaccompanied by the required intent is rewarded. . . . [S]uccess as a finder is measured solely in terms of obtaining possession of specific property; . . . mere contribution by one party to another's successful efforts to obtain possession earns no compensation.
>
> Would-be finders are encouraged by these rules to act secretly, and to hide their recoveries, in order to avoid claims of prior owners or other would-be finders that could entirely deprive them of the property. . . .

In sharp contrast to "the harsh, primitive, and inflexible nature of the law of finds" is the law of salvage . . . [which] encourages less competitive and secretive forms of conduct. . . . The primary concern of salvage law is the preservation of property on oceans and waterways. Salvage law specifies the circumstances under which a party may . . . [acquire] the right to take possession of property (e.g., vessels, equipment, and cargo) for the purpose of saving it from destruction, damage, or loss, and to retain it until proper compensation has been paid.

Salvage law assumes that the property . . . has not been abandoned. Admiralty courts have adhered to the traditional and realistic premise that property previously owned but lost at sea has been taken involuntarily out of the owner's possession and control . . . ; property may not be "salvaged" under admiralty law unless it is in some form of peril. . . .

Salvage law requires that . . . a party have the intention and the capacity to save the property involved, but the party need not have the intention to acquire it. Furthermore, although the law of salvage, like the law of finds, requires a salvor to establish possession over property before obtaining the right to exclude others, "possession" means something less . . . than in finds law. In the salvage context, only the right to compensation for service, not the right to title, usually results; "possession" is therefore more readily found than under the law of finds. . . . Moreover, unlike the would-be finder, who is either a keeper or a loser, the salvor receives a payment, depending on the value of the service rendered, that may go beyond quantum meruit.[28] Admiralty's equitable power to make an award for salvage—recognized since ancient times in maritime civilizations—is a corollary to the assumption of nonabandonment and has been applied irrespective of the owner's express refusal to accept such service. . . .

Today, finds law is applied to previously owned sunken property only when that property has been abandoned by its previous owners. . . . There are only a handful of cases which have applied the law of finds, all of which fit into two categories. First, there are cases where owners have expressly and publicly abandoned their property. In the second type of case, items are recovered from ancient shipwrecks and no owner appears in court to claim them. Such circumstances may give rise to an inference of abandonment, but should an owner appear in court and there be no evidence of an express abandonment, the law of salvage must be applied. . . .

The case below appears to be the only reported decision involving salvaged treasure from ancient shipwrecks wherein a court has applied the law of finds despite the fact that the previous owner appeared in court. In all other finds law cases, no prior owner has appeared. One example is the *Treasure Salvors* set of cases, all of which involved the salvage of Spanish treasure ships sunk off the Florida Keys in 1622. Widely quoted is the Fifth Circuit's phrase that "[disposition of a wrecked vessel whose very location has been lost for centuries as though its owner were still in existence stretches a fiction to absurd lengths." Treasure Salvors, Inc. v. The Unidentified Wrecked and Abandoned Sailing Vessel, 569 F.2d 330 (5th Cir. 1978). Yet the Court there also took the trouble to note that it had been stipulated by all parties involved that the original owners had abandoned the wrecks, and the district court also made mention of the fact that, "The

---

28. Quantum meruit is measured by the value of the service rendered and has no element of providing a reward.—Eds.

modern day government of Spain has expressed no interest in filing a claim in this litigation as a successor-owner." Another Spanish wreck, this time from the 1715 Plate Fleet, was involved in Cobb Coin Co., Inc. v. The Unidentified, Wrecked and Abandoned Sailing Vessel, 525 F. Supp. 186 (S.D. Fla. 1981), and there the Spanish government again made no claim of ownership. . . .

In maintaining the position that previous owners can abandon sunken vessels even without any affirmative acts, Columbus-America relies especially on two state supreme court cases decided before the Civil War, Eads v. Brazelton, 22 Ark. 499 (1861) and Wyman v. Hurlburt, 12 Ohio 81 (1843). . . . [Court's discussion in which it discounts and distinguishes these cases omitted.—EDS.]

In conclusion, when sunken ships or their cargo are rescued from the bottom of the ocean by those other than the owners, courts favor applying the law of salvage over the law of finds. Finds law should be applied, however, in situations where the previous owners are found to have abandoned their property. Such abandonment must be proved by clear and convincing evidence, . . . such as an owner's express declaration abandoning title. Should the property encompass an ancient and longlost shipwreck, a court may infer an abandonment. Such an inference would be improper, though, should a previous owner appear and assert his ownership interest; in such a case the normal presumptions would apply and an abandonment would have to be proved by strong and convincing evidence.

Before addressing whether the district court correctly found that the insured shipments of gold were abandoned by the underwriters, several points should be noted. First, the CENTRAL AMERICA herself was self-insured, and successors in interest to the U.S. Mail and Steamship Company have made no attempt to claim an ownership interest in the wreck. Also, there appears to have been a fairly significant amount of passenger gold aboard, but this case, almost surprisingly, has failed to see descendants of any of the passengers attempt to gain a share of the treasure. Thus, an abandonment may be found, and Columbus-America may be declared the finder and sole owner, as to any recovered parts of the ship, all passenger possessions, and any cargo besides the insured shipments.[6]

As for the insured gold, to "prima facially" prove their ownership interests at trial, the underwriters produced several original documents: entries from the Atlantic Mutual's Vessel Disasters Book concerning the disaster (one of which contained the scribbled notation, "e[stimated] l[oss] $150,000"); records of Board resolutions to pay claims; minutes from an underwriters' board meeting discussing the CENTRAL AMERICA; a study prepared by the New York Board of Underwriters regarding the disaster; and the salvage contract between the underwriters and Brutus de Villeroi. The insurers also produced a great many period newspaper articles. These discussed the amount of treasure on board; the insurers of this treasure and the amounts they insured; the willingness of the insurers to pay off claims; the general satisfaction the insureds received from having their claims promptly settled; and the salvage negotiations between the underwriters and the Boston Submarine Armor Company. . . .

---

6.   Should Columbus-America be able to prove, for example from a location on the ocean floor inconsistent with the bulk of the treasure, that certain gold was, more likely than not, passenger gold, rather than part of the insured shipment, this gold should be awarded to Columbus-America in its entirety. Also, should more than $1,219,189 (1857 valuation) of gold be rescued, Columbus-America should be found the owner of any surplus.

Despite finding that the underwriters owned the gold in 1857, the district court applied the law of finds and awarded Columbus-America the entire treasure. This was because at some point the insurers had abandoned their interests in the gold. . . . [T]he Court ruled as it did because . . . the underwriters did nothing to recover the gold after 1858, and they supposedly destroyed all documentation they had regarding payment of claims for the gold.

During trial, the underwriters did not produce any of the original insurance contracts with the insureds, statements from shippers that goods were aboard, bills of lading, or canceled checks or receipts from paying off the claims. While such documents would have existed in 1857, none could be located in 1990. Thus, because an insurance executive testified that the usual practice today is for insurance companies to destroy worthless documents after five years, the district court found that the above documentation concerning the CENTRAL AMERICA must have been intentionally destroyed in the ordinary course of business. Such destruction, coupled with 130 years of nonuse, equaled, according to the Court, an abandonment. . . .

Contrary to the district court, we cannot find any evidence that the underwriters intentionally or deliberately destroyed any of their documents about the CENTRAL AMERICA. Instead, the only evidence we have is that after 134 years, such documents that may have once existed can no longer be located. With such a passing of time, it seems as, if not more, likely that the documents were lost or unintentionally destroyed, rather than being intentionally destroyed.

. . . It is undoubtedly true that in our case some of the insurance documents from 134 years ago are missing. Yet, the underwriters did present several other original documents from their files concerning this case, and in at least one instance all the documents in an insurer's file on the CENTRAL AMERICA were stolen by a would-be salvor. Also, almost all of the evidence in the record actually seems to indicate a specific predisposition on the underwriters' part not to abandon the treasure.

Shortly after the disaster, the underwriters negotiated with a salvage company about rescuing the gold, and the next year a salvage contract was formed between two of the insurers and Brutus de Villeroi. Nothing came of these efforts, and the issue lay dormant for 120 years. Still, it appears that the gold was not totally forgotten, for when the Atlantic Mutual Insurance Company ("Atlantic Mutual") wrote its official history in 1967, it devoted a couple of pages to the CENTRAL AMERICA tragedy and the company's salvage contract with de Villeroi.

Because of drastic advances in deep water salvage, the late 1970s witnessed a good many would-be salvors contacting various underwriters regarding the CENTRAL AMERICA. Atlantic Mutual and The Insurance Company of North America ("INA") opened their archives to these salvors, and several in turn sought to form salvage arrangements with the insurers. . . . [A]t no time did the insurers ever agree to abandon their ownership interests in the gold. . . . As late as 1987, INA was negotiating a salvage contract with Boston Salvage Consultants, Inc., whereby INA would receive two percent of any treasure recovered—before the parties could enter into a contract, though, the district court enjoined . . . these and other salvors from working in the area where it was then thought the wreck lay. In addition, not only the American insurers, but also the British, entered into various salvage negotiations, the latter through their Salvage Association.

. . . In conclusion, . . . we are unable to find the requisite evidence that could lead a court to conclude that the underwriters affirmatively abandoned their interest in the gold. . . . Accordingly, the case is remanded to the district court for further proceedings.

On remand, the district court is to apply the law of salvage, and in so doing it must determine what percentage of the gold each underwriter insured. Equally, if not more, important, the Court must also determine the proper salvage award for Columbus-America. Although this is a decision that must be left to the lower court, we are hazarding but little to say that Columbus-America should, and will, receive by far the largest share of the treasure.

. . . As for the logistics in making a salvage award, we believe that in a case such as this, an award in specie would be proper. *See, e.g., Cobb Coin*, 525 F. Supp. at 198 (when items salvaged are "uniquely and intrinsically valuable beyond their monetary worth, an award in specie is more appropriate"). Also, because salvaging efforts have not been completed, the lower court might want to consider denominating the award as a percentage of the total recovery, rather than as a set monetary amount—should a specific monetary award be set too high, the underwriters could end up receiving nothing, while if an award is set too low, Columbus-America would have a disincentive to completely recovering the gold.

No matter what exact award is given, though, we are confident that Columbus-America will be justly rewarded for its extensive efforts in salvaging the CENTRAL AMERICA.

Reversed and remanded.

WIDENER, C.J., dissenting: . . . In my opinion, both the district court's finding of abandonment and its specific finding that the underwriters intentionally destroyed the documents are amply supported by the evidence.[2] The majority's holding, by necessary implication, must be that abandonment can only be shown by an express statement by the owner indicating his intention to abandon. This holding, in my opinion, cannot be reconciled with established precedent. Abandonment may be inferred from all of the relevant facts and circumstances and may be determined on the basis of circumstantial evidence.

. . . The obvious, most logical, and clearly permissible inference from the fact that the insurance companies did not retain any documents pertaining to the CENTRAL AMERICA is that, at some point during the past hundred and

---

2.   The majority makes much of the fact that the documents may have been lost or stolen. . . . I think the evidence establishes that the most likely inference is that the documents were destroyed, in the regular course of business, as worthless. In any event, I believe resolution of the question of whether the documents were destroyed or lost is unnecessary to a finding of abandonment. The insurance companies affirmatively abandoned any property interest they had in the cargo of the CENTRAL AMERICA by not maintaining the indicia of ownership they may have had at one time pertaining to the cargo on the CENTRAL AMERICA. We cannot know, more than 100 years after the fact, why the relevant documents are no longer in the possession of the insurance companies. However, we do know that any documentation that may have existed was in the control of the insurance companies and they no longer have these documents. Had they believed that a situation would arise where they would need to prove that they had paid claims on the cargo, they certainly would have taken steps to maintain and protect the documents. . . . The fact that the companies do not know when the documents were last in their possession or the circumstances of their removal is sufficient evidence that they viewed the documents as worthless. The obvious inference . . . is that they had abandoned their claims to the property.

thirty-odd years, the companies, giving up any expectation of ever recovering the property, destroyed their documents and, in so doing, evidenced their abandonment of their claims to the CENTRAL AMERICA. . . .

Also, it is interesting that, even after the technology for recovering the CENTRAL AMERICA became available, the insurers did not enter into any salvage contracts concerning its recovery. They did nothing to recover the property, just as they had done for the past 130-plus years. . . .

Notes and Questions

1. On remand, the district court found that the Columbus-America Discovery Group was entitled to 90 percent of the insurance companies' gold recovered as a salvage award and awarded it exclusive rights to market the gold. The salvage award was upheld on appeal, but the case was remanded to require the insurance companies to prove the amount each had paid out in claims. *Columbus-America Discovery Group, Inc. v. Atlantic Mutual Insurance Co.*, 56 F.3d 556 (4th Cir. 1995).

In upholding the salvage award, the court rejected the argument that the "moiety rule" (moiety means half or a portion), which had been developed to give a salvor 50 percent of the value of the cargo, imposed a ceiling on the recovery, and described the salvage effort, masterminded by Tommy Thompson, as follows (56 F.3d at 572):

> Thompson, a man of modest means, became fascinated with the CENTRAL AMERICA and its history and resolved to find it. When he could not obtain financing from traditional sources, he made his pitch locally, stringing together a syndicate of small investors. Faced with searching in waters well over a mile deep, he hired a company with access to some of the best sonar equipment available. To find an exceedingly small needle in a dauntingly large haystack, he painstakingly researched the available information and consulted a leading expert in mathematical search theory. Upon discovering that no existing machine would allow an efficient recovery of items from the ocean bottom while simultaneously maintaining the integrity of even the smallest of those items, Thompson's response was in effect, "No problem—we'll build one." . . . In short, we cannot imagine anyone demonstrating more diligence, skill, and energy than Columbus-America has shown here. Its efforts provide a standard against which all others should be judged.

Gary Kinder's *Ship of Gold in the Deep Blue Sea* (Vintage Books 1999) gives a spellbinding account of Thompson's quest to develop technology for deep-ocean exploration and recovery, which led to his finding the *Central America* and his subsequent legal battles to obtain title to the treasure.

2. How does the law of finds as described by the court differ from the law of salvage? What are the advantages of applying salvage law instead of finders law? Are the two really inconsistent, or does salvage law simply provide something finders law does not, namely, an established right to share in the value of the property salvaged? Should salvage law principles be adopted to resolve cases of things found on land where both the landowner and the finder have meritorious claims?

3. The court mentions that the government of Spain did not assert any interest in the litigation involving salvage of Spanish treasure ships sunk off the Florida Keys in 1622. Its attitude later changed and Spain successfully asserted ownership of the Nuestra Señora de Las Mercedes, a Spanish warship sunk by a British Squadron in 1805. The ship was discovered by Odyssey Marine Exploration, Inc. in 3,600 feet of water 100 miles west of the Straits of Gibraltar. In *Odyssey Marine Exploration, Inc. v. The Unidentified Shipwrecked Vessel*, 657 F.3d 1159 (11th Cir. 2011), the court held that the ship was entitled to sovereign immunity as property of a foreign state, the U.S. federal courts had no jurisdiction over the action, and it ordered Odyssey to release the ship and its cargo (595,000 gold and silver coins and 17 cannons) to Spain.

4. *United States v. Steinmetz*, 763 F. Supp. 1293 (D.N.J. 1991), pitted an antique dealer who bought the ship's bell from the Confederate Warship *Alabama* from an antique dealer in Hastings, England against the U.S. Navy. The bell was apparently salvaged by a diver in 1936, from the ship, which had been sunk in 1864 by the U.S.S. Kearsarge outside Cherbourg, France, in international waters. It hung over a bar in Guernsey until the bar was destroyed by British bombs in World War II. Steinmetz brought the bell back to the United States in 1979 and offered it to the Naval Academy, which refused to buy it. When he put it up for auction in 1990, naval authorities spotted the ad in the catalog and demanded return of the bell. The court awarded the bell to the United States on the ground that it had acquired the vessel *Alabama* by capture in war and never abandoned title. Steinmetz was awarded nothing, either for the value of his services, or on the grounds of unjust enrichment. Why hadn't Steinmetz acquired title to the bell by adverse possession? As you will see in the next chapter, title to property cannot ordinarily be obtained from the government by adverse possession.

5. The items recovered from the *Central America*, like those recovered from many other sunken ships, have substantial historical importance and archaeological value. Although the Columbus-America Discovery Group took extraordinary measures to protect and record the integrity of the site and to preserve the artifacts it retrieved, many treasure hunters are not able or willing to make such efforts. Should the public's interest in conserving its heritage be protected?

6. Concern that the wreck of the *Titanic*, which was found in 1985 in more than 10,000 feet of water, was rapidly disintegrating due to both natural forces and human activities, led the United States to enter an agreement with Canada, the United Kingdom, and France to protect what was left. Scientists from the NOAA (National Oceanic and Atmospheric Administration) surveyed the wreck in 2003 in an effort to determine what should be done. *See* William J. Broad, *Scientists Warn That Visitors Are Loving Titanic to Death*, N.Y. Times, Aug. 9, 2003. For NOAA's continuing role in protecting the Titanic, see http://www.noaa.gov/titanic/noaasrole.html. On the 100th anniversary of the disaster, April 15, 2012, the wreck became a UNESCO World Heritage Site, see http://www.unesco.org/new/en/culture/themes/underwater-cultural-heritage/the-heritage/did-you-know/titanic/.

The Abandoned Shipwreck Act of 1987[29]

Reacting to fears that rapidly increasing numbers of shipwreck recoveries would lead to destruction of important underwater historical sites and dispersal of

---

29.   43 U.S.C. §§ 2101 *et seq.*

treasure that should be part of the nation's cultural heritage, Congress passed the Abandoned Shipwreck Act of 1987, which lays claim to many abandoned shipwrecks in the submerged waters[30] of the United States and transfers title to the states in whose waters they are found. The Act declares that it is the policy of Congress that the states take responsibility for management of shipwrecks for a variety of purposes, including habitat protection, providing opportunities for sport diving and tourism, and allowing appropriate public- and private-sector recovery of shipwrecks consistent with the protection of historical values and environmental integrity. Finally, it declares that the law of salvage and the law of finds do not apply to shipwrecks covered by the Act.

To be covered by the Act, a shipwreck must be abandoned, as that term is used in admiralty law,[31] and either embedded in the submerged lands of a state, embedded in coralline formations protected by a state on submerged lands of the state; or on submerged lands of a state that are included in or determined eligible for inclusion in the National Register.

For a highly critical view of the Act, which the author concludes has no demonstrable benefit and perversely may benefit the few treasure hunters of prominence, who are the only ones with the resources to navigate cumbersome state bureaucracies to secure a favorable award for salvage operations, see Sabrina L. Mclaughlin, *Roots, Relics and Recovery: What Went Wrong with the Abandoned Shipwreck Act of 1987*, 19 Colum.-VLA J.L. & Arts 149 (1995). The Act does not apply to ships like the *Central America* that went down in international waters. For an article reviewing the effect of international law on shipwrecks, see Sean R. Nicholson, *Mutiny as to the Bounty: International Law's Failing Preservation Efforts Regarding Shipwrecks and Their Artifacts Located in International Waters*, 66 UMKC L. Rev. 135 (1997).

A hotly contested case involving California gold recovered from the wreck of the *Brother Jonathan*, which sank off the north coast of California in 1865,[32] settled after[33] the United States Supreme Court decided that the question whether the ship had been abandoned would be determined in federal court using admiralty law principles. Deep Sea Research, which located the wreck and recovered the gold, kept more than 1,007 gold coins; the state lands commission received

30.   These are generally lands under navigable bodies of water and under the ocean within three miles of the coast.

31.   California v. Deep Sea Research, Inc., 523 U.S. 491, 493 (1998).

In Sea Hunt, Inc. v. The Unidentified Shipwrecked Vessel or Vessels, 221 F.3d 634 (4th Cir. 2000), *cert. denied*, 531 U.S. 1144 (2001), Maritime Salvage Corporation, operating under salvage permits issued by the State of Virginia, which claimed ownership under the Abandoned Shipwreck Act, brought an in rem action against two Spanish ships wrecked off the coast of Virginia in 1750 and 1802. The United States intervened on behalf of the government of Spain, which subsequently filed a claim of ownership to the vessels. Both governments claimed that the ships, which were serving as vessels of the Royal Navy when they sank, were covered by the 1902 Treaty of Friendship and General Relations between the United States and Spain under which vessels belonging to both Spain and the United States may be abandoned only by express acts. Noting that the treaty creates reciprocal immunities "essential to protecting United States shipwrecks and gravesites," the court held that Sea Hunt had not proved by clear and convincing evidence that the Kingdom of Spain had expressly abandoned the vessels. The court also denied a salvage award to Sea Hunt on the ground that the owner may refuse unwanted salvage and that Sea Hunt knew the ships were Spanish and that Spain might make a claim of ownership and decline salvage.

32.   California v. Deep Sea Research, *supra* n.31, held that the case was properly within the federal court's admiralty jurisdiction and remanded for reconsideration of the abandonment issue.

33.   This account is based on an article that appeared in the Los Angeles Times on March 18, 1999.

200 coins and the right to oversee historical preservation efforts. Any future recoveries were to be shared 80 percent to Deep Sea Research, 20 percent to the state. Most of the coins were sold at auction for $6.3 million. Much of the gold aboard the ship has not been recovered. *See* http://humboldtsentinel. com/2012/02/25/tragedy-treasure-and-the-brother-jonathan/.

UNESCO Convention on Protection of the Underwater Cultural Heritage[34]

In November 2001, UNESCO adopted its fourth convention on protection of cultural heritage, the Convention on the Protection of the Underwater Cultural Heritage, which entered into force on January 2, 2009. States that sign on to the convention agree to take steps to protect underwater cultural heritage, defined as "traces of human existence having a cultural, historical or archaeological character which have been partially or totally under water, periodically or continuously, for at least 100 years . . . ." The convention requires that signatory states consider preservation *in situ* as the first option and that underwater cultural heritage not be commercially exploited. Article 2 §§ 5, 7. Not surprisingly, this convention has drawn strong opposition from the commercial treasure hunters. As of March 2014, 47 countries, which do not include either the United States or the United Kingdom, have become parties to the Convention.

For additional reading on this fascinating area of the law, see Valentina Vadi, *War, Memory, and Culture: The Uncertain Legal Status of Historic Sunken Warships Under International Law*, 37 Tul. Mar. L.J. 333 (2013); Amber Crosman Cheng, *All in the Same Boat? Indigenous Property Rights in Underwater Cultural Heritage*, 32 Hous. J. Int'l L. 695 (2010); Liza J. Bowman, *Oceans Apart over Sunken Ships: Is the Underwater Cultural Heritage Convention Really Wrecking Admiralty Law?*, 42 Osgood Hall L.J. 1 (2004); Craig Forrest, *A New International Regime for the Protection of Underwater Cultural Heritage*, 51 Int'l & Comp. L.Q. 511 (2002); Mark A. Wilder, *Application of Salvage Law and the Law of Finds to Sunken Shipwreck Discoveries*, 67 Defense Counsel J. 92 (2000); M. June Harris, *Who Owns the Pot of Gold at the End of the Rainbow? A Review of the Impact of Cultural Property on Finders and Salvage Laws*, 14 Ariz. J. Int'l & Comp. L. 223 (1997); Lawrence J. Kahn, *Sunken Treasures: Conflicts Between the Historic Preservation Law and the Maritime Law of Finds*, 7 Tul. Envtl. L.J. 595 (1994); Bob Holmes, *Mutiny over the Bounty: At the Bottom of the Oceans Lie Shipwrecks Laden with Golden Treasure and Historical Artefacts. Who Owns the Rights to This Priceless Heritage?*, New Scientist, July 19, 2003, p. 10.

---

34.   The text of the convention is available at http://www.unesco.org/culture/legal-protection/water/images/engconv.doc.

CHAPTER 3

Acquisition of Property by Conquest, Adverse Possession, and Prescription

In this chapter you learn how property can be taken away from the owners for both private and public purposes without their consent and without compensation. We look first at acquisition by conquest and then turn to acquisition of property by adverse possession and prescription. In Chapter 13 we take up the subject of governmental acquisition of property by exercise of the eminent domain power, which differs in that the acquisition must be for a public use and the government must pay just compensation.

A. CONQUEST

> *The hunter or savage state requires a greater extent of territory to sustain it than is compatible with the progress and just claims of civilized life, and must yield to it.*
>
> *The earth was given to mankind to support the greatest number of which it is capable, and no tribe or people have the right to withhold from the wants of others more than is necessary for their own support and comfort.*
>
> James Monroe, President of the United States[1]

> *[T]o most twentieth-century Americans, the legacy of slavery was serious business, while the legacy of conquest was not. . . . The Civil War, Reconstruction, the migration of Southern blacks into other regions, and the civil rights movement all guaranteed that the nation would recognize the significance of slavery and the South.*
>
> *Conquest took another route into national memory. In the popular imagination, the reality of conquest dissolved into stereotypes of noble savages and noble pioneers*

---

1. Quoted in Eric Kades, *History and Interpretation of the Great Case of Johnson v. M'Intosh*, 19 Law & Hist. Rev. 67, 73 (2001), and Eric Kades, *The Dark Side of Efficiency: Johnson v. M'Intosh and the Expropriation of Indian Lands*, 148 U. Pa. L. Rev. 1065, 1076 (2000). The first comes from a letter to Andrew Jackson dated Oct. 5, 1817, cited in Francis Paul Prucha, American Indian Policy in the Formative Years, The Indian Trade & Intercourse Acts, 1790-1834, at 248 (1962); the second comes from 6 The Territorial Papers of the United States 106-13 (Clarence Edwin Carter ed., 1939).

143

struggling quaintly in the wilderness. . . . The subject of slavery was the domain of serious scholars . . . ; the subject of conquest was the domain of mass entertainment. . . . Children happily played "cowboys and Indians" but stopped short of "masters and slaves."

Patricia Nelson Limerick, *The Legacy of Conquest* at 18-19 (1987)

JOHNSON AND GRAHAM'S LESSEE v. M'INTOSH

Supreme Court of the United States
21 U.S. 543 (1823)

[Action in ejectment[2] for possession of 11,560 acres in Illinois claimed by the plaintiffs under a purchase and conveyance from the Illinois and the Piankeshaw Indians in 1775 and by the defendant under an 1819 grant from the United States. The plaintiffs appeal from a judgment given for the defendant on the agreed statement of facts. The following information appears in the statement of facts that precedes the opinion in the case.

The plaintiffs are successors to two groups of investors, one represented by William Murray, the other by Louis Viviat.[3] The conferences in which the sales by the Illinois and the Piankeshaws were agreed on were publicly held for the space of a month, one at the post of Kaskasias, the other at the post of Vincennes, or post St. Vincent, and were attended by many individuals of all the tribes of Illinois Indians and of the Piankeshaw nation of Indians,[4] besides the chiefs named as grantors in the deed. According to the statement, "the whole transaction was open, public, and fair, and the deed fully explained to the grantors and other Indians, by skilful interpreters, and fully understood by them before it was executed." The equivalent of 55,000 U.S. Dollars (in current, i.e., about 1823 value) was paid to the Illinois and the Piankeshaws for the two tracts of land.[5]

On May 6, 1776, the colony of Virginia declared independence from Great Britain, claiming all the land granted the colony by James I in 1609 (which included all the land lying west of 400 miles of the seacoast to the Mississippi River). In 1783, the state of Virginia ceded all its territory lying northwest of the

---

2.   An action in ejectment is an action to recover possession of real property. Originally developed as an action in which a lessee could recover possession from the lessor in the event of a wrongful eviction, the action proved so much superior to the forms of action then available to fee owners, that the practice of naming a fictitious lessee as plaintiff arose to allow landowners, generally, to use the action to recover possession of land. No longer necessary, the practice of naming a fictitious lessee was still in use when this case was brought.

3.   Kades reports that the plaintiffs were successors to two closely related land speculation ventures that arose out of a group of Philadelphia merchants and grew to include the Governor of Virginia. Despite the long-observed rule that private purchases of Indian land were prohibited, and express warning from local British officials, the speculators made the purchases. Kades suggests they felt emboldened by a British Attorney General's opinon affirming the rights of individuals to buy land from rajahs in British India, or the prospect of a possible revolution and change of regime in America, or possibly, that they believed legislators could be bribed with land grants to enact legislation validating their titles. Eric Kades, *The Dark Side of Efficiency: Johnson v. M'Intosh and the Expropriation of Indian Lands*, 148 U. Pa. L. Rev. 1065 at n.43 (2000).

4.   In fact, it appears that there were relatively few of the Illinois tribes left, their numbers having fallen from around 12,000 in 1680 to 1,720 in 1756, to 500 in 1800. *Id.* at n.46.

5.   Apparently the two tracts included over 3 million acres. *See id.* at n.87.

Ohio River to the United States by a deed executed by Thomas Jefferson, Samuel Hardy, Arthur Lee, and James Monroe, four of its delegates to Congress.

The plaintiffs' predecessors were prevented from taking possession of the land by the war of the American Revolution. From 1781 until 1816, the plaintiffs and their predecessors repeatedly petitioned the Congress of the United States to acknowledge and confirm their title but without success. In 1819, the United States conveyed to William M'Intosh 11,560 acres of the land conveyed by the Piankeshaws to the investors, and this lawsuit followed.[6]—EDS.]

Mr. Chief Justice MARSHALL delivered the opinion of the Court. The plaintiffs in this cause claim the land, in their declaration mentioned, under two grants, purporting to be made, the first in 1773, and the last in 1775, by the chiefs of certain Indian tribes, constituting the Illinois and the Piankeshaw nations; and the question is, whether this title can be recognised in the Courts of the United States?

The facts, as stated in the case agreed, show the authority of the chiefs who executed this conveyance, so far as it could be given by their own people; and likewise show, that the particular tribes for whom these chiefs acted were in rightful possession of the land they sold. The inquiry, therefore, is, in a great measure, confined to the power of Indians to give, and of private individuals to receive, a title which can be sustained in the Courts of this country.

As the right of society, to prescribe those rules by which property may be acquired and preserved is not, and cannot be drawn into question; as the title to lands, especially, is and must be admitted to depend entirely on the law of the nation in which they lie; it will be necessary, in pursuing this inquiry, to examine, not singly those principles of abstract justice, which the Creator of all things has impressed on the mind of his creature man, and which are admitted to regulate, in a great degree, the rights of civilized nations . . . ; but those principles also which our own government has adopted in the particular case, and given us as the rule for our decision.

On the discovery of this immense continent, the great nations of Europe were eager to appropriate to themselves so much of it as they could respectively acquire. Its vast extent offered an ample field to the ambition and enterprise of all; and the character and religion of its inhabitants afforded an apology for considering them as a people over whom the superior genius of Europe might claim an ascendency. The potentates of the old world found no difficulty in convincing themselves that they made ample compensation to the inhabitants of the new, by bestowing on them civilization and Christianity, in exchange for unlimited independence. But, as they were all in pursuit of nearly the same object, it was necessary, in order to avoid conflicting settlements, and consequent war with each other, to establish a principle, which all should acknowledge as the law by which the right of acquisition, which they all asserted, should be regulated as between themselves. This principle was, that discovery gave title to the government by whose subjects, or by whose authority, it was made,

---

6. Because M'Intosh obtained his patents on April 24, 1815, and the only claims then allowable were limited to 160 acres per person, Kades speculates that he either engaged in massive fraud, or accumulated claims from clients in return for legal services rendered in helping them establish their claims. It also appears that the parties did not in fact have overlapping claims, but feigned their dispute because everyone wanted a Supreme Court decision on the validity of private purchases from the Indians. *See* Eric Kades, *History and Interpretation of the Great Case of Johnson v. M'Intosh,* 19 Law & Hist. Rev. 67, 98-99 (2001).

against all other European governments, which title might be consummated by possession.

The exclusion of all other Europeans, necessarily gave to the nation making the discovery the sole right of acquiring the soil from the natives, and establishing settlements upon it. . . . It was a right which all asserted for themselves, and to the assertion of which, by others, all assented. Those relations which were to exist between the discoverer and the natives, were to be regulated by themselves. The rights thus acquired being exclusive, no other power could interpose between them.

In the establishment of these relations, the rights of the original inhabitants were, in no instance, entirely disregarded; but were necessarily, to a considerable extent, impaired. They were admitted to be the rightful occupants of the soil, with a legal as well as just claim to retain possession of it, and to use it according to their own discretion; but their rights to complete sovereignty, as independent nations, were necessarily diminished, and their power to dispose of the soil at their own will, to whomsoever they pleased, was denied by the original fundamental principle, that discovery gave exclusive title to those who made it.

While the different nations of Europe respected the right of the natives, as occupants, they asserted the ultimate dominion to be in themselves; and claimed and exercised, as a consequence of this ultimate dominion, a power to grant the soil, while yet in possession of the natives. These grants have been understood by all, to convey a title to the grantees, subject only to the Indian right of occupancy.

The history of America, from its discovery to the present day, proves, we think, the universal recognition of these principles. [Lengthy discussion of the activities and claims of Spain, France, the Netherlands, and Portugal in North America omitted. — EDS.]

No one of the powers of Europe gave its full assent to this principle more unequivocally than England. . . . So early as the year 1496, her monarch granted a commission to the Cabots, to discover countries then unknown to Christian people, and to take possession of them in the name of the king of England. Two years afterwards, Cabot proceeded on this voyage, and discovered the continent of North America, along which he sailed as far south as Virginia. To this discovery the English trace their title.

In this first effort made by the English government to acquire territory on this continent, we perceive a complete recognition of the principle which has been mentioned. The right of discovery given by this commission, is confined to countries "then unknown to all Christian people"; and of these countries Cabot was empowered to take possession in the name of the king of England. Thus asserting a right to take possession, notwithstanding the occupancy of the natives, who were heathens, and, at the same time, admitting the prior title of any Christian people who may have made a previous discovery.

[Conflicting claims of England and France as to the extent of their rights acquired by discovery] . . . produced a long and bloody war, which was terminated by the conquest of the whole country east of the Mississippi. In the treaty of 1763, France ceded and guarantied to Great Britain, all Nova Scotia, or Acadie, and Canada, with their dependencies; and it was agreed, that the boundaries between the territories of the two nations, in America, should be irrevocably fixed by a line drawn from the source of the Mississippi, through the middle of that river and the lakes Maurepas and Ponchartrain, to the sea. This treaty expressly cedes, and has always been understood to cede, the whole country, on the English side of the dividing line, between the two nations, although a great and valuable part of it was occupied by the Indians. Great Britain, on her part, surrendered to France all her pretensions to the country west of the Mississippi. It has never been supposed that she surrendered nothing, although she was not in actual possession of a foot of land. She surrendered all right to acquire the country; and any after attempt to purchase it from the Indians, would have been considered and treated as an invasion of the territories of France. . . .

Thus, all the nations of Europe, who have acquired territory on this continent, have asserted in themselves, and have recognised in others, the exclusive right of the discoverer to appropriate the lands occupied by the Indians. Have the American States rejected or adopted this principle?

By the treaty which concluded the war of our revolution, Great Britain relinquished all claim, not only to the government, but to the "propriety and territorial rights of the United States," whose boundaries were fixed in the second article. By this treaty, the powers of government, and the right to soil, which had previously been in Great Britain, passed definitively to these States. We had before taken possession of them, by declaring independence; but neither the declaration of independence, nor the treaty confirming it, could give us more than that which we before possessed, or to which Great Britain was before entitled. It has never been doubted, that either the United States, or the several States, had a clear title to all the lands within the boundary lines described in the treaty, subject only to the Indian right of occupancy, and that the exclusive power to extinguish that right, was vested in that government which might constitutionally exercise it.

Virginia, particularly, within whose chartered limits the land in controversy lay, passed an act, in the year 1779, declaring her "exclusive right of pre-emption from the Indians, of all the lands within the limits of her own chartered territory, and that no person or persons whatsoever, have, or ever had, a right to purchase any lands within the same, from any Indian nation, except only persons duly authorized to make such purchase; formerly for the use and benefit of the colony, and lately for the Commonwealth." The act then proceeds to annul all deeds made by Indians to individuals, for the private use of the purchasers. . . .

In pursuance of the same idea, Virginia proceeded, at the same session, to open her land office, for the sale of that country which now constitutes Kentucky, a country, every acre of which was then claimed and possessed by Indians, who maintained their title with as much persevering courage as was ever manifested by any people.

The States, having within their chartered limits different portions of territory covered by Indians, ceded that territory, generally, to the United States, on conditions expressed in their deeds of cession, which demonstrate the opinion, that they ceded the soil as well as jurisdiction, and that in doing so, they granted a productive fund to the government of the Union. The lands in controversy lay within the chartered limits of Virginia, and were ceded [to the United States] with the whole country northwest of the river Ohio. . . .

The ceded territory was occupied by numerous and warlike tribes of Indians; but the exclusive right of the United States to extinguish their title, and to grant the soil, has never, we believe, been doubted. . . .

The magnificent purchase of Louisiana, was the purchase from France of a country almost entirely occupied by numerous tribes of Indians, who are in fact independent. Yet, any attempt of others to intrude into that country, would be considered as an aggression which would justify war. Our late acquisitions from Spain are of the same character; and the negotiations which preceded those acquisitions, recognise and elucidate the principle which has been received as the foundation of all European title in America.

The United States, then, have unequivocally acceded to that great and broad rule by which its civilized inhabitants now hold this country. They hold, and assert in themselves, the title by which it was acquired. They maintain, as all others have maintained, that discovery gave an exclusive right to extinguish the Indian title of occupancy, either by purchase or by conquest; and gave also a right to such a degree of sovereignty, as the circumstances of the people would allow them to exercise. . . .

We will not enter into the controversy, whether agriculturists, merchants, and manufacturers, have a right, on abstract principles, to expel hunters from the territory they possess, or to contract their limits. Conquest gives a title which the Courts of the conqueror cannot deny, whatever the private and speculative opinions of individuals may be, respecting the original justice of the claim which has been successfully asserted. . . . It is not for the Courts of this country to question the validity of this title, or to sustain one which is incompatible with it.

Although we do not mean to engage in the defence of those principles which Europeans have applied to Indian title, they may, we think, find some excuse, if not justification, in the character and habits of the people whose rights have been wrested from them.

The title by conquest is acquired and maintained by force. The conqueror prescribes its limits. Humanity, however, acting on public opinion, has established, as a general rule, that the conquered shall not be wantonly oppressed, and that their condition shall remain as eligible as is compatible with the objects of the conquest. Most usually, they are incorporated with the victorious nation, and become subjects or citizens of the government with which they are connected. The new and old members of the society mingle with each other; the distinction between them is gradually lost, and they make one people. Where this incorporation is practicable, humanity demands, and a wise policy requires, that the rights of the conquered to property should remain unimpaired; that the new subjects should be governed as equitably as the old, and that confidence in their security should gradually banish the painful sense of being separated from their ancient connexions, and united by force to strangers. . . .

But the tribes of Indians inhabiting this country were fierce savages, whose occupation was war, and whose subsistence was drawn chiefly from the forest. To leave them in possession of their country, was to leave the country a wilderness; to govern them as a distinct people, was impossible, because they were as brave and as high spirited as they were fierce, and were ready to repel by arms every attempt on their independence.

What was the inevitable consequence of this state of things? The Europeans were under the necessity either of abandoning the country, and relinquishing their pompous claims to it, or of enforcing those claims by the sword, and by the adoption of principles adapted to the condition of a people with whom it was impossible to mix, and who could not be governed as a distinct society, or of remaining in their neighbourhood, and exposing themselves and their families to the perpetual hazard of being massacred. . . .

That law which regulates, and ought to regulate in general, the relations between the conqueror and conquered, was incapable of application to a people under such circumstances. The resort to some new and different rule, better adapted to the actual state of things, was unavoidable. . . .

However extravagant the pretension of converting the discovery of an inhabited country into conquest may appear; if the principle has been asserted in the first instance, and afterwards sustained; if a country has been acquired and held under it; if the property of the great mass of the community originates in it, it becomes the law of the land, and cannot be questioned. So, too, with respect to the concomitant principle, that the Indian inhabitants are to be considered merely as occupants, to be protected, indeed, while in peace, in the possession of their lands, but to be deemed incapable of transferring the absolute title to others. However this restriction may be opposed to natural right, and to the usages of civilized nations, yet, if it be indispensable to that system under which the country has been settled, and be adapted to the actual condition of the two people, it may, perhaps, be supported by reason, and certainly cannot be rejected by Courts of justice. . . .

This opinion conforms precisely to the principle which has been supposed to be recognized by all European governments, from the first settlement of America. . . .

Another view has been taken of this question, which deserves to be considered. The title of the crown, whatever it might be, could be acquired only by a conveyance from the crown. If an individual might extinguish the Indian title for his own benefit, or, in other words, might purchase it, still he could acquire only that title. . . . [The land acquired would be] held under them, by a title dependent on their laws. . . . [I]f they choose to resume it, and make a different disposition of the land, the Courts of the United States cannot interpose for the protection of the title. . . . If they annul the grant, we know of no tribunal which can revise and set aside the proceeding. . . .

By the treaties concluded between the United States and the Indian nations, whose title the plaintiffs claim, the country comprehending the lands in controversy has been ceded to the United States, without any reservation of their title. These nations had been at war with the United States, and had an unquestionable right to annul any grant they had made to American citizens. Their cession of the country, without a reservation of this land, affords a fair presumption, that they considered it as of no validity. . . .

According to the theory of the British constitution, all vacant lands are vested in the crown, as representing the nation; and the exclusive power to grant them is admitted to reside in the crown, as a branch of the royal prerogative. It has been already shown, that this principle was as fully recognised in America as in . . . Great Britain. . . . In Virginia . . . as well as elsewhere in the British dominions, the complete title of the crown to vacant lands was acknowledged. . . . So far as respected the authority of the crown, no distinction was taken between vacant lands and lands occupied by the Indians. . . .

After bestowing on this subject a degree of attention which was more required by the magnitude of the interest in litigation, and the able and elaborate arguments of the bar, than by its intrinsic difficulty, the Court is decidedly of opinion, that the plaintiffs do not exhibit a title which can be sustained in the Courts of the United States; and that there is no error in the judgment which was rendered against them in the District Court of Illinois.

Judgment affirmed, with costs.

Notes and Questions

1. This opinion was written during a period of increasing political turmoil over the relationships between the state and federal governments with respect to Indian policy and the removal of the Indians to lands west of the Mississippi River. The Supreme Court was in the thick of it as Marshall sought to maintain the Court's constitutional powers while protecting some property rights of the Indians. The basic problem was caused by the expanding European population's need for more land and the absence of any power sufficient to stop the settlers from taking it. The southern states, particularly, exerted enormous pressure to drive the Indians west of the Mississippi River. Despite the Supreme Court's efforts to protect them, the removal was effected by the forced march of the Cherokees, known as the "Trail of Tears," in 1834. For assessments of Marshall's role, and the impact of his opinion in *Johnson v. M'Intosh,* and two other cases, called the Cherokee cases, see Nell Jessup Newton, *Compensation, Reparations, and Restitution: Indian Property Claims in the United States,* 28 Ga. L. Rev. 453 (1994); Rennard Strickland & William M. Strickland, *A Tale of Two Marshalls: Reflections on Indian Law and Policy, the Cherokee Cases, and the Cruel Irony of Supreme Court Victories,* 47 Okla. L. Rev. 111 (1994); and Ronald A. Berutti, *The Cherokee Cases: The Fight to Save the Supreme Court and the Cherokee Indians,* 17 Am. Indian L. Rev. 291 (1992). For more recent scholarship focusing on *Johnson v. M'Intosh,* see Blake Watson, *The Doctrine of Discovery and the Elusive Definition of Indian Title,* 15 Lewis & Clark L. Rev. 995 (2011), and Blake Watson, *Buying America from the Indians: Johnson v. McIntosh and the History of Indian Land Rights* (2012).

2. What is the source of the rule that government had a monopoly on the power to acquire land from the Indians?

3. How important was the rule confirmed in *Johnson v. M'Intosh*? Eric Kades concludes that the rule provided an important part of a process for European expropriation of Indian lands at really cheap prices. He explains:[7]

> European agricultural colonization undoubtedly presented the possibility of enormous gains from trade. . . . Europeans had a wide variety of manufactured goods of great value to Indians in their traditional way of life, *e.g.,* guns, metal tools, cooking utensils, and warmer fabrics . . . . The only question was, which side would garner the lion's share of the gains from this trade? In a system of purely voluntary exchange, without any coercion either way, we might have expected to see the European farmers buy off relatively small corners of Indian hunting grounds for relatively large amounts of trade goods. American land could still have been much cheaper for settlers than in heavily populated Europe. The land-rich Indians, while preserving their way of life, would have been glad to part with a modicum of their territory for novel and useful manufactures. . . .
>
> This, of course, is not what happened. Instead, the United States obtained virtually every acre of Indian lands at astoundingly low prices. . . . The [*M'Intosh*] decision stifled bidding by Americans for Indian land, and . . . left the Indians facing a single buyer assured of no competition. [In addition] the willingness of the Europeans to use threats, and rarely, force, to obtain land at bargain prices . . . set a ceiling on what the United States had to pay . . . . [And] the United States . . . had

---

7. Kades, *The Dark Side of Efficiency, supra* n.1 at 1104-05.

a number of techniques for lowering the price of Indian lands without resorting to violence, or even threats. The most powerful technique was . . . settlement on the frontier. Settlers killed relatively few Indians in . . . massacres . . . ; they killed many more by spreading endemic diseases like smallpox. Perhaps even more importantly, by clearing forests for agriculture, introducing European animals, and hunting at prodigious rates, they thinned the game animals on which the Indians depended for food, clothing, and other necessities.

4. Is the discovery and conquest theory applied in *Johnson v. M'Intosh* similar to the capture theory applied in *Pierson v. Post*? Does the "Indian title of occupancy" differ from the title to wild animals gained by "occupancy"? What justification did Marshall give for the Europeans' settlement of the Americas without regard to the consent of the inhabitants? Can you think of other justifications that might have been offered? Compare these with the justifications offered for adverse possession in the cases that follow.

B.   ADVERSE POSSESSION AND PRESCRIPTION OF INTERESTS IN LAND

A person can acquire good title to property owned by someone else by holding possession of the property "adversely" to the true owner for the period specified in the statute of limitations governing an action to recover possession of the particular kind of property, real or personal.[8] The doctrine, which is called "prescription" when the property acquired is an easement,[9] is ancient, and reflects several different doctrinal strands that have merged into modern law.[10] One strand recognizes that long-continued enjoyment of property, in and of itself, creates an entitlement to the property. Another recognizes that a flawed title may be perfected by continued use or possession of the property. Yet a third strand is based on the idea that long-continued use or possession is evidence of a title previously granted by a ceremony or document now lost.[11] The final strand is the idea that the time for asserting legal claims should be limited. This idea is embodied in the statutes of limitations.

---

8.   Statutes of limitations bar legal actions on claims if suit has not been commenced within a specified period of time, which varies depending on the cause of action and the jurisdiction. The time to bring an action for personal injury is often limited to one or two years; the time to bring an action on a written contract is often six years. Limitations periods for actions to recover real property vary from five to 60 years or more, depending on the state and whether the land is privately or publicly owned.

9.   An easement is the right to use property belonging to someone else for a limited purpose, like maintaining a utility line or a driveway. We study easements in Chapter 12.

10.   *See Restatement (Third) of Property, Servitudes* (2000) § 2.17 cmt. *b,* Historical note: theoretical bases of prescription doctrine.

11.   Before the days of public land records, loss of deeds was not uncommon. In societies lacking widespread literacy, ceremonies rather than written documents may have been used to transfer property entitlements. In England, for example, a ceremony called feoffment with livery of seisin was required to transfer an estate in land. Although often memorialized by a charter, the written document was not necessary and, alone, was not sufficient to transfer title.

What lies behind these various strands of doctrine? Here are the views of two prominent legal scholars in the early part of the 20th century:

A thing which you have enjoyed and used as your own for a long time, whether property or an opinion, takes root in your being and cannot be torn away without your resenting the act and trying to defend yourself, however you came by it. The law can ask no better justification than the deepest instincts of man. . . . If he [the owner] knows that another is doing acts which on their face show that he is on the way toward establishing such an association, I should argue that in justice to that other he was bound at his peril to find out whether the other was acting under his permission, to see that he was warned, and, if necessary, stopped.[12]

The statute has not for its object to reward the diligent trespasser for his wrong nor yet to penalize the negligent and dormant owner for sleeping upon his rights; the great purpose is automatically to quiet all titles which are openly and consistently asserted, to provide proof of meritorious titles, and correct errors in conveyancing.[13]

Are there other reasons for limiting the time within which legal claims may be asserted? The dimming of memories and loss of evidence as time goes by are often thought to be good reasons. Can you think of others?

Although statutes of limitations purport to bar claims to regain possession of land after a certain period of time has elapsed, without regard to the activities of the person in possession, courts drew on the earlier strands of prescription doctrine to limit their operation. Variations are found with respect to some requirements, but courts everywhere refuse to apply the statute of limitations to bar a landowner from regaining possession unless the following requirements have been met by the person in possession:

1. *Actual and exclusive possession.* The possessor must have taken actual possession of all or part of the land claimed and held it to the exclusion of possession by others.
2. *Adverse or "hostile" possession.* The possessor must not hold subserviently to the owner of the property, as for example, under a lease from the owner. Usually, the possessor's occupation must be wrongful as to the owner, so that possession by one co-owner is not adverse to another co-owner unless the co-owner in possession refuses to allow entry by the other ("ousts" the other, to use the technical term).
3. *Claim of right.* Various meanings are given to the requirement that the possessor have a claim of right. In some states, it means no more than that the possessor must be acting as an owner of the property, rather than as a transient, or casual trespasser, might act. Other states go further and require either a good-faith (but mistaken) belief that the possessor owns the property, or they go to the opposite extreme and require that the possessor intentionally act to acquire property he or she does not own. These three views are known as the "objective" standard, the "good-faith" standard, and the "aggressive trespasser" or "bad-faith" standard.[14]

---

12. Oliver Wendell Holmes, *The Path of the Law*, 10 Harv. L. Rev. 457, 477 (1897).
13. Henry W. Ballantine, *Title by Adverse Possession*, 32 Harv. L. Rev. 135 (1918).
14. *See* Margaret J. Radin, *Time, Possession, and Alienation*, 64 Wash. U. L.Q. 739, 746-47 (1986).

4. *Open and notorious.* The possessor must "fly his flag," to use an old phrase, so that the owner has the opportunity to see that someone appears to be claiming rights to use the property in violation of the owner's rights. As you can imagine, challenging problems are posed by underground uses like natural gas storage, caves, and buried utility lines. Courts are torn between wanting to protect the rights of the owner who realistically has little way of discovering the adverse use and wanting to prevent the waste that is likely to result from enjoining the adverse use. Is this a situation where a "liability rule" rather than a "property rule"[15] might be appropriate? It would allow the use to continue but award the property owner compensation for the value of the interest taken. It would also solve the bilateral monopoly problem that might otherwise place the adverse user in a very disadvantageous bargaining position.

5. *Continuous.* The possession must be maintained throughout the statutory period, which is the period set by the applicable statute of limitations. Continuity does not mean, however, that the adverse possessor must be present on the land all the time. Seasonal use or intermittent use may be sufficient so long as the use is similar to that which would be made by an ordinary owner of property like that in dispute. If there is a break in the possession caused by the owner's reentry, or acquisition of title by the government, the adverse possessor may have to start over, building a new statutory period after regaining possession. A break caused by a third-party intrusion, however, does not usually defeat the continuity requirement if the adverse possessor manages to regain possession from the intruder.

6. *For the statutory period.* The statutory period is set by the applicable statute of limitations. Periods range from the very short five years in California to 21 years in Ohio; 10-, 15-, and 20-year periods are common. Much longer periods may be required for certain kinds of property, like wild and unenclosed lands, or land held for public or quasi-public uses, like schools or railroads. In many states, public land cannot be acquired by adverse possession under any circumstances.

The requirements for acquiring an easement by prescription are generally the same as for acquiring a possessory interest by adverse possession.[16] However, there is no requirement that a prescriptive use be exclusive (the owner and adverse user can both use a private road, for example), and there is no requirement that the use be made in good faith, even in states that apply a good-faith requirement to claimants of title by adverse possession.

There is a substantial, and even surprising,[17] amount of litigation involving claims by adverse possession and prescription. In the materials that follow, we will look more closely at the requirements and limitations of the doctrine. As you study these cases, think about how well the courts have balanced society's interest in protecting property owners against the interests that the prescription

---

15. *See* note on Property Rules and Liability Rules in Chapter 2.

16. Prescription is extensively treated in the *Restatement (Third) of Property, Servitudes* §§ 2.16-2.17 (2000).

17. Professor Helmholz found 850 appellate opinions on adverse possession in cases decided between 1966 and 1983. *See* R.H. Helmholz, *Adverse Possession and Subjective Intent*, 61 Wash. U. L.Q. 331, 333 n.7 (1983).

doctrines were designed to protect. We begin with a leading case decided shortly after the death of Chief Justice John Marshall, author of the opinion in *Johnson v. M'Intosh.*

1. Adverse Possession

EWING v. BURNET[18]
Supreme Court of the United States
36 U.S. 41 (1837)

[This was an action in ejectment brought in the federal district court for Ohio by James Ewing to recover possession of a vacant lot measuring approximately 100 by 200 feet located on the corner of Third and Vine Streets in Cincinnati, Ohio. Ewing inherited the title from Samuel Williams, who died in 1824. Williams had acquired title from Samuel Forman in 1798. Forman acquired title from John Cleves Symmes,[19] the original grantee of the United States to all the land on which Cincinnati was then located. Forman's deed was dated June 11, 1798.

Jacob Burnet also had a deed from Symmes, but it was dated May 21, 1803. Burnet claimed title by adverse possession.

The lot which sloped steeply down away from Third Street was not fenced, and people in the area crossed over it at will. Burnet, who lived in a mansion on the other side of Third Street (an unopened street) dug sand and gravel from the lot, gave permission to others to do the same, and refused permission to still others. At different times, he leased the property to others to take sand and gravel. He brought trespass actions against people who removed sand and gravel without his permission. Burnet claimed to own the lot from 1803 on and paid the taxes on it from 1810 until 1834. Several witnesses testified that Burnet was in possession of the lot.

There was evidence that Williams, who also lived in Cincinnati, knew of the 1803 deed to Burnet but made no effort to enter the land or demand possession before his death in 1824. One witness testified, however, that Williams repeatedly said, even on his deathbed, that the lot was his and he intended to claim and improve it when he was able. However, Williams was very poor. The same

---

18. It will not surprise you to learn that the full title of this case is Lessee of Ewing v. Burnet. *See supra* n.2 in Johnson and Graham's Lessee v. M'Intosh. — EDS.

19. John Cleves Symmes was a Revolutionary War veteran who secured from the federal government in 1792 the Miami Purchase, running northward from the Ohio River between the Miami and Little Miami Rivers. This included the site of Losantiville, later renamed Cincinnati. Washington appointed Symmes a judge of the Northwest Territory. Symmes maintained a constant state of warfare with the territorial governor, St. Clair. Symmes sold to settlers large tracts of land that were not within the federal grant to him; and, as this case indicates, he sold some land twice. St. Clair issued proclamations warning the settlers against him. Sued by numerous settlers to whom he purported to make sales, Symmes tried to get Congress to bail him out by making further grants; but this effort, though supported by Symmes' son-in-law, William Henry Harrison, failed. Washington, Hamilton, and Jefferson were continually pestered by this business; finally some relief was given to the settlers, but not by Symmes, by preemption rights. The conclusion has been drawn that Symmes was "a far-sighted pioneer, somewhat careless in details, but not intentionally dishonest," Bond, The Civilization of the Old Northwest 85 (1934).

witness also said that Burnet was informed that Williams owned the lot after Burnet purchased it but before he received his deed.

Ewing appeals from a jury verdict in favor of Burnet.

The Ohio statute provided substantially as follows:

> An action to recover the title to or possession of real property shall be brought within twenty-one years after the cause of action accrued, but if a person entitled to bring the action is, at the time the cause of action accrues, within the age of minority or of unsound mind, the person, after the expiration of twenty-one years from the time the cause of action accrues, may bring the action within ten years after the disability is removed.[20]—EDS.]

[handwritten margin note: 21 years to claim adverse possession in Ohio]

BALDWIN, J. . . . An entry by one man on the land of another, is an ouster of the legal possession arising from the title, or not, according to the intention with which it is done; if made under claim and color of right, it is an ouster, otherwise, it is a mere trespass; in legal language, the intention guides the entry and fixes its character. That the evidence in this case justified the jury in finding an entry by the defendant on this lot, as early as 1804, cannot be doubted; nor that he claimed the exclusive right to it, under colour of title, from that time till suit [was] brought. There was abundant evidence of the intention with which the first entry was made, as well as of the subsequent acts related by the witnesses, to justify a finding that they were in assertion of a right in himself; so that the only inquiry is, as to the nature of the possession kept up.

[handwritten margin note: Δ claimed land as his own.]

It is well settled, that to constitute an adverse possession, there need not be a fence, building or other improvement made; it suffices for this purpose, that visible and notorious acts of ownership are exercised over the premises in controversy, for twenty-one years, after an entry under claim and color of title. So much depends on the nature and situation of the property, the uses to which it can be applied, or to which the owner or claimant may choose to apply it, that it is difficult to lay down any precise rule, adapted to all cases. But it may with safety be said, that where acts of ownership have been done upon land, which, from their nature, indicate a notorious claim of property in it, and are continued for twenty-one years, with the knowledge of an adverse claimant, without interruption, or an adverse entry by him, for twenty-one years; such acts are evidence of an ouster of a former owner, and an actual adverse possession against him; if the jury shall think, that the property was not susceptible of a more strict or definite possession than had been so taken and held.

Neither actual occupation, cultivation nor residence, are necessary to constitute actual possession, when the property is so situated as not to admit of any permanent useful improvement, and the continued claim of the party has been evidenced by public acts of ownership, such as he would exercise over property which he claimed in his own right, and would not exercise over property which he did not claim. Whether this was the situation of the lot in question, or such was the nature of the acts done, was the peculiar province of the jury; the evidence, in our opinion, was legally sufficient to draw the inference that such were the facts of the case, and if found specially, would have entitled the defendant to the judgment of the court in his favor; they, of course, did not err

[handwritten margin note: holding]

---

20. Ohio Rev. Code Ann. § 2305.04. This is substantially equivalent to the statute in effect in 1834.

in refusing to instruct the jury that the evidence was not sufficient to make out an adverse possession.

Notes and Questions

1. Adverse possession is often justified on the ground that it penalizes the owner who sleeps on his rights and rewards those who make productive use of the land. If it was true that Williams was too poor to bring an action of ejectment against Burnet, is it fair that he should lose title to his property? Can the result be justified on other grounds?

2. Notice that Ewing did not acquire a right of action in ejectment until he inherited the property in 1824. Why is his claim barred by the statute? Notice, too, that Williams died in 1824, one year before the statute ran as to his claim. Why is Burnet entitled to treat the two causes of action (Williams's and Ewing's) as if they were a single cause of action? If that weren't the law, how useful would the statute of limitations be?

3. Note the distinction the court draws between "ouster" and "a mere trespass" in this context. What is the difference and why is this distinction useful?

4. *Actual possession.* It is usually said that to obtain title, the claimant must establish that her possession was actual and exclusive. Did Burnet meet those requirements? What does "exclusive" mean in this context?

5. *Payment of taxes.* Payment of property taxes is not usually required to acquire title by adverse possession, but it is often a strong factor in favor of the possessor. Failure to pay taxes may work against the claimant, either because it disposes the court to look unfavorably on the claim, or because it weakens the case for "actual possession" where the property is not enclosed, cultivated, or built on, as in the principal case. Failure to pay taxes may also weaken a claim of good-faith belief in ownership of the property in states where that is required. In some of the western states, like California, statutes require payment of taxes as a condition of acquiring title by adverse possession.

Problems in Applying the Statute of Limitations: Tacking

An adverse possessor may transfer his or her interest in the property to another, who may continue the adverse possession. If both have met the other requirements for acquiring title by adverse possession, they may "tack" the two (or more) periods together to make up the statutory period. To tack to a prior adverse possessor, the successor must show that there was a transfer and that the periods of possession were consecutive. In working through the following problems, assume that the applicable statute of limitations is similar to the Ohio statute. You can probably work your way through these problems using the information you have been given so far, your common sense, and considering the purposes of adverse possession, but if you need additional help, you can consult 3 *American Law of Property* § 15.10 (Casner ed. 1952). If you are interested in the English view of adverse possession, which places more emphasis on penalizing the owner who sleeps on her rights than on rewarding the possessor who meets the requirements, a good source is Charles Harpum, Stuart Bridge

& Martin Dixon, *Megarry & Wade, The Law of Real Property* §§ 35-021 – 35-023 p. 1470 (8th ed. 2012).

1. AP[1] takes possession of Blackacre, which belongs to O[1], in 1990. In 1995, O[1] conveys her interest in Blackacre to O[2]. In 1994, AP[1] transfers his interest to AP[2]. When will AP[2] acquire title if both he and AP[1] have met the other requirements for adverse possession?

2. AP takes possession of Blackacre, which belongs to O, in 1985. In 1995, while AP is out of town on a two-week vacation, B takes possession of Blackacre. When AP returns, B refuses to leave. Knowing he doesn't own Blackacre, AP moves away. If B remains in possession, when will she acquire title?

3. Same facts as in question 2, but AP comes back in six months and brings an action in ejectment against B. Is AP entitled to possession? Can B defeat AP's claim by demonstrating that title is in O? If AP is successful in regaining possession, when will his possession ripen into title?

NOME 2000 v. FAGERSTROM

Supreme Court of Alaska
799 P.2d 304 (Alaska 1990)

MATTHEWS, Chief J. [On July 24, 1987, Nome 2000 filed suit to eject Charles and Peggy Fagerstrom from a tract of land measuring approximately seven and one-half acres, overlooking the Nome River. The disputed parcel is included in a larger tract known as "mineral survey 1161," owned of record by Nome 2000. The Fagerstroms counterclaimed that through their use of the parcel they had acquired title by adverse possession. The Alaska statutory period is 10 years. . . .[21]—EDS.] . . .

After Nome 2000 presented its case, the jury found that the Fagerstroms had adversely possessed the entire parcel. The court then entered judgment in favor of the Fagerstroms. On appeal, Nome 2000 contests the trial court's denial of its motion for a directed verdict and the sufficiency of the evidence in support of the jury verdict.[2] . . .

The disputed parcel is located in a rural area known as Osborn. During the warmer seasons, property in Osborn is suitable for homesites and subsistence and recreational activities. During the colder seasons, little or no use is made of Osborn property. Charles Fagerstrom's earliest recollection of the disputed parcel is his family's use of it around 1944 or 1945. At that time, he and his family used an abandoned boy scout cabin present on the parcel as a subsistence base camp during summer months. Around 1947 or 1948, they moved their summer campsite to an area south of the disputed parcel. However, Charles and his family continued to make seasonal use of the disputed parcel for subsistence and recreation.

---

21.   Alaska Stat. § 09.10.030. Section 09.25.050 provides a seven-year period when possession is under "color and claim of title." The Fagerstroms did not claim their possession was under color of title.

2.   Because Nome 2000 challenges the trial court's denial of its motion for a directed verdict, and the sufficiency of the evidence underlying the jury verdict, we are constrained to view the evidence in a light most favorable to the Fagerstroms. Our statement of the facts is made from this viewpoint.

In 1963, Charles and Peggy Fagerstrom were married and, in 1966, they brought a small quantity of building materials to the north end of the disputed parcel. They intended to build a cabin. In 1970 or 1971, the Fagerstroms used four cornerposts to stake off a twelve acre, rectangular parcel for purposes of a Native Allotment application.[3] The northeast and southeast stakes were located on or very near mineral survey 1161. The northwest and southwest stakes were located well to the west of mineral survey 1161. The overlap constitutes the disputed parcel. The southeast stake disappeared at an unknown time.

Also around 1970, the Fagerstroms built a picnic area on the north end of the disputed parcel. The area included a gravel pit, beachwood blocks as chairs, firewood and a 50-gallon barrel for use as a stove.

About mid-July 1974, the Fagerstroms placed a camper trailer on the north end of the disputed parcel. The trailer was leveled on blocks and remained in place through late September. Thereafter, until 1978, the Fagerstroms parked their camper trailer on the north end of the disputed parcel from early June through September. The camper was equipped with food, bedding, a stove and other household items. About the same time that the Fagerstroms began parking the trailer on the disputed parcel, they built an outhouse and a fish rack on the north end of the parcel. Both fixtures remained through the time of trial in their original locations. The Fagerstroms also planted some spruce trees, not indigenous to the Osborn area, in 1975-76.

During the summer of 1977, the Fagerstroms built a reindeer shelter on the north end of the disputed parcel. The shelter was about 8 x 8 feet wide, and tall enough for Charles Fagerstrom to stand in. Around the shelter, the Fagerstroms constructed a pen which was 75 feet in diameter and 5 feet high. The shelter and pen housed a reindeer for about six weeks and the pen remained in place until the summer of 1978.

During their testimony, the Fagerstroms estimated that they were personally present on the disputed parcel from 1974 through 1978, "every other weekend or so" and "[a] couple times during the week . . . if the weather was good." When present they used the north end of the parcel as a base camp while using the entire parcel for subsistence and recreational purposes. Their activities included gathering berries, catching and drying fish and picnicking. Their children played on the parcel. The Fagerstroms also kept the property clean, picking up litter left by others.

While so using the disputed parcel, the Fagerstroms walked along various paths which traverse the entire parcel. The paths were present prior to the Fagerstroms' use of the parcel and, according to Peggy Fagerstrom, were free for use by others in connection with picking berries and fishing. On one occasion, however, Charles Fagerstrom excluded campers from the land. They were burning the Fagerstroms' firewood.

Nome 2000 placed into evidence the deposition testimony of Dr. Steven McNabb, an expert in anthropology, who stated that the Fagerstroms' use of the disputed parcel was consistent with the traditional Native Alaskan system of land use. According to McNabb, unlike the non-Native system, the traditional

3.   Federal law authorizes the Secretary of the Interior to allot certain non-mineral lands to Native Alaskans. . . . As a result of her application, Peggy was awarded two lots (lots 3 and 12) which border the disputed parcel along its western boundary.

Native system does not recognize exclusive ownership of land. Instead, customary use of land, such as the Fagerstroms' use of the disputed parcel, establishes only a first priority claim to the land's resources. The claim is not exclusive and is not a matter of ownership, but is more in the nature of a stewardship. That is, other members of the claimant's social group may share in the resources of the land without obtaining permission, so long as the resources are not abused or destroyed. McNabb explained that Charles' exclusion of the campers from the land was a response to the campers' use of the Fagerstroms' personal property (their firewood), not a response to an invasion of a perceived real property interest.[5]

Nevertheless, several persons from the community testified that the Fagerstroms' use of the property from 1974 through 1977 was consistent with that of an owner of the property. For example, one Nome resident testified that since 1974 "[the Fagerstroms] cared for [the disputed parcel] as if they owned it. They made improvements on it as if they owned it. It was my belief that they did own it."

During the summer of 1978, the Fagerstroms put a cabin on the north end of the disputed parcel. Nome 2000 admits that from the time that the cabin was so placed until the time that Nome 2000 filed this suit, the Fagerstroms adversely possessed the north end of the disputed parcel. . . .

[I]f the Fagerstroms adversely possessed the disputed parcel, or any portion thereof, for ten consecutive years, then they have acquired title to that property. . . . Because the Fagerstroms' use of the parcel increased over the years, and because Nome 2000 filed its complaint on July 24, 1987, the relevant period is July 24, 1977 through July 24, 1987.

We recently described the elements of adverse possession as follows: "In order to acquire title by adverse possession, the claimant must prove, by clear and convincing evidence, . . . that for the statutory period 'his use of the land was continuous, open and notorious, exclusive and hostile to the true owner.'" Smith v. Krebs, 768 P.2d 124 (Alaska 1989). The first three conditions—continuity, notoriety and exclusivity—describe the physical requirements of the doctrine. See R. Cunningham, W. Stoebuck and D. Whitman, *The Law of Property* § 11.7 (1984). The fourth condition, hostility, is often imprecisely described as the "intent" requirement.

On appeal, Nome 2000 argues that as a matter of law the physical requirements are not met absent "significant physical improvements" or "substantial activity" on the land. Thus, according to Nome 2000, only when the Fagerstroms placed a cabin on the disputed parcel in the summer of 1978 did their possession become adverse. For the prior year, so the argument goes, the Fagerstroms' physical use of the property was insufficient because they did not construct "significant structure[s]" and their use was only seasonal. Nome 2000 also argues that the Fagerstroms' use of the disputed parcel was not exclusive because "[o]thers were free to pick the berries, use the paths and fish in the area." We reject these arguments.

---

5.   However, Charles Fagerstrom testified that when he excluded the campers he felt that they were "on our property." He also testified that during the mid to late 70's he would have "frown[ed]" upon people camping on "my property."

Whether a claimant's physical acts upon the land are sufficiently continuous, notorious and exclusive does not necessarily depend on the existence of significant improvements, substantial activity or absolute exclusivity. Indeed, this area of law is not susceptible to fixed standards because the quality and quantity of acts required for adverse possession depend on the character of the land in question. Thus, the conditions of continuity and exclusivity require only that the land be used for the statutory period as an average owner of similar property would use it. . . . Peters v. Juneau-Douglas Girl Scout Council, 519 P.2d 826 (Alaska 1974) ("[P]ossession need not be absolutely exclusive; it need only be a type of possession which would characterize an owner's use."). Where, as in the present case, the land is rural, a lesser exercise of dominion and control may be reasonable. See (Cooper v. Carter Oil Co., 316 P.2d 320 (Utah 1957) "pasturing of sheep for three weeks a year is sufficient where land is suitable only for grazing"); (Monroe v. Rawlings, 49 N.W.2d 55 (Mich. 1951) "6 visits per year to hunting cabin plus some timber cutting found sufficient where land was wild and undeveloped"); (Pulcifer v. Bishop, 225 N.W. 3 (Mich. 1929) exclusivity is not destroyed as to beach property commonly used by others).

exclusivity not necessary

The character of the land in question is also relevant to the notoriety requirement. Use consistent with ownership which gives visible evidence of the claimant's possession, such that the reasonably diligent owner "could see that a hostile flag was being flown over his property," is sufficient. Shilts v. Young, 567 P.2d 769 (Alaska 1977). Where physical visibility is established, community repute is also relevant evidence that the true owner was put on notice.[7]

Holding:

Applying the foregoing principles to this case, we hold that the jury could reasonably conclude that the Fagerstroms established, by clear and convincing evidence, continuous, notorious and exclusive possession for ten years prior to the date Nome 2000 filed suit.[8] We point out that we are concerned only with the first year, the summer of 1977 through the summer of 1978, as Nome 2000 admits that the requirements of adverse possession were met from the summer of 1978 through the summer of 1987.

The disputed parcel is located in a rural area suitable as a seasonal homesite for subsistence and recreational activities. This is exactly how the Fagerstroms used it during the year in question. On the premises throughout the entire year were an outhouse, a fish rack, a large reindeer pen (which, for six weeks, housed a reindeer), a picnic area, a small quantity of building materials and some trees not indigenous to the area. During the warmer season, for about 13 weeks, the Fagerstroms also placed a camper trailer on blocks on the disputed parcel. The Fagerstroms and their children visited the property several times during the warmer season to fish, gather berries, clean the premises, and play. In total, their conduct and improvements went well beyond "mere casual and occasional trespasses" and instead "evince[d] a purpose to exercise exclusive dominion over the property." *See Peters*, 519 P.2d at 830. That others were free to pick berries and fish is consistent with the conduct of a hospitable landowner,

7. The function of the notoriety requirement is to afford the true owner an opportunity for notice. However, actual notice is not required; the true owner is charged with knowing what a reasonably diligent owner would have known. . . .

8. Neither the trial court's denial of Nome 2000's motion for a directed verdict nor the jury's verdict should be disturbed if reasonable jurors could have concluded that the requirements for adverse possession were met. . . .

and undermines neither the continuity nor exclusivity of their possession. *See id.* at 831 (claimant "merely acting as any other hospitable landowner might" in allowing strangers to come on land to dig clams).

With respect to the notoriety requirement, a quick investigation of the premises, especially during the season in which it was best suited for use, would have been sufficient to place a reasonably diligent landowner on notice that someone may have been exercising dominion and control over at least the northern portion of the property. Upon such notice, further inquiry would indicate that members of the community regarded the Fagerstroms as the owners. Continuous, exclusive, and notorious possession were thus established. ———— *

Nome 2000 also argues that the Fagerstroms did not establish hostility. It claims that "the Fagerstroms were required to prove that they intended to claim *[π claims no hostility.]* the property as their own." According to Nome 2000, this intent was lacking as the Fagerstroms thought of themselves not as owners but as stewards pursuant to the traditional system of Native Alaskan land usage. We reject this argument and hold that all of the elements of adverse possession were met.

What the Fagerstroms believed or intended has nothing to do with the question whether their possession was hostile. . . . Hostility is . . . determined by application of an objective test which simply asks whether the possessor "acted toward the land as if he owned it," without the permission of one with legal authority to give possession. . . . [T]he Fagerstroms' actions toward the property were consistent with ownership of it, and Nome 2000 offers no proof that the Fagerstroms so acted with anyone's permission. That the Fagerstroms' objective manifestations of ownership may have been accompanied by what was described as a traditional Native Alaskan mind-set is irrelevant. To hold otherwise would be inconsistent with precedent and patently unfair.

Having concluded that the Fagerstroms established the elements of adverse possession, we turn to the question whether they were entitled to the entire disputed parcel. Specifically, the question presented is whether the jury could reasonably conclude that the Fagerstroms adversely possessed the southerly portion of the disputed parcel. *[issue over whole parcel]*

Absent color of title,[10] only property actually possessed may be acquired by adverse possession. . . . Here, from the summer of 1977 through the summer of 1978, the Fagerstroms' only activity on the southerly portion of the land included use of the pre-existing trails in connection with subsistence and recreational activities, and picking up litter. They claim that these activities, together *[Δ's claim.]* with their placement of the cornerposts, constituted actual possession of the southerly portion of the parcel. Nome 2000 argues that this activity did not constitute actual possession and, at most, entitled the Fagerstroms to an easement *[π's claim.]* by prescription across the southerly portion of the disputed parcel.

Nome 2000 is correct. The Fagerstroms' use of the trails and picking up of litter, although perhaps indicative of adverse use, would not provide the reasonably diligent owner with visible evidence of another's exercise of dominion and control. To this, the cornerposts add virtually nothing. Two of the four posts are located well to the west of the disputed parcel. Of the two that were allegedly

---

10.   "Color of title exists only by virtue of a written instrument which purports to pass title to the claimant, but which is ineffective because of a defect in the means of conveyance or because the grantor did not actually own the land he sought to convey." *Hubbard,* 684 P.2d at 847. . . .

placed on the parcel in 1970, the one located on the southerly portion of the parcel disappeared at an unknown time. . . . Thus, we conclude that the superior court erred in its denial of Nome 2000's motion for a directed verdict as to the southerly portion. This case is remanded to the trial court, with instructions to determine the extent of the Fagerstroms' acquisition in a manner consistent with this opinion.

Affirmed in part, reversed in part, and remanded.

Notes and Questions

1. Assume that Nome 2000 is a large landholder with many tracts of rural and wilderness land. How can it protect itself from adverse possessors? The California adverse possession statutes are qualified by the following proviso, adopted at the behest of the railroads,[22] which owned enormous tracts of undeveloped land:

> Provided, however, that in no case shall adverse possession be considered established under the provisions of any section or sections of this Code, unless it shall be shown that the land has been occupied and claimed for the period of five years continuously, and the party or persons, their predecessors and grantors, have paid all the taxes, State, county, or municipal, which have been levied and assessed upon such land. [Cal. Civ. Proc. Code § 325.]

2. At which of the adverse possession requirements was Dr. Steven McNabb's testimony aimed? Contrast the court's treatment of the character and importance of the Fagerstroms' activities on the land with that in *Johnson v. M'Intosh*, and in *Tee-Hit-Ton Indians v. United States*, 348 U.S. 272 (1955). The Tee-Hit-Tons, a clan of the Tlingit Tribe, claimed a right under the Fifth Amendment to compensation for timber taken from 350,000 acres in the Tongass National Forest, land they claimed to own on the ground that they and their tribal predecessors had continually claimed, occupied, and used the land from time immemorial. The Chief testified that he had learned the boundaries of the Tee-Hit-Ton area from hunting and fishing with his uncle, and that the tribe had both winter and summer villages in the area, that ownership was not individual but tribal (any member may use any portion he wishes as long as he uses it, but when he stops using it, other members of the tribe are free to use it), and that they fished and hunted the land. Claims were carved on totem poles. In addition, various articles by experts on tribal groups confirmed that land claims among the Tlingits were "wholly tribal." From this the court concluded that the Tee-Hit-Tons "were in a hunting and fishing stage of civilization" and used the land "like . . . the nomadic tribes of the States Indians." Therefore, the Indians' claim was more a claim of sovereignty than ownership and could be extinguished by the government at will without payment of compensation unless Congress had specifically recognized the tribe's rights as "ownership." If record title to the property claimed by the Tee-Hit-Tons had been in private hands, rather than

---

22. *See* Averill Q. Mix, *Payment of Taxes as a Condition of Title by Adverse Possession: A Nineteenth-Century Anachronism,* 9 Santa Clara L. Rev. 244, 246-49 (1969). Other large landowners also supported adoption of the statute.

in the government and they sued for trespass or conversion, would their claim have been more likely to succeed?

3. In *Karuk Tribe of California v. Ammon*, 209 F.3d 1366 (Fed. Cir. 2000), *cert. denied* (2001), the court held that only an Act of Congress can grant a right of "permanent" as opposed to "permissive" occupancy to Indians and that Indian occupancy rights may be extinguished by Congress without any compensation unless an Act of Congress "has specifically recognized the Indians' ownership rights." Thus no compensation was due Karuk and Yurok Indians, previously entitled to reservation rights, who were excluded from the Hoopa Valley Reservation timber revenues by the 1988 Hoopa-Yurok Settlement Act. The dissent begins: "It is not tenable, at this late date in the life of the Republic, to rule that Native Americans living on a Reservation are not entitled to the constitutional protections of the Fifth Amendment. . . . The jurisprudence of conquest, set forth in *Johnson v. M'Intosh*, has no applicability to this case. . . . It is a case of first impression; and its holding is incorrect as well as unjust."

LAWRENCE v. TOWN OF CONCORD

Supreme Judicial Court of Massachusetts
788 N.E.2d 546 (2003)

SPINA, J. Perhaps as late as 1997, the town of Concord (town) became aware that it had received a specific devise of land located at 1586 Main Street in Concord (locus), under a will that was probated in 1942. Albert J. Lawrence claimed title to the same locus through a specific devise from Joseph Frazier, a prior occupant of the locus whom Lawrence claims perfected title through adverse possession. The town's response was to exercise its power of eminent domain as to the locus but pay Lawrence no damages. Lawrence brought an action for damages under G.L. c. 79 . . . .[1]

On cross motions for summary judgment a Superior Court judge concluded that Lawrence failed to establish title to the locus through Frazier's adverse possession because "Frazier's possession could not have been notorious or adverse where the [t]own did not have notice of its ownership" of the locus. The Appeals Court affirmed . . . [holding] that the "evidence was ample, and essentially uncontradicted" that, from 1965 until Frazier died in 1996, his possession was "exclusive, continuous, and adverse to the town's ownership for a period of at least twenty years." However, the Appeals Court determined that the occupation was "not open and notorious" because the town had no knowledge that it owned the property. . . . We granted Lawrence's application for further appellate review. We conclude that the town's lack of knowledge as to its ownership did not defeat Frazier's claim of title by adverse possession, and remand to the Superior Court for a determination of the damages owed to Lawrence arising from the town's eminent domain proceeding.

---

1.   General Laws c. 79 in general treats the issue of takings of real property by eminent domain. Section 12 allows for the payment of compensation for property taken by eminent domain . . . .

1. *Facts.* The following uncontradicted facts are found in the record.[2] In a properly executed and witnessed holographic will dated August 27, 1941, Mary J. Burke left the locus, her home and real estate, to her daughter, Helen E. Burke Boyer,

> never to be sold. After she goes I wish to have my home go to my adopted daughter Harriet Burke Frazier. If no children survive said Harriet Burke Frazier I wish to have my home with land theron [sic] go to the town [Concord] to be used as they [sic] see fit and proceeds from same to be used for better education of some deserving children.

Mary J. Burke died on August 4, 1942, and her will was allowed on September 14, 1942. On November 30, 1964, Helen E. Burke Boyer conveyed her life interest in the locus to Harriet Burke Frazier. . . . Harriet Burke Frazier had married Joseph Frazier on December 5, 1937. On May 18, 1965, Harriet Burke Frazier died, survived by Joseph Frazier, but without issue.

Subsequent to his wife's death, Joseph Frazier rented the locus for a period of years while he lived at another site in Concord where he and his late wife had run a small store. The first rental that is shown in the record was to a Michael DiPietro, and is evidenced by a summary process action in the District Court of Central Middlesex brought by Frazier against DiPietro for possession and unpaid rent. The action was successful and a writ of possession and execution was delivered to Frazier on May 17, 1968, covering rents due from September 5, 1967, through February 1, 1968. The record also shows that Margaret and Raymond Dornig lived at the locus between 1969 and 1973. From at least 1969 until his death in 1996, Joseph Frazier received and paid all of the real estate tax bills on the locus.[3]

The annual "street lists" of the town . . . showed that Joseph Frazier lived at the locus on January 1, 1965 (with his wife and sister-in-law), and also from January 1, 1974, until he died on December 24, 1996. Uncontradicted affidavits filed in support of Lawrence's motion for summary judgment indicate that Frazier occupied the locus from as early as 1966, and certainly from the mid 1970's until his death. Neighbors and friends visited Frazier at his home at the locus, joined him for drinks, sat with him or saw him on his porch, and watched him gardening. One affiant, the executrix of Frazier's estate, reported that Frazier was "aware that the property at 1586 Main Street did not belong to him. [He was] nervous that the [t]own would find out that he did not own the property and kick him out."

On April 28, 1997, after Frazier's death, a lawyer for his estate contacted the town to bring the town's potential interest in the locus to its attention, and to

---

2. Although the town disputes some portions of the factual record, it has failed to create a genuine issue of material fact by setting forth "specific facts" in an affidavit or otherwise. . . .

3. From 1965 to 1972 the bills were addressed to "Harriet Burke Frazier." From 1973 to 1980 the bills were addressed to the "Estate of Harriet Burke Frazier." From 1980 until 1996 the bills were addressed to "Joseph G. Frazier." Shortly before Frazier died, he gave Lawrence all the tax bills from 1969 to 1996. The town disputes whether Joseph Frazier paid the bills over the time period stated above, arguing that there is no proof that he paid them. However, the town has failed to provide any evidence to contradict the reasonable inference that the bills, which had been stamped "paid" and were in Frazier's possession, were paid by Frazier, or on his behalf. "Payment of taxes evidences a claim of ownership." Bernard v. Nantucket Boys' Club, Inc., 391 Mass. 823, 826, 465 N.E.2d 236 (1984).

inform the town that Lawrence, to whom Frazier devised the locus, was asserting that Frazier had acquired title to the locus by adverse possession.[4] In an attempt to clear title to the locus, the town's board of selectmen, on June 22, 1998, and pursuant to town meeting authorization, took the locus by eminent domain, "in fee simple . . . on behalf of the [t]own of Concord for municipal purposes, including the future sale thereof." Because the selectmen claimed to own the locus, they determined that "no damages have been sustained and none are awarded." . . .

2. *The town's lack of knowledge.* Lawrence contends that Frazier satisfied all of the elements of adverse possession and that the doctrine does not protect parties who are ignorant of their interest. The town argues that, because it did not know that it owned the locus, it could not defend its title, and in these circumstances it would be inequitable to allow Frazier to acquire title by adverse possession. The town further argues, and the Superior Court judge and the Appeals Court agreed, that Frazier's possession of the property was not sufficiently "open" and "notorious" to place the town on actual notice of its ownership interest in the locus.

The Appeals Court reasoned that Frazier's "use was not open because the true owner, the town, neither knew nor reasonably should have known of its ownership or that the nature of Frazier's use changed when Harriet died, becoming adverse to the town's ownership," and that "[n]othing in Frazier's conduct or use should have alerted the town, or anyone else, to the town's interest." . . . In reaching its conclusion, the Appeals Court relied on Foot v. Bauman, 129 N.E.2d 916 (Mass. 1955), where this court adopted the rule in 2 *American Law of Property* § 8.56 (Casner ed. 1952), which states: "To be open the use must be made without attempted concealment. To be notorious it must be known to some who might reasonably be expected to communicate their knowledge to the owner if he maintained a reasonable degree of supervision over his premises. It is not necessary that the use be actually known to the owner for it to meet the test of being notorious." The reference to knowledge in § 8.56 pertains to the owner's knowledge of the adverse possessor's use of the property, not the owner's knowledge of ownership.

Moreover, Foot v. Bauman did not involve an owner who had no knowledge of his interest in the subject property. The focus of the case was a neighbor's use of the property and the owner's actual or constructive knowledge of that use. The neighbor and his predecessors had maintained a sewer line below the surface of the property, unbeknownst to the owner, who had purchased the property after the sewer line had been installed. The owner did not discover the sewer line until after it had been in use for more than twenty years. When the owner sued to enjoin its use, the neighbor claimed an easement by prescription. The owner contended that the neighbor's use was not open and notorious because

4. Although the town states that this letter was the first notice received by the town of its interest in the locus, the tax bills from the town in the record show that in 1990 and 1991, the bills were addressed to Joseph G. Frazier with the notation "old bill before deed history." Starting in 1992 and until 1999, the bills remain addressed to Joseph G. Frazier, but with a second address line replacing the above notation with "c/o Town Manager — Town of Concord." The significance of this change is not clear, but it may indicate that at least some arm of town government was aware of the town's ownership interest in the locus as of 1992. Because the critical time period for the success of Frazier's claim of adverse possession is from at least December 9, 1967, until December 9, 1987, the issue is not necessary to our decision, and can safely be disregarded. . . .

the sewer line had been concealed from view. A master found facts from which the court concluded that the owner could have ascertained the existence of the sewer line through a reasonable degree of supervision of the property, and determine that the use of the sewer was sufficiently open and notorious to create an easement by prescription.

. . . The burden of proving adverse possession is on the person claiming title thereby and "extends to all of the necessary elements of such possession." Mendonca v. Cities Serv. Oil Co. of Pa., 237 N.E.2d 16 (Mass. 1968). . . .

The purpose of the requirement of "open and notorious" use is to place the true owner "on notice of the hostile activity of the possession so that he, the owner, may have an opportunity to take steps to vindicate his rights by legal action." Ottavia v. Savarese, 155 N.E.2d 432 (Mass. 1959). There is no requirement that the true owner be given explicit notice of adverse use. ("Where the user has acted, without license or permission of the true owner, in a manner inconsistent with the true owner's rights, the acts alone . . . may be sufficient to put the true owner on notice of the nonpermissive use.") *See also* . . . Samuels v. Borrowscale, 104 Mass. 207 (1870) ("All that is necessary . . . is actual, adverse and exclusive possession, so open and notorious that it may be presumed to have been known to the rightful owner. . . . Special notice to the [true owner], either by act or word, that the [adverse possessor] held in defiance of or repudiated his title, was not necessary"); Poignard v. Smith, 23 Mass. 172 (1828) (where true owners were both out of Commonwealth, adverse possession was still made out because "acts of notoriety, such as building a fence round the land or erecting buildings upon it, are notice to all the world").

Open and notorious use of a property is thus deemed to place the true owner on constructive notice of such use, and it is immaterial whether the true owner actually learns of that use or not. The elements of "open and notorious" use, central to this case, are descriptive of the adverse possessor's acts of possession and use. An owner's knowledge of its interest is not an element of proof of a claim of adverse possession, and an owner's lack of knowledge of ownership is not a defense to such a claim. *See* Kendall v. Selvaggio, 602 N.E.2d 206 (neither mutual mistake nor unilateral misunderstanding concerning boundary location, examples of ignorance of ownership, will defeat claim of adverse possession).

Finally, we reject the argument that the owner must have knowledge of its interest for the same reason that we have rejected a requirement of actual knowledge of the adverse use. It "would deprive the principle of [adverse possession] of much of its value in quieting controversy and giving sanction to long continued usages." Foot v. Bauman. "Long dormant claims to title could rise from the dust bin of history and many titles would become unsettled." Allen v. Batchelder, 459 N.E.2d 129 (Mass. App. Ct. 1984).

The town next alleges that Frazier took steps to conceal his lack of ownership, and thus his possession was atypical of the open and notorious possession needed to sustain the burden of proof.[6] There is no evidence that Frazier perpetrated a fraud on the town, as the Appeals Court correctly concluded. . . . To

---

6. For example, the town claims that the information contained in the street lists only shows that Frazier lived at the locus on January 1 of each of the years between 1974 and 1996, and not between January 2 and December 31 of those years. Although this is one possible interpretation, it is not a reasonable one, and the town provides no facts to contradict the affidavits of the neighbors that represent that Frazier lived on the property as a normal neighbor. . . .

the eyes of the world around him, Frazier's possession and use had all the usual indicia of ownership. His possession and use provided sufficient notice to support a claim of adverse possession. He had no duty to disclose his lack of ownership or to enlighten the town as to its interests.

The town also argues that Frazier's failure to include the locus as property of his wife on an inheritance tax form he filled out after her death is an indication of wilful and possibly fraudulent misrepresentation. Because his wife had only ever had a life estate in the locus, it was in fact accurate to state that after her death she did not own the locus, or have the power to dispose of the locus in her own will. . . . .

In addition, the town points to Frazier's unwillingness to have a title search run on the property as an indication that he was afraid that his adverse possession would be discovered. That may be, and as stated above, adverse possessors may live in trepidation of discovery before the statutory period has run. But Frazier had no obligation to run a title search and his failure to do so has no probative value for any live issue in this case.

Finally, the town claims that Frazier's failure to have the town change the names under which the tax bills on the locus were sent "suggest[s] that Frazier attempted to avoid alerting the Town to its interest in the parcel." A taxpayer is under no affirmative obligation to see to it that the assessors properly address tax bills, unless requested by the assessors to submit the name and address of the true owner. . . . Here there was no evidence of any such request of Frazier by the town's assessors. When the bills arrived at the property Frazier paid them. He fulfilled all the responsibilities that were required of him. Moreover, beginning in 1980, the bills were addressed to him.

Adverse possession as a doctrine assumes that the adverse possessor may be acting with the hope and even the intent to conceal that he has no valid interest in the property. Because his use is open to the world to see and he appears to be acting as though he were a true owner, the inner workings of his mind are irrelevant. . . . "So long as a man is in possession of land claiming title, however wrongfully, and with whatever degree of knowledge that he has no right, so long the real owner is out of possession in a constructive as well as an actual sense. It is of the nature of the statute of limitations when applied to civil actions, in effect, to mature a wrong into a right, by cutting off the remedy." Humbert v. Rector, Churchwardens & Vestrymen of Trinity Church in the City of N.Y., 24 Wend. 587 (N.Y. 1840). Ignorance by the true owners of the fact that a wrong is being committed against them is not among the "disabilities enumerated by the statute of limitations . . . ." "The statute [on its terms] bars the man who has been out of possession for twenty years, and no one is the less out of possession, because the man who is in may know that his possession is tortious."

An adverse possessor has no burden to reveal his intentions to the true owner absent a special relationship between the parties, as, for example, between a licensor and licensee, where a repudiation of the earlier relationship is necessary to establish a claim of adverse possession. Where a special relationship exists the putative adverse possessor is required to give actual notice to the true owner of the change in status from permissive to adverse. . . . There was no special relationship here.

The Appeals Court points to Begg v. Ganson, 609 N.E.2d 1225 (Mass. App. Ct. 1993), for the proposition that Frazier's use was initially permissive (as husband to his wife) and that, in those circumstances the burden of showing that the use has shifted from permissive to adverse is heightened. . . . The *Begg* case, however, is distinguishable. It . . . involved a landlord-tenant relationship. The tenant had occupied the property for thirty-seven years under a written agreement. When the landlord attempted to terminate the agreement, the tenant claimed adverse possession by virtue of his continuous breach of certain terms of the agreement for over twenty years. The court disagreed and said that where possession is initially permissive, the one claiming adverse possession has a "heavy burden" to show that the character of the possession changed so drastically as to put an owner on notice that "he should take steps to protect his rights." . . . Here, as between the town and Frazier, there was no special relationship, and the town did not give Frazier specific permission to occupy the locus. The town was aware, as reflected by tax bills addressed to the "Estate of Harriet Burke Frazier," that Frazier's wife had died. Frazier's use of the locus was adverse to the interests of the town from the moment of his wife's death.

The statute of limitations to recover possession of land runs against the true owner after twenty years if the adverse possessor satisfies the elements of adverse possession. All that was required of Frazier was that he occupy the locus without the permission of the true owner, continuously for twenty years, exclusively, openly, notoriously, and adversely to the true owner, thereby giving notice to the world of his possession.[7]

3. *Statutory bar to adverse possession against the town.* The town argues that, because the locus was given to the town and held for a public purpose it is exempt from adverse possession, under G.L. c. 260, § 31,[8] and that Frazier's claim of adverse possession fails because he had not occupied the locus for the requisite twenty years prior to December 9, 1987. The Appeals Court determined that Frazier's possession was "exclusive, continuous and adverse to the town's ownership for a period of at least twenty years. The evidence was ample, and essentially uncontradicted, that, from 1965 until Frazier's death in 1996, it was each of these things." We agree.

The town argues that Frazier was not in possession of the parcel from December 9, 1967, until December 9, 1987 . . . . The town points to the fact that the street lists show Margaret and Raymond Dornig as the occupants of the locus from January 1, 1969, until at least January 1, 1973. In addition, Frazier's name appeared on the street lists as occupying another house from January, 1966, through January 1, 1973. . . .

A person claiming title by adverse possession need not personally occupy the land for twenty years. He may rely on the possession of his tenants . . . .

The town argues that . . . the fact that Frazier needed to go to court to obtain a judgment against his tenant (DiPietro) fundamentally changes the situation, and that DiPietro remaining on the property effected an ouster of Frazier that

---

7.   As both parties point out, the laws in the Commonwealth have changed, requiring the executor of an estate to notify the beneficiaries of contingent interests set forth in a will of their interest within three months of the allowance of the will, thus rendering the facts presented by this case unlikely to be repeated. ... .

8.   General Laws c. 260, § 31, inserted by St. 1987, c. 564, § 54, states in relevant part: "[T]his section shall not bar any action by . . . any political subdivision [of the Commonwealth], for the recovery of land . . . held for [a] public purpose." Statute 1987, c. 564, § 46, states: "The provisions of [§ 54] of this act shall not be construed to abrogate the rights of any person in an action to establish title by adverse possession who has seized or possessed real property . . . for no less than twenty years pursuant to [G.L. c. 260, § 31,] prior to the effective date of this act."

interrupted his possession for twenty years. The town is incorrect, however, because all that DiPietro (or the Dornigs) could have claimed was a leasehold estate as a tenant, whereas Frazier's claim is to the fee simple in the locus. Thus, even if DiPietro or the Dornigs interrupted Frazier's use of the property, they did not interrupt Frazier's underlying claim to ownership of the fee simple in the property. . . .

4. *Conclusion.* Frazier satisfied all the requirements for a claim of adverse possession of the locus. He occupied the locus for more than twenty continuous years, openly, notoriously, exclusively, and adversely to the true owner and without that owner's permission. At the end of that twenty years, he owned the locus and his devise to Lawrence was effective. As a result of the taking by the town, Lawrence is entitled to damages. We reverse the judgment of the Superior Court and remand for a determination of the damages owed to Lawrence arising from the town's eminent domain proceeding.

Notes and Questions

1. *Open and notorious.* In the principal case, the disputed property was an entire house lot and the court held that Frazier's possession was open and notorious even though the city did not know it owned the property. What if the dispute had involved a small encroachment instead? *Mannillo v. Gorski,* 255 A.2d 258 (N.J. 1969), involved a concrete walk and steps that encroached 15 inches onto plaintiff's lot, which was 25' wide x 100' deep. The court held that a minor encroachment along a common boundary is not open and notorious unless the true owner has actual knowledge of the location of the boundary. It reasoned from two premises: (1) the moral justification for adverse possession is that a landowner who has slept on her rights may properly be penalized; and (2) open and notorious use of the property creates a presumption that the owner has knowledge of an adverse occupancy. It concluded:

> when the encroachment of an adjoining owner is of a small area and the fact of an intrusion is not clearly and self-evidently apparent to the naked eye but requires an on-site survey . . . such a presumption is fallacious and unjustified. . . . Therefore, to permit a presumption of notice to arise in the case of minor border encroachments not exceeding several feet would fly in the face of reality and require the true owner to be on constant alert for possible small encroachments. The only method of certain determination would be by obtaining a survey each time the adjacent owner undertook any improvement at or near the boundary, and this would place an undue and inequitable burden upon the true owner.

Compare the *Mannillo* court's reasoning with that in *Lawrence,* the principal case. How would you predict that the Massachusetts court would resolve a similar case?

2. *Underground uses.* The court discussed *Foot v. Bauman,* 129 N.E.2d 916 (Mass. 1955), in which a prescriptive easement for an underground sewer was acquired even though the landowner purchased the property after the sewer was installed and had no knowledge of its existence. The court concluded that the use was open and notorious based on evidence that the defendant–adverse user's house was up the hill, the town sewer was below, and there were three manhole covers on the plaintiff's land between the house and the town sewer. Compare this case with *Van Sandt v. Royster* in Chapter 12, which found an underground sewer line "apparent."

In 1883, the entrance to Marengo Cave was discovered, and within a week, the cave was explored and widely publicized. Shortly thereafter, the owner of the land where the mouth of the cave was located took possession of the cave, set it up for exhibition purposes, and began to charge admission. John Ross first visited the cave in 1895 and purchased a parcel of land about 700 feet away from the cave entrance in 1908. Twenty-one years later, in 1929, Ross sued to quiet title to that part of the cave that lay under his land. A court-ordered survey determined where the boundary line between the two tracts ran through the cave. Ross claimed not to have known that part of the cave ran under his property until the survey. Defendant, Marengo Cave Company, claimed that it had acquired title to the entire cave by adverse possession because it and its predecessors had continuously exhibited the cave since 1883. Was defendant's use open and notorious? *See Marengo Cave Co. v. Ross*, 10 N.E.2d 917 (Ind. 1937) (no, the use was not open and notorious; Ross had no reasonable means to discover that his land was being used).

3. *State of mind.* The court in *Lawrence* says that if the adverse possessor "appears to be acting as though he were a true owner, the inner workings of his mind are irrelevant." Most courts and commentators agree that the subjective intent and belief of the adverse possessor should not affect the outcome of the claim to have acquired title. However, some courts disagree. A few courts have followed *Preble v. Maine Cent. R. Co.*, 27 A. 149 (Me. 1893), which held that in boundary line disputes, possession pursuant to a mistaken belief as to the location of the boundary was not adverse; the claimant must intend "to claim title to all land within a certain boundary on the face of the earth, whether it shall eventually be found to be the correct one or not." However, most courts have rejected the "Maine doctrine" (also called the "aggressive trespasser rule") in favor of the "Connecticut doctrine" that originated in *French v. Pearce*, 8 Conn. 439 (1831), which declared a mistake as to ownership to be immaterial if the claimant conducted himself as the owner. Some courts that had earlier adopted the Maine doctrine have overruled the old cases, *see, e.g., Mannillo v. Gorski*, 255 A.2d 258 (N.J. 1969), and the Maine legislature has attempted to overturn it, *see Striefel v. Charles-Keyt-Leaman Partnership*, 733 A.2d 984 (Me. 1999) (attempt may have failed because legislature mistakenly assumed mistake went to hostility requirement rather than to claim of right requirement). Criticism of the Maine doctrine centers on the fact that it rewards the intentional wrongdoer and punishes the honest, mistaken possessor.

Other courts take the position that only good-faith claimants may be rewarded with title by adverse possession. Although most commentators take the position that the objective standard is the prevailing position in the United States, R.H. Helmholz claims that courts, in fact, take good faith into account and are much more likely to find for a good-faith trespasser than an aggressive trespasser, *Adverse Possession and Subjective Intent*, 61 Wash. U. L.Q. 331 (1983). His conclusion sparked a debate. *See* Roger A. Cunningham, *Adverse Possession and Subjective Intent: A Reply to Professor Helmholz*, 64 Wash. U. L.Q. 1 (1986); R.H. Helmholz, *More on Subjective Intent: A Response to Professor Cunningham*, 64 Wash. U. L.Q. 65 (1986); Roger A. Cunningham, *More on Adverse Possession: A Rejoinder to Professor Helmholz*, 64 Wash. U. L.Q. 1167 (1986).

4. *Payment?* Should a successful adverse possessor or prescriptive user be required to pay the previous owner for the value of the property interest acquired? In *Warsaw v. Chicago Metallic Ceilings, Inc.*, 676 P.2d 584 (Cal. 1984), the California Supreme Court reversed a decision of the court of appeal that had awarded compensation to the landowner who lost the right to prevent a neighbor from backing trucks over his land after five years of prescriptive use.

Requiring bad-faith trespassers to pay compensation for the interests they acquire has appealed to some commentators as a solution that would carry out the salutary functions of adverse possession doctrine while at the same time punishing wrongful conduct. Notice that this solution would convert the protection accorded the right to exclude, and even ownership, from a "property rule" to a "liability rule." For the landowner in an objective standard, or aggressive trespasser state, of course, a compensation requirement would be an improvement. *See* Thomas W. Merrill, *Property Rules, Liability Rules, and Adverse Possession*, 79 Nw. U. L. Rev. 1122 (1984); Comment, *Compensation for the Involuntary Transfer of Property Between Private Parties: Application of a Liability Rule to the Law of Adverse Possession*, 79 Nw. U. L. Rev. 759 (1984). Another alternative, proposed in Richard A. Epstein, *Past and Future: The Temporal Dimension in the Law of Property*, 64 Wash. U. L.Q. 667 (1986), is to require a longer period of time for bad-faith adverse possessors. Statutes that allow a shorter time period for claims under color of title probably reflect the notion that claims under color of title are less likely to be made by bad-faith possessors.

Problems in Applying the Statute of Limitations: Tolling for Disability

Every state has some provision for protecting the property rights of an owner who is under a disability when an adverse possessor takes possession of his or her land. There are two different types of statutes. One type is illustrated by the Ohio statute of limitations, which provides:

> [I]f a person entitled to bring the action is, at the time the cause of action accrues, within the age of minority or of unsound mind, the person, after the expiration of twenty-one years from the time the cause of action accrues, may bring the action within ten years after the disability is removed.

A New Jersey statute illustrates the other type:

> If any person entitled to any of the actions or proceedings specified in . . . [the statute of limitations for various actions] or to a right or title of entry under section 2A:14-6, is or shall be, at the time of any such cause of action or right or title accruing, under the age of 21 years, or insane, such person may commence such action or make such entry, within such time as limited by said sections, after his coming to or being of full age or of sane mind.

Provisions like these, which are called "tolling" provisions, are often difficult to read. In applying these statutes, there are two things you need to know: Usually, the only disability that counts is a disability that exists when the adverse possessor takes possession of the property; and the benefit of the statute extends not only to the original adverse possessor but also to that person's successors. To see if you understand how they work, try applying each of these statutes to the following situations assuming that the statute of limitations for an action in ejectment is 10 years:

1. Assume that O owns Blackacre in 1975 and that AP takes possession adversely to O on July 1, 1975. When does AP acquire title in each of the following scenarios?

  a. O is insane on July 1, 1975, and dies intestate[23] in 1980. H is his heir and has no disability.
  b. O is insane on July 1, 1975, and dies intestate in 1995. H is his heir and has no disability.
  c. O has no disability in 1975 and dies intestate on July 3, 1975. H, his heir, is six years old at the time of O's death. What difference if O had died June 30, 1975, instead? What difference if the statutory period is 10 years instead of 21?
  d. O is insane on July 1, 1975, and dies intestate in 1995. H, his heir, is two years old at the time of his death.
  e. O is 10 years old on July 1, 1975; in 1982 he is convicted of a felony and imprisoned until 2000.

2. Georgianna Smith died intestate in 1921 owning three parcels of land. Her heirs were two sons, two daughters, and Camille, her granddaughter. The two sons and two daughters sold and conveyed all three parcels to third parties in 1922 and 1923. The deeds purported to convey the entire title to the grantees, who took possession of the land. No mention was made of Camille's one-fifth interest. Camille reached age 21 on June 26, 1929. When did the grantees obtain title to Camille's interest? *See Braue v. Fleck*, 127 A.2d 1 (N.J. 1956). The answer is what you would expect from reading the New Jersey statute printed above, but the opinion is worth reading if you are a history buff, or if you run across puzzling redundancies in a state's statutes of limitations on actions to recover real property. The New Jersey Supreme Court's opinion explains the existence of the three different New Jersey statutes (with two different tolling provisions) by reference to the development of the action in ejectment and its gradual displacement of the older "writ of right," and the application of different adverse possession requirements to the two forms of action from the 17th through the 19th centuries in England and New Jersey.

3. You represent D, who wants to buy a piece of property from AP. AP can prove that she has been in possession of the property and paid the taxes since 1975. The land records show that O is the owner of the property. Despite your best efforts, you have been unable to locate O. What advice will you give D?

---

23. Intestate means without a will. The property of a person who dies intestate passes to the heirs, persons who are determined under the intestate succession statute (sometimes called the statute of descent and distribution). Modernly, heirs are the spouse, children, and other descendants, and if there are no children, or other direct lineal descendants, heirs may include parents, and collateral relatives (brothers and sisters, nieces and nephews, aunts, uncles, and cousins).

Color of Title

Two advantages are conferred on the adverse possessor whose claim is based on a deed or other written instrument that purports to give her title to the land: The period required to establish title by adverse possession is often shorter; and she is regarded as having constructive possession of all the property described in the deed, so long as the deed covers a single parcel. If the deed covers more than one lot or parcel, the constructive possession ordinarily extends only to the boundaries of the lot the adverse possessor has actually taken partial possession of. Even in a state that does not otherwise require a good-faith claim of right, an adverse possessor must have entered the property in the good-faith belief that the deed conveyed what it purported to convey to obtain the advantage of color of title.[24] Do you see why?

KIOWA CREEK LAND & CATTLE CO. v. NAZARIAN
Court of Appeals of Nebraska
554 N.W.2d 175 (Neb. Ct. App. 1996)

HANNON, J. Kiowa Creek Land & Cattle Co., Inc. (Kiowa), filed this . . . action [on March 30, 1994] to obtain a declaration that it held an easement of access across a section of land that was formerly school land but which had been purchased by the . . . Nazarians . . . from the Nebraska Board of Educational Lands and Funds (NBEL & F) by a quitclaim deed dated September 24, 1990 . . . . The district court granted the Nazarians a summary judgment of dismissal on the grounds that the land had been owned by the State of Nebraska until it deeded the land to the Nazarians less than 10 years before, and therefore, since the statute of limitations does not run against the state and the land had been in private ownership for less than 10 years, Kiowa could not have acquired rights by prescription regardless of the use it might have made of an access way across the land. We agree and affirm the trial court's judgment.

The Nazarians had rented the school land from the NBEL & F from January 1, 1982, until they purchased it. Kiowa owned land to the west of the Nazarians' land, and for purposes of this opinion we will assume that Kiowa traveled across the school land for such time and in such a manner as to establish an easement by prescription if the state had not been the owner of the school land until 1990. . . .

The trial court and the Nazarians rely principally upon the case Topping v. Cohn, 99 N.W. 372 (Neb. 1904). In that case, two lots of school land to which accretion land[25] attached itself as a river slowly changed its course were sold to the defendant in 1901. The *Topping* court concluded that the land in question accreted to the school land while it was owned by the State and stated: "That no title by adverse possession can be acquired against the state or general

---

24.   *See, e.g.,* Braue v. Fleck, 127 A.2d 1 (N.J. 1956). The fact that the public land records show that title is in someone other than the grantor does not deprive the grantee of good-faith status unless the grantee is aware of the record title.

25.   As a river gradually changes course, parcels bounded by the river increase by accretion and decrease by erosion. — EDS.

government is elementary. Land cannot be the subject of adverse possession while the title is in the state." . . .

Union Mill & Min. Co. v. Ferris et al., 24 F. Cas. 594 (C.C.D. Nev. 1872), considers the question with respect to a claim of . . . [a prescriptive right to use water in a stream based] upon use during the time that title was in the government. . . . [T]he court stated:

> [The] statutes of limitation do not run against the state, so that no use of water
> while the title to the land is in the government, can avail the defendant, as a foun-
> dation of title by prescription, or defeat, or modify the title conveyed to the grantee
> by his patent.

. . . Kiowa seeks to avoid the effect of these holdings by relying upon Test v. Reichert, 14 N.W.2d 853 (Neb. 1944). . . . Test's wife owned land that adjoined land owned by the federal government, and Test planted wheat on 10 acres of the adjoining government land. Test's wife's land was purchased by Reichert, but Reichert refused to buy the crops on the adjoining government land. Over Test's objection, Reichert harvested the 10 acres of wheat on the government land. Test then brought a conversion action to recover the value of the wheat. Reichert defended upon the basis that the law . . . prohibited the public from acquiring rights to public lands. The court held that the right to a crop which is growing upon unenclosed public land lies in the one who has planted it and looked after it, rather than in one who forcibly takes possession against the will of the planter. In the discussion of the *Test* case, the court quoted 1 Am. Jur. *Adverse Possession* § 104 at 849 (1936): "[O]ne may acquire rights in public lands by adverse occupancy against all third persons, and this is true even though the claimant admits the government's ownership; in other words, the claimant's possession may be adverse without being hostile to the government." If this rule applied to this case, it would give Kiowa an easement across the Nazarians' land. The primary reason that the *Test* case has no application to the case at hand is that in *Test*, neither party traced his rights to the government, whereas in the case at hand, the Nazarians acquired their right to the land from the state.

On a practical level, the state rarely, if ever, uses its school lands itself. Such lands are almost always leased for a period of 12 years. If the *Test* rule were applied . . . no one could purchase that land from the government without the land being subject to the possibility of an easement immediately upon sale. The state's title to its land would be subject to the statute of limitations whenever the state sold or leased its land. Such a rule has no support in the cases and would seriously hamper the state's rights indirectly by injuring those who buy land from it. For these reasons, we affirm the trial court's judgment.

Affirmed.

Notes and Questions

1. What justifies the rule that land cannot be taken from the government by adverse possession or prescription? The usual justifications are that the government does not have the resources to monitor all its landholdings for signs of adverse claims, government employees may not have sufficient incentives to take actions against adverse claimants, and may even collude to defraud the government, and the public's interest in public lands should not be subject to loss by inadvertence. Do any of these justifications apply to the decision reached in this case, or the other cases where the adverse claims are established against private possessors who ultimately acquire title to the property?

2. *Relation back.* Until an adverse possessor succeeds in acquiring title, he or she is liable for trespass and "mesne profits." Mesne profits are the profits realized by the adverse possessor between the date the possession began and the lawsuit (or the period as to which the statute of limitations—often six years on an action for mesne profits—has not run). However, once title has been acquired, it "relates back" to the date of the adverse possessor's entry, and, magically, the causes of action for trespass and mesne profits are barred along with the action in ejectment. *See* Restatement of Property § 224, comment *c*, § 465. Could the court have used the relation-back concept to protect Kiowa's interest in the access easement?

3. What happens if the government acquires title to property that is in the hands of an adverse possessor? Ordinarily, that stops the adverse possession. However, if the government then transfers the property back into private hands, does the adverse possessor take up where he or she left off, or does the period start all over again? The answer is that it depends. If the government's ownership was not really for governmental or public use, but simply a transition from one private ownership to another, the adverse possession may be regarded as continuing without interruption, or merely suspended during the period of government ownership. *See, e.g., Stump v. Whibco,* 715 A.2d 1006 (N.J. Super. Ct. App. Div. 1998) (fact that Small Business Administration held title to the property for part of 1974 did not interrupt adverse possession). *See also* J. H. Crabb, Annotation, *Tax Sales or Forfeitures by or to Governmental Units as Interrupting Adverse Possession,* 50 A.L.R.2d 600 (1956); *Camp Clearwater, Inc. v. Plock,* 146 A.2d 527 (N.J. Super. Ct. 1959), *aff'd,* 157 A.2d 15 (N.J. Super. App. Div. 1960).

4. Although most jurisdictions follow the common-law rule that adverse possession and prescription do not run against the government (the old maxim was "*nullum tempus occurit regis*"—no time runs against the king), the rule is not universally followed, and there is considerable variation in whether it applies to land held by railroads and public utilities that are not owned by the government.

5. The court in *Kiowa* offers a "practical" justification for its holding: that otherwise, the school district lands would be subject to loss through the failure of its lessees to stop adverse possessors and prescriptive users. Is the court correct? Read on.

2. *Prescription*

DIETERICH INTERNATIONAL TRUCK SALES, INC. v. J.S. & J. SERVICES, INC.

California Court of Appeal
5 Cal. Rptr. 2d 388 (Ct. App.), rev. denied (1992)

[J.S. & J. Services, which does business as Terminal Station, leases its premises from landlord Brown for a 49-year term that began in 1956. Terminal Station is a truck stop, coffee shop, general store, and fueling station. Dieterich is a truck sales and repair operation located on adjacent premises that services large trucks, school buses, and vans.

Since Dieterich began operations in 1967, he has used an approximately 50-foot-wide stretch of the Terminal Station property to allow his customers' trucks to gain access to his service bays. The property is laid out in such a way that big trucks cannot get in and out without crossing the Terminal Station property, and to service trucks longer than 50 feet, part of the truck must extend onto that property.

The two businesses complemented each other, and no problem arose until the county Department of Health Services ordered Terminal to replace its leaking underground storage tanks in 1988. Installation of the new tanks, which were placed squarely in the area used by Dieterich, required erection of barriers that blocked access to the service bays. Dieterich filed a complaint for injunctive and declaratory relief and to quiet title to an easement.

The trial court held that Dieterich had acquired an easement by prescription against both Terminal Station and landlord Brown. Both appealed. The appellate court affirmed the decision as to Terminal in an unpublished part of the opinion. Its decision as to landlord Brown follows. — EDS.]

McDANIEL, A.J. . . . Defendant Brown . . . [contends]: A future interest, such as a landlord's reversion cannot be the subject of a prescriptive easement because the statutory period for acquiring the easement runs only against a possessory interest. Actions for ejectment or trespass, which are the usual method for preventing an easement by prescription, require that the owner have a present possessory interest in the property he seeks to protect. Because Brown, as landlord, is not in possession . . . (the lease runs until the year 2005), he is legally unable to bring the necessary action to obstruct plaintiff's use by prescription. . . .

In response, plaintiff . . . cites section 826 of the Civil Code, which enables landlords to maintain actions to protect their property during the term of a lease: "A person having an estate in fee, in remainder *or reversion,* may maintain an action for any injury done to the inheritance, *notwithstanding an intervening estate for* . . . years . . . ." (Italics added.) Plaintiff argues that section 826 empowers landlords to sue to protect their inheritance,[26] which would include preventing plaintiff from acquiring an easement by prescription . . . .

An analogous problem was addressed in Smith v. Cap Concrete, Inc. (1982) 133 Cal. App. 3d 769, in which the landlords brought an action in trespass against a third-party concrete company for depositing "broken concrete wash-out" on the landlords' property at the behest of the tenants' sublessee. In its defense, the concrete company argued that the landlords were not in possession and could not bring an action for trespass. The court recognized that the landlords were legally unable to bring an action for trespass as trespass "is designed to protect possessory — not necessarily ownership — interests in land from unlawful

---

26. Inheritance as used here means the landlord's interest in the land, which is inheritable from him in the event he dies intestate still owning it. This is one of the defining characteristics of the basic unit of landownership — the fee simple estate, which you will study in Chapter 5. The landlord's inheritance is his right to regain possession of the land when the lease terminates, a right that can be inherited from him. He can also sell it or give it away, if he wants to, or lose it to creditors if he does not pay his debts. — EDS.

interference." Yet the court reversed the judgment for defendant, holding that the landlords had a claim for "injury done to the inheritance" pursuant to section 826 because the disposed concrete constituted waste. . . .

. . . [W]e adopt the distinction . . . between a suit to protect an "ownership interest" under Civil Code section 826 on the one hand, and a suit to protect possessory interests, such as an action in trespass on the other hand. . . .

. . . [H]ere, the interest which defendant Brown seeks to protect is wholly and essentially the right to possession. It is that stick in the bundle of rights which gives Brown the power to prevent others from entering his property—*quare clausum fregit*.[27] The injury to be prevented is entry onto defendant's property for the period of the prescription, causing plaintiff's use to ripen into a right. To protect that interest, defendant must bring an action in trespass or ejectment. . . .

. . . [A]ll of the cases dealing with section 826 of the Civil Code construe "injury done to the inheritance" as transitory, physical injury to the land itself, such as the laying of railroad tracks (Thompson v. Pacific Electric Ry. Co. (Cal. 1928) 265 P. 220); the diversion of water causing crops to wither (Heilbron v. Water Ditch Co. (Cal. 1888) 17 P. 65); and the dumping of concrete wash-out (Smith v. Cap Concrete, Inc., *supra*). Such is not the type of harm asserted here. Indeed, in *Thompson*, the court contemplated, just as we do here, that an injury under Civil Code section 826 would be physical harm to the land, stating that section 826 had no applicability for the landlord because "There is no conclusive presumption that if the [railroad] tracks are removed or abandoned on the falling in of the life estate, an injury has resulted to the inheritance."

Thus, Brown, lacking a present possessory interest in the property, was legally unable to bring an action to prevent plaintiff from gaining the easement by prescription. . . .

The judgment appealed from is affirmed as against defendant Terminal Station, but reversed as to defendant Brown. Each party shall bear its own costs on appeal. Otherwise, it is a pleasure to compliment counsel on both sides for the excellent briefing they provided the court. Such quality is rare these days.

Notes and Questions

1. *Future interests and the law of waste.* This case gives you a preview of a subject you will study in more depth in Chapters 5 and 6. Although you may find some of the concepts difficult at this point, the case is included here because it illustrates so clearly the principle that the adverse possessor acquires no more than what the person entitled to possession had at the time the adverse possessor went into possession of the property, or began using the property in the case of a prescriptive easement. If the adverse possessor has the misfortune to possess or use property held by a lessee or life tenant, the adverse possessor will get no more than the balance of the lease term or life estate. A life estate is the right to possess property

---

27.   *Quare clausum fregit* in Latin literally means "whereby he broke the close." It is used to describe trespass committed by making an unauthorized entry on land in possession of another. — EDS.

during someone's lifetime (that person is called the life tenant). When the life tenant dies, the "remaindermen" or "reversioners" have the right to possession.

The law of waste is designed to protect the landlord's or remainderman's interest in future possession—to prevent the lessee or life tenant from using up the value of the property by, for example, cutting the timber, extracting the minerals, or destroying the buildings on the property. Waste is an old, fairly crude, body of law designed to protect the capital value of the property, not to allow the landlord to interfere with the tenant's decisions to ignore or acquiesce in the use of the property by others during the lease term.

2. To test your understanding of the principle underlying *Dieterich,* suppose that O died in 1980, leaving Blackacre to her husband for life, with remainder on his death to their children. AP took possession of Blackacre in 1985. Assume that the statute of limitations is 10 years, and that the husband is still alive. What does AP have? What will happen when the husband dies?

Suppose, instead, that AP took possession of Blackacre, owned by O, in 1990. In 1995, O died, leaving Blackacre to her husband for life, with remainder on his death to their children. When will AP acquire title to Blackacre?

3. Why did Dieterich claim an easement rather than a possessory interest? There are two reasons. First, adverse possession normally requires use that excludes use by the owner of the property, and Terminal Station's customers were using the same area that Dieterich used throughout the prescriptive period. Second, successful claims of adverse possession in California require payment of property taxes for the five-year statutory period. Cal. Civ. Proc. Code § 325. As a result, few claims of adverse possession are made. However, the requirement does not apply to acquisition of more limited use rights (easements) by prescription. Recent cases have rebuffed attempts to subvert the tax payment requirement by claiming prescriptive easements that would give use rights equivalent to possession. *See, e.g., Silacci v. Abramson,* 53 Cal. Rptr. 2d 37 (Ct. App. 1996) (no prescriptive easement for 1,600 square feet of neighbor's property fenced in and used as backyard).

4. The principle that an adverse possessor or prescriptive user cannot acquire more than the interest of the person presently entitled to possession of the property also applies to easements and covenants that burden the property. For example, if AP acquires title to Blackacre, which was subject to an easement giving the owner of Whiteacre the right to use the driveway across Blackacre, the title AP acquires is subject to that easement. The same is true if Blackacre is subject to a covenant prohibiting nonresidential use of the property. The only way AP can take free of these servitudes (the generic name for easements and covenants) is to obstruct the easement or violate the covenant for the statutory period. By the same token, however, AP also acquires the benefits of servitudes that are "appurtenant" to Blackacre. (Appurtenant servitudes are ones that are created to benefit particular land; the benefit runs right along with the title of the property into the hands of subsequent purchasers and other successors.) So, if there was an easement giving the holder of Blackacre the right to maintain an electric utility line across Whiteacre, and a covenant giving the holder of Blackacre the right to prevent use of Whiteacre for nonresidential uses when AP entered, AP would get those too, along with title to Blackacre at the end of the statutory period.

C. ADVERSE POSSESSION OF CHATTELS AND PRESERVATION OF CULTURAL HERITAGE

AUTOCEPHALOUS GREEK-ORTHODOX CHURCH OF CYPRUS v. GOLDBERG & FELDMAN FINE ARTS, INC.

United States Court of Appeals, Seventh Circuit
917 F.2d 278 (7th Cir. 1990), cert. denied, 502 U.S. 941 (1991)

BAUER, C.J.

> There is a temple in ruin stands,
> Fashion'd by long forgotten hands;
> Two or three columns, and many a stone,
> Marble and granite, with grass o'ergrown!
> Out upon Time! it will leave no more
> Of the things to come than the things before!
> Out upon Time! who for ever will leave
> But enough of the past and the future to grieve
> O'er that which hath been, and o'er that which must be:
> What we have seen, our sons shall see;
> Remnants of things that have pass'd away,
> Fragments of stone, rear'd by creatures of clay!

from *The Siege of Corinth*, George Gordon (Lord Byron)[1]

Byron, writing here of the Turkish invasion of Corinth in 1715, could as well have been describing the many churches and monuments that today lie in ruins on Cyprus . . . . In this appeal, we consider the fate of several tangible victims of Cyprus' turbulent history; specifically, four Byzantine mosaics created over 1400 years ago. The district court awarded possession of these extremely valuable mosaics to plaintiff-appellee, the Autocephalous Greek-Orthodox Church of Cyprus ("Church of Cyprus" or "Church"). Defendants-appellants, Peg Goldberg and Goldberg & Feldman Fine Arts, Inc. (collectively "Goldberg"), . . . [appeal]. We affirm.

I. BACKGROUND

In the early sixth century, a.d., a large mosaic was affixed to the apse of the Church of the Panagia Kanakaria ("Kanakaria Church") in the village of Lythrankomi, Cyprus. The mosaic, made of small bits of colored glass, depicted Jesus Christ as a young boy in the lap of his mother, the Virgin Mary, who was seated on a throne. Jesus and Mary were attended by two archangels and surrounded by a frieze depicting the twelve apostles. The mosaic was displayed in the Kanakaria Church for centuries, where it became, under the practices of Eastern Orthodox Christianity, sanctified as a holy relic. It survived both the

---

1. *Reprinted in* The Complete Poetical Works of Bryon 384-96 (Cambridge ed. 1933).

vicissitudes of history, . . . (the period of Iconoclasm during which many religious artifacts were destroyed), and, thanks to restoration efforts, the ravages of time.[2]

Testimony before Judge Noland established that the Kanakaria mosaic was one of only a handful of such holy Byzantine relics to survive into the twentieth century. Sadly, however, war came to Cyprus in the 1970s . . . .

The Cypriot people have long been a divided people, approximately three-fourths being of Greek descent and Greek-Orthodox faith, the other quarter of Turkish descent and Muslim faith.[3] No sooner had Cyprus gained independence from British rule in 1960 than . . . [c]ivil disturbances erupted between Greek and Turkish Cypriots, necessitating the introduction of United Nations peacekeeping forces in 1964. . . . Through the 1960s, the Greek Cypriots, concentrated in the southern part of the island, became increasingly estranged from the Turkish Cypriots, concentrated in the north.[4]

The tensions erupted again in 1974. . . . In July, 1974, the civil government of the Republic of Cyprus was replaced by a government controlled by the Greek Cypriot military. In apparent response, on July 20, 1974, Turkey invaded Cyprus from the north. By late August, the Turkish military forces had advanced to occupy approximately the northern third of the island. The point at which the invading forces stopped is called the "Green Line." To this day, the heavily-guarded Green Line bisects Nicosia, the capital of the Republic, and splits the island from east to west. . . .

Lythrankomi is in the northern portion of Cyprus that came under Turkish rule. Although the village and the Kanakaria Church were untouched by the invading forces in 1974, the villagers of Greek ancestry were soon thereafter "enclaved" by the Turkish military. Despite the hostile environment, the pastor and priests of the Kanakaria Church continued for two years to conduct religious services for the Greek Cypriots who remained in Lythrankomi. . . . [T]hese clerics, and virtually all remaining Greek Cypriots, were forced to flee to southern Cyprus in the summer of 1976. . . .

When the priests evacuated the Kanakaria Church in 1976, the mosaic was still intact. . . . In November, 1979, a resident of northern Cyprus brought word to the Republic's Department of Antiquities that . . . [v]andals had plundered the church, removing anything of value from its interior. The mosaic, or at least its most recognizable and valuable parts, had been forcibly ripped from the apse of the church. Once a place of worship, the Kanakaria Church had been reduced to a stable for farm animals.

Upon learning of the looting of the Kanakaria Church and the loss of its mosaics (made plural by the vandals' axes), the Republic of Cyprus took immediate steps to recover them[,] . . . contacting and seeking assistance from many organizations and individuals, including the United Nations Educational, Scientific and Cultural Organization ("UNESCO"); the International Council

---

2.   For more on the history, significance and restoration of the Kanakaria mosaic, *see* A. Megaw & E. Hawkins, The Church of the Panagia Kanakaria at Lythrankomi in Cyprus: Its Mosaics and Frescoes (1977).

3.   For a full treatment of the pre-independence history of Cyprus, *see* Hill, A History of Cyprus (4 vols.) (1949).

4.   This anxious period of Cypriot history is examined in T. Ehrlich, *Cyprus, the "Warlike Isle": Origins and Elements of the Current Crisis*, 18 Stan. L. Rev. 1021 (1996).

of Museums; the International Council of Museums and Sites; Europa Nostra (an organization devoted to the conservation of the architectural heritage of Europe); the Council of Europe; international auction houses such as Christie's and Sotheby's; Harvard University's Dumbarton Oaks Institute for Byzantine Studies; and the foremost museums, curators and Byzantine scholars throughout the world. The Republic's United States Embassy also routinely disseminated information about lost cultural properties to journalists, U.S. officials and scores of scholars, architects and collectors in this country, asking for assistance in recovering the mosaics. The overall strategy behind these efforts was to get word to the experts and scholars who would probably be involved in any ultimate sale of the mosaics. These individuals, it was hoped, would be the most likely (only?) actors in the chain of custody of stolen cultural properties who would be interested in helping the Republic and Church of Cyprus recover them.

The Republic's efforts have paid off. In recent years, the Republic has recovered and returned to the Church of Cyprus several stolen relics and antiquities. The Republic has even located frescoes and other works taken from the Kanakaria Church, including the four mosaics at issue here. These four mosaics, each measuring about two feet square, depict the figure of Jesus, the busts of one of the attending archangels, the apostle Matthew and the apostle James. . . .

Peg Goldberg is an art dealer and gallery operator. Goldberg and Feldman Fine Arts, Inc., is the Indiana corporation that owns her gallery in Carmel, Indiana. In the summer of 1988, Peg Goldberg went to Europe to shop for works for her gallery. Although her main interest is 20th century paintings, etchings and sculptures, Goldberg was enticed while in The Netherlands by Robert Fitzgerald, another Indiana art dealer and "casual friend" of hers, to consider the purchase of "four early Christian mosaics." In that connection, Fitzgerald arranged a meeting in Amsterdam for July 1st. At that meeting, Fitzgerald introduced Goldberg to Michel van Rijn, a Dutch art dealer, and Ronald Faulk, a California attorney. . . . All she knew about them was what she learned in their few meetings, which included the fact that van Rijn, a published expert on Christian icons (she was given a copy of the book), had been convicted by a French court for art forgery; that he claimed to be a descendant of both Rembrandt and Rubens; and that Faulk was in Europe to represent Fitzgerald and van Rijn.

At that first meeting . . . van Rijn showed Goldberg photographs of the four mosaics at issue in this case and told her that the seller wanted $3 million for them. Goldberg testified that she immediately "fell in love" with the mosaics. Van Rijn told her that the seller was a Turkish antiquities dealer who had "found" the mosaics in the rubble of an "extinct" church in northern Cyprus while working as an archaeologist "assigned (by Turkey) to northern Cyprus." (Goldberg knew of the Turkish invasion of Cyprus and of the subsequent division of the island.) As to the seller, Goldberg was also told that he had exported the mosaics to his home in Munich, Germany with the permission of the Turkish Cypriot government, and that he was now interested in selling the mosaics quickly because he had a "cash problem." Goldberg was not initially given the seller's identity. Goldberg also learned that Faulk, on behalf of Fitzgerald and van Rijn, had already met with this as-yet-unidentified seller to discuss the sale of these mosaics. Her interest quite piqued, Goldberg asked Faulk to return to Munich and tell the seller—whose identity, she would eventually learn, was Aydin Dikman—that she was interested.

Faulk dutifully took this message to Dikman in Munich, and returned to Amsterdam the following day . . . with a contract he signed as agent for van Rijn to purchase the mosaics from Dikman for $350,000. When Goldberg met with Faulk on July 2, she was not told of this contract . . . . Faulk merely informed her that Dikman still had the mosaics (though he was "actively negotiating with another buyer"), and that, in Faulk's opinion the export documents he had been shown by Dikman were in order. Faulk apparently showed Goldberg copies of a few of these documents, none of which, of course, were genuine, and at least one of which was obviously unrelated to these mosaics.

The next day . . . the principals gathered again in Amsterdam. Goldberg, van Rijn, Fitzgerald and Faulk agreed to "acquire the mosaics for their purchase price of $1,080,000 (U.S.)." The parties agreed to split the profits from any resale of the mosaics as follows: Goldberg 50%; Fitzgerald 22.5%; van Rijn 22.5%; and Faulk 5%. A document to this effect was executed on July 4, 1988. . . .

. . . Goldberg contacted Otto N. Frenzel III, a friend and high-ranking officer at the Merchants National Bank of Indianapolis ("Merchants"), and requested a loan from Merchants of $1.2 million for the purchase of the mosaics. She told Frenzel that she needed $1,080,000 to pay van Rijn and the others, and she required the additional $120,000 to pay for expenses, insurance, restoration and the like. Merchants assured her that financing could be arranged, if she could provide appraisals and other documents substantiating the transaction. With Fitzgerald's and van Rijn's help, Goldberg obtained the appraisals (all three of which valued the mosaics at between $3 and $6 million), and sent them to Merchants. That done, she and Fitzgerald hurried to Geneva, Switzerland, for the transfer of the mosaics, which was to take place on July 5. After arriving in Switzerland, Goldberg learned that her requested loan had been approved by Merchants and the money would be forthcoming, though a few days behind schedule. Her financing secured, Goldberg proceeded to the July 5 meeting as scheduled. She could not yet turn over the money, but she wanted to get a look at what she was buying.

The July 5 meeting was held in the "free port" area of the Geneva airport, an area reserved for items that have not passed through Swiss customs. Faulk and Dikman arrived from Munich with the mosaics, which were stored in crates. Dikman introduced himself to Goldberg and then left; this brief exchange was the only time the two would meet. Goldberg then inspected the four mosaics. She testified that she "was in awe," and that, despite some concern about the mosaics' deteriorating condition, she wanted them "more than ever."

During the few days that Goldberg waited in Switzerland for the money to arrive from Merchants, she placed several telephone calls concerning the mosaics. She testified that she wanted to make sure the mosaics had not been reported stolen, and that no treaties would prevent her from bringing the mosaics into the United States. She called UNESCO's office in Geneva and inquired as to whether any treaties prevented "the removal of items from northern Cyprus in the mid- to late-1970s to Germany," but did not mention the mosaics. She claims also to have called, on advice from an art dealer friend of hers in New York, the International Foundation for Art Research ("IFAR"), an organization that collects information concerning stolen art. She testified that she asked IFAR whether it had any record of a claim to the mosaics, and that, when she called back later as instructed, IFAR told her it did not. Judge Noland clearly doubted the credibility of this testimony, noting, among other things, that neither Goldberg nor

IFAR have any record of any such search. (A formal IFAR search involves a fee and thus generates a bill that would serve as proof that a search was performed.) Judge Noland also questioned Goldberg's testimony that she telephoned customs officials in the United States, Switzerland, Germany and Turkey. The only thing of which Judge Noland was sure was that Goldberg did not contact the Republic of Cyprus or the TRNC [Turkish Republic of Northern Cyprus] (from one of whose lands she knew the mosaics had come); the Church of Cyprus; "Interpol," a European information-sharing network for police forces; nor "a single disinterested expert on Byzantine art."

However Goldberg occupied her time from July 5 to July 7, on the latter date the money arrived. Goldberg took the $1.2 million, reduced to $100 bills and stuffed into two satchels, and met with Faulk and Fitzgerald at the Geneva airport. As arranged, Goldberg kept $120,000 in cash and gave the remaining $1,080,000 to Faulk and Fitzgerald in return for the mosaics. . . . Along with the mosaics, Goldberg received a "General Bill of Sale" issued by Dikman to Goldberg and Feldman Fine Arts, Inc. The following day, July 8, 1988, Goldberg returned to the United States with her prize.

. . . Her friends and business associates in Indiana soon took quite an interest in her purchase; literally. For large sums of money, Frenzel, Goldberg's well-placed friend at Merchants, and another Indiana resident named Dr. Stewart Bick acquired from van Rijn and Fitzgerald substantial interests in the profits from any resale of the mosaics.

Peg Goldberg's efforts soon turned to . . . the resale of these valuable mosaics. She worked up sales brochures about them, and contacted several other dealers to help her find a buyer. Two of these dealers' searches led them . . . to Dr. Marion True of the Getty Museum in California. When told of these mosaics and their likely origin, the aptly-named Dr. True explained to the dealers that she had a working relationship with the Republic of Cyprus and that she was duty-bound to contact Cypriot officials about them. Dr. True called . . . the Director of the Republic's Department of Antiquities and one of the primary Cypriot officials involved in the worldwide search for the mosaics . . . [who] verified that the Republic was in fact hunting for the mosaics . . . and he set in motion the investigative and legal machinery that ultimately resulted in the Republic learning that they were in Goldberg's possession in Indianapolis.

After their request for the return of the mosaics was refused by Goldberg, the Republic of Cyprus and the Church of Cyprus (collectively "Cyprus") brought this suit in the Southern District of Indiana for the recovery of the mosaics. Judge Noland bifurcated the possession and damages issues and held a bench trial on the former. In a detailed, thorough opinion (that occupies thirty-one pages in the *Federal Supplement*), Judge Noland awarded possession of the mosaics to the Church of Cyprus. Goldberg filed a timely appeal.

II.   ANALYSIS . . .

B.   Choice of Law

As a federal court sitting in diversity, the district court was obligated to (and did) apply the law of the state in which it sat—Indiana. This included Indiana law as to which body of substantive law to apply to the case, *i.e.*, Indiana's choice of law rules. . . . Because we find Judge Noland's analysis under Indiana law to be free of error, we affirm his conclusion that Indiana law applies without reaching his discussion of Swiss law.

The district court properly considered Cyprus' suit to recover the mosaics a replevin action . . . .

C.   *Statute of Limitations*

With great zeal, Goldberg . . . challenged the timeliness of Cyprus' complaint. Under Indiana's statute of limitations . . . Cyprus had six years from the time its cause of action accrued . . . to sue for the recovery of the mosaics. . . . Though the exact date of the looting of the Kanakaria Church is unknown, it is agreed that Cyprus first learned of the theft of their mosaics in November, 1979. It is also agreed that Cyprus first learned that the mosaics were in Goldberg's possession in late 1988. If Cyprus' cause of action accrued on the former date, their complaint, filed in March, 1989, was untimely. If . . . it accrued on the latter date (or at any other point after March, 1983), their complaint was timely. . . . [W]hen did Cyprus' cause of action "accrue" . . . [?]

. . . Indiana courts start with the following general rule: A cause of action accrues when the plaintiff ascertains, or by due diligence could ascertain, actionable damages. Several Indiana decisions have recognized, as a corollary to this general rule, a "discovery rule" for the accrual of a cause of action; to wit, "the statute of limitations commences to run 'from the date plaintiff knew or should have discovered that she suffered an injury or impingement, and that it was caused by the product or act of another.'" . . .

Apart from but related to the discovery rule, Indiana recognizes, by both statute and case law, the doctrine of fraudulent concealment. Under this doctrine, a defendant who has by deceit or fraud prevented a potential plaintiff from learning of a cause of action cannot take advantage of his wrongdoing by raising the statute of limitations as a bar to plaintiff's action. . . .[11] Central to both the discovery rule and the doctrine of fraudulent concealment is the determination of the plaintiff's diligence in investigating the potential cause of action. . . .

Applying these Indiana rules and principles to this case, and unguided by any directly analogous Indiana precedent, Judge Noland concluded that an Indiana court would find that Cyprus' action was timely filed. His primary ground . . . was his determination that, under a discovery rule, Cyprus' cause of action did not accrue until Cyprus learned from Dr. True that the mosaics were in Goldberg's possession in Indiana. In so holding, he looked not only to Indiana cases but also to general discovery rule principles . . . and to O'Keeffe v. Snyder, 416 A.2d 862 (N.J. 1980), a decision of the New Jersey Supreme Court addressing the accrual of a cause of action in the context of a replevin action involving a work of art. (In *O'Keeffe*, the court held that artist Georgia O'Keeffe's cause

---

11.   Judge Noland also discusses the doctrine, recognized by Indiana courts, of equitable estoppel. As this doctrine is identical in all respects relevant here to the statutory doctrine of fraudulent concealment . . . and as the application of the discovery rule alone adequately resolves the issue in this case, we will not explore further this equitable doctrine.

of action for replevin of three paintings stolen from a gallery in 1946 accrued "when she first knew, or reasonably should have known through the exercise of due diligence, of the cause of action, including the identity of the possessor of the paintings.") Further, Judge Noland found, as a necessary precondition to the application of the discovery rule, that Cyprus exercised due diligence in searching for the mosaics. Thus, Judge Noland ruled that Cyprus was not, nor reasonably should have been, on notice as to the possessor or location of the mosaics until late 1988.

Goldberg attacks Judge Noland's discovery rule analysis on two grounds. First, she charges that in applying the discovery rule in this case Judge Noland "announced a new rule of Indiana law in conflict with established Indiana limitations principles." Not so. Judge Noland applied legal principles set out in Indiana cases, and generally accepted elsewhere, to a new situation not yet addressed by the Indiana courts, exactly what a district court sitting in diversity is obligated to do when presented with a novel issue under state law. . . . Further, his conclusion that in this case the operative "discovery" had to include the identity of the holder of the mosaics is eminently sound. In the context of a replevin action for particular, unique and concealed works of art, a plaintiff cannot be said to have "discovered" his cause of action until he learns enough facts to form its basis, which must include the fact that the works are being held by another and who, or at least where, that "other" is. Further, we note that any "laziness" this rule might at first blush invite on the part of plaintiffs is heavily tempered by the requirement that, all the while, the plaintiff must exercise due diligence to investigate the theft and recover the works.

Second, Goldberg attacks Judge Noland's due diligence finding. Specifically, she argues that Cyprus failed to contact several organizations it should have, particularly IFAR and Interpol. She also repeats the argument she made to Judge Noland that events occurring before the end of 1983[12] should have started the clock ticking on Cyprus' cause of action, with particular emphasis on an article that appeared in a Turkish newspaper. We note first that the due diligence determination is . . . highly "fact-sensitive and must be decided on a case-by-case basis." Although Goldberg cites some support for a de novo standard of review on this issue, *see* DeWeerth v. Baldinger, 836 F.2d 103 (2d Cir. 1987), *cert. denied*, 486 U.S. 1056 (1988), we ordinarily review determinations such as this, which involve the application of law to facts, under the "clearly erroneous" standard. . . . Under any standard of review, however, Judge Noland's due diligence determination must be affirmed.

The record evidence . . . makes it clear that, although the Republic of Cyprus may not have contacted all the organizations Goldberg in hindsight would require, it took substantial and meaningful steps, from the time it first learned of the disappearance of the mosaics, to locate and recover them. The efforts by the Republic's officials, targeted at the likely points of sale of the mosaics, were sweeping and consistent with trade practices. Indeed, one expert, a curator from The Walters Art Gallery in Baltimore, Maryland, testified at trial that Cyprus "stands

---

12.   Note that any events occurring after 1983, including the acquisition in 1984 by the Menil Foundation in Texas of other Kanakaria mosaic fragments and frescoes from Dikman (of which Goldberg makes much), even if they triggered the accrual of Cyprus' six-year statute of limitations, would not make Cyprus' March, 1989 complaint untimely.

apart" in its efforts to recover stolen cultural properties. As to Goldberg's repetition here of her arguments regarding the article in the Turkish publication and the other events, the record adequately supports Judge Noland's conclusion that these events did not nor should not have put Cyprus on notice as to a possible cause of action. The article, which fingered Dikman as a man wanted in Cyprus and Turkey for smuggling artifacts and later mentioned the mosaics from the Kanakaria Church, did not reveal that Dikman might be in possession of the mosaics . . . . What's more, the record reveals that, upon learning of such Turkish press reports, Cyprus redoubled its efforts at notification and recovery. . . . Judge Noland's conclusion that Cyprus was duly diligent and should not have discovered its cause of action before late 1988 stands on firm factual footing. Goldberg's fervent attack on this conclusion at most establishes that an alternative view of the evidence was plausible, which is not enough to merit our disturbing it.

D.   The Merits of the Replevin Claim

Under Indiana law, replevin is an action at law . . . . To recover the item sought to be replevied, (which is the primary remedy in a replevin action), the plaintiff must establish three elements: "his title or right to possession, that the property is unlawfully detained, and that the defendant wrongfully holds possession." 25 I.L.E. *Replevin* § 42.

Judge Noland applied these elements to the facts of this case and determined that Cyprus had met its burden as to each. Our review of this application of Indiana law to the facts convinces us that it is free of error: 1) the Kanakaria Church was and is owned by the Holy Archbishopric of the Church of Cyprus, a self-headed (hence "Autocephalous") church associated with the Greek-Orthodox faith; 2) the mosaics were removed from the Kanakaria Church without the authorization of the Church or the Republic (even the TRNC's unsuccessful motion to intervene claimed that the mosaics were improperly removed); and 3) Goldberg, as an ultimate purchaser from a thief, has no valid claim of title or right to possession of the mosaics.

We note that Judge Noland . . . backstopped his conclusion, . . . conducting an alternative analysis under Swiss substantive law. Briefly, the court concluded that the Church had superior title under Swiss law as well, because Goldberg could not claim valid title under the Swiss "good faith purchasers" notion having only made a cursory inquiry into the suspicious circumstances surrounding the sale of the mosaics. (Under Indiana law, such considerations are irrelevant because, except in very limited exceptions not applicable here, a subsequent purchaser (even a "good faith, bona fide purchaser for value") who obtains an item from a thief only acquires the title held by the thief; that is, no title.) [Because] Indiana law controls every aspect of this action, . . . Judge Noland's extensive (and quite interesting) discussion of Swiss law, as well as Goldberg's lengthy attack thereon, need not be reviewed. . . .

III.   CONCLUSION

As Byron's poem laments, war can reduce our grandest and most sacred temples to mere "fragments of stone." Only the lowest of scoundrels attempt to reap personal gain from this collective loss. Those who plundered the churches and monuments of war-torn Cyprus, hoarded their relics away, and are now smuggling and selling them for large sums, are just such blackguards. The Republic of Cyprus, with diligent effort and the help of friends like Dr. True, has been able to locate several of these stolen antiquities; items of vast cultural, religious (and, as this case demonstrates, monetary) value. . . . Unfortunately, when these mosaics surfaced they were in the hands not of the most guilty parties, but of Peg Goldberg and her gallery. . . . [T]he district court determined that Goldberg must return the mosaics to their rightful owner: the Church of Cyprus. Goldberg's tireless attacks have not established reversible error in that determination, and thus, for the reasons discussed above, the district court's judgment is AFFIRMED.

Lest this result seem too harsh, we should note that those who wish to purchase art work on the international market, undoubtedly a ticklish business, are not without means by which to protect themselves. Especially when circumstances are as suspicious as those that faced Peg Goldberg, prospective purchasers would do best to do more than make a few last-minute phone calls. As testified to at trial, in a transaction like this, "All the red flags are up, all the red lights are on, all the sirens are blaring." In such cases, dealers can (and probably should) take steps such as a formal IFAR search; a documented authenticity check by disinterested experts; a full background search of the seller and his claim of title; insurance protection and a contingency sales contract; and the like. If Goldberg would have pursued such methods, perhaps she would have discovered in time what she has now discovered too late: The Church has a valid, superior and enforceable claim to these Byzantine treasures, which therefore must be returned to it.

CUDAHY, C.J., concurring. . . . A second and unrelated, but important, aspect of this case involves the treatment of the cultural heritage of foreign nations under international and United States law. The United States has both acceded to international agreements and enacted its own statutes regarding the importation of cultural property. These regulatory efforts have encompassed transfers of property during both wartime and peacetime and apply whether the property was originally stolen or "merely" illegally exported from the country of origin. The two most significant international agreements that attempt to protect cultural property are the 1954 Convention on the Protection of Cultural Property in the Event of Armed Conflict (the "1954 Hague Convention") . . . and the UNESCO Convention on the Means of Prohibiting and Preventing the Illicit Transport, Export and Transfer of Ownership of Cultural Property . . . .

Under both these multinational treaties, as well as under the United States' Convention on Cultural Property Implementation Act, 19 U.S.C. § 2601 et seq. (1983), the Cypriot mosaics would be considered cultural property warranting international protection. . . . The UNESCO Convention and the Cultural Property Implementation Act constitute an effort to instill respect for the cultural property and heritage of all peoples. The mosaics before us are of great intrinsic beauty. They are the virtually unique remnants of an earlier artistic period and should be returned to their homeland and their rightful owner. This is the case not only because the mosaics belong there, but as a reminder that greed and callous disregard for the property, history and culture of others cannot be countenanced by the world community or by this court.

Notes and Questions

1. If Peg Goldberg had been a good-faith purchaser—for example, if she had purchased the mosaics from a reputable dealer with assurances that they had been legally obtained—would she, or should she, have been protected?

2. *International protection of cultural heritage.* UNESCO manages the 1954 Hague Convention (the Convention for the Protection of Cultural Property in the Event of Armed Conflict), and its Protocols, the 1970 Convention on the Means of Prohibiting and Preventing the Illicit Import, Export and Transfer of Ownership of Cultural Property, and the 1972 Convention on Protection of the World Cultural and Natural Heritage. *See* Anthi Helleni Poulos, *The 1954 Hague Convention for the Protection of Cultural Property in the Event of Armed Conflict: An Historic Analysis,* 28 Int'l J. Legal Info. 1 (2000). For a review of common law, civil law, and the UNIDROIT convention for the international protection of cultural property, see Adina Kurjatko, *Are Finders Keepers? The Need for a Uniform Law Governing the Rights of Original Owners and Good Faith Purchasers of Stolen Art,* 5 U.C. Davis J. Int'l L. & Pol'y 59 (1999).

3. Protecting and returning items of cultural heritage to their places of origin has generated an enormous amount of interest since the decision in the Kanakaria mosaics case. Greece, Italy, Egypt, Turkey, Cambodia and other source countries have increasingly pressed claims against museums and auction houses in the United States and Europe to return objects they claim were looted or otherwise unlawfully removed from their place of origin. One of the earlier and most famous claims is for the return of the Elgin marbles taken from the Parthenon in the early 19th century and purchased for the British Museum in 1816. Seeking return of antiquities held by the Getty Museum in Los Angeles, the Italian government pressed criminal charges against Dr. Marion True. The trial began in 2005 and continued until dismissed when the Italian statute of limitations ran out in 2010. The Getty ultimately returned 40 pieces to Italy. Jason Felch and Ralph Frammolino, then reporters for the Los Angeles Times, wrote a book about the Getty's questionable practices in acquiring antiquities and about Dr. True's role as the museum's curator of antiquities, *Chasing Aphrodite, The Hunt for Looted Antiquities at the World's Richest Museum* (2011), and now maintain a website at www.chasingaphrodite.com that reports on the hunt for looted antiquities in the world's museums.

4. There is a very substantial literature on protection of cultural property. If you are interested in pursuing the subject, you might start with John Henry, *Thinking About the Elgin Marbles: Critical Essays on Cultural Property, Art and Law* (2000), and Patty Gerstenblith, *Art, Cultural Heritage, and the Law* (3d ed. 2012). The Lawyers' Committee for Cultural Heritage Preservation maintains a website with current information about activities in the field at www.culturalheritagelaw.org.

SOLOMON R. GUGGENHEIM FOUNDATION v. LUBELL

Court of Appeals of New York
567 N.Y.S.2d 623 (N.Y. 1991)

The backdrop for this replevin action is the New York City art market, where masterpieces command extraordinary prices at auction and illicit dealing in stolen merchandise is an industry all its own. The Solomon R. Guggenheim Foundation, which operates the Guggenheim Museum in New York City, is seeking to recover a Chagall gouache worth an estimated $200,000 [which it] . . . believes . . . was stolen from its premises by a mailroom employee some-time in the late 1960s. The appellant Rachel Lubell and her husband, now deceased, bought the painting from a well-known Madison Avenue gallery in 1967 and have displayed it in their home for more than 20 years. Mrs. Lubell claims that before the Guggenheim's demand for its return in 1986, she had no reason to believe that the painting had been stolen.

On this appeal, we must decide if the museum's failure to take certain steps to locate the gouache is relevant to the appellant's Statute of Limitations defense. . . . [T]he appellant argues that the museum had a duty to use reasonable diligence to recover the gouache, that it did not do so, and that its cause of action in replevin is consequently barred by the Statute of Limitations. The Appellate Division rejected the appellant's argument. We agree with the Appellate Division that the timing of the museum's demand for the gouache and the appellant's refusal to return it are the only relevant factors in assessing the merits of the Statute of Limitations defense. We see no justification for undermining the clarity and predictability of this rule by carving out an exception where the chattel to be returned is a valuable piece of art. Appellant's affirmative defense of laches remains viable, however, and her claims that the museum did not undertake a reasonably diligent search for the missing painting will enter into the trial court's evaluation of the merits of that defense. . . .

New York case law has long protected the right of the owner whose property has been stolen to recover that property, even if it is in the possession of a good-faith purchaser for value . . . . There is a three-year Statute of Limitations for recovery of a chattel. The rule in this State is that a cause of action for replevin against the good-faith purchaser of a stolen chattel accrues when the true owner makes demand for return of the chattel and the person in possession of the chattel refuses to return it . . . . Until demand is made and refused, possession of the stolen property by the good-faith purchaser for value is not considered wrongful. Although seemingly anomalous, a different rule applies when the stolen object is in the possession of the thief. In that situation, the Statute of Limitations runs from the time of the theft . . . even if the property owner was unaware of the theft at the time that it occurred . . . .

In DeWeerth v. Baldinger, [836 F.2d 103 (2d Cir.)], which the trial court in this case relied upon in granting Mrs. Lubell's summary judgment motion, the Second Circuit took note of the fact that New York case law treats thieves and good-faith purchasers differently and looked to that difference as a basis for imposing a reasonable diligence requirement on the owners of stolen art. Although the court acknowledged that the question posed by the case was an open one, it declined to certify it to this Court . . . stating that it did not think that it "[would] recur with sufficient frequency to warrant use of the certification procedure." Actually, the issue has recurred several times in the three years since DeWeerth was decided (see, e.g., Republic of Turkey v. Metropolitan Museum of Art, [S.D.N.Y. July 16, 1990]), including the case now before us. We have reexamined the relevant New York case law and we conclude that the Second Circuit should not have imposed a duty of reasonable diligence on the owners of stolen art work for purposes of the Statute of Limitations.

While the demand and refusal rule is not the only possible method of measuring the accrual of replevin claims, it does appear to be the rule that affords the most protection to the true owners of stolen property. Less protective measures would include running the three-year statutory period from the time of the theft even where a good-faith purchaser is in possession of the stolen chattel, or, alternatively, calculating the statutory period from the time that the good-faith purchaser obtains possession of the chattel . . . . Other States that have considered this issue have applied a discovery rule to these cases . . . .

New York has already considered—and rejected—adoption of a discovery rule. In 1986, both houses of the New York State Legislature passed Assembly Bill 11462-A, which would have modified the demand and refusal rule and instituted a discovery rule in actions for recovery of art objects brought against certain not-for-profit institutions. This bill provided that the three-year Statute of Limitations would run from the time these institutions gave notice, in a manner specified by the statute, that they were in possession of a particular object. Governor Cuomo vetoed the measure, however, on advice of the United States Department of State, the United States Department of Justice and the United States Information Agency . . . . In his veto message, the Governor expressed his concern that the statute "[did] not provide a reasonable opportunity for individuals or foreign governments to receive notice of a museum's acquisition and take action to recover it before their rights are extinguished." The Governor also stated that he had been advised by the State Department that the bill, if it went into effect, would have caused New York to become "a haven for cultural property stolen abroad since such objects [would] be immune from recovery under the limited time periods established by the bill."

The history of this bill and the concerns expressed by the Governor in vetoing it, when considered together with the abundant case law spelling out the demand and refusal rule, convince us that that rule remains the law in New York and that there is no reason to obscure its straightforward protection of true owners by creating a duty of reasonable diligence. Our case law already recognizes that the true owner, having discovered the location of its lost property, cannot unreasonably delay making demand upon the person in possession of that property . . . . Here, however, where the demand and refusal is a substantive and not a procedural element of the cause of action . . . it would not be prudent to extend that case law and impose the additional duty of diligence before the true owner has reason to know where its missing chattel is to be found.

Further, the facts of this case reveal how difficult it would be to specify the type of conduct that would be required for a showing of reasonable diligence. . . . [T]he parties hotly contest whether publicizing the theft would have turned up the gouache. According to the museum, some members of the art community believe that publicizing a theft exposes gaps in security and can lead to more thefts; the museum also argues that publicity often pushes a missing painting further underground. In light of the fact that members of the art community have apparently not reached a consensus on the best way to retrieve stolen art . . . it would be particularly inappropriate for this Court to spell out arbitrary rules of conduct that all true owners of stolen art work would have to follow to . . . preserve their right to pursue a cause of action in replevin. . . . The value of the property stolen, the manner in which it was stolen, and the type of institution from which it was stolen will all necessarily affect the manner in which a true owner will search for missing property. . . . [I]t would be difficult, if not impossible, to craft a reasonable diligence requirement that could take into account all of these variables and that would not unduly burden the true owner.

Further, our decision today is in part influenced by our recognition that New York enjoys a worldwide reputation as a preeminent cultural center. To place the burden of locating stolen artwork on the true owner and to foreclose the rights of that owner to recover its property if the burden is not met would, we believe, encourage illicit trafficking in stolen art. Three years after the theft, any purchaser, good faith or not, would be able to hold onto stolen art work unless the true owner was able to establish that it had undertaken a reasonable search for the missing art. This shifting of the burden onto the wronged owner is inappropriate. In our opinion, the better rule gives the owner relatively greater protection and places the burden of investigating the provenance of a work of art on the potential purchaser.

. . . [O]ur holding today should not be seen as either sanctioning the museum's conduct or suggesting that the museum's conduct is no longer an issue in this case. We agree with the Appellate Division that the arguments raised in the appellant's summary judgment papers are directed at the conscience of the court and its ability to bring equitable considerations to bear in the ultimate disposition of the painting. . . . [A]lthough appellant's Statute of Limitations argument fails, her contention that the museum did not exercise reasonable diligence in locating the painting will be considered by the Trial Judge in the context of her laches defense. The conduct of both the appellant and the museum will be relevant to any consideration of this defense at the trial level, and prejudice will also need to be shown . . . . On the limited record before us there is no indication that the equities favor either party. . . .

We agree with the Appellate Division, for the reasons stated by that court, that the burden of proving that the painting was not stolen properly rests with the appellant Mrs. Lubell. . . . [T]he order of the Appellate Division should be affirmed, with costs, and the certified question answered in the affirmative.

Notes and Questions

1. Why does the New York Court of Appeal reject the discovery rule adopted by the New Jersey Supreme Court in *O'Keeffe v. Snyder*, 418 A.2d 862 (N.J. 1980), and applied by the court in the Kanakaria mosaics case? Which is the better rule, the discovery rule or the demand rule?

2. California adopted a discovery rule by statute. Cal. Civ. Proc. Code § 338(c)(2), which sets a three-year limit on an action for taking, detaining, or injuring any goods or chattels, including actions for the specific recovery of personal property, provides: "The cause of action in the case of theft . . . of any article of historical, interpretive, scientific, or artistic significance is not deemed to have accrued until the discovery of the whereabouts of the article by the aggrieved party, his or her agent, or the law enforcement agency which originally investigated the theft." In 2010, § 338(c)(3)(A) was added to the statute, providing a six-year period for bringing actions to recover works of fine art, but only for actions filed before December 31, 2017. The period begins to run only after actual discovery of the identity and whereabouts of the work and information "sufficient to indicate that the claimant has a claim for a possessory interest in the work . . . ." The statute specifies that actual knowledge does not include any constructive knowledge imputed by law.

3. These decisions have sparked a fair amount of scholarly interest. A few of the articles include Patricia Youngblood Reyhan, *A Chaotic Palette: Conflict of Laws in Litigation Between Original Owners and Good-Faith Purchasers of Stolen Art,* 50 Duke L.J. 955 (2001); Ashton Hawkins et al., *A Tale of Two Innocents: Creating an Equitable Balance Between the Rights of Former Owners and Good Faith Purchasers of Stolen Art,* 64 Fordham L. Rev. 49 (1995); Alexandre A. Montagu, *Recent Cases on the Recovery of Stolen Art — The Tug of War Between Owners and Good Faith Purchasers Continues,* 18 Colum.-VLA J.L. & Arts 75 (1993-94); Steven A. Bibas, Note, *The Case Against Statutes of Limitations for Stolen Art,* 103 Yale L.J. 2437 (1994); Andrea E. Hayworth, Note, *Stolen Artwork: Deciding Ownership Is No Pretty Picture,* 43 Duke L.J. 337 (1993).

4. Peg Goldberg took a big risk when she purchased the mosaics in the Geneva airport, but Mrs. Lubell clearly was a good-faith purchaser from an established art gallery. Is there anything more Mrs. Lubell could have done to protect herself? What protection does the court's ruling offer her? As you will see when you study transactions in land, substantial protection is routinely afforded to good-faith purchasers through the public land records, the recording acts, and title insurance. A person who buys land may obtain a search of the records to determine outstanding claims and takes free of claims that are not recorded. Purchasers of automobiles are afforded even more protection because claims are listed right on the title. An Art Loss Register, which has been operating in the United States since 1991, lists stolen art that has been reported to the police and is uniquely describable, and conducts searches. Should this register be treated like the land records so that theft victims who register their losses can recover from subsequent purchasers, and purchasers take free of unregistered claims? *See* Tarquin Preziosi, *Applying a Strict Discovery Rule to Art Stolen in the Past,* 49 Hastings L.J. 225 (1997), for a review and critique of current treatment of art theft. *See also* Kenneth Hamma, *Finding Cultural Property Online,* 19 Cardozo Arts & Ent. L.J. 125 (2001).

5. In the early 1970s, master recordings of performances by New Orleans musician "Professor Longhair" (Henry Roeland Byrd) came into the possession of Bearsville, located in Woodstock, N.Y. Byrd representatives made several requests for return of the tapes, but Bearsville apparently did not respond and retained possession. In 1987 and 1991 albums from the Byrd recordings, produced under license from Bearsville, were released. Songbyrd, Inc., a successor to Byrd's interests, sued in 1995, claiming that New York's three-year statute of limitations had not run because Bearsville had never refused its demands. Held: *Guggenheim* did not apply; the statute began to run when Bearsville converted the recordings because there was no evidence that Bearsville was a good-faith purchaser. *Songbyrd, Inc. v. Estate of Albert B. Grossman,* 23 F. Supp. 2d 219 (N.D.N.Y. 1998). Does treating the wrongdoer better than the good-faith purchaser make sense?

As the court in *Guggenheim* notes, the statute also favors a thief. Does this make sense? Does the thief acquire title at the end of three years? In most states, fraudulent concealment of the property either delays the beginning of the limitations period, or creates a separate cause of action with a separate statute that does not begin until the property is transferred to a bona fide purchaser. If the statute has run in favor of the thief, however, but the thief has not acquired title, what happens next?

6. As a practical matter, does anyone ever acquire title to personal property by adverse possession, even in states that hold the statute of limitations begins to run at the time of the theft or conversion? When the property has been stolen, the answer is often no, either because the possession is not open and notorious, or because the statute did not begin to run while the item was fraudulently concealed. However, if the property has passed into the hands of a bona fide purchaser, who holds openly for the statutory period, the purchaser may win. For an attempt to make sense of this area, see Patty Gerstenblith, *Adverse Possession of Personal Property*, 37 Buff. L. Rev. 119 (1989). She concludes that, apart from the recent discovery rule cases, the primary focus is on the behavior of the possessor, and that good faith and reasonable reliance are the most important elements in establishing adverse possession of personal property. This focus accomplishes two goals: "encouraging ethical conduct and fostering commercial activity." *See also* R.H. Helmholz, *Wrongful Possession of Chattels: Hornbook Law and Case Law*, 80 Nw. U. L. Rev. 1221, 1237 (1986).

ROSNER v. UNITED STATES

United States District Court, S.D. Florida
231 F. Supp. 2d 1202 (2002)

ORDER ON DEFENDANT'S MOTION TO DISMISS

SEITZ, District Judge. THIS CAUSE is before the Court on Defendant's Motion to Dismiss. . . . Plaintiffs bring this class action lawsuit on behalf of Hungarian Jews, and their descendants, whose personal property and valuables they believe were stolen and loaded onto the "Hungarian Gold Train" by the pro-Nazi Hungarian government during World War II, and later seized by the United States Army outside of Salzburg, Austria. Specifically, Plaintiffs' Complaint alleges three counts: (1) unconstitutional taking in violation of the Fifth Amendment to the United States Constitution; (2) breach of an implied-in-fact contract of bailment; and (3) violation of conventional and customary international law.

The Government moves to dismiss on the following grounds: (1) Plaintiffs' Complaint is untimely, and therefore, barred in its entirety by sovereign immunity; (2) Plaintiffs' claim of international law violations (Count III) is barred because Congress has not waived sovereign immunity for such a claim; (3) Plaintiffs' Fifth Amendment claim (Count I) fails to state a claim upon which relief can be granted; and (4) Plaintiffs' claim for breach of an implied-in-fact contract of bailment (Count II) fails to state a claim upon which relief can be granted.

After hearing oral argument on August 22, 2002, and for the reasons stated below, the Government's motion is granted in-part and denied in-part. Specifically, the Court rules as follows: (1) based on the allegations in the Complaint, Plaintiffs' viable claims are not time-barred under the principles of equitable tolling; (2) to the extent that Plaintiffs seek nonmonetary relief pursuant to the Administrative Procedure Act, the international law claim (Count III) is viable; (3) Plaintiffs' Fifth Amendment claim (Count I) fails to state a claim upon which relief can be granted, and thus, will be dismissed with prejudice; and (4) Plaintiffs' claim for breach of an implied-in-fact contract of bailment (Count II) does state a claim upon which relief can be granted.

BACKGROUND

On March 19, 1944, towards the end of World War II, Germany invaded Hungary. Soon thereafter, through a series of discriminatory decrees, the pro-Nazi Hungarian government forced all Jews to turn over their gold, silver, gems, and other personal valuables to the authorities. Ultimately, the Hungarian government decreed that all Jewish-owned wealth and property belonged to the Hungarian government. In the fall and winter of 1944-45, as the prospect of Germany's defeat loomed larger, the Hungarian government, at the direction of the Nazis, loaded the stolen Jewish property onto a train bound for Germany. Because of the value of the train's cargo, the train became known as the "Gold Train." The lengthy train, consisting of over forty cars, made its way from Hungary into Austria, but never made it to German territory.

On or about May 11, 1945, the U.S. Army seized the Gold Train from pro-Nazi Hungarian troops outside of Salzburg, Austria. Due to the war-ravaged conditions of Europe's rail system, the Gold Train remained south of Salzburg, under guard of American troops, for close to three months. In late July 1945, after the railway system was marginally repaired, the train was moved, via U.S. Army locomotive, to the Maglan suburb of Salzburg. From there, the assets on the Gold Train were moved by truck to storage facilities in Salzburg. According to Plaintiffs, the majority of the assets, with the exception of the 1200 paintings, were stored in the Military Government Warehouse. The artwork was stored elsewhere in Salzburg.

Plaintiffs maintain that the property on the Gold Train was identifiable. The items on the train were in locked containers with the names and addresses of the owners on the outside. The Jewish families placed their items in such containers, along with other identifying marks, to enable them to reclaim their belongings.

Additionally, Plaintiffs claim that the Government was in possession of overwhelming circumstantial evidence that the property on the Gold Train belonged to Hungarian Jews and that such property was identifiable. Yet, notwithstanding such evidence, and despite repeated requests from the Hungarian Jewish community, Plaintiffs allege that in the summer of 1946, the United States Government declared that it was not possible to identify either the individual owners of the property or even the appropriate country of ownership. Thereafter, unbeknownst to Plaintiffs or the public, the Government sold, distributed and/or requisitioned the property from the Gold Train. According to Plaintiffs, a majority of the property was sold through the Army Exchange Service or donated to international refugee services, some of the property was used by U.S. military officers as home and office furnishings, and a substantial amount of property was looted from the warehouse in Salzburg.

Plaintiffs do not know the ultimate disposition of the property. Because of the amount of time that has elapsed, combined with the classification of many official documents pertaining to their property, most, if not all of the putative class could not have known about the facts giving rise to this lawsuit. These Plaintiffs maintain it was only in October 1999, when the Presidential Advisory Commission on Holocaust Assets released its Report on the Gold Train, that many of the facts presented in their Complaint came to light.

LEGAL STANDARD

. . . [A] court may dismiss a complaint for failure to state a claim only if it is clear that no relief could be granted under any set of facts that could be proved consistent with the allegations. . . .

LEGAL ANALYSIS

A.   *Sovereign Immunity*

1.   *Statute of Limitations*

As a sovereign, the United States cannot be sued in its own courts unless Congress explicitly authorizes such suit. . . . The applicable statute of limitations for Plaintiffs' claims is six years. . . . Accordingly, the Government argues that because Hungarian Jews knew by at least 1947 that the United States Army had possession of the Gold Train, the limitations period expired no later than 1953. In response, Plaintiffs make two arguments: (1) under the continuing violation doctrine the limitations period has not yet run; and (2) the limitations period should be tolled based on principles of equitable tolling. The continuing violation doctrine is not applicable in this case. Equitable tolling, however, is warranted and thus the Complaint as pled is timely. . . .

(b)   *Equitable Tolling*

The equitable tolling doctrine allows plaintiffs to sue after the expiration of the applicable statute of limitations, provided they have been prevented from doing so due to inequitable circumstances. . . . The Government maintains that because Plaintiffs have not alleged that they were tricked into allowing the filing deadline to pass, and because they did not pursue judicial remedies within the original six-year limitations period, equitable tolling is not permissible. In response, Plaintiffs . . . argue that they have alleged that the Government has kept them ignorant of vital information necessary to pursue their claims, without any fault or lack of due diligence of their part. Alternatively, Plaintiffs maintain that the brutal reality of the Holocaust, and the resulting extraordinary circumstances that Plaintiffs were forced to endure, merits application of equitable tolling in this case.

Recently, the United States Supreme Court stated, "limitations periods are customarily subject to equitable tolling, unless tolling would be inconsistent with the text of the relevant statute." Young v. United States, 535 U.S. 43 (2002) . . . . In particular, the Court stated that equitable tolling is permitted in situations "where the claimant has actively pursued his judicial remedies by filing a defective pleading during the statutory period, *or* where the complainant has been induced or tricked by his adversary's misconduct into allowing the filing deadline to pass." The Court also suggested, however, that "tolling might be appropriate in other cases" as well. Thus, in addition to satisfying one of the Supreme Court's tests mentioned above, equitable tolling may also be warranted based upon certain extraordinary circumstances.

The allegations of the Complaint satisfy the second Supreme Court test, namely, that Plaintiffs were induced or tricked by the Government's misconduct into allowing the filing deadline to pass. Because this issue is arising on a motion to dismiss, the Court must accept as true that "[p]laintiffs and other members of the class have been kept in ignorance of vital information essential to pursue their claims, without any fault or lack of diligence on their part." In particular, Plaintiffs allege that in addition to seizing and subsequently not returning the Gold Train property, the United States Government has also continued to wrongfully claim that the property on the Gold Train was unidentifiable and thus unreturnable. Moreover, Plaintiffs allege that the Government essentially turned a deaf ear to Plaintiffs' repeated requests for information about their property. "It was only in October 1999, when the Presidential Advisory Commission on Holocaust Assets released its report on the Gold Train" that the facts necessary to file their Complaint came to light.[8] (Complaint, ¶ 90).

Taken as true, these allegations present the Court with a set of circumstances that warrant equitable tolling of the limitations period. In addition, the Court notes that, for the majority of Plaintiffs, the years following World War II were particularly difficult. This, combined with the fact that the Government cannot benefit from its own alleged misconduct, tips the balance in favor of tolling the limitations period. Accordingly, at this stage of the proceedings, given the equitable considerations at play in this case, Plaintiffs are entitled to the benefit of equitable tolling and their Complaint is timely. . . .

C. Breach of an Implied-in-Fact Contract of Bailment

. . . Both parties agree that the elements of an implied-in-fact contract are inferred from the parties' conduct and need not be expressly stated. . . . As such, Plaintiffs have alleged that the Government: (1) accepted possession of Plaintiffs' property with the express knowledge that the property belonged to Plaintiffs; (2) never claimed to be the owner of the property; (3) took possession of the property with the express intent of undertaking to return the property to its rightful owners; (4) stored and guarded the property in warehouses for protection so that it could be returned to its rightful owners; (5) indicated, expressly and through applicable laws, that any identifiable property from the Gold Train would be returned in accordance with U.S. policy and custom; and (6) falsely declared that the property was unidentifiable, thus breaching the agreement. Based on these allegations, and without deciding whether Plaintiffs can eventually prove their claim, the Court finds Plaintiffs have alleged sufficient facts to survive a motion to dismiss. Moreover, given the fact intensive

---

8. Accordingly, the limitations period began to run in 1999 and would have expired in 2005.

nature of such a claim, such is more appropriately addressed on summary judgment. . . . Accordingly, at this stage of the proceedings, drawing all reasonable inferences in the nonmovant's favor, the Court must deny the Government's motion to dismiss Count II for failure to state a claim. . . .

Notes and Questions

1. *Equitable tolling.* Compare the discovery, demand and refusal, and equitable tolling approaches to protecting the interests of the true owner. Which of them strikes the best balance between the interests of the owner and the adverse possessor?

2. *Looting and destruction of art during the Nazi era.* To understand the horrendous scope of the Nazi looting and destruction of art before and during World War II, read Lynn H. Nicolas, *The Rape of Europa* (1994), and see both the 2006 documentary of the same name, and the 2014 film *Monuments Men*. Holocaust victims and their descendants have brought many cases in recent years seeking return of looted art. The cases are complicated because they not only involve questions whether they are time-barred, but also questions of foreign sovereign immunity and preemption under the act of state and foreign affairs doctrines that are too complicated to go into in this course. If you are interested, they are covered in courses on art and museum law.

Current Controversies Challenge the Capture, Conquest, and Prescription Doctrines

At the beginning of the 21st century, the western industrialized nations are confronted by situations and claims that challenge the doctrines we have studied in these first two chapters. The capture doctrine, coupled with development of factory fishing boats with miles-long nylon nets and advanced electronic surveillance technology, has led to critical depletion of the ocean's resources. Two-thirds of the world's major fishing areas and stocks are now exhausted or seriously depleted.[28] Rights to land taken from Native American tribes under the doctrines of discovery and conquest, as well as by fraud and treaty manipulation, are increasingly contested by their descendants, who seek return of land, as well as compensation. Cultural artifacts held in both private and public collections are increasingly claimed by victims of the Holocaust, Native American tribes,[29] and countries such as Greece, Italy, Egypt, Turkey, India, Cambodia, and

---

28.   William J. Broad & Andrew C. Revkin, *Has the Sea Given Up Its Bounty?*, N.Y. Times, Science, July 29, 2003 ("More than 70 percent of commercial fish stocks are now considered fully exploited, overfished or collapsed. Sea birds and mammals are endangered. And a growing number of marine species are reaching the precariously low levels where extinction is considered a real possibility." Gary Polakovic, *Saving a Place for Marine Life*, L.A. Times, Aug. 27, 1999, pp. A1, A20, A22, attributes the figure to the United Nations Food and Agriculture Organization. The article reports on a proposal to expand the "no-take" zones in Channel Islands National Park to 25,000 acres to provide essential breeding grounds for fish.

29.   The Native American Grave Protection and Repatriation Act of 1990, 25 U.S.C. §§ 3001-3013, requires museums to return sacred objects and objects of cultural patrimony to a direct lineal descendant of the owner, or to a tribe that can show the object was owned or controlled by the tribe, unless the museum can show that its possession was obtained with the voluntary consent of an individual or group that had authority to transfer it.

Thailand. Particularly knotty problems were presented by the collapse of communist regimes in Eastern Europe, with the attendant return of property confiscated by the state to private ownership. Do the ideas behind prescription—that long-continued possession creates expectations the law should protect; that the law should bring repose by refusing to hear "stale" claims—provide any help in resolving these challenges?

As you might expect, these challenges have not gone unnoticed in the scholarly press. Just a few of the articles to be found in the legal literature are listed here. If you are interested in the subject, you can find many more. On Native American land claims, see Gus P. Coldebella & Mark S. Puzella, *The Landowner Defendants in Indian Land Claims: Hostages to History*, 37 New Eng. L. Rev. 585 (2003); Inbal Sansani, *American Indian Land Rights in the Inter-American System: Dann v. United States*, 10 Human Rights 2 (2003); Nell Jessup Newton, *Compensation, Reparations, and Restitution: Indian Property Claims in the United States*, 28 Ga. L. Rev. 453 (1994); Christine A. Klein, *Treaties of Conquest: Property Rights, Indian Treaties, and the Treaty of Guadalupe Hidalgo*, 26 N.M. L. Rev. 201 (1996); Robert A. Williams, Jr., *The American Indian in Western Legal Thought* (1990); Patricia Nelson Limerick, *The Legacy of Conquest* (1982); Francis Paul Prucha, *American Indian Policy in the Formative Years* (1962); Felix S. Cohen, *Handbook of Federal Indian Law* (1942). On protection and repatriation of cultural artifacts, see Kevin F. Jowers, Comment, *International and National Legal Efforts to Protect Cultural Property: The 1970 UNESCO Convention, The United States, and Mexico*, 38 Tex. Int'l L.J. 145 (2003); John H. Merryman, Thinking About the Elgin Marbles, 83 Mich. L. Rev. 1881 (1985); Stephanie O. Forbes, *Securing the Future of Our Past: Current Efforts to Protect Cultural Property*, 9 Transnat'l Law. 235 (1996); Patty Gerstenblith, *Identity and Cultural Property: The Protection of Cultural Property in the United States*, 75 B.U. L. Rev. 559 (1995); Peter K. Tompa, *Ancient Coins as Cultural Property: A Cause for Concern?*, 4 J. Int'l Legal Stud. 69 (1998); Note, *International Art Theft and the Illegal Import and Export of Cultural Property: A Study of Relevant Values, Legislation, and Solutions*, 15 Suffolk Transnat'l L. Rev. 609 (1992). There is a Symposium on *The Native American Graves Protection and Repatriation Act of 1990 and State Repatriation-Related Legislation* in 24 Ariz. St. L.J. at xi-562. *See also* Steven Platzman, *Objects of Controversy: The Native American Right to Repatriation*, 41 Am. U. L. Rev. 517 (1992).

On reprivatization and restitution efforts in Eastern Europe, see George Bogdan, *The Economic and Political Logic of Mass Privatization in Czechoslovakia and Poland*, 4 Cardozo J. Int'l & Comp. L. 43 (1996); William R. Youngblood, *Poland's Struggle for a Restitution Policy in the 1990s*, 9 Emory Int'l L. Rev. 645 (1995); Richard W. Crowder, *Restitution in the Czech Republic: Problems and Prague-Nosis*, 5 Ind. Int'l & Comp. L. Rev. 237 (1994); Ann Gelpern, *The Laws and Politics of Reprivatization in East-Central Europe: A Comparison*, 14 U. Pa. J. Int'l Bus. L. 315 (1993).

CHAPTER 4

Property Rights in Creative Works

Intellectual property has become the Dodge City of property—wild and out of control but wonderfully exciting and innovative.

— Carol M. Rose, *The Several Futures of Property: Of Cyberspace and Folk Tales, Emission Trades and Ecosystems,* 83 Minn. L. Rev. 129 (1998)

Outright copying is often a civilizing rather than a cannibalizing folkway. The world would be a duller place without the originators, but it would not work without the copyists.

— B. H. Bunn Co. v. AAA Replacement Parts Co., 451 F.2d 1254, 1259 (5th Cir. 1971)

How much protection should be given to celebrity personas, ideas, designs, performances, computer code, and the products of biological research? We can only hope to scratch the surface of these fascinating and hotly debated questions in this basic Property course, but if you find this interesting, you can pursue the subject in the Intellectual Property and Unfair Trade and Competition courses offered in the advanced curriculum.

A. PROPERTY RIGHTS IN PERSONAS AND THE RIGHT OF PUBLICITY

A relatively new property right, the right of publicity, protects a person's interest in the commercial exploitation of her name, likeness, and identity. The right is recognized by statute or as a matter of common law in more than half the states[1] and by § 46 of the *Restatement of Unfair Competition* (1995). Its legal roots may be found in doctrines of trademark, unfair competition, copyright, and the right of privacy. Its roots in privacy law are somewhat ironic. As noted by Judge Posner, "Paradoxically, this branch of the right of privacy is most often invoked

---

1. J. Thomas McCarthy, The Rights of Publicity and Privacy § 6.3 (2d ed. 2013).

by celebrities avid for publicity . . . ; they just want to make sure they get the highest possible price for the use of their name and picture in advertising."[2]

THE HUMAN PERSONA AS COMMERCIAL PROPERTY: THE RIGHT OF PUBLICITY

J. Thomas McCarthy, The Spring 1995 Horace S. Manges Lecture, 19 Colum.-VLA J.L. & Arts 129, 130-31 (1995)

What is this thing called the right of publicity? I think that the answer is quite simple. There is nothing abstruse or complicated about it. The right of publicity is simply the right of every person to control the commercial use of his or her identity.[5]

This means that it is illegal under the right of publicity to use without a license the identity of a real person to attract attention to an advertisement or product.

It should be made clear at the outset what the right of publicity can do and what it cannot do. It can give every person the right either to prevent or to permit for a fee, the use of his or her identity in an advertisement to help sell someone's product. But the right of publicity cannot be used to prevent someone's name in news reporting.[6] It cannot be used to prevent the use of identity in an unauthorized biography.[7] It cannot prevent use of identity in an entertainment parody or satire, such as that of Rich Little or Saturday Night Live.[8] . . .

While some criticize the right of publicity as posing the danger of invading our free speech rights, in fact, for all practical purposes, the only kind of speech impacted by the right of publicity is commercial speech—advertising. Not news, not stories, not entertainment and not entertainment satire and parody—only advertising and similar commercial uses.

Both the concept and the label "right of publicity" were created . . . in New York City. On February 16, 1953, Judge Jerome Frank, writing the opinion for the federal court of appeals in the seminal *Haelan* baseball trading card case held that under the law of the state of New York there was something called a "right of publicity" that was separate and apart from the right of privacy.[9]

The right of publicity is not a kind of trademark. It is not just a species of copyright. And it is not just another kind of privacy right. It is none of these things, although it bears some family resemblance to all three. The right of publicity is a wholly different and separate legal right.

---

2.   Richard A. Posner, Economic Analysis of Law 57 (8th ed. 2011).
5.   *See* McCarthy, The Rights of Publicity and Privacy § 1.1(A)(1) (Rev. 1995).
6.   *See, e.g.,* Stephano v. News Group Publications, Inc., 474 N.E.2d 580 (N.Y. 1984) (On Fall Fashions in New York magazine using plaintiff's photo was held to be a non-actionable story of public interest, not an actionable advertisement in disguise).
7.   Matthews v. Wozencraft, 1 F.3d 432, 439 (5th Cir. 1994) (The publication of an unauthorized book about events in the plaintiff's life was not an infringement of plaintiff's rights of either publicity or privacy. Most of the facts were public and apart from the fictionalization, the basic facts in defendant's book were true. The court found that defendant's book and possible movie version would not damage plaintiff's own factual book about the same story.).
8.   *See* McCarthy, The Rights of Publicity and Privacy § 8.15(b) (Rev. 1995).
9.   Haelan Laboratories, Inc. v. Topps Chewing Gum, Inc., 202 F.2d 866 (2d Cir.), *cert. denied,* 346 U.S. 816 (1953).

ZACCHINI v. SCRIPPS-HOWARD BROADCASTING CO.

Supreme Court of the United States
433 U.S. 562 (1977)

Mr. Justice WHITE delivered the opinion of the ·Court. Petitioner, Hugo Zacchini, is an entertainer. He performs a "human cannonball" act in which he is shot from a cannon into a net some 200 feet away. Each performance occupies some 15 seconds. In August and September 1972, petitioner was engaged to perform his act on a regular basis at the Geauga County Fair in Burton, Ohio. He performed in a fenced area, surrounded by grandstands, at the fair grounds. Members of the public attending the fair were not charged a separate admission fee to observe his act.

On August 30, a freelance reporter for Scripps-Howard Broadcasting Co., the operator of a television broadcasting station and respondent in this case, attended the fair. He carried a small movie camera. Petitioner noticed the reporter and asked him not to film the performance. The reporter did not do so on that day; but on the instructions of the producer of respondent's daily newscast, he returned the following day and videotaped the entire act. This film clip approximately 15 seconds in length, was shown on the 11 o'clock news program that night, together with favorable commentary.[1]

Petitioner then brought this action for damages, alleging that he is "engaged in the entertainment business," that the act he performs is one "invented by his father and . . . performed only by his family for the last fifty years," that respondent "showed and commercialized the film of his act without his consent," and that such conduct was an "unlawful appropriation of plaintiff's professional property." Respondent answered and moved for summary judgment, which was granted by the trial court.

The Court of Appeals of Ohio reversed. The majority held that petitioner's complaint stated a cause of action for conversion and for infringement of a common-law copyright, and one judge concurred in the judgment on the ground that the complaint stated a cause of action for appropriation of petitioner's "right of publicity" in the film of his act. All three judges agreed that the First Amendment did not privilege the press to show the entire performance on a news program without compensating petitioner for any financial injury he could prove at trial.

Like the concurring judge in the Court of Appeals, the Supreme Court of Ohio rested petitioner's cause of action under state law on his "right to the publicity value of his performance." The opinion syllabus . . . declared first that one may not use for his own benefit the name or likeness of another, whether or not the use or benefit is a commercial one, and second that respondent would be liable for the appropriation over petitioner's objection and in the absence of license or privilege, of petitioner's right to the publicity value of his

---

1.   The script of the commentary accompanying the film clip read as follows: "This . . . is the story of a *true spectator sport* . . . the sport of human cannonballing . . . in fact, the great Zacchini is about the only human cannonball around, these days . . . just happens that, where he is, is the Great Geauga County Fair, in Burton . . . and believe me, although it's not a long act, it's a thriller . . . and you really need to see it in person . . . to appreciate it . . . ."

performance. The court nevertheless gave judgment for respondent because, in the words of the syllabus:

> A TV station has a privilege to report in its newscasts matters of legitimate public interest which would otherwise be protected by an individual's right of publicity, unless the actual intent of the TV station was to appropriate the benefit of the publicity for some non-privileged private use, or unless the actual intent was to injure the individual.

We granted certiorari to consider an issue unresolved by this Court: whether the First and Fourteenth Amendments immunized respondent from damages for its alleged infringement of petitioner's state law "right of publicity." Insofar as the Ohio Supreme Court held that the First and Fourteenth Amendments of the United States Constitution required judgment for respondent, we reverse the judgment of that court.

If the judgment below rested on an independent and adequate state ground, the writ of certiorari should be dismissed as improvidently granted . . . . We are confident, however, that the judgment below did not rest on an adequate and independent state ground and that we have jurisdiction to decide the federal issue presented in this case.

There is no doubt that petitioner's complaint was grounded in state law and that the right of publicity which petitioner was held to possess was a right arising under Ohio law. It is also clear that respondent's claim of constitutional privilege was sustained. . . . It is clear . . . from the opinion of the Ohio Supreme Court . . . that in adjudicating the crucial question of whether respondent had a privilege to film and televise petitioner's performance, the court placed principal reliance on Time, Inc. v. Hill, 385 U.S. 374 (1967), a case involving First Amendment limitations on state tort actions. It construed the principle of that case, along with that of New York Times Co. v. Sullivan, 376 U.S. 254 (1964), to be that "the press has a privilege to report matters of legitimate public interest even though such reports might intrude on matters otherwise private," and concluded, therefore, that the press is also "privileged when an individual seeks to publicly exploit his talents while keeping the benefits private." . . .

The Ohio Supreme Court held that respondent is constitutionally privileged to include in its newscasts matters of public interest that would otherwise be protected by the right of publicity, absent an intent to injure or to appropriate for some nonprivileged purpose. If . . . respondent had merely reported that petitioner was performing at the fair and described or commented on his act, with or without showing his picture on television, we would have a very different case. But petitioner['s] . . . complaint is that respondent filmed his entire act and displayed that film on television for the public to see and enjoy. This, he claimed, was an appropriation of his professional property. The Ohio Supreme Court agreed that petitioner had "a right of publicity" that gave him "personal control over commercial display and exploitation of his personality and the exercise of his talents." This right of "exclusive control over the publicity given to his performances" was said to be such a "valuable part of the benefit which may be attained by his talents and efforts" that it was entitled to legal protection. It was also observed, or at least expressly assumed, that petitioner had not abandoned his rights by performing under the circumstances present at the Geauga County Fair Grounds.

The Ohio Supreme Court nevertheless held that the challenged invasion was privileged, saying that the press "must be accorded broad latitude in its choice of how much it presents of each story or incident, and of the emphasis to be given to such presentation. No fixed standard which would bar the press from reporting or depicting either an entire occurrence or an entire discrete part of a public performance can be formulated which would not unduly restrict the 'breathing room' in reporting which freedom of the press requires." Under this view, respondent was thus constitutionally free to film and display petitioner's entire act.[5] . . .

[T]he State's interest in permitting a "right of publicity" is in protecting the proprietary interest of the individual in his act in part to encourage such entertainment. . . . [T]he State's interest is closely analogous to the goals of patent and copyright law, focusing on the right of the individual to reap the reward of his endeavors and having little to do with protecting feelings or reputation. . . . An entertainer such as petitioner usually has no objection to the widespread publication of his act as long as he gets the commercial benefit of such publication. Indeed, in the present case petitioner did not seek to enjoin the broadcast of his act; he simply sought compensation for the broadcast in the form of damages. . . .

It is evident . . . that petitioner's state-law right of publicity would not serve to prevent respondent from reporting the newsworthy facts about petitioner's act.[11] Wherever the line in particular situations is to be drawn between media reports that are protected and those that are not, we are quite sure that the First and Fourteenth Amendments do not immunize the media when they broadcast a performer's entire act without his consent. The Constitution no more prevents a State from requiring respondent to compensate petitioner for broadcasting his act on television than it would privilege respondent to film and broadcast a copyrighted dramatic work without liability to the copyright owner . . . or to film and broadcast a prize fight . . . or a baseball game . . . where the promoters or the participants had other plans for publicizing the event. There are ample reasons for reaching this conclusion. . . .

5. The court's explication was as follows:

The proper standard must necessarily be whether the matters reported were of public interest, and if so, the press will be liable for appropriation of a performer's right of publicity only if its actual intent was not to report the performance, but, rather, to appropriate the performance for some other private use, or if the actual intent was to injure the performer. It might also be the case that the press would be liable if it recklessly disregarded contract rights existing between the plaintiff and a third person to present the performance to the public, but that question is not presented here.

11. W. Prosser, Law of Torts 806-807 (4th ed. 1971), generalizes on the cases:

The New York courts were faced very early with the obvious fact that newspapers and magazines, to say nothing of radio, television and motion pictures, are by no means philanthropic institutions, but are operated for profit. As against the contention that everything published by these agencies must necessarily be "for purposes of trade," they were compelled to hold that there must be some closer and more direct connection, beyond the mere fact that the newspaper itself is sold; and that the presence of advertising matter in adjacent columns, or even the duplication of a news item for the purpose of advertising the publication itself, does not make any difference. Any other conclusion would in all probability have been an unconstitutional interference with the freedom of the press. Accordingly, it has been held that the mere incidental mention of the plaintiff's name in a book or a motion picture is not an invasion of his privacy; nor is the publication of a photograph or a newsreel in which he incidentally appears.

The broadcast of a film of petitioner's entire act poses a substantial threat to the economic value of that performance. . . . [T]his act is the product of petitioner's own talents and energy, the end result of much time, effort, and expense. Much of its economic value lies in the "right of exclusive control over the publicity given to his performance"; if the public can see the act free on television, it will be less willing to pay to see it at the fair.[12] The effect of a public broadcast of the performance is similar to preventing petitioner from charging an admission fee. "The rationale for [protecting the right of publicity] is the straightforward one of preventing unjust enrichment by the theft of good will. No social purpose is served by having the defendant get free some aspect of the plaintiff that would have market value and for which he would normally pay." Kalven, *Privacy in Tort Law — Were Warren and Brandeis Wrong?*, 31 Law & Contemp. Prob. 326, 331 (1966). Moreover, the broadcast of petitioner's entire performance, unlike the unauthorized use of another's name for purposes of trade or the incidental use of a name or picture by the press, goes to the heart of petitioner's ability to earn a living as an entertainer. Thus, in this case, Ohio has recognized what may be the strongest case for a "right of publicity" involving, not the appropriation of an entertainer's reputation to enhance the attractiveness of a commercial product, but the appropriation of the very activity by which the entertainer acquired his reputation in the first place.

Of course, Ohio's decision to protect petitioner's right of publicity here rests on more than a desire to compensate the performer for the time and effort invested in his act; the protection provides an economic incentive for him to make the investment required to produce a performance of interest to the public. This same consideration underlies the patent and copyright laws long enforced by this Court. As the Court stated in Mazer v. Stein, 347 U.S. 201 (1954):

> The economic philosophy behind the clause empowering Congress to grant patents and copyrights is the conviction that encouragement of individual effort by personal gain is the best way to advance public welfare through the talents of authors and inventors in "Science and useful Arts." Sacrificial days devoted to such creative activities deserve rewards commensurate with the services rendered. . . .

There is no doubt that entertainment, as well as news, enjoys First Amendment protection. It is also true that entertainment itself can be important news. But it is important to note that neither the public nor respondent will be deprived of the benefit of petitioner's performance as long as his commercial stake in his act is appropriately recognized. Petitioner does not seek to enjoin the broadcast of his performance; he simply wants to be paid for it. Nor do we think that a state-law damages remedy against respondent would represent a species of liability without fault contrary to the letter or spirit of Gertz v. Robert Welch, Inc., 418 U.S. 323 (1974). Respondent knew that petitioner objected to televising his act, but nevertheless displayed the entire film.

---

12. It is possible, of course, that respondent's news broadcast increased the value of petitioner's performance by stimulating the public's interest in seeing the act live. In these circumstances, petitioner would not be able to prove damages and thus would not recover. But petitioner has alleged that the broadcast injured him to the extent of $25,000 and we think the State should be allowed to authorize compensation of this injury if proved.

We conclude that although the State of Ohio may as a matter of its own law privilege the press in the circumstances of this case, the First and Fourteenth Amendments do not require it to do so. Reversed.

[Dissenting opinion of Justice POWELL, joined in by Justices BRENNAN and MARSHALL omitted.]

Notes and Questions

1. The court emphasizes that Zacchini did not seek to enjoin the broadcast, merely to be paid for it. Can you think of any reason why Zacchini's right of publicity should not be protected by a "property rule" (an injunction)? Why it should be?

2. The complaint alleged that Zacchini's father invented the human cannon-ball act and it had been performed only by his family for the last 50 years.[3] If other people began performing a human cannonball act, would Zacchini be entitled to enjoin them? Should he be entitled to royalties? Does the right of publicity cover this situation?

3. Does the right of publicity apply only to celebrities? The court in *Memphis Development Foundation v. Factors Etc., Inc.*, 616 F.2d 956 (6th Cir.), *cert. denied* (1980), described the right by saying: "[T]he famous have an exclusive legal right during life to control and profit from the commercial use of their name and personality." But § 46 of the *Restatement (Third) of Unfair Competition* (1995) states:

> One who appropriates the commercial value of a person's identity by using without consent the person's name, likeness, or other indicia of identity for purposes of trade is subject to liability. . . .
>
> Comment *a*. . . . The appropriation of another's identity for purposes of trade can result in injury to both commercial and personal interests. This Restatement deals with rules affording relief against unfair methods of competition, and the rules stated in this Topic are therefore limited to the redress of commercial injuries. The interest protected by these rules is often described as the "right of publicity." Relief is also generally available under the law of torts for injuries to personal interests caused by the unauthorized commercial use of another's identity. The protection of these personal interests is often described as an aspect of the "right of privacy."

3.   Wikipedia reports that the first human cannonball was a 14-year old girl launched in London from a spring-driven cannon invented by a Canadian known as "The Great Farini." Hugo Zacchini's father, Ildebrando, invented a compressed air cannon first used by the Zacchini family in 1922. Five sons of Ildebrando Zacchini, owner of the Circus Olympia in Italy, became the Flying Zacchinis and were brought to America in 1929 by John Ringling. The last of the brothers, Mario, whose acts included being blasted over two Ferris wheels, died at age 87 in February 1999. The second generation of Zacchinis, including Hugo, the plaintiff in this case, began performing in the 1950s. Hugo's final flight was in 1991. Pittsburgh Post-Gazette, Feb. 8, 1999. The cannon used by the Flying Zacchinis can be seen in the circus museum at the Ringling estate in Sarasota, Florida.

The Cleveland Plain Dealer of March 29, 1998, reports that opening day of the baseball season in 1974 was postponed for a day because the weather was too cold for featured attraction, Hugo Zacchini. He refused to be shot from the cannon at temperatures below 40° F because his range increased too much.

Current human cannonballs include the David Smith family. David, listed in the Guinness Book of World Records as holding the record at 185 feet, and all three of his children perform. Daughter Rebecca, who decided to go into the business at age 15, said "I make a great living. . . . It's the only thing I have to do. I've never had a normal job." Dallas Morning News, Aug. 26, 1999.

4. *Is there a right of publicity after death? Elvis Presley Int'l Memorial Found. v. Crowell,* 733 S.W.2d 89 (Tenn. App. 1987), held that the right of publicity, exploited during lifetime, is inheritable at death. The court reasoned that when people invest in their names and images during life, they create a capital asset that should be transferable at death, just like other intangible assets in which they invest time and money. To allow others to make free use of the name or image after death would be unjust enrichment. In *Lugosi v. Universal Pictures,* 603 P.2d 425 (Cal. 1979), the court held that Bela Lugosi's lifetime right to exploit his fame and likeness for commercial purposes, which he did not choose to exploit, did not survive his death. The court, troubled by the unbounded nature of the claimed right, asked where the line was to be drawn, and questioned whether drawing such a line was within the scope of judicial authority. The California legislature responded in 1984 with Cal. Civ. Code § 3444.1, which extends the right of publicity for 70 years after death. Other states have similar measures. *See, e.g.,* Ind. Code § 32-13-1-8 (1999) (100 years), Ky. Rev. Stat. Ann. § 391.170 (Banks-Baldwin 1998) (50 years), Nev. Rev. Stat. § 597.790 (1997) (50 years).

5. The protection afforded by the right of publicity also extends to an imitation of a person's voice. In *Midler v. Ford Motor Co.,* 849 F.2d 460 (9th Cir. 1988), the Ford Motor Company and its advertising agency violated the right of publicity by hiring a singer to perform "Do You Want to Dance" in a voice and style intended to "sound as much as possible like the Bette Midler record." The court said that "when a distinctive voice of a professional singer is widely known and is deliberately imitated in order to sell a product, the sellers have appropriated what is not theirs." Midler was awarded $400,000 in damages against Young & Rubicam, Inc., *see* 944 F.2d 909 (9th Cir. 1991), *cert. denied* (1992).

6. *Invoking the image of a celebrity.* In *Carson v. Here's Johnny Portable Toilets, Inc.,* 698 F.2d 831 (6th Cir. 1982), the court found a violation of the right of publicity in use of the phrase "Here's Johnny." In using the phrase, which was closely associated with Carson for much of his career, the defendants intended to evoke his image and appropriate it for commercial purposes. The Court explained: "If the celebrity's identity is commercially exploited, there has been an invasion of his right whether or not his 'name or likeness' is used."

White v. Samsung Electronics America, Inc., 971 F.2d 1395 (9th Cir. 1992), held that a robot that evoked the identity of Vanna White, the wheel turner on "Wheel of Fortune," violated her right of publicity. *Wendt v. Host International, Inc.,* 197 F.3d 1284 (9th Cir. 1999), went further in holding that Paramount Pictures, which held the copyright to "Cheers," could be liable for licensing the use of robots that invoked the identities of the actors who played Norm and Cliff on the show. Judge Kozinski wrote sharp dissents in both cases raising the question whether the court had gone too far in curtailing the public domain.

WHITE v. SAMSUNG ELECTRONICS AMERICA, INC.

United States Court of Appeals, Ninth Circuit
989 F.2d 1512 (1993)

KOZINSKI, Circuit Judge, with whom Circuit Judges O'SCANNLAIN and KLEINFIELD join, dissenting from the order rejecting the suggestion for rehearing en banc.

. . . Something very dangerous is going on here. Private property, including intellectual property, is essential to our way of life. It provides an incentive for investment and innovation; it stimulates the flourishing of our culture; it protects the moral entitlements of people to the fruits of their labors. But reducing too much to private property can be bad medicine. Private land, for instance, is far more useful if separated from other private land by public streets, roads and highways. Public parks, utility rights-of-way and sewers reduce the amount of land in private hands, but vastly enhance the value of the property that remains.

So too it is with intellectual property. Overprotecting intellectual property is as harmful as underprotecting it. Creativity is impossible without a rich public domain. Nothing today, likely nothing since we tamed fire, is genuinely new: Culture, like science and technology, grows by accretion, each new creator building on the works of those who came before. Overprotection stifles the very creative forces it's supposed to nurture.

The panel's opinion is a classic case of overprotection. Concerned about what it sees as a wrong done to Vanna White, the panel majority erects a property right of remarkable and dangerous breadth: Under the majority's opinion, it's now a tort for advertisers to *remind* the public of a celebrity. Not to use a celebrity's name, voice, signature or likeness; not to imply the celebrity endorses a product; but simply to evoke the celebrity's image in the public's mind. This Orwellian notion withdraws far more from the public domain than prudence and common sense allow. It conflicts with the Copyright Act and the Copyright Clause. It raises serious First Amendment problems. It's bad law, and it deserves a long, hard second look.

Questions

Is Judge Kozinksi right that these cases extended the right of publicity too far? When is property rights protection necessary to encourage people to invest in creating valuable performances and personas and when does it interfere with useful creative activity? For an excellent article exploring the ramifications of the increasing range of intellectual property rights, see James Boyle, *The Second Enclosure Movement and the Construction of the Public Domain*, 66 Law & Contemp. Prob. 33 (2003).

KELLER v. ELECTRONIC ARTS, INC.

United States Court of Appeals
724 F.3d 1268 (9th Cir. 2013)

BYBEE, Circuit Judge: Video games are entitled to the full protections of the First Amendment, because "[l]ike the protected books, plays, and movies that preceded them, video games communicate ideas—and even social messages—through many familiar literary devices (such as characters, dialogue, plot, and music) and through features distinctive to the medium (such as the player's interaction with the virtual world)." Brown v. Entm't Merchs. Ass'n, 131 S. Ct. 2729 (2011). Such rights are not absolute, and states may recognize the right of publicity to a degree consistent with the First Amendment. Zacchini v.

Scripps-Howard Broad. Co., 433 U.S. 562 (1977). In this case, we must balance the right of publicity of a former college football player against the asserted First Amendment right of a video game developer to use his likeness in its expressive works.

The district court concluded that the game developer, Electronic Arts ("EA"), had no First Amendment defense against the right-of-publicity claims of the football player, Samuel Keller. We affirm. Under the "transformative use" test developed by the California Supreme Court, EA's use does not qualify for First Amendment protection as a matter of law because it literally recreates Keller in the very setting in which he has achieved renown. . . .

I

Samuel Keller was the starting quarterback for Arizona State University in 2005 before he transferred to the University of Nebraska, where he played during the 2007 season. EA is the producer of the *NCAA Football* series of video games, which allow users to control avatars representing college football players as those avatars participate in simulated games. In *NCAA Football*, EA seeks to replicate each school's entire team as accurately as possible. Every real football player on each team included in the game has a corresponding avatar in the game with the player's actual jersey number and virtually identical height, weight, build, skin tone, hair color, and home state. EA attempts to match any unique, highly identifiable playing behaviors by sending detailed questionnaires to team equipment managers. Additionally, EA creates realistic virtual versions of actual stadiums; populates them with the virtual athletes, coaches, cheerleaders, and fans realistically rendered by EA's graphic artists; and incorporates realistic sounds such as the crunch of the players' pads and the roar of the crowd.

EA's game differs from reality in that EA omits the players' names on their jerseys and assigns each player a home town that is different from the actual player's home town. However, users of the video game may upload rosters of names obtained from third parties so that the names do appear on the jerseys. In such cases, EA allows images from the game containing athletes' real names to be posted on its website by users. Users can further alter reality by entering "Dynasty" mode, where the user assumes a head coach's responsibilities for a college program for up to thirty seasons, including recruiting players from a randomly generated pool of high school athletes, or "Campus Legend" mode, where the user controls a virtual player from high school through college, making choices relating to practices, academics, and social life.

In the 2005 edition of the game, the virtual starting quarterback for Arizona State wears number 9, as did Keller, and has the same height, weight, skin tone, hair color, hair style, handedness, home state, play style (pocket passer), visor preference, facial features, and school year as Keller. In the 2008 edition, the virtual quarterback for Nebraska has these same characteristics, though the jersey number does not match, presumably because Keller changed his number right before the season started.

Objecting to this use of his likeness, Keller filed a putative class-action complaint in the Northern District of California asserting, as relevant on appeal, that EA violated his right of publicity under California Civil Code § 3344 and

California common law.[2] EA moved to strike the complaint as a strategic lawsuit against public participation ("SLAPP") under California's anti-SLAPP statute, Cal. Civ. Proc. Code § 425.16, and the district court denied the motion. . . .[3]

II

California's anti-SLAPP statute is designed to discourage suits that "masquerade as ordinary lawsuits but are brought to deter common citizens from exercising their political or legal rights or to punish them for doing so." . . . The statute provides:

> A cause of action against a person arising from any act of that person in further-ance of the person's right of petition or free speech under the United States Consti-tution or the California Constitution in connection with a public issue shall be sub-ject to a special motion to strike, unless the court determines that the plaintiff has established that there is a probability that the plaintiff will prevail on the claim.

We have determined that the anti-SLAPP statute is available in federal court. . . .

We evaluate an anti-SLAPP motion in two steps. First, the defendant must "make a prima facie showing that the plaintiff's suit arises from an act by the defendant made in connection with a public issue in furtherance of the defen-dant's right to free speech under the United States or California Constitution." Keller does not contest that EA has made this threshold showing. Indeed, there is no question that "video games qualify for First Amendment protection," . . . or that Keller's suit arises from EA's production and distribution of *NCAA Football* in furtherance of EA's protected right to express itself through video games.

Second, we must evaluate whether the plaintiff has "establish[ed] a reason-able probability that the plaintiff will prevail on his or her . . . claim." . . . EA did not contest before the district court and does not contest here that Keller has stated a right-of-publicity claim under California common and statutory law.[4] Instead, EA raises four affirmative defenses derived from the First Amendment: the "transformative use" test, the *Rogers* test, the "public interest" test, and the "public affairs" exemption. EA argues that, in light of these defenses, it is not reasonably probable that Keller will prevail on his right-of-publicity claim. . . .

---

2. There are actually nine named plaintiffs, all former National Collegiate Athletic Associa-tion ("NCAA") football or basketball players . . . . EA's NCAA basketball games are also implicated in this appeal. Because the issues are the same for each plaintiff, all of the claims are addressed through our discussion of Keller and *NCAA Football*.

3. We review *de novo* the district court's denial of a motion to strike under California's anti-SLAPP statute. . . .

4. The elements of a right-of-publicity claim under California common law are: "(1) the defen-dant's use of the plaintiff's identity; (2) the appropriation of plaintiff's name or likeness to defen-dant's advantage, commercially or otherwise; (3) lack of consent; and (4) resulting injury." Stewart v. Rolling Stone LLC, 181 Cal. App. 4th 664 (internal quotation marks omitted). The same claim under California Civil Code § 3344 requires a plaintiff to prove "all the elements of the common law cause of action" plus "a knowing use by the defendant as well as a direct connection between the alleged use and the commercial purpose."

A

The California Supreme Court formulated the transformative use defense in Comedy III Productions, Inc. v. Gary Saderup, Inc., 21 P.3d 797 (Cal. 2001). The defense is "a balancing test between the First Amendment and the right of publicity based on whether the work in question adds significant creative elements so as to be transformed into something more than a mere celebrity likeness or imitation." The . . . [c]ourt explained that "when a work contains significant transformative elements, it is not only especially worthy of First Amendment protection, but it is also less likely to interfere with the economic interest protected by the right of publicity." The court rejected the wholesale importation of the copyright "fair use" defense into right-of-publicity claims, but recognized that some aspects of that defense are "particularly pertinent." . . .

Comedy III gives us at least five factors to consider in determining whether a work is sufficiently transformative to obtain First Amendment protection. *See* J. Thomas McCarthy, *The Rights of Publicity and Privacy* § 8:72 (2d ed. 2012). First, if "the celebrity likeness is one of the 'raw materials' from which an original work is synthesized," it is more likely to be transformative than if "the depiction or imitation of the celebrity is the very sum and substance of the work in question." Second, the work is protected if it is "primarily the defendant's own expression"—as long as that expression is "something other than the likeness of the celebrity." This factor requires an examination of whether a likely purchaser's primary motivation is to buy a reproduction of the celebrity, or to buy the expressive work of that artist. Third, to avoid making judgments concerning "the quality of the artistic contribution," a court should conduct an inquiry "more quantitative than qualitative" and ask "whether the literal and imitative or the creative elements predominate in the work." Fourth, the California Supreme Court indicated that "a subsidiary inquiry" would be useful in close cases: whether "the marketability and economic value of the challenged work derive primarily from the fame of the celebrity depicted." Lastly, the court indicated that "when an artist's skill and talent is manifestly subordinated to the overall goal of creating a conventional portrait of a celebrity so as to commercially exploit his or her fame," the work is not transformative.

We have explained that "[o]nly if [a defendant] is entitled to the [transformative] defense *as a matter of law* can it prevail on its motion to strike," because the California Supreme Court "envisioned the application of the defense as a question of fact." As a result, EA "is only entitled to the defense as a matter of law if no trier of fact could reasonably conclude that the [game] [i]s not transformative."

California courts have applied the transformative use test in relevant situations in four cases. First, in *Comedy III* itself, the California Supreme Court applied the test to T-shirts and lithographs bearing a likeness of The Three Stooges and concluded that it could "discern no significant transformative or creative contribution." The court reasoned that the artist's "undeniable skill is manifestly subordinated to the overall goal of creating literal, conventional depictions of The Three Stooges so as to exploit their fame." "[W]ere we to decide that [the artist's] depictions were protected by the First Amendment," the court continued, "we cannot perceive how the right of publicity would remain a viable right other than in cases of falsified celebrity endorsements."

Second, in Winter v. DC Comics, the California Supreme Court applied the test to comic books containing characters Johnny and Edgar Autumn, "depicted as villainous half-worm, half-human offspring" but evoking two famous brothers, rockers Johnny and Edgar Winter. 69 P.3d 473 (Cal. 2003). The court held that "the comic books are transformative and entitled to First Amendment protection." It reasoned that the comic books " . . . contain significant expressive content other than plaintiffs' mere likenesses." "To the extent the drawings of the Autumn brothers resemble plaintiffs at all, they are distorted for purposes of lampoon, parody, or caricature." Importantly, the court relied on the fact that the brothers "are but cartoon characters . . . in a larger story, which is itself quite expressive."

Third, in Kirby v. Sega of America, Inc., the California Court of Appeal applied the transformative use test to a video game in which the user controls the dancing of "Ulala," a reporter from outer space allegedly based on singer Kierin Kirby, whose " 'signature' lyrical expression . . . is 'ooh la la.' " 144 Cal. App. 4th 47 (2006). The court held that "Ulala is more than a mere likeness or literal depiction of Kirby," pointing to Ulala's "extremely tall, slender computer-generated physique," her "hairstyle and primary costume," her dance moves, and her role as "a space-age reporter in the 25th century," all of which were "unlike any public depiction of Kirby." "As in Winter, Ulala is a 'fanciful, creative character' who exists in the context of a unique and expressive video game."

Finally, in No Doubt v. Activision Publishing, Inc., the California Court of Appeal addressed Activision's Band Hero video game. 192 Cal. App. 4th 1018 (2011) . . . . In Band Hero, users simulate performing in a rock band in time with popular songs. Users choose from a number of avatars, some of which represent actual rock stars, including the members of the rock band No Doubt. Activision licensed No Doubt's likeness, but allegedly exceeded the scope of the license by permitting users to manipulate the No Doubt avatars to play any song in the game, solo or with members of other bands, and even to alter the avatars' voices. The court held that No Doubt's right of publicity prevailed despite Activision's First Amendment defense because the game was not "transformative" under the Comedy III test. It reasoned that the video game characters were "literal recreations of the band members," doing "the same activity by which the band achieved and maintains its fame." According to the court, the fact "that the avatars appear in the context of a videogame that contains many other creative elements does not transform the avatars into anything other than exact depictions of No Doubt's members doing exactly what they do as celebrities." The court concluded that "the expressive elements of the game remain manifestly subordinated to the overall goal of creating a conventional portrait of No Doubt so as to commercially exploit its fame."

We have also had occasion to apply the transformative use test. In Hilton v. Hallmark Cards, we applied the test to a birthday card depicting Paris Hilton in a manner reminiscent of an episode of Hilton's reality show The Simple Life. 599 F.3d [894 (9th Cir. 2010)]. We observed some differences between the episode and the card, but noted that "the basic setting is the same: we see Paris Hilton, born to privilege, working as a waitress." We reasoned that "[w]hen we compare Hallmark's card to the video game in Kirby, which transported a 1990s singer (catchphrases and all) into the 25th century and transmogrified her into a space-age reporter, . . . the card falls far short of the level of new expression added in the video game." As a result, we concluded that "there is enough doubt as to whether Hallmark's card is transformative under our case law that we cannot say Hallmark is entitled to the defense as a matter of law."

With these cases in mind as guidance, we conclude that EA's use of Keller's likeness does not contain significant transformative elements such that EA is entitled to the defense as a matter of law. The facts of *No Doubt* are very similar to those here. EA is alleged to have replicated Keller's physical characteristics in *NCAA Football*, just as the members of No Doubt are realistically portrayed in *Band Hero*. Here, as in *Band Hero*, users manipulate the characters in the performance of the same activity for which they are known in real life . . . . The context in which the activity occurs is also similarly realistic . . . . As the district court found, Keller is represented as "what he was: the starting quarterback for Arizona State" and Nebraska, and "the game's setting is identical to where the public found [Keller] during his collegiate career: on the football field."

EA argues that the district court erred in focusing primarily on Keller's likeness and ignoring the transformative elements of the game as a whole. Judge Thomas, our dissenting colleague, suggests the same. We are unable to say that there was any error, particularly in light of *No Doubt*, which reasoned much the same as the district court in this case: "that the avatars appear in the context of a videogame that contains many other creative elements does not transform the avatars into anything other than exact depictions of No Doubt's members doing exactly what they do as celebrities." . . .

The Third Circuit came to the same conclusion in Hart v. Electronic Arts, Inc., 717 F.3d 141 (3d Cir. 2013). In *Hart*, EA faced a materially identical challenge under New Jersey right-of-publicity law, brought by former Rutgers quarterback Ryan Hart. Though the Third Circuit was tasked with interpreting New Jersey law, the court looked to the transformative use test developed in California . . . (noting that the right-of-publicity laws are "strikingly similar" . . .). Applying the test, the court held that "the *NCAA Football* . . . games at issue . . . do not sufficiently transform [Hart]'s identity to escape the right of publicity claim," reversing the district court's grant of summary judgment to EA.

. . . . [T]he district court was correct in concluding that EA cannot prevail as a matter of law based on the transformative use defense at the anti-SLAPP stage. . . .

B

EA urges us to adopt for right-of-publicity claims the broader First Amendment defense that we have previously adopted in the context of false endorsement claims under the Lanham Act: the *Rogers* test. *See* Brown v. Elec. Arts, 724 F.3d [1235] (applying the *Rogers* test to a Lanham Act claim brought by former NFL player Jim Brown relating to the use of his likeness in EA's *Madden NFL* video games). . . .

Rogers v. Grimaldi is a landmark Second Circuit case balancing First Amendment rights against claims under the Lanham Act. 875 F.2d 994 (2d Cir. 1989). The case involved a suit brought by the famous performer Ginger Rogers against the producers and distributors of *Ginger and Fred*, a movie about two fictional Italian cabaret performers who imitated Rogers and her frequent performing partner Fred Astaire. Rogers alleged both a violation of the Lanham

Act for creating the false impression that she endorsed the film and infringement of her common law right of publicity.

The *Rogers* court recognized that "[m]ovies, plays, books, and songs are all indisputably works of artistic expression and deserve protection," but that "[t]he purchaser of a book, like the purchaser of a can of peas, has a right not to be misled as to the source of the product." "Consumers of artistic works thus have a dual interest: They have an interest in not being misled and they also have an interest in enjoying the results of the author's freedom of expression." The *Rogers* court determined that titles of artistic or literary works were less likely to be misleading than "the names of ordinary commercial products," and thus that Lanham Act protections applied with less rigor when considering titles of artistic or literary works than when considering ordinary products. The court concluded that "in general the Act should be construed to apply to artistic works only where the public interest in avoiding consumer confusion outweighs the public interest in free expression." The court therefore held:

> In the context of allegedly misleading titles using a celebrity's name, that balance will normally not support application of the [Lanham] Act unless the title has no artistic relevance to the underlying work whatsoever, or, if it has some artistic relevance, unless the title explicitly misleads as to the source or the content of the work.

We first endorsed the *Rogers* test for Lanham Act claims involving artistic or expressive works in Mattel, Inc. v. MCA Records, Inc., 296 F.3d 894 (9th Cir. 2002). We agreed that, in the context of artistic and literary titles, "[c]onsumers expect a title to communicate a message about the book or movie, but they do not expect it to identify the publisher or producer" . . . . Then, in E.S.S. Entertainment 2000, Inc. v. Rock Star Videos, Inc., we considered a claim by a strip club owner that video game maker Rock Star incorporated its club logo into the game's virtual depiction of East Los Angeles, violating the club's trademark right to that logo. 547 F.3d 1095 (9th Cir. 2008). We held that Rock Star's use of the logo and trade dress was protected by the First Amendment and that it therefore could not be held liable under the Lanham Act. In so doing, we extended the *Rogers* test slightly, noting that "[a]lthough this test traditionally applies to uses of a trademark in the title of an artistic work, there is no principled reason why it ought not also apply to the use of a trademark in the body of the work."

. . . EA argues that we should extend this test . . . to right-of-publicity claims because it is "less prone to misinterpretation" and "more protective of free expression" than the transformative use defense. Although we acknowledge that there is some overlap between the transformative use test formulated by the California Supreme Court and the *Rogers* test, we disagree that the *Rogers* test should be imported wholesale for right-of-publicity claims. Our conclusion on this point is consistent with the Third Circuit's rejection of EA's identical argument in *Hart.* As the history and development of the *Rogers* test makes clear, it was designed to protect consumers from the risk of consumer confusion—the hallmark element of a Lanham Act claim. The right of publicity, on the other hand, does not primarily seek to prevent consumer confusion. . . . Rather, it primarily "protects a form of intellectual property [in one's person] that society deems to have some social utility." . . .

The right of publicity protects the *celebrity*, not the *consumer*. Keller's publicity claim is not founded on an allegation that consumers are being illegally misled into believing that he is endorsing EA or its products. . . . Keller's claim is that EA has appropriated, without permission and without providing compensation, his talent and years of hard work on the football field. The reasoning of the *Rogers* and *Mattel* courts—that artistic and literary works should be protected unless they explicitly mislead consumers—is simply not responsive to Keller's asserted interests here. *Cf. Hart*, 717 F.3d at 157 ("Effectively, [EA] argues that [Hart] should be unable to assert a claim for appropriating his likeness as a football player precisely because his likeness was used for a game about football. Adopting this line of reasoning threatens to turn the right of publicity on its head."). . . .

C

California has developed two additional defenses aimed at protecting the reporting of factual information under state law. One of these defenses only applies to common law right-of-publicity claims while the other only applies to statutory right-of-publicity claims. Montana v. San Jose Mercury News, Inc., 34 Cal. App. 4th 790 (1995). Liability will not lie for common law right-of-publicity claims for the "publication of matters in the public interest." Similarly, liability will not lie for statutory right-of-publicity claims for the "use of a name, voice, signature, photograph, or likeness in connection with any news, public affairs, or sports broadcast or account, or any political campaign." Cal. Civ. Code § 3344(d). Although these defenses are based on First Amendment concerns, . . . they are not coextensive with the Federal Constitution, New Kids on the Block v. News Am. Publ'g, Inc., 971 F.2d 302 (9th Cir. 1992), and their application is thus a matter of state law.

EA argues that these defenses give it the right to "incorporate athletes' names, statistics, and other biographical information" into its expressive works, as the defenses were "designed to create 'extra breathing space' for the use of a person's name in connection with matters of public interest." Keller responds that the right of publicity yields to free use of a public figure's likeness only to the extent reasonably required to report information to the public or publish factual data, and that the defenses apply only to broadcasts or accounts of public affairs, not to EA's *NCAA Football* games, which do not contain or constitute such reporting about Keller.

California courts have generally analyzed the common law defense and the statutory defense separately, but it is clear that both defenses protect only the act of publishing or reporting. By its terms, § 3344(d) is limited to a "broadcast or account," and we have confirmed that the common law defense is about a publication or reporting of newsworthy items. *Hilton*, 599 F.3d at 912. However, most of the discussion by California courts pertains to whether the subject matter of the communication is of "public interest" or related to "news" or "public affairs," leaving little guidance as to when the communication constitutes a publication or reporting.

For instance, in Dora v. Frontline Video, Inc., a wellknown surfer sued the producer of a documentary on surfing entitled "The Legends of Malibu," claiming misappropriation of his name and likeness. 15 Cal. App. 4th 536 (1993). The court held that the documentary was protected because it was "a fair comment on real life events which have caught the popular imagination." The court explained that surfing "has created a lifestyle that influences speech, behavior, dress, and entertainment," has had "an economic impact," and "has also had a significant influence on the popular culture," such that "[i]t would be difficult to conclude that a surfing documentary does not fall within the category of public affairs." Similarly, in Gionfriddo v. Major League Baseball, retired professional baseball players alleged that Major League Baseball violated their right of publicity by displaying "factual data concerning the players, their performance statistics, and verbal descriptions and video depictions of their play" in game programs and on its website. 94 Cal. App. 4th 400 (2001). The court reasoned that "[t]he recitation and discussion of factual data concerning the athletic performance of these plaintiffs command a substantial public interest, and, therefore, is a form of expression due substantial constitutional protection." And in Montana v. San Jose Mercury News, Inc., former NFL quarterback Joe Montana brought a right-of-publicity action against a newspaper for selling posters containing previously published pages from the newspaper depicting the many Super Bowl victories by Montana and the San Francisco 49ers. The court found that "[p]osters portraying the 49'ers' [sic] victories are . . . a form of public interest presentation to which protection must be extended."

We think that, unlike in *Gionfriddo, Montana,* and *Dora,* EA is not publishing or reporting factual data. EA's video game is a means by which users can play their own virtual football games, not a means for obtaining information about real-world football games. Although EA has incorporated certain actual player information into the game (height, weight, etc.), its case is considerably weakened by its decision not to include the athletes' names along with their likenesses and statistical data. EA can hardly be considered to be "reporting" on Keller's career at Arizona State and Nebraska when it is not even using Keller's name in connection with his avatar in the game. Put simply, EA's interactive game is not a publication of facts about college football; it is a game, not a reference source. These state law defenses, therefore, do not apply.[12]

---

12.   We similarly reject Judge Thomas's argument that Keller's right-of-publicity claim should give way to the First Amendment in light of the fact that "the essence of *NCAA Football* is founded on publicly available data." Judge Thomas compares *NCAA Football* to the fantasy baseball products that the Eighth Circuit deemed protected by the First Amendment in the face of a right-of-publicity claim in C.B.C. Distribution and Marketing, 505 F.3d at 823-24. But there is a big difference between a video game like *NCAA Football* and fantasy baseball products like those at issue in *C.B.C.* Those products merely "incorporate[d] the names along with performance and biographical data of actual major league baseball players." *NCAA Football,* on the other hand, uses virtual likenesses of actual college football players. It is seemingly true that each likeness is generated largely from publicly available data—though, as Judge Thomas acknowledges, EA solicits certain information directly from schools—but finding this fact dispositive would neuter the right of publicity in our digital world. Computer programmers with the appropriate expertise can create a realistic likeness of any celebrity using only publicly available data. If EA creates a virtual likeness of Tom Brady using only publicly available data—public images and videos of Brady—does EA have free reign [sic] to use that likeness in commercials without violating Brady's right of publicity? We think not, and thus must reject Judge Thomas's point about the public availability of much of the data used given that EA produced and used actual likenesses of the athletes involved.

III

Under California's transformative use defense, EA's use of the likenesses of college athletes like Samuel Keller in its video games is not, as a matter of law, protected by the First Amendment. We reject EA's suggestion to import the *Rogers* test into the right-of-publicity arena, and conclude that state law defenses for the reporting of information do not protect EA's use.

AFFIRMED.

THOMAS, Circuit Judge, dissenting:

Because the creative and transformative elements of Electronic Arts' *NCAA Football* video game series predominate over the commercial use of the athletes' likenesses, the First Amendment protects EA from liability. Therefore, I respectfully dissent. . . .

Notes and Questions

1. Electronic Arts and the Collegiate Licensing Company settled this case by paying $40 million. The case continued against the NCAA, which later settled for $20 million on the day the *O'Bannon* case seeking an order blocking the NCAA policy that prevents sharing licensing revenues with student players went to trial (O'Bannon v. National Collegiate Athletic Ass'n, 7 F. Supp. 3d 955 (N.D. Calif. 2014)). By settling the video games case, the NCAA apparently hoped to preclude evidence that EA was willing to pay for the likenesses of players, but was prevented from doing so by NCAA rules. *See* Kevin Trahan, SBNation, *How $20 Million Video Games Settlement Could Change* O'Bannon, http://www.sbnation.com/college-football/2014/6/9/5793556/keller-lawsuit-ncaa-settlement-money-obannon (June 9, 2014); *see also* Ben Strauss & Steve Eder, *N.C.A.A. Settles One Video Game Suit for $20 Million as a Second Begins*, N.Y. Times, June 9, 2014, http://www.nytimes.com/2014/06/10/sports/ncaafootball/ncaa-settles-sam-keller-video-game-suit-for-20-million.html.

2. Electronic Arts responded to this suit by discontinuing its games, but has indicated that it may revive them if it can pay the players. *See* Kevin Trahan, *EA Sports Might Bring Back College Football Game If It Can Pay Players*, June 18, 2014, http://www.sbnation.com/college-football/2014/6/18/5822084/ea-sports-ncaa-football-video-game-return/in/4340045.

Problems: Right of Publicity and the First Amendment

1. In March 1997, Los Angeles Magazine published the "Fabulous Hollywood Issue!" An article from this issue entitled "Grand Illusions" used computer technology to alter 16 famous film stills to make it appear that the actors were wearing Spring 1997 fashions. The final shot was a still from the 1982 movie *Tootsie*, which starred Dustin Hoffman playing an actor who dressed as a woman to get a part on a TV soap. The original showed Hoffman in character in a red long-sleeved sequined evening dress and high heels, posing in front of an American flag. The still carried the text, "What do you get when you cross a hopelessly straight, starving actor with a dynamite red sequined dress? You get America's hottest new actress." In the magazine, the American flag and Hoffman's head remained as they appeared in the original, but Hoffman's body and his long-sleeved red sequined dress were replaced by the body of a male model in the same pose, wearing a spaghetti-strapped, cream-colored, silk evening dress and high-heeled sandals. Instead of the original caption, the text identified the still as from the movie *Tootsie*, and read, "Dustin Hoffman isn't a drag in a butter-colored silk gown by Richard Tyler and Ralph Lauren heels."

Is the magazine's use of the photo protected by the First Amendment? *See Hoffman v. Capital Cities/ABC, Inc.*, 255 F.3d 1180 (9th Cir. 2001).

2. Rick Rush has painted many famous athletes in his project of "painting America through sports." In 1997, he went to the Masters golf tournament in Augusta to paint Tiger Woods. Rush produced a series of prints called "The Masters of Augusta" with Woods in the foreground and other famous golfers in the background, and through Jireh Publishing, offered a limited edition of 250 serigraphs at $700 and 5,000 lithographs at $100 each.[4] ETW Corp. filed suit in federal court in Cleveland against Jireh in June 1998, alleging violations of the Lanham Act and of Woods' common law right of publicity. The president of ETW Corp. was Tiger Woods' father, Earl. ETW, represented by Squire, Sanders & Dempsey, a firm with 750 lawyers in 26 offices around the world, sought an order requiring destruction of the remaining prints, a share of profits from previous sales, triple damages, attorneys' fees and costs. Dennis Niermann, a Cleveland lawyer who specialized in sexual harassment and employment law,[5] represented Jireh Publishing.

Is Jireh protected by the First Amendment? *See ETW Corporation v. Jireh Publishing, Inc.*, 332 F.3d 915 (6th Cir. 2003).

Three articles by Marcia Chambers in the New York Times on June 21, 2003, July 3, 2002, and Feb. 16, 1999, trace the history of this litigation and the intense national interest it engendered. Amicus briefs on behalf of ETW were filed by the estates of Frank Sinatra and Elvis Presley, the players associations of the NFL and Major League Baseball, and the Screen Actors Guild. Briefs supporting Rush were filed by the New York Times, the Newspaper Association of America, a group of 73 law professors, the Reporters Committee on Freedom of the Press, the American Society of Media Photographers, the Volunteer Lawyers for the Arts, and the Society of Professional Journalists. An article by J. Thomas McCarthy and Paul M. Anderson, *Protection of the Athlete's Identity: The Right of Publicity, Endorsements and Domain Names*, 11 Marq. Sports L. Rev. 195 (2001), puts the Tiger Woods painting controversy in historical context and, in addition to the right of publicity, discusses the related area of false endorsement under federal law and the federal and California laws on cybersquatting of personal names.

---

4.   The New York Times reports they were sold for $15 each, *see* N.Y. Times, Feb. 16, 1999 and July 3, 2002; the Sixth Circuit opinion says $100 each, 332 F.3d at 919.

5.   *See* his website at http://www.sex-harassment.info/.

B. COPYRIGHT

The Congress shall have power . . . To promote the progress of science and useful arts, by securing for limited times to authors and inventors the exclusive right to their respective writings and discoveries.

U.S. Const. Art. I, §8, Cl. 8

COPYRIGHT ACT, 17 U.S.C. § 106

Subject to sections 107 through 122, the owner of copyright under this title has the exclusive rights to do and to authorize any of the following:

(1) to reproduce the copyrighted work in copies or phonorecords;

(2) to prepare derivative works based upon the copyrighted work;

(3) to distribute copies or phonorecords of the copyrighted work to the public by sale or other transfer of ownership, or by rental, lease, or lending;

(4) in the case of literary, musical, dramatic, and choreographic works, pantomimes, and motion pictures and other audiovisual works, to perform the copyrighted work publicly;

(5) in the case of literary, musical, dramatic, and choreographic works, pantomimes, and pictorial, graphic, or sculptural works, including the individual images of a motion picture or other audiovisual work, to display the copyrighted work publicly; and

(6) in the case of sound recordings, to perform the copyrighted work publicly by means of a digital audio transmission.

1. Purpose of Copyright and the Fair Use Doctrine

SUNTRUST BANK v. HOUGHTON MIFFLIN COMPANY

United States Court of Appeals, Eleventh Circuit
268 F.3d 1257 (2001)

BIRCH, Circuit Judge: In this opinion, we decide whether publication of The Wind Done Gone ("TWDG"), a fictional work admittedly based on Margaret Mitchell's Gone With the Wind ("GWTW"), should be enjoined from publication based on alleged copyright violations. The district court granted a preliminary injunction against publication . . . . We VACATE the injunction and REMAND for consideration of the remaining claims. . . .

A. History and Development of the Copyright Clause

The Copyright Clause finds its roots in England, where, in 1710, the Statute of Anne "was designed to destroy the booksellers' monopoly of the booktrade and to prevent its recurrence." L. Ray Patterson, *Understanding the Copyright Clause*, 47 J. Copyright Soc'y USA 365, 379 (2000). This Parliamentary statute assigned copyright in books to authors, added a requirement that only a new work could be copyrighted, and limited the duration, which had been perpetual, to two fourteen-year terms. 8 Anne, C.19 (1710), *reprinted in* 8 Melville B. Nimmer & David Nimmer, *Nimmer on Copyright* § 7-5 (2001). It is clear that the goal of the Statute of Anne was to encourage creativity and ensure that the public would have free access to information by putting an end to "the continued use of copyright as a device of censorship." Patterson at 379. The Framers of the U.S. Constitution relied on this statute when drafting the Copyright Clause of our Constitution . . . . Congress directly transferred the principles from the Statute of Anne into the copyright law of the United States in 1783, first through a recommendation to the states to enact similar copyright laws, and then in 1790, with the passage of the first American federal copyright statute.

The Copyright Clause was intended "to be the engine of free expression." To that end, copyright laws have been enacted to achieve three main goals: the promotion of learning, the protection of the public domain, and the granting of an exclusive right to the author.

1.   Promotion of Learning

In the United States, copyright has always been used to promote learning by guarding against censorship.[8] Throughout the nineteenth century, the copyright in literature was limited to the right "to publish and vend books." The term "copy" was interpreted literally; an author had the right only to prevent others from copying and selling her particular literary work. *See* Stowe v. Thomas, 23 F. Cas. 201 (C.C.E.D. Pa.1853) (holding that a translation of *Uncle Tom's Cabin* into German was not a copyright infringement because it was not a copy of the work as it was published).[9] This limited right ensured that a maximum number of new works would be created and published. It was not until the 1909 Act, which codified the concept of a derivative work, that an author's right to protect his original work against imitation was established. This change more closely represents current statutory copyright law and is consistent with copyright's constitutional mandate.

As a further protection of the public interest, until 1976, statutory copyright law required that a work be published before an author was entitled to a copyright in that work. Therefore, in order to have the sole right of publication for the statutory period, the author was first required to make the work available to the public. In 1976, copyright was extended to include any work "fixed in any tangible medium of expression" in order to adapt the law to technological advances. § 102(a). Thus, the publication requirement was removed, but the fair use right was codified to maintain the constitutionally mandated balance to ensure that the public has access to knowledge.

The Copyright Act promotes public access to knowledge because it provides an economic incentive for authors to publish books and disseminate ideas to the public. . . . Without the limited monopoly, authors would have little economic

---

8.   *See* Jane C. Ginsburg, *Creation and Commercial Value: Copyright Protection in Works of Information*, 90 Colum. L. Rev. 1865, 1873 (1990) . . . .

9.   Under modern copyright, such a right to translate would enjoy protection as a "derivative work." §§ 101 and 106. In Folsom v. Marsh, 9 F. Cas. 342 (C.C. Mass.1841), Justice Story created the concept of "fair use," which actually expanded the copyright monopoly, since until that time a translation or abridgement was not considered an infringement.

incentive to create and publish their work. Therefore, by providing this incentive, the copyright law promotes the public access to new ideas and concepts.

2. Protection of the Public Domain

The second goal of the Copyright Clause is to ensure that works enter the public domain after an author's rights, exclusive, but limited, have expired. Parallel to the patent regime, the limited time period of the copyright serves the dual purpose of ensuring that the work will enter the public domain and ensuring that the author has received "a fair return for [her] labors." . . . The public is protected in two ways: the grant of a copyright encourages authors to create new works . . . , and the limitation ensures that the works will eventually enter the public domain, which protects the public's right of access and use.

3. Exclusive Rights of the Author

Finally, the Copyright Clause grants the author limited exclusive rights in order to encourage the creation of original works. Before our copyright jurisprudence developed, there were two separate theories of copyright in England—the natural law copyright, which was the right of perpetual publication, and the statutory copyright, which was the limited-time copyright. The natural law copyright . . . implied an ownership in the work itself . . . . [I]n 1774, the House of Lords ruled that the natural law copyright, that is, the ownership of the work itself, expires upon publication of the book, when the statutory copyright attaches. . . .

This bifurcated system was carried over into our copyright law. As of the 1909 Act, an author had "state common law protection [that] persisted until the moment of general publication." Estate of Martin Luther King, Jr. v. CBS, Inc., 194 F.3d 1211 (11th Cir. 1999). After the work was published, the author was entitled to federal statutory copyright protection if she had complied with certain federal requirements (i.e., publication with notice). If not, the work was released into the public domain. . . . The system illustrates that the author's ownership is in the copyright, and not in the work itself, for if the author had an ownership interest in the work itself, she would not lose that right if she published the book without complying with federal statutory copyright requirements. Compliance with the copyright law results in the guarantee of copyright to the author for a limited time, but the author never owns the work itself. § 202 ("Ownership of a copyright, or of any of the exclusive rights under a copyright, is distinct from ownership of any material object in which the work is embodied.").

This has an important impact on modern interpretation of copyright, as it emphasizes the distinction between ownership of the work, which an author does not possess, and ownership of the copyright, which an author enjoys for a limited time. In a society oriented toward property ownership, it is not surprising to find many that erroneously equate the work with the copyright in the work and conclude that if one owns the copyright, they must also own the work. However, the fallacy of that understanding is exposed by the simple fact that the work continues to exist after the term of copyright associated with the work has expired. . . .

B. The Union of Copyright and the First Amendment

The Copyright Clause and the First Amendment, while intuitively in conflict,[12] were drafted to work together to prevent censorship; copyright laws were enacted in part to prevent private censorship and the First Amendment was enacted to prevent public censorship.[13] There are "[c]onflicting interests that must be accommodated in drawing a definitional balance" between the Copyright Clause and the First Amendment. 1 Nimmer § 1.10[B][1]. In establishing this balance "[o]n the copyright side, economic encouragement for creators must be preserved and the privacy of unpublished works recognized. Freedom of speech[, on the other hand,] requires the preservation of a meaningful public or democratic dialogue, as well as the uses of speech as a safety valve against violent acts, and as an end in itself."

In copyright law, the balance between the First Amendment and copyright is preserved, in part, by the idea/expression dichotomy and the doctrine of fair use. . . .

1. The Idea/Expression Dichotomy

Copyright cannot protect an idea, only the expression of that idea. . . . The result is that "copyright assures authors the right to their original expression, but encourages others to build freely upon the ideas and information conveyed by the work." . . . It is partly through this idea/expression dichotomy that copyright law embodies the First Amendment's underlying goal of encouraging open debate and the free exchange of ideas. . . . Holding an infringer liable in copyright for copying the expression of another author's ideas does not impede First Amendment goals because the public purpose has been served—the public already has access to the idea or the concepts. A new author may use or discuss the idea, but must do so using her own original expression.

2. Fair Use

First Amendment privileges are also preserved through the doctrine of fair use. Until codification of the fair-use doctrine in the 1976 Act, fair use was a judge-made right developed to preserve the constitutionality of copyright legislation by protecting First Amendment values. Had fair use not been recognized as a right under the 1976 Act, the statutory abandonment of publication as a condition of copyright that had existed for over 200 years would have jeopardized the constitutionality of the new Act because there would be no statutory guarantee that new ideas, or new expressions of old ideas, would be accessible

---

12. While the First Amendment disallows laws that abridge the freedom of speech, the Copyright Clause calls specifically for such a law.

13. *See* Rebecca Tushnet, *Copyright as a Model for Free Speech Law: What Copyright Has in Common with Anti-Pornography Laws, Campaign Finance Reform, and Telecommunications Regulation,* 42 B.C. L. Rev. 1, 2 (2000) ("The First Amendment gets government off speakers' backs, while the Copyright Act enables speakers to make money from speaking and thus encourages them to enter the public marketplace of ideas.").

to the public. Included in the definition of fair use are "purposes such as criticism, comment, news reporting, teaching . . . , scholarship, or research." § 107. The exceptions carved out for these purposes are at the heart of fair use's protection of the First Amendment, as they allow later authors to use a previous author's copyright to introduce new ideas or concepts to the public. Therefore, within the limits of the fair-use test, any use of a copyright is permitted to fulfill one of the important purposes listed in the statute.

Because of the First Amendment principles built into copyright law through the idea/expression dichotomy and the doctrine of fair use, courts often need not entertain related First Amendment arguments in a copyright case.

Notes and Questions

1. The Court of Appeals in the *Suntrust* case vacated the district court's preliminary injunction against publication of *The Wind Done Gone*, a parody of *Gone with the Wind*, finding First Amendment concerns, the likelihood of a successful fair use defense, and a lack of irreparable injury. The court concluded there was no need to address other factors "except to stress that the public interest is always served in promoting First Amendment values and in preserving the public domain from encroachment." The fair use defense is taken up in *Campbell v. Acuff-Rose Music, Inc.*, which follows.

2. *Duration of copyright.* Since the first U.S. copyright act, the duration of copyright has been dramatically extended, most recently by the highly controversial Sonny Bono Copyright Term Extension Act of 1998. That Act added 20 years to the term of existing copyrights, preventing many classic motion pictures and other works from passing into the public domain. At present, most copyrights for works created after 1978 last for the lifetime of the author plus 70 years. The U.S. Supreme Court rejected claims that this extension of the copyright term violates the Constitution's mandate that exclusive rights granted to authors be for "limited times" in *Eldred v. Ashcroft*, 537 U.S. 186 (2003). Professor Lawrence Lessig, a strong advocate of the value of a robust public domain and the First Amendment, represented Eldred in the case. He has written a book on the subject, *Free Culture: How Big Media Uses Technology and the Law to Lock Down Culture and Control Creativity* (2004).

3. *Duration of copyright and the Berne Convention.* The Berne Convention for the Protection of Literary and Artistic Works, which governs international copyright relations among its 164 member states, requires protection of copyrighted works unless the copyright has expired in the country of origin or the country where protection is claimed. Before joining the Berne Convention in 1989, the United States granted copyright protection only to foreign authors whose works were published in the United States and whose countries granted reciprocal rights to American authors. As a result many foreign works were in the public domain even though protected abroad. To comply with the Agreement on Trade-Related Aspects of Intellectual Property Rights, Congress granted copyright protection to preexisting works from Berne member countries that had previously been in the U.S. public domain. In response to a challenge by orchestra conductors, musicians, publishers, and others, the Supreme Court upheld the retroactive copyright protection, holding that it did not exceed Congress's power under the Copyright Clause, in *Golan v. Holder*, 132 S. Ct. 873 (2012).

4. *Termination of copyright licenses and assignments after 35 years.* Except in the case of works made for hire, the author, or a deceased author's spouse and children (and children of deceased children) have the right to terminate any transfer or license of a copyright or copyright rights executed after January 1, 1978, during a five-year period beginning between 35 and 40 years after the transfer or license under 17 U.S.C. § 203. A lengthy battle over attempts by the heirs of Superman's creators, Joe Shuster and Jerry Siegal, to terminate rights now held by Warner Brothers Entertainment appears to have ended unsuccessfully due to earlier settlement agreements with their estates. *See Larson v. Warner Bros. Entertainment,* 504 Fed. Appx. 586 (9th Cir. 2013).

5. *Copyright and the First Amendment.* The tension between copyright and the First Amendment is explored in an interesting article by Jed Rubenfeld, *The Freedom of Imagination: Copyright's Constitutionality,* 112 Yale L.J. 1 (2002). Professor Rubenfeld filed an amicus brief in the *Suntrust* case supporting Alice Randall, author of *The Wind Done Gone.*

6. The United States Copyright Office maintains a website with useful information about copyrights and copyright law at www.copyright.gov.

CAMPBELL v. ACUFF-ROSE MUSIC, INC.

Supreme Court of the United States
510 U.S. 569 (1994)

Justice SOUTER delivered the opinion of the Court.

We are called upon to decide whether 2 Live Crew's commercial parody of Roy Orbison's song, "Oh, Pretty Woman," may be a fair use within the meaning of the Copyright Act of 1976, 17 U.S.C. § 107 . . . .

I

In 1964, Roy Orbison and William Dees wrote a rock ballad called "Oh, Pretty Woman" and assigned their rights in it to respondent Acuff-Rose Music, Inc. . . . Acuff-Rose registered the song for copyright protection.

Petitioners Luther R. Campbell, Christopher Wongwon, Mark Ross, and David Hobbs are collectively known as 2 Live Crew, a popular rap music group. In 1989, Campbell wrote a song entitled "Pretty Woman," which he later described in an affidavit as intended, "through comical lyrics, to satirize the original work . . . ." 2 Live Crew's manager informed Acuff-Rose that 2 Live Crew had written a parody of "Oh, Pretty Woman," that they would afford all credit for ownership and authorship of the original song to Acuff-Rose, Dees, and Orbison, and that they were willing to pay a fee for the use they wished to make of it. Enclosed with the letter were a copy of the lyrics and a recording of 2 Live Crew's song. Acuff-Rose's agent refused permission, stating that "I am aware of the success enjoyed by 'The 2 Live Crews', but I must inform you that we cannot permit the use of a parody of 'Oh, Pretty Woman.'" Nonetheless, . . . 2 Live Crew released records, cassette tapes, and compact discs of "Pretty Woman" in a collection of songs entitled "As Clean As They Wanna Be." The albums and compact discs identify the authors of "Pretty Woman" as Orbison and Dees and its publisher as Acuff-Rose.

Almost a year later, after nearly a quarter of a million copies of the recording had been sold, Acuff-Rose sued 2 Live Crew and its record company, Luke Skyywalker Records, for copyright infringement. The District Court granted summary judgment for 2 Live Crew, reasoning that the commercial purpose of 2 Live Crew's song was no bar to fair use; that 2 Live Crew's version was a parody, which "quickly degenerates into a play on words, substituting predictable lyrics with shocking ones" to show "how bland and banal the Orbison song" is; that 2 Live Crew had taken no more than was necessary to "conjure up" the original in order to parody it; and that it was "extremely unlikely that 2 Live Crew's song could adversely affect the market for the original." . . .

The Court of Appeals for the Sixth Circuit reversed and remanded. Although it assumed for the purpose of its opinion that 2 Live Crew's song was a parody . . . , the Court of Appeals thought the District Court had put too little emphasis on the fact that "every commercial use . . . is presumptively . . . unfair," Sony Corp. of America v. Universal City Studios, Inc., 464 U.S. 417, (1984), and it held that "the admittedly commercial nature" of the parody "requires the conclusion" that the first of four factors relevant under the statute weighs against a finding of fair use. Next, the Court of Appeals determined that, by "taking the heart of the original and making it the heart of a new work," 2 Live Crew had, qualitatively, taken too much. Finally, after noting that the effect on the potential market for the original (and the market for derivative works) is "undoubtedly the single most important element of fair use," Harper & Row, Publishers, Inc. v. Nation Enterprises, 471 U.S. 539 (1985), the Court of Appeals faulted the District Court for "refus[ing] to indulge the presumption" that "harm for purposes of the fair use analysis has been established by the presumption attaching to commercial uses." In sum, the court concluded that its "blatantly commercial purpose . . . prevents this parody from being a fair use."

We granted certiorari to determine whether 2 Live Crew's commercial parody could be a fair use.

II

It is uncontested here that 2 Live Crew's song would be an infringement of Acuff-Rose's rights in "Oh, Pretty Woman," under the Copyright Act of 1976 but for a finding of fair use through parody. From the infancy of copyright protection, some opportunity for fair use of copyrighted materials has been thought necessary to fulfill copyright's very purpose, "[t]o promote the Progress of Science and useful Arts . . . ." For as Justice Story explained, "[i]n truth, in literature, in science and in art, there are, and can be, few, if any, things, which in an abstract sense, are strictly new and original throughout. Every book in literature, science and art, borrows, and must necessarily borrow, and use much which was well known and used before." Emerson v. Davies, 8 F. Cas. 615 (CCD Mass.1845). . . . In copyright cases brought under the Statute of Anne of 1710, English courts held that in some instances "fair abridgements" would not infringe an author's rights, see W. Patry, The Fair Use Privilege in Copyright Law 6-17 (1985); Leval, *Toward a Fair Use Standard*, 103 Harv. L. Rev. 1105 (1990) (hereinafter Leval), and although the First Congress enacted our initial copyright statute . . . without any explicit reference to "fair use," as it later came to be known, the doctrine was recognized by the American courts nonetheless.

In Folsom v. Marsh, 9 F. Cas. 342 (CCD Mass. 1841), Justice Story distilled the essence of law and methodology from the earlier cases: "look to the nature and objects of the selections made, the quantity and value of the materials used, and the degree in which the use may prejudice the sale, or diminish the profits, or supersede the objects, of the original work." Thus expressed, fair use remained exclusively judge-made doctrine until the passage of the 1976 Copyright Act, in which Justice Story's summary is discernible:

"§ 107. Limitations on exclusive rights: Fair use

"Notwithstanding the provisions of sections 106 and 106A, the fair use of a copyrighted work, including such use by reproduction in copies or phonorecords or by any other means specified by that section, for purposes such as criticism, comment, news reporting, teaching (including multiple copies for classroom use), scholarship, or research, is not an infringement of copyright. In determining whether the use made of a work in any particular case is a fair use the factors to be considered shall include—

"(1) the purpose and character of the use, including whether such use is of a commercial nature or is for nonprofit educational purposes;

"(2) the nature of the copyrighted work;

"(3) the amount and substantiality of the portion used in relation to the copyrighted work as a whole; and

"(4) the effect of the use upon the potential market for or value of the copyrighted work. . . .

Congress meant § 107 "to restate the present judicial doctrine of fair use, not to change, narrow, or enlarge it in any way" and intended that courts continue the common-law tradition of fair use adjudication. . . . The fair use doctrine thus "permits [and requires] courts to avoid rigid application of the copyright statute when, on occasion, it would stifle the very creativity which that law is designed to foster." Stewart v. Abend, 495 U.S. 207 (1990) . . . .

The task is not to be simplified with bright-line rules, for the statute, like the doctrine it recognizes, calls for case-by-case analysis. . . . The text employs the terms "including" and "such as" in the preamble paragraph to indicate the "illustrative and not limitative" function of the examples given, . . . which thus provide only general guidance about the sorts of copying that courts and Congress most commonly had found to be fair uses. Nor may the four statutory factors be treated in isolation, one from another. . . . See Leval 1110-1111; Patry & Perlmutter, *Fair Use Misconstrued: Profit, Presumptions, and Parody*, 11 Cardozo Arts & Ent. L.J. 667, 685-687 (1993) (hereinafter Patry & Perlmutter).[10]

10. Because the fair use enquiry often requires close questions of judgment as to the extent of permissible borrowing in cases involving parodies (or other critical works), courts may also wish to bear in mind that the goals of the copyright law, "to stimulate the creation and publication of edifying matter" are not always best served by automatically granting injunctive relief when parodists are found to have gone beyond the bounds of fair use. . . . Leval 1132 (while in the "vast majority of cases, [an injunctive] remedy is justified because most infringements are simple piracy," such cases are "worlds apart from many of those raising reasonable contentions of fair use" where "there may be a strong public interest in the publication of the secondary work [and] the copyright owner's interest may be adequately protected by an award of damages for whatever infringement is found") . . . .

A

The first factor . . . is "the purpose and character of the use, including whether such use is of a commercial nature or is for nonprofit educational purposes." . . . The enquiry here may be guided by the examples given in the preamble to § 107, looking to whether the use is for criticism, or comment, or news reporting, and the like. The central purpose of this investigation is to see, in Justice Story's words, whether the new work merely "supersede[s] the objects" of the original creation ("supplanting" the original), or instead adds something new, with a further purpose or different character, altering the first with new expression, meaning, or message; it asks, in other words, whether and to what extent the new work is "transformative." Although such transformative use is not absolutely necessary for a finding of fair use,[11] the goal of copyright, to promote science and the arts, is generally furthered by the creation of transformative works. Such works thus lie at the heart of the fair use doctrine's guarantee of breathing space within the confines of copyright . . . . [T]he more transformative the new work, the less . . . the significance of other factors, like commercialism, that may weigh against a finding of fair use.

. . . [P]arody has an obvious claim to transformative value . . . . [I]t can provide social benefit, by shedding light on an earlier work, and, in the process, creating a new one. . . . The germ of parody lies in the definition of the Greek *parodeia*, quoted in Judge Nelson's Court of Appeals dissent, as "a song sung alongside another," quoting 7 Encyclopedia Britannica 768 (15th ed. 1975). Modern dictionaries . . . describe a parody as a "literary or artistic work that imitates the characteristic style of an author or a work for comic effect or ridicule" . . . . For the purposes of copyright law, . . . the heart of any parodist's claim to quote from existing material is the use of some elements of a prior author's composition to create a new one that, at least in part, comments on that author's works. . . . If, on the contrary, the commentary has no critical bearing on the substance or style of the original composition, which the alleged infringer merely uses to get attention or to avoid the drudgery in working up something fresh, the claim to fairness in borrowing from another's work diminishes accordingly (if it does not vanish), and other factors, like the extent of its commerciality, loom larger.[14] Parody needs to mimic an original to make its point, and so has some claim to use the creation of its victim's . . . imagination, whereas satire can stand on its own two feet and so requires justification for the very act of borrowing.[15] See Bisceglia, *Parody and Copyright Protection: Turning the Balancing Act Into a Juggling Act*, in ASCAP, Copyright Law Symposium, No. 34, p. 25 (1987).

The fact that parody can claim legitimacy for some appropriation does not, of course, tell either parodist or judge much about where to draw the line. Like a

11. The obvious statutory exception to this focus on transformative uses is the straight reproduction of multiple copies for classroom distribution.

14. . . . [W]hen there is little or no risk of market substitution, whether because of the large extent of transformation of the earlier work, the new work's minimal distribution in the market, the small extent to which it borrows from an original, or other factors, taking parodic aim at an original is a less critical factor in the analysis, and looser forms of parody may be found to be fair use, as may satire with lesser justification for the borrowing than would otherwise be required.

15. Satire has been defined as a work "in which prevalent follies or vices are assailed with ridicule," 14 Oxford English Dictionary at 500, or are "attacked through irony, derision, or wit," American Heritage Dictionary.

book review quoting the copyrighted material criticized, parody may or may not be fair use, and petitioners' suggestion that any parodic use is presumptively fair has no more justification in law or fact than the equally hopeful claim that any use for news reporting should be presumed fair. The Act has no hint of an evidentiary preference for parodists over their victims, and no workable presumption for parody could take account of the fact that parody often shades into satire when society is lampooned through its creative artifacts, or that a work may contain both parodic and nonparodic elements. Accordingly, parody, like any other use, has to work its way through the relevant factors, and be judged case by case, in light of the ends of the copyright law.

Here, the District Court held, and the Court of Appeals assumed, that 2 Live Crew's "Pretty Woman" contains parody, commenting on and criticizing the original work, whatever it may have to say about society at large. . . . Judge Nelson, dissenting below, came to the . . . conclusion, that the 2 Live Crew song "was clearly intended to ridicule the white-bread original" and "reminds us that sexual congress with nameless streetwalkers is not necessarily the stuff of romance and is not necessarily without its consequences. The singers (there are several) have the same thing on their minds as did the lonely man with the nasal voice, but here there is no hint of wine and roses." . . .

We have less difficulty in finding that critical element in 2 Live Crew's song than the Court of Appeals did, although having found it we will not take the further step of evaluating its quality. The threshold question when fair use is raised in defense of parody is whether a parodic character may reasonably be perceived.[16] Whether, going beyond that, parody is in good taste or bad does not and should not matter to fair use. As Justice Holmes explained, "[i]t would be a dangerous undertaking for persons trained only to the law to constitute themselves final judges of the worth of [a work], outside of the narrowest and most obvious limits . . . ." Bleistein v. Donaldson Lithographing Co., 188 U.S. 239 (1903) (circus posters have copyright protection); cf. Yankee Publishing Inc. v. News America Publishing, Inc., 809 F. Supp. 267 (SDNY 1992) (Leval, J.) ("First Amendment protections do not apply only to those who speak clearly, whose jokes are funny, and whose parodies succeed") (trademark case).

While we might not assign a high rank to the parodic element here, we think it fair to say that 2 Live Crew's song reasonably could be perceived as commenting on the original or criticizing it, to some degree. 2 Live Crew juxtaposes the romantic musings of a man whose fantasy comes true, with degrading taunts, a bawdy demand for sex, and a sigh of relief from paternal responsibility. The later words can be taken as a comment on the naiveté of the original of an earlier day, as a rejection of its sentiment that ignores the ugliness of street life and the debasement that it signifies. It is this joinder of reference and ridicule that marks off the author's choice of parody from the other types of comment and criticism that traditionally have had a claim to fair use protection as transformative works.

---

16. The only further judgment, indeed, that a court may pass on a work goes to an assessment of whether the parodic element is slight or great, and the copying small or extensive in relation to the parodic element, for a work with slight parodic element and extensive copying will be more likely to merely "supersede the objects" of the original. . . .

The Court of Appeals, however, immediately cut short the enquiry into 2 Live Crew's fair use claim by confining its treatment of the first factor essentially to one relevant fact, the commercial nature of the use. The court then inflated the significance of this fact by applying a presumption . . . that "every commercial use of copyrighted material is presumptively . . . unfair . . . ." In giving virtually dispositive weight to the commercial nature of the parody, the Court of Appeals erred.

The language of the statute makes clear that the commercial or nonprofit educational purpose of a work is only one element of the first factor enquiry into its purpose and character. . . . Congress resisted attempts to narrow the ambit of this traditional enquiry by adopting categories of presumptively fair use, and it urged courts to preserve the breadth of their traditionally ample view of the universe of relevant evidence. . . . Accordingly, the mere fact that a use is educational and not for profit does not insulate it from a finding of infringement, any more than the commercial character of a use bars a finding of fairness. If, indeed, commerciality carried presumptive force against a finding of fairness, the presumption would swallow nearly all of the illustrative uses listed in the preamble paragraph of § 107, including news reporting, comment, criticism, teaching, scholarship, and research, since these activities "are generally conducted for profit in this country." Congress could not have intended such a rule, which certainly is not inferable from the common-law cases, arising as they did from the world of letters in which Samuel Johnson could pronounce that "[n]o man but a blockhead ever wrote, except for money." 3 Boswell's Life of Johnson 19 (G. Hill ed. 1934).

. . . [T]he "fact that a publication was commercial as opposed to nonprofit is a separate factor that tends to weigh against a finding of fair use." But that is all, and the fact that even the force of that tendency will vary with the context is a further reason against elevating commerciality to hard presumptive significance. The use, for example, of a copyrighted work to advertise a product, even in a parody, will be entitled to less indulgence under the first factor of the fair use enquiry than the sale of a parody for its own sake, let alone one performed a single time by students in school. . . .[18]

B

The second statutory factor, "the nature of the copyrighted work," draws on Justice Story's expression, the "value of the materials used." This factor calls for recognition that some works are closer to the core of intended copyright protection than others, with the consequence that fair use is more difficult to establish when the former works are copied. See, *e.g.*, Stewart v. Abend (contrasting

18. Finally, regardless of the weight one might place on the alleged infringer's state of mind, . . . we reject Acuff-Rose's argument that 2 Live Crew's request for permission to use the original should be weighed against a finding of fair use. Even if good faith were central to fair use, 2 Live Crew's actions do not necessarily suggest that they believed their version was not fair use; the offer may simply have been made in a good-faith effort to avoid this litigation. If the use is otherwise fair, then no permission need be sought or granted. Thus, being denied permission to use a work does not weigh against a finding of fair use.

fictional short story with factual works); *Harper & Row* (contrasting soon-to-be-published memoir with published speech); *Sony* (contrasting motion pictures with news broadcasts); *Feist* (contrasting creative works with bare factual compilations); 3 M. Nimmer & D. Nimmer, Nimmer on Copyright § 13.05[A][2] (1993) (hereinafter Nimmer); Leval 1116. We agree with both the District Court and the Court of Appeals that the Orbison original's creative expression for public dissemination falls within the core of the copyright's protective purposes. This fact, however, is not much help in this case, or ever likely to help much in separating the fair use sheep from the infringing goats in a parody case, since parodies almost invariably copy publicly known, expressive works.

C

The third factor asks whether "the amount and substantiality of the portion used in relation to the copyrighted work as a whole" . . . are reasonable in relation to the purpose of the copying. Here, attention turns to the persuasiveness of a parodist's justification for the particular copying done, and the enquiry will harken back to the first of the statutory factors, for, as in prior cases, we recognize that the extent of permissible copying varies with the purpose and character of the use. See *Sony* (reproduction of entire work "does not have its ordinary effect of militating against a finding of fair use" as to home video-taping of television programs); *Harper & Row* ("[E]ven substantial quotations might qualify as fair use in a review of a published work or a news account of a speech" but not in a scoop of a soon-to-be-published memoir). The facts bearing on this factor will also tend to address the fourth, by revealing the degree to which the parody may serve as a market substitute for the original or potentially licensed derivatives.

The District Court considered the song's parodic purpose in finding that 2 Live Crew had not helped themselves overmuch. The Court of Appeals disagreed, stating that "[w]hile it may not be inappropriate to find that no more was taken than necessary, the copying was qualitatively substantial . . . . We conclude that taking the heart of the original and making it the heart of a new work was to purloin a substantial portion of the essence of the original."

The Court of Appeals is of course correct that this factor calls for thought not only about the quantity of the materials used, but about their quality and importance, too. In *Harper & Row*, for example, the Nation had taken only some 300 words out of President Ford's memoirs, but we signaled the significance of the quotations in finding them to amount to "the heart of the book," the part most likely to be newsworthy and important in licensing serialization. We also agree with the Court of Appeals that whether "a substantial portion of the infringing work was copied verbatim" from the copyrighted work is a relevant question, for it may reveal a dearth of transformative character or purpose under the first factor, or a greater likelihood of market harm under the fourth; a work composed primarily of an original, particularly its heart, with little added or changed, is more likely to be a merely superseding use, fulfilling demand for the original.

Where we part company with the court below is in applying these guides to parody . . . . Parody presents a difficult case. Parody's humor, or . . . its comment, necessarily springs from recognizable allusion to its object through distorted imitation. Its art lies in the tension between a known original and its parodic twin. When parody takes aim at a particular original work, the parody must be able to "conjure up" at least enough of that original to make the object of its critical wit recognizable. What makes for this recognition is quotation of the original's most distinctive or memorable features, which the parodist can be sure the audience will know. Once enough has been taken to assure identification, how much more is reasonable will depend, say, on the extent to which the song's overriding purpose and character is to parody the original or, in contrast, the likelihood that the parody may serve as a market substitute for the original. But using some characteristic features cannot be avoided.

. . . [T]he Court of Appeals was insufficiently appreciative of parody's need for the recognizable sight or sound when it ruled 2 Live Crew's use unreasonable as a matter of law. It is true, of course, that 2 Live Crew copied the characteristic opening bass riff (or musical phrase) of the original, and true that the words of the first line copy the Orbison lyrics. But if quotation of the opening riff and the first line may be said to go to the "heart" of the original, the heart is also what most readily conjures up the song for parody, and it is the heart at which parody takes aim. Copying does not become excessive in relation to parodic purpose merely because the portion taken was the original's heart. If 2 Live Crew had copied a significantly less memorable part of the original, it is difficult to see how its parodic character would have come through.

This is not, of course, to say that anyone who calls himself a parodist can skim the cream and get away scot free. In parody, as in news reporting, context is everything, and the question of fairness asks what else the parodist did besides go to the heart of the original. It is significant that 2 Live Crew . . . thereafter departed markedly from the Orbison lyrics for its own ends. 2 Live Crew not only copied the bass riff and repeated it, but also produced otherwise distinctive sounds, interposing "scraper" noise, overlaying the music with solos in different keys, and altering the drum beat. This is not a case where "a substantial portion" of the parody itself is composed of a "verbatim" copying of the original. . . . [T]he parody is [not] so insubstantial, as compared to the copying, that the third factor must be resolved as a matter of law against the parodists.

. . . [A]s to the lyrics, . . . the Court of Appeals correctly suggested that "no more was taken than necessary," but just for that reason, we fail to see how the copying can be excessive in relation to its parodic purpose, even if the portion taken is the original's "heart." As to the music, we express no opinion whether repetition of the bass riff is excessive copying, and we remand to permit evaluation of the amount taken, in light of the song's parodic purpose and character, its transformative elements, and considerations of the potential for market substitution . . . .

D

The fourth fair use factor is "the effect of the use upon the potential market for or value of the copyrighted work." It requires courts to consider not only the extent of market harm caused by the particular actions of the alleged infringer, but also "whether unrestricted and widespread conduct of the sort engaged in by the defendant . . . would result in a substantially adverse impact on the potential market" for the original. . . . The enquiry "must take account not only of harm to the original but also of harm to the market for derivative works."

Since fair use is an affirmative defense, its proponent would have difficulty carrying the burden of demonstrating fair use without favorable evidence about relevant markets.[21] In moving for summary judgment, 2 Live Crew left themselves at just such a disadvantage when they failed to address the effect on the market for rap derivatives, and confined themselves to uncontroverted submissions that there was no likely effect on the market for the original. They did not, however, thereby subject themselves to the evidentiary presumption applied by the Court of Appeals. In assessing the likelihood of significant market harm, the Court of Appeals quoted from language in *Sony* that " '[i]f the intended use is for commercial gain, that likelihood may be presumed. But if it is for a noncommercial purpose, the likelihood must be demonstrated.' " The court reasoned that because "the use of the copyrighted work is wholly commercial, . . . we presume that a likelihood of future harm to Acuff-Rose exists." In so doing, the court resolved the fourth factor against 2 Live Crew, just as it had the first, by applying a presumption about the effect of commercial use, a presumption which as applied here we hold to be error.

No "presumption" or inference of market harm that might find support in *Sony* is applicable to a case involving something beyond mere duplication for commercial purposes. *Sony*'s discussion of a presumption contrasts a context of verbatim copying of the original in its entirety for commercial purposes, with the noncommercial context of *Sony* itself (home copying of television programming). In the former circumstances, what *Sony* said simply makes common sense: when a commercial use amounts to mere duplication of the entirety of an original, it clearly "supersede[s] the objects," of the original and serves as a market replacement for it, making it likely that cognizable market harm to the original will occur. But when, on the contrary, the second use is transformative, market substitution is at least less certain, and market harm may not be so readily inferred. Indeed, as to parody pure and simple, it is more likely that the new work will not affect the market for the original . . . by acting as a substitute for it. . . . [T]he parody and the original usually serve different market functions. . . .

We do not, of course, suggest that a parody may not harm the market at all, but when a lethal parody, like a scathing theater review, kills demand for the original, it does not produce a harm cognizable under the Copyright Act. . . . [T]he role of the courts is to distinguish between "[b]iting criticism [that merely] suppresses demand [and] copyright infringement[, which] usurps it."

This distinction between potentially remediable displacement and unremediable disparagement is reflected in the rule that there is no protectible derivative market for criticism. The market for potential derivative uses includes only

---

21. Even favorable evidence, without more, is no guarantee of fairness. Judge Leval gives the example of the film producer's appropriation of a composer's previously unknown song that turns the song into a commercial success; the boon to the song does not make the film's simple copying fair. Leval 1124, n. 84. This factor, no less than the other three, may be addressed only through a "sensitive balancing of interests." Market harm is a matter of degree, and the importance of this factor will vary, not only with the amount of harm, but also with the relative strength of the showing on the other factors.

those that creators of original works would in general develop or license others to develop. Yet the unlikelihood that creators of imaginative works will license critical reviews or lampoons of their own productions removes such uses from the very notion of a potential licensing market. "People ask . . . for criticism, but they only want praise." S. Maugham, Of Human Bondage 241 (Penguin ed. 1992). Thus, to the extent that the opinion below may be read to have considered harm to the market for parodies of "Oh, Pretty Woman," the court erred.

In explaining why the law recognizes no derivative market for critical works, including parody, we have, of course, been speaking of the later work as if it had nothing but a critical aspect . . . . But the later work may have a more complex character, with effects not only in the arena of criticism but also in protectible markets for derivative works, too. In that sort of case, the law looks beyond the criticism to the other elements of the work, as it does here. 2 Live Crew's song comprises not only parody but also rap music, and the derivative market for rap music is a proper focus of enquiry. . . . Evidence of substantial harm to it would weigh against a finding of fair use, because the licensing of derivatives is an important economic incentive to the creation of originals. . . . Of course, the only harm to derivatives that need concern us, as discussed above, is the harm of market substitution. The fact that a parody may impair the market for derivative uses by the very effectiveness of its critical commentary is no more relevant under copyright than the like threat to the original market.[24]

Although 2 Live Crew submitted uncontroverted affidavits on the question of market harm to the original, neither they, nor Acuff-Rose, introduced evidence or affidavits addressing the likely effect of 2 Live Crew's parodic rap song on the market for a nonparody, rap version of "Oh, Pretty Woman." And while Acuff-Rose would have us find evidence of a rap market in the very facts that 2 Live Crew recorded a rap parody of "Oh, Pretty Woman" and another rap group sought a license to record a rap derivative, there was no evidence that a potential rap market was harmed in any way by 2 Live Crew's parody, rap version. . . . The District Court essentially passed on this issue, observing that Acuff-Rose is free to record "whatever version of the original it desires," the Court of Appeals went the other way by erroneous presumption. Contrary to each treatment, it is impossible to deal with the fourth factor except by recognizing that a silent record on an important factor bearing on fair use disentitled the proponent of the defense, 2 Live Crew, to summary judgment. The evidentiary hole will doubtless be plugged on remand.

III

It was error for the Court of Appeals to conclude that the commercial nature of 2 Live Crew's parody of "Oh, Pretty Woman" rendered it presumptively unfair.

---

24. In some cases it may be difficult to determine whence the harm flows. In such cases, the other fair use factors may provide some indicia of the likely source of the harm. A work whose overriding purpose and character is parodic and whose borrowing is slight in relation to its parody will be far less likely to cause cognizable harm than a work with little parodic content and much copying.

No such evidentiary presumption is available to address either the first factor, the character and purpose of the use, or the fourth, market harm, in determining whether a transformative use, such as parody, is a fair one. The court also erred in holding that 2 Live Crew had necessarily copied excessively from the Orbison original, considering the parodic purpose of the use. We therefore reverse the judgment of the Court of Appeals and remand the case for further proceedings consistent with this opinion.

Justice KENNEDY, concurring. I agree that remand is appropriate and join the opinion of the Court, with these further observations about the fair use analysis of parody.

. . . It is not enough that the parody use the original in a humorous fashion, however creative that humor may be. The parody must target the original, and not just its general style, the genre of art to which it belongs, or society as a whole (although if it targets the original, it may target those features as well). . . . This prerequisite confines fair use protection to works whose very subject is the original composition and so necessitates some borrowing from it. . . . It also protects works we have reason to fear will not be licensed by copyright holders who wish to shield their works from criticism. . . .

As to the fourth factor (the effect of the use on the market for the original), the Court acknowledges that it is legitimate for parody to suppress demand for the original by its critical effect. What it may not do is usurp demand by its substitutive effect. . . . Creative works can compete with other creative works for the same market, even if their appeal is overlapping. Factor four thus underscores the importance of ensuring that the parody is in fact an independent creative work, which is why the parody must "make some critical comment or statement about the original work which reflects the original perspective of the parodist—thereby giving the parody social value beyond its entertainment function."

. . . Fair use is an affirmative defense, so doubts about whether a given use is fair should not be resolved in favor of the self-proclaimed parodist. We should not make it easy for musicians to exploit existing works and then later claim that their rendition was a valuable commentary on the original. Almost any revamped modern version of a familiar composition can be construed as a "comment on the naiveté of the original," because of the difference in style and because it will be amusing to hear how the old tune sounds in the new genre. Just the thought of a rap version of Beethoven's Fifth Symphony or "Achy Breaky Heart" is bound to make people smile. If we allow any weak transformation to qualify as parody, however, we weaken the protection of copyright. And underprotection of copyright disserves the goals of copyright just as much as overprotection, by reducing the financial incentive to create.

While I am not so assured that 2 Live Crew's song is a legitimate parody, the Court's treatment . . . leaves room for the District Court to determine on remand that the song is not a fair use. As future courts apply our fair use analysis, they must take care to ensure that not just any commercial takeoff is rationalized *post hoc* as a parody.

APPENDIX A TO OPINION OF THE COURT

"Oh, Pretty Woman"
by Roy Orbison and William Dees

Pretty Woman, walking down the street,

Pretty Woman, the kind I like to meet,

Pretty Woman, I don't believe you, you're not the truth,

No one could look as good as you Mercy

Pretty Woman, won't you pardon me,

Pretty Woman, I couldn't help but see,

Pretty Woman, that you look lovely as can be

Are you lonely just like me?

Pretty Woman, stop a while,

Pretty Woman, talk a while,

Pretty Woman give your smile to me

Pretty Woman, yeah, yeah, yeah

Pretty Woman, look my way,

Pretty Woman, say you'll stay with me

'Cause I need you, I'll treat you right

Come to me baby, Be mine tonight

Pretty Woman, don't walk on by,

Pretty Woman, don't make me cry,

Pretty Woman, don't walk away,

Hey, O.K.

If that's the way it must be, O.K.

I guess I'll go on home, it's late

There'll be tomorrow night, but wait!

What do I see

Is she walking back to me?

Yeah, she's walking back to me!

Oh, Pretty Woman.

APPENDIX B TO OPINION OF THE COURT

"Pretty Woman"
as Recorded by 2 Live Crew

Pretty woman walkin' down the street

Pretty woman girl you look so sweet

Pretty woman you bring me down to that knee

Pretty woman you make me wanna beg please

Oh, pretty woman

Big hairy woman you need to shave that stuff

Big hairy woman you know I bet it's tough

Big hairy woman all that hair it ain't legit

Cause you look like 'Cousin It'

Big hairy woman

Bald headed woman girl your hair won't grow

Bald headed woman you got a teeny weeny afro

Bald headed woman you know your hair could look nice

Bald headed woman first you got to roll it with rice

Bald headed woman here, let me get this hunk of biz for ya

Ya know what I'm saying you look better than rice a roni

Oh bald headed woman

Big hairy woman come on in

And don't forget your bald headed friend

Hey pretty woman let the boys Jump in

Two timin' woman girl you know you ain't right

Two timin' woman you's out with my boy last night

Two timin' woman that takes a load off my mind

Two timin' woman now I know the baby ain't mine

Oh, two timin' woman

Oh pretty woman

Notes and Questions

1. *Parody used to advertise a product.* In rejecting a presumption that commercial use cannot be fair use, the court emphasized the importance of context, stating that "use, for example, of a copyrighted work to advertise a product, even in a parody, will be entitled to less indulgence under the first factor of the fair use enquiry than the sale of a parody for its own sake . . . ." GoldieBlox, a toy company that makes construction toys "from a female perspective" aims "to disrupt the pink aisle and inspire the future generation of female engineers." In a video made to advertise their products, three girls reject "princess" play and build a complex Rube Goldberg contraption to the tune of the Beastie Boys song "Girls, Girls, Girls," but with completely different lyrics. Instead of portraying girls as household help and sex objects, the GoldieBlox version portrays them as builders of space ships, coders of apps, as engineers. After the video went viral, Beastie Boys claimed the video infringed their copyright. GoldieBlox filed a declaratory action seeking a ruling that their parody was fair use, but the case was settled before any decision was reached. If the case had gone to trial, how should it have come out?

2. *Parody of the author fair use?* In *Salinger v. Colting*, 607 F.3d 68 (2d Cir. 2010), the court upheld grant of a preliminary injunction against publication of *60 Years Later: Coming Through the Rye*, a purported sequel to *The Catcher in the Rye*. As described by the court, "60 Years Later tells the story of a 76-year-old Holden Caulfield, referred to as 'Mr. C,' in a world that includes Mr. C's 90-year-old author, a 'fictionalized Salinger.' The novel's premise is that Salinger has been haunted by his creation and now wishes to bring him back to life in order to kill him. Unsurprisingly, this task is easier said than done. As the story progresses, Mr. C becomes increasingly self-aware and able to act in ways contrary to the will of Salinger. After a series of misadventures, Mr. C travels to Cornish, New Hampshire, where he meets Salinger in his home. Salinger finds he is unable to kill Mr. C and instead decides to set him free. The novel concludes with Mr. C reuniting with his younger sister, Phoebe, and an estranged son, Daniel."

The court found that the work was neither sufficiently transformative nor a parody of *Catcher in the Rye*. Although it did contain a parody of Salinger, to qualify for fair use, the parody must be of the work itself.

3. *Visual arts and fair use.* Contemporary artists increasingly face questions about the uses they can make of existing images and sometimes find themselves in copyright litigation. Shepard Fairey's use of an Associated Press photo for his iconic "Hope" campaign poster for Barack Obama, Richard Prince's use of French photographer Patrick Cariou's portraits of Rastafarians in his "Canal Zone" collages, and Jeff Koons's sculpture based on Art Rogers's photo "Puppies" all led to litigation.

As part of the College Art Association's Fair-Use Initiative, Professors Patricia Aufderheide and Peter Jaszi have interviewed visual arts professionals about their use of materials created by others and convened meetings of groups of visual arts professionals in New York, Dallas, Washington, D.C., Chicago, and Los Angeles to explore situations in which fair use allows use of such materials. Their first published report, *Copyright, Permissions, and Fair Use Among Visual Artists and the Academic and Museum Visual Arts Communities,* found widespread misunderstanding of the fair use doctrine that leads to substantial constraints and self-censorship in the artists' work. *See* http://www.collegeart. org/news/2014/06/25/update-on-the-caa-fair-use-initiative/, and Ben Mauk, *Who Owns This Image?*, The New Yorker, Feb. 14, 2014.

2. *What Can Be Copyrighted?*

COPYRIGHT ACT, 17 U.S.C. § 102

(a) Copyright protection subsists, in accordance with this title, in original works of authorship fixed in any tangible medium of expression, now known or later developed, from which they can be perceived, reproduced, or otherwise communicated, either directly or with the aid of a machine or device. Works of authorship include the following categories:
(1) literary works;
(2) musical works, including any accompanying words;
(3) dramatic works, including any accompanying music;
(4) pantomimes and choreographic works;
(5) pictorial, graphic, and sculptural works;
(6) motion pictures and other audiovisual works;
(7) sound recordings; and
(8) architectural works.
(b) In no case does copyright protection for an original work of authorship extend to any idea, procedure, process, system, method of operation, concept, principle, or discovery, regardless of the form in which it is described, explained, illustrated, or embodied in such work.

ODDZON PRODUCTS, INC v. OMAN

United States Court of Appeals, District of Columbia Circuit
924 F.2d 346 (1991)

RUTH BADER GINSBURG, Circuit Judge. The Copyright Office, in September 1988, refused to register a claim to copyright in a work of soft sculpture titled KOOSH ball. On judicial review under the Administrative Procedure Act . . . the district court determined, by summary judgment, that the refusal to register was not an abuse of discretion. . . . We agree. . . . We underscore, however, that neither our decision, nor that of the district court, in any way precludes a determination, in an infringement action, that the KOOSH ball is indeed copyrightable. . . .

The KOOSH ball is a patented, trademarked product formed of hundreds of floppy, wiggly, elastomeric filaments radiating from a core. Originally developed to teach youngsters with poor eye-to-hand coordination how to play catch, the KOOSH ball has a soft, snugly feel, and is easily grasped if it contacts any portion of a person's hand. Copyright claimant [toymaker] OddzOn Products, Inc., . . . describes the KOOSH as a "loveable, laughable ball," fun for ages three and up. OddzOn sought copyright registration for the KOOSH ball to block importation of less expensive "knockoffs." *See* 17 U.S.C. §§ 602, 603 (copyright owners may request the Customs Service to seize infringing copies); 19 C.F.R. § 133.31 ("Claims to copyright which have been registered . . . may be recorded with Customs for import protection."); *cf.* 19 U.S.C. § 1337(a)(1)(B) (prescribing more cumbersome procedure before U.S. International Trade Commission to stop importation of articles that "infringe a valid and enforceable United States patent").

The Copyright Office addressed both the visual character and the "tactility" or feel of the KOOSH ball. As to the former, the examiners regarded the KOOSH ball as a familiar symbol or design; the ball's filaments, the Chief of the Examining Division said, "basically define a sphere, and there is no copyrightable authorship in producing such a familiar shape." . . . The feel of the object was comprehended by the examiners as a functional part of the work, and therefore not a basis for registration. . . .

The district court . . . similarly turned first to the visual aspect of the KOOSH ball. The district judge indicated that it would have been arbitrary for the Copyright Office to deny registration "simply because [the KOOSH ball's] shape approximates a sphere."[1] . . . The judge then sensibly read the registration refusal letters from the Copyright Office to say: "[I]t is not merely that the KOOSH ball approximates a sphere, it is also that there is not enough additional creative work beyond the object's basic shape to warrant a copyright."

The district court went on to consider whether the KOOSH ball's feel demonstrated the requisite creative authorship so clearly as to mark the refusal to register an abuse of discretion. The district judge looked to the Copyright Act definition of "pictorial, graphic, and sculptural works"; such works include works of artistic craftsmanship insofar as their form but not their mechanical or utilitarian aspects are concerned; the design of a useful article . . . shall be considered a pictorial, graphic, or sculptural work only if, and only to the extent that, such design incorporates pictorial, graphic or sculptural features that can be identified separately from, and are capable of existing independently of, the utilitarian aspects of the article. 17 U.S.C. § 101. . . . [T]he district court held that it was not an abuse of discretion for the Copyright Office to rank the tactile qualities of the KOOSH ball as dependent upon, and inseparable from, the utilitarian features of the object, and hence not protectable by copyright. . . .

As we stated in Atari Games Corp. v. Oman, 888 F.2d 878 (D.C. Cir. 1989), . . . [w]e review the Copyright Office decision under a deferential, "abuse of discretion" standard . . . (Silberman, J., concurring) (distinguishing deferential review of registration decisions from "an infringement action in which the court [is] not obliged to defer to an agency's action or interpretation"). . . .

In this case, . . . [t]he visual aspect of the KOOSH ball, according to the examiners, did not reflect the minimal degree of creativity required for a copyright. The tactility of the KOOSH ball could not be taken into account in the creativity assessment, the examiners indicated, because the KOOSH ball is a useful article and its feel is inseparable from its utilitarian function.

If the KOOSH ball is properly classified as a "useful article,"[4] its registration presented the Copyright Office with "[o]ne of the most difficult issues arising under the Copyright Act." See Perlmutter, Conceptual Separability and Copyright in

---

1. . . . The judge asked counsel for the Copyright Office: "If Picasso had painted a round object on a canvas, would you say because it depicts a familiar subject—namely, something that's round—it can't be copyrighted?". . . .

4. The Copyright Act defines "useful article" as one "having an intrinsic utilitarian function that is not merely to portray the appearance of the article or to convey information. An article that is normally a part of the useful article is considered a 'useful article.'" 17 U.S.C. § 101.

the Designs of Useful Articles, 37 J. Copyr. Soc. 339 (1990). Congress excluded the design of useful articles from the realm of copyright except when, "and only to the extent that, such design incorporates [artistic] features that can be identified separately from, and are capable of existing independently of the utilitarian aspects of the article." 17 U.S.C. § 101 . . . . In its report on the bill that became the Copyright Act of 1976, the House Judiciary Committee amplified:

> [A]lthough the shape of an industrial product may be aesthetically satisfying and valuable, the Committee's intention is not to offer it copyright protection under the bill. Unless the shape of an automobile, airplane, ladies' dress, food processor, television set, or any other industrial product contains some element that, physically or conceptually, can be identified as separable from the utilitarian aspects of the article, the design would not be copyrighted under the bill. . . .

OddzOn does not argue that the feel of the KOOSH ball is physically separable from the ball's function. Is the ball's tactility "conceptually . . . separable from the utilitarian aspects of th[e] article?" That is a question we do not answer given the limited nature of our review of registration decisions. . . . It suffices to point out that there is a notable lack of agreement among courts and commentators on the very meaning of "conceptual separability." . . .

At oral argument, we asked OddzOn's counsel how the KOOSH ball would fare if we applied to it the "conceptual separability" test employed by the panel majority in Brandir Int'l, Inc. v. Cascade Pacific Lumber Co., 834 F.2d 1142 (2d Cir. 1987). In that case, a divided Second Circuit panel held uncopyrightable a work originally created as a wire sculpture, and later modified for mass production as a bicycle rack. We set out the exchange with counsel for OddzOn:

Court: How do you distinguish this case from the bicycle rack case, the *Brandir* case, that is cited in [the district court's] opinion . . . ?
Counsel: Well, I say [*Brandir*] was wrong.
Court: But if we were to follow that case, then you lose?
Counsel: I think that's correct.

We reserve appraisal of *Brandir* and competing tests of "conceptual separability" for a case that obliges us to enter the "conceptual separability" fray. We are satisfied, however, that the Copyright Office was not arbitrary in adhering to a line similar to the one taken by our sister circuit.

Was the KOOSH ball correctly classified as "a useful article" and therefore properly held subject to the separability test? The Copyright Office so treated the ball, and OddzOn did not challenge the "utilitarian object" categorization during the application process or in the district court. In its brief on appeal, however, OddzOn added a footnote raising "a point admittedly not raised heretofore." . . . OddzOn called our attention to Gay Toys, Inc. v. Buddy L. Corp., 703 F.2d 970 (6th Cir. 1983), a decision holding that a toy airplane is not a "useful article" and therefore is protectable, if minimally creative, without first passing a separability test.[5] Because the classification question was not raised in

---

5.   The Sixth Circuit understood the House Report . . . to show that the exclusion of utilitarian articles from copyright protection was meant for "industrial products such as automobiles, food processors, and television sets." "The function of toys," in that court's view, "is much more similar to that of works of art than it is to the 'intrinsic utilitarian function' of industrial products."

the application proceedings, that question is not appropriately before us for review.

In conclusion, we again emphasize that we decide simply and only that the refusal of the Copyright Office to register the KOOSH ball, in the circumstances here presented, does not constitute an abuse of discretion. We do not decide on the copyrightability of the item, and we intimate no opinion on the decision we would reach if the matter came before us in an infringement action.[6] . . .

Notes and Questions

1. *Registration.* Why did OddzOn seek copyright registration for its KOOSH ball? Registration is not necessary to obtain copyright protection, which exists from the time the work is created. However, proper application for registration is necessary to bring an action for infringement and provides other advantages. Registration makes a public record of the copyright and provides a certificate of registration, and, most importantly for OddzOn, registration allows the copyright holder to obtain from the Customs Service notice of the importation of articles that appear to be copies of the work. *See* 17 U.S.C.A. § 602.

2. Why did Congress refuse to extend copyright protection to useful articles—those that have "an intrinsic utilitarian function that is not merely to portray the appearance of the article or to convey information" (17 U.S.C. § 101)? *See Mazer v. Stein*, 347 U.S. 201 (1954) (mass-produced sculptures of Balinese dancers intended for use as lamp bases were copyrightable as to their form, but not as to their mechanical or utilitarian features). The purpose of the exception is to prevent the monopolization through copyright of everyday items such as spoons, toasters, lamps, or automobiles.

3. *Enforcing copyrights.* Actions to enforce copyrights are within the exclusive jurisdiction of the federal district courts. 28 U.S.C.A. § 1338(a). How did the action in the principal case differ from an infringement action?

FEIST PUBLICATIONS, INC. v. RURAL TELEPHONE SERVICE CO.

Supreme Court of the United States
499 U.S. 340 (1991)

O'CONNOR, J., delivered the opinion of the Court, in which REHNQUIST, C.J., and WHITE, MARSHALL, STEVENS, SCALIA, KENNEDY, and SOUTER, JJ., joined. BLACKMUN, J., concurred in the judgment. . . .

Rural Telephone Service Company, Inc., is a certified public utility that provides telephone service to several communities in northwest Kansas. It is subject to a state regulation that requires all telephone companies operating in Kansas to issue annually an updated telephone directory. Accordingly, as a condition of its monopoly franchise, Rural publishes a typical telephone directory, consisting

---

6. Counsel for the Register stated at oral argument on appeal that if a court of appeals in an infringement action held that the KOOSH ball was copyrightable, the Copyright Office would then be obliged to register the copyright. . . .

of white pages and yellow pages. The white pages list in alphabetical order the names of Rural's subscribers, together with their towns and telephone numbers. The yellow pages list Rural's business subscribers alphabetically by category and feature classified advertisements of various sizes. Rural distributes its directory free of charge to its subscribers, but earns revenue by selling yellow pages advertisements.

Feist Publications, Inc., is a publishing company that specializes in area-wide telephone directories. Unlike a typical directory, which covers only a particular calling area, Feist's area-wide directories cover a much larger geographical range, reducing the need to call directory assistance or consult multiple directories. . . . Like Rural's directory, Feist's is distributed free of charge and includes both white pages and yellow pages. Feist and Rural compete vigorously for yellow pages advertising.

As the sole provider of telephone service in its service area, Rural obtains subscriber information quite easily. Persons desiring telephone service must apply to Rural and provide their names and addresses; Rural then assigns them a telephone number. Feist is not a telephone company . . . and therefore lacks independent access to any subscriber information. To obtain white pages listings for its area-wide directory, Feist approached each of the 11 telephone companies operating in northwest Kansas and offered to pay for the right to use its white pages listings.

Of the 11 telephone companies, only Rural refused to license its listings to Feist. Rural's refusal created a problem for Feist, as omitting these listings would have left a gaping hole in its area-wide directory, rendering it less attractive to potential yellow pages advertisers. . . .

Unable to license Rural's white pages listings, Feist used them without Rural's consent. . . . 1,309 of the 46,878 listings in Feist's 1983 directory were identical to listings in Rural's 1982-1983 white pages. Four of these were fictitious listings that Rural had inserted into its directory to detect copying.

Rural sued for copyright infringement in the District Court for the District of Kansas taking the position that Feist . . . could not use the information contained in Rural's white pages. Rural asserted that Feist's employees were obliged to travel door-to-door or conduct a telephone survey to discover the same information for themselves. Feist responded that such efforts were economically impractical and, in any event, unnecessary because the information copied was beyond the scope of copyright protection. The District Court granted summary judgment to Rural, explaining that "[c]ourts have consistently held that telephone directories are copyrightable" citing a string of lower court decisions. In an unpublished opinion, the Court of Appeals for the Tenth Circuit affirmed . . . . We granted *certiorari* to determine whether the copyright in Rural's directory protects the names, towns, and telephone numbers copied by Feist.

This case concerns the interaction of two well-established propositions. The first is that facts are not copyrightable; the other, that compilations of facts generally are. Each of these propositions possesses an impeccable pedigree. That there can be no valid copyright in facts is universally understood. The most fundamental axiom of copyright law is that "[n]o author may copyright his ideas or the facts he narrates." Harper & Row, Publishers, Inc. v. Nation Enterprises, 471 U.S. 539 (1985). Rural wisely concedes this point. . . . At the same time, however, it is beyond dispute that compilations of facts are within the subject matter of copyright. Compilations were expressly mentioned in the Copyright Act of 1909, and again in the Copyright Act of 1976.

There is an undeniable tension between these two propositions. Many compilations consist of nothing but raw data—*i.e.,* wholly factual information not accompanied by any original written expression. On what basis may one claim a copyright in such a work? Common sense tells us that 100 uncopyrightable facts do not magically change their status when gathered together in one place. Yet copyright law seems to contemplate that compilations that consist exclusively of facts are potentially within its scope.

The key to resolving the tension lies in understanding why facts are not copyrightable. The *sine qua non* of copyright is originality. To qualify for copyright protection, a work must be original to the author. Original, as the term is used in copyright, means only that the work was independently created by the author (as opposed to copied from other works), and that it possesses at least some minimal degree of creativity. 1 M. Nimmer & D. Nimmer, *Copyright* § 2.01 (1990) (hereinafter Nimmer). To be sure, the requisite level of creativity is extremely low; even a slight amount will suffice. The vast majority of works make the grade quite easily, as they possess some creative spark, "no matter how crude, humble or obvious" it might be. Originality does not signify novelty; a work may be original even though it closely resembles other works so long as the similarity is fortuitous, not the result of copying. . . .

Originality is a constitutional requirement. The source of Congress' power to enact copyright laws is Article I, § 8, cl. 8, of the Constitution, which authorizes Congress to "secur[e] for limited Times to Authors . . . the exclusive Right to their respective Writings." In two decisions from the late 19th century—The Trade-Mark Cases, 100 U.S. 82 (1879); and Burrow-Giles Lithographic Co. v. Sarony, 111 U.S. 53 (1884)—this Court defined the crucial terms "authors" and "writings." In so doing, the Court made it unmistakably clear that these terms presuppose a degree of originality.

In The Trade Mark Cases, . . . [t]he Court explained that originality requires independent creation plus a modicum of creativity . . . . In *Burrow Giles*, . . . [t]he Court defined "author," in a constitutional sense, to mean "he to whom anything owes its origin; originator; maker." As in The Trademark Cases, the Court emphasized the creative component of originality. It described copyright as being limited to "original intellectual conceptions of the author," and stressed the importance of requiring an author who accuses another of infringement to prove "the existence of those facts of originality, of intellectual production, of thought, and conception."

The originality requirement . . . remains the touchstone of copyright protection today. . . . Leading scholars agree on this point. As one pair of commentators succinctly puts it: "The originality requirement is *constitutionally mandated* for all works." Patterson & Joyce, *Monopolizing the Law: The Scope of Copyright Protection for Law Reports and Statutory Compilations*, 36 UCLA L. Rev. 719, 763, n. 155 (1989) (emphasis in original) (hereinafter Patterson & Joyce). *Accord,* Nimmer § 1.06[A] ("[Originality is a statutory as well as a constitutional requirement") . . . .

It is this bedrock principle of copyright that mandates the law's seemingly disparate treatment of facts and factual compilations. . . . The distinction is one between creation and discovery: The first person to find and report a particular fact has not created the fact; he or she has merely discovered its existence. . . .

Census takers, for example, do not "create" the population figures that emerge from their efforts; in a sense, they copy these figures from the world around them. Denicola, *Copyright in Collections of Facts: A Theory for the Protection of Nonfiction Literary Works*, 81 Colum. L. Rev. 516, 525 (1981) (hereinafter Denicola). . . . The same is true of all facts—scientific, historical, biographical, and news of the day. "[T]hey may not be copyrighted and are part of the public domain available to every person."

Factual compilations, on the other hand, may possess the requisite originality. The compilation author typically chooses which facts to include, in what order to place them, and how to arrange the collected data so that they may be used effectively by readers. These choices as to selection and arrangement, so long as they are made independently by the compiler and entail a minimal degree of creativity, are sufficiently original that Congress may protect such compilations through the copyright laws. . . . [E]ven a directory that contains . . . only facts, meets the constitutional minimum for copyright protection if it features an original selection or arrangement.

This protection is subject to an important limitation. The mere fact that a work is copyrighted does not mean that every element of the work may be protected. . . . [C]opyright protection may extend only to those components of a work that are original to the author. Patterson & Joyce 800-802; Ginsburg, *Creation and Commercial Value: Copyright Protection of Works of Information*, 90 Colum. L. Rev. 1865, 1868, and n. 12 (1990) (hereinafter Ginsburg). . . . [I]f the compilation author clothes facts with an original collocation of words, he or she may be able to claim a copyright in this written expression. Others may copy the underlying facts from the publication, but not the precise words used to present them. In *Harper & Row*, for example, we explained that President Ford could not prevent others from copying bare historical facts from his autobiography, but that he could prevent others from copying his "subjective descriptions and portraits of public figures." Where the compilation author adds no written expression but . . . lets the facts speak for themselves, the expressive element is more elusive. The only conceivable expression is the manner in which the compiler has selected and arranged the facts. . . . No matter how original the format, however, the facts themselves do not become original through association.

This inevitably means that the copyright in a factual compilation is thin. Notwithstanding a valid copyright, a subsequent compiler remains free to use the facts contained in another's publication to aid in preparing a competing work, so long as the competing work does not feature the same selection and arrangement. . . .

It may seem unfair that much of the fruit of the compiler's labor may be used by others without compensation. As Justice Brennan has correctly observed, however, this is not "some unforeseen byproduct of a statutory scheme." *Harper & Row* (dissenting opinion). It is, rather, "the essence of copyright," and a constitutional requirement. The primary objective of copyright is not to reward the labor of authors, but "[t]o promote the Progress of Science and Useful Arts." To this end, copyright assures authors the right to their original expression, but encourages others to build freely upon the ideas and information conveyed by a work. This principle, known as the idea/expression or fact/expression dichotomy, applies to all works of authorship. As applied to a factual compilation, assuming the absence of original written expression, only the compiler's selection and arrangement may be protected; the raw facts may be copied at will. . . .

[Section] 101 of the 1976 Act . . . defines a "compilation" in the copyright sense as "a work formed by the collection and assembling of preexisting materials or of data *that* are selected, coordinated, or arranged *in such a way that* the resulting work as a whole constitutes an original work of authorship" (emphasis added).

The purpose of the statutory definition is to emphasize that collections of facts are not copyrightable per se. . . . The third requirement emphasizes that a compilation, like any other work, is copyrightable only if it satisfies the originality requirement ("an original work of authorship"). Although § 102 states plainly that the originality requirement applies to all works, the point was emphasized with regard to compilations to ensure that courts would not repeat the mistake of the "sweat of the brow" courts by concluding that fact-based works are treated differently and measured by some other standard. . . .

The key to the statutory definition is the second requirement. It instructs courts that, in determining whether a fact-based work is an original work of authorship, they should focus on the manner in which the collected facts have been selected, coordinated, and arranged. . . . [T]o merit protection, the facts must be selected, coordinated, or arranged "in such a way" as to render the work as a whole original. [T]he statute envisions that there will be some fact-based works in which the selection, coordination, and arrangement are not sufficiently original to trigger copyright protection. . . .

[T]he originality requirement is not particularly stringent. . . . Originality requires only that the author make the selection or arrangement independently (*i.e.,* without copying that selection or arrangement from another work), and that it display some minimal level of creativity. Presumably, the vast majority of compilations will pass this test, but not all will. There remains a narrow category of works in which the creative spark is utterly lacking or so trivial as to be virtually nonexistent. . . .

There is no doubt that Feist took from the white pages of Rural's directory a substantial amount of factual information. . . . The question is whether . . . Feist, by taking 1,309 names, towns, and telephone numbers from Rural's white pages, cop[ied] anything that was "original" to Rural? . . . Rural may have been the first to discover and report the names, towns, and telephone numbers of its subscribers, but . . . these bits of information are uncopyrightable facts; they existed before Rural reported them and would have continued to exist if Rural had never published a telephone directory. . . . Section 103(b) states explicitly that the copyright in a compilation does not extend to "the preexisting material employed in the work."

The question that remains is whether Rural selected, coordinated, or arranged these uncopyrightable facts in an original way. . . . Rural's white pages are entirely typical. . . . Rural simply takes the data provided by its subscribers and lists it alphabetically by surname. The end product is a garden-variety white pages directory, devoid of even the slightest trace of creativity.

Rural's selection of listings could not be more obvious: It publishes the most basic information—name, town, and telephone number—about each person who applies to it for telephone service. This is "selection" of a sort, but it lacks the modicum of creativity necessary to transform mere selection into copyrightable expression. Rural expended sufficient effort to make the white pages directory useful, but insufficient creativity to make it original. . . .

Nor can Rural claim originality in its coordination and arrangement of facts. The white pages do nothing more than list Rural's subscribers in alphabetical

order. This arrangement may, technically speaking, owe its origin to Rural . . . .
But there is nothing remotely creative about arranging names alphabetically in
a white pages directory. . . .

As a constitutional matter, copyright protects only those constituent elements
of a work that possess more than a *de minimis* quantum of creativity. . . . As a statutory matter, 17 U.S.C. § 101 does not afford protection from copying to a collection of facts that are selected, coordinated, and arranged in a way that utterly
lacks originality. Given that some works must fail, we cannot imagine a more
likely candidate. Indeed, were we to hold that Rural's white pages pass muster,
it is hard to believe that any collection of facts could fail.

. . . This decision should not be construed as demeaning Rural's efforts in
compiling its directory, but rather as making clear that copyright rewards originality, not effort. . . .

The judgment of the Court of Appeals is *Reversed.*

Notes and Questions

1. *Copyrightable materials.* The 1909 Copyright Act extended copyright protection to "all writings of an author," which led to controversy over the copyrightability of compilations of fact and other writings produced by mere "sweat of
the brow." Congress clarified the law in the 1976 Act by replacing "all writings"
with "original works of authorship." What is the utility of the originality requirement? Is it fair to allow free copying of facts discovered by others without compensating them for their initiative, time, and effort?

2. What is the likely impact of *Feist* on the creation, design, and management
of electronic databases? For a taste of the literature and legislative proposals
Feist provoked, see Miriam Bitton, *Protection for Informational Works After Feist
Publications, Inc. v. Rural Telephone Service Co.,* 21 Fordham Intellectual Prop.
Media & Ent. L.J. 611 (2011); Marc K. Temin, *The Irrelevance of Creativity:* Feist's
Wrong Turn and the Scope of Copyright Protection for Factual Works, 111 Penn St. L.
Rev. 263 (2006); Victoria Smith Ekstrand, *Drawing Swords After* Feist: *Efforts to
Legislate the Database Pirate,* 7 Comm. L. & Pol'y 317 (2002); J. Ryan Mitchell, *If
At* Feist *You Don't Succeed, Try, Try Again: An Evaluation of the Proposed Collections
of Information Antipiracy Act,* 78 Neb. L. Rev. 900 (1999); Benjamin B. Thorner,
Copyright Protection for Computer Databases: The Threat of Feist *and a Proposed Solution,*
1 Va. J.L. & Tech. 5 (1997).

3. *Copyright and computers.* A work of original authorship is protected by copyright from the time it is fixed in any tangible medium of expression. How does
this apply to works on computers? *Mai v. Peak,* 991 F.2d 511 (9th Cir. 1993),
held that loading copyrighted software into a computer's RAM (random access
memory) constitutes a fixation. Thus, anything created and stored, or viewed,
on a computer is sufficiently fixed to be given copyright protection, and conversely, may constitute infringement by copying. The Business Software Alliance,
a trade group whose members include Microsoft, Adobe, Apple, and other big
software companies, has a power of attorney to enforce its members' claims for
copyright infringement. It maintains a web page at http://www.bsa.org/ with
a "Report Piracy" button. It recruits informants through Facebook and other
media. *See* Ernesto, *Hundreds of Paid Informants Help to Rat Out Software Pirates,*

June 26, 2014, https://torrentfreak.com/bsa-gets-hundreds-paid-informants-rat-software-pirates-140626/.

4. *Inclusion of previously published works in electronic databases.* Are the copyrights of freelance authors who write for publications such as the New York Times infringed when the Times, without their consent, licenses the articles to Mead Data Central Corp. to include in its NEXIS database? The Copyright Act, in 17 U.S.C. § 201(c), creates a presumption that the author of a work who has consented to its inclusion in a collective work or compilation has also granted the owner of the copyright in the collective work "the privilege of reproducing and distributing the contribution as part of that particular collective work, any revision of that collective work, and any later collective work in the same series." *See New York Times v. Tasini*, 533 U.S. 483 (2001) (publication in electronic database is not a revision or later collective work in the same series; electronic databases reproduce and distribute articles standing alone and not in context, not "as part of that particular collective work" to which the author contributed; author's consent is required).

5. *Copyright in tattoos.* Tattoos are often original works of the tattoo artist fixed in a tangible medium of expression—human skin—and thus should be entitled to copyright protection. But what rights should that give the tattoo artist? In 2011, tattoo artist Victor Whitmill sued Warner Bros. for using a copy of boxer Mike Tyson's Maori-inspired facial tattoo in the film *The Hangover: Part II*. In another case, Stephen Allen, a tattoo artist, sued video game maker Electronic Arts and former Miami Dolphins running back Ricky Williams over a tattoo Allen put on Williams' bicep. The tattoo appeared on the cover of EA's "NFL Street" video game. Both cases settled before trial, but the NFL players association has warned players to get copyright waivers from their tattoo artists. *See* Yolanda M. King, *The Challenges Facing Copyright Protection for Tattoos*, 92 Or. L. Rev. 129 (2013); Kal Raustiala & Christopher Sprigman, *Whose Tattoo is It Anyway?*, L.A. Times, Oct. 6, 2013, http://www.latimes.com/opinion/op-ed/la-oe-raustiala-tattoo-copyright-20131006-story.html.

Copyright and the First Sale Doctrine

Section 109(a) of the Copyright Act provides that "the owner of a particular copy or phonorecord lawfully made under this title . . . is entitled, without the authority of the copyright owner, to sell or otherwise dispose of the possession of that copy or phonorecord." Does this apply to copyrighted items published abroad? John Wiley & Sons, a textbook publisher, often assigns rights to publish, print, and sell foreign editions of its English language textbooks to its wholly owned foreign subsidiary. The foreign editions state that they are to be used only in certain areas and are not to be exported.

Supap Kirtsaeng, who came to the United States from Thailand as a student, had his friends and family buy textbooks in Thailand, where they cost much less than in the United States, and mail them to him. He partially financed his education by reselling the textbooks. John Wiley & Sons, Inc. sued him for copyright infringement under § 106(3), which gives exclusive distribution rights to the copyright holder, and § 602(a)(1), which prohibits importing a copy made abroad without permission of the copyright holder. The court held that the first sale doctrine applies to copies lawfully made abroad, as well as to copies lawfully made in the United States. *Kirtsaeng v. John Wiley & Sons, Inc.*, 133 S. Ct. 1351 (2013).

3.   *Copyright and the Internet*

AMERICAN BROADCASTING COS., INC. v. AEREO, INC.

Supreme Court of the United States
134 S. Ct. 2498 (2014)

BREYER, J., delivered the opinion of the Court, in which ROBERTS, C.J., and KENNEDY, GINSBURG, SOTOMAYOR, and KAGAN, JJ., joined. SCALIA, J., filed a dissenting opinion, in which THOMAS and ALITO, JJ., joined.

Justice BREYER delivered the opinion of the Court.

The Copyright Act of 1976 gives a copyright owner the "exclusive righ[t]" to "perform the copyrighted work publicly." The Act's Transmit Clause defines that exclusive right as including the right to

> "transmit or otherwise communicate a performance . . . of the [copyrighted] work . . . to the public, by means of any device or process, whether the members of the public capable of receiving the performance . . . receive it in the same place or in separate places and at the same time or at different times." § 101.

We must decide whether respondent Aereo, Inc., infringes this exclusive right by selling its subscribers a technologically complex service that allows them to watch television programs over the Internet at about the same time as the programs are broadcast over the air. We conclude that it does.

I

A

For a monthly fee, Aereo offers subscribers broadcast television programming over the Internet, virtually as the programming is being broadcast. Much of this programming is made up of copyrighted works. Aereo neither owns the copyright in those works nor holds a license from the copyright owners to perform those works publicly.

Aereo's system is made up of servers, transcoders, and thousands of dime-sized antennas housed in a central warehouse. It works roughly as follows: First, when a subscriber wants to watch a show that is currently being broadcast, he visits Aereo's website and selects, from a list of the local programming, the show he wishes to see.

Second, one of Aereo's servers selects an antenna, which it dedicates to the use of that subscriber (and that subscriber alone) for the duration of the selected show. A server then tunes the antenna to the over-the-air broadcast carrying the show. The antenna begins to receive the broadcast, and an Aereo transcoder translates the signals received into data that can be transmitted over the Internet.

Third, rather than directly send the data to the subscriber, a server saves the data in a subscriber-specific folder on Aereo's hard drive. In other words, Aereo's system creates a subscriber-specific copy—that is, a "personal" copy—of the subscriber's program of choice.

Fourth, once several seconds of programming have been saved, Aereo's server begins to stream the saved copy of the show to the subscriber over the Internet. (The subscriber may instead direct Aereo to stream the program at a later time, but that aspect of Aereo's service is not before us.) The subscriber can watch the streamed program on the screen of his personal computer, tablet, smart phone, Internet-connected television, or other Internet-connected device. The streaming continues, a mere few seconds behind the over-the-air broadcast, until the subscriber has received the entire show. . . .

Aereo emphasizes that the data that its system streams to each subscriber are the data from his own personal copy, made from the broadcast signals received by the particular antenna allotted to him. Its system does not transmit data saved in one subscriber's folder to any other subscriber. When two subscribers wish to watch the same program, Aereo's system activates two separate antennas and saves two separate copies of the program in two separate folders. It then streams the show to the subscribers through two separate transmissions—each from the subscriber's personal copy.

B

Petitioners are television producers, marketers, distributors, and broadcasters who own the copyrights in many of the programs that Aereo's system streams to its subscribers. They brought suit against Aereo for copyright infringement . . . [seeking] a preliminary injunction, arguing that Aereo was infringing their right to "perform" their works "publicly," as the Transmit Clause defines those terms.

The District Court denied the preliminary injunction. . . . [A] divided panel of the Second Circuit affirmed. In the Second Circuit's view, Aereo does not perform publicly within the meaning of the Transmit Clause because it does not transmit "to the public." . . . We granted certiorari.

II

This case requires us to answer two questions: First, in operating in the manner described above, does Aereo "perform" at all? And second, if so, does Aereo do so "publicly"? We address these distinct questions in turn.

Does Aereo "perform"? See . . . § 101 ("To *perform* . . . a work 'publicly' means [among other things] to transmit . . . a performance . . . of the work . . . to the public . . . . ". . . In Aereo's view, it . . . does no more than supply equipment that "emulate[s] the operation of a home antenna and [digital video recorder (DVR)]." . . . Aereo's equipment simply responds to its subscribers' directives. So it is only the subscribers who "perform" when they use Aereo's equipment to stream television programs to themselves. Considered alone, the language of the Act does not clearly indicate when an entity "perform[s]" (or "transmit[s]") and when it merely supplies equipment that allows others to do so. But when read in light of its purpose, the Act is unmistakable: An entity that engages in activities like Aereo's performs.

A

History makes plain that one of Congress' primary purposes in amending the Copyright Act in 1976 was to overturn this Court's determination that community antenna television (CATV) systems (the precursors of modern cable systems) fell outside the Act's scope. In Fortnightly Corp. v. United Artists Television, Inc., 392 U.S. 390 (1968), the Court considered a CATV system that carried local television broadcasting . . . [and] held that the provider did not "perform" at all. . . . The Court drew a line: "Broadcasters perform. Viewers do not perform." And a CATV provider "falls on the viewer's side of the line." . . . "Essentially," the Court said, "a CATV system no more than enhances the viewer's capacity to receive the broadcaster's signals [by] provid[ing] a well-located antenna with an efficient connection to the viewer's television set." Viewers do not become performers by using "amplifying equipment," and a CATV provider should not be treated differently for providing viewers the same equipment.

In Teleprompter Corp. v. Columbia Broadcasting System, Inc., 415 U.S. 394 (1974), the Court considered the copyright liability of a CATV provider that carried broadcast television programming into subscribers' homes from hundreds of miles away. Although the Court recognized that a viewer might not be able to afford amplifying equipment that would provide access to those distant signals, it nonetheless found that the CATV provider was more like a viewer than a broadcaster. . . .

B

In 1976 Congress amended the Copyright Act in large part to reject the Court's holdings in *Fortnightly* and *Teleprompter*. . . . Congress enacted new language that erased the Court's line between broadcaster and viewer, in respect to "perform[ing]" a work. . . . Under this new language, *both* the broadcaster *and* the viewer of a television program "perform" . . . . Congress also enacted the Transmit Clause, which specifies that an entity performs publicly when it "transmit[s] . . . a performance . . . to the public." § 101 (defining "[t]o 'transmit' a performance" as "to communicate it by any device or process whereby images or sounds are received beyond the place from which they are sent"). . . . The Clause . . . makes clear that an entity that acts like a CATV system itself performs, even if when doing so, it simply enhances viewers' ability to receive broadcast television signals.

Congress further created a new section of the Act to regulate cable companies' public performances of copyrighted works. Section 111 creates a complex, highly detailed compulsory licensing scheme that sets out the conditions, including the payment of compulsory fees, under which cable systems may retransmit broadcasts. . . .

C

This history makes clear that Aereo is not simply an equipment provider. Rather, Aereo, and not just its subscribers, "perform[s]" (or "transmit[s]"). Aereo's activities are substantially similar to those of the CATV companies that Congress amended the Act to reach. . . .

We recognize, and Aereo and the dissent emphasize, one particular difference between Aereo's system and the cable systems at issue in *Fortnightly* and *Teleprompter*. The systems in those cases transmitted constantly . . . . In contrast, Aereo's system remains inert until a subscriber indicates that she wants to watch a program. Only at that moment, in automatic response to the subscriber's request, does Aereo's system activate an antenna and begin to transmit the requested program.

This is a critical difference, says the dissent. It means that Aereo's subscribers, not Aereo, "selec[t] the copyrighted content" that is "perform[ed]," and for that reason they, not Aereo, "transmit" the performance. . . . Given Aereo's overwhelming likeness to the cable companies targeted by the 1976 amendments, this sole technological difference between Aereo and traditional cable companies does not make a critical difference here. . . . [T]his difference means nothing to the subscriber. It means nothing to the broadcaster. . . .

In other cases involving different kinds of service or technology providers, a user's involvement in the operation of the provider's equipment and selection of the content transmitted may well bear on whether the provider performs within the meaning of the Act. But the many similarities between Aereo and cable companies, considered in light of Congress' basic purposes in amending the Copyright Act, convince us that this difference is not critical here. We conclude that Aereo is not just an equipment supplier and that Aereo "perform[s]."

III

Next, we must consider whether Aereo performs petitioners' works "publicly." . . . One and only one subscriber has the ability to see and hear each Aereo transmission. The fact that each transmission is to only one subscriber, in Aereo's view, means that it does not transmit a performance "to the public."

In terms of the Act's purposes, these differences do not distinguish Aereo's system from cable systems, which do perform "publicly." Viewed in terms of Congress' regulatory objectives, why should any of these technological differences matter? They concern the behind-the-scenes way in which Aereo delivers television programming to its viewers' screens. They do not render Aereo's commercial objective any different from that of cable companies. Nor do they significantly alter the viewing experience of Aereo's subscribers. Why would a subscriber who wishes to watch a television show care much whether images and sounds are delivered to his screen via a large multisubscriber antenna or one small dedicated antenna, whether they arrive instantaneously or after a few seconds' delay, or whether they are transmitted directly or after a personal copy is made? And why, if Aereo is right, could not modern CATV systems simply continue the same commercial and consumer-oriented activities, free of copyright restrictions, provided they substitute such new technologies for old? Congress would as much have intended to protect a copyright holder from the unlicensed activities of Aereo as from those of cable companies. . . .

IV

Aereo and many of its supporting *amici* argue that to apply the Transmit Clause to Aereo's conduct will impose copyright liability on other technologies, including new technologies, that Congress could not possibly have wanted to reach. We agree that Congress, while intending the Transmit Clause to apply broadly to cable companies and their equivalents, did not intend to discourage or to control the emergence or use of different kinds of technologies. But we do not believe that our limited holding today will have that effect. . . .

We cannot now answer more precisely how the Transmit Clause or other provisions of the Copyright Act will apply to technologies not before us. We agree with the Solicitor General that "[q]uestions involving cloud computing, [remote storage] DVRs, and other novel issues not before the Court, as to which 'Congress has not plainly marked [the] course,' should await a case in which they are squarely presented." And we note that, to the extent commercial actors or other interested entities may be concerned with the relationship between the development and use of such technologies and the Copyright Act, they are of course free to seek action from Congress. . . .

In sum, having considered the details of Aereo's practices, we find them highly similar to those of the CATV systems in *Fortnightly* and *Teleprompter*. . . . We therefore reverse the contrary judgment of the Court of Appeals, and we remand the case for further proceedings consistent with this opinion. It is so ordered.

Justice SCALIA, with whom Justice THOMAS and Justice ALITO join, dissenting.

This case is the latest skirmish in the long-running copyright battle over the delivery of television programming. . . . The Networks sued Aereo for several forms of copyright infringement, but we are here concerned with a single claim: that Aereo violates the Networks' "exclusive righ[t]" to "perform" their programs "publicly." That claim fails at the very outset because Aereo does not "perform" at all. The Court manages to reach the opposite conclusion only by disregarding widely accepted rules for service-provider liability and adopting in their place an improvised standard ("looks-like-cable-TV") that will sow confusion for years to come. . . .

Notes and Questions

1. The decision in *Aereo* was a big win for the traditional broadcast industry against a startup that threatened its business model. What will be the impact of the decision on future innovation? Did the Court act appropriately in closing the loophole in the 1976 copyright act, or should it have let Congress deal with the question, as the dissent argued?

2. Although the dissent would not have found Aereo liable for direct copyright infringement, it left open the possibility that it might be liable for secondary infringement, which it described as follows:

Secondary liability . . . is a means of holding defendants responsible for infringement by third parties, even when the defendants "have not themselves engaged in the infringing activity. It applies when a defendant "intentionally induc[es] or encourag[es]" infringing acts by others or profits from such acts "while declining to exercise a right to stop or limit [them]." *Metro-Goldwyn-Mayer Studios Inc. v. Grokster, Ltd.*, 545 U.S. 913 (2005).

Grokster distributed free software for peer-to-peer file sharing, encouraging users to share material it knew was copyrighted. It made money by streaming ads to its users. The Supreme Court overturned lower court decisions that followed *Sony Corp. of America v. Universal City Studios, Inc.*, 464 U.S. 417 (1984), in holding Grokster not liable because its software could be used for non-infringing uses on the ground that Grokster encouraged use of its software to download copyrighted works.

3. The Digital Millennium Copyright Act, adopted in 1998, offers a safe harbor against copyright liability to internet service providers for material uploaded by users under a variety of conditions, if the service provider responds expeditiously to notices to remove claimed infringing material. *See* 17 U.S.C. § 512. For the long-running battle over some 79,000 clips of material copyrighted by Viacom posted to YouTube, see *Viacom International Inc. v. YouTube, Inc.*, 676 F.3d 19 (2d Cir. 2012), 940 F. Supp. 2d 110 (S.D.N.Y. 2013) (YouTube entitled to safe harbor; plaintiff lacked specific proof that provider had knowledge of any specific infringement; content provider was not willfully blind to infringements).

Misappropriation and Common-Law Unfair Trade Doctrines

Works that are not protected by copyright may be protected by judicially created doctrines of misappropriation and unfair competition. The Supreme Court, in *International News Service v. Associated Press*, 248 U.S. 215 (1918), upheld the issuance of an injunction prohibiting International News Service from copying uncopyrighted news items from early editions of Associated Press Newspaper bulletin boards on the East Coast and selling them either bodily or after rewriting to International's customers on the West Coast. Because of the time difference, INS customers could compete equally with AP customers on the West Coast. The basis for the Court's decision was unfair competition:

. . . [A]lthough we may and do assume that neither party has any remaining property interest as against the public in uncopyrighted news matter after the moment of its first publication, it by no means follows that there is no remaining property interest in it as between themselves. For to both of them alike, news matter, however little susceptible of ownership or dominion in the absolute sense, is stock in trade, to be gathered at the cost of enterprise, organization, skill, labor, and money, and to be distributed and sold to those who will pay money for it, as for any other merchandise. Regarding the news, therefore, as but the material out of which both parties are seeking to make profits at the same time and in the same field, we hardly can fail to recognize that for this purpose, and as between them, it must be regarded as quasi property, irrespective of the rights of either as against the public. . . .

[I]n a court of equity, where the question is one of unfair competition, if that which complainant has acquired fairly at substantial cost may be sold fairly at substantial profit, a competitor who is misappropriating it for the purpose of disposing of it to his own profit and to the disadvantage of complainant cannot be heard to say that it is too fugitive or evanescent to be regarded as property. It has all the attributes of property necessary for determining that a misappropriation of it by a competitor is unfair competition because contrary to good conscience.

It is to be observed that the view we adopt does not result in giving to complainant the right to monopolize either the gathering or the distribution of the news, . . . but only postpones participation by complainant's competitor in the processes of distribution and reproduction of news that it has not gathered, and only to the extent necessary to prevent that competitor from reaping the fruits of complainant's efforts and expenditure, to the partial exclusion of complainant. . . .

It is said that the elements of unfair competition are lacking because there is no attempt by defendant to palm off its goods as those of the complainant, characteristic of the most familiar, if not the most typical, cases of unfair competition. But we cannot concede that the right to equitable relief is confined to that class of cases. In the present case the fraud upon complainant's rights is more direct and obvious. Regarding news matter as the mere material from which these two competing parties are endeavoring to make money, and treating it, therefore, as quasi property for the purposes of their business because they are both selling it as such, defendant's conduct differs from the ordinary case of unfair competition in trade principally in this that, instead of selling its own goods as those of complainant, it substitutes misappropriation in the place of misrepresentation, and sells complainant's goods as its own.

Although the "hot news" doctrine of *International News*, as federal common law, was abrogated by *Erie Railroad Co. v. Tompkins*, 304 U.S. 64 (1938), and has been criticized, *see, e.g.*, Leo J. Raskind, *The Misappropriation Doctrine as a Competitive Norm of Intellectual Property Law*, 75 Minn. L. Rev. 875 (1991), it proved useful as a basis for providing a theory for state-law protection against piracy of sound recordings before copyright protection became available under the Sound Recording Act of 1972. *See, e.g., Mercury Record Productions, Inc. v. Economic Consultants, Inc.*, 218 N.W.2d 705 (Wis. 1974); *CBS, Inc. v. Garrod*, 622 F. Supp. 532 (M.D. Fla. 1985). However, it has very narrow scope in protecting materials that are or could be copyrighted because § 301 of the 1976 Copyright Act provides that state law is preempted that protects the type of work, or seeks to vindicate "legal or equitable rights that are equivalent" to the exclusive rights, protected by copyright law. *See* Shyamkrishna Balganesh, *The Uncertain Future of "Hot News" Misappropriation After Barclays Capital v. Theflyonthewall.com*, 112 Colum. L. Rev. 134 (2012).

C.   TRADEMARK AND TRADE DRESS

Trademarks identify the source of goods and services. Trademark law is part of a larger body of law known as unfair competition law, which includes federal and state statutes and common law that protect consumers and producers alike:

The purpose underlying any trade-mark statute is twofold. One is to protect the public so it may be confident that, in purchasing a product bearing a particular trade-mark which it favorably knows, it will get the product which it asks for and wants to get. Secondly, where the owner of a trade-mark has spent energy, time, and money in presenting to the public the product, he is protected in his investment from its misappropriation by pirates and cheats. This is the well-established rule of law protecting both the public and the trade-mark owner.[6]

In this chapter we focus on federal law that is based on the Lanham Act, 15 U.S.C. §§ 1051-1141.

LANHAM ACT, 15 U.S.C. § 1125(a)

(1) Any person who, on or in connection with any goods or services, or any container for goods, uses in commerce any word, term, name, symbol, or device, or any combination thereof, or any false designation of origin, false or misleading description of fact, or false or misleading representation of fact, which—

(A) is likely to cause confusion, or to cause mistake, or to deceive as to the affiliation, connection, or association of such person with another person, or as to the origin, sponsorship, or approval of his or her goods, services, or commercial activities by another person, or

(B) in commercial advertising or promotion, misrepresents the nature, characteristics, qualities, or geographic origin of his or her or another person's goods, services, or commercial activities,

shall be liable in a civil action by any person who believes that he or she is or is likely to be damaged by such act.

1. Trademark

QUALITEX CO. v. JACOBSON PRODUCTS CO.

Supreme Court of the United States
514 U.S. 159 (1995)

BREYER, J., delivered the opinion for a unanimous Court.

The question in this case is whether the Trademark Act of 1946 (Lanham Act), 15 U.S.C. §§ 1051-1127, permits the registration of a trademark that consists, purely and simply, of a color. We conclude that, sometimes, a color will meet ordinary legal trademark requirements. And, when it does so, no special legal rule prevents color alone from serving as a trademark.

The case before us grows out of petitioner Qualitex Company's use (since the 1950's) of a special shade of green-gold color on the pads that it makes and sells to dry cleaning firms for use on dry cleaning presses. In 1989, respondent Jacobson Products (a Qualitex rival) began to sell its own press pads to dry cleaning firms; and it colored those pads a similar green gold. In 1991, Qualitex registered the special green-gold color on press pads with the Patent and Trademark Office as a trademark. . . .

Qualitex won the lawsuit in the District Court. But, the Court of Appeals for the Ninth Circuit set aside the judgment . . . because, in the Circuit's view, the Lanham Act does not permit Qualitex . . . to register "color alone" as a

---

6. S. Rep. No. 1333, 79th Cong., 2d Sess., 3 (1946), quoted in Two Pesos, Inc. v. Taco Cabana, Inc., 505 U.S. 763, 782, n.15 (1992) (Stevens, concurring).

trademark. The Courts of Appeals have differed as to whether or not the law recognizes the use of color alone as a trademark. . . . Therefore, this Court granted *certiorari*.

The Lanham Act gives a seller or producer the exclusive right to "register" a trademark, and to prevent his or her competitors from using that trademark. Both the language of the Act and the basic underlying principles of trademark law would seem to include color within the universe of things that can qualify as a trademark. The language of the Lanham Act describes that universe in the broadest of terms. It says that trademarks "includ[e] any word, name, symbol, or device, or any combination thereof." Since human beings might use as a "symbol" or "device" almost anything at all that is capable of carrying meaning, this language, read literally, is not restrictive. The courts and the Patent and Trademark Office have authorized for use as a mark a particular shape (of a Coca-Cola bottle), a particular sound (of NBC's three chimes), and even a particular scent (of plumeria blossoms on sewing thread). . . . If a shape, a sound, and a fragrance can act as symbols why, one might ask, can a color not do the same?

A color is also capable of satisfying the more important part of the statutory definition of a trademark, which requires that a person "us[e]" or "inten[d] to use" the mark

> "to identify and distinguish his or her goods, including a unique product, from those manufactured or sold by others and to indicate the source of the goods, even if that source is unknown." § 1127.

True, a product's color is unlike "fanciful," "arbitrary," or "suggestive" words or designs, which almost automatically tell a customer that they refer to a brand. . . . [O]ver time, customers may come to treat a particular color on a product or its packaging (say, a color that in context seems unusual, such as pink on a firm's insulating material or red on the head of a large industrial bolt) as signifying a brand. And, if so, that color would have come to identify and distinguish the goods — *i.e.,* "to indicate" their "source" — much in the way that descriptive words on a product (say "Trim" on nail clippers . . .) can come to indicate a product's origin. In this circumstance, trademark law says that the word . . . , although not inherently distinctive, has developed "secondary meaning." *See* Inwood Laboratories, Inc. v. Ives Laboratories, Inc., 456 U.S. 844 (1982). ("[S]econdary meaning" is acquired when "in the minds of the public, the primary significance of a product feature . . . is to identify the source of the product rather than the product itself"). Again, one might ask, if trademark law permits a descriptive word with secondary meaning to act as a mark, why would it not permit a color, under similar circumstances, to do the same?

We cannot find in the basic objectives of trademark law any obvious theoretical objection to the use of color alone as a trademark, where that color has attained "secondary meaning" and therefore identifies and distinguishes a particular brand (and thus indicates its "source"). In principle, trademark law, by preventing others from copying a source-identifying mark, "reduce[s] the customer's costs of shopping and making purchasing decisions," 1 J. McCarthy, *McCarthy on Trademarks and Unfair Competition* § 2.01 [2] (3d ed. 1994) (hereinafter McCarthy), for it quickly and easily assures a potential customer that *this* item — the item with this mark — is made by the same producer as other similarly marked items that he or she liked (or disliked) in the past. At the same time, the law helps assure a producer that it (and not an imitating competitor) will reap the financial, reputation-related rewards associated with a desirable product. The law thereby "encourage[s] the production of quality products, and simultaneously discourages those who hope to sell inferior products by capitalizing on a consumer's inability quickly to evaluate the quality of an item offered for sale. It is the source-distinguishing ability of a mark—not its ontological status as color, shape, fragrance, word, or sign—that permits it to serve these basic purposes. And, for that reason, it is difficult to find, in basic trademark objectives, a reason to disqualify absolutely the use of a color as a mark.

Neither can we find a principled objection to the use of color as a mark in the important "functionality" doctrine of trademark law. The functionality doctrine prevents trademark law, which seeks to promote competition by protecting a firm's reputation, from instead inhibiting legitimate competition by allowing a producer to control a useful product feature. It is the province of patent law, not trademark law, to encourage invention by granting inventors a monopoly over new product designs or functions for a limited time, after which competitors are free to use the innovation. If a product's functional features could be used as trademarks, however, a monopoly over such features could be obtained without regard to whether they qualify as patents and could be extended forever (because trademarks may be renewed in perpetuity) . . . . Functionality doctrine therefore would require, to take an imaginary example, that even if customers have come to identify the special illumination-enhancing shape of a new patented light bulb with a particular manufacturer, the manufacturer may not use that shape as a trademark, for doing so, after the patent had expired, would impede competition—not by protecting the reputation of the original bulb maker, but by frustrating competitors' legitimate efforts to produce an equivalent illumination-enhancing bulb. This Court has explained that, "[i]n general terms, a product feature is functional," and cannot serve as a trademark, "if it is essential to the use or purpose of the article or if it affects the cost or quality of the article," that is, if exclusive use of the feature would put competitors at a significant non-reputation-related disadvantage. Although sometimes color plays an important role (unrelated to source identification) in making a product more desirable, sometimes it does not. And, this latter fact—the fact that sometimes color is not essential to a product's use or purpose and does not affect cost or quality—indicates that the doctrine of "functionality" does not create an absolute bar to the use of color alone as a mark.

It would seem, then, that color alone, at least sometimes, can meet the basic legal requirements for use as a trademark. It can act as a symbol that distinguishes a firm's goods and identifies their source, without serving any other significant function. . . . The green-gold color acts as a symbol. Having developed secondary meaning (for customers identified the green-gold color as Qualitex's), it identifies the press pads' source. And, the green-gold color serves no other function. (Although it is important to use some color on press pads to avoid noticeable stains, the court found "no competitive need in the press pad industry for the green-gold color, since other colors are equally usable.") Accordingly, unless there is some special reason that convincingly militates against the use of color alone as a trademark, trademark law would protect Qualitex's use of the green-gold color on its press pads.

Respondent Jacobson Products says that there are four special reasons why the law should forbid the use of color alone as a trademark. We shall explain, in turn, why we, ultimately, find them unpersuasive.

First, Jacobson says that, if the law permits the use of color as a trademark, it will produce uncertainty and unresolvable court disputes about what shades of a color a competitor may lawfully use. Because lighting (morning sun, twilight mist) will affect perceptions of protected color, competitors and courts will suffer from "shade confusion" as they try to decide whether use of a similar color on a similar product does, or does not, confuse customers and thereby infringe a trademark. Jacobson adds that the "shade confusion" problem is "more difficult" and "far different from" the "determination of the similarity of words or symbols." . . .

We do not believe, however, that color, in this respect, is special. Courts traditionally decide quite difficult questions about whether two words or phrases or symbols are sufficiently similar, in context, to confuse buyers. They have had to compare, for example, such words as "Bonamine" and "Dramamine" (motion-sickness remedies); "Huggies" and "Dougies" (diapers); "Cheracol" and "Syrocol" (cough syrup); "Cyclone" and "Tornado" (wire fences); and "Mattres" and "1-800-Mattres" (mattress franchisor telephone numbers). . . . We do not see why courts could not apply those standards to a color, replicating, if necessary, lighting conditions under which a colored product is normally sold. Indeed, courts already have done so in cases where a trademark consists of a color plus a design, i.e., a colored symbol such as a gold stripe (around a sewer pipe), a yellow strand of wire rope, or a "brilliant yellow" band (on ampules). . . .

Second, Jacobson argues . . . that colors are in limited supply. . . . Jacobson claims that, if one of many competitors can appropriate a particular color for use as a trademark, and each competitor then tries to do the same, the supply of colors will soon be depleted. Put in its strongest form, this argument would concede that "[h]undreds of color pigments are manufactured and thousands of colors can be obtained by mixing." L. Cheskin, *Colors: What They Can Do For You* 47 (1947). But, it would add that, in the context of a particular product, only some colors are usable. By the time one discards colors that, say, for reasons of customer appeal, are not usable, and adds the shades that competitors cannot use lest they risk infringing a similar, registered shade, then one is left with only a handful of possible colors. And, under these circumstances, to permit one, or a few, producers to use colors as trademarks will "deplete" the supply of usable colors to the point where a competitor's inability to find a suitable color will put that competitor at a significant disadvantage.

This argument is unpersuasive, however, largely because it relies on an occasional problem to justify a blanket prohibition. When a color serves as a mark, normally alternative colors will likely be available for similar use by others. . . . Moreover, if that is not so—if a "color depletion" or "color scarcity" problem does arise—the trademark doctrine of "functionality" normally would seem available to prevent the anticompetitive consequences that Jacobson's argument posits, thereby minimizing that argument's practical force.

The functionality doctrine, as we have said, forbids the use of a product's feature as a trademark where doing so will put a competitor at a significant disadvantage because the feature is "essential to the use or purpose of the article" or "affects [its] cost or quality." . . . The functionality doctrine thus protects competitors against a disadvantage (unrelated to recognition or reputation) that trademark protection might otherwise impose, namely, their inability reasonably to replicate important non-reputation-related product features. For example, this Court has written that competitors might be free to copy the color of a medical pill where that color serves to identify the kind of medication (e.g., a type of blood medicine) in addition to its source. . . . And, the federal courts have demonstrated that they can apply this doctrine in a careful and reasoned manner, with sensitivity to the effect on competition. Although we need not comment on the merits of specific cases, we note that lower courts have permitted competitors to copy the green color of farm machinery (because customers wanted their farm equipment to match) and have barred the use of black as a trademark on outboard boat motors (because black has the special functional attributes of decreasing the apparent size of the motor and ensuring compatibility with many different boat colors). . . .

The upshot is that, where a color serves a significant nontrademark function—whether to distinguish a heart pill from a digestive medicine or to satisfy the "noble instinct for giving the right touch of beauty to common and necessary things," G. Chesterton, *Simplicity and Tolstoy* 61 (1912)—courts will examine whether its use as a mark would permit one competitor (or a group) to interfere with legitimate (nontrademark-related) competition through actual or potential exclusive use of an important product ingredient. That examination should not discourage firms from creating esthetically pleasing mark designs, for it is open to their competitors to do the same. . . . But, ordinarily, it should prevent the anticompetitive consequences of Jacobson's hypothetical "color depletion" argument, when, and if, the circumstances of a particular case threaten "color depletion." . . .

Fourth, Jacobson argues that there is no need to permit color alone to function as a trademark because a firm already may use color as part of a trademark, say, as a colored circle or colored letter or colored word, and may rely upon "trade dress" protection,[7] under § 43(a) of the Lanham Act, if a competitor copies its color and thereby causes consumer confusion regarding the overall appearance of the competing products or their packaging. . . . The first part of this argument begs the question. One can understand why a firm might find it difficult to place a usable symbol or word on a product (say, a large industrial bolt that customers normally see from a distance); and, in such instances, a firm might want to use color, pure and simple, instead of color as part of a design. Neither is the second portion of the argument convincing. Trademark law helps the holder of a mark in many ways that "trade dress" protection does not. *See* 15 U.S.C. § 1124 (ability to prevent importation of confusingly similar goods); § 1072 (constructive notice of ownership); § 1065 (incontestible status); § 1057(b) (prima facie evidence of validity and ownership). Thus, one can easily find reasons why the law might provide trademark protection in addition to trade dress protection.

Having determined that a color may sometimes meet the basic legal requirements for use as a trademark and that respondent Jacobson's arguments do not justify a special legal rule preventing color alone from serving as a trademark

---

7. Trade dress traditionally referred to the packaging or labeling of a product, but it has been extended to the total image of the product, and may include features like size, shape, color, color combinations, textures, or graphics. John Harland Co. v. Clarke Checks, Inc., 711 F.2d 966, 980 (11th Cir. 1983).—Eds.

(and, in light of the District Court's here undisputed findings that Qualitex's use of the green-gold color on its press pads meets the basic trademark requirements), we conclude that the Ninth Circuit erred in barring Qualitex's use of color as a trademark. For these reasons, the judgment of the Ninth Circuit is *Reversed. . . .*

Notes and Questions

1. *What is a trademark?* "A trademark is a word, phrase, symbol or design, or a combination of words, phrases, symbols or designs, that identifies and distinguishes the source of the goods of one party from those of others. A service mark is the same as a trademark, except that it identifies and distinguishes the source of a service rather than a product." U.S. Patent and Trademark Office, www.uspto.gov. What was the trademark obtained by Qualitex Co. and how did it get it?

2. *Descriptive marks.* Descriptive terms receive trademark protection only if they become sufficiently identified with a particular product to acquire a secondary meaning. Bank of America, for example, has acquired sufficient secondary meaning that it will be protected, while "LA" for low alcohol beer has not. *See G. Heileman Brewing Co. v. Anheuser-Busch, Inc.*, 873 F.2d 985 (7th Cir. 1989).

3. *Can color serve as a trademark in the fashion industry?* Christian Louboutin S.A. obtained a registered trademark for red soles on women's high fashion designer footwear in 2008. Yves Saint Laurent included four all-red shoes, including red soles, in its 2011 Cruise collection and Christian Louboutin sued for trademark infringement. The district court denied a preliminary injunction against selling the shoes on the ground that color is functional in the fashion world and thus color alone cannot serve as a trademark. The Second Circuit disagreed but held that Louboutin's mark had acquired secondary meaning only as to shoes with uppers of a contrasting color, not as to all-red shoes, 696 F.3d 206 (2012). The decision is criticized in Rhojonda A. Debrow Cornett, Note, *Seeing Red: A Critical Analysis of Christian Louboutin S.A. v. Yves St. Laurent America, Inc.*, 65 Ala. L. Rev. 539 (2013), which agrees that color alone can serve as a trademark in the fashion industry but argues that the Louboutin mark should have been upheld for all shoes with red soles in Louboutin's signature color.

4. *Scandalous marks.* Marks are also not registrable if they are immoral or scandalous. 15 U.S.C. § 1052(a). However, the offensiveness of the mark must be judged in the context in which it is used, and must be immoral or scandalous from the standpoint of the general public. *See, e.g., In re Old Glory Condom Corp.*, 26 U.S.P.Q.2d (BNA) 1216 (1993) (mark with design of condom imprinted with American flag held not scandalous); *In re Hershey*, 6 U.S.P.Q.2d (BNA) 1470 (T.T.A.B. 1988) (Big Pecker Brand shown with a design of a bird not scandalous).

5. *Disparaging marks.* Section 1052(a) also prevents registration of marks that "*disparage or falsely suggest a connection with* persons, living or dead, institutions, beliefs, or national symbols, or bring them into contempt, or disrepute." In June 2014, the U.S. Patent and Trademark Office cancelled trademarks of the Washington Redskins after the Trademark Trial and Appeal Board determined that the name Redskins was disparaging to Native Americans. The decision will be appealed.

6. *Celebrity trademarks.* Names and images of celebrities can serve as trademarks when they identify the source of goods or services, but trademark protection does not extend to other images of the celebrity that are not used to sell goods. *See* J. Thomas McCarthy, *McCarthy on Trademarks and Unfair Competition* § 10.39 (4th ed. 2012), citing the following cases where court found there was no trademark in particular celebrity images used: *ETW Corp. v. Jireh Publ'g, Inc.*, 332 F.3d 915 (6th Cir. 2003 (Tiger Woods); *Fifty-Six Hope Road Music, Ltd. v. A.V.E.L.A., Inc.*, 688 F. Supp. 2d 1148 (D. Nev. 2010) (Bob Marley); *Presley's Estate v. Russen*, 513 F. Supp. 1339 (D.N.J. 1981) (Elvis Presley); *Pirone v. MacMillan, Inc.*, 894 F.2d 579 (2d Cir. 1990) (Babe Ruth). *See also In re Elvis Presley Enterprises Inc.*, 50 U.S.P.Q.2d 1632 (T.T.A.B. 1999) (application to register as a mark the "likeness and image of Elvis Presley" without specifying which image of Presley was being registered rejected as too broad). Celebrity images are protectible by the right of publicity, but right of publicity gives less protection because it is state, not federal, law. Only about half of the states recognize the right, and the extent of protection varies among those that do. Matt Whibley argues that courts should give more protection to celebrity images in *Celebrity and Trademarks: Why Courts Should Recognize a Celebrity-Likeness-Mark*, 43 Sw. L. Rev. 121 (2013).

7. *Duration of trademarks.* Unlike copyrights and patents, trademarks do not have constitutionally mandated time limits. A certificate of registration for a trademark remains in force for 10 years, on the condition that the owner of the mark file an affidavit after six years showing that the mark is still in use. Registrations may be renewed every 10 years so long as the mark remains in use. 15 U.S.C. §§ 1058-1059. Why is the protection given to trademarks unlimited as to time?

8. *Federal registration.* Unlike copyrights, trademarks are protected by both state and federal law, but like copyright, registration is not needed to obtain a trademark. As in other areas of the common law, first-in-time, determined by use of a distinctive mark to identify a seller's goods or services, normally determines priority of rights. As in copyright, federal registration confers significant advantages to a trademark holder. Registration provides:

- constructive notice to the public of the registrant's claim of ownership of the mark;
- a legal presumption of the registrant's ownership of the mark and the registrant's exclusive right to use the mark nationwide on or in connection with the goods and/or services listed in the registration;
- the ability to bring an action concerning the mark in federal court;
- the use of the U.S registration as a basis to obtain registration in foreign countries; and
- the ability to file the U.S. registration with the U.S. Customs Service to prevent importation of infringing foreign goods.

Registration also gives the trademark owner the right to use the ® symbol, which may carry significant deterrent effect. "TM" and "SM" may be used to give notice of a claim of ownership without registration of the mark.

9. For more information on trademark and unfair competition law, see J. Thomas McCarthy, *McCarthy on Trademarks and Unfair Competition* (4th ed. 2012), and *Restatement (Third) Unfair Competition* (1995).

2. *Trade Dress*

TRAFFIX DEVICES, INC. v. MARKETING DISPLAYS, INC.

Supreme Court of the United States
532 U.S. 23 (2001)

Justice KENNEDY delivered the opinion of the Court.

Temporary road signs with warnings like "Road Work Ahead" or "Left Shoulder Closed" must withstand strong gusts of wind. An inventor named Robert Sarkisian obtained two utility patents for a mechanism built upon two springs (the dual-spring design) to keep these and other outdoor signs upright despite adverse wind conditions. The holder of the now-expired Sarkisian patents, respondent Marketing Displays, Inc. (MDI), established a successful business in the manufacture and sale of sign stands incorporating the patented feature. MDIs stands for road signs were recognizable to buyers and users (it says) because the dual-spring design was visible near the base of the sign.

This litigation followed after the patents expired and a competitor, TrafFix Devices, Inc., sold sign stands with a visible spring mechanism that looked like MDI's. MDI and TrafFix products looked alike because they were. When TrafFix started in business, it sent an MDI product abroad to have it reverse engineered, that is to say copied. Complicating matters, TrafFix marketed its sign stands under a name similar to MDI's. MDI used the name "WindMaster," while TrafFix, its new competitor, used "Wind-Buster."

MDI brought suit under the Trademark Act of 1946 (Lanham Act) against TrafFix for trademark infringement (based on the similar names), trade dress infringement (based on the copied dual-spring design), and unfair competition. TrafFix counterclaimed on antitrust theories. After the . . . District Court . . . considered cross-motions for summary judgment, MDI prevailed on its trademark claim for the confusing similarity of names and was held not liable on the antitrust counterclaim; those two rulings, affirmed by the Court of Appeals, are not before us. . . .

The District Court ruled against MDI on its trade dress claim. . . . After determining that the one element of MDI's trade dress at issue was the dual-spring design, . . . it held that "no reasonable trier of fact could determine that MDI has established secondary meaning" in its alleged trade dress. . . . In other words, consumers did not associate the look of the dual-spring design with MDI. As a second, independent reason to grant summary judgment in favor of TrafFix, the District Court determined the dual-spring design was functional. On this rationale secondary meaning is irrelevant because there can be no trade dress protection in any event. In ruling on the functional aspect of the design, the District Court noted that Sixth Circuit precedent indicated that the burden was on MDI to prove that its trade dress was nonfunctional, and not on TrafFix to show that it was functional (a rule since adopted by Congress . . .), and then went on to consider MDI's arguments that the dual-spring design was subject to trade dress protection. Finding none of MDI's contentions persuasive, the District Court concluded MDI had not "proffered sufficient evidence which would enable a reasonable trier of fact to find that MDI's vertical dual-spring design is non-functional." . . . Summary judgment was entered against MDI on its trade dress claims.

The Court of Appeals for the Sixth Circuit reversed the trade dress ruling . . . [holding that] the District Court had erred in ruling MDI failed to show a genuine issue of material fact regarding whether it had secondary meaning in its alleged trade dress, . . . and . . . in determining that MDI could not prevail in any event because the alleged trade dress was in fact a functional product configuration. . . . The Court of Appeals suggested the District Court committed legal error by looking only to the dual-spring design when evaluating MDI's trade dress. Basic to its reasoning was the . . . observation that it took "little imagination to conceive of a hidden dual-spring mechanism or a tri or quad-spring mechanism that might avoid infringing [MDI's] trade dress." . . . The Court of Appeals explained that "[i]f TrafFix or another competitor chooses to use [MDI's] dual-spring design, then it will have to find *some other way* to set its sign apart to avoid infringing [MDI's] trade dress." . . . It was not sufficient, according to the Court of Appeals, that allowing exclusive use of a particular feature such as the dual-spring design in the guise of trade dress would "hinde[r] competition somewhat." Rather, "[e]xclusive use of a feature must 'put competitors at a *significant* non-reputation-related disadvantage' before trade dress protection is denied on functionality grounds." . . . (quoting Qualitex Co. v. Jacobson Products Co.). . . . [T]he Court of Appeals took note of a split . . . in various other Circuits on the issue whether the existence of an expired utility patent forecloses the possibility of the patentee's claiming trade dress protection in the product's design. . . . To resolve the conflict, we granted certiorari. . . .

It is well established that trade dress can be protected under federal law. The design or packaging of a product may acquire a distinctiveness which serves to identify the product with its manufacturer or source; and a design or package which acquires this secondary meaning, assuming other requisites are met, is a trade dress which may not be used in a manner likely to cause confusion as to the origin, sponsorship, or approval of the goods. In these respects protection for trade dress exists to promote competition. . . . [V]arious Courts of Appeals have allowed claims of trade dress infringement relying on the general provision of the Lanham Act which provides a cause of action to one who is injured when a person uses "any word, term name, symbol, or device, or any combination thereof . . . which is likely to cause confusion . . . as to the origin, sponsorship, or approval of his or her goods." Congress confirmed this statutory protection for trade dress by amending the Lanham Act to recognize the concept. Title 15 U.S.C. § 1125(a)(3) provides: "In a civil action for trade dress infringement under this chapter for trade dress not registered on the principal register, the person who asserts trade dress protection has the burden of proving that the matter sought to be protected is not functional." This burden of proof gives force to the well-established rule that trade dress protection may not be claimed for product features that are functional. And in *Wal-Mart* [v. Samara Bros., Inc., 529 U.S. 205 (2000)], we were careful to caution against misuse or overextension of trade dress. We noted that "product design almost invariably serves purposes other than source identification." . . .

Trade dress protection must subsist with the recognition that in many instances there is no prohibition against copying goods and products. In general, unless an intellectual property right such as a patent or copyright protects an item, it will be subject to copying. As the Court has explained, copying is not always discouraged or disfavored by the laws which preserve our competitive economy. Bonito Boats, Inc. v. Thunder Craft Boats, Inc., 489 U.S. 141 (1989). Allowing competitors to copy will have salutary effects in many instances. "Reverse engineering of chemical and mechanical articles in the public domain often leads to significant advances in technology."

The principal question in this case is the effect of an expired patent on a claim of trade dress infringement. A prior patent, we conclude, has vital significance in resolving the trade dress claim. A utility patent is strong evidence that the features therein claimed are functional. If trade dress protection is sought for those features the strong evidence of functionality based on the previous patent adds great weight to the statutory presumption that features are deemed functional until proved otherwise by the party seeking trade dress protection. Where the expired patent claimed the features in question, one who seeks to establish trade dress protection must carry the heavy burden of showing that the feature is not functional, for instance by showing that it is merely an ornamental, incidental, or arbitrary aspect of the device.

In the case before us, the central advance claimed in the expired utility patents (the Sarkisian patents) is the dual-spring design; and the dual-spring design is the essential feature of the trade dress MDI now seeks to establish and to protect. The rule we have explained bars the trade dress claim, for MDI did not, and cannot, carry the burden of overcoming the strong evidentiary inference of functionality based on the disclosure of the dual-spring design in the claims of the expired patents.

The dual springs shown in the Sarkisian patents were well apart (at either end of a frame for holding a rectangular sign when one full side is the base) while the dual springs at issue here are close together (in a frame designed to hold a sign by one of its corners). . . . [T]his makes little difference. The point is that the springs are necessary to the operation of the device. The fact that the springs in this very different-looking device fall within the claims of the patents is illustrated by MDI's own position in earlier litigation. In the late 1970's, MDI engaged in a long-running intellectual property battle with a company known as Winn-Proof. Although the precise claims of the Sarkisian patents cover sign stands with springs "spaced apart," . . . the Winn-Proof sign stands (with springs much like the sign stands at issue here) were found to infringe the patents. . . . Sarkisian v. Winn-Proof Corp., 697 F.2d 1313 (1983). Although the Winn-Proof traffic sign stand (with dual springs close together) did not appear . . . to infringe the literal terms of the patent claims (which called for "spaced apart" springs), the Winn-Proof sign stand was found to infringe the patents under the doctrine of equivalents, which allows a finding of patent infringement even when the accused product does not fall within the literal terms of the claims. . . . In light of this past ruling—a ruling procured at MDI's own insistence—it must be concluded the products here at issue would have been covered by the claims of the expired patents.

The rationale for the rule that the disclosure of a feature in the claims of a utility patent constitutes strong evidence of functionality is well illustrated in this case. . . . [The] statements made in the patent applications and in the course of procuring the patents demonstrate the functionality of the design. MDI does not assert that any of these representations are mistaken or inaccurate, and this is further strong evidence of the functionality of the dual-spring design. . . .

In finding for MDI on the trade dress issue the Court of Appeals gave insufficient recognition to the importance of the expired utility patents, and their evidentiary significance, in establishing the functionality of the device. The error likely was caused by its misinterpretation of trade dress principles in other respects. . . . [E]ven if there has been no previous utility patent the party asserting trade dress has the burden to establish the nonfunctionality of alleged trade dress features. MDI could not meet this burden. . . .

The Court has allowed trade dress protection to certain product features that are inherently distinctive. *Two Pesos* [v. Taco Cabana, Inc.,] 505 U.S. 763. . . . In *Two Pesos*, however, the Court at the outset made the explicit analytic assumption that the trade dress features in question (decorations and other features to evoke a Mexican theme in a restaurant) were not functional. . . . The trade dress in those cases did not bar competitors from copying functional product design features. In the instant case, beyond serving the purpose of informing consumers that the sign stands are made by MDI (assuming it does so), the dual-spring design provides a unique and useful mechanism to resist the force of the wind. Functionality having been established, whether MDI's dual-spring design has acquired secondary meaning need not be considered. . . . The dual-spring design is not an arbitrary flourish in the configuration of MDI's product; it is the reason the device works. Other designs need not be attempted.

. . . The Lanham Act does not exist to reward manufacturers for their innovation in creating a particular device; that is the purpose of the patent law and its period of exclusivity. The Lanham Act, furthermore, does not protect trade dress in a functional design simply because an investment has been made to encourage the public to associate a particular functional feature with a single manufacturer or seller. The Court of Appeals erred in viewing MDI as possessing the right to exclude competitors from using a design identical to MDI's and to require those competitors to adopt a different design simply to avoid copying it. MDI cannot gain the exclusive right to produce sign stands using the dual-spring design by asserting that consumers associate it with the look of the invention itself. Whether a utility patent has expired or there has been no utility patent at all, a product design which has a particular appearance may be functional because it is "essential to the use or purpose of the article" or "affects the cost or quality of the article." *Inwood*, 456 U.S. [844] . . . .

. . . The judgment of the Court of Appeals is reversed, and the case is remanded for further proceedings consistent with this opinion.

Notes and Questions

1. *Generic marks.* In addition to the functional element of a product's shape or packaging, which cannot be protected, generic labels for products or services may not be protected as trademarks. When a mark becomes so identified in the public mind with a product that it becomes a generic label, it loses trademark protection. Aspirin, thermos, escalator, cellophane, and shredded wheat are trademarks that passed into such widespread use that they "committed genericide."

2. *Designs.* Designers may be able to secure trademark protection against knockoffs if the design is not functional. In *PAF S.r.l. v. Lisa Lighting Co.*, 712 F. Supp. 394 (S.D.N.Y. 1989), the Italian manufacturer and exclusive U.S. distributor of the highly acclaimed, award-winning "DOVE" lamp were awarded injunctive relief, the defendant's profits, and attorneys' fees against a Delaware corporation that imported 1,000 copies from Taiwan that it marketed as the

"SWAN" lamp. The DOVE lamp sold for between $160 and $200; the SWAN, for $120. The DOVE was entitled to protection because it was "a highly distinctive, aesthetically appealing lamp, not a predominantly functional lamp," and the fact that the defendant copied it established that its trade dress (its design) had acquired a secondary meaning. "[T]he crux of the doctrine of secondary meaning 'is that the mark comes to identify not only the goods but the source of those goods,' even though the relevant consuming public might not know the name of the producer."

3.   Trademark Dilution

Most trademark law is directed at preventing confusion among consumers as to the source of a product or service, and prohibits use of similar marks only when confusion is likely to occur. That is why the owner of the Acme Bakery probably cannot stop the Acme Carwash from using the term *Acme*, even if the bakery used it first. However, another branch of trademark law protects "famous" trademarks, even when no confusion is likely to occur. Originally protected only by state law, Congress adopted the Federal Trademark Dilution Act in 1995. That Act added § 1125(c) to the Lanham Act, which, as amended, provides in part:

> Subject to the principles of equity, the owner of a famous mark that is distinctive, inherently or through acquired distinctiveness, shall be entitled to an injunction against another person who, at any time after the owner's mark has become famous, commences use of a mark or trade name in commerce that is likely to cause dilution by blurring or dilution by tarnishment of the famous mark, regardless of the presence or absence of actual or likely confusion, of competition, or of actual economic injury . . . .

The statute defines the two types of dilution as follows:

> "dilution by blurring" is association arising from the similarity between a mark or trade name and a famous mark that impairs the distinctiveness of the famous mark. . . .
>
> "dilution by tarnishment" is association arising from the similarity between a mark or trade name and a famous mark that harms the reputation of the famous mark.

One of the advantages to having a federally registered mark is that in the event of a conflict, a registered mark prevails over an unregistered mark, even though the unregistered mark is famous. First Amendment concerns led to inclusion in the dilution statute at 15 U.S.C. § 1125(c)(3) of exemptions for:

- any fair use, including a nominative or descriptive use of a famous mark by another person other than as a designation of source for the person's own goods or services, including use in connection with
  - advertising or promotion that permits consumers to compare goods or services; or
  - identifying and parodying, criticizing, or commenting upon the famous mark owner or the goods and services of the famous mark owner;
- all forms of news reporting and news commentary; and
- any noncommercial use of a mark.

In *Moseley v. V Secret Catalogue, Inc.*, 537 U.S. 418 (2003), the Supreme Court undertook a thorough review of the background of the federal anti-dilution statute and concluded that, unlike its state counterparts, the federal act requires proof of actual dilution, rather than a "mere likelihood" of dilution. In the course of its opinion, the court noted from the congressional hearings that the purpose of the statute was "to protect famous trademarks from subsequent uses that blur the distinctiveness of the mark or tarnish or disparage it, even in the absence of a likelihood of confusion." Examples of dilution that would be actionable included DUPONT shoes, BUICK aspirin, and KODAK pianos. The concept of dilution includes both uses that blur the distinctiveness of a mark and uses that "tarnish or disparage" it. The court reversed the grant of an injunction to the owner of the Victoria's Secret mark against the Moseleys' use of the name "Victor's Little Secret" for the adult novelty store they ran in a strip mall in Elizabethtown, Kentucky. The court remanded because summary judgment had been granted without any evidence of actual injury to the economic value of the mark or of any lessening of the capacity of the mark to identify and distinguish goods and services sold in the Victoria's Secret stores or catalogs. The court explained what it meant by actual dilution:

> . . . [T]he mere fact that consumers mentally associate the junior user's mark with a famous mark is not sufficient to establish actionable dilution. . . . [S]uch mental association will not necessarily reduce the capacity of the famous mark to identify the goods of its owner . . . . [E]ven though Utah drivers may be reminded of the circus when they see a license plate referring to the "greatest snow on earth," it by no means follows that they will associate "the greatest show on earth" with skiing or snow sports, or associate it less strongly or exclusively with the circus. "Blurring" is not a necessary consequence of mental association. (Nor, for that matter, is "tarnishing.") . . .

The statute expressly exempts parodies from trademark dilution claims, but only if the parody is not used as a designation of source for the parodist's own goods or services. When the brand itself is a parody, courts have reached inconsistent results in cases involving "Chewy Vuiton" dog toys, a "Gucci Goo" diaper bag, "Charbucks" coffee, "Lardache" plus size jeans, and the "Velvet Elvis Bar." These cases and others are discussed in Stacey L. Dogan & Mark A. Lemley, *Parody As Brand*, 47 U.C. Davis L. Rev. 473 (2013), who conclude:

> Brand parodies serve useful social purposes and are unlikely to interfere with any legitimate interests of trademark owners. But the fact that they are both parodies and brands means that their legal status is unclear. We think brand parodies deserve clear legal protection, and that existing law can provide that protection if it is properly understood.

4. *Cyberpiracy*

Section 1125(d) was added to the Lanham Act (15 U.S.C.) in 1999 to address abuse of domain names. Labeled "Cyberpiracy Prevention," it provides in part:

> (1) (A) A person shall be liable in a civil action by the owner of a mark, including a personal name that is protected as a mark under this section, if, without regard to the goods or services of the parties, that person

(i) has a bad faith intent to profit from that mark, including a personal name which is protected as a mark under this section; and

(ii) registers, traffics in, or uses a domain name that—

(I) in the case of a mark that is distinctive at the time of registration of the domain name, is identical or confusingly similar to that mark;

(II) in the case of a famous mark that is famous at the time of registration of the domain name, is identical or confusingly similar to or dilutive of that mark . . . .

TOYOTA MOTOR SALES, U.S.A., INC. v. TABARI

United States Court of Appeals, Ninth Circuit
610 F.3d 1171 (2010)

Opinion by Chief Judge KOZINSKI. . . .

FACTS

Farzad and Lisa Tabari are auto brokers—the personal shoppers of the automotive world. They contact authorized dealers, solicit bids and arrange for customers to buy from the dealer offering the best combination of location, availability and price. Consumers like this service, as it increases competition among dealers, resulting in greater selection at lower prices. For many of the same reasons, auto manufacturers and dealers aren't so keen on it, as it undermines dealers' territorial exclusivity and lowers profit margins. Until recently, the Tabaris offered this service at buy-a-lexus.com and buyorleaselexus.com.

Toyota Motor Sales U.S.A. ("Toyota") is the exclusive distributor of Lexus vehicles in the United States, and jealous guardian of the Lexus mark. A Toyota marketing executive testified at trial that Toyota spends over $250 million every year promoting the Lexus brand. In the executive's estimation, "Lexus is a very prestigious luxury brand and it is an indication of an exclusive luxury experience." No doubt true.

Toyota objected to the Tabaris' use on their website of copyrighted photography of Lexus vehicles and the circular "L Symbol Design mark." Toyota also took umbrage at the Tabaris' use of the string "lexus" in their domain names, which it believed was "likely to cause confusion as to the source of [the Tabaris'] web site." The Tabaris removed Toyota's photography and logo from their site and added a disclaimer in large font at the top. But they refused to give up their domain names. Toyota sued, and the district court found infringement after a bench trial. It ordered the Tabaris to cease using their domain names and enjoined them from using the Lexus mark in any other domain name. Pro se as they were at trial, the Tabaris appeal.

NOMINATIVE FAIR USE

When customers purchase a Lexus through the Tabaris, they receive a genuine Lexus car sold by an authorized Lexus dealer, and a portion of the proceeds ends up in Toyota's bank account. Toyota doesn't claim the business of brokering Lexus cars is illegal or that it has contracted with its dealers to pro-hibit selling through a broker. Instead, Toyota is using this trademark lawsuit to make it more difficult for consumers to use the Tabaris to buy a Lexus.

The district court applied the eight-factor test for likelihood of confusion articulated in AMF Inc. v. Sleekcraft Boats, 599 F.2d 341 (9th Cir.1979), and found that the Tabaris' domain names—buy-a-lexus.com and buyorleaselexus. com—infringed the Lexus trademark. But we've held that the *Sleekcraft* analysis doesn't apply where a defendant uses the mark to refer to the trademarked good itself. *See* Playboy Enters., Inc. v. Welles, 279 F.3d 796 (9th Cir.2002); New Kids on the Block v. News Am. Publ'g, Inc., 971 F.2d 302, 308 (9th Cir.1992). The Tabaris are using the term Lexus to describe their business of brokering Lexus automobiles; when they say Lexus, they mean Lexus. We've long held that such use of the trademark is a fair use, namely nominative fair use. And fair use is, by definition, not infringement. The Tabaris did in fact present a nominative fair use defense to the district court.

In cases where a nominative fair use defense is raised, we ask whether (1) the product was "readily identifiable" without use of the mark; (2) defendant used more of the mark than necessary; or (3) defendant falsely suggested he was sponsored or endorsed by the trademark holder.

This test "evaluates the likelihood of confusion in nominative use cases." It's designed to address the risk that nominative use of the mark will inspire a mis-taken belief on the part of consumers that the speaker is sponsored or endorsed by the trademark holder. The third factor speaks directly to the risk of such con-fusion, and the others do so indirectly: Consumers may reasonably infer spon-sorship or endorsement if a company uses an unnecessary trademark or "more" of a mark than necessary. But if the nominative use satisfies the three-factor *New Kids* test, it doesn't infringe. If the nominative use does not satisfy all the *New Kids* factors, the district court may order defendants to modify their use of the mark so that all three factors are satisfied; it may not enjoin nominative use of the mark altogether.

A. The district court enjoined the Tabaris from using "any . . . domain name, service mark, trademark, trade name, meta tag or other commercial indication of origin that includes the mark LEXUS." A trademark injunction, particularly one involving nominative fair use, can raise serious First Amendment concerns because it can interfere with truthful communication between buyers and sellers in the marketplace. Accordingly, "we must [e]nsure that [the injunction] is tai-lored to eliminate only the specific harm alleged." To uphold the broad injunc-tion entered in this case, we would have to be convinced that consumers are likely to believe a site is sponsored or endorsed by a trademark holder whenever the domain name contains the string of letters that make up the trademark.

In performing this analysis, our focus must be on the "'reasonably prudent consumer' in the marketplace." The relevant marketplace is the online market-place, and the relevant consumer is a reasonably prudent consumer accustomed to shopping online; the kind of consumer who is likely to visit the Tabaris' web-site when shopping for an expensive product like a luxury car. Unreasonable, imprudent and inexperienced web-shoppers are not relevant.

The injunction here is plainly overbroad—as even Toyota's counsel grudg-ingly conceded at oral argument—because it prohibits domain names that on their face dispel any confusion as to sponsorship or endorsement. The Tabaris are prohibited from doing business at sites like independent-lexus-broker.com and we-are-definitely-not-lexus.com, although a reasonable consumer wouldn't believe Toyota sponsors the websites using those domains. Prohibition of such truthful and non-misleading speech does not advance the Lanham Act's purpose of protecting consumers and preventing unfair competition; in fact, it undermines that rationale by frustrating honest communication between the Tabaris and their customers.

Even if we were to modify the injunction to exclude domain names that expressly disclaim sponsorship or endorsement (like the examples above), the injunction would still be too broad. The Tabaris may not do business at lexus-broker.com, even though that's the most straightforward, obvious and truthful way to describe their business. The nominative fair use doctrine allows such truthful use of a mark, even if the speaker fails to expressly disavow association with the trademark holder, so long as it's unlikely to cause confusion as to sponsorship or endorsement. . . . Speakers are under no obligation to provide a disclaimer as a condition for engaging in truthful, non-misleading speech.

Toyota argues it is entitled to exclusive use of the string "lexus" in domain names because it spends hundreds of millions of dollars every year making sure everyone recognizes and understands the word "Lexus." But "[a] large expenditure of money does not in itself create legally protectable rights." . . . Indeed, it is precisely because of Toyota's investment in the Lexus mark that "[m]uch useful social and commercial discourse would be all but impossible if speakers were under threat of an infringement lawsuit every time they made reference to [Lexus] by using its trademark." . . .[8]

On remand, Toyota must bear the burden of establishing that the Tabaris' use of the Lexus mark was *not* nominative fair use. A finding of nominative fair use is a finding that the plaintiff has failed to show a likelihood of confusion as to sponsorship or endorsement. . . .[11] And, as the Supreme Court has unambiguously instructed, the Lanham Act always places the "burden of proving likelihood of confusion . . . on the party charging infringement." In this case, that party is Toyota. "[A]ll the [Tabaris] need[ ] to do is to leave the factfinder unpersuaded."

. . . A defendant seeking to assert nominative fair use as a defense need only show that it used the mark to refer to the trademarked good, as the Tabaris undoubtedly have here. The burden then reverts to the plaintiff to show a likelihood of confusion.

We vacate and remand for proceedings consistent with this opinion. At the very least, the injunction must be modified to allow some use of the Lexus mark in domain names by the Tabaris. Trademarks are part of our common language, and we all have some right to use them to communicate in truthful, non-misleading ways.

---

8.   "Words . . . do not worm their way into our discourse by accident." Alex Kozinski, *Trademarks Unplugged*, 68 N.Y.U. L. Rev. 960, 975 (1993). Trademark holders engage in "well-orchestrated campaigns intended to burn them into our collective consciousness." Although trademark holders gain something by pushing their trademark into the lexicon, they also inevitably lose a measure of control over their mark.

11.   . . . [U]nlike classic fair use, nominative fair use is not specifically provided for by statute. A court may find classic fair use despite "proof of infringement" because the Lanham Act authorizes that result. *See* 15 U.S.C. § 1115(b)(4). Nominative fair use, on the other hand, represents a finding of no liability under that statute's basic prohibition of infringing use.

Many of the district court's errors seem to be the result of unevenly-matched lawyering, as Toyota appears to have taken advantage of the fact that the Tabaris appeared pro se. To avoid similar problems on remand, the district court might consider contacting members of the bar to determine if any would be willing to represent the Tabaris at a reduced rate or on a volunteer basis.

D. PATENT LAW PROTECTION

A patent is a property right granted by the Government of the United States of America to an inventor "to exclude others from making, using, offering for sale, or selling the invention throughout the United States or importing the invention into the United States" for a limited time in exchange for public disclosure of the invention when the patent is granted.

http://www.uspto.gov/inventors/patents.jsp

The Patent Act of 1952, 35 U.S.C. §§ 1-376, was enacted by Congress under the grant of authority found in the Constitution, Article I, Section 8, Clause 8, known as the Copyright Clause. To be eligible for patent protection, an invention must be novel, useful, non-obvious in nature, and not offensive to public morality. In addition, the inventor's claim must be clear and definite, and the invention must be described sufficiently that a person of ordinary skill in the art can make and use the invention.

There are three main types of patents: utility patents, design patents, and plant patents. Utility patents are issued for any new, or improved, useful machine, manufacture, process, or composition of matter. Design patents are issued for any new, original, and ornamental design for an item of manufacture, where it is only the appearance that is protected and not the actual item. Plant patents are issued for any new asexually reproducing plant.

Patents have a much shorter duration than either copyright or trademark. The term of a patent begins on the date when the patent issues and ends 20 years from the date on which the patent application was filed.[8] If the Patent and Trademark Office fails to issue the patent within three years from the date of filing, the term of the patent may be extended one day for each day of delay beyond the three-year period. Unlike other patents, the term of design patents is limited to 14 years from the date the patent issues.[9] Patents are not renewable, which allows the patented invention or discovery to be available for public use much sooner than copyrighted works.

A patent grants the right to prevent all others from making, using, or selling the patented product or process. A patent holder also has rights to prevent others from inducing domestic infringement, from selling components for assembly of the patented invention abroad, and to prevent others from importing into the United States articles manufactured with a patented process. 35 U.S.C.

8. 35 U.S.C. § 154.
9. 35 U.S.C. § 173.

§ 271. Appeals in patent cases are handled exclusively in the Court of Appeals for the Federal Circuit.

1. Patent Eligibility

DIAMOND v. CHAKRABARTY
Supreme Court of the United States
447 U.S. 303 (1980)

Mr. Chief Justice BURGER delivered the opinion of the Court. We granted certiorari to determine whether a live, human-made micro-organism is patentable subject matter under 35 U.S.C. § 101. . . .

In 1972, respondent Chakrabarty, a microbiologist, filed a patent application, assigned to the General Electric Co. The application asserted 36 claims related to Chakrabarty's invention of "a bacterium from the genus *Pseudomonas* containing therein at least two stable energy-generating plasmids, each of said plasmids providing a separate hydrocarbon degradative pathway."[1] This human-made, genetically engineered bacterium is capable of breaking down multiple components of crude oil. Because of this property, which is possessed by no naturally occurring bacteria, Chakrabarty's invention is believed to have significant value for the treatment of oil spills.

Chakrabarty's patent claims were of three types: first, process claims for the method of producing the bacteria; second, claims for an inoculum comprised of a carrier material floating on water, such as straw, and the new bacteria; and third, claims to the bacteria themselves. The patent examiner allowed the claims falling into the first two categories, but rejected claims for the bacteria. His decision rested on two grounds: (1) that micro-organisms are "products of nature," and (2) that as living things they are not patentable subject matter under 35 U.S.C. § 101.

Chakrabarty appealed the rejection of these claims to the Patent Office Board of Appeals, and the Board affirmed the Examiner on the second ground.[3] Relying on the legislative history of the 1930 Plant Patent Act, in which Congress extended patent protection to certain asexually reproduced plants, the Board concluded that § 101 was not intended to cover living things such as these laboratory created micro-organisms. . . .

The Constitution grants Congress broad power to legislate to "promote the Progress of Science and useful Arts, by securing for limited Times to Authors and Inventors the exclusive Right to their respective Writings and Discoveries." Art. I, § 8, cl. 8. The patent laws promote this progress by offering inventors

---

1.   . . . In the work represented by the patent application at issue here, Chakrabarty discovered a process by which four different plasmids, capable of degrading four different oil components, could be transferred to and maintained stably in a single *Pseudomonas* bacterium, which itself has no capacity for degrading oil.

3.   The Board concluded that the new bacteria were not "products of nature," because *Pseudomonas* bacteria containing two or more different energy-generating plasmids are not naturally occurring.

exclusive rights for a limited period as an incentive for their inventiveness and research efforts. . . .

The question before us in this case is a narrow one of statutory interpretation requiring us to construe 35 U.S.C. § 101, which provides:

> Whoever invents or discovers any new and useful process, machine, manufacture, or composition of matter, or any new and useful improvement thereof, may obtain a patent thereof, subject to the conditions and requirements of this title.

Specifically, we must determine whether respondent's micro-organism constitutes a "manufacture" or "composition of matter" within the meaning of the statute. . . .

[T]his Court has read the term "manufacture" in § 101 in accordance with its dictionary definition to mean "the production of articles for use from raw or prepared materials by giving to these materials new forms, qualities, properties, or combinations, whether by hand-labor or by machinery." . . . Similarly, "composition of matter" has been construed consistent with its common usage to include "all compositions of two or more substances and . . . all composite articles, whether they be the results of chemical union, or of mechanical mixture, or whether they be gases, fluids, powders or solids." . . . In choosing such expansive terms as "manufacture" and "composition of matter," modified by the comprehensive "any," Congress plainly contemplated that the patent laws would be given wide scope.

The relevant legislative history also supports a broad construction. The Patent Act of 1793, authored by Thomas Jefferson, defined statutory subject matter as "any new and useful art, machine, manufacture, or composition of matter, or any new or useful improvement [thereof]." . . . In 1952, when the patent laws were recodified, Congress replaced the word "art" with "process," but otherwise left Jefferson's language intact. The Committee Reports accompanying the 1952 Act inform us that Congress intended statutory subject matter to "include anything under the sun that is made by man." . . .

This is not to suggest that § 101 has no limits or that it embraces every discovery. The laws of nature, physical phenomena, and abstract ideas have been held not patentable. *See* Parker v. Flook, 437 U.S. 584 (1978); Gottschalk v. Benson, 409 U.S. 63 (1972); Funk Brothers Seed Co. v. Kalo Inoculant Co., 333 U.S. 127 (1948); O'Reilly v. Morse, 15 How. 62 (1854); Le Roy v. Tatham, 14 How. 156 (1853). Thus, a new mineral discovered in the earth or a new plant found in the wild is not patentable subject matter. Likewise, Einstein could not patent his celebrated law that $E = mc^2$; nor could Newton have patented the law of gravity. Such discoveries are "manifestations of . . . nature, free to all men and reserved exclusively to none." . . .

Judged in this light, respondent's micro-organism plainly qualifies as patentable subject matter. His claim is not to a hitherto unknown natural phenomenon, but to a nonnaturally occurring manufacture or composition of matter — a product of human ingenuity "having a distinctive name, character [and] use." . . . The point is underscored dramatically by comparison of the invention here with that in *Funk*. There, the patentee had discovered that there existed in nature certain species of root-nodule bacteria which did not exert a mutually inhibitive effect on each other. He used that discovery to produce a mixed culture capable of inoculating the seeds of leguminous plants. Concluding that the patentee had discovered "only some of the handiwork of nature," the Court ruled the product nonpatentable. . . . Here, by contrast, the patentee has produced a new bacterium with markedly different characteristics from any found in nature and one having the potential for significant utility. His discovery is not nature's handiwork, but his own; accordingly it is patentable subject matter under § 101. . . .

We have emphasized in the recent past that "[o]ur individual appraisal of the wisdom or unwisdom of a particular [legislative] course . . . is to be put aside in the process of interpreting a statute." . . . Our task, rather, is the narrow one of determining what Congress meant by the words it used in the statute; once that is done our powers are exhausted. Congress is free to amend § 101 so as to exclude from patent protection organisms produced by genetic engineering. *Cf.* 42 U.S.C. § 2181(a), exempting from patent protection inventions "useful solely in the utilization of special nuclear material or atomic energy in an atomic weapon." Or it may chose to craft a statute specifically designed for such living things. But, until Congress takes such action, this Court must construe the language of § 101 as it is. The language of that section fairly embraces respondent's invention.

Accordingly, the judgment of the Court of Customs and Patent Appeals is *Affirmed.*

BILSKI v. KAPPOS
Supreme Court of the United States
130 S. Ct. 3218 (2010)

Justice KENNEDY. The question in this case turns on whether a patent can be issued for a claimed invention designed for the business world. The patent application claims a procedure for instructing buyers and sellers how to protect against the risk of price fluctuations in a discrete section of the economy. Three arguments are advanced for the proposition that the claimed invention is outside the scope of patent law: (1) it is not tied to a machine and does not transform an article; (2) it involves a method of conducting business; and (3) it is merely an abstract idea. The Court of Appeals ruled that the first mentioned of these, the so-called machine-or-transformation test, was the sole test to be used for determining the patentability of a "process" under the Patent Act.

I

Petitioners' application seeks patent protection for a claimed invention that explains how buyers and sellers of commodities in the energy market can protect, or hedge, against the risk of price changes. The key claims are claims 1 and 4. Claim 1 describes a series of steps instructing how to hedge risk. Claim 4 puts the concept articulated in claim 1 into a simple mathematical formula. Claim 1 consists of the following steps:

"(a) initiating a series of transactions between said commodity provider and consumers of said commodity wherein said consumers purchase said commodity at a fixed rate based upon historical averages, said fixed rate corresponding to a risk position of said consumers;

"(b) identifying market participants for said commodity having a counter-risk position to said consumers; and

"(c) initiating a series of transactions between said commodity provider and said market participants at a second fixed rate such that said series of market participant transactions balances the risk position of said series of consumer transactions."

The remaining claims explain how claims 1 and 4 can be applied to allow energy suppliers and consumers to minimize the risks resulting from fluctuations in market demand for energy. . . .

The patent examiner rejected petitioners' application, explaining that it "is not implemented on a specific apparatus and merely manipulates [an] abstract idea and solves a purely mathematical problem without any limitation to a practical application, therefore, the invention is not directed to the technological arts." The Board of Patent Appeals and Interferences affirmed . . . .

The United States Court of Appeals for the Federal Circuit heard the case en banc and affirmed. The case produced five different opinions. . . .

II

A

. . . Section 101 . . . specifies four independent categories of inventions or discoveries that are eligible for protection: processes, machines, manufactures, and compositions of matter. "In choosing such expansive terms . . . modified by the comprehensive 'any,' Congress plainly contemplated that the patent laws would be given wide scope." Diamond v. Chakrabarty (1980). Congress took this permissive approach to patent eligibility to ensure that " 'ingenuity should receive a liberal encouragement'" (quoting 5 Writings of Thomas Jefferson 75-76 (H. Washington ed. 1871)).

The Court's precedents provide three specific exceptions to § 101's broad patent-eligibility principles: "laws of nature, physical phenomena, and abstract ideas." While these exceptions are not required by the statutory text, they are consistent with the notion that a patentable process must be "new and useful." And, in any case, these exceptions have defined the reach of the statute as a matter of statutory *stare decisis* going back 150 years. . . . The concepts covered by these exceptions are "part of the storehouse of knowledge of all men . . . free to all men and reserved exclusively to none." Funk Brothers Seed Co. v. Kalo Inoculant Co., 333 U.S. 127 (1948).

The § 101 patent-eligibility inquiry is only a threshold test. Even if an invention qualifies as a process, machine, manufacture, or composition of matter, . . . the claimed invention must also satisfy "the conditions and requirements of this title." Those requirements include that the invention be novel, see § 102, nonobvious, see § 103, and fully and particularly described, see § 112.

The present case involves an invention that is claimed to be a "process" . . . .

The Court first considers two proposed categorical limitations on "process" patents under § 101 that would, if adopted, bar petitioners' application in the present case: the machine-or-transformation test and the categorical exclusion of business method patents.

B

1

. . . This Court has "more than once cautioned that courts "should not read into the patent laws limitations and conditions which the legislature has not expressed." In patent law, as in all statutory construction, "[u]nless otherwise defined, 'words will be interpreted as taking their ordinary, contemporary, common meaning.'" . . .

Adopting the machine-or-transformation test as the sole test for what constitutes a "process" (as opposed to just an important and useful clue) violates these statutory interpretation principles. Section 100(b) provides that "[t]he term 'process' means process, art or method, and includes a new use of a known process, machine, manufacture, composition of matter, or material." The Court is unaware of any "ordinary, contemporary, common meaning," . . . of the definitional terms "process, art or method" that would require these terms to be tied to a machine or to transform an article. . . .

This Court's precedents establish that the machine-or-transformation test is a useful and important clue, an investigative tool, . . . [but] is not the sole test for deciding whether an invention is a patent-eligible "process."

2

It is true that patents for inventions that did not satisfy the machine-or-transformation test were rarely granted in earlier eras, especially in the Industrial Age. . . . But times change. . . . The machine-or-transformation test may well provide a sufficient basis for evaluating processes similar to those in the Industrial Age. . . . But there are reasons to doubt whether the test should be the sole criterion for determining the patentability of inventions in the Information Age. As numerous *amicus* briefs argue, the machine-or-transformation test would create uncertainty as to the patentability of software, advanced diagnostic medicine techniques, and inventions based on linear programming, data compression, and the manipulation of digital signals. . . .

It is important to emphasize that the Court today is not commenting on the patentability of any particular invention, let alone holding that any of the above-mentioned technologies from the Information Age should or should not receive patent protection. This Age puts the possibility of innovation in the hands of more people and raises new difficulties for the patent law. With ever more people trying to innovate and thus seeking patent protections for their inventions, the patent law faces a great challenge in striking the balance between protecting inventors and not granting monopolies over procedures that others would discover by independent, creative application of general principles. Nothing in this opinion should be read to take a position on where that balance ought to be struck.

C

1

Section 101 similarly precludes the broad contention that the term "process" categorically excludes business methods. The term "method," which is within § 100(b)'s definition of "process," at least as a textual matter and before consulting other limitations in the Patent Act and this Court's precedents, may include at least some methods of doing business. . . . The Court is unaware of any argument that the "ordinary, contemporary, common meaning" of "method" excludes business methods. Nor is it clear how far a prohibition on business method patents would reach, and whether it would exclude technologies for conducting a business more efficiently. . . .

2

Interpreting § 101 to exclude all business methods simply because business method patents were rarely issued until modern times revives many of the previously discussed difficulties. At the same time, some business method patents raise special problems in terms of vagueness and suspect validity. See eBay Inc. v. MercExchange, L.L.C., 547 U.S. 388 (2006) (KENNEDY, J., concurring). The Information Age empowers people with new capacities to perform statistical analyses and mathematical calculations with a speed and sophistication that enable the design of protocols for more efficient performance of a vast number of business tasks. If a high enough bar is not set when considering patent applications of this sort, patent examiners and courts could be flooded with claims that would put a chill on creative endeavor and dynamic change.

In searching for a limiting principle, this Court's precedents on the unpatentability of abstract ideas provide useful tools. Indeed, if the Court of Appeals were to succeed in defining a narrower category or class of patent applications that claim to instruct how business should be conducted, and then rule that the category is unpatentable because, for instance, it represents an attempt to patent abstract ideas, this conclusion might well be in accord with controlling precedent. But beyond this or some other limitation consistent with the statutory text, the Patent Act leaves open the possibility that there are at least some processes that can be fairly described as business methods that are within patentable subject matter under § 101.

Finally, even if a particular business method fits into the statutory definition of a "process," that does not mean that the application claiming that method should be granted. . . . [T]o receive patent protection, any claimed invention must be novel, nonobvious, and fully and particularly described. These limitations serve a critical role in adjusting the tension, ever present in patent law, between stimulating innovation by protecting inventors and impeding progress by granting patents when not justified by the statutory design.

III

Even though petitioners' application is not categorically outside of § 101 under the two broad and atextual approaches the Court rejects today, that does not mean it is a "process" under § 101. Petitioners seek to patent both the concept of hedging risk and the application of that concept to energy markets. Rather than adopting categorical rules that might have wide-ranging and unforeseen impacts, the Court resolves this case narrowly on the basis of this Court's decisions in *Benson, Flook*, and *Diehr*, which show that petitioners' claims are not patentable processes because they are attempts to patent abstract ideas. Indeed, all members of the Court agree that the patent application at issue . . . claims an abstract idea.

In *Benson* [1972], the Court considered whether a patent application for an algorithm to convert binary-coded decimal numerals into pure binary code was a "process" under § 101. The Court first explained that "'[a] principle, in the abstract, is a fundamental truth; an original cause; a motive; these cannot be patented, as no one can claim in either of them an exclusive right.'" The Court then held the application at issue was not a "process," but an unpatentable abstract idea. "It is conceded that one may not patent an idea. But in practical effect that would be the result if the formula for converting . . . numerals to pure binary numerals were patented in this case." A contrary holding "would wholly pre-empt the mathematical formula and in practical effect would be a patent on the algorithm itself."

In *Flook* [1978], the Court considered the next logical step after *Benson*. The applicant there attempted to patent a procedure for monitoring the conditions during the catalytic conversion process in the petrochemical and oil-refining industries. The application's only innovation was reliance on a mathematical algorithm. *Flook* held the invention was not a patentable "process." The Court conceded the invention at issue, unlike the algorithm in *Benson*, had been limited so that it could still be freely used outside the petrochemical and oil-refining industries. Nevertheless, *Flook* rejected "[t]he notion that post-solution activity, no matter how conventional or obvious in itself, can transform an unpatentable principle into a patentable process." The Court concluded that the process at issue there was "unpatentable under § 101, not because it contain[ed] a mathematical algorithm as one component, but because once that algorithm [wa]s assumed to be within the prior art, the application, considered as a whole, contain[ed] no patentable invention." As the Court later explained, *Flook* stands for the proposition that the prohibition against patenting abstract ideas "cannot be circumvented by attempting to limit the use of the formula to a particular technological environment" or adding "insignificant postsolution activity."

Finally, in *Diehr* [*Diamond v. Diehr*, 450 U.S. 175 (1981)], the Court established a limitation on the principles articulated in *Benson* and *Flook*. The application in *Diehr* claimed a previously unknown method for "molding raw, uncured synthetic rubber into cured precision products," using a mathematical formula to complete some of its several steps by way of a computer. *Diehr* explained that while an abstract idea, law of nature, or mathematical formula could not be patented, "an *application* of a law of nature or mathematical formula to a known structure or process may well be deserving of patent protection." *Diehr* emphasized the need to consider the invention as a whole, rather than "dissect[ing] the claims into old and new elements and then . . . ignor[ing] the presence of the old elements in the analysis." Finally, the Court concluded that because the claim was not "an attempt to patent a mathematical formula, but rather [was] an industrial process for the molding of rubber products," it fell within § 101's patentable subject matter.

In light of these precedents, it is clear that petitioners' application is not a patentable "process." . . . "Hedging is a fundamental economic practice long prevalent in our system of commerce and taught in any introductory finance class." . . . The concept of hedging, described in claim 1 and reduced to a mathematical formula in claim 4, is an unpatentable abstract idea, just like the algorithms at issue in *Benson* and *Flook*. Allowing petitioners to patent risk hedging would pre-empt use of this approach in all fields, and would effectively grant a monopoly over an abstract idea. . . .

Today, the Court once again declines to impose limitations on the Patent Act that are inconsistent with the Act's text. The patent application here can be rejected under our precedents on the unpatentability of abstract ideas. The Court, therefore, need not define further what constitutes a patentable "process," beyond pointing to the definition of that term provided in § 100(b) and looking to the guideposts in *Benson*, *Flook*, and *Diehr*.

And nothing in today's opinion should be read as endorsing interpretations of § 101 that the Court of Appeals for the Federal Circuit has used in the past. . . . In disapproving an exclusive machine-or-transformation test, we by no means foreclose the Federal Circuit's development of other limiting criteria that further the purposes of the Patent Act and are not inconsistent with its text.

The judgment of the Court of Appeals is affirmed.

Justice STEVENS, with whom Justice GINSBURG, Justice BREYER, and Justice SOTOMAYOR join, concurring in the judgment.

In the area of patents, it is especially important that the law remain stable and clear. The only question presented in this case is whether the so-called machine-or-transformation test is the exclusive test for what constitutes a patentable "process". . . . It would be possible to answer that question simply by holding, as the entire Court agrees, that although the machine-or-transformation test is reliable in most cases, it is not the *exclusive* test.

I agree with the Court that, in light of the uncertainty that currently pervades this field, it is prudent to provide further guidance. But I would take a different approach. Rather than making any broad statements about how to define the term "process" in § 101 or tinkering with the bounds of the category of unpatentable, abstract ideas, I would restore patent law to its historical and constitutional moorings.

For centuries, it was considered well established that a series of steps for conducting business was not, in itself, patentable. In the late 1990's, the Federal Circuit and others called this proposition into question. Congress quickly responded to a Federal Circuit decision with a stopgap measure designed to limit a potentially significant new problem for the business community. It passed the First Inventors Defense Act of 1999 (codified at 35 U.S.C. § 273), which provides a limited defense to claims of patent infringement, for "method[s] of doing or conducting business." Following several more years of confusion, the Federal Circuit changed course, overruling recent decisions and holding that a series of steps may constitute a patentable process only if it is tied to a machine or transforms an article into a different state or thing. This "machine-or-transformation test" excluded general methods of doing business as well as, potentially, a variety of other subjects that could be called processes.

The Court correctly holds that the machine-or-transformation test is not the sole test for what constitutes a patentable process; rather, it is a critical clue. But the Court is quite wrong, in my view, to suggest that any series of steps that is not itself an abstract idea or law of nature may constitute a "process" within the meaning of § 101. The language in the Court's opinion to this effect can only cause mischief. The wiser course would have been to hold that petitioners' method is not a "process" because it describes only a general method of engaging in business transactions—and business methods are not patentable. More precisely, although a process is not patent-ineligible simply because it is useful for conducting business, a claim that merely describes a method of doing business does not qualify as a "process" under § 101.

. . . If business methods could be patented, then many business decisions, no matter how small, could be *potential* patent violations. Businesses would either live in constant fear of litigation or would need to undertake the costs of searching through patents that describe methods of doing business, attempting to decide whether their innovation is one that remains in the public domain. . . .

These many costs of business method patents not only may stifle innovation, but they are also likely to "stifle competition[.]" Even if a business method patent is ultimately held invalid, patent holders may be able to use it to threaten litigation and to bully competitors, especially those that cannot bear the costs of a drawn out, fact-intensive patent litigation. That can take a particular toll on small and upstart businesses. Of course, patents always serve as a barrier to competition for the type of subject matter that is patented. But patents on business methods are patents on business itself. Therefore, unlike virtually every other category of patents, they are by their very nature likely to depress the dynamism of the marketplace. . . .

Accordingly, while I concur in the judgment, I strongly disagree with the Court's disposition of this case.

Justice BREYER, with whom Justice SCALIA joins as to Part II, concurring in the judgment.

I

I agree with Justice STEVENS that a "general method of engaging in business transactions" is not a patentable "process" within the meaning of 35 U.S.C. § 101. This Court has never before held that so-called "business methods" are patentable, and, in my view, the text, history, and purposes of the Patent Act make clear that they are not. I would therefore decide this case on that ground, and I join Justice STEVENS' opinion in full.

I write separately, however, to highlight the substantial *agreement* among many Members of the Court on many of the fundamental issues of patent law raised by this case. In light of the need for clarity and settled law in this highly technical area, I think it appropriate to do so.

In addition to the Court's unanimous agreement that the claims at issue here are unpatentable abstract ideas, it is my view that the following four points are consistent with both the opinion of the Court and Justice STEVENS' opinion concurring in the judgment:

First, although the text of § 101 is broad, it is not without limit. . . . "[T]he underlying policy of the patent system [is] that 'the things which are worth to the public the embarrassment of an exclusive patent,' . . . must outweigh the restrictive effect of the limited patent monopoly." . . . (quoting Letter from Thomas Jefferson to Isaac McPherson (Aug. 13, 1813), in 6 Writings of Thomas Jefferson 181 (H. Washington ed.)). The Court has thus been careful in interpreting the Patent Act to "determine not only what is protected, but also what is free for all to use." In particular, the Court has long held that "[p]henomena of nature, though just discovered, mental processes, and abstract intellectual concepts are not patentable" . . . since allowing individuals to patent these fundamental principles would "wholly pre-empt" the public's access to the "basic tools of scientific and technological work." . . .

Second, in a series of cases that extend back over a century, the Court has stated that "[t]ransformation and reduction of an article to a different state or thing is *the clue* to the patentability of a process claim that does not include particular machines." . . . Application of this test, the so-called "machine-or-transformation test," has thus repeatedly helped the Court to determine what is "a patentable 'process.'"

Third, while the machine-or-transformation test has always been a "useful and important clue," it has never been the "sole test" for determining patentability. . . . Rather, the Court has emphasized that a process claim meets the requirements of § 101 when, "considered as a whole," it "is performing a function which the patent laws were designed to protect (*e.g.*, transforming or reducing an article to a different state or thing)." The machine-or-transformation test is thus an *important example* of how a court can determine patentability under § 101, but the Federal Circuit erred in this case by treating it as the *exclusive test.*

Fourth, although the machine-or-transformation test is not the only test for patentability, this by no means indicates that anything which produces a "'useful, concrete, and tangible result,'" State Street Bank & Trust Co. v. Signature Financial Group, Inc., 149 F.3d 1368, 1373 (C.A.Fed.1998), is patentable. "[T]his Court has never made such a statement and, if taken literally, the statement would cover instances where this Court has held the contrary." . . . Indeed, the introduction of the "useful, concrete, and tangible result" approach to patentability, associated with the Federal Circuit's *State Street* decision, preceded the granting of patents that "ranged from the somewhat ridiculous to the truly absurd." In re Bilski, 545 F.3d 943, 1004 (C.A.Fed.2008) (Mayer, J., dissenting) (citing patents on, *inter alia*, a "method of training janitors to dust and vacuum using video displays," a "system for toilet reservations," and a "method of using color-coded bracelets to designate dating status in order to limit 'the embarrassment of rejection'") . . . . To the extent that the Federal Circuit's decision in this case rejected that approach, nothing in today's decision should be taken as disapproving of that determination. . . .

Notes and Questions

1. By recognizing that living organisms and business methods could be eligible for patents, *Diamond v. Chakrabarty* and *Bilski v. Kappos* significantly expanded the types of patents granted and gave rise to substantial debate about what should be eligible to receive patent protection. Neither decision gave much guidance as to the scope of the judicially created exceptions to patent eligibility for laws of nature, naturally occurring phenomena, or abstract ideas.

2. *Natural phenomena.* For over 30 years after the decision in *Chakrabarty*, patents were issued for the isolation or purification of genes, genetic sequences, and other naturally occurring products. The biotech sector grew enormously and, with it, controversies over attempts to monopolize and profit from diagnostic testing and biological research. The Supreme Court reentered the field in 2012 and has somewhat clarified what is patent eligible in its decisions in *Mayo Collaborative Services, Inc. v. Prometheus Laboratories, Inc.*, 132 S. Ct. 1289 (2012), and *Association for Molecular Pathology v. Myriad Genetics, Inc.*, 133 S. Ct. 2107 (2013).

3. *Business methods and abstract ideas.* The Supreme Court also addressed some of the questions left open in *Bilski* about the exception for abstract ideas and the patentability of methods for applying ideas in *Mayo Collaborative Services, Inc. v. Prometheus Laboratories, Inc.*, 132 S. Ct. 1289 (2012), and *Alice Corp. Pty. Ltd. v. CLS Bank International*, 134 S. Ct. 2347 (2014).

ASSOCIATION FOR MOLECULAR PATHOLOGY v. MYRIAD GENETICS, INC.

Supreme Court of the United States
133 S. Ct. 2107 (2013)

Justice THOMAS delivered the opinion of the Court.

Respondent Myriad Genetics, Inc. (Myriad), discovered the precise location and sequence of two human genes [BRCA1 and BRCA2], mutations of which can substantially increase the risks of breast and ovarian cancer. Myriad obtained a number of patents based upon its discovery. This case . . . requires us to resolve whether a naturally occurring segment of deoxyribonucleic acid (DNA) is patent eligible . . . by virtue of its isolation from the rest of the human genome. We also address the patent eligibility of synthetically created DNA known as complementary DNA (cDNA), which contains the same protein-coding information found in a segment of natural DNA but omits portions within the DNA segment that do not code for proteins. . . .

I

A

. . . Scientists can . . . extract DNA from cells using well known laboratory methods. These methods allow scientists to isolate specific segments of DNA—for

instance, a particular gene or part of a gene—which can then be further studied, manipulated, or used. It is also possible to create DNA synthetically through
processes similarly well known in the field of genetics. . . . This synthetic DNA
created in the laboratory . . . is known as complementary DNA (cDNA). . . .

B

. . . Before Myriad's discovery of the BRCA1 and BRCA2 genes, scientists knew
that heredity played a role in establishing a woman's risk of developing breast
and ovarian cancer, but they did not know which genes were associated with
those cancers.

. . . Knowledge of the location of the BRCA1 and BRCA2 genes allowed
Myriad to determine their typical nucleotide sequence. That information, in
turn, enabled Myriad to develop medical tests that are useful for detecting mutations in a patient's BRCA1 and BRCA2 genes and thereby assessing whether the
patient has an increased risk of cancer. . . .

C

Myriad's patents would, if valid, give it the exclusive right to isolate an individual's BRCA1 and BRCA2 genes (or any strand of 15 or more nucleotides within
the genes) by breaking the covalent bonds that connect the DNA to the rest of
the individual's genome. The patents would also give Myriad the exclusive right
to synthetically create BRCA cDNA. In Myriad's view, manipulating BRCA DNA
in either of these fashions triggers its "right to exclude others from making" its
patented composition of matter under the Patent Act. . . .

But isolation is necessary to conduct genetic testing, and Myriad was not the
only entity to offer BRCA testing after it discovered the genes. . . . Myriad . . .
filed patent infringement suits against other entities that performed BRCA testing, resulting in settlements in which the defendants agreed to cease all allegedly infringing activity. . . . Myriad, thus, solidified its position as the only entity
providing BRCA testing.

Some years later, petitioner Ostrer, along with medical patients, advocacy
groups, and other doctors, filed this lawsuit seeking a declaration that Myriad's
patents are invalid . . . . The District Court then granted summary judgment to
petitioners on the composition claims at issue in this case based on its conclusion that Myriad's claims, including claims related to cDNA, were invalid because
they covered products of nature. . . . The Federal Circuit reversed . . . and this
Court granted the petition for certiorari, vacated the judgment, and remanded
the case in light of Mayo Collaborative Services v. Prometheus Laboratories,
Inc., 566 U.S. ___ (2012). . . .

On remand, the Federal Circuit affirmed the District Court in part and
reversed in part, with each member of the panel writing separately. . . . [T]he
court held that both isolated DNA and cDNA were patent eligible under § 101.
The central dispute among the panel members was whether the act of *isolating*
DNA—separating a specific gene or sequence of nucleotides from the rest of
the chromosome—is an inventive act that entitles the individual who first iso-
lates it to a patent. . . .

Although the judges expressed different views concerning the patentability of isolated DNA, all three agreed that patent claims relating to cDNA met the patent eligibility requirements of § 101. . . .

II . . .

B

It is undisputed that Myriad did not create or alter any of the genetic information encoded in the BRCA1 and BRCA2 genes. The location and order of the nucleotides existed in nature before Myriad found them. Nor did Myriad create or alter the genetic structure of DNA. Instead, Myriad's principal contribution was uncovering the precise location and genetic sequence of the BRCA1 and BRCA2 genes . . . . The question is whether this renders the genes patentable.

Myriad recognizes that our decision in *Chakrabarty* is central to this inquiry. . . . The *Chakrabarty* bacterium was new "with markedly different characteristics from any found in nature," . . . due to the additional plasmids and resultant "capacity for degrading oil." . . . In this case, by contrast, Myriad did not create anything. To be sure, it found an important and useful gene, but separating that gene from its surrounding genetic material is not an act of invention.

Groundbreaking, innovative, or even brilliant discovery does not by itself satisfy the § 101 inquiry. . . . Myriad's patent descriptions highlight the problem with its claims. . . . [They] simply detail the "iterative process" of discovery by which Myriad narrowed the possible locations for the gene sequences that it sought. . . . Myriad seeks to import these extensive research efforts into the § 101 patent-eligibility inquiry. . . . But extensive effort alone is insufficient . . . .

Nor are Myriad's claims saved by the fact that isolating DNA from the human genome severs chemical bonds and thereby creates a nonnaturally occurring molecule. Myriad's claims are simply not expressed in terms of chemical composition, nor do they rely in any way on the chemical changes that result from the isolation of a particular section of DNA. Instead, the claims understandably focus on the genetic information encoded in the BRCA1 and BRCA2 genes. If the patents depended upon the creation of a unique molecule, then a would-be infringer could arguably avoid at least Myriad's patent claims on entire genes . . . by isolating a DNA sequence that included both the BRCA1 or BRCA2 gene and one additional nucleotide pair. Such a molecule would not be chemically identical to the molecule "invented" by Myriad. But Myriad obviously would resist that outcome because its claim is concerned primarily with the information contained in the genetic *sequence*, not with the specific chemical composition of a particular molecule.

Finally, Myriad argues that the PTO's past practice of awarding gene patents is entitled to deference . . . . We disagree. . . .[7]

---

7. Myriad also argues that we should uphold its patents so as not to disturb the reliance interests of patent holders like itself. . . . Concerns about reliance interests arising from PTO determinations, insofar as they are relevant, are better directed to Congress. . . .

C

cDNA does not present the same obstacles to patentability as naturally occurring, isolated DNA segments. . . . Petitioners concede that cDNA differs from natural DNA in that "the non-coding regions have been removed." . . . They nevertheless argue that cDNA is not patent eligible because "[t]he nucleotide sequence of cDNA is dictated by nature, not by the lab technician." . . . That may be so, but the lab technician unquestionably creates something new when cDNA is made. cDNA retains the naturally occurring exons of DNA, but it is distinct from the DNA from which it was derived. As a result, cDNA is not a "product of nature" and is patent eligible under § 101, except insofar as very short series of DNA may have no intervening introns to remove when creating cDNA. In that situation, a short strand of cDNA may be indistinguishable from natural DNA.[9]

III

It is important to note what is *not* implicated by this decision. First, there are no method claims before this Court. Had Myriad created an innovative method of manipulating genes while searching for the BRCA1 and BRCA2 genes, it could possibly have sought a method patent. But the processes used by Myriad to isolate DNA were well understood by geneticists at the time of Myriad's patents . . . and are not at issue in this case.

Similarly, this case does not involve patents on new *applications* of knowledge about the BRCA1 and BRCA2 genes. Judge Bryson [of the Federal Circuit] aptly noted that, "[a]s the first party with knowledge of the [BRCA1 and BRCA2] sequences, Myriad was in an excellent position to claim applications of that knowledge. Many of its unchallenged claims are limited to such applications." . . .

Nor do we consider the patentability of DNA in which the order of the naturally occurring nucleotides has been altered. Scientific alteration of the genetic code presents a different inquiry, and we express no opinion about the application of § 101 to such endeavors. We merely hold that genes and the information they encode are not patent eligible under § 101 simply because they have been isolated from the surrounding genetic material.

. . . [T]he judgment of the Federal Circuit is affirmed in part and reversed in part.

ROBERTS, C.J., and KENNEDY, GINSBURG, BREYER, ALITO, SOTOMAYOR, and KAGAN, JJ., joined the opinion of the Court. Justice SCALIA concurred in part and concurred in the judgment.

Notes and Questions

1. *Will the cost of genetic testing come down?* Shortly after the decision in this case, Myriad filed suit against Ambrey Genetics, which had announced that it

---

9.   We express no opinion whether cDNA satisfies the other statutory requirements of patentability. . . .

would provide lower-cost testing for mutations of the BRCA1/BRCA2 genes. The suit alleges infringement of 10 patents involving cDNA claims. *See* Dennis Crouch, *Myriad Seeks to Enforce Its BRCA1/BRCA2 Gene Patents,* PatentlyO Blog, July 9, 2013, http://patentlyo.com/patent/2013/07/myriad-seeks-to-enforce-its-brca1rca2-gene-patents.html. Crouch opined that Myriad has a strong case, but that there might be a question whether the public interest in access to diagnostic tools for breast cancer might lead the judge to deny an injunction.

2. *Another avenue for avoiding cDNA patents?* In *Patents Without Teeth: Whole Genome Sequencing and Gene Patent Infringement After AMP v. Myriad,* 54 Jurimetrics J. 65 (2013), Blake Atkinson argues that whole genome sequencing, a new technology "poised to become commonplace . . . in the next few years," will avoid the need to use patented cDNA to test for BRCA and other genes.

ALICE CORPORATION PTY. LTD. v. CLS BANK INTERNATIONAL

Supreme Court of the United States
134 S. Ct. 2347 (2014)

Justice THOMAS delivered the opinion of the Court.

The patents at issue in this case disclose a computer-implemented scheme for mitigating "settlement risk" (*i.e.,* the risk that only one party to a financial transaction will pay what it owes) by using a third-party intermediary. The question presented is whether these claims are patent eligible under 35 U.S.C. § 101, or are instead drawn to a patent-ineligible abstract idea. We hold that the claims at issue are drawn to the abstract idea of intermediated settlement, and that merely requiring generic computer implementation fails to transform that abstract idea into a patent-eligible invention. . . .

I

A

Petitioner Alice Corporation is the assignee of several patents that disclose schemes to manage certain forms of financial risk. . . . In particular, the claims are designed to facilitate the exchange of financial obligations between two parties by using a computer system as a third-party intermediary. The intermediary creates "shadow" credit and debit records (*i.e.,* account ledgers) that mirror the balances in the parties' real-world accounts at "exchange institutions" (*e.g.,* banks). The intermediary updates the shadow records in real time as transactions are entered, allowing "only those transactions for which the parties' updated shadow records indicate sufficient resources to satisfy their mutual obligations." At the end of the day, the intermediary instructs the relevant financial institutions to carry out the "permitted" transactions in accordance with the updated shadow records, thus mitigating the risk that only one party will perform the agreed-upon exchange.

In sum, the patents in suit claim (1) the foregoing method for exchanging obligations (the method claims), (2) a computer system configured to carry out the method for exchanging obligations (the system claims), and (3) a computer-readable medium containing program code for performing the method of exchanging obligations (the media claims). . . .

B

Respondents CLS Bank International and CLS Services Ltd. (together, CLS Bank) operate a global network that facilitates currency transactions. In 2007, CLS Bank filed suit against petitioner, seeking a declaratory judgment that the claims at issue are invalid, unenforceable, or not infringed. Petitioner counterclaimed, alleging infringement. Following this Court's decision in Bilski v. Kappos, 561 U.S. 593 (2010), the parties filed cross-motions for summary judgment on whether the asserted claims are eligible for patent protection . . . . The District Court held that all of the claims are patent ineligible because they are directed to the abstract idea of "employing a neutral intermediary to facilitate simultaneous exchange of obligations in order to minimize risk."

A divided panel of the United States Court of Appeals for the Federal Circuit reversed, holding that it was not "manifestly evident" that petitioner's claims are directed to an abstract idea. The Federal Circuit granted rehearing en banc, vacated the panel opinion, and affirmed the judgment of the District Court in a one-paragraph *per curiam* opinion. . . .

We granted certiorari and now affirm.

II

Section 101 of the Patent Act defines the subject matter eligible for patent protection. It provides:

> "Whoever invents or discovers any new and useful process, machine, manufacture, or composition of matter, or any new and useful improvement thereof, may obtain a patent therefor, subject to the conditions and requirements of this title."

"We have long held that this provision contains an important implicit exception: Laws of nature, natural phenomena, and abstract ideas are not patentable." *Association for Molecular Pathology v. Myriad Genetics, Inc.* . . .

We have described the concern that drives this exclusionary principle as one of pre-emption. See, *e.g.,* *Bilski* (upholding the patent "would pre-empt use of this approach in all fields, and would effectively grant a monopoly over an abstract idea"). Laws of nature, natural phenomena, and abstract ideas are "the basic tools of scientific and technological work." *Myriad, supra.* "[M]onopolization of those tools through the grant of a patent might tend to impede innovation more than it would tend to promote it," thereby thwarting the primary object of the patent laws. . . . We have "repeatedly emphasized this . . . concern that patent law not inhibit further discovery by improperly tying up the future use of" these building blocks of human ingenuity.

At the same time, we tread carefully in construing this exclusionary principle lest it swallow all of patent law. At some level, "all inventions . . . embody, use, reflect, rest upon, or apply laws of nature, natural phenomena, or abstract ideas." Thus, an invention is not rendered ineligible for patent simply because it involves an abstract concept. See Diamond v. Diehr, 450 U.S. 175 (1981). "[A]pplication[s]" of such concepts "'to a new and useful end,'" we have said, remain eligible for patent protection. *Gottschalk v. Benson*, 409 U.S. 63 (1972).

Accordingly, in applying the § 101 exception, we must distinguish between patents that claim the "'buildin[g] block[s]'" of human ingenuity and those that integrate the building blocks into something more, thereby "transform[ing]" them into a patent-eligible invention. The former "would risk disproportionately tying up the use of the underlying" ideas, and are therefore ineligible for patent protection. The latter pose no comparable risk of pre-emption, and therefore remain eligible for the monopoly granted under our patent laws.

III

In Mayo Collaborative Services v. Prometheus Laboratories, Inc., 566 U.S. ___ (2012), we set forth a framework for distinguishing patents that claim laws of nature, natural phenomena, and abstract ideas from those that claim patent-eligible applications of those concepts. First, we determine whether the claims at issue are directed to one of those patent-ineligible concepts. If so, we then ask, "[w]hat else is there in the claims before us?" To answer that question, we consider the elements of each claim both individually and "as an ordered combination" to determine whether the additional elements "transform the nature of the claim" into a patent-eligible application. We have described step two of this analysis as a search for an "'inventive concept'"—*i.e.,* an element or combination of elements that is "sufficient to ensure that the patent in practice amounts to significantly more than a patent upon the [ineligible concept] itself."

We must first determine whether the claims at issue are directed to a patent-ineligible concept. We conclude that they are: These claims are drawn to the abstract idea of intermediated settlement.

The "abstract ideas" category embodies "the longstanding rule that '[a]n idea of itself is not patentable.'" . . . In *Benson*, for example, this Court rejected as ineligible patent claims involving an algorithm for converting binary-coded decimal numerals into pure binary form, holding that the claimed patent was "in practical effect . . . a patent on the algorithm itself." And in Parker v. Flook, 437 U.S. 584 (1978), we held that a mathematical formula for computing "alarm limits" in a catalytic conversion process was also a patent-ineligible abstract idea.

We most recently addressed the category of abstract ideas in Bilski v. Kappos. The claims at issue in *Bilski* described a method for hedging against the financial risk of price fluctuations. . . . "[A]ll members of the Court agree[d]" that the patent at issue in *Bilski* claimed an "abstract idea." . . . The Court explained that "[h]edging is a fundamental economic practice long prevalent in our system of commerce and taught in any introductory finance class." "The concept of hedging" as recited by the claims in suit was therefore a patent-ineligible "abstract idea, just like the algorithms at issue in *Benson* and *Flook*."

It follows from our prior cases, and *Bilski* in particular, that the claims at issue here are directed to an abstract idea. . . . Like the risk hedging in *Bilski*, the concept of intermediated settlement is "a fundamental economic practice long prevalent in our system of commerce." [S]ee, *e.g.*, Emery, Speculation on the Stock and Produce Exchanges of the United States, in 7 *Studies in History, Economics and Public Law* 283, 346-356 (1896) (discussing the use of a "clearing-house" as an intermediary to reduce settlement risk). The use of a third-party intermediary . . . is also a building block of the modern economy. . . . Thus, intermediated settlement, like hedging, is an "abstract idea" beyond the scope of § 101.

Petitioner acknowledges that its claims describe intermediated settlement, but rejects the conclusion that its claims recite an "abstract idea." Drawing on the presence of mathematical formulas in some of our abstract-ideas precedents, petitioner contends that the abstract-ideas category is confined to "preexisting, fundamental truth[s]" that "'exis[t] in principle apart from any human action,'" . . . (quoting *Mayo*).

Bilski belies petitioner's assertion. The concept of risk hedging we identified as an abstract idea in that case cannot be described as a "preexisting, fundamental truth." . . . Although hedging is a longstanding commercial practice, it is a method of organizing human activity, not a "truth" about the natural world "that has always existed." One of the claims in *Bilski* reduced hedging to a mathematical formula, but the Court did not assign any special significance to that fact, much less the sort of talismanic significance petitioner claims. Instead, the Court grounded its conclusion that all of the claims at issue were abstract ideas in the understanding that risk hedging was a "fundamental economic practice." . . .

B

Because the claims at issue are directed to the abstract idea of intermediated settlement, we turn to the second step in *Mayo*'s framework. We conclude that the method claims, which merely require generic computer implementation, fail to transform that abstract idea into a patent-eligible invention.

1

. . . A claim that recites an abstract idea must include "additional features" to ensure "that the [claim] is more than a drafting effort designed to monopolize the [abstract idea]." *Mayo* made clear that transformation into a patent-eligible application requires "more than simply stat[ing] the [abstract idea] while adding the words 'apply it.'"

Mayo itself is instructive. The patents at issue in *Mayo* claimed a method for measuring metabolites in the bloodstream in order to calibrate the appropriate dosage of thiopurine drugs in the treatment of autoimmune diseases. The respondent in that case contended that the claimed method was a patent-eligible application of natural laws that describe the relationship between the concentration of certain metabolites and the likelihood that the drug dosage will be harmful or ineffective. But methods for determining metabolite levels were already "well known in the art," and the process at issue amounted to "nothing significantly more than an instruction to doctors to apply the applicable laws when treating their patients." "Simply appending conventional steps, specified at a high level of generality," was not "*enough*" to supply an "inventive concept."

The introduction of a computer into the claims does not alter the analysis at *Mayo* step two. In *Benson*, for example, we considered a patent that claimed an algorithm implemented on "a general-purpose digital computer." Because the algorithm was an abstract idea, the claim had to supply a " 'new and useful' " application of the idea in order to be patent eligible. But the computer implementation did not supply the necessary inventive concept; the process could be "carried out in existing computers long in use." We accordingly "held that simply implementing a mathematical principle on a physical machine, namely a computer, [i]s not a patentable application of that principle."

Flook is to the same effect. There, we examined a computerized method for using a mathematical formula to adjust alarm limits for certain operating conditions (*e.g.*, temperature and pressure) that could signal inefficiency or danger in a catalytic conversion process. Once again, the formula itself was an abstract idea, and the computer implementation was purely conventional. . . . In holding that the process was patent ineligible, we rejected the argument that "implement[ing] a principle in some specific fashion" will "automatically fal[l] within the patentable subject matter of § 101." Thus, "*Flook* stands for the proposition that the prohibition against patenting abstract ideas cannot be circumvented by attempting to limit the use of [the idea] to a particular technological environment."

In *Diehr*, by contrast, we held that a computer-implemented process for curing rubber was patent eligible, but not because it involved a computer. The claim employed a "well-known" mathematical equation, but it used that equation in a process designed to solve a technological problem in "conventional industry practice." The invention in *Diehr* used a "thermocouple" to record constant temperature measurements inside the rubber mold—something "the industry ha[d] not been able to obtain." The temperature measurements were then fed into a computer, which repeatedly recalculated the remaining cure time by using the mathematical equation. These additional steps, we recently explained, "transformed the process into an inventive application of the formula." *Mayo*. In other words, the claims in *Diehr* were patent eligible because they improved an existing technological process, not because they were implemented on a computer.

These cases demonstrate that the mere recitation of a generic computer cannot transform a patent-ineligible abstract idea into a patent-eligible invention. Stating an abstract idea "while adding the words 'apply it' " is not enough for patent eligibility. Nor is limiting the use of an abstract idea "to a particular technological environment." Stating an abstract idea while adding the words "apply it with a computer" simply combines those two steps, with the same deficient result. . . . This conclusion accords with the pre-emption concern that undergirds our § 101 jurisprudence. Given the ubiquity of computers, wholly generic computer implementation is not generally the sort of "additional featur[e]" that provides any "practical assurance that the process is more than a drafting effort designed to monopolize the [abstract idea] itself." *Mayo*.

. . . There is no dispute that a computer is a tangible system (in § 101 terms, a "machine"), or that many computer-implemented claims are formally addressed to patent-eligible subject matter. But if that were the end of the § 101 inquiry, an applicant could claim any principle of the physical or social sciences by reciting a computer system configured to implement the relevant concept. Such a result would make the determination of patent eligibility "depend simply on the draftsman's art," thereby eviscerating the rule that "'[l]aws of nature, natural phenomena, and abstract ideas are not patentable,'" *Myriad*.

2

The representative method claim in this case recites the following steps: (1) creating" shadow records for each counterparty to a transaction; (2) obtaining" start-of-day balances based on the parties' real-world accounts at exchange institutions; (3) adjusting" the shadow records as transactions are entered, allowing only those transactions for which the parties have sufficient resources; and (4) issuing irrevocable end-of-day instructions to the exchange institutions to carry out the permitted transactions. Petitioner principally contends that the claims are patent eligible because these steps "require a substantial and meaningful role for the computer." As stipulated, the claimed method requires the use of a computer to create electronic records, track multiple transactions, and issue simultaneous instructions; in other words, "[t]he computer is itself the intermediary."

. . . [T]he relevant question is whether the claims here do more than simply instruct the practitioner to implement the abstract idea of intermediated settlement on a generic computer. They do not.

. . . Using a computer to create and maintain "shadow" accounts amounts to electronic recordkeeping—one of the most basic functions of a computer. . . . The same is true with respect to the use of a computer to obtain data, adjust account balances, and issue automated instructions; all of these computer functions are "well-understood, routine, conventional activit[ies]" previously known to the industry. . . .

Considered "as an ordered combination," the computer components of petitioner's method "ad[d] nothing . . . that is not already present when the steps are considered separately." . . . The method claims do not, for example, purport to improve the functioning of the computer itself. . . . Nor do they effect an improvement in any other technology or technical field. Instead, the claims at issue amount to "nothing significantly more" than an instruction to apply the abstract idea of intermediated settlement using some unspecified, generic computer. Under our precedents, that is not "*enough*" to transform an abstract idea into a patent-eligible invention.

C

Petitioner's claims to a computer system and a computer-readable medium fail for substantially the same reasons. . . . As to its system claims, petitioner emphasizes that those claims recite "specific hardware" configured to perform "specific computerized functions." But what petitioner characterizes as specific hardware—a "data processing system" with a "communications controller" and "data storage unit," for example—is purely functional and generic. Nearly every computer will include a "communications controller" and "data storage unit" capable of performing the basic calculation, storage, and transmission functions required by the method claims. As a result, none of the hardware recited by the system claims "offers a meaningful limitation beyond generally linking 'the use of the [method] to a particular technological environment,' that is, implementation via computers." . . .

Because petitioner's system and media claims add nothing of substance to the underlying abstract idea, we hold that they too are patent ineligible under § 101.

For the foregoing reasons, the judgment of the Court of Appeals for the Federal Circuit is affirmed.

Justice SOTOMAYOR, with whom Justice GINSBURG and Justice BREYER join, concurring.

I adhere to the view that any "claim that merely describes a method of doing business does not qualify as a 'process' under § 101." Bilski v. Kappos, 561 U.S. 593, 614 (2010) (Stevens, J., concurring in judgment); see also In re Bilski, 545 F.3d 943, 972 (C.A.Fed.2008) (Dyk, J., concurring) ("There is no suggestion in any of th[e] early [English] consideration of process patents that processes for organizing human activity were or ever had been patentable"). As in *Bilski*, however, I further believe that the method claims at issue are drawn to an abstract idea. I therefore join the opinion of the Court.

Notes and Questions

1. What guidance does the *Alice* opinion provide on what constitutes an abstract idea and how much must be added to make the idea patentable? Donald Chisum, author of *Chisum on Patents*, a multi-volume treatise on patent law, in a guest commentary on the PatentlyO blog concludes that "the *Alice* opinion supports the following proposition: a novel and unobvious solution to a technical problem is *not* an 'abstract idea,' and a claim drawn to such a solution, even if broad, is not subject to the *Mayo* framework . . . ." *The Supreme Court's Alice Decision on Patent Eligibility of Computer-Implemented Inventions: Finding an Oasis in the Desert,* June 23, 2014, http://patentlyo.com/patent/2014/06/eligibility-implemented-inventions.html.

2. *Guidance from the U.S. Patent Office on patent eligibility.* Before the Supreme Court issued its opinion in the *Alice* case, the Patent Office issued for comment new guidelines on patent eligibility requirements in light of the decisions in *Mayo* and *Myriad. See* http://www.uspto.gov/patents/announce/myriad-mayo.jsp. Additional guidelines were announced shortly after the *Alice* decision, *see* http://www.uspto.gov/patents/announce/alice_pec_25jun2014.pdf.

Patent Trolls and the Supreme Court

Entities that amass patent portfolios solely for the purpose of obtaining licensing fees and settlements from other companies, known as patent trolls, non-practicing entities (NPEs), or patent assertion entities (PAEs), account for an increasing amount of patent infringement litigation (over 2,500 cases, 62 percent of all infringement suits in 2012). They have often taken advantage of uncertainty about the scope and validity of software-related patents to threaten both established companies and startups and obtain licensing fees or settlements paid because the costs of litigation are so high, not because the patent was valid or there was actual infringement. For an assessment of the costs to innovation and the economy, see Executive Office of the President, *Patent Assertion and U.S. Innovation,* a 2013 Report Prepared by the President's Council of Economic Advisers, the National Economic Council, and the Office of Science and Technology Policy, available at http://www.whitehouse.gov/sites/default/files/docs/patent_report.pdf.

Three 2014 decisions of the Supreme Court will make it easier to resist the claims of patent trolls. *Alice Corp. Pty. Ltd. v. CLS Bank International* (2014) makes it clear that using computers to implement ideas, alone, is not enough to qualify for patent eligibility. The decision has been hailed as a major blow to patent trolls, see Klint Finley, *Supreme Court Deals Major Blow to Patent Trolls,* Wired, http://www.wired.com/2014/06/supreme-court-deals-major-blow-to-patent-trolls/. Companion decisions in *Octane Fitness, LLC v. Icon Health & Fitness, Inc.,* 134 S. Ct. 1749 (2014), and *Highmark, Inc. v. Allcare Health Management System, Inc.,* 134 S. Ct. 1744 (2014), will make it easier for defendants in abusive infringement suits to obtain attorneys' fee awards. *See* Daniel Nazer, *Watch Out Trolls: Supreme Court Expands Fee Shifting in Patent Cases,* Apr. 29, 2014, Electronic Frontier Foundation, https://www.eff.org/deeplinks/2014/04/watch-out-trolls-supreme-court-expands-fee-shifting-patent-cases.

2.   Plant Patents

Patents may be issued for newly developed plants under the Plant Protection Act of 1930, 35 U.S.C. §§ 161-164, but that Act is limited to plants that reproduce asexually. Other plants may be protected under the Plant Variety Protection Act, 7 U.S.C. § 2321, but that Act provides exemptions for research and for farmers to save their seed for replanting. In 1985, five years after the decision in *Chakrabarty,* the Patent and Trademark Office began issuing utility patents for new plants shown to be useful and non-obvious. Patent holders on hybrid corn began selling seed subject to licenses that prohibited farmers from saving seeds from their crops for replanting. In an infringement action brought against a seed reseller, the validity of the utility patents was challenged. In *J.E.M. Ag Supply, Inc. v. Pioneer Hi-Bred International, Inc.,* 534 U.S. 124 (2002), the Supreme Court upheld the validity of the patents, rejecting the claim that the more specific plant protection statutes provided the exclusive method of plant protection. In the case that follows, the court took up the question whether farmers could be prevented from saving and replanting seed from crops grown from patented seeds.

BOWMAN v. MONSANTO COMPANY

Supreme Court of the United States
133 S. Ct. 1761 (2013)

Justice KAGAN delivered the opinion for a unanimous Court.

Under the doctrine of patent exhaustion, the authorized sale of a patented article gives the purchaser, or any subsequent owner, a right to use or resell that article. Such a sale, however, does not allow the purchaser to make new copies of the patented invention. The question in this case is whether a farmer who buys patented seeds may reproduce them through planting and harvesting without the patent holder's permission. We hold that he may not.

I

Respondent Monsanto invented a genetic modification that enables soybean plants to survive exposure to glyphosate, the active ingredient in many herbicides (including Monsanto's own Roundup). Monsanto markets soybean seed containing this altered genetic material as Roundup Ready seed. . . . Two patents issued to Monsanto cover various aspects of its Roundup Ready technology, including a seed incorporating the genetic alteration. . . .

Monsanto sells, and allows other companies to sell, Roundup Ready soybean seeds to growers who assent to a special licensing agreement. . . . That agreement permits a grower to plant the purchased seeds in one (and only one) season. He can then consume the resulting crop or sell it as a commodity, usually to a grain elevator or agricultural processor. . . . But under the agreement, the farmer may not save any of the harvested soybeans for replanting, nor may he supply them to anyone else for that purpose. . . . [A] single Roundup Ready seed can grow a plant containing dozens of genetically identical beans, each of which, if replanted, can grow another such plant—and so on and so on. The agreement's terms prevent the farmer from co-opting that process to produce his own Roundup Ready seeds, forcing him instead to buy from Monsanto each season.

Petitioner Vernon Bowman is a farmer in Indiana . . . . He purchased Roundup Ready each year, from a company affiliated with Monsanto, for his first crop of the season. In accord with the agreement just described, he used all of that seed for planting, and sold his entire crop to a grain elevator . . . .

Bowman, however, devised a less orthodox approach for his second crop of each season. Because he thought such late-season planting "risky," he did not want to pay the premium price that Monsanto charges for Roundup Ready seed. . . . He therefore went to a grain elevator; purchased "commodity soybeans" intended for human or animal consumption; and planted them in his fields.[1] Those soybeans came from prior harvests of other local farmers. And because most of those farmers also used Roundup Ready seed, Bowman could anticipate that many of the purchased soybeans would contain Monsanto's patented technology. When he applied a glyphosate-based herbicide to his fields, . . . a significant proportion of the new plants survived the treatment, and produced in their turn a new crop of soybeans with the Roundup Ready trait. Bowman saved seed from that crop to use in his late-season planting the next year—and then the next, and the next, until he had harvested eight crops in that way. . . .

---

1.   Grain elevators . . . purchase grain from farmers and sell it for consumption; under federal and state law, they generally cannot package or market their grain for use as agricultural seed. . . . But because soybeans are themselves seeds, nothing (except, as we shall see, the law) prevented Bowman from planting, rather than consuming, the product he bought from the grain elevator.

·After discovering this practice, Monsanto sued . . . . Bowman raised patent exhaustion as a defense, arguing that Monsanto could not control his use of the soybeans because they were the subject of a prior authorized sale (from local farmers to the grain elevator). The District Court rejected that argument, and awarded damages to Monsanto of $84,456. The Federal Circuit affirmed. . . .

We granted certiorari to consider the important question of patent law raised in this case . . . and now affirm.

II

The doctrine of patent exhaustion limits a patentee's right to control what others can do with an article embodying or containing an invention. Under the doctrine, "the initial authorized sale of a patented item terminates all patent rights to that item." And by "exhaust[ing] the [patentee's] monopoly" in that item, the sale confers on the purchaser, or any subsequent owner, "the right to use [or] sell" the thing as he sees fit. We have explained the basis for the doctrine as follows: "[T]he purpose of the patent law is fulfilled with respect to any particular article when the patentee has received his reward . . . by the sale of the article"; once that "purpose is realized the patent law affords no basis for restraining the use and enjoyment of the thing sold." . . .

Consistent with that rationale, the doctrine restricts a patentee's rights only as to the "particular article" sold; it leaves untouched the patentee's ability to prevent a buyer from making new copies of the patented item. . . . [S]ee Wilbur-Ellis Co. v. Kuther, 377 U.S. 422 (1964) (holding that a purchaser's "reconstruction" of a patented machine "would impinge on the patentee's right *to exclude others from making*' . . . the article" . . .). Rather, "a second creation" of the patented item "call[s] the monopoly, conferred by the patent grant, into play for a second time." That is because the patent holder has "received his reward" only for the actual article sold, and not for subsequent recreations of it. . . . If the purchaser of that article could make and sell endless copies, the patent would effectively protect the invention for just a single sale. . . .

Unfortunately for Bowman, that principle decides this case against him. Under the patent exhaustion doctrine, Bowman could resell the patented soybeans he purchased from the grain elevator; so too he could consume the beans himself or feed them to his animals. . . . But the exhaustion doctrine does not enable Bowman to make *additional* patented soybeans without Monsanto's permission (either express or implied). . . .[3]

Were the matter otherwise, Monsanto's patent would provide scant benefit. . . .

---

3.   This conclusion applies however Bowman acquired Roundup Ready seed: The doctrine of patent exhaustion no more protected Bowman's reproduction of the seed he purchased for his first crop (from a Monsanto-affiliated seed company) than the beans he bought for his second (from a grain elevator). The difference between the two purchases was that the first—but not the second—came with a license from Monsanto to plant the seed and then harvest and market one crop of beans. We do not here confront a case in which Monsanto (or an affiliated seed company) sold Roundup Ready to a farmer without an express license agreement. . . . [W]e think that case unlikely to arise. . . . And in the event it did, the farmer might reasonably claim that the sale came with an implied license to plant and harvest one soybean crop.

Bowman principally argues that exhaustion should apply here because seeds are meant to be planted. . . . Bowman . . . is merely using them in the normal way farmers do. Bowman thus concludes that allowing Monsanto to interfere with that use would "creat[e] an impermissible exception to the exhaustion doctrine" for patented seeds and other "self-replicating technologies." . . .

But it is really Bowman who is asking for an unprecedented exception — to . . . the "well settled" rule that "the exhaustion doctrine does not extend to the right to 'make' a new product." . . .

Still, Bowman has another seeds-are-special argument: that soybeans naturally "self-replicate or 'sprout' unless stored in a controlled manner," and thus "it was the planted soybean, not Bowman" himself, that made replicas of Monsanto's patented invention. . . . But we think that blame-the-bean defense tough to credit. Bowman was not a passive observer of his soybeans' multiplication; . . . the seeds he purchased (miraculous though they might be in other respects) did not spontaneously create eight successive soybean crops. . . . [I]t was Bowman, and not the bean, who controlled the reproduction (unto the eighth generation) of Monsanto's patented invention.

Our holding today is limited — addressing the situation before us, rather than every one involving a self-replicating product. We recognize that such inventions are becoming ever more prevalent, complex, and diverse. In another case, the article's self-replication might occur outside the purchaser's control. Or it might be a necessary but incidental step in using the item for another purpose. Cf. 17 U.S.C. § 117(a)(1) ("[I]t is not [a copyright] infringement for the owner of a copy of a computer program to make . . . another copy or adaptation of that computer program provide[d] that such a new copy or adaptation is created as an essential step in the utilization of the computer program"). We need not address here whether or how the doctrine of patent exhaustion would apply in such circumstances. In the case at hand, Bowman planted Monsanto's patented soybeans solely to make and market replicas of them, thus depriving the company of the reward patent law provides for the sale of each article. Patent exhaustion provides no haven for that conduct. We accordingly affirm the judgment of the Court of Appeals for the Federal Circuit.

PART II

OWNERSHIP INTERESTS
IN PROPERTY

Our legal system divides interests in property into those considered "ownership" interests and others. The others, like mortgages, easements, covenants, and licenses, are described as "encumbrances" or "appurtenances" rather than as "ownership" interests. Generally speaking, ownership interests carry the right to possession; the others are regarded as non-possessory. Although this statement is not completely accurate, it is good enough to provide a rough demarcation between the interests covered in this part and those we study in Part III (contracts to buy and sell land and mortgages) and Part IV (easements, licenses, and covenants).

In this part, we study both the kinds of ownership interests permitted in our system and the ways those interests can be shared by more than one owner. Ownership can be shared successively, with one owner having the right to possession now and another the right to possession in the future, or ownership can be shared concurrently with all owners simultaneously enjoying the right to possession. Chapters 5 and 6 explore the world of successive ownership; Chapter 7 explores the world of concurrent ownership.

CHAPTER 5

Possessory Estates and Future Interests

Traditionally, English land law in the feudal period and the law of estates and future interests that grew out of the complicated land settlements developed by the English landed aristocracy during the period leading up the World War I formed a core part of the first year Property course. Fortunately for students in the 21st century, much of that law is better left to courses in legal history and the law of trusts, where complicated dynastic wealth transfers are now to be found. Our focus in this chapter is on ownership interests that are not in trust and the way they are used in current American law.

The system of ownership used in American law, which was built on a base of English law, allows property ownership to be divided among holders of present estates and future interests and allows titles to be split into simultaneously held legal and equitable titles. Present estates carry the right to possession of the property; future interests carry the right to possession in the future. Titles are split when trusts are created: The trustee holds legal title for the beneficiaries, who hold equitable title.

Rights to possession may be absolute or subject to conditions. The ultimate ownership is contained in the *fee simple estate*, which grants the right to possession into the future, forever. Even though the owner of a fee simple may be a human who will not live forever, the owner can transfer the fee simple to someone else, who in turn, can transfer it to another, and so on endlessly. If the owner dies, the fee simple passes under her will, or if she dies intestate (without a will), the property passes to her heirs.

The owner of a fee simple estate may, and usually does, have the right to present possession, but if lesser estates have also been created in the property, the fee simple is a future interest, a right to possession in the future. Lesser estates, so called because the duration of the rights to possession they grant falls short of "forever," are the following:

- *Fee tail estate.* This estate, no longer in use in the United States, was inheritable only by the lineal descendants of the person to whom it was granted. If the line of lineal descendants died out, the estate expired and the right to possession passed to the owner of the next estate, who was often the owner of the fee simple.
- *Life estate.* This estate grants the right to possession to someone for the duration of a person's life, usually the person to whom it is granted. When that person dies, the estate expires.

- *Term of years.* This estate, more commonly known as a lease, expires at a specified date. Although conceptualized as less than a life estate, leases can in fact be granted for long terms. Because a largely separate body of law has grown up around the landlord-tenant relationship involved in leases, they are treated in Chapter 6.

The fee simple differs from the fee tail in that it can be inherited by any of the holder's heirs; the *fee tail* can be inherited only by heirs "of the body" (the lineal descendants). The fee simple is thus said to be an estate of "general inheritability" while the fee tail is an estate of "limited inheritability."

Every piece of land in our system has a fee simple owner, whether an individual, a corporation, a governmental body, or the public.[1] Lesser estates do not exist, however, unless specifically created by the owner of the fee simple. When the fee simple owner creates and transfers a lesser estate to someone else, she basically gives up the right to possession for a period of time. Why would an owner want to do that?

- *Term of years*: The owner leases the property to another to get an income stream (rent) from someone who places a higher value on the right to possess and use the property than the owner does. The right to possession reverts to the owner of the fee simple on termination of the lease. Leases are widely used.
- *Life estate*: The owner might give a life estate to an elderly parent to provide a place to live, or might give the fee simple to the owner's children but retain a life estate in the property for the rest of his life, or by his will might give a life estate to his wife for life, and the fee simple (to become possessory after her death) to his children. Life estates are used in estate planning, rather than in commercial transactions. Most life estates today are found in trusts.
- *Fee tail*: This estate was used by the English landed aristocracy to keep property in the family. As fans of Jane Austen and "Downton Abbey" know, succession to entailed family estates could be quite complicated. The fee tail was not much used in America and has been modified by statutes that convert it into some form of life estate followed by a fee simple. Trusts now provide the primary vehicle for maintaining particular land or—more often—wealth accumulations in families.

Whenever a lesser estate is created, there is a future interest—the right to possession when the lesser estate terminates. If possession returns to the person who created the lesser estate, as in the typical lease, the future interest is called a **reversion**. If possession passes on to a third person, as after the typical life estate, the future interest is called a **remainder**. In some other cases, as we will see, the future interest may be called an **executory interest**. The same present estates and future interests can be created in the equitable title as in the legal title (fee simple, life estate, term of years, reversions, remainders, executory interests).

In this chapter we study the way that landowners use legal estates and future interests to control use of land and to provide for their families and loved ones—and, sometimes, to control them, too. We will also take a peek at trust

---

1. Personal property may have no owner because ownership of personal property, unlike land, may be abandoned.

law and the dreaded Rule Against Perpetuities, which featured prominently in the plots of two films, *The Descendants* (2011) and *Body Heat* (1981). Trusts and the Rule are covered in depth in upper class courses on wills and trusts and estate planning.

But first, some background information.

Language Used to Create Estates: Words of Limitation and Words of Purchase

The common law developed verbal formulas to indicate whether a grantee was to receive an inheritable estate, and if so, whether it was inheritable only by lineal descendants, or whether it was inheritable generally. If no inheritance rights were intended, no formula was necessary. A conveyance "to Gerry" gave Gerry a life estate. If limited inheritance rights were intended, the grantor created a fee tail by conveying "to Gerry and the heirs of his body" or "to Gerry and the heirs male of his body." To convey an estate of general inheritance, the grantor conveyed "to Gerry and his heirs." Over time these formulas became rigid requirements, and for many centuries, the only way to convey a fee simple to a person was to use the formula "and his heirs" after the person's name.[2] To convey a fee simple to a non-human entity, the phrase "its successors and assigns" was used instead of "and his heirs."

In the 20th century, the old rigidity disappeared as courts became willing to give effect to the intent manifested in the deed. Today, a conveyance is usually presumed to include the entire estate owned by the grantor, whatever that may be. A grantor who intends to convey only a life estate should be careful to spell out that the conveyance is "to Gerry for life."

The word *limitation* is sometimes used in place of the word *estate*, a usage that probably grew out of the idea that estates are differentiated by limitations on their duration. The words that identify the particular estate granted are called *words of limitation*. By contrast, the words that identify the grantee are called *words of purchase*. The word *heirs* is usually a word of limitation, rather than of purchase, but not always. In the standard formula, "to Gerry and his heirs," Gerry receives the full fee simple and Gerry's heirs receive nothing. Gerry does not need the consent of the heirs apparent to sell the property or to leave it someone else by will.[3] They inherit only if he has not otherwise disposed of the property before his death.

If a transfer is made to heirs of a deceased person, however, the word *heirs* serves both to identify the takers and to indicate that they take the property in fee simple. Here, the term serves as both a word of purchase and a word of limitation. In the unlikely event that a gift was made to the heirs of a deceased person "for life," the word *heirs* would serve solely as a word of purchase. The most likely situation in which you will encounter a conveyance to heirs is in a gift such as "to Gerry for life, and at his death, to his heirs." In this case, Gerry

---

2. This rule was not applied to wills. The court would give effect to the testator's intent as expressed in the will whether or not the proper formula was used.

3. No one has heirs until they die. Heirs, by definition, are those people, identified by statute, who take the property owned at death of a person who dies without a will.

would have the right to possession for his lifetime, and at his death, the right to possession would pass to his heirs, who would own the fee simple.[4]

Problems

Identify the words of purchase and the words of limitation in the following conveyances:

1. O conveys "to A for 10 years, remainder to B for life, remainder to the First Baptist Church, its successors and assigns."

2. O conveys "to A for life, remainder to the heirs of B."

3. O conveys "to A and his heirs, but if A shall die without issue living at the time of his death, to B and his heirs."

Who Are the Heirs? Inheritance of Property

The heirs are the people who take the "probate estate"[5] of a person who dies "intestate" (without a valid will). State law varies in the details, but in nearly every state the heirs include the surviving spouse of the decedent, the decedent's issue (lineal descendants to all degrees), and if there are no issue, the decedent's ascendants (parents, grandparents, etc.) and other blood relatives, who are known as "collaterals."[6] If the decedent is survived by both spouse and issue, the spouse usually receives between one-third and one-half, and the issue take the rest. If there are issue, but no spouse, the issue take it all. Only if the decedent has no living lineal descendants do the ascendants or collaterals take any of the property.

At one time, the "heirs" of a decedent, who inherited the land, were different from the "next of kin," who inherited the personal property. Once primogeniture was abolished, however, the differences generally disappeared, and today, the same people inherit both real and personal property from the decedent. Another old doctrine that disappeared with primogeniture is the "ancestral property" doctrine,[7] under which property inherited from one side of the family returned to the collateral heirs on that side of the family rather than being shared by all the collateral heirs. Thus, if O had inherited Blackacre from his mother, on O's death intestate and without surviving spouse or issue, the property would go to O's cousins on his mother's side to the exclusion of the cousins

---

4. In a jurisdiction where the Rule in Shelley's Case was in force at the time of the conveyance, "his heirs" would be treated as words of limitation, without regard to the grantor's intention. That Rule, which has been abolished nearly everywhere, is discussed in Section D of this chapter.

5. The probate estate is the property that the decedent owns at the time of death. It does not include property that was held in joint tenancy with right of survivorship, or property held in a "living" trust, life insurance policies payable to a named beneficiary, or property held in bank accounts or brokerage accounts with a "POD" (Pay on Death) designation. These are called "non-probate" assets because they pass according to the various beneficiary designations rather than under the decedent's will or the intestate succession statute.

6. If you look at a typical table of consanguinity, you will see why they are called collaterals.

7. This doctrine was known as the "blood of the first purchaser" doctrine at common law. Under it, property passing to collaterals went only to those who were "of the blood of the first purchaser."

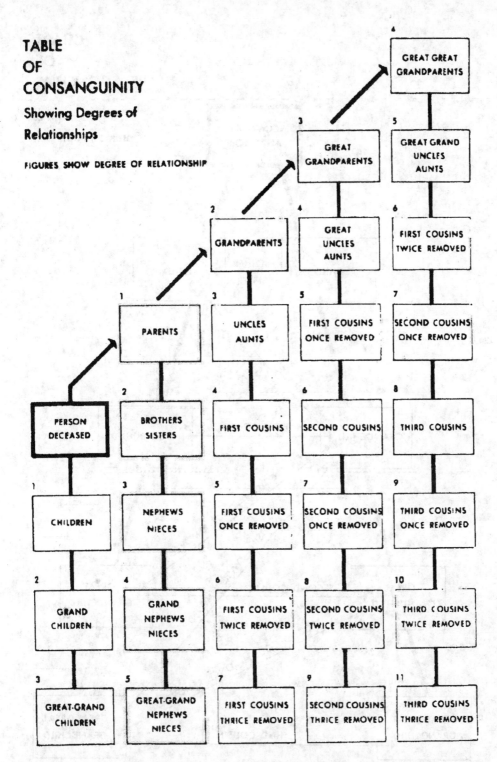

TABLE
OF
CONSANGUINITY

Showing Degrees of
Relationships

FIGURES SHOW DEGREE OF RELATIONSHIP

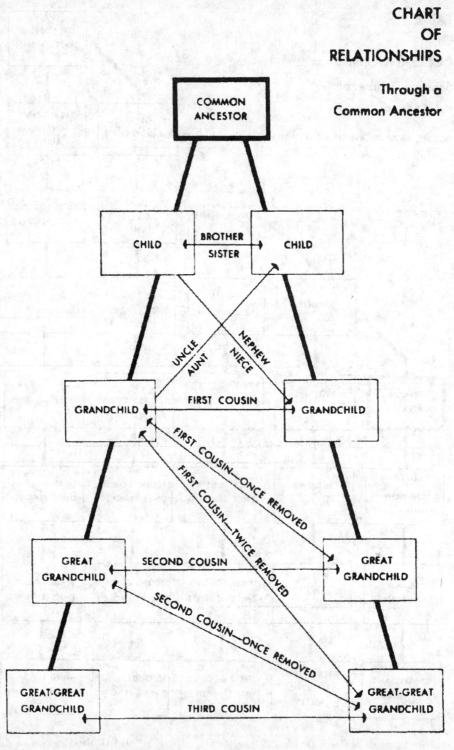

CHART OF RELATIONSHIPS

Through a Common Ancestor

on his father's side of the family. Odd remnants of the old doctrine persist in some states.[8]

What If There Are No Heirs? Escheat

If a person dies owning property, does not leave a valid will, and has no heirs, does the fee simple come to an end? The answer is no. The fee simple "escheats" to the state in which the property is located. The state then owns the property in fee simple.

[margin handwritten note: escheats — fee simple becomes the State's property.]

A. THE DEFEASIBLE FEE SIMPLE: CONTROLLING LAND USE AND BEHAVIOR BY THREAT OF FORFEITURE

Since the early days of the common law, landowners have attached conditions to the grants of fee simple estates as a way of coercing desired behavior or dealing with changed situations. If the condition happens, the grantee's estate is forfeited and the grantor gets the land back, or it goes to someone else. Because a fee simple granted on condition was subject to being defeated by occurrence of the condition, it came to be known as a "defeasible" fee. Although defeasible fees may be terminated, they are not regarded as lesser estates, like the life estate or term of years, because, if the condition does not happen, they will go on forever. For historical reasons, the future interests held by those who will have the right to possession if the condition happens are not called reversions or remainders. Defeasible fees today are primarily used in gifts of land for charitable or municipal purposes, and occasionally to control ownership within a family.

A fee simple estate that is not subject to a condition is labeled a fee simple "absolute." There are three categories of defeasible fees:

- *Fee simple determinable.* The grantee holds the fee simple "until" a condition happens, when the grantee's estate terminates and the fee simple automatically returns to the grantor. Until the condition happens, the grantor's interest is called a *possibility of reverter.*
- *Fee simple on condition subsequent.* The grantee holds the fee simple estate, "but if" a condition happens, the grantor has the right to reenter the land and take back the fee simple estate. Until the grantor has taken back the fee simple, the grantor's interest is called a *right of entry* or *power of termination.* It may also be called a *right of reentry.*
- *Fee simple on executory limitation.* The grantee holds the fee simple estate, but if a condition happens, the fee simple automatically vests in a named third party. Until the condition happens, the named third party's interest is called an *executory interest* or an *executory limitation.*

---

8. California retains a semblance of the old doctrine in its Probate Code § 6402.5, which provides that, under certain circumstances, community property received from a predeceasing spouse goes to the relatives of the predeceased spouse rather than to the relatives of the decedent.

The difference between a fee simple determinable and a fee simple on condition subsequent is that the fee simple determinable terminates automatically
when the condition happens. The fee on condition subsequent does not terminate until the grantor reenters and takes possession, or gives notice to the
grantee and sues for possession. To decide which has been created, courts look
to the language of the grant. Language that typically signals a fee simple determinable is that the estate is conveyed to the grantee "so long as" the property
is used for a specified purpose, or "until" the grantee does a specified thing.
Language that signals a fee on condition subsequent is that the estate is conveyed to the grantee, "but if" a condition occurs, the grantor has the right to
reenter and terminate. Either "so long as" or "but if" language may be used to
create a fee subject to an executory limitation — its distinguishing characteristic
is that, on forfeiture, the estate passes to a third party. If the condition happens,
the estate passes automatically to the third party.

> *Example 1:* O, the owner of Blackacre, conveys it to A in fee simple. *Result:* A
> has a fee simple absolute and O has nothing.
>
> *Example 2:* O, the owner of Blackacre, conveys it to A in fee simple *so long as*
> the property is used for a public school, and in the event the property ceases
> being used as a public school, Blackacre *shall revert* to O. *Result:* A has a fee
> simple determinable, and O has a possibility of reverter.
>
> *Example 3:* O, the owner of Blackacre, conveys it to A and his heirs, *but if* the
> property is not used for a public school, O shall have the *right to reenter and
> terminate* the estate granted. *Result:* A has a fee simple subject to a condition
> subsequent. O has a right of entry (which can also be called a right of reentry,
> or a power of termination).
>
> *Example 4:* O, the owner of Blackacre, conveys it to Son-in-Law, his daugh-
> ter's widower, "so long as he remains unmarried." *Result:* Son-in-Law has a fee
> simple determinable. O has a possibility of reverter.
>
> *Example 5:* O, the owner of Blackacre, conveys it to A in fee simple, *but if*
> the property is not used for a public school at any time within the next 90
> years, Blackacre *shall become the property of State University. Result:* A has a fee
> simple subject to an executory limitation (or executory interest), and State
> University has an executory interest.
>
> *Example 6:* O, the owner of Blackacre, conveys it to A and his heirs *so long as*
> the property is used for a public school, and in the event the property ceases
> being used as a public school within the next 90 years, Blackacre *shall become
> the property of State University. Result:* A has a fee simple on an executory limita-
> tion and State University has an executory interest.[9]
>
> *Example 7:* O, the owner of Blackacre, conveys it to Son-in-Law and his heirs,
> but if Son-in-Law remarries, to B and C, the children of O's deceased daugh-
> ter A. *Result:* Son-in-Law has a fee simple subject to an executory interest and
> B and C have an executory interest.

---

9. Sometimes this is labeled a "fee simple determinable followed by an executory interest,"
but this seems an unnecessary refinement (as well as an unwieldy mouthful) since the forfeiture is
always automatic in favor of an executory interest (unlike the situation where the future interest
is retained by the grantor). Examples 5 and 6 assume that Blackacre is located in a state that has
enacted the Uniform Statutory Rule Against Perpetuities.

[handwritten margin note: Courts look toward language of the grant to determine which category of defeasible fee.]

Why all these labels? The reasons are partly functional and partly historical. Notice the difference in language between the fee simple determinable and the fee on a condition subsequent. If the condition occurs, the fee simple determinable automatically comes to an end and the property reverts to the grantor in fee simple absolute (or to the grantor's heirs if the grantor has died). By contrast, the grantor must reenter and terminate a fee on a condition subsequent to get the fee simple back. If the grantor does nothing, the fee simple remains with the grantee. When would this matter? It might matter when the question is whether the holder of the defeasible fee has gained a fee simple absolute by adverse possession (when does the possession become hostile?). It might matter if a statute in the jurisdiction treats a possibility of reverter differently from a right of entry. It might matter if, for some reason (environmental contamination perhaps?), the holder of the defeasible fee wants to get rid of the property and the holder of the future interest does not want it.

The reason for the difference in labels when the "divesting interest" is held by a third party, rather than the grantor, is purely historical. Before 1536, such an interest was void as a legal interest if held by a third party. After 1536 (the Statute of Uses),[10] such interests in the legal title could be held by third parties. The difference in labels probably persists, however, because there is a functional difference. Executory interests (created in third parties) are subject to the Rule Against Perpetuities (of which more later), but rights of entry and possibilities of reverter (interests retained by grantors) are not. As a practical matter, this means that a time limit must ordinarily be specified for the duration of the condition when an executory interest is used, whereas no time limit is required with a right of entry or possibility of reverter. Whether these differences make sense in the modern world is another matter.

As you read the following cases, consider whether the benefits of these devices are worth the complexity they introduce into the law, and whether there might be a simpler way to do it. California has simplified its laws by converting all defeasible fees into fees simple subject to a condition subsequent, and possibilities of reverter and executory interests into powers of termination.[11] The statute of limitations on exercising a power of termination is five years after occurrence of the condition. Should other states consider something similar?

STATION ASSOCIATES, INC. v. DARE COUNTY

Supreme Court of North Carolina
513 S.E.2d 789 (N.C. 1999)

PARKER, J. This title dispute to approximately 10 acres of land at the northern tip of Hatteras Island, Dare County, originates in an 1897 deed. In that year

---

10. The Statute of Uses was enacted primarily to restore land-based revenues to Henry VIII, which had been reduced by complex conveyancing practices employing "uses," which were something like trusts. *See* discussion in Section C of this chapter and at http://en.wikipedia.org/wiki/Statute_of_Uses for an explanation.

11. Cal. Civ. Code §§ 885.010 *et seq.* Kentucky has a similar statute, Ky. Rev. Stat. § 381.218.

Jessie B. Etheridge conveyed the land in issue (hereinafter "the property") to the United States in the following deed:

Treasury Department Life-Saving Service-Form No. 12.

Whereas, The SECRETARY OF THE TREASURY has been authorized by law to establish the LIFE-SAVING STATION herein described;

And whereas, Congress, by Act of March 3, 1875, provided as follows, viz.: "And the Secretary of the Treasury is hereby authorized, whenever he shall deem it advisable, to acquire, by donation or purchase, [o]n behalf of the United States, the right to use and occupy sites for life-saving or life-boat stations, houses of refuge, and sites for pier-head Beacons, the establishment of which has been, or shall hereafter be, authorized by Congress;"

And whereas, the said Secretary of the Treasury deems it advisable to acquire, on behalf of the United States, the right to use and occupy the hereinafter-described lot of land as a site for a Life-Saving Station, as indicated by his signature hereto:

Now, [this Indenture between Jessie B. Etheridge, party of the first part, and the United States, represented by the Secretary of the Treasury, party of the second part, WITNESSETH that the said party of the first part, in consideration of the sum of two hundred dollars by these presents grant[s], demise[s], release[s], and convey[s] unto the said United States] all that certain lot of land situate in Nags Head township, County of Dare and State of North Carolina, and thus described and bounded: Beginning at a cedar post bearing from the South West corner of the Oregon Life Saving Station South 40° West and distant 28.24 chains[12] from said post South 68° West 10 chains to post, thence South 22° E. 10 chains to post, thence North 68° E. 10 chains to post, thence North 22° W. 10 chains to first Station containing 10 acres, be the contents what they may, with full right of egress and ingress thereto in any direction over other lands of the grantor by those in the employ of the United States, on foot or with vehicles of any kind, with boats or any articles used for the purpose of carrying out the intentions of Congress in providing for the establishment of Life-Saving Stations, and the right to pass over any lands of the grantor in any manner in the prosecution of said purpose; and also the right to erect such structures upon the said land as the United States may see fit, and to remove any and all such structures and appliances at any time; the said premises to be used and occupied for the purposes named in said Act of March 3, 1875:

To have and to hold the said lot of land and privileges unto the United States from this date.

And the said party of the first part for himself, executors, and administrators do[es] covenant with the United States to warrant and defend the peaceable possession of the above-described premises to the United States, for the purposes above named for the term of this covenant, against the lawful claims of all persons claiming by, through, or under Jessie B. Etheridge.

---

12.   A chain is 66 feet long, the length of a surveyor's chain with 100 links. In descriptions using chains as a measure, you may also find rods, which are 16.5 feet long. There are four rods to a chain.—EDS.

And it is further stipulated, that the United States shall be allowed to remove all buildings and appurtenances from the said land whenever it shall think proper, and shall have the right of using other lands of the grantor for passage over the same in effecting such removal.

In witness whereof, the parties hereto have set their hands and seals this 8th day of March, A.D. eighteen hundred and ninety-seven.

Signed, sealed, and delivered in presence of

s/J.B. Etheridge   s/L.J. Gage
                          Secretary of the Treasury

The United States took possession and duly established a life-saving station on the property operated by the Life-Saving Service, a part of the United States Treasury Department. The United States Coast Guard was thereafter created; and sometime prior to 1915 the Coast Guard took over operation of the station, which was then named the Oregon Inlet Coast Guard Station. In December of 1989, the U.S. Coast Guard abandoned the station. On 17 July 1992, the United States quitclaimed its interest in the property to Dare County.

Plaintiffs, who are the heirs of the original grantor, Jessie B. Etheridge, along with a corporation that purchased from the heirs an ownership interest in the land, claimed title to the property and instituted this action against Dare County.

The trial court granted judgment on the pleadings to defendant Dare County, concluding as a matter of law that Dare County had title to the property in fee simple absolute. The Court of Appeals reversed and remanded holding that the United States was granted only a fee simple determinable by the 1897 deed and that a genuine issue of fact existed as to whether a condemnation proceeding by the United States in 1959 extinguished plaintiffs' reversionary interest. We now reverse the Court of Appeals and reinstate the judgment of the trial court.

Before this Court defendant argues that the 1897 deed conveyed to the United States a fee simple absolute, but even if the estate conveyed was a fee simple determinable with a possibility of reverter, in 1959, when the United States created the Cape Hatteras National Seashore Recreation Area by condemning properties along the outer banks, plaintiffs' possibility of reverter in the property was extinguished by the condemnation. We do not need to address the second part of defendant's argument as we conclude that the 1897 deed conveyed to the United States not a fee simple determinable, but a fee simple absolute.

An estate in fee simple determinable is created by a limitation in a fee simple conveyance which provides that the estate shall automatically expire upon the occurrence of a certain subsequent event. "The law does not favor a construction of the language in a deed which will constitute a condition subsequent unless the intention of the parties to create such a restriction upon the title is clearly manifested." Washington City Bd. of Educ. v. Edgerton, 94 S.E.2d 661 (N.C. 1956). "Ordinarily a clause in a deed will not be construed as a condition subsequent, unless it contains language sufficient to qualify the estate conveyed and provides that in case of a breach the estate will be defeated, and this must appear in appropriate language sufficiently clear to indicate that this was the intent of the parties." Ange v. Ange, 71 S.E.2d 19 (N.C. 1952).

This Court has declined to recognize reversionary interests in deeds that do not contain express and unambiguous language of reversion or termination upon condition broken. *Washington City* (habendum clause contained expression of intended purpose — "for school purposes"; held fee simple because no power of termination or right of reentry was expressed); *Ange* (habendum clause contained the language "for church purposes only"; nevertheless held to be an indefeasible fee since there was "no language which provides for a reversion of the property to the grantors or any other person in case it ceases to be used as church property"); Shaw Univ. v. Durham Life Ins. Co., 53 S.E.2d 656 (N.C. 1949) (property and the proceeds therefrom were to be "perpetually devoted to educational purposes"; held fee simple absolute since there was "nothing in the . . . deed to indicate the grantor intended to convey a conditional estate," and there was "no clause of re-entry, no limitation over or other provision which was to become effective upon condition broken"); Lassiter v. Jones, 1 S.E.2d 845 (N.C. 1939) (deed conveyed property "for the exclusive use of the Polenta Male and Female Academy; it shall be used exclusively for school purposes"; held to have conveyed a fee simple "for the reason that nowhere in the deed is there a reverter or reentry clause"); *First Presbyterian*, 157 S.E. at 438-39 (. . . property was to be used for church purposes only; held to be an indefeasible fee simple; . . . there was "no language showing an intent that the property shall revert to the grantor . . . or that the grantor . . . shall have the right to reenter"); Hall v. Quinn, 130 S.E. 18, 19-20 (N.C. 1925) (granting clause and habendum clause both indicated that the property was "to be used for the purposes of education" only; held to be an estate in fee simple because there was "no clause of re-entry; no forfeiture of the estate upon condition broken"); *Braddy*, 60 S.E. at 508 (recitals that the grantor was to improve the property did not create an estate upon condition since there was an absence of an express reservation in the deed of a right of reentry).

We have stated repeatedly that a mere expression of the purpose for which the property is to be used without provision for forfeiture or reentry is insufficient to create an estate on condition and that, in such a case, an unqualified fee will pass.

However, in those cases in which the deed contained express and unambiguous language of reversion or termination, we have construed a deed to convey a determinable fee or fee on condition subsequent. Mattox v. State, 186 S.E.2d 378 (N.C. 1972) (habendum clause contained condition that if the grantee failed to continuously and perpetually use the property as a Highway Patrol Radio Station and Patrol Headquarters, the land "shall revert to, and title shall vest in the Grantor"); City of Charlotte v. Charlotte Park & Rec. Comm'n, 178 S.E.2d 601 (N.C. 1971) (habendum clause contained language that "upon condition that whenever the said property shall cease to be used as a park . . . , then the same shall revert to the party of the first part"); Lackey v. Hamlet City Bd. of Educ., 128 S.E.2d 806 (N.C. 1963) (deed contained paragraph providing, "It is also made a part of this deed that in the event of the school's disabandonment (failure) . . . this lot of land shall revert to the original owners"); Charlotte Park & Rec. Comm'n v. Barringer, 88 S.E.2d 114 (N.C. 1955) (deed indicated that in the event the lands were not used solely for parks and playgrounds, the "said lands shall revert in fee simple to the undersigned donors"), *cert. denied*, 350 U.S. 983 (1956); Pugh v. Allen, 102 S.E. 394 (N.C. 1920) (deed contained provision that "in case the said James H. Pugh should die without an heir the following gift shall revert to the sole use and benefit of my son"); Smith v. Parks, 97 S.E. 209 (N.C. 1918) (deed indicated that "should [grantor] die without leaving such heir or heirs, then the same is to revert back to her nearest kin"); Methodist Protestant Church of Henderson v. Young, 40 S.E. 691 (N.C. 1902) (deed expressed that if the church shall "discontinue the occupancy of said lot in manner as aforesaid, then this deed shall be null and void and the said lot or parcel of ground shall revert to [the grantor]").

Applying this law to the deed in the present case, we note that the 1897 document is completely devoid of any language of reversion or termination. . . . Plaintiffs contend, however, that the deed contains certain phrases expressive of the parties' intent that the estate was to be of limited duration: first, that the granting clause gives the United States the right only to "use and occupy" the property for the stated purposes; and second, that the word "term" within the warranty clause, in which the grantor warrants peaceable possession of the property "for the purposes above named for the term of this covenant," is sufficient to indicate that the parties intended that the United States' occupancy of the property would be for a limited duration. We disagree with plaintiffs' arguments. The use of the words "use and occupy" and "term" in this deed is not the equivalent of a clear expression that the property shall revert to the grantor or that the estate will automatically terminate upon the happening of a certain event.

[margin note: π's argue language for fee simple determinable]

Plaintiffs also state that for over one hundred years, the proper construction of deeds has focused on the intent of the parties and that a narrow focus on "technical" or "magic" words is inappropriate. They argue that the language of purpose contained within the deed, coupled with the language permitting the United States to "erect such structures on the said land as the United States may see fit, and to remove any and all such structures at any time," is inconsistent with the grant of a fee simple absolute. Such language of purpose and license, the argument runs, would be surplusage if a fee simple absolute were intended; thus, it follows that the deed conveys only a determinable fee since, "[if] possible, effect must be given to every part of a deed" and "no clause, if reasonable intendment can be found, shall be construed as meaningless." In making this argument, plaintiffs rely on the reasoning employed by the District Court for the Eastern District of North Carolina in Etheridge v. United States, 218 F. Supp. 809 (E.D.N.C. 1963). In *Etheridge*, the court attempted to apply North Carolina law in construing a deed nearly identical to the deed in this case; using a methodology of focusing on the parties' intent and giving effect to all parts of the deed, the court held that the deed conveyed a fee simple determinable. This Court is not bound by decisions of a United States District Court interpreting or applying North Carolina law.

[margin note: π argue intent.]

While discerning the intent of the parties is the ultimate goal in construing a deed, we disagree with plaintiffs' characterization of the test, requiring express and unambiguous language of reversion or termination, as a test that relies on "rigid technicality" and ignores the intent of the parties. Under our case law the use of some express language of reversion or termination is the usual manner in which parties intending to create a fee simple determinable manifest that intent. The language of termination necessary to create a fee simple determinable need not conform to any "set formula." Rather, "any words expressive of the grantor's intent that the estate shall terminate on the occurrence of the event" or that "on the cessation of [a specified] use, the estate shall end," will be sufficient to create a fee simple determinable. In this case, however, no such language or expression can be found from which the Court can conclude, without speculation and conjecture, that "it is plainly intended by the conveyance or some part thereof, that the grantor meant to convey an estate of less dignity." N.C.G.S. § 39-1 (1984).[13]

Accordingly, we reverse the decision of the Court of Appeals and remand to that court for further remand to the Superior Court, Dare County, for reinstatement of the judgment of the Superior Court. REVERSED.

Notes and Questions

1. The choice facing the court in this case was between a fee simple absolute and a fee simple determinable. Which do you think was intended? If you had been representing Etheridge at the time of the conveyance, which would you have recommended? What concerns might Etheridge have had? What purpose would a fee simple determinable have served? What alternatives might you have considered using—a lease? a restrictive covenant?

2. If you had been representing the Treasury Department, under what circumstances would you have been willing to recommend accepting a fee simple determinable instead of a fee simple absolute?

3. The full list of cases cited by the court illustrating language construed to create either a fee simple absolute or a defeasible fee has been left in the opinion, rather than edited out, so that you can get a feel for the types of cases in which defeasible fees are likely to be used. Do you see any common threads in these cases?

RED HILL OUTING CLUB v. HAMMOND

Supreme Court of New Hampshire
722 A.2d 501 (N.H. 1998)

HORTON, J. The defendants, David and Elizabeth Hammond and their son, Robert Hammond, appeal the Superior Court's decision denying them right of re-entry and possession of land they deeded to the plaintiff, Red Hill Outing Club (club), subject to a condition subsequent. We affirm.

David Hammond purchased land in Moultonboro in 1956 known as Red Hill, which was subsequently cleared for use as a ski slope. Hammond installed a rope tow and participated in forming the club for the purpose of operating the ski slope. From 1969 to 1979, the club leased Red Hill. During this period, it operated the rope tow and provided free ski lessons to members and Moultonboro residents.

---

13. This statute provides: "When real estate is conveyed to any person, the same shall be held and construed to be a conveyance in fee, whether the word 'heir' is used or not, unless such conveyance in plain and express words shows, or it is plainly intended by the conveyance or some part thereof, that the grantor meant to convey an estate of less dignity."—EDS.

In 1979, David and Elizabeth Hammond conveyed Red Hill by quitclaim deed to the club for nominal consideration. The deed contained the following condition:

> The Grantee . . . covenants and agrees that the within described premises shall be maintained and made available to residents of Moultonboro as a ski slope in accordance with its now existing by-laws. If the Grantee fails to provide such skiing facilities to Moultonboro residents for a period of two consecutive years then a breach of this covenant has occurred, provided such failure was not caused by reason of an act of God, such as inadequate snowfall. In the event the Grantee . . . breach[es this covenant], the Grantor shall have the right to reenter and take possession of said premises . . . .

[handwritten margin note: fs subject to condition subsequent]

From 1979 to the mid-eighties use of the ski slope grew. But the popularity of other ski areas, changing interests of families who had previously frequented the slope, inadequate snowfall in some years, and the waning leadership of the club resulted in a noticeable decline in its use after 1988. Consequently, the club ceased offering free ski lessons after the winter of 1988-1989, and did not obtain a rope tow permit for the ski seasons of 1992-1993 and 1993-1994. Red Hill was closed to all skiing during the winter of 1993-1994. *[handwritten margin note: Ski business declines]*

In October 1994, the defendants filed a notice of re-entry and possession, claiming that the club had breached its condition by failing to provide skiing facilities at Red Hill for two consecutive years. In response, the club brought action against the Hammonds, seeking, *inter alia*, declaratory judgment regarding the parties' relative rights. *[handwritten margin note: Δ claims (right to reentry). π claims]*

After a bench trial, which included a view, the trial court determined that the condition subsequent should be strictly construed. Therefore, to comply with its obligation to provide Red Hill as "skiing facilities," the club needed only to "maintain and make available the premises . . . as a ski slope." Accordingly, the court found that the club had not substantially breached the condition because it had remained in existence as a club and continued to maintain and offer use of the hill as a ski slope. It found that any failure of the club to provide ski facilities from February 1993 to October 1994 was not sufficient in duration to constitute a breach. . . . *[handwritten margin note: TCT]*

The defendants first argue . . . that by strictly interpreting the condition to refer only to maintaining and making available the ski slope, the trial court ignored the parties' original intent to include the operation of a licensed ski tow and provision of free ski instruction within the club's obligation to provide "skiing facilities." Although the defendants acknowledge that strict construction of conditions subsequent has long been the rule in this State, they urge us to update this rule consistent with the modern trend in contract interpretation. *[handwritten margin note: Δ argues. looking for modernization.]*

The construction of deeds is an issue of law for this court. The general rule in interpreting a deed is to determine the parties' intent at the time of conveyance in light of the surrounding circumstances. As the defendants correctly note, formalistic requirements in real estate conveyancing have largely given way to effectuating the manifest intent of the parties, absent contrary public policy or statute. Thus, for example, when the interests of a changing society persuaded us that restrictive covenants were valuable land use planning devices rather than restraints on the use of land, we discarded the rule of strict construction in favor of ascertaining the parties' intent in light of the surrounding circumstances at the time of a covenant's creation. . . .

We are not convinced, however, that we should apply the general rule of construction to conditions subsequent. "The [grantor of a fee simple subject to condition subsequent] shall have his exact legal right, but no more." Emerson v. Simpson, 43 N.H. 475 (1862). "[T]o defeat an estate of his own creation, [he] must bring the [grantee] clearly within its letter." . . . Because of the drastic consequence of a breach, we have traditionally viewed conditions subsequent with disfavor.

The passage of time has failed to increase the social value of conditions subsequent. Unlike restrictive covenants, conditions subsequent continue to be viewed with disfavor because of their potential to cause a forfeiture of land. . . . We disagree with the defendants that the consequences of a forfeiture are "no greater" than those of specific performance of a contract or an attachment on property. A forfeiture by nature is a drastic remedy because in most cases it is widely disproportionate to the breach. See Korngold, *For Unifying Servitudes and Defeasible Fees: Property Law's Functional Equivalents*, 66 Tex. L. Rev. 533, 551 (1988). In addition, restricted use of the land for a potentially indefinite duration substantially diminishes the land's marketability and development, ultimately to the detriment of the community. See Powell, *Defeasible Fees and the Nature of Real Property*, 40 Kan. L. Rev. 411, 418-19 (1992). Neither specific performance, an equitable remedy at the court's discretion, nor attachment, applied to secure payment of judgment should a plaintiff prevail, evokes the hardships associated with a condition subsequent. . . .

The overwhelming majority of courts in other jurisdictions also have continued to strictly construe conditions subsequent in deeds with regard to their capacity to work a forfeiture. . . . Our position conforms to the great weight of authority from our sister States.

Our decision today does not abrogate the guiding rule that the intent of the parties to a deed is to be determined and effectuated when possible. . . . When it is a condition subsequent that must be construed, however, the rule of strict construction operates to confine the determination of intent to the face of the deed and resolve all ambiguities against forfeiture. We therefore hold that the trial court did not err in construing the club's obligation as limited to maintaining and making the hill available as a ski area. It was not required to import meanings not apparent on the face of the deed such as obligations to provide a rope tow or ski instruction. . . .

The trial court correctly found that the club's substantial compliance with the express language in the deed would satisfy the terms of the condition. Substantial compliance will avoid a breach of a condition subsequent. . . .

"We will not substitute our own judgment for that of the trier of fact if it is supported by the evidence, especially when he has been assisted in reaching his conclusions by a view." Here, evidence showed that Red Hill was cleared in the fall from 1991 to 1993 during club work sessions in preparation for skiing, that people skied on the property for a few days in February 1993, and that current facilities at Red Hill include a rope tow, clubhouse, storage shed, lights, and snow-packing equipment. Although it is true the club failed after 1991 to operate a rope tow with a permit in compliance with statutory requirements, . . . that fact is not dispositive of whether it provided ski facilities under the plain terms of the deed. Since we hold that the club was not required under the deed to provide a tow, its failure to obtain a permit to operate one may have violated a statute but did not breach the condition. Ample evidence in the record supports the trial court's conclusion that the club did not abandon the property and thus substantially complied with the condition subsequent. . . .

Notes and Questions

1. The Hammonds used a fee simple on a condition subsequent in their conveyance to the club. If you had been representing them when the conveyance was made, what would you have recommended?

2. If you were going to draft a deed for the Hammonds, knowing what you know now, what would you have included?

3. The modern inclination is to construe deeds to reflect the intent of the parties rather than to follow formalistic rules construing them against the grantor or in favor "of the free use of land." Do you agree with the court that more restrictive rules are appropriate where the sanction for failure to use the land as provided results in forfeiture? If the Hammonds had chosen to impose a use restriction (the property shall be used for a ski hill) or an affirmative covenant (the Club shall maintain a rope tow and provide free ski lessons during ski season), the remedies available to them would not have included forfeiture. Instead, they would have been able to seek an injunction requiring compliance with the covenants or damages for breach of covenant. Why do you suppose they chose to use the fee on a condition subsequent instead?

Restraints on Alienation and Unenforceable Conditions

Absolute restraints on alienation of a fee simple estate are usually void. Thus, a conveyance "to A in fee simple, but if A transfers the property without the grantor's consent, the grantor shall have the right to reenter and terminate the estate granted" gives A a fee simple absolute. The condition is void. Restraints on alienation are disfavored because they tend to discourage improvement of the land and prevent the owner from making the land available for its most valuable use. They keep property off the market, and they keep the owner's creditors from reaching the land in satisfaction of his debts.

Partial restraints are often void, but they may be held valid if the restraint has a legitimate purpose and its impact and duration are reasonably limited. Thus, a provision requiring the owner of Blackacre to offer it to his grantor at the same price and terms on which he is willing to sell it to another (a right of first refusal) is usually valid if the grantor has a limited time within which to exercise the right. A provision limiting transfer of "affordable" housing to persons who meet certain income or wealth requirements is likely to be valid, whereas a condition prohibiting transfer to anyone other than a member of the grantor's family is likely to be void.

Defeasible fees often severely limit alienability by requiring a highly specific—and often not profitable—use of the premises on pain of forfeiture. Property that can only be used for a park, a particular type of church, a school, a ski hill that gives free lessons, or a railroad maintenance yard is not likely to be very marketable. Conditions imposing use restrictions of this sort, however, are very seldom held invalid as unreasonable restraints on alienation. By contrast, the conditions that testators impose on their devisees are more likely to be held invalid.

In *In re Romero's Estate*, 847 P.2d 319 (N.M. Ct. App. 1993), for example, the testator devised his residence to his fiancée "so long as she remained unmarried and did not cohabit with an unrelated adult male" and to his minor sons "so long as their mother did not reside with them." The court held that if the primary purpose of the devise to the fiancée was to separate the testator's sons from their mother, it was void, and the property passed directly to his sons, but if his primary intent was to benefit his fiancée, only the condition designed to prevent the sons from living with their mother was void. The case was remanded for a factual determination as to the testator's intent. Conditions designed to prevent a first marriage or to cause a divorce are void, but conditions designed to shift property ownership on remarriage are normally valid. Contrast *Casey v. Casey*, 700 S.W.2d 46 (Ark. 1985), in which a condition that land devised to the testator's son would be forfeited if the son's daughter were ever to own, possess, or be a guest on the land for more than one week per year was held invalid, with *Babb v. Rand*, 345 A.2d 496 (Me. 1975), in which a condition that the grantee shall never deny access or occupation of the land to the testator's other children was held valid.

Problem

In *Cast v. National Bank of Commerce, Trust & Savings Ass'n*, 183 N.W.2d 485 (Neb. 1971), the court invalidated a condition that the devisee, Richard Cast, or one of his children "shall occupy the farm as his or her residence for 25 years" on pain of forfeiting the estate. The court held the condition void as a restraint on alienation. In *Falls City v. Missouri Pacific Railway*, 453 F.2d 771 (8th Cir. 1971), the question was whether land reverted to the city when the railroad moved its headquarters out of Falls City. Falls City had conveyed the land to the railroad so long as the property was used as the railroad company's divisional headquarters, and if it ceased to use the land for that purpose, the land was to revert to the city. The court held that the railroad owned the property in fee simple absolute because the condition was an invalid restraint on alienation. It said:

> We find that the recent decision of the Nebraska Supreme Court in *Cast v. National Bank of Commerce, Trust and Savings Association of Lincoln* . . . is controlling. In *Cast*, the court held . . . that a condition attached to a defeasible fee simple is an [unenforceable] indirect restraint against alienation "if it materially affects marketability adversely." . . . In limiting the use of the property by the Railroad to use as its divisional headquarters only, the City, in practical effect, completely restricted alienation of the land to other grantees.

Was the court correct in characterizing the decision in *Cast* as controlling precedent?[14] (A federal court sitting in a case like this is bound to apply law of

---

14. The Nebraska Supreme Court has subsequently criticized application of *Cast* to other fact situations. *See* Spanish Oaks, Inc. v. Hy-Vee, Inc., 655 N.W.2d 390 (Neb. 2003); Occidental Sav. & Loan Ass'n v. Venco Partnership, 293 N.W.2d 843 (Neb. 1980).

the relevant state, which in this case was Nebraska.) If you had represented the city, what arguments would you have made?

CITY OF PALM SPRINGS v. LIVING DESERT RESERVE
Court of Appeal, Fourth District, Division 2, California
82 Cal. Rptr. 2d 859 (Ct. App.), *review denied* (1999)

McKinster, J. Not infrequently, wealthy individuals, intending both to promote the common weal and to memorialize themselves, give property to a city on the condition that it be used in perpetuity for some specified purpose. With disturbing regularity, however, the city soon tires of using the donated property for the purpose to which it agreed when it accepted the gift, and instead seeks to convert the property to some other use. . . .

In June of 1986, the Bank of America, as trustee of the McCallum Desert Foundation under the will of Pearl M. McManus, deceased, executed a grant deed, conveying 30 acres of land to the City. The Deed provides:

> THIS DEED IS MADE AND ACCEPTED ON THE EXPRESS CONDITION that the land hereby conveyed be used solely as the site of the McCALLUM DESERT PRESERVE AND EQUESTRIAN CENTER, and that grantee, its successors or assigns shall forever use the land and premises for the purpose of maintaining a public park for the exposition of desert fauna and flora, named as the McCALLUM DESERT PRESERVE AND EQUESTRIAN CENTER.

> In the event that the property is not used solely and perpetually as the site of the McCALLUM DESERT PRESERVE AND EQUESTRIAN CENTER, then the interest in the land and premises herein conveyed shall pass to the Living Desert Reserve, Palm Desert, California, and grantee shall forfeit all rights thereto.

The City expressly accepted the grant in October of 1986. Less than three years later, however, the City decided that it would rather build a golf course on the Land. Believing that the golf course would be inconsistent with the condition in the Deed, the City asked the Living Desert for permission to buy other property for use as a preserve instead of the Land. Those negotiations continued periodically without success. The City's final offer was made in November of 1992, when it offered to buy the Living Desert's reversionary interest in the Land for $200,000 and threatened to take the interest by eminent domain if the Living Desert did not agree.

After the Living Desert declined that offer, the City adopted a resolution of necessity . . . by which it found that the public health, safety and welfare required the acquisition of the Living Desert's reversionary interest in the Land for the purpose of expanding the City's municipal golf course. In March of 1993, the City filed a complaint in eminent domain . . . . Simultaneously, the City applied for an order for immediate possession of the reversionary interest within 30 days, relying on an appraisal valuing that interest at $200,000. . . . The trial court granted the application and issued the order for immediate possession.

In October of 1993, the Living Desert recorded a notice of breach of condition subsequent. (Civ. Code, § 885.050.) . . . [T]he Living Desert cross-complained against the City to quiet title to the Land. It alleged that, as a result of the City's breach of the conditions and the notice of that breach, the fee simple interest of the City in the Land had reverted to the Living Desert.

The parties stipulated that the issues of whether (1) the reversionary interest held by the Living Desert is a compensable interest and (2) the City had breached the conditions of the Deed would be bifurcated from and tried before the issue of the amount of any compensation due for the reversionary interest.

At the beginning of trial, the City moved for judgment on the pleadings. The trial court granted the motion as to the cross-complaint, finding that the interest of the Living Desert is measured as of the date the complaint in eminent domain was filed, that as of that date the City had not yet changed the use of the Land or otherwise violated the Deed, and that the Living Desert therefore owned only a reversionary interest, not the fee title to the Land. . . . Following an evidentiary bench trial, the trial court . . . ruled that the reversionary interest was not a compensable interest . . . , and entered judgment in favor of the City.

The Living Desert appeals. The Attorney General of the State of California appears as an *amicus curiae*. . . .

. . . Living Desert . . . contends that the trial court erred by relying on Code of Civil Procedure section 1265.410, subdivision (a)(1), to determine that the reversionary interest was not compensable. Specifically, it argues that the statute does not apply to efforts by a condemnor to relieve itself of the obligation to comply with conditions accompanying a gift of property, and that if it does, the statute permits the taking of property without just compensation, in violation of the federal and state constitutions. . . .

Challenging the assumptions under which the case was tried below, the Attorney General contends that the Foundation gave the Land to the City in a charitable trust, not in fee simple subject to a condition subsequent. . . .

A gift of property in fee subject to a condition subsequent differs from a gift of that same property in trust. . . . [T]he transferee [unlike a trustee] has no enforceable duties. The breach of condition may result in the termination of the transferee's interest, but it does not subject the transferee to actions for damages or to enforce the condition. . . .

The question . . . is whether (1) the donor intended to provide that if the property were not used for the designated charitable purposes it should revert either to the donor's estate or to a contingent donee, or (2) the donor intended to impose an enforceable obligation on the trustees to devote it to those purposes.

Courts favor the construction of a gift as a trust over a conditional gift . . . . Because forfeiture is a harsh remedy, any ambiguity is resolved against it. Moreover, the transferor's objective is to use the transfer to confer a benefit upon the public. To ensure that the benefit is conferred as intended, the transferor ordinarily wants the intended beneficiary to be able to enforce that intent. Because the only remedy for the breach of a condition is a forfeiture, a condition is not a very effective method of accomplishing those goals. For both of those reasons, courts will generally construe a conveyance as one upon trust rather than upon condition.

However, if the donor clearly manifests an intention to make a conditional gift, that intention will be honored. . . . The Deed expressly states the Foundation's intent that, in the event of a breach of the condition, the transferee (City) shall forfeit its interest in favor of a third party (the Living Desert). Accordingly, the Deed must be construed as granting to the City a fee simple subject to a condition subsequent, and assigning to the Living Desert a power of termination. . . .

The general rule in California is that, when a condemnor takes property the ownership of which is split into an estate in fee simple subject to a condition subsequent and a power of termination, the owner of the future interest is not entitled to any compensation unless the condition has been breached as of the date of valuation. If no such breach has yet occurred, then the possibility of a reversion is too remote and speculative to be valued, and the reversionary interest is deemed to be valueless for purposes of condemnation.

However, the general rule denying compensation to the holder of the reversionary interest applies only "in the absence of exceptional circumstances . . . ." One of the exceptions is that the reversionary interest is compensable if the reversion would have been likely to occur within a reasonably short time. That exception is described in the *Restatement of Property*, section 53, comment *c*, and has been recognized in California since at least 1951. That exception was codified in 1975 as section 1265.410(a)(1), which provides: "Where the acquisition of property for public use violates a use restriction coupled with a contingent future interest granting a right to possession of the property upon violation of the use restriction: . . . If violation of the use restriction was otherwise reasonably imminent, the owner of the contingent future interest is entitled to compensation for its value, if any."

The trial court found that this exception did not apply because a violation of the restriction by the City was not reasonably imminent. It reasoned (1) that the City did not intend to violate the condition until it was relieved from the obligation of complying with it, either by agreement with Living Desert or by eminent domain, and (2) that the City's preparation to exercise its power of eminent domain cannot be considered in determining whether a violation was reasonably imminent. . . . To the contrary, the undisputed evidence demonstrates that the violation was imminent. Therefore, the exception to the general rule did apply, and the Living's Desert's interest was compensable. . . .

The trial court relied upon its factual finding that "the last thing the City wanted to do was 'violate' the restriction and lose its fee." Obviously, the City did not want to suffer the consequences of violating the restriction while it was still in effect. But that fact, although undeniable, is irrelevant to the question whether a violation of the condition was reasonably imminent.

Reasonableness is an objective test. Hence, the relevant inquiry is not whether the defendant regards the action as reasonable, but whether reasonably prudent persons generally, looking at the circumstances impartially and objectively, would consider it to be reasonable. . . . To the extent that the trial court relied on the City's subjective understanding, it erred.

. . . [T]he imminence of the violation is to be evaluated "from the time of the commencement of an eminent domain proceeding, and [without] taking into account any changes in the use of the land sought to be condemned which may result as a consequence of such proceeding. . . ." (Rest., Property, § 53, comment *c*, p. 188 . . .)].) Consideration of the effect of the condemnation is excluded because it would generally cause the owner of the present interest to suffer an unfair forfeiture. . . . [I]f further use of the property by the grantee in conformance with the use restriction is prevented by the divestiture of the grantee's title through eminent domain, the failure to perform is excused as being involuntary on the part of the grantee, and the future interest is not compensated.

In short, the statutory rule contemplates a situation in which the grantee of the conditional deed intends to continue to comply with the condition indefinitely, but is prevented from doing so because a paramount authority seizes title to the property through the power of eminent domain. And because it is designed to apply in situations in which the intentions and desires of the grantee of the present interest are contrary to and frustrated by the condemnor, it necessarily assumes that the grantee and the condemnor are separate entities dealing at arm's length.

The circumstances before us are radically different from those assumed by the statutory rule, for two reasons.

First, the grantee of the present interest and the condemnor are one and the same entity: the City. . . . Second, the condemnation of the future interest did not divest the City of its present interest in the Land, and thus did not prevent the City from continuing to use the Land in conformance with the use restriction. That it did not plan to do so was not a decision forced upon it by the condemnation, but rather was its own voluntary choice, for which it should be held accountable. . . .

The City . . . has been unfaithful both to the Foundation's intent and to the spirit of the conditions under which it accepted the Foundation's gift. . . . [W]hether the City's policymakers genuinely believed that the law might permit it to keep the Land without either complying with the Foundation's wishes or paying fair compensation—indeed, without paying any compensation whatsoever—the decision to assert that position did not display the high degree of fairness, justice, and virtue that should characterize public entities. We cannot condone such inequitable behavior. . . .

[T]he trial court's conclusions that the violation was not reasonably imminent and that the Living Desert's power of termination was not compensable must be reversed. However, no retrial on that issue is necessary, because the evidence establishing the imminence of the violation is both undisputed and indisputable. . . .

Had the condition been violated before the City commenced its condemnation action, the measure of compensation payable to the Living Desert would have been the fair market value of an estate in fee simple absolute. The violation here had not yet occurred when this action was filed but was reasonably imminent. . . . Under that circumstance, the trial court should apply the same measure of compensation to determine the value of Living Desert's power of termination, *i.e.*, 100 percent of the value of the unrestricted fee in the Land.

Notes and Questions

1. The grantor in this case, Bank of America, is a professional trustee, and made the conveyance in its capacity as trustee of a charitable trust (the McCallum Desert Foundation). Why might it have used a defeasible fee rather than a charitable trust? Is there any advantage to placing control of the land (and responsibility) in the city's hands rather than creating a charitable trust or conveying it to Living Desert in the first place?

2. Why does the court characterize the City's interest as a fee simple subject to a condition subsequent and Living Desert's interest as a power of termination? Under the common-law rules, Living Desert's interest would be an executory interest and the City's would be a fee simple subject to an executory limitation because Living Desert was a third party. Did the court make a mistake? *See* Cal. Civ. Code § 885.010(a)(2):

> "Power of termination" includes the power created in a transferee to terminate a fee simple estate in real property to enforce a restriction on the use of the real property in the form of a limitation or condition subsequent to which the fee simple estate is subject, whether the power is characterized in the instrument that creates or evidences it as an executory interest, executory limitation, or otherwise, and includes the interest known at common law as an executory interest preceded by a fee simple determinable.

3. California follows the Restatement rule that the owner of the defeasible fee receives all the condemnation proceeds unless violation of the condition is imminent, which makes sense in light of the rule that the owner holds the funds received subject to the same condition. If the state had condemned the McCallum Desert Preserve to build a highway, for example, the city would have received the condemnation proceeds but would have been required to use them to maintain a park called the McCallum Desert Preserve and Equestrian Center. If the city was unwilling or unable to meet the condition, the funds would have been forfeited to the Living Desert Reserve.

The Restatement rule was rejected in *Ink v. City of Canton,* 212 N.E.2d 574 (Ohio 1965). In that case, the state highway department condemned all but 6.5 acres of a 33.5-acre park held by the city on condition that the property be used as a public park named in memory of Harry H. Ink. Instead of awarding all of the proceeds to the city (which had not planned to convert any of the park land to other purposes), the court held the city was entitled only to the value of the land as restricted to use as a park and subject to a condition of forfeiture. Not only were Ink's heirs held entitled to the difference between that value and the value of the land in fee simple absolute, but the heirs also retained their possibility of reverter in the proceeds awarded to the city (in the event the proceeds were not used to maintain Ink Park) and in the remaining 6.5 acres of Ink Park. The court's rationale was that the city would get a windfall if awarded the value of a fee simple absolute and that it deserved no more because it had not paid for the land (it was a gift from the Inks). Which rule makes more sense, the Restatement/California rule or the Ohio rule?

Differences Among the Defeasible Fees: Adverse Possession, Alienability, and Duration

Does it make a difference which type of defeasible fee is used? In the cases you have read so far, the answer is no—the same result would have been reached, regardless of the defeasible fee used. But sometimes it does make a difference.

Adverse possession. When the condition occurs, the holder of a possibility of reverter or executory interest immediately and automatically becomes the owner of the property in fee simple absolute, and the possessor becomes an adverse possessor. By contrast, title held in fee simple on a condition subsequent does not change until the grantor exercises the power of termination. Even after occurrence of the condition, the holder of the fee simple on condition subsequent remains a rightful possessor. This difference is often more apparent than real, however, either because the holder of the right of entry who delays exercising the power for the period of the statute of limitations is likely to be found to have waived the power, or to be guilty of laches, or because the state has enacted a special statute of limitations that applies the same period to exercising a power of termination as it does to recovering possession pursuant to a possibility of reverter or executory interest.

For example, Md. Code Ann., Real Prop. § 6-103, provides:

> No person may commence an action for the recovery of land, nor make an entry on it, by reason of a breach of a condition subsequent, or by reason of the termination of an estate of fee-simple determinable, unless the action is commenced or entry is made within seven years after breach of the condition or from the time when the fee-simple determinable estate terminates. . . . Possession of land after breach of a condition subsequent or after termination of an estate of fee-simple determinable is adverse and hostile from the first breach of a condition subsequent or from the occurrence of the event terminating the fee-simple determinable estate.[15]

In *Sligh v. Plair*, 569 S.W.2d 58 (Ark. 1978), the court held that the grantor had waived his right of reentry by waiting 34 years after breach of the condition that the grantee live on the property and 10 years after breach of the condition that the grantee not sell or mortgage the property before he declared a forfeiture. It does not appear that anyone argued that these conditions were invalid restraints on alienation, but given the court's holding, this apparent oversight was harmless.

Alienability. The common-law rules on alienability of the possibility of reverter and right of entry were the same: Both passed to the grantor's heirs at death, neither was alienable inter vivos. In a few states, the attempt to transfer a possibility of reverter was simply void, but an attempt to transfer a right of entry destroyed it. In many states, alienability is now governed by statute. In Illinois, neither interest is alienable or devisable, Ill. Stat. ch. 765 330/1, but in other states these interests have become alienable inter vivos and devisable by will. *See, e.g.,* Md. Code Ann., Real Prop. § 6-104; N.C. Gen. Stat. § 39-6.3.

Duration. At common law, possibilities of reverter and powers of termination retained by the grantor had potentially unlimited duration because they were not subject to the Rule Against Perpetuities. Executory interests, by contrast, were subject to the rule, which destroyed them if the condition was not certain to occur or become impossible of occurrence within 21 years, or within 21 years after the death of a specified person (or group of people) living when the defeasible fee was created. Statutes in many states have changed this situation.

In some states, the conditions expire after a specified period of time, leaving the holder of the defeasible fee with a fee simple absolute. Illinois, for example, terminates conditions after 40 years.[16] Minnesota is unusual in applying the statute only to fees simple determinable,[17] but statutes in other states may apply their flat time limit only to interests retained by the grantor, leaving the duration

---

15. Similar statutes include N.Y. Real Prop. Acts. Law § 612 (10 years) and Va. Code Ann. § 8.01-255.1 (10 years). California's statutory period is five years. Cal. Civ. Code § 885.030.

16. Ill. Stat. ch. 765, 330/4. In North Carolina, the time limit is 60 years. N.C. Gen. Stat. § 41-32. The time limit does not apply to interests held by a charity or governmental body or to interests in oil, gas, or minerals. In Maryland, the limit is 30 years. Md. Code Ann., Real Prop. § 6-101.

17. *See* Hiller v. County of Anoka, 529 N.W.2d 426 (Minn. Ct. App. 1995).

of executory interests to be controlled by the Rule Against Perpetuities. Maine has reached a similar result as a matter of common law, rather than by statute. In *Mildram v. Town of Wells*, 611 A.2d 84 (Me. 1992), the court held that a condition imposed in 1905 that a lot given to the town be used for a "Town House" was satisfied by the town's use of the property for the Town Hall until 1988. The court reasoned as follows:

> The . . . deed . . . contains no reference to duration. . . . [N]othing in the language of the condition suggests that Georgia Mildram's purpose was to require the perpetual maintenance of the property as a "Town House" regardless of all the changes that might occur in the town of Wells.

In other states, the common-law durational rules continue to apply, but it is necessary to record a notice of intent to preserve the interest at regular intervals to keep possibilities of reverter, rights of entry, and executory interests alive. New York, for example, requires recording between 27 and 30 years after the interest is created and re-recording every 9 to 10 years thereafter.[18] California requires recording at 30-year intervals.[19]

The Uniform Statutory Rule Against Perpetuities continues the common-law distinction between interests retained by the grantor, which are exempt from the Rule, and executory interests, which are subject to the Rule. It does enact a broad exemption for future interests that are not created in donative transfers, but that may not affect many executory interests attendant on defeasible fees because most are created in donative transactions.

We end this section with the question we asked earlier: Is all this complexity worth it? Why not have just one estate available for use when the grantor is willing to donate his property for a charitable or civic purpose but wants it back if the donee is no longer able or willing to use it as intended?

B. LIFE ESTATES AND REMAINDERS

Much of the common law of estates and future interests developed out of the efforts of the English landed aristocracy to keep land in the family over many generations. Although the social conditions that drove much of that development have greatly changed, property owners continue to look for ways to provide a secure future for their families. To this end, they often create estate plans built around one or more life estates followed by remainders and executory interests. Usually, these interests are created in trusts that mainly hold financial assets like stocks and bonds, but sometimes life estates are created in the family home or a valuable work of art without establishing a trust.

18. N.Y. Real Prop. Acts. Law § 345.
19. Cal. Civ. Code § 885.030.

1. Life Estates

Life estates are usually created to provide someone with income or a place to live, or both, during their lifetime, while assuring that on the life tenant's death, the property will go to persons selected by the grantor.

NELSON v. PARKER

Supreme Court of Indiana
687 N.E.2d 187 (Ind. 1997)

issue: BOEHM, J. The issue in this case is whether a deed "subject to a life estate" in a third person validly creates that life estate. We hold that it does and overrule earlier authority to the contrary.

Russell Nelson died in August 1994, three months after executing a warranty deed containing the following language:

Convey and warrant to

RUSSELL H. NELSON, DURING HIS LIFETIME, AND UPON HIS DEATH, SHALL PASS TO DANIEL NELSON.

SUBJECT TO: EASEMENTS, LIENS, ENCUMBRANCES, LIFE ESTATE IN IRENE PARKER, AND RESTRICTIONS OF RECORD.

Daniel was Russell's son. Irene Parker had lived with Russell for thirteen years prior to his death and remained on the property after he died. In September 1994 Daniel initiated this action to eject Parker, asserting that the deed did not effectively grant Parker a life estate. On cross-motions for summary judgment, the trial court agreed with Parker that she held a valid life estate and granted her motion for summary judgment. The court concluded that the object of deed construction is to ascertain the intent of the parties. Looking at the language of the deed as a whole, the court found that Russell intended to create a life estate in Parker. Daniel appealed.

In the trial court, both parties based their contention on their view of the grantor's intent. In the Court of Appeals Daniel made a new argument. He characterized the "subject to a life estate" language as improperly "reserving" an interest in a stranger to the deed. A "reservation" is "[a] clause in a deed or other instrument of conveyance by which the grantor creates, and reserves to himself, some right, interest, or profit in the estate granted, which had no previous existence as such, but is first called into being by the instrument reserving it; such as rent, or an easement." *BLACK'S LAW DICTIONARY* 1307 (6th ed. 1990). As the definition suggests, at common law a grantor could reserve an interest only for the grantor, but <u>not</u> for a third person, or "stranger" to the deed.[1] Words of reservation were not considered to be words of "grant" and so could not create an interest in another. Daniel cited this Court's decision in Ogle v. Barker, 68 N.E.2d 550 (Ind. 1946) which upheld this common law rule. Because Parker was a "stranger to the deed," Daniel argued, the reservation of a life estate to her was void.

The Court of Appeals accepted Daniel's characterization of the "subject to" language as a reservation but declined to follow the common law rule. Rather, . . . the court found the grantor's intent to be controlling. In affirming judgment for Parker, the court found that Russell's intent to create a life estate in Parker was clear from the deed's language and the surrounding circumstances at the time of the deed's execution. More importantly, the court analyzed and rejected the rule upheld in *Ogle* that a grantor cannot by reservation convey a life estate in real property to a party who is a stranger to the deed. The court noted that the rule's validity had already been questioned in Brademas v. Hartwig, 369 N.E.2d 954 (Ind. Ct. App. 1977). In *Brademas*, the court followed § 472 of the *Restatement of Property* and held that a reservation in a deed of an easement to a third party was valid when the intention of the parties was "patently evident." In rejecting Daniel's argument, the Court of Appeals also commented that the common law rule was derived from efforts, dating back to feudal times, to limit conveyance by deed as a substitute for livery by seisin. *Nelson*, 670 N.E.2d at 964 (citing Willard v. First Church of Christ Scientist, Pacifica, 498 P.2d 987, 989 (Cal. 1972) (explaining the history of the rule and concluding that "it is clearly an inapposite feudal shackle today")). Noting that other jurisdictions had also decided against the wisdom of the rule, the court held that Russell's intent to create a life estate in Parker trumped application of the common law rule. We granted transfer because of the apparent conflict between the Court of Appeals opinion and the decision of this Court in *Ogle*.

. . . In view of the plain language of the deed, the fact that the life estate language was underscored, and the circumstance that Parker had lived in the house as Russell's companion for thirteen years, we agree with the trial court and the Court of Appeals that Russell's intent to create a life estate in Parker is clearly reflected in this record. The question then becomes whether *stare decisis* requires adherence to *Ogle*.

Although it is arguable whether the "subject to" language created a "reservation" in the first place, we agree with the Court of Appeals that the common law rule upheld in *Ogle* serves no practical purpose today. It is a trap for the unwary and if enforced serves only to frustrate the intent of the grantor. Inadvertent use of the word "reservation," or other clumsy effort to grant an interest in land should not frustrate an otherwise clear intent based on mindless adherence to a formal and outdated rule. . . .

Not all courts agree. . . . Estate of Thomson v. Wade, 509 N.E.2d 309 (N.Y. 1987), appears to be the case most frequently cited in support of the common

---

1.   At common law, a "reservation" is distinct from an "exception." A reservation carves out a new interest in the property for the grantor, for example a life estate or an easement. An exception excludes part of the property from the conveyance, retaining the interest for the grantor, for example, a conveyance of Blackacre except for 30 acres on the northeast corner. In modern cases, the terms "reservation" and "exception" have become interchangeable, with no penalty for incorrect usage. Roger A. Cunningham et al., The Law of Property 718 & n.55 (1984).

law rule. In that case, the New York Court of Appeals upheld the rule, noting that any frustration it caused to the grantor's intent could easily be avoided by a direct conveyance. A grantor could first convey an easement to a "third person" and then convey the fee, literally "subject to" an already existing easement. Although this procedure avoids frustrating the grantor's intent, there is no reason to force the grantor to do in two steps what could otherwise be done in one. Further, as the Indiana Court of Appeals remarked in *Brademas,* the *Ogle* rule did not prevent the grantor from first reserving to himself then conveying the reserved interest to a third party. Thus, under *Ogle,* Russell could have "reserved" a life estate to himself, and then simply conveyed it to Parker without encountering any legal impediment. The sum of this is that the rule functions solely as an obstacle to conveying interests in land, but serves no purpose. This is not a function consistent with our modern preference for effecting the grantor's clear intent.

Estate of Thomson concluded that the common law rule protects the rights of bona fide purchasers and avoids conflicts of ownership. But the court did not explain how the rule served these ends. In this case, Daniel's interest appears from the deed to be a fee simple interest subject to a life estate. We see no reason and no policy to be furthered by imposing an artificial and unintended result on the parties. A bona fide purchaser of an identical interest would have reasonably believed that the interest was, as the deed said, "subject to" a life estate. Any examiner of an abstract or title policy for this property is fairly notified of Parker's interest. Thus, as the *Willard* court noted, a purchaser faced with this language would assume it to be at least potentially valid and pay less for property erroneously encumbered by "reservation" or by "subject to" language, only to receive a windfall if the interest is later deemed void because of the common law rule. In addition to working this sort of inequitable result generally, the rule would work an unfair, if not inequitable, result in this case. Daniel presumably knew the contents of the deed and knew of Russell's intentions when the deed was drafted in May, but did not contest Parker's interest until after the alleged error became uncorrectable by reason of Russell's death in August. As to the concern expressed in *Estate of Thomson* for conflicts of ownership, the rule as relied upon by Daniel fueled an otherwise nonexistent conflict.

Finally, *Estate of Thomson* relied on the public policy favoring certainty in the area of property law: "[where] settled rules are necessary and necessarily relied upon, stability and adherence to precedent are generally more important than a better or even a 'correct' rule of law." We recognize the importance of settled rules in property law. Stability is desirable so planners can predict the outcome of the use of formulaic language and rely on achieving the conventional result. But it is hard to imagine who reasonably and in good faith could rely on a failed reservation clause to obliterate an apparently intended interest. This Court is not persuaded that the public policy of promoting settled rules requires adherence to a vestige of ancient conveyancing law that has only pernicious effects. To the extent *Ogle* holds otherwise, it is overruled.[4]

The trial court's grant of summary judgment in favor of Parker is affirmed.

---

4. Daniel argues that *Brademas,* and other cases circumventing or rejecting the common law rule, primarily concerned easements and not life estates and that the rule should still apply to life estates. The distinction is relevant, he contends, because conveyance of an easement does not create an ownership interest in the property whereas a life estate does. Although this may be true, it is of little significance. All the reasons for rejecting the rule as applied to easements are of equal validity as applied to life estates. . . .

Notes and Questions

1. How should Russell Nelson have structured the gift to Irene Parker to avoid the problem presented by the old common-law rule?

2. What was the purpose of using the life estates here? Are there any circumstances under which Russell might have wanted Daniel to be able to take possession of the property before Irene's death? If so, he could have made the life estate subject to conditions. A life estate, like a fee simple, may be made defeasible.

3. *State of the title.* During the three months after the deed became effective and before he died, Russell had a life estate, followed by a remainder for life in Irene, and a remainder in fee simple absolute in Daniel. When Russell died, Irene's life estate became possessory (no longer a remainder) and Daniel continued to hold a remainder in fee simple absolute. When Irene dies, Daniel's estate will become a present possessory fee simple absolute.

4. *Irene's life estate.* Like most other interests in property, Irene's life estate is alienable. She can rent out the property to others during her lifetime, or transfer her life estate to someone else if she wants to. Of course, whatever she transfers to someone else, whether by lease or otherwise, terminates when she dies. If she does transfer her entire life estate to another, the transferee is said to have an "estate *pur autre vie,*" which means an estate for the life of another.

5. *Daniel's remainder.* He owns the fee simple estate, but he is not entitled to possession until Irene Parker's death. What happens if Daniel dies before Irene? Because his remainder is in fee simple, it does not terminate at his death and passes either under his will, or by intestacy if he has no will. Like Irene's life estate, Daniel's remainder is alienable. He can sell it or give it away, and if he does so, his transferee will get the right to possession at Irene's death and the fee simple absolute.

IN RE ESTATE OF JACKSON

Supreme Court of South Dakota
508 N.W.2d 374 (S.D. 1993)

PER CURIAM. Ileane Brosnan appeals a probate court order . . . relating to the distribution of insurance proceeds stemming from hail damage to the decedent's house. . . .

In February of 1968, Mary Jackson . . . conveyed certain real property, including a house, to Iola Miller . . . and Ileane Brosnan . . . . However, Jackson retained a life estate in the real property and lived in the house until 1989 when she entered a nursing home. While she was in the nursing home, Jackson (or her guardian) continued to pay taxes and purchase insurance on the house.

A hail storm during May of 1991 caused substantial damage to the house. Jackson's insurance company examined the damage and began to process the claim. Jackson died on June 1, 1991. Miller was appointed executrix of Jackson's estate. Acting upon advice from the estate's attorney, Miller distributed the insurance proceeds ($5,713.50) between herself and Brosnan. . . . Miller and Brosnan sold the house to Darrel Jackson for $7,000.

We deduce from the record that the estate's attorney changed his mind and decided the insurance proceeds belonged to the estate and should be distributed among the residuary beneficiaries. Brosnan objected when the estate's final accounting was presented for court approval. Brosnan filed a claim against the estate for necessary repairs due to the hail damage. Thereupon, the circuit court, acting as the probate court, approved the final accounting holding that the insurance proceeds belonged to Jackson's estate. Brosnan appeals.

Miller and Brosnan owned the house except for the life estate retained by Jackson. Jackson, as a life tenant, could use the property in any manner except that she could "do no act to the injury of the inheritance." SDCL 43-8-1. As a life tenant, Jackson also had the obligation to "keep the buildings and fences in repair from ordinary waste, and must pay the taxes and other annual charges, and a just proportion of the extraordinary assessments benefitting the whole inheritance." SDCL 43-8-2. In other words, Jackson was responsible to make necessary repairs to the house. . . . If she failed to make such repairs, the remaindermen . . . would have been able to institute an action against her alleging waste. *See* Annotation, *Right of Contingent Remaindermen to Maintain Action for Damages for Waste*, 56 A.L.R. 3d 677 (Supp. 1992).

When Jackson died, the life estate ended. The probate court is specifically authorized to "fully and effectually adjudicate" the termination of a life estate. However, the probate court focused only on the issue of who was entitled to receive the insurance proceeds. The probate court correctly concluded that since Jackson would have received those insurance proceeds if she had lived, her estate should receive them upon her death. The probate court failed to consider Jackson's responsibility to repair the life estate property. Since the house was damaged during her life estate, Jackson had an obligation to make necessary repairs. After her death, her estate was responsible to fulfill that obligation. We reverse.

Notes and Questions

1. What purpose did Mary Jackson's February 1968 transfer to Miller and Brosnan serve? If her purpose was to allow the house to pass to them on her death without probate, was the transfer a good idea? What if Mary Jackson had decided she needed to sell the house to raise money? What if Miller or Brosnan had died before Jackson and Jackson had decided she wanted to leave the property to someone else? As you will learn in wills and trusts, a revocable inter vivos trust is a far better vehicle for avoiding probate than a deeded transfer of fee simple with retained life estate.

2. If Jackson had not carried insurance that covered the hail damage, should she have been liable to make the repairs? The usual rule is that the life tenant is liable for ordinary repairs, but not to make extraordinary repairs or to rebuild structures damaged or destroyed without her fault. But how helpful is this rule? Surely, the hail storm that caused the damage in this case was not Mary Jackson's fault. On the other hand, the repairs may have been "ordinary" in the sense that the ordinary owner of a house like this one would have repaired the damage rather than abandoning the house, or tearing it down and building a new one.

3. Would it make more sense to conceptualize the life tenant's duty as a duty to act as a reasonable person would under similar circumstances? The question then might become whether an ordinary reasonable person holding a life estate in a house would make the repairs or would carry casualty insurance that covers the loss in question. But, does it make sense to ask what the ordinary life tenant would do? Life estates like this are relatively rare, and the kinds of repairs that a rational life tenant would make would depend very much on how long the life tenant believes he or she will be around to enjoy them. Measured by that standard, Mary Jackson almost certainly would not have done anything other than board up the holes to keep rain and intruders out.

Would it make more sense, then, to require the life tenant to act as an ordinary fee simple owner of this kind of property would act? If the ordinary owner would make the repairs or carry casualty insurance that covered the losses, the life tenant should be liable for damage that results to the remaindermen from her failure to do so. But is this fair to the life tenant? Isn't she being forced to pay for something that may outlast her life interest? Should the remaindermen be charged with the value they receive from any excess value created by the life tenant? At what point do the costs of complexity in the law outweigh the benefits gained in achieving fairness between the present and future interest holders?

Waste

The creator of a life estate is free to specify the rights and obligations of the life tenant. To the extent that he or she fails (or chooses not) to do so, the law of waste provides the default rules governing the life tenant's responsibilities for care and conservation of the property. The *Jackson* case applies generally accepted rules about the life tenant's responsibility to make repairs, but as you can see, the rules are not terribly satisfactory. A lesson you should take from this is that if you are going to draft or review an instrument that creates a life estate, you should pay careful attention to the provisions spelling out the life tenant's responsibilities.

Kinds of waste. Waste may be classified as "voluntary" or "involuntary." The *Jackson* case involved involuntary or "permissive waste," which results from failure to make repairs or pay the ordinary carrying charges of the property (taxes, mortgage payments, etc.). Voluntary waste, by contrast, results from intentional acts of the life tenant that cause substantial change to the value or character of the property. The basic idea is that the remaindermen or reversioners are entitled to receive the property more or less in the same state that it was in when the life tenant received it. The life tenant is not entitled to damage "the inheritance" by trashing the house, stripping the top soil, harvesting healthy timber, or depleting oil and gas reservoirs. However, there are exceptions. If the property was already being used for mining or oil and gas production before creation of the life estate, the life tenant is entitled to continue working the open mines and wells but is generally not entitled to open new ones. This is called the "open mine doctrine." Similarly, the life tenant is entitled to cut wood for firewood, fences, and other domestic use on the premises.

If the life tenant increases the value of the property by making permanent changes in its use, substantially altering structures, or building additional structures on the property, the activity is called "ameliorative" or "meliorating" waste. Although there is no monetary damage, the future interest holders may be entitled to enjoin the life tenant from making threatened changes or to require restoration of the property to its previous state, if possible. However, there is substantial authority that the life tenant is entitled to make changes that are necessary to permit a reasonable use of the property so long as the value of the property is not diminished.

Forfeiture for waste. In *Town of Stratford v. Mudre,* 1993 WL 489500 (Conn. Super. Ct. 1993), the property was sold at a tax foreclosure sale after the life tenant failed to pay the real property taxes. A surplus of $77,000 remained after the taxes and costs had been paid. The remaindermen claimed all of it on the grounds that the life tenant had forfeited her estate by failing to pay the taxes. The court disagreed, ordering that the proceeds be placed in a federally insured interest-bearing account and that the interest be paid to the life tenant during her lifetime. The court noted that the life estate is forfeited for waste only where expressly provided for by statute.

A North Carolina statute, N.C. Gen. Stat. § 1-538, provides:

> In all cases of waste, when judgment is against the defendant, the court may give judgment for treble the amount of the damages assessed by the jury, and also that the plaintiff recover the place wasted, if the damages are not paid on or before a day to be named in the judgment.

The remedies provided by the North Carolina statute are the same as those provided in England by the Statute of Gloucester, which was enacted in 1278. In some states, the Statute of Gloucester may be regarded as part of the common law "received" into the state's common law. In others, as noted in *Town of Stratford, supra,* additional statutory authority like that provided in North Carolina is required.

For more information on the law of waste, a good beginning point is the quite extensive treatment in Chapter 4 of William B. Stoebuck & Dale Whitman, *The Law of Property* (3d ed. 2000). That chapter, titled "Relations Between Owners of Present and Future Estates and Interests in the Same Realty or Personalty," also covers waste by lessees and holders of defeasible fee simple estates.

Alienability of Life Estates; Sale to Support Life Tenant

A life estate is fully alienable unless subject to a valid restraint on alienation, but the life tenant cannot convey more than she has—an estate that ends when she dies. If she does transfer it, the recipient has an "estate *pur autre vie*" (law French for an estate for the life of another). As a practical matter, few people want to buy an estate *pur autre vie*—they want a fee simple absolute. Realistically, then, the life tenant can't sell the property unless the remaindermen or reversioners are willing to join in the conveyance. If they refuse, there may be nothing the life tenant can do about it.

However, if the property cannot generate sufficient income to pay the carrying charges or make repairs necessary to maintain its value, a court may exercise its inherent equitable powers to order sale of the property to preserve the interests of both the life tenant and the future interest holders, even in the absence of statute. Statutes in many states do authorize such sales, although the circumstances in which the sale may be ordered vary substantially.

In *Baker v. Weedon*, 262 So. 2d 641 (Miss. 1972), the court ordered sale of part of a 152-acre farm to provide funds to care for the life tenant, who was 73 years old and in economic distress. She had been given the life estate in 1932 by her husband's will. The remaindermen resisted sale of the property because the property's value was significantly appreciating. Even though the farm still generated sufficient income to pay the carrying charges (it was rented for $1,300 per year), the court held the sale was necessary to provide for the reasonable needs of the life tenant. The estimated market value of the property at the time of trial was $168,500. The case was remanded to order a sale of so much of the property as would be necessary to generate a fund that, invested, would yield sufficient income to provide for the reasonable needs of the life tenant.

Another impediment to the sale of the property may arise if some of the remaindermen or reversioners have not yet been born or identified. For example, if the remainder is to the life tenant's issue surviving her, *per stirpes*, the issue who will take cannot be determined until the death of the life tenant. Similarly, if the reversion passes through the residuary clause of the grantor's will, it might go to a trust for the grantor's descendants living 90 years after the date of the grantor's death. If the court orders a sale of the property, the interests of the unborn and unidentified future interest holders are safeguarded by an order that the proceeds be held in trust and invested to pay the income to the life tenant and, on her death, to distribute the proceeds to whoever is entitled.

[handwritten margin note: future interest of unborn child protected throughout the sale.]

Sometimes the life tenant would prefer a lump-sum distribution to receiving the income generated by the proceeds over her lifetime. It is possible to value a life estate by estimating the remaining life expectancy of the life tenant and estimating the market interest rate that will prevail over the rest of the life tenant's life expectancy, but the valuation is likely to prove quite different from what would happen if the funds were retained and invested. Predictions based on actuarial tables will not predict how long this life tenant will live and assumptions as to future interest rates are often wrong. One poor soul bought the remainder in a French apartment held by an elderly life tenant. The life tenant lived to be 120, outlasting the remainderman by a considerable number of years. For these reasons, courts are usually reluctant to order a lump-sum distribution. However, they occasionally do so, particularly if there is some indication that the grantor's intent would not be frustrated by such a disposition. *See, e.g., Estate of Hewitt*, 721 A.2d 1082 (Pa. 1998).

2.   Remainders, Reversions, and Executory Interests

When a grantor gives a life estate to someone, the grantor usually also gives away the remainder, by specifying who is to get the property at the death of the life tenant. If the grantor fails to do so, or if the remainder the grantor creates fails for some reason, the grantor still owns an interest in the property—the right to possession after the life tenant's death, in fee simple absolute. When held by the grantor, this future interest is called a reversion. For historical reasons, a reversion is always deemed to be a vested interest, even though it may or may not ever become possessory.

Life estates that are not in trust are usually followed by very simple remainders, as in both *Nelson v. Parker* and *Estate of Jackson*, or occasionally by a reversion in the grantor. Usually, no provision is made for the death of the remainderman before the life tenant, or other contingencies that might change what the grantor would want to do with the property, like bankruptcy, divorce, marriage, or birth of children, for example. All of these contingencies could be dealt with by conditions that would transfer the property to someone else on various contingencies, but legal life estates like this are usually created without benefit of counsel, and in any event, are usually much better handled by using a trust. Revocable inter vivos trusts, sometimes called "living trusts" are now very commonly used to hold family property and will transfer it at death without incurring the expense of probate. The kinds of conditions that can be attached to legal remainders, and in fact, are often attached to future interests in trust are briefly described here. You will want to familiarize yourself with the basic concepts and vocabulary, but can leave detailed study of the use of these interests to a course in wills and trusts.

When conditions are attached to remainder interests, more labels come into play. A remainder that is subject to no conditions is called an **indefeasibly vested remainder**. A remainder subject to a condition precedent is a **contingent remainder**. In talking about remainders, it is important to distinguish between **vesting in interest** and **vesting in possession**. A remainder is vested in interest if there is no unfulfilled condition precedent attached to the interest, but does not vest in possession until the life estate terminates.

A condition (which is something that might or might not happen) may be either precedent or subsequent. A **condition precedent** is something that has to happen before someone gets an interest. A remainder with a condition precedent is called a **contingent remainder**. If the condition happens, the remainder vests. If the condition precedent never happens, the contingent remainder never **vests** and the holder will never be entitled to possession. The right to possession on death of the life tenant will pass to an alternate contingent remainderman, if there is one, or, if none, to the holder of the reversion.

A **condition subsequent** is something that, if it happens, will take away the remainder and the interest will either return to the grantor or pass to someone else. A remainder subject to a condition subsequent is called a **remainder subject to complete divestment**. If the condition becomes impossible while the life tenant is still alive, the remainder becomes an indefeasibly vested remainder. If the condition has not happened before the life tenant dies, the remainder vests in possession and, usually, the condition expires and the holder will have a present interest in fee simple absolute. (If the condition does not expire on the life tenant's death, and can still happen, the holder has a present fee simple on condition subsequent.)

- *Example:* To Irene for life, remainder to Daniel *if he survives her.* This is a condition precedent. Daniel has a contingent remainder and the grantor has a reversion, which will become possessory on Irene's death if Daniel in fact predeceases her. Since Russell is dead, the reversion will pass to his heirs or under his will.
- *Example:* To Irene for life, remainder to Daniel, *but if he dies before* Irene, to First Church. This is a condition subsequent. Daniel's remainder is a fee simple subject to an executory interest, but it is called a vested remainder subject to complete divestment. First Church has an executory interest.

Remainders are commonly given to children or issue (lineal descendants) of the grantor or other relatives. If the parent of the possible children, or parents of possible issue, are alive, this remainder is called a **class gift**, and so long as it is possible that more children or issue will be born before the remainder vests in possession, the remainder is described as **subject to open** or **subject to partial divestment** because, if additional children are born, they, too will be entitled to a share, which will decrease the shares of the previously born children.

- *Example:* To Susana for life, remainder to Susana's children. At the time of the gift, Susana is alive has two children, Maria and Kathy. *Result:* Maria and Kathy have *vested remainders subject to partial divestment* by the birth of additional children.

If a class gift is contingent, it is not usually described as also being subject to partial divestment or subject to open, even though in fact the interests of existing class members will be cut down in size if additional members come into the class.

For historical reasons, no longer relevant, the law has distinguished between remainders and **executory interests**. Even though contingent remainders and contingent executory interests are treated exactly the same in modern law, judges and lawyers still use the labels. The difference between them is that a future interest is a remainder only if it can vest immediately on expiration of a life estate. If it divests a fee simple interest, it is an executory interest.

- *Example:* To A for life, remainder to B if B survives A. *Result:* B has a contingent remainder because the remainder can vest immediately on A's death if B is still alive.
- *Example:* To A for life, remainder to B if B survives A by 30 days. B has a contingent executory interest because the remainder cannot vest until 30 days after A's death. In the interim, the grantor's reversion becomes possessory in fee simple subject to the condition subsequent that if B survives for 30 days, B's interest will divest the reversion.

Note: The Importance of Classifying Future Interests

For the Rule Against Perpetuities, it is important to classify interests into those retained by the grantor, and, among those given to others, to classify interests into vested, contingent, and class gifts (vested subject to partial divestment). Interests retained by the grantor (reversions, possibilities of reverter, rights of entry) are not subject to the Rule, even if contingent (they are deemed vested). Of the interests given to others, indefeasibly vested interests and vested interests subject to complete divestment are not subject to the Rule. Only contingent interests (not retained by the grantor) and class gifts are subject to the Rule Against Perpetuities.

In determining whether creditors have the right to reach future interests, it may be important to distinguish between vested and contingent interests. The same may be true in determining whether a particular beneficiary has an interest that can be transferred during life or by will. Whether an interest is vested or contingent may also affect a determination whether the holder of a future interest may go into possession after termination of the prior estates but before the occurrence of a condition.

- *Example:* O to A for life, remainder to B at his age of 21. But if B fails to reach 21, to revert to O. A dies when B is 19. *Result:* If B's interest is construed to be contingent on reaching 21, the property reverts to O, subject to divestment if B reaches 21. If B's interest is vested subject to complete divestment, B is entitled to possession immediately, subject to divestment if he dies under 21.

Up through the end of the 19th century, and for some time into the 20th century, it was important to distinguish between contingent remainders and executory interests because contingent remainders were destructible while executory interests were not. Since the doctrine of destructibility of remainders was abolished, however, there has been no reason to differentiate a contingent remainder from a contingent executory interest. They are treated the same for all important purposes. It is only from habit that lawyers and judges continue to identify them as two separate interests.

C. THE TRUST

The trust is a device that allows you to split the title of property into two parallel and simultaneous titles called the "legal" title and the "equitable" title. The legal title is given to the trustee, who is charged with the responsibility of holding and managing the property for the sole benefit of the beneficiaries, who hold the equitable title. The same present estates and future interests can be created in the equitable title as in the legal title. Trusts are very useful whenever unified management is desirable for an asset in which several people have interests. They provide an excellent way to manage property for the benefit of minors, incompetents, spendthrifts, and other folks who either don't want or aren't capable of the responsibility for investing and caring for their assets.

Trusts are also very commonly used as a will substitute to pass property on at death without having it go through probate. The owner of the property declares himself to be the trustee of the property for the benefit of himself for life, with remainder to another. The owner retains a power to amend or revoke the trust, thus retaining flexibility in disposing of the property during his life. This type of trust is called a **revocable inter vivos trust**. In a typical situation, a couple will declare themselves trustees of family property for themselves for their lifetimes, and on the death of the survivor, to their then living children and issue of deceased children. If Russell Parker and Mary Jackson had been well advised, they would have used this type of trust, rather than granting their beneficiaries indefeasible fee simple interests subject to legal life estates.

The concept of parallel legal and equitable titles to land, and other assets, traces back to the medieval practice of conveying land "to uses," a conveyance to someone (the *feoffee to uses*) with a provision that the land would be held for the use (*ad opus*) of a beneficiary (the *cestui que use*).[20] Various explanations are offered for the practice, including the Crusades, which took landowners out of the country; the vows of poverty of Franciscan Friars, which prevented them from holding title in their own names; dishonesty (keeping assets from a creditor, or from being forfeited for treason); and avoidance of feudal dues. The common-law courts did not recognize the interests of the *cestui*, but by the 15th century, the King's Chancellor had begun to protect the interests of the *cestui* and to develop some consistent principles for dealing with uses. When Henry VIII needed additional funds[21] after breaking with Rome, he managed to persuade Parliament to enact the Statute of Uses in 1536. That statute had the effect of transferring the legal title to the beneficiary, but within a short time, it was decided that if the feoffee to uses had active duties to perform for the *cestui*, the Statute did not apply. Thus was born the modern trust, which is still within the jurisdiction of equity (or Chancery, the separate court system that grew up around the King's Chancellor). The old feoffee to uses has become the trustee, who holds the legal title, and the *cestui* has become the beneficiary, who holds the equitable title.

Trusts are very frequently used in estate planning — the process of arranging a person's assets so that they provide maximum flexibility and protection for the owner and the owner's family during life and provide an orderly mechanism for transmitting wealth on to future generations. "Dynastic" trusts — trusts wealthy people set up for their descendants or other relatives to last as long as the law allows — seem to be gaining in popularity in recent years, in part because of a substantial exemption in the federal generation-skipping tax (a companion to the federal estate and gift tax, which taxes property given away during life and property owned at death). Recent changes in the Rule Against Perpetuities, which we take up next, have made it possible — at least for now — to set up perpetual dynastic trusts in several states, and 90-year trusts in others.

One other point about trusts is that the usual rules about restraints on alienation do not apply. The trustee can be directed not to sell the trust property, and the beneficiary's interest can be subjected to a "spendthrift" clause that prohibits the beneficiary from transferring or borrowing against his interest and prevents his creditors from reaching the trust assets. You will learn more about trusts if you take a course in trusts and wills, trusts and estates, or estate planning.

---

20. The beneficiary is still sometimes referred to as the "*cestui*" in modern law. The name comes from the law French phrase "*cestui a que use le feoffment fuit fait*," which means the person for whose use the conveyance was made. Feoffment was about the only legal method used for transferring title to land until the Statute of Uses in 1536, and remained in use until the Statute of Frauds, which required a writing, was enacted in 1677.

21. The King's revenues were substantially impacted by uses because he was entitled, as feudal overlord, to feudal dues. By getting rid of uses, he was able to restore the value of his dues. To understand how all this worked, you will need to consult one of the works on the history of English law, like A.W. Brian Simpson, Uses and the Statute, in An Introduction to the History of the Land Law ch. VIII (2d ed. 1986).

D. THE RULES AGAINST PERPETUITIES AND OTHER DOCTRINES THAT DESTROY FUTURE INTERESTS

In many states, time limits are imposed on the length of time that the ownership of property can remain split up into present and future interests, because split interests make it difficult to sell the property and often limit the amount of investment that will be made in the property because it is difficult to get loans to make improvements and because a present possessor with a limited interest is not likely to want to make investments that benefit others. There is also a sentiment that property should be controlled by the living, not by "the dead hand"—the decisions as to ownership made by previous owners now long gone or long dead (usually, both).

Over the centuries, the common law developed several different devices that had the effect of reuniting the present possessory interest and the fee simple absolute. By the 15th century, two methods for converting a fee tail into a fee simple were recognized (the "fine" and the "common recovery"). The **Rule in Shelley's Case**, developed in the 14th century, converted a remainder in the heirs of the grantee into a vested remainder in the grantee. Thus, a conveyance to "A for life, remainder to A's heirs" gave A the fee simple absolute. The **Doctrine of Worthier Title** operated similarly on a remainder to the grantor's heirs, converting it to a reversion in the grantor. Thus, a conveyance from O "to A for life, remainder to O's heirs" resulted in a life estate in A and a reversion in O.

Another doctrine that worked serious havoc on future interests was the **Destructibility of Contingent Remainders Doctrine**. It destroyed remainders that were still subject to a condition precedent when the prior estate terminated.

> *Example 1:* O to A for life, remainder to A's children who reach 21. A dies when his children are ages 17 and 18. The remainders are destroyed because they are still subject to a condition precedent. *Result:* O's reversion becomes possessory and O owns the property in fee simple absolute.

The Destructibility Doctrine could be combined with the "merger" doctrine to destroy contingent remainders even before the prior estate terminated. The merger doctrine (which still exists) is that if one person holds two estates in the same piece of property, and there are no intervening estates held by someone else, the two estates will merge into the larger estate. The wrinkle added by the Destructibility Doctrine was that two vested estates held by the same person could merge even if they were separated by a contingent remainder—the contingent remainder was destroyed.

> *Example 2:* O to A for life, remainder to A's children who reach 21. O subsequently transfers O's reversion to A. *Result:* The contingent remainders are destroyed, and A's life estate and reversion merge to give A the present possessory fee simple absolute.
>
> *Example 3:* O to A for life, remainder to B's children who survive A. O and A convey their interests to C and his heirs. *Result:* C's life estate and reversion merge and C has a present possessory fee simple absolute.

Lawyers eventually found ways around all of these old rules (except merger), often by using leasehold estates and executory interests instead of life estates and contingent remainders, and the rules were either too old and enshrined in tradition to be adapted to meet the new conveyancing forms, or loopholes were tolerated because the rules operated to frustrate intent so often in situations that were not particularly threatening to the common good. Eventually, a more comprehensive method was developed—the **Rule Against Perpetuities**—which took its modern form in the 18th century. Even though the old rules became unnecessary at that point, they persisted well into the 20th century. However, they have all been pretty well abolished now, although some of them fairly recently (e.g., North Carolina abolished the Rule in Shelley's Case effective October 1, 1987). Since most of them were abolished by statutes that operated prospectively only, you may have to grapple with them, but we are not going to attempt to go into their intricacies here. You will find plenty of old treatises and cases that can teach you all you need to know if the need arises.

The Rule Against Perpetuities controls the dead hand by imposing a time limit on contingent interests and class gifts that are subject to open. Contingent interests you have already met—they are interests subject to a condition precedent (contingent remainders and executory interests). Class gifts you have also met—they are gifts made to a group of people who are defined by their relationship to somebody else, like the grantor, or the life tenant. Thus, a gift to the children of A is a class gift. So, too, are gifts to A's issue, to the descendants of the testator living 20 years after the date of his death, and to the grantor's siblings who survive the life tenant. The interesting thing about class gifts from the perpetuities viewpoint is that you can't tell how many people are going to become class members until the parents of possible class members are dead. This creates a problem because existing class members cannot join with the life tenant to convey a complete fee simple absolute to a prospective purchaser. Somebody else may later become a class member and demand his or her share of the property.

The Rule Against Perpetuities also applies to the beneficial interests in trusts, even though the trustee owns the legal fee simple title and usually has power to sell and borrow to make the trust property productive. The concern about dead hand control in trusts is that the beneficiaries are not able to make full use of their property, or make decisions as to its disposition, while it is in the hands of the trustee.

The Rule Against Perpetuities applies to contingent interests and class gifts, but not to reversionary interests. In its "pure" common-law form, the Rule destroys all contingent interests and class gifts that will not vest within 21 years after the death of an identifiable person who is alive at the time the future interest is created. (Identifiable people, known technically as "lives in being," must be identifiable at the time of the conveyance.) The Rule is very effective in reuniting all the elements of a fee simple absolute in the hands of people who are identified and have indefeasibly vested interests, that they can sell or partition[22] at least every 120 years or so (and often earlier). It also assures that

---

22. When two or more persons share a possessory estate in land, they are entitled to the court's help in dividing up the land either physically, or by ordering a sale and division of the proceeds. The action is known as an action for partition.

property held in trust will be distributed to the beneficiaries within the same time frame.

Although the Rule is very effective, it was too effective in its pure common-law form. Like the older doctrines it replaced, it often destroyed perfectly sensible family wealth transmission arrangements that posed no threat whatsoever to the public welfare.

Example 1: O conveyed to A for life, then to A's children who reach age 25. The class gift to A's children violates the Rule (and consequently is destroyed) because A might die leaving a child born after the date of the conveyance who is under the age of four at the time of A's death, and all of A's other children might die before that afterborn child reaches the age of four.

Why does this violate the Rule? If that happened and the afterborn child went on to reach age 25, that child would join the class and take a share that would cut down the size of the shares owned by A's other children who had already reached the age of 25. The class gift is void because, looked at from the date of O's conveyance, it is not certain that the class members will be able to convey a full fee simple absolute within 21 years after the death of A, or O, or A's children who were alive at the date of the conveyance.

But what if A doesn't have a child born after the date of the conveyance who is under the age of four when A dies? The children who reach 25 will be able to sell somebody a full fee simple absolute less than 21 years after A's death, but it doesn't matter. The class gift is still void. Why? The pure common-law form of the Rule, developed in the 18th century, and relentlessly applied throughout the 19th century and well into the 20th century, pays no attention to anything that happened after the date of the conveyance. What matters is certainty, as of the date of the creation of the future interest, that it cannot, under any circumstances, remain contingent for more than 21 years after the death of some identifiable person who was alive at the time the future interest was created.

Example 2: O conveyed to Mary for life, then to Mary's children and the survivor or survivors of them until the death of Mary's last child, and then to the then surviving daughters of John and Elizabeth. At the time of the conveyance, Mary had no children and John and Elizabeth, who were 80 years old, had four daughters.

The class gift to Mary's children is valid because the whole class will be identified (and able to convey the entire life estate) by the time of Mary's death, but the class gift to John and Elizabeth's daughters is void. Why? John and Elizabeth might have another daughter after the date of the conveyance. And Mary might have a child or children after the date of the conveyance. And Mary's last surviving child might live longer than 21 years after the deaths of O, Mary, John, Elizabeth, and the four daughters of John and Elizabeth who were alive at the date of the conveyance. And then the afterborn daughter of John and Elizabeth might live longer than all of Mary's children. If all of those things happened, the remainder in fee simple absolute would not vest until more than 21 years after the death of any life in being.

Does it matter that, in fact, Mary died five years after the date of the conveyance without having had children, the four daughters of John and Elizabeth were then alive, and John and Elizabeth died without having any more daughters? Absolutely not. The pure common-law Rule looked only to what might have happened given the facts that existed on the date of the conveyance. Does it matter that John and Mary were physically incapable of having any more children on that date? No. The pure common-law Rule presumed, irrebuttably, that a person could live to any age, could die at any time, and could have children at any time until he or she died, regardless of age or physical condition.

> *Example 3:* O to A for life, then to A's widow for life, then to A's issue living at the time of the widow's death. At the time of the conveyance A is married to B and has three children. The widow's interest is valid because she will be identified by the time of A's death, but the class gift to A's issue is void. Why? A's wife might die after the date of the gift, or A might get a divorce, and then A might marry someone who was born after the date of the gift, and she might be his widow. A's afterborn widow might live more than 21 years longer than A and A's three children. At the time of her death, the remainder could vest in descendants of A who were all born after the date of the gift.

What if it turns out that A never gets divorced and his wife survives him? Or he indeed remarries, but he marries someone who was alive at the time the gift was made? You know the answer: It doesn't matter.

The absurdity of cases like these led Professors Leach and Casner, the original authors of this casebook, to lead a crusade to reform the Rule by adopting the "wait and see" principle, culminating in its adoption by the American Law Institute in the *Restatement, Second, of Property, Donative Transfers* (1983).[23] The wait-and-see principle is stated in § 1.4 of that Restatement. Although several versions of the wait-and-see principle can be found in various state statutes, the basic idea is that you wait to see what happens before deciding whether an interest is void. How long do you wait? At least until the death of the life tenant, and maybe until the deaths of the parents of potential class members, if the parents were lives in being. Maybe longer. What do you wait for? To see whether any of the interests vest, or become certain to vest (or fail), within 21 years after the death of a life in being. What if they don't? The interests are void.

What happens to interests that violate the Rule? Under the common-law Rule, they are destroyed. In modern law, they are often reformed to comply with the Rule, using the *cy pres* principle. (That means the court rewrites the instrument creating the future interest so that the interest will vest within 21 years after the death of a life in being, sticking as close as possible to the grantor's intended disposition.)

---

23. *See, e.g.,* W. Barton Leach, *Perpetuities in Perspective: Ending the Rule's Reign of Terror,* 65 Harv. L. Rev. 721, 739-45 (1952). "Wait and see" was adopted by the Institute only after heated debates at the 1978 and 1979 Annual Meetings. Those debates pitted Professor Powell, Reporter for the First Restatement of Property, against Professor Casner, Reporter for the Second Restatement, in what Professor Donahue called the Battle of the Titans, *Continuation of Discussion of Restatement of the Law, Second, Property, Tentative Draft No. 1,* 55 A.L.I. Proc. 289 (1979). It is interesting to remember that Professor Powell brought Professor Casner into the American Law Institute in 1935 to work as an associate reporter for the First Restatement while Casner was still a graduate student at Columbia. Siding with Powell in the debates were Professors Lusky, Berger, and Rohan. Professors Stein, Donahue, Maudsley, and Heckerling sided with Casner. *Discussion of Restatement of the Law, Second, Property, Tentative Draft No. 1—Part 1,* 56 A.L.I. Proc. 466 (1980). The debates are reproduced verbatim in the Proceedings.

Some additional reforms have been introduced in some states by statutes that create irrebuttable presumptions that the surviving spouse of a life in being will also be a life in being, and that people below and above certain ages won't have children after the date the future interest is created.

In 1986, the National Conference of Commissioners on Uniform State Laws promulgated a statutory rule against perpetuities that incorporates elements of all the earlier reforms: wait and see, an irrebuttable presumption that a widow is a life in being, and reformation. It also provides an alternative 90-year vesting period. Although sharply criticized by leading scholars in the field,[24] the uniform act (USRAP) has been adopted by at least 29 states. Its principal provisions are as follows:

UNIFORM STATUTORY RULE AGAINST PERPETUITIES (USRAP)[25]

1. A nonvested property interest is invalid unless one of the following conditions is satisfied:

(a) When the interest is created, it is certain to vest or terminate no later than 21 years after the death of an individual then alive.

(b) The interest either vests or terminates within 90 years after its creation.

In determining whether a nonvested property interest . . . is valid under this article, the possibility that a child will be born to an individual after the individual's death is disregarded.

2. In determining the validity of a nonvested property interest . . . an individual described as the spouse of an individual alive at the commencement of the perpetuities period shall be deemed to be an individual alive when the interest is created, whether or not the individual so described was then alive.

3. On petition of an interested person, a court shall reform a disposition in the manner that most closely approximates the transferor's manifested plan of distribution and is within the 90 years allowed . . . if any of the following conditions is satisfied:

(a) A nonvested property interest . . . becomes invalid under the statutory rule against perpetuities. . . .

(b) A class gift is not but might become invalid under the statutory rule against perpetuities . . . , and the time has arrived when the share of any class member is to take effect in possession or enjoyment.

(c) A nonvested property interest that is not [valid under the common-law Rule] . . . can vest but not within 90 years of its creation.

---

24. *See, e.g.*, Jesse Dukeminier, *The Uniform Statutory Rule Against Perpetuities: Ninety Years in Limbo*, 34 UCLA L. Rev. 1023 (1987); Ira M. Bloom, *Perpetuities Refinement: There Is an Alternative*, 62 Wash. L. Rev. 23 (1987); Susan F. French, *Ending the Perpetuities Wars of the Late Twentieth Century: A Better Reform Package*, in *Perpetuities: Three Essays in Honor of My Father*, 65 Wash. L. Rev. 323 (1990).

Professors Waggoner, author of USRAP, and Dukeminier engaged in a heated debate that can be found in Lawrence W. Waggoner, *Perpetuity Reform*, 81 Mich. L. Rev. 1718 (1983); Dukeminier, *Perpetuities: The Measuring Lives*, 85 Colum. L. Rev. 1648 (1985); Waggoner, *Perpetuities: A Perspective on Wait-and-See*, 85 Colum. L. Rev. 1714 (1985); Dukeminier, *A Response by Professor Dukeminier*, 85 Colum. L. Rev. 1730 (1985); Waggoner, *A Rejoinder by Professor Waggoner*, 85 Colum. L. Rev. 1739 (1985); and Dukeminier, *A Final Comment by Professor Dukeminier*, 85 Colum. L. Rev. 1742 (1985). The exchange grew more heated with Dukeminier, *The Uniform Statutory Rule Against Perpetuities: Ninety Years in Limbo*, *supra*, and Waggoner, *The Uniform Statutory Rule Against Perpetuities: The Rationale of the 90-Year Waiting Period*, 73 Cornell L. Rev. 157 (1988).

25. These provisions have been numbered for ease of presentation and several provisions of the Uniform Act have been omitted.

Criticism of USRAP has focused primarily on the 90-year period, which may lead to increased use of long-term trusts, and on the inability to reform future interests other than class gifts until 90 years have passed.

The most remarkable recent development in perpetuities law is the move to abolish it, at least for trusts where the trustee has the power to sell the assets. In the early 1980s, South Dakota and Wisconsin replaced the Rule Against Perpetuities with a rule invalidating future interests that suspend the power of alienation[26] for more than lives in being plus 30 years. If the trustee is given a power to sell the trust's assets, there is no time limit on when the beneficiaries' interests must vest. *See* S.D. Codified Laws Ann. §§ 43-5-1, 43-5-8 (adopted 1983) and Wis. Stat. Ann. § 700.16 (adopted 1981). Since 1986, when the generation-skipping tax with its then $1 million exemption (raised to $5 million and indexed for inflation beginning in 2012)[27] was enacted, at least 17 more states have exempted trusts from the Rule Against Perpetuities. In most states the exemption is conditioned on the trustee's having a power of sale, but giving the trustee a power of sale is routine. In 1999, Rhode Island abolished the Rule altogether, as did Idaho in 2008.[28] In addition to South Dakota, Idaho, Rhode Island, and Wisconsin, states in which perpetual trusts can now be created include Alaska, Arizona, Delaware, the District of Columbia, Illinois, Maine, Maryland, Missouri, Ohio, and Virginia. In addition, Wyoming allows 1,000-year trusts, Florida has extended the USRAP wait-and-see period to 360 years, and Washington allows 150-year trusts.[29] Driven by institutions offering professional trustee services and estate planners eager to capitalize on the opportunity to sell perpetual multi-million-dollar trusts, it appears that the limits on trust duration have been effectively abolished for wealthy people.

A front-page story in the Wall Street Journal[30] reported that estate plans of the newly wealthy increasingly include incentives for children to behave in ways in which parents approve. Atlanta Braves pitcher, Tom Glavine, for example, was said to be considering a provision that would pay his daughter a substantial amount if she becomes a stay-at-home mom. Other parents are reportedly including provisions to penalize children who do not use prenuptial agreements, who fail periodic drug tests, receive traffic tickets, or fail to engage in charitable work. Although the wealthy have always attached conditions to the family trusts, these new incentive trusts promise to give new meaning to the phrase "dead hand control." Have the reformers who abolished the Rule for trusts, but left it in place for other interests, gotten it all wrong?

---

26. "The power of alienation is suspended when there are no persons in being who, alone or in combination with others, can convey an absolute fee in possession of land, or full ownership of personalty." Wis. Stat. Ann. § 700.16(2).

27. Although most transfers in trust are subject to an estate or generation-skipping tax when property moves from one generation to the next, Congress has provided that each person can transfer a certain amount free of the tax. Once established, these trusts can go on for as long as the law allows without paying death or transfer taxes.

28. R.I. Gen. Laws § 34-11-38; Idaho Code § 55-111.

29. *See* Jesse Dukeminier & James E. Krier, *The Rise of the Perpetual Trust*, 50 UCLA L. Rev. 1303 (2003).

30. Monica Langley, *Trust Me, Baby: The House, the Money—It'll All Be Yours; There's Just One Thing*, Wall St. J., Nov. 17, 1999, at A1, right col.

Exemptions from the Common-Law Rule Against Perpetuities

The common-law Rule has never applied to future interests held by governmental or charitable organizations so long as the property vests in some qualified organization within the common-law period.

> *Example 1:* O conveys Blackacre to State University, but if State University fails to use Blackacre for agricultural research purposes, Blackacre shall pass to the Nature Conservancy. *Result:* The executory interest given to the Nature Conservancy is valid because the Nature Conservancy is a charitable organization and the present fee simple is vested in another charitable organization.

> *Example 2:* O conveys Blackacre to A, but if Blackacre is not used for agricultural purposes, then to the Nature Conservancy. *Result:* The executory interest given to the Nature Conservancy is void because A is not a charitable organization and the condition vesting the executory interest will not necessarily occur within lives in being plus 21 years.

The common law also exempts possibilities of reverter and rights of entry from the Rule, a position that probably never made very much sense, and certainly makes no sense today. As we saw in the section on defeasible fees, this exemption has led to a variety of other measures designed to limit the duration of these interests. USRAP continues this exemption.

Although the Rule Against Perpetuities is very poorly suited to addressing problems caused by commercial options to buy property in the future ("options in gross"), the common-law Rule has frequently been applied to invalidate them. Lawyers who draft options should know enough to limit the period in which the option can be exercised to 21 years, or to within 21 years of some specified person's death, but, unfortunately, the Rule is more familiar to trusts and estates lawyers than to commercial real estate lawyers, and, of course, many options are drawn up without involving lawyers at all. USRAP addresses this problem by exempting most future interests created in non-donative transactions from the Rule.

SYMPHONY SPACE, INC. v. PERGOLA PROPERTIES, INC.

Court of Appeals of New York
669 N.E.2d 799 (N.Y. 1996)

KAYE, Chief J. This case presents the novel question whether options to purchase commercial property are exempt from the prohibition against remote vesting embodied in New York's Rule against Perpetuities (EPTL 91.1 [(b)]). Because an exception for commercial options finds no support in our law, we decline to exempt all commercial option agreements from the statutory Rule against Perpetuities.[31]

---

31.   New York's statutory rule is not USRAP, which does exempt commercial options. — eds.

[W]e agree with the trial court and Appellate Division that the option defendants seek to enforce violates the statutory prohibition against remote vesting and is therefore unenforceable.

I.   FACTS

The subject of this proceeding is a two-story building situated on the Broadway block between 94th and 95th Streets on Manhattan's Upper West Side. In 1978, Broadwest Realty Corporation owned this building, which housed a theater and commercial space. Broadwest had been unable to secure a permanent tenant for the theater—approximately 58% of the total square footage of the building's floor space. Broadwest also owned two adjacent properties, Pomander Walk (a residential complex) and the Healy Building (a commercial building). Broadwest had been operating its properties at a net loss.

Plaintiff Symphony Space, Inc., a not-for-profit entity devoted to the arts, had previously rented the theater for several one-night engagements. In 1978, Symphony and Broadwest engaged in a transaction whereby Broadwest sold the entire building to Symphony for the below-market price of $10,010 and leased back the income-producing commercial property, excluding the theater, for $1 per year. Broadwest maintained liability for the existing $243,000 mortgage on the property as well as certain maintenance obligations. As a condition of the sale, Symphony, for consideration of $10, also granted Broadwest an option to repurchase the entire building. Notably, the transaction did not involve Pomander Walk or the Healy Building.

The purpose of this arrangement was to enable Symphony, as a not-for-profit corporation, to seek a property tax exemption for the entire building—which constituted a single tax parcel—predicated on its use of the theater. The sale-and-leaseback would thereby reduce Broadwest's real estate taxes by $30,000 per year, while permitting Broadwest to retain the rental income from the leased commercial space in the building, which the trial court found produced $140,000 annually. The arrangement also furthered Broadwest's goal of selling all the properties, by allowing Broadwest to postpone any sale until property values in the area increased and until the commercial leases expired. Symphony, in turn, would have use of the theater at minimal cost, once it received a tax exemption.

Thus, on December 1, 1978, Symphony and Broadwest—both sides represented by counsel—executed a contract for sale of the property from Broadwest to Symphony for the purchase price of $10,010. The contract specified that $10 was to be paid at the closing and $10,000 was to be paid by means of a purchase-money mortgage.

The parties also signed several separate documents, each dated December 31, 1978: (1) a deed for the property from Broadwest to Symphony; (2) a lease from Symphony to Broadwest of the entire building except the theater for rent of $1 per year and for the term January 1, 1979 to May 31, 2003, unless terminated earlier; (3) a 25-year, $10,000 mortgage and mortgage note from Symphony as mortgagor to Broadwest as mortgagee, with full payment due on December 31, 2003; and (4) an option agreement by which Broadwest obtained from Symphony the exclusive right to repurchase all of the property, including the theater.

It is the option agreement that is at the heart of the present dispute. Section 3 of that agreement provides that Broadwest may exercise its option to purchase the property during any of the following "Exercise Periods":

(a) at any time after July 1, 1979, so long as the Notice of Election specifies that the Closing is to occur during any of the calendar years 1987, 1993, 1998 and 2003;

(b) at any time following the maturity of the indebtedness evidenced by the Note and secured by the Mortgage, whether by acceleration or otherwise;

(c) during the ninety days immediately following any termination of the Lease by the lessor thereof other than for nonpayment of rent or any termination of the Lease by the lessee thereof . . .

(d) during the ninety days immediately following the thirtieth day after Broadwest shall have sent Symphony a notice specifying a default by Symphony of any of its covenants or obligations under the Mortgage.

Section 1 states that "Broadwest may exercise its option at any time during any Exercise Period." That section further specifies that the notice of election must be sent at least 180 days prior to the closing date if the option is exercised pursuant to section 3(a) and at least 90 days prior to the closing date if exercised pursuant to any other subdivision.

The following purchase prices of the property, contingent upon the closing date, are set forth in section 4: $15,000 if the closing date is on or before December 31, 1987; $20,000 if on or before December 31, 1993; $24,000 if on or before December 31, 1998; and $28,000 if on or before December 31, 2003.

Importantly, the option agreement specifies in section 5 that "Broadwest's right to exercise the option granted hereby is . . . unconditional and shall not be in any way affected or impaired by Broadwest's performance or nonperformance, actual or asserted, of any obligation to be performed under the Lease or any other agreement or instrument by or between Broadwest and Symphony," other than that Broadwest was required to pay Symphony any unpaid rent on the closing date. Finally, section 6 established that the option constituted "a covenant running with the land, inuring to the benefit of heirs, successors and assigns of Broadwest."

Symphony ultimately obtained a tax exemption for the theater. In the summer of 1981, Broadwest sold and assigned its interest under the lease, option agreement, mortgage and mortgage note, as well as its ownership interest in the contiguous Pomander Walk and Healy Building, to defendants . . . for $4.8 million. . . .

Subsequently, defendants initiated a cooperative conversion of Pomander Walk, which was designated a landmark in 1982, and the value of the properties increased substantially. An August 1988 appraisal of the entire blockfront, including the Healy Building and the unused air and other development rights available from Pomander Walk, valued the property at $27 million assuming the enforceability of the option. By contrast, the value of the leasehold interest plus the Healy Building without the option were appraised at $5.5 million.

Due to Symphony's alleged default on the mortgage note, defendant Swett served Symphony with notice in January 1985 that it was exercising the option on behalf of all defendants. The notice set a closing date of May 6, 1985. Symphony, however, disputed . . . that it was in default. . . . According to Symphony, moreover, it then discovered that the option agreement was possibly invalid. Consequently, in March 1985, Symphony initiated this declaratory judgment action against defendants, arguing that the option agreement violated the New York statutory prohibition against remote vesting. . . .

The trial court . . . concluded that the Rule Against Perpetuities applied to the commercial option contained in the parties' agreement, that the option violated the Rule and that Symphony was entitled to exercise its equitable right to redeem the mortgage. . . .

. . . [T]he Appellate Division likewise determined that the commercial option was unenforceable under the Rule Against Perpetuities and . . . certified the following question to us: "Was the order of the Supreme Court, as affirmed by this Court, properly made?" We conclude that it was and now affirm.

II. STATUTORY BACKGROUND

The Rule Against Perpetuities evolved from judicial efforts during the 17th century to limit control of title to real property by the dead hand of landowners reaching into future generations. Underlying both early and modern rules restricting future dispositions of property is the principle that it is socially undesirable for property to be inalienable for an unreasonable period of time. These rules thus seek "to ensure the productive use and development of property by its current beneficial owners by simplifying ownership, facilitating exchange and freeing property from unknown or embarrassing impediments to alienability" (Metropolitan Transp. Auth. v. Bruken Realty Corp., 492 N.E.2d 379, citing De Peyster v. Michael, 6 N.Y. 467).

The traditional statement of the common law Rule Against Perpetuities was set forth by Professor John Chipman Gray: "No interest is good unless it must vest, if at all, not later than twenty-one years after some life in being at the creation of the interest."

In New York, the rules regarding suspension of the power of alienation and remoteness in vesting—the Rule Against Perpetuities—have been statutory since 1830. Prior to 1958, the perpetuities period was two lives in being plus actual periods of minority. Widely criticized as unduly complex and restrictive, the statutory period was revised in 1958 and 1960, restoring the common law period of lives in being plus 21 years. . . .

New York's current statutory Rule Against Perpetuities is found in EPTL 9-1.1. Subdivision (a) sets forth the suspension of alienation rule and deems void any estate in which the conveying instrument suspends the absolute power of alienation for longer than lives in being at the creation of the estate plus 21 years. The prohibition against remote vesting is contained in subdivision (b), which states that "[n]o estate in property shall be valid unless it must vest, if at all, not later than twenty-one years after one or more lives in being at the creation of the estate and any period of gestation involved." This Court has described subdivision (b) as "a rigid formula that invalidates any interest that may not vest within the prescribed time period" and has "capricious consequences" (Wildenstein & Co. v. Wallis, 595 N.E.2d 828). Indeed, these rules are predicated upon the public policy of the State and constitute non-waivable, legal prohibitions . . . .

In addition to these statutory formulas, New York also retains the more flexible common law rule against unreasonable restraints on alienation. Unlike the statutory Rule Against Perpetuities, which is measured exclusively by the passage of time, the common law rule evaluates the reasonableness of the restraint based on its duration, purpose and designated method for fixing the purchase price. . . .

III. VALIDITY OF THE OPTION AGREEMENT

Defendants proffer three grounds for upholding the option: that the statutory prohibition against remote vesting does not apply to commercial options; that the option here cannot be exercised beyond the statutory period; and that this Court should adopt the "wait and see" approach to the Rule Against Perpetuities. We consider each in turn.

A. Applicability of the Rule to Commercial Options

Under the common law, options to purchase land are subject to the rule against remote vesting (Simes and Smith, *Future Interests* § 1244 [2d ed.]; Leach, *Perpetuities in a Nutshell*, 51 Harv. L. Rev. 638, 660 . . .). Such options are specifically enforceable and give the option holder a contingent, equitable interest in the land (Dukeminier, *A Modern Guide to Perpetuities*, 74 Cal. L. Rev. 1867, 1908; Leach, *Perpetuities in Perspective: Ending the Rule's Reign of Terror*, 65 Harv. L. Rev. 721, 736-737). This creates a disincentive for the landowner to develop the property and hinders its alienability, thereby defeating the policy objectives underlying the Rule against Perpetuities . . . .

Typically, however, options to purchase are part of a commercial transaction. For this reason, subjecting them to the Rule Against Perpetuities has been deemed "a step of doubtful wisdom." . . . Professor W. Barton Leach, has explained,

> "[t]he Rule grew up as a limitation on family dispositions; and the period of lives in being plus twenty-one years is adapted to these gift transactions. The pressures which created the Rule do not exist with reference to arm's-length contractual transactions, and neither lives in being nor twenty-one years are periods which are relevant to business men and their affairs" (Leach, *Perpetuities: New Absurdity, Judicial and Statutory Correctives*, 73 Harv. L. Rev. 1318, 1321-1322).

Professor Leach, however, went on to acknowledge that, under common law, "due to an overemphasis on concepts derived from the nineteenth century, we are stuck with the application of the Rule to options to purchase," urging that "this should not be extended to other commercial transactions."

It is now settled in New York that, generally, EPTL 9-1.1 (b) applies to options. In Buffalo Seminary v. McCarthy, 86 A.D.2d 435 . . . , the court held that an unlimited option in gross to purchase real property was void under the statutory rule against remote vesting, and we affirmed the Appellate Division. . . . Since then, we have reiterated that options in real estate are subject to the statutory rule (*see, e.g.,* Wildenstein & Co. v. Wallis, 595 N.E.2d 828 . . .).

Although the particular option at issue in *Buffalo Seminary* was part of a private transaction between neighboring landowners, the reasoning employed in that case establishes that EPTL 9-1.1 (b) applies equally to commercial purchase options. In reaching its conclusion in *Buffalo Seminary*, the court explained that, prior to 1965, New York's narrow statutory rule against remote vesting did not encompass options. A review of the history of the broad provision enacted in 1965, however, established that the Legislature specifically intended to incorporate the American common law rules governing perpetuities into the New York statute.

Because the common law rule against remote vesting encompasses purchase options that might vest beyond the permissible period, the court concluded that EPTL 9-1.1 (b) necessarily encompasses such options. Inasmuch as the common law prohibition against remote vesting applies to both commercial and noncommercial options, it likewise follows that the Legislature intended EPTL 9-1.1 (b) to apply to commercial purchase options as well.

Consequently, creation of a general exception to EPTL 9-1.1 (b) for all purchase options that are commercial in nature, as advocated by defendants, would remove an entire class of contingent future interests that the Legislature intended the statute to cover. While defendants offer compelling policy reasons—echoing those voiced by Professor Leach—for refusing to apply the traditional rule against remote vesting to these commercial option contracts, such statutory reformation would require legislative action similar to that undertaken by numerous other State lawmakers . . . .

Our decision in Metropolitan Transp. Auth. v. Bruken Realty Corp., is not to the contrary. In *Bruken*, we held that EPTL 9-1.1 (b) did not apply to a preemptive right in a "commercial and governmental transaction" that lasted beyond the statutory perpetuities period. In doing so, we explained that, unlike options, preemptive rights (or rights of first refusal) only marginally affect transferability:

> An option grants to the holder the power to compel the owner of property to sell it whether the owner is willing to part with ownership or not. A preemptive right, or right of first refusal, does not give its holder the power to compel an unwilling owner to sell; it merely requires the owner, when and if he decides to sell, to offer the property first to the party holding the preemptive right so that he may meet a third-party offer or buy the property at some other price set by a previously stipulated method.

Enforcement of the preemptive right in the context of the governmental and commercial transaction, moreover, actually encouraged the use and development of the land, outweighing any minor impediment to alienability.

Bruken merely recognized that the Legislature did not intend EPTL 9-1.1(b) to apply to those contingent future interests in real property that encourage the holder to develop the property by insuring an opportunity to benefit from the improvements and to recapture any. In these limited circumstances, enforcement would promote the purposes underlying the rule.

. . . [W]e have since emphasized that options to purchase are to be treated differently than preemptive rights, underscoring that preemptive rights impede alienability only minimally whereas purchase options vest substantial control over the transferability of property in the option holder . . . . We have also clarified that even preemptive rights are ordinarily subject to the statutory rule against remote vesting (*see*, Morrison v. Piper, 566 N.E.2d 643, . . .). Only where the right arises in a governmental or commercial agreement is the minor restraint on transferability created by the preemptive right offset by the holder's incentive to improve the property.

Here, the option agreement creates precisely the sort of control over future disposition of the property that we have previously associated with purchase options and that the common law rule against remote vesting—and thus EPTL 9-1.1 (b)—seeks to prevent. . . . [T]he option grants its holder absolute power to purchase the property at the holder's whim and at a token price set far below market value. This Sword of Damocles necessarily discourages the property owner from investing in improvements to the property. Furthermore, the option's existence significantly impedes the owner's ability to sell the property to a third party, as a practical matter rendering it inalienable.

That defendants, the holder of this option, are also the lessees of a portion of the premises does not lead to a different conclusion here.

Generally, an option to purchase land that originates in one of the lease provisions, is not exercisable after lease expiration, and is incapable of separation from the lease is valid even though the holder's interest may vest beyond the perpetuities period (*see*, Berg, *Long-Term Options and the Rule Against Perpetuities*, 37 Cal. L. Rev. 1, 21; Leach, *Perpetuities: New Absurdity, Judicial and Statutory Correctives*, 73 Harv. L. Rev. 1320; Simes and Smith, *Future Interests* § 1244). Such options known as options "appendant" or "appurtenant" to leases—encourage the possessory holder to invest in maintaining and developing the property by guaranteeing the option holder the ultimate benefit of any such investment. Options appurtenant thus further the policy objectives underlying the rule against remote vesting and are not contemplated by EPTL 9-1.1 (b).

To be sure, the option here arose within a larger transaction that included a lease. Nevertheless, not all of the property subject to the purchase option here is even occupied by defendants. The option encompasses the entire building—both the commercial space and the theater—yet defendants are leasing only the commercial space. With regard to the theater space, a disincentive exists for Symphony to improve the property, since it will eventually be claimed by the option holder at the predetermined purchase price. . . .

Put simply, the option here cannot qualify as an option appurtenant and significantly deters development of the property. If the option is exercisable beyond the statutory perpetuities period, refusing to enforce it would thus further the purpose and rationale underlying the statutory prohibition against remote vesting.

B. Duration of the Option Agreement

. . . Where, as here, the parties to a transaction are corporations and no measuring lives are stated in the instruments, the perpetuities period is simply 21 years. Section 1 of the parties' agreement allows the option holder to exercise the option "at any time during any Exercise Period" set forth in section three. Section 3(a) . . . expressly provides that the option may be exercised "at any time after July 1, 1979," so long as the closing date is scheduled during 1987, 1993, 1998 or 2003.

Even factoring in the requisite notice, . . . the option could potentially be exercised as late as July 2003—more than 24 years after its creation in December 1978. . . .

Nor can EPTL 9-1.3—the "saving statute"—be invoked to shorten the duration of the exercise period . . . . That statute mandates that, "[u]nless a contrary intention appears," certain rules of construction govern with respect to any matter affecting the Rule Against Perpetuities. The specified canons of construction include that "[i]t shall be presumed that the creator intended the estate to be valid" and "[w]here the duration or vesting of an estate is contingent upon . . . the occurrence of any specified contingency, it shall be presumed that the creator of such estate intended such contingency to occur, if at all, within twenty-one years from the effective date of the instrument creating such estate."

By presuming that the creator intended the estate to be valid, the statute seeks to avoid annulling dispositions due to inadvertent violations of the Rule Against Perpetuities. The provisions of EPTL 9-1.3, however, are merely rules of construction. While the statute obligates reviewing courts, where possible, to avoid constructions that frustrate the parties' intended purposes, it does not authorize courts to rewrite instruments that unequivocally allow interests to vest outside the perpetuities period (*compare*, EPTL 9-1.2 [reducing age contingency to 21 years, where interest is invalid because contingent on a person reaching an age in excess of 21 years]).

Indeed, by their terms, the rules of construction apply only if "a contrary intention" does not appear in the instrument. . . . The unambiguous language of the agreement here expresses the parties' intent that the option be exercisable "at any time" during a 24-year period pursuant to section 3(a). The section thus does not permit a construction that the parties intended the option to last only 21 years.

Given the contrary intention manifested in the instrument itself, the saving statute is simply inapplicable. . . .

C. "Wait and See" Approach

Defendants next urge that we adopt the "wait and see" approach to the Rule Against Perpetuities: An interest is valid if it actually vests during the perpetuities period, irrespective of what might have happened. The option here would survive under the "wait and see" approach since it was exercised by 1987, well within the 21-year limitation.

This Court, however, has long refused to "wait and see" whether a perpetuities violation in fact occurs. As explained in Matter of Fischer, 120 N.E.2d 688, "[i]t is settled beyond dispute that in determining whether a will has illegally suspended the power of alienation, the courts will look to what might have happened under the terms of the will rather than to what has actually happened since the death of the testator" (*see also*, Matter of Roe, 24 N.E.2d 322).

The very language of EPTL 9-1.1, moreover, precludes us from determining the validity of an interest based upon what actually occurs during the perpetuities period. Under the statutory rule against remote vesting, an interest is invalid "unless it must vest, if at all, not later than twenty-one years after one or more lives in being." . . .

We note that the desirability of the "wait and see" doctrine has been widely debated . . . . Its incorporation into EPTL 9-1.1, in any event, must be accomplished by the Legislature, not the courts.

We therefore conclude that the option agreement is invalid under EPTL 9-1.1 (b). . . .

IV. REMEDY

As a final matter, defendants argue that, if the option fails, the contract of sale conveying the property from Broadwest to Symphony should be rescinded due to the mutual mistake of the parties. We conclude that rescission is inappropriate. . . .

. . . [D]efendants maintain that neither Symphony nor Broadwest realized that the option violated the Rule Against Perpetuities at the time they entered into the agreement and that both parties intended the option to be enforceable. . . . Here, the parties' mistake amounts to nothing more than a misunderstanding as to the applicable law . . . .

The remedy of rescission, moreover, lies in equity and is a matter of discretion. . . . Defendants' plea that the unenforceability of the option is contrary to the intent of the original parties ignores that the effect of the Rule Against Perpetuities—which is a statutory prohibition, not a rule of construction—is always to defeat the intent of parties who create a remotely vesting interest. As explained by the Appellate Division, there is "an irreconcilable conflict in applying a remedy which is designed to void a transaction because it fails to carry out the parties' true intent to a transaction in which the mistake made by the parties was the application of the Rule Against Perpetuities, the purpose of which is to defeat the intent of the parties."

The Rule Against Perpetuities reflects the public policy of the State. Granting the relief requested by defendants would thus be contrary to public policy, since it would lead to the same result as enforcing the option and tend to compel performance of contracts violative of the Rule. . . .

Accordingly, the order of the Appellate Division should be affirmed, with costs, and the certified question answered in the affirmative.

Notes and Questions

1. How should the option agreement have been drafted to avoid problems with the Rule? Both parties to the option agreement were represented by counsel. Should counsel for Broadwest be liable to the defendants for their loss?

2. The Rule Against Perpetuities applies to the vesting of contingent interests in land. Why is an option to purchase—a contract—subject to the Rule Against Perpetuities? Although contract rights are generally not subject to the Rule, an option to purchase is specifically enforceable. On exercise of the option, the option holder becomes entitled to a decree in equity ordering the property owner to convey it to the option holder, which will divest the fee simple holder's title and vest title in the option holder. The option holder is regarded as having a contingent equitable interest in the land, which is subject to the Rule.

3. Are there advantages to applying the Rule Against Perpetuities to an option in gross rather than the rule against unreasonable restraints on alienation? Should an option that complies with the Rule Against Perpetuities also be subject to invalidation as an unreasonable restraint on alienation?

4. How should judges treat statutes that are enacted to codify the common law—like common-law rules that judges can and should continue to adapt to current conditions, or like statutes that only the legislature can change?

5. The Supreme Court of Mississippi held that a 25-year trust was valid, even though it would have been invalid under the strict common-law Rule Against Perpetuities, by applying wait and see in *In re Estate of Anderson*, 541 So. 2d 423 (Miss. 1989). Responding to the argument that allowing a 25-year trust would make a shambles of the Rule, the court stated:

> But a moment's reflection reveals that an adept lawyer can tie up property "for an unconscionable period—*viz.*, twenty-one years after the deaths of a dozen or so babies chosen from families noted for longevity, a term which, in the ordinary course of events, will add up to about a century."[21] If this be so, what sense does it make that the mere twenty-five years the Anderson trust will last are too much?[22] Moreover, the twenty-five years these trust assets will be dominated by Charles Maurice Anderson's dead hand pale into insignificance when compared with the ninety year wait-and-see period which is the centerpiece of the new Uniform Statutory Rule Against Perpetuities promulgated in 1986 by the National Conference of Commissioners on Uniform State Laws.[23]

21.   6 American Law of Property § 24.16, at 52 (Casner ed. 1952).

22.   . . . We know of no rule more infected with the twin diseases of over-inclusiveness and under-inclusiveness than the Rule.

23.   It is no exaggeration to suggest that "there is agreement among virtually all of the commentators and experts in the field that the Rule Against Perpetuities is in need of reform." Waggoner, *Perpetuity Reform*, 81 Mich. L. Rev. 1718 (1983). Out of exasperation with the continuing power of the dead hand of John Chipman Gray, many states have opted for statutory reform of the Rule, the new Uniform Statutory Rule being only the latest and most prominent of such efforts. With the three judicial ameliorations in being in this state—wait-and-see, abolition of all-or-nothing in class gifts, and implied savings clause—there would appear no need here for legislation on the subject. *See* Dukeminier, *The Uniform Statutory Rule Against Perpetuities: Ninety Years in Limbo*, 34 UCLA L. Rev. 1023 (1987); Smith, *Perpetuities in New Jersey: A Plea for Judicial Supremacy*, 24 Rutgers L. Rev. 80 (1969).

CHAPTER 6

Landlord-Tenant

Leases divide the right to present possession, held by the tenant (lessee), from the right to future possession, held by the landlord (lessor). The tenant's interest is called the leasehold estate, or "term"; the landlord's interest is called the reversion. Although it is possible to use leases in family wealth transmission and to follow a leasehold estate with a future interest in someone other than the grantor (lessor), the vast majority of leases are used in commercial transactions in which the future interest is retained by the lessor.

Early in the common-law period, leases were used as a financing device. Because lending money at interest was forbidden by the Catholic Church as usury, a borrower would convey a leasehold estate to the lender, who would then take the profits from the property to repay the loan and provide compensation for use of the money. Unlike life estates, leases were not regarded as "freehold" estates and instead were classified as "chattels real," a label that is still sometimes encountered today, even though the differences that used to be attached to a non-freehold estate have largely disappeared.

Leases today are used by people who do not have sufficient capital to buy an asset outright, or who do not want to deploy their capital in purchasing a fee simple. Many people rent apartments instead of buying condominiums, for example, because they don't have the money to buy or because they are not ready to buy, or because they would rather spend their money on other things. Leases with options to purchase allow renters to occupy and improve premises while they amass sufficient capital, or wait to make a decision as to whether to buy the fee simple.

When a property is developed with multiple residential or commercial units, four different models may be used: (1) The developer can retain ownership of the fee simple and lease out the units, perhaps retaining full ownership of the common areas subject to easements held by the tenants. (2) The developer can create a condominium, selling fee simple title to the units to individual buyers and the common areas to an organization comprised of the unit owners. (3) The developer can create a cooperative corporation and sell stock in the corporation to owners accompanied by a proprietary lease to an individual unit. (4) A group of people may take title to the property as tenants in common and create contractual rights to exclusive use of individual units.

Model (1) where the developer retains ownership of the fee simple to the entire property provides the simplest management structure. The landlord is in charge, choosing the lease terms, selecting tenants, maintaining the common areas, and controlling whatever profits the development generates. In model (2), the organization of unit owners, often called a condominium or community association, usually operates through an elected board of directors, which manages the property, often through a hired management company. The association is not designed to make a profit. Model (3), the cooperative, operates much like a condominium, usually with an elected board that manages the property. Model (4), the tenancy in common, has no built-in management structure. In the absence of a management structure created by contract, partition is the remedy available if the owners disagree.

Model (1), the apartment house, is governed by the law of landlord and tenant, which we study in this chapter. Model (2), the condominium, is governed by the law of common interest communities, which we touch on in Chapter 12. Model (3), the cooperative, is governed by a mix of landlord-tenant law and common interest community law, and model (4), the TIC, is governed by the law of concurrent interests, which is covered in Chapter 7, Section A.

A.   THE LANDLORD-TENANT RELATIONSHIP

1.   *The Leasehold Estates*

There are four common-law leasehold estates, or tenancies:

Estate for years.   Sometimes called a "term of years," an estate for years is a tenancy with a fixed duration. Whether the term is one day or 20 years, it is an estate for years because measured by a fixed time period. An estate for years terminates automatically at the end of the period. It is expressly created by the parties and, under the Statute of Frauds in most jurisdictions, must be in writing if the period exceeds one year.

Periodic tenancy.   Under a periodic tenancy, the tenant holds for the initial period and for successive periods of the same duration until either the landlord or the tenant terminates the lease by giving an appropriate notice. Week-to-week, month-to-month, and year-to-year leases are periodic tenancies. The key feature is that the tenancy is continuous—it automatically rolls over from period to period.

A periodic tenancy may be created expressly, but most are created by implication. Consider these examples:

1. L leases to T without specifying the term of the lease. This creates a tenancy at will. Then T pays rent to L on a monthly basis. In most states, this transforms the tenancy into one from month to month.
2. L leases to T for one year. At the end of the year, T holds over and sends L a check for the usual monthly rent. L cashes the check. In most states, T becomes a tenant from year to year.

Care must be taken in giving notice to terminate a periodic tenancy. The notice period is six months for a tenancy from year to year unless a shorter notice is permitted by statute. For any period less than a year, the required notice equals the length of the period—e.g., a tenancy from month to month can be terminated only by one month's notice. As to the time of termination, the notice must terminate the tenancy at the end of a period, not in the middle of a period.

Estate at will.   If L leases to T with a provision that either may terminate the arrangement at will, this is a tenancy at will. So also is any other arrangement whereby T takes possession of L's land with L's permission, express or implied. *See Providence Land Services, LLC v. Jones*, 353 S.W.3d 538 (Tex. Ct. App. 2011).

At common law, an estate at will could be terminated at any time by either party without notice. However, statutes now commonly provide that notice equivalent to the period between rent payments is required to terminate a tenancy at will.[1] The tenancy at will is automatically terminated if either party dies or if the landlord conveys the landlord's interest, but statutes frequently provide that in this situation the tenant cannot be evicted for some stipulated period.

Estate at sufferance.   An estate at sufferance is really not an estate like the other common-law estates. Rather, it is a way to describe the wrongful possession of land by a tenant who improperly holds over at the end of his lease. The estate at sufferance is a valuable fiction for the landlord since she has a choice to treat the holdover tenant as a trespasser subject to eviction or as a tenant for a new valid tenancy who must pay rent.

On the different tenancies, see *Restatement (Second) of Property—Landlord and Tenant* §§ 1.4-1.6 (1977); R. Schoshinski, *American Law of Landlord and Tenant* §§ 2.1-2.23 (1980).

PROVIDENCE LAND SERVICES, LLC v. JONES

Court of Appeals of Texas
353 S.W.3d 538 (2011)

TERRY MCCALL, Justice. This appeal arises from a dispute between a landlord and its tenants concerning residential lake lots located at Lake Colorado City. . . . After a bench trial, the trial court determined that . . . [the] leases constituted ninety-nine year leases . . . .

BACKGROUND FACTS

Graydon M. and Inez Howell previously owned the land . . . . Beginning in the 1970s, the Howells began to lease individual lots to people who wanted lake property. The lake lots were known as the "Howell Properties," and they consisted of forty-three total lots. The underlying litigation involved twenty-five of these lots.

The Howells and their tenants executed written lease agreements for each of the lots. The terms of the leases were drafted by the Howells without the aid of an attorney. With respect to the duration of the leases, the leases can be classified into three categories: (1) leases that expressly provided that they were

---

1.   *See, e.g.,* Mass. Gen. Laws ch. 186, § 12.
2.   *See, e.g.,* Mass. Gen. Laws ch. 186, § 13.

"indefinite"; (2) leases with no express end date; and (3) leases with fixed termination dates. . . .

Graydon Howell died in 1988. After his death, Inez Howell continued to administer Howell Properties until her death in 1996. The Howells' daughter, Carolyn Howell, assumed control of Howell Properties after her mother's death. She continued to administer the lots until her death in 2007.

There were no disputes concerning the duration of the leases during the lifetimes of Graydon, Inez, and Carolyn. The events giving rise to this . . . action occurred when control of Howell Properties passed to Carolyn's brother, Rex Glenn Howell, at her death in 2007. Rex conveyed the lots to appellant, Providence Land Services, LLC, in January 2008. Soon after acquiring the lake lots, Providence sent new leases to the tenants proposing new lease terms including thirty-day termination provisions and higher lease payments. Providence . . . [asserted] that the leases signed by the tenants and the Howells were tenancies at will. The tenants . . . [sued] Providence in an effort to establish that their original leases were long-term leases as a result of written and verbal agreements that they had made with the Howells.

Indefinite Term Leases

. . . These leases provided as follows with respect to their duration:

> For the sum of $ ____, the receipt of which is hereby acknowledged, a like annual rental of $ ____ payable each year on or before _____, Lessor will lease to Lessee the following described lot or parcel of ground on shores of Lake Colorado City, for residential purposes only, for the period from this date until *Indefinite*, under the following stipulations, agreements, and restrictions. [Indefinite was handwritten onto a preprinted form.]

The trial court determined that the use of the word "indefinite" to define the end date of the leases' duration was ambiguous as a matter of law. Accordingly, the trial court considered the oral testimony and documentary evidence submitted by the tenants to the effect that they and the Howells intended to create long-term leases by the use of the term "indefinite." The tenants presented a great deal of evidence regarding their work to clear the lake lots for occupancy and the substantial improvements that they made on the lake lots based upon the expectancy of being there many years. The trial court ultimately interpreted the duration of the Indefinite Term Leases to be ninety-nine years from the date when they were entered. . . .

. . . [A] contract is only ambiguous if its language is subject to two or more reasonable interpretations. . . . The tenants contend that "indefinite" is subject to two meanings: a "legal definition" of uncertain or vague, and a layperson's definition of "not limited." . . . [T]he tenants contend that . . . "indefinite" . . . indicates that their duration was ninety-nine years or longer.

We disagree . . . . "Indefinite" is not synonymous with "infinity," "perpetual," or "forever." . . . The use of "indefinite" in the leases has a definite and certain legal meaning; the leases, as written, have no end date. As a matter of law, the leases are not ambiguous. Accordingly, parol evidence . . . is not admissible to alter the construction of the meaning of "indefinite."

A lease contract must, as to its duration, be certain as to time or refer to a certainty. If the tenant is holding the premises for no certain time . . . , he is merely a tenant at will, and the tenancy may be terminated at the will of either party. . . . Accordingly, the tenants . . . are tenants at will.

The tenants additionally argue on appeal that Providence is barred under the doctrine of promissory estoppel from enforcing the leases as tenancies at will. . . . The tenants contend that they detrimentally relied on the representations made by the Howells that they could stay as long as they wanted on the lake lots by making significant, permanent improvements to the lots.

π further argue.

A lease of real estate for a term longer than one year must be in writing . . . . [T]o satisfy the statute of frauds, there must be a written memorandum that is complete . . . and that contains all of the essential elements of the agreement so that the contract can be ascertained from the writing without resort to oral testimony. . . . [A]ny oral agreement or representation by the Howells regarding the duration of the leases would be barred by the statute of frauds.

SoF

The tenants are . . . attempting to either create a new lease agreement with an unlimited duration or alter the legal effect of the existing lease. When promissory estoppel is raised to bar the application of the statute of frauds, there is a requirement that the promisor promised to sign a written document complying with the statute of frauds. Nagle v. Nagle, 633 S.W.2d 796, 800 (Tex. 1982). . . . The record does not reflect that the Howells promised to sign another lease agreement with different terms pertaining to its duration. . . .

. . . We conclude that these leases constituted tenancies at will as a matter of law. . . . [The court reached the same conclusion as to the "no end" leases.]

Notes and Questions

1. Why would the Howells use leases in a situation like this? Why would the lessees invest in the properties if their leases could be terminated at will?

2. If the Howells had orally agreed to sell these properties at a particular price and the buyers had taken possession and begun to make payments, most courts would enforce the contract under the part performance doctrine (covered in Chapter 9) on the theory that the performance is sufficient evidence of the contract. Why wouldn't that doctrine apply here?

3. If the court had been willing to interpret "indefinite" as a reasonable time or to supply a reasonableness term in the "no end" leases, how should it have determined what a reasonable term would be?

2. Themes in Current Landlord-Tenant Law

We develop various themes in our exploration of the law of landlord and tenant. Sometimes courts directly address them, but often they lurk beneath the surface of the opinions. These themes include:

Conveyance or contract? Traditionally, courts and commentators have viewed a leasing transaction as a conveyance of an estate in land, subject to distinct property law concepts and rules. More recently, various courts and scholars have seen the lease as a contract between the landlord and tenant for the purchase of space and services. Applying contract principles to leases, these courts have often reached results different from those reached under traditional property rules. *See Fox Grain Cattle Co. v. Maxwell,* 885 P.2d 432 (Mont. 1994) (holding contract damages proper for breach of implied covenant of good faith and fair dealing in farm lease).

Others maintain that leases have a dual nature, incorporating features of both conveyances and contracts. *See, e.g., Kendall v. Ernest Pestana, Inc.,* 709 P.2d 837, 843 (Cal. 1985) (implying an obligation of commercial reasonableness in a landlord's refusal to approve an assignment of a lease). Still others argue that in reality there are many similarities between the property and contract analyses. *See* Edward Chase & E. Hunter Taylor, *Landlord and Tenant: A Study in Property and Contract,* 30 Vill. L. Rev. 571 (1985); Robert H. Kelley, *Any Reports on the Death of the Property Law Paradigm for Leases Have Been Greatly Exaggerated,* 41 Wayne L. Rev. 1563 (1995).

Statutes.   There has been an increase in legislation governing the law of landlord-tenant. In her groundbreaking article, Professor Mary Ann Glendon writes:

> It is generally acknowledged that the 1960s and 1970s saw a revolution of sorts in American landlord-tenant law, but the nature of that revolution is disputed. To many, the essence of the change has seemed to be a shift of the basis of lease law from principles of property to principles of contract. This view is particularly noticeable in the opinions of judges who have been instrumental in bringing about fundamental alterations in the common law of landlord-tenant, and it also seems to have been central to the thinking of the draftsmen of the Uniform Residential Landlord and Tenant Act (URLTA). In fact, however, landlord-tenant case law was already deeply pervaded by contract notions by the end of the nineteenth century. . . .
>
> What is new, if not revolutionary, in the past 20 years, is that residential and commercial landlord-tenant law have gradually diverged, the former more influenced by developments in consumer law, the latter by commercial law. The decisive element in the transformation of the residential landlord-tenant relationship has been its subjection to pervasive, mostly statutory, regulation of its incidents. Contrary to a widespread belief among jurists, this process has been less the product of highly publicized court decisions establishing implied warranties of habitability in residential leases, than of steadily proliferating legislation. Together, legislative and judicial treatment of leases of dwellings now make it plain that the movement in residential lease law has been not from one area of private law to another, but from private ordering to public regulation. In this process of transition from private to public law, the habitability issue, which has dominated residential landlord-tenant law for the past two decades, is now yielding center stage to developments even more far-reaching in their implications: rent regulation, security of tenure for the tenant, and the qualification of the landlord's traditional rights to alienate the freehold or to convert it to another use.

Mary Ann Glendon, *The Transformation of American Landlord-Tenant Law,* 23 B.C. L. Rev. 503-05 (1982).

Is change of the law best achieved by judicial decision or legislation? Does legislation limiting the landlord's return from the property and increasing obligations on the landlord violate the rights of landowners? *See Chicago Board of Realtors v. City of Chicago,* 819 F.2d 732 (7th Cir. 1987) (challenge to Uniform Residential Landlord and Tenant Act provisions limiting late payment charges to $10 a month, mandating that landlords pay interest on tenant security deposits, limiting restrictions on assignments and subleases, and shifting the repair obligation from tenants to landlords did not violate the Takings, Due Process, or Equal Protection Clauses of the United States Constitution).

Residential/commercial dichotomy.   In recent years, courts and legislatures have distinguished between residential and commercial leases in a number of situations. At times, they have given special recognition to residential tenants in disputes with landlords, reflecting a desire to provide habitable shelter and to regulate evictions of tenants from their homes. This view often reflects a *Residential lease.* (not always accurate) assumption that a landlord has greater economic power and skill than the residential tenant. *See* Edward H. Rabin, *The Revolution in Residential Landlord-Tenant Law: Causes and Consequences*, 69 Cornell L. Rev. 517 (1984) (finding that changes were brought about by social, political, and intellectual currents in the 1960s); Charles J. Meyers, *The Covenant of Habitability and the American Law Institute*, 27 Stan. L. Rev. 879, 882 (1975) (criticizing the motive in residential lease law as "the moral principle of redistribution of wealth from landlord to tenant"); Daniel B. Bogart, *Good Faith and Fair Dealing in Commercial Leasing: The Right Doctrine in the Wrong Transaction*, 41 J. Marshall L. Rev. 275 (2008) (arguing that these doctrines should be applied differently in the heavily negotiated commercial law arena than in residential leases); Lawrence Berger, *The New Residential Tenancy Law—Are Landlords Public Utilities?*, 60 Neb. L. Rev. 707 (1981); Comment, *No Easy Way Out: Making the Summary Eviction Process a Fairer and More Efficient Alternative to Landlord Self-Help*, 41 UCLA L. Rev. 759, 767-68 (1994) ("Contrary to the stereotype of the greedy landlord running large apartment complexes, small-scale operators dominate the private rental housing market.").

In contrast, a commercial lease is typically viewed as a free market transaction between parties with equal bargaining power and skill (again, another assumption that does not always comport with reality) that should generally be enforced *commercial lease.* as any other consensual arrangement.

Trumping the bargaining process.   As a related matter, courts are sometimes faced with a choice between enforcing a lease agreement as written or altering or voiding its terms out of concerns for fairness. Which side a court will come down upon depends on the legal standards of the jurisdiction, judicial attitude and philosophy, and the particular facts of the case before it.

Various theories support the enforcement of the exact terms of the lease contract: Free market allocations of goods and services best serve the public interest; parties have relied on the written agreement; and moral considerations require that one be bound by one's undertakings. These ideas are often encapsulated in the phrase "freedom of contract." *See O'Callaghan v. Wallwer & Beckwith Realty Co.*, 155 N.E.2d 545 (Ill. 1958) (enforcing a clause exculpating landlord from liability for negligence).

On the other hand, courts may make a direct attack on lease provisions and refuse to enforce them because they are unconscionable. Factors showing unconscionability include a party's relative lack of bargaining power or sophistication; no meaningful alternatives due to standardized lease provisions, or a shortage of alternative housing; and terms that are unreasonably favorable to the other party. A lease may also be voided because it violates public policy. *See, e.g., North American Investment Co. v. Lawson*, 854 P.2d 384 (Okla. Ct. App. 1993) ($60 monthly late penalty on residence with monthly base rental of $150 unconscionable); *Nylen v. Park Doral Apartments*, 535 N.E.2d 178, 184 (Ind. Ct. App. 1989) ($2-a-day late fee not unconscionable even though lease was standardized and favored the landlord; agreement was not one that "no sensible person not under delusion, duress or in distress would make, and one that no honest and fair person would accept"); *Calef v. West*, 652 N.W.2d 496 (Mich. Ct. App. 2002) (exculpatory clause in residential lease void as contrary to public policy); *Bedrosky v. Hiner*, 430 N.W.2d 535 (Neb. 1988) (exculpatory clause in negotiated commercial lease enforceable).

Even when the courts are not dealing with a direct assault on a lease provision on grounds of unconscionability or violation of public policy, the themes inherent in such decisions—freedom of contract, inequality of bargaining power, lack of alternatives, substandard housing, and overreaching—temper decisions and influence opinions overtly or indirectly.

Drafting and counseling. Good drafting may avoid many landlord-tenant disputes. As you study this chapter, consider who should bear the burden of negotiation and drafting as well as how you would have drafted the document and counseled the tenant and landlord. Consider as well the widespread use of standardized forms. What are the costs and benefits of form leases? *See* Gary Goldman, *A Uniform National Lease: A Worthy Goal*, 7 Prob. & Prop. 15 (Mar./Apr. 1993); Jeremy E. Goldstein, *Taking the Bite Out of Form Leases*, 8 Prob. & Prop. 22 (Jan./Feb. 1994); Bailey Kuklin, *On the Knowing Inclusion of Unenforceable Contract and Lease Terms*, 56 U. Cin. L. Rev. 845 (1988).

For further discussion of these themes, see Gerald Korngold, *Whatever Happened to Landlord-Tenant Law?*, 77 Neb. L. Rev. 703 (1998).

B. LANDLORD'S OBLIGATIONS AND TENANT'S REMEDIES

1. Duty to Deliver Possession

TEITELBAUM v. DIRECT REALTY CO.

Supreme Court of New York, Nassau County
172 Misc. 48, 13 N.Y.S.2d 886 (1939)

LOCKWOOD, J. This action tried by the Court without a jury, is to recover $25,000, plaintiff's alleged damages for defendant's failure to deliver possession of the store at 61 Main Street, Hempstead, N.Y., under a written lease dated February 10, 1938.

At the time the lease was made, the store was occupied by Abe and Dorothy Fergang under a lease expiring June 30, 1938. For many years, plaintiff had operated a drugstore a few doors away from the leased premises. Plaintiff was to take possession on July 1, 1938, make the necessary alterations and installations and open his new drugstore on August 1, 1938.

On July 1, 1938, the Fergangs refused to move out claiming a renewal of their lease by an alleged oral agreement. Defendant brought a summary processing in the District Court and the jury rendered a verdict in favor of the Fergangs. Defendant appealed to the Appellate Term, which reversed the order, and directed a new trial. On the retrial, the Fergangs defaulted. They vacated the premises in January 1939.

Upon the undisputed facts, the Fergangs wrongfully withheld possession of the premises from the plaintiff. Defendant did not refuse to put plaintiff in possession, nor was plaintiff's possession withheld or hindered by any act of the defendant. In fact, defendant did more than it was legally required to do. It attempted to dispossess the Fergangs and was finally successful. . . . Plaintiff was not kept out of possession by anyone holding under authority of the defendant, landlord, or by one having a title paramount to his.

Plaintiff places great reliance upon Friedland v. Myers, 139 N.Y. 432, where plaintiff-lessee was refused possession because the tenant then in possession was entitled to remain under a lease made by the landlord prior to the making of plaintiff's lease. It had previously been held in a dispossess proceeding that the tenant's possession was rightful.

However, the present case is not one where the landlord covenanted to give possession when he had no authority to do so. Plaintiff could have had possession but for the wrongful act of the Fergangs.

It is said in "New York Law of Landlord and Tenant," Vol. 1, Sec. 316, page 639:

> . . . [C]ontrary to the view taken in England and in many jurisdictions in this country, it is held in our state in a number of cases in the lower courts, that the extent of the landlord's implied agreement is that he has a good title and can give a free and unincumbered lease for the term demised, and that if, at the time of the commencement of the term, the possession is held by a trespasser, not holding with the sanction of the landlord there is no implied obligation on the part of the landlord to oust such trespasser to enable the tenant to enter, and that consequently his failure to do so does not render him liable in damages to the lessee. . . . Wilson, Ch. J., speaking for the Supreme Court in a leading case, says:
>
> > It is not the duty of the landlord, when the demised premises are wrongfully held by a third person, to take the necessary steps to put his lessee in possession. The latter being clothed with the title by virtue of the lease, it belongs to him to pursue such legal remedies as the law provided for gaining it, whether few or many. . . .
>
> The same view is taken where a prior tenant of the landlord or a sublessee of such tenant, after the expiration of his term, wrongfully and without the sanction of the landlord, retains the possession. . . . Proof merely that a third person was in possession of the demised premises at the commencement of the term, without further proof of his right to retain possession does not show a breach of the landlord's implied obligation to give possession. . . .

Admittedly, plaintiff is a month-to-month tenant in his old place at $200 a month and could have moved into the new place when it was vacated last January and could have used the new fixtures which he now claims are a total loss. It might well be that on reflection, he found the rent he agreed to pay for the new property too high.

Defendant's motion for judgment is granted and judgment shall be entered in favor of the defendant, dismissing the complaint.

Notes and Questions

1. There has been a divergence in the United States on the question whether the landlord must put the tenant into possession of the premises if the lease is silent on the issue. Some jurisdictions follow the "American rule," which implies a lease term that the landlord must only give the tenant the legal right to possession, thus obligating the tenant to remove holdover tenants. Other states follow the "English rule," which implies a term requiring the landlord to ensure that the tenant can take physical possession at the start of the term. *See* Robert Schoshinski, *American Law of Landlord and Tenant* § 3.1 (1980). What theory supports the American rule? Is it viable today? What policies support the English rule?

Over recent years, the trend has favored the English rule, with new statutes accounting for much of the momentum. For example, § 2.103 of the Uniform Residential Landlord and Tenant Act requires that the landlord "deliver possession" to the tenant at the start of the term.

2. Courts have traditionally found a landlord in breach if a third party has a paramount title that prevents the tenant from taking possession or enjoying her leasehold. This obligation is sometimes called an implied covenant of title or an implied covenant of power to demise. Thus, a landlord is in breach if another person holds better title to the property, whether it is a fee simple interest or a lesser interest such as a paramount lease to a third party. *See Restatement (Second) of Property—Landlord and Tenant* §§ 4.1, 4.2.

Should a landlord be deemed in breach of the implied covenant of title if it is discovered that there is a paramount title even though it has not yet been asserted?

Problem

L rents an apartment to T2, the term to begin at the expiration of T1's term, and T1 wrongfully holds over. In a jurisdiction that has adopted the American rule, L sues T1 to recover possession of the apartment. T1 defends on the ground that since L has executed a lease with T2, L is no longer entitled to possession of the apartment, and therefore L does not have the legal capacity to maintain the proceeding. What decision? *See Eells v. Morse*, 101 N.E. 803 (N.Y. 1913).

2. *Duty to Protect the Tenant's Quiet Enjoyment: Constructive Eviction*

BLACKETT v. OLANOFF

Supreme Judicial Court of Massachusetts
371 Mass. 714, 358 N.E.2d 817 (1977)

WILKINS, J. The defendant in each of these consolidated actions for rent successfully raised constructive eviction as a defense against the landlords' claim. The judge found that the tenants were "very substantially deprived" of quiet enjoyment of their leased premises "*for a substantial* time." He ruled that the tenants' implied warranty of quiet enjoyment was violated by late evening and early morning music and disturbances coming from nearby premises which the landlords leased to others for use as a bar or cocktail lounge. The judge further found that, although the landlords did not intend to create the conditions, the landlords "had it within their control to correct the conditions which . . . amounted to a constructive eviction . . . ." He also found that the landlords promised each tenant to correct the situation, that the landlords made some attempt to remedy the problem, but they were unsuccessful, and that each tenant vacated his apartment within a reasonable time. Judgment was entered for each tenant; the landlords appealed; and we transferred the appeals here. We affirm the judgments.

The landlords argue that they did not violate the tenants' implied covenant of quiet enjoyment because they are not chargeable with the noise from the lounge. The landlords do not challenge the judge's conclusion that the noise emanating from the lounge was sufficient to constitute a constructive eviction, if that noise could be attributed to the landlords,[3] nor do the landlords seriously argue that a constructive eviction could not be found as matter of law because the lounge was not on the same premises as the tenants' apartments. . . . The landlords' principal contention is that they are not responsible for the conduct of the proprietors, employees, and patrons of the lounge.

Our opinions concerning a constructive eviction . . . sometimes have stated that the landlord must perform some act with the intent of depriving the tenant of the enjoyment and occupation of the whole or part of the leased premises. See Katz v. Duffy, 158 N.E. 264 (Mass. 1927), and cases cited. There are occasions, however, where a landlord has not intended to violate a tenant's rights, but there was nevertheless a breach of the landlord's covenant of quiet enjoyment which flowed as the natural and probable consequence of what the landlord did, what he failed to do, or what he permitted to be done. Charles E. Burt, Inc. v. Seven Grand Corp., 163 N.E.2d 4 (Mass. 1959) (failure to supply light, heat, power, and elevator services). Westland Housing Corp. v. Scott, 44 N.E.2d 959 (Mass. 1942) (intrusions of smoke and soot over a substantial period of time due to a defective boiler). Shindler v. Milden, 184 N.E. 673 (Mass. 1933) (failure to install necessary heating system, as agreed). Case v. Minot, 33 N.E. 700 (Mass. 1893) (landlord authorizing another lessee to obstruct the tenant's light and air, necessary for the beneficial enjoyment of the demised premises). Skally v. Shute, 132 Mass. 367 (1882) (undermining of a leased building rendering it unfit for occupancy). Although some of our opinions have spoken of particular action or inaction by a landlord as showing a presumed intention to evict, the landlord's conduct, and not his intentions, is controlling. . . .

The judge was warranted in ruling that the landlords had it within their control to correct the condition which caused the tenants to vacate their apartments. The landlords introduced a commercial activity into an area where they leased premises for residential purposes. The lease for the lounge expressly provided

---

3.   There was evidence that the lounge had amplified music (electric musical instruments and singing, at various times) which started at 9:30 P.M. and continued until 1:30 A.M or 2 A.M., generally on Tuesdays through Sundays. The music could be heard through the granite walls of the residential tenants' building, and was described variously as unbelievably loud, incessant, raucous and penetrating. The noise interfered with conversation and prevented sleep. There was also evidence of noise from patrons' yelling and fighting.

that entertainment in the lounge had to be conducted so that it could not be heard outside the building and would not disturb the residents of the leased apartments. The potential threat to the occupants of the nearby apartments was apparent in the circumstances. The landlords complained to the tenants of the lounge after receiving numerous objections from residential tenants. From time to time, the pervading noise would abate in response to the landlords' complaints. We conclude that, as matter of law, the landlords had a right to control the objectionable noise coming from the lounge and that the judge was warranted in finding as a fact that the landlords could control the objectionable conditions.

This situation is different from the usual annoyance of one residential tenant by another, where traditionally the landlord has not been chargeable with the annoyance. *See* Katz v. Duffy, *supra* (illegal sale of alcoholic beverages). DeWitt v. Pierson, 112 Mass. 8 (1873) (prostitution).[4] Here we have a case more like Case v. Minot, 33 N.E. 700 (Mass. 1893), where the landlord entered into a lease with one tenant which the landlord knew permitted that tenant to engage in activity which would interfere with the rights of another tenant. There, to be sure, the clash of tenants' rights was inevitable, if each pressed those rights. Here, although the clash of tenants' interests was only a known potentiality initially, experience demonstrated that a decibel level for the entertainment at the lounge, acoustically acceptable to its patrons and hence commercially desirable to its proprietors, was intolerable for the residential tenants.

Because the disturbing condition was the natural and probable consequence of the landlords' permitting the lounge to operate where it did and because the landlords could control the actions at the lounge, they should not be entitled to collect rent for residential premises which were not reasonably habitable. Tenants such as these should not be left only with a claim against the proprietors of the noisome lounge. To the extent that our opinions suggest a distinction between nonfeasance by the landlord, which has been said to create no liability, and malfeasance by the landlord, we decline to perpetuate that distinction where the landlord creates a situation and has the right to control the objectionable conditions.

Judgments affirmed.

4. The general, but not universal, rule in this country is that a landlord is not chargeable because one tenant is causing annoyance to another (A. H. Woods Theatre v. North American Union, 246 Ill. App. 521 (1927) (music from one commercial tenant annoying another commercial tenant's employees)), even where the annoying conduct would be a breach of the landlord's covenant of quiet enjoyment if the landlord were the miscreant. *See* . . . 1 American Law of Property § 3.53 (A. J. Casner ed. 1952); Annot., 38 A.L.R. 250 (1925). *Contra* Kesner v. Consumers Co., 255 Ill. App. 216 (1929) (storage of flammables constituting a nuisance); Bruckner v. Helfaer, 222 N.W. 790 (Wis. 1929) (residential tenant not liable for rent where landlord, with ample notice, does not control another tenant's conduct).

The rule in New York appears to be that the landlord may not recover rent if he has had ample notice of the existence of conduct of one tenant which deprives another tenant of the beneficial enjoyment of his premises and the landlord does little or nothing to abate the nuisance. *See* Cohen v. Werner, 378 N.Y.S.2d 868 (N.Y. App. T. 1975). . . . A tenant with sufficient bargaining power may be able to obtain an agreement from the landlord to insert and to enforce regulatory restrictions in the leases of other, potentially offending, tenants. . . .

landlord

WESSON v. LEONE ENTERPRISES, INC.

Supreme Judicial Court of Massachusetts
437 Mass. 708, 774 N.E.2d 611 (2002)

CORDY, J. In this case, we abandon the common-law rule of independent covenants in commercial leases in favor of the modern rule of mutually dependent covenants as reflected in the *Restatement (Second) of Property (Landlord and Tenant)* § 7.1 (1977)....

1. *Background.* The plaintiff landlord, John T. Wesson, . . . owned a multi-tenanted commercial building located in Danvers (Wesson building), in which the defendant tenant, Leone Enterprises, Inc., a financial printing company, rented space. The lease ran for five years, commencing on March 31, 1988.[3]

The tenant first complained to the landlord about "significant leaks in the roof" in April, 1991.[4] The parties met soon afterward and the tenant pointed out "more than one," but less than five, leaks in the premises. The landlord agreed to fix the roof and called on his son, Wayne Wesson, who periodically managed the building, to oversee the repairs. Wayne patched the roof himself. The leaks reappeared later that spring, and the landlord hired a professional roofing contractor to make further repairs.

complaint of leak,

leaks fixed

reappear

In early August, 1991, the roof began leaking in some of the same places previously repaired. The tenant complained several times to the landlord and Wayne about the leaks, and claimed that he and his subtenant[5] were "forced to take necessary precautions to protect [their] businesses from more water damage."[6] After these leaks were repaired by the landlord, the tenant notified him of another leak "in a different location" on September 6, 1991. This particular leak, however, was caused by a defective electrical conduit connected to the roof-top air conditioning unit, the maintenance of which was the tenant's responsibility under the lease.[7] The landlord had the roof inspected the next day by a professional roofer, who sealed the leak. There was no evidence at trial of any additional leaks or complaints of leaks after September 7, 1991.

leak by Ac but tenant's responsibility. Landlord Seals the leak.

On November 4, 1991, the tenant notified the landlord that he would be "vacating the premises on or before December 31, 1991,"[9] for reasons "well

---

3.   The initial rent for the 12,000 square foot space was $8,186 per month ($6,250 per month in base rent plus thirty-four per cent of the operating fees and expenses of the Wesson building). The tenant was required to indemnify the landlord "against all loss of rent and other payments which the LESSOR may incur" if the lease was terminated.

4.   At trial, the tenant testified that there had been leaks before this time but that he had not complained "because [he] never thought they were a problem or an issue that [he] should be worried about."

5.   MicroNational Inc. sublet one-half of the tenant's space in the Wesson Building. . . .

6.   The evidence at trial of "precautions" taken by the tenant was the covering of his equipment and stock with plastic sheeting. There was no evidence introduced of any precautions taken by the subtenant.

7.   The lease required the tenant to "maintain all equipment of any nature located within the demised area including, but without limitation, lighting, heating, air conditioning, plumbing, and the air conditioning units which service the demised premises and are located on the roof of the building of which the demised premises is a part. The LESSEE shall be responsible for the heating and air conditioning of the demised premises."

9.   The tenant leased alternative space in Ipswich in November, 1991. The new lease, for 7,200 square feet at $3,000 per month, became effective on November 1, 1991.

known to you. The constant lack of minimal heat as well as the serious leakage problem."[10] The tenant also paid rent in full through the end of 1991.

The landlord filed a complaint . . . alleging breach of contract and damage to the demised premises.[11] . . . The tenant filed counterclaims for constructive eviction and deceptive business practices under G.L. c. 93A, § 11. The landlord then amended his complaint to add a claim against the tenant for interference with advantageous relations.[12]

. . . After hearing testimony from the landlord, Wayne Wesson, the tenant, and the architect who designed the Wesson Building, the judge found the tenant's testimony "regarding the frequency of his complaints about the leaky roof, the danger it posed upon his equipment and inventory and that he was forced to move out to be credible." In contrast, the judge found the testimony of Wayne Wesson and the landlord "regarding their reasonable responses to whatever complaints they received about the leaking roof not credible." The judge further found that "the roof was in a state of disrepair and needed more than spot repairs"; that "whether Wayne or a professional roofer attempted the repairs, the methods used were shoddy and unsuccessful"; and that, "from April 1991 through November of 1991 . . . [the tenant] complained to both [the landlord] and [Wayne] by telephone and by letter that the roof leaked and put his business at risk." Based on these findings, the judge concluded that the tenant had been constructively evicted . . . . Alternatively, she held that, even if the tenant had not been constructively evicted, the tenant could have lawfully withheld the rent under the dependent covenants rule, where the landlord had failed to provide a "dry space," a service "essential" to the lease.

Judgment entered in favor of the defendant tenant on the plaintiff landlord's breach of contract claim and on the tenant's counterclaim of constructive eviction. Relocation damages in the amount of $1,063 were awarded to the tenant. The landlord appealed . . . . We transferred the case to this court on our own motion.

We affirm . . . but for reasons different from those of the Superior Court judge. The judge's finding of constructive eviction was in error, but because we adopt the rule of mutually dependent covenants for commercial leases and conclude that the plaintiff landlord breached his covenant to maintain the roof, the tenant was entitled to terminate the lease and recover relocation costs. . . .

3. Constructive eviction. The landlord bases his claim that the judge erred in finding a constructive eviction on two alternative grounds: first, that the lease required the tenant, not the landlord, to maintain the roof . . . ;[14] and second,

---

10.   In addition to leaks, the tenant had also complained about problems with the building's heating system from September, 1989, through January, 1990. In January and February, 1991, attorneys for the plaintiff and the tenant exchanged correspondence about the heating system problems and the tenant's request for a rent reduction. Effective March 1, 1991, the parties agreed to reduce the total monthly rent to $7,000 through the end of the lease. The problems with the heating system are not an issue on appeal because, "while the parties litigated the issue of whether or not the lack of heat constituted a constructive eviction, [the tenant] conceded at the close of the evidence that the reduction in rent resolved this issue."

11.   The landlord alleged $5,500 in physical damages to the premises, including "damage . . . caused by a forklift, and ink stains on the floor." The judge found that the actual cost to repair the damages was "unclear," and that the damage sustained was not "beyond normal 'wear and tear.'"

12.   According to the landlord, tenant threatened to inform the landlord's mortgagee of "various alleged breaches of the mortgage covenants" and "alleged statements made by [the landlord] . . . to induce the mortgagee to make the loan" if the landlord did not dismiss the complaint. Although the landlord presented evidence of this claim at trial, no damages were proved and the judge dismissed the claim.

that even if the lease required the landlord to maintain the roof, his actions or failures did not rise to the level of constructive eviction.

The landlord's contention that the terms of the lease make the tenant responsible for maintaining the roof is an argument made first on appeal and is therefore waived. In any event, the judge's implicit finding that it was the landlord's obligation under the lease to keep the roof in good repair is fully supported by the evidence . . . .

. . . A constructive eviction is any "act of a permanent character, done by the landlord, or by his procurement, with the intention and effect of depriving the tenant of the enjoyment of the premises demised, or of a part thereof, to which he yields and abandons possession," . . . "within a reasonable time." Stone v. Sullivan, [300 Mass.] at 455. It is the tenant's burden to prove that he was constructively evicted. . . .

In ascertaining whether there has been a constructive eviction, it is "the landlord's conduct," and not his subjective intention, that "is controlling." Blackett v. Olanoff, 358 N.E.2d 817 (Mass. 1977). Therefore, a constructive eviction may be found even where a landlord did not intend to violate a tenant's rights, as the law assumes that the landlord intends "the natural and probable consequence of what [he] did, what he failed to do, or what he permitted to be done." However, not every act or failure to act on the part of the landlord that causes disruption to a tenant rises to the level of a constructive eviction. To constitute a constructive eviction, the act must have "some degree of substance and permanence of character." Tracy v. Long, 3 N.E.2d 789 (Mass. 1936). Thus, a landlord's failure to provide a service that is essential to the use and enjoyment of the demised premises may qualify as a constructive eviction.[15] Yet, conduct that does "not make the premises untenantable for the purposes for which they were used" will not constitute constructive eviction. A.W. Banister Co. v. P.J.W. Moodie Lumber Corp., 190 N.E. 727 (Mass. 1934) (landlord's breach of express covenant to supply steam to dry lumber "simply made the use [of the leased premises] less convenient and more expensive" and "[d]amages for breach of covenant . . . afforded an adequate remedy").[16]

14.   "In the absence of express agreement by a lessor to make repairs on leased premises not in his control, a failure to do so does not give the lessee the right to quit or to refuse to pay the rent, even though for lack of repair the leased premises became . . . unfit for the use for which they were leased." Stone v. Sullivan, 15 N.E.2d 476 (Mass. 1938).

15.   See Charles E. Burt, Inc. v. Seven Grand Corp., 163 N.E.2d 4 (Mass. 1959) (. . . electric power, heat, and elevator services, for six-month period . . .); Shindler v. Milden, 184 N.E. 673 (Mass. 1933) (. . . landlord failed to provide promised heating system; leased premises rendered unfit for intended use as restaurant); Rome v. Johnson, 174 N.E. 716 (Mass. 1931) (manufacturer constructively evicted by landlord's failure to provide sufficient heat over four-month period resulting in such extreme cold that "oil used in the machines slowed up their operation" and "at times . . . the [employees] had to stand around and could not do their work"); Boston Veterinary Hosp. v. Kiley, 107 N.E. 426 (Mass. 1914) (shutting off tenant's water rendered leased stables "unsuitable for the purposes for which they were hired"); Brown v. Holyoke Water-Power Co., 25 N.E. 966 (Mass. 1890) (. . . permanently disconnecting all power to machinery).

16.   See Sims v. Mason, 281 N.E.2d 608 (Mass. 1972) (lessors' failure to make promised improvements, to provide proper cleaning services, and to furnish suitable heat and air conditioning "not . . . sufficient to amount to a constructive eviction" of leased office space); Capp v. Chamberlain Real Estate, Inc., 242 N.E.2d 756 (Mass. 1968) (no constructive eviction from apartment leased for commercial use as studio where wiring adequate for normal use but inadequate to run air conditioners installed by lessee); Gateway Co. v. Charlotte Theatres, Inc., 297 F.2d 483 (1st Cir. 1961) (applying Massachusetts law and expressing "considerable doubt" as to whether "delay in failure to install the air conditioning could ever be regarded as a constructive eviction" that requires breach "of a fundamental nature, not just something that costs some money").

In this case, the . . . tenant was . . . required to prove that the leaks made "the premises untenantable for the purposes for which they were used." On this point, the tenant's evidence was inadequate as a matter of law.

The evidence of untenantability at trial consisted of testimony that (1) there were leaks "right on top" of one of the "high-tech," expensive cameras and that after "the camera got wet" it was covered with plastic sheeting so it would not get wet again; (2) a customer's preprinted paper stock was protected with plastic sheeting after a leak had "dampened the top portion" of his "skids of paper"; and (3) at times "the ceiling tiles got so wet that they . . . crumbled and fell out." There was no evidence that the leaks caused work stoppages, resulted in missed or delayed customer deliveries, or otherwise prevented the tenant from carrying on business. The tenant continued to conduct business from the time it first complained of the leaks in April, 1991, through the time the tenant moved out sometime after November 4, 1991. While the landlord's breach of his covenant to repair may have made the tenant's operation less convenient and more expensive . . . , it did not rise to the level of a constructive eviction.

4. *Application of the dependent covenants rule.* At common law, covenants in leases were considered "independent, in the absence of clear indications to the contrary, and the lessee [was] relieved from performance of his covenants only by actual or constructive eviction." Barry v. Frankini, 191 N.E. 651 (Mass. 1934). *See Restatement (Second) of Property (Landlord and Tenant)* Introductory Note to c. 7 (1977) ("At old common law the promises made by a landlord in a lease were independent obligations, so that the failure of the landlord to perform them did not give the tenant any right to disregard his obligations under the lease."). The independent covenants rule applied to both residential and commercial leases and was based on the assumption that "a lease is primarily a conveyance of an interest in real estate," Boston Hous. Auth. v. Hemingway, 293 N.E.2d 831 (Mass. 1973), and "reflected the parties' expectations in a rural agrarian society where the right to possession of the land constituted the chief element of the exchange." "The theory of a lease as a conveyance . . . fitted in well with the ancient farm lease. The lease was essentially of land; the house was incidental. Tenant got no services from landlord and expected none. Tenant was there, landlord absent. Tenant had tools that he was well versed in using. He could make such repairs as might be necessary." 1 M.R. Friedman, Leases § 1.1 at 5-6 (4th ed. 1997). As a result, "[e]ven if the landlord made express maintenance promises in the lease, courts often held that the landlord's breach of these 'secondary' obligations did not affect the tenant's obligation to pay rent." This apparent unfairness was balanced under the same doctrine by the inability of the landlord to recover possession of his property from a tenant even if the tenant breached its covenant to pay rent. Both lessor and lessee were limited in their remedies to seeking damages for breach of the lease covenants. *See* Note, *Modernizing Commercial Lease Law: The Case for an Implied Warranty of Fitness,* 19 Suffolk U. L. Rev. 929, 934 (1985). Any equilibrium that may have existed in this application of the rule was lost with the enactment of statutory dispossession actions, permitting landlords to regain possession of the premises if the tenant failed to pay rent even though the landlord may have breached express covenants within the lease. . . .

Exceptions to the independent covenants rule first emerged in the context of residential leases at the end of the Nineteenth Century. In 1892, this court held that the rule did not apply to the lease of "a furnished room or a furnished house for a few days or a few weeks or months." Ingalls v. Hobbs, 31 N.E. 286 (Mass. 1892). The rationale for this exception "rested on the broader premise that we would not apply the independent covenants rule in those cases where the essential purpose of the lease was not the transfer of an interest in land but the use of the demised premises for immediate occupation." Boston Hous. Auth. v. Hemingway, *supra*. As it applied to residential leases, the independent covenants rule was completely supplanted in 1973, when we recognized that a residential "lease is essentially a contract between the landlord and the tenant wherein the landlord promises to deliver and maintain the demised premises in habitable condition and the tenant promises to pay rent for such habitable premises." "These promises constitute interdependent and mutual considerations."

That decision was consistent with the national trend in residential leases away from interpretations based on classic property law doctrine that treated leases as "conveyances," and toward modern notions of leases as contracts for the possession of property, and modern notions of consumer protection. . . .

The development of the law of commercial leases has followed divergent paths. . . . Some courts interpret commercial leases as they would any other commercial contract; while others have taken a step in that direction by abolishing the independent covenants rule in favor of a rule of mutually dependent covenants. Still other courts have acted at the extremes, either by continuing strictly to apply the independent covenants rule, or by moving to the other end of the spectrum and recognizing an implied warranty of suitability in commercial leases. While we conclude that there is a need to move away from the rule of independent covenants, we continue to recognize that there are significant differences between commercial and residential tenancies and the policy considerations appropriate to each.

The landlord claims that the judge erred by applying the dependent covenants rule to the parties' lease and concluding that the landlord's failure "to provide an essential service, a dry space" would have permitted the tenant "lawfully [to withhold] rent had he not vacated the Wesson building." . . . As noted previously, the premise underlying the continued viability of the independent covenants rule is that a commercial lease is a conveyance of property where the right to possession of the land constitutes the chief element of the exchange. This premise no longer comports with the reality of the typical modern commercial lease, which is intended to secure the right to occupy improvements to the land rather than the land itself, and which usually contemplates a continuing flow of necessary services from landlord to tenant, services that are normally under the landlord's control. . . .

We conclude that the better rule is the rule of mutually dependent covenants set forth in the *Restatement (Second) of Property (Landlord and Tenant)* § 7.1 (1977), the principles of which we adopt to the extent necessary to resolve the issues in this case. Specifically, we adopt so much of the Restatement that provides as follows:

> Except to the extent the parties to a lease validly agree otherwise, if the landlord fails to perform a valid promise contained in the lease to do, or to refrain from doing, something . . . and as a consequence thereof, the tenant is deprived of a significant inducement to the making of the lease, and if the landlord does not perform his promise within a reasonable period of time after being requested to do so, the tenant may (1) terminate the lease . . . ."

"The rule of this section . . . is based on a logical extension of the position taken by a significant number of judicial decisions which have applied the [dependence of obligations] doctrine in connection with the failure of the landlord to fulfill his obligations in regard to the condition of the leased property." *Restatement* § 7.1 . . . Reporter's Note at 252. It also reflects our view of the better reasoned path to follow in modernizing the law of commercial leases.

Having adopted a rule of mutually dependent covenants, we now consider whether the tenant was entitled to vacate the premises prior to the lease termination date in light of our earlier conclusion that no constructive eviction occurred.[26]

The requirements of the rule we have adopted today are different from the requirements necessary to demonstrate a constructive eviction. For example, the rule does not require that the premises be "untenantable for the purposes for which they were used," in order for the tenant to terminate the lease and vacate the premises. It is sufficient for the tenant to demonstrate the landlord's failure, after notice, to perform a promise that was a significant inducement to the tenant's entering the lease in the first instance. We interpret this language to include promises that constitute a substantial benefit understood at the time the lease was entered to be significant to the purpose thereof. Richard Barton Enters., Inc. v. Tsern, 928 P.2d 368 (Utah 1996) (covenant to pay rent dependent on lessor's performance of covenants that were significant inducement to enter lease or significant to "the purpose for which the lessee entered into the lease"). Here that substantial benefit was a dry space necessary to safely conduct the high technology printing business for which the landlord knew the premises were to be used. In other cases, it might include promises having little to do with the condition of the premises, such as an agreement not to lease space in the same building to competing businesses. *See* Teodori v. Werner, 415 A.2d 31 (Pa. 1980) (landlord's noncompetition promise critical to commercial lease agreement).

Based on the judge's findings of fact, all of the requirements of the rule have been met in this case: the landlord breached his covenant to maintain the roof by failing to adequately repair its chronic leaking; the breach directly interfered with the tenant's business by depriving it of a substantial benefit significant to the purpose of the lease; and, after adequate notice, the landlord's efforts to

---

26.   Ordinarily, judicial changes to contract and property law are applied prospectively only, "[p]rimarily because of concern for litigants and others who have relied on existing precedents." Payton v. Abbott Labs, 437 N.E.2d 171 (Mass. 1982). *See* Johnson Controls, Inc. v. Bowes, 409 N.E.2d 185 (Mass. 1980) (insurance contracts); Whitinsville Plaza, Inc. v. Kotseas, 390 N.E.2d 243 (Mass. 1979) (covenants not to compete in deeds and leases). Such concerns are compelling where "the change of existing laws involves a previously unquestioned aspect of . . . law, in which reliance interests exert a strong influence." Johnson Controls, Inc. v. Bowes, 409 N.E.2d 185. These are not the circumstances of the rule we adopt in this case. The abandonment of the rule of independent covenants in commercial leases has been foreshadowed at least since our 1973 decision in Boston Hous. Auth. v. Hemingway, supra, in which we abandoned the rule in residential leases. In the interim, the *Restatement (Second) of Property (Landlord and Tenant)* (1977) adopted the rule of dependent covenants, and the lack of continued vitality in Massachusetts of the rule of independent covenants has been foreshadowed in cases decided by the Appeals Court, Holmes Realty Trust v. Granite City Storage Co., *supra*, and by the Federal court, Reed v. United States Postal Serv., *supra*. In these circumstances, commercial landlords and tenants have had ample warning and opportunity to anticipate such a change and to incorporate appropriate provisions in their lease agreements. The concern for reliance on unquestioned precedent is simply not present here. Consequently, we apply the rule to the lease in this case.

correct the problem were both "shoddy and unsuccessful." The tenant was entitled to terminate the lease and recover relocation costs in the amount determined by the judge. . . .

Notes and Questions

1. Implied into every lease is a covenant of quiet enjoyment. The covenant protects against disturbance of the tenant's possession by the landlord or persons claiming under him. The covenant is breached when the landlord actually evicts the tenant in violation of the leasehold, such as by locking the tenant out of the premises. *See Turks Head Realty Trust v. Shearson Lehman Hutton, Inc.*, 736 F. Supp. 422 (D.R.I. 1990). It has long been recognized in American law that the covenant of quiet enjoyment is also breached when the tenant is constructively evicted from the premises even though the landlord did not physically oust the tenant. The tenant could bring an action for damages against the landlord for breach of the implied covenant of quiet enjoyment.

As detailed in *Wesson*, the doctrine of independent covenants traditionally prevailed in landlord and tenant law. Unlike contract law, where covenants are dependent, the breach by the landlord of a material covenant in the lease did not generally give the tenant the right to cease performance. So, for example, the failure of the landlord to fulfill an express covenant to repair did not allow the tenant to stop, or reduce, rent payments. A key exception, however, was the implied covenant of quiet enjoyment, where the courts found that an actual or constructive eviction excused the tenant from the rent obligation. As a result, tenants (such as in *Blackett*) could defend actions by landlords seeking rent by showing an actual or constructive eviction. *See* Mary Ann Glendon, *The Transformation of American Landlord-Tenant Law*, 23 B.C. L. Rev. 503, 511-14 (1982).

[handwritten margin note: constructive eviction = defense for not paying rent!]

As an example of facts permitting the court to find a constructive eviction by the landlord, see *Bermuda Avenue Shopping Center v. Rappaport*, 565 So. 2d 805 (Fla. Dist. Ct. App. 1990) (after tenant moved into space within shopping mall, landlord began mall renovation causing dirt, dust, and construction debris to intrude into tenant's space and also blocking nearby parking spaces and sidewalks). For a complete discussion of actual and constructive eviction, see Robert Schoshinski, *American Law of Landlord and Tenant* §§ 3.3-3.8 (1980).

2. How did the court find that the landlord breached the implied covenant of quiet enjoyment in *Blackett* even though it was not the landlord's music that caused the disturbance? Is the court's distinction between malfeasance and misfeasance viable? Should the result have been different if the landlord had rented to the lounge before renting to the defendants? What policies support finding a constructive eviction when the tenant is disturbed by other tenants? Consider *Restatement (Second) of Property—Landlord and Tenant* § 6.1 cmt. *d*:

> d. *Conduct of a third person outside of leased property that is attributable to landlord.* The conduct of a third person outside of the leased property that is performed on property in which the landlord has an interest, which conduct could be legally controlled by him, is attributable to the landlord for the purposes of applying the rule of this section. Conduct of a third person outside the leased property, no matter

where it is carried on, will be attributable to the landlord for the purposes of the rule of this section if the landlord is a contributing factor to the conduct.

As the court in *Blackett* notes, courts usually refuse to find a constructive eviction when other tenants, not the landlord, cause the disturbance. *See* Annotation, *Landlord and Tenant: Constructive Eviction by Another Tenant's Conduct,* 1 A.L.R. 4th 849 (1980). What is the theory behind that view?

3. The *Blackett* court indicates that the landlord could have forced the bar to stop disturbing the other tenants. Where the lease is silent, the Uniform Residential Landlord and Tenant Act § 3.101(7) provides:

landlord has a course to take —

> A tenant shall . . . conduct himself and require other persons on the premises with his consent to conduct themselves in a manner that will not disturb his neighbors' peaceful enjoyment of the premises.

Are there any benefits in granting such express or legislative power over tenants to landlords? Are there disadvantages?

A tenant may be in breach of her lease for certain disturbances even in the absence of a relevant lease provision. Under common-law principles, if a tenant undertakes an illegal use of the property and the landlord is not a party to the illegality, the tenant may be liable in damages and subject to an injunction. Robert Schoshinski, *American Law of Landlord and Tenant* § 5:12 (1980). Statutes in many jurisdictions also permit eviction for illegal use. *See, e.g.,* Minn. Stat. § 504B.171 (inserting in all leases a covenant by tenant barring unlawful controlled substances in premises, common areas, and surroundings); N.Y. Real Prop. Acts. Law § 711(5) (premises cannot be used for any illegal trade or manufacture or other illegal business); N.Y. Real Prop. Acts. Law § 715 (barring illegal drug activity). Tough issues arise. For example, the United States Supreme *example* Court upheld a lease provision allowing a tenant in public housing to be evicted if any member of the tenant's household, the tenant's guest, or other person under the tenant's control engaged in drug-related criminal activity on or near the premises. Such provisions were required by Congress in leases involving HUD housing, under the Anti-Drug Abuse Act of 1988, 42 U.S.C. § 1437d. The Court rejected the "innocent" tenant defense and permitted eviction even if the tenant was not personally aware of the drug activity, finding that the "plain meaning" of the statute did not provide for an exception. *Department of Housing and Urban Development v. Rucker,* 535 U.S. 125 (2002).

Other antisocial behavior may also breach the lease. For example, under a 1982 New York statute, a tenant in cities with more than 1 million people may be evicted if the tenant removes the batteries from a smoke detector or otherwise makes it inoperable and does not cure the default within 30 days after receiving a court notice of such violation. N.Y. Real Prop. Acts. Law § 711(6).

Finally, general nuisance principles may be brought to bear against a disturbing tenant and may be used, under some statutes, as the basis of an eviction. One court evicted a tenant from his apartment in the "fashionable Mayflower Hotel" where he had lived for 16 years because of the behavior of the tenant's nephew (and ward) who lived with the tenant. The nephew suffered from chronic schizophrenia and engaged in "detailed incidents of nudity in public places in the hotel; verbal abuse, profanity and vulgarity toward hotel guests and staff; hazard to health and safety of others by maintenance of unsanitary conditions and lack of attention to personal hygiene; and veiled threats of physical and sexual assault." The nephew's behavior could be controlled by medication, but he neglected to take it. The court found that the landlord was entitled to relief based on the nuisance that had already occurred. The court held that it was proper since there was no way to ensure that the nephew would take his medication and the nephew could return to the building to visit his uncle even if the nephew were to live in another place. "The safety and domestic tranquility of the other tenants in the building, to say nothing of [the landlord's] staff, demand protection of the law in the form of the eviction of [the tenant], whose conduct permitted and condoned the nuisance, and whose tenancy itself, in all likelihood, will encourage the nuisance to continue unabated." *Frank v. Park Summit Realty Corp.*, 573 N.Y.S.2d 655 (App. Div. 1991).

What about second-hand smoke seeping into one tenant's apartment from another? *See Poyck v. Bryant*, 820 N.Y.S.2d 774 (Civ. Ct. N.Y. 2006).

4. What standards does the *Wesson* court articulate for the tenant to succeed in a constructive eviction claim as opposed to the dependent covenant defense? Is there a viable distinction between the two standards? Are those standards breached on the facts of *Wesson*?

Can a constructive eviction be found on the following facts? A gynecologist, whose practice included performing elective abortions, leased space for his medical practice in an office building. A few months into the lease, antiabortion protesters began picketing outside and inside the building on Saturdays (the day on which the doctor performed abortions). The protesters sang and chanted, distributed literature, and approached patients to speak to them. Sometimes the protesters occupied the stairs or the doctor's waiting room, preventing patients from reaching the office. The doctor vacated the premises, after the protests continued for six months. Would the result differ if the lease required the landlord to provide a security guard seven days a week but none were ever provided for weekends? If the sheriff's office refused the doctor's request to arrest the protesters under criminal trespass laws unless the landlord, as owner of the building, also requested sheriff involvement? *See Fidelity Mutual Life Insurance Co. v. Kaminsky*, 768 S.W.2d 818 (Tex. Ct. App. 1989).

5. Courts have generally held that in order to prevail on a claim of constructive eviction, the tenant must move out. This requirement, however, places an especial burden on lower-income residential tenants, since the shortage of habitable, low-cost housing makes it unlikely that a vacating tenant can find alternative accommodations. *See generally* Edward H. Rabin, *The Revolution in Residential Landlord-Tenant Law: Causes and Consequences*, 69 Cornell L. Rev. 517, 540-54 (1984).

Moreover, the move-out requirement puts all tenants in a difficult legal position. If the tenant moves out in order to assert constructive eviction and rents new premises, and a court subsequently finds that there was no breach of the implied covenant of quiet enjoyment, the tenant will be liable on two leases. The move-out rule forces tenants to make difficult economic choices based on inadequate information and guesses about future court determinations. Consider how the attorney might help in such situations.

Are there any current justifications for the requirement that the tenant must move out? How would you construct an argument against the rule?

There have been a few judicial decisions in limited circumstances that reject the move-out requirement. *See, e.g., Charles E. Burt, Inc. v. Seven Grand Corp.*, 163

N.E.2d 4 (Mass. 1959) (finding an "equitable constructive eviction and requiring a commercial tenant who stayed in possession to pay only a reduced rent). *The Restatement (Second) of Property—Landlord and Tenant* § 6.1 Reporter's note 5 rejects the requirement that the tenant move out to claim constructive eviction and permits the tenant to remain in possession with an abatement of rent for the landlord's breach. *Accord Echo Consulting Services, Inc. v. North Conway Bank*, 669 A.2d 227 (N.H. 1995) (tenant can recover for reduction of value of leasehold due to breach of implied covenant of quiet enjoyment even though interference did not severely interfere with right to possession).

Problems: Constructive Eviction

1. INT executed a five-year lease to be a tenant in an office building. One year later, the landlord leased a suite of offices across the hall from INT to JELC, a day care center. INT is a nonprofit organization that provides translations of the liturgical book of the Roman Catholic Church. INT believes that its work requires a scholarly and professional environment. There was some noise caused by the children at JELC that could, at times, be heard in INT's office. INT's first communication with the landlord about this situation was by a letter to the landlord asserting that INT was moving out because of the noise from JELC. INT moved to new quarters the next month. Can INT successfully defend an action for rent by the landlord for the rest of the lease term? *See International Commission on English in the Liturgy v. Schwartz*, 573 A.2d 1303 (D.C. Ct. App. 1990); *Restatement (Second) of Property—Landlord and Tenant* § 6.1.

2. Infinity leased space in a Chicago office building, with the lease stating that the space would be used by Infinity to operate a radio station. The lease also granted a license to Infinity to install an antenna on the roof. Landlord subsequently announced plans to build a 64-story building on land that it owned next to the building in which Infinity leased space. Infinity informed Landlord that the new building would interfere with the broadcasts from its antenna. Landlord built the new building, and it did indeed reduce the reception from Infinity's station to some extent. Could Infinity successfully claim a constructive eviction? *See Infinity Broadcasting Corp. v. Prudential Insurance Co.*, 869 F.2d 1073 (7th Cir. 1989).

3. Condition of the Premises: The Warranty of Habitability

Landlord

JAVINS v. FIRST NATIONAL REALTY CORP.

United States Court of Appeals, District of Columbia Circuit
428 F.2d 1071 (D.C. Cir. 1970)

WRIGHT, J. These cases present the question whether housing code violations which arise during the term of a lease have any effect upon the tenant's obligation to pay rent. . . .

Because of the importance of the question presented, we granted appellants' petitions for leave to appeal. We now reverse and hold that a warranty of habitability, measured by the standards set out in the Housing Regulations for the District of Columbia, is implied by operation of law into leases of urban dwelling units covered by those Regulations and that breach of this warranty gives rise to the usual remedies for breach of contract.

holding

I

. . . By separate written leases, each of the appellants rented an apartment in a three-building apartment complex in Northwest Washington known as Clifton Terrace. The landlord, First National Realty Corporation, filed separate actions in the Landlord and Tenant Branch of the Court of General Sessions on April 8, 1966, seeking possession on the ground that each of the appellants had defaulted in the payment of rent due for the month of April. The tenants, appellants here, admitted that they had not paid the landlord any rent for April. However, they alleged numerous violations of the Housing Regulations as "an equitable defense or [a] claim by way of recoupment or set-off in an amount equal to the rent claim." . . . They offered to prove "[t]hat there are approximately 1500 violations . . . some affecting the premises of this Defendant directly, others indirectly, and all tending to establish a course of conduct of violation of the Housing Regulations to the damage of Defendants. . . ." . . . Appellants conceded at trial, however, that this offer of proof reached only violations which had arisen since the term of the lease had commenced. The Court of General Sessions refused appellants' offer of proof and entered judgment for the landlord. The District of Columbia Court of Appeals affirmed, rejecting the argument made by appellants that the landlord was under a contractual duty to maintain the premises in compliance with the Housing Regulations. . . .

Facts.

Δ seeks.

π argue.

π appellant argues violations after lease began.

— PP

II

Since, in traditional analysis, a lease was the conveyance of an interest in land, courts have usually utilized the special rules governing real property transactions to resolve controversies involving leases. However, as the Supreme Court has noted in another context, "the body of private property law . . . , more than almost any other branch of law, has been shaped by distinctions whose validity is largely historical." Courts have a duty to reappraise old doctrines in the light of the facts and values of contemporary life—particularly old common law doctrines which the courts themselves created and developed. As we have said before, "[T]he continued vitality of the common law . . . depends upon its ability to reflect contemporary community values and ethics."

old rule is changed.

common law depends on today.

The assumption of landlord-tenant law, derived from feudal property law, that a lease primarily conveyed to the tenant an interest in land may have been reasonable in a rural, agrarian society; it may continue to be reasonable in some leases involving farming or commercial land. In these cases, the value of the lease to the tenant is the land itself. But in the case of the modern apartment dweller, the value of the lease is that it gives him a place to live. The city dweller who seeks to lease an apartment on the third floor of a tenement has little interest in the land 30 or 40 feet below, or even in the bare right to possession within the four walls of his apartment. When American city dwellers, both rich and poor, seek "shelter" today, they seek a well known package of goods and services—a package which includes not merely walls and ceilings, but also adequate heat, light and ventilation, serviceable plumbing facilities, secure windows and doors, proper sanitation, and proper maintenance. . . .

Some courts have realized that certain of the old rules of property law governing leases are inappropriate for today's transactions . . . [and] have been gradually introducing more modern precepts of contract law in interpreting leases. Proceeding piecemeal has, however, led to confusion where "decisions are frequently conflicting, not because of a healthy disagreement on social policy, but because of the lingering impact of rules whose policies are long since dead."

In our judgment the trend toward treating leases as contracts is wise and well considered. Our holding in this case reflects a belief that leases of urban dwelling units should be interpreted and construed like any other contract.[13]

III

Modern contract law has recognized that the buyer of goods and services in an industrialized society must rely upon the skill and honesty of the supplier to assure that goods and services purchased are of adequate quality. In interpreting most contracts, courts have sought to protect the legitimate expectations of the buyer and have steadily widened the seller's responsibility for the quality of goods and services through the implied warranties of fitness and merchantability. Thus without any special agreement a merchant will be held to warrant that his goods are fit for the ordinary purposes for which such goods are used and that they are at least of reasonably average quality. Moreover, if the supplier has been notified that goods are required for a specific purpose, he will be held to warrant that any goods sold are fit for that purpose. These implied warranties have become widely accepted and well established features of the common law, supported by the overwhelming body of case law. Today most states as well as the District of Columbia have codified and enacted these warranties into statute, as to the sale of goods, in the Uniform Commercial Code.

Implied warranties of quality have not been limited to cases involving sales. The consumer renting a chattel, paying for services, or buying a combination of goods and services must rely upon the skill and honesty of the supplier to at least the same extent as a purchaser of goods. Courts have not hesitated to find implied warranties of fitness and merchantability in such situations. In most areas product liability law has moved far beyond "mere" implied warranties running between two parties in privity with each other.

---

13.   This approach does not deny the possible importance of the fact that land is involved in a transaction. The interpretation and construction of contracts between private parties has always required courts to be sensitive and responsive to myriad different factors. We believe contract doctrines allow courts to be properly sensitive to all relevant factors in interpreting lease obligations.

We also intend no alteration of statutory or case law definitions of the term "real property" for purposes of statutes or decisions on recordation, descent, conveyancing, creditors' rights, etc. We contemplate only that contract law is to determine the rights and obligations of the parties to the lease agreement, as between themselves. The civil law has always viewed the lease as a contract, and in our judgment that perspective has proved superior to that of the common law. *See* 2 M. Planiol, Treatise on the Civil Law § 1663 *et seq.* (1959); 11 La. Stat. Ann., Civil Code, Art. 2669 (1952).

The rigid doctrines of real property law have tended to inhibit the application of implied warranties to transactions involving real estate. Now, however, courts have begun to hold sellers and developers of real property responsible for the quality of their product.[21] For example, builders of new homes have recently been held liable to purchasers for improper construction on the ground that the builders had breached an implied warranty of fitness.[22] In other cases courts have held builders of new homes liable for breach of an implied warranty that all local building regulations had been complied with.[23] And following the developments in other areas, very recent decisions[24] and commentary[25] suggest the possible extension of liability to parties other than the immediate seller for improper construction of residential real estate.

[margin note: warranties inhibited by Real Property Law.]

Despite this trend in the sale of real estate, many courts have been unwilling to imply warranties of quality, specifically a warranty of habitability, into leases of apartments. Recent decisions have offered no convincing explanation for their refusal; rather they have relied without discussion upon the old common law rule that the lessor is not obligated to repair unless he covenants to do so in the written lease contract. However, the Supreme Courts of at least two states, in recent and well reasoned opinions, have held landlords to implied warranties of quality in housing leases. Lemle v. Breeden, S. Ct. Hawaii, 462 P.2d 470 (1969); Reste Realty Corp. v. Cooper, 251 A.2d 268 (N.J. 1969). *See also* Pines v. Perssion, 111 N.W.2d 409 (Wis. 1961). In our judgment, the old no-repair rule cannot coexist with the obligations imposed on the landlord by a typical modern housing code, and must be abandoned in favor of an implied warranty of habitability. In the District of Columbia, the standards of this warranty are set out in the Housing Regulations.

[margin note: Old rule: must be in lease to fix (Landlords not often held to implied warranty)]

IV

A. In our judgment the common law itself must recognize the landlord's obligation to keep his premises in a habitable condition. This conclusion is compelled by three separate considerations. First, we believe that the old rule was ① based on certain factual assumptions which are no longer true; on its own terms, it can no longer be justified. Second, we believe that the consumer protection ② cases discussed above require that the old rule be abandoned in order to bring residential landlord-tenant law into harmony with the principles on which those

---

21.   *See generally* Bearman, *Caveat Emptor in Sale of Realty — Recent Assaults Upon the Rule*, 14 Vand. L. Rev. 541 (1961); Dunham, *Vendor's Obligation as to Fitness of Land for a Particular Purpose*, 37 Minn. L. Rev. 108 (1953).

22.   *See* Waggoner v. Midwestern Development, Inc., S.D., 154 N.W.2d 803 (1967); Bethlahmy v. Bechtel, 91 Idaho 55, 415 P.2d 698 (1969); Schipper v. Levitt & Sons, Inc., [44 N.J. 70, 207 A.2d 314 (1965)]; Carpenter v. Donohoe, 154 Colo. 78, 388 P.2d 399 (1964); Loraso v. Custom Built Homes, Inc., La. App., 144 So. 2d 459 (1962). Other cases still continue the older limitation on the vendor's liability to homes sold before construction is complete. *See, e.g.,* Hoye v. Century Builders, 52 Wash. 2d 830, 329 P.2d 474 (1958).

23.   *See* Schiro v. W. E. Gould & Co., 18 Ill. 2d 538, 165 N.E.2d 286 (1960); Annot., 110 A.L.R. 1048 (1937).

24.   Connor v. Great Western Savings and Loan Ass'n, 69 Cal. 2d 850, 73 Cal. Rptr. 369, 447 P.2d 609 (1968) (in bank) (Traynor, Ch. J.). Chief Justice Traynor's excellent opinion utilizes tort doctrines to extend liability beyond the immediate seller.

25.   Comment, *Liability of the Institutional Lender for Structural Defects in New Housing*, 35 U. Chi. L. Rev. 739 (1968).

cases rest. Third, we think that the nature of today's urban housing market also dictates abandonment of the old rule.

The common law rule absolving the lessor of all obligation to repair originated in the early Middle Ages.[30]

Court decisions in the late 1800s began to recognize that the factual assumptions of the common law were no longer accurate in some cases. For example, the common law, since it assumed that the land was the most important part of the leasehold, required a tenant to pay rent even if any building on the land was destroyed. Faced with such a rule and the ludicrous results it produced, in 1863 the New York Court of Appeals declined to hold that an upper story tenant was obliged to continue paying rent after his apartment building burned down. The court simply pointed out that the urban tenant had no interest in the land, only in the attached building.

Another line of cases created an exception to the no-repair rule for short term leases of furnished dwellings. The Massachusetts Supreme Judicial Court, a court not known for its willingness to depart from the common law, supported this exception . . . .[37]

. . . Today's urban[39] tenants, the vast majority of whom live in multiple dwelling houses, are interested, not in the land, but solely in "a house suitable for occupation." Furthermore, today's city dweller usually has a single, specialized skill unrelated to maintenance work; he is unable to make repairs like the "jack-of-all-trades" farmer who was the common law's model of the lessee. Further, unlike his agrarian predecessor who often remained on one piece of land for his entire life, urban tenants today are more mobile than ever before. A tenant's tenure in a specific apartment will often not be sufficient to justify efforts at repairs. In addition, the increasing complexity of today's dwellings renders them much more difficult to repair than the structures of earlier times. In a multiple dwelling repair may require access to equipment and areas in the control of the landlord. Low and middle income tenants, even if they were interested in making repairs, would be unable to obtain any financing for major repairs since they have no long-term interest in the property.

. . . The landlord sells housing as a commercial businessman and has much greater opportunity, incentive and capacity to inspect and maintain the condition of his building. Moreover, the tenant must rely upon the skill and bona

---

30. The rule was "settled" by 1485. 3 W. Holdsworth, A History of English Law 122-123 (6th ed. 1934). The common law rule . . . originated in the even older rule prohibiting the tenant from committing waste. The writ of waste expanded as the tenant's right to possession grew stronger. Eventually, . . . to protect the landowner's reversionary interest, the tenant became obligated to make repairs and liable to eviction and damages if he failed to do so.

The land was so central to the original common law conception of a leasehold that rent was viewed as "issuing" from the land: "[T]he governing idea is that the land is bound to pay the rent. . . . We may almost go to the length of saying that the land pays it through [the tenant's] hand." 2 F. Pollock & F. Maitland, The History of English Law 131 (2d ed. 1923).

Even the old common law courts responded with a different rule for a landlord-tenant relationship which did not conform to the model of the usual agrarian lease. Much more substantial obligations were placed upon the keepers of inns (the only multiple dwelling houses known to the common law). Their guests were interested solely in shelter and could not be expected to make their own repairs. . . . [Footnotes 30, 31, and 33 in the opinion have been combined.—EDS.]

37. Ingalls v. Hobbs, 156 Mass. 348, 31 N.E. 286 (1892).

39. In 1968 more than two thirds of America's people lived in the 228 largest metropolitan areas. Only 5.2% lived on farms. The World Almanac 1970 at 251 (L. Long ed.). More than 98% of all housing starts in 1968 were non-farm. Id. at 313.

fides of his landlord at least as much as a car buyer must rely upon the car man-ufacturer. In dealing with major problems, such as heating, plumbing, electri-cal or structural defects, the tenant's position corresponds precisely with "the ordinary consumer who cannot be expected to have the knowledge or capacity or even the opportunity to make adequate inspection of mechanical instrumen-talities, like automobiles, and to decide for himself whether they are reasonably fit for the designed purpose." Henningsen v. Bloomfield Motors, Inc., 161 A.2d 69 (N.J. 1960).[42]

Since a lease contract specifies a particular period of time during which the tenant has a right to use his apartment for shelter, he may legitimately expect that the apartment will be fit for habitation for the time period for which it is rented. We point out that in the present cases there is no allegation that appellants' apartments were in poor condition or in violation of the housing code at the commencement of the leases.[43] Since the lessees continue to pay the same rent, they were entitled to expect that the landlord would continue to keep the premises in their beginning condition during the lease term. It is precisely such expectations that the law now recognizes as deserving of formal, legal protection.

Even beyond the rationale of traditional products liability law, the relation-ship of landlord and tenant suggests further compelling reasons for the law's protection of the tenants' legitimate expectations of quality. The inequality in bargaining power between landlord and tenant has been well documented. Tenants have very little leverage to enforce demands for better housing. Various impediments to competition in the rental housing market, such as racial and class discrimination and standardized form leases, mean that landlords place tenants in a take it or leave it situation. The increasingly severe shortage of ade-quate housing further increases the landlord's bargaining power and escalates the need for maintaining and improving the existing stock. Finally, the findings by various studies of the social impact of bad housing has led to the realization that poor housing is detrimental to the whole society, not merely to the unlucky ones who must suffer the daily indignity of living in a slum.

Thus we are led by our inspection of the relevant legal principles and pre-cedents to the conclusion that the old common law rule imposing an obligation upon the lessee to repair during the lease term was really never intended to apply to residential urban leaseholds. Contract principles established in other areas of the law provide a more rational framework for the apportionment of landlord-tenant responsibilities; they strongly suggest that a warranty of habit-ability be implied into all contracts[49] for urban dwellings.

42.   Nor should the average tenant be thought capable of "inspecting" plaster, floorboards, roofing, kitchen appliances, etc. To the extent, however, that some defects are obvious, the law must take note of the present housing shortage. Tenants may have no real alternative but to accept such housing with the expectation that the landlord will make necessary repairs. Where this is so, caveat emptor must of necessity be rejected.

43.   In Brown v. Southall Realty Co., 237 A.2d 834 (1968), the District of Columbia Court of Appeals held that unsafe and unsanitary conditions existing at the beginning of the tenancy and known to the landlord rendered any lease of those premises illegal and void.

49.   We need not consider the provisions of the written lease governing repairs since this implied warranty of the landlord could not be excluded. See Henningsen v. Bloomfield Motors, Inc., [32 N.J. 358, 161 A.2d 69 (1960)]; Kay v. Cain, 81 U.S. App. D.C. 24, 25, 154 F.2d 305, 306 (1946). . . .

B. We believe, in any event, that the District's housing code requires that a warranty of habitability be implied in the leases of all housing that it covers. . . . The . . . Regulations provide a comprehensive regulatory scheme setting forth in some detail: (a) the standards which housing in the District of Columbia must meet; (b) which party, the lessor or the lessee, must meet each standard; and (c) a system of inspections, notifications and criminal penalties. The Regulations themselves are silent on the question of private remedies.

Two previous decisions of this court, however, have held that the Housing Regulations create legal rights and duties enforceable in tort by private parties. In Whetzel v. Jess Fisher Management Co., 282 F.2d 943 (D.C. App. 1960), we followed the leading case of Altz v. Lieberson, 134 N.E. 703 (N.Y. 1922), in holding (1) that the housing code altered the common law rule and imposed a duty to repair upon the landlord, and (2) that a right of action accrued to a tenant injured by the landlord's breach of this duty. As Judge Cardozo wrote in *Lieberson*:

> . . . We may be sure that the framers of this statute, when regulating tenement life, had uppermost in thought the care of those who are unable to care for themselves. The Legislature must have known that unless repairs in the rooms of the poor were made by the landlord, they would not be made by any one. The duty imposed became commensurate with the need. The right to seek redress is not limited to the city or its officers. The right extends to all whom there was a purpose to protect. . . .

The District of Columbia Court of Appeals gave further effect to the Housing Regulations in Brown v. Southall Realty Co., 237 A.2d 834 (1968). There the landlord knew at the time the lease was signed that housing code violations existed which rendered the apartment "unsafe and unsanitary." Viewing the lease as a contract, the [court] held that the premises were let in violation of Sections 2304 and 2501 of the Regulations and that the lease, therefore, was void as an illegal contract. In the light of *Brown*, it is clear not only that the housing code creates privately enforceable duties as held in *Whetzel*, but that the basic validity of every housing contract depends upon substantial compliance with the housing code at the beginning of the lease term. The *Brown* court relied particularly upon Section 2501 of the Regulations which provides:

> Every premises accommodating one or more habitations shall be maintained and kept in repair so as to provide decent living accommodations for the occupants. This part of this Code contemplates more than mere basic repairs and maintenance to keep out the elements; its purpose is to include repairs and maintenance designed to make a premises or neighborhood healthy and safe.

By its terms, this section applies to maintenance and repair during the lease term. Under the *Brown* holding, serious failure to comply with this section before the lease term begins renders the contract void. We think it untenable to find that this section has no effect on the contract after it has been signed. To the contrary, by signing the lease the landlord has undertaken a continuing obligation to the tenant to maintain the premises in accordance with all applicable law.

This principle of implied warranty is well established. Courts often imply relevant law into contracts to provide a remedy for any damage caused by one party's illegal conduct. In a case closely analogous to the present ones, the Illinois Supreme Court held that a builder who constructed a house in violation of the Chicago building code had breached his contract with the buyer:

> . . . [T]he law existing at the time and place of the making of the contract is deemed a part of the contract, as though expressly referred to or incorporated in it. . . .
>
> The rationale for this rule is that the parties to the contract would have expressed that which the law implies "had they not supposed that it was unnecessary to speak of it because the law provided for it." . . . Consequently, the courts, in construing the existing law as part of the express contract, are not reading into the contract provisions different from those expressed and intended by the parties, . . . but are merely construing the contract in accordance with the intent of the parties.[56]

We follow the Illinois court in holding that the housing code must be read into housing contracts—a holding also required by the purposes and the structure of the code itself. The duties imposed by the Housing Regulations may not be waived or shifted by agreement if the Regulations specifically place the duty upon the lessor.[58] Criminal penalties are provided if these duties are ignored. This regulatory structure was established by the Commissioners because, in their judgment, the grave conditions in the housing market required serious action. Yet official enforcement of the housing code has been far from uniformly effective. Innumerable studies have documented the desperate condition of rental housing in the District of Columbia and in the nation. In view of these circumstances, we think the conclusion reached by the Supreme Court of Wisconsin as to the effect of a housing code on the old common law rule cannot be avoided:

> . . . [T]he legislature has made a policy judgment—that it is socially (and politically) desirable to impose these duties on a property owner—which has rendered the old common law rule obsolete. To follow the old rule of no implied warranty of habitability in leases would, in our opinion, be inconsistent with the current legislative policy concerning housing standards. . . .[60]

56.   Schiro v. W. E. Gould & Co., *supra* [n.]23, 18 Ill. 2d at 544, 165 N.E.2d at 290. As a general proposition, it is undoubtedly true that parties to a contract intend that applicable law will be complied with by both sides. We recognize, however, that reading statutory provisions into private contracts may have little factual support in the intentions of the particular parties now before us. But, for reasons of public policy, warranties are often implied into contracts by operation of law in order to meet generally prevailing standards of honesty and fair dealing. When the public policy has been enacted into law like the housing code, that policy will usually have deep roots in the expectations and intentions of most people. *See* Costigan, *Implied-in-Fact Contracts and Mutual Assent,* 33 Harv. L. Rev. 376, 383-385 (1920).

58.   Any private agreement to shift the duties would be illegal and unenforceable. The precedents dealing with industrial safety statutes are directly in point:

> . . . [T]he only question remaining is whether the courts will enforce or recognize as against a servant an agreement express or implied on his part to waive the performance of a statutory duty of the master imposed for the protection of the servant, and in the interest of the public, and enforceable by criminal prosecution. We do not think they will. To do so would be to nullify the object of the statute. . . . Narramore v. Cleveland, C, C. & St. L. Ry. Co., 6 Cir., 96 F. 298 (1899). *See* W. Prosser, Torts § 67 at 468-469 (3d ed. 1964) and cases cited therein.

60.   Pines v. Perssion, 111 N.W.2d 409 (Wis. 1961). *Accord,* Buckner v. Azulai, 251 Cal. App. 2d Supp. 1013 (1967).

We therefore hold that the Housing Regulations imply a warranty of habitability, measured by the standards which they set out, into leases of all housing that they cover.

V

In the present cases, the landlord sued for possession for nonpayment of rent. Under contract principles,[61] however, the tenant's obligation to pay rent is dependent upon the landlord's performance of his obligations, including his warranty to maintain the premises in habitable condition. In order to determine whether any rent is owed to the landlord, the tenants must be given an opportunity to prove the housing code violations alleged as breach of the landlord's warranty.[62]

At trial, the finder of fact must make two findings: (1) whether the alleged violations[63] existed during the period for which past due rent is claimed, and (2) what portion, if any or all, of the tenant's obligation to pay rent was suspended by the landlord's breach. If no part of the tenant's rental obligation is found to have been suspended, then a judgment for possession may issue forthwith. On the other hand, if the Jury determines that the entire rental obligation has been extinguished by the landlord's total breach, then the action for possession on the ground of nonpayment must fail.[64]

The jury may find that part of the tenant's rental obligation has been suspended but that part of the unpaid back rent is indeed owed to the landlord. In these circumstances, no judgment for possession should issue if the tenant agrees to pay the partial rent found to be due. If the tenant refuses to pay the partial amount, a judgment for possession may then be entered.

The Judgment of the District of Columbia Court of Appeals is reversed and the cases are remanded for further proceedings consistent with this opinion.[67]

---

61. In extending all contract remedies for breach to the parties to a lease, we include an action for specific performance of the landlord's implied warranty of habitability.

62. To be relevant, of course, the violations must affect the tenant's apartment or common areas which the tenant uses. Moreover, the contract principle that no one may benefit from his own wrong will allow the landlord to defend by proving the damage was caused by the tenant's wrongful action. However, violations resulting from inadequate repairs or materials which disintegrate under normal use would not be assignable to the tenant. Also we agree with the District of Columbia Court of Appeals that the tenant's private rights do not depend on official inspection or official finding of violation by the city government. Diamond Housing Corp. v. Robinson, 257 A.2d 492, 494 (1969).

63. The jury should be instructed that one or two minor violations standing alone which do not affect habitability are de minimis and would not entitle the tenant to a reduction in rent.

64. As soon as the landlord made the necessary repairs rent would again become due. Our holding, of course, affects only eviction for nonpayment of rent. The landlord is free to seek eviction at the termination of the lease or on any other legal ground.

67. Appellants in the present cases offered to pay rent into the registry of the court during the present action. We think this is an excellent protective procedure. If the tenant defends against an action for possession on the basis of breach of the landlord's warranty of habitability, the trial court may require the tenant to make future rent payments into the registry of the court as they become due; such a procedure would be appropriate only while the tenant remains in possession. The escrowed money will, however, represent rent for the period between the time the landlord files suit and the time the case comes to trial. In the normal course of litigation, the only factual question at trial would be the condition of the apartment during the time the landlord alleged rent was due and not paid.

As a general rule, the escrowed money should be apportioned between the landlord and the tenant after trial on the basis of the finding of rent actually due for the period at issue in the suit. To

N.Y. REAL PROP. LAW § 235-B (ADDED 1975, AS AMENDED 1976)

1. In every written or oral lease or rental agreement for residential premises the landlord or lessor shall be deemed to covenant and warrant that the premises so leased or rented and all areas used in connection therewith in common with other tenants or residents are fit for human habitation and for the uses reasonably intended by the parties and that the occupants of such premises shall not be subjected to any conditions which would be dangerous, hazardous or detrimental to their life, health or safety. . . .

2. Any agreement by a lessee or tenant of a dwelling waiving or modifying his rights as set forth in this section shall be void as contrary to public policy.

Notes and Questions

1. Until the 1960s, the common law provided that a landlord had no implied duty to deliver the premises in fit or habitable condition. Moreover, the landlord had no implied duty to maintain or repair the property during the lease term. Exceptions to these doctrines were limited, such as when there was a short-term lease of furnished premises. *See* Mary Ann Glendon, *The Transformation of American Landlord-Tenant Law,* 23 B.C. L. Rev. 503, 514-17 (1982).

The warranty of habitability has been imposed in some jurisdictions by judicial decision. In other states, the warranty was first established by legislation. Still other jurisdictions enacted legislation to codify, implement, or adjust a judicially recognized warranty. *See Young v. Morrisey,* 329 S.E.2d 426 (S.C. 1985) (rejecting the warranty), *superseded by* S.C. Code Ann. §§ 27-40-10 to -90 (1991) (imposing the warranty as to residential properties only). A leading statute is the Uniform Residential Landlord and Tenant Act, currently adopted in 15 jurisdictions. Are the issues so complex that legislatures, not courts, should institute the warranty? *See* Mary Ann Glendon, *Transformation of American Landlord-Tenant Law,* 23 B.C. L. Rev. 503 (1982). The *Restatement (Second) of Property — Landlord and Tenant* imposes a warranty of habitability in §§ 5.1-5.6.

What type of tenants and properties fall under the warranty? Compare *Javins* and the New York statute. Since *Javins,* the broader approach of the New York statute has become the general rule. *See Pole Realty Co. v. Sorrells,* 417 N.E.2d 1297 (Ill. 1981) (extending warranty from apartment units to single-family homes). Moreover, the warranty typically encompasses the condition of the premises both at the beginning and during the term. *See* Robert Schoshinski, *American Law of Landlord and Tenant* §§ 3.16, 3.18 (1980).

2. What does Judge Wright offer as the bases for finding an implied warranty of habitability in *Javins?* Do these suggest that the warranty should be irrelevant in commercial leases? *See* Robert W. Gray, *The Applicability of Constructive Eviction,*

---

insure fair apportionment, however, we think either party should be permitted to amend its complaint or answer at any time before trial, to allege a change in the condition of the apartment. In this event, the finder of fact should make a separate finding as to the condition of the apartment at the time at which the amendment was filed. This new finding will have no effect upon the original action; it will only affect the distribution of the escrowed rent paid after the filing of the amendment.

Implied Warranty of Habitability, Common-Law Fraud, and the Consumer Fraud Act to Omissions of Material Fact in a Commercial Lease, 38 J. Marshall L. Rev. 1289 (2005); Comment, *An Economic Analysis of Implied Warranties of Fitness in Commercial Leases*, 94 Colum. L. Rev. 658 (1994).

3. Will the warranty of habitability improve the plight of lower-income tenants? Will it lead to increased quality and quantity of rental housing? At the time *Javins* was decided, various commentators argued that imposing the warranty would not improve the plight of lower-income tenants and would not result in increased availability of quality housing. Dean Charles Meyers, in criticizing the warranty of habitability in the *Restatement (Second) of Property — Landlord and Tenant*, wrote:

> In summary, the economic consequences of the Restatement rules on habitability are likely to be the following:
>
> 1) Some proportion of the substandard rental housing stock would be upgraded and rents would be raised to cover the added costs. Tenants formerly occupying the housing would either be forced out or be required to pay a higher proportion of their income for rent. Those tenants who are unable or unwilling to pay for the upgraded housing will move out, creating an increased demand for lower-priced, lower-quality housing.
>
> 2) For some proportion of the substandard rental housing stock, rents could not be raised, but landlords could still upgrade the housing without incurring a deficit. In these cases the tenants would enjoy a short-term wealth transfer, for they would enjoy better housing at no increase in rent. But low-income tenants as a class would not benefit in the long run, for the covenant of habitability will retire this component of the housing stock sooner than would otherwise be the case and will discourage new investment in low-rent housing.
>
> 3) The third portion of the substandard housing stock will be abandoned as soon as the owner determines that income will not cover the expenses of Restatement repairs and concludes that this deficit is likely to persist.

Charles J. Meyers, *The Covenant of Habitability and the American Law Institute*, 27 Stan. L. Rev. 879, 893 (1975). For similar views, see Lawrence Berger, *The New Residential Tenancy Law — Are Landlords Public Utilities?*, 60 Neb. L. Rev. 707, 746-49 (1981) (arguing that the warranty may lead to inefficient repairs); Note, *The Implied Warranty of Habitability as a Mechanism for Redistributing Income: Good Goal, Bad Policy*, 40 Case W. Res. L. Rev. 525 (1989-1990) (asserting that governmental housing subsidies paid directly to the poor are a more effective tool for increasing lower-income housing). Other commentators, however, have rejected this view, at least in part:

> The specific landlord behavior involved I call "milking." I mean by milking the decision to reduce maintenance below the level necessary to keep a building in existence as a residential unit. In other words, the milking landlord treats his property as a wasting rather than a renewable asset. He adopts a strategy of renting for what the market will bear as the building deteriorates, fully understanding that within some relatively short period of time he will be out of business. Either tenants will no longer pay him anything, or the authorities will close the building. At that point, he expects the building to have no market value. He will walk away from it, give it away, or lose it to tax foreclosure. . . .
>
> Assume that we are trying to improve the housing conditions of the poor without increasing rent at all. Under the conditions of the model we have been working with, it would make sense to try to identify those buildings that are *about to be* milked, and enforce the warranty to the extent necessary to prevent that outcome.

We would ignore (a) those buildings in such bad condition that their owners would abandon rather than comply with the warranty, and (b) those buildings that would stay in the stock after upgrading to the renewable level, but at higher rents.

Duncan Kennedy, *The Effect of the Warranty of Habitability on Low Income Housing: "Milking" and Class Violence*, 15 Fla. St. U. L. Rev. 485, 489, 500 (1987). *See* Bruce A. Ackerman, *Regulating Slum Housing Markets on Behalf of the Poor: Of Housing Codes, Housing Subsidies and Income Redistribution Policy*, 80 Yale L.J. 1093 (1971).

Empirical studies of the effect of the warranty of habitability have begun. Professor Edward Rabin examined the impact of increased tenants' rights, including the warranty among others, on the supply of rental housing in the 1970s:

> Regardless of any change in consumer preferences, the long-term trend toward improved housing conditions and living standards continued. Also, during the seventies there was a massive increase in housing subsidies for the poor. *If the revolution in landlord-tenant law affected the supply of rental housing detrimentally, the countervailing combination of generally improving living standards, increased housing subsidies, and changes in consumer preferences provided a more significant beneficial effect.*

Edward H. Rabin, *The Revolution in Residential Landlord-Tenant Law: Causes and Consequences*, 69 Cornell L. Rev. 517, 562 (1984). *See* David A. Super, *The Rise and Fall of the Implied Warranty of Habitability*, 99 Cal. L. Rev. 389 (2011) (threat of evictions and lack of decent housing alternatives have limited the effectiveness of the warranty); Werner Z. Hirsch, *Effect of Habitability and Anti-Speedy Eviction Laws on Black and Aged Indigent Tenant Groups: An Economic Analysis*, 3 Int'l Rev. L. & Econ. 121 (1983) (concluding that as of the mid-1970s, habitability laws had a statistically adverse effect on the welfare of African-American, indigent tenants and no statistically significant effect on the welfare of aged indigent tenants).

Was the effect of the decision on lower-income housing a concern of the court in *Javins*? Should it have been a concern? Should courts decide cases like *Javins* even though they lack hard data on the underlying social problem and the likely effect of their decisions? What if the future does not turn out to be as the court predicted?

4. Why do you think the tenants' complaint in *Javins* alleged that the defects arose only after the leases commenced? What if the defects were present at the time the leases were signed? What if the leases expressly provided that the tenant waived the warranty? How do the *Javins* opinion and N.Y. Real Prop. Law § 235-b address this issue? Compare these approaches to the view of comment *c* of § 5.1 and § 5.6 of the *Restatement (Second) of Property—Landlord and Tenant*, which prefers a construction avoiding waiver but ultimately allows it unless the waiver is unconscionable. *See P.H. Investment v. Oliver*, 818 P.2d 1018 (Utah 1991) (adopting the Restatement position). Other courts typically agree with the *Javins* view on waiver. *See also* Uniform Residential Landlord and Tenant Act § 2.104 (permitting the parties to place the burden of repair, except for compliance with building and housing codes affecting health and safety, on the tenant).

What does it mean for the landlord if waiver of the warranty is prohibited, especially if the landlord cannot adjust the price for leasing upwards because of market conditions or rent controls? Is that appropriate?

5. What is required by the warranty of habitability in the *Javins* opinion and N.Y. Real Prop. Law § 235-b? Section 2.104 of the Uniform Residential Landlord and Tenant Act provides:

§ 2.104. [Landlord to Maintain Premises]

(a) A landlord shall

 (1) comply with the requirements of applicable building and housing codes materially affecting health and safety;

(2) make all repairs and do whatever is necessary to put and keep the premises in a fit and habitable condition;

(3) keep all common areas of the premises in a clean and safe condition;

(4) maintain in good and safe working order and condition all electrical, plumbing, sanitary, heating, ventilating, air-conditioning, and other facilities and appliances, including elevators, supplied or required to be supplied by him;

(5) provide and maintain appropriate receptacles and conveniences for the removal of ashes, garbage, rubbish, and other waste incidental to the occupancy of the dwelling unit and arrange for their removal; and

(6) supply running water and reasonable amounts of hot water at all times and reasonable heat [between October 11 and May 1] except where the building that includes the dwelling unit is not required by law to be equipped for that purpose, or the dwelling unit is so constructed that heat or hot water is generated by an installation within the exclusive control of the tenant and supplied by a direct public utility connection.

Assess the strengths and weaknesses of these standards. Consider in this regard *Belanger v. Mulholland*, 30 A.3d 836 (Me. 2011) (pipes burst in premises and no longer provided water and toilet stopped working): Would this violate the *Javins*, New York, or Uniform Act warranty?

6. How does the *Javins* court's concept of a lease affect the remedies that are permitted to the defendant/tenants? How do the tenants' options differ from those available under constructive eviction?

The legislatures and courts have developed various remedies for the tenant for breach of the warranty. These include rescission of the lease; specific performance of the landlord's habitability obligation; rent abatement to the extent of the breach; rent withholding, permitting the tenant to place rent in escrow until the landlord eliminates the defect; a separate action for damages; and repair and deduct remedies, permitting the tenant to correct the condition and subtract the cost from the rent. *See* James Charles Smith, *Tenant Remedies for Breach of Habitability: Tort Dimensions of a Contract Concept*, 35 U. Kan. L. Rev. 505 (1987) (providing a comprehensive critique); Robert Schoshinski, *American Law of Landlord and Tenant* §§ 3.19-3.26, 3.32 (1980); Unif. Residential Landlord and Tenant Act §§ 4.101-4.107.

There has been disagreement as to how damages—either for the purpose of rent abatement or a separate damages action—should be calculated. *See Glasoe v. Trinkle*, 479 N.E.2d 915, 921 (Ill. 1985):

[S]everal methods for measuring such damages have been suggested by various courts and authors. These include "difference in value" and "percentage reduction in use."

There are two varieties of the "difference in value" approach. Under the first variety the tenant's damages are measured by the difference between the fair rental value of the premises if they had been as warranted and their fair value during their occupancy by the tenant in the unsafe, unsanitary, or unfit condition. Under the second variety the tenant's damages are measured by the difference between the agreed rent and the fair rental value of the premises during their occupancy by the tenant in the unsafe, unsanitary or unfit condition.

The "percentage reduction in use" approach reduces the tenant's rent by a percentage reflecting the diminution in the value and enjoyment of the premises by reason of the existence of defects which give rise to the breach of the implied warranty of habitability.

[handwritten margin note: measure rent amount to damage amount]

The *Restatement (Second) of Property — Landlord and Tenant* provides for rent abatement in § 11.1 Rent Abatement:

> If the tenant is entitled to an abatement of the rent, the rent is abated to the amount of that proportion of the rent which the fair rental value after the event giving the right to abate bears to the fair rental value before the event. Abatement is allowed until the default is eliminated or the lease terminates, whichever first occurs.

[handwritten margin note: how much the rent should have been]

Which damages measure is preferable? What damages will result when there is a rental of substandard housing at the market rate for substandard premises, and both the landlord and tenant are aware when making the lease that the premises will be substandard?

In an action for damages, the tenant may also recover reasonable expenditures for improvements made prior to the breach, reasonable relocation costs, and lost business profits that are proved to a reasonable degree of certainty and that the landlord could have foreseen would result from the breach. *Restatement (Second) of Property — Landlord and Tenant* § 10.2.

7. Does the warranty apply when a governmental entity is the landlord? Courts have refused to imply a warranty of habitability in projects sponsored by the federal Department of Housing and Urban Development, finding that Congress did not intend to impose such a duty on private parties or on HUD operating such projects. *Alexander v. United States Department of Housing & Urban Development*, 555 F.2d 166 (7th Cir. 1977); *Kingston Square Tenants Ass'n v. Tuskegee Gardens, Ltd.*, 792 F. Supp. 1566 (S.D. Fla. 1992) (refusing a damages remedy against former private owners). It has been found, though, that while the state's warranty of habitability will not be imposed on HUD leases, Congress intended that when HUD actually administers a residential project, it must maintain the property in safe and sanitary condition. *See Conille v. Secretary of Housing & Urban Development*, 840 F.2d 105 (1st Cir. 1988) (HUD as mortgagee in possession). Moreover, it has been held that state-administered housing is subject to the warranty. *See Department of Housing Preservation & Development of the City of New York v. Sartor*, 487 N.Y.S.2d 1 (App. Div. 1985).

[handwritten margin note: Government housing = no implied warranty of habit.]

[handwritten margin note: BUT must be maintain.]

Problems: Warranty of Habitability

1. T leased an apartment in a multi-tenant building from L. For 17 days, there was a city-wide strike by unionized maintenance and janitorial staff of residential buildings. Only a few of L's staff did not join the strike. As a result, trash piled up in front of L's building and in the trash rooms, routine maintenance was not performed, no regular exterminating was performed, leading to an increase in vermin, and common areas were uncleaned. The strike has ended. Does T have any rights against L as a result of the strike? Does the result change if the printed lease contained a provision excusing the landlord for breaches "by reason of any cause beyond Landlord's reasonable control"? *See Park West Management Corp. v. Mitchell*, 404 N.Y.S.2d 115 (App. Div. 1978), *aff'd*, 391 N.E.2d 1288 (N.Y. 1979).

2. A physician leased office space in a building for use as a medical office. Soon after moving in, the doctor noted that the air conditioning and lights did not always work, vermin and rodents infested the office, and there were various incidents of burglary and vandalism in the building. The doctor ceased paying her rent and did not communicate with the landlord. The landlord has just called the doctor insisting on rent payments. Advise the doctor on her rights and on her different courses of action. *See Davidow v. Inwood North Professional Group*, 747 S.W.2d 373 (Tex. 1988). But see *Chausse v. Coz*, 540 N.E.2d 667 (Mass. 1989).

3. The landlord of a luxury high-rise apartment building failed to provide certain amenities appropriate to such buildings. The tenants claimed a breach of the statutory warranty of habitability and withheld rent pursuant to a statutory remedy for such breaches. Is this a breach under N.Y. Real Prop. Law § 235-b (set out above)? *See Solow v. Wellner*, 658 N.E.2d 1005 (N.Y. 1995). Could the tenants claim failure of consideration or breach of a dependent covenant?

4.   Landlord's Tort Liability

Under the traditional rule, a landlord was not liable for injuries suffered by the tenant or her guests on the leased property. This position was consistent with the earlier view that as the transferee of an estate in land, the tenant had full ownership responsibilities as far as the quality and safety of the premises. Some courts, however, found some results under the common-law rule harsh. As a result, although the common law did not develop a global duty of care, certain exceptions to the rule of nonliability of the landlord were developed:

1. *Areas under control of landlord.* The landlord is liable for injuries in areas under his control where the injury arises from a failure to use reasonable care to keep the area reasonably safe. Typical cases involve injuries in common areas, such as a hallway or staircase.
2. *Latent defects.* Where a landlord is aware of the existence of a hazardous condition in the premises that could not be discovered by the tenant in a reasonable inspection, the landlord is liable for injuries caused by the condition if the landlord does not disclose the problem. The landlord is not responsible to repair the problem under this rule. Some courts have also held a landlord liable under this exception if she had reason to know of the condition even though she did not have actual knowledge.
3. *Negligent performance of a repair.* If a landlord makes a repair to the premises, voluntarily or pursuant to a contractual obligation, he will be liable for injuries arising from a negligent repair.
4. *Public use exception.* Where it is contemplated that the tenant will admit members of the public to the leased premises, the landlord is liable for injuries to third parties caused by dangerous conditions if the landlord knew or reasonably could have known of the condition and the landlord failed to repair the problem. Initially, courts construed the exception narrowly,

applying it to premises where a large number of the public would be admitted, such as a sports arena. Later, some courts required admission of only a few members of the public, as to a physician's office.

5. *Breach of statutory duty.* Courts have differed significantly on the question of whether the breach of a statutory or administrative code leading to personal injury can be the basis of a tort recovery. The breach has been treated by various courts as irrelevant to the tort action, providing evidence of negligence, or demonstrating negligence per se.

Additionally, the courts have generally held that the landlord's duty extends not only to the tenant but also to persons on the property with the consent of the tenant.[3]

On the liability of landlords for personal injuries in general, see *Restatement (Second) of Property—Landlord and Tenant* §§ 17.1-17.7; Robert Schoshinski, *American Law of Landlord and Tenant* §§ 4.1-4.7 (1980).

As one might expect, the tort liability of the landlord for an injury to the tenant was revisited by many courts in the era following the rejection of caveat emptor in *Javins v. First National Realty Corp.* and similar cases.

MILLER v. DAVID GRACE, INC.

Supreme Court of Oklahoma
212 P.3d 1223 (2009)

COLBERT, J. . . . This is a negligent maintenance and construction action initiated by a tenant against her landlord and a contractor after the tenant fell from her second story balcony due to a defectively installed balcony railing. The district court granted the landlord's and contractor's motions for summary judgment based on the traditional common law rule that holds a landlord harmless for injuries occurring on the leased premises and held that the danger was open and obvious. The appellate court affirmed the judgment in favor of the landlord but reversed the judgment in favor of the contractor because factual questions remain as to the tenant's knowledge of the dangerous condition and whether the danger was open and obvious. We hold that summary judgment was inappropriate as to both defendants and adopt the view embraced by other jurisdictions which imposes a general duty of care upon landlords to maintain the leased premises in a reasonably safe condition, including areas under the tenant's exclusive control or use.

I.   BACKGROUND AND PROCEDURAL HISTORY

On July 29, 2002, Plaintiff, Lora Ann Miller (Tenant) moved into the River Chase Apartments owned and operated by First Choice Management (Landlord). The unit was located on the second floor and contained a wooden balcony deck and U-shaped metal guardrail. At Landlord's request, Tenant was instructed to inspect the unit to determine if "anything was wrong with [the unit]" and

3.   *See* Ford v. Ja-Si, 420 A.2d 184 (Del. Super. Ct. 1980).

convey her findings to Landlord. During Tenant's inspection, Tenant discovered the balcony railing was loose.

Tenant testified by deposition that she believed her balcony was dangerous and "maybe somebody was going to fall." According to Tenant, the balcony railing was loose because it was missing a screw and the railing was not "metaled" to the wall. Tenant advised the apartment manager of the defects on at least two occasions. Allegedly, the manager advised Tenant that "she would help [Tenant] take care of it"; however, no repairs were ever made. Unbeknownst to Tenant, the railing was also missing additional screws on the other side of the balcony and the balcony flooring was cracked in the very spot where the railing should have been attached by screws to the wooden deck.

On August 18, 2002, Tenant, while standing on the balcony, placed her hand on the defective railing, leaned forward, and the entire U-shaped railing along with Tenant fell from the second floor, landing on the ground below. She sustained multiple injuries.

In September 2001, just eleven months prior to Tenant's fall, Landlord employed David Grace, Inc. (Contractor) to "rebuild all balconies as per city code." According to Contractor, Landlord did not notify Contractor of any problems with the repair work.

Tenant initiated a negligent maintenance and construction action against Landlord and Contractor, respectively. Tenant asserts that Landlord owed her a duty to repair the defective railing. In addition, she contends the dangerous condition was not an open and obvious hazard and therefore, she was unable to fully appreciate the risk. As to Contractor, Tenant contends that Contractor "owed a duty to construct and install a safe balcony railing." . . .

Without explanation, the trial court granted summary judgment to both defendants. Tenant appealed. The appellate court affirmed judgment in favor of Landlord, but reversed the judgment in favor of Contractor because Tenant's negligence action stems from an improperly installed railing, not from Contractor's alleged duty to warn her of the defective condition. Tenant urges this Court to overrule Godbey, Alfe v. New York Life Ins. Co., 1937 OK 67 P.2d 947, and similar cases; and to adopt the view embraced by a majority of other states which removes a veil of landlord immunity and instead treats the landlord as any other property owner imposed with a general duty of care of their premises. . . .

III.   ANALYSIS

Tenant urges that the Oklahoma Legislature abrogated the common law landlord tort immunity rule with its enactment of Okla. Stat. tit. 41, § 118 (2001). She contends the immunity rule articulated in *Alfe* and *Godbey* is out of sync with Oklahoma's landlord tenant laws. Those cases centered around Okla. Stat. tit. 41, §§ 31 and 32, which was repealed by section 118 in 1978.

This Court, however, cannot agree with Tenant's contention. Absent the Legislature's expressed intent to the contrary, the common law remains intact. Tate v. Browning-Ferris, Inc., 1992 OK 833 P.2d 1218. Although the Oklahoma Landlord Tenant Act imposes a duty upon the landlord to "[m]ake all repairs and do whatever is necessary to put and keep the tenant's dwelling unit and premises in a fit and habitable condition," it does not create a tort remedy for personal injuries sustained as a result of a landlord's breach of those duties. It merely regulates the contractual rights and obligations of the residential parties and does not enlarge the landlord's duty under common law. *See* Okla. Stat. tit. 41, §§ 103(A) & 121 (2001).

Landlord and Contractor insist no duty is owed to Tenant in light of the holdings articulated in *Godbey*, 1939 OK 86 P.2d 621, and *Alfe*, 1937 OK 67 P.2d 947. In *Godbey*, the tenant-plaintiff sued the landlord-defendant for the drowning death of tenant-plaintiff's infant son. The infant fell into an open cistern located on the leased premises. Prior to the accident, the tenant-plaintiff discovered the open cistern which was concealed by tall weeds. The doctrine of caveat emptor controlled because no lessor-lessee covenant to repair existed, the tenant-plaintiff was in exclusive control of the demised premises, and the tenant-plaintiff was aware of the condition's existence long before the fatal accident.

Alfe presents a landlord's failure to adhere to the statutorily prescribed obligations to lease a premises in a fit and habitable condition. [T]he landlord leased residential property to a tenant in unhabitable condition. Subsequently, the tenant was injured as a result of the hazardous and dangerous condition. That court however, held the only liability imposed upon a landlord is derived by statute and any remedies for breach of those duties are confined exclusively to those enumerated therein.

In the area of landlord tort liability, Oklahoma currently follows the common law maxim of "caveat emptor," which states:

> the right of possession and enjoyment of the leased premises passes to the lessee, in the absence of concealment or fraud by the landlord as to some defect in the premises known to him and unknown to the tenant, the rule of caveat emptor applies and the tenant takes the premises in whatever condition they may be in, thus assuming all risk of personal injury from defects therein.

Over the years, Oklahoma has carved out several exceptions to this rule. For instance, in Buck v. Miller, 1947 OK 181 P.2d 264, this Court imposed liability on a landlord where the landlord negligently made repairs or improvements. Next, this Court attached liability to a landlord who failed to maintain common areas under the landlord's control. In Arnold v. Walters, the court noted that:

> Where the owner of an apartment house leases parts thereof to different tenants and expressly or impliedly reserves other parts thereof, such as entrances, halls, stairways, porches, walks, etc., for the common use of different tenants it is the owner's duty to exercise reasonable care to keep safe such parts of which he so reserves control, and if he is negligent in this regard and a personal injury results by reason thereof to a tenant, he is liable, provided the injury occurs while such part of the premises is being used in the manner intended. 1950 OK 224 P.2d 261.

And most recently, this Court's jurisprudence pierced the "landlord immunity veil" . . . finding a landlord liable when the landlord's acts or omissions enabled a third party to commit criminal acts upon a tenant in Lay v. Dworman, 1986 OK 732 P.2d 455. In *Lay*, the plaintiff was assaulted and raped after an intruder gained access to her apartment due to a defective lock on a sliding glass door. Although the tenant previously complained of the defective lock on the sliding glass door, the landlord failed to make the necessary repairs. The *Lay* court imposed a duty upon the landlord "to use reasonable care to maintain the common areas of the premises in such a manner as to insure that the likelihood of criminal activity is not unreasonably enhanced by the condition of those common premises." In so doing, the *Lay* court noted that "the landlord faces potential liability when the circumstances are such that a reasonable man would realize that a failure to act would render one relying on those actions susceptible to criminal acts." Therefore, any tenant injured as a result of a landlord's failure to act has no redress currently unless that tenant can successfully frame a cause of action to fit into one of this Court's recognized exceptions. The end result discourages repairs and rewards inattentive landlords with immunity from suit while impeding a tenant's recovery for a landlord's utter disregard for a tenant's health, safety, and welfare.

At present, Oklahoma's adherence to the caveat emptor doctrine obscures rather than illuminates the proper considerations which govern a court's determination of a residential landlord's duty. Instead, reasonableness and foresight should be paramount. No tenant's life or limb is less worthy of Oklahoma's protection simply because the tenant is in possession of the landlord's premises. It is unreasonable to allow a landlord to seek refuge under the cloak of immunity after intentionally turning a deaf ear to a tenant's pleas to make necessary repairs. . . .

Before the accident, the landlord's insurance company advised the landlord that the unit's railing was dangerous and cancelled the landlord's liability insurance. The landlord however, failed to make the necessary repairs but purchased the repair materials and warned the tenant of the danger. Although the landlord made no express agreement to keep the premises in repair, the landlord testified that he considered it his obligation to do so. . . .

IV.

The evolving nature of residential leases demand the reformation of an archaic rule, and today this Court supplants the caveat emptor doctrine of landlord tort immunity. In its place, this Court imposes a general duty of care upon landlords to maintain the leased premises, including areas under the tenant's exclusive control or use, in a reasonably safe condition. This duty requires a landlord to act reasonably when the landlord knew or reasonably should have known of the defective condition and had a reasonable opportunity to make repairs.

It is clear from the totality of the record that Landlord knew or should have known that the balcony railing was unsafe. . . . However, Landlord remained complacent and failed to make the necessary repairs or at a minimum, investigate Tenant's concerns. Upon Tenant's notice to Landlord of the dangerous condition, Landlord had a duty to exercise reasonable care to restore Tenant's balcony to a safe condition. To the extent that *Godbey*, *Alfe*, and other similar cases are inconsistent with this Court's finding that a landlord owes a general duty of care to the tenant, those cases are overruled.

. . . The expectation that a landlord act reasonably is inherent in contemporary residential leases. One . . . legitimate expectation includes proper installation and maintenance of a balcony guardrail, especially when its predominate function is to prevent a person from falling. . . .

The landlord's knowledge is key in triggering the duty to maintain the leased premises in a reasonably safe condition. Although, the landlord's right to reenter areas of the leased premises under the tenant's exclusive control are limited to the tenant's consent, cases of emergency, abandonment, or court injunctive relief, Okla. Stat. tit. 41 § 128(D), today's pronouncement does not make the landlord an insurer of the tenant's safety. Rather, this Court imposes a duty upon the landlord to act reasonably when the landlord knew or by the exercise of reasonable diligence would have known, of the defective condition, *see* Schlender v. Andy Jansen Co., 1962 OK 380 P.2d 523, and had a reasonable opportunity to make repairs. Only in the presence of a duty neglected or violated will a landlord's negligence be actionable. By the same token, the landlord's liability, as any other tortfeasor, may be reduced or absolved by the tenant's contributory negligence. The question of liability should be submitted to the jury to decide.

[handwritten margin note: also consider contributory negligence.]

V.

The law is well-settled that a landowner has a duty to keep the premises in a reasonably safe condition, Jack Healey Linen Ser. Co. v. Travis, 1967 OK 434 P.2d 924, and to warn others of any "hidden dangers, traps, snares, pitfalls, and the like." Excepted from this duty is the necessity of protecting from dangers so "open and obvious" as to reasonably expect others to detect them for themselves.

In the instant case, the lower court failed to consider evidence that there were dangerous latent defects in the guardrail. . . . These latent defects present material issues of fact which preclude summary judgment. Additionally, these facts are relevant to whether the dangerous condition was open and obvious and whether such danger and risk was imperceptible to Tenant.

Despite Tenant's familiarity with the general physical condition of the railing, such familiarity cannot transform a defective condition into an apparent appreciable risk. *Jack Healey, supra.* Likewise, it does not follow that unknown hidden defects are open and obvious. The openness and obviousness of the dangerous condition and whether Tenant appreciated those risk are questions for the jury. The trial court erred in removing these issues from the jury's consideration. . . . [Discussion of rejection of Contractor's "no duty defense" omitted.—Eds.]

VI. CONCLUSION

Today this Court recognizes a landlord's duty to exercise reasonable care. We express no opinion on whether Tenant may be able to ultimately recover against either Landlord or Contractor for negligence. However, because the existence of disputed material facts remain as to (1) whether the Landlord's duty of care was breached; and (2) the open and obvious character of the balcony railing so as to relieve Landlord and Contractor of liability, the orders granting summary judgment are reversed.

Notes and Questions

1. Since the declaration of the implied warranty of habitability, courts have taken different positions on landlords' tort liability. At least some courts have continued to follow the traditional rule of nonliability, subject only to the traditional exceptions discussed above. *See, e.g., Casey v. Estes*, 657 So. 2d 845 (Ala. 1995); *Trotter v. Chicago Housing Authority*, 516 N.E.2d 684 (Ill. App. 1987); *Broughton v. Maes*, 378 N.W.2d 134 (Minn. Ct. App. 1985). Moreover, while some courts such as *Miller* increased duties in residential leases, that new rule does not necessarily extend to commercial tenants. *See Bishop v. TES Realty Trust*, 942 N.E.2d 173 (Mass. 2011) (applying statute requiring reasonable care on landlords to commercial leases, settling a previously disputed question among cases).

[handwritten margin note: new rule does not apply to commercial leases]

A growing number of courts, like *Miller*, have found landlords subject to a general duty of reasonable care to prevent injuries to tenants and others due to unsafe conditions. *Sargent v. Ross*, 308 A.2d 528 (N.H. 1973), is a leading case of this group. Plaintiff's four-year-old daughter was being cared for by a tenant of a second-floor apartment. The child fell from an outdoor stairway used to reach the apartment. The court rejected the plaintiff's attempt to find the landlord liable under the common area and negligent repair exceptions to the common-law rule, refusing to "broaden one of the existing exceptions and hence perpetuate an artificial and illogical rule" or to "expand the fiction" and finding it "more realistic instead to consider reversing the general rule of nonliability." For similar decisions, see *Mansur v. Eubanks*, 401 So. 2d 1328 (Fla. 1981); *Pagelsdorf v. Safeco Insurance Co.*, 284 N.W.2d 55 (Wis. 1979).

The California Supreme Court took a different approach in *Becker v. IRM Corp.*, 698 P.2d 116 (Cal. 1985), by holding that a residential landlord may be held strictly liable for injuries to a tenant caused by a defective condition in the premises. *Becker* supported its holding with the same theories that courts apply in other examples of strict liability in tort: Landlords are part of the enterprise of producing and marketing shelter to renters and so should bear corresponding costs of injuries; strict liability provides the best mechanism to spread costs and ensure that injured plaintiffs are compensated; and landlords have superior knowledge of the product and ability to inspect. *Becker* was overruled, however, in *Peterson v. Superior Court*, 899 P.2d 905 (Cal. 1995), which applied a general negligence standard to landlords. *Peterson* found that strict liability was inappropriate since landlords only have limited influence on design and manufacture of products; there is not the same expectation of safety with a use product such as a residence; and risk spreading alone is not a sufficient justification for strict liability. Other jurisdictions have expressly rejected the strict products liability position. *See, e.g., George Washington University v. Weintraub*, 458 A.2d 43 (D.C. 1983); *Armstrong v. Cione*, 738 P.2d 79 (Haw. 1987).

[handwritten margin note: Strict liability inappropriate]

Other jurisdictions find a landlord liable for torts arising out of a breach of the warranty of habitability, as described in Note 2.

For analyses of tort liability of the landlord, see Olin Browder, *The Taming of a Duty—The Tort Liability of Landlords*, 81 Mich. L. Rev. 99 (1982); Jean Love, *Landlord's Liability for Defective Premises: Caveat Lessee, Negligence, or Strict Liability?*, 1975 Wis. L. Rev. 19; Melissa T. Lonegrass, *Convergence in Contort: Landlord Liability for Defective Premises in Comparative Perspective*, 85 Tul. L. Rev. 413 (2010); Michael Davis & Phillip DeLaTorre, *A Fresh Look at Premises Liability as Affected by the Warranty of Habitability*, 59 Wash. L. Rev. 141 (1984); Joan Neisser, *The Tenant as Consumer: Applying Strict Liability Principles to Landlords*, 64 St. John's L. Rev. 527 (1990).

2. The warranty of habitability may also play a direct role in finding a landlord liability for tenant injuries. *Restatement (Second) of Property—Landlord and Tenant* § 17.6 Landlord Under Legal Duty to Repair Dangerous Condition provides:

A landlord is subject to liability for physical harm caused to the tenant and others upon the leased property with the consent of the tenant or his subtenant by a dangerous condition existing before or arising after the tenant has taken possession, if he has failed to exercise reasonable care to repair the condition and the existence of the condition is in violation of:

(1) an implied warranty of habitability; or

(2) a duty created by statute or administrative regulation.

Would there have been liability in *Miller* under the Restatement standard? What role does the statutory warranty of habitability have in the court's decision in *Miller*? Some cases expressly rely on breach of an implied warranty of habitability as the basis of finding liability for personal injuries. *See, e.g., Houston v. York*, 755 So. 2d 495 (Miss. Ct. App. 1999); *Johnson v. Scandia Associates, Inc.*, 771 N.E.2d 24 (Ind. 1999) (perplexingly finding liability for personal injuries for express warranties but not implied). Consider, as well, statutory warranties such as Unif. Residential Landlord and Tenant Act § 2.104(a)(2): "A landlord shall . . . make all repairs and do whatever is necessary to put and keep the premises in a fit and habitable condition." *See Newton v. Magill*, 872 P.2d 1213 (Alaska 1994) (Uniform Act abrogated traditional rules of premises liability); *New Haverford Partnership v. Stroot*, 772 A.2d 792 (Del. 2001); *Sikora v. Wenzel*, 727 N.E.2d 1277 (Ohio 2000).

What are the respective strengths and weaknesses of the various approaches toward personal injury—retention of the common law and its exceptions, the broad negligence standard of *Miller*, liability based on a breach of the warranty of habitability, and strict products liability? Is there a viable distinction between residential and commercial leases? Should liability extend to damage to the tenant's property? *See Weiler v. Hooshiari*, 19 A.3d 124 (Vt. 2011).

3. Consider whether the landlord would be liable in the following situations under negligence theory, warranty of habitability theory, and common-law exceptions, and whether the result is desirable:

a. Four days after the tenant leased the downstairs unit of a duplex, she died as a result of asphyxiation due to leaking carbon monoxide fumes from the gas heater. The venting system was not functioning properly. There was evidence of rust and physical deterioration on the venting system pipes. Would the result change if there were no evidence of rust or deterioration on the pipes or if the deterioration of the venting system had not occurred until 10 months into the lease? *See Kilmer v. Browning*, 806 S.W.2d 75 (Mo. Ct. App. 1991); *Bradley v. Wachovia Bank & Trust Co.*, 369 S.E.2d 86 (N.C. 1988).

b. The tenant was injured as a result of the explosion of a gas stove in an apartment unit that was in the basement of a house owned and otherwise occupied by the landlord. The explosion was due to a defect in the assembly of the unit that could only have been found by a skilled technician and only after taking the stove apart. *See Old Town Development Co. v. Langford*, 349 N.E.2d 744 (Ind. Ct. App. 1976).

4. *Liability for acts of criminals.* In the groundbreaking case of *Kline v. 1500 Massachusetts Avenue Apartment Corp.*, 439 F.2d 477 (D.C. Cir. 1970), the plaintiff, a tenant in a 585-unit apartment building, was assaulted and robbed in the common hallway outside her apartment unit. The 24-hour security that had been in place when the plaintiff leased her unit had been discontinued, and the landlord had notice of prior crimes committed in the building. The United States Court of Appeals for the District of Columbia Circuit held that the landlord was liable to the tenant on the facts, requiring a standard of "reasonable care in all the circumstances":

> The rationale of the general rule exonerating a third party from any duty to protect another from a criminal attack has no applicability to the landlord-tenant relationship in multiple dwelling houses. The landlord is no insurer of his tenants' safety, but he certainly is no bystander. And where, as here, the landlord has notice of repeated criminal assaults and robberies, has notice that these crimes occurred in the portion of the premises exclusively within his control, has every reason to expect like crimes to happen again, and has the exclusive power to take preventive action, it does not seem unfair to place upon the landlord a duty to take those steps which are within his power to minimize the predictable risk to his tenants. . . .

> Having said this, it would be well to state what is not said by this decision. We do not hold that the landlord is by any means an insurer of the safety of his tenants. His duty is to take those measures of protection which are within his power and capacity to take, and which can reasonably be expected to mitigate the risk of intruders assaulting and robbing tenants. The landlord is not expected to provide protection commonly owed by a municipal police department; but as illustrated in this case, he is obligated to protect those parts of his premises which are not usually subject to periodic patrol and inspection by the municipal police.

A number of courts have rejected the finding of landlord liability to tenants for the criminal acts of third parties. What reasons support that position? *See, e.g., Miller v. Whitworth,* 455 S.E.2d 821 (W. Va. Ct. App. 1995) (deliberate criminal act of a third person is the intervening cause of harm; difficulty determining the foreseeability of criminal acts; vagueness of the standard owner must meet; economic consequences; protecting citizens is duty of government, not the private sector).

Under *Kline,* would a landlord be liable for a criminal assault against a tenant in his apartment when the intruder gained access to the tenant's second-floor apartment by placing a ladder against the side of the building and breaking a window? If access was achieved through the unit door and the lock on the door had been broken for a week? *See Rodgers v. Rosen,* 737 P.2d 562 (Okla. 1987) (no); *Walls v. Oxford Management Co.,* 137 N.H. 653, 633 A.2d 103 (1993) (yes, if landlord created or was responsible for known defective condition that foreseeably enhanced risk of criminal attack); *Ward v. Inashmaan Associates Ltd. Partnership,* 931 A.2d 1235 (N.H. 2007) (no general duty to protect tenant from criminal attacks but landlord liable if landlord created the condition or there was "overriding foreseeability" of attack); Deborah J. La Fetra, *A Moving Target: Property Owners' Duty to Prevent Criminal Acts on the Premises,* 28 Whittier L. Rev. 409 (2006).

The City of Newark, New Jersey, has taken a more direct approach. A local ordinance provides that for residential buildings with more than 100 units, landlords must provide armed security guards for 8 hours a day and unarmed guards for the remaining 16 hours. The New Jersey Supreme Court rejected a challenge to the ordinance, finding no arbitrary exercise of the police power, no denial of equal protection by an exemption of condominiums, and no improper

[handwritten margin note: LL has power over land & can expect crimes, duty to prevent (w/ his power to do so)]

delegation of the city's duty to provide police enforcement. *515 Associates v. City of Newark*, 623 A.2d 1366 (N.J. 1993). In what ways may this ordinance increase the costs for landlords?

Problems: Landlord Liability for Personal Injuries

1. Star had conducted a meat-packing business. It leased its building and equipment to Serv-U for five years to conduct a meat-packing business on the premises. After Serv-U began operations on the property, a vat installed on the premises containing ammonia gas exploded, causing severe injuries to an employee of Serv-U. An investigation after the accident revealed that a weld had given way. Is Star liable to the employee? Compare the relative liability of Star and Serv-U. *See Mora v. Baker Commodities, Inc.*, 210 Cal. App. 3d 771 (1989).

2. Tenant leased an apartment in a 100-unit building. Tenant opened a window in the living room, leaving the window screen in place, and left the room. Tenant's six-year-old child climbed into the window and fell through the screen, severely injuring herself. The screen was properly installed but was inadequate to hold a child's weight. Over the past two years, similar events had happened with three other children. The local ordinance requires that window screens be sufficient to keep out insects. Is Landlord liable for the child's injuries? Is this a matter better resolved by a legislature rather than a court? *See Lamkin v. Towner*, 563 N.E.2d 449 (Ill. 1990); *Best v. Services for Cooperative & Condominium Communities*, 629 N.E.2d 123 (Ill. Ct. App. 1993); *Mudsar v. V.G. Murray Co.*, 396 S.E.2d 325 (N.C. Ct. App. 1990).

[handwritten margin note: contributory negligence? w/ should have known by LL]

5.   Duty Not to Discriminate in Leasing

As a starting proposition, a landlord, as owner of her property, has the right to choose whether or to whom she will lease the property. Clearly, landlords daily reject potential tenants for lack of financial ability or a poor track record as a resident, although some concerns have been raised about the compilation of data by tenant-screening companies that are hired by landlords to provide reports about potential tenants.[4]

Courts have validated landlords' rejection of tenants for other reasons as well. For example, a landlord was upheld in rejecting an attorney as a tenant because the landlord was concerned that the attorney was "attuned to her legal rights" and the landlord preferred a tenant "who was likely to be less informed and more passive."[5]

Over recent years, however, federal and state legislation have limited the landlord's right to reject tenants and have required the landlord in some situations to take specific steps to make the premises accessible to the handicapped. Discrimination in housing is covered in Chapter 10.

---

4.   *See* Gary Williams, *Can Government Limit Tenant Blacklisting?*, 24 Sw. U. L. Rev. 1077 (1995); Robert R. Stauffer, Note, *Tenant Blacklisting: Tenant Screening Services and the Right to Privacy*, 24 Harv. J. on Legis. 239 (1987).

5.   Kramarsky v. Stahl Management, 401 N.Y.S.2d 943 (Sup. Ct. 1977).

C.   TENANT DUTIES AND LANDLORD REMEDIES

1.   *Tenant Duties*

a.   Duty to Preserve the Premises ☆

SIGSBEE HOLDING CORP. v. CANAVAN
Civil Court of the City of New York, Bronx County
39 Misc. 2d 465, 240 N.Y.S.2d 900 (Civ. Ct. 1963)

WACHTEL, J. The landlord seeks a final order of eviction on the ground that the tenant replaced old, used cabinets, with new ones, and contends that this constitutes waste and a violation of a substantial obligation of the tenancy. The importance of this matter cannot of course be disregarded. Countless tenants would be affected by the decision in this case, for if this were a basis for eviction of tenants the door would be opened to evictions in almost every case where a landlord refuses to permit the tenant to improve the apartment, perhaps even to drive nails into the wall to hang shelves, pictures, curtains or medicine cabinets. The law obviously cannot permit such a *reductio ad absurdum*. Nor is this the law.

"It is the well-settled rule that a tenant, in the absence of restrictions contained in a lease, may occupy and use the demised premises in any lawful way not materially different from the way in which they are usually employed, to which they are adapted and for which they were constructed. The right to exclusive occupation granted to a tenant by a lease entitles him to use the premises in the same manner that the owner might have used them. However, the tenant must not do anything that injures the inheritance or which constitutes waste." (Rasch, New York Landlord and Tenant, Vol. 1, Section 354 . . . .) The real inquiry in all cases involving alterations made by the tenant is whether there is damage done which injures the reversion (Agate v. Lowenbein, 57 N.Y. 604). If a lessee makes extensive alterations, takes down and removes a number of partitions and doors, gas fixtures, chandeliers, and plumbing in order to convert the premises into a hotel, causing serious injury to the reversion and substantially diminishing the value of the property he commits waste. At common law if he materially and permanently changes the nature and character of the building, as where he completely changes the interior arrangement of a portion of the premises by removing some partitions and erecting others, by placing the wooden framework for a store frame in the place where brick piers had previously stood, it is waste even if the value of the property is enhanced (McDonald v. O'Hara, 192 N.Y.S. 545), particularly where such alterations "render it impossible for him to restore the same premises substantially at the expiration of the term." (Winship v. Pitts, 3 Paige 259.) But if a tenant leases a factory and requires an engine in good working order to run the machinery, and without the owner's consent removes the old, worn-out and dangerous engine, and installs a new one, he does not commit waste and does not violate the clause of the lease prohibiting alterations without the consent of the landlord if such replacement is done

[handwritten marginalia top: can have change w/o waste as long as no injury incurred.]

without injury either to the foundation or to the building, or to the old engine. (Andrews v. Day Button Co., 132 N.Y. 348.) For in such a case "no substantial alteration was made in the situation, condition, or nature of the premises, but . . . on removal of the new engine the old one could be restored to the foundation from which it was taken."

Similarly, where the tenant leases the premises to conduct a restaurant the installation by him of three air-conditioning units, each weighing 750 pounds not attached to the floor or walls, standing on their own support, requiring no new or additional power lines, does not constitute "alteration" or such substantial change which varies the form or nature of the building (Leong Won v. Snyder, Supreme Court, Kings County, 1949, 94 N.Y.S.2d 247), but is a permissible exercise of the tenant's "right to the use and enjoyment of the premises for the express purpose of the leasing." So, also, where a tenant removes the landlord's sink and stove (Lansis v. Meklinsky, 198 N.Y.S.2d 247), or the landlord's refrigerator (Parker v. Johnson, 206 N.Y.S.2d 594) and replaces them with his own without the landlord's consent, he does not violate the covenant of the lease prohibiting "alteration" without the landlord's consent nor does he violate a substantial obligation of the tenancy under subdivision 1 section 52 of the State Rent and Eviction Regulations . . . . Following these authorities it has been held that in the absence of a specific covenant in the lease prohibiting the use of washing machines without the landlord's consent, the use of a movable washing machine not permanently attached or affixed to the existing plumbing or electric lines, but connected during use by rubber hoses with the sink faucets and drain, does not constitute a violation of a substantial obligation of the tenancy, for it is a reasonable and proper exercise of the tenant's "use and enjoyment." . . .

[marginalia right: examples of no violation. "of alteration"]

[marginalia right: need express/ specific covenant in lease.]

. . . [T]here is no proof that the improvement made by the tenant in the course of the proper use and enjoyment of the premises involved an injury to the reversion. It in fact enhanced its value. Nor is there any proof that it constitutes a substantial and permanent change in the nature and character of the building premises. The tenant testified the old cabinets hung only on two nails and there was a hole in the ceiling above it with an exposed BX cable. . . .

[marginalia right: tenants did not alter/injure/ or permanently change apartment.]

Accordingly, petition is dismissed on the merits.

Notes and Questions

1. Why might the landlord want to evict the tenant in a situation like this?

2. As indicated in the discussion of the implied warranty of habitability and tort liability, at common law the landlord had no duty to repair leased premises. Rather, the lease contained an implied duty on the tenant to make repairs. The tenant's duty to repair was limited, however, even under earlier doctrine, to minor repairs necessary to prevent degradation of the property, and the lessee was not required to make substantial repairs. This duty to repair may also be understood as part of the general obligation of a holder of a present estate not to commit permissive waste (although there are some questions whether tenants for years were bound by the doctrine of permissive waste under early English precedent). Permissive waste occurs when a present interest holder fails to take reasonable steps to preserve the property for the owner of the future interest.

[marginalia right: Permissive waste]

Thus, if a tenant did not replace a window broken in a storm so that water damage later resulted to the interior walls, the tenant would be liable under the implied duty to repair or permissive waste concept. Robert Schoshinski, *American Law of Landlord and Tenant* § 5:18 (1980).

Was the tenant's implied duty to repair a reasonable common-law rule? Is the exception for substantial repairs sensible? Should the implied duty to repair be modified in light of decisions like *Javins v. First National Realty Corp.*? What obligation should the tenant have? Consider the approach of the Uniform Landlord and Tenant Act § 2.104, set out above and the following § 3.101 [Tenant to Maintain Dwelling Unit]:

A Tenant shall

(1) comply with all obligations primarily imposed upon tenants by applicable provisions of building and housing codes materially affecting health and safety;

(2) keep that part of the premises that he occupies and uses as clean and safe as the condition of the premises permit;

(3) dispose from his dwelling unit all ashes, garbage, rubbish, and other waste in a clean and safe manner;

(4) keep all plumbing fixtures in the dwelling unit or used by the tenant as clear as their condition permits;

(5) use in a reasonable manner all electrical, plumbing, sanitary, heating, ventilating, air-conditioning, and other facilities and appliances including elevators in the premises;

(6) not deliberately or negligently destroy, deface, damage, impair, or remove any part of the premises or knowingly permit any person to do so; and

(7) conduct himself and require other persons on the premises with his consent to conduct themselves in a manner that will not disturb his neighbors' peaceful enjoyment of the premises.

3. The tenant's duty to repair may be limited or enlarged by express agreement. The tenant's obligation may be found in an express repair clause or in the surrender clause that specifies the condition of the premises at the termination of the lease. M. Friedman, *Friedman on Leases* § 10.601 (3d ed. 1990).

Provisions imposing a duty to repair often present problems of interpretation as to whether a particular repair is included. Moreover, since the language varies from lease to lease and because different jurisdictions have varying interpretations of the same language, the precedential value of these decisions may be limited. Essentially, the court must engage in contract interpretation and attempt to determine the parties' intent in light of the language, circumstances, and constructional rules. What factors should be relevant in such a decision? Consider a five-year lease for commercial property that provides that the tenant will "maintain roof, foundations, and exterior walls." Should the tenant be responsible for structural repairs to the roof due to rotting beams in the amount of $35,000? *See Jacobi v. Timmers Chevrolet, Inc.*, 296 S.E.2d 777 (Ga. Ct. App. 1982); *see also Shapiro v. Valmont Industries, Inc.*, 982 F.2d 237 (7th Cir. 1992); *Mobil Oil Credit Corp. v. DST Realty, Inc.*, 689 S.W.2d 658 (Mo. Ct. App. 1985); M. Friedman, *Friedman on Leases* § 10.601 (3d ed. 1990).

Different courts have reached different interpretations of the same or very similar language, perhaps due to light shed by other indicia of the parties' intent. Thus, a covenant obligating a tenant "to keep the premises in repair" has been viewed by some courts to expand the common-law implied duty only to the extent that damage from reasonable wear and tear must be included but viewed by other courts as a "general" covenant to repair, including an obligation to rebuild the premises if they are destroyed by fire or other calamity. Robert Schoshinski, *American Law of Landlord and Tenant* § 5:20 (1980). Some courts have held that a requirement to keep premises in "good" repair obligates the tenant to return the property in a repaired state even if it were not in a good condition at the beginning of the term, while others rule that the tenant is obligated only to keep the premises in the same condition as they were at the start of the term. Which are the better interpretations? Can a tenant adequately protect herself in light of these distinctions?

4. Did the tenant in *Sigsbee* commit *permissive* waste? Was *Sigsbee* correctly decided? Did the court strike an appropriate balance between the landlord and the tenant? Should the *Sigsbee* result have been the same if the landlord were a teacher and had leased her home to a tenant for a two-year term while the landlord was away on sabbatical leave? What if the tenant had remodeled the entire kitchen and replaced the appliances since the kitchen was 30 years old and barely functional?

Compare *Melms v. Pabst Brewing Co.*, 79 N.W. 738 (Wis. 1899), where a brewing company owned a life estate *per autre vie* in a property occupied by a large house. This property adjoined others used by the company in its brewing operations, and over the years the surrounding area had become predominately industrial. The brewing company razed the house and graded the lot down to street level in order to use the lot as part of the brewing business. The owners of the reversion brought an action claiming waste. The brewing company defended by the doctrine of ameliorating waste, which provides that technical waste is not actionable where the tenant's actions increase the value of the property. The court permitted the defense on the facts, stating:

> The evidence shows that the property became valueless for the purpose of residence property as the result of the growth and development of a great city. Business and manufacturing interests advanced and surrounded the once elegant mansion, until it stood isolated and alone, standing upon just enough ground to support it, and surrounded by factories and railway tracks, absolutely undesirable as a residence, and incapable of any use as business property.

See Melms v. Pabst Brewing Co. and the Doctrine of Waste in American Property Law, 94 Marq. L. Rev. 1055 (2011). On ameliorating waste, see R. Powell, Real Property ¶ [640[2].

In this regard, consider:

N.Y. Real Prop. Acts. Law § 803:

> 1. When a person having an estate for life or for years in land proposes to make an alteration in, or a replacement of a structure or structures located thereon, then the owner of a future interest in such land can neither recover damages for, nor enjoin the alteration or replacement, if the person proposing to make such alteration or replacement complies with the requirements hereinafter stated as to the giving of security and establishes the following facts:

a. That the proposed alteration or replacement is one which a prudent owner of an estate in fee simple absolute in the affected land would be likely to make in view of the conditions existing on or in the neighborhood of the affected land; and

b. That the proposed alteration or replacement, when completed, will not reduce the market value of the interests in such land subsequent to the estate for life or for years; and

c. That the proposed alteration or replacement is not in violation of the terms of any agreement or other instrument regulating the conduct of the owner of the estate for life or for years or restricting the land in question; and

d. That the life expectancy of the owner of the estate for life or the unexpired term of the estate for years is not less than five years; and

e. That the person proposing to make such alteration or replacement, not less than thirty days prior to commencement thereof, served upon each owner of a future interest, who is in being and ascertained, a written notice of his intention to make such alteration or replacement, specifying the nature thereof, which notice was served personally or by registered mail sent to the last known address of each such owner of a future interest.

2. When the owner of a future interest in the affected land demands security that the proposed alteration or replacement, if begun, will be completed and that he be protected against responsibility for expenditures incident to the making of the proposed alteration or replacement, the court in which the action to recover damages or to enjoin the alteration or replacement is pending, or if no such action is pending, the supreme court, on application thereto, on such notice to the interested parties as the court may direct, shall fix the amount and terms of the security reasonably necessary to satisfy such demand. The furnishing of the security so fixed shall be a condition precedent to the making of the proposed alteration or replacement.

3. This section applies only to estates for life or for years created on or after September 1, 1937.

To a large extent, the New York statute codifies case law delineating the requirements of a successful ameliorating waste defense. What goals do such requirements, as reflected in the New York legislation, serve?

5. Would the result have been different in *Sigsbee* if the case had been brought after expiration of the lease and the landlord sought damages for the cost of reinstallation of the original cabinets? What should the measure of damages be? *See Gabin v. Goldstein*, 497 N.Y.S.2d 984 (Civ. Ct. 1986) (after tenants abandoned, landlord awarded $1,500 for cost of removal of built-in furniture installations in single-family home rented by absentee owner to tenant under a four-year lease).

Under statutes in about one-half of the jurisdictions, a landlord may recover multiple damages for waste. *See, e.g.,* Mo. Stat. Ann. § 537.420 (treble damages); Wash. Rev. Code Ann. § 64.12.030 (treble damages). Statutes in many states permit the landlord to terminate (i.e., forfeit) the remaining term of the lease if the tenant commits waste. *See, e.g.,* Ind. Code § 32-30-4-1; N.C. Gen. Stat. § 1-533; *Rowe v. Wells Fargo Realty Services, Inc.*, 166 Cal. App. 3d 310 (1985) (damage to thermostats and temperature controls did not cause a substantial decrease in value to permit termination of lease for waste).

6. Permissive waste will not be found for degradation to the property due to ordinary wear and tear. *United States Gypsum Co. v. Schiavo Bros.*, 668 F.2d 172 (3d Cir. 1981). What reasons support this rule?

An express repair provision may contain express language excepting damages for ordinary wear and tear from the tenant's obligation. *See, e.g., Fisher Properties, Inc. v. Arden-Mayfair, Inc.*, 726 P.2d 8 (Wash. 1986) ("in as good state and condition as reasonable use and wear . . . will permit"). Conversely, an express repair provision may obligate the tenant to repair damage due to ordinary wear and tear. *See, e.g., Santillanes v. Property Management Services, Inc.*, 716 P.2d 1360 (Idaho Ct. App. 1986).

7. The law of fixtures determines whether, at the end of the term, the tenant has the right to remove articles affixed by her to the property or whether they should remain for the landlord. Property will be found to be a fixture, and thus the property of the landlord, if it is attached to the realty by the tenant with the intent to make it a permanent part of the land. Because an objective intent standard is used and because the ordinary tenant does not intend to increase the value of the property for the benefit of the landlord, courts do not readily find property to be fixtures. Robert Schoshinski, *American Law of Landlord and Tenant* § 5:29 (1980). Additionally, if a fixture is a trade fixture, such as machinery used in a business, the property may be removed by the tenant without resort to the objective intent test. *See also Brown v. DuBosi*, 532 N.E.2d 223 (Ohio Mun. Ct. 1988) (track lighting used in retail business was trade fixture). On fixtures in general, see Note, *Fixtures in the Landlord-Tenant Relationship*, 34 U. Chi. L. Rev. 617 (1967); Michael Haley, *Compensation for Tenants' Improvements: A Valediction?*, 11 Legal Stud. 119 (1991).

The tenant may be barred from removing an otherwise removable item, however, if substantial damage to the premises will result. *See, e.g.,* Idaho Code Ann. § 55-308. Under Restatement § 12.2 cmt. *s*, however, removal is permitted as long as the tenant restores the property within a limited time. What reasons support this Restatement position?

These judicial and statutory rules on fixtures may be, and in the commercial context commonly are, altered by contract. *See, e.g., Alexander v. Cooper*, 843 S.W.2d 644 (Tex. App. 1992) (car wash machinery could not be removed by tenant where lease provided that all alterations were to be left on expiration of lease).

Problems: Waste

1. Tenant leased an old warehouse from Landlord for 10 years with the understanding that the property would be used for a retail home-improvement store. To provide a more efficient and aesthetic sales floor, Tenant removed various nonsupport walls that had divided a portion of the space into offices. Tenant also installed numerous plumbing fixtures on the sales floor to provide realistic displays for shoppers. Can Landlord successfully claim waste by Tenant? Will Tenant have any liability to Landlord at the end of the term when Tenant vacates and Landlord leases the property to a carpet retailer? *See Restatement (Second) of Property—Landlord and Tenant* § 12.1 illus. 6, 24, 26.

2. Landlord leased premises to Tenant for use as a candle-making factory. When Tenant vacated at the end of the term, a wax residue remained on the walls and ceiling even after the Tenant's efforts to clean it. Does Tenant have any liability to Landlord? *See Chew v. International Society for Krishna Consciousness of Colorado New Barsana Farm Community, Inc.*, 738 P.2d 57 (Colo. Ct. App. 1987).

3. Landlord leased a drive-in theater to Tenant for a five-year term. The lease contained a clause requiring Tenant to "keep the leased premises in good repair." A few months into the term, the county health department notified the Tenant that the well water on the site was contaminated. Tenant was able to obtain a one-year postponement of enforcement by the county. To address the problem, a new well had to be dug or a reverse osmosis plant had to be installed on the old well. This was not done, and 19 months into the term, the county ordered the theater closed. Tenant vacated the premises and stopped paying rent. Does Landlord have any remedies against Tenant? *See Portal Enterprises, Inc. v. Cahoon*, 715 P.2d 1324 (Nev. 1986).

b. Duty to Operate

PIGGLY WIGGLY SOUTHERN, INC. v. HEARD
Supreme Court of Georgia
261 Ga. 503, 405 S.E.2d 478 (1991)

HUNT, J. This case involves the construction of a shopping center store lease. Both the trial court and the Court of Appeals held the lease contained an express continued use covenant as well as an implied covenant of continued operation. We granted the writ of certiorari to determine whether the Court of Appeals was correct in its construction of the parties' lease, and reverse.

In 1963, the parties executed a lease in which appellees' predecessor agreed to construct a supermarket for appellant according to plans prepared by appellant. Appellant drafted the lease, which began in 1964 for a term of 15 years, and called for an annual base rent of $29,053.60 as well as a percentage rent of annual gross sales exceeding $2,000,000. The lease was renewed on the same terms for an additional seven years in 1979, with options to renew for two additional three-year terms. Appellant exercised both renewal options and, after it was acquired by a new corporation, one month into the second three-year term, closed its store, vacated the premises, and moved its grocery store operation to a nearby shopping center belonging to its new owner. While appellant continued to pay the annual base rent to appellees, it refused to sublease the vacant store, despite the interest of other supermarkets in the abandoned space. Appellees filed suit seeking damages for appellant's alleged breach of the lease.

We agree with appellant that the lease agreement between the parties does not contain an express covenant of continuous operation. Rather, the language of the agreement is plainly to the contrary, and, therefore, the trial court, the Court of Appeals, and this court are not authorized to construe it otherwise. . . . The language of the agreement expressly negates a requirement of continuous operation:

> . . . LESSEE'S use of the leased building and the leased property shall not be limited nor restricted to such purposes [use as a supermarket, etc.], and said building and property may be used *for any other lawful business*, without the consent of LESSOR (emphasis supplied).

See Kroger Co. v. Bonny Corp., 216 S.E.2d 341 (Ga. Ct. App. 1975).[1]

Nor does the lease agreement contain any provision which would create an *implied* covenant of continuous operation. Rather, the contract, read as a whole, indicates otherwise. The agreement's provision for free assignability by the tenant, without consent of the lessor, weighs strongly against a construction of the contract which would require the tenant to continue its business throughout the term of the lease. Kroger Co. v. Bonny Corp., *supra*. Likewise, the existence of a substantial minimum base rent, in addition to the provision for percentage rental payments, suggests the absence of an implied covenant of continuous operation. *See also* 38 A.L.R.2d Annot., p. 1113 *et seq., Construction and Application of Provision in Lease Under Which Landlord is to Receive Percentage of Lessee's Profits or Receipts.*

The parties did not agree to nor bargain for appellant's continuous operation of the premises, and we are not authorized to rewrite the contract to create such a provision. . . .[2]

BENHAM, J., dissenting. . . . In addition to the facts set out in the majority opinion, it should be noted that the complete text of the lease provision on which appellees rely reads as follows:

> Lessee is leasing the leased building for use as a supermarket and other parts of the leased property for parking and other uses incident to a supermarket business, but LESSEE'S use of the leased building and the leased property shall not be limited nor restricted to such purposes, and said building and property may be used for any other lawful business, without the consent of LESSOR.

Although the language of this lease with regard to appellant's obligation to continue business operations in the leased premises during the term of the lease is not as clear as the language in non-abandonment clauses such as those quoted in Kroger Co. v. Bonny Corp., 216 S.E.2d 341 (Ga. Ct. App. 1975),[3] any ambiguity is dispelled by application of the rules governing the construction of contracts. One of the rules pertinent to this matter is that an ambiguity in a document should be construed against its draftsman.

. . . [S]ince the lease with which this case is concerned was drafted by appellant, it must be construed most strongly against appellant. Another applicable rule . . . require[s] that a contract be considered in its entirety.

In considering the entirety of the lease contract in the present case, I note that in addition to the provision for appellant using the premises for a supermarket

---

1. In Kroger Co. v. Bonny Corp., the Court of Appeals rejected the contention that language in the lease agreement providing the tenant "use said premises in a lawful manner" created a covenant of continuous operation.

2. *See generally* 40 A.L.R.3d Annot., p. 971 *et seq., Lease of Store as Requiring Active Operation of Store*, which states the general rule that

> . . . the courts take the position that the lessee is under no obligation, in the absence of a specific provision therefor, to occupy or use, or continue to use, the leased premises, even though one of the parties, or both, expected and intended that they would be used for the particular purpose to which they seemed to be adapted or for which they seemed to be constructed.

Id. at 975.

3. "'[L]essee agrees not to abandon or vacate leased premises during the period of this lease.'" *Id.* at 838.

business or any other lawful business, the lease provides for percentage rental payments . . . .

Considering the percentage rental provision together with the provision quoted above relating to business use, which includes a right to assignment of the lease without consent of the lessor, and construing the lease most strongly against appellant as the drafter of the lease, I conclude, as did the trial court and the Court of Appeals, that the lease contains an express covenant by appellant that it would conduct business operations in the leased premises during the entire period of the lease.

Appellant and the majority rely on Kroger Co. v. Bonny Corp., *supra*, for the proposition that the provision in the lease for use of the premises for a business other than operating a supermarket does not amount to an express covenant of continuous operation. There is, however, an essential difference between the language used in the lease in *Bonny* and the language used in the lease in this case. In *Bonny*, the pertinent language provided only that the tenant would "use said premises in a lawful manner." Paying the base rent and keeping the premises empty would certainly constitute using the premises "in a lawful manner." The lease in the present case, in contrast, requires that appellant use the premises for a "lawful business." Holding the premises empty cannot reasonably be construed as using the premises for a "business." . . .

The majority rejects the possibility of the existence of an implied covenant with the simplistic assertion that the base rent provided for in the lease is "substantial." What are the standards to be applied in determining whether the base rent is a "substantial" amount? Is substantiality of the base rent the only factor to be considered? These questions go unanswered in the majority opinion. A more reasoned approach than simply declaring that the base rent is substantial and that there cannot, therefore, be an implied covenant of continuous operation would be to apply the conditions enumerated by the Arizona Court of Appeals in First American Bank & Co. v. Safeway Stores, 729 P.2d 938, 940 (Ariz. 1986):

> [C]ertain conditions must be satisfied before a covenant will be implied: "(1) the implication must arise from the language used; (2) it must appear from the language used that it was so clearly within the contemplation of the parties that they deemed it unnecessary to express it; (3) implied covenants can only be justified on the grounds of legal necessity; (4) a promise can be implied only where it can be rightfully assumed that it would have been made if attention had been called to it; (5) there can be no implied covenant where the subject is completely covered by the contract."

I am persuaded that adoption of those standards in this state would lead to more certainty in the drafting and interpretation of commercial leases, and that the application of those standards to the present case would result in the conclusion that there was an implied covenant of continuous operation in the lease under consideration. Since that conclusion would require affirmance of the judgment of the Court of Appeals, I . . . dissent . . . .

Notes and Questions

1. There are various forms of "percentage leases" used in leases for retail establishments. The most common requires the tenant to pay as rent a set percentage of monthly gross receipts of the business, with the landlord entitled to a guaranteed minimum of rent. Some leases provide only for percentage rent, without the minimum. Other leases may calculate the rent as a percentage of the profits (or net receipts) rather than gross receipts. *See* Richard Thigpen, *Good Faith Performance Under Percentage Leases*, 51 Miss. L.J. 315 (1980-1981); Note, *Resolving Disputes Under Percentage Leases*, 51 Minn. L. Rev. 1139 (1967). Use of percentage rent in shopping centers "is virtually universal. In other retail establishments its use is hardly less." Milton Friedman, *Friedman on Leases* § 6.1, at 189 (3d ed. 1990).

Why are percentage rent clauses so widely used? What functions do they serve? How else can a landlord provide for inflation and a tenant for recession or other reversal of fortune in a long-term lease?

2. Why does a landlord, like the one in *Piggly Wiggly*, seek to have the tenant bound by a continuous operation covenant? What reasons may be behind the tenant's cessation of operations? *See* Francis Mastroianni, *Caveat Lessor: Courts' Unwillingness to Find Implied Covenants of Continuous Use in Commercial Real Estate Leases*, 24 Real Est. L.J. 236 (1996); Comment, *Commercial Leasing: Implied Covenants of Operation in Shopping Center Leases*, 95 Dick. L. Rev. 383 (1991). What is likely to happen when an anchor tenant in a shopping center goes dark?

3. Would *Piggly Wiggly* have been decided differently if the lease had provided for no minimum rent? The court accurately states the prevailing attitude of the courts that "the existence of substantial minimum base rent" is a strong factor against implying a covenant of continuous operation. Why is this so?

How much rent is "substantial"? One court stated that " 'a substantial minimum' cannot be precisely defined and factual information on this issue must be examined before a covenant will be implied." *College Block v. Atlantic Richfield Co.*, 206 Cal. App. 3d 1376 (1988). In another case, the court concluded:

> [W]e find that the [tenant] paid a substantial fixed base rent. This is evident from the fact that the [tenant] paid $6,438.17 a month, and had paid $885,416.01 in base rent through the end of 1985; whereas, the [tenant] had paid only $283,830.59 in percentage payment clause over the thirteen-year period involved.

Thompson Development, Inc. v. Kroger Co., 413 S.E.2d 137 (W. Va. 1991). Is this decision correct? *See generally* Comment, *Percentage Leases: Is There a Need to Imply a Covenant of Continuous Operation?*, 72 Marq. L. Rev. 559 (1989).

4. In addition to percentage rent, courts have relied on the presence of other factors in finding or rejecting an implied covenant of continuous operation. Consider whether the following factors, some of which are mentioned in *Piggly Wiggly*, are relevant and why:

- The lease provides an express right to assign or sublet without consent.
- The lease contains a "use clause," i.e., the tenant "will use the premises for [*operation of a retail supermarket*]."
- The lease grants the tenant an exclusive right to the use in a shopping center.
- The cost of improvements made by the landlord for this particular tenant.
- The lease was actively negotiated between the parties.
- There were discussions between the parties during negotiations about continuous operation.

5. Courts have struggled over the remedies for the breach of an express or implied covenant of continuous operation. Should damages be available, and how should they be calculated? Is injunctive relief appropriate? What if the tenant's store is operating at a loss? Can the landlord terminate the lease? Which remedies does the landlord prefer and in what situations? *See Hornwood v. Smith's Food King No. 1*, 772 P.2d 1284 (Nev. 1989) (diminution in value of shopping center); *New Park Forest Associates II v. Rogers Enterprises, Inc.*, 552 N.E.2d 1215 (Ill. Ct. App. 1990) (contract not to vacate could not be specifically enforced).

Problems: Continuous Operation Clauses

1. You represent the developer of a shopping center with 15 small stores and a large space that the developer wants to lease to a supermarket. Draft a continuous operation clause for the lease. What issues do you need to address? What modifications will the tenant seek? How should the differences be resolved?

2. Landlord and Tenant entered into a five-year lease for a store in a high-crime area of the city. Both Landlord and Tenant were aware of the nature of the neighborhood when the lease was made, and the rental amount was consistent with the fair market rental for such premises. The lease did not contain an express continuous operation clause. Tenant seeks to move out after one year but is willing to continue paying rent. Landlord is concerned that vandals will destroy the store if it is unoccupied. Should a court imply a continuous operation covenant? If so, what remedy should the court give Landlord? *See Asling v. McAllister-Fitzgerald Lumber Co.*, 244 P. 16 (Kan. 1926).

c.   Duty to Pay Rent

(i)   *Destruction of the Premises*

ALBERT M. GREENFIELD & CO. v. KOLEA
Supreme Court of Pennsylvania
475 Pa. 351, 380 A.2d 758 (1977)

MANDERINO, J. Appellee (lessor) . . . sued appellant (lessee) for breach of two lease agreements. The trial court awarded appellee $7,200.00. . . . We reverse.

The appellee's claim in this case is based on two separate, but related, lease agreements. The first lease, executed on March 20, 1971, covered ". . . all that certain one story garage building and known as 5735-37 Wayne Avenue, extending to Keyser Street in the rear [Philadelphia] . . . to be used and occupied as storage of automobiles. . . ." This lease, executed for a term of two years beginning May 1, 1971, provided for an annual rental of $4,800.00. The second lease, covering adjoining property, was also executed on March 20, 1971. The second lease covered . . . all those certain lots or pieces of ground known as 5721-33 Wayne Avenue . . . to be used and occupied for the sale and storage of automobiles . . . ." The second lease, also executed for a two-year term beginning May 1, 1971, provided for an annual rental of $2,500.00. There was no building located on the real estate covered by the second lease. Neither lease contained a provision with respect to the tenant's obligations in the event of destruction of the building.

On May 1, 1972, after the appellant had occupied the premises for one year, fire completely destroyed the building covered by lease number one. The fire was labeled as accidental by the Fire Marshall's office. The day after the fire the remaining sections of the exterior walls were razed by the lessor, and barricades were placed around the perimeter of the premises covered by both leases. Appellant thereafter refused to pay rent under either of the leases.

The general rule has been stated that in the absence of a lease provision to the contrary, a tenant is not relieved from the obligation to pay rent despite the total destruction of the leased premises. . . .

The reason for the rule has been said to be that although a building may be an important element of consideration for the payment of rent, the interest in the soil remains to support the lease despite destruction of the building. It has also been said that since destruction of the building is usually by accident, it is only equitable to divide the loss; the lessor loses the property and the lessee loses the term. . . .

Two exceptions designed to afford relief to the tenant from the harshness of the common law principle have been created. These exceptions reflect the influence of modern contract principles as applied in the landlord-tenant relationship.

The first exception provides that where only a portion of a building is leased, total destruction of the building relieves the tenant of the obligation to pay rent. . . . This exception recognizes that in the leasing of a part of a building there is no implication that any estate in land is granted. . . . [T]he parties have *bargained for* a part of a building and not the land beneath.

The influence of contract principles of bargained for exchange is also apparent in the second exception to the general common law rule. The second exception is based on the doctrine of *impossibility of performance*, and is stated in Greenburg v. Sun Shipbuilding Co., 121 A. 63, 64 (Pa. 1923):

> Where a contract relates to the use and possession of specific property, the existence of which is necessary to the carrying out of the purpose in view, a condition is implied by law, as though written in the agreement that the impossibility of performance arising from the destruction of the property without fault of either party, shall end all contractual obligations relating to the thing destroyed.

See also Rest. Contracts, § 460, 6 *Corbin on Contracts*, § 1337.

As was said in West v. Peoples First National Bank & Trust Co., 378 Pa. 275, 106 A.2d 427 (1954),

> . . . where a contract relates to specific property the existence or maintenance of which is necessary to the carrying out of the purpose of the agreement, the condition is implied by law, just as though it were written into the agreement, that the impossibility of performance or the frustration of purpose arising from the destruction of the property or interference with its use, without the fault of either party, ends all contractual obligations relating to the property. Moreover, impossibility in that connection means not only strict impossibility but impracticability because of extreme and unreasonable difficulty, expense, or loss involved. . . .

The Rest. Contracts § 454, also applies the test of impracticability rather than strict impossibility: " . . . [i]mpossibility means not only strict impossibility but *impracticability* because of extreme and unreasonable difficulty, expense, injury, or loss involved." (Emphasis added.)

In the instant case, it is apparent that when the building was destroyed by fire it became impossible for the appellee to furnish the agreed consideration— ". . . all that one story garage building. . . ." Nothing in the first lease implies that any interest in the land itself was intended to be conveyed. It is also obvious that the purpose of the lease with respect to the appellant was thereby frustrated. As noted in the lease, the parties contemplated that appellant would use the building for the repair and sale of used motor vehicles. Without a building appellant could no longer carry on a used car business as contemplated by the parties at the time they entered into the lease agreement. It became extremely impracticable for the appellant to continue using the adjoining lot when his business office and repair stations were destroyed by the fire. Additionally, because of the dangerous condition created by the fire, the city required appellee to barricade the property covered by both leases, thus preventing appellant from entering the property.

In reaching our decision that the accidental destruction of the building by fire excused the parties from further performance . . . , we are cognizant of the fact that we are allocating the risk to be assumed by the parties. Such an allocation of risk can be accomplished in one of two ways. First, the parties could specifically provide for risk assumption with respect to certain possible contingencies. In the absence of an express recognition and assumption by the parties, the court is left with the task of determining what the parties would have done had the issue arisen in the contract negotiations. . . . In reaching such a decision a court must consider many factors. As stated in 6 Corbin on Contracts § 1325:

> There is no rule of law by which the issue can be deductively determined; it depends upon the practices and customs of men in like cases, upon the prevailing mores of the time.

In reaching a decision involving the landlord-tenant relationship, too often courts have relied on outdated common law property principles and presumptions . . . . In this case, for example, if we applied the general rule and ignored the realities of the situation, we would bind the appellant to paying rent for barren ground when both parties to the lease contemplated that the building would be used for the commercial enterprise of repair and sale of used motor vehicles.

The trial court's decision to bind the lessee to the lease was simply an application of an outdated common law presumption. . . . It is no longer reasonable to *assume* that in the absence of a lease provision to the contrary the lessee should bear the risk of loss in the event of total destruction of the building. Where the parties do not expressly provide for such a catastrophe, the court should analyze the facts and the lease agreement as any other contract would be analyzed. Following such an analysis, if it is evident to the court that the parties bargained for the existence of a building, and no provision is made as to who bears the risk of loss if the building is destroyed, the court should relieve the parties of their respective obligations when the building no longer exists.

Accordingly, we reverse the order of the Superior Court, and remand to the trial court with directions to grant the appellant's motion for judgment n.o.v.

Notes and Questions

1. What is the theory behind the common-law rule that a tenant was not relieved of the duty to pay rent when there was a sudden destruction of the building on the leased premises where there was no fault by the tenant?

2. Many jurisdictions have rejected the common-law rule by statute. *See, e.g.,* N.Y. Real Prop. Law § 227; N.C. Gen. Stat. § 42-12; Unif. Residential Landlord and Tenant Act § 4.106. These statutes may automatically terminate the tenancy upon sudden destruction, give the tenant an option to do so, or keep the lease in place but suspend rent until repairs are made. Robert Schoshinski, *American Law of Landlord and Tenant* § 10:7 (1980).

Could the tenant have forced the landlord to rebuild the building in *Albert M. Greenfield? See Farnham v. Windle*, 918 F.2d 47 (7th Cir. 1990) (no, termination is only remedy).

(ii) Rent Controls

The earliest rent control legislation, enacted in Washington, D.C., was a reaction to the housing shortages and escalating prices during the First World War.[6] Today's powerful and pervasive rent regulation structure in New York City has its origins in legislation passed during the Second World War, again, in response to a severe housing shortage.[7]

More recent rent regulation responded to a perceived shortage of affordable, decent rental housing. In 1969, New York passed legislation expanding rent regulation to buildings built after World War II but also providing for inflationary increases in rent and allowing other flexibility in the system.[8] In the 1970s, approximately 100 municipalities in New Jersey adopted rent controls.[9] Massachusetts passed legislation enabling municipalities to enact rent controls, although a statewide ballot initiative passed in November 1994 and subsequent legislation have eliminated rent controls in the state, with a phaseout for units occupied by the poor, elderly, and disabled.[10] Rent control ordinances were passed in numerous California municipalities during the 1970s and 1980s. 1986 figures indicated that more than 200 municipalities in the United States had some form of rent control.[11]

While the rent control ordinances differ from one another, some generalizations are possible. Although some of the older rent control legislation did not permit any increase in rental fees over the years, the modern provisions typically provide for a "fair rate of return" on the property. This return is usually set from time to time by an administrative or legislative body. Some regimes allow extra

---

6. *See* Block v. Hirsh, 256 U.S. 135 (1921).

7. *See* Comment, *Residential Rent Control in New York City*, 3 Colum. J.L. & Soc. Probs. 30 (1967).

8. *See* Stephen Dobkin, *Confiscating Reality: The Illusion of Controls in the Big Apple*, 54 Brook. L. Rev. 1249, 1254-59 (1989).

9. *See* Kenneth K. Baar, *Rent Control in the 1970s: The Case of the New Jersey Tenants' Movement*, 28 Hastings L.J. 631 (1977).

10. 1994 Mass. Adv. Legis. Serv. 282.

11. Anthony Downs, *Residential Rent Controls* 3 (1988). *See also* Fla. Stat. § 125.0103 (setting state limitations on local rent control regulations).

increases in rent when a new tenant moves in, while other jurisdictions provide for the decontrol of a unit when it becomes vacant. In light of this incentive for landlords to replace old tenants with new ones, the statutes typically give the tenant a right to renew the lease perpetually unless the tenant is in substantial breach. Moreover, tenants may be evicted only for cause, and the legislation may limit conversions of rental buildings to condominiums or other withdrawals from the rental market. Some jurisdictions exempt new construction from the regulations (or at least provide less stringent regulation). For an excellent treatment of rent control, see Robert Schoshinski, *American Law of Landlord and Tenant* §§ 7.1-7.10 (1980).

There are differing views on the question whether rent control is a good policy.

RENT CONTROL AND THE THEORY OF EFFICIENT REGULATION

Richard A. Epstein,
54 Brook. L. Rev. 741, 767-70 (1988)

C.   Long-term Investment

The gap between market and regulated rents also has an effect upon both the long-term operation of the rental housing supply, and upon the operation of the political process. A rent control statute is in part a form of price control, and like all price controls, it results in a systematic gap between the large quantity of goods demanded (because the price is low) and the small quantity of goods supplied (for the same reason). Without regulation, the price would rise, the demand would ease, and the supply would increase until the market was back in equilibrium, as happened in San Francisco after the [1906] earthquake. But with the obvious form of redress effectively controlled, some other forms of conduct are necessary to narrow the gap between supply and demand. . . . Even if new construction is exempt from the statute, existing rent control laws give a loud and clear signal that old policies may be reversed so that future units may be subject to similar restrictions. That prospect is, moreover, far from negligible because once those units are occupied, their residents add a new class of voters to the rolls whose interests can no longer be ignored in the political calculus. All rent control statutes thus depress the future total return of any investment. Reduced returns mean reduced investments, so that rent control statutes only exacerbate the housing shortages they are said to alleviate.

D.   The Political Dimension

As hinted above, the rent control statutes also have very powerful and unfortunate political overtones. The gap between regulated and market rentals is not fixed by an act of nature. It must be determined in political markets. But the operation of these markets differs in a notable way from that of ordinary rental markets. In the usual private market, both landlord and tenant have made

specific investments in an ongoing relationship that is subject to the risk of strategic behavior at renewal. The tenant must incur the costs of finding new premises if the landlord raises the rental above market, while the landlord faces the
costs of finding a new tenant if the present tenant will not agree to any increase.
Yet in the private market, both landlord and tenant are reluctant to exploit the
vulnerability of the other side for fear of retaliation. A quick and easy agreement
on renewal spares both sides the risk and cost of protracted conflict, and is the
norm in most housing markets, where present tenants usually face increases
similar to those required of newly arriving tenants. The bilateral holdout problem is effectively controlled by increasing the number of alternative opportunities available. "Thick" markets work more smoothly than "thin" ones.

The situation is far more complex with rent control because some collective
decision is necessary to decide the permissible level of rent increases. Instead of
having competitive markets make the decision, the law must necessarily introduce political formulas whereby the majority of voters within the jurisdiction,
subject only to loose constitutional rate of return constraints, determine the formula for allowable increases. The political battles are often ugly, acrimonious,
and uncivilized. The costs are extensive, given the very wide bargaining range
between the market and the minimum allowable regulated rents. Factional struggle can dissipate the gains that are otherwise generated by voluntary exchange.
The 1942 New York law, like other older statutes, was so rigid and oppressive
that it decimated the housing stock of New York for a generation by forcing
the abandonment of many units. More modern stabilization statutes constantly
speak of "fair rates" of return on the model of public utility regulation. But even
here there is always the danger that the regulations will overshoot their mark,
so that some landlords will find it profitable to first milk and then abandon
their units, which become a source of urban plight and public mismanagement.
While the law may require some reasonable rate of return, there is many a slip
between cup and lip. The restrictions on rents, coupled with increases in taxes,
may force many landlords into bankruptcy.

RESIDENTIAL RENT CONTROLS: AN EVALUATION 1-2
Anthony Downs (1988)

As a general rule, residential rent regulation makes economic sense if, and
only if, two conditions occur simultaneously in the market and are both expected
to last for some time. Demand for rental units must rise sharply at the same time
that new construction of such units has been legally restricted in order to con-
serve resources—as during wartime. In the absence of these conditions, rent
controls are neither an appropriate nor an effective response to perceived housing shortages. On the contrary, they generally exacerbate such shortages. . . .

[It] is important to note the difficult normative policy choices reflected in the
decision to impose rent controls. Much evidence indicates that all rent controls,
even temperate controls, transfer income from owners to tenants or between
various classes of tenants. In addition, many of the short-term benefits of rent
controls (reduced rents) aid affluent rather than poor households, and some
of the costs (reduced access to vacant units) must be borne by very poor households. Where rent is eliminated as a basis for distinguishing among potential

tenants, owners often use other factors such as credit-worthiness, race, sex, or ethnicity in allocating scarce rental units—even though most such discrimination is illegal.

. . . The conclusion of this study is that the social and economic costs and disadvantages of rent controls—especially over the long run—almost always outweigh any perceived short-term benefits they provide, in the absence of the two justifying conditions described earlier.

RESIDENTIAL RENT CONTROL
Margaret Jane Radin, 15 Phil. & Pub. Aff. 350, 359-60, 361, 362 (1986)

Most of us . . . feel that a tenant's interest in continuing to live in an apartment that she has made home for some time seems somehow a stronger or more exigent claim than a commercial landlord's interest in maintaining the same scope of freedom of choice regarding lease terms and in maintaining a high profit margin. Where rising rents are forcing out tenants and where landlords have significant economic rents, that is, one feels the tenant's claim is stronger than the landlord's. Even where significant economic rents are not present, so that some landlords are forced to leave the business, one may still feel that the tenant's expectation or desire to continue in her home is more important than the commercial landlord's expectation or desire to continue in the landlord business over some other business that will yield a better return. We do not recognize any general right to remain in a specific business such that regulation of the industry would be prohibited if regulation would operate to force some of the less efficient suppliers out of that market and into others.

The intuitive general rule is that preservation of one's home is a stronger claim than preservation of one's business, or that noncommercial personal use of an apartment as a home is morally entitled to more weight than purely commercial landlording. . . .

Let me refer to the situation where the tenant stands to lose an established home and the landlord is purely commercial as "standard circumstances." To the extent there does exist the intuitive appeal for preserving the tenant's home in standard circumstances that I postulate here, it can be understood in terms of the distinction between personal and fungible property that I elaborated in an earlier article. Property that is "personal" in this philosophical sense is bound up with one's personhood, and is distinguishable from property that is held merely instrumentally or for investment and exchange and is therefore purely commercial or "fungible." . . .

Personal property describes specific categories in the external world in which holders can become justifiably self-invested, so that their individuality and selfhood become intertwined with a particular object. The object then cannot be replaced without pain by money or another similar object of equivalent market value; the particular object takes on unique value for the individual. Only a few special objects or categories of objects are personal property. Other property items, which can be replaced by their equivalents or money at no pain to the holder, are merely fungible, that is not bound up with personhood. . . .

HOME IS WHERE THE HEART IS: A BRIEF REPLY TO PROFESSOR EPSTEIN

Curtis J. Berger, 54 Brook. L. Rev. 1239,
1241-43, 1246-47 (1989)

Unless one agrees with Professor Epstein that from the moment of constitutional ratification, the incidents of legal estates became frozen and virtually immune from regulatory change—a view that few others entertain—the law must be ready to adjust legal relationships to their evolving economic and social environment. . . .

Professor Epstein, as do most economists, makes the further point that regulation causes a chronic rental shortage, which ultimately injures the entire class of tenants. It is one of those academic arguments which . . . has yet to be proven empirically. I have seen studies purporting to show a direct correlation between rental vacancies in a community and the presence or absence of controls, but it is the very condition of shortage which helps to explain the controls. I have also seen rent control blamed for high abandonment rates of rental properties; but here again, the evidence is inconclusive. Abandonment rates are also high in many cities that have not had controls since the end of World War II, and in New York City many (possibly most) buildings at the time of their abandonment could not command the controlled rental from the tenants who chose to live there.

Notes and Questions

1. *Policy considerations.* There has been significant debate in the literature on the question whether rent control is good social policy. Proponents of rent control feel that it is a necessity in light of a declining stock of affordable housing, with lower-income people paying a very high proportion of their income for the rental of substandard housing. Moreover, proponents argue that the regulation also protects moderate-income tenants who otherwise would "be subject to extreme rent fluctuations in tight housing markets." W. Dennis Keating, *Commentary on Rent Control and the Theory of Efficient Regulation*, 54 Brook. L. Rev. 1223, 1224 (1989). Further, others assert that rising rents in areas that are becoming gentrified cause homelessness since current tenants cannot afford the increased payments. Jorge O. Elorza, *Absentee Landlord, Rent Control and Healthy Gentrification: A Policy Proposal to Deconcentrate the Poor in Urban America*, 17 Cornell J.L. & Pub. Pol'y 1 (2007); Note, *Reassessing Rent Control: Its Economic Impact in a Gentrifying Housing Market*, 101 Harv. L. Rev. 1835 (1988). Do these arguments provide an adequate basis for the imposition of rent controls?

Are the positions of Professor Epstein and Mr. Downs convincing? Will rent regulations actually cause a lack of supply of rental housing? Does it make a difference if the statute is one of the older types that bars all rent increases or a modern one that permits limited increases and that exempts new construction? *See* George Fallis & Lawrence B. Smith, *Uncontrolled Prices in a Controlled Market: The Case of Rent Controls*, 74 Am. Econ. Rev. 193, 199 (1984) (theoretical analysis and empirical study show that rent for exempted newly constructed units is above what the rent would be in the absence of the rent control ordinance); Michael J. Mandel, *Does Rent Control Hurt Tenants?: A Reply to Epstein*, 54 Brook. L. Rev. 1267 (1989); Phillip Weitzman, *Economics and Rent Regulation: A Call for a New Perspective*, 13 N.Y.U. Rev. L. & Soc. Change 975 (1984-1985) (arguing that increased rents do not always yield increased supply of rental housing); James C. Smith, *The Dynamics of Landlord Tenant Law and Residential Finance: The Comparative Economics of Home Ownership*, 44 Wash. U. J. Urb. & Contemp. L. 3 (1993) (comparing the British and the American experiences). Do rent controls adversely affect the demand for housing? *See* Edward H. Rabin, *The Revolution in Residential Landlord-Tenant Law: Causes and Consequences*, 69 Cornell L. Rev. 517, 581-82 (1984).

Who has the better argument as to the "fairness" and social gains or losses attributable to rent regulation? Do you accept Professor Radin's dichotomy between personal and commercial property? What about the effect of rent control on people wishing to move into the city but who cannot find housing because of low supply due to rent control?

2. *Eviction protection.* As indicated in the introductory note to this section, rent control ordinances typically protect the tenant's right to renew the lease and limit eviction during the term to certain substantial breaches. These include failure to pay rent, failure to cure a violation of the lease after written notice from the landlord, conduct causing substantial damage or substantial interference with the quiet enjoyment of other tenants, illegal use of the premises, refusal to provide the landlord with reasonable access for repairs, subleasing without the landlord's consent, permanent removal of the unit from the rental market, intent to use the premises for the landlord's or the landlord's immediate family's own use, and other "just cause" not in conflict with the rent control ordinance. Kenneth K. Baar, *Guidelines for Drafting Rent Control Laws: Lessons for a Decade*, 35 Rutgers L. Rev. 723, 833-34 (1983).

What kinds of incentives does a rent control ordinance create for the landlord? For the tenant? Is a court likely to treat an eviction case differently if the unit is subject to rent control?

3. Rent control ordinances have been challenged on the ground that they take the landlord's property without compensation contrary to the protections afforded by the Fifth and Fourteenth Amendments to the United States Constitution, which we study in Chapter 13. *See, e.g., Dawson v. Higgins*, 588 N.Y.S.2d 93 (Sup. Ct. 1992), *aff'd*, 197 A.D.2d 127, *appeal dismissed*, 640 N.E.2d 143 (N.Y. 1994), *cert. denied*, 513 U.S. 1077 (1995) (finding no regulatory taking by New York City rent control regulations; landlord's investment-backed expectations were not disappointed as landlord knew property was regulated before buying).

For differing views on whether rent control effects a taking, see Richard A. Epstein, *Rent Control and the Theory of Efficient Regulation*, 54 Brook. L. Rev. 741, 742-59 (1988); W. Dennis Keating, *Commentary on Rent Control and the Theory of Efficient Regulation*, 54 Brook. L. Rev. 1223, 1227-30 (1989); R.S. Radford, *Why Rent Control Is a Regulatory Taking*, 6 Forham Envtl. L.J. 755 (1995); Timothy L. Collins, *"Fair Rents" or "Forced Subsidies" Under Rent Regulation: Finding a Regulatory Taking Where Legal Fictions Collide*, 59 Alb. L. Rev. 1293 (1996); Karl Manheim, *Rent Control in the New Lochner Era*, 23 UCLA J. Envtl. L. & Pol'y 211 (2005).

2. Landlord's Remedies

a. Recovery of Possession

(i) Forfeiture

Eviction for nonpayment of rent has become so commonplace that it may have surprised you to learn that, at common law, a landlord had no right to terminate a lease absent an express termination clause. The idea of independent covenants reigned (landlord's covenant of quiet enjoyment was independent of tenant's covenant to pay rent). To give themselves termination rights, landlords resorted to conditions. Using forms similar to those used for fee simple estates, leasehold estates could be set up either as determinable estates, which terminated automatically on occurrence of the condition (breach of a lease covenant), or as estates subject to a power of termination, which gave the landlord the power to terminate on occurrence of the condition. Today, legislation in many, but not all, states gives landlords the right to terminate on the tenant's default, but the legislation varies. Some statutes grant the right of termination only for rent defaults; others extend the right for other material defaults. In states that have adopted the idea that lease covenants—like other contractual undertakings—should be regarded as dependent, is there still a need for express lease clauses, or statutes, granting landlords the right to forfeit for tenants' breach of covenant? *See Cain Partnership, Ltd. v. Pioneer Investment Services Co.*, 914 S.W.2d 452 (Tenn. 1996) (case remanded to apply Restatement (Second) principle of mutuality of remedies where lease contained no express forfeiture clause).

Although the landlord's right to evict for nonpayment of rent is routinely available, many statutes require that the landlord give the tenant notice of default and that eviction proceedings will be commenced unless the tenant vacates within a specified time. Some statutes also grant the tenant an opportunity to cure the default within a specified time and require that the notice of default include a statement of the tenant's right to cure. Courts' traditional reluctance to enforce forfeitures leads to strict enforcement of notice requirements and refusal to allow actions for possession if the notice was deficient. *See, e.g., Liberty Manor v. Rinnels*, 487 N.W.2d 324 (Iowa 1992) (action for possession dismissed because the landlord's notice stated that statutory 14-day cure period would not be given because of tenant's repeated breaches of lease covenants). *See also Bevill v. Zoura*, 32 Cal. Rptr. 2d 635 (Ct. App. 1994) (notice that stated tenant owed $40,033.28, rather than the $21,958 actually owed, held defective). In the absence of statute, should courts require landlords to give notice and opportunity to cure before terminating the lease and bringing an action for possession? In *Bouwkamp v. McNeill*, 902 P.2d 725 (Wyo. 1995), the court held that the landlord had the right to terminate a commercial lease for the tenants' failure to maintain insurance, even though the tenants offered to cure, because the lease, which was drafted by the tenants, permitted forfeiture without notice of default. If the landlord had drafted the lease, should the result have been different? Despite lease terms and court procedures, do landlords represented by counsel usually have an unfair advantage over tenants without representation? *See* Raymond H. Brescia, *Sheltering Counsel: Toward a Right to a Lawyer in Eviction Proceedings*, 25 Touro L. Rev. 187 (2009).

The courts' traditional reluctance to enforce forfeitures also leads to ready find-ings that a landlord has waived a tenant's breach of covenant, often by accepting payments of back rent without giving the tenant notice that the landlord intends to terminate the lease. Courts may be more likely to find waiver in residen-tial leases, but landlords are not given free rein in the commercial area either. *Compare* the decisions in *Davidson v. Doyle*, 825 P.2d 1227 (Nev. 1992) (landlord did not waive right to terminate commercial lease by accepting rent from tenant after informing tenant that she had breached lease by failing to keep property in good repair) *with Community Housing Alternatives, Inc. v. Latta*, 362 S.E.2d 1 (N.C. Ct. App. 1987) (landlord waived right to terminate for tenant's prior vio-lations by accepting tenant's rent). Does it matter that the lease provides that failure to declare a default, or pursue other remedies, immediately, does not waive the landlord's right to declare the tenant in default later? *Compare Dunbar Housing Authority v. Nesmith*, 400 S.E.2d 296 (W. Va. 1990) (landlord at feder-ally subsidized housing project did not waive right to evict tenant for breach of lease by accepting rent after initial notice to vacate was issued) *with Winslow v. Dillard Department Stores, Inc.*, 849 S.W.2d 862 (Tex. Ct. App. 1993) (lessor waived breach by accepting rent for five years without notifying lessee that lessor con-sidered lease terminated by lessee's failure to obtain guarantor's written con-sent to lease renewal; nonwaiver provision in lease — that failure to immediately declare default did not waive default — did not preclude waiver of nonwaiver provision). *See generally* Matthew Sackel, *Pay Up or Get Out: The Landlord's Guide to the Perfect Eviction*, 66 U. Miami L. Rev. 973 (2012); Larry Weiser & Matthew W. Treu, *Adding Injury to Injury: Inadequate Protection of Tenants' Property During Eviction and the Need for Reform*, 20 Loy. Consumer L. Rev. 247 (2008).

The Uniform Residential Landlord and Tenant Act requires landlords to give notice and a 14-day opportunity to pay overdue rent before forfeiture (§ 4.201) and provides in § 4.204:

> Acceptance of rent with knowledge of a default by the tenant or acceptance of per-formance by him that varies from the terms of the rental agreement constitutes a waiver of the landlord's right to terminate the rental agreement for that breach, unless otherwise agreed after the breach has occurred.

(ii)   Self-Help

NO EASY WAY OUT: MAKING THE
SUMMARY EVICTION PROCESS A FAIRER AND
MORE EFFICIENT ALTERNATIVE TO LANDLORD SELF-HELP

Comment, Randy G. Gerchick,
41 UCLA L. Rev. 759, 774-77 (1994)

After centuries of allowing parties to take or regain possession of real property by force, it became clear that such use of force contributed greatly to breaches of the peace. In response to the need for preventing violent clashes, King Richard II adopted a statute in 1381 making forcible entry to take possession a crime. The party seeking possession was no longer permitted to use unlimited force when conducting a self-help eviction. Despite the statute's criminal penalties,

[handwritten: tenant had no civil action.]

the English courts initially found that the statute did not establish a civil action of trespass for the ousted tenant. The courts held that having no right to possession, the ousted tenant sustained no legal injury when deprived of possession by the landlord. Thus, the landlord who forcibly removed a tenant could not be liable for civil trespass if she was entitled to possession. As for injuries to a tenant or to his personal property caused by the landlord's forcible entry and repossession, early English courts held that a landlord could be liable in tort. In 1920, however, the English courts overruled themselves and held that a landlord rightfully entitled to possession would not be liable in tort for injuries to the tenant's person or damages to the tenant's personal property. Under the resultant English Rule, so long as she uses no more force than is reasonably necessary to effect the entry, a landlord entitled to possession is not civilly liable for ejecting a tenant without resort to the legal process, even though her actions may constitute a crime.

B. United States History

Arising out of the somewhat confused development of the English common law, landlord-tenant law in the United States is, not surprisingly, similarly muddled. Although a variety of legal remedies were made available to landlords to regain possession, for most of this country's history, a majority of states allowed landlords to use self-help to regain their properties from tenants.

Early U.S. common law often permitted the landlord to forcibly enter and expel the tenant without holding the landlord civilly liable for damages. The landlord could resort to self-help or pursue the legal remedy known as ejectment. Arising out of the common law, ejectment statutes required the landlord to prove she held title to the disputed land. Because the landlord had to show title superior not only to the tenant's, but also to everyone else's, the action for ejectment was a relatively slow, fairly complex, and substantially expensive procedure. *[handwritten: ejectment]*

Recognizing the potential for violent conflict when a landlord sought to forcibly remove a tenant and seeking to prevent such conflicts, states enacted forcible entry and detainer ("FED") statutes. An important aspect of these statutes was to make it a criminal offense for a party to forcibly oust another from possession of real property and to provide a judicial remedy for a tenant that had been wrongfully put out of possession. The other common element of FED statutes was to provide the landlord with a summary judicial proceeding—an alternative to the cumbersome ejectment action—to deter the landlord's impulse to evict a tenant by force. If not contained within the FED statute, summary judicial proceedings often were established through unlawful detainer ("UD") statutes under which the landlord could file a civil action claiming the tenant was unlawfully detaining the disputed premises.

[handwritten: to prevent violent eviction.]
[handwritten: tenant given remedy for violent eviction]
[handwritten: LL given summ judicial proceeding]

C. Current Status

Today all jurisdictions have enacted FED or UD statutes designed to peaceably settle disputes over possession. Such statutes protect the tenant's interest in maintaining possession by ensuring him an opportunity to challenge the landlord's legal grounds for eviction while furthering the landlord's interests by enabling her to expeditiously evict a holdover or nonpaying tenant through summary judicial proceedings. With the availability of a speedy remedy for landlords, the majority of states have banned self-help evictions, requiring resort to legal process instead.

JORDAN v. TALBOT

Supreme Court of California
55 Cal. 2d 597, 361 P.2d 20 (1961)

TRAYNOR, J. Plaintiff was a tenant in defendant's apartment house. The lease provided that the lessor had a right of re-entry upon the breach of any condition in the lease and a lien upon all personal effects, furniture, and baggage in the tenant's apartment to secure the rents and other charges. One of the conditions was the payment of $132.50 rent on the first of each month. Plaintiff paid the rent for eight months. After she was two months in arrears in rent, defendant, without her consent and during her temporary absence, unlocked the door of her apartment, entered and removed her furniture to a warehouse, and refused to allow her to re-occupy the apartment. Thereupon plaintiff filed this action for forcible entry and detainer and for conversion of her furniture and other personal property.

The jury returned a verdict of $6,500 for forcible entry and detainer and for conversion and $3,000 punitive damages. Plaintiff appeals from an order granting defendant's motion for a new trial. . . .

Defendant contends that: (1) his entry was not unlawful, since he had a right of re-entry; (2) he did not violate subdivision 1 of [Code of Civil Procedure] section 1159, since he did not use force to enter the premises; . . . (4) he did not violate subdivision 1 of [Code of Civil Procedure] section 1160, since he neither unlawfully nor forcibly detained possession to the apartment; and that (5) in any case his entry was privileged by virtue of his lien on the property in the apartment.

Defendant's Right of Re-Entry Is Not a Defense to an Action for Forcible Entry

In defining forcible entry section 1159 . . . refers to "every person," thereby including owners as well as strangers to the title. Under section 1172 of the Code of Civil Procedure the plaintiff "shall only be required to show, in addition to the forcible entry or forcible detainer complained of, that he was peaceably in the actual possession at the time of the forcible entry, or was entitled to the possession at the time of the forcible detainer. The defendant may show in his defense that he or his ancestors, or those whose interest in such premises he claims, have been in the quiet possession thereof for the space of one whole year together next before the commencement of the proceedings, and that his interest therein is not ended or determined; and such showing is a bar to the proceedings." Nowhere is it stated that a right of re-entry is a defense to an action for forcible entry or detainer.

Nor can such a defense be implied from the historical background or purpose of the statute. Both before and after the enactment of the present forcible entry and detainer statutes this court held that ownership or right of possession to the property was not a defense to an action for forcible entry. In McCauley v. Weller, 1859, 12 Cal. 500, 524 [decided before the enactment of sections 1159 through 1179a of the Code of Civil Procedure] and in Voll v. Hollis, 1882, 60 Cal. 569, 573 [decided after the enactment of the foregoing sections] it was held that evidence of defendant's ownership of the land was irrelevant to the question of liability for a forcible entry and detainer. "[T]he action of forcible entry and detainer is a summary proceeding to recover possession of premises forcibly or unlawfully detained. The inquiry in such cases is confined to the actual peaceable possession of the plaintiff and the unlawful or forcible ouster or detention by defendant—the object of the law being to prevent the disturbance of the public peace, by the forcible assertion of a private right. Questions of title or right of possession cannot arise; a forcible entry upon the actual possession of plaintiff being proven, he would be entitled to restitution, though the fee-simple title and present right of possession are shown to be in the defendant. The authorities on this point are numerous and uniform."

[margin note: Question for forcible entry cases.]

In Lasserot v. Gamble[, 46 P. 917 (Cal. 1896)]; Kerr v. O'Keefe[, 71 P. 447 (Cal. 1903)]; California Products, Inc. v. Mitchell[, 52 Cal. App. 312 (1921)], and Martin v. Cassidy[, 149 Cal. App. 2d 106, (1957)], the landlord entered pursuant to a lease granting him a right of re-entry similar to defendant's right of re-entry in the present case. In each case the court held that absent a voluntary surrender of the premises by the tenant, the landlord could enforce his right of re-entry only by judicial process, not by self-help. Under section 1161 of the Code of Civil Procedure a lessor may summarily obtain possession of his real property within three days. This remedy is a complete answer to any claim that self-help is necessary.

As in the foregoing cases, the lease herein is silent as to the method of enforcing the right of re-entry. In any event a provision in the lease expressly permitting a forcible entry would be void as contrary to the public policy set forth in section 1159. . . . [Regardless of who has the right to possession, orderly procedure and preservation of the peace require that the actual possession shall not be disturbed except by legal process. ✗

[margin note: express term in lease is not in accord w/ public policy.]

Defendant Was Guilty of Forcible Entry

Section 1159 Subdivision 1 prohibits an entry by means of breaking open doors or windows. Defendant violated this section when he unlocked plaintiff's apartment without her consent and entered with the storage company employees to remove her furniture, even though there was no physical damage to the premises or actual violence. . . .

In Winchester v. Becker, 4 Cal. App. 382, defendant also used a key to unlock the tenant's door in the absence of the tenant. The court held that any unauthorized opening of a closed door is a breaking open of the door within the meaning of this subdivision. The words "breaking open" in section 1159 were given

[margin note: 1159 subdivision 1]

[handwritten: look towards ↓]

the meaning they had in the common law of burglary. Likewise in McNeil v. Higgins, *supra,* the court held that an entry through an open window was an entry "gained by exercise of unlawful force" . . . in violation of section 1159. . . .

In Illinois, under a statute similar to 5 Richard 11c. 7., force has been defined as an entry against the consent of the occupant. The court there stated that an entry by force means "no more than the term '*vi et armis*' means at common law; that is, 'with either actual or implied force.'" Phelps v. Randolph, 147 Ill. 335, 35 N.E. 243; *see also Prosser on Torts* 100 (2d ed.). . . .

[handwritten margin: 1159 Subdivision 2]

Even if we were to interpret the first subdivision of section 1159 as being inapplicable unless a door or window was physically damaged or threats of violence actually occurred, the evidence in the instant case would nevertheless support a finding of forcible entry as defined by subdivision 2 of section 1159. Under that subdivision a forcible entry is completed if, after a peaceable entry, the occupant is excluded from possession by force or threats of violence. The removal of plaintiff's furniture without her consent rendered the apartment unsuitable for residence and forced her to seek shelter elsewhere. Moreover, when plaintiff returned to her apartment at 1:30 A.M. and inquired about her belongings defendant's employee ordered her to "Get the hell out of here. You're out of this place. Don't talk to me about it. Call Mr. Talbot." The jury could reasonably conclude that plaintiff was justified in believing that any attempt on her part to reinstall her furniture would be met by force. It has long been settled that there is a forcible entry under subdivision 2 if a show of force is made that causes the occupant to refrain from re-entering. . . .

Defendant Was Guilty of a Forcible Detainer

[handwritten margin: 1160 Subdivision 1]

Subdivision 1 of section 1160 provides that a person is guilty of a forcible detainer if he "*[b]y force or by menaces and threats of violence unlawfully* holds and keeps the possession of any real property, whether the same was acquired peaceably or otherwise." (Italics added.) In the present case there is evidence that the apartment was withheld by force and menace and that such withholding was unlawful.

Force and menace can be implied from defendant's agent's removal of plaintiff's furniture and his admonishment to "Get the hell out of here. You're out. . . ." The detention was unlawful, for a person who obtains possession to property by a forcible entry does not have the right to retain possession. . . .

Defendant Was Not Authorized to Enforce His Lien by Entering Plaintiff's Home

The provision in the lease granting defendant a lien does not specify a means of enforcement. In Childs Real Estate Co. v. Shelburne Realty Co., 23 Cal. 2d 263, where the lessor had a similar lien, we stated "in the absence of provisions in the lease for enforcement, equitable action would be necessary to make the lien operative [citations]." . . . Even if the lease had authorized a forcible entry it would be invalid as violating the policy of the forcible entry and detainer statutes. . . .

[handwritten margin: even if provision in lease allowing forcible entry would be void b/c violates public policy.]

We conclude therefore that the evidence supports the verdict of forcible entry and detainer. Since the policy of these sections [1159 and 1160] is the preservation of the peace, the rights thereunder may not be contracted away; thus defendant's right of re-entry and his lien on personal property in the apartment did not justify his entry into the apartment.

cannot contract around public policy.

Defendant Did Not Convert Plaintiff's Goods

Defendant stored most of the items removed from plaintiff's apartment in a warehouse in plaintiff's name. The items that the warehousemen had difficulty removing were stored in the lessor's basement and held for the plaintiff. The lessor did not use any of plaintiff's belongings or make any claim of ownership to them. In Zaslow v. Kroenert, 29 Cal. 2d 541, we held that the removal of another's property and storing it in the owner's name without any other exercise of dominion or control is not a conversion. We there stated that "[w]here the conduct complained of does not amount to a substantial interference with the possession or the right thereto, but consists of intermeddling with or use of or damages to the personal property, the owner has a cause of action for trespass or case, and may recover only the actual damages suffered by reason of the impairment of the property or the loss of its use." . . . Plaintiff is therefore entitled only to actual damages in an amount sufficient to compensate her for any impairment of the property or loss of its use. . . .

Furthermore, plaintiff had a duty to minimize damages. . . . She knew that the property was being held in storage in her name. If she had the funds, or could obtain them by a lien on the property held, she was under a duty to recover her goods as soon as possible and is entitled only to costs of storage for whatever time is reasonable to make new arrangements. Plaintiff would have had to move to new quarters under any circumstances since she was in arrears in her rent and defendant had the right to re-enter pursuant to legal process. There was testimony that additional loans could have been obtained on the furniture. On retrial, however, plaintiff may show that she was without funds or means of obtaining them to pay the storage costs. In that case she would not be under a duty to recover the furniture to minimize damages. "The duty to minimize damages does not require an injured person to do what is unreasonable or impracticable, and, consequently, when expenditures are necessary for minimization of damages, the duty does not run to a person who is financially unable to make such expenditures." Valencia v. Shell Oil Co., 23 Cal. 2d 840.

The verdict for conversion was as a matter of law unsupported by the evidence. The new trial was therefore properly granted. . . .

Notes and Questions

1. The great majority of American jurisdictions today have case law or statutes that bar any type of self-help in residential leases and require landlords to use the legal process to remove a residential tenant. *See* Unif. Residential Landlord and Tenant Act § 4.207 (prohibiting repossession of a dwelling unit except as permitted by the legal remedies set out in the Act). A few jurisdictions still allow self-

help for residential tenancies, although most allow only "peaceful" measures. *See, e.g., Moriarty v. Dziak,* 435 So. 2d 35 (Ala. 1983); Alaska Stat. § 09.45.690 (1983). Many states permit peaceful self-help in commercial leases, finding that the statutory judicial process for eviction was not intended to supplant private remedies. *See, e.g., Sol de Ibiza, LLC v. Panjo Realty, Inc.,* 911 N.Y.S.2d 567 (App. Term. 2010); *PRC Kentron, Inc. v. First City Center Associates, II,* 762 S.W.2d 279 (Tex. App. 1988); *contra Simpson v. Lee,* 499 A.2d 889 (D.C. Ct. App. 1985).

Should all self-help be prohibited? Consider views of the landlord, tenant, and the public. Does it matter if it is commercial as opposed to residential property?

On the issue of self-help, see Luis Jorge DeGraffe, *The Development of Unlawful Evictions and Tenant Remedies for Injurious Conduct in New York,* 41 Syracuse L. Rev. 1179 (1990); Thomas W. Earnhardt, *Peaceful Padlocking in a Perfect World,* 13 N.C. Cent. L.J. 195 (1982); Comment, *Landlord Eviction Remedies Act—Legislative Overreaction to Landlord Self-Help,* 18 Wake Forest L. Rev. 25 (1982); Ralph E. Boyer & Daniel S. Grable, *Reform of Landlord-Tenant Statutes to Eliminate Self-Help in Evicting Tenants,* 22 U. Miami L. Rev. 800 (1968).

2. Even if self-help is permitted, what are "peaceful" actions? What would the court in *Jordan v. Talbot* consider peaceful? Was there a breach of the peace where a landlord reentered the premises of a restaurant tenant after business hours and changed the locks to keep the tenant out? *See Rucker v. Wynn,* 441 S.E.2d 417 (Ga. Ct. App. 1994) (landlord had right under lease to reenter without notice or resort to legal proceedings).

3. Where a landlord improperly uses self-help, remedies may include an action to regain possession, damages for improper eviction, and tort claims for injury to person or property. Punitive damages may also be awarded in some jurisdictions. *See Ladeas v. Carter,* 845 S.W.2d 45 (Mo. Ct. App. 1992).

A residential tenant who was behind one month in his rent informed his landlord that he was going away for two days and would return. The tenant did not in fact return for eight weeks, during which time he paid no rent and did not contact the landlord. After the tenant had been absent for six weeks, the landlord entered the premises, removed the tenant's possessions and stored them, and re-rented the apartment. Is the landlord liable for improper self-help? *See Martinez v. Steinbaum,* 623 P.2d 49 (Colo. 1981) (no, inference that tenant had abandoned premises justified reentry).

example where self-help warranted

Problem

CWA operated a transitional housing facility for battered women and their children. The program was not to simply provide emergency housing but was to provide support to families seeking to make a transition to a life independent of their former abusers. CWA provided participants with apartments; in return, the women were expected either to work or attend school and to participate in regularly scheduled counseling and vocational guidance sessions. One resident, upset with the quality of the counseling sessions, refused to attend. After attempts at resolution failed, CWA changed the locks on the resident's apartment door. Was this improper self-help? *See Serreze v. YWCA of Western Massachusetts, Inc.,* 572 N.E.2d 581 (Mass. Ct. App. 1991).

(iii)   *Summary Process*

Some form of summary process by which a landlord can recover possession from a tenant in default is available in every state. The process is described in the following excerpt from Randy G. Gerchick's Comment, *No Easy Way Out: Making the Summary Eviction Process a Fairer and More Efficient Alternative to Landlord Self-Help*, 41 UCLA L. Rev. 759, 792 (1994):

> Prior to filing a summary proceeding, the landlord usually must serve the tenant with a notice, which informs the tenant of the landlord's reasons for seeking possession. After the notice period expires, the landlord may file a summary eviction claim. The landlord must then serve the tenant with a notice of the summons and complaint, and upon receipt the tenant will have between two and five days to respond to the landlord's complaint. If the tenant fails to answer the complaint, the landlord may request the court clerk to enter the tenant's default, and upon proof of service of the summons and complaint, the court will issue a writ of possession to the landlord. If the tenant answers the complaint, the landlord may request a trial date. If the landlord wins at trial, the court will also issue a writ of possession to the landlord.
>
> Upon receipt of the writ of possession, the landlord must file the writ with the sheriff or marshal. In some jurisdictions, the marshal will evict the tenant immediately upon receipt of the writ of possession. In other jurisdictions, the tenant will be given a few days to cure his breach (by paying the rent due, for example) or to locate new living quarters. At the end of that period, the marshal will conduct the eviction and turn over possession to the landlord or her representative. Just as the time requirements at each stage of the process may vary between jurisdictions, the total duration of the process may also vary. . . .

To make summary eviction proceedings quick and efficient, statutes generally limit the scope of the action to the question whether the landlord is entitled to possession and may limit relief available to recovery of possession but not rent. When lease covenants were treated as independent, the only relevant questions were whether the tenant was in default on a covenant to pay rent, or other covenant, and whether the landlord had the right to terminate for breach of the covenant. The only defenses available to a tenant were that the rent had been paid or that no rent was owed because the landlord had breached the covenant of quiet enjoyment. With recognition of the warranty of habitability and growing recognition of the dependence of material covenants, the allowed defenses in many states have expanded.

Lindsey v. Normet, 405 U.S. 56 (1972), rejected equal protection and due process challenges to provisions of the Oregon summary eviction statute that required trial within six days of service of the eviction complaint and also limited defenses that could be raised by the tenant. The Court did hold a requirement that a tenant wishing to appeal must post a bond for double the rent expected to accrue during pendency of the appeal. On the hurdles facing tenants in summary eviction, see Mary Spector, *Tenant Stories: Obstacles and Challenges Facing Tenants Today*, 40 J. Marshall L. Rev. 407 (2007).

When the government is the landlord, such as in a public housing project, termination decisions must afford the tenant due process of law. *See, e.g., Hinojosa v. Housing Authority*, 896 S.W.2d 833 (Tex. App. 1995) (adequate process in termination decision since tenant received notice, had opportunity to have counsel and cross-examine witnesses, called witnesses, and participated in two infor-mal grievance hearings and jury trial). *See also* Note, *Section 8 Existing Housing Evictions*, 27 Wash. U.J. Urb. & Contemp. L. 417 (1984).

How long does it take for before a landlord recovers possession using a sum-mary eviction proceeding? The answer varies from jurisdiction to jurisdiction, of course, but from a landlord's standpoint the process often must seem less than speedy. The California process is described in Randy G. Gerchick's Comment, *No Easy Way Out: Making the Summary Eviction Process a Fairer and More Efficient Alternative to Landlord Self-Help*, 41 UCLA L. Rev. 759, 807-09 (1994). Gerchick finds that while the California statutes allow a landlord to obtain possession within as little as 17 days, one study across the state indicates that in actuality it requires 51.4 days on average and another study shows that in Los Angeles it requires 108 days on average.

In New York, the availability of summary process depends on whether the leasehold estate terminates automatically on the tenant's breach (the estate is determinable) or whether the landlord must exercise a power of termination (the estate is on a condition subsequent). Summary process is only allowed for the determinable leasehold estate, which may also be called an estate on a con-ditional limitation. If the estate is on condition subsequent, the landlord must proceed in the lengthier ejectment action. *See Perrotta v. Western Regional Off-Track Betting Corp.*, 469 N.Y.S.2d 504 (App. Div. 1983); N.Y. Real Prop. Acts. Law § 711; and Stephen Ross, *Converting Nonpayment to Holdover Summary Proceedings: The New York Experience with Conditional Limitations Based upon Nonpayment of Rent*, 15 Fordham Urb. L.J. 289 (1987).

(iv)   Security in Tenure: Retaliatory Conduct

ELK CREEK MANAGEMENT COMPANY v. GILBERT

Supreme Court of Oregon
353 Or. 565, 303 P.3d 929 (2013)

WALTERS, J. ORS 90.385 prohibits a landlord from "retaliat[ing] by" serving notice to terminate a tenancy after the tenant has made a complaint that is in good faith and related to the tenancy. In this case, we conclude that, to prove retaliation under ORS 90.385, a tenant must establish that the landlord served the notice of termination because of the tenant's complaint. The tenant need not prove, in addition, that the complaint caused the landlord actual or perceived injury or that the landlord intended to cause the tenant equivalent injury in return. We reverse the decision of the Court of Appeals, and the judgment of the circuit court, and we remand the case to the circuit court for further proceedings.

This case concerns a month-to-month tenancy pursuant to a written rental agreement. After the landlord gave the tenants a 30-day no-cause notice of termi-nation of tenancy and the tenants failed to vacate the premises, the landlord filed an action for possession. The tenants filed an answer denying that the landlord was entitled to possession and alleging that the landlord had given notice of ter-mination because of the tenants' legitimate complaints. The trial court rejected the tenants' defense and made written Findings of Fact and Conclusions of Law, which serve as the basis for our recitation of the underlying facts[:]

At some time before May 19, 2009, the tenants "made some sort of general complaint(s) to [the owner] about the electrical system on the property." The manager also had noticed a bent service mast and had become concerned about the property's electrical service. On May 19, the landlord gave the tenants written notice that the owner wanted to do a "walk-through" of the premises. That notice stated that the owner was going to "check out the breaker box and want[ed] to see the floor in the bathroom." After the initial walk-through, the manager advised the tenants that she wanted to do another walk-through on June 16. A licensed electrician accompanied the owner and the manager on that second walk-through, and, at its conclusion, the electrician recommended that the owner make repairs to the electrical system. It was apparent "to everyone" that those repairs would "involve a cost to the owner." The manager called the tenants the next afternoon and informed them that the owner had decided to terminate their lease. The following day, the tenants received a 30-day no-cause termination notice and a note from the manager, which stated:

> "I am sorry that I have to give you the thirty days notice. [The owner] has several repairs including updating the electrical. If there is anything I can do please let me know."

At trial, the manager testified that she had issued the notice of eviction based on instructions from the owner. The owner did not testify.

. . . [T]he trial court recognized that "[i]t is a landlord's duty during a tenancy to 'maintain the dwelling unit in a habitable condition' and [to maintain the] 'electrical lighting with wiring and electrical equipment * * * in good working order.' ORS 90.320(1)(e)." The court found that the electrical system . . . was not in good working order. The court further found that (1) it was "a reasonable inference that [the tenant's] conversations with [the owner] as well as [the manager's] concern with the service mast caused [the owner] to want to do the initial walk-through on May 19th"; and (2) there was no evidence of the owner's reason for termination other than that expressed in the note sent by the manager—that the owner "has several repairs including updating the electrical." The court concluded, however, that the tenants had not established that the tenancy termination constituted "retaliation" by the owner . . . .

We allowed the tenants' petition for review to consider the tenants' argument that the Court of Appeals incorrectly interpreted ORS 90.385 when it declared that "[t]he concept of retaliation . . . involves an intention on the part of the landlord to cause some sort of disadvantage to the tenant, motivated by an injury (or perceived injury) that the tenant has caused the landlord." . . . The tenants contend that, to prove retaliation . . . , a tenant must prove only that a landlord took one of the actions specified in ORS 90.385 . . . ; no additional proof of injury or intent to harm is required. . . .

ORS 90.385(1) prohibits a landlord from "retaliat[ing] by" taking certain described acts "after" a tenant has engaged in certain described activities.[4]

---

4. ORS 90.385(1) provides:

"Except as provided in this section, a landlord may not retaliate by increasing rent or decreasing services, by serving a notice to terminate the tenancy or by bringing or threatening to bring an action for possession after:

A landlord may not retaliate by (1) "increasing rent or decreasing services"; (2) "serving a notice to terminate the tenancy"; or (3) "bringing or threatening to bring an action for possession," after a tenant has (1) made or expressed an intent to make specified complaints, including a complaint that is "in good faith and related to the tenancy"; (2) "organized or become a member of a tenants' union or similar organization"; (3) "testified against the landlord in any judicial, administrative or legislative proceeding"; (4) with certain exceptions, "successfully defended an action for possession brought by the landlord within the previous six months"; or (5) "performed or expressed intent to perform any other act for the purpose of asserting, protecting or invoking the protection of any right secured to tenants under any federal, state or local law."

The tenant activities that the statute protects are acts that a tenant has a right to take. For instance, ORS 90.360 expressly permits a tenant to give a landlord notice of a failure to materially comply with ORS 90.320, the statute that requires that landlords maintain leased premises in a habitable condition, and ORS 105.137 permits a tenant to defend against a landlord's action for possession. The final subparagraph of ORS 90.385(1), subparagraph (f), protects a tenant from retaliation after a tenant has performed "*any other act* for the purpose of asserting, protecting or invoking the protection of any right secured to tenants under any federal, state or local law." (Emphasis added.) That subparagraph recognizes that there are many laws that grant tenant rights and indicates a legislative intent to protect tenants from retaliation when they exercise those rights. The legislature's use of the phrase any "other act" in subparagraph (f) refers back to the acts specifically listed in the preceding subparagraphs and suggests that they too describe acts that a tenant has the right to take. Thus, ORS 90.385 describes two categories of acts: those that a landlord is prohibited from taking in retaliation and those that a tenant has the right to take and that the legislature protects against retaliation.

"(a) The tenant has complained to, or expressed to the landlord in writing an intention to complain to, a governmental agency charged with responsibility for enforcement of any of the following concerning a violation applicable to the tenancy:

"(A) A building, health or housing code materially affecting health or safety;

"(B) Laws or regulations concerning the delivery of mail; or

"(C) Laws or regulations prohibiting discrimination in rental housing;

"(b) The tenant has made any complaint to the landlord that is in good faith and related to the tenancy;

"(c) The tenant has organized or become a member of a tenants' union or similar organization;

"(d) The tenant has testified against the landlord in any judicial, administrative or legislative proceeding;

"(e) The tenant successfully defended an action for possession brought by the landlord within the previous six months . . . ; or

"(f) The tenant has performed or expressed intent to perform any other act for the purpose of asserting, protecting or invoking the protection of any right secured to tenants under any federal, state or local law."

ORS 90.385 does not expressly require that a tenant demonstrate that the tenant's protected acts caused injury to the landlord or that the landlord perceived the tenant's acts as causing injury. ORS 90.385 also does not expressly require that a tenant demonstrate that a landlord took one of the prohibited acts with an intent to cause injury to the tenant. . . . [T]he question before us is whether the legislature nevertheless intended to impose those requirements, and, if not, what requirement or requirements the legislature did intend to impose.

The trial court and the Court of Appeals discovered the requirements of injury and intention to impose injury in return in the word "retaliate." The trial court interpreted that word to capture the concept of "lex talionis," which the court described as having ancient foundations and as being easily understood in metaphors such as "an eye for an eye" or "a tooth for a tooth."[5] The essence of that concept, as the trial court described it, is that, "when one suffers a real or perceived wrong, a like injury will be inflicted upon the one who did the initial real or perceived harm."[6]

ORS 90.385 obviously does not require that a landlord punish a tenant according to the wrong inflicted by the tenant. It could, however, prohibit a landlord's exercise of lex talionis, and that is the construction that the Court of Appeals apparently adopted. . . . The court reasoned that, when the legislature prohibited a landlord from retaliating against a tenant, it intended to prohibit a landlord that suffers injury from causing a tenant injury in kind. . . .

The correct construction of ORS 90.385 does not, however, turn only on the dictionary definition of one of its words. We also must consider the context in which the legislature used the word "retaliate" and other indicators of the legislature's intent. . . . When we do so, we conclude . . . that the legislature did not intend to require that a tenant prove that the tenant's protected act caused the landlord actual or perceived injury or that the landlord intended to cause the tenant injury in return; rather, the statute is satisfied if the landlord made the decision to act because of the tenant's protected activity.

First . . . , a tenant who takes one of the actions referenced in ORS 90.385(1) takes an action that the tenant has a right to take and that the legislature intends to protect. For instance, a tenant has a right to notify a landlord of necessary repairs. . . . A tenant's exercise of that right provides the landlord with information that enables it to meet its statutory obligation to maintain leased premises in habitable condition. Thus, when the legislature prohibits the landlord from retaliating, the legislature advances two interconnected interests: an interest in allowing tenants to assert their statutory rights, and an interest in having landlords fulfill their statutory obligations. It would be inconsistent with those interests for the legislature to impose a requirement that the tenant prove that his or her exercise of those rights caused the landlord injury.

---

5.   Those phrases appear in the Book of Exodus: "[T]hou shalt give life for life, eye for eye, tooth for tooth[.]" Exodus 21:23-24 (King James).

6.   The ancient law of lex talionis may have served to limit vengeful retribution. The Code of Hammurabi provided for a system of punishment proportional to the crime, and Hebrew law restricted compensation to the value of the loss. See W. Gunther Plaut & David E. Stein eds., The Torah: A Modern Commentary, 528-29 (rev. 2005). Thus, the concept of lex talionis might more properly be described as only one eye for one eye. See also Thomas A. Balmer, Some Thoughts on Proportionality, 87 Or. L. Rev. 783, 784-85 (2008).

Second, . . . [t]he Oregon Residential Landlord and Tenant Act (ORLTA), which includes ORS 90.385, . . . enacted in 1973, . . . was modeled on the Uniform Residential Landlord and Tenant Act (1972) (URLTA), [A]s originally enacted, ORS 90.385 mirrored section 5-101 of that Uniform Act. Both acts prohibited a landlord from "retaliat[ing] by" taking specified actions after a tenant had engaged in protected activities, including complaining of a landlord's violation of statutory habitability requirements, and both acts included a "disputable presumption" that the landlord had engaged in retaliation if the landlord acted within a specified period after the tenant's protected activity. Under the URLTA, that period was one year; under the ORLTA, that period was six months.

Section 5-101 of the URLTA included a comment . . . that, before the adoption of either act, courts in seven states and the District of Columbia had "upheld the defense of retaliatory eviction" and that other states had recognized that defense by statute. Chronologically, the first of the cited cases was Edwards v. Habib, 397 F.2d 687 (D.C. Cir. 1968). In that case, the court held that, although a landlord is entitled to "evict for any legal reason or for no reason at all," the landlord may not "evict in retaliation for his tenant's report of housing code violations to the authorities." The court explained that implementation of the District of Columbia housing codes depends on private individuals taking initiative and reporting violations. . . . [P]ermitting the eviction of tenants who make such reports would frustrate the codes' effectiveness and violate public policy. The court observed that trial courts could determine the reason for a landlord's eviction in the same way that they decide other questions of fact. . . . [Discussion of cases that followed *Edwards v. Habib* and statutes enacted in their wake omitted. —EDS.]

When [the National Conference of Commissioners on Uniform State Laws adopted 5-101 they were aware of the varying approaches taken in different states and] . . . deliberately chose not to include a requirement, such as that included in the Minnesota statute, that the landlord intend its action as a penalty for the tenant's conduct. Instead, the drafters chose to require proof that the landlord had "retaliate[d] by" taking action after a tenant engaged in protected activity, consistent with the New Jersey formulation. The New Jersey Supreme Court had decided that the New Jersey statute did not require proof of a landlord's "malice or hostility." If the URLTA framers had wanted to include such a requirement in their "retaliatory eviction" defense, it is likely that they would have done so explicitly or used an alternative formulation that more clearly incorporated that concept.

. . . [W]hen the Oregon Legislature enacted ORS 90.385 in 1973, it adopted Section 5-101 of the URLTA nearly verbatim and had before it the URLTA comment to that section. . . . We therefore conclude that the Oregon Legislature's original intent was consistent with the intent of the drafters of the URLTA; when the Oregon Legislature used the word "retaliate" in ORS 90.385, it did not intend to invoke the ancient concept of "lex talionis."

The legislature's amendment of the ORLTA in 1979 and its deletion of the disputable presumption does not change our conclusion. . . . Before the amendment, the disputable presumption allowed the tenant to shift the burden of persuasion to the landlord so that the landlord was required to prove that its action, if taken within six months of the tenant's protected activity, was not retaliatory. . . . Under the current statute, the tenant no longer can shift the burden of proof to the landlord. That does not mean, however, that the tenant must now prove that the landlord suffered injury and intended injury in return. As amended, ORS 90.385 continues to require a tenant to demonstrate that the landlord acted because of a tenant's engagement in protected activity. . . .

A question remains, however, about the height of the causal bar that the Oregon Legislature requires Oregon tenants to clear. Did the Oregon Legislature intend to require tenants to prove that a tenant's protected activity was the sole reason for the landlord's action, or did it intend to impose some other causal standard? . . . [T]he drafters of both the URLTA and the ORLTA chose a statutory framework similar to the New Jersey framework and declined to expressly require, as Connecticut and California had, that the tenant prove that the tenant's protected activity was the "sole" or "dominant" reason for the landlord's prohibited action. It is therefore likely that the drafters did not intend to impose either of those more strictly stated causal requirements. . . .

We believe that the legislature instead intended to require a tenant to prove that the tenant's protected activity was a factor that made a difference in the landlord's decision. . . . [T]hat requirement is consistent with the New Jersey Supreme Court's interpretation of the New Jersey statute used as a format for the URLTA and the ORLTA, and, as we will explain, that requirement also is consistent with this court's articulation of causal requirements in other contexts. [Explanation omitted. — EDS.]

. . . We conclude that ORS 90.385 requires a tenant to prove that, "but for" the tenant's protected activity, the landlord would not have made the decision that it did. In the circumstance in which . . . two causes concur, but either operating alone would have been sufficient to cause the result, a tenant also may prevail by proving that the tenant's protected activity was a "material and substantial factor" in the landlord's decision. The tenant need not prove that the tenant's protected activity was the "sole" or "dominant" reason for the landlord's decision.

Having construed ORS 90.385, we now must determine its effect on the judgment in this case. . . .

Although the trial court decided that the tenants' complaints were one of the reasons that the owner decided to conduct the initial walk-through, the court did not explicitly decide whether the tenants' complaints also were one of the reasons that the owner decided to serve the notice of termination; the trial court speculated that the owner may have given that notice for other "valid business reasons." Without explicitly elaborating on what those "valid business reasons" may have been, the trial court discussed whether the tenants had inflicted harm on the owner and whether the owner had attempted to harm the tenants by terminating their tenancy. The court observed that the owner had spent considerable sums on repairs in the past and described the conduct of both parties as "innocuous." However, . . . whether the owner was thankful, threatened, or neutral when the tenants notified her of electrical problems, and whether the owner considered the costs of improving the electrical system injurious or simply necessary, ORS 90.385 prohibited the owner from serving the tenants with notice of termination because of the tenants' complaints. If the tenants' complaints were one of the factors that the owner considered in making her decision to evict, and the owner would not have made that decision "but for" the tenant's complaints, then the owner was prohibited from making that decision. That is true even if there also were other factors that the owner considered in arriving at her conclusion. If the owner had two different, independent reasons for deciding to evict the tenants, and either alone would have caused the owner to make the decision to evict, the owner also was prohibited from deciding to do so if the tenant's protected activity was one of those independent reasons.

In applying that test, it is important to recognize that a landlord has a statutory obligation to maintain leased premises in a habitable condition. . . . ORS 90.385(4)(d) . . . permits a landlord to evict a tenant where compliance with the applicable building or housing code requires alteration, remodeling, or demolition which would effectively deprive the tenant of use of the dwelling unit. Except in that instance, the fact that repairs and their associated cost are statutorily compelled means that they cannot be a lawful reason for a landlord's decision to evict a tenant; or, said another way, the cost of statutory compliance cannot be a legitimate reason for a landlord to take a statutorily prohibited act against a tenant who exercises a statutorily protected right.

That does not mean, of course, that a landlord must continue to lease property that it owns or that a landlord always is prohibited from evicting a tenant after the tenant complains about the condition of a dwelling. For example, if the landlord offers evidence that it made the decision to serve a notice of termination for some reason unrelated to the tenant's complaint, such as that the tenant failed to pay rent or violated other terms of the lease, or that it made its decision to evict before the tenant complained, a factfinder may conclude that the tenant's complaint was not a factor that made a difference in the landlord's decision.

In this case, the trial court could have inferred, from the temporal connection between the tenants' complaint and the owner's decision to evict them, that the tenants' complaints made a difference in the owner's decision. However, the trial court did not do so and instead speculated that the owner may have had other "valid business reasons" for her action. Although the record does not reveal any such reasons, we hesitate to decide what conclusion the trial court would have reached had it applied the correct legal standard. We therefore reverse and remand for further proceedings consistent with this decision. . . .

Notes and Questions

1. Although there is broad agreement that tenants should be protected against retaliatory eviction, the extent of the protection varies among the states.[12] Areas in which there are differences include:

- what tenant conduct is protected (e.g., reporting a housing code violation, asserting the warranty of habitability, joining a tenants group)
- whether the tenant is protected not only from an eviction or nonrenewal but also from other retaliation, such as a decrease in services by the landlord[13]
- whether the tenant must first notify the landlord of a violation and give a reasonable opportunity for cure before reporting the violation

---

12.   *See* Deborah Hodges Bell, *Providing Security of Tenure for Residential Tenants: Good Faith as a Limitation on a Landlord's Right to Terminate*, 19 Ga. L. Rev. 483 (1985); Richard E. Blumberg & Brian Quinn Robbins, *Beyond URLTA: A Program for Achieving Real Tenant Goals*, 11 Harv. C.R.-C.L. L. Rev. 1 (1976); Frank I. Michelman, *Property as a Constitutional Right*, 38 Wash. & Lee L. Rev. 1097 (1981).

13.   *See* 9 Vt. Stat. Ann § 4465(a) (barring "changing the terms of a rental agreement").

- whether the retaliatory action should be permitted if the landlord had other non-retaliatory motives
- whether the tenant or the landlord has the burden of proof
- whether and how the landlord, after being found guilty of retaliatory action, can evict the tenant in the future
- whether a tenant can sue landlord for damages based on retaliation action rather than seeking to get back into possession
- whether the doctrine applies to non-merchant landlords
- whether commercial tenants are protected.[14]

2. Some jurisdictions go further and provide security of tenure by permitting eviction of residential tenants only for good cause.[15] Do such statutes provide needed protections to tenants, or do they improperly dilute the ownership rights of landlords?[16] *See* Florence Wagman Roisman, *The Right to Remain: Common Law Protections for the Security of Tenure*, 86 N.C. L. Rev. 817 (2008) (arguing that security of tenure is a fundamental human need and can be implied from the implied covenant of fair dealing in contracts); *see generally* Andrea B. Carroll, *The International Trend Toward Requiring Good Cause for Tenant Eviction: Dangerous Portents for the United States?*, 38 Seton Hall L. Rev. 427 (2008).

b. Monetary Damages

(i) *The Calculus of Remedies*

The landlord may wish to recover money damages for breach of the lease when there is a forfeiture and the landlord evicts the tenant or where the tenant abandons the premises.

Forfeiture. Where the landlord terminates the lease pursuant to a forfeiture clause and evicts the tenant, the landlord may wish to preserve the benefits of the lease agreement, especially when the rent reserved in the lease is higher than the current market rate. The theoretical problem for the landlord, however, is that because the lease has been terminated, the landlord cannot recover this amount as "rent." Thus, landlords typically include a provision in the lease that permits them to re-rent the premises upon termination and recover damages from the tenant in the amount of the difference between the rent reserved in the lease and the new rent.[17] Even in the absence of such a provision, should the landlord be able to recover those damages?[18]

---

14. *Compare Restatement (Second) of Property—Landlord and Tenant* § 14.8 (reflecting the rule of virtually all statutes and cases limiting the defense to residential tenants), *with* Custom Parking, Inc. v. Superior Court, 138 Cal. App. 3d 90, 187 Cal. Rptr. 674 (1982) (permitting a commercial tenant to raise the defense of retaliatory eviction). *See* Murphy v. Smallridge, 468 S.E.2d 167 (W.Va. 1996) (permitting action for damages).

15. *See, e.g.,* N.J. Stat. Ann. § 2A: 18-61.1.

16. *See* Karl Manheim, *Tenant Eviction Protection and the Takings Clause*, 1989 Wis. L. Rev. 925; Note, *Are Landlords Being Taken by the Good Cause Eviction Requirement?*, 62 S. Cal. L. Rev. 321 (1988).

17. *See* Robert Schoshinski, American Law of Landlord and Tenant § 6:1 (1980).

18. *See* Cal. Civ. Code § 1951.2 (providing statutory remedy to landlord); *Restatement (Second) of Property—Landlord and Tenant* § 13.1 cmts. *k, l,* and *m.*

Abandonment. When a tenant abandons the leased premises without justifiable excuse, what are the possible positions the landlord might take, assuming there is no contractual clause in the lease covering the situation? The following are typical:[19]

1. Take back the leased premises and forget about the tenant as rapidly as possible. All courts agree that the landlord may do this, thereby accepting a surrender of the leased premises from the tenant and terminating the lease for all purposes. The tenant is relieved of any liability for rent that has not yet become due.

2. Ignore the tenant's abandonment and continue to hold the tenant liable under the terms of the lease as though the tenant had remained in possession. Can the landlord collect for sums not yet due? Must the landlord undertake to mitigate the damage?

3. Relet the leased premises and hold the tenant liable for the difference in the amount of rent reserved in the lease and the amount of rent received on the reletting. The difficulty with this position is that the reletting by the landlord looks like such an assumption of control over the leased premises as to amount to an acceptance of the tenant's surrender. The traditional inquiry is whether the landlord intended to accept the surrender, and this intention may be expressed or implied.

[Margin annotation: Surrender]

Problem

Tenant leased retail space in a mall and subsequently abandoned the premises without paying the rent due for the remainder of the term. Landlord permitted the Las Cruces Museum of Natural History to use the space rent free to promote good community relations. Can Landlord recover the unpaid rent from Tenant for the remainder of the term? *See Mesilla Valley Mall Co. v. Crown Industries,* 808 P.2d 633 (N.M. 1991).

(ii)   Landlord's Duty to Mitigate

AUSTIN HILL COUNTRY REALTY, INC. v. PALISADES PLAZA

Supreme Court of Texas
948 S.W.2d 293 (1997)

SPECTOR, J. . . . The issue in this case is whether a landlord has a duty to make reasonable efforts to mitigate damages when a tenant defaults on a lease. The court of appeals held that no such duty exists at common law. We hold today that a landlord has a duty to make reasonable efforts to mitigate damages. Accordingly, we reverse the judgment of the court of appeals and remand for a new trial.

[Margin annotations: Issue 1 ; Holding 1]

19.   *See* Sarajane Love, *Landlord's Remedies When the Tenant Abandons: Property, Contract, and Leases,* 30 U. Kan. L. Rev. 533 (1982); Note, *New Approach to Adjudicating Tenant's Abandonment of Premises,* 9 Cardozo L. Rev. 1811 (1988) (arguing that abandonment should be based on outwardly visible facts only and not on tenant's subjective intent).

I

Palisades Plaza, Inc., owned and operated an office complex consisting of four office buildings in Austin. Barbara Hill, Annette Smith, and David Jones sold real estate in Austin as a Re/Max real estate brokerage franchise operating through Austin Hill Country Realty, Inc. On September 15, 1992, the Palisades and Hill Country executed a five-year commercial office lease for a suite in the Palisades' office complex. An addendum executed in connection with the lease set the monthly base rent at $3,128 for the first year, $3,519 for the second and third years, and $3,910 for the fourth and fifth years. The parties also signed an improvements agreement that called for the Palisades to convert the shell office space into working offices for Hill Country. The lease was to begin on the "commencement date," which was defined in the lease and the improvements agreement as either (1) the date that Hill Country occupied the suite, or (2) the date that the Palisades substantially completed the improvements or would have done so but for "tenant delay." All parties anticipated that the lease would begin on November 15, 1992.

By the middle of October 1992, the Palisades had nearly completed the improvements. Construction came to a halt on October 21, 1992, when the Palisades received conflicting instructions about the completion of the suite from Hill on one hand and Smith and Jones on the other. By two letters, the Palisades informed Hill Country, Hill, Smith, and Jones that it had received conflicting directives and would not continue with the construction until Hill, Smith, and Jones collectively designated a single representative empowered to make decisions for the trio. Hill, Smith, and Jones did not reply to these letters.

Breach bk no representative chosen.

In a letter dated November 19, 1992, the Palisades informed Hill Country, Hill, Smith, and Jones that their failure to designate a representative was an anticipatory breach of contract. The parties tried unsuccessfully to resolve their differences in a meeting. The Palisades then sued Hill Country, Hill, Smith, and Jones (collectively, "Hill Country") for anticipatory breach of the lease.

At trial, Hill Country attempted to prove that the Palisades failed to mitigate the damages resulting from Hill Country's alleged breach. In particular, Hill Country introduced evidence that the Palisades rejected an offer from Smith and Jones to lease the premises without Hill, as well as an offer from Hill and another person to lease the premises without Smith and Jones. Hill Country also tried to prove that, while the Palisades advertised for tenants continuously in a local newspaper, it did not advertise in the commercial-property publication "The Flick Report" as it had in the past. Hill Country requested an instruction asking the jury to reduce the Palisades' damage award by "any amount that you find the [Palisades] could have avoided by the exercise of reasonable care." The trial judge rejected this instruction, stating, "Last time I checked the law, it was that a landlord doesn't have any obligation to try to fill the space." The jury returned a verdict for the Palisades for $29,716 in damages and $16,500 in attorney's fees. The court of appeals affirmed that judgment.

Hill claims.

Jury instruction.

Tct. = for Palisades COA affirm.

II

In its only point of error, Hill Country asks this Court to recognize a landlord's duty to make reasonable efforts to mitigate damages when a tenant breaches a lease. . . .

The traditional common law rule regarding mitigation dictates that landlords have no duty to mitigate damages. . . . This rule stems from the historical concept that the tenant is owner of the property during the lease term; as long as the tenant has a right to possess the land, the tenant is liable for rent. . . . Under this rule, a landlord is not obligated to undertake any action following a tenant's abandonment of the premises but may recover rents periodically for the remainder of the term. . . .

In Texas, the traditional common law rule was first adopted in Racke v. Anheuser-Busch Brewing Ass'n, 42 S.W. 774 (Tex. Civ. App.—Galveston 1897, no writ). In *Racke*, a landlord sued to determine the extent of the tenant's liability for holding over past the lease term. Concluding that the holdover rendered the tenant liable under a new tenancy for one year, the Court of Civil Appeals held that the landlord could not "be subjected to damages for failing to let the premises to another, to prevent rents accruing the [tenant]."

Texas courts have consistently followed this no-mitigation rule in cases involving a landlord's suit for past due rent. . . .

III

In discerning the policy implications of a rule requiring landlords to mitigate damages, we are informed by the rules of other jurisdictions. Forty-two states and the District of Columbia have recognized that a landlord has a duty to mitigate damages in at least some situations: when there is a breach of a residential lease, a commercial lease, or both. [Citations omitted.—EDS.]

Only six states have explicitly held that a landlord has no duty to mitigate in any situation. [Citations omitted.—EDS.] In South Dakota, the law is unclear.

Those jurisdictions recognizing a duty to mitigate have emphasized the change in the nature of landlord-tenant law since its inception in medieval times. At English common law, the tenant had only contractual rights against the landlord and therefore could not assert common-law real property causes of action to protect the leasehold. Over time, the courts recognized a tenant's right to bring real property causes of action, and tenants were considered to possess an estate in land. 2 R. POWELL, THE LAW OF REAL PROPERTY § 221[1], at 16-18 (1969). The landlord had to give the tenant possession of the land, and the tenant was required to pay rent in return. As covenants in leases have become more complex and the structures on the land have become more important to the parties than the land itself, courts have begun to recognize that a lease possesses elements of both a contract and a conveyance. Under contract principles, the lease is not a complete conveyance to the tenant for a specified term such that the landlord's duties are fulfilled upon deliverance of the property to the tenant. Rather, a promise to pay in a lease is essentially the same as a promise to pay in any other contract, and a breach of that promise does not necessarily end the landlord's ongoing duties. Because of the contractual elements of the modern lease agreement, these courts have imposed upon the landlord the contractual duty to mitigate damages upon the tenant's breach.

Public policy offers further justification for the duty to mitigate. First, requiring mitigation in the landlord-tenant context discourages economic waste and encourages productive use of the property. As the Colorado Supreme Court has written:

Under traditional property law principles a landlord could allow the property to remain unoccupied while still holding the abandoning tenant liable for rent. This encourages both economic and physical waste. In no other context of which we are aware is an injured party permitted to sit idly by and suffer avoidable economic loss and thereafter to visit the full adverse economic consequences upon the party whose breach initiated the chain of events causing the loss.

Schneiker v. Gordon, 732 P.2d 603, 610 (Colo. 1987). A mitigation requirement thus returns the property to productive use rather than allowing it to remain idle. Public policy requires that the law "discourage even persons against whom wrongs have been committed from passively suffering economic loss which could be averted by reasonable efforts." Wright v. Baumann, 398 P.2d 119, 121 (Or. 1965) (quoting C. McCORMICK, HANDBOOK ON THE LAW OF DAMAGES, § 33 (1935)). *[handwritten: economic waste]*

Second, a mitigation rule helps prevent destruction of or damage to the leased property. If the landlord is encouraged to let the property remain unoccupied, "the possibility of physical damage to the property through accident or vandalism is increased." *Schneiker*, 732 P.2d at 610. *[handwritten: physical damage]*

Third, the mitigation rule is consistent with the trend disfavoring contract penalties. Courts have held that a liquidated damages clause in a contract must represent a reasonable estimate of anticipated damages upon breach. *See, e.g.,* Warner v. Rasmussen, 704 P.2d 559 (Utah 1985). "Similarly, allowing a landlord to leave property idle when it could be profitably leased and forcing an absent tenant to pay rent for that idled property permits the landlord to recover more damages than it may reasonably require to be compensated for the tenant's breach. This is analogous to imposing a disfavored penalty upon the tenant." *[handwritten: disfavor contract damages]*

Finally, the traditional justifications for the common law rule have proven unsound in practice. Proponents of the no-mitigation rule suggest that the landlord-tenant relationship is personal in nature, and that the landlord therefore should not be forced to lease to an unwanted tenant. *See* Wohl v. Yelen, 161 N.E.2d 339 (Ill. App. Ct. 1959). Modern lease arrangements, however, are rarely personal in nature and are usually business arrangements between strangers. Edwin Smith, Jr., Comment, *Extending the Contractual Duty to Mitigate Damages to Landlords when a Tenant Abandons the Lease*, 42 BAYLOR L. REV. 553, 559 (1990). Further, the landlord's duty to make reasonable efforts to mitigate does not require that the landlord accept replacement tenants who are financial risks or whose business was precluded by the original lease. Note, *Landlord and Tenant—Mitigation of Damages*, 45 WASH. L. REV. 218, 225 (1970). *[handwritten: common law rule does not work]* *[handwritten: no financial risk having new tenants]*

The overwhelming trend among jurisdictions in the United States has thus been toward requiring a landlord to mitigate damages when a tenant abandons the property in breach of the lease agreement. Those courts adopting a mitigation requirement have emphasized the contractual elements of a lease agreement, the public policy favoring productive use of property, and the practicalities of the modern landlord-tenant arrangement as supporting such a duty. *[handwritten: ||*]*

IV

We are persuaded by the reasoning of those courts that recognize that landlords must mitigate damages upon a tenant's abandonment and failure to pay rent. . . .

V

To ensure the uniform application of this duty by the courts of this state, and to guide future landlords and tenants in conforming their conduct to the law, we now consider several practical considerations that will undoubtedly arise. We first consider the level of conduct by a landlord that will satisfy the duty to mitigate. The landlord's mitigation duty has been variously stated in other jurisdictions: . . . ("objective commercial reasonableness"); . . . ("reasonable efforts"); . . . ("reasonably and in a good-faith effort"). Likewise, the courts of this state have developed differing language regarding a party's duty to mitigate in other contexts. *See* City of San Antonio v. Guidry, 801 S.W.2d 142, 151 (Tex. App. 1990) (collecting cases). We hold that the landlord's duty to mitigate requires the landlord to use objectively reasonable efforts to fill the premises when the tenant vacates in breach of the lease.

We stress that this is not an absolute duty. The landlord is not required to simply fill the premises with any willing tenant; the replacement tenant must be suitable under the circumstances. Nor does the landlord's failure to mitigate give rise to a cause of action by the tenant. Rather, the landlord's failure to use reasonable efforts to mitigate damages bars the landlord's recovery against the breaching tenant only to the extent that damages reasonably could have been avoided. Similarly, the amount of damages that the landlord actually avoided by releasing the premises will reduce the landlord's recovery.

Further, we believe that the tenant properly bears the burden of proof to demonstrate that the landlord has mitigated or failed to mitigate damages and the amount by which the landlord reduced or could have reduced its damages. The traditional rule in other contexts is that the breaching party must show that the nonbreaching party could have reduced its damages. . . . In the landlord-tenant context, although there is some split of authority, many other jurisdictions have placed the burden of proving mitigation or failure to mitigate upon the breaching tenant. . . .

When the tenant contends that the landlord has actually mitigated damages, the breaching tenant need not plead the landlord's actual mitigation as an affirmative defense. Rather, the tenant's evidence of the landlord's mitigation tends to rebut the measure of damages under the landlord's claim of breach and may be admitted under a general denial. . . . The tenant's contention that the landlord failed to mitigate damages, in contrast, is similar to an avoidance defense; evidence of failure to mitigate is admissible only if the tenant pleads the failure to mitigate as an affirmative defense. . . .

The final issue to resolve regarding the duty to mitigate is to which types of actions by the landlord the duty will apply. Traditionally, Texas courts have regarded the landlord as having four causes of action against a tenant for breach of the lease and abandonment. *See* Speedee Mart v. Stovall, 664 S.W.2d 174 (Tex. App. 1983); Jerry D. Johnson, Landlord Remedies in Texas: Confusion Reigns Where Certainty Should Prevail, 33 S. TEX. L. REV. 417, 419-20 (1992). First, the landlord can maintain the lease, suing for rent as it becomes due. Second, the landlord can treat the breach as an anticipatory repudiation, repossess, and sue for the present value of future rentals reduced by the reasonable cash market value of the property for the remainder of the lease term. Third, the landlord can treat the breach as anticipatory, repossess, release the property, and sue the tenant for the difference between the contractual rent and the amount received from the new tenant. Fourth, the landlord can declare the lease forfeited (if the lease so provides) and relieve the tenant of liability for future rent.

The landlord must have a duty to mitigate when suing for anticipatory repudiation. Because the cause of action is contractual in nature, the contractual duty to mitigate should apply. The landlord's option to maintain the lease and sue for rent as it becomes due, however, is more troubling. To require the landlord to mitigate in that instance would force the landlord to reenter the premises and thereby risk terminating the lease or accepting the tenant's surrender. . . . We thus hold that, when exercising the option to maintain the lease in effect and sue for rent as it becomes due following the tenant's breach and abandonment, the landlord has a duty to mitigate only if (1) the landlord actually reenters, or (2) the lease allows the landlord to reenter the premises without accepting surrender, forfeiting the lease, or being construed as evicting the tenant. *See* Robinson Seed & Plant Co. v. Hexter & Kramer, 167 S.W. 749 (Tex. Civ. App. 1914); 21 A.L.R.3d at 556-63. A suit for anticipatory repudiation, an actual reentry, or a contractual right of reentry subject to the above conditions will therefore give rise to the landlord's duty to mitigate damages upon the tenant's breach and abandonment.

Risky form of LL mitigating damages.

with sue for rent duties

VI

In their first amended answer, Hill Country and Barbara Hill specifically contended that the Palisades failed to mitigate its damages. Because the court of appeals upheld the trial court's refusal to submit their mitigation instruction, we reverse the judgment of the court of appeals and remand for a new trial.

Restatement (Second) of Property—
Landlord and Tenant § 12.1(3)

(3) Except to the extent the parties to the lease validly agree otherwise, if the tenant abandons the leased property, the landlord is under no duty to attempt to relet the leased property for the balance of the term of the lease to mitigate the tenant's liability under the lease, including his liability for rent, but the landlord may:

   (a) accept the tenant's offer of surrender of the leased property, which is inherent in the abandonment, and thereby terminate the lease, leaving the tenant liable only for rent accrued before the acceptance and damage caused by the abandonment; or

   (b) notify the tenant that he will undertake to relet the leased property for the tenant's account, thereby relieving the tenant of future liabilities under the lease, including liability for future rent, to the extent the same are performed as a result of a reletting on terms that are reasonable.

UNIFORM RESIDENTIAL LANDLORD AND TENANT ACT § 4.203(C)

(c) If the tenant abandons the dwelling unit, the landlord shall make reasonable efforts to rent it at a fair rental. If the landlord rents the dwelling unit for a term beginning before the expiration of the rental agreement, it terminates as of the date of the new tenancy. If the landlord fails to use reasonable efforts to rent the dwelling unit at a fair rental or if the landlord accepts the abandonment as a surrender,

if relet before 1st lease is up, 1st lease ends at date 2nd starts.

the rental agreement is deemed to be terminated by the landlord as of the date the landlord has notice of the abandonment. If the tenancy is from month-to-month or week-to-week, the term of the rental agreement for this purpose is deemed to be a month or a week, as the case may be.

Notes and Questions

1. As *Austin Hill* indicates, the vast majority of states now find a duty to mitigate on the landlord, although this may be limited to residential leases. The traditional rule that the landlord has no obligation to mitigate remains in force in at least some major jurisdictions. *Holy Properties, Ltd. v. Kenneth Cole Productions, Inc.*, 661 N.E.2d 694, 696 (N.Y. 1995), rejected mitigation for commercial leases:

> Parties who engage in transactions based on prevailing law must be able to rely on the stability of such precedents. In business transactions, particularly, the certainty of settled rules is often more important than whether the established rule is better than another or even whether it is the "correct" rule. This is perhaps true in real property more than any other area of the law, where established precedents are not lightly to be set aside.

Rios v. Carrillo, 861 N.Y.S.2d 129 (App. Div. 2008), confirmed that mitigation also is not required in residential leases in New York. Pennsylvania also rejects mitigation. *Stonehedge Square Ltd. Partnership v. Movie Merchants, Inc.*, 715 A.2d 1082 (Pa. 1998).

What policies support a landlord's duty to mitigate? What reasoning underlies the traditional rule? Is it sensible to require mitigation in residential leases but not in commercial? *See generally* John A. Humbach, *The Common-Law Conception of Leasing: Mitigation, Habitability, and Dependence of Covenants*, 60 Wash. U. L.Q. 1213 (1983); Comment, *Extending the Contractual Duty to Mitigate Damages to Landlords When a Tenant Abandons the Lease*, 42 Baylor L. Rev. 553 (1990); Note, *Illinois Landlords' New Statutory Duty to Mitigate Damages: Ill. Rev. Stat. Ch. 110, § 9-213.1*, 34 DePaul L. Rev. 1033 (1985).

2. In evaluating the costs and benefits of a mitigation rule, consider exactly what a "duty to mitigate" would require a landlord to do. What standard does the court require in *Austin Hill*? What actions did the landlord take and what should it take? What burdens would that impose? If this were a residential lease, what is the landlord's obligation under § 4.203(c) of the Uniform Residential Landlord and Tenant Act set out above? What if the leased premises are the upstairs of a duplex, and the landlord's only other realty is the downstairs unit in which she lives?

Austin Hill indicated that the mitigation obligation can be waived by agreement. The Texas legislature reversed this, however, barring such waivers. Tex. Prop. Code Ann. § 91.006(b). Why might waivers have been prohibited?

3. What effect should the landlord's failure to mitigate have on his action for damages? What does *Austin Hill* indicate? What would the result be under § 4.203(c) of the Uniform Residential Landlord and Tenant Act, *supra*? *See* Robert Schoshinski, *American Law of Landlord and Tenant* § 12:8 (1980); Glen Weissenberger, *The Landlord's Duty to Mitigate Damages on the Tenant's Abandonment: A Survey of Old Law and New Trends*, 53 Temp. L. Rev. 1, 31-32 (1980).

There is also a timing issue where there is a duty to mitigate raised in *Austin Hill*. Suppose the tenant abandons with half of the term remaining, and the landlord immediately brings suit for damages; how much should the court award the landlord at that time since the lease and the duty to mitigate are ongoing? *See* Roberta Rosenthal Kwall, *Retained Jurisdiction in Damage Actions Based on Anticipatory Breach: A Missing Link in Landlord-Tenant Law*, 37 Case W. Res. L. Rev. 273 (1987).

4. Should it make a difference whether the tenant has the right to assign or sublet? *See* Cal. Civ. Code § 1951.4 (lessor may do nothing after tenant's abandonment and continue to recover rent if, but only if, the lease expressly provides for this remedy and the tenant is allowed to assign or sublet).

5. Assume the landlord in *Austin Hill* had another office unit available in the building. After the defaulting tenant abandons, a prospective tenant approaches the landlord and is interested in leasing a unit in the building of the type that was abandoned. Must the landlord rent the abandoned unit to the new tenant, or may the landlord rent another vacant unit?

6. Consider whether the landlord met the mitigation obligation in the following scenarios:

a. The landlord re-rented the abandoned premises at a rent lower than that provided in the original lease. *See Ruud v. Larson*, 392 N.W.2d 62 (N.D. 1986).

b. The landlord unsuccessfully offered the abandoned premises at a rent higher than that provided in the original lease. *See Polster, Inc. v. Swing*, 164 Cal. App. 3d 427 (1985).

c. The landlord unsuccessfully offered the abandoned premises with an added lease term that the landlord could terminate the lease on 60 days' notice. *See Danada Square LLC v. KFC Nat'l Management Co.*, 913 N.E.2d 33 (Ill. Ct. App. 2009).

Problem

Landlord leased office premises under a 10-year lease to Tenant. After seven years, Tenant defaulted on the rent payment and abandoned the premises. Landlord would like to reenter the premises to repaint them, something that he feels is necessary to attract a new tenant. Landlord also wants to make other physical improvements that he believes are necessary to make the premises more attractive to a new tenant since the market in the area has become more upscale over the past several years. Landlord wants to know whether he can recover the costs for repainting and remodeling. He also wants to know whether he can raise or decrease the amount of rent as compared to the rent amount in the lease with the abandoning tenant.

What would you advise Landlord about his plans? Can you suggest steps that he might now take so that he can achieve his goals? Do you have any advice on how he might avoid these issues when making future leases? *See Reid v. Mutual of Omaha Insurance Co.*, 776 P.2d 896 (Utah 1989); *MXL Industries, Inc. v. Mulder*, 623 N.E.2d 369 (Ill. Ct. App. 1993).

(iii)   Acceleration Clauses

Landlords often include acceleration clauses in leases. These clauses provide that rent for the entire term is immediately due if the tenant defaults on a rent installment or if the tenant breaches any other provision of the lease. The courts are divided on the enforceability of these clauses.

AURORA BUSINESS PARK ASSOCIATES v. MICHAEL ALBERT, INC.

Supreme Court of Iowa
548 N.W.2d 153 (Iowa 1996, en banc)

ANDREASEN, J. The district court entered judgment for the landlord on its action for the recovery of past unpaid rent and for future rent as damages under an acceleration clause in the parties' lease. The tenant contends that the acceleration clause constitutes an unenforceable penalty and that the court failed to award the proper damages. We affirm as modified and remand.

I.   BACKGROUND FACTS AND PROCEEDINGS

The defendants, Michael Albert, Inc. and Michael L. Albert (Albert), and the plaintiff, Aurora Business Park Associates, L.P. (Aurora), entered into a lease agreement in which Albert agreed to lease office and warehouse space in the Aurora Business Park. The lease term was from March 1, 1991 until February 28, 1996. Albert took possession of the property after signing the lease but vacated the premises some time in June or July of 1993. No June rent payment was made and notice of default was given to Albert. Shortly thereafter, Aurora served a notice to quit and retook possession of the premises. Aurora was unsuccessful in reletting the property.

The lease includes the following provision:

> In the event of termination of this Lease by reason of a violation of its terms by the Lessee, Lessor shall be entitled to prove claim for and obtain judgment against Lessee for the balance of the rent agreed to be paid for the term herein provided, plus all expenses of Lessor in regaining possession of the premises and the reletting thereof, including attorneys' fees and court costs, crediting against such claim, however, any amount obtained by reason of any such reletting.

In August 1993, Aurora brought an action to recover past unpaid rent and the balance of rent for the remaining term of the lease. . . . At the end of Aurora's case, Albert moved for a dismissal claiming Aurora failed to establish that it used reasonable diligence in attempting to relet the premises. The motion was denied. Albert also asserted that an award of future rent would be improper because the acceleration clause constituted an unenforceable penalty and, alternatively, that the court was required to offset any future rent by the reasonable value of the use of the premises to the landlord or a reasonable amount for rent the landlord would actually receive during the remaining term of the lease.

On August 31, [1994], the court entered judgment in favor of Aurora and against Albert in the amount of $221,692.28 with interest plus attorney fees and court costs. The court concluded that Albert had breached the lease by abandoning the property without giving notice and by defaulting on the rental payments. The court found the acceleration clause to be a valid liquidated damages provision rather than an unenforceable penalty. The court also found that Aurora had used reasonable diligence in attempting to relet the property. The court awarded damages for the remaining term of the lease without offset for a reasonable value of the use of the premises to Aurora or for rent which may be received from reletting the property during the remaining term of the lease. The court did not reduce the amount for future rent to its present value.

Albert filed a motion for a new trial. The court . . . partially sustained Albert's motion by reducing the future accelerated rent payments to their present value. The court entered judgment for $215,251.90 with interest plus attorney fees and costs.

Our review is for correction of errors at law. . . . Whether a contract provision is a valid liquidated damages clause or an unenforceable penalty is a question of law for the court. . . .

II. ENFORCEABILITY OF THE ACCELERATION CLAUSE

Albert contends that the judgment not only allows Aurora to recover the amount of rent due under the terms of the lease, but also allows Aurora to retain possession of the premises for its own use or relet the premises and retain any rents collected. Consequently, Aurora is placed in a better position than if the lease had been performed. Albert claims this not only violates the general principles of law against double recovery, but also violates the terms of the lease which specifically states that actual rents collected are to be offset against the amount of the claim. Additionally, Albert contends that the acceleration clause is an unenforceable penalty.

Some jurisdictions have held that provisions for the acceleration of payments of rent are invalid as unenforceable penalties. 49 Am. Jur. 2d *Landlord & Tenant* §§ 716-17 (1995); *see, e.g.,* Kothe v. R.C. Taylor Trust, 280 U.S. 224 (1930) (lease provision that lessee's bankruptcy terminates lease and lessor is entitled to damages equal to rent for remainder of term is an unenforceable penalty); Ricker v. Rombough, 120 Cal. App. 2d Supp. 912 (1953) (rent acceleration provision in real property lease is unenforceable and void). Other jurisdictions, however, find specific acceleration clauses to be valid and enforceable. 49 Am. Jur. 2d *Landlord & Tenant* §§ 716-17; *see, e.g.,* W & G Seaford Assocs. v. Eastern Shore Mkts., 714 F. Supp. 1336 (D. Del. 1989) (acceleration clause for rent under commercial lease is valid liquidated damages provision); Amacker v. Wedding, 363 So. 2d 223 (La. Ct. App. 1978) (landlord entitled to liquidated damages equal to rent for one year pursuant to commercial lease clause); Frank Nero Auto Lease, Inc. v. Townsend, 411 N.E.2d 507, 512 (Ohio Ct. App. 1979) (weight of authority recognizes right of parties to contractually provide for repossession and acceleration of future rents where damages bear reasonable relationship to actual damages or lessor has obligation to mitigate damages); Woodhaven Apartments v. Washington, 907 P.2d 271 (Utah Ct. App. 1995) (liquidated damages clause in residential lease is valid). The American Law Institute has recognized rent acceleration clauses as a valid expansion of a landlord's remedy:

> The parties may provide in the lease that if the tenant defaults in the payment of rent or fails in some other way to perform his obligations under the lease, the total amount of rent payable during the term of the lease shall immediately become due and payable.

Restatement (Second) of Property Landlord & Tenant § 12.1 cmt. *k* (1977). . . .

A landlord and tenant may agree to the landlord's remedies if the tenant abandons the property and fails to pay rent, as long as the provision does not constitute a penalty. *See Restatement (Second) of Property Landlord & Tenant* § 12.1 cmt. *j; see also* Benson v. Iowa Bake-Rite Co., 221 N.W. 464, 467 (Iowa 1928) ("The law seems quite settled . . . that parties to a lease may, by mutual consent, terminate the same, and if they do the tenant is not liable for future rent unless the same is stipulated for in the agreement terminating the lease."). We recognized the trend of favoring liquidated damages clauses in *Rohlin*:

> In the past, we disfavored the use of liquidated damage clauses and favored interpretation of contracts that make stipulated sums penalties. Later, we relaxed this penalty rule and recognized that parties may fix damages by contract when the amount of damages is uncertain and the amount fixed is fair.

Rohlin, 476 N.W.2d at 79. We adopted the following test:

> Damages for breach by either party may be liquidated in the agreement but only at an amount that is reasonable in the light of the anticipated or actual loss caused by the breach and the difficulties of proof of loss. A term fixing unreasonably large liquidated damages is unenforceable on grounds of public policy as a penalty.

(quoting *Restatement (Second) of Contracts* § 356(1) (1981)); *see also* Engel v. Vernon, 215 N.W.2d 506 (Iowa 1974) ("if the sum stipulated is out of reasonable proportion to the loss or injury actually sustained or reasonably to be anticipated, it will be treated as a penalty"). . . .

We first address whether the amount of actual damages resulting from a breach of the lease was uncertain. If a breach occurs, the ability to obtain another suitable tenant for the property is unknown. If Aurora was able to relet the property shortly after the breach, the resulting damages would be reduced. There is no guarantee, however, that Aurora would be able to relet the premises at any time during the remainder of the lease term. Under this scenario, Aurora would suffer substantial damages. Furthermore, the damages will vary depending upon when the breach occurs. We find there is considerable uncertainty as to the actual amount of damages resulting from a breach of the lease two and one-half years before the end of its agreed term.

We next address whether the amount of liquidated damages under the acceleration clause is reasonable. The amount . . . "is reasonable to the extent that it approximates the loss anticipated at the time of the making of the contract, even though it may not approximate the actual loss." *Restatement (Second) of Contracts* § 356 cmt. *b* (1981) . . . . Albert contends that the proper measure of damages is the remaining rent due under the lease less the reasonable fair market value of the premises for the remainder of the term. Although other courts have utilized this formula, . . . we have not adopted this approach. In *Becker*, we rejected the tenants' argument that they "were entitled to credit on the rent due for the reasonable rental value of the use of the premises by [landlords] for the unexpired term." 293 N.W. at 20-21.

A landlord is entitled to recover from a tenant the damages sustained as a result of the tenant's abandonment and nonpayment of rent. . . . In general, the purpose behind the allowance of damages for breach of a contract "is to place the injured party in the position he or she would have occupied if the contract had been performed." . . . In Iowa "we are committed to the doctrine that when a tenant wrongfully abandons leased premises, the landlord is under a duty to show reasonable diligence has been used to relet the property at the best obtainable rent and thereby obviate or reduce the resulting damage." . . . Consequently, a landlord is entitled to damages equal to the amount of rent reserved in the lease, plus any other consequential damages, less amounts received in reletting the property. *See* Roberts v. Watson, 195 N.W. 211, 212-13 (Iowa 1923) (affirming judgment for landlord for full amount of unpaid rent plus subsequently accruing rent under five year lease less receipts from reletting); CHR Equip. Fin., Inc. v. C & K Transp., Inc., 448 N.W.2d 693 (Iowa App. 1989) (allowing recovery of future rent payments, reduced to present value, under equipment lease which provided for reasonable damages); *see also* Vibrant Video, Inc. v. Dixie Pointe Assocs., 567 So. 2d 1003 (Fla. Dist. Ct. App. 1990) (award of future rent for balance of commercial lease term less amount due from reletting must be reduced to present value).

The acceleration clause at issue here places Aurora in the position it would have occupied had Albert performed the entire lease. Furthermore, it takes into account the landlord's duty to mitigate damages by offsetting any claim by amounts received in reletting the property. We believe the acceleration clause reasonably approximates the anticipated or actual loss that resulted from Albert's abandonment and breach of the lease. Consequently, we hold that the acceleration clause is a valid and enforceable liquidated damages provision.

CREDIT FOR RENT RECEIVED BY RELETTING

Albert urges the court should at least set off against the judgment any rents actually received by reletting the premises during the remainder of the lease. We agree. The acceleration clause explicitly provided a credit against the balance of the future rent for "any amount by reason of any such reletting." Furthermore, if a landlord regains possession of property abandoned by a tenant, courts "agree that a landlord may not keep both the accelerated rent and rent received from renting to a new tenant." *Restatement (Second) of Property Landlord & Tenant* § 12.1 n. 10; *see also* W & G Seaford, 714 F. Supp. at 1347 (Landlord "concedes that a lessor cannot recover possession of the premises and an amount representing solely accelerated rent."); Quintero-Chadid Corp. v. Gersten, 582 So. 2d 685, 689 (Fla. Dist. Ct. App. 1991) ("If the landlord goes back into possession and relets the premises, he must give the tenant credit for the rents received."); *see also* 22 Am. Jur. 2d *Damages* § 712 (1988) (acceleration clause imposes a penalty "if it allows one party to repossess and resell, while still collecting the entire unpaid rental for the rest of the term").

DISPOSITION

We affirm the district court's judgment upholding the acceleration clause in the parties' lease as a valid liquidated damages provision. We modify the court's decision to provide for a credit against the judgment for rents received from reletting the property during the remainder of the lease term. We remand the case for the district court to determine if the property was relet during the remainder of the lease term. If so, Aurora must credit Albert for the rents obtained. Costs of appeal are taxed one-fourth against Aurora and three-fourths against Albert. . . .

Note and Questions

1. Under traditional landlord-tenant doctrine, the landlord could not accelerate rent in the absence of an express clause in the lease since no debt for rent became due until the tenant had enjoyed possession for the stated period. 2 Milton R. Friedman, *Friedman on Leases* § 5.101 (3d ed. 1990). Under the modern view of a lease as a contract, should a landlord be able to accelerate rent in the absence of a specific clause?

2. Assume that the clause in *Aurora* simply provided that all sums due under the lease would be due upon breach by the tenant. Should acceleration be permitted? How does it compare to the use of liquidated damages in other contracts? What policies support the respective positions of the landlord and tenant? Does the landlord have a better argument for the enforceability of the acceleration clause where the tenant misses a few months' rent payments, does not abandon the property, and instead wants to continue in possession? A typical statement of the requirements for a valid liquidated damages clause provides:

> [A] liquidated damages clause must meet three criteria to be upheld: (1) because of the nature or subject matter of the agreement, damages arising from a breach would be difficult to calculate accurately; (2) the sum fixed as liquidated damages must reflect a reasonable estimate of likely damages; and (3) the provision must be intended solely to compensate the nonbreaching party and not as a penalty for breach or as an incentive to perform.

Highgate Associates, Ltd. v. Merryfield, 597 A.2d 1280 (Vt. 1991).

Compare the analysis in *Aurora* with *Ott v. Vineville Market, Ltd.,* 416 S.E.2d 362, 364 (Ga. Ct. App. 1992), where an acceleration clause in a lease for a store in a shopping center was upheld:

> Ott's contention that the accelerated lease payments constitute a penalty is also without merit. As this was not a liquidated damage provision, there was no need to satisfy the test for enforceability of liquidated damages.

3. Why did the *Aurora* court reject the usual rule that deducts from the landlord's recovery the fair market value of the premises for the rest of the term and instead provide a credit for rent actually received from a reletting?

Problems: Acceleration Clauses

1. Tenant leased premises for use as an auto parts store for a 20-year term, at a rent of $2,000 a month. The printed lease form contained an acceleration clause upon failure of Tenant to pay sums due under the lease. Tenant made the first three rental payments, then missed the next two months' rent. Tenant did not respond to Landlord's requests for payment but has continued in possession, running its business. Can Landlord enforce the acceleration clause and require Tenant to pay the full amount of the rent now (i.e., $474,000)? In answering this question, consider whether Landlord's and Tenant's economic positions are better before or after the acceleration. *See Fifty States Management Corp. v. Pioneer Auto Parks, Inc.*, 389 N.E.2d 113 (N.Y. 1979).

2. Tenant executed a one-year lease containing an acceleration clause in the event that Tenant defaulted in payment of rent. Two months into the term, Tenant abandoned the premises and stopped paying rent. Landlord ignored the abandonment and seeks to hold Tenant liable for the rent. Can Landlord exercise the acceleration clause and insist that tenant pay all of the rent for the remainder of the term now?

(iv)   Recovery Devices

Landlords have employed various devices in an attempt to ensure that they will be able to collect sums owed to them by tenants. These include late fees, security deposits, and distraint.

Late fees. Whether a late fee clause is enforceable usually depends on whether the court views it as a valid liquidated damages provision or as a void penalty. Landlords maintain that they are damaged by late payment of rent in various ways: It creates extra work for management to send late notices and to contact the tenant until rent is paid; the landlord's cash flow necessary to pay fixed costs is interrupted; the landlord may lose interest income when rent is delinquent.[20]

Security deposits.   Leases typically require the tenant to make a security deposit at the inception of the lease to secure payment of rent and the tenant's other obligations. Various questions have arisen as to the parties' rights and obligations concerning the security deposit. In the absence of a specific lease provision or statute addressing these issues, courts require the landlord to return the deposit when the tenant has satisfied her obligations under the lease. The landlord may deduct unpaid rent and damages before returning the deposit.[21]

Over recent years, many jurisdictions have passed statutes regulating security deposits, especially concerning residential tenancies. Section 2.101 of the Uniform Residential Landlord and Tenant Act addresses many of the typical issues:

---

20.   *See* Nylen v. Park Doral Apartments, 535 N.E.2d 178 (Ind. Ct. App. 1989) ($2-a-day late fee in a residential lease a valid liquidated damages clause); *but see* North Am. Inv. Co. v. Lawson, 854 P.2d 384 (Okla. Ct. App. 1993) ($2-a-day late fee in a residential lease void since rent in lease was only $150 a month).

21.   *See* Robert Schoshinski, American Law of Landlord and Tenant §§ 6:31-6:38 (1980).

(a) A landlord may not demand or receive security, however denominated, in an amount or value in excess of [1] month['s] periodic rent.

(b) Upon termination of the tenancy property or money held by the landlord as security may be applied to the payment of accrued rent and the amount of damages which the landlord has suffered by reason of the tenant's noncompliance with Section 3.101 all as itemized by the landlord in a written notice delivered to the tenant together with the amount due [14] days after termination of the tenancy and delivery of possession and demand by the tenant.

(c) If the landlord fails to comply with subsection (b) or if he fails to return any prepaid rent required to be paid to the tenants under this Act the tenant may recover the property and money due him together with damages in an amount equal to [twice] the amount wrongfully withheld and reasonable attorney's fees.

(d) This section does not preclude the landlord or tenant from recovering other damages to which he may be entitled under this Act.

(e) The holder of the landlord's interest in the premises at the time of the termination of the tenancy is bound by this section.

Other statutes also require the landlord to retain the deposit in a separate bank account and to pay interest earned on the account to the tenant.[22]

If a statute requires return of the tenant's security deposit within 30 days after the landlord regains possession of the premises and allows the landlord to retain an amount sufficient to "remedy tenant defaults in the payment of rent," can the landlord retain amounts to cover future rent? *See 250 L.L.C. v. Photopoint Corp. (USA)*, 131 Cal. App. 4th 703, *review denied* (2005) (no, past due rent only).

Distraint. One of the oldest of the common-law remedies available to a landlord for the collection of rent was called "distraint." This feudal right allowed the landlord to go to the demised premises and seize *anything* that might be found there (whether belonging to the tenant or a stranger) and hold it until the rent was paid. In many jurisdictions, distraint for rent either has been expressly abolished by statute or has been deemed by the courts to be abolished by implication through the adoption of other statutes relating to speedy remedies for the recovery of rent. Because the landlord's self-help remedy requires no prior judicial approval or subsequent supervision, there have been concerns about whether such a remedy violates fundamental procedural due process rights.[23] More recent decisions, however, have found that no state action is involved in landlord distraint, thus avoiding due process claims.[24]

---

22.   *See, e.g.*, 68 Pa. Stat. Ann. § 250.511b. *See generally* Lee Harris, *Judging Tenant Protections: The Evidence from Enforcement of Landlord Penalties*, 42 U Mem. L. Rev. 149 (2011).

23.   *See* Gerald Korngold, *Can Distraint Stand Up as a Landlord's Remedy?*, 5 Real Est. L.J. 242 (1977).

24.   *See, e.g.*, Luria Bros. & Co. v. Allen, 672 F.2d 347 (3d Cir. 1982).

D. SUCCESSION TO RIGHTS AND OBLIGATIONS: ASSIGNMENTS AND SUBLEASES

1. Liability for Rent and Other Covenants

a. Assignments

KELLY v. TRI-CITIES BROADCASTING, INC.

Court of Appeal, California
147 Cal. App. 3d 666, 195 Cal. Rptr. 303 (1983)

STANIFORTH, Acting P.J. This court is called upon to review an order to arbitrate and an order confirming the arbitrator's award.

In 1975, Tri-Cities Broadcasting, Inc. purchased a radio business from Far West Broadcasting Corp. The radio business operated on land leased from the father of Robert Pat Kelly and Richard C. Kelly. Tri-Cities purchased the lease as a part of the purchase of the business.

This appeal is taken from the trial court's order correcting and confirming an arbitration award and judgment thereon. However, both sides agree to this court's review of the initial order to arbitrate.

In the order to arbitrate controversy the trial court found Tri-Cities and Jeffrey Chandler, president of Tri-Cities, "assumed the lessees' obligations under the terms of that certain 'Lease Agreement' executed in 1965 . . . ."

The relevant facts begin with the entry into a lease to run for 20 years from February 1, 1965, between S. L. Kelly, the deceased father of the Kellys, and Gordon and Irene B. Bambrick (the Bambricks), doing business as Carlsbad Broadcasters. The lease was for a parcel of real property in Carlsbad on which the Bambricks placed a radio tower, antenna and transmitter. The lease provides: "In consideration of the lease hereby granted to Lessee by Lessor, Lessee hereby agrees to provide Lessor with five minutes of radio program time per day, seven days a week, which program time shall be utilized to advertise business enterprises and activities of S. L. Kelly and/or assigns."

In 1970, the Bambricks sold the station to Far West. Far West was aware of the rent provision of the lease and provided radio time when it was requested in accordance with the lease.

In 1975, after several years of nonuse, the radio station was sold by Far West to Tri-Cities. Tri-Cities became the owner of all the assets of the radio station. For a period of at least nine months, Tri-Cities operated a radio station at the site covered by the original lease. The sale was consummated in July 1975; the leased premises, a transmitter site, was abandoned in late June 1977.

The addendum to the purchase agreement between Far West, Jeffrey Chandler and Tri-Cities provides: "6. *Land lease assignment.* Seller acknowledged the [existence] of a land lease covering the real property on which the broadcasting transmitter is located. Such lease should be included as an asset of the corporation on Exhibit 'A,' being effectively transferred to Buyer. However, the assignability of such lease will be subject to its terms." Exhibit A, item 10, to the purchase agreement lists: "Land Lease covering real property on which broad-casting transmitter is located. (Assignability of such Lease will be subject to its terms.)" The bill of sale involving the Far West, Tri-Cities transaction lists as number 10: "Land Lease covering real property on which broadcasting trans-mitter is located."

Paragraph VII of the original lease agreement states: "Lessor hereby agrees that in the event Lessee shall form a corporation for the purpose of operating Radio Station KCLB, that this lease may be assigned to said corporation; or if Radio Station KCLB shall be sold to any party other than Lessor, under the terms of this Lease Agreement, that this lease may be assigned by Lessee to said buyer without further obligation on the part of Lessee. However, Lessee hereby warrants and represents that in the event said assignment shall ever take place, the assignee therein shall assume all of the liabilities and obligations assumed by Lessee in this Lease Agreement.

The original lease further provides in paragraph IX: "The assigns and/or heirs of both parties shall carry out the terms of this Lease Agreement." Neither Chandler nor any other representative of Tri-Cities read or reviewed the lease before completing the purchase of Far West's assets. Tri-Cities did not expressly agree to pay rent for the balance of the lease term.

At the time the petition to order arbitration was considered, the trial court file contained a verified complaint on behalf of the Kellys, a declaration under penalty of perjury of Jeffrey Chandler, various pleadings and points and author-ities on both sides.

The declaration of Jeffrey Chandler states he is the president and chief oper-ating officer of Tri-Cities, as such he had entered into negotiations with Far West to purchase all the assets of Far West, and: (1) he was not sure a written lease existed, (2) no written assignment of the lease was executed to Far West at the time of its 1970 purchase or thereafter, (3) Far West was aware of the rent and had provided radio time to the lessor on demand in the first years of its ownership, (4) during the last years of Far West's ownership, and until 1979 no demand for radio time had been made, (5) Tri-Cities did not assume the lease because it intended to move the transmitter to other property, (6) Tri-Cities' interest in the lease was limited to the period of time it was waiting for FCC approval of its new site and station, and (7) when approval was received, Tri-Cities moved the transmitter and abandoned the site.

The Kellys' verified petition to compel arbitration alleges: (1) Tri-Cities paid property taxes on the radio tower, (2) Tri-Cities named the Kellys as additional insureds on Tri-Cities' policy of liability insurance covering the leased property, (3) Jeffrey Chandler stated to Robert Kelly in a conversation in 1977, "I guess I will have to honor the lease provision," and (4) the Far West, Tri-Cities purchase agreement, the lease and the possession of the property by Tri-Cities are proof of Tri-Cities' assumption of the lease.

The lease agreement expressly provides for arbitration of any dispute which "the parties hereto or their assignees shall be unable to resolve . . . ." Such arbi-tration is to be before the American Arbitration Association and the decision is to be "final and binding."

The arbitrator expressly found "That I am bound to follow the Superior Court finding that the lease was assumed by the Respondent Jeff Chandler and that the Superior Court finding of assumption is conclusive." . . .

II

Turning now to the merits of the appeal, we heed this first rule: The facts must be viewed in the light most favorable to the judgment. Even so, no conclusion can be drawn but that Tri-Cities did not expressly assume the terms of the lease. In every case examined where there has been an express assumption, the assignee has stated specifically either orally or in writing that he agrees to be bound by the terms of the lease including the covenant to pay rent. [Discussion of cases omitted.—EDS.]

The evidence submitted before the trial court contains no evidence, either oral or in writing, meeting the requirements for an express assumption of the lease terms. Although the addendum says "[s]uch lease should be included as an asset of the corporation" and "[h]owever, the assignability of such lease will be subject to its terms," these words cannot be stretched into an express assumption of all the terms in the lease. This is plainly an *assignment*, not an *assumption*, of the lease to Tri-Cities as an asset.

The addendum's last sentence, "However the assignability of such lease will be subject to its terms," does not patently or covertly constitute an express assumption of the lease. That sentence was included because the assignor did not have a copy of the lease and did not know whether he had authority to assign it. The language "the assignability of such lease will be subject to its terms" is a reference to the uncertainty as to its *assignability*. It is not an agreement to assume the obligation of the lease.

III

The second provision of paragraph VI of the lease provides a *warranty by the lessor* to the lessee. If the leased premises are sold at any time the buyer will assume responsibility to perform all the terms of the lease. *This warranty by the lessor to the lessee* does not impose any obligation upon the original lessee. It could not impose any obligation upon an assignee of the original lessee.

Nor does the language of paragraph VII impose any duty upon a nonassuming assignee. Paragraph VII authorizes an assignment with this proviso: "However, Lessee hereby warrants and represents that in the event said assignment shall ever take place, the assignee therein shall assume all of the liabilities and obligations assumed by the Lessee in this Lease Agreement." These plain words impose a duty on the *lessee*, not the assignee. If the lessee failed to perform the duty, then an obligation may arise on his or her part, but certainly absent an express assumption this language creates no privity of contract with Tri-Cities. "An occupant of real property who holds by virtue of a bare assignment of the lease and without entering into any contract, either with his assignor or the lessor, affirmatively binding himself to fulfill the covenants of the lease, *is subject only to such obligations as he impliedly assumes by entry and taking possession of the leased premises.*" (Realty & Rebuilding Co. v. Rea (1920) 184 Cal. 565 italics added.)

Thus, taking possession, without more, does not constitute sufficient evidence to support the finding of an assumption of the lease. Occupation gives rise to an obligation for "covenants which run with the land." (Ellingson v. Walsh, O'Connor & Barneson, *supra*, 15 Cal. 2d 673.)

Nor does the provision in paragraph IX of the lease, "The assigns and/or heirs of both parties shall carry out the terms of this Lease Agreement," constitute an express assumption of the terms of the lease. Paragraph IX is a contractual obligation of the original lessor and lessee to obtain assumption agreements insofar as are necessary to perform the terms of the lease. It creates no privity of contract with Tri-Cities.

The documents presented to the trial court at the hearing on petition to arbitrate — the purchase and sales agreement, the addendum to the purchase [and] sales agreement and the bill of sale — do not show Tri-Cities to be a party to the lease.

We conclude as a matter of law no evidence was presented to the trial court, documentary or otherwise, to substantiate the conclusion Tri-Cities had assumed the lease. The evidence on point is to the contrary.

IV

Absent an express assumption of the obligations of the lease there is no privity of contract between the original landlords, the Kellys, and the assignee Tri-Cities. An assignee who takes possession under an assignment without an express assumption of the obligation of the lease is not bound by the contractual obligations of the lease. In Treff v. Gulko (1931) 214 Cal. 591, 595 [7 P.2d 697], the Supreme Court said: "The assignment of the lease here involved . . . contains no covenant on the part of the assignee to pay the rent, and in accepting the same the assignee did not even impliedly agree to pay the rent. He was, of course, liable for the rent so long as he remained in possession of the leased premises, but without any agreement express or implied he could not be held beyond the time of his actual occupation of the premises." . . . In Ellingson v. Walsh, O'Connor & Barneson, 15 Cal. 2d 673, the Supreme Court said: "The lease has a dual character; it is a conveyance of an estate for years, and a contract between lessor and lessee. The result is that dual obligations arise — contractual obligations from the terms of the lease, and obligations under the law from the creation of the tenancy. As it is sometimes expressed, there are dual obligations arising from 'privity of contract' and 'privity of estate.' [Citation.]

"This dual character of the obligations of a tenant may be illustrated by an assignment of the tenant's right without any assumption of the obligations by the assignee. The assignee who does not assume is not liable on the lease, that is to say, is not bound by its contractual obligations. But the nonassuming assignee who occupies the premises is liable by reason of his tenancy, and his obligation, arising out of privity of estate, continues at least through the period of his occupancy. Likewise, where the new tenant comes in without even a written assignment, but takes over possession of the old lessee with the consent of the lessor, he is liable for rent." This rule . . . is followed by all modern authorities on real property in California. See 4 Miller & Starr, Current Law of Real Estate (§ 27.89, pp. 408-409): "An assignee who takes possession under an assignment without an express assumption of the obligations of the lease is not bound by the contractual obligations of the lease. . . . As long as he remains in possession the nonassuming assignee is bound to pay the rent, maintain the insurance, make repairs, and pay the taxes, if the lease so provides. However, these obligations terminate when the assignee terminates his possession. In the absence of an express assumption of the lease by the assignee there is no privity of contract between the assignee and the landlord, and the assignee is not liable for the covenants which are not otherwise binding under the privity of estate." . . .

Equally in point and positive are the authorities Johnson-Moskovitz, 6 *California Real Estate Law and Practice,* section 172.31, page 172.20, where the authors said: "Unless the assignee specifically assumes all of the contractual obligations incident to the lease, his relationship with the original landlord is based only on privity of estate." And point out further: "Should the assignee abandon the premises or reassign the lease, his privity of estate with the landlord would be divested. Therefore, for example, the assignee's liability for continued rental payments would cease. *Although some commentators have criticized that result, the rule's vitality remains.*" And the *Restatement Second of Property,* section 16.1, subdivision (2), states: "A transferee of an interest in leased property is obligated to perform an express promise contained in the lease if:

(a) the promise creates a burden that touches and concerns the transferred interest;

(b) the promisor and promisee intend that the burden is to run with the transferred interest;

(c) the transferee is not relieved of the obligation by the person entitled to enforce it; and

(d) the transfer brings the transferee into privity of estate with the person entitled to enforce the promise.

The chief authority on real property in the United States, Thompson, states in volume 3A *Thompson on Real Property,* section 1216 (1959 rev.) page 98: "[I]n the absence of [an] express covenant on his part he [the assignee] is liable only for such covenants as run with the land and only during such time as he holds the term."

California law is clear: An assignee, in the absence of an express assumption, is liable only for covenants which run with the land and only during the period of his occupancy. His liability "ceases with cessation of possession." (*See* Lutton v. Rau, 37 Cal. App. 429 . . . . The assignee has the obligation to pay the stated rental provided in the lease and not merely the reasonable value of the use . . . .)

We recognize there is a contrary view. The holding in *Treff* is criticized in 3 Witkin, *Summary of California Law, Real Property,* section 484, pages 2165-2166. Witkin reasons as follows: The "privity of estate" between landlord and tenant does not terminate by mere abandonment, it requires the landlord accept a surrendering of the leasehold. . . . Witkin . . . cites the inherent unfairness of a rule forcing a landlord to scrupulously observe the rights of assignees so long as they remain in possession, but allowing assignees to terminate their obligations at their pleasure. This is alleged to be equivalent to a fixed term on the landlord's side and a mere tenancy at will on the tenant's side. Whatever merit there is to this argument, we are bound to follow Supreme Court precedent.

Moreover, the hardship to which Witkin alludes is easily avoided in commercial leases. These are, as was this one, normally prepared to the landlord's specifications and may contain restrictions on assignment without landlord approval to prevent problems such as this. It is the contractual oversight, not the law, which imposes whatever hardship the landlord has incurred.[2]

V

Two covenants are here sought to be enforced against Tri-Cities, the covenant for rent and the covenant to submit to arbitration. There is no question the lessee's agreement to pay rent is a covenant running with the land, binding upon the assigns of the lessee. An express contractual assumption of an obligation for rent is unnecessary. . . .

As to the nature of a covenant to submit to arbitration, case authority is sparse. The only authority found is Abbott v. Bob's U-Drive (1960) 222 Ore. 147 [352 P.2d 598]. The *Abbott* court held: "In the case at bar the covenant to arbitrate is invoked to require the lessee to submit to arbitration a matter relating to rental payments under the lease. A covenant to pay rent clearly 'touches and concerns' the land. It would seem to follow that a covenant to arbitrate a question with respect to rental payments should also be required as relating to the property interests of the original covenanting parties as lessor and lessee. As stated in Clark page 99 [Clark, *Covenants and Interests Running with Land*], 'there would seem to be no reason for applying the rules of touching and concerning in an overtechnical manner, which is unreal from the standpoint of the parties themselves.'" The Oregon Supreme Court concluded a covenant to arbitrate was a covenant running with the land. We agree and would treat it as similar to a covenant to pay rent upon which it rests for the conclusion that such a covenant "touches and concerns the land."

The rule relied on in 3A *Thompson on Real Property, supra*, is again applicable to the covenant to arbitrate. "In the absence of an express covenant on his part he [the assignee] is liable only for such covenants as run with the land and only during such time as he holds the term." (§ 1216, p. 98.)

This rule is based upon privity of estate, not privity of contract. When the privity of estate no longer exists, those covenants running with the land, based upon that privity, are no longer enforceable. Thus the covenant to arbitrate is binding upon a nonassuming assignee only as to matters arising during the term or period that the assignee was bound by privity of estate. No authorities predict an agreement to arbitrate could be stretched to require arbitration of a claim for rent due after the premises had been abandoned, after the privity of the estate has been broken.

The evidence before the trial court as to Tri-Cities' period of occupancy of the leased plot was, at most, "from September, 1975, to late June, 1977." The arbitrator, proceeding on the erroneous premise there had been an "assumption" of the lease term by Tri-Cities, made no award for the period of actual occupancy but awarded prospective damages "for rent from January 1979 to September 30, 1980" of $16,500 and "for the remaining term of the lease" the arbitrator awarded a monthly charge of $800 . . . .

---

2. Apparently the landlord believed the contractual remedy of holding the original lessee to its warranty to obtain an assumption by its assignee was sufficient security. It should have been except for the lessee's later insolvency. Had the lessee never assigned, its insolvency would have left the landlord in the same position it is now.

On all counts, the arbitrator's award was contrary to law, the errors are patent on the face of the award. Tri-Cities can be held responsible only during such time as it held the term. That liability is limited to the *then* (Sept. 1975-June 1977) dollar value of the radio time agreed to be given in lieu of a monetary rent and only for the months of actual occupancy.

Judgment reversed with directions to deny confirmation of the arbitrator's award.

Notes and Questions

1. Would the Bambricks (T1) be liable for rent in *Kelly* and, if so, under what theory? Does the assignment by the Bambricks (T1) to Far West (T2) affect the liability of T1? If you had represented T1 at the time of the proposed sale to T2, could you have done anything to protect T1 from future liability?

2. Why does the court conclude that Tri-Cities (T3) is not liable under the lease?

The court's conclusion that Tri-Cities did not assume the lease obligations is consistent with the general pattern of cases. In *Reid v. Weissner & Sons Brewing Co.*, 40 A. 877, 879 (Md. 1898), for example, T1 executed an assignment of a lease "with all its covenants, terms and conditions" to T2. The court held that this was not sufficient to bind T2 under privity of contract to the landlord:

> These words, "with all its covenants, terms and conditions," add nothing to the legal effect of the assignment. They certainly are not contractual words of the assignee. They embody no promise by [T2] to the lessor. They are simply words of description, and not words of contract. . . .

Most courts, however, would not find that Tri-Cities (T3) effectively terminated its privity of estate. Compare the steps that T2 took to end privity of estate with the actions of T3. Did the court correctly decide that T3 was no longer in privity of estate? Should privity of estate end for T3

b/c simply abandoned the premise

  (a) if T3 assigns to a financially irresponsible T4? *See Shadeland Development Corp. v. Meek*, 489 N.E.2d 1192 (Ind. Ct. App. 1986) (no duty to exercise reasonable care in assignment of lease).
  (b) if T3 retains possession of the premises after an assignment to T4 pursuant to a sublease from T4 to T3? *See OTR v. Flakey Jake's, Inc.*, 770 P.2d 629 (Wash. 1989).
  (c) if the landlord relets the premises to T4 after T3 abandoned the property? *See First American National Bank of Nashville v. Chicken System of America, Inc.*, 616 S.W.2d 156 (Tenn. Ct. App. 1980).

What steps can you advise landlord clients to take to counter the loss of liability under privity of estate rules?

3. Is Far West (T2) liable in *Kelly* under either privity of estate or privity of contract?

4. As *Kelly* indicates, an assignee in privity of estate with the landlord is liable not only for rent but also for all covenants that run with the leasehold estate. Following requirements set down in *Spencer's Case*, 5 Co. 16a, 77 Eng. Rep. 72

(1583), a covenant will run with the land if the original landlord and tenant intended that the burdens and benefits of the covenant would pass down to future assignees and if the covenant "touches and concerns" the land. The intent to run is usually presumed if the covenant affects the use and enjoyment of the property, although some older decisions require the express binding of "assigns." The touch-and-concern requirement has been justified as a means to prevent promises that are "collateral" to ownership of the property from binding future owners. For a covenant to touch and concern the property interests, it must increase or decrease the use and enjoyment or value of the property. Thus, a covenant to repair the property is found to touch and concern. *See* 2 *American Law of Property* §§ 9.1-9.7; Robert Schoshinski, *American Law of Landlord and Tenant* § 8:2 (1980). Note how the court in *Kelly* did not use a formalistic approach in deciding that the arbitration covenant ran with the land.

Covenants running between owners in fee are addressed in Chapter 12.

5. Assume that T1 is liable under privity of contract for rent and T2 is liable under privity of estate. The landlord may choose to sue either T1 or T2 and collect from either one of them (but not both). As between T1 and T2 themselves, however, T2 is primarily liable and T1 is secondarily liable as a surety. So if the landlord successfully recovers from T1, T1 may use the principle of subrogation to recover from T2 the amount T1 had to pay to the landlord. What explains the relative liability of T1 and T2? *See* 1 *American Law of Property* §§ 3.61, 3.64; 1 Milton R. Friedman, *Friedman on Leases* §§ 7.501d, 7.502.

6. The landlord's interest in the lease can also be assigned. The transferee receives the landlord's future right of possession (reversion) and the benefits and burdens of covenants that run with the lease. *See* Robert Schoshinski, *American Law of Landlord and Tenant* § 8:4 (1980).

Problem

Landlord leased commercial premises to T1. T1 assigned to T2. Landlord and T2 agreed to increase the amount of rent. Is T1 still liable for the rent? Would the result be the same if Landlord and T2 had agreed to reduce the rent? *See St. Louis Twin Oaks Associates v. Executive Office Network, Ltd.*, 804 F. Supp. 1127 (E.D. Mo. 1992).

b. Subleases

AMERICAN COMMUNITY STORES CORP. v. NEWMAN

Supreme Court of Nebraska
441 N.W.2d 154 (1989)

HASTINGS, Chief Justice. This appeal involves three cases consolidated for trial, briefing, and argument. Plaintiffs, tenants under three separate leases for buildings housing grocery stores, filed petitions for declaratory judgments . . . [seeking] a determination as to whether they violated the terms of the individual store leases which prohibit assignment of the leases without the prior written consent of the landlord, but permit subletting without permission.

Defendants counterclaimed for possession based on alleged assignments of the leases without prior written consent. Both parties filed cross motions for summary judgment. Defendants now appeal from the order of the trial court ruling that the leases had not been violated because no prohibited assignments had been entered into which remained in effect beyond the period which existed for the curing of defaults as provided for in the leases. Summary judgments were granted in favor of the plaintiffs, and defendants' counterclaims were dismissed. . . .

American Community Stores Corporation (ACS), which operated Hinky Dinky stores in Nebraska, held leases with the various landlords on grocery store buildings in Columbus, Auburn, and Omaha. The leases generally were for 20-year terms with options to renew or extend for multiple 5-year leasing periods. Due to labor difficulties, ACS announced sometime in January of 1985 that it was closing its stores in Nebraska. The Columbus store was closed at the beginning of December 1984, and the Auburn and Omaha stores in mid-February of 1985. Each store was reopened under different management the day after it closed. The Auburn store was reopened and operated by Hinky Dinky Auburn, Inc., the Columbus store was reopened and operated by Russ' Super Foods, Inc., and the Omaha store was reopened and operated by Gro-Mor, Inc.

The agreements between ACS and the various parties were originally structured such that ACS would assign the leases to Nash-Finch Company, a grocery wholesaler, and Nash-Finch would in turn sublease the stores to the operators. Assignment agreements were signed and placed in the files of the companies.

Shortly after the public announcement of the closings, ACS, through its owner, Cullum Companies, Inc., contacted the trustees for the landlords, requesting permission to assign leases to Nash-Finch. In the case of the Columbus store, a representative of Nash-Finch wrote the trustee a letter dated December 31, 1984, giving notice of the assignment between ACS and Nash-Finch effective December 1, 1984, and of the fact that Nash-Finch was subletting the store to Russ' Super Foods.

By separate letter for each store, each letter dated February 8, 1985, one of the trustees for the landlords notified ACS that the landlord did not consent to assignment of the leases for the Auburn and Omaha stores. Furthermore, if ACS proceeded to assign the lease without written consent, the letter was to constitute the notice of default required in article X of each lease. By separate letter also dated February 8, the trustee notified ACS that unless he heard otherwise from ACS within 2 weeks, he would assume that the transfer of the Columbus store to Nash-Finch was by assignment without consent. In the event Nash-Finch's possession was by assignment, the letter was notice of default. Houston E. Holmes, Jr., vice president and general counsel of Cullum Companies, Inc., notified the trustee for the landlords by letter dated February 14, 1985, that the stores would be *sublet*.

Article IX of each of the leases provided in part:

SECTION 1. Tenant may not assign or transfer this lease without the written consent of Landlord first had and obtained; however, without obtaining such consent, Tenant may sublet the leased premises or portions thereof for purposes and upon provisions not inconsistent with the terms and provisions of this lease.

Article X of the same leases provides:

SECTION 1. If, at any time during the term of this lease . . . (a) Tenant shall default . . . (ii) In the observance or performance of any of Tenant's other covenants, agreements or obligations hereunder for a period of twenty (20) days after Landlord shall have given Tenant written notice specifying such default or defaults . . . Landlord shall have the right, at its election, at any time thereafter while such default or defaults continue, to re-enter and take complete and peaceable possession of the leased premises . . . and to declare said term ended. . . .

In an apparent effort to cure these claimed defaults, Jon Solberg, in-house counsel for Nash-Finch, and Holmes, on behalf of ACS, agreed during a telephone conversation in mid-February that the assignment agreements would be removed from the various files and replaced with subleases.

change assignments to subleases

The term of each sublease ends 2 days prior to the end of ACS's term under the prime lease with the defendants. In addition, Nash-Finch, as sublessee, was granted the right to "exercise the remaining option periods granted by the Prime Lease."

In granting plaintiffs' motion for summary judgment, the trial court made the following findings of fact:

T ct's reasoning

1. That although there may be a question of fact as to whether an assignment was executed and then destroyed prior to closing of the sale, a sublease was executed thereafter and within 20 days of notice of default given by defendant.

2. That the sublease agreement executed is in fact and law a sublease and not an assignment and therefore does not require the consent of the defendant and is not in violation of any provisions of the original lease. This conclusion is based upon the following:

   a) The original lease permitted a sublease for all as well as a portion of the leased premises.

   b) The sublease expired prior to the term of the original lease thus retaining in the lessee a right of reversion.

   c) The lessee retained a right of reentry for a condition broken which is also a right of reversion.

   d) The fact that options given to the sublessee would purport to run as long if not longer than the expiration of the original lease is not, as a matter of law, valid so as to make the sublease for the same term as the original lease. The option can only begin to run from the expiration of the basic term of the sublease, not the original lease. Further, the sublessee cannot be granted more than the prime lessee has to offer under the original lease.

Δ argue:

Appellants argue that the original assignments are still in effect because there is nothing in the record that the agreements were canceled or altered. They further argue that even though the assignment documents were destroyed, which fact is not disputed, they still bind ACS and Nash-Finch because they were never formally rescinded or the subject of reassignment from Nash-Finch to ACS.

That reasoning is erroneous. In Nebraska, an assignment by a lessee of an interest in a lease which prohibits such assignment without the lessor's consent is ineffective without such consent. Moritz v. S & H Shopping Centers, Inc., 247 N.W.2d 454 (Neb. 1976). . . . In *Moritz* . . . this court stated:

> Defendant had no authority to assign the lease without the consent of plaintiff. Such consent was never given or received and defendant's contention that it transferred certain interests in the lease is necessarily immaterial as no valid rights could have been transferred or acquired in the absence of plaintiff's consent.

The assignments between ACS and Nash-Finch were not valid because the landlords refused to consent to them, and therefore they are not still in effect in continuing violation of the leases. It was not necessary for the parties to formally rescind the assignments or for Nash-Finch to reassign the leases to ACS before the parties could attempt to enter into valid subleases.

Nevertheless, the assignments without consent, even though invalid, were still violations of the covenants in the leases. However, appellants overlook the fact that the leases provided ACS with 20 days to cure a default after being notified of the default by the landlord. This was done if, in fact, the documents later executed were subleases.

In Nebraska, covenants in a lease against assignment or subletting are not favorably regarded by the courts and are liberally construed in favor of the lessee. Jamson v. Poulos, 168 N.W.2d 526 (Neb. 1969). . . . This means that the scope of a covenant against assignment will not be enlarged by the courts, and the covenant will not be considered violated by any technical transfer that is not fairly and substantially an assignment. Chesnut v. Master Laboratories, [27 N.W.2d 541 (Neb. 1947)].

The generally accepted test for determining whether a transfer is an assignment or a sublease is set out in 2R. Powell, *The Law of Real Property*, ¶ 246[1] at 372.92-.93 (1986), as follows:

> When the transfer is for the whole balance of the unexpired term, with respect to all of the originally leased premises and on exactly the same terms as those under which the main lessee held the transaction is inescapably an "assignment." When the transfer is for a period shorter than the unexpired balance of the term, and relates to a physical part only of the originally leased premises and is on terms materially different from those stipulated in the main lease, the transaction is inescapably a "sublease." To state the test in a slightly different manner, the question is whether if by the transaction the lessee conveys his entire term, or whether he retains a reversionary interest. If by the transaction the tenant conveys the entire term and thereby parts with all reversionary interest in the property, the transaction is construed to be an assignment, whereas if there remains a reversionary interest in the estate, it is a sublease.

Appellants contend that the subleases are really assignments because ACS did not reserve a reversionary interest at the end of the option terms. According to appellants, contrary to the trial court's ruling, the right of reentry for condition broken is not a reversionary interest. . . . [Citations omitted. — EDS.] However, there is authority for the position that the right of reentry is a reversionary interest sufficient to qualify a transfer as a sublease rather than an assignment. *See, Restatement (Second) of Property § 15.1*, comment *i*. (1977) . . . . [Additional citations omitted. — EDS.]

We adopt the reasoning of the latter authorities and declare that a right of reentry is a reversionary interest sufficient to qualify a transfer of rights under a lease agreement as a sublease rather than an assignment.

Quite apart from the question of the right of reentry, ACS did retain a reversionary interest by reason of the expiration of the term of the sublease prior to that of the basic lease. It is generally accepted that the retained reversionary interest need not be for a substantial period of time in order for an agreement to be considered a sublease. Agreements calling for the surrender of possession only 1 day prior to the expiration of the term of the main lease have been held to be subleases rather than assignments. *See* Bostonian Shoe Co. of New York v. Wulwick Associates, 501 N.Y.S.2d 393 (App. Div. 1986); F.W. Woolworth Co. v. Plaza North, Inc., 493 N.E.2d 1304 (Ind. App. 1986); Warnert v. MGM Properties, 362 N.W.2d 364 (Minn. App. 1985).

In each agreement at issue in this appeal, Nash-Finch's tenancy ends 2 days prior to the end of ACS's tenancy under the prime lease. Under the common-law distinction between assignments and subleases, this is a sufficient reversionary interest to constitute the transfer a sublease.

Appellants argue that even though the agreements between ACS and Nash-Finch reserve a portion of the initial term to ACS, the so-called subleases between Nash-Finch and its operators are contractually inconsistent; i.e., the Auburn and Omaha subleases between Nash-Finch and the operators provide for termination of the operator's lease on the same day that ACS's term expires under the prime lease. Appellants insist that this is evidence that the real intent of ACS and Nash-Finch was to assign the leases. Contrary to this contention, it seems only to indicate that the subleases between Nash-Finch and the operators were not changed to reflect the change from assignments to subleases between ACS and Nash-Finch.

In Nebraska, a sublessee has no greater rights against the original lessor than were given by the original sublessor to the original sublessee. Thus, despite the provisions in the subleases between Nash-Finch and the operators of the Omaha and Auburn stores, the tenancy of the operators will end when the term of Nash-Finch ends, 2 days prior to the expiration of ACS's term under the prime lease.

Appellants also contend that ACS transferred the premises for the entire remainder of its term because it granted Nash-Finch the right to exercise the remaining renewal options in the prime lease. It is reasonable to conclude that ACS was granting Nash-Finch options to renew the subleases in order to extend their terms by 5 years each for the number of times ACS could extend the prime lease, rather than granting Nash-Finch the right to actually extend the prime lease pursuant to ACS's option to renew. Since under a sublease there is no privity of contract between the original lessor and the sublessee, Nash-Finch as sublessee could not exercise ACS's option to renew. . . .

In F.W. Woolworth Co. v. Plaza North, Inc., *supra*, the court found that an agreement which allowed the transferee to occupy the premises during the extended period of a renewable prime lease permitting the original lessee to extend the lease for five successive terms of 5 years, which gave the transferee options to extend, and which expired 1 day before the expiration of the second and third extended periods of the prime lease, was a permitted sublease and not a prohibited assignment. The facts in that case as to the extension options are strikingly similar to the instant case.

To the same effect is Joseph Bros. Co. v. F.W. Woolworth Co., 641 F. Supp. 822 (N.D. Ohio 1985), *aff'd* 844 F.2d 369 (6th Cir. 1988). The issue also facing that court was whether the agreement constituted an assignment or a sublease. According to the court,

> [t]he effect of the agreement was that each term of the Woolco-Hills agreement expired one day before the expiration of the corresponding term of the Joseph Brothers-Woolco agreement. If each party extended its lease to the limits, the Joseph Brothers-Woolco lease would expire one day after the Woolco-Hills lease.

The court noted that once a lease renewal option has been exercised, the term of the original lease is deemed to be enlarged to encompass the option period. Therefore, the issue was whether the same was true if a sublease is entered into before the renewal option is exercised. The court found that Woolco clearly acted with the intention in good faith of exercising its option to extend the lease, evidenced by the fact that Woolco did so 1 month after the agreement with Hills and 52 years before it was necessary. Accordingly, the court found that "reasonable minds could only conclude that it was the intention of Woolco to sublease the premises to Hills, that Woolco made a good faith attempt to enter into a sublease, and that the agreement meets the legal requirements to constitute it as a sublease rather than an assignment." *Id.* at 825.

Recently, this court in International Harvester Credit Corp. v. Lech, 438 N.W.2d 474 (Neb. 1989), reiterated the well-established law in this state that "the interpretation given to a contract by the parties themselves while engaged in the performance of it is one of the best indications of true intent and should be given great, if not controlling, influence." ACS and Nash-Finch, while engaged in the performance of the agreements, appear to have interpreted the renewal option to mean Nash-Finch will inform ACS if it wishes to extend the term and ACS in turn will then exercise its option under the prime lease by notifying the landlord. Nash-Finch's right to extend the subleases is dependent upon ACS's exercise of its options to renew the prime leases. The effect is that each term of the subleases expires 2 days before the expiration of the corresponding term of the prime lease. If ACS and Nash-Finch each extend their leases to the limits, the prime leases will expire 2 days after the subleases.

Appellants cite to this court the rule of Jaber v. Miller, 239 S.W.2d 760 (Ark. 1951), that the intention of the parties is to govern in determining whether an instrument is an assignment or a sublease. . . . Tennessee also follows the intention rule. The court in Ernst v. Conditt, 390 S.W.2d 703 (Tenn. Ct. App. 1964), quoting Williams v. Williams, 84 Tenn. 164 (1885), stated, " 'We have most wisely abandoned technical rules in the construction of conveyances in this State, and look to the intention of the instrument alone for our guide, that intention is to be arrived at from the language of the instrument read in the light of the surrounding circumstances.' " . . .

Reading the language of the agreements between ACS and Nash-Finch in the light of the surrounding circumstances and taking into consideration the motives which induced the agreement, the only reasonable interpretation of the agreements is that they are and were intended to be subleases. ACS was informed that the landlord would not consent to assignments and considered

ACS to be in default. ACS, having the object and purpose of transferring its interest in the premises while not violating the leases and forfeiting its interest in the premises, clearly intended to enter into subleases, which it could do without permission. To this end, ACS entered into agreements that satisfy the common-law requirements of a sublease.

There is no genuine issue as to any material fact or as to the ultimate inferences that may be drawn therefrom, and the appellees are entitled to judgment in their favor as a matter of law. The judgments of the district court are affirmed.

Holding

Notes and Questions

1. In *American Community Stores*, why does it matter whether the agreements between ACS and Nash-Finch created assignments or subleases?

2. *Distinguishing between an assignment and a sublease.* The Nebraska court in *American Community Stores* follows the usual rule in holding that a transfer of less than the remaining term of the lease creates a sublease, even if the transfer is for just one day less. An assignment requires transfer of the entire remaining term of the lease. There is a split of authority on the question whether the transferor's retention of a right of entry or power to terminate the estate granted on the occurrence of a condition (such as failure to pay rent) results in a sublease. Because a right of entry or power of termination is not regarded as an estate in land, the majority of courts hold that the entire leasehold estate is transferred and an assignment results. The Nebraska court adopts the minority view in the principal case.

The Nebraska court also takes a minority position in its expressed willingness to consider the intent of the parties rather than looking solely to the characteristics of the estate transferred in determining whether the transferee is an assignee or sublessee.

minority position = characteristic of the transfer.

3. *What is the difference between a sublease and an assignment?* An assignment simply results in substitution of the assignee in the place of the tenant, and so long as the assignee remains in privity of estate, the landlord has the right to enforce the lease covenants that run with the land against the assignee. By contrast, a sublease creates a new lease relationship in which the tenant becomes the landlord of the sublessee. The prime landlord has no right to collect rent, or enforce the other lease covenants against the sublessee, and instead must look to the tenant or assignee. Of course, if the prime lessee fails to pay the rent, the landlord can terminate the prime lease and the sublessee's only recourse is against the sublessor. Why do people use subleases? What is the utility of an arrangement that insulates the sublessee from liability on the covenants in the prime lease?

4. What are the rights of the various parties in *American Community Stores* with respect to exercise of the options to renew the lease?

5. If a court has adopted the view that intent of the parties controls whether a transfer effects an assignment or a sublease, what conclusion might it draw from the fact that the transferee is paying rent directly to the landlord rather than to the tenant/transferor?

2. Power to Assign or Sublet

tenants · *LL*

JULIAN v. CHRISTOPHER

Court of Appeals of Maryland
320 Md. 1, 575 A.2d 735 (1990)

CHASANOW, J. In 1961, this Court decided the case of Jacobs v. Klawans, 169 A.2d 677 (Md. 1961), and held that when a lease contained a "silent consent" clause prohibiting a tenant from subletting or assigning without the consent of the landlord, landlords had a right to withhold their consent to a subletting or assignment even though the withholding of consent was arbitrary and unreasonable.

In 1983, in The Citizens Bank & Tr. v. Barlow Corp., 456 A.2d 1283 (Md. 1983), we noted that the issue was not preserved for appeal, but "[i]f the common law rule applied in *Klawans* is to be reconsidered, it will have to be done on a record which preserves the question for review." We now have before us the issue of whether the common-law rule applied in *Klawans* should be changed. *issue.*

In the instant case, the tenants, Douglas Julian and William J. Gilleland, III, purchased a tavern and restaurant business, as well as rented the business premises from landlord, Guy D. Christopher. The lease stated in clause ten that the premises, consisting of both the tavern and an upstairs apartment, could not be assigned or sublet "without the prior written consent of the landlord." Sometime after taking occupancy, the tenants requested the landlord's written permission to sublease the upstairs apartment. The landlord made no inquiry about the proposed sublessee, but wrote to the tenants that he would not agree to a sublease unless the tenants paid additional rent in the amount of $150.00 per month. When the tenants permitted the sublessee to move in, the landlord filed an action in the District Court of Maryland in Baltimore City requesting repossession of the building because the tenants had sublet the premises without his permission. *LL claims.*

need written consent of the LL for assign or sublease.

when request sublease LL wants more $

At the district court trial, the tenants testified that they specifically inquired about clause ten, and were told by the landlord that the clause was merely included to prevent them from subletting or assigning to "someone who would tear the apartment up." The district court judge refused to consider this testimony. He stated in his oral opinion that he would "remain within the four corners of the lease, and construe the document strictly," at least as it pertained to clause ten. Both the District Court and, on appeal, the Circuit Court for Baltimore City found in favor of the landlord. The circuit judge noted: "If you don't have the words that consent will not be unreasonably withheld, then the landlord can withhold his consent for a good reason, a bad reason, or no reason at all in the context of a commercial lease, which is what we're dealing with." We granted certiorari to determine whether the *Klawans* holding should be modified in light of the changes that have occurred since that decision.

PP

District Ct & COA for LL.

issue

While we are concerned with the need for stability in the interpretation of leases, we recognize that since the *Klawans* case was decided in 1961, the foundations for that holding have been substantially eroded. The *Klawans* opinion cited *Restatement of Property* § 410 as authority for its holding. The current *Restatement (Second) of Property* § 15.2 rejects the *Klawans* doctrine and now takes the position that:

Klawans has eroded

Restatement [handwritten]

A restraint on alienation without the consent of the landlord of the tenant's interest in the leased property is valid, but the landlord's consent to an alienation by the tenant cannot be withheld unreasonably, unless a freely negotiated provision in the lease gives the landlord an absolute right to withhold consent.

Another authority cited in *Klawans* in support of its holding was 2 R. Powell, *Powell on Real Property*. The most recent edition of that text now states:

Thus, if a lease clause prohibited the tenant from transferring his or her interest without the landlord's consent, the landlord could withhold consent arbitrarily. This result was allowed because it was believed that the objectives served by allowing the restraints outweighed the social evils implicit in them, inasmuch as the restraints gave the landlord control over choosing the person who was to be entrusted with the landlord's property and was obligated to perform the lease covenants.

It is doubtful that this reasoning retains full validity today. Relationships between landlord and tenant have become more impersonal and housing space (and in many areas, commercial space as well) has become scarce. These changes have had an impact on courts and legislatures in varying degrees. Modern courts almost universally adopt the view that restrictions on the tenant's right to transfer are to be strictly construed. (Footnotes omitted.)

2 R. Powell, *Powell on Real Property* § 248[1] (1988).

Finally, in support of its decision in *Klawans*, this Court noted that, "although it, apparently, has not been passed upon in a great number of jurisdictions, the decisions of the courts that have determined the question are in very substantial accord." This is no longer true. Since *Klawans*, the trend has been in the opposite direction.[1] "The modern trend is to impose a standard of reasonableness on the landlord in withholding consent to a sublease unless the lease expressly states otherwise." Campbell v. Westdahl, 715 P.2d 288 (Ariz. Ct. App. 1985).

In his article, *Correctly Interpreting Long-Term Leases Pursuant to Modern Contract Law: Toward a Theory of Relational Leases*, 74 Va. L. Rev. 751, 761-63 (1988), Alex M. Johnson, Jr., tracks the development of what he calls the "burgeoning minority position." Professor Johnson notes that:

In 1963 Louisiana became the first state to adopt the minority position on alienability by holding in Gamble v. New Orleans Housing Mart, Inc. [154 So. 2d 625 (La. Ct. App. 1963)] that lessors must act reasonably in situations requiring the lessor's consent to a transfer.

Following Louisiana's lead, two common law jurisdictions, Ohio and Illinois, rejected the common law view and adopted the holding and rationale in *Gamble*. In

[handwritten left margin: modern trend = LL must be reasonable in not consenting to sublease unless otherwise stated]

---

1. At present the following courts have adopted the minority rule: Homa-Goff Interiors, Inc. v. Cowden, 350 So. 2d 1035 (Ala. 1977); Hendrickson v. Freericks, 620 P.2d 205 (Alaska 1980); Tucson Medical Center v. Zoslow, 712 P.2d 459 (Ariz. Ct. App. 1985); Warmack v. Merchants Nat. Bank of Fort Smith, 612 S.W.2d 733 (Ark. 1981); Kendall v. Ernest Pestana, Inc., 709 P.2d 837 (Cal. 1985); Basnett v. Vista Village Mobile Home Park, 699 P.2d 1343 (Colo. Ct. App. 1984), *rev'd on other grounds*, 731 P.2d 700 (Colo. 1987); Warner v. Konover, 553 A.2d 1138 (Conn. 1989); 1010 Potomac Assoc. v. Grocery Manufacturers, 485 A.2d 199 (D.C. 1984); Fernandez v. Vazquez, 397 So. 2d 1171 (Fla. Dist. Ct. App. 1981); Funk v. Funk, 633 P.2d 586 (Idaho 1981); Jack Frost Sales v. Harris Trust & Sav. Bank, 433 N.E.2d 941 (Ill. Ct. App. 1982); First Federal Sav. Bank v. Key Markets, 532 N.E.2d 18 (Ind. Ct. App. 1988); Gamble v. New Orleans Housing Mart, Inc., 154 So. 2d 625 (La. Ct. App. 1963); Newman v. Hinky Dinky Omaha-Lincoln, Inc., 427 N.W.2d 50 (Neb. 1988); Boss Barbara, Inc. v. Newbill, 638 P.2d 1084 (N.M. 1982).

1977 the Alabama Supreme Court addressed the lessor's right to withhold consent unreasonably in a frequently cited opinion, Homa-Goff Interiors, Inc. v. Cowden [350 So. 2d 1035 (Ala. 1977)] and concluded that the common law view was archaic in today's urban society. The Alabama court was the first to base its decision on the policy of alienability. The court balanced the right of the lessor to withhold consent unreasonably against society's interest in the alienability of commercial leaseholds, concluding that the "reasonable" alienation of commercial leasing space is paramount and predominates over any attempt by the lessor to restrict alienability arbitrarily.

Since *Homa-Goff*, fourteen states have reexamined their law on this issue. Six states have adopted or reaffirmed their adoption of the common law view, while eight states have rejected the common law view and restricted, either in whole or in part, the lessor's right to restrain alienability arbitrarily. The eight states that have adopted the minority position were influenced by the position taken recently by the American Law Institute (ALI).

The ALI endorses the minority position that a lessor must act reasonably when withholding consent to alienate the lease, absent express terms to the contrary. (Footnotes omitted.)

Traditional property rules favor the free and unrestricted right to alienate interests in property. Therefore, absent some specific restriction in the lease, a lessee has the right to freely alienate the leasehold interest by assignment or sublease without obtaining the permission of the lessor.[2] R. Schoshinski, *American Law of Landlord and Tenant* § 5:6 (1980); 1 *American Law of Property* §3.56 (1952).

Contractual restrictions on the alienability of leasehold interests are permitted. R. Cunningham, W. Stoebuck, and D. Whitman, *The Law of Property* § 12.40 (1984). Consequently, landlords often insert clauses that restrict the lessee's common law right to freely assign or sublease. Probably the most often used clause is a "silent consent" clause similar to the provision in the instant case, which provides that the premises may not be assigned or sublet without the written consent of the lessor.

In a "silent consent" clause requiring a landlord's consent to assign or sublease, there is no standard governing the landlord's decision. Courts must insert a standard. The choice is usually between (1) requiring the landlord to act reasonably when withholding consent, or (2) permitting the landlord to act arbitrarily and capriciously in withholding consent.

Public policy requires that when a lease gives the landlord the right to withhold consent to a sublease or assignment, the landlord should act reasonably, and the courts ought not to imply a right to act arbitrarily or capriciously. If a landlord is allowed to arbitrarily refuse consent to an assignment or sublease, for what in effect is no reason at all, that would virtually nullify any right to assign or sublease.

Because most people act reasonably most of the time, tenants might expect that a landlord's consent to a sublease or assignment would be governed by standards of reasonableness. Most tenants probably would not understand that

---

2.   The common-law right may have some limitations. For example, a lessee may not sublet or assign the premises to be used in a manner which is injurious to the property or inconsistent with the terms of the original lease.

a clause stating "this lease may not be assigned or sublet without the landlord's written consent" means the same as a clause stating "the tenant shall have no right to assign or sublease." Some landlords may have chosen the former wording rather than the latter because it vaguely implies, but does not grant to the tenant, the right to assign or sublet.

There are two public policy reasons why the law enunciated in *Klawans* should now be changed. The first is the public policy against restraints on alienation. The second is the public policy which implies a covenant of good faith and fair dealing in every contract.

Because there is a public policy against restraints on alienation, if a lease is silent on the subject, a tenant may freely sublease or assign. Restraints on alienation are permitted in leases, but are looked upon with disfavor and are strictly construed. If a clause in a lease is susceptible of two interpretations, public policy favors the interpretation least restrictive of the right to alienate freely. Interpreting a "silent consent" clause so that it only prohibits subleases or assignments when a landlord's refusal to consent is reasonable, would be the interpretation imposing the least restraint on alienation and most in accord with public policy.

Since the *Klawans* decision, this Court has recognized that in a lease, as well as in other contracts, "there exists an implied covenant that each of the parties thereto will act in good faith and deal fairly with the others." Food Fair v. Blumberg, 200 A.2d 166, 174 (Md. 1964). When the lease gives the landlord the right to exercise discretion, the discretion should be exercised in good faith, and in accordance with fair dealing; if the lease does not spell out any standard for withholding consent, then the implied covenant of good faith and fair dealing should imply a reasonableness standard.

We are cognizant of the value of the doctrine of *stare decisis*, and of the need for stability and certainty in the law. However, as we noted in Harrison v. Montgomery Co. Bd. of Educ., 456 A.2d 894, 903 (Md. 1983), a common law rule may be modified "where we find, in light of changed conditions or increased knowledge, that the rule has become unsound in the circumstances of modern life, a vestige of the past, no longer suitable to our people." The *Klawans* common law interpretation of the "silent consent" clause represents such a "vestige of the past," and should now be changed.

Reasonableness of Withheld Consent

In the instant case, we need not expound at length on what constitutes a reasonable refusal to consent to an assignment or sublease. We should, however, point out that obvious examples of reasonable objections could include the financial irresponsibility or instability of the transferee, or the unsuitability or incompatibility of the intended use of the property by the transferee. We also need not expound at length on what would constitute an unreasonable refusal to consent to an assignment or sublease. If the reasons for withholding consent have nothing to do with the intended transferee or the transferee's use of the property, the motivation may be suspect. Where, as alleged in this case, the refusal to consent was solely for the purpose of securing a rent increase, such refusal would be unreasonable unless the new subtenant would necessitate additional expenditures by, or increased economic risk to, the landlord.

the lack of consent in this case is unreasonable unless financial risk, which there was none.

Prospective Effect

The tenants ask us to retroactively overrule *Klawans,* and hold that in all leases with "silent consent" clauses, no matter when executed, consent to assign or sublease may not be unreasonably withheld by a landlord. We decline to do so. In the absence of evidence to the contrary, we should assume that parties executing leases when *Klawans* governed the interpretation of "silent consent" clauses were aware of *Klawans* and the implications drawn from the words they used. We should not, and do not, rewrite these contracts.

Don't overturn Klawan.

In appropriate cases, courts may "in the interest of justice" give their decisions only prospective effect. Contracts are drafted based on what the law is; to upset such transactions even for the purpose of improving the law could be grossly unfair. Overruling prospectively is particularly appropriate when we are dealing with decisions involving contract law. The courts must protect an individual's right to rely on existing law when contracting.

Ordinarily decisions which change the common law apply prospectively, as well as to the litigants before the court. What is meant by "prospectively" may depend on the fairness of applying the decision to cases or events occurring after the effective date of the decision. *See, e.g.,* Boblitz v. Boblitz, 462 A.2d 506 (Md. 1983) (abrogating interspousal immunity in negligence cases—decision applicable to the case before the court and causes of action accruing or discovered after the date of the decision); Kelley v. R.G. Industries, Inc., 497 A.2d 1143 (Md. 1985) (imposing strict liability on manufacturer of "Saturday Night Specials"—decision applicable to the case before the court as well as retail sales after the date of the mandate). It is reasonable to assume that landlords may have relied on the *Klawans* interpretation when entering into leases with "silent consent" clauses. This reliance should be protected. Contracts should be interpreted based on the law as it existed when they were entered into. Therefore, whether the *Klawans* case or the instant case governs the interpretation of a "silent consent" clause depends on whether the lease being interpreted was executed before or after the mandate in this case.

Silent clauses interpretation depends on timing.

For leases with "silent consent" clauses which were entered into before the mandate in this case, *Klawans* is applicable, and we assume the parties were aware of the court decisions interpreting a "silent consent" clause as giving the landlord an unrestricted right to withhold consent.

For leases entered into after the mandate in this case, if the lease contains a "silent consent" clause providing that the tenant must obtain the landlord's consent in order to assign or sublease, such consent may not be unreasonably withheld. If the parties intend to preclude any transfer by assignment or sublease, they may do so by a freely negotiated provision in the lease. If the parties intend to limit the right to assign or sublease by giving the landlord the arbitrary right to refuse to consent, they may do so by a freely negotiated provision of the lease clearly spelling out this intent. For example, the clause might provide, "consent may be withheld in the sole and absolute subjective discretion of the lessor."

after this case —Rule.

can contract around rule in clause showing intent

The final question is whether the tenants in the instant case, having argued successfully for a change in the law, should receive the benefit of the change. There should be some incentive to challenge an infirm doctrine or seek reversal of unsound precedent. As the Supreme Court of Illinois has stated:

> At least two compelling reasons exist for applying the new rule to the instant case while otherwise limiting its application to cases arising in the future. First, if we were to merely announce the new rule without applying it here, such announcement would amount to mere *dictum.* Second, and more important, to refuse to apply the new rule here would deprive appellant of any benefit from his effort and expense in challenging the old rule which we now declare erroneous. Thus there would be no incentive to appeal the upholding of precedent since appellant could not in any event benefit from a reversal invalidating it.

Molitor v. Kaneland Community Unit District No. 302, 163 N.E.2d 89, 97 (Ill. 1959).

For these reasons, even though a decision is to have only prospective effect, this Court has applied the new rule to the case before it, unless it would be unfair to do so.

The tenants in the instant case should get the benefit of the interpretation of the "silent consent" clause that they so persuasively argued for, unless this interpretation would be unfair to the landlord. We note that the tenants testified they were told that the clause was only to prevent subleasing to "someone who would tear the apartment up." Therefore, we will reverse the judgment of the Circuit Court with instructions to vacate the judgment of the District Court and remand for a new trial. At that trial, the landlord will have the burden of establishing that it would be unfair to interpret the "silent consent" clause in accordance with our decision that a landlord must act reasonably in withholding consent. He may establish that it would be unfair to do so by establishing that when executing the lease he was aware of and relied on the *Klawans* interpretation of the "silent consent" clause. We recognize that we may be giving the tenants a benefit that other tenants with leases entered into before our mandate will not receive. The reasons why we do so were well stated, though in a slightly different context, by Justice Brennan in Stovall v. Denno, 388 U.S. 293 (1967):

> Sound policies of decisionmaking, rooted in the command of Article III of the Constitution that we resolve issues solely in concrete cases or controversies, and in the possible effect upon the incentive of counsel to advance contentions requiring a change in the law, militate against denying [these litigants] the benefit of today's decisions. Inequity arguably results from according the benefit of a new rule to the parties in the case in which it is announced but not to other litigants similarly situated in the trial or appellate process who have raised the same issue. But we regard the fact that the parties involved are chance beneficiaries as an insignificant cost for adherence to sound principles of decision-making. (Footnotes omitted.)

JUDGMENT OF THE CIRCUIT COURT FOR BALTIMORE CITY REVERSED, AND CASE REMANDED TO THAT COURT WITH DIRECTIONS TO VACATE THE JUDGMENT OF THE DISTRICT COURT OF MARYLAND IN BALTIMORE CITY AND TO REMAND THE CASE TO THAT COURT FOR FURTHER PROCEEDINGS NOT INCONSISTENT WITH THIS OPINION. COSTS TO BE PAID BY RESPONDENT.

Notes and Questions

1. Cases continue to split on the question whether a reasonableness require-ment should be read into a clause requiring a landlord's consent before an assignment or a sublease. *See, e.g., 21 Merchants Row Corp. v. Merchants Row, Inc.*, 587 N.E.2d 788 (Mass. 1992) (no reasonableness requirement will be implied); *Park Place Center Enterprises, Inc. v. Park Place Mall Associates*, 836 S.W.2d 113 (Tenn. Ct. App. 1992) (imposing a reasonableness requirement). Those cases implying a reasonableness requirement state that it applies equally to assign-ments and subleases. *See, e.g., Kendall v. Ernest Pestana, Inc.*, 709 P.2d 837 (Cal. 1985) (consent may be withheld in a commercial lease only for a commercially reasonable objection), *codified in* Cal. Civ. Code § 1995.260. Which party should bear the burden of negotiating or drafting a provision governing existence of a reasonableness limitation on the landlord's right to withhold consent?

Why should the landlord be concerned with the identity of an assignee or subtenant of the tenant?

2. What policies support the traditional rule and the *Julian* approach? Which view is correct? Should a reasonableness standard be imposed where the land-lord is leasing the top half of a two-family home, which is the only real estate owned by the landlord, and the landlord lives in the bottom unit? Should a tenant be able to expressly waive the reasonableness provision? *See Pacific First Bank v. New Morgan Park Corp.*, 876 P.2d 761 (Or. 1994) (yes).

On consent clauses, in addition to Professor Johnson's article cited in *Julian*, see William G. Coskran, *Assignment and Sublease Restrictions: The Tribulations of Leasehold Transfers*, 22 Loy. L.A. L. Rev. 405 (1989); Note, *Withholding Consent to Alienate: If Your Landlord Is in a Bad Mood, Can He Prevent You from Alienating Your Lease?*, 43 Duke L.J. 671 (1993); Note, Pacific First Bank v. New Morgan Park Corporation: *Reasonable Withholding of Consent to Commercial Lease Assignments*, 31 Willamette L. Rev. 713 (1995); Note, Kendall v. Pestana, Inc.: *Standard of Reasonableness Applied to Commercial Assignment Clauses*, 18 Pac. L.J. 327 (1986).

What should be the relationship between the landlord's right to withhold consent and the landlord's duty to mitigate damages? Consider § 12.1(3) and § 15.2 of the *Restatement (Second) of Property—Landlord and Tenant*. Does it make sense to relieve the landlord of the duty to mitigate damages if the tenant can freely assign or sublet as allowed under Cal. Civ. Code § 1951.4 if the landlord's rights are clearly spelled out in the lease?

3. Even in jurisdictions that do not imply a reasonableness requirement, the consent clause in a lease may expressly require that the landlord's consent may not be unreasonably withheld. *See, e.g., Maxima Corp. v. Cystic Fibrosis Foundation*, 568 A.2d 1170 (Md. 1990). Thus, courts are confronted—either as a matter of law or based on an express clause—with the question whether the landlord's refusal was reasonable in light of specific facts. What guidelines does *Julian* sug-gest on this issue? Consider the following situations:

   (a) T1's proposed sublease to T2 was at a rent that exceeded the amount of rent in L's lease with T1, and L wanted to make a new lease directly with T2. *See Toys "R" Us, Inc. v. NBD Trust Co. of Illinois*, 904 F.2d 1172 (7th Cir. 1990).

   (b) T1 sought assignment of a lease that included percentage rental to L based on the gross sales from the store premises, and the proposed

T2 was comparatively inexperienced in the retail business. *See Jonas v. Prutaub Joint Venture*, 567 A.2d 230 (N.J. Super. App. Div. 1989).
(c) The business of the proposed assignee T2 would compete with a store operated by L in the same shopping center. *See Pay 'N Pak Stores, Inc. v. Miller*, 210 Cal. App. 3d 1404 (1989).

4. Various constructional issues are involved in consent clauses. Some courts avoid the issue of the reasonableness of withholding consent by finding that no consent is needed under the language of the clause. *See, e.g., American Community Stores Corp. v. Newman*, 441 N.W.2d 154 (Neb. 1989) (prohibition against assignment without consent did not apply to sublease).

One ancient doctrine also helped prevent many conflicts over consent clauses. The rule in *Dumpor's Case*, 76 Eng. Rep. 1110 (1603), provides that once a landlord consents to an assignment of a lease pursuant to a consent clause in the lease, the consent clause is deemed to be permanently waived. No consent is therefore required for subsequent reassignments. This rule apparently still applies in a number of American jurisdictions. *See* Robert Schoshinski, *American Law of Landlord and Tenant* § 8:17 (1980). Is the rule in *Dumpor's Case* a sensible rule? If you represented a landlord, could you avoid the application of the rule?

5. Consent clauses have been addressed by statutes in a number of jurisdictions. The California legislature codified the rule of *Kendall v. Ernest Pestana, Inc.*, 709 P.2d 837 (Cal. 1985), at Cal. Civ. Code §§ 1995.010-.340. *See* Susan Myster, *Protecting Landlord Control of Transfers: The Status of "Sole Discretion" Clauses in California Commercial Leases*, 35 Santa Clara L. Rev. 845 (1995). Like *Kendall*, the statute only injects a reasonableness standard in commercial leases. The New York legislature took a somewhat different approach, providing rules for assignment and subletting of residences. N.Y. Real Prop. Law § 226-b attempts to accommodate the reasonable interests of both landlords and tenants. With respect to assignments, the statute provides that a tenant cannot assign without the landlord's consent, and that the landlord may withhold consent without cause. However, if the landlord unreasonably withholds consent, the tenant is released from the lease on 30 days' notice. If consent is reasonably withheld, the tenant may not assign and is not released. With respect to subletting, a tenant has the right to sublet with the consent of the landlord, which may not be unreasonably withheld. Tenants are required to submit written proposals for subleases. The landlord's consent will be presumed if the landlord does not respond within 30 days. If the landlord reasonably withholds consent, the sublease is ineffective and the original tenant continues to be bound. Where refusal is unreasonable, however, the tenant may proceed with the sublease. Subleases or assignments not complying with the statute may be the basis for an eviction action—thus giving landlords a powerful weapon to prevent under-the-table arrangements by tenants. To complete the protection for all sides, lease provisions waiving the statute are declared to be void.

Problems: Consent to Assignment

1. L, a religious denomination, leased space in an office building to T1. The lease contained a provision requiring consent by L prior to an assignment or sublease; state law imposes a reasonableness requirement on L's decisions. T1 proposes to sublease the property to Planned Parenthood (T2), and provides evidence of that organization's financial security and good track record as a tenant. L refuses consent since its members are strictly opposed to birth control of any type. Should a court uphold L's refusal? *See Restatement (Second) of Property—Landlord and Tenant* § 15.2 illus. 6; *American Book Co. v. Yeshiva University Development Foundation, Inc.*, 297 N.Y.S.2d 156 (Sup. Ct. 1969). No, b/c the sublessee is capable of renting the apt. unreasonably withhold of consent b/c has nothing to do w/ apt.

2. A lease for space in an office building contained a provision permitting Landlord to terminate the lease if Tenant requested consent to sublease the premises. If Landlord exercised its rights under the clause, Tenant would have no further obligations under the lease and no right to excess rent received by Landlord upon reletting the premises. Is such a clause valid? *See Carma Developers (California), Inc. v. Marathon Development California, Inc.*, 826 P.2d 710 (Cal. 1992).

CHAPTER 7

Concurrent Estates and
Marital Property

In Chapters 5 and 6, we studied the ways in which property ownership can be split among people whose rights to possession are successive. In this chapter, we look at four ways to divide property ownership so that the rights to possession are concurrent: tenancy in common, joint tenancy with right of survivorship, tenancy by the entirety, and community property. Anyone can own property as tenants in common or as joint tenants. Until recently, only married couples could own property as tenants by the entirety or community property, and in most states that may still be the case. California Family Code § 297.5, adopted in 2003, provides that registered domestic partners have the same rights under statutes and the common law as those granted to spouses, which means they can own community property. In Section D, we also look at property treated as "marital property" even though it is not held in one of the marital tenancies.

concurrent possession

Whenever the right to present possession of property is owned by more than one person, the owners are tenants in common unless they have acquired title in some other form. Tenancies in common are widespread. They arise when property passes by intestate succession, when couples divorce without a property settlement dividing their jointly owned property, and whenever people buy property together without going to the expense of creating a corporation, partnership, or trust to hold title. Friends buying vacation cabins, business associates buying an "investment" property, unmarried couples buying property together, usually take title as tenants in common. Increasingly, relative strangers who can't afford houses in high-priced real estate markets pool resources to buy multiunit housing for their own residential use, and take title as tenants in common, rather than going to the expense of creating a condominium or cooperative.

The possibilities for conflict among cotenants are great because of the many decisions that must be made about the use, maintenance, improvement, and possible sale of the property. Carefully drawn agreements can provide mechanisms for sensible property management and disposition of the parties' shares in the event of divorce, death, or desire to cash out the investment, but all too often, there is no such agreement. The cotenants are left to the default rules provided by law either because they had no choice, as with inherited property, or because they were unaware of the need for an agreement, or they were unable or unwilling to incur the financial and emotional costs of negotiating and drafting an agreement.

The default rules that govern concurrent estates are the subject of this chapter.

A. AN OVERVIEW OF THE CONCURRENT ESTATES: ALIENABILITY

The default rules governing alienability of concurrent estates are, fortunately, very clear, and for the most part readily variable by agreement.

Tenancy in common is what we might call the residual form of ownership—if no other form of ownership is specified, the owners hold as tenants in common, unless they are trustees, who hold title as joint tenants with right of survivorship.[1] The interests of tenants in common are fully alienable: Tenants in common can transfer their interests independently of one another during life, and their interests pass by their wills, or by intestate succession, at death.

Interests of joint tenants with right of survivorship are fully alienable inter vivos but inalienable at death. Instead of passing to the cotenant's heirs or devisees, the property "remains" with the survivor. Since the 13th century, each joint tenant has been regarded as owning the whole rather than a fractional interest in the property. When a joint tenant dies, the effect is conceptualized as the extinguishment of a burden from the other joint tenants' interests rather than as a passing of the deceased tenant's interest to the survivors. Thus, the claims that usually can be made against the property of a decedent by tax collectors, creditors, and family members may be avoided by using a joint tenancy.[2] Joint tenants can transfer their interests independently during life, but if they do so, they convert their interest into a tenancy in common, destroying the survivorship right. Joint tenancy property cannot be transferred by will and does not pass by intestate succession.

Tenancy by the entirety is like the joint tenancy in that there is a right of survivorship, but it is unlike either the tenancy in common or the joint tenancy in that the cotenants cannot transfer their interests independently.[3] Without getting a divorce, tenants by the entirety cannot acquire the right to sell their individual interests in the property or to dispose of them by will without joinder of both spouses.

Community property, like tenancy by the entirety property, is open only to married couples or registered domestic partners in California. Like tenancy by

---

1. There are practical and historical reasons for this distinction. Before the Statute of Uses, landowners often conveyed property to feoffees to uses (the precursors of the modern trustee) to avoid having the property descend to their heirs by inheritance. This allowed landowners to transfer the property by will before the Statute of Wills was enacted in 1540 and to avoid the feudal incidents of relief, wardship, and marriage. To make this work, landowners enfeoffed several people at a time as joint tenants with right of survivorship. As each tenant died, ownership continued in the rest. When the number became too small, the feoffees to uses would add additional joint tenants to the group. Partly because of this practice, a presumption developed that property conveyed to more than one person was intended to be held in joint tenancy. That presumption has been reversed today for most conveyances to more than one owner, but it remains in force as to trustees. It continues to play a practical role. When one of several trustees dies, the legal title to the property remains with the surviving trustees rather than becoming entangled in the deceased trustee's estate.

2. Legislatures can, of course, change this result and have often done so for death taxes. Federal estate taxes, and many, but not all, state inheritance and estate taxes do apply to property held in joint tenancy. Joint tenancy property has also been subjected to claims of a surviving spouse, as you will learn in a course on wills and trusts or estate planning.

3. This is the majority rule. There are some states where each spouse has the ability to transfer the property inter vivos.

the entirety property, land held as community property can only be transferred inter vivos if both spouses join in the conveyance. Unlike tenancy by the entirety property, or joint tenancy property, however, community property can be disposed of by will.

Example 1: A and B own Blackacre in fee simple absolute as tenants in common. A dies leaving a will transferring his property in trust for the benefit of his spouse and issue. *Result:* An undivided one-half interest in Blackacre passes under A's will. The trustee and B hold Blackacre as tenants in common.

Example 2: A and B own Blackacre as joint tenants with right of survivorship. A dies leaving a spouse and children. A's will leaves all his property in trust for the benefit of his spouse and issue. *Result:* B owns all of Blackacre. No interest in Blackacre passes under A's will.

Example 3: A and B own Blackacre as joint tenants with right of survivorship. B transfers her interest in Blackacre to C. *Result:* A and C own Blackacre as tenants in common.

Example 4: O conveys Blackacre to A, B, and C as Trustees, to hold for the benefit of O's spouse for life, then to O's issue. A dies. *Result:* B and C own Blackacre as Trustees. No interest in Blackacre passes through A's estate. — B/c dead.

Example 5: H and W own Blackacre as tenants by the entirety. H transfers his interest in Blackacre to C. H then dies. H's will leaves all his property to State University. *Result:* W owns Blackacre. H has no power to transfer Blackacre either inter vivos or by will unless W joins in the transfer.   W must agree.

Example 6: H and W own Blackacre as community property. H transfers his interest in Blackacre to C. H then dies. H's will leaves all his property to State University. *Result:* State University and W own Blackacre as tenants in common. H cannot unilaterally transfer his interest in Blackacre during life but can transfer it by will.

B.   PROBLEMS WITH SHARING POSSESSION

Unfortunately, the default rules governing shared possession of property held by cotenants are both murky and defective, as Evelyn Lewis convincingly demonstrates in *Struggling with Quicksand: The Ins and Outs of Cotenant Possession Value Liability and a Call for Default Rule Reform,* 1994 Wis. L. Rev. 331. Why do they remain so unsatisfactory after centuries of development (concurrent estates have been with us since at least the 13th century)? She speculates that "cotenant conflicts receive little attention from property law reformers" because they involve "'one-shotters'—parties who rarely litigate, who are predominantly members of the obedient middle-class and who suffer quietly the rules of law they were too unsophisticated to know or consider in advance of the conflict."[4]

---

4.   1994 Wis. L. Rev. at 341.

Cotenants own "undivided" shares in the land, which means that each cotenant has the right to possess and enjoy all the land, not just a specific geographic portion, and none of them has the right to exclude the others. Management problems are likely to arise because—unlike a trust, corporation, or condominium—no one is legally in charge, and a cotenant who assumes responsibility for managing the property is not entitled to compensation.[5] Each cotenant is entitled to possession of the entire property and responsible for his or her share of necessary maintenance expenses, but there is no mechanism for collective decision making.

The law offers almost no help to tenants by the entirety and community property owners: If they can't agree on management or disposition of the marital property, the court will divide it between them on divorce.[6] The law offers only a little more to tenants in common and joint tenants. Each cotenant can sell his or her share of the property, individually, but they all have to agree to sell the whole thing. If they cannot agree, the court will, on petition of any cotenant, either physically divide the property among them, or order the property sold and divide the proceeds in an action of partition. Short of partition, the only help the law affords a cotenant is an action for accounting for rents or profits received by another cotenant, or an action for contribution for advances made to pay another cotenant's share of taxes, mortgage payments, and necessary maintenance expenses. Any cotenant can make improvements to the property, but the others are not required to contribute. An action for waste may be available for damage done to the property by one cotenant, but exploitation of natural resources ordinarily gives rise to an action for accounting for profits rather than an action for waste.[7]

Some of the most difficult problems in tenancies in common and joint tenancies surround the question whether a cotenant who uses or occupies the property has to account to the others for the value of her use or occupation. The majority rule is that she does not, unless she "ousts" the other cotenants.

MARTIN v. MARTIN

Court of Appeals of Kentucky
878 S.W.2d 30 (Ky. Ct. App. 1994)

JOHNSTONE, J. Garis and Peggy Martin appeal from a judgment of the Pike Circuit Court which required them to pay rent to the cotenants of certain real estate. Reluctantly, we reverse.

Garis and Peggy own an undivided one-eighth interest in a tract of land in Pike County. This interest was conveyed to Garis by his father, Charles Martin, in 1971. Appellees, Charles and Mary Martin, own a life estate in the undivided seven-eighths of the property for their joint lives, with remainder to appellants.

---

5.   *See, e.g.*, Combs v. Ritter, 223 P.2d 505 (Cal. Ct. App. 1950).

6.   This is the traditional rule, but it may have been modified in some states. The extent to which the state will intervene to settle disputes between married couples is the subject of courses in family law or marital property.

7.   A cotenant, unlike a life tenant, usually is an owner in fee simple and has the right to exploit the natural resources on the property.

Charlie improves property

In 1982, Charles Martin improved a portion of the property and developed a four-lot mobile home park which he and Mary rented. In July of 1990, Garis and Peggy moved their mobile home onto one of the lots. It is undisputed that Garis and Peggy expended no funds for the improvement or maintenance of the mobile home park, nor did they pay rent for the lot that they occupied.

Garis moved on land improved, paid no rent. or $ for improve

In 1990, Garis and Peggy filed an action which sought an accounting of their claimed one-eighth portion of the net rent received by Charles and Mary from the lots. The accounting was granted; however, the judgment of the trial court required appellants to pay "reasonable rent" for their occupied lot. It is that portion of the judgment from which this appeal arises.

Garis wanted to renue portion of their rent

PP

The sole issue presented is whether one cotenant is required to pay rent to another cotenant. Appellants argue that absent an agreement between cotenants, one cotenant occupying premises is not liable to pay rent to a co-owner. Appellees respond that a cotenant is obligated to pay rent when that cotenant occupies the jointly owned property to the exclusion of his co-owner.

issue.
Garis argued.
Charles = pay rent if coowner excluded.

Appellants and appellees own the subject property as tenants in common. The primary characteristic of a tenancy in common is unity of possession by two or more owners. Each cotenant, regardless of the size of his fractional share of the property, has a right to possess the whole.

|||

The prevailing view is that an occupying cotenant must account for outside rental income received for use of the land, offset by credits for maintenance and other appropriate expenses. See Barnes v. Kidwell, 245 Ky. 740, 54 S.W.2d 331 (1932). The trial judge correctly ordered an accounting and recovery of rent in the case *sub judice.*

However, the majority rule on the issue of whether one cotenant owes rent to another is that a cotenant is not liable to pay rent, or to account to other cotenants respecting the reasonable value of the occupancy, absent an ouster or agreement to pay. 51 A.L.R.2d 413 § 8; *see also* Taylor v. Farmers and Gardeners Market Association, 295 Ky. 126, 173 S.W.2d 803 (1943)....

majority rule?

The appellees reason that the award of rent was proper upon the premise that Garis and Mary [Peggy? — EDS.] ousted their cotenants. While the proposition that a cotenant who has been ousted or excluded from property held jointly is entitled to rent is a valid one, we are convinced that such ouster must amount to exclusive possession of the entire jointly held property. We find support for this holding in *Taylor, supra,* in which the Court stated, 173 S.W.2d at 807-08:

> But, however this may be, running throughout all the books will be found two essential elements which must exist before the tenant sought to be charged is liable. These are: (a) That the tenant sought to be charged and who is claimed to be guilty of an ouster must assert *exclusive* claim to the property in himself, thereby necessarily including a denial *of any* interest or any right or title in the supposed ousted tenant; (b) he must give notice to this effect to the ousted tenant, or his acts must be so open and notorious, positive and assertive, as to place it beyond doubt that he is claiming the *entire* interest in the property. (Emphasis in original.)

① exclusive claim to property,
② notice of ouster

We conclude that appellants' occupancy of one of the four lots did not amount to an ouster. To hold otherwise is to repudiate the basic characteristic of a tenancy in common that each cotenant shares a single right to possession of the entire property and each has a separate claim to a fractional share. 4a Richard R. Powell, *Powell on Real Property* § 601 (1986).

Holding

Accordingly, the judgment of the Pike Circuit Court is reversed as to the award of rent to the appellees.

Notes and Questions

1. Why should Garis and Peggy be entitled to rents received from the mobile home lots that Charles and Mary developed? The English Statute of Anne, enacted in 1704, is generally followed in the United States, either as part of the received common law or because a similar statute has been enacted. The statute, which changed the earlier rule that a cotenant was not liable to the other cotenants for rents received, authorizes actions of account by any cotenant against another cotenant "for receiving more than comes to his just share or proportion."

2. In the accounting, Garis and Peggy sought one-eighth of the "net rent." What expenses should be deducted in arriving at net rent? Should they be charged with one-eighth of the costs of developing the mobile home park? The usual rule is that a cotenant is not entitled to contribution from the other cotenants for the costs of improving the property. However, on partition, the improving cotenant is entitled either to the part of the property that has been improved or to the increase in value of the property due to the improvement. Should that rule be applied in this situation?

3. The court follows the majority rule that a cotenant in possession is not liable to pay rent or account for the reasonable value of his occupancy unless he ousts the other cotenant. Can you think of any justifications for this rule other than the formal argument that each cotenant has the right to possession? If Charles and Mary, rather than Garis and Peggy, lived on one of the lots, should they have to pay rent? If Charles and Mary also paid all the taxes, and other carrying charges for the property, should Garis be entitled to deduct the value of Charles and Mary's use and occupation from the amount he and Peggy are required to contribute?

ESTATE OF HUGHES v. PATTON

California Court of Appeal
5 Cal. App. 4th 1607, 7 Cal. Rptr. 2d 742 (1992)

WIENER, Acting Presiding Justice. When Kathryn Marlow Hughes died on February 12, 1975, she and her husband George Ervin Hughes had been living in her separate property residence at 3438 Browning Street in San Diego. The house was worth about $45,000. Upon her death George, as a spouse omitted from Kathryn's November 15, 1965, will admitted to probate, acquired a one-third interest in the property pursuant to then Probate Code section 70. . . .[8] The named beneficiaries under the will, Kathryn's two children, Victoria Wiseman and Charles Marlow, received the balance in equal shares. George, and later when he remarried, with his wife Sylvia, continued to live in the residence. Although they paid the monthly installments on the note secured on

---

8.   Spouse not named or provided for in will took an intestate share of the estate. — EDS.

the property they paid no additional rent. When George died on November 26, 1986, Sylvia remained in the house until July 31, 1988, living there rent-free until July 22, 1987, when the court ordered her to pay a monthly rental of $350.

This appeal . . . questions the [probate] court's determination that Sylvia Hughes, both individually and in her fiduciary capacity as Executrix of the Estate of George E. Hughes, was not liable for the rent. . . . [W]e disagree with its ruling that the conduct of George as a cotenant in possession of the residence never constituted an ouster of the remaining cotenants . . . [and] reverse the order for further proceedings consistent with this opinion.

I

No particular purpose is served by our setting out the lengthy procedural history of this case and the inordinate time it has taken to determine the interest of a surviving spouse in a residence owned by his deceased wife. One can only ponder why it has taken about 15 years to determine that as a pretermitted heir George, and now his estate, is entitled to a one third interest in Kathryn's net estate when that conclusion appears to have been self-evident shortly after Kathryn died. Perhaps what occurred here only proves the spirit of Dickens' *Bleak House* and its celebrated case of Jarndyce v. Jarndyce is still with us, notwithstanding court delay reduction statutes and revised probate procedures. But rather than ruminating on the delay, . . . we are better served by examining the report filed . . . [by the referee appointed] to assist the court with respect to the various issues raised by the pleadings . . . .

II

. . . The report reflects that had a reasonable rental been charged against George, his one-third interest in Kathryn's estate would have been reduced by $84,275.87. And even though Kathryn's modest residence was reappraised in January 1990 at $256,000, about 5 times its value 15 years earlier, the court's decision not to offset the accrued rent from George's one third interest materially affected Kathryn's two children, the other beneficiaries of her estate who have since assigned their interest to James M. Kinder,[9] the aggrieved party for whose benefit . . . [the administrator] appeals. . . .

. . . Absent an ouster a cotenant out of possession has no right to recover the rental value of the property from a cotenant in possession . . . . Thus the crucial issue here is whether the probate court correctly decided George's conduct, including both his occupancy of the property and the court proceedings he instituted, did not constitute an ouster.

---

9. Googling James M. Kinder turns up information about someone of that name who owns a car rental business in San Diego and has been labeled a vexatious litigant because he brings so many frivolous claims. *See* http://www.sandiegoreader.com/weblogs/financial-crime-politics/2010/oct/19/vexatious-litigant-loses-appeal/. *See also* Kinder v. Allied Interstate, Inc., 2010 WL 2993958 (Cal. Ct. App. 2010), *cert. denied,* 131 S. Ct. 2447 (2011) (upholding finding that he is a vexatious litigant) and Loshonkohl v. Kinder, 135 Cal. Rptr. 2d 114 (Cal. Ct. App. 2003), *cert. denied* (2004) (judgment for $350,000 for defaming a police officer upheld) — EDS.

III

A

"An ouster, in the law of tenancy in common, is the wrongful dispossession or exclusion by one tenant of his cotenant or cotenants from the common property of which they are entitled to possession." . . . Whether there has been an ouster is a legal question. . . .

Sometimes the facts will make it clear an ouster has occurred. For example in Zaslow v. Kroenert, . . . [Cal. 1946] the trial court and later the appellate court had no difficulty deciding that changing the locks on the doors, posting "no trespassing" signs on the property and denying the cotenant admittance on demand was an ouster. . . . The facts, however, are not always so easy and sometimes it is quite difficult for the cotenant in possession to decide whether there is an obligation to account to a cotenant or cotenants not in possession. "The practical borderline between privileged occupancy of the whole by a single cotenant and unprivileged greedy grabbing which subjects the greedy one to liability to his cotenants is not crystal clear." (4A R. Powell, *The Law of Real Property*, § 603, p. 610 (1982).)

The problems associated with the difficulty of establishing an ouster prompted the California Law Revision Commission in 1983 to recommend a statutory procedure to simplify the process. . . . Adopting the recommendation in 1984 the Legislature enacted Civil Code section 843 permitting a cotenant out of possession to make a written demand for concurrent possession of the property. An ouster is established if within 60 days after service of the demand, "the tenant in possession does not offer and provide unconditional concurrent possession of the property to the tenant out of possession." . . .

Our discussion of the legislative history of Civil Code section 843 is not to criticize the . . . beneficiaries for failing to use this provision, but rather to emphasize the difficulties associated with determining when an ouster has occurred. The decision is particularly difficult in a case like the one before us where the conduct of the cotenant in possession for a substantial period consisted solely of his residing in the estate property, manifesting neither an intent to share possession nor to deprive other cotenants from sharing possession. In this . . . setting where the cotenants out of possession have the burden of establishing an ouster, the referee and later the court properly decided that absent any evidence George actually excluded Victoria or Charles, it could not find an ouster. . . . We therefore agree with the court that "George . . . did not physically oust VICTORIA and CHARLES nor [was there] any request to permit them to occupy the premises with him . . . ."

IV

The more troublesome question is whether the referee and later the court correctly analyzed the effect of George's community property petition filed on September 15, 1982 . . . , alleging that because the residence was community property he was entitled to 100 percent of the property as the surviving spouse. Under this theory Kathryn's two children did not acquire any interest in the property. The referee dealt with this issue in the following manner:

"... [D]oes the fact that GEORGE filed a petition seeking to have the entire property set aside to him as community property amount to ouster or exclusion? Although no cases were found dealing with this question, it is difficult to see how it could do so, on policy grounds. Where a co-tenant has an unquestioned right to an undivided part interest in property and a colorable claim to the entire property it is difficult to see how he could proceed more reasonably than to seek a judicial resolution of the matter. He should be encouraged not to resort to self-help and should not be penalized (by being held liable to his co-tenants for rent) by seeking (even unsuccessfully) to establish his claim to the entire property in a peaceable manner."

Although there is a certain appeal to the referee's rationale we believe it is at odds with the underlying concept of ouster. . . . [A]t common law ouster was established by a cotenant's unambiguous conduct manifesting an intent to exclude another cotenant from gaining or sharing possession of jointly owned property. Here George manifested a similar intent by categorically alleging in his petitions that he was the sole owner of the property and that Kathryn's two children had no interest in the property. . . . [W]e conclude the petitions were the functional equivalent of changing locks or posting "no trespassing" signs telling a cotenant out of possession that he or she may not enter the premises. It is one thing for the cotenant in possession to remain silent, but quite another for the cotenant to seek legal redress claiming entitlement to all the property to the exclusion of other claimants. . . .

In reaching this conclusion we disagree with the referee's observation that interpreting George's action in this manner penalizes the cotenant in possession because it will trigger an obligation to pay rent. Whenever an ouster occurs the rental obligation accrues. Consequently the manner of its accrual is irrelevant provided the cotenant in possession reasonably understands the effect of his or her behavior. In this case where George was represented by counsel when he filed his petition we believe he should suffer the detriment in addition to receiving any potential benefit associated with his petition.

In addition, the fact that ouster may occur in a peaceful, non-aggressive manner through lawful means is consistent with the policy underlying the 1984 legislation . . . . More significantly, however, ouster furnishes the tenant in possession a reciprocal benefit since it starts the time in which the tenant in possession will hold the property adversely. "While there is a presumption that the possession of one cotenant is amicable and permissive, and not adverse to his cotenants, this presumption is not conclusive. Thus, under certain circumstances, the exclusive possession of one cotenant can 'ripen' into title against the other cotenants if the occupying cotenant otherwise satisfies the requirements for title by adverse possession." (5 Miller & Starr, *Cal. Real Estate* 2d, § 12:9, p. 113.) . . .

Our conclusion . . . does not necessarily mean that his estate and/or Sylvia are liable for the rental accruing from the date the community property petition was filed. There may be other facts which will be presented to the trial court on remand which will affect the outcome of this case. The court may establish an equitable estoppel or waiver in light of the heirs' failure to seek a partition of the property, particularly where the delay and the substantial increase in the property's value have conferred an unexpected benefit to Kinder. There is, of course, the further possibility that George's estate may take a different tactical position on retrial, asserting his right to the property on a theory of adverse possession since he began to hold the property in a hostile manner from the date he filed his community property petition. If it should prevail, the matter of rent, the subject of this appeal, will become moot. . . .

Notes and Questions

1. All cotenants are usually required to contribute their share of the carrying charges on the property (taxes, mortgage payments, repairs, etc.) but most states allow the cotenants not in possession to claim a credit, or offset, for the value of the occupying cotenant's use or occupation of the property. The court in *Yakavonis v. Tilton*, 968 P.2d 908 (Wash. Ct. App. 1998), refused to adopt the offset rule because it is "contrary to the basic rights of cotenancy ownership," which give each cotenant the right to occupy the whole regardless of the size of his or her undivided share. Which is the better rule?

2. As the court says, it is sometimes difficult to know whether an ouster has occurred. From an examination of the cases, Evelyn Lewis concluded that the ouster concept has proved almost infinitely malleable, allowing courts to reach diametrically opposed conclusions on similar facts. To illustrate her point, she compares *Mauch v. Mauch*,[10] where the cotenants in possession of the family farm were held to have ousted their widowed sister-in-law by telling her they "didn't want to have her on the place" and that she "was not to come back," with *Fitzgerald v. Fitzgerald*,[11] where an ex-wife did not oust her ex-husband by telling him to leave the family home and that "she'd call the law." She also cites *Spiller v. Mackereth*, 338 So. 2d 859 (Ala. 1976) (lock change was not ouster), and *Morga v. Friedlander*, 680 P.2d 1267 (Ariz. Ct. App. 1984) (lock change was ouster), as evidence that courts use ouster to engage in the "equitable second-guessing that so often blurs crystalline rules."

Drawing further support from cases in which courts have developed and applied concepts of constructive and presumptive ouster, she concludes that the law of ouster is much less clear than the picture usually presented by legal treatises and judges' recitals of the law. The overall effect of the flexible ouster rules coupled with the majority rule allowing offset of the value of the occupying cotenant's possession in an action for contribution is practically to nullify the rule that any cotenant may occupy the premises rent free regardless of the size of his or her economic stake in the property. Evelyn Alicia Lewis, *Struggling with Quicksand: The Ins and Outs of Cotenant Possession Value Liability and a Call for Default Rule Reform*, 1994 Wis. L. Rev. 331, 360-80.

DELFINO v. VEALENCIS

Supreme Court of Connecticut
436 A.2d 27 (Conn. 1980)

HEALEY, J. The central issue in this appeal is whether the Superior Court properly ordered the sale . . . of property owned by the plaintiffs and the defendant . . . .

---

10. 418 P.2d 941 (Okla. 1966).
11. 558 So. 2d 122 (Fla. Dist. Ct. App. 1990).

   The plaintiffs, Angelo and William Delfino, and the defendant, Helen C. Vealencis, own, as tenants in common, real property . . . consist[ing] of an approximately 20.5 acre parcel of land and the dwelling of the defendant thereon. The plaintiffs own an undivided 99/144 interest in the property, and the defendant owns a 45/144 interest. The defendant occupies the dwelling and a portion of the land, from which she operates a rubbish and garbage removal business. Apparently, none of the parties is in actual possession of the remainder of the property. The plaintiffs, one of whom is a residential developer, propose to develop the property, upon partition, into forty-five residential building lots.

   In 1978, the plaintiffs brought an action . . . seeking a partition of the property by sale with a division of the proceeds according to the parties' respective interests. The defendant moved for a judgment of in-kind partition . . . . The trial court . . . concluded that a partition in kind could not be had without "material injury" to the respective rights of the parties, and therefore ordered that the property be sold at auction . . . and that the proceeds be paid into the court for distribution to the parties. . . .

   [The defendant appeals.]

   General Statutes § 52-495 authorizes courts of equitable jurisdiction to order, upon the complaint of any interested person, the physical partition of any real estate held by tenants in common, and to appoint a committee for that purpose.[7] When, however, in the opinion of the court a sale of the jointly owned property "will better promote the interests of the owners," the court may order such a sale under § 52-500. . . .

   It has long been the policy of this court, as well as other courts, to favor a partition in kind over a partition by sale. . . . The first Connecticut statute that provided for an absolute right to partition by physical division was enacted in 1720 . . . , the substance of which remains virtually unchanged today. Due to the possible impracticality of actual division, this state, like others, expanded the right to partition to allow a partition by sale under certain circumstances.[10] . . . The early decisions of this court that considered the partition-by-sale statute emphasized that "(t)he statute giving the power of sale introduces . . . no new principles; it provides only for an emergency, when a division cannot be well made, in any other way. . . . The court later expressed its reason for preferring partition in kind when it stated: "(A) sale of one's property without his consent is an extreme exercise of power warranted only in clear cases." Ford v. Kirk, 41 Conn. 9 (1874). Although under General Statutes § 52-500 a court is no longer required to order a partition in kind even in cases of extreme difficulty or hardship . . . , it is clear that a partition by sale should be ordered only when two conditions are satisfied: (1) the physical attributes of the land are such that a partition in kind is impracticable or inequitable; . . . and (2) the interests of the owners would better be promoted by a partition by sale. . . . Since our law has for many years presumed that a partition in kind would be in the best interests of the owners, the burden is on the party requesting a partition by sale to demonstrate that such a sale would better promote the owners' interests. . . .

   7.   If the physical partition results in unequal shares, a money award can be made from one tenant to another to equalize the shares. 4A Powell, Real Property P 612, pp. 653-54; 2 American Law of Property, Partition § 6.26, p. 113.

   10.   Connecticut's statute was passed in 1844. Public Acts 1844, c. XIII.

Under the test set out above, the court must first consider the practicability of physically partitioning the property in question. The trial court concluded that due to the situation and location of the parcel of land, the size and area of the property, the physical structure and appurtenances on the property, and other factors,[11] a physical partition of the property would not be feasible. An examination of the subordinate findings of facts and the exhibits, however, demonstrates that the court erred in this respect.

It is undisputed that the property in question consists of one 20.5 acre parcel, basically rectangular in shape, and one dwelling, located at the extreme western end of the property. Two roads, Dino Road and Lucien Court, abut the property and another, Birch Street, provides access through use of a right-of-way. Unlike cases where there are numerous fractional owners of the property to be partitioned, and the practicability of a physical division is therefore drastically reduced, in this case there are only two competing ownership interests: the plaintiffs' undivided 99/144 interest and the defendant's 45/144 interest. These facts, taken together, do not support the trial court's conclusion that a physical partition of the property would not be "feasible" in this case. Instead, the above facts demonstrate that the opposite is true: a partition in kind clearly would be practicable under the circumstances of this case.

Although a partition in kind is physically practicable, it remains to be considered whether a partition in kind would also promote the best interests of the parties. In order to resolve this issue, the consequences of a partition in kind must be compared with those of a partition by sale.

The trial court concluded that a partition in kind could not be had without great prejudice to the parties since the continuation of the defendant's business would hinder or preclude the development of the plaintiffs' parcel for residential purposes, which the trial court concluded was the highest and best use of the property. The court's concern over the possible adverse economic effect upon the plaintiffs' interest in the event of a partition in kind was based essentially on four findings: (1) approval by the city planning commission for subdivision of the parcel would be difficult to obtain if the defendant continued her garbage hauling business; (2) lots in a residential subdivision might not sell, or might sell at a lower price, if the defendant's business continued; (3) if the defendant were granted the one-acre parcel, on which her residence is situated and on which her business now operates, three of the lots proposed in the plaintiffs' plan to subdivide the property would have to be consolidated and would be lost; and (4) the proposed extension of one of the neighboring roads would have to be rerouted through one of the proposed building lots if a partition in kind were ordered. The trial court also found that the defendant's use of the portion of the property that she occupies is in violation of existing zoning regulations. The court presumably inferred from this finding that it is not likely that the defendant will be able to continue her rubbish hauling operations from this property in the future. The court also premised its forecast that the planning commission would reject the plaintiffs' subdivision plan for the

11.   These other factors included the present use and the expected continued use by the defendant of the property, the property's zoning classification, and the plaintiffs' proposed subdivision plans. We consider these factors later in the opinion.

remainder of the property on the finding that the defendant's use was invalid. These factors basically led the trial court to conclude that the interests of the parties would best be protected if the land were sold as a unified unit for residential subdivision development and the proceeds of such a sale were distributed to the parties. . . .

[Before considering whether these reasons were sufficient to overcome the preference for partition in kind, the court reviewed the evidence and concluded that there was not sufficient support for the court findings that defendant's use of the property violated existing zoning regulations, that she would not likely to be able to continue her business on the premises, and that the planning commission was not likely to approve plans for a residential subdivision if her business continued because she only used the property to store garbage trucks and dumpsters—no garbage was brought there.—Eds.]

The court's remaining observations relating to the effect of the defendant's business on the probable fair market value of the proposed residential lots, the possible loss of building lots to accommodate the defendant's business and the rerouting of a proposed subdivision road, which may have some validity, are not dispositive of the issue. It is the interests of all of the tenants in common that the court must consider . . . and not merely the economic gain of one tenant, or a group of tenants. The trial court failed to give due consideration to the fact that one of the tenants in common has been in actual and exclusive possession of a portion of the property for a substantial period of time; that the tenant has made her home on the property; and that she derives her livelihood from the operation of a business on this portion of the property, as her family before her has for many years. A partition by sale would force the defendant to surrender her home and, perhaps, would jeopardize her livelihood. It is under just such circumstances, which include the demonstrated practicability of a physical division of the property, that the wisdom of the law's preference for partition in kind is evident. . . .

Since the property in this case may practicably be physically divided, and since the interests of all owners will better be promoted if a partition in kind is ordered, we conclude that the trial court erred in ordering a partition by sale, and that, under the facts as found, the defendant is entitled to a partition of the property in kind.

Notes and Questions

1. *Favoring the cotenant attached to the land.* In deciding how to partition land, it is not unusual for a court to give more weight to the interests of a cotenant who has a particular attachment to the land than to one who does not. In *Eli v. Eli*, 557 N.W.2d 405 (S.D. 1997), the court ordered partition in kind of a 112-acre parcel of unimproved farmland over the objection of two of the three cotenants. Even though the trial court found that the land would sell for $50 to $100 more per acre if sold as a whole, the third cotenant wanted to keep a portion of land that had been in the family for almost a century, and had indicated a willingness to compensate the others if the remaining properties in fact sold for less. When partitioning property in kind, courts are also inclined to award cotenants

parcels that are adjacent to other land they own or that include improvements made by the cotenant. *See, e.g., Anderson v. Anderson,* 560 N.W.2d 729 (Minn. Ct. App. 1997) (cotenant awarded parcel on which cotenant had built a house); *Barth v. Barth,* 901 P.2d 232 (Okla. Ct. App. 1995) (cotenant's ownership of adjacent land properly considered).

In Louisiana, the rule is different. By statute, partition in kind is not allowed unless parcels of equal value can be created, and parcels must be drawn by lot. In *McNeal v. McNeal,* 732 So. 2d 663 (La. Ct. App. 1999), Lemmie McNeal and his second wife, Vela, owned 14 acres of property. When Lemmie died, his half passed to his 21 children, subject to Vela's usufruct (similar to a life estate) in the whole. Through various intra family conveyances, his son Elbert came to own 76 percent and ten other children, 24 percent. The children with 24 percent aggregated their interests and sued for partition. Elbert claimed the property could not be divided in kind, and the appellate court agreed. Because the parcel with the house was worth more than the rest, division could only be made by awarding Elbert the parcel with the house. This would violate the statutory requirement that four parcels of roughly equal value be created and distributed by having Elbert draw three and the other heirs draw one.

2. *Zoning and planning considerations.* The court in the principal case did not give much weight to the plaintiff's concerns about getting approval to subdivide the land. However, if partition in kind would result in lots that violate the applicable zoning ordinance, partition by sale will be ordered. *See, e.g., Friend v. Friend,* 964 P.2d 1219 (Wash. Ct. App. 1998). In *Withee v. Garnett,* 705 A.2d 1119 (Me. 1998), the court refused to allow partition in kind in favor of a cotenant who wanted to keep a piece of the land in the Garnett family because his portion of the lot would not meet the town's minimum lot size requirement.

3. *Owelty.* Partition in kind may be ordered even though the parcels are of unequal value if the differences can be compensated with offsetting payments, called owelty. In *Anderson v. Anderson,* 560 N.W.2d 729 (Minn. Ct. App. 1997), the court ordered parcels 1 and 2, with a combined fair market value of $614,000, set off to Bernhard and Lucille Anderson, who had built a house and garage on those parcels, and awarded parcels 3 and 4, with a combined market value of $261,900, to the other cotenants. The award to Bernhard and Lucille was conditioned on payment of $176,050 to the others. The other cotenants appealed, complaining that the trial court erred in refusing to include an adjustment for the capital gains taxes they would incur on account of the owelty payment. The court affirmed, holding that tax consequences should not be taken into account. The court reasoned that Bernhard and Lucille would themselves face capital gains taxes should they decide to sell their parcels.

4. Can a cotenant owning a very small share of the property force a partition by sale? The Connecticut Supreme Court, in *Fernandes v. Rodriguez,* 761 A.2d 1283 (Conn. 2000), overturned a Court of Appeal decision allowing the cotenant with the major interest, who wanted to keep the property, to buy out the tenant with the minor interest for the value of his equity. The Supreme Court held that under the Connecticut statutes, courts had no power to grant any remedy other than partition in kind or to order a sale followed by division of the proceeds.

LEG INVESTMENTS v. BOXLER

California Court of Appeal
183 Cal. App. 4th 484, 107 Cal. Rptr. 3d 519 (2010)

CANTIL-SAKAUYE, J. LEG Investments (LEG) owns a 50 percent undivided interest in a vacation home at Lake Tahoe as cotenant with Thomas and Donalee Boxler (the Boxlers). After disputes arose between the cotenants and LEG unsuccessfully tried to sell its interest, LEG sought a partition by sale. The trial court determined the right of first refusal in the tenancy in common (TIC) agreement waived the right to partition. . . . The court also awarded the Boxlers $86,955 in attorney fees based on the attorney fee provision in the TIC agreement.

LEG appeals . . . . We agree and reverse.

In 1976, Carl and Judith Bumpass and the Boxlers purchased . . . lakefront property at . . . Carnelian Bay, California . . . . Each couple owned a 50 percent undivided interest . . . as cotenants. In 1993, the Bumpasses transferred their interest in the Property to Raymond and Sharon Schwerdtfeger. The Schwerdtfegers and the Boxlers entered into the TIC agreement . . . .

Paragraph 6.1 provided in part: "If and when either Owner decides to sell their [i]nterest in the Property and that Owner receives a bona fide offer for its purchase from any other person or entity, the other Owner shall have the first right of refusal to purchase the selling Owner's Interest in the Property for the price and on the terms provided for in such bona fide offer." The remainder of paragraph 6.1 spelled out the procedure for accepting or refusing the right of first refusal. If the right was refused, "the selling Owner may enter into an agreement to sell the Interest to the offeror at the price and under terms no less favorable than those set forth in the notice of offer given to the other Owner."

The term of the TIC agreement was for 30 years from execution, with automatic five-year extensions until termination was agreed to by the owners. Paragraph 7.8 of the TIC agreement provided: "This Agreement shall be binding upon and inure to the benefit of the parties hereto, their heirs, devisees, transferees, executors, administrators, successors, assigns, and all other persons hereafter holding an Interest in the Property. The covenants herein shall be deemed to run with the land, both as to benefit and burden."

The TIC agreement provided the prevailing party in "any action between the parties seeking enforcement or interpretation of any of the terms and conditions of this Agreement" shall be awarded court costs and reasonable attorney fees. . . . A memorandum of the TIC agreement was recorded in Placer County.

In 1998, LEG purchased the Schwerdtfegers' interest in the property. LEG is a general partnership. Eppie Johnson is a general partner of LEG. . . .

Johnson claimed there were disputes and problems with the Boxlers as co-owners almost immediately after LEG's purchase. The Boxlers or their guests often failed to clean the Property and the Boxlers refused to pay for reasonable and necessary landscaping, maintenance, cleaning and repairs. In 2003, LEG offered to sell its interest in the Property or purchase the Boxlers' interest for $750,000. The Boxlers declined both offers.

In 2005, C.R. Gibb, a sophisticated real estate investor with many years of experience in the Lake Tahoe real estate market, offered to purchase LEG's interest in the Property for $1.4 million, subject to his approval of the Boxlers as co-owners. Pursuant to paragraph 6.1 of the TIC agreement, LEG transmitted

Gibb's offer to the Boxlers and offered them a right of first refusal to purchase LEG's interest on the same terms. The Boxlers declined. "We will not be exercising our right of first refusal for your bona fide offer of $1,400,000.00." After meeting with the Boxlers, Gibb determined they were unwilling to contribute to renovations and repairs. Gibb would not approve the Boxlers as co-owners and withdrew his offer to purchase.

In March 2006, LEG demanded the Boxlers agree to list the Property for sale or purchase LEG's interest. If neither option was acceptable, LEG would file an action for partition by sale. In response, counsel for the Boxlers stated his clients "would consider purchasing LEG Investments' one-half interest based upon an appraisal, provided there was an appropriate discount in the appraisal attributable to ownership of a fractional interest." . . .

In May 2006, LEG filed a complaint for partition by sale. . . . The complaint alleged partition by sale was more equitable than division in kind because it was impracticable to physically divide the Property. It further alleged, "The relationship between the parties has so deteriorated that the absolute right to partition by sale is the only available remedy. [D]efendants have refused to pay for and provide reasonable and necessary maintenance, cleaning, and repairs . . . ."

In the prayer, the complaint sought partition by sale of the property, expenses for litigation guarantee, title reports and partition, an accounting of expenses incurred, appointment of a receiver or broker for sale of the Property, and a preliminary and permanent injunction against waste.

The Boxlers . . . asserted four affirmative defenses: failure to state a cause of action; express contractual waiver of the right to partition; implied waiver of the right to partition; and unfairness. The affirmative defenses of waiver were based on the original parties' intention that the Property be used as a long-term vacation home and the provisions in the TIC agreement, particularly the right of first refusal. The Boxlers alleged partition was unfair because LEG had acquired the Property at a discount reflecting their fractional interest. A partition sale of the entire Property at nondiscounted value would result in a windfall to LEG and resulting unfairness to the Boxlers. . . .

[In support of its motion for summary adjudication or summary judgment], LEG . . . provided Johnson's declaration, in which he outlined the problems with the Boxlers, including their failure to clean the Property or to pay reasonable expenses, and LEG's attempts to sell their interest. Johnson declared that in 2003, the Boxlers refused to buy LEG's interest in the property or sell their interest for $750,000. In a 2006 deposition, Thomas Boxler testified that in 2003 he asked a realtor to determine the fair market value of the Property and the realtor determined its value was $3 million at that time. Johnson stated that the relationship between LEG and the Boxlers had so deteriorated that partition was the only remedy. He believed that due to "the difficulty of co-ownership of the property with the Boxlers, [no] potential buyer [would] approve the Boxlers as co-owners or purchase LEG's interest in the property for anywhere near [fair] market value."

In opposition, the Boxlers disputed LEG's interpretation of the TIC agreement. . . . They . . . argued their interpretation . . . [that it waived the right to partition] was supported by the historic conduct of the owners — always complying with the right of first refusal for every sale and not suing for partition.

In support of their motion [for summary adjudication or summary judgment], Thomas Boxler declared that "with the exception of the privately arranged purported contract between LEG and Mr. Gibbs [*sic*], no effort has been made by

Eppie Johnson or any other partner or representative of LEG to make the public aware of its desire to sell its one-half interest in the Property at the fair market value of that interest."

In opposition, LEG provided evidence that Boxler had been abusive to the prior owners, the Schwerdtfegers . . . . After the Boxlers refused to buy the Schwerdtfegers' interest for what they had paid for it, the Schwerdtfegers listed it for sale. The Boxlers refused to cooperate; Boxler even threatened to shoot a realtor. A potential sale fell through when the purchaser refused to approve the Boxlers as co-owners. During the sale to LEG, the Boxlers demanded the Schwerdtfegers return their personal property to the Property and extracted $15,000 from the Schwerdtfegers to close escrow. A realtor with 17 years' experience in the Lake Tahoe area declared Boxler "is the most difficult property owner I have ever encountered in my real estate career."

LEG also provided evidence that the Schwerdtfegers and their attorney, who drafted the TIC agreement, did not intend the right of first refusal to waive the right to partition. . . .

The [trial] court found the right of first refusal waived the statutory right to partition and granted the Boxlers' motion[s] for summary adjudication [and attorney fees] . . . .

DISCUSSION

. . . A co-owner of property has an absolute right to partition unless barred by a valid waiver. . . . "An agreement giving rights of first refusal to the other tenants implies an agreement not to bring a partition action in lieu of a sale to the cotenants." (Harrison v. Domergue (1969) 78 Cal. Rptr. 797.) . . .

[None] of the many cases cited by the parties present the factual situation found here: a cotenant desires to sell his interest and receives an offer from a third party; the selling cotenant complies with the right of first refusal, but the other cotenant declines to exercise the right; after the proposed sale falls through, the selling cotenant seeks partition. . . . [W]e must determine whether the right of first refusal absolutely waives the right of partition for the term of the TIC or whether the right of first refusal merely modifies the right of partition to require the selling cotenant to first offer to sell to the nonselling cotenant on terms as favorable as those offered by a prospective buyer.

. . . In Harrison v. Domergue, the court found the "apparent purpose" of a similar right of first refusal was "to retain for [the original parties] control of the admission of new co-owners." The Boxlers offer a second purpose. They contend the right of first refusal gave the nonseller cotenant the right to purchase the selling cotenant's interest at the price of a fractional interest. The trial court . . . adopted this reasoning . . . .

Interpreting the right of first refusal in the TIC agreement to permit partition after the nonselling cotenant has declined to exercise the right of first refusal and the proposed sale to a third party has fallen through would not be contrary to either of these purposes. The nonseller could control ownership of the property by exercising its right of first refusal. Further, exercising the right of first refusal would give the nonseller the right to purchase the selling cotenant's interest at the market price for a fractional interest; that price would be set by the third party bona fide purchaser.

. . . The trial court expressed concern the selling cotenant could set up a bogus third party sale. This concern can be addressed by the nonseller challenging the bona fide nature of the third party offer. The Boxlers failed to make that challenge. . . .

Construing the right of first refusal as a perpetual—at least for the term of the TIC agreement—implied waiver of the right to partition is a disfavored interpretation. . . . Construing the implied waiver as continuing throughout the term of the TIC agreement, despite compliance with the right of first refusal, would restrict alienation of the Property. . . . LEG presented evidence to support its position that Mr. Boxler was a difficult owner and no potential purchaser would approve the Boxlers as co-owners, thereby preventing LEG from selling its interest in the Property. The policy behind a partition action is to permanently end all disputes about property and to remove all obstructions to its free enjoyment. . . . The interpretation of the implied waiver advanced by the Boxlers and accepted by the trial court would defeat this policy. . . .

DISPOSITION

The judgment and the order awarding the Boxlers attorney fees are reversed. The trial court is directed . . . to enter a new order granting LEG's motion for summary adjudication on its first cause of action for partition by sale . . . [and] to enter an interlocutory judgment directing partition of the Property by sale. LEG shall recover its costs on appeal. . . .

Notes and Questions

1. The Boxlers argued that LEG will receive an undeserved windfall if allowed to partition the property by sale. Were they correct?

2. What concerns would you raise with someone considering buying a recreational property with co-owners? What advice would you give about how to handle those concerns?

3. Concerned over the conversion of rental units by home buyers acquiring multiunit buildings as TIC with agreements giving each owner an exclusive right of occupancy (ERO) of a particular unit, San Francisco adopted an ordinance forbidding ERO agreements and providing that all owners had a right of access to all units. The ordinance was held unconstitutional as a violation of California's right of privacy in *Tom v. City and County of San Francisco*, 16 Cal. Rptr. 3d 13 (Ct. App. 2004).

C.   JOINT TENANCY WITH RIGHT OF SURVIVORSHIP: CREATION AND SEVERANCE

Although joint tenancy is a very old form of ownership and fell into disfavor a century or two ago, it is very popular today because it provides a cheap and accessible will substitute: It passes property to the surviving joint tenant without the expense or hassle of probate proceedings. In addition, it usually passes the property free of any debts created by the deceased joint tenant. It does, however, suffer from drawbacks, which are often insufficiently appreciated. If the owner of property places it into joint tenancy with another, except in the case of joint bank accounts, an immediate gift is ordinarily made of an undivided one-half interest in the property. In the absence of a contrary agreement, the donee can immediately sell or transfer his or her interest in the property, or seek partition, regardless of the interests of the donor. A creditor of the donee may also reach the donee's interest in satisfaction of a judgment lien during the donee's lifetime. The donor who is interested in avoiding probate but does not really want to make a present gift of an interest in the property is well advised to use a "POD" (pay on death) designation in the many states where those are now recognized[12] and a revocable inter vivos trust where they are not.[13]

In situations where the owner of property does intend to make a present gift, or the parties purchase the property together, joint tenancy may work very well. However, there is another drawback: The survivorship right may be susceptible to destruction in unexpected ways. Any joint tenant can deliberately destroy the survivorship right as to his or her share by converting his or her interest to a tenancy in common, but this is not necessarily a problem.[14] The problem is that by entering into a lease or mortgage without the joinder of the other cotenants, one cotenant can destroy the survivorship right without intending to and without understanding that the destruction has occurred until it is too late to do anything about it (i.e., the tenant's death). The ability to destroy a joint tenancy (resulting in conversion of the relationship to a tenancy in common) arises out of the "four unities"—requirements for creating and maintaining a joint tenancy that were formulated in the 14th century.[15]

- Time—the interests of the joint tenants must vest at the same time.
- Title—the joint tenants must acquire their interests by the same instrument.
- Interest—the joint tenants must have estates of the same type and duration.[16]
- Possession—the joint tenants must have undivided interests in the whole.

In addition to the four unities, 19th century statutes adopted to reverse the old common-law presumption that a conveyance to two or more grantees created a

---

12.   A POD designation is a perfect will substitute because it creates no present interest in the named beneficiary, is fully revocable, and passes the property to the named beneficiary without going through probate.

13.   Revocable inter vivos trusts are described in Chapter 5.

14.   Wills, too, are fully revocable until death. If the parties want an irrevocable right of survivorship, they can either make a contract to that effect or create an irrevocable trust.

15.   *See* Anne L. Spitzer, *Joint Tenancy with Right of Survivorship: A Legacy from Thirteenth Century England*, 16 Tex. Tech. L. Rev. 629 (1985).

16.   The unity of interest has often been misunderstood by modern writers who believe it means that joint tenants must have equal economic shares in the property. Blackstone, citing Coke on Littleton, explains that unity of interest means: "they must have one and the same interest. One joint-tenant cannot be entitled to one period of duration or quantity of interest in lands, and the other to a different: one cannot be tenant for life, and the other for years: one cannot be tenant in fee, and the other in tail." 2 Commentaries 181 (Legal Classics Library Special Ed. 1983).

joint tenancy sometimes trip up people who try to create joint tenancies without good legal advice. However, modern courts usually are able to effectuate the parties' intent to create a joint tenancy so long as they have complied with the Statute of Frauds.[17]

DOWNING v. DOWNING
Court of Appeals of Maryland
606 A.2d 208 (Md. 1992)

CHASANOW, J. In 1948, Helen Downing and her husband John Downing bought an 88-acre farm in Carroll County, Maryland. They had two children, John Robert Downing and Bonnie Lynn Downing. When John Sr. died, Helen became the sole owner of the family farm.

On August 7, 1972, several years after John Sr.'s death, Helen conveyed the farm to a "straw man,"[1] Stanford Hoff, "his heirs and assigns forever in fee simple." Hoff immediately reconveyed the property "unto HELEN S. DOWNING, widow, and JOHN ROBERT DOWNING, as joint tenants, their heirs and assigns, forever in fee simple." . . .

Prior to the conveyances of August 7, 1972, Helen, assisted by John Jr., negotiated an oral agreement with John Myers (Myers) whereby Myers was permitted to grow and harvest crops on arable portions of the property in exchange for payments to Helen. This agreement did not entitle Myers to exclusive possession of the farm, only to raise and harvest crops on the land. The deed to Hoff is silent about this arrangement, as is the deed from Hoff to Helen and John Jr. Following the August 1972 conveyances, with John Jr.'s concurrence, Helen continued to receive all of the farm rent payments from Myers. From time to time John Jr. consulted with Myers about his cultivation methods to make sure the land was being properly cared for. Myers continues to raise crops there to this day.

Helen subsequently married Gordon Cullison. On October 31, 1985, Helen and John Jr. executed a mortgage of the property in favor of the Union National Bank. . . .

Helen died on January 15, 1987. In her will, she made specific bequests to various family members, including her second husband and her descendants, but made no mention of the farm. The residue of the estate was to go half to John Jr. and half to Bonnie. . . . Bonnie, as personal representative of her mother's estate, filed a complaint seeking to have the 1972 deed construed as creating a tenancy in common. Under such an arrangement, the family farm would not go solely to her brother, but an undivided one-half would be placed in her mother's estate.

---

17. To create or transfer an interest in land, a written instrument is required.

1. "The old common law rule that a grantor could not create a joint tenancy by conveying to himself and another (or others), or by conveying an undivided interest to another, generally has been evaded by conveying the entire estate to a third party 'straw man' who, by prearrangement, then conveys the estate back to the entire group of intended joint tenants (including the grantor)." Roger A. Cunningham, The Law of Property, § 5.3, at 206 (1984). *But see* Maryland Code (1974, 1988 Repl. Vol., 1991 Cum. Supp.), Real Property Article, § 4-108 abolishing the need for straw deeds in certain cases.

[An evidentiary hearing was held before a master.—EDS.] . . . The master concluded that no joint tenancy ever came into being because "[t]he chief incident of a joint tenancy is the right of survivorship. Such is not spelled out in this deed." The master also noted that the mortgage and farming arrangement would have destroyed a joint tenancy in any event.

. . . The circuit court concluded that the deed created a joint tenancy but that the subsequent mortgage executed by both joint tenants severed the joint tenancy. Therefore, the court agreed with the master that the family farm is "owned by John R. Downing and the Estate of Helen S. Downing (Cullison) as tenants in common." John Jr. appealed from this order to the Court of Special Appeals. We granted certiorari on our own motion prior to consideration by the Court of Special Appeals. . . .

Joint tenancy means that each joint tenant owns an undivided share in the whole estate, has an equal right to possess, use, and enjoy the property, and has the right of survivorship. . . . At common law, there were four unities necessary for the creation of a valid joint tenancy. . . .

For the purposes of this case, the crucial distinction between a joint tenancy and a tenancy in common is the right of survivorship identified with a joint tenancy. . . .

"At common law it was presumed that a conveyance to two or more persons created a joint tenancy." Alexander v. Boyer, 253 A.2d at 363 [1969]. Chapter 162 of the Acts of 1822 reversed the common law and declared joint tenancy to be disfavored in Maryland . . . . Chapter 162's embodiment in effect at the time of the August 7, 1972 deed was Maryland Code Article 50, § 9, which provided, "No deed, devise or other instrument of writing shall be construed to create an estate in joint tenancy, unless in such deed, devise or other instrument of writing it is expressly provided that the property hereby conveyed is to be held in joint tenancy."

[handwritten margin note: at common law changed.]

Bonnie tells us that she has found no Maryland decision that "flatly states that the term, 'joint tenants,' standing alone, is sufficient to overcome the disfavor with which joint tenancies are viewed in Maryland." This Court has held that in the case of a joint tenancy, it must be so clearly expressed as to leave no doubt about the parties' intention. . . . However, we believe that when a deed uses the words "joint tenants," as does the instrument in the instant case, this language can be sufficient to establish that the property granted is to be held in joint tenancy.[5]

In McManus v. Summers, 430 A.2d 80 (Md. 1981), we held that although joint tenancies are disfavored, a clear manifestation of intent to create a joint tenancy will be effectuated. In *McManus*, Dollie Collins went to Texas to procure

---

5.   Bonnie does not argue that the words "heirs and assigns" are at odds with the right of survivorship associated with a joint tenancy and therefore create an ambiguity. The Court of Special Appeals, in Gardner v. Gardner, 25 Md. App. 638, 335 A.2d 157, *cert. denied*, 275 Md. 748 (1975), concluded the words "heirs and assigns" are not ambiguous. Chief Judge Robert C. Murphy of this Court, specially assigned to the intermediate appellate court in the *Gardner* case, wrote, "[t]he words are merely descriptive of the estate conveyed—a fee simple. . . . The words 'heirs and assigns,' as one New York court has noted, 'are the usual technical words of conveyance granting a title in fee simple. At common law they were essential to the conveyance. They are unnecessary for that or any purpose . . . but when used in wills or deeds such is their meaning. They are merely words of limitation used to describe the nature of the estate given. . . .'" *Id.* 25 Md. App. at 644, 335 A.2d at 161 (*quoting In re* Denari's Will, 165 Misc. 450, 300 N.Y.S. 1279, 1283 (1937)). . . .

a divorce, later found to be invalid. Her husband, O. Thaxter Smith, believing the divorce to be valid, married Mary Smith. They subsequently purchased real estate in Montgomery County. "The deed referred to the 'parties of the second part' as 'O. THAXTER SMITH and MARY R. SMITH, his wife. . . .' The land in question was conveyed 'unto the said parties of the second part, in fee simple, as TENANTS BY THE ENTIRETY. . . . '" Upon the husband's death, his children by the first marriage argued that because the subsequent marriage was invalid, this property was owned as tenants in common. We reasoned that

> "a tenancy by the entirety cannot be established unless the grantees are legally married." . . . It is true that under the predecessor of [Real Property Article] § 2-117 joint tenancies have been viewed with disfavor. . . . Although viewed with disfavor, it must be remembered that as to the formula for creation of joint tenancies . . . "[t]he [statutory] requirement is only one of clear manifestation of intention, not one of particular words . . .".

We held that "a conveyance to two persons described in that deed as husband and wife, which conveyance purported to be to them as tenants by the entirety, created a joint tenancy if the grantees in fact were not legally married." *McManus* concluded that a right of survivorship existed even when no right of survivorship was mentioned in the deed because the parties' intent was clear.

Helen and John Jr., in the instrument now before this Court, indicated that they intended to hold the property as joint tenants by language used in both the granting clause and the habendum clause. By using the words, "as joint tenants," they satisfied the requirements of the Real Property Article. The Court need look no further than the deed itself to conclude that a valid joint tenancy came into being.[6]

We now turn to the unities of time, title, interest, and possession required for the existence of a valid joint tenancy. Bonnie, in her brief, concedes that the unities of time and title are satisfied, but she argues that letting Myers farm the land destroyed the unities of interest and possession. Bonnie contends that because of the pre-existing farming agreement with Myers, the unity of interest was never met, and if met, was destroyed by the next annual renewal of the "lease" to Myers. Bonnie also argues that because the farming rights had been assigned to Myers, John Jr.'s right to possession was frustrated, and the unity of possession was destroyed.

The simple answer to Bonnie's contention with respect to the unity of interest is that the mere fact that Helen might have given Myers the right to farm the land does not preclude a joint tenancy. What Helen conveyed to Hoff and Hoff reconveyed to Helen and John Jr. was the fee simple estate subject to Myers' right to farm. Regardless of whether we categorize this farming right as a lease, license, or profit, it would not preclude a joint tenancy. A joint tenancy can be created in an estate less than an unencumbered fee simple estate. . . .

Nor does Helen's receipt of the rents, with John Jr.'s consent, destroy the unities of interest or possession. *See* Roger A. Cunningham et al., *The Law of Property* § 5.3 n. 38.5 (Supp. 1987). "[C]ourts have frequently held that the 'unity of

---

6. Had the author of the deed employed such language as, "as joint tenants with the right of survivorship" or "as joint tenants and not as tenants in common," the intent to create a joint tenancy would have been more readily apparent. . . .

possession' may exist even though by express agreement between the joint tenants one of them retains the exclusive right to the possession of, and/or income from, the jointly owned property." *See also* Porter v. Porter, 472 So. 2d 630 (Ala. 1985) . . . : "The mere temporary division of property held by joint tenants, without an intention to partition, will not destroy the unity of possession and amount to a severance of the joint tenancy."

The circuit court was wrong in concluding that the mortgage on the property by Helen and John Jr. destroyed the joint tenancy. A mortgage by a single joint tenant does destroy the unities of interest and title and this destroys the joint tenancy. . . . However, where all joint tenants join in the mortgage, none of the unities are destroyed, and there is no reason why the joint tenancy should not continue. . . .

Judgment of the circuit court for Carroll County reversed. . . .

Notes and Questions

1. Why did Mrs. Downing use a strawman when she wanted to put the farm into joint tenancy with her son John? Is there any reason why a modern court should insist that joint tenants take their title by the same instrument?

2. Sometimes people put their property, particularly bank accounts, into joint tenancy because they want someone else to be able to manage or have access to the property for their benefit in case they become ill or otherwise unable to handle their affairs. In such cases, the joint tenancy is said to be "for convenience" only and passes no beneficial interest in the property to the donee. Is this such a case?

3. The court holds that the mortgage did not sever the joint tenancy (destroy the survivorship right) because both joint tenants joined. It says, however, that if either joint tenant had acted alone to mortgage his or her interest in the farm, the joint tenancy would have been destroyed. Why should this be? If, indeed, Helen had decided to borrow money against her interest in the farm (and someone was willing to lend it to her), would that indicate that she didn't want the farm to go to John on her death? If she had retained sole ownership of the farm, and mortgaged it after making a will in which she left the farm to John, the devise to John would not be revoked. Why should it be different if she decides to use a joint tenancy instead of a will?

PEOPLE v. NOGARR

California District Court of Appeal
330 P.2d 858, 67 A.L.R.2d 992 (Cal. Dist. Ct. App. 1958)

NOURSE, J. *pro tem.* . . . The appellant, Elaine R. Wilson and Calvert S. Wilson, were husband and wife. On April 10, 1950, they acquired the real property in question as joint tenants and the record title remained in them as joint tenants until the death of Calvert. In July 1954 Elaine and Calvert separated. On October 11, 1954, Calvert executed his promissory note [in the sum of $6,440] to his parents, the respondents, Frank H. and Alice B. Wilson. . . . At the same time he executed and delivered to respondents a mortgage upon the real property in question. Elaine did not have knowledge of or give her consent to the execution of this mortgage. On June 23, 1955, Calvert died.

On May 8, 1956, the People of the State of California commenced an action to condemn the subject real property. By its complaint the condemner alleged that Elaine R. Wilson was the owner of the subject real property and that respondents were mortgagees thereof. By her answer Elaine alleged that she was the owner of the property, that respondents had no right, title or interest therein. Respondents by their answer alleged that they were the owners and holders of the mortgage executed by Calvert and prayed that the mortgage be satisfied from the proceeds of the condemnation award. By agreement the fair market value of the property was fixed at $13,800 and that amount together with interest was paid into court by the condemner. Thereafter trial was had as to the rights and interests of Elaine and the respondents. No formal findings were made by the court but by a memorandum ruling the court found that there was owing to respondents the sum of $6,440 upon the promissory note executed by Calvert and secured by the aforesaid mortgage and ordered that sum plus interest disbursed to respondents out of 50 per cent of the funds remaining in the hands of the trustee (the county clerk) after the payment of certain liens which were concededly a charge upon the joint estate. Judgment was entered accordingly. . . .

It is appellant's contention that execution of the mortgage by Calvert did not operate to terminate the joint tenancy and sever his interest from that of Elaine but that the mortgage was a charge or lien upon his interest as a joint tenant only and that therefore upon his death his interest having ceased to exist the lien of the mortgage terminated and that Elaine was entitled to the distribution of the entire award exclusive of the sums distributed to other lienholders.

We have reached the conclusion that appellant's contention must be sustained. . . . It is undisputed in the present case that a joint tenancy in fee simple existed between Elaine and Calvert at the time of the execution of the mortgage, that at that time there existed all of the four unities, that consequently Elaine upon the death of Calvert became the sole owner of the property in question and under the doctrine of equitable conversion to the entire award in condemnation, unless the execution by Calvert of the mortgage destroyed one of the unities and thus severed the joint tenancy and destroyed the right of survivorship.

Under the law of this state a mortgage is but a hypothecation of the property mortgaged. It creates but a charge or lien upon the property hypothecated without the necessity of a change of possession and without any right of possession in the mortgagee and does not operate to pass the legal title to the mortgagee. Civ. Code, § 2920. . . .

Inasmuch as the mortgage was but a lien or charge upon Calvert's interest and as it did not operate to transfer the legal title, or any title to the mortgagees, or entitle the mortgagees to possession, it did not destroy any of the unities and, therefore, the estate in joint tenancy was not severed and Elaine and Calvert did not become tenants in common. It necessarily follows that as the mortgage lien attached only to such interest as Calvert had in the real property, when his interest ceased to exist the lien of the mortgage expired with it.

In Zeigler v. Bonnell, [126 P.2d 118, Cal. Ct. App.,] it was directly held that a judgment lien upon the interest of a joint tenant terminated on the death of the judgment debtor joint tenant. In so holding the court said:

> The right of survivorship is the chief characteristic that distinguishes a joint tenancy from other interests in property. The surviving joint tenant does not secure that right from the deceased joint tenant, but from the devise or conveyance by which the joint tenancy was first created. While both joint tenants are alive each has a specialized form of a life estate, with what amounts to a contingent remainder in the fee, the contingency being dependent upon which joint tenant survives. The judgment lien of respondent could attach only to the interest of his debtor, William B. Nash. That interest terminated upon Nash's death. After his death there was no interest to levy upon. Although the title of the execution purchaser dates back to the date of his lien, that doctrine only applies when the rights of innocent third parties have not intervened. Here the rights of the surviving joint tenant intervened between the date of the lien and the date of the sale. On the latter date the deceased joint tenant had no interest in the property, and his judgment creditor has no greater rights. . . . This rule is sound in theory and fair in its operation. When a creditor has a judgment lien against the interest of one joint tenant he can immediately execute and sell the interest of his judgment debtor, and thus sever the joint tenancy, or he can keep his lien alive and wait until the joint tenancy is terminated by the death of one of the joint tenants. If the judgment debtor survives, the judgment lien immediately attaches to the entire property. If the judgment debtor is the first to die, the lien is lost. If the creditor sits back to await this contingency, as respondent did in this case, he assumes the risk of losing his lien.

We are unable to distinguish between the effect of a judgment lien and of a lien of a mortgage executed by one joint tenant only. The only distinction between the two liens is that the mortgage lien is a lien upon specific property while the judgment lien is a general lien upon all real property of the judgment debtor. . . .

Respondents have directed our attention to decisions of other jurisdictions which they assert support their contention that a joint tenant has a right to mortgage his interest and that this operates to sever the joint tenancy. Examination of each of the cases relied upon by respondents discloses that all except one of them were rendered in jurisdictions where a mortgage operated not merely as a lien or charge upon the mortgagor's interest but as a transfer or conveyance of his interest, the conveyance being subject to defeasance upon the payment of the mortgage debt. It is evident that in those jurisdictions where a mortgage operates to convey title to the mortgagee, the unity of title is destroyed and in those jurisdictions where it operates not only to transfer title but the right of possession to the mortgagee, both the unity of title and of possession are destroyed and that in either case there is a severance of the joint tenancy. . . .

There is nothing inequitable in holding that the lien of respondents' mortgage did not survive the death of the mortgagor. Their note was payable upon demand and they could have enforced the lien and mortgage by foreclosure and sale prior to the death of the mortgagor and thus have severed the joint tenancy. If they chose not to do so but to await the contingency of which joint tenant died first they did so at their own risk. Under that event the lien that they had expired. If the event had been otherwise and the mortgagor had been the survivor the security of their lien would have been doubled.

The judgment is reversed.

Notes and Questions

1. Why does the surviving joint tenant take free from the mortgage? If Elaine and Calvert had held the property as tenants in common, and he had left her his interest in the property by will, she would have taken it subject to the mortgage. Is there any justification for allowing this special creditor exemption to people who choose to use joint tenancies rather than other forms of passing property at death?

2. What can a prospective lender to one joint tenant do to protect his or her security interest in the property in the event the borrower dies before paying off the loan?

3. Creditors of a joint tenant, like creditors of a tenant in common, can reach the assets of the cotenant during lifetime, and unless the asset is exempt from execution, the cotenant's interest can be sold to pay the debt. The effect of such a sale is to destroy the joint tenancy right of survivorship: The purchaser at the foreclosure sale becomes a tenant in common with the other owners of the property. Does this make sense? Would it make sense to destroy the right of survivorship when the debt was contracted rather than at the time of foreclosure?

4. When a prospective lender requires that both joint tenants assume liability for the debt, the creditor's lien is not affected by the death of either. While both debtors are alive, however, questions may arise as to the extent of the creditor exemptions they are entitled to. In *Commerce Bank v. Odell*, 827 P.2d 1205 (Kan. Ct. App. 1992), a creditor holding a judgment against two people sought execution against 240 acres of land they owned as joint tenants. Each joint tenant claimed a 120-acre homestead and claimed that the entire 240 acres was exempt from execution. The applicable statute provided:

> A homestead to the extent of 160 acres of farming land, or of one acre within the limits of an incorporated town or city, or a manufactured home or mobile home, occupied as a residence by the owner or by the family of the owner, or by both the owner and family thereof, together with all the improvements on the same, shall be exempted from forced sale under any process of law.

The court disagreed, holding that, together, they could only claim a total of 160 acres. Would the joint tenants have been well advised to partition the 240 acres voluntarily before filing their homestead claims?

SMOLEN v. SMOLEN
Supreme Court of Nevada
956 P.2d 128 (Nev. 1998)

PER CURIAM. Martin Smolen and respondent Roslyn Smolen married on March 1, 1970. In 1990, doctors diagnosed Martin with a brain tumor. Martin's physical health began to deteriorate. To protect their assets from liability for extensive, anticipated medical costs, the parties consulted a lawyer, who advised them to divorce.

On February 8, 1994, the district court entered a Decree of Divorce terminating the marriage and dividing the parties' property. In this decree, the district court ordered that "the following community property of the parties shall remain in joint tenancy: (i) Real property located at 3676 Pecos Road, Las Vegas, Nevada." This language reflects the parties' desire that the survivor retain ownership of the residence.

Martin and Roslyn lived together for nine months after the divorce, during which time Martin's health continued to deteriorate. In August 1994, doctors diagnosed Martin with degenerative brain disease, dementia, and atypical Parkinson's disease. In November 1994, Roslyn obtained temporary legal guardianship of Martin without his knowledge or consent.

On December 8, 1994, Roslyn put Martin in a group home, against his wishes. Martin . . . wished to remain at the couple's Las Vegas residence. Martin contacted his nephew, appellant Jason Smolen, an attorney in Virginia. Jason hired a Nevada attorney . . . ; this attorney filed a motion with the district court seeking to terminate Roslyn's temporary guardianship. Based on an April 19, 1995 hearing, the district court revoked Roslyn's temporary guardianship and found Martin competent to manage his person and estate.

On May 26, 1995, Martin established a revocable trust naming Jason sole beneficiary and successor trustee . . . [and] instructed Jason as to his wishes regarding the remainder of his estate. Martin executed a deed, dated May 31, 1995, by which he transferred his interest in the Las Vegas residence to this new trust. On July 4, 1995, Martin apparently suffered a stroke, which rendered him incapacitated and dependant upon life support.

Between Martin's July 4th stroke and his death on October 15, 1995, Martin resided at Sunrise Hospital. While Martin was . . . [there], Roslyn discovered that Martin had deeded his interest in the Las Vegas residence to Jason. She contacted Jason numerous times in an effort to compel him to deed Martin's interest in the property back to her. Jason claims that he offered several compromise proposals to Roslyn, in an attempt to resolve her concerns while carrying out his uncle's clearly articulated wishes. Roslyn rejected Jason's offers, including the opportunity to remain in the residence, cost free, for the rest of her life. On October 29, 1995, Roslyn retained counsel to assist her in this matter.

On December 29, 1995, Roslyn moved to cancel the May 31, 1995 deed. . . . [After a hearing,] the district court cancelled the . . . deed, . . . and ordered that ". . . [the Las Vegas residence] is to be returned to the community and deeded to the Plaintiff [Roslyn] as the survivor." Jason appealed . . . .

In her motion to cancel Martin's . . . deed, Roslyn successfully argued that upon entering into the divorce, Martin and Roslyn had an agreement that the surviving spouse would own 100 percent of the Las Vegas residence. Roslyn now argues that the district court's order that the property "shall remain in joint tenancy" reflects this understanding. Roslyn also argues that the district court's order expressly preserves the joint tenancy, and thus, impliedly prohibits its destruction. Consequently, Roslyn argues, the deed . . . violated the divorce decree and, therefore, was void. . . .

. . . [T]he district court's order stating that the property "shall remain in joint tenancy" created a joint tenancy replete with all characteristics attributable to this estate under the common law. One such characteristic is the power of any joint tenant to unilaterally transfer his interest and terminate the estate. The language of the divorce decree does not prohibit future transfer or alienation of the property. Thus, Martin severed the joint tenancy when he conveyed his interest in the Las Vegas residence to the new trust. This transfer . . . also created a tenancy in common between Roslyn and the new Martin Smolen trust. Upon

Martin's death, his interest in the Las Vegas property passed through the trust to Jason, rendering Jason a tenant in common with Roslyn.

Martin and Roslyn, like all joint tenants, possessed not only an interest in the joint tenancy but also the power to transfer such interest and sever the tenancy. Martin's transfer . . . did not violate the common law or the divorce decree.

Therefore, we conclude that the district court's order of February 9, 1996, cancelling the deed effecting Martin's transfer, contradicts the common law rule that such transfer is valid. Accordingly, we reverse . . . .

Notes and Questions

1. If you had represented Roslyn Smolen in the divorce proceeding, how could you have protected her survivorship interest in the house? Should the law have protected Roslyn's expectancy interest in Martin's half of the house? If so, how could that be done?

2. What are Roslyn's rights with respect to the house now? What advice would you give her?

3. *Effect of divorce on joint tenancy.* If the divorce decree had said nothing about the house, would the divorce have severed the joint tenancy? Technically, a decree of divorce need not affect title to land other than property held as tenants by the entirety or community property, but courts have seldom relied on the continued existence of the four unities in resolving the question. Although cases go both ways, most decisions are based on the intent of the parties rather than the four unities. *See* R.H. Helmholz, *Realism and Formalism in the Severance of Joint Tenancies,* 77 Neb. L. Rev. 1, 21 (1998). Statutes in most states provide that will provisions in favor of a spouse are revoked by divorce. Should these statutes be extended to survivorship rights in jointly held property?

4. *Unilateral severance of joint tenancies.* Martin destroyed the joint tenancy by making a conveyance in trust for himself for life with remainder to Jason. If his will left his property to Jason, could he have accomplished the same thing by executing a declaration of intent to terminate the joint tenancy, or a deed to himself? In *Riddle v. Harmon,* 162 Cal. Rptr. 530 (Ct. App. 1980), the court held that Frances Riddle had terminated a joint tenancy between herself and her husband by a deed that granted herself an undivided one-half interest in the property as tenant in common and recited that the purpose of the deed was to terminate the joint tenancy with her husband. Noting that she could have done the same thing by using a strawman, the court said:

> In view of the rituals that are available to unilaterally terminate a joint tenancy, there is little virtue in steadfastly adhering to cumbersome feudal law requirements. "It is revolting to have no better reason for a rule of law than that so it was laid down in the time of Henry IV. It is still more revolting if the grounds upon which it was laid down have vanished long since, and the rule simply persists from blind imitation of the past." (Justice Oliver Wendell Holmes, *Collected Legal Papers* (1920) p. 187.) Common sense as well as legal efficiency dictate that a joint tenant should be able to accomplish directly what he or she could otherwise achieve indirectly by use of elaborate legal fictions.

If the law permits, as it does, the revocation of wills, is there any reason to prohibit the revocation of survivor designations on joint tenancies or other kinds of will substitutes (life insurance, revocable trusts, POD designations)? Is there any reason to require notice to the erstwhile joint tenant or other beneficiary?

In response to the decision in *Riddle v. Harmon*, the California legislature enacted Cal. Civ. Code § 683.2:

> (c) Severance of a joint tenancy of record by deed, written declaration, or other written instrument pursuant to subdivision (a) [conveying title to a third person or executing a declaration of intent to sever the joint tenancy] is not effective to terminate the right of survivorship of the other joint tenants as to the severing joint tenant's interest unless one of the following requirements is satisfied:
>
> > (1) Before the death of the severing joint tenant, the deed, written declaration, or other written instrument effecting the severance is recorded in the county where the real property is located.
> >
> > (2) The deed, written declaration, or other written instrument effecting the severance is executed and acknowledged before a notary public by the severing joint tenant not earlier than three days before the death of that joint tenant and is recorded in the county where the real property is located not later than seven days after the death of the severing joint tenant.

Similar statutes are in effect in New York (N.Y. Real Prop. Law § 240-c(2) (McKinney)) and Minnesota (Minn. Stat. Ann. § 500.19(5)). They are designed, in part at least, to prevent a joint tenant from secretly executing a deed of severance and leaving it where it will be found at the time of death if he or she dies first but where it can be retrieved and destroyed if the other joint tenant dies first. Is this a good idea?

Modern Role of the Four Unities

Do the four unities in fact play any role in modern joint tenancy law? Should they? After examining cases decided since the 1950s, R.H. Helmholz concludes that although they are routinely mentioned in the cases, the four unities seldom play a decisive role in the cases if the intent of the parties can be ascertained: "The four unities continue to be invoked, but not where they would make a difference in the outcome. . . . [I]n the main, the four unities have been used . . . simply to reach an outcome that would also have been reached by enforcing the intent of the parties or applying some other legal rule."[18]

D.   MARITAL PROPERTY

The states may be divided roughly into two groups: (1) the "common law" states, which regard each person's earnings as his or her own, regardless of marital status, and (2) the "community property" states, which regard the earnings of

18.   R.H. Helmholz, *Realism and Formalism in the Severance of Joint Tenancies*, 77 Neb. L. Rev. 1, 7-8 (1998).

married people as belonging to the "community" comprised of the married couple. The community property system, introduced into the United States from the laws of Spain and France, is in effect in nine states: Arizona, California, Idaho, Louisiana, Nevada, New Mexico, Texas, Washington, and Wisconsin. In the common-law states, married people own their property individually (in severalty, to use the old term) unless they choose to put it into tenancy in common, joint tenancy, or tenancy by the entirety.[19] In the community property states, all property acquired by married people during marriage, except that acquired by gift, devise, or inheritance,[20] is community property, unless they choose to convert it into separate property and hold it individually, as tenants in common, or as joint tenants. The spouses hold equal undivided interests in community property. The underlying theory is that a marriage is a cooperative enterprise in which both spouses contribute directly or indirectly to the acquisition of property. Although spouses may convert community property into separate property (and vice versa), there is a strong presumption that any property possessed during the marriage belongs to the community.

Before 1948, residents of community property states enjoyed substantial income tax advantages, which led a number of common-law states to switch to community property systems. However, they switched back when the tax advantages were eliminated in 1948. More recently, the concept of marriage as a shared enterprise has had some appeal. The National Conference of Commissioners on Uniform State Laws promulgated the Uniform Marital Property Act in 1983, which is based on community property principles although it uses language of "marital property" instead of community property. Under the Act, which was adopted in Wisconsin in 1986, each spouse owns an undivided half of all property acquired from earnings during the marriage and may dispose of half the marital property by will. Even in states that have not adopted the community property concept of shared ownership during the marriage, many have adopted some form of equitable division of assets on divorce and provide a surviving spouse some share of the deceased spouse's assets at death.

Interesting questions sometimes arise as to what constitutes marital property. A number of cases have considered whether the value of professional degrees earned during marriage is subject to division on divorce. The answer generally has been "no" although the sacrifice of a spouse who supported the family while the other spouse went to school, coupled with the increased earning power of the spouse with the degree, may entitle the spouse to additional spousal support. *See, e.g., Simmons v. Simmons*, 708 A.2d 949 (Conn. 1998) (medical degree); *Martinez v. Martinez*, 818 P.2d 538 (Utah 1991). In New York, the value of celebrity status, as well as professional degrees, acquired during marriage may be taken into account in dividing a divorcing couple's assets. *See, e.g., Elkus v. Elkus*, 572 N.Y.S.2d 901 (App. Div. 1991) (celebrity value of opera star, Frederica von Stade); *O'Brien v. O'Brien*, 489 N.E.2d 712 (N.Y. 1985) (medical degree).

Other interesting questions arise with respect to the treatment of frozen ova, sperm, and embryos. In *Davis v. Davis*, 842 S.W.2d 588 (Tenn. 1992), the

19. Tenancy by the entirety is not recognized in many common-law states; nor is it recognized in any community property state.

20. States differ as to the status of the income from separate (noncommunity) property. In most of the states, the income remains separate, but in Idaho, Louisiana, and Texas, it is community property.

divorcing parties fought over the disposition of seven frozen embryos left over from unsuccessful in vitro fertilization attempts. The wife asked for custody so that she could make them available for adoption by others; the husband wanted them awarded to him so that they could destroyed. The court decided that they were neither children nor property, but an interim category entitled to "special respect because of their potential for human life." However, the husband's "right of procreational autonomy," his desire not to become a parent, prevailed. In *Hecht v. Superior Court*, 20 Cal. Rptr. 2d 275 (Ct. App. 1993), the court held that the decedent had the right to leave his frozen sperm by will to the woman he had lived with for five years; his former wife and children were not entitled to an order directing its destruction.

Rights of creditors of one spouse to collect against marital assets vary from state to state depending on the type of marital property recognized. The most protection is conferred by tenancy by the entirety regimes. *See, e.g., Sawada v. Endo*, 561 P.2d 1291 (Haw. 1977) (tenancy by the entirety property not subject to creditors of one spouse without consent of the other); *Keene v. Edie*, 935 P.2d 588 (Wash. 1997) (tort creditors of one spouse can reach community property if tortfeasor's separate property not sufficient to satisfy judgment); *Harris v. Crowder*, 322 S.E.2d 854 (W. Va. 1984) (judgment creditor of one spouse can reach that spouse's interest in family home held in joint tenancy and force partition only if the interest of the other spouse will not be prejudiced). Arkansas allows a judgment debtor to levy upon and sell a debtor's right of survivorship and entitlement to half the rents and profits from property owned in tenancy by the entirety with the debtor's spouse, but the creditor is not entitled to partition, and the spouse retains the right of possession. *Morris v. Solesbee*, 892 S.W.2d 281 (Ark. Ct. App. 1995).

At common law (the old English common law), a wife's rights at the death of her husband were determined by "dower" and a husband's rights at the death of his wife were determined by "curtesy." Dower gave the wife the right to a life estate in one-third of the lands of which her husband had been "seised" at any time during the course of the marriage. If her dower lands had not been specified at the church door before the marriage, the heir had 40 days after his father's death to designate the lands in which she had dower. Curtesy gave the husband a life estate in all of the wife's lands, but only if issue capable of inheriting the lands had been born alive. Although dower is often described as providing the primary source of support for widows, a very interesting recent study concludes that few women actually enjoyed dower rights after the 17th century:

> While the legal profession devoted considerable thought to the development of the law of dower between 1660 and 1833, an important object of its activity was to ensure that at least among the classes who married only after taking good legal advice, women could not claim dower. Some of the legal devices by which this was accomplished were capable of arousing the highest degrees of professional enthusiasm as "extremely ingenious," "skillful contrivances," and "masterstrokes of ingenuity." Toward the end of the period, when claims of dower were made they were frequently thought to be the unfortunate result either of drafting mistakes in settlements or deeds to real property or of women being misled by unscrupulous advice. Dower was, even in 1700, barrable in so many different ways and was apparently so often successfully barred (that is, the right of dower was prevented from attaching to the property) that it seems symptomatic of the general archaism

of eighteenth-century legal learning that so much is said [in the law books] about dower attaching.[21]

Dower and curtesy have been replaced in the United States by gender-neutral "forced" or "elective" shares in the deceased spouse's assets. The modern shares differ from the old common-law rights in that they apply to both real and personal property, but they apply to property owned at death rather than to all property owned during the marriage. In community property states, there is no forced share, but each spouse owns half of the community property accumulated during the marriage. Under the forced share statutes in effect in the common-law states,[22] a surviving spouse can elect to take against the deceased spouse's will and take a specified fraction of the estate instead. In most states, the share is one-third or one-half without regard to the length of the marriage, but the Uniform Probate Code now provides a sliding scale based on the length of the marriage.

Lawyers in the 20th century, like lawyers before them, have exercised a great deal of ingenuity to limit the ability of spouses to claim their statutory rights, but their efforts may be frustrated by the courts or legislatures. The Uniform Probate Code uses the concept of an "augmented estate" to subject to the surviving spouse's claims a variety of assets transferred by inter vivos transfers designed to bypass the probate process. Revocable inter vivos trusts no longer provide an easy way to avoid spousal claims.[23] Outright gifts before marriage often work, but they may be challenged.[24]

Premarital agreements limiting or waiving the unpropertied spouse's claims to spousal support or inheritance rights have long been used, and often successfully, but they, too, are sometimes challenged successfully. Shortly after the California Supreme Court upheld a prenuptial agreement in which Barry Bonds's wife signed away her rights to community property and spousal support a few hours before the wedding, *Marriage of Bonds*, 5 P.3d 815 (Cal. 2000), the California legislature amended Fam. Code § 1615 to provide stringent new protections for spouses not represented by independent legal counsel.

If these materials on marital property have piqued your curiosity, you will be able to learn more about these subjects in courses on wills and trusts, estate planning, and family law.

---

21. Susan Staves, Married Women's Separate Property in England, 1660-1833 at 28 (1990).

22. Georgia is the only non-community property state that does not provide the surviving spouse with an elective share.

23. *See, e.g.,* Sullivan v. Burkin, 460 N.E.2d 571 (Mass. 1984) (assets transferred by husband to revocable inter vivos trust will, in the future, be subject to claims of surviving spouse); Seifert v. Southern Nat'l Bank of S.C., 409 S.E.2d 337 (S.C. 1991) (surviving spouse entitled to elective share in assets transferred by husband to revocable inter vivos trust).

24. *See, e.g.,* Strong v. Wood, 306 N.W.2d 737 (Iowa 1981) (76-year-old farmer conveyed his farm to his children, reserving a life estate to himself, one month before marrying 66-year-old widow; widow's claim rejected for lack of proof that she relied on prospective property rights as inducement to marriage).

PART III

VOLUNTARY TRANSFERS
OF PROPERTY

The ability to transfer property is one of its most important attributes, giving the owner the means to make gifts or to make exchanges for investment and consumption purposes. Chapter 8 opens up the subject of lifetime gifts, introducing the basic concepts, and looking in some detail at outright inter vivos gifts and gifts made in contemplation of death. Chapter 8 touches on the trust and the will—two important gift-making mechanisms—but leaves more detailed treatment to the courses in trusts, wills, and estate planning. Chapter 9 covers the modern land transaction, tracing a typical real estate deal from initial contract through financing and closing. Chapter 9 also covers recording systems and title insurance, as well as other methods of protecting the buyer of real estate against defects in the seller's title.

Although property owners are generally free to transfer their property to whom they please, antidiscrimination law imposes important constraints on their ability to refuse to sell or rent their property to potential purchasers or renters on a variety of grounds including race, religion, marital status, sex, and handicap. The ability to enforce restrictive covenants and zoning laws that adversely affect people on these bases is also constrained. Chapter 10 explores these constraints.

CHAPTER 8

Lifetime Gifts That
Are Not in Trust

The law of lifetime gifts is part of a broader category known as "donative transfers," which also includes the law of wills, trusts, and will substitutes, subjects touched on in Chapters 5 and 7, which are covered in specialized courses in the usual law school curriculum. Although the word "gift" may properly be used to include testamentary transfers and transfers in trust,[1] as used in this chapter, it means a present outright[2] transfer of an interest in property made without consideration.[3]

All that is required to make an effective gift is that the donor transfer the property to the donee with the intention of making a gift. If the property is land, the intention to transfer the property must appear in a writing signed by the donor; otherwise, the intention may be expressed orally or inferred from the circumstances surrounding the transfer. For, example, if you leave a package wrapped in "Happy Birthday" paper on your friend's desk on her birthday, it will be readily inferred that you intended to make a gift. On the other hand, if you leave the same package on the checkout counter of the cafeteria, substantial additional circumstances would be required to show that you intended to make a gift to the cashier.

Complications arise when the available evidence does not clearly indicate whether or not a gift was intended and when the donor does something other than hand over either the property itself or a signed writing that transfers title to the property to the donee. Competing claims to the property frequently arise after the donor has died or become incapacitated, but sometimes arise when the transferor wants the property back. If the claimed donor transferred possession of the property to the claimed donee, the estate's (or rarely, the transferor's) claim is based on lack of donative intent. If the claimed donor did something other than transfer possession to the claimed donee, the estate's claim may be based either on lack of donative intent or on failure to comply with the formalities required for a donative transfer.

The law of inter vivos gifts lies between two doctrines that limit its scope: the doctrine that gratuitous promises (promises to make gifts) are not enforceable;

---

1. A transfer in trust means a transfer of property to a trustee to be held in trust for specified purposes or beneficiaries.
2. Outright in this context means that the transfer is not in trust.
3. Consideration, a concept studied in the law of contracts, basically means an identified quid pro quo. A transfer for consideration is an exchange, made as the result of an explicit bargain. A gift is a transfer made without an agreed-upon exchange.

and the doctrine that transfers taking effect at death (testamentary transfers) must be made by will. Although there has been substantial erosion of the latter doctrine in recent years as a wider range of will substitutes has become accepted, an oral gift of property to be effective "when I die" is still invalid. Much of the litigation over claimed lifetime gifts occurs at the margins of these two doctrines.

We begin with a look at cases exploring two fundamental propositions: Something more than intention is required to make a gift; and a gift, once made, is irrevocable unless an express or implied power to revoke has been reserved.

A. ORAL GIFTS

Although oral gifts of land have been invalid since adoption of the Statute of Frauds in 1677, oral gifts of personal property continue to be valid. Of course, if large sums are involved, or the terms are at all complicated, a written instrument should always be used. Whether or not an instrument of gift is used, however, something more is always needed to give effect to the intent to make a gift. That something more is described as "delivery."

IRONS v. SMALLPIECE
King's Bench
106 Eng. Rep. 467 (1819)

Trover for two colts. Plea, not guilty. The defendant was the executrix and residuary legatee of the plaintiff's father, and the plaintiff claimed the colts, under a verbal gift made to him by the testator twelve months before his death. The colts however continued to remain in possession of the father until his death.

It appeared further that about six months before the father's death, the son having been to a neighbouring market for the purpose of purchasing hay for the colts, and finding the price of that article very high, mentioned the circumstance to his father, and that the latter agreed to furnish for the colts any hay they might want at a stipulated price, to be paid by the son. None however was furnished to them till within three or four days before the testator's death. Upon these facts, Abbot[t], C.J. was of opinion, that the possession of the colts never having been delivered to the plaintiff, the property therein had not vested in him by the gift; but that it continued in the testator at the time of his death, and consequently that it passed to his executrix under the will; and the plaintiff was therefore non-suited.

ABBOTT, C.J. I am of the opinion that by the law of England, in order to transfer property by gift there must be either a deed or instrument of gift, or there must be an actual delivery of the thing to the donee. Here the gift is merely verbal, and differs from a *donatio causa mortis*[4] only in this respect, that the latter is subject to a condition, that if the donor live the thing shall be restored to him.

---

4. *Donatio causa mortis* means a gift in contemplation of death. — EDS.

Now it is a well established rule of law, that a *donatio causa mortis* does not transfer the property without an actual delivery. The possession must be transferred, in point of fact; and the late case of Bunn v. Markham, 2 Marsh. 532, where all the former authorities were considered, is a very strong authority upon that subject. There Sir G. Clifton had written upon the parcels containing the property the names of the parties for whom they were intended, and had requested his natural son to see the property delivered to the donees. It was therefore manifestly his intention that the property should pass to the donees; yet as there was no actual delivery, the court of Common Pleas held that it was not a valid gift. I cannot distinguish that case from the present, and therefore think that this property in the colts did not pass to the son by the verbal gift: and I cannot agree that the son can be charged with the hay which was provided for these colts three or four days before the father's death; for I cannot think that that tardy supply can be referred to the contract which was made so many months before.

HOLROYD, J. I am also of the same opinion. In order to change the property by a gift of this description, there must be a change of possession: here there has been no change of possession. If indeed it could be made out that the son was chargeable for the hay provided for the colts, then the possession of the father might be considered as the possession of the son. Here however no hay is delivered during a long interval from the time of the contract, until within a few days of the father's death; and I cannot think that the hay so delivered is to be considered as delivered in execution of that contract made so long before, and consequently the son is not chargeable for the price of it.

Notes and Questions

1. Although a physical delivery requirement seems consistent with what we know of "primitive" conveyancing practices, like the feoffment with livery of seisin, and probably was required in post-conquest English law, a dictum of Lord Coke in a 1675 case[5] cast doubt on the existence of a delivery requirement. The dictum was contradicted by the holding in *Irons v. Smallpiece* that there was a delivery requirement for inter vivos gifts (as well as gifts *causa mortis*), and the doubts were finally laid to rest in 1890 in *Cochrane v. Moore.*[6]

2. What is the significance of the discussion about the hay in *Irons v. Smallpiece?* What difference would it have made if the son had paid the expenses of keeping the colts after the claimed gift?

3. Was this decision fair to the son? To the father? What policies, if any, were advanced by the decision?

Function of the Delivery Requirement

Why require delivery? Although the delivery requirement probably originated with medieval notions of seisin, 19th and 20th century writers have constructed

---

5. Wortes v. Clifton, 1 Rol. Rep. 61, 81 Eng. Rep. 328 (1675).
6. 25 Q.B.D. 57 (1890).

a functional rationale for the requirement. Professor Phillip Mechem, in *Gifts of Chattels and of Choses in Action Evidenced by Commercial Instruments*, 21 Ill. L. Rev. 341, 348 (1926), and Professors Ashbel G. Gulliver and Catherine J. Tilson in *Classification of Gratuitous Transfers*, 51 Yale L.J. 1 (1941), suggested that delivery fulfills the following functions:

- *The Ritual Function*: It makes the significance of the gift vivid and concrete to the donor; and
- *The Evidentiary Function*: It provides unequivocal evidence of the gift to the actual witnesses of the transaction, and provides the donee with prima facie evidence in favor of the alleged gift.

The authors of both articles suggest that if other factors fill the functions performed by the delivery requirement, courts should uphold the gift even in the absence of delivery.

How well does the delivery requirement work in protecting property owners against fraudulent claims and careless statements? How well does it work in sorting out intended gifts from other transactions? Consider the following case notes:

Problem and Notes: Delivery

1. O bought a grand piano with his separate funds and placed it in the living room of the family home. Shortly thereafter, he said to his wife, "Dear, I give you the piano." The piano remained in the living room until O's death. O's children from a prior marriage claim the piano should be included in his estate. Who owns the piano?

In *Robinson v. Hoalton*, 2 P.2d 34 (Cal. 1931), the father delivered a deed to the farm to the son and orally gave him the personal property on the farm. The father retained a life estate in the farm and continued to reside there with the son until his death. The court held there was a valid delivery of the personal property. "The rule as to delivery is not so strictly applied to transactions between members of a family living in the same house, the law in such cases accepting as a delivery acts which would not be so regarded if the transactions were between strangers living in different places. It is not required that the thing given should be removed from their common residence."

In *Newman v. Bost*, 29 S.E. 848 (N.C. 1898), the decedent called his nurse and his housekeeper into his sickroom shortly before his death and handed his keys to the housekeeper, saying that he wanted her to have everything in the house. The housekeeper had been in his employ in the 10 years since his wife's death, and there was evidence that the decedent may have contemplated marriage to her. The gift failed as to all items in the house except items of furniture locked by the keys and the furniture with which decedent had furnished her bedroom. Despite evidence that decedent had always called the piano located in the parlor "Miss Julia's piano," the court held there had been no gift for lack of delivery.

2. O recorded a cattle brand in the name of his daughter, A. O then branded some of his cattle with A's brand, intending to make a gift to A. O kept the cattle and made no attempt to turn them over to A. On O's death, is A entitled to the cattle branded with her brand? *Hillebrant v. Brewer*, 6 Tex. 45 (1851), held there was a sufficient delivery to consummate the gift, the acts of recording and branding affording "as satisfactory evidence of the intention of the donor to part with the dominion and ownership of the property as the nature of the case would admit of. It is analogous to a gift by deed or writing, which, as between donor and donee, has been held tantamount to a delivery."

3. Beginning in 1946, O, the owner of an incorporated business, occasionally issued stock certificates in the corporation in the names of his children but required the children to endorse the certificates in blank and retained possession of them. The children were listed as shareholders on the corporate records. After a falling out in 1982, plaintiff sued O for her share of the stock, claiming that he had told her he was giving the children the stock but retaining the certificates "for safekeeping." *Lichetenstein v. Eljohnan, Inc.*, 555 N.Y.S.2d 331 (App. Div. 1990), held that no gift had been made because there was no actual or constructive delivery.

4. Shortly before his death, Andrew directed that two checks be drawn and issued to his grandson Sean, one for $2,000, the other for $15,000. After his death, and the death of his widow, Margaret, the administrators of their estates claimed that the money given to Sean was a loan, not a gift. The only evidence was testimony of Sean's father that the grandfather told him he had let Sean have some money and it was forgiven, testimony from another relative that Margaret had not wanted Andrew to give Sean the money, and a notation written by Margaret in the check register for the $15,000 check that said "loan." Held: loan not gift. *Sleigh v. Sleigh*, 445 S.E.2d 509 (W. Va. 1994).

5. After O's death, O's executor claims that A holds $1,000,000 in bearer bonds belonging to the estate. A claims that O originally delivered the bonds to her for safekeeping but then later decided to make a gift of them to A. A produces a witness who testifies that O said to A in his presence, "I hereby give to you the bearer bonds you have been safekeeping for me." Who is entitled to the bonds? *In re Mills*, 172 A.D. 530, 158 N.Y.S. 1100, *aff'd*, 219 N.Y. 642, 114 N.E. 1072 (1916), held that A owned the bonds.

6. Mother and father loaned daughter A $16,000. After her father had died and a conservator had been appointed for her mother, A was sued by the two estates to recover the loan. A claimed that her parents had forgiven the indebtedness, and offered as evidence an entry in her mother's diary—"Dad doesn't want her sending checks to repay us." Although the court accepted that the parents in fact intended to make a gift by forgiving the debt, the court held that no gift had been made because there was no delivery. *Gartin v. Taylor*, 577 N.W.2d 410 (Iowa 1998).

Acceptance

To complete a transfer of property, acceptance by the transferee is required. However, if the transfer is beneficial to the transferee, acceptance will ordinarily be assumed, subject to the donee's right to reject or disclaim it:

> Although the issue of acceptance is rarely litigated, the authority that does exist indicates that, given a valid delivery, acceptance will be implied if the gift is unconditional and beneficial to the donee. The presumption of acceptance may apply

even if the donee does not learn of the gift until after the donor's death. A donee cannot be expected to accept or reject a gift until he learns of it and unless a gift is rejected when the donee is informed of it, the presumption of acceptance is not defeated.[7]

Worrell v. Lathan[8] tells a sad and cautionary tale. Barbara Worrell, a longtime friend of Elizabeth Brisendine, drove Elizabeth to and from the hospital and doctors' appointments during her terminal illness. On several occasions, Elizabeth tried to give Barbara money, but she never accepted it. In early September 1993, Elizabeth tried to give a check to Barbara. Barbara refused the check without looking at it, telling Elizabeth that she looked after her out of friendship and did not desire payment for helping a friend. Elizabeth later told her the check would be in the mail.

Elizabeth died in October. Barbara heard nothing further about the check until January 1994, when Henry Meyer, who handled Elizabeth's finances, contacted her to say that some third party had signed her name to the check and tried to cash it. When Barbara learned that the check was for $10,000, she decided that she would like to have it after all. Henry confirmed that the check was written during Elizabeth's lifetime and that Elizabeth said she was going to mail the check to Barbara. Is it too late? The South Carolina Court of Appeals thought so:

> We are . . . unable to find any evidence reasonably tending to show any form of delivery of the check. No evidence was presented to show the check was mailed or in the hands of an agent. No reasonable explanation has been provided for the whereabouts of the check between the time Brisendine initially attempted to deliver it to Worrell, when the gift was declined, and the subsequent reappearance of the check. . . . Without evidence of delivery, the facts of this case are insufficient to establish a gift regardless of the donor's intent. . . .
>
> Acceptance by the donee of a gift inter vivos or *causa mortis* is generally held to be an essential element of a gift. Acceptance is sufficient if the gift is accepted before revocation by the donor, or before revocation by the death of the donor. In this case, the unexplained circumstances surrounding Worrell's not receiving the check could indicate Brisendine either revoked or intended to revoke the gift before her death. In any event, Brisendine's death effectively revoked the gift.[9]

Can you construct a plausible argument in favor of letting Barbara Worrell have $10,000 from Elizabeth Brisendine's estate?

Revocability

The *Worrell* court correctly says that a gift may be revoked before it is accepted. What about revocation of a gift after it has been accepted? Can the donor get the property back if the donor has a subsequent falling out with the donee or

---

7.   Scherer v. Hyland, 380 A.2d 698 (N.J. 1977).
8.   478 S.E.2d 287 (S.C. Ct. App. 1996).
9.   478 S.E.2d at 288-89.

discovers a need for the property? In *Gonzales v. Zerda*,[10] Frank Zerda sued Adela Gonzales in conversion, seeking return of funds collected under a $67,000 certificate of deposit Zerda had given Gonzales in 1987. Zerda claimed that his gift was revocable because made in contemplation of death (a gift *causa mortis*). Although the court agreed that a gift *causa mortis* is revocable by the donor, it held that Zerda's gift was inter vivos rather than *causa mortis*. Inter vivos gifts are not generally revocable.[11]

Zerda's gift was not *causa mortis* because, although he was 80 years old, "was feeling pretty sick," and thought he might die if he went into the hospital,[12] he in fact had no plans to enter the hospital at the time he made the gift. The court said:

> To hold the gift as one *causa mortis*, it must be shown to have been in contemplation of death from present illness or anticipated peril. The circumstances must be such as to show that the donor intended the gift to take effect if he should die shortly afterwards, but if he should recover, that the property should be restored to him. . . . From portions of the evidence it may be inferred that the plaintiff was in sickness at the time of making the deed; but this cannot affect the irrevocable character of the gift, unless sickness can be shown to be so imminently dangerous as to justify the belief that it will be fatal in its termination.[13]

NEWELL v. NATIONAL BANK OF NORWICH

Supreme Court, Appellate Division, New York
212 N.Y.S. 158 (App. Div. 1925)

COCHRANE, P.J. Emory S. Reynolds, the defendant's testator, was a childless widower. For many years he had been an intimate friend of plaintiff. About March 1, 1918, he was seriously ill with pneumonia and expected to die. He sent for the plaintiff and gave him a diamond ring, the title to which is the question to be determined herein. He caused the ring to be delivered to plaintiff. The circumstances are described as follows by a nurse in attendance:

> He told Mr. Newell why he sent for him that morning. He had everything seen to and was ready to go; had all his affairs seen to, with the exception of handing over the ring to him. He was ready to go, or ready to die, and that his other business was all straightened up.

Mr. Reynolds recovered from his illness and lived more than four years thereafter.

Viewed as a gift *causa mortis*, the gift cannot be sustained, because it is well established that the recovery to health of the donor works per se a revocation

---

10. 802 S.W.2d 794 (Tex. Ct. App. 1990).

11. Whether an inter vivos gift may be made revocable by express retention of a power to revoke is not altogether clear from the authorities.

12. However, plaintiff was not hospitalized in either 1986 or 1987. He also testified that at the time he signed the lost certificate affidavit allowing Adela to withdraw the money, he felt as well as he ever had.

13. 802 S.W.2d at 795.

of the gift. Curtiss v. Barrus, 38 Hun (N.Y.) 165 . . . Basket v. Hassell, 107 U.S. 602 . . . .

The trial court has found that there was a gift inter vivos. Such a gift may exist, although at the time of making it the donor was under the apprehension of death. In 28 *Corpus Juris*, p. 622, the rule is stated as follows:

> The test whether the gift is one inter vivos or one *causa mortis* is not the mere fact that the donor is *in extremis*, and expects to die, and does die of that illness, but whether he intended the gift to take effect *in praesenti*, irrevocably and unconditionally, whether he lives or dies. . . .

There can be no doubt that the expectation of death is frequently the inducement for a gift inter vivos.

The question then is: Does the evidence sustain the finding that a gift inter vivos was intended? We approach that question with the rule in mind that the presumption is otherwise, and that the burden is on the plaintiff to establish such a gift. We have already alluded to the testimony of the nurse. There is also some testimony given by her tending to show that the testator wanted the plaintiff to have the ring, regardless of whether the testator lived or died. It clearly appears that, after the restoration of the testator to health, plaintiff did not want to wear the ring, and was willing to return it to the testator for his use as long as he lived. He so expressed himself, verbally and by letter. The testator was equally insistent that plaintiff should retain the ring. Finally, several months after he got well, the testator summoned a witness to the office of plaintiff, and, speaking to this witness in the presence of the plaintiff, said:

> Frank [the plaintiff] wants me to wear this ring, but I don't think I should do it. I gave him that ring, and I want him to have it; but he insists upon my wearing it, now that I am able to be around again. Under only one consideration will I agree to wear it, and I want it thoroughly understood that this ring belongs to Frank, and when I die I want it understood that it belongs to him, and that he shall have it.

Thereafter the testator had the ring in his possession and wore it until his death. Other witnesses testify to substantially the same statement at different times by the testator. The transaction in the office of the plaintiff is insufficient to constitute a gift to him by the testator, because it left the donor in possession of the property; but we think it reflects the mental attitude of the testator at the time when, during his illness, he delivered the ring to the plaintiff. He had no near relatives. The most of his property at that time had been willed to charitable purposes, as the evidence discloses. His business and social relations with plaintiff were very intimate. The circumstances surrounding the transaction, and his attitude thereafter and subsequent declarations, indicate quite clearly that when, during his illness, he gave the ring to the plaintiff, he did so irrespective of whether he lived or died, although at the time he was apprehensive of death. If that was his purpose, absolute title then vested in the plaintiff, and the subsequent possession and use thereof by the testator was that merely of a bailee. We think the findings of the trial court are fairly sustained by the evidence.

The judgment should be affirmed, with costs. . . .

Notes and Questions

1. The fact that a gift is made in contemplation of imminent death gives rise to an implied power of revocation. What is the basis for implication of the power? Intent? Public policy?

2. Discussions of gifts *causa mortis* are frequently unclear on the question whether the gift is automatically revoked if the donor lives through the illness or peril that led to the making of the gift, or whether the donor simply has the power to revoke.[14] Which construction makes more sense? If you had been in a position to decide the *Newell* case, how would you have analyzed the situation?

3. What other circumstances should give rise to an inference that the donor intends that the gift be subject to defeasance? Wedding gifts are often thought to be revoked if the wedding fails to occur, but not if the couple subsequently divorces. What about engagement gifts and other gifts made in contemplation of marriage? Should revocation be automatic in these situations or require exercise of a power to revoke? Are there other situations you can think of that should be treated similarly?

B. GIFTS MADE BY CHECK

Gifts made by check often run into problems if the donor dies before the check is cashed. The problem arises because a check falls squarely between the two basic doctrines that a promise to make a gift has no legal effect,[15] but a present transfer of a right to receive money in the future gives the donee an enforceable claim. These two doctrines can be illustrated as follows:

> *Example 1:* O promises to give A $500 for her birthday next December. O dies in November. *Result:* A has no claim against O's estate for the $500.

> *Example 2:* O assigns to A the right to $500 to be paid next December. O dies in November. *Result:* A has a valid claim against O's estate for $500.

A check is a direction to the donor's bank to pay money to the holder of the check when it is presented for payment. By the terms of the donor's contract with the bank, the donor has the right to stop payment on the check until it is presented. Do you see how this causes trouble for the donee?

Another problem intertwined throughout the cases involving gifts *causa mortis* is the distinction drawn in our legal system between lifetime and testamentary

---

14. This discussion should remind you of the difference between a fee simple determinable and a fee on condition subsequent.

15. *See* Jane B. Baron, *Gifts, Bargains, and Form,* 64 Ind. L.J. 155 (1988-89), for a critique of the distinction drawn between gifts and bargains in Anglo-American law. Bargains (promises to make exchanges) are enforced without any formality requirement; gifts (transfers without a specified exchange or quid pro quo) require delivery or other formalities that prevent enforcement of promises to make future gifts. *See* Melvin Aron Eisenberg, *The World of Contract and the World of Gift,* 85 Cal. L. Rev. 821 (1997), for a critique of Baron's article.

gifts. Lifetime gifts of personalty can be made orally; testamentary gifts must be made in a signed writing that is either in the testator's handwriting or attested by two witnesses.[16] A lifetime gift is one that presently transfers some interest in property to the donee. A testamentary gift transfers nothing until the death of the donor; before that happens, the donee has only an "expectancy," which is not an interest in property and creates no enforceable claims against the donor's estate.

IN RE ESTATE OF SMITH

Superior Court of Pennsylvania
694 A.2d 1099 (Pa. Super. Ct. 1997)

DEL SOLE, J.: . . . On May 7, 1994, Appellant's husband, Alfred E. Smith (Decedent), committed suicide in the basement of the couple's home. Prior to his suicide, Decedent took the following steps in an effort to attend to several of his personal affairs. On May 5, 1994, Decedent drafted four checks in various amounts to four individuals: Joy Youpa (Decedent's girlfriend), Carol Sandt (Ms. Youpa's sister), Barbara Kressley (Decedent's sister), and Diana Kressley (Decedent's niece). On May 6, 1994 Decedent prepared and executed a holographic will.[17] The will contained the following contested provision: "I want Willard Kressley to have the option of buying my '66 Corvette from Jean [Appellant] for $12,000." Also on May 6, 1994, Decedent mailed the checks to his sister and niece accompanied with a suicide note.[1] On May 7, 1994, before committing suicide, Decedent delivered the checks to his girlfriend and her sister by leaving the checks under a pizza box on their kitchen table. The two mailed checks and the note were received on May 9, 1994, two days after the suicide. Each of the recipients knew of Decedent's death at the time she cashed her check.

After Appellant, as administratrix of Decedent's estate, discovered that Decedent had written the four checks, she requested that the funds be returned by the recipients to the estate. The four recipients refused and Appellant commenced a civil action alleging conversion and seeking restitution. . . . The court entered a decree holding that the four checks to the donees were valid gifts *causa mortis*. . . . These appeals followed. . . .

---

16.   These are the basic requirements for making a valid will but not the only ones. The document must be executed with "testamentary intent" and may be subject to additional requirements. Holographic wills (wills made in the testator's handwriting without witnesses) are not allowed in some states. Oral wills are practically not allowed in modern law. Prior to the Statute of Frauds, oral wills were allowed. The Statute of Frauds required written attested wills except that oral wills of personal property worth up to £30 were allowed. In addition, soldiers on active duty and mariners at sea were permitted to make oral wills.

18.   A holographic will is handwritten by the testator and is valid without the formalities required for printed wills. — EDS.

1.   The note stated:

I know this is a hell of a mess and I am truly sorry for the embarrassment, but I can't go on. I know there will be legal questions about the will, but they are my intentions. I know the estate taxes for the state could have been avoided, but I don't have time. I'm sorry. I'm sorry. I'm sorry. Good-bye. Alfred

Barbara, The checks are [to] use at your discretion. Alfred

To establish a gift *causa mortis*, it must be shown that at the time of the alleged gift, the decedent intended to make a gift, the decedent apprehended death, the res of the intended gift was either actually or constructively delivered, and death actually occurred. It is not necessary that the donor expressly say he knows or believes he is dying; that may be inferred from the attendant circumstances. It will suffice if at the time the gift was made, the donor believed he was going to die, that he was likely to die soon; and death did actually ensue within a reasonable time thereafter.

The facts of the instant case support a finding of a gift *causa mortis*. . . . Therefore, the lower court was correct in refusing to revoke the checks.[2] . . .

CIRILLO, President Judge Emeritus, concurring and dissenting. . . . I vehemently disagree . . . .

Because the intention to commit suicide may be readily abandoned at one's own will, courts from other jurisdictions have taken the position that the contemplated or intended suicide of a donor is not a "peril, ailment or disease" which can serve as the foundation of a gift *causa mortis* 60 A.L.R.2d § 2 at 577; *see also* Ray v. Leader Federal Savings & Loan Assoc., 292 S.W.2d 458, 467 (Tenn. Ct. App. 1953) ("[s]ickness, peril and danger, as used in definitions of donations *causa mortis* we believe to mean something other than a determination of an individual who is presumed to be well, physically and mentally, to take his life").[4] Courts, therefore, have found that gifts made in contemplation of suicide are against public policy and should not be enforced.

The Pennsylvania Supreme Court has held that the law does not look with favor upon gifts *causa mortis*; these gifts are often made without the regular safeguards afforded by the law for the disposition of property in an executed will. In keeping with this view, strict proof is required to find that such gifts exist.

Without any instructive guide from case law of this jurisdiction on the issue of gifting in contemplation of suicide, I am forced to broaden my search and delve into Pennsylvania's general public policy with regard to condoning the commission of suicide. My research locates a case which briefly discusses this jurisdiction's view on suicide. In Commonwealth v. Root, 156 A.2d 895 (Pa. Super. 1959), the court, in dicta, outlined the civil ramifications of suicide and the general policy concerns behind taking life at one's own hands. The *Root* court stated:

> If a man's negligence contributes to his injury or death, he, or those claiming under him, cannot recover damages in a civil suit. It has long been the policy of

2.   We believe that by considering gifts made in contemplation of suicide to be gifts *causa mortis*, we further the public policy against suicide since the donor may retrieve the gifts if the suicide is not completed. As our courts have held, a gift *causa mortis* differs from other gifts only in that it is made when the donor believes he is about to die, and, is revocable should he survive. Titusville Trust Co. v. Johnson, at 497-498, 100 A.2d at 96. *See, In re* Brown's Estate, 489 Pa. 199, 413 A.2d 1083 (1980).

4.   I recognize that there are jurisdictions that would find that contemplation of suicide is sufficient for purposes of proving an element of a gift *causa mortis*. *See* Scherer v. Hyland, 75 N.J. 127, 380 A.2d 698 (1977); *see also* Berl v. Rosenberg, 169 Cal. App. 2d 125, 336 P.2d 975 (1959) (public policy against suicide will not invalidate an otherwise valid gift *causa mortis*); *In re* Van Wormer's Estate, 255 Mich. 399, 238 N.W. 210 (1931) (melancholia ending in suicide sufficient to sustain a gift *causa mortis*). These courts have focused on the fact that according to modern human psychological principles, the utter despair attendant upon one contemplating suicide may reasonably be viewed as even more imminent than a person struggling with a fatal physical illness. Such reasoning is attenuated, at best, in light of this Commonwealth's consistent views disfavoring suicide.

the common law that one who fails to look out for his own safety is not entitled to demand in court that he be compensated for the consequences of his failure. . . . The policy of the law is to protect human life, even the life of a person who wishes to destroy his own.

Pennsylvania's policy of protecting human life is further evidenced by the criminalization of assisted suicide in our Criminal Code. By upholding and validating gifts made in contemplation of suicide, the majority rewards the donor and his or her donees for the intended and successful completion of a self-destructive act. . . . The majority's holding cuts against the notion that courts prefer the reliable disposition of property through a will or by the well-expressed intentions in a living person's inter vivos transfer. . . .

Notes and Questions

1. What are the dissent's concerns about allowing the donees to keep the proceeds of the checks left for them by the decedent? Is it that decedent did not intend to make the gifts? That the decedent did not choose the proper form for making the gift? That the decedent should not be allowed to give away property that would otherwise have gone to his wife? That the decedent lacked capacity to make a gift? Do you agree that the majority has "rewarded" the donor and the donees for his successful commission of suicide?

2. Should a person be allowed to give his property away just before death? Until relatively recently, a number of states had so-called mortmain (dead hand) statutes that invalidated testamentary gifts to charity if the will was executed within a certain period before death (six months, for example).[18] The theory behind the statutes was that thoughts of impending death were likely to distort the testator's judgment and divert assets from the testator's family. Should a similar rule be applied to gifts made in contemplation of death? Within a certain time before death? Should it make any difference whether the gift is made by will, by delivery, or by a deed of gift?

WOO v. SMART

Supreme Court of Virginia
442 S.E.2d 690 (Va. 1994)

COMPTON, J. Born in China, the decedent [William D. Yee] and the donee [S. Hing Woo] met in connection with the operation of a Richmond-area restaurant that was established by her father in the 1970s. The decedent, age 51 when he died, had a high school education; she, age 39 when he died, had "finished" college. He became manager of the restaurant and she assisted him in its operation. They were "like husband and wife," occasionally living together, and

---

18.   Of the 11 jurisdictions that had mortmain statutes in 1970, all have repealed or invalidated them. *See, e.g.,* Shriners' Hosp. for Crippled Children v. Zrillic, 563 So. 2d 64 (Fla. 1990) (statute unconstitutional because denied charitable beneficiary equal protection and due process of law). The last state was Georgia, which repealed its statute in 1998, Ga. Code Ann. § 53-2-10.

maintained a close relationship that lasted for 19 years. In 1985, he was diagnosed with coronary heart disease.

The decedent had brothers and sisters living in Hong Kong, Canada, and New York, from some of whom he was estranged. He resided in a small house near the restaurant with a younger brother; she resided with her mother and two brothers at a different location. . . .

On March 27, 1989, two days before his death, the decedent complained to the donee "that he was feeling terribly bad" and that he believed death was imminent. Against her advice "to stay home and take a rest," he came to the restaurant "to take care of some money in his bank." During the evening, he "gave" her the $42,700.00 check drawn on Signet Bank to "close out" his account there. The "same night," he "gave" her the $80,000.00 check drawn on Central Fidelity Bank to represent the value of "various" savings accounts at that bank. During the next day, March 28, 1989, still "feeling badly," the decedent returned to the restaurant and handed the donee the $1,900.00 check to "close out" his checking account at Central Fidelity Bank. These checks were given to the donee so that she would be "provided for"; the decedent told her that he "wanted" her "to have the money if he died."

The decedent died in a hospital emergency room on March 29, 1989; none of the checks had been cashed. The donee received the proceeds of the two checks on the day after death. The check for $80,000.00 was never presented because it represented funds in savings accounts and there were insufficient funds in the checking account to cover it.

[In this action, the administrator of Yee's estate sought a declaratory judgment that the three checks were not effective gifts because they were not presented for payment and paid prior to the decedent's death, and asked for judgment against the donee in the amount of $44,600 representing the sum of the two checks that were cashed. Woo claimed the checks were valid gifts *causa mortis*. After an *ore tenus* hearing,[19] the chancellor ruled that no gift was made and awarded judgment against Woo for $44,600. She appealed. — EDS.] . . .

[T]he trial court determined that the donee had established all but one of the essential elements [of a gift *causa mortis*]. The court found that the decedent fully intended to make gifts of money to the donee; the evidence clearly showed the decedent wanted to provide for her if he died and the checks were handed to her for that purpose. The court also ruled that the attempted gifts . . . were made while the decedent was under the apprehension of immediate death and upon condition that the property belong to the donee if the decedent died as expected. The trial court found, however, that the gifts failed "because delivery of the checks did not constitute delivery of the object of the gifts themselves; that is, the money in the bank." . . .

The narrow question presented is whether . . . possession . . . was delivered to the donee at the time of the alleged gift. . . . [T]he inquiry is whether a check can be the proper subject of a gift *causa mortis*, a question of first impression for this Court.

We adopt the majority rule elsewhere that a donor's own check drawn on a personal checking account is not, prior to acceptance or payment by the bank, the subject of a valid gift *causa mortis*. . . . Generally, although there is contrary

---

19.   An *ore tenus* hearing is one at which oral testimony is taken. — EDS.

authority, the determination whether delivery of the donor's own check is such a gift depends upon "whether the transaction is regarded as amounting to an assignment of the portion of the deposit indicated by the check." . . .

The Uniform Commercial Code (U.C.C.) makes clear that transfer of a check does not operate as an assignment of money on deposit. Former Code § 8.3-409(1) (now in substance § 8.3A-408), applicable to this dispute, provided: "A check or other draft does not of itself operate as an assignment of any funds in the hands of the drawee[20] available for its payment, and the drawee is not liable on the instrument until he accepts it." Because the check does not operate as an assignment of the funds, mere delivery of a check does not place the gift beyond the donor's power of revocation and the check simply becomes an unenforceable promise to make a gift.

In addition, the required delivery must be "actual and complete, such as deprives the donor of all further control and dominion." . . . Until the check is paid, the donor retains control and dominion over the funds and the gift is incomplete; the donor could stop payment or write another check for the funds payable to a third person, or the donor may die, thus revoking the donor-drawer's command to the drawee bank to pay the money. . . . Accordingly, as the trial court ruled, while three checks were delivered by the decedent to the donee, "no money was delivered." Because no money was delivered, no money successfully can be claimed by the donee as a gift *causa mortis*.

We reject the donee's contention that the foregoing section of the U.C.C. "was meant to protect banks against a holder of a check, not to address the rights of other non-bank parties as to the funds on deposit in the account." The statute is clear and unambiguous; it is not limited as the donee suggests. And, contrary to the donee's argument, the Official Comment to the section does not require these gifts to be validated. After noting that "a check or other draft does not of itself operate as an assignment in law or equity," the Comment states that an "assignment may, however, appear from other agreements, express or implied; and when the intent to assign is clear the check may be the means by which the assignment is effected." The donee argues, "If one could never use a check for an assignment, this official comment has no meaning." But it is the statute that would be rendered meaningless if the Comment were applied to authenticate the gifts in this case, in which there is the effort to validate the gratuitous promise of a deceased donor. . . .

Notes and Questions

1. How does the *Woo* court conceptualize the gift *causa mortis*? Does it reject the standard view that a gift *causa mortis* is a present transfer subject to a power of revocation? Does it take the view that a gift *causa mortis* is in reality an oral will validated by the formality of transferring possession of the gift during life rather than the usual signed writing that is either in the testator's handwriting or attested by two witnesses? Which view of the gift *causa mortis* makes more sense?

---

20.   The drawee is the bank, or other financial institution, on which the check is drawn. —EDS.

2. Courts split on the question whether delivery of a check is effective to make a gift of money from a bank account. Some, like the *Smith Estate* court, have no trouble finding that delivery of a check is effective. Others, like the *Woo* court, hold that no gift is made until the donee cashes the check. Why? As the court said in *Woo*, the donor can stop payment on the check. Why does that matter? It wouldn't if the gift was made when the check was delivered (stopping payment would be wrongful, just as taking back the birthday present you've given your friend would be wrongful). The explanation lies in a conceptualization of the check itself as a "mere" promise to pay money rather than as an assignment of funds in the account or constructive delivery of the funds in the account. The court relied on the Uniform Commercial Code in reaching the conclusion that delivery of the check did not accomplish a present transfer. Is a rule designed for commercial transactions necessarily appropriate to determine whether an effective donative transfer has been made? Which conceptualization of the check transaction better accords with ordinary people's expectations in a gift situation?

3. *Constructive delivery.* When the subject matter of an oral gift is not readily available or capable of manual tradition (being physically handed over), courts usually recognize gifts effected by delivery of the means of gaining access to the subject matter. For example, a gift of the furnishings in a house was effectuated by handing over the key to the house in *Libel v. Corcoran,* 452 P.2d 832 (Kan. 1969), and a gift of a car was made by handing over the keys to the car in *Estate of Lines,* 201 N.Y.S.2d 290 (Sur. Ct. 1959). Disclosure of the location of the item may also serve as delivery. In *Waite v. Grubbe,* 73 P. 206 (Or. 1903), the testator made a valid gift by disclosing the location of buried cash, and in *Teague v. Abbott,* 100 N.E. 27 (Ind. Ct. App. 1912), a gift was made by disclosing the combination to a safe. Why wasn't delivery of Yee's check constructive delivery of the funds in the accounts?

4. *Delivery of check as gift* causa mortis. Accepting the *Woo* court's view that the problem with the checks was that the donor could revoke them, should that make any difference in a gift *causa mortis*? Given the court's statement referred to in Note 1, which suggests that a gift *causa mortis* does not take effect until the donor's death anyway, should it matter that Yee had the power to stop the check until he died? Since he did not stop the check, why not let Woo have the money? Why do you think the court came out as it did?

Symbolic Delivery and Delivery to Third Person

Instead of delivering the subject matter of the gift, or the keys or other means of acquiring possession, donors sometimes deliver a symbol. Commonly used symbols include instruments of title, like title to an automobile, corporate stock certificates, and bank books. If the donative intent is clear, a court may uphold a gift of a chattel by symbolic delivery even though the donor retains a life estate. In *Beck v. Givens,*[21] for example, a gift of sheep was made by delivering an instrument purporting to be a bill of sale to the donee, even though the donor retained possession during his lifetime.

---

21. 309 P.2d 715 (Wyo. 1957).

An effective gift may also be made by delivering the subject matter to a third person with instructions to deliver it to the donee immediately or at some time in the future. Except as the gift is otherwise revocable (as a gift *causa mortis*, or a gift in contemplation of marriage), an attempt by the donor to retain a power to revoke is likely to cause trouble. Standard doctrine is that the gift fails for lack of delivery if the donor retains an express power to revoke. However, the standard doctrine seems questionable since presumably, the donor could accomplish the same thing by making the delivery to the third person "as trustee." Revocable trusts are valid, and unless there is a contrary statute, oral trusts of personal property are valid. If convinced that the donor intended to make a revocable gift by transferring property to a third party to hold for the donee, a modern court should be willing to uphold it as a revocable trust.

C.   DEEDS OF GIFT

Gifts other than simple outright transfers and gifts of substantial value should always be made, or at least evidenced by, a written instrument to avoid questions about the donor's intent and the terms of the gift. Gifts of land can only be made by instrument of transfer, and the best, and sometimes the only way, to make a gift of an intangible or a future interest is to use an instrument of transfer. The gift is effectuated by delivering the instrument, which should identify the parties, spell out the donor's intent to make a gift, identify the property transferred to the donee, and bear the donor's signature.

Generally, the same considerations apply in determining whether an instrument of transfer has been delivered as in determining whether a chattel has been delivered. However, because there is often less ambiguity when an instrument of transfer is used, courts are generally more willing to accept other evidence of intent as a substitute for actually handing over the deed. But if it is not clear that the donor intended a written transfer to be effective, the gift will fail in the absence of delivery. In *Lauerman v. Destocki*,[22] for example, Robert Frazier signed certain stock certificates in blank and directed his attorney to type in the names of five employees of his company, intending to make a gift. When the attorney returned to his hospital room, Frazier was too tired to review the certificates, and he died the next day. The court held no gift had been made.

In addition to the inevitable questions that can arise over the meaning of a written instrument (which are covered in the wills and trusts course, not here), three kinds of questions may arise when a written instrument of transfer is used. The first is whether a written instrument can be used to make the gift without physical delivery of the subject matter of the gift. The second is whether there has been sufficient delivery of the instrument of transfer to effectuate the gift. The third, which usually accompanies the second, is whether the donor will be allowed to use an inter vivos transfer to avoid probate.

---

22.   622 N.E.2d 1122 (Ohio Ct. App. 1993).

The first question—whether a gift of a chattel can be made by delivery of an instrument of transfer—seems surprising since transfers of land by written instrument have been possible since the Statute of Uses (1536) and required since the Statute of Frauds (1677). However, as you will see in the next case, 20th century lawyers and judges still entertained with apparently straight faces the argument that a gift of a chattel could only be made by something equivalent to the medieval livery of seisin.

The second and third questions—whether there has been sufficient delivery and whether the instrument presently transfers an interest in the property—require courts to grapple with the distinction between valid inter vivos transfers and invalid attempts to make testamentary transfers without making a will.

GRUEN v. GRUEN
Court of Appeals of New York
496 N.E.2d 869, 83 A.L.R. 4th 955 (N.Y. 1986)

SIMONS, J. Plaintiff commenced this action seeking a declaration that he is the rightful owner of a painting which he alleges his father, now deceased, gave to him. . . . The subject of the dispute is a work entitled "Schloss Kammer am Attersee II" painted by a noted Austrian modernist, Gustav Klimt. It was purchased by plaintiff's father, Victor Gruen, in 1959 for $8,000. On April 1, 1963 the elder Gruen, a successful architect with offices and residences in both New York City and Los Angeles during most of the time involved in this action, wrote a letter to plaintiff, then an undergraduate student at Harvard, stating that he was giving him the Klimt painting for his birthday but that he wished to retain the possession of it for his lifetime. This letter is not in evidence, apparently because plaintiff destroyed it on instructions from his father. Two other letters were received, however, one dated May 22, 1963 and the other April 1, 1963. Both had been dictated by Victor Gruen and sent together to plaintiff on or about May 22, 1963. The letter dated May 22, 1963 reads as follows:

Dear Michael:

I wrote you at the time of your birthday about the gift of the painting by Klimt.

Now my lawyer tells me that because of the existing tax laws, it was wrong to mention in that letter that I want to use the painting as long as I live. Though I still want to use it, this should not appear in the letter. I am enclosing, therefore, a new letter and I ask you to send the old one back to me so that it can be destroyed.

I know this is all very silly, but the lawyer and our accountant insist that they must have in their possession copies of a letter which will serve the purpose of making it possible for you, once I die, to get this picture without having to pay inheritance taxes on it.

Love,

s/Victor

Enclosed with this letter was a substitute gift letter, dated April 1, 1963, which stated:

> Dear Michael:
>
> The 21st birthday, being an important event in life, should be celebrated accordingly. I therefore wish to give you as a present the oil painting by Gustav Klimt of Schloss Kammer which now hangs in the New York living room. You know that Lazette and I bought it some 5 or 6 years ago, and you always told us how much you liked it.
>
> Happy birthday again.
>
> > Love,
> >
> > s/Victor

Plaintiff never took possession of the painting nor did he seek to do so. Except for a brief period between 1964 and 1965 when it was on loan to art exhibits and when restoration work was performed on it, the painting remained in his father's possession, moving with him from New York City to Beverly Hills and finally to Vienna, Austria, where Victor Gruen died on February 14, 1980. Following Victor's death plaintiff requested possession of the Klimt painting and when defendant [plaintiff's stepmother] refused, he commenced this action.

The issues framed for appeal are whether a valid inter vivos gift of a chattel may be made where the donor has reserved a life estate in the chattel and the donee never has had physical possession of it before the donor's death and, if it may, which factual findings on the elements of a valid inter vivos gift more nearly comport with the weight of the evidence in this case, those of Special Term or those of the Appellate Division. The latter issue requires application of two general rules. First, to make a valid inter vivos gift there must exist the intent on the part of the donor to make a present transfer; delivery of the gift, either actual or constructive to the donee; and acceptance by the donee. Second, the proponent of a gift has the burden of proving each of these elements by clear and convincing evidence.

Donative Intent

There is an important distinction between the intent with which an inter vivos gift is made and the intent to make a gift by will. An inter vivos gift requires that the donor intend to make an irrevocable present transfer of ownership; if the intention is to make a testamentary disposition effective only after death, the gift is invalid unless made by will . . . .

Defendant contends that the trial court was correct in finding that Victor did not intend to transfer any present interest in the painting to plaintiff in 1963 but only expressed an intention that plaintiff was to get the painting upon his death. The evidence is all but conclusive, however, that Victor intended to transfer ownership of the painting to plaintiff in 1963 but to retain a life estate in it and that he did, therefore, effectively transfer a remainder interest in the painting to plaintiff at that time. Although the original letter was not in evidence, testimony of its contents was received along with the substitute gift letter and its covering letter dated May 22, 1963. The three letters should be considered together as a single instrument (*see*, Matter of Brandreth, 169 N.Y. 437, 440, 62 N.E. 563) and when they are they unambiguously establish that Victor Gruen intended to make a present gift of title to the painting at that time. But there was other evidence for after 1963 Victor made several statements orally and in writing indicating that he had previously given plaintiff the painting and that plaintiff owned it. Victor Gruen retained possession of the property, insured it, allowed others to exhibit it and made necessary repairs to it but those acts are not inconsistent with his retention of a life estate. Furthermore, whatever probative value could be attached to his statement that he had bequeathed the painting to his heirs, made 16 years later when he prepared an export license application so that he could take the painting out of Austria, is negated by the overwhelming evidence that he intended a present transfer of title in 1963. Victor's failure to file a gift tax return on the transaction was partially explained by allegedly erroneous legal advice he received, and while that omission sometimes may indicate that the donor had no intention of making a present gift, it does not necessarily do so and it is not dispositive in this case.

Defendant contends that even if a present gift was intended, Victor's reservation of a lifetime interest in the painting defeated it. She relies on a statement from Young v. Young, 80 N.Y. 422 that "'[a]ny gift of chattels which expressly reserves the use of the property to the donor for a certain period, or . . . as long as the donor shall live, is ineffectual'" (*id.*, at p. 436, quoting 2 Schouler, *Personal Property*, at 118). The statement was dictum, however, and the holding of the court was limited to a determination that an attempted gift of bonds in which the donor reserved the interest for life failed because there had been no delivery of the gift, either actual or constructive (*see id.*, at p. 434; *see also*, Speelman v. Pascal, 10 N.Y.2d 313, 319-320, . . . 178 N.E.2d 723). The court expressly left undecided the question "whether a remainder in a chattel may be created and given by a donor by carving out a life estate for himself and transferring the remainder" (Young v. Young, *supra*, at p. 440). We answered part of that question in Matter of Brandreth, 169 N.Y. 437, 441-442, 62 N.E. 563, *supra*) when we held that "[in] this state a life estate and remainder can be created in a chattel or a fund the same as in real property." The case did not require us to decide whether there could be a valid gift of the remainder.

Defendant recognizes that a valid inter vivos gift of a remainder interest can be made not only of real property but also of such intangibles as stocks and bonds. Indeed, several of the cases she cites so hold. That being so, it is difficult to perceive any legal basis for the distinction she urges which would permit gifts of remainder interests in those properties but not of remainder interests in chattels such as the Klimt painting here. The only reason suggested is that the gift of a chattel must include a present right to possession. The application of *Brandreth* to permit a gift of the remainder in this case, however, is consistent with the distinction, well recognized in the law of gifts as well as in real property law, between ownership and possession or enjoyment. Insofar as some of our cases purport to require that the donor intend to transfer both title and possession immediately to have a valid inter vivos gift, they state the rule too broadly and confuse the effectiveness of a gift with the transfer of the possession of the subject of that gift. The correct test is "'whether the maker intended the [gift] to have *no effect* until after the maker's death, or whether he intended it to transfer *some present interest*'" (McCarthy v. Pieret, 281 N.Y. 407, 409, 24 N.E.2d 102 . . .

[emphasis added]). As long as the evidence establishes an intent to make a present and irrevocable transfer of title or the right of ownership, there is a present transfer of some interest and the gift is effective immediately. Thus, in *Speelman v. Pascal (supra)*, we held valid a gift of a percentage of the future royalties to the play "My Fair Lady" before the play even existed. There, as in this case, the donee received title or the right of ownership to some property immediately upon the making of the gift but possession or enjoyment of the subject of the gift was postponed to some future time.

Defendant suggests that allowing a donor to make a present gift of a remainder with the reservation of a life estate will lead courts to effectuate otherwise invalid testamentary dispositions of property. The two have entirely different characteristics, however, which make them distinguishable. Once the gift is made it is irrevocable and the donor is limited to the rights of a life tenant not an owner. Moreover, with the gift of a remainder title vests immediately in the donee and any possession is postponed until the donor's death whereas under a will neither title nor possession vests immediately. Finally, the postponement of enjoyment of the gift is produced by the express terms of the gift not by the nature of the instrument as it is with a will.

Delivery

. . . Defendant contends that when a tangible piece of personal property such as a painting is the subject of a gift, physical delivery of the painting itself is the best form of delivery and should be required. Here, of course, we have only delivery of Victor Gruen's letters which serve as instruments of gift. Defendant's statement of the rule as applied may be generally true, but it ignores the fact that what Victor Gruen gave plaintiff was not all rights to the Klimt painting, but only title to it with no right of possession until his death. Under these circumstances, it would be illogical for the law to require the donor to part with possession of the painting when that is exactly what he intends to retain.

Nor is there any reason to require a donor making a gift of a remainder interest in a chattel to physically deliver the chattel into the donee's hands only to have the donee redeliver it to the donor. As the facts of this case demonstrate, such a requirement could impose practical burdens on the parties to the gift while serving the delivery requirement poorly. Thus, in order to accomplish this type of delivery the parties would have been required to travel to New York for the symbolic transfer and redelivery of the Klimt painting which was hanging on the wall of Victor Gruen's Manhattan apartment. Defendant suggests that such a requirement would be stronger evidence of a completed gift, but in the absence of witnesses to the event or any written confirmation of the gift it would provide less protection against fraudulent claims than have the written instruments of gift delivered in this case.

Acceptance

Acceptance by the donee is essential to the validity of an inter vivos gift, but when a gift is of value to the donee, as it is here, the law will presume an acceptance on his part. Plaintiff did not rely on this presumption alone but also presented clear and convincing proof of his acceptance of a remainder interest in the Klimt painting by evidence that he had made several contemporaneous statements acknowledging the gift to his friends and associates, even showing some of them his father's gift letter, and that he had retained both letters for over 17 years to verify the gift after his father died. Defendant relied exclusively on affidavits filed by plaintiff in a matrimonial action with his former wife, in which plaintiff failed to list his interest in the painting as an asset. These affidavits were made over 10 years after acceptance was complete and they do not even approach the evidence in Matter of Kelly (285 N.Y. 139, 148-149, 33 N.E.2d 62 [dissenting in part opn.], *supra*) where the donee, immediately upon delivery of a diamond ring, rejected it as "too flashy." We agree with the Appellate Division that interpretation of the affidavit was too speculative to support a finding of rejection and overcome the substantial showing of acceptance by plaintiff.

Accordingly, the judgment appealed from and the order of the Appellate Division brought up for review should be affirmed, with costs.

Notes and Questions

1. Is there any reason the widow should have been allowed to retain the painting given to the son? If Victor had used a will to transfer the painting to his son on death, the widow would have been able to include its value in calculating the value of her elective share. Is it fair that her rights should depend on the form of transfer chosen by Victor?

2. If Victor had retained an express power to revoke the gift of the painting, would the attempted gift have been ineffective? If Victor had used an inter vivos trust rather than an outright gift, he could have retained a power to revoke. If he had retained a power to revoke in the letters he wrote Michael, would the court have upheld the gift? Should courts treat differently situations where the power to revoke is included in a written instrument of gift and where it is created orally?

3. When Michael Gruen finally received the painting from Victor's fourth wife and widow, Kamija, he consigned it to Sotheby's in London, which sold it at auction for £3,300,000 (approximately $5,336,000) on June 30, 1987. The London dealer Marlborough Fine Art bought the painting at a record price for Klimt's work.[23] Ten years later, Christie's auctioned the painting in London for £14,500,000 (approximately $23,500,000).[24] The painting, at that time the only one of the five Schloss Kammer paintings that was not already in a museum,[25] ended up in the Galleria Nazionale d'Arte Moderna in Rome.[26]

4. For the story behind the *Gruen* case, see Susan F. French, Gruen v. Gruen: *A Tale of Two Stories*, in *Property Stories* (2004).

23.   The Financial Times (London), July 1, 1987, Section 1; The Arts, p. 21.
24.   *Id.*, Oct. 10, 1997, Section News-UK, p. 9.
25.   *Id.*
26.   You can find a picture of *Schloss Kammer am Attersee II* at the Gustav Klimt museum at www.expo-klimt.com.

D.   DELIVERY TO A THIRD PARTY

Delivery can be made to a third party if made with the intent that the gift be immediately effective and the donor does not intend to retain a power to revoke. A donor who wants to retain the ability to revoke a gift needs to use a revocable trust, rather than delivering the deed to a third party with instructions to deliver it to the grantee at some future time. Although it can be effective, making a gift by delivery to a third party on the grantor's death often leads to litigation.

CHANDLER v. CHANDLER

Supreme Court of Alabama
409 So. 2d 780 (1982)

JONES, J. Appellants . . . are six of the eight children of J. W. and Maggie Chandler. Appellee, J. P. Chandler . . . , is a brother of Appellants. In June, 1964, the Chandler parents executed a deed purportedly conveying to Maggie an undivided one-half interest in 270 acres for life, reserving unto J. W. an undivided one-half interest for life, with right of survivorship for the lifetime of the survivor, and with remainder in fee simple to their son, J. P. The father and mother lived on the subject property for many years, until they died in 1972 and 1975, respectively.

In May, 1980, this action was commenced, seeking to set aside the deed on grounds of undue influence, mental incapacity of the father (grantor), and "no legal delivery" of the deed. This appeal is from the trial court's judgment upholding the validity of the deed.

Appellants . . . state the issue presented for our review:

Whether there is a valid delivery of a deed where the deed is held by a third party depositary "for safekeeping," subject to be returned to the grantors upon request, to be transferred to the grantee upon the death of the grantors.

If we accept the ". . . subject to be returned to the grantors upon request . . ." portion of Appellants' statement of the issue, unquestionably the trial court committed reversible error. The reserved right of a grantor, who has left the deed with a third party, to retrieve the instrument, and thus revoke the grant, voids delivery of the deed which is essential to its validity as a conveyance.

Appellants' brief correctly sets forth the applicable "lack of delivery" rules:

Delivery of a deed is essential to its validity as a conveyance. Delivery is the final act which consummates the deed, signifying that it is in operation and effect. Generally, where the deed is not delivered during the life of the grantor, no right or title is conferred on the grantee. An exception to the general rule is where the grantor delivers a deed to a third party to be delivered to the grantee after the death of the grantor. However, there is no delivery when the deed is merely given to the third party for safekeeping. If the deed is subject to be recalled by the grantor before delivery to the grantee, there is no effectual delivery by the grantor. . . .

Urging our application of these rules to the evidence of record before us, Appellants conclude:

> The deed in this case was held by the Dozier bank "for safekeeping," according to the head cashier of the bank. . . . The grantor had the right to go back to the bank and recover the deed. . . . The trial court failed to recognize the well-established principles of delivery in upholding the sufficiency of delivery, and, thus, ruled incorrectly that the conveyance was valid.

The well-settled, and equally well-understood, "sufficiency of delivery" principle, where delivery is made to a person other than the grantee or his agent, is discussed in Fitzpatrick v. Brigman, 30 So. 500 (Ala. 1900):

> (T)he delivery must be so effectual as to deprive the grantor of the right to revoke it. For so long as he reserves to himself the *locus penitentiae*[27] there is no delivery—no present intention to divest himself of the title to the property. . . . (T)he grantor need not expressly reserve to himself this right to repent, but if his act upon which a delivery is predicated does not place the deed beyond his control, as a matter of law, then his right of revocation is not gone.
>
> . . . "The law does not presume, when a deed is handed to a third person, that it has been with the intention to pass title to the grantee. In order to make such an act a delivery to the grantee, the intention of the grantor must be expressed at the time in an unmistakable manner." . . .

We look to the record, then, to test the Appellants' assertion that ". . . grantors unquestionably did not place the deed beyond their complete control since the third party depositary would have returned the deed had the grantors requested it; thus, the right of revocation was not gone."

In support of their "lack of delivery" contention, Appellants accurately summarize the evidence:

> The deed in question was not transferred directly to the defendant-grantee, but rather was transferred to the bank vault of the Dozier bank by J. W. Chandler sometime in 1965. Ms. Sport (the head cashier) testified there was only one packet in the Dozier bank vault belonging to J. W. Chandler. She testified that she personally received instructions from J. W. Chandler at the time the deed was put in the vault, . . . (and) that the deed was given to the defendant, pursuant to instructions on a note attached to the deed instructing that the deed be delivered to J. P. Chandler upon the death of J. W. Chandler. . . . Ms. Sport testified that on most of the "stuff" the bank keeps, since it has no safety deposit boxes, "you have got to have some kind of instructions as to who to deliver certain items to." Questioned further, Ms. Sport stated that, "(I)f I delivered the documents to J. P. Chandler, there was some information attached to it . . . ." Pressed further about the presence of a note, she was asked, "Do you remember whether or not there was any . . . ?" to which Ms. Sport responded, "There was or I wouldn't have delivered them to J. P." Asked again, whether she, in fact, remembers a note, she replied, "Yes." Finally, referring to the presence of a note with instruction, she stated, "I told you very distinctly that

---

27. Locus poenitentiae, literally meaning place of repentance, is used to mean an opportunity to change your mind before it is too late. Mellinkoff's Dictionary of American Legal Usage 388 (1992).—Eds.

if I delivered them, that it was on there." She stated that instructions on the note were typed out by another employee of the bank, Mr. Merrill.

Ms. Sport testified that when a person, such as J. W. Chandler, leaves a deed with the bank, that person has a right to go back and pick that deed up at any time he desires. She was asked whether "Mr. Chandler or any other person for that matter (would) have had the right or control to go get the paper from the time that he put them in there at any time prior to (his) death," and (she) responded that he would have the right to go to the bank and take back the document. Asked the purpose of having this service such as was provided J. W. Chandler when he transferred his deed to the Dozier bank, Ms. Sport replied, "Just for safekeeping."

The question for our resolution is whether the trial court erred, in the face of Ms. Sport's testimony . . . in finding a valid delivery of the deed. We hold that the trial court did not err in concluding from Ms. Sport's testimony, when considered along with the totality of the circumstances, that J. W. Chandler, at the time he delivered the deed to the bank for "safekeeping," possessed the requisite intent to relinquish control over the deed and have it take effect as a present conveyance.

Indeed, we are of the opinion that J. W. Chandler's unequivocal instruction to the third party to deliver the deed, upon his death, to his son J. P., absent any expression or conduct on the part of the father relative to his right to retrieve the deed, or otherwise exercise control thereof, precluded a contrary finding on the part of the trial court. The policy of the bank in permitting those who left papers in its vault to take such papers back from the bank is not determinative of the grantor's surrender of control of the instrument in question. The fact of delivery rests in the grantor's intention, which is an issue of fact to be determined from all the attendant circumstances at the time.

Here the grantor, for a valuable consideration expressed in the deed, granted a life estate in a one-half interest to his wife, reserved to himself a life estate in the remaining one-half interest (expressly creating a joint tenancy with right of survivorship), with the remainder to his son J. P. He delivered the deed to the bank with express instructions (both written and oral) to deliver the deed to J. P. upon the grantor's death. The bank's policy of freely returning such papers upon its customers' requests is grounded in the nature of the bank's service to, and relationship with, its customers. Such policy, grounded on institutional good will considerations, is not determinative of the legal requisite of the grantor's intention to so surrender control of the deed as to effectuate the conveyance. . . .

Central to our holding is the undisputed fact that the grantor gave express, unequivocal instructions to the third party for delivery of the deed to the named grantee upon a certain future event—the death of the grantor. Given this fact, along with the other attendant circumstances, including the absence of words or conduct reserving the grantor's right of revocation, the inference of completed delivery, fully executed, is amply sustainable, and in accord with our case law cited above.

Moreover, the trial judge was warranted under the evidence in finding the requisite delivery as between the grantors and the life tenants without reference to any issue of delivery as between the grantors and the remainderman. Nevertheless, we have addresssed the issue of "delivery" as between the grantor (the father) and the remainderman (the son) in the context of the issue as framed by the pleadings and tried before the trial court and as presented and argued to this Court.

AFFIRMED. . . .

TROBERT, C.J. I dissent. While the majority correctly set out the law as it has evolved in Alabama, they misapply this law to the facts of this case. The majority states that the testimony of Ms. Sport, an officer of the First National Bank of Dozier, "along with the totality of the circumstances," shows that J. W. Chandler "possessed the requisite intent to relinquish control over the deed" to have it operate as a valid conveyance. This is simply not the case. . . .

While J. W. Chandler did leave instructions to the bank to deliver the deed upon his death, it is without doubt that the bank held the deed only for safekeeping and that he retained control over the deed. Ms. Sport testified that the deed was in a file at the bank under the name of Mr. J. W. Chandler at the time of his death in 1972. She stated that this was done as part of the normal service rendered by the banks in that area, since these banks do not have safe deposit boxes. When specifically questioned about the issue of control, the following ensued:

> *Q.* Ms. Sport, I will ask you ma'am, would Mr. Chandler or any other person, for that matter, have the right or control to go get the papers from the time that he put them in there at any time prior to their death?
>
> *A.* Why, sure.
>
> *Q.* Would you tell the Court the purpose of your bank having this for your customers, please?
>
> *A.* Just for safekeeping.
>
> *Q.* Thank you.

From this testimony, it is quite obvious that Mr. Chandler did not place the deed beyond his control. Thus, as a matter of law his right of revocation was not gone and no finding of a valid delivery could have been made. . . .

Had J. W. Chandler deposited the deed into a personal safe deposit box, there is no question that the delivery would not have been complete. Here, however, the bank had no safe deposit boxes, but held documents in special files for its customers. Ms. Sport's testimony shows that these files are the functional equivalent of safe deposit boxes. Therefore, there can be no doubt that J. W. Chandler still had the deed within his control and possession. . . .

Notes and Questions

1. Why would Mr. Chandler have left the deed at the bank rather than delivering it to his son if not to retain the ability to change his mind? In *Vasquez v. Vasquez*, 973 S.W.2d 330 (Tex. Ct. App. 1998), there was a valid delivery where the donor delivered the deed to his lawyer with instructions to keep the deed secret until the donor's death.

2. If the donor gives a photocopy of the deed to the grantee but retains the original for safekeeping, has there been a delivery? Would this qualify as a symbolic delivery? *See Evans v. Waddell*, 689 So. 2d 23 (Ala. 1997) (summary judgment improper because facts raised material issues as to delivery).

3. The dissent says that if Mr. Chandler had put the deed into his safety deposit box there would have been no delivery, but the law is not so clear. There are many cases where donors have placed deeds or valuables in safe deposit boxes with written directions for delivery to the grantee or a named donee on the death of the owner and the results go all over the place. Sometimes a valid inter vivos gift is found if the donee had access to the box, sometimes not. Would it make sense to treat delivery to a safe deposit box like a gift on condition subsequent—a valid transfer subject to revocation by the donor before death? *Compare Lenhart v. Desmond*, 705 P.2d 338 (Wyo. 1985) (grantor entitled to have deed placed in safe deposit box and withdrawn and recorded by grantee invalidated; grantor testified he never intended grantee to have the property before his death; placing deed in box did not constitute delivery), *with Chalmers v. Chalmers*, 937 S.W.2d 171 (Ark. 1997) (note and mortgage placed in joint safe deposit box with assignment in favor of wife was valid gift; delivery to safe deposit box was sufficient even though wife knew nothing of it until after husband's death).

4. What happens if the donor changes the deed after delivery to the third party? *In Brevdy v. Singer*, 259 P.2d 1087 (Wyo. 1953), Julius Brevdy executed deeds to two parcels of land on June 4, 1947, one to each of his daughters, and delivered them to his attorney, Howard Black, with written instructions directing Black to deliver the deeds on Julius's death. On May 1, 1950, Julius advised Black that he had sold one of the parcels, and instructed him to add the name of his other daughter to the deed to the remaining parcel, which Black did. Julius then signed a new letter of instruction directing delivery of the remaining deed to both daughters on his death. On June 19, 1947, Julius married Edna, who became his widow when he died in an automobile accident on December 5, 1950. The widow claimed that the remaining parcel of land was part of Julius's estate. Who won? The daughters did, the court holding that the amended deed was valid and the delivery to Black was effective.

E.   JOINT BANK ACCOUNTS AND DONATIVE INTENT

Joint bank accounts with right of survivorship have given rise to lots of litigation because people often use them for a variety of purposes that are not adequately reflected on the signature card. The signature card typically provides that any party to the account may withdraw all the funds and that on the death of one, the remaining funds belong to the survivor or survivors. A few examples will illustrate the range of situations that may arise. Let's assume that O deposits $25,000 in an account in her name and A's name as joint tenants with right of survivorship and that the courts in the local jurisdiction will admit evidence in addition to the signature card as to O's intent.

> *Example 1:* O intends to make an immediate gift to A of half the money in the account and that on O's death the balance shall belong to A. *Result:* This is what might be called a "true" joint tenancy.

Example 2: O does not intend that A have any right to withdraw funds during O's lifetime but intends that the balance shall go to A on O's death. *Result:* This is what might be called a will substitute, or non-probate transfer. A has no interest in the account during O's life, but if anything remains at O's death, A will be entitled to it. What O should use if it is available in the jurisdiction[28] is a "pay on death" account rather than a joint account.

Example 3: O intends to give A access to the funds to pay O's bills in the event O becomes incapacitated but does not intend that the balance of the funds go to A on O's death. *Result:* This is a "convenience" account in which A has no beneficial interest. What O should use is a power of attorney account, but banks are often resistant and try to steer depositors toward joint tenancy accounts because their liability exposure is less. If A has O's power of attorney, A is O's agent with authority to act on her behalf, but that authority ceases on O's death. The bank would be liable for making payments after O's death, whereas with a joint tenancy account, it may safely make payments to the survivor.

Litigation tends to arise over joint bank accounts when the non-depositor withdraws money from the account for purposes other than paying the depositor's bills and after the depositor's death when the heirs and devisees claim that the account was created for convenience only. In jurisdictions following the Uniform Probate Code, lifetime withdrawal rights are based on the net contributions of the parties; in other jurisdictions each party may be entitled to withdraw an equal share of the account. After death of the depositor, most states allow the estate to claim the balance of the account on proof by clear and convincing evidence that a convenience account was intended. In a few states, however, the presumption that the survivorship rights were intended is conclusive.

---

28.   Pay on death accounts have been accepted in many states since authorized by the Uniform Probate Code, which was promulgated in 1969.

CHAPTER 9

The Modern Real Estate Transaction

The sale and transfer of real property—whether a bit of raw land worth a few thousand dollars or a commercial development costing tens of millions—involves a large cast of characters, legal complexity, and complicated documentation. The effort involved far exceeds that required for the sale and transfer of personal property or intangibles of far greater value.

This chapter examines the steps and issues in a basic real estate transaction and the roles of the different players. As you study these materials, consider whether the degree of complexity is necessary: Does it serve the parties' expectations, provide needed protections, result in an efficient land transfer system, or merely reflect devotion to historical practices originating in feudal England?

A. INTRODUCTION TO THE REAL ESTATE TRANSACTION

1. Overview of a Transaction

RESIDENTIAL REAL ESTATE TRANSACTIONS: THE LAWYER'S PROPER ROLE—SERVICES—COMPENSATION

14 Real Prop. Prob. & Tr. J. 581, 581-607 (1979)

SCOPE OF THIS PAPER

The concerns of the organized bar considered in this Paper are:

1. whether the parties to the home-buying transaction receive adequate legal services;

2. whether they pay more for these services than they should; and,

3. whether, in any event, existing procedures can be modified in such a fashion as to afford the parties necessary services at a reasonable cost.

A HYPOTHETICAL HOME PURCHASE TRANSACTION

Before the concerns mentioned above can be addressed it is important to inquire what steps are needed to consummate a routine purchase and sale of a home financed by a mortgage given by an institutional lender. In the description which follows, this Paper consciously resorts to what may seem to be over-generalization. It does so because differences in practice and nomenclature lead many otherwise knowledgeable conveyancers and laymen, at one extreme, to look upon procedures used in their communities as unique, and at the other, as universal. In fact, while there is diversity in the details of practice, there is fundamental unity in the underlying problems facing conveyancers everywhere.

A.   The Brokerage Contract

Initially a seller . . . enter[s] . . . a brokerage contract with a real estate agent. In many jurisdictions this contract is not required to be in writing with all of the usual dangers of unwritten contracts. A special peril faced by sellers who have not had the advantage of legal counsel is that they may employ more than one broker and, in the absence of a clear understanding concerning the conditions under which the brokerage fee is earned, the seller may become liable to pay more than one fee.

In practice, a high percentage of brokerage contracts are in writing. A common assumption is that the contract is simple and standardized. In fact, a properly drawn contract will anticipate a number of legal problems of some complexity, such as the right of the seller to negotiate on the seller's own behalf, the effect of multiple listings, the disposition of earnest money if the buyer defaults, the rights of the broker if the seller is unable to proffer a marketable title, the duration of any exclusive listing and . . . the point at which the brokerage fee is earned. Most of the terms are negotiable and, in theory, a new contract should be drawn each time a broker is employed.

Standardized forms, where carefully drawn, have certain advantages. There are no objections to form contracts per se, as used by either brokers or other participants in the land transfer transaction. The objections to form contracts are that they may be inappropriate to the particular transaction, badly drawn initially or incorrectly filled in.

Any seller signing such a contract should have it approved by the seller's lawyer before signing. The seller should have the lawyer explain its meaning and be on hand to see that it is properly executed. (It is presumed that if the seller consults a lawyer, the lawyer will advise against entering into any oral agreement.) In other words, the seller needs the traditional legal services embraced in the expression "advice, representation and drafting." The broker needs similar services at one time or another and receives them from the broker's own lawyer. . . . In routine transactions the broker is sufficiently familiar with the details to be able to handle the matter without resort to professional assistance.

B.   The Preliminary Negotiations

When the broker has found a potential buyer, negotiations between the buyer and the seller will begin, with the broker acting in the role of intermediary. In some cases the seller will leave to the broker all the work of negotiation and will merely ratify the agreement reached with the buyer.

It is generally thought that neither the buyer nor the seller needs a lawyer in the course of the negotiations. In theory this assumption is correct because neither party is bound until a written sales contract is signed. In fact, a great deal of trouble can be avoided if both the buyer and the seller consult their own lawyers during the course of the negotiations. If they are to make a proper bargain, they must know what to bargain about.

Aside from the . . . price, which seems paramount in the minds of both parties, they should consider such problems as the mode of paying the purchase price and the tax consequences . . . , the status of various articles as fixtures or personal property, the time set for occupancy and the effect of loss by casualty pending the closing.

They can make whatever agreement they want, but they should anticipate all important questions and be certain a complete understanding has been reached. Failure to do so in the preliminary negotiations may mean, at the time for signing a contract, that they will have to start negotiations all over again. Worse, they may enter into a contract highly disadvantageous to one or the other, so uncertain as to require litigation to determine its meaning, or so ambiguous as to be void for indefiniteness.

C. The Commitment for Financing

Before entering into a sales contract, it would be desirable for the buyer to obtain as much of a commitment as possible for necessary financing. Many lenders, however, refuse to make the necessary inspections, appraisals and credit investigations to make such a commitment until the buyer can exhibit a signed purchase and sale agreement, and many buyers are reluctant to risk losing the property to a higher offer by deferring the execution of the purchase and sale agreement. All of this leads to the common practice of including in the agreement a "subject to financing" clause which should be examined by the lawyers for the parties before the contract is signed.

Finding a willing lender is not part of a lawyer's professional duties. In practice a lawyer . . . may be able to render this service. Legal expertise is exercised when the lawyer advises the buyer about problems the buyer should anticipate in coming to terms with the lender. . . . [For example], the buyer will seldom . . . understand the potential effect of an acceleration clause. . . . The buyer should also obtain an estimate of the closing costs . . . and should obtain legal advice as to all items found in the estimate.

The commitment contract between the lender and buyer will normally be prepared by the lender's lawyer. Before it is accepted, the buyer's lawyer should ascertain that it properly anticipates all important contingencies, comports with the oral agreement previously reached and binds the lender. Normally the lender has much greater financial expertise than the buyer. This advantage may not have been of as much importance formerly as it is today, because the financing of homes has in many instances become extremely complex. For this reason, when dealing with the lender the buyer is in need of legal assistance.

D. The Contract of Sale

Once an informal agreement has been reached, the buyer and the seller will enter into a formal contract of sale. The importance of this document cannot be overemphasized. Once it is signed, the rights and obligations of the parties are fixed. Each transaction is unique and, in theory, a contract should be specially drafted for each.

The interested parties are the broker, the buyer and the seller. The contract should . . . [cover] the broker's commission. The buyer and the seller want assurance that the writing reflects their understanding. If they have not received legal advice during the preliminary negotiations, they will need to know what questions should have been anticipated and whether firm and advantageous provisions are found in the document. When the instrument is executed, their lawyers should be present to assure that the proper formalities are observed to make it binding. Here again the parties need legal services . . . .

This need is not avoided by the use of forms. Even if the form is properly drawn, the printed portion may not adequately express the particular agreement made between the parties, or the words used in filling in blanks may distort its effectiveness. . . . Whenever forms are used, any insertion should be carefully checked by the buyer's and seller's lawyers, and the appropriateness of the form for the particular transaction should be determined by the buyer's and seller's lawyers. The buyer and the seller are often unaware of what the contract means, what they should anticipate, and what steps are needed to make the instrument binding. They should be advised by their own legal counsel.

. . . [Before] the contract is signed, the buyer and the seller should have detailed advice about many legal aspects of the transaction. For example, they . . . need to anticipate the question of who bears the loss or damage to, or destruction of, buildings on the premises between the time the contract is signed and the time of closing. They also may . . . [need to know] whether the contract so changes the interest of the seller as to affect insurance policies; whether either the buyer or seller, or both, should execute new wills; whether federal and state gift and death tax matters are involved; whether joint tenancies or tenancies by the entireties will be affected; and the like.

E. Determining the Status of the Title

After the contract of sale is executed, the state of the seller's title must be determined to the satisfaction of both the buyer and the lender. This is generally the most important legal work connected with the transaction. The initial examination will be made by the lawyer for the buyer, the seller, the lender, or the title insurer, relying upon the official land title records or an abstract thereof, or a title plant maintained by a title insurance company. Where a lawyer's certificate is relied upon, either the lender or the buyer, or both, may desire additional protection in the form of a title insurance policy.

Whoever makes the title examination, the buyer's lawyer should inform the buyer of the limitations, if any, which impair the title. The buyer should also receive formal protection by a written opinion from the lawyer, an owner's title insurance policy, or both. If the buyer applies for title insurance, the buyer's lawyer should negotiate the provisions to be included or excluded from the policy. The lawyer should also make clear to the buyer what the policy means . . . , particular[ly], the exceptions to coverage. The use of standardized exceptions is common to title insurance. They are complex and restrictive and are frequently not understood by the layman.

. . . The buyer must first be made aware of the existence of these exceptions and must then be made to understand them. If the exception is to a $10,000 mortgage and the buyer sees the provision, the buyer will probably not mistake its meaning. But if the exception is to "all of the conditions and restrictions found in deed of X to Y, recorded in the office of the clerk of the court of Z County, in Deed Book 309 at page 873," the buyer will not, in the first place, realize that the exception is important, or, if the buyer does, will not understand its meaning without assistance from the lawyer.

F. The Survey

. . . At some time prior to the approval of title the buyer, the lender, or the title insurance company may demand a survey . . . to find whether the legal description of the land conforms to the lines laid down on the ground. An additional purpose may be to determine whether structures on the premises violate restrictive covenants or zoning ordinances or constitute an encroachment. . . . [T]he parties should have their lawyers advise them about any legal implications of the surveyor's findings and the scope and extent of the surveyor's certification. . . .

I. Drafting Instruments

. . . [T]he deed, mortgage and the bond or note secured by the mortgage . . . are commonly drafted by the mortgagee's attorney, although the representative of either of the other parties is equally qualified. Whoever does the work, the product should be examined by lawyers for . . . the other . . . parties and the title insurance company, and they should be advised whether the instruments are effective and create the interests intended.

The drafting of these instruments is sometimes considered merely routine work. This is not true. For example, the description of the parties must be so phrased as to prevent confusion, and the description of the land must be complete and accurate. The importance of the form of warranties is often overlooked. By way of illustration, if the title is encumbered by equitable covenants or utility easements, either or both may be acceptable to the buyer and lender, but they should be excepted from the warranty.

How title is to be taken should have been provided in the initial contract between the buyer and the seller, and the buyer should be advised as to the tax and other effects of the manner in which title is taken.

Of equal importance are other special agreements reached earlier in the transaction. The controlling law may provide that the deed supersedes prior understandings so that if they are not embraced in the deed they are nullified. Each deed must therefore be examined to determine whether it carries out what has been agreed upon.

K. Obtaining Title Insurance

Where a title insurance policy for the buyer is based on the certificate of a lawyer not employed by a title insurance company, the lawyer may make an application for the initial binder and, after closing, send in a final certificate and procure a policy. This is work for which the lawyer normally, and properly, should be paid by the client to the extent the lawyer is not paid for these services as the agent of the title company. The lawyer should not accept compensation from a title insurance company solely for referring business to that company. This is . . . clearly improper and contrary to the . . . position of the American Bar Association. The Real Estate Settlement Procedures Act specifically prohibits the acceptance of . . . "kickbacks" from the title insurance company.

L. Closing

A closing statement is generally prepared prior to final closing. The statement . . . indicate[s] the allocation of debits and credits to the various parties. In some cases it is prepared by a layman, in others by a lawyer. The buyer's and seller's lawyers should make certain their clients understand the nature and amount of all closing costs. The American Bar Association supported the adoption of legislation requiring a uniform closing statement in all government-related mortgage transactions. . . . Even a standard closing form in itself is not sufficient, unless the parties are assured by their own lawyers of the appropriateness of each item.

Unless there is an escrow closing, a further check of title should be made immediately prior to closing. If this check is not made, it is possible that the parties will be unaware that the title has been impaired between the time of the original examination and the closing date. This further check will generally be carried out by the lawyer, abstracter or title insurance company certifying or insuring title.

The closing is the proceeding at which the parties exchange executed instruments, make required payments, and conclude the formal aspects of the transaction. . . . [T]he buyer, the seller, and the lender should be represented by their own lawyers. They require advice and may need representation if a disagreement arises. They should be assured that the legal documents they exchange create the interests intended, that they receive the protection to which they are entitled and that correct payments have been made to those entitled to receive them.

As a part of the closing, arrangements must be made for insurance, taxes, and other incidents of ownership. Instruments must be recorded and a final check of title made. Disbursements must be made and documents distributed to the parties entitled to receive them. Title insurance policies, where called for, must be procured. If a lawyer handles the closing, the lawyer will attend to all or virtually all of these details.

THE CONFLICTS OF INTEREST

At every step set out above it has been said that buyers and sellers should have representation, advice and draftsmanship. This is to say, each needs separate legal representation and should not rely on services rendered by a lawyer for some other party. Why, it will be asked, is so much legal service needed to consummate a routine, uncontested transaction? No two transactions are identical, and none is simple. Because of the complexity of property law a "minor" slip may cause great expense and inconvenience. To the buyer, at least, the purchase of a house may be the most important legal and financial transaction of a lifetime.

All of the parties have conflicting interests. . . . Houses are bought and sold by the inexperienced as well as by the sophisticated. The buyer and seller, without representation, will usually not have as much knowledge of conveyancing as the other parties. Only their own attorneys will be motivated to explain fully the transaction.

It is sometimes said the parties require disinterested advice. This misstates the case. Instead of disinterested advice, each requires the assistance of someone dedicated to that person's interest and equipped with sufficient skill to protect that person. The escrow company used in some sections of the country is theoretically disinterested. Actually its primary loyalty usually is to the institutions which are the sources of its business.

A. Broker and Seller

. . . [T]he initial step in selling a house will probably be the signing of a brokerage contract. Upon the signing of the contract the broker becomes the seller's agent. The broker and seller will have a common interest in obtaining a maximum price from the buyer. So, of course, will the lawyer for the seller. The lawyer has an interest in seeing to it that all other terms of the sale are as favorable to the seller as possible. An apprehension that the signing of the sales contract may be jeopardized by an overmeticulous attention to the other terms sometimes makes the broker reluctant to submit a proposed contract of sale to the seller's lawyer. On the other hand, many brokers realize that the seller's lawyer can help to prepare a contract that is specifically enforceable by the seller. This relieves the broker of the risk that the broker's commission will be nullified by the collapse before the closing of a contract improperly drawn. This may happen when qualifications on the seller's title have not been properly expressed.

It has been indicated that a fear of delay or disruption of the transaction often makes the broker somewhat less than enthusiastic about advising the buyer to submit a proposed contract to a lawyer. The lawyer who lets the contract of sale gather dust does much to foster this feeling. The lawyer should not surrender the client's vital interests, but should remember that the client wants the house, and should not unnecessarily impede the closing. Lawyers are trained in the art of finding fair and reasonable solutions to what might otherwise be deadlocks. . . .

B. Buyer and Seller

The interests of the buyer and the seller conflict in the sense that one wants a minimum and the other a maximum price. They do not need lawyers to advise them on this point. What they do not realize is that the contract of sale does or should contain a multitude of provisions relative to the mode of payment and to other important terms of the sale. These provisions are freely negotiable. If future dispute and possibly litigation are to be avoided the parties must be made aware of the need for true negotiation before a contract is signed. They must also be made aware that the drafting of a contract clearly expressing their agreement is a complex undertaking. In particular, they should not sign "standard form" contracts without the advice of their own lawyers.

C. Broker and Lender

Except in unusual circumstances there will be no conflict between the interests of the broker and the lender. The real danger is that their common interest will conflict with that of the buyer. If the buyer, as frequently happens, leaves financing to the broker, the broker may resort to a lending institution with which the broker normally does business. The arrangement between these two may be highly beneficial to them but disadvantageous to the buyer, who, if properly counseled, may shop around for better terms. Many sellers of homes do not rely on brokers or, even if they do, have their own sources of credit to which they direct buyers. In these cases similar conflicts of interest arise.

D. Buyer and Lender

The buyer wants to obtain money from the lender at as low an interest rate as possible. It is frequently assumed that, once the interest rate and the amount of monthly payments are agreed upon, the buyer and the lender have only common concerns. This is not true. In the first place, the terms of the financing agreement can be framed in such a way as to be beneficial to one at the expense of the other. For example, an acceleration clause wanted by the lender may be onerous to the buyer. By contrast, an anticipation clause beneficial to the buyer may be objectionable to the lender.

In the second place, the title requirements of the lender and buyer are dissimilar. The buyer wants assurance of maximum enjoyment of the property and freedom from post-settlement claims from third parties. The lender wants assurance that title is not impaired to the point where its value will be reduced below the amount of an outstanding indebtedness. A restrictive covenant or zoning ordinance increasing the value of the property may also prevent an intended use by the buyer. The lender would not object to the restriction; the buyer would find it unacceptable.

In another type of case, where the examiner makes a mistake, either by overlooking a partial impairment of title or by making an incorrect legal judgment about marketability, the error, in theory, adversely affects both the buyer and the lender. In practice, if the error relates to a matter which does not impair the value of the land to the point where the value is less than the amount of the mortgage indebtedness, the lender will suffer no loss. If the lawyer represents only the lender, the loss will therefore fall on the buyer. The lender's lawyer is not the buyer's lawyer and owes allegiance only to the lender. [*See Page v. Frazier*, 445 N.E.2d 148 (Mass. 1983).]

The buyer's and the lender's interests may also conflict at the time of closing. The buyer wants to keep costs to a minimum because the buyer generally pays the major portion. The lender conventionally pays none of the closing costs and has little or no concern in reducing them other than as a business expedient.

E. The Title Insurer and Buyer or Lender

It is sometimes [wrongly] assumed there is no conflict between the interests of the title insurer, on the one hand, and the buyer and lender on the other. . . . The insurer wants minimum risk; the other parties maximum protection. In no event is the insurer liable for any loss exempted by the terms of the policy. (In most policies, exemptions are listed under the heading "Schedule B.") Where there is no exemption, its liability is confined to situations where there has been loss to the policyholder.

If the policy runs to the mortgagee alone, even an unexpected impairment of title may result in no loss to the mortgagee. In such a case the insurer incurs no liability and the buyer without coverage must pay the cost.

The fact that the lender and the insurance company deal at arm's length is well understood by both. What is not understood by the buyer is that, by the nature of the contract, the buyer's interests are in conflict with those of the insurer. The two can enter into a binding agreement giving protection spelled out and limited by the terms of the contract. The inherent conflict, however, between the interests of the parties stands in the way of the insurer either advising or representing the insured. Although the insurer has no fiduciary relation to the lender, it looks upon the lender as a primary source of business and may render special services for purely economic reasons. However, dealings with buyers are usually one-time transactions and insurers have no inducement to offer concessions.

An individual lawyer has the same need to be protected by exceptions in the lawyer's title opinion. The lawyer must advise the buyer as to the significance of such exceptions—whether they can be accepted, if the buyer really wants the property, without undue risk of dispossession or financial loss. The lawyer can explain the difference between a good record title, a marketable title, and a merchantable title. If there is title insurance, the lawyer can negotiate for assurance that, notwithstanding a record defect that goes to marketability, the buyer's possession will not be disturbed. There is no duty on the title insurance company to explain the exceptions to its customer.

HOW THE SYSTEM WORKS IN PRACTICE

What has gone before is a largely theoretical explanation of the steps taken in completing a residential real estate transaction, the conflicts of interest engendered in the process and the need for the legal services created by these conflicts. To what extent does this explanation comport with what actually takes place?

A great variety of practices are employed throughout the country and generalizations should be expressed with caution. However, it is probably safe to say that in a high percentage of cases the seller is unrepresented and signs the contracts of brokerage and sale on the basis of faith in the broker. The buyer does not employ a lawyer. The contract of sale is signed without reading it and, once financing has been obtained, the details of title search and closing are left to the lender or broker. In many closings no lawyer will appear.

THE REDUCTION IN COST

A.   Title Examination Costs

Title examination often is expensive because of the excessive labor input under the present system. This high labor input is the result of the following major causes: (1) Condition of public land title records; (2) Lack of marketable title legislation; and (3) Lack of title curative legislation. . . .

IMPLEMENTATION OF AN EFFECTIVE PROGRAM

The basic premise of this Paper is that legal costs in home buying transactions can be reduced at the same time services to the public are enlarged. A number of remedial measures have been suggested. They are not self-implementing. Precisely what is needed to put them into effect?

Top priority should be given to a three-pronged program designed to create a useable system of public land records, to shorten the period of title search, and to quickly purge the records of technical defects. Any study of the recording system should include a consideration of how all public records affecting land titles can be consolidated in a single office and how matters arising out of federal law can be better incorporated in the local recording system. Such a program can be implemented fully only by state legislatures, acting in some instances with federal assistance. If they are to be induced to act, it will be necessary to think in both technical and political terms. The first task will be to furnish workable model statutes. Drafting should be done initially at the national level to insure the best possible product and, at the same time, to avoid costly duplication. These national models can later be modified or enlarged to meet particular local conditions. . . .

COMPENSATION OF LAWYERS

The belief has been expressed that lawyers receive excessive fees for handling residential real estate transactions and that the system of pricing is inequitable. However, the general feeling of the profession is that title work is relatively poorly rewarded and that the great danger is not that the lawyers will make too much money but that they will cease to render needed but unprofitable services. As has been indicated, in many instances present charges can be reduced. But, except in limited areas where clear abuses exist, any such reduction can come only after basic reforms have been put into operation.

Complaints against the pricing system have generally been directed against fees based on a percentage of the amount of the sales price or the mortgage debt. It is often asserted that charging on the basis of work performed will produce more equitable results. A third formula, whereby fees are computed by making specific charges for each item of work, is little used. It tends to inflate cost unduly and is justifiably unpopular.

Justification for the percentage system can be based on the fact that the risk assumed by the lawyer and the lawyer's malpractice insurer is greater or less in proportion to the value of the property. Since the examination of title to an inexpensive home may be as arduous as that for a mansion, if a percentage formula is used, the lawyer can "average out" and can render service to the small buyer at a price that otherwise would not be possible. On the other hand, pricing on the basis of the amount of work done appeals to the ordinary man's sense of justice. Although no one formula is entirely equitable, fees should be based at least on work performed and responsibility assumed.

TITLE INSURANCE

In some sections of the country the use of title insurance has eliminated the lawyer from conveyancing or drastically reduced the lawyer's role. . . . The value of some form of title insurance is recognized. . . . So long as . . . [the] present system of recording evidence of title is used, national mortgage lenders may insist upon title insurance in addition to the certificate or opinion conventionally furnished by an examining lawyer. Although the national mortgage market is the primary source of demand for title insurance, a lesser but increasing demand comes from local lenders and from home buyers who want owner coverage. The insurance can be provided by commercial companies or by bar-related title insurers. . . .

A legitimate question is whether the public can be better served by commercial title companies or the bar. . . . The role of the title company should be confined to title insurance. Conveyancing should be left to independent lawyers. The independent lawyer in private practice will protect the client's interests at each stage of the transaction and provide the necessary counseling when any difficulties arise. The objective is to provide needed legal services to the buyer and seller by their own lawyers at reasonable cost. . . .

CONCLUSIONS AND RECOMMENDATIONS

The lawyer should play a primary role in the residential real estate transaction because no one else is in a position to furnish needed legal services. At the present and for years past, the lawyer's role has steadily declined and in some places the lawyer plays no role at all. This trend should be reversed. At the same time the cost to the home buyer should be reduced. Both these objectives are practicable but can be achieved only by a systematic, long-range program of reform. The major measures required, and the part to be played by various groups if success is to be anticipated, have been set out in this Paper. . . .

Notes and Questions

Professor Michael Braunstein questions the need for lawyer involvement in residential real estate transactions and offers empirical evidence that lawyers' participation has been reduced in such transactions:

> Lawyers have tended to become marginalized in the residential real estate transaction, and it is very unlikely that this tendency will be reversed. The cause of the marginalization is not hard to identify. The . . . process by which the real estate purchaser is assured of good title is the most difficult and abstract part of the residential conveyance. Once title insurance companies took over this part of the residential real estate transaction, it was inevitable that the simpler and more routine parts of the transaction would be handled by others as well. If a lawyer was not needed for the hard part, it would not take the buyers and sellers of real property long to realize that the lawyer was probably not needed for the easier parts of the transaction either.

> There is a certain irony in all this. It is hard to imagine that the structural changes wrought by the federal government at the conclusion of World War II were intended to displace lawyers from residential conveyancing. The creation of the secondary mortgage market was designed to further national goals of affordable and plentiful housing. The secondary market accomplished these goals, in part, by demanding that participants in the market conform their transactions to standardized forms and assure the validity and priority of residential mortgages with title insurance. As the transaction became more standardized and title insurance became more prevalent, the marginalization of the residential real estate lawyers was assured: an unintended and yet unavoidable consequence of fundamental structural changes in the residential real estate transaction.

> Notwithstanding how obvious it is, the legal profession, both academic and practicing, has been slow to realize what has happened. Academics publish casebooks that seem mired in the past and continue to portray the role of the lawyer in the residential transaction as more important and more central to the transaction than it really is. Practicing lawyers continue to resist the imperialism of title insurance in the courts and legislatures. These lawyers make claims about the importance of their work to the public, but the public is largely unimpressed because claims are alternately vague, trivial and implausible.

> Finally, in a larger sense, this research sheds light not just on why lawyers were marginalized in a particular transaction, but on how the demand for professional services is formed. The demand for professional services is not created by the professions themselves. . . . The best explanation for the demand for professional services is that the professions respond to structural change in the society. Structural change which has the effect of routinizing what had been professional activity, creates opportunities for others outside the profession to perform the activity. To the extent that the newcomers are more accessible, efficient, or less expensive than the profession which was performing the service, the newcomers will thrive and the profession will perish. Certainly this is the lesson to be learned from the experience of the legal profession in residential real estate conveyancing.

Structural Change and Inter-Professional Competitive Advantage: An Example Drawn from Residential Real Estate Conveyancing, 62 Mo. L. Rev. 241, 278-79 (1977).

Others disagree. *See* Aurora Abella-Austriaco, Llewellyn Chin, Joanne Elliott & K.F. Boackle, *A Busy Residential Real Estate Market Means More Work for Lawyers,*

84 A.B.A. J. 55 (July 1998) (describing increased complexity of residential real estate transactions, due to recent changes in the law including environmental regulation, new disclosure statutes and case law, complex tax implications, new mortgage vehicles, and increased lender demands for documentation).

As you study this chapter, consider what functions lawyers should have in residential transactions. Should lawyers be involved in the contract, deed, financing, or title stages? Do buyers and sellers need greater lawyer involvement in more sophisticated residential transactions or commercial deals? Who should determine when lawyers should participate, and how and when should that choice be made?

2. The Lawyer's Professional Responsibility

IN RE CONDUCT OF BAER

Supreme Court of Oregon
298 Or. 29, 688 P.2d 1324 (1984)

PER CURIAM. The Oregon State Bar instituted disciplinary proceedings against the accused, Peter E. Baer, charging him with violations of the disciplinary rules in his dealings with Mr. and Mrs. Larry G. Peterson. A hearing was held before the Trial Board and the accused was found guilty of violating Disciplinary Rules 5-101(A) (refusing employment when the interests of the lawyer may impair his independent professional judgment); 5-104(A) (limiting business relations with a client); and 5-105(A)-(C) (refusing to accept or continue employment if the interest of another client may impair the independent professional judgment of the lawyer). The Trial Board recommended that the accused receive a public reprimand and be required to take and pass the legal ethics examination required of new admittees. The Disciplinary Review Board concurred in the findings but disagreed as to sanctions. The Disciplinary Review Board recommended that the accused be suspended for 30 days and be required to take and pass the legal ethics examination.

We find that in September, 1980, Mr. and Mrs. Larry G. Peterson owned a home in Boring, Oregon. Mrs. Peter Baer, the then wife of the accused, visited the Peterson residence and became interested in purchasing the property. Mrs. Baer returned to the home with the accused to inspect it and Mrs. Baer again expressed her desire to purchase the property. Within a few days, the Petersons and the Baers commenced negotiations for the sale of the house. The accused suggested to the Petersons that by letting him do the legal work necessary to close the transaction they would save several thousand dollars. The original sales price was $62,500. This price was lowered to $59,500 to reflect the savings in legal costs. The accused participated fully in negotiating the sales price and terms, and in other discussions relating to the property transaction. The accused did not disclose that he was representing only his wife's interests, but instead merely told the Petersons they could have another attorney check his work if they chose to do so. He did not clarify the need for independent legal advice nor did he inform the Petersons he was not representing them. The Petersons believed the accused was representing all parties to the transaction.

Thereupon, the Petersons accepted Mrs. Baer's offer to purchase the house with the understanding that the accused would perform all the legal services necessary to close the transaction. The Petersons asked questions about the legal aspects of the transaction and the accused answered their questions. He also offered them tax advice pertaining to the sale. Pursuant to the understanding of the parties, the accused prepared an earnest money agreement, an amended earnest money agreement, an addendum to the amended earnest money agreement, a warranty deed and escrow instructions.

The accused acted as escrow agent in closing the sale of the property. Mrs. Peterson questioned whether it was appropriate for Mr. Baer to handle the escrow and questioned him as to the legal rights of the Petersons in the event the transaction was not handled correctly. The accused responded that the Petersons could look to his malpractice insurance.

Pursuant to the amended earnest money agreement, Mrs. Baer was to make a down payment at closing, assume the Petersons' mortgage, and pay the remaining balance of approximately $29,500 no later than April 2, 1981. Upon payment of the $29,500, Mrs. Baer was to receive a warranty deed previously signed by the Petersons and left in escrow with the accused. The Petersons asked the accused what would happen if the final payment was not made. The accused told them that they would get their house back and would keep the money. As it turned out, accused's wife was unable to sell her former residence and thus was not able to make the final $29,500 payment. The Petersons attempted to repossess the house but were advised by the accused that the agreement was not a contract of sale as the Petersons thought, but rather was a simple earnest money agreement. The accused further advised the Petersons that the accused's wife now held a part ownership interest in the house and if the Petersons wanted the house back they would have to sell it and refund the accused's wife her money.

In April, 1981, the Petersons hired an attorney to protect their interests. The Petersons' counsel reviewed the matter and wrote accused advising him that he had "a severe conflict of interest" and suggested the accused settle the matter immediately. The accused responded by filing suit on behalf of his wife . . . for rescission of the purchase agreement, alleging fraud on the part of the Petersons due to certain defects in the house. . . .

DR 5-101(A) provides:

> Except with the consent of his client after full disclosure, a lawyer shall not accept employment if the exercise of his professional judgment on behalf of his client will be or reasonably may be affected by his own financial, business, property, or personal interests.

DR 5-104(A) provides:

> A lawyer shall not enter into a business transaction with a client if they have differing interests therein and if the client expects the lawyer to exercise his professional judgment therein for the protection of the client, unless the client has consented after full disclosure.

The accused argues that the Trial Board and the Disciplinary Review Board erred in finding him guilty . . . because his only client was his wife—he did not accept employment from the Petersons nor did he enter into a business transaction with them. We disagree. The accused suggested and the Petersons agreed that he perform the legal work necessary to close the real estate transaction. He prepared the documents associated with the sale of the property. The price of the home was reduced by approximately $3,000 to reflect the savings of attorney fees to the Petersons. Due to his wife's participation in the transaction, the accused's interests differed with the Petersons' and his professional judgment reasonably might have been affected by his own financial, business and personal concerns. Although the accused told the Petersons they could have another attorney check his work, this falls short of the full disclosure requirement:

> " 'To satisfy the requirement of full disclosure by a lawyer before undertaking to represent two conflicting interests, it is not sufficient that both parties be informed of the fact that the lawyer is undertaking to represent both of them, but *he must explain to them the nature of the conflict of interest in such detail so that they can understand the reasons why it may be desirable for each to have independent counsel,* with undivided loyalty to the interests of each of them.' " *See* Wise, *Legal Ethics* 77 (2d ed. 1970); Patterson and Cheatham, *The Profession of Law* 232, 235 (1971); Drinker, *supra* at 121 [*Legal Ethics* (1953)] . . . .

We find the accused guilty of violating DR 5-101(A) and DR 5-104(A).

The accused was also charged with violating DR 5-105 for his representation of the Petersons and his wife in the real estate transaction and for filing suit against the Petersons. DR 5-105 provides in pertinent part:

> (A) A lawyer shall decline proffered employment if the exercise of his independent professional judgment in behalf of a client will be or is likely to be adversely affected by the acceptance of the proffered employment, except to the extent permitted under DR 5-105(C).
>
> (B) A lawyer shall not continue employment if the exercise of his independent professional judgment in behalf of a client will be or is likely to be adversely affected by his representation of another client, except to the extent permitted under DR 5-105(C).
>
> (C) In the situations covered by DR 5-105(A) and (B), a lawyer may represent multiple clients if it is obvious that he can adequately represent the interest of each and if each consents to the representation after full disclosure of the possible effect of such representation on the exercise of his independent professional judgment on behalf of each. . . .

In *In re* Porter, *supra*, 283 Or. at 523, we said:

> ". . . [I]f the representation of multiple clients is such that the lawyer's independent professional judgment on behalf of one client *will be* adversely affected (an 'actual' conflict), or *is likely to be* adversely affected (a 'potential' conflict), the representation is improper unless the exception provided in DR 5-105(C) applies." (Original emphasis.)

A conflict of interest existed when the accused undertook the representation of both sides in the real estate transaction. . . . The requirement . . . for full disclosure was not met by the accused. We find the accused violated DR 5-105. . . .

The accused is suspended from the practice of law for not less than 60 days beginning on November 1, 1984, and thereafter until he has taken and successfully completed the professional responsibility examination. . . . The Oregon State Bar is awarded its actual and necessary costs and disbursements. . . .

Notes and Questions

1. What are the costs and benefits of dual representation? What disclosure would have been adequate for the court in *Baer*? What precise words should Attorney Baer have used with the Petersons?

2. Rule 1.7 of the Model Rules of Professional Conduct, adopted by the American Bar Association in 2002, provides:

> (a) Except as provided in paragraph (b), a lawyer shall not represent a client if the representation involves a concurrent conflict of interest. A concurrent conflict of interest exists if:
>
> (1) the representation of one client will be directly adverse to another client; or
>
> (2) there is a significant risk that the representation of one or more clients will be materially limited by the lawyer's responsibilities to another client, a former client or a third person or by a personal interest of the lawyer.
>
> (b) Notwithstanding the existence of a concurrent conflict of interest under paragraph (1), a lawyer may represent a client if:
>
> (1) the lawyer reasonably believes that the lawyer will be able to provide competent and diligent representation to each affected client;
>
> (2) the representation is not prohibited by law;
>
> (3) the representation does not involve the assertion of a claim by one client against another client represented by the lawyer in the same litigation or other proceeding before a tribunal; and
>
> (4) each affected client gives informed consent, confirmed in writing.

Would *Baer* have been decided differently if the Model Rules, rather than the earlier Code of Professional Responsibility relied on by the court, had been in effect?

3. The New Jersey Supreme Court has a long line of cases addressing the issue of multiple representation in real estate transactions. In a concurring opinion in *In re Lanza*, 322 A.2d 445 (N.J. 1974), Justice Pashman maintained that dual representation of buyers and sellers should never be permitted. He stated that "[i]t is virtually impossible for one attorney in any manner and under any circumstances to faithfully and with undivided allegiance represent both a buyer and seller." Moreover, "[n]either buyer nor seller can ever possibly fully appreciate all the complexities involved. This is precisely the reason why full disclosure and informed consent are illusory."

In *Baldasarre v. Butler*, 625 A.2d 458, 467 (N.J. 1993), the court barred dual representation in "complex commercial real estate transaction[s]." This rule is necessary "where large sums of money are at stake, where contracts contain complex contingencies, or where options are numerous."

Should all dual representation be barred? Is the residential-commercial distinction valid? *See* Philip W. Bolus, Comment, *One for All Is Worth Two in the Bush: Mixing Metaphors Creates Lawyer Conflict of Interest Problems in Residential Real Estate*

Transactions, 56 U. Cin. L. Rev. 639 (1987); Kevin McMunigal, *Rethinking Attorney Conflict of Interest Doctrine*, 5 Geo. J. Legal Ethics 823 (1992); Bruce A. Green, *Conflicts of Interest in Legal Representation: Should the Appearance of Impropriety Rule Be Eliminated in New Jersey — Or Revived Everywhere Else?*, 28 Seton Hall L. Rev. 315 (1997).

Problem

Lawyer engaged in a dual representation of Buyer and Seller of a home. At closing, Buyer lacked adequate funds and offered a postdated check to Seller. Lawyer indicated to Seller that this was no problem. Did Lawyer breach DR 5-105, set out in *Baer*? *See In re Lanza*, 322 A.2d 445 (N.J. 1974).

3.   Brokers

TRISTRAM'S LANDING, INC. v. WAIT

Supreme Judicial Court of Massachusetts
367 Mass. 622, 327 N.E.2d 727 (1975)

TAURO, C.J. This is an action in contract seeking to recover a brokerage commission . . . . The judge found for the plaintiffs in the full amount of the commission. The defendant filed exceptions to that finding and appealed.

. . . The plaintiffs are real estate brokers doing business in Nantucket. The defendant owned real estate on the island which she desired to sell. In the past, the plaintiffs acted as brokers for the defendant when she rented the same premises.

The plaintiffs heard that the defendant's property was for sale, and in the spring of 1972 the plaintiff Van der Wolk telephoned the defendant and asked for authority to show it. The defendant agreed that the plaintiffs could act as brokers, although not as exclusive brokers, and told them that the price for the property was $110,000. During this conversation there was no mention of a commission. The defendant knew that the normal brokerage commission in Nantucket was five per cent of the sale price.

In the early months of 1973, Van der Wolk located a prospective buyer, Louise L. Cashman . . . . Her written offer of $100,000, dated April 29, was conveyed to the defendant. Shortly thereafter, the defendant's husband and attorney wrote to the plaintiffs that "a counter-offer of $105,000 with an October 1st closing" should be made to Cashman. Within a few weeks, the counter offer was orally accepted, and a purchase and sale agreement was drawn up by Van der Wolk.

The agreement was executed by Cashman and was returned to the plaintiffs with a check for $10,500, representing a ten percent down payment. The agreement was then presented by the plaintiffs to the defendant, who signed it after reviewing it with her attorney. The down payment check was thereafter turned over to the defendant.

The purchase and sale agreement signed by the parties called for an October 1, 1973, closing date. On September 22, the defendant signed a 15 day extension of the closing date, which was communicated to Cashman by the plaintiffs.

Cashman did not sign the extension. On October 1, 1973, the defendant appeared at the registry of deeds with a deed to the property. Cashman did not appear . . . and thereafter refused to go through with the purchase. No formal action has been taken . . . to enforce the agreement or to recover damages for its breach, although the defendant has retained the down payment.

Van der Wolk presented the defendant with a bill for commission in the amount of $5,250, five percent of the agreed sales price. The defendant, through her attorney, refused to pay, stating that "[t]here has been no sale and consequently the 5% commission has not been earned." The plaintiffs then brought this action . . . .

In the course of dealings between the plaintiffs and the defendant there was no mention of commission. The only reference to commission is found in the purchase and sale agreement signed by Cashman and the defendant, which reads as follows: "It is understood that a broker's commission of five (5) percent on the said sale is to be paid to . . . [the broker] by the said seller." The plaintiffs contend that, having produced a buyer who was ready, willing and able to purchase the property, and who was in fact accepted by the seller, they are entitled to their full commission. The defendant argues that no commission was earned because the sale was not consummated. We agree with the defendant, and reverse the finding by the judge below.

1. The general rule . . . is that, absent special circumstances, the broker "is entitled to a commission if he produces a customer ready, able, and willing to buy upon the terms and for the price given the broker by the owner." In the past, this rule has been construed to mean that once a customer is produced by the broker and accepted by the seller, the commission is earned, whether or not the sale is actually consummated. . . . Furthermore, execution of a purchase and sale agreement is usually seen as conclusive evidence of the seller's acceptance of the buyer. . . .

Despite these well established and often cited rules, we have held that "[t]he owner is not helpless" to protect himself from these consequences. "He may, by appropriate language . . . [provide] that no commission is to become due until the customer actually takes a conveyance and pays therefor."

In the application of these rules to the instant case, we believe that the broker here is not entitled to a commission. We cannot construe the purchase and sale agreement as an unconditional acceptance by the seller of the buyer, as the agreement itself contained conditional language. The purchase and sale agreement provided that the commission was to be paid "on the said sale," and we construe this language as requiring that the said sale be consummated before the commission is earned.

While we recognize that there is a considerable line of cases indicating that language providing for payment of a commission when the agreement is "carried into effect" or "when title is passed" does not create a condition precedent, but merely sets a time for payment to be made, Alvord v. Cook, 54 N.E. 499 (Mass. 1899); Rosenthal v. Schwartz, 101 N.E. 1070 (Mass. 1913); Lord v. Williams, 156 N.E. 421 (Mass. 1927); Canton v. Thomas, 162 N.E. 769 (Mass. 1928), we do not think the course of events and the choice of language in this case fall within the *Alvord* case and its progeny. This is not a case, like Canton v. Thomas, where a separate agreement was made between the seller and the broker wherein the broker would receive a commission " 'in consideration of . . . procuring a purchaser.' " Similarly, Rosenthal v. Schwartz, *supra*, is distinguishable on its facts, as there the seller himself defaulted, thus depriving the broker of a commission by his own acts. . . .

To the extent that there are cases . . . , unique on their facts, which may appear inconsistent with this holding and seem to indicate a contrary result, we choose not to follow them.

In light of what we have said, we construe the language "on the said sale" as providing for a "special agreement," or as creating "special circumstances" wherein consummation of the sale became a condition precedent for the broker to earn his commission. . . . Accordingly, . . . the plaintiffs were not entitled to recover . . . .

2. Although what we have said to this point is determinative of the rights of the parties, we note that the relationship and obligations of real estate owners and brokers inter se has been the "subject of frequent litigation" . . . . In two of the more recent cases where we were faced with this issue, we declined to follow the developing trends in this area, holding that the cases presented were inappropriate for that purpose. . . . We believe, however, that it is both appropriate and necessary at this time to clarify the law, and we now join the growing minority of States who have adopted the rule of Ellsworth Dobbs, Inc. v. Johnson, 236 A.2d 843 (N.J. 1967).[6]

In *Ellsworth,* the New Jersey court faced the task of clarifying the law regarding the legal relationships between sellers and brokers in real estate transactions. In order to formulate a just and proper rule, the court examined the realities of such transactions. The court noted that "ordinarily when an owner of property lists it with a broker for sale, his expectation is that the money for the payment of commission will come out of the proceeds of the sale." It quoted with approval from the opinion of Lord Justice Denning, in Dennis Reed, Ltd. v. Goody, [1950] 2 K.B. 277, where he stated: "When a house owner puts his house into the hands of an estate agent, the ordinary understanding is that the agent is only to receive a commission if he succeeds in effecting a sale. . . . The common understanding of men is . . . that the agent's commission is payable out of the purchase price . . . . The house-owner wants to find a man who will actually buy his house and pay for it. He does not want a man who will only make an offer or sign a contract. He wants a purchaser 'able to purchase and able to complete as well.'"

The court went on to say that the principle binding "the seller to pay commission if he signs a contract of sale with the broker's customer, regardless of the customer's financial ability, puts the burden on the wrong shoulders. Since the broker's duty to the owner is to produce a prospective buyer who is financially able to pay the purchase price and take title, a right in the owner to assume such capacity when the broker presents his purchaser ought to be recognized." Reason and justice dictate that it should be the broker who bears the burden of producing a purchaser who is not only ready, willing and able at the time of the negotiations, but who also consummates the sale at the time of closing.

6. Both Kansas and Oregon have adopted the *Ellsworth* rule in its entirety. . . . Additionally, Vermont, Connecticut and Idaho have cited the case with approval. . . . Other States and the District of Columbia also have similar, but more limited rules . . . adopted prior to the *Ellsworth* case. . . .

Thus, we adopt the following rules:

When a broker is engaged by an owner of property to find a purchaser for it, the broker earns his commission when (a) he produces a purchaser ready, willing and able to buy on the terms fixed by the owner, (b) the purchaser enters into a binding contract with the owner to do so, and (c) the purchaser completes the transaction by closing the title in accordance with the provisions of the contract. If the contract is not consummated because of lack of financial ability of the buyer to perform or because of any other default of his . . . there is no right to commission against the seller. On the other hand, if the failure of completion of the contract results from the wrongful act or interference of the seller, the broker's claim is valid and must be paid.

. . . In view of the waiver of the counts in quantum meruit, we do not now consider the extent to which the broker may be entitled to share in a forfeited deposit or other benefit received by the seller as a result of the broker's efforts.

We recognize that this rule could be easily circumvented by language to the contrary in purchase and sale agreements or in agreements between sellers and brokers. In many States a signed writing is required for an agreement to pay a commission to a real estate broker. . . . Such a requirement may be worthy of legislative consideration, but we do not think we should establish such a requirement by judicial decision. Informal agreements fairly made between people of equal skill and understanding serve a useful purpose. But many sellers, unlike brokers, are involved in real estate transactions infrequently, perhaps only once in a lifetime, and are thus unfamiliar with their legal rights. In such cases agreements by the seller to pay a commission even though the purchaser defaults are to be scrutinized carefully. If not fairly made, such agreements may be unconscionable or against public policy. . . .

Judgment for the defendant.

Notes and Questions

1. Consider the role brokers play in real estate transactions. What value do they add to the transaction, from the perspectives of the buyer, the seller, and the system?

2. The rule of *Tristram's Landing* has been embraced by a number of courts over recent years, although some modern courts still follow the traditional (and probably still majority) rule. *See, e.g., Sticht v. Shull,* 543 So. 2d 395 (Fla. Dist. Ct. App. 1989). What reasons support the rule in *Tristram's Landing*? Does it allow a commission in all cases? What limits are there to the rule? Why might courts refuse to follow *Tristram's Landing*?

3. Different forms of listing agreements create differing rights and liabilities for the broker and the seller: an open listing (or non-exclusive listing) entitles the broker to payment only if she procures a ready, willing, and able buyer; an exclusive agency entitles the broker to payment if the property is sold by anyone other than the seller; and an exclusive right to sell gives the broker the right to a commission if *anyone,* including the seller, finds a buyer.

Which type of agreement would a seller prefer? What risks are created for a seller under an exclusive agency or exclusive right to sell? What protections can the law provide for the seller?

Courts often have to determine whether the key requirements for earning a commission in non-exclusive agreements—if a broker is the "procuring cause" and if a buyer is "ready, willing, and able"—have been met. These are essentially fact-based determinations and also often depend on whether the seller acted in good faith. *See, e.g., Gilmer v. Fauteux*, 723 A.2d 1150 (Vt. 1998) (contacting purchaser four times over four-year period was not procuring cause); *Blackstone v. Thalman*, 949 S.W.2d 470 (Tex. Ct. App. 1997) (buyer who made counter-offer contingent on appraisal was not ready, willing, and able to purchase at terms stated in listing agreement).

4. What type of obligation and liability should the broker have to the seller? In what ways could their interests diverge? What does each have a right to expect?

Is it improper (and actionable) if the broker purchases the property for herself without disclosing to the sellers that she is the buyer? *See Kirkruff v. Wisegarver*, 697 N.E.2d 406 (Ill. App. Ct. 1998) (broker breached fiduciary duty; seller entitled to damages measured by net profit on subdivision of land). If the broker fails to disclose that the buyer was also negotiating to buy a neighboring property? *See Olsen v. Vail Associates Real Estate, Inc.*, 935 P.2d 975 (Colo. 1997) (no breach of fiduciary duty).

Should a broker be liable to the buyer for misrepresenting facts about the property? Does it matter whether (a) the broker was only repeating information that the seller told the broker and the broker did not know that the information was false? *See Robinson v. Grossman*, 57 Cal. App. 4th 634 (1997) (listing broker had no duty to verify or disclaim sellers' representation that cracks in stucco were only "cosmetic" problem); (b) the broker did not inspect the property before repeating incorrect information from the seller? (Cal. Civ. Code § 2079(a) (broker has duty to make reasonably competent visual inspection and disclose material facts to buyer); (c) the broker made no false statement but failed to disclose important information? *See Enright v. Jonassen*, 931 P.2d 1212 (Idaho 1997) (broker breached duty to discover and disclose that property was located in floodplain; buyer entitled to extra expense due to floodplain designation but not to disgorgement of broker's fee). *See* Marianne Jennings, *Agent Liability and Seller's Representations*, 27 Real Est. L.J. 308 (1999).

5. Statutes in many jurisdictions require that a brokerage agreement be in writing; otherwise, the broker may not collect a commission. *See Fred Ezra Co. v. Pedas*, 682 A.2d 173 (D.C. Ct. App. 1996) (permitting broker to recover commission despite statute under common-law implied-in-fact contract). Many states allow a commission only to licensed brokers. What policies support such regulations?

Problems: Agent's Commission

1. Is Broker entitled to a commission when (a) Seller refuses to close because Buyer cannot obtain mortgage financing to make the purchase or (b) Buyer refuses to close because the title to the property is not marketable?

2. Seller enters into non-exclusive listing agreements with B1, B2, and B3 for the sale of the property at $10,000. B1 produces a customer who is ready, willing, and able to buy at $10,000. Before a sales agreement is signed with the customer, B2 brings in a customer at $11,000; Seller refuses to sign with B1's customer and instead signs a sales contract with B2's customer. B2's customer suffers financial reverses and cannot close the transaction. B3 then shows up with a customer for $9,500. Seller is so disgusted with the whole business that she signs a contract with B3's customer, and the deal closes. To whom does Seller owe a commission?

B. CONTRACT OF SALE

The usual residential or commercial transaction has two key documents—the contract (or agreement) of sale, containing the promises by the buyer and seller to buy and sell the land, followed by the deed, which passes title from the seller to the buyer. In addition, the contract of sale contains various express and implied conditions to the sale.

Typically (although there are exceptions, some of which are discussed in these materials), the contract provides for a period of time (usually somewhere between 30 and 90 days) between the execution of the contract and the delivery of the deed. This interim period allows the parties to check the status of the title to the property, permits the buyer to obtain mortgage financing, and allows the parties to take other steps necessary to close the deal.

This section examines the contract of sale, including the requisite formalities, conditions to closing, expectations of the parties, and remedies for breach.

1. Statute of Frauds

The Statute of Frauds in the various American jurisdictions sets out the requisite formalities to create a binding contract of sale for real property. The current American versions closely track the provisions of the 1677 English Statute of Frauds, which, among many other things, declared that no freehold estate could be created or transferred except by an instrument in writing signed by the grantor. It thus made documentary transfer compulsory and established the basis for a workable system of title security.

a. Contracts for Sale of Land Under the Statute

Section 4(4) of the English Statute of Frauds, which generally has been copied almost word for word into current American law, provides:

> No action shall be brought . . . upon any contract or sale of lands, tenements or hereditaments, of any interest in or concerning them . . . unless the agreement upon which such action shall be brought, or some memorandum or note thereof, shall be in writing, and signed by the party to be charged therewith, or some other person thereunto by him lawfully authorized.

The purpose of the statute was, and remains, to protect property holders from trumped-up claims that others owned interests in their property. This effectively made land ownership more secure and increased its value as a commercial asset.

Degree of definiteness. The courts will usually find that the contract is sufficiently definite for specific performance if it identifies the parties, the property, the price, and the time for closing. *See, e.g., Povey v. Clow*, 934 P.2d 528 (Or. Ct. App. 1997) (other terms not material). While most courts are flexible on the issue of adequacy of the property's description and permit the use of a street address to describe the property, some require a full legal description. *See, e.g., Lafayette Place Assocs. v. Boston Redevelopment Auth.*, 694 N.E.2d 820 (Mass. 1998), *cert. denied* (1999) (description of property as the "Hayward Parcel" sufficient); *but see Halbert v. Forney*, 945 P.2d 1137 (Wash. Ct. App. 1997) (street address insufficient).

The doctrine of part performance. The courts have created an exception to the Statute of Frauds, based not on the language of the statute but on equitable principles. Under this doctrine of partial performance, the courts have ruled that a party to an oral agreement who has made part performance of such type as to indicate the existence and general content of the agreement may secure specific performance. The courts maintain that the actual performance satisfies concerns over fraudulent claims of ownership.

The taking of possession by the buyer is seen by the courts as sufficient part performance, and for some courts is the only act sufficient to satisfy the doctrine. *See Pate v. Billy Boyd Realty & Constr., Inc.*, 699 So. 2d 186 (Ala. Civ. App. 1997) (possession required). Some courts, however, permit indicia of part performance without possession. *See, e.g., Johnson Farms v. McEnroe*, 568 N.W.2d 920 (N.D. 1997) (payment of consideration, collaboration on subdivision sufficient to show part performance).

b. The Statute and Deeds

The statute also provides that no estate in land can be created or transferred except by an instrument in writing signed by the grantor. Any other attempted conveyance creates an estate at will only. An exception is made for leases not exceeding three years, if there is a rent reserved equal to at least two-thirds of the rental value of the property (sections 1 to 3). This portion of the statute is the basis of today's requirement of a deed to convey realty. The statute's exception for leases continues as well, except today usually leases under a year are excepted.

2. *Contract Conditions*

The following materials examine the implied and express conditions in a contract of sale for realty, as well as the remedies of the parties in the event of breach. In studying these materials, consider how these conditions serve the legitimate expectations of the parties and whether they promote an efficient and active real estate transactions system. Note as well the interaction between the conditions themselves and the remedies for their breach.

a. Marketable Title

CONKLIN v. DAVI

Supreme Court of New Jersey
76 N.J. 468, 388 A.2d 598 (1978)

MOUNTAIN, J. Plaintiffs contracted to sell and convey to defendants a residential property in Ridgewood. The purchasers refused to consummate the sale, alleging defects in title and misrepresentations . . . [by] sellers. Plaintiffs . . . [sued] for specific performance; defendants counterclaimed for rescission. Before the trial commenced, plaintiffs abandoned their claim for specific performance, and the case proceeded solely . . . on the counterclaim . . . seeking rescission, . . . to secure return of the down payment.

At the conclusion of the purchasers' case, the court granted the sellers' motion for judgment. The purchasers appealed, and the Appellate Division . . . reversed . . . . Instead of remanding for a new trial, however, the Appellate Division ordered that judgment be entered in favor of the purchasers. . . . Although we agree with the Appellate Division that the trial court erred in granting vendors' motion, we think its entry of judgment in purchasers' favor to have been clearly erroneous. There must be a new trial.

The reversal by the Appellate Division was in effect a ruling that the trial court had erred in failing to deny the sellers' motion. Had the trial judge, rather than the Appellate Division, denied the motion, the sellers unquestionably could then have offered evidence to support their position. . . . The vendors cannot be denied this right simply because the adverse ruling emanated from an appellate court rather than the trial court.

Since there must be a new trial, it may be helpful for us to comment upon certain statements and contentions appearing in the opinions filed below as well as in the briefs. Because the sellers have had no opportunity to present their case, some of the facts we here assume necessarily rest upon inference if not conjecture.

. . . [T]he validity of the title to a portion of the premises . . . is sought to be sustained by the sellers upon a claim of adverse possession. The purchasers take the position that this being so, they were justified in repudiating the agreement; that the sellers could not force such a title upon them, but should have perfected the record title prior to the date of closing. This, they add, should have been done either by securing a deed from the present record title holder, or by means of an action to quiet title. While we readily concede that the sellers would have been well advised to have followed such a course, we do not agree that their failure to do so imperiled their position to the extent urged by the purchasers.

When a prospective seller's title is grounded upon adverse possession, or contains some apparent flaw of record, he has a choice of options. He may at once take whatever steps are necessary to perfect the record title, including resort to an action to quiet title, an action to cancel an outstanding encumbrance, or whatever other appropriate step may be necessary to accomplish the purpose. In the alternative he may, believing his title to be marketable despite the fact that it rests on adverse possession or is otherwise imperfect of record, choose to enter into a contract of sale, hoping to convince the purchaser or, if necessary, a court, that his estimate of the marketability of his title is justified. That is the course the sellers seem to have followed here. It must be borne in mind that this latter course is available only where the contract of sale does not require the vendor to give a title valid of record, but provides for a less stringent requirement, such as marketability or insurability. Such is the case here. Of course "[a] buyer is entitled to the kind of title stipulated for in the contract of sale." Friedman, *Contracts and Conveyances of Real Property* (3d ed. 1975) § 4.2, p. 259. . . . Here the contract . . . [stated]:

> Title to be conveyed shall be marketable and insurable, at regular rates, by any reputable title insurance company licensed to do business in the State of New Jersey, subject only to the encumbrances hereinabove set forth.

It will be seen at once that . . . there is no requirement that it be a perfect title of record. Many titles, imperfect of record, are nonetheless marketable. Justice Cardozo, then Chief Judge of the New York Court of Appeals, observed:

> The law assures to a buyer a title free from reasonable doubt, but not from every doubt. . . . If "the only defect in the title" is "a very remote and improbable contingency," a "slender possibility only," a conveyance will be decreed. . . . [Norwegian Evangelical Free Church v. Milhauser, 169 N.E. 134 (N.Y. 1929)]

Incidentally, the law will imply that title must be marketable, even where the contract is silent upon the point. . . . The purchasers are accordingly in error in insisting that nothing less than a good record title will suffice. A title that is marketable and insurable, though imperfect of record, will meet the terms of the contract.

Having thus chosen to rely upon marketability of the title to so much of their land as they claim by adverse possession, and upon it clearly appearing that the purchasers would not, under such conditions, perform the contract, sellers instituted an action for specific performance. [P]urchasers answered and filed a counterclaim for relief by way of rescission, seeking the return of their down payment as well as damages and attorneys fees. . . . Thereafter, . . . the sellers abandoned their suit for specific performance, leaving for trial only the issue raised by the purchasers' counterclaim for rescission. Purchasers assert that they have been in some way improperly prejudiced by the sellers having abandoned their suit for specific performance. We fail to see how this can be. The criterion, in a case such as this, is the same whether the seller seeks specific performance or the purchaser sues for the return of his deposit. The determinative issue in each case is whether or not the seller had marketable title. . . .

The purchasers also advanced the contention that the validity of the title must be assessed as of the specified closing date, and not at some later time. But established doctrine refutes this contention. Where, because of an alleged title defect, vendor and vendee litigate the issue, it will be the title as it exists at the time of final decree or judgment that will control, not the title the vendor may have had when the suit was commenced. . . .

> In all cases where the vendor seeks to force a title upon the vendee, it is the latter's position, not at the commencement of the suit, but at its termination, which is to be regarded. The question is, not what kind of a title the vendor has, but what

kind of a title the vendee will get if the court of chancery or the court of errors and appeals, after reviewing the decree of the court of chancery, forces the offered title upon him. [Barger v. Gery, 64 N.J. Eq. 263 (Ch. 1902)]

In the last-cited case Vice Chancellor Stevenson went on to say,

> Where the alleged doubt in regard to the offered title relates to a matter of law, a decision of the court in the suit for specific performance undertaking to establish what the law is must, of necessity, have some effect either to strengthen or dispel the doubt.

There the court granted specific performance, but noting that most of the evidence in support of complainant's otherwise defective title had been first brought forward during the trial, it denied complainant his costs.

> In this case the evidence to support the offered title was not presented by the vendor to the vendee; a very important part of it was obtained by the vendor after this suit was commenced.

To recapitulate, in an action for specific performance by a vendor or for rescission by a vendee, where the issue is marketability of title, the vendor is entitled to a judgment if, at the conclusion of the suit, the court holds title to be marketable, even though the decision in favor of marketability rests upon facts adduced for the first time at trial or upon legal rulings made during the course of the proceedings.

The purchasers have also advanced the contention that they were entitled to rescind the contract because, contrary to the contractual proviso, title was not insurable by a reputable title insurance company. Generally, provisions requiring title insurance as a condition precedent to acceptance of title are enforceable. . . . This condition may already have been satisfied, for a Vice-President of New Jersey Realty Title Insurance Company testified to a willingness to insure the purchasers' possession against claims of third persons. Under these circumstances it would appear that the contractual condition had probably been met, but the point can be fully explored at the retrial.

. . . [W]e agree with the Appellate Division that the trial court erred in granting the sellers' motion at the conclusion of the purchasers' case. The purchasers had shown that the sellers did not have record title to one tract of the entire parcel. The contract of sale provided that title must be marketable and insurable. It did not provide, however, . . . that the sellers would be required to produce a clear title of record without reliance upon adverse possession. It is well settled in New Jersey that title resting in adverse possession, if clearly established, will be held marketable. . . . This rule represents the great weight of authority. . . . Accordingly, if the sellers could prove that they did in fact hold title to the tract in question by virtue of adverse possession, they would have met their contractual obligation, at least insofar as marketability is concerned. Although the trial judge indicated that he believed the sellers could readily establish title by adverse possession, they had not yet done so. Therefore their motion should have been denied and they should have been directed to go forward with their proofs.

We note that it is not necessary for the sellers to join as parties all possible claimants with outstanding interests, as would be the case in an action to quiet title. In many, if not most, cases of this sort the claimants who may hold adverse interests are not joined; very often they are not known. It follows, as the purchasers here correctly point out, that a judgment in the action will not be *res judicata* as to such claimants. And yet virtually all courts agree that in such a suit there may be, and often is, a judgment of marketability leading to affirmative relief by way of specific performance or to a denial of a vendee's claim to rescind. . . . [T]o reach this result the court must conclude (1) that the outstanding claimants could not succeed were they in fact to assert a claim, and (2) that there is no real likelihood that any claim will ever be asserted. . . .

Although there are statements in some of the cases to the contrary, we think that in a suit such as this, where the purchaser seeking rescission has shown that record title is outstanding in some person other than the seller, the burden should then shift to the seller to establish his title by adverse possession. . . .

Notes and Questions

1. The warranty of marketable title is implied in every contract for sale of real property. Like the covenant of quiet enjoyment implied in leases, the term is added by courts to protect the legitimate expectations of buyers. Does the court's decision in *Conklin* meet the legitimate expectations of buyers? Of sellers? Does it promote an efficient land transfer system? What would happen if courts required that sellers produce a perfect chain of title going back to a grant from a sovereign?

2. Although usually defined in terms of a title free from "reasonable doubt," marketability is typically treated as an issue of law decided by the court, rather than an issue of fact decided by the jury. Marketability issues arise in several contexts. *Conklin* illustrates the problem that arises when the seller lacks good record title. Another problem arises when the seller is a cotenant and the other cotenants have not joined in the contract of sale. *See, e.g., Warner v. Denis*, 933 P.2d 1372 (Haw. Ct. App. 1997) (seller, husband, held property in joint tenancy with wife who did not sign contract; husband liable for breach of contract when unable to convey wife's interest). What if the property is landlocked? Courts' views vary. *Compare Myerberg, Sawyer & Rue P.A. v. Agee*, 446 A.2d 69 (Md. Ct. App. 1982) (property without access is unmarketable), *with Sinks v. Karleskint*, 474 N.E.2d 767 (Ill. Ct. App. 1985) (lack of access affects value, not title).

Another set of marketability problems arises when the property is subject to an encumbrance such as an easement, restrictive covenant, or mortgage not mentioned in the sales contract. The general rule is that existence of an encumbrance renders the title unmarketable, although an exception is sometimes made for easements that are readily visible, such as electric power lines or roadways. *See, e.g., Haisfield v. Lape*, 570 S.E.2d 794 (Va. 2002) (title not marketable; line of sight easement was not open, visible, physical encumbrance of the property that must have been taken into account in fixing price of the property). Does this exception make sense? Remember that the result of finding the title unmarketable is that the seller must remove the encumbrance or let the buyer out of the contract, refunding the earnest money or down payment, and that the theory behind the marketability term is that it protects the buyer's legitimate expectations.

3. The implied warranty is a default rule that may be altered or eliminated by the parties who may agree that the title must be a good *record* title or merely an *insurable* title. Sometimes, the parties may agree that the buyer will purchase whatever interest the seller has, even if it turns out to be no title at all. The implied warranty of marketable title shifts the burden of negotiation to the buyer who wants good record title, and, perhaps, a title free of easements for visible encumbrances. It shifts the burden of negotiation to the seller who is only willing or able to provide less than a marketable title. In settling on the implied warranty of marketability, did the courts strike the appropriate balance between the interests of buyers and sellers?

4. *Insurable title.* Insurable title is a title that a reputable title insurance company would be willing to insure at regular rates. If the court in *Conklin* had concluded that a title based on adverse possession is not marketable as a matter of law, the seller's title might still have been insurable. By insuring the title, the title company promises to pay the costs of defending any subsequent claims brought against the insured by a party claiming superior title and to indemnify the insured in case it loses. If it believes the buyer would prevail and the risk or costs of having to defend a quiet title action are relatively low, the title company may be willing to issue the insurance. What concerns should you raise with a client who has been offered a title that is insurable but not marketable? *See Nelson v. Anderson*, 676 N.E.2d 735 (Ill. Ct. App. 1997) (purchaser not required to accept title even though title insurance company agreed for extra premium to insure present and future purchasers against loss due to violation of restrictive covenant prohibiting construction within 10 feet of any boundary).

5. *Public land use restrictions.* The existence of zoning and other public land use regulations affecting the property generally do not render the title unmarketable, even if the regulations severely restrict or prevent development of the property. *See, e.g., Truck South, Inc. v. Patel*, 528 S.E.2d 424 (S.C. 2000) (discovery of water on the property resulting in designation as federally protected wetlands after contract was signed did not render title unmarketable—presence of marsh may be a burden, but it is not a lien, easement, or other encumbrance). Although the existence of a public regulation is not an encumbrance, existing violations of public regulations do render the title unmarketable. Does this make sense? *See* Allison Dunham, *The Effect on Title of Violations of Building Covenant's and Zoning Ordinances*, 27 Rocky Mtn. L. Rev. 255 (1955). Interestingly, however, the presence of hazardous waste on the property does not render the title unmarketable. *See* J. David Reitzel, *CERCLA and Marketable Title: Is Toxic Contamination a Cloud?*, Real Est. L.J. (Winter 1998), and Pamela A. Harbeson, Comment, *Toxic Clouds on Titles: Hazardous Waste and the Doctrine of Marketable Title*, 19 B.C. Envtl. Aff. L. Rev. 355 (1991).

Note: Installment Land Contracts

A different type of contract of sale, known variously as an installment land contract, contract for deed, or installment sale contract, is a device to finance the purchase of land. Under this contract, the buyer goes into possession immediately and is obligated to pay installments of the purchase price from time to time. Upon completion of all of the payments—usually stretched out over a number of years—the seller delivers a deed to the buyer. This differs from a typical executory contract of sale, which provides for a shorter period between contract and deed, requires payment (except for a deposit) only when the deed is delivered at closing, and primarily serves to allocate the rights and obligations of the parties during the interim period. The installment land contract is often used by buyers who lack the financial resources to obtain a mortgage and provide the down payment for an executory contract of sale.

The seller under an installment land contract retains title to the land as security to force full payment of the price. This can lead to harsh results. Suppose the buyer under an installment land contract pays 119 of 120 monthly payments over a 10-year period and defaults on the last payment. Under the contract, the seller can retain the purchase price already paid by the buyer as well as the title. Do the courts allow sellers to get away with such forfeitures?

Historically, many courts allowed the seller to do just that. *See, e.g., Russell v. Richards*, 702 P.2d 993 (N.M. 1985) (forfeiture allowed after six years of payments). Over recent years, courts and legislators have intervened, on different theories and with different remedies. *See, e.g., Wilson v. Taylor*, 577 N.W.2d 100 (Mich. 1998) (limiting forfeiture to sums still owing); *Lamberth v. McDaniel*, 506 S.E.2d 295 (N.C. Ct. App. 1998) (buyer has right to redeem its interest on default by paying remaining debt). The *Restatement of Property (Third) — Mortgages* § 3.4(b) (1997) has adopted the position of many of these modern decision makers and states that "a contract for deed creates a mortgage." This means that the substantive and procedural rules and protections of mortgage law will apply. On default the property will be sold, and the seller will only be entitled to the remaining balance of the price plus related expenses. Think about the installment land contract again when you read the materials on mortgages. On various topics in installment land contracts, see Grant S. Nelson, *The Contract for Deed as a Mortgage: The Case for the Restatement Approach*, 1998 BYU L. Rev. 1111; Eric Freyfogle, *Vagueness and the Rule of Law: Reconsidering Installment Land Contract Forfeitures*, 1988 Duke L.J. 609.

Problem

Buyer signs a contract of sale for a single-family home in a fully residential area. Can Buyer refuse to close when she learns that the property is subject to a restrictive covenant limiting the use of the property to residential purposes? Is the result different if the local zoning ordinance also limits use to residential purposes? *See Bull v. Burton*, 124 N.E. 111 (N.Y. 1919). If time for closing has not yet arrived, but Buyer learns that Seller himself had filed a plan of restrictions creating the residential-only limitation? *See Hinkell v. Adams*, 378 S.E.2d 621 (Va. 1989).

b.   Equitable Conversion/Risk of Loss

BRYANT v. WILLISON REAL ESTATE CO.

Supreme Court of Appeals of West Virginia
350 S.E.2d 748 (W. Va. 1986)

MILLER, Chief J. . . . This case was heard . . . without a jury . . . . The facts are that on January 4, 1980, the plaintiffs entered into a contract to purchase the

O.J. Morrison Building in Clarksburg for $175,000. As required by the sales contract, they paid $10,000 to Willison Real Estate Company, the agent for the vendors, at the time the contract was signed. The balance was to be paid upon delivery of the deed, at which time the purchasers would take possession of the property. No date was set for the closing.

On February 18, 1980, before the delivery of the deed, a water line broke in the sprinkler system, permitting water to run throughout the building and into two adjoining businesses. The purchasers had planned to extensively renovate the building for use as a medical office building. The purchasers were informed by an architect and an engineer who inspected the damage that the remodeling of the Morrison Building could be delayed by as much as four to six weeks because the building had to be properly dried out. The purchasers asked the vendors to correct the water damage or to permit the contract to be rescinded. The vendors declined to repair the damage and sold the building to another purchaser in July of 1980 for $140,000. The purchasers then instituted this action for rescission of the contract and return of their down payment. The trial court ruled that the purchasers must bear the risk of loss both to the Morrison Building and for the water damage to the adjoining property owned by third parties.

The purchasers contend that the trial court placed undue reliance on the doctrine of equitable conversion and rejected language in the sales contract placing the risk of loss on the vendors.[1] Our law on the doctrine of equitable conversion . . . is rather minimal. The doctrine . . .[2] provides that where an executory contract for the sale of real property does not contain a provision allocating the risk of loss and the property is damaged by fire or some other casualty not due to the fault or neglect of the vendor,[3] the risk of loss is on the purchaser. This assumes the vendor has good title.

Our main case is Maudru v. Humphreys, 98 S.E. 259 (W. Va. 1919), where the purchaser was in possession of the property under an executory contract of sale. A fire destroyed a building on the property and this Court found the purchaser to have borne the risk of loss, stating . . . :

> . . . In such case there is no implied warranty that the condition of the property at the time of sale shall continue until after deed is made.

---

1.   The . . . sales contract . . . [provided]: "It is also understood and agreed that the owner is responsible for said property until the Deed has been delivered to said purchaser."

2.   . . . [On the] doctrine of equitable conversion . . . [see] 6A R. Powell, Powell on Real Property ¶ 925(6) (1984)[:] the doctrine was first introduced in "Anglo-American jurisprudence in the landmark English case of Paine v. Meller, 31 Eng. Rep. 1088 (Ch. 1801)"; . . . it rests on the "concept that 'equity regards as done that which is agreed or ought to be done.'" Thus, at the time the real estate contract is signed, the purchaser becomes the equitable owner and the seller retains a right to possession and legal title as security for the payment of the balance of the purchase price. . . . [S]ome courts have rejected the doctrine. . . . [S]everal states have adopted the Uniform Vendor and Purchaser Risk Act which generally relieves the purchaser from the contract if he is not in possession and if the property is materially destroyed without fault on the part of the purchaser. The Uniform Act recognizes that risk of loss can be settled by an express provision in the sales contract. He also points out that the Paine case has been rejected in England by the Law of Property Act of 1925.

3.   . . . [W]here the risk of loss is on the purchaser and the damage to the property is caused by negligence of the vendor, the vendor must bear the risk of loss. . . . M. Friedman, Contracts & Conveyances of Real Property § 4.11 at 438 (4th ed. 1984).

... The Court in *Maudru* did not make an extensive analysis ... but did state that "[t]here is no warranty or condition in the contract ... that the property should be in the same condition when the transaction is completed as it was when the contract was made." This appears to be an implied recognition that the parties may allocate the risk of loss in a sales contract and thereby alter the doctrine of equitable conversion.

It is rather universally recognized that the parties ... may allocate the risk of loss for fire or other casualty occurring before the actual transfer of the legal title. If the contract allocates the risk to the vendor, then the doctrine of equitable conversion, which places the risk of loss on the purchaser, is no longer applicable. ...

The trial court was of the view that the contract language stating that "the owner is responsible for said property until the Deed has been delivered to said purchaser" was not sufficient to cast the responsibility on the vendors. This conclusion was based, in part, on testimony of the sales agent for the vendor that this language pertained only to vandalism.

We disagree .... The contract was on a printed form and the language is free from ambiguity. Cases in other jurisdictions have held language of similar import to place the ... risk of loss on the vendor.

To permit this language to be restricted to acts of vandalism cuts across the plain meaning of its wording and would be contrary to the general rule that forecloses oral modification of contract language which is free from ambiguity. ...

Apparently, the trial court also relied on language in the sales contract which provided: "Purchaser to carry enough fire insurance to protect Self." We do not believe that this provision can be read to place the risk of loss on the purchasers. This provision is nothing more than an acknowledgment of the general rule that both parties to an executory contract for the sale of real property have an insurable interest. ...

The trial court also referred to the sentence in the contract that "[t]his contract is also subject to 'As Is' condition" as indicating an intention not to deliver the building in a specific condition. We agree with this conclusion insofar as it would dispel any claim by the purchasers to require the vendors to make any improvements to the building from the condition it was in at the time the contract was signed. There was apparently no dispute that the building had been unoccupied for some period of time and was somewhat deteriorated.

However, we do not agree that this language can be read to remove the risk of loss from the vendors. ... [U]se of an "as is" provision ... is generally intended to negate the existence of any warranty as to the particular fitness or condition of the property. ... [It] simply means that the purchaser must take the premises ... in its present condition as of the date of the contract. ... M. Friedman, *Contracts & Conveyances of Real Property* § 1.2(n) at 69 (4th ed. 1984).

Having determined that the vendors bore the risk of loss under the contract, we believe the purchasers had the right to ... return of the initial down payment once the vendors refused to consider an abatement in the sale price ... and then sold the property to a third party.

The particular remedies that may be available where there has been partial destruction or damage ... are not easily categorized as they depend upon particular facts and circumstances. It may be generally stated that where the risk of loss is on the vendor and the casualty damage to the property is not substantial, the purchaser is entitled to sue for specific performance, and the purchase price is abated to the extent the property was damaged. . . . [W]here the risk of loss is on the vendor and there is substantial damage to the property, the appropriate remedy ordinarily is to terminate the contract and return the down payment to the purchaser. *See* . . . 3A A. Corbin, Contracts § 668 (1960); M. Friedman, *supra* at § 4.11.[5]

We have recognized that a purchaser may have specific performance of his contract to purchase real estate with an abatement in the purchase price where the vendor cannot fully perform his agreement.[6] Lathrop v. Columbia Collieries Co., 73 S.E. 299 (W. Va. 1911). However, it appears that we have not had occasion to speak to the remedy where the risk of loss is on the vendor and damage has been done to the building.

The purchasers . . . sued only to recover their down payment. The vendors counterclaimed for the difference in the sales price on the original contract and what they obtained from the subsequent sale of the Morrison Building. The trial court rejected the vendors' counterclaim for reasons that are not entirely clear. However, in view of the risk of loss being placed on the vendors, the trial court's ruling with regard to the vendors' counterclaim would be correct for two reasons.

First, the vendors having the risk of loss for the water damage could not require the purchasers to pay the full purchase price. Consequently, the vendors were wrong in concluding that the purchasers had breached the sales contract when they refused to pay the full purchase price. As a result of this erroneous conclusion, the vendors breached the contract when they sold the property to the third party.[7] If the water damage had not been substantial, the vendors could have sued the purchasers for specific performance while offering an abatement in the purchase price.

As a second alternative, if the vendors had concluded that the damages were substantial, they could have terminated the sales contract and returned the purchasers' down payment. . . .

Under the particular facts of this case, we conclude that where a contract places the risk of loss on the vendor and insubstantial damage to the property occurs without the fault of either party, the purchaser may recover his down payment where the vendor refuses to repair the damage or to give an abatement in the purchase price.[8] . . .

. . . [W]e were somewhat handicapped on this appeal because the parties did not supply a transcript of the testimony, but submitted the findings of fact and conclusions of law made by the trial court which were most thorough. It would appear that the purchasers would be entitled to a judgment for the amount of their down payment and interest, but in view of the lack of a complete

---

5.   New York's highest court has concluded in Lucenti v. Cayuga Apartments, Inc., 399 N.E.2d 918 (N.Y. 1979), that where the risk of loss is on the vendor and substantial damage has occurred to the building, the purchaser may obtain specific performance with an abatement in the purchase price. Since the purchasers do not raise the issue of specific performance, we decline to address this issue.

6.   This is the general rule elsewhere. . . . M. Friedman, *supra*, at § 4.11.

7.   For a general discussion of a purchaser's remedies where the vendor transfers property to a third party, *see* 77 Am. Jur. 2d *Vendor and Purchaser* §§ 380-86 (1975); 92 C.J.S. *Vendor & Purchaser* § 299 (1955); M. Friedman, *supra* at § 12.2(a)1.

8.   We have assumed for purposes of this case that the damages to the building were insubstantial.

record, we are reluctant to enter such judgment here. . . . We, therefore, reverse
. . . and remand the case for further proceedings not inconsistent with this
opinion. . . .

Notes and Questions

1. *Risk of loss.* When the contract is silent, which party should bear the risk
of loss due to damage or destruction of the property between the signing of
the contract and the time for closing? Ordinarily, the owner bears the risk of
loss, but who is the owner? Technically, the seller is the owner until the deed
is delivered to the buyer. On the other hand, the buyer is entitled to specific
performance of the seller's obligation to deliver the deed if the buyer pays the
agreed-on price. If oil is discovered underlying the property after the contract
is signed, the buyer is entitled to the increased value of the property—not the
seller. If the buyer is entitled to appreciation after the contract date, should it
also be subject to depreciation due to damage and destruction, as well as to
changes in the market?

Courts have given different answers to the question. There is the group, probably still the majority, that takes the position taken in *Bryant*—depreciation by
damage and destruction is treated the same as appreciation and depreciation
due to a falling market: It belongs to the buyer if the sale is completed, either
voluntarily, or through the grant of specific performance. Other courts treat
damage and destruction by fire, flood, and other catastrophes differently: The
seller bears the risk of loss until closing.

The Uniform Vendor and Purchaser Risk Act, adopted in 13 states (California,
Hawaii, Illinois, Michigan, Nevada, New Mexico, New York, North Carolina,
Oklahoma, Oregon, South Dakota, Texas, and Wisconsin), places the risk of
loss on the seller until delivery of possession or title to the buyer, whichever is
earlier.

Which is the best of the three rules? What are the strengths and weaknesses
of each? What factors should we use to evaluate which is best? What remedies
are available to the buyer if the risk is on the seller and to the seller if the risk
is on the buyer?

2. As *Bryant* indicates, the parties may avoid the default rule by expressly providing for risk of loss. Was the drafting adequate in *Bryant?* How would you have
drafted a provision?

3. Either, neither, or both parties may have insured the property. If the majority rule applies, placing risk on the buyer, and only the seller has casualty insurance on the property, who is entitled to the proceeds? *See In re Gay,* 213 B.R.
500 (E.D. Ky. 1997) (purchaser was equitable owner, but did not receive benefit
of insurance); *King v. Dunlap,* 945 S.W.2d 736 (Tenn. Ct. App. 1996) (contract
purchaser); *Gossett v. Farmers Insurance Co. of Washington,* 948 P.2d 1264 (Wash.
1997) (buyers entitled to proceeds to the extent of improvements they had
made; seller entitled to balance).

4. Equitable conversion is also applied by the courts to solve other real estate
matters. For example, assume S and B sign a contract providing for B to buy
Blackacre from S. Before closing, both S and B die. S's will leaves her realty to
S1 and personalty to S2, and B's will leaves his realty to B1 and personalty to B2.

Who is entitled to Blackacre, who must pay for it, and who will receive the sales proceeds? Does rigid application of equitable conversion to this situation yield a good result? *See Moses Bros. v. Johnson,* 7 So. 146 (Ala. 1890) (seller may prevent contract vendee from compromising seller's security interest by cutting timber); *Clapp v. Tower,* 93 N.W. 862 (N.D. 1903) (proceeds on resale of real property after executors cancelled contract made by decedent must be accounted for as personal property of estate).

Problem

Seller and Buyer signed a contract for sale of a house. The contract provided for Buyer to have access to the house before closing to remodel the kitchen and bathrooms, and Seller gave Buyer a key for that purpose. A few days before closing, the house was almost totally destroyed by fire. Who bore the risk of loss under each of the three rules? What remedies do the parties have? Have you changed your view on the allocation rule you prefer in light of this problem?

c. Quality of the Property

STAMBOVSKY v. ACKLEY

Supreme Court, Appellate Division of New York
169 A.D.2d 254, 572 N.Y.S.2d 672 (1991)

RUBIN, J. Plaintiff, to his horror, discovered that the house he had recently contracted to purchase was widely reputed to be possessed by poltergeists, reportedly seen by defendant seller and members of her family on numerous occasions over the last 9 years. Plaintiff promptly commenced this action seeking rescission of the contract . . . . Supreme Court reluctantly dismissed the complaint . . . .

The unusual facts of this case, as disclosed by the record, clearly warrant a grant of equitable relief to the buyer who, as a resident of New York City, cannot be expected to have any familiarity with the folklore of the Village of Nyack. Not being a "local," plaintiff could not readily learn that the home . . . is haunted. Whether the source of the spectral apparitions seen by defendant seller are parapsychic or psychogenic, having reported their presence in both a national publication (Reader's Digest) and the local press (in 1977 and 1982, respectively), defendant is estopped to deny their existence and, as a matter of law, the house is haunted. More to the point, however, no divination is required to conclude that it is defendant's promotional efforts in publicizing her close encounters with these spirits which fostered the home's reputation in the community. In 1989, the house was included in five-home walking tour of Nyack and described in a November 27th newspaper article as "a riverfront Victorian (with ghost)." The impact of the reputation thus created goes to the very essence of the bargain between the parties, greatly impairing both the value of the property and its potential for resale. The extent of this impairment may be presumed for the purpose of reviewing the disposition of this motion to dismiss the cause of action for recission . . . and represents merely an issue of fact for resolution at trial.

While I agree with Supreme Court that the real estate broker, as agent for the seller, is under no duty to disclose to a potential buyer the phantasmal reputation of the premises and that, in his pursuit of a legal remedy for fraudulent misrepresentation against the seller, plaintiff hasn't a ghost of a chance, I am nevertheless moved by the spirit of equity to allow the buyer to seek rescission of the contract of sale and recovery of his down payment. New York law fails to recognize any remedy for damages incurred as a result of the seller's mere silence, applying instead the strict rule of caveat emptor. Therefore, the theoretical basis for granting relief, even under the extraordinary facts of this case, is elusive if not ephemeral.

"Pity me not but lend thy serious hearing to what I shall unfold" (William Shakespeare, Hamlet, Act I, Scene V [Ghost]).

From the perspective of a person in the position of plaintiff herein, a very practical problem arises with respect to the discovery of a paranormal phenomenon: "Who you gonna' call?" as a title song to the movie "Ghostbusters" asks. Applying the strict rule of caveat emptor to a contract involving a house possessed by poltergeists conjures up visions of a psychic or medium routinely accompanying the structural engineer and Terminix man on an inspection of every home subject to a contract of sale. It portends that the prudent attorney will establish an escrow account lest the subject of the transaction come back to haunt him and his client—or pray that his malpractice insurance coverage extends to supernatural disasters. In the interest of avoiding such untenable consequences, the notion that a haunting is a condition which can and should be ascertained upon reasonable inspection of the premises is a hobgoblin which should be exorcised from the body of legal precedent and quietly laid to rest.

It has been suggested by a leading authority that the ancient rule which holds that mere nondisclosure does not constitute actionable misrepresentation "finds proper application in cases where the fact undisclosed is patent, or the plaintiff has equal opportunities for obtaining information which he may be expected to utilize, or the defendant has no reason to think that he is acting under any misapprehension" (Prosser, *Torts* § 106, at 696 [4th ed. 1971]). However, with respect to transactions in real estate, New York adheres to the doctrine of caveat emptor and imposes no duty upon the vendor to disclose any information concerning the premises . . . unless there is a confidential or fiduciary relationship between the parties . . . or some conduct on the part of the seller which constitutes "active concealment" (see, 17 E. 80th Realty Corp. v. 68th Assocs.,—A.D.2d—[1st Dept., May 9, 1991] [dummy ventilation system constructed by seller]; Haberman v. Greenspan, 82 Misc. 2d 263 [foundation cracks covered by seller]). Normally, some affirmative misrepresentation (e.g., Tahini Invs. v. Bobrowsky, 99 A.D.2d 489 [industrial waste on land allegedly used only as farm]; Jansen v. Kelly, 11 A.D.2d 587 [land containing valuable minerals allegedly acquired for use as campsite]) or partial disclosure (Junius Constr. Corp. v. Cohen, 257 N.Y. 393 [existence of third unopened street concealed]; Noved Realty Corp. v. A. A. P. Co., 250 App. Div. 1 [escrow agreements securing lien concealed]) is required to impose upon the seller a duty to communicate undisclosed conditions affecting the premises (*contra*, Young v. Keith, 112 A.D.2d 625 [defective water and sewer systems concealed]).

Caveat emptor is not so all-encompassing a doctrine of common law as to render every act of nondisclosure immune from redress, whether legal or equitable. "In regard to the necessity of giving information which has not been asked, the rule differs somewhat at law and in equity, and while the law courts would permit no recovery of *damages* against a vendor, because of mere concealment of facts *under certain circumstances,* yet if the vendee refused to complete the contract because of the concealment of a material fact on the part of the other, equity would refuse to compel him so to do, because equity only compels the specific performance of a contract which is fair and open, and in regard to which all material matters known to each have been communicated to the other" (Rothmiller v. Stein, 143 N.Y. 581 [emphasis added]). Even as a principle of law, long before exceptions were embodied in statute law (*see, e.g.,* UCC 2-312 . . . [et seq.], the doctrine was held inapplicable to contagion among animals, adulteration of food, and insolvency of a maker of a promissory note and of a tenant substituted for another under a lease . . . . Common law is not moribund. *Ex facto jus oritur* (law arises out of facts). Where fairness and common sense dictate that an exception should be created, the evolution of the law should not be stifled by rigid application of a legal maxim.

The doctrine of caveat emptor requires that a buyer act prudently to assess the fitness and value of his purchase and operates to bar the purchaser who fails to exercise due care from seeking the equitable remedy of rescission . . . . For the purposes of the instant motion to dismiss . . . plaintiff is entitled to every favorable inference which may reasonably be drawn from the pleadings . . . specifically, . . . that he met his obligation to conduct an inspection of the premises and a search of available public records with respect to title. It should be apparent, however, that the most meticulous inspection and the search would not reveal the presence of poltergeists at the premises or unearth the property's ghoulish reputation in the community. Therefore, there is no sound policy reason to deny plaintiff relief for failing to discover a state of affairs which the most prudent purchaser would not be expected to even contemplate. . . .

The case law in this jurisdiction dealing with the duty of a vendor of real property to disclose information to the buyer is distinguishable . . . . The most salient distinction is that existing cases invariably deal with the physical condition of the premises (e.g., London v. Courduff [use as a landfill]; Perin v. Mardine Realty Co., 5 A.D.2d 685, *aff'd* 6 N.Y.2d 920 [sewer line crossing adjoining property without owner's consent]), defects in title (e.g., Sands v. Kissane, 282 App. Div. 140 [remainderman]), liens against the property (e.g., Noved Realty Corp. v. A. A. P. Co.), expenses or income (e.g., Rodas v. Manitaras, . . . 159 A.D.2d 341 [gross receipts]) and other factors affecting its operation. No case has been brought to this court's attention in which the property value was impaired as the result of the reputation created by information disseminated to the public by the seller (or, for that matter, as a result of possession by poltergeists).

Where a condition which has been created by the seller materially impairs the value of the contract and is peculiarly within the knowledge of the seller or unlikely to be discovered by a prudent purchaser exercising due care with respect to the subject transaction, nondisclosure constitutes a basis for rescission as a matter of equity. Any other outcome places upon the buyer not merely the obligation to exercise care in his purchase but rather to be omniscient with respect to any fact which may affect the bargain. No practical purpose is served by imposing such a burden upon a purchaser. To the contrary, it encourages predatory business practice and offends the principle that equity will suffer no wrong to be without a remedy.

Defendant's contention that the contract of sale, particularly the merger or "as is" clause, bars recovery of the buyer's deposit is unavailing. Even an express disclaimer will not be given effect where the facts are peculiarly within the knowledge of the party invoking it . . . . Moreover, a fair reading of the merger clause reveals that it expressly disclaims only representations made with respect to the physical condition of the premises and merely makes general reference to representations concerning "any other matter or things affecting or relating to the aforesaid premises." As broad as this language may be, a reasonable interpretation is that its effect is limited to tangible or physical matters and does not extend to paranormal phenomena. Finally, if the language of the contract is to be construed as broadly as defendant urges to encompass the presence of poltergeists in the house, it cannot be said that she has delivered the premises "vacant" in accordance with her obligation under the provisions of the contract rider.

To the extent New York law may be said to require something more than "mere concealment" to apply even the equitable remedy of rescission, the case of Junius Constr. Corp. v. Cohen (257 N.Y. 393, *supra*), while not precisely on point, provides some guidance. In that case, the seller disclosed that an official map indicated two as yet unopened streets which were planned for construction at the edges of the parcel. What was not disclosed was that the same map indicated a third street which, if opened, would divide the plot in half. The court held that, while the seller was under no duty to mention the planned streets at all, having undertaken to disclose two of them, he was obliged to reveal the third. . . .

. . . [D]efendant seller deliberately fostered the public belief that her home was possessed. Having undertaken to inform the public-at-large, to whom she has no legal relationship, . . . she may be said to owe no less a duty to her contract vendee. It has been remarked that the occasional modern cases which permit a seller to take unfair advantage of a buyer's ignorance so long as he is not actively misled are "singularly unappetizing" (Prosser, *Torts* § 106, at 696 [4th ed. 1971]). Where, as here, the seller not only takes unfair advantage of the buyer's ignorance but has created and perpetuated a condition about which he is unlikely to even inquire, enforcement of the contract (in whole or in part) is offensive to the court's sense of equity. Application of the remedy of rescission, within the bounds of the narrow exception to the doctrine of caveat emptor set forth herein, is entirely appropriate to relieve the unwitting purchaser from the consequences of a most unnatural bargain.

Accordingly, the judgment which dismissed the complaint should be modified . . . and the first cause of action seeking rescission of the contract reinstated, without costs.

SMITH, J. (dissenting). . . . "It is settled law in New York State that the seller of real property is under no duty to speak when the parties deal at arm's length. The mere silence of the seller, without some act or conduct which deceived the purchaser, does not amount to a concealment that is actionable as a fraud . . . The buyer has the duty to satisfy himself as to the quality of his bargain pursuant to the doctrine of caveat emptor, which in New York State still applies to real estate transactions." . . .

The parties herein were represented by counsel and dealt at arm's length. This is evidenced by the contract of sale which, *inter alia*, contained various riders and a specific provision that all prior understandings and agreements between the parties were merged into the contract, that the contract completely expressed their full agreement and that neither had relied upon any statement by anyone else not set forth in the contract. There is no allegation that defendants, by some specific act, other than the failure to speak, deceived the plaintiff. Nevertheless, a cause of action may be sufficiently stated where there is a confidential or fiduciary relationship creating a duty to disclose and there was a failure to disclose a material fact, calculated to induce a false belief. However, plaintiff herein has not alleged and there is no basis for concluding that a confidential or fiduciary relationship existed between these parties . . . . In addition, there is no allegation that defendants thwarted plaintiff's efforts to fulfill his responsibilities fixed by the doctrine of caveat emptor.

Finally, if the doctrine of caveat emptor is to be discarded, it should be for a reason more substantive than a poltergeist. The existence of a poltergeist is no more binding upon the defendants than it is upon this court. . . .

Notes and Questions

1. Caveat emptor was long the dominant rule in sales of real property. Although an active misrepresentation by the seller about the property was actionable, *see, e.g., Janinda v. Lanning*, 390 P.2d 826 (Idaho 1964) (as to quality of water supply), simple failure to disclose a defect known to the seller did not expose the seller to liability. This rule still controls, as you see in *Stambovsky*, for physical defects in New York and in other jurisdictions as well. *See, e.g., Urman v. S. Boston Savings Bank*, 674 N.E.2d 1078 (Mass. 1997) (no duty to disclose defects in the absence of a fiduciary duty).

In recent years, however, an increasing number of courts have rejected the nondisclosure rule in cases involving sales of residences:

> [W]here the seller of a home knows of facts materially affecting the value of the property which are not readily observable and are not known to the buyer, the seller is under a duty to disclose them to the buyer. *Johnson v. Davis*, 480 So. 2d 625 (Fla. 1985).

What is the utility of the doctrine of caveat emptor? What accounts for the modern trend away from the doctrine? Are there good reasons to shift the burden from the buyer to the seller? Does the limitation in *Johnson*, to facts not readily observable that materially affect the value of the property, make sense?

Jurisdictions that have adopted a disclosure rule in residential property transactions have usually refused to extend the doctrine to sales of commercial land. *See, e.g., Futura Realty v. Lone Star Building Centers (Eastern), Inc.*, 578 So. 2d 363 (Fla. Dist. Ct. App. 1991) (no duty to disclose pollution problems). Is the residential-commercial dichotomy supportable? *See generally* Kathleen McNamara Tomcho, Note, *Commercial Real Estate Buyer Beware: Sellers May Have the Right to Remain Silent*, 70 S. Cal. L. Rev. 1571 (1997); John V. Orth, *Sale of Defective Houses*, 6 Green Bag 2d 163 (2003).

2. Is the *Stambovsky* court serious? Does it believe in ghosts, and is that relevant? Is the distinction between nondisclosure of physical conditions and disclosure of "possession by poltergeists" viable?

What should the buyer's remedies be in the event that there is an actionable nondisclosure by seller?

3. Statutes in various jurisdictions impose a duty of disclosure on sellers of residences. California's includes a detailed disclosure checklist that must be completed by the seller. Cal. Civ. Code §§ 1102 *et seq.* What are the benefits and disadvantages of a legislative rather than a judicial approach? Is it a good idea to have statutes mandate use of specific forms? *See Engelhart v. Kramer,* 570 N.W.2d 550 (S.D. 1997) (under S.D. Codified Laws § 43-4-44, seller liable for damages when he only stated that there were "some spots" with cracks and "some crumbling" when foundation was severely cracked and disintegrating).

Other statutes relieve a seller from disclosing that the property was previously inhabited by a person with AIDS or that a felony was committed in the house. *See, e.g.,* Cal. Civ. Code § 1710.2; Tenn. Code Ann. § 66-5-110. Are these statutes consistent with the court's decision in *Stambovsky?* What reasons support such statutes?

4. Can a judicially imposed disclosure obligation be waived? Consider the court's discussion in *Stambovsky* concerning the "as is" clause.

5. A major exception to caveat emptor, embodied in recent case law or statutes in virtually all jurisdictions, makes builder/vendors of new homes liable to purchasers for defects under a theory of implied warranty of fitness. *See, e.g.,* N.Y. Gen. Bus. Law § 36-B; *McDonald v. Mianecki,* 398 A.2d 1283 (N.J. 1979) (builder/vendor liable for non-potable well water). Is this a good idea?

Suppose the original purchaser from a builder/vendor sells the property after a few months, and a construction defect then becomes apparent. Can the new purchaser recover from the builder/vendor under the implied warranty? How should the rule be crafted? *See Blagg v. Fred Hunt Co.,* 612 S.W.2d 321 (Ark. 1981) (if resale occurs within a reasonable time, second owner has cause of action against builder/vendor).

6. In 1980, Congress enacted CERCLA, the Comprehensive Environmental Response, Compensation and Liability Act, 42 U.S.C. §§ 9601-9675, which makes property owners strictly liable for hazardous materials on their property, even if they did not discharge the materials. While the buyer may be able to sustain a cause of action against the seller for failing to disclose an environmental problem, *see, e.g., Timm v. Clement,* 574 N.W.2d 368 (Iowa Ct. App. 1997) (no disclosure of leaking underground tanks), the buyer will still be liable under CERCLA if sued by neighbors or the federal government for the (huge) cost of cleaning up the property. It is thus imperative for buyers to make an independent assessment of the environmental condition of the property before purchasing. *See* Albert Slap & Samuel Israel, *Private CERCLA Litigation: How to Avoid It? How to Handle It?,* 25 Real Prop. Prob. & Tr. J. 705 (1991); Comment, Scott Seiler, *The Environmental Due Diligence Defense and Contractual Protection Devices,* 49 La. L. Rev. 1405 (1989).

Problems: Caveat Emptor

1. After purchasing residential property from Seller and moving in, Buyer learns that there are major neighborhood noise problems, including loud neighbors and excessive traffic on the streets at night. Can Buyer recover from

Seller for failure to disclose these problems? *See Alexander v. McKnight*, 7 Cal. App. 4th 973 (1992).

2. Before purchasing farmland from Seller, Buyer—a petroleum engineer—ascertained that the property had expansive oil reserves. Seller did not know this, and Buyer did not tell Seller. Seller accepted a price that reflected the market price for use of the property as agricultural land but that was significantly below the market price for oil-bearing property. Was Buyer obligated to disclose the existence of the oil to Seller before negotiating the contract? *See Zaschak v. Traverse Corp.*, 333 N.W.2d 191 (Mich. Ct. App. 1983) (no).

d.   Contract Remedies

Buyer's remedies. A buyer is entitled either to specific performance or to damages for a seller's breach of a contract to sell real property.

Specific performance. Because the courts assume that land is unique, buyers have an automatic right to specific performance and need not show special facts to receive an equitable remedy. *See, e.g., Coale v. Hilles*, 976 S.W.2d 61 (Mo. Ct. App. 1998) (specific performance ordered; language of contract was not unclear or indefinite). Moreover, courts usually permit the buyer to have specific performance with an abatement in price reflecting the decreased value of the bargain due to the seller's breach. *See, e.g., Milkes v. Smith*, 91 Cal. App. 2d 79 (1949) (acreage less than contract provided); *Kelley v. Leucadia Financial Corp.*, 846 P.2d 1238 (Utah 1992) (same). What advantages and risks does specific performance offer to the buyer? When will the buyer seek that remedy?

Damages. A buyer is entitled to damages equal to the difference between the contract price and the market price for the property. What are the advantages and risks to the buyer with the damages remedy? When will the buyer choose to recover damages?

Seller's remedies. Paralleling the buyer's remedies, the seller is entitled to specific performance or damages when the buyer breaches a real estate contract.

Specific performance. The seller has a right to specific performance by the buyer as a matter of course. The seller will tender the deed, and the buyer will be ordered to pay the price. What are the advantages and limitations of the specific performance remedy from the seller's perspective? In what type of situations will the seller seek this remedy?

Damages. The seller is entitled to damages for the buyer's failure to perform under the contract. The rule applied almost universally entitles the seller to the difference between the contract price and the value of the property at the time of the breach. A few cases have held that the seller should receive the difference between the contract price and the price received by the seller on reselling the property. *See, e.g., Kuhn v. Spatial Design, Inc.*, 585 A.2d 967 (N.J. Super. App. Div. 1991). Which measure is appropriate in light of the parties' expectations and the nature of real estate transfers? *See* Gerald Korngold, *Seller's Damages from a Defaulting Buyer of Realty: The Influence of the Uniform Land Transactions Act on the Courts*, 20 Nova L. Rev. 1069 (1996).

What are the advantages and disadvantages to the seller of the damages remedy? When should this remedy be sought?

Additional remedies. Sometimes the contract of sale may grant the parties additional remedies, limit the parties to certain remedies, or do both. For example, some clauses grant the seller the right to retain the deposit (usually 5 to 10 percent of the purchase price) upon the buyer's breach as liquidated damages. (Retention of the deposit may also be permitted by some courts as an implied remedy.) Courts will uphold liquidated damages clauses as long as they are not "penalties." The jurisdictions split fairly evenly, however, on the question whether the court should look only at the time the contract was made to determine whether the clause was a reasonable attempt to forecast damages or whether it should take a "second look" at the time of breach to determine whether the clause was reasonable as of that time. *See Kelly v. Marx*, 705 N.E.2d 1114 (Mass. 1999) (overruling "second look" precedent).

Clauses limiting the seller's remedies to retention of the deposit have been upheld in the absence of fraud, duress, or unconscionability. *See, e.g., Roscoe-Gill v. Newman*, 937 P.2d 673 (Ariz. Ct. App. 1996) ($5,000 liquidated damages upheld even though seller could only obtain price $80,000 below contract price on resale). Similarly, clauses limiting the buyer's remedies, perhaps to the return of the deposit, are upheld. *See generally Kessler v. Tortoise Development, Inc.*, 937 P.2d 417 (Idaho 1997) (buyer limited to return of deposit when title was not marketable).

C. THE DEED

1. Overview

If all goes well the parties will proceed to "close" the sale transaction. The seller as "grantor" will deliver the deed to the buyer as "grantee" in exchange for the buyer's paying the balance due under the contract. As discussed above, the Statute of Frauds requires a deed for the transfer of real property.

Deeds are classified according to the degree of title protection the grantor gives to the grantee:

1. *A general warranty deed:* The grantor warrants the title against defects arising before and during the time the grantor was connected with the land.

2. *A special warranty deed:* The grantor warrants the title against defects arising during the grantor's association with the land but not against defects arising before that time. To illustrate: Suppose A purchases land in 1984 and conveys to B in 1987. B conveys to C in 1992 by deed of special warranty. If it later appears that the title is defective due to a mortgage given by B in 1989 or an attachment levied against B's property in 1990, the warranty has been broken; but if the defect is due to a mortgage given by A in 1984 or an attachment levied against A's property in 1985, there is no breach. By contrast, a general warranty deed would cover all these defects.

3. *A quitclaim deed:* The grantor warrants nothing; the grantor merely transfers what title the grantor has, if any.

Nineteenth century deeds were prolix, lengthy documents. Conveyancers were disinclined to take the risks of shortening them; they knew the standard forms worked and felt they could not be equally sure of any other. To individual grantors and grantees this made little difference; but it caused registries of deeds in heavily populated areas to be unnecessarily bulky. For this reason, short-form statutes were passed in many states. They provide statutory forms of deeds and declare that certain short expressions therein—e.g., "warranty covenants"—have the effect of whole paragraphs of long-form language. In many states, the short form is habitually used; but in some others the old long form persists.

Problem

Seller and Buyer sign a contract of sale. At closing, Seller tenders a quitclaim deed to Buyer. Buyer insists on a general warranty deed. What type of deed is required?

2. Delivery

Unlike in gift situations, there is seldom any question whether the deed has been delivered when land is sold. In states where an escrow is used to close a sale, documents and money are delivered to an escrow agent who completes the transaction by delivering the deed to the buyer and the sale price to the seller after determining that all steps specified in the escrow instructions have been taken. The seller delivers the deed to the agent subject to the condition that it be delivered to the buyer only when the buyer has paid the purchase price. In other states, the parties have a "round the table" closing, where the parties meet and exchange documents and money face to face.

Suppose a seller delivers a deed to an escrow agent with instructions to release the deed to the buyer upon payment of the price to the agent. The agent, however, releases the deed without payment, and the buyer quickly conveys the property to X for consideration. Who has title—the seller or X? Although the cases are mixed, the prevailing view holds for seller even though X is a bfp (bona fide purchaser), 32 Am. Jur. 2d *Escrows* § 33. *See Powell v. Goldsmith,* 152 Cal. App. 3d 746 (1984) (escrow released deed before recording purchase money mortgage, causing it to be junior to mortgage held by appellants; held that failure to comply with condition would not elevate appellants' mortgage even assuming they were bona fide purchasers); *but see Mays v. Shields,* 45 S.E. 68 (Ga. 1903) (when grantor knows deed was improperly released by escrow agent and fails to take curative action, bona fide purchaser prevails against grantor for title). Which approach is preferable, and why? *See* Gerald Korngold, *Resolving the Intergenerational Conflicts of Real Property Law: Preserving Free Markets and Personal Autonomy for Future Generations,* 56 Am. U. L. Rev. 1525, 1562-64 (2007).

Notes and Questions

1. *Forged deeds.* The law consistently provides that a forged deed is void and the grantee receives no title. *See, e.g., First National Bank in Albuquerque v. Enriquez,* 634 P.2d 1266 (N.M. 1981). So, if O owns Blackacre and X forges a deed from O to himself, records it, and then conveys a deed to A for consideration, O prevails for title against A. Is that a good result?

2. *Merger doctrine.* The doctrine of merger by deed provides that upon delivery of the deed, the contract of sale merges into the deed and disappears unless the parties provide otherwise. One key exception states collateral promises are not merged.

What reasons support the merger doctrine? Can it easily be applied? Consider whether the following are "collateral" promises: a builder's express warranty to construct a house in good and workmanlike manner, *Davis v. Tazewell Place Associates*, 492 S.E.2d 162 (Va. 1997) (collateral undertaking, no merger); a seller's promise to place the mortgage it receives from the buyer in a position subordinate to other mortgages, *40 North Corp. v. Morrell*, 964 P.2d 423 (Wyo. 1998) (clause merged into deeds); a provision giving the seller the option to repurchase the property, *Bruggeman v. Jerry's Enterprises, Inc.*, 583 N.W.2d 299 (Minn. Ct. App. 1998), *aff'd and remanded*, 591 N.W.2d 705 (Minn. 1999) (collateral, no merger); and a warranty that plumbing, heating, electrical, and air-conditioning systems would be in working order on the date of possession, *Lanterman v. Edwards*, 689 N.E.2d 1221 (Ill. Ct. App. 1998) (collateral, no merger).

3. Description

Under the Statute of Frauds, a deed is not effective to pass an interest in land unless it adequately describes the land conveyed. How detailed must the description be for the deed to be valid? The test seems to be whether the land can be located by referring to the deed and admissible extrinsic evidence. The evidence that may be introduced to support the description in the deed must show that from the circumstances, the words could refer to only one piece of land. Thus, if the deed conveys "my farm," the land records will give meaning to the description if the grantor owns only one farm. If the grantor owns two farms, however, the deed furnishes no basis for identifying the land and is ineffective even though there is evidence as to which farm the grantor intended to convey.

In commercial land transactions, the deeds tend to be very detailed in describing the land because the purchaser's attorney will not be satisfied with anything less than a full and complete description. In a donative transaction, however, the donee normally is not given an opportunity to examine the deed and make suggestions, and thus the descriptions tend to be less exact. In wills, devises of real estate are often phrased in such terms as "all the real property I may own at my death." The description of the real property devised is in these general terms because the will does not become legally operative until the transferor dies, and he or she cannot know for certain now what land will be owned at that time.

In undertaking a detailed description of land, the drafter may have several different methods available. One is referring to the survey of public land made by the federal government. In the 18th century, the United States government began surveying the public lands. This survey divided the public lands into rectangular tracts located with reference to a baseline running east and west on a true parallel of latitude, and a principal meridian running along a longitude. At every six miles along both the baseline and the meridian, perpendicular lines are run. These lines intersect to form townships that are tracts six miles square and contain about 23,040 acres. A line of townships running north and south is called a range, and the ranges are numbered east and west from the meridian. Each township in a range also is numbered north and south from the baseline. Each township is divided into 36 sections, each one mile square. The sections are numbered consecutively beginning in the northeast corner of the township and proceeding west to the range line, and in the next row proceeding west to east. This is continued, alternately proceeding west and east, until reaching section 36, which is in the southeast corner of the township. The sections in turn are divided into half sections and quarter sections; the quarter sections into quarter-quarter sections. A given quarter-quarter section (consisting of about 40 acres) may be identified as the NW quarter of the NE quarter of section 13 of township 2N, range 3W, principal meridian. Draw a diagram and see if you can plot this tract.

The rectangular system developed by the government for the public lands is very commonly used to describe agricultural land. It is not adaptable to describing small city lots.

Another method is to describe the land by metes and bounds. This means that the land is described with reference to identifiable and permanent objects or locations that either are part of the boundary or are terminal points of lines that are the boundary. Normally, a description by metes and bounds makes use of monuments—i.e., tangible, permanent landmarks. A house, a street, a river, or stake lines run by surveyors are some of the things that may be used as monuments.

Related to the description of land by metes and bounds is a description by courses and distances. This is done by giving a starting place and the direction and length of the lines to be run.

The owner of a tract of land may divide it into lots and make a map showing the boundaries of each lot. Each lot is given a number on the map. This map usually is called a plat and in most states can be recorded.

Thereafter, a lot may be described by referring to the plat and number of the lot. Other types of maps may also be utilized in describing land. Many cities have made official surveys, and the maps and field notes are available. Sometimes private maps are used.

Sometimes the person drafting the instrument of transfer uses a combination of descriptions. This creates no difficulty unless the descriptions used conflict. To resolve such conflicts when they exist, courts have developed various rules of construction. These rules are designed to give effect to what the parties most likely intended. A boundary based on paper calculations is normally controlled by a boundary based on physical conditions. Accordingly, monuments referred to prevail over anything else on the theory that the premises were bought in reliance on what could be seen. The accepted order seems to be natural monuments, artificial monuments, maps, courses and distances, and area. You must keep in mind that these are rules of construction, not of law, and you may be able to overcome them in particular cases. Thus, the title examiner in checking the various deeds in the chain of title cannot rely too heavily on these rules of construction if any of the back deeds contain conflicting descriptions.

When the land is described by reference to monuments having width, such as a street or stream, and the grantor owns part or all of the street subject to the right-of-way in the public, or owns part or all of the bed of the stream, the question may arise whether the description includes any part of the monument itself. The extensive litigation on this point usually does not come up until many years after the deed was executed, when the public street is abandoned, or the stream changes course, and it becomes important for the first time to decide who owns the street or bed of the stream. Some rules of construction have been adopted to aid in resolving these disputes. If the grantor owned to the center of the street, as is usual, and owned no land on the other side of the street, it will be presumed that the grantor intended to convey to the grantee title in the street that was referred to as a monument in describing the land. A good drafter who uses monuments having width to describe the boundaries of land makes it unequivocally clear what the grantee is to receive. A title examiner must carefully notice references to monuments in past deeds because it may be important to the purchaser to know the status of his or her rights with respect to streets, the bed of a stream, and the like.

A court may reform a mistake in a legal description. For example, an appellate court ordered reformation of a mortgage deed on the theory of mutual mistake where the attorney used the legal description for property other than that intended by the parties in *Derby Savings Bank v. Oliwa*, 714 A.2d 1278 (Conn. Ct. App. 1998).

4. Covenants for Title

A grantee may protect his ownership rights by use of the recording system and protect against superior titles by purchasing title insurance (discussed *infra*). The grantee can also obtain title covenants—a warranty that the grantee's title is good—from the grantor.

The covenants for title in common usage are classified either as present covenants or future covenants. A present covenant for title guarantees that a described situation exists at the time the covenant is made; that situation either exists or it doesn't, so the covenant is broken when it is made or it is never broken. The standard present covenants for title are the following:

1. *Covenant for seisin (seizin).* If the grantor covenants that he or she is lawfully seised of the land, this is normally construed to mean that the grantor guarantees that he or she owns the estate he or she is purporting to convey. The fact that the land conveyed is subject to a mortgage or is subject to some restriction as to its use does not cause a breach of this covenant.

2. *Covenant of the right to convey.* If the grantor covenants that he or she has the right to convey the land involved, the grantor has guaranteed practically the same thing as when giving a covenant for seisin. There is, however, one difference. The grantor may have the right to convey and not be the owner of the estate he or she is purporting to convey, as when he or she is conveying the land under a power.

3. *Covenant against encumbrances.* If the grantor covenants against encumbrances, he or she is guaranteeing that there are no mortgages, tax liens, judgment liens, easements, covenants restricting the use of the land, etc., outstanding against the land conveyed.

The standard future covenants for title are the following:

1. *Covenant of quiet enjoyment and covenant of general warranty.* These two covenants are for all practical purposes the same and mean that the grantor guarantees that the purchaser will not be disturbed in the future by the grantor or by some paramount claim existing at the date of the conveyance. In other words, these covenants are not broken until there has been a disturbance. The disturbance may be the result of an ouster from possession by one having a paramount title, by the foreclosure of a mortgage, by the enforcement of a covenant restricting the use of the land, etc. If the purchaser pays off an outstanding mortgage on the land, this may be a disturbance even though the purchaser is not in fact ousted from possession.

2. *Covenant for further assurances.* This covenant simply guarantees that the grantor will do such further acts as are within the grantor's power to make the purchaser's title good.

SEYMOUR v. EVANS

Supreme Court of Mississippi
608 So. 2d 1141 (Miss. 1992)

McRae, J. . . . Appellees are purchasers of real property who, after accepting deeds and obligating themselves to pay, discovered that zoning ordinances prevented them from using the property as they had intended. The chancellor set aside the deeds, finding that they violated the seller's implied warranties. He further ordered the return of the appellees' purchase payments and awarded consequential damages and attorney's fees to the appellees. On appeal, the seller assigns several issues for review. We address two. . . .

FACTS AND PROCEEDINGS

The events leading up to this appeal began when appellant Edna C. Seymour decided to sell part of the land she owned in Jackson County, Mississippi. On August 22, 1983, she conveyed by warranty deed a three-acre parcel to John M. and Katherine McDonnell . . . . The McDonnells executed a promissory note and deed of trust in favor of Seymour for the deferred portion of the purchase price. On September 13, 1983, the McDonnells conveyed by warranty deed this same three-acre tract to Jerry W. and Bonnie Ann Coleman. . . . The Colemans assumed the McDonnells' indebtedness to Seymour.

Two couples, Larry and Gina Evans . . . and Dudley and Lori Cruse . . . , expressed an interest in purchasing another tract containing five and one half acres which Seymour offered for sale. They requested that the property be divided equally and conveyed to them separately. Accordingly, Seymour executed two warranty deeds on April 20, 1984. One conveyed to the Evans a parcel of land containing about 2.75 acres; the other conveyed to the Cruses a parcel of equal size. Seymour also conveyed to each couple an easement across her unsold property for purposes of ingress and egress. The Evans and the Cruses executed promissory notes and deeds of trust in favor of Seymour.

The Colemans, the Evans, and the Cruses all intended to use their . . . properties for residential purposes. The land was unimproved, so, after receiving their deeds, the grantees cleared the property of underbrush and began to make improvements thereon.

. . . [A]bout two years later, the Cruses filed an application . . . for a permit to locate a mobile home on their tract. . . . [The] Assistant Director of the Jackson County Planning Department, told them that a permit could not be issued because the division of April 20, 1984 violated the Jackson County subdivision ordinances. As [he] explained it, the property could be brought into compliance only by procuring plat approval and by paving a road for ingress and egress. The Cruses informed the Evans of their difficulties, and both couples contacted Seymour. Seymour said there was nothing she could do.

The appellees subsequently met on several occasions with officials of the Jackson County Planning Department and the Planning Commission. At each meeting, they were told that no permits could be issued until the properties were brought into compliance with the subdivision regulations. . . . The Colemans and the Evans took the various county officials at their word and never filed for permits. The parties agree that Seymour was unaware of the subdivision regulations at the time when she conveyed the subject properties.

On April 13, 1988, the appellees filed a complaint in chancery court against Seymour, John Phillips and Associates (Seymour's realtor), Century 21-K Realty (the Evans' and the Cruses' realtor), the McDonnells, and Jackson County. The two real estate agencies were subsequently dismissed as part of a negotiated settlement. The county was dismissed with prejudice . . . . The chancellor entered judgment against Seymour and the McDonnells . . . . The decree set aside the warranty deed from Seymour to the Evans, the warranty deed from Seymour to the Cruses, and the warranty deed from the McDonnells to the Colemans. The decree also required Seymour to reimburse the Evans and the Cruses for all payments made on the property together with their down payments, taxes, surveyors fees, forestry fees, loss of wages, closing costs, and attorney's fees.

LAW

I.   Did Seymour Violate the Common Law Seller's Warranties by Conveying Land in a Manner Which Violated County Subdivision Regulations?

The Evans, the Cruses, and the Colemans each received their respective tracts by warranty deed. According to Miss. Code Ann. § 89-1-33:

> The word "warrant" without restrictive words in a conveyance shall have the effect of embracing all of the five covenants known to common law, to wit: seisin, power to sell, freedom from encumbrance, quiet enjoyment and warranty of title.

The chancellor found that the conveyances by which appellees acquired their interests in the subject properties "Violate[d] the common law covenants of warranty granted under section 89-1-33, especially power to sell." His Findings of Fact and Conclusions of Law does not disclose the analysis he employed in reaching this outcome. . . . [W]e first . . . address a threshold question: Did the Seymour conveyances in fact violate the Jackson County subdivision ordinances, and if so, would the appellees have been unable to obtain variances? If the appellees could have obtained either permits or variances, then the basis for their complaint would have disappeared.

A.   Were Appellees in Fact Unable to Obtain Permits or Variances?

Seymour argues that the subject conveyances do not fall within the scope of the ordinance. Thus, she maintains, the county should have granted the requested permits. Section 106.1 of the Jackson County subdivision ordinance provides in pertinent part:

> These regulations and development standards shall apply to the following forms of land subdivisions:
>
> a. The division of land into two or more tracts, lots, sites, or parcels, any part of which, when subdivided, shall contain less than three (3) acres in area.

According to Seymour, the Colemans' parcel does not fall within the scope of § 106.1 since the Colemans' parcel contained three — not less than three — acres. This argument ignores the clear language of § 106.1 (a). Subsection (a) does not exclude all parcels not containing less than three acres; rather, the subsection excludes subdivisions which contain *no* parcels of less than three acres. The parcels conveyed to the Evans and the Cruses, along with other previous conveyances to which the record refers, all contain less than three acres. Since the Colemans' tract is part of the same division out of which the Evans and the Cruses acquired their respective interests, subsection (a) applies to the Colemans' parcel.

Seymour next argues that even if subsection (a) places her conveyances within the scope of the ordinance, § 106.1(f) takes them out. Subsection (f) provides:

> The provisions of this ordinance shall not apply to a sale or conveyance of a parcel of land constituting a part of a larger unplatted tract where such conveyance is made by a metes and bounds description, and no dedication, vacation, or reservation of any public or private street or easement is made within such larger unplatted tract subsequent to the effective date of this ordinance.

The ordinance went into effect in 1970. It is unquestioned that the parcels conveyed to the appellees constitute parts of "a larger unplatted tract" retained by Seymour. It is also undisputed that the appellees have access to their tracts by way of an easement across the "larger unplatted tract." The only real issue, then, is whether the easement was created subsequent to 1970. If so, then the conveyances will not fall under the § 106.1(f) exception.

Seymour contends that the property contained within the easement was surveyed for the purpose of building a county road in 1966. The county, however, never acquired an interest in the property. All the relevant conveyances appearing in the record occurred subsequent to 1970. The chancellor did not err in finding that Seymour's conveyances to the appellees were governed by the Jackson County subdivision ordinances.

It is thus clear that Seymour's conveyances conflicted with the Jackson County subdivision ordinances. It is not clear, however, that the appellees would have been unable to obtain hardship variances if they had sought them. If they had obtained variances, then the whole controversy now before the Court would have evaporated. The chancellor apparently assumed that the county would not have granted a variance, but the record does not provide a solid foundation for this assumption. Various county officials testified that the planning commission rarely grants variances and that the appellees probably could not have obtained one, but such testimony amounts to little more than mere speculation. Speculative evidence, standing alone, is generally insufficient to support a chancellor's finding of fact. On the other hand, we hesitate to require parties like the appellees to fight a losing battle to the bitter end just to prove what is already a foregone conclusion. In Knight v. McCain, 531 So.2d 590 (Miss. 1988), we considered an analogous case and concluded:

> The [purchasers] did everything possible to secure a permit but actually apply; the only reason they did not actually apply for a permit was because they were told not to do so by the building permit office because it would not be issued. The law does not require the doing of a futile act.

Whether the chancellor in the instant case could reasonably have concluded that the appellees "did everything possible" is a close question. It is also a question that we need not decide. Even if the county had conclusively refused to grant the appellees building permits, the chancellor would still have erred in ruling that Seymour's conveyances violated the § 89-1-33 seller's warranties. [W]e . . . separately discuss each warranty . . . .

B.   Covenants of Seisen [sic] and Power to Sell

First are the covenants of seisin and power to sell. The distinction between these two warranties is largely one of only historical significance. As a practical matter, they are identical in content and scope. *See* 6A R. Powell, *Real Property* ¶ 900 [2] [b] (P. Rohan rev. ed. 1989); . . . . The purpose of both is to provide assurance that the grantor has the estate he purports to convey. . . . The record before us contains nothing to indicate that Seymour's estate . . . was anything less than fee simple absolute. No third party has ever asserted a conflicting claim or interest. More to the point, the Jackson County subdivision regulations did not in any wise diminish Seymour's estate. . . .

Appellees concede that Seymour's title was impeccable, but they insist that the conveyances nevertheless violated Seymour's warranty of power to sell because Seymour did not have the "power" to sell land in violation of the county subdivision ordinances. This novel argument must fail for two reasons. First, to define "power to sell" in such terms expands the scope of the warranty beyond its traditional focus on the estate of the grantor. Secondly, a deed which runs afoul of subdivision regulations is perfectly valid despite the violation. In Sienkiewicz v. Smith, 649 P.2d 112 (Wash. 1982), a trial court ruled that an earnest money contract was unenforceable since the conveyance it secured would violate a subdivision platting statute. On appeal, the Supreme Court of Washington disagreed:

> Although we have long held that generally an agreement violating a statute or municipal ordinance is void . . . , this is not necessarily true where the agreement is neither immoral nor criminal in nature and the statute or ordinance subjects violators merely to a penalty without more. . . . In Marriott [Financial Services, Inc. v. Capital Funds, Inc., 217 S.E.2d 551 (N.C. 1975)], the North Carolina Supreme Court refused to grant rescission to a purchaser on the grounds that the vendor

had not complied with a city platting ordinance. In so ruling, the court looked to the language and purpose of the statute and asserted that since the contract was neither immoral nor criminal, the penalty for violation is limited to the penalties expressly provided for in the statute. Rescission was not included among those penalties. This sentiment is echoed is echoed [*sic*] in Gilmore v. Hershaw, 521 P.2d 934 (Wash. 1974), wherein we refused to grant rescission for a violation of [a subdivision statute] on the grounds that the Legislature specifically provided remedies other than rescission . . . .

The holdings of the Washington and North Carolina courts appear to represent the majority view. . . . Further, the propositions set out in *Sienkiewicz* and *Marriott* harmonize with this Court's position on analogous points of law. In Rast v. Sorrell, 127 So. 2d 435 (Miss. 1961), the seller of a pool hall sued for damages after the buyer refused to go through with the contract. The buyer argued that the contract was void since the business had been operated in violation of a licensing statute. We held:

> The contract here involved is not declared void and unenforceable by the statute. It is not a contract *malum in se*, it is a contract *malum prohibitum*, and the penalty, which is alone a criminal penalty, is imposed for the sole purpose of protecting the public revenue. There is no inherent infirmity or illegality in such a contract. The Legislature intended to rely alone on the penalty provided in the statute for the protection of the revenue of the state.

We addressed a similar matter in Gardner v. Reed, 42 So. 2d 206 (Miss. 1949). . . . [A] buyer defended against the enforcement of a contract for . . . fertilizer on grounds that the seller, a commercial fertilizer dealer, had not complied with statutory registration, inspection, and notice requirements. In holding for the buyer, we noted that "[t]he contract covered the purchase of a lawful commodity, and was not malum in se but merely malum prohibitum." . . . "[T]here is no statutory provision declaring such a contract void and unenforceable for failure to comply with the provisions thereof, but makes such failure a criminal offense instead."

Rast and *Gardner* implicate that the conveyances from Seymour to appellees are valid and enforceable so long as the ordinances they are alleged to violate regulate actions which are merely malum prohibitum. In Mississippi State Highway Commission v. Wagley, 231 So. 2d 507 (Miss. 1970), we noted that violation of a zoning restriction is malum prohibitum so long as the proscribed use does not involve "inherent evil." There is nothing inherently evil about selling small tracts of land without platting them and without constructing paved streets for ingress and egress. Accordingly, Seymour's conveyances were not invalid . . . .

C. *Covenant Against Encumbrances*

. . . As a general rule, zoning and other public restrictions on the use of land do not in and of themselves constitute breaches of a covenant against encumbrances. *See Powell on Real Property*, ¶ [900[2]; . . . *see also* Dover Pool & Racquet Club, Inc. v. Brooking, 322 N.E.2d 168 (Mass. 1975) ("In general building and zoning laws in existence at the time a land contract is signed are not treated as encumbrances"); Laand Corp. v. Firsching, 534 P.2d 916, 918 (Nev. 1975) (existing subdivision ordinance does not constitute encumbrance); Pamerqua Realty Corp. v. Dollar Service Corp., 461 N.Y.S.2d 393 (App. Div. 1983) (purchaser is deemed to have entered contract subject to laws and ordinances). This is true even though the regulation renders one's title unmarketable. *See Thompson on Real Property* § 5354 n.22. Professor Powell cogently explains the state of the law:

> Encumbrances can usually be classified as one of three types: (1) servitudes, (2) . . . liens or charges on the land, and (3) present or future estates which may be carved out of the estate conveyed.
>
> A servitude generally affects the land or its use and enjoyment in some physical way. It reduces the value of the land because a purchaser will not pay as much for a parcel of land which is limited in its usage as he or she would for an unencumbered one. Thus, easements . . . and covenants . . . are encumbrances. . . .
>
> However, the existence of a zoning ordinance which limits the use of the land, even though its effect may be substantially similar to that of a restrictive covenant, is not considered a violation of the covenant. The attitude of the courts seems to be that these restrictions are public regulations equally applicable to all land in the district and are equally open for the grantor and grantee to investigate. Therefore, the purchaser takes title with the risk that such a regulation may exist.

The law becomes a bit murky where property is not merely subject to a zoning restriction but is actually in violation of the restriction at the time of conveyance. The jurisdictions are not in agreement, but a majority seems generally to regard an existing violation as a breach of the covenant against encumbrances. . . . Professor Powell explains [*Real Property* ¶ 900 [2][c][3]:

> [C]ourts will not presume that a purchaser intended to use land in violation of a regulation. This interpretation of the distinction is supported by the fact that where construction on, or use of, the premises at the time of the conveyance already violates a restriction, the purchaser may assume that it is permitted and a breach of the covenant will occur.

The Seymour conveyances obviously do not fall within the scope of the general rule that existing violations breach the implied covenant against encumbrances:

---

3. The Powell rationale is, of course, inapplicable where the violation is not apparent. If the purchaser cannot discern the violation, then he cannot logically "assume" that the nonconformity is permitted. Many courts have therefore recognized an exception to the general rule where latent violations exist. *See, e.g.,* Frimberger v. Anzellotti, 594 A.2d 1029 (Conn. 1991); . . . *Frimberger* concludes that such an exception is justified since

> a conceptual enlargement of the covenant against encumbrances [to include latent, existing violations of restrictive land use ordinances] would create uncertainty and confusion in the law of conveyancing and title insurance because neither a title search nor a physical examination of the premises would disclose the violation.

[*S*]ee also Comment, *Public Land Use Regulations & Marketability of Title*, 1958 Wis. L. Rev. 128.
A few courts have recognized a second exception to the general rule where an extant violation of a land use ordinance is easily remediable. *See* FFG, Inc. v. Jones, 6 Haw. App. 35, 708 P.2d 836 (Hawaii Ct. App. 1985) (zoning law violation which merely required the redesigning and repainting of parking lot on commercial property did not constitute encumbrance). The rationale for this exception is that minor non-conformities do not substantially diminish the value of the property and thus do not qualify as encumbrances.

The purported violations were not "existing" at the time of the conveyance. Rather, the conveyances themselves *gave rise to the violations.* The purchaser is not entitled to assume that a violation is permissible where there has been no history of tacit assent. . . . We therefore find that the alleged violations of the Jackson County subdivision ordinances do not abridge Seymour's covenant against encumbrances.

D.   Covenant of Quiet Enjoyment

. . . According to Bridges v. Heimburger, 360 So.2d 929, 931 (Miss. 1978), the warranty of quiet enjoyment is breached where "there ha[s] been a judicial determination of loss of title or some other hostile action equivalent to eviction." The appellees claim that the county's refusal to grant permits was an action "equivalent to eviction."

The law does not precisely define the "equivalent" of eviction, but at least in the context of conveyance by warranty deed, it is clear that a grantee may claim constructive eviction only where his title suffers from an infirmity which endangers his right to possess the property. According to Powell, the covenant of quiet enjoyment "assures the grantee that his or her quiet possession or enjoyment will not be disrupted by the grantor or anyone else with paramount title." *Powell on Real Property* ¶ 900[2] [e]. *Cf. Bridges*, 360 So.2d at 931 (covenant of quiet enjoyment not breached where grantee had good title and where grantee's "possession was never disturbed or even threatened"). In practical effect, therefore, this covenant operates "as the fraternal, if not identical, twin of the covenant of warranty." . . . In the instant case, the record reveals no blemish on the appellees' title. Further, the appellees have demonstrated no infringement upon their right to possess the tracts in question; they merely assert that the violations of the subdivision ordinance prevent them from using the properties in the manner they intended.[6] In the absence of an impediment to good title or the right to possession, there can be no breach of the covenant of quiet enjoyment.

We hold that Seymour did not breach the warranties implied in her deeds to the appellees by conveying the subject properties in contravention to county subdivision ordinances.

---

6.   The appellees cite no authority to support their proposition that a frustration of intended use amounts to a breach of the covenant of quiet enjoyment. Courts in other jurisdictions have regarded "constructive eviction" as including the legal inability to use a *leasehold* as one intended. *See* Park West Mgmt. Corp. v. Mitchell, 391 N.E.2d 1288 N.Y. (1979) (covenant of quiet enjoyment includes a duty to refrain from act or omission which would render premises unusable by leasehold tenant); Polk v. Armstrong, 540 P.2d 96 (Nev. 1975) (commercial tenant's inability to obtain operating license due to landlord's failure to bring premises into compliance with law amounted to constructive eviction). These cases are readily distinguishable from the instant case, however. First and most obviously, the case *sub judice* does not involve a leasehold. Seymour retained no control over the parcels she conveyed and assumed no responsibility for facilitating the appellees' use thereof. Secondly, unlike the litigants in *Mitchell and Polk*, the parties here entered no agreement contemplating the appellees' intended use of the properties. There is nothing in either the contracts of sale or the warranty deeds to indicate that the appellees intended to use the tracts for any particular purpose. Where the parties do not specify the purpose for which property is to be used, the grantor certainly cannot be viewed as having guaranteed the property's suitability for a particular use. . . .

II. Whether the Chancellor Erred in Granting Damages and Attorney's Fees to the Appellees?

The chancellor based his award of damages and fees on his finding that Seymour had breached her implied warranties by selling property in violation of the Jackson County subdivision ordinances. . . .

CONCLUSION

The record does not clearly and conclusively indicate that the appellees could not have obtained the permits or variances they needed in order to use their properties in the manner they intended. We find, however, that even if the county had officially denied the appellees both permits and variances, the denials would not have given rise to breaches of Seymour's implied warranties. The covenants of seisen [*sic*], power to sell, title, and quiet enjoyment all require some infringement on title or the right to possess. No such infringement occurred here. The violation of a subdivision ordinance breaches a covenant against encumbrances only where the violation already exists at the time of conveyance. The violation at issue here did not preexist the conveyance. . . . Reversed and Rendered.

Questions

When is a present covenant breached? When is a future covenant breached? Does it make sense to limit when a grantee can recover under a future covenant? Assume that after taking title, the grantee discovers in a title search that his grantor only had a seven-eighths interest in the property—does it matter in an action by the grantee on a covenant of general warranty whether (a) the owner of the outstanding one-eighth interest is unaware of her rights; (b) the owner of the one-eighth interest is aware but has not taken any action; (c) the grantee has a potential buyer that refuses to proceed because of the one-eighth interest?

Problems: Covenants for Title

1. A received a deed with a general warranty covenant from O. It appeared that X, a predecessor in title of O, had given a prior deed to B. B asserted ownership in the land, and A entered into a settlement agreement splitting the property evenly with B. Can A successfully bring a covenant action against O? *See Garcia v. Herrera*, 959 P.2d 533 (N.M. Ct. App. 1998).

2. Grantor gave Grantee a deed with a covenant of general warranty. Grantee subsequently brought an action claiming that the land was subject to an easement by adverse use, allowing neighbors to use a roadway across Grantee's land. For years, including during the time the sale was negotiated, the roadway was openly and consistently used by the neighbors. Can Grantee successfully maintain a covenant of title action against Grantor? Assume that Grantee never brought an action and conveyed the land 10 years later to X. Could X successfully sue Grantor on the general warranty? *See Sinks v. Karleskint*, 474 N.E.2d 767 (Ill. Ct. App. 1985); *Richitt v. Southern Pine Plantations, Inc.*, 491 S.E.2d 528 (Ga. Ct. App. 1997).

3. A conveys Blackacre to B with a covenant of quiet enjoyment for $80,000. B then conveys the property to C by quitclaim for $90,000. X, with a superior title, evicts C from possession; at that time, Blackacre is worth $100,000. From whom can C recover, and how much?

D. THE MORTGAGE

The mortgage is the vehicle by which buyers finance the purchase of real property or the means through which an owner can secure a non-purchase-related loan. Various mortgage issues are addressed in portions of this chapter dealing with the contract of sale, deed, and recording system. A full examination of the intricacies of mortgage law is best left for an advanced course in real estate transactions or secured transactions. The following materials introduce you to some key concepts and the cast of characters in a basic mortgage transaction.

1. *Glossary and Cast of Characters*

Let us take a simple transaction.

The owner of land worth $10,000 wants to borrow $6,000; the lender wants security. So the owner—whom we shall call MR for mortgagor—executes a promissory note to ME, the mortgagee, by which MR promises to pay $6,000 to ME, three years from date, with 12 percent interest, payable semiannually. At the same time, MR gives to ME a mortgage on the land to secure the obligations of the note. The mortgage is a document, varying in form according to local law and custom, which gives to ME a claim against the land for repayment of the loan. The mortgage will be recorded in the appropriate registry of deeds. The note will not be recorded because it does not create any interest in land; it is not a document of title but merely a promise. Thus, the first point to master is this: The usual modern mortgage transaction involves two documents, (1) the note, a document which establishes an obligation from MR to ME, and (2) the mortgage, a document by which MR gives to ME a security interest in the land to assure performance of the obligation.

At this stage MR is said to hold the "equity" in the land, whereas before giving the mortgage MR held "title." "Equity" is a shortened form of "equity of redemption" and means simply title-subject-to-a-mortgage. We shall later examine the question whether it is accurate to call MR's interest an equity; but there is no question that it is standard terminology.

Transfer of the equity. MR, holding the equity, may want to sell it. If the value of the land is sound, the equity is worth $4,000. MR finds a buyer, whom we shall call PE, for purchaser of equity, and upon payment of $4,000 gives to PE a deed of the land that recites that the land is "subject to a mortgage of $6,000 to ME."

Is PE liable on the note for $6,000? Certainly not; PE has made no promise to pay anything to anybody. Only MR is liable. However, ME can enforce ME's security interest in the land—which means in substance that after default ME can compel a sale of the land and take the first $6,000 of the proceeds of sale; and this possibility, as a practical matter, compels PE to pay the $6,000 when it falls due to protect the equity in the land. But suppose ME chooses to collect the note from MR, ignoring ME's rights against the land since MR is perfectly solvent; doesn't this cause a net loss to MR and give a windfall profit to PE? It would, were it not for the doctrine of subrogation, which we shall later discuss.

Since the three-party situation involving MR, ME, and PE causes difficulties by separating the obligation on the note and the ownership of the equity, MR usually tries to have PE assume the personal obligation of the note at the time PE buys the equity—i.e., MR tries to get PE to promise to pay the note and to save MR harmless. Better still, MR tries to arrange a novation by which MR is released from the obligation on the note and PE becomes sole obligor. Thus, to summarize, where MR sells the equity to PE, the transaction usually takes one of three forms:

1. sale of the equity subject to the mortgage—MR being still liable on the note and PE not being personally liable

2. sale of the equity subject to the mortgage, which the purchaser promises to pay—both MR and PE being liable on the note to ME, but PE being obligated to indemnify MR

3. sale of the equity with the mortgagor being discharged from liability on the note and the purchaser becoming the sole obligor.

Assignment of the mortgage. ME, holding a note of MR for $6,000 secured by mortgage on the land, may want to get this money out; and ME may find someone willing to take over the investment. If so, ME endorses the note and assigns the mortgage to A-ME, assignee of the mortgage. Thereafter all obligations of MR run to A-ME, and the latter holds the security interest in the land; the assignment should be recorded in the registry of deeds.

Second mortgages. After MR has given a $6,000 mortgage to ME, MR may want to borrow more money on the land. MR has an equity worth $4,000 and can possibly find someone who will lend $2,000 upon a second mortgage—i.e., a mortgage on the equity, or a mortgage subject to the first mortgage. In that case MR gives to ME-2 a note for $2,000, usually at a higher rate of interest to compensate for the increased risk, and also gives ME-2 a mortgage on the land that recites that it is "subject to a first mortgage to ME." Third, fourth, and later mortgages can be given in the same way.

Reduction of the mortgage. As payments of interest or principal are made, the practice is for ME to endorse payments on the back of the note. No corresponding entry is made in the registry of deeds; therefore, if the registry shows an outstanding mortgage of $6,000, this may represent a lien on the land of $6,000 plus a lot of accrued interest, or it may represent a lien for a very small sum because of large amounts of principal having been paid.

When the note is paid in full, ME surrenders the note to MR and executes a *discharge* of the mortgage, which is recorded.

2. Function of a Mortgage

To the mortgagor, the mortgage represents financing; to the mortgagee, it represents security for an investment. If MR wants to buy a house for $100,000, MR rarely has the full price at the time of purchase; the mortgage enables MR to purchase upon a down payment and then to pay off the balance by partial payments on the principal of the mortgage that ME takes.[1] In this type of transaction, ME is often a bank that is seeking investments that will (1) produce the yield required to meet interest requirements of savings deposits, and (2) involve relatively low risk of loss of the principal invested. Today, the mortgage may likely be resold in a bundle of mortgages in the secondary market.

When MR buys a piece of real estate, it may be that the vendor will take back a *purchase money mortgage* to secure unpaid installments of the agreed purchase price.

Where MR has land and wants to build on it, the *construction loan mortgage* provides a convenient method. Assume that MR has land worth $30,000 on which MR wants to put a $120,000 house; MR has only $20,000 toward the cost of building. MR gives to ME a mortgage covering the land and the building to be erected. The total amount to be advanced by ME is $100,000; but this will be turned over to MR in stated installments only as the house progresses to various stages, e.g., when foundations are complete, when roof is on, when exterior finish is complete and plumbing installed, when the house is complete except for grading. Thus, as the building "feeds the mortgage," the amount of the mortgage is stepped up. In this situation, ME has to be careful that, as ME advances installments of the loan, statutory liens of contractors and laborers for work on the property (known as mechanics' liens) are discharged, for these liens may be senior to the mortgage, and the builder, working on a shoestring, may not be trusted to pay off these claims.

1. *Various methods of financing land purchases.* If O owns Blackacre and P wishes to acquire it but lacks the purchase price of a fee simple, a number of methods exist for financing the project. All, or nearly all, are available everywhere; but local custom tends to make some of them popular in one state, others in another. Here are a number of the common devices:

a. The bank mortgage. This is described in the text.

b. The purchase money mortgage. Here the mortgagee is the vendor rather than a bank.

c. The installment land contract. This is described in the section on contracts for sale. The vendor keeps title until the full purchase price is paid; but the purchaser takes possession upon paying the first installment.

d. The escrow agreement. The vendor delivers a deed to a third person under irrevocable instructions to (a) deliver the deed to the purchaser if the latter pays the price in accordance with the contract, or (b) to redeliver the deed to the vendor if the purchaser defaults. This is simply a deferred payment or installment contract, the purchaser having additional protection against the vendor's failure to convey.

e. The long-term lease. Instead of buying a fee simple from O, P takes a 100-year lease, renewable forever; P makes a lump-sum payment comparable in amount to what P would pay out of P's own funds if P was financing the purchase under a mortgage, and the rent is fixed at an amount that will give to O an appropriate return off of the unpaid purchase price. Of course, the parties provide for a "net lease" under which P pays taxes, insurance, repairs, and all other expense. From P's point of view, this arrangement has great advantages: Not only is the initial outlay minimal, but also there will never be a time in the future when P will be faced with the necessity of raising a large principal sum.

3.   Deeds of Trust

The deed of trust, which is widely used in California and some other states, is functionally similar to a mortgage. Structurally, however, it is different in that a third party—the trustee—is added to the transaction. The borrower (trustor) conveys title to the lender's nominee (trustee) as security for repayment of the debt. The lender is the beneficiary of the trust. If the note is paid, the trustee reconveys title to the borrower; if it is not, the trustee at the beneficiary's request will hold a public sale of the land. The trustee will distribute the proceeds to the beneficiary to satisfy the debt. The surplus, if any, will be distributed to the borrower.

The deed of trust became popular because mortgages traditionally could not be foreclosed without judicial process. Under the deed of trust, the trustee is required to give notice of default and pending sale to the debtor and the debtor can cure the default up to the time of sale, but no judicial process is involved and there is no redemption period after the sale. The advantages of the deed of trust have now been removed in the majority of states that by statute now allow mortgages to include powers of non-judicial sale. The law now treats these two forms of security the same and they are addressed interchangeably in this chapter.

4.   Security Interests Other Than Real Estate Mortgages and Deeds of Trust

To put the real estate mortgage in its setting, it is worthwhile to mention other members of the family to which it belongs. Other security interests in real estate include:

1. *Attachments.* At the commencement of a legal proceeding, the plaintiff, sometimes and in some states, attaches real estate of the defendant as security for payment of such judgment as may be obtained.

2. *Judgment liens.* In some states, the rendition or docketing of a judgment against A constitutes a lien on A's real estate even though there has been no attachment.

3. *Municipal taxes and assessments.* These constitute liens upon the real estate with reference to which they are levied, and such liens are usually senior to all others.

4. *Mechanics' liens.* These have already been mentioned with reference to construction loan mortgages. It is usually provided by statute that contractors, materialmen, and laborers who perform construction services on real estate have liens to secure payment, provided that they give public notice as prescribed. This notice usually consists of giving written notice in the city hall as to, first, the contract covering the transaction and, later, the amount due thereunder; time limitations for such notice are prescribed.

Closely related to security transactions are those in which the personal obligation of the principal debtor is buttressed by the personal obligation of a surety. For example, S endorses A's promissory note to B, or S guarantees that A will complete a construction contract with B. The principles governing the relationship between the creditor, the principal obligor, and the surety make up the law of *suretyship*, which is related to but still apart from the law of security transactions with which we are here concerned.

5.   The Real Estate Mortgage as It Was Developed in the Courts

Now back to our principal object of concern. It will be useful to indicate how the mortgage and its incidents grew up in the courts; then to point out the principal types of statutory variations that bring it about that mortgage practice differs substantially from state to state in this country. Let us designate as the classic mortgage the institution that grew up in the courts.

The classic mortgage was a deed from MR to ME in the usual form of a straight conveyance, plus a defeasance clause that provided that if the obligations of the note were performed (i.e., if the interest was paid periodically, the taxes on the property paid, the property kept insured for the benefit of ME in an appropriate amount, and the principal paid at maturity) the deed should thereupon become void and of no effect. In other words, the mortgage was a conveyance to the mortgagee subject to a condition subsequent. The note or mortgage usually contained an acceleration clause, declaring that if the minor obligations of MR (interest, taxes, insurance) should not be performed, the principal would thereupon become due at the option of ME. The mortgage usually contained a provision that until default MR should remain in possession. If MR paid on time, the property automatically reverted to MR under the defeasance clause. But it was customary for ME to give MR a written discharge as evidence of performance of the obligations and (in the United States) to record in the registry of deeds so that MR would thenceforth have a clear record title.

Redemption. Suppose MR did not pay the note at maturity—i.e., at the "law day" provided in the mortgage? At law, MR's rights in the property were ended, for ME held a deed subject to a condition subsequent that could no longer happen. However, if MR later offered to pay the principal, plus interest, plus expenses to which ME may have been put as a result of MR's default, the courts of equity required ME to accept payment and reconvey the property. A usual basis for involving equity jurisdiction has always been relief against forfeiture; and, because the value of the property often exceeded by a substantial margin the obligation secured, retention of the property by ME often constituted a windfall profit to ME at the expense of MR. So MR would bring a "bill to redeem," alleging the facts, stating a willingness to pay principal, interest, and expenses, depositing the money in court, and praying that ME be directed to reconvey the property on payment. The equity court entered a decree to that effect as a matter of course. ME was thereby made whole by recovering the amount of the debt, interest, and expenses; and MR got the property back.

Foreclosure. The possibility of redemption made things difficult for ME when MR had defaulted. ME had title to the land to be sure, but if the land should rise in value or if MR should come into money, there was always a chance that MR would redeem in equity. This made the land unsalable and thereby defeated the security function of the mortgage. The equity courts provided the antidote in the "bill to foreclose." ME would bring a bill in equity against MR, alleging the facts and praying that MR be enjoined from bringing a bill to redeem. One form of decree was that MR should be so enjoined unless MR should pay up within a specified period, say three months; this was called strict foreclosure, in that it cut off all rights of MR and made ME the outright owner of the property. However, if there was reason to believe that the property was worth more than the amount due to ME, the court would direct that the property be sold by an officer of the court and the proceeds of the sale devoted to paying expenses of the sale, satisfying ME's claims, and paying the balance to MR; this was called foreclosure by sale. ME and MR could protect their respective interests by bidding at the sale; and, indeed, in the normal course of events ME was the principal, perhaps sole, bidder. For reasons that will shortly appear, foreclosure by sale became the standard method even when the property was clearly worth less than the amount due.

Two questions as to common terminology:

1. How about the propriety of calling MR's interest an "equity"? After default, yes; before default, no. Before default, the legal rights of MR under the defeasance clause of the mortgage are fully adequate to protect MR if MR meets the obligations of the note; MR has a legal future interest in the property. However, the practice is universal to call MR's interest an "equity" at all times.

2. How about the propriety of the expression "foreclosing a mortgage"? Obviously meaningless. "Foreclose" means "shut out" or "debar." The thing that is foreclosed is the mortgagor's right to redeem, not the mortgage. Foreclosure matures or enlarges the mortgagee's security interest into an absolute title. Yet the accepted practice is to talk of foreclosing a mortgage.

Deficiency judgment. To whatever extent foreclosure puts value into ME's hands, the debt of MR to ME is discharged; but as to any deficiency, ME still holds an unsecured personal claim against MR. The best way to establish the amount of deficiency, if any, is by sale of the property at which both ME and MR are free to bid or produce bidders; and it is for this reason that foreclosure by sale is customarily used where the property is insufficient in value to pay the debt and MR is of sufficient financial worth to make a judgment against MR worth having. Theoretically, after a strict foreclosure, a deficiency judgment can be obtained in an action at law on the basis of testimony as to the value of the property, but this is not done as a matter of practice. Deficiency judgments can be ruinous; a sudden break in the stock market, such as occurred in 1929 and 1930, can force lenders to call their real estate loans (many mortgages are allowed to run as "open" mortgages—not to be confused with "open end" mortgages—long after they are due). By causing numerous forced sales of land at a time when buyers are nonexistent, foreclosures depress salable values to a small fraction of the face amount of what was considered a sound mortgage. Legislation may limit deficiency judgments in certain situations.

6. *The Mortgagee's Security Interest: Title Theory, Lien Theory*

The classic mortgage gave ME title to the property, subject to a condition subsequent. Yet this was always recognized in equity, and often at law, as a security interest only. For example:

1. If ME took possession either before or after default but before foreclo-sure, ME had to apply the net rents to the claims against MR.

2. If ME died, the property went to ME's executor or administrator (being treated as personal property), not to ME's heir or devisee (who is entitled to real property).

3. MR's spouse had dower, but ME's spouse had no dower rights.

4. If ME assigned the debt to A but did not assign the mortgage, equity treated the mortgage as nevertheless assigned. "The mortgage follows the debt."

5. If before mortgaging the property, MR had made covenants that would ordinarily "run with the land" and be binding upon a grantee from MR — e.g., a covenant to maintain a road over the land in repair, or a cov-enant not to use the premises for industrial purposes — ME was not liable upon these covenants, at least in the usual case where ME did not take possession.

Moreover, courts of equity developed a series of rules designed to prevent ME from imposing on MR by realizing more than ME's security interest in the land. For example,

6. No matter how clearly it was stated in the mortgage that MR should have no right to redeem unless MR paid, MR could still redeem.

7. If ME took a straight deed with no defeasance clause but the purpose was to assure future payment of a debt (as distinguished from the property being taken in satisfaction of the debt), this created an "equitable mort-gage," and MR was allowed to redeem.

So, in most substantive respects, the mortgagee's interest was *treated* as a lien though it was *called* title. The "title theory," therefore, must always be adjusted to the idea that the mortgagee has a security interest only.

It is for this reason that the difference between "title-theory states" and "lien-theory states" is a good deal less important in the practice of the profession than it has been in academic discussion.

Some states have by judicial decision on specific points so eliminated any trace of the mortgagee's "title" that they consider themselves lien-theory states. Other states have enacted statutory reforms on the same specific points or expressly declare that the mortgagee's interest is a lien only.

7. *Foreclosure in Modern Practice*

The most common method of foreclosure in the various states is by judicial sale. Usually, the procedure is minutely regulated by statute and is cut and dried, eliminating any discretion on the part of the court or its functionaries. Sale is made by a special master, referee, or sheriff. The requirements as to notice to various parties, advertisement, time and place of sale, etc., are strict, and a fail-ure to comply with them subjects the foreclosure to attack.

In other states, the practice is to include in the mortgage a paragraph declaring that upon default ME may sell the property, satisfy himself or herself out of the proceeds, and pay the balance, if any, to MR. Some states prescribe this method by statute; others permit it if a power of sale is included in the mortgage; a few forbid it by requiring foreclosure by judicial sale. States that permit it regulate the procedure of conducting the sale and jealously protect the mortgagor against violation of rules designed for the mortgagor's benefit. Most permit the mortgagee to purchase at his or her own sale; a few do not.

WILLIAMS v. KIMES
Supreme Court of Missouri
949 S.W.2d 899 (Mo. 1997)

BENTON, J. Is the holder of a recorded contingent remainder an "owner" entitled to notice of a power of sale foreclosure under Sec. 443.325.3(2)?[1] The circuit court answered in the negative. This Court has jurisdiction because the appeal involves the validity of a statute. . . .

I

In his will, Aubra Robert Wrather devised 72 acres of real property to his daughter "Reba Wrather LaFont, and her bodily heirs, in fee simple." The probate court distributed the property to "Reba Wrather LaFont and her bodily heirs." By this language, LaFont received a life estate, her presumptive bodily heirs received a contingent remainder during her lifetime, and her bodily heirs, living at the time of her death, would receive a fee simple absolute. Sec. 442.470; Easter v. Ochs, 837 S.W.2d 516 (Mo. banc 1992); Willard Eckhardt and Paul Peterson, *Possessory Estates, Future Interests and Conveyances in Missouri*, Sec. 19 at 19-20 (1986).

During probate, the executor and LaFont borrowed money from Farmers Bank, mortgaging the 72 acres and other property. Upon default, Farmers Bank foreclosed on the 72 acres in 1988. The executor and LaFont both received a Notice of Trustee's Sale by certified mail, return receipt requested. The presumptive bodily heirs in 1988—Anita Kay Williams, James G. LaFont, Heather Maria Hobbs, and Lesley Suzanne Hobbs—did not receive actual notice of the foreclosure sale.

At the power of sale foreclosure in 1988, Sherman D. Kimes, Elaine Kimes, Albert W. Kimes, and Nina Mae Kimes purchased the 72 acres. In 1990 the Kimeses conveyed the 72 acres to a family trust.

LaFont died on October 13, 1993. Two of her three children, appellants Anita Kay Williams and James G. LaFont, survived her. The third passed away in 1986, survived by Heather Maria Hobbs and Lesley Suzanne Hobbs, who in 1994 sold their interest to Anita Kay Williams and appellant W.A. Williams. Since LaFont's death, the Kimeses have remained in possession of the 72 acres.

---

1.   All references are to *RSMo 1994*.

II

The dispositive issue is whether Anita Kay Williams, James G. LaFont, Heather Maria Hobbs, and Lesley Suzanne Hobbs were "owners" 40 days before the power of sale foreclosure. Sec. 443.325, subd. 3(2) provides:

> In the event of foreclosure under a power of sale, the foreclosing mortgagee or trustee shall, not less than twenty days prior to the scheduled date of the sale, cause to be deposited in the United States mail an envelope certified or registered, and with postage prepaid, enclosing a notice containing the information required in the published notice of sale referred to in section 443.320, addressed . . . .

> (2) To the person shown by the records in the office of the recorder of deeds to be *the owner of the property as of forty days prior to the scheduled date of foreclosure sale* at the foreclosing mortgagee's last known address for said record owner; . . . .

This Court has broadly defined an owner to include "any person beneficially interested in property." Siemer v. Schuermann Building and Realty Co., 381 S.W.2d 821 (Mo. 1964). *The Restatement of Property* [Sec. 10 at 25 (1936)], similarly defines an owner as "a person who has one or more interests" in real estate. . . . Most importantly, Missouri has long authorized the conveyance of contingent remainders. Sec. 442.020, *see* Grimes v. Rush, 197 S.W.2d 310 (Mo. 1946); McNeal v. Bonnel, 412 S.W.2d 167 (Mo. 1967).

The records in the recorder of deeds' office showed the owners of the property 40 days before the foreclosure sale to be "LaFont Wrather LaFont and her bodily heirs." The holders of the contingent remainder—Anita Kay Williams, James G. LaFont, Heather Maria Hobbs, and Lesley Suzanne Hobbs—had an interest capable of conveyance, and were thus "owners" entitled to actual notice. . . .

III

The Kimeses raise three contrary points.

A

The Kimeses note that the identity of LaFont's "bodily heirs" could not be ascertained until her death in 1993. True, at the time of the foreclosure sale in 1988, LaFont's presumptive heirs possessed a contingent remainder subject to being defeated if they died before LaFont. . . . However, a contingent remainder is an ownership interest sufficient to require notice of a foreclosure. . . .

The Kimeses' practical concern is that notice to the known contingent remainder holders never assures that the eventual bodily heirs receive notice, and that this uncertainty will chill lending and power of sale foreclosing. To the extent that this concern is valid, the parties should consider judicial foreclosure. . . .

B

The Kimeses assert that Anita Kay Williams, James G. LaFont, Heather Maria Hobbs, and Lesley Suzanne Hobbs were required to file the statutory request in order to receive notice of the foreclosure sale. . . . As owners, they were entitled to actual notice under sec. 443.325, subd. 3(2), and were not required to file a request for notice under sec. 443.325, subd. 1.

C

The Kimeses argue that the presumptive heirs' receipt of constructive notice through publication, and actual notice to the life tenant and the executor of the estate, was sufficient. Constructive notice through weekly newspaper publication is insufficient for owners. . . . There is no proof that the contingent remainder holders received actual notice of the foreclosure sale until after LaFont's death.

IV

The remaining issue is the appropriate remedy for failure to provide actual notice. Only substantial irregularities will invalidate a foreclosure sale. Kennon v. Camp, 353 S.W.2d 693 (Mo. 1962). However, where owners receive no notice and are prejudiced, there is no substantial compliance. *See* I.P.I. Liberty Village Associates v. Spalding Corners Associates, 751 S.W.2d 120 (Mo. App. 1988) . . . .

A buyer at a statutory sale takes subject to the interests of those who were entitled to notice but did not receive it. Lohr v. Cobur Corporation, 654 S.W.2d 883 (Mo. Banc 1983) (holding that a tax sale for delinquent county real estate taxes did not extinguish the deed of trust because notice by publication was insufficient); Anheuser-Busch Employees' Credit Union v. Davis, 899 S.W.2d 868, 870 (Mo. banc 1995) (finding that constructive notice, unaccompanied by written notice, was insufficient to extinguish the deed of trust at a tax sale). This Court holds that the presumptive heirs' interest was not extinguished by the power of sale foreclosure. The Kimeses purchased only LaFont's life estate.

The contingent remainder became a fee simple absolute upon LaFont's 1993 death. Appellants are entitled to immediate possession of the 72 acres. Regarding the claims for damages, credits, and other relief, this case is remanded to the trial court . . . .

V

The judgment of the circuit court is reversed, and the case remanded for further proceedings consistent with this opinion.

Note and Questions

1. You can see from *Williams v. Kimes* that it is critically important to give notice to all owners of the property in a foreclosure proceeding. Do you see why notice to future interest holders as well as to present possessors is required? As a practical matter, how could the lender have given notice to the LaFont bodily heirs? Should the lender have limited the amount of its loan to the value of a life estate in the property? How could it have gotten a security interest in the remainder?

2. What about the Kimes? Do they have any recourse against the lender, or against the bodily heirs? On a second appeal after the remand, the Supreme Court held they were entitled to a recoupment of their purchase price and the imposition of an equitable lien in the amount of $86,400 on the property to secure payment. It also held that the remaindermen were entitled to the value of the land for the period of time they were wrongfully deprived of its possession and use on account of the void foreclosure sale. *Williams v. Kimes*, 25 S.W.3d 150 (Mo. 2000).

3. To learn more about mortgage foreclosures, see *Restatement of the Law of Property (Third)—Mortgages*; Debra Pogrund Stark, *Facing the Facts: An Empirical Study of the Fairness and Efficiency of Foreclosures and a Proposal for Reform*, 30 U. Mich. J.L. Reform 639 (1997); Marshall E. Tracht, *Renegotiation and Secured Credit: Explaining the Equity of Redemption*, 52 Vand. L. Rev. 599 (1999).

E.   THE RECORDING SYSTEM

1.   Introduction

The recording system was designed to resolve the following scenario: O conveys Blackacre to A for consideration; the next day, O conveys Blackacre to B for consideration (sometimes O is a rogue, sometimes he is simply a bumbler). Who as between A and B has title to Blackacre?

Prior to the recording acts, the common-law rule was "first in time, first in right." That old rule still applies when there is no applicable recording statute. The recording acts attempt to resolve the competing claims of As and Bs in Blackacre. The interests asserted by A and B may be mutually exclusive (i.e., both cannot be fee owners of Blackacre). Or the interests may exist simultaneously in Blackacre (e.g., mortgages, easements, restrictive covenants, or the like), but the issue may be which has priority, or whether a subsequent purchaser is bound at all by the other interest.

The recording acts determine the validity and priority of conflicting interests. The acts function by creating a record system that will reflect who owns what interests in any given piece of realty. Potential purchasers can search the records to determine ownership; purchasers can thus avoid paying good money for bad title. In order to encourage people to record documents in the system and to conduct searches, the laws in the various states generally punish those who fail to follow standard recording and searching procedures.

Another set of questions is outside the recording acts—i.e., whether A or B can recover from O for creating conflicting interests, either based on covenants for title or tort (especially where O is of the rogue variety). The recording acts are only about who has title to Blackacre.

As you study these materials, try to discern the policy underlying the recording acts. In deciding how to resolve difficult cases, focus on the language of the statute, what result will serve the policy of the statute, whether the parties were following standard recording and searching procedures, and who best could have avoided the loss in question.

For a general discussion of the recording acts, see Barbara Taylor Mattis, *Recording Acts: Anachronistic Reliance*, 25 Real Prop. Prob. & Tr. J. 17 (1990). For an analysis of how a title search may be conducted most efficiently, see Matthew Baker, Thomas J. Miceli, C.F. Sirmans & Geoffrey K. Turnbull, *Optimal Title Search*, 31 J. Leg. Stud. 139 (2002).

a. The Mechanics of Recording: The Grantor-Grantee Index and the Tract System

It is essential to an understanding of the system of recording documents affecting the title to land that you have some knowledge of what may be called the "mechanics" of title examinations. That is, you must know how you locate on the public records the recorded documents that must be evaluated to determine the state of the record title. To put it another way, a purchaser of land ought not to be compelled to take subject to claims against the land set forth on the public records unless a reasonable search of the records will reveal them. You cannot determine what a purchaser of land may reasonably be expected to find on the public records without knowing something about the mechanical job of locating recorded documents.

Surprisingly, perhaps even shockingly, recording systems have remained stuck in the paper age despite the many advantages of digital records. Although electronic records and searches are now available in some counties, particularly large ones like Los Angeles County, much of the law and practice in this area still reflects the traditional operation of the public records systems described in this chapter.

When you take a document of title to the recorder's office, that document is copied in full (in some localities a photo copy may be made), and the copy is placed in a bound volume.[2] That bound volume contains many other copies of instruments affecting land in the county. When one volume is filled with copies of instruments, another volume is started. If you are looking for a particular document, you might take months to locate it if you had to turn the pages of all the volumes in which the documents are copied in full. It should be obvious to you that some kind of index must be kept that will enable you to obtain a reference to the volume and page in which the document you are interested in is copied. But what kind of index will do the job?

---

2. The bound volumes referred to in the text take up a great amount of space. To solve the space problem, documents are now being recorded on microfilm. A print may be made from the microfilm when needed. *See* Robert N. Cook (assisted by Frederick M. Lombardi), *American Land Law Reform: Modernization of Recording Statutes*, 13 Case W. Res. L. Rev. 639, 664 (1962).

Grantor-grantee index. The recorder's office keeps what is called a grantor-grantee index. This simply means that every recorded document is indexed both by the name of the grantor in the document and by the name of the grantee. The names of the grantors and the grantees are arranged in the index in alphabetical order. Thus, if you are buying land from Adams, you can go to the recorder's office of the county in which the land is located and, by starting with the latest index book containing the names of grantees whose names begin with A (you start with the grantee book because Adams, from whom you are buying, was a grantee in the deed that conveyed the property to Adams), you can trace back until you find indexed a conveyance to Adams. When you find an index reference of such conveyance, you will find opposite the name of Adams the volume and page at which the deed to Adams is copied in full. The index also gives a brief description of the property conveyed to Adams and the name of Adams's grantor. You can then repeat this process in the appropriate grantee index that applies to the name of the grantor of Adams and find the deed by which Adams's grantor obtained title, and so on.

The grantor index is used to ascertain whether a particular owner of property made any conveyances that will prevail over the conveyance under which you will be claiming if you buy. Thus, when you are buying from Adams, you use the grantee index to ascertain where Adams got the property; but you use the grantor index to ascertain whether Adams has made conveyances that will prevail over you if you buy the property.

Tract index. Some states have authorized the establishment of another type of index, which is called a "tract"[3] or "block" index. A tract index is keyed to the description of the land conveyed rather than to the names of the parties involved in a conveyance.

In order for a tract index to be established, the area covered by the index (the area normally is a county, but may be a city if the index is established only on a citywide basis) is divided into small segments, usually referred to as blocks, and each block is given a number. These blocks are not necessarily all the same size. Each block then is divided into smaller segments, usually called lots. Each lot is bounded so as to include within it an area under single ownership (or possibly concurrent ownership) at the time the index is established. The lots thus marked off are given numbers.

A map of the county, or city, showing the boundaries and number of each block and the boundaries and number of each lot within a block, is located in the recorder's office. An index is established for each block, and a separate page in that index is devoted exclusively to conveyances of each lot within the block. Thus, when you are examining the title to a particular tract of land, you go to the recorder's office and look at the map of the county, or city, determine the number of the block in which your land is located, ascertain the number of your lot within the block, go to the index volume for conveyances of land in your block, turn to the page containing references of conveyances of your numbered lot, and on that one page you find a list of the conveyances of your lot from the

---

3.   Robert N. Cook (assisted by Frederick M. Lombardi), *American Land Law Reform: Modernization of Recording Statutes,* 13 Case W. Res. L. Rev. 639, 649 (1962), lists in a footnote the following states as requiring the keeping of a tract index: Nebraska, North Dakota, Oklahoma, South Dakota, Utah, Washington, and Wyoming.

date the index was established. Opposite each listed conveyance is a reference to the volume and page where the document concerning that conveyance is copied in full.

The description of the tract index given above is that of an ideal index. You must examine the local situation to determine to what extent the tract index as established falls short of this ideal.

Combination tract and grantor-grantee index. A combination tract and grantor-grantee index may be established. Under such a combination index, the county is divided into numbered blocks as in the tract index, and you locate first the numbered block in which your particular land is located. The conveyances of land in that block, however, are indexed by the names of the parties, so that you locate your references by the grantor-grantee index method. This combination speeds up the use of the grantor-grantee index because the area covered by each index is much smaller than the countywide index used in most localities. This tends to cut down the number of grantors and grantees with names similar to the ones you are running in the index.

Descent or devise of land. Neither the grantor-grantee index nor the tract index, as they now exist, make any provision for indexing the passage of title to land on death of the owner. Thus, under either index system, if your indexed chain of ownership contains a gap, it is probably due to the fact that title has passed at some time by descent or devise.

Determining land owned by particular person. It may be important, for some purposes, to go to the land records and locate all the real property owned of record by an individual in a particular county. You can do this under a grantor-grantee index system very easily. It would be an almost impossible task under a tract index. Do you see why?

For a discussion of beginning steps to computerized and online recording, see Arthur R. Gaudio, *Real Estate Records: A Model for Action*, 24 W. New Eng. L. Rev. 271 (2002); Phyllis Slesinger & Daniel McLaughlin, *Mortgage Electronic Registration System*, 31 Idaho L. Rev. 805 (1995); Dale Whitman, *Digital Recording of Real Estate Conveyances*, 32 J. Marshall L. Rev. 227 (1999). Also consider how emerging economies might develop recording systems from scratch, and which system would be most effective. *See* Tim Hanstad, *Designing Land Registration Systems for Developing Countries*, 13 Am. U. J. Int'l L. & Pol'y 647 (1998); Lev Batalov, Comment, *The Russian Title Registration System for Realty and Its Effect on Foreign Investors*, 73 Wash. L. Rev. 989 (1998).

b.   Classification of Recording Acts

The extent to which a subsequent purchaser is protected against a prior unrecorded deed depends on the type of statute in the local jurisdiction. There are four distinct types of statutes.

1. *Notice* statutes, which place no premium on the race to the recorder's office and protect the bona fide purchaser whether he or she records first or not.

2. *Race-notice* statutes, which place a premium on the race to the recorder's office and protect the bona fide purchaser only if he or she records first.

3. *Period-of-grace* statutes, which give the prior grantee a period of time in which to record, and protect the bona fide purchaser only if the prior grantee does not record in the time allowed by the statute.

4. *Race* statutes, which place a premium on the race to the recorder's office and protect the purchaser, whether the purchaser has notice or not, if he or she records first.

The following are illustrations of each of the four types of statutes mentioned above.

(i) Notice

MASS. GEN. LAWS ANN. CH. 183, § 4

A conveyance of an estate in fee simple, fee tail or for life, or a lease for more than seven years from the making thereof, or an assignment of rents or profits from an estate or lease, shall not be valid as against any person, except the grantor or lessor, his heirs and devisees and persons having actual notice of it, unless it, or an office copy as provided in section thirteen of chapter thirty-six, or, with respect to such a lease or an assignment of rents or profits, a notice of lease or a notice of assignment of rents or profits, as hereinafter defined, is recorded in the registry of deeds for the county or district in which the land to which it relates lies. . . .

(ii) Race-Notice

MICH. COMP. LAWS § 565.29

Every conveyance of real estate within the state hereafter made, which shall not be recorded as provided in this chapter, shall be void as against any subsequent purchaser in good faith and for a valuable consideration, of the same real estate or any portion thereof, whose conveyance shall be first duly recorded. . . .

(iii) Period of Grace

DEL. CODE ANN. TIT. 25, § 153[4]

If a deed concerning lands or tenements is not recorded in the proper office within 15 days after the day of the sealing and delivery thereof, the deed shall not avail against a subsequent fair creditor, mortgagee or purchaser for a valuable consideration unless it appears that such creditor when giving the credit, or such mortgagee or purchaser, when advancing the consideration, had notice of such deed.

---

4. This statute was repealed in 1968, but is included here because it illustrates the period-of-grace concept, which is a key feature of mechanics' lien statutes in many states. Under these statutes, persons providing labor or materials on a construction project are permitted to record a lien for unpaid amounts due them by the owner. The lien takes priority on the date the project commenced, or the work was done, or the materials were delivered, provided it is recorded within the grace period allowed by the statute. *See, e.g.,* 49 Pa. Stat. Ann. § 1508 (date construction project began); Iowa Code Ann. § 572.18 (date the particular claimant began his or her work). Interests recorded during the grace period lose priority to the mechanics' lien. Currently, there is no jurisdiction that uses a grace period in its general recording act. For a discussion of period-of-grace statutes, see American Law of Property § 17.32 (A. James Casner ed. 1952).

This provision shall not extend to a lease under a fair rent for a term not exceeding 21 years, when the possession accompanies the lease, or the lessee is to come into possession within one year after the making of it.

(iv)   Race

N.C. GEN. STAT. § 47-18

No (i) conveyance of land, or (ii) contract to convey, or (iii) option to convey, or (iv) lease of land for more than three years shall be valid to pass any property as against lien creditors or purchasers for a valuable consideration from the donor, bargainor or lessor, but from the time of registration thereof within the county where the land lies . . . .

c.   Types of "Notice"

A person (B) may receive notice of A's prior interest in Blackacre in one of three ways:

1. *Actual* notice. B actually knows of O's prior conveyance to A.

2. *Record* notice. If a document is recorded in the chain of title for Blackacre, all people in the world are deemed to have record notice of its terms. So, if A records his deed from O before B receives her deed, B is said to have record notice of A's interest whether or not B searched the record and found the instrument. B is punished, therefore, for failure to search. Section 2 below defines record notice and the "chain of title" concept.

3. *Inquiry* notice. The law requires a person to make a reasonable physical inspection of property before taking an interest in it and to make reasonable inquiries about ownership that such an inspection would trigger. Again, this knowledge is imputed to B whether or not he makes the actual inspection, and so the law punishes failure to follow this procedure. Inquiry notice is also sometimes called inspection notice. Inquiry notice is examined in Section 3 below.

The term *constructive* notice is somewhat slippery — it is used sometimes synonymously with record notice, sometimes synonymously with inquiry notice, and sometimes to encompass both record and inquiry notice. It is, therefore, to be used carefully and examined critically.

Problems: Recording

1. O conveys Blackacre to A in fee simple, and A does not record. O then conveys Blackacre to B, who is unaware of A's deed, in fee simple; B does not record. A records, then B records. Who has title to Blackacre under the Massachusetts statute?

2. O conveys Blackacre to A in fee simple, and A does not record. O then conveys Blackacre to B, who is aware of A's deed, in fee simple. B records, then A records. Who has title to Blackacre under the North Carolina statute?

3. O conveys Blackacre to A in fee simple, and A does not record. O then conveys Blackacre to B, who is unaware of A's deed, in fee simple; B does not record. A records, then B records. Who has title to Blackacre under the Michigan statute?

4. O conveys Blackacre to A in fee simple, and A does not record. O then conveys Blackacre to B, who is unaware of A's deed, in fee simple; B does not record. B learns of A's deed. B records, then A records. Who has title to Blackacre under the Michigan statute? Under the Massachusetts statute? Under the North Carolina statute?

5. O conveys Blackacre to A in fee simple, and A does not record. O then conveys Blackacre to B, who is unaware of A's deed, in fee simple; B does not record. A records; A then conveys Blackacre to C, who is unaware of B's deed, in fee simple. Who has title to Blackacre under the Massachusetts statute? Under the Michigan statute? Under the North Carolina statute?

6. O conveys Blackacre to A in fee simple, and A does not record. O then conveys Blackacre to B, who is aware of A's deed, in fee simple; B records. B then conveys Blackacre to C, who is unaware of B's deed, in fee simple. A then records, and then C records. Who has title to Blackacre under the Massachusetts statute? Under the Michigan statute? Under the North Carolina statute?

7. If you are representing a buyer in a notice jurisdiction, what should you do before giving the purchase funds to the grantor to ensure that your client will prevail over prior deeds and other instruments executed by the grantor and that have not been recorded? In a race-notice jurisdiction? In a race jurisdiction? In a period-of-grace jurisdiction?

2. Record Notice

One is deemed to have record notice of instruments properly recorded within the "chain of title" of a property—i.e., those documents that are discoverable by a reasonable search of the records. One does not have record notice of documents outside the chain of title. So, the chain of title concept both determines the extent of the title search that must be conducted and identifies those documents that give record notice.

The chain of title concept may be set by statute or require judicial definition. The following cases indicate the boundaries of the chain of title concept and record notice.

RYCZKOWSKI v. CHELSEA TITLE & GUARANTY CO.

Supreme Court of Nevada
449 P.2d 261 (Nev. 1969)

By the Court, THOMPSON, J. This is an action for damages by the record owners of land against the title insurance company for its failure to list on the policy of title insurance a recorded easement as an encumbrance upon the owners' title. The controlling issue is whether that recorded easement, granted by a predecessor in interest while the equitable owner of state land and before his acquisition of patent thereto, falls within the coverage of a policy of title insurance written for the present owners who are successors in interest of the patentee. The title insurance policy does not insure against loss or damage by reason of "easements, claims of easement, or encumbrances which are not shown by the public records." Although the easement was physically of record, the district court ruled that since the easement was recorded before the grantor of the ease-ment acquired title to the land by patent, the recorded easement was a "wild" document, not within the chain of title, and excluded from the coverage of the title insurance policy. Accordingly, judgment was entered for the title insurance company.

. . . In 1946 one J. J. Cleary entered into a land sale contract with the State of Nevada . . . and, in 1952, acquired title from the state by patent . . . . The pat-ent contained the land sale contract number in the upper right-hand corner of the document. The land sale contract, however, was not recorded. In 1949, while enjoying his equitable interest in the land, and before acquiring legal title thereto by patent, Cleary granted a power line easement over a portion of the property to the Sierra Pacific Power Company, which document the company caused to be recorded. The easement embraced about 2.1 acres upon which the company placed its poles and power lines. Title to the patented land thereafter passed from Cleary to various persons and finally, in 1964, to the present own-ers. Title Guaranty (now defunct) was engaged to search the record for defects in title, and Chelsea Title to insure title to the land. The title search by Title Guaranty stopped with the 1952 recorded patent from the state. Consequently, the 1949 power company easement was not discovered, and was not listed in the title insurance policy issued by Chelsea as an encumbrance upon the owners' title. Hence, this litigation.

Snow v. Pioneer Title Insurance Company, [444 P.2d 125 (Nev. 1968)], estab-lished the rule for Nevada that an instrument executed by an owner which is recorded before acquisition or after relinquishment of title is outside the chain of title.[1] Consequently, the title searcher is not liable for its failure to discover such an instrument, and the title insurer is not liable since such an instrument falls within the exclusion of the insurance policy of "easements, liens or encumbrances not shown by the public records." We there noted that such rule is preferred in the states which use the grantor-grantee indexing sys-tem, and is justified by the practical considerations which attend title record searching.

The 1952 patent from the state to Cleary was the original source of title and the first link in the chain of title for the purposes of title searching. Thompson, *Abstracts and Titles*, 2d ed., §§ 817, 125.[2] A patent is the first instrument by which title passes from the sovereign to an individual. . . . Accordingly, the power com-pany easement which was executed and recorded before the issuance of patent by the state was a "wild" document, not within the chain of title, and not "shown

1. The chain of title is constituted by conveyances made by successive holders of the record title but made by them while respectively holders thereof. Philbrick, *Limits of Record Search and Therefore of Notice*, 93 U. Pa. L. Rev. 125, 178.

2. The owners suggest that the original source of title was not the 1952 patent, but was the 1946 land sale contract, and contend that when patent issued it "related back" to the 1946 contract. The suggestion is meaningless since the 1946 contract was not placed on record. In any event, none of the cases cited by them for the "relation back" doctrine involves the issue with which we are here concerned.

by the public records." . . . Since Snow v. Pioneer Title Insurance Company is dispositive of this case, we do not consider other arguments advanced to support the judgment below, nor other contentions seeking to invalidate it.

Affirmed.

MORSE v. CURTIS
Supreme Judicial Court of Massachusetts
2 N.E. 929 (Mass. 1885)

MORTON, C.J. This is a writ of entry. Both parties derive their title from one Hall. On August 8, 1872, Hall mortgaged the land to the demandant. On September 7, 1875, Hall mortgaged the land to one Clark, who had notice of the earlier mortgage. The mortgage to Clark was recorded on January 31, 1876. The mortgage to the demandant was recorded on September 8, 1876. On October 4, 1881, Clark assigned his mortgage to the tenant, who had no actual notice of the mortgage to the demandant. The question is which of these titles has priority.

The same question was directly raised and adjudicated in the two cases of Connecticut v. Bradish, 14 Mass. 296, and Trull v. Bigelow, 16 Mass. 406. These adjudications establish a rule of property which ought not to be unsettled, except for the strongest reasons.

It is true, that, in the later case of Flynt v. Arnold, 2 Met. 619, Chief Justice Shaw expresses his individual opinion against the soundness of these decisions; but in that case the judgment of the court was distinctly put upon another ground, and his remarks can only be considered in the light of dicta, and not as overruling the earlier adjudications.

Upon careful consideration, the reasons upon which the earlier cases were decided seem to us the more satisfactory, because they best follow the spirit of our registry laws and the practice of the profession under them. The earliest registry laws provided that no conveyance of land shall be good and effectual in law "against any other person or persons but the grantor or grantors, and their heirs only, unless the deed or deeds thereof be acknowledged and recorded in manner aforesaid." St. 1783, c. 37, Sec. 4.

Under this statute, the court, at an early period, held that the recording was designed to take the place of the notorious act of livery of seisin; and that, though by the first deed the title passed out of the grantor, as against himself, yet he could, if such deed was not recorded, convey a good title to an innocent purchaser who received and recorded his deed. But the court also held that a prior unrecorded deed would be valid against a second purchaser who took his deed with a knowledge of the prior deed, thus engrafting an exception upon the statute. . . .

This exception was adopted on the ground that it was a fraud in the second grantee to take a deed, if he had knowledge of the prior deed. As Chief Justice Shaw forcibly says, in Lawrence v. Stratton, 6 Cush. 163, the rule is "put upon the ground, that a party with such notice could not take a deed without fraud, the objection was not to the nature of the conveyance, but to the honesty of the taker; and, therefore, if the estate had passed through such taker to a bona fide purchaser, without fraud, the conveyance was held valid."

This exception by judicial exposition was afterwards engrafted upon the statutes, and somewhat extended, by the Legislature. . . . It is to be observed that, in each of these revisions, it is provided that an unrecorded prior deed is not valid against any persons except the grantor, his heirs and devisees, "and persons having actual notice" of it. The reasons why the statute requires actual notice to a second purchaser, in order to defeat his title, is apparent: its purpose is that his title shall not prevail against the prior deed, if he has been guilty of a fraud upon the first grantee; and he could not be guilty of such fraud, unless he had actual notice of the first deed.

Now, in the case before us, it is found as a fact that the tenant had no actual knowledge of the prior mortgage to the demandant at the time he took his assignment from Clark; but it is contended that he had constructive notice, because the demandant's mortgage was recorded before such assignment.

It was held in Connecticut v. Bradish, *ubi supra*, that such record was evidence of actual notice, but was not of itself enough to show actual notice, and to charge the assignee of the second deed with a fraud upon the holder of the first unrecorded deed. This seems to us to accord with the spirit of our registry laws, and with the uniform understanding of and practice under them by the profession.

These laws not only provide that deeds must be recorded, but they also prescribe the method in which the records shall be kept and indexes prepared for public inspection and examination. . . . There are indexes of grantors and grantees, so that, in searching a title, the examiner is obliged to run down the list of grantors, or run backward through the list of grantees. If he can start with an owner who is known to have a good title, as, in the case at bar, he could start with Hall, he is obliged to run through the index of grantors until he finds a conveyance by the owner of the land in question. After such conveyance, the former owner becomes a stranger to the title, and the examiner must follow down the name of the new owner to see if he has conveyed the land, and so on. It would be a hardship to require an examiner to follow in the indexes of grantors the names of every person who, at any time, through perhaps a long chain of title, was the owner of the land.

We do not think this is the practical construction which lawyers and conveyancers have given to our registry laws. The inconveniences of such a construction would be much greater than would be the inconvenience of requiring a person, who has neglected to record his prior deed for a time, to record it, and to bring a bill in equity to set aside the subsequent deed, if it was taken in fraud of his rights.

The better rule, and the one least likely to create confusion of titles, seems to us to be, that, if a purchaser, upon examining the registry, finds a conveyance from the owner of the land to his grantor, which gives him a perfect record title completed by what the law, at the time it is recorded, regards as equivalent to a livery of seisin, he is entitled to rely upon such record title, and is not obliged to search the records afterwards, in order to see if there has been any prior unrecorded deed of the original owner.

This rule of property, established by the early case of Connecticut v. Bradish, ought not to be departed from, unless conclusive reasons therefor be shown. We are therefore of opinion, that, in the case at bar, the tenant has the better title; and, according to the terms of the report, the verdict ordered for the demandant must be set aside, and a

New trial granted.

GENOVESE DRUG STORES, INC. v. CONN. PACKING CO., INC.

United States Court of Appeals for the Second Circuit
732 F.2d 286 (1984)

NEWMAN, Circuit Judge. Fotomat Corporation appeals from an order of the District Court for the District of Connecticut granting a motion by Genovese Drug Stores, Inc. for a preliminary injunction barring Fotomat from operating a film processing business from a kiosk constructed in the parking lot of a shopping center in which Genovese rents space for operation of a drug store. The injunction was issued to enforce a restrictive covenant in Genovese's lease. Since the undisputed facts establish that Fotomat had neither actual nor constructive notice of the restrictive covenant at the time it leased the portion of the parking lot on which its kiosk stands, we vacate the injunction and direct that judgment enter in favor of Fotomat. . . .

The litigation concerns a shopping center in Bloomfield, Connecticut. The property on which the shopping center is located was purchased in 1947 by defendant Connecticut Packing Company, Inc. ("Copaco"), a Connecticut corporation. . . . In 1970 Copaco conveyed a portion of the Bloomfield property to Bercrose Associates, a Connecticut partnership composed of . . . three of the four owners of Copaco. . . .

On October 16, 1971, Bercrose leased a portion of its part of the shopping center property to Genovese for the operation of a retail drug store. The Bercrose-Genovese lease contained a restrictive covenant in which Bercrose agreed that it would not demise any portion of the shopping center to any "drive-in operation whose principal business is the receipt and processing of photographic film for development, including, but not limited to, drive-ins known as 'Foto-Mat'." Concurrent with the execution of the lease, Irving Bercowetz, acting in his capacity as president of Copaco, executed a statement entitled "Consent and Agreement" ("Consent"), in which Copaco agreed to be bound by the lease terms with respect to the portions of the shopping center owned by Copaco. The Consent was appended to the Bercrose-Genovese lease. On March 10, 1972, pursuant to *Conn. Gen. Stat. § 47-19* (1977) which provides for the recording of a "notice of lease" in lieu of the lease document, a Memorandum of Lease was recorded on the Bloomfield land records and indexed under the name of Bercrose as grantor and Genovese as grantee. As required by *section 47-19*, the Memorandum of Lease states the location where the lease is on file, in this case, the offices of Bercrose's attorneys. The Memorandum of Lease makes no mention of the restrictive covenant prohibiting drive-in photo kiosks nor of the Consent in which Copaco agreed to be bound by the terms of the Bercrose-Genovese lease.

In 1982 Fotomat negotiated with Philip Johnson, who was in charge of leasing for both Copaco and Bercrose . . . . Ultimately they agreed upon the leasing of space for a drive-in kiosk in the parking lot of the shopping center. The kiosk was initially planned to be located on the Bercrose portion of the shopping center property, but was finally decided to be placed on the portion owned by Copaco. In June of 1982, Copaco, acting by its president Irving Bercowetz, executed a lease with Fotomat for a 36-square-foot portion of parking lot owned by Copaco. At no time during the lease negotiations did Johnson, Irving Bercowetz, or anyone else inform Fotomat of the restrictive covenant in the Bercrose-Genovese lease. Fotomat did not make a title search of the land records concerning the 36-square-foot area it was leasing, relying instead on a guarantee from Copaco that there were no restrictions on Fotomat's use of the property for operation of a drive-in kiosk.

Fotomat began site preparation and, on September 16, 1982, placed on its leased space a prefabricated kiosk. Eight days later Genovese made demand upon Johnson to have the kiosk removed and on November 9, 1982, filed suit in the District Court against Copaco, Bercrose, and Fotomat. Operation of the kiosk has been prohibited since that date, initially by a temporary restraining order, which was extended by stipulation, and ultimately by the preliminary injunction challenged on this appeal.

DISCUSSION

In issuing the preliminary injunction, the District Court made several determinations, but in resolving this appeal, we need consider only the Court's conclusion that Fotomat had constructive notice of the restrictive covenant in the Bercrose-Genovese lease. . . . It is undisputed that Fotomat had no actual notice of the restrictive covenant.

. . . Judge Clarie ruled that the recordation of the Memorandum of Lease in compliance with *Conn. Gen. Stat. § 47-19* provided adequate notice of all the terms of the Bercrose-Genovese lease, including the restrictive covenant. . . .

We start from two premises of real estate law that enjoy support in Connecticut and elsewhere. First, since restrictive covenants, especially those endeavoring to restrict commercial activity for competitive advantage, are not favorites of the law, those who seek to benefit from them must expect that their terms and effectiveness will be strictly construed. . . . Second, the rules concerning land records and the constructive notice they provide should be relatively uncomplicated and should promote a high degree of certainty as to the extent of searching necessary to afford protection to buyers. . . .

With these premises in mind, we turn to the issue of whether the Bloomfield land records gave Fotomat constructive notice of Genovese's restrictive covenant. We are not as certain as Judge Clarie that Connecticut courts, which appear not yet to have faced the issue, will construe *section 47-19* to mean that recordation of a notice of lease provides constructive notice of a restrictive covenant contained in that lease, at least a covenant burdening property other than the leased premises by restricting commercial activity for competitive advantage. Other states construing similar statutes have obliged the beneficiaries of restrictive covenants to record them, ruling that notices of lease provide constructive notice only of terms that do not implicate the rights of third parties, unless they are endeavoring to acquire an interest in property subject to the notice of lease. *See, e.g.,* Howard D. Johnson Co. v. Parkside Development Corp., 348 N.E.2d 656, 661 (Ind. Ct. App. 1976). *See generally* 3 Friedman, *Friedman on Leases* § 31.2; Report of Special Committee on Leases, *Some Considerations to be Observed in the Recording of Leases*, 12 Real Prop., Prob. & Trust J. 256, 264-67 (1977).

We need not construe the application of *section 47-19* to restrictive covenants, however, because we disagree with the District Court's view that Fotomat had a duty to search the Bercrose chain of title, in which the Memorandum of Lease was recorded. The traditional rule is that a purchaser or lessee of property is charged with constructive notice only of those encumbrances that appear in his direct chain of title. Hawley v. McCabe, 169 A. 192, 194 (Conn. 1933); . . . *see* 3 Friedman, *Friedman on Leases* § 28.601; Clark, *Real Covenants* at 183; *Connecticut Standards of Title* § 2.3 (Ct. Bar Ass'n 1980); Philbrick, *Limits of Record Search and Therefore of Notice*, 93 U. Pa. L. Rev. 125, 174 (1944). As a lessee of Copaco, Fotomat had no obligation, as a general matter, to search the chain of title of any entity other than Copaco. . . .

. . . Genovese, as it was obliged to do as a first step toward protection from competitive activity on Copaco's property, secured the written agreement of Copaco to the terms of the Bercrose-Genovese lease. What Genovese failed to do was take the required second step of recording Copaco's restriction upon its own property in Copaco's chain of title, where it would give constructive notice to a lessee of Copaco.[1] . . .

Injunction vacated and case remanded for further proceedings consistent with this opinion. Fotomat may recover its costs on appeal.

Notes and Questions

There is some contrary authority to the three principal cases. *Ryczkowski* is the predominant view, but there is some contrary authority (*see, e.g., Ayer v. Philadelphia & Boston Face Brick Co.*, 34 N.E. 177 (Mass. 1893) (tenant without notice of mortgage given before mortgagor obtained title is subordinate to the mortgage when mortgagor subsequently obtains title)); *Morse* is the predominant view, with a rare case holding differently (*see, e.g., Woods v. Garnett*, 16 So. 390 (Miss. 1894) (specifically rejecting *Morse* and finding duty to search record for subsequently recorded instruments showing prior interests)); and there are a significant number of jurisdictions reaching the view opposite from *Genovese* (*see, e.g., Finley v. Glenn*, 154 A. 299 (Pa. 1931) (defendant lot purchasers had constructive notice of restrictive covenants contained in deeds from common grantor to other lots in subdivision that also burdened their lot)); *see American Law of Property* § 17.24 (A. James Casner ed., 1952) (stating that cases are evenly split).

In evaluating whether these decisions are correct, consider whether the court's rule protects people who follow standard recording and searching procedure and punishes those who do not; what costs and efforts are required under the court's rule, compared to the contrary result; whether the court's decision supports the establishment and operation of an efficient and cost-effective recording system; who could have best avoided the loss in question and how?

---

1. There is some variation among states as to whether lessee or purchaser must search all chains of title from a common grantor. *Compare* Guillette v. Daly Dry Wall, Inc., 325 N.E.2d 572 (Mass. 1975) (must search all conveyances from common grantor), *with* Buffalo Academy of the Sacred Heart v. Boehm Bros., 196 N.E. 42, 45 (N.Y. 1935) (need search only land records covering specific parcel conveyed). Dick v. Sears-Roebuck & Co., 160 A. 432 (Conn. 1932), has been cited for the proposition that a tenant must "examine the contents of all the deeds given by his grantor (and presumably of all his predecessors in title)." Note, *Restrictive Covenants in Shopping Center Leases*, 34 N.Y.U. L. Rev. 940, 946 & n.48 (1959). Properly read, that case merely requires a lessee to examine the deed his grantor received from his predecessor in title. Even if read broadly, that decision would not require Fotomat to search the chain of Bercrose, which was not its lessor. [Footnote relocated. — EDS.]

See generally William Ryckman, Jr., *Notice and the "Deeds Out" Problem*, 64 Mich. L. Rev. 421 (1966).

Problems: Chain of Title

1. L.J. Smith conveys Blackacre to A in fee simple. A immediately takes his deed to the recorder's office. The recorder improperly indexes the deed under the name S.J. Smith. L.J. Smith then conveys Blackacre to B in fee simple. Who has title to Blackacre? Would the result differ if the grantor's name was L.J. Korngold? If the recorder indexed the L.J. Smith deed under the name L.J. Jones? *See Keybank N.A. v. NBD Bank*, 699 N.E.2d 322 (Ind. Ct. App. 1998); *Prouty v. Marshall*, 225 Pa. 570, 74 A. 550 (1909), *questioned in First Citizens National Bank v. Sherwood*, 879 A.2d 118 (Pa. 2005) (positing that 16 Pa. Stat. § 356 may have abrogated *Prouty*).

2. O conveys Blackacre to A on August 1, 1980, and A records on June 1, 1982. O conveys Blackacre to B on September 1, 1981, and B has notice of the prior unrecorded deed. B records immediately. A now learns of O's deed to B. What steps should A take in a state following *Morse* in order to prevent B from defeating A's rights in Blackacre by a conveyance to a bona fide purchaser?

3.   Inquiry Notice

Although a subsequent purchaser may not have actual notice, he may have inquiry notice of prior claims. The following case examines the concept of inquiry notice.

SANBORN v. McLEAN
Supreme Court of Michigan
233 Mich. 227, 206 N.W. 496 (1925)

WIEST, J. Defendant Christina McLean owns the west 35 feet of lot 86 of Green Lawn subdivision, at the northeast corner of Collingwood Avenue and Second Boulevard, in the city of Detroit, upon which there is a dwelling house, occupied by herself and her husband, defendant John A. McLean. The house fronts Collingwood Avenue. At the rear of the lot is an alley. Mrs. McLean derived title from her husband and, in the course of the opinion, we will speak of both as defendants. Mr. and Mrs. McLean started to erect a gasoline filling station at the rear end of their lot, and they and their contractor, William S. Weir, were enjoined by decree from doing so and bring the issues before us by appeal. . . .

Collingwood Avenue is a high-grade residence street between Woodward Avenue and Hamilton Boulevard, with single, double and apartment houses, and plaintiffs who are owners of land adjoining, and in the vicinity of defendants' land, and who trace title, as do defendants, to the proprietors of the subdivision, claim that the proposed gasoline station will be a nuisance per se, is in violation of the general plan fixed for use of all lots on the street for residence purposes only, as evidenced by restrictions upon 53 of the 91 lots fronting on Collingwood Avenue, and that defendants' lot is subject to a reciprocal negative easement barring a use so detrimental to the enjoyment and value of its neighbors. Defendants insist that no restrictions appear in their chain of title and they purchased without notice of any reciprocal negative easement, and deny that a gasoline station is a nuisance per se. We find no occasion to pass upon the question of nuisance, as the case can be decided under the rule of reciprocal negative easement.

This subdivision was planned strictly for residence purposes, except lots fronting Woodward Avenue and Hamilton Boulevard. The 91 lots on Collingwood Avenue were platted in 1891, designed for and each one sold solely for residence purposes, and residences have been erected upon all of the lots. Is defendants' lot subject to a reciprocal negative easement? If the owner of two or more lots, so situated as to bear the relation, sells one with restrictions of benefit to the land retained, the servitude becomes mutual, and, during the period of restraint, the owner of the lot or lots retained can do nothing forbidden to the owner of the lot sold. For want of a better descriptive term this is styled a reciprocal negative easement. It runs with the land sold by virtue of express fastening and abides with the land retained until loosened by expiration of its period of service or by events working its destruction. It is not personal to owners but operative upon use of the land by any owner having actual or constructive notice thereof. It is an easement passing its benefits and carrying its obligations to all purchasers of land subject to its affirmative or negative mandates. It originates for mutual benefit and exists with vigor sufficient to work its ends. It must start with a common owner. Reciprocal negative easements are never retroactive; the very nature of their origin forbids. They arise, if at all, out of a benefit accorded land retained, by restrictions upon neighboring land sold by a common owner. Such a scheme of restrictions must start with a common owner; it cannot arise and fasten upon one lot by reason of other lot owners conforming to a general plan. If a reciprocal negative easement attached to defendants' lot it was fastened thereto while in the hands of the common owner of it and neighboring lots by way of sale of other lots with restrictions beneficial at that time to it. This leads to inquiry as to what lots, if any, were sold with restrictions by the common owner before the sale of defendants' lot. While the proofs cover another avenue we need consider sales only on Collingwood.

December 28, 1892, Robert J. and Joseph R. McLaughlin, who were then evidently owners of the lots on Collingwood Avenue, deeded lots 37 to 41 and 58 to 62, inclusive, with the following restrictions:

"No residence shall be erected upon said premises, which shall cost less than $2,500 and nothing but residences shall be erected upon said premises. Said residences shall front on Helene (now Collingwood) Avenue and be placed no nearer than 20 feet from the front street line."

July 24, 1893, the McLaughlins conveyed lots 17 to 21 and 78 to 82, both inclusive, and lot 98 with the same restrictions. Such restrictions were imposed for the benefit of the lands held by the grantors to carry out the scheme of a residential district, and a restrictive negative easement attached to the lots retained, and title to lot 86 was then in the McLaughlins. Defendants' title, through mesne conveyances, runs back to a deed by the McLaughlins dated September 7, 1893, without restrictions mentioned therein. Subsequent deeds to other lots were executed by the McLaughlins, some with restrictions and some without. Previous to September 7, 1893, a reciprocal negative easement had attached to lot 86 by acts of the owners, as before mentioned, and such easement is still attached and may now be enforced by plaintiffs, provided defendants, at the time of their purchase, had knowledge, actual or constructive, thereof. The plaintiffs run back with their title, as do defendants, to a common owner. This common owner, as before stated, by restrictions upon lots sold, had burdened all the lots retained with reciprocal restrictions. Defendants' lot and plaintiff Sanborn's lot, next thereto, were held by such common owner, burdened with a reciprocal negative easement and, when later sold to separate parties, remained burdened therewith and right to demand observance thereof passed to each purchaser with notice of the easement. The restrictions were upon defendants' lot while it was in the hands of the common owners, and abstract of title to defendants' lot showed the common owners and the record showed deeds of lots in the plat restricted to perfect and carry out the general plan and resulting in a reciprocal negative easement upon defendants' lot and all lots within its scope, and defendants and their predecessors in title were bound by constructive notice under our recording acts. The original plan was repeatedly declared in subsequent sales of lots by restrictions in the deeds, and while some lots sold were not so restricted the purchasers thereof, in every instance, observed the general plan and purpose of the restrictions in building residences. For upward of 30 years the united efforts of all persons interested have carried out the common purpose of making and keeping all the lots strictly for residences, and defendants are the first to depart therefrom.

When Mr. McLean purchased on contract in 1910 or 1911, there was a partly built dwelling house on lot 86, which he completed and now occupies. He had an abstract of title which he examined and claims he was told by the grantor that the lot was unrestricted. Considering the character of use made of all the lots open to a view of Mr. McLean when he purchased, we think he was put thereby to inquiry, beyond asking his grantor whether there were restrictions. He had an abstract showing the subdivision and that lot 86 had 97 companions; he could not avoid noticing the strictly uniform residence character given the lots by the expensive dwellings thereon, and the least inquiry would have quickly developed the fact that lot 86 was subjected to a reciprocal negative easement, and he could finish his house and, like the others, enjoy the benefits of the easement. We do not say Mr. McLean should have asked his neighbors about restrictions, but we do say that with the notice he had from a view of the premises on the street, clearly indicating the residences were built and the lots occupied in strict accordance with a general plan, he was put to inquiry, and had he inquired he would have found of record the reason for such general conformation, and the benefits thereof serving the owners of lot 86 and the obligations running with such service and available to adjacent lot owners to prevent a departure from the general plan by an owner of lot 86.

While no case appears to be on all fours with the one at bar the principles we have stated, and the conclusions announced, are supported by . . . [cases from Michigan, New York, Wisconsin, and New Jersey are cited].

We notice the decree in the circuit directed that the work done on the building be torn down. If the portion of the building constructed can be utilized for any purpose within the restrictions it need not be destroyed. With this modification the decree in the circuit is affirmed, with costs to plaintiffs.

Notes and Questions

1. In *Sanborn*, what did the later purchasers know (and how), and when did they know it? Does the court place reasonable burdens on the later purchasers? Are other considerations influencing the court's delineation of inquiry notice and the obligation of later purchasers to inquire?

2. Another type of inquiry notice arises from references, in recorded documents, that are insufficient to give record notice but put the reader on notice to inquire as to the existence of prior unrecorded interests. *See, e.g., Municipal Trust & Savings Bank v. United States*, 114 F.3d 99 (7th Cir. 1997) (recitation in deed that land's title was subject to federal taxation put parties on notice to investigate for federal tax liens); *Winkworth Fuel & Supply Co. v. Bloomsbury Corp.*, 253 N.W. 304 (Mich. 1934) (subsequent lienor had notice of unrecorded first mortgage mentioned in recorded second mortgage). Were there any references in recorded documents in *Sanborn* that could create inquiry notice of the existence of a prior interest?

Problem

B sought to purchase Blackacre from O. In searching the title, B found a recorded 20-year lease from O to A, which was due to expire by its own terms. B visited the property and saw A in possession before B took his deed. After taking his deed from O, B sought to move in on the day A's lease was to expire. A refused, showing B an unrecorded fee simple deed from O to A predating B's deed. Who has title to Blackacre? *See generally Grose v. Sauvageau*, 942 P.2d 398 (Wyo. 1997).

4.   Marketable Title Acts and Similar Solutions

In the examination of the land records, there is no point at which the examiner can stop and be able to say with complete certainty that nothing might appear on the land records earlier than the date at which the examiner stops that will affect the title. This imposes a tremendous burden on the examiner if the examiner does a complete job in searching for possible defects in the title.

Some states have adopted comprehensive solutions to the issue, following the Model Marketable Title Act, the Uniform Marketable Title Act, or their own template. Essentially, these statutes provide that an interest in real property will be lost if it is not re-recorded every 30 years. Thus, an owner can establish marketable title by showing 30 years of an unbroken record chain of title. *See, e.g.,* Unif. Marketable Tit. Act § 3; Fla. Stat. §§ 712.10 *et seq.* In states that have not enacted general marketable title acts, title searches may be somewhat simplified by statutes that extinguish certain kinds of interests, such as rights of entry and possibilities of reverter, or covenants that run with the land, if not re-recorded before a specified date, or periodically. *See, e.g.,* Mass. Gen. Laws ch. 260 § 31A (possibilities of reverter, rights of entry created before 1955 will not be enforced unless recorded before 1964), Mass. Gen. Laws ch. 184 §§ 26-30 (covenants must be re-recorded periodically), Cal. Civ. Code §885.030 (rights of entry expire unless notice recorded every 30 years). It should be noted, however, that a statute somewhat like the Massachusetts one on possibilities of reverter and rights of entry ran into constitutional difficulties in New York in *Board of Education v. Miles*,[5] but survived a constitutional attack in Illinois in *Trustees of Schools of Township No. 1 v. Batdorf*.[6]

Other states prescribe an absolute limit on the duration of possibilities of reverter and rights of entry. *See, e.g.,* 765 Ill. Comp. Stat. 330/4 (duration of 40 years); Ky. Rev. Stat Ann. §§ 381.218 and 381.219 (duration of 30 years). *See generally* L. Simes & C. Taylor, *Improvement of Conveyancing by Legislation (1960)*; Walter E. Barnett, *Marketable Title Acts — Panacea or Pandemonium?*, 53 Cornell L. Rev. 45 (1967).

F.   TITLE PROTECTION

1.   *The Torrens System*

The recording acts, as we have seen, provide for the recording of instruments of conveyance, and it is up to the purchaser through her attorney and title searcher to examine the instruments on the record and formulate conclusions as to their effect on the title. *Title registration*, however, is different — it is designed to provide a public record of the state of the title itself, so that the purchaser of land is not called upon to formulate conclusions in this regard.

The difference between the recording acts and title registration was explained by Chief Justice Start of Minnesota in *State ex rel. Douglas v. Westfall*[7] as follows:

> The basic principle of this system is the registration of the title of land, instead of registering, as the old system requires, the evidence of such title. In the one case only the ultimate fact or conclusion that a certain named party has title to a particular tract of land is registered, and a certificate thereof delivered to him. In the other the entire evidence, from which proposed purchasers must, at their peril, draw such conclusion, is registered.

The use of title registration by the English-speaking countries was started by Sir Richard Torrens in Australia, and the title registration acts are sometimes called the Torrens acts. Torrens had been in the office concerned with the registration of the title of ships, and when his interests were transferred to land titles, he evidently conceived the idea of registering the title to land in the same manner as the title to a ship was registered.

Only 19 American jurisdictions ever enacted title registration statutes.[8] In all of these states, however, title registration was permitted but not required, and the traditional recording system was left intact. Moreover, over one-half of the

---

5. 207 N.E.2d 181 (N.Y. 1965).
6. 130 N.E.2d 111 (Ill. 1955).
7. 85 Minn. 437, 438, 89 N.W. 175 (1902).
8. John McCormack, *Torrens and Recording: Land Title Assurance in the Computer Age*, 18 Wm. Mitchell L. Rev. 61, 72 (1992).

jurisdictions that enacted title registration have since repealed their statutes, including Illinois in 1992.[9] Only five states have any substantial title registration today, with only Massachusetts and Hawaii having statewide use.[10] No state or locality has a majority of land under a Torrens system.[11] Thus, even in states that enacted Torrens statutes, the old system continues to predominate in connection with conveyances of land.

The language of the local statute that permits the registration of the title to land must be carefully examined to ascertain the method of obtaining a registered title, the effect it has on possible claimants of an interest in the land, and the steps to be taken to transfer a title once it is registered.

When the necessary steps have been taken to register the title to land, a certificate of title is issued. The original is kept on file, and a duplicate is issued to the owner. All future transactions with respect to the registered land will be noted on the certificate of title. When a transfer is made of the registered land, the transferor's certificate of title is canceled and a new certificate of title is issued to the transferee.

If a purchaser can rely on the certificate of title held by the seller, the purchaser receives much greater protection than when unregistered land is the subject of the sale. To the extent that interests in others that are not noted on the certificate of title can be asserted against the purchaser, an examination of some kind must be made outside the certificate of title in order for the purchaser to know the real state of the title. The following case raises issues about the reliability of the certificate of title from the standpoint of the purchaser of registered land.

COMMONWEALTH ELECTRIC CO. v. MacCARDELL

Supreme Judicial Court of Massachusetts
876 N.E.2d 405 (Mass. 2007)

IRELAND, J. On September 23, 2002, the plaintiff, Commonwealth Electric Company, filed a petition in the Land Court seeking an amendment to the defendant's certificate of title on one parcel of land owned by the defendant that would note its alleged utility easement. On January 21, 2005, the Land Court entered judgment in favor of the defendant and dismissed the plaintiff's petition. The plaintiff appealed. The Appeals Court affirmed . . . . We granted the plaintiff's application for further appellate review. The plaintiff argues that the defendant had actual knowledge of the utility easement by virtue of the fact that the poles were on her property and supplied electricity to her residence; therefore, the Land Court improperly dismissed its petition to amend the defendant's title. Because we conclude that the plaintiff failed to establish that the defendant had "actual knowledge" of the utility easement, we affirm the decision of the Land Court dismissing the plaintiff's petition to amend the defendant's title.

---

9. 765 Ill. Comp. Stat. 35/110.3.
10. McCormack, 18 Wm. Mitchell L. Rev. at 73.
11. *Id.*

Facts. The judge found the following facts. Thomas Murray owned two parcels of land on Plum Hill Avenue in Duxbury. On June 5, 1936, Murray granted an easement to the plaintiff's predecessor, Plymouth County Electric Company, for the installation of transmission lines. The easement deed did not provide compass directions, it merely mentioned that the land was located in Duxbury and that the pole lines could "enter from land now or formerly of Plum Hill Avenue and cross to land now or formerly of Chester L. Churchill."

On April 13, 1944, William T. Reagan, administrator of the Murray estate, filed an action in the Land Court in order to register and confirm the title to the two parcels of land on Plum Hill Avenue. The smaller parcel, Lot 1, is located on the north side of Plum Hill Avenue and the larger parcel, Lot 2, is located on the south side of Plum Hill Avenue. On October 25, 1944, the Land Court entered a decree that confirmed and registered the two lots to Reagan. After the decree had been entered, the Plymouth registry district of the Land Court issued a certificate of title to Reagan. Both the certificate of title and the Land Court decree of registration state that "*lot 2* is subject to pole easements as set forth in a deed given by Thomas Murray to the Plymouth County Electric Co., dated June 5, 1936, duly recorded." However, the defendant inhabits and owns Lot 1, which contains the actual poles. The poles supply electricity to both the defendant's property and the adjacent property owned by Alec and Leah Petro. Neither certificate of title refers to the poles or utility easement that the plaintiff is claiming.

The present dispute arose when Petro requested that the plaintiff increase the level of electrical service to his home. The plaintiff determined that, in order to effectuate this increase in service, a transformer might need to be installed on a pole located on the defendant's property. When it conducted a search of the records to discern whether it had an easement, the plaintiff found that there was an easement on the certificate of title for Lot 2 but no easement on the certificate of title for Lot 1. Consequently, it petitioned the Land Court . . . to amend the defendant's certificate of title for Lot 1 to hold the easement. The plaintiff contends that in 1944 the registration decree imposed the easement on the wrong lot, Lot 2 rather than Lot 1. The defendant argues that she purchased a title with no encumbrances and allowing the plaintiff to amend her certificate would impair that title.[2]

The Land Court title examiner selected to conduct the title search of the properties found that the easement granted by Murray to Plymouth County Electric Company in 1944 should have been registered as an encumbrance on Lot 1 and not Lot 2.

Discussion. The principal reason for establishing a land title registration system . . . is to provide individuals with a means of ensuring that titles to land are indefeasible and certain. Feinzig v. Ficksman, 674 N.E.2d 1329 (Mass. Ct. App. 1997). . . . The statutory mechanism for amending an error in the certificate of title is prescribed by *G. L. c. 185, § 114*. It is well established that certificate of title holders and subsequent purchasers of registered land for value and in good faith take "free from all encumbrances except those noted on the

---

2.   The defendant contended that amending the certificate would impair her title because she would then be subject to at least a five-to-ten foot pole height increase and trees would have to be cut.

certificate." *G. L. c. 185, § 46.* Furthermore, with respect to easements, the general rule is that "[i]n order to affect registered land as the servient estate, an easement must appear on the certificate of title." Tetrault v. Bruscoe, 497 N.E.2d 275 (Mass. 1986). . . . However, the court has carved out two exceptions to the general rule: "(1) if there were facts described on his certificate of title which would prompt a reasonable purchaser to investigate further other certificates of title, documents, or plans in the registration system; or (2) if the purchaser has actual knowledge of a prior unregistered interest." It is undisputed that the utility easement was not noted on the defendant's certificate of title or referenced within other documents within the registration system. Therefore, we need only consider the "actual knowledge" exception.

The "actual knowledge" exception is based on the statutory good faith requirement in *G. L. c. 185, § 46.* Essentially, this means that for a title holder to benefit from the protections afforded by the land registration system, the title holder must be a good faith purchaser and must not possess actual knowledge of unregistered interests, i.e., easements.[3] Calci v. Reitano, 846 N.E.2d 1164 (Mass. Ct. App. 2006). A party seeking to encumber an owner's registered land on the ground that he or she had actual knowledge of the unregistered interest bears the burden of proving the actual knowledge. . . .

The actual knowledge exception was first applied in Killam v. March, 55 N.E.2d 945 (Mass. 1944), where the court held that a purchaser of registered land was subject to the encumbrance of an unregistered lease when the purchaser had actual notice through a reference to the lease in the purchase and sale agreement. Registered land owners forfeit the protections afforded by the registration system when they have actual notice because the "Legislature did not intend to give certificate holders . . . an indefeasible title as against interests of which they had actual notice."

One way to satisfy the actual knowledge exception is through "documentation, whether registered or unregistered." Calci v. Reitano, *supra*. In the *Calci* case, the defendant purchased registered land that had a certificate of title free of any encumbrances; however, the plaintiff claimed an easement over the defendant's land. The Appeals Court stated, "To fulfil the actual notice exception to a recorded easement, it is not enough that the holder of registered title know that the land has been used in a . . . way that might indicate an easement, because this could be . . . [either] adverse use, which" is not allowed under *G. L. c. 185, § 53,* or permissive use. The Appeals Court held that no actual knowledge existed because there was no documentation registered or unregistered of the easement and no evidence that the defendant knew of any such documents.

Essentially, the standard for determining actual knowledge is whether there is "[i]ntelligible information of a fact, either verbally or in writing," or in documentation that can be registered or not. Emmons v. White, 788 N.E.2d 558 (Mass. Ct. App. 2003), quoting George v. Kent, 89 Mass. 16 (1863). This standard makes sense in light of the statute's over-all purpose, which is to establish indefeasible titles for good faith purchasers who are unaware of unregistered encumbrances attached to their registered land.

In the present case, the plaintiff argues that Feldman v. Souza, 538 N.E.2d 64 (Mass. Ct. App. 1989), is the controlling case. We disagree. There, the plaintiffs

---

3.   The plaintiff conceded at the hearing that the defendant was a good faith purchaser.

sought to amend the defendants' certificate of title to include an easement. The easement was noted on the plaintiffs' transfer certificate of title but was not on the defendants' certificate. However, before the defendants purchased the property Feldman told Souza that he had an easement. In addition, on the original registration plan and subsequent revisions there was an unlabelled strip that "looks like a right of way." The Appeals Court concluded that the defendants had actual knowledge of the easement. Unlike in the *Feldman* case, the defendant was not explicitly forewarned by the plaintiff that there was a utility easement before she purchased Lot 1. Moreover, no documents existed that explicitly reference an easement on Lot 1. In fact, if the defendant had tracked down the original certificate of title granted to Reagan in 1944, it would have referenced an easement on Lot 2, not Lot 1. Therefore, we disagree with the plaintiff's assertion that the *Feldman* case controls.

The plaintiff has not presented any proof that the defendant had actual knowledge of the easement and thus has not met its burden of proof. The plaintiff did not depose the defendant nor was she questioned during the Land Court proceeding. Instead, the plaintiff relies on the presence of utility poles on the defendant's property, the fact that she can turn her lights on every morning, and the fact that she receives a monthly utility bill to prove that the defendant had actual knowledge. Moreover, the plaintiff argues that "[u]nlike an access case . . . it is inconceivable that a utility company's installation and use of poles" would ever be permissive rather than a claim of right. These arguments are unpersuasive. To meet the actual notice exception it is insufficient merely to claim that the holder of registered title knew that the land was being used in a way that might indicate an easement. The use may be adverse, which does not create an easement under *G. L. c. 185, § 53*, or a registered owner might have granted permissive use. The plaintiff provided no evidence to support its assertion that the installation of poles would never be granted through permissive use. Moreover, the mere presence of a utility pole does not automatically place a registered landowner on notice that his or her property might be encumbered because the actual owner of a utility pole is not readily ascertainable and the average lay person may be unaware of the exact boundaries of the property.[4] To meet the actual knowledge exception, there must be some intelligible oral or written information that indicates the existence of an encumbrance or prior unregistered interest.

Conclusion. For the reasons set forth above, we affirm the Land Court's decision, dismissing the plaintiff's petition to amend the defendant's title. *So ordered.*

Notes

As described in the note preceding *MacCardell*, title registration has been a failure in the United States. *MacCardell* illustrates one reason—when off-the-

---

4. At oral argument the plaintiff urged us to adopt a constructive knowledge test that would impute actual knowledge on a purchaser of registered land where there is sufficient evidence of the possible existence of an easement which would alert a reasonable purchaser to investigate further. We decline to do so. A constructive knowledge test would not help the plaintiff because ownership of a utility pole is not readily ascertainable. An utility pole could be owned by a municipality or an utility company. See, e.g., *G. L. c. 164, § 34A (a)* (allowing municipalities to purchase light poles). See Cambridge v. Department of Telecomm. & Energy, 449 Mass. 868, 872, 874 N.E.2d 1110 (2007). Such a test would also subvert the goals of the land registration system.

record items are allowed to affect the quality of the purchaser's title under a Torrens system, the advantage of Torrens disappears. Moreover, as with so much in life, inertia is a powerful force. Given the historical and social importance of land in the Anglo-American legal system and the large percentage of average Americans' savings invested in their homes, there is an understandable skepticism about changes that may undermine ownership interests. There have been quite sharp debates between the proponents and critics of this "newfangled" system. *See, e.g.,* Richard Powell, *Registration of the Title to Land in the State of New York* (1938) (favoring the old system), and Myres McDougal & John Brabner-Smith, *Land Title Transfer: A Regression,* 48 Yale L.J. 1125 (1939) (condemning Professor Powell's conclusions).

Other explanations for the failure of "Torrenization" in the United States include the high cost of initial registration and the cost of ongoing administration of the system. John McCormack, *Torrens and Recording: Land Title Assurance in the Computer Age,* 18 Wm. Mitchell L. Rev. 61, 64 (1992). Others have suggested that the opposition of the title insurance industry prevented title registration, although that is debated. *See* C. Dent Bostick, *Land Title Registration: An English Solution to an American Problem,* 63 Ind. L.J. 55 (1988); Comment, Barry Goldner, *The Torrens System of Title Registration: A New Proposal for Effective Implementation,* 29 UCLA L. Rev. 661 (1982).

Whatever the reason, little land has actually been brought under the Torrens system. As the Colorado Supreme Court observed: "Although lauded by legal scholars as a promising alternative to traditional title registration methods, practitioners have been less than enthusiastic in adopting the Torrens system. In fact, Torrens actions are so rare in Colorado that none of the three real estate experts testifying at trial had ever participated in a Torrens proceeding." *Lobato v. Taylor,* 70 P.3d 1152 n.4 (Colo. 2003).

2. *Title Insurance*

SOMERSET SAVINGS BANK v. CHICAGO TITLE INSURANCE CO.

Supreme Judicial Court of Massachusetts
649 N.E.2d 1123 (1995)

LYNCH, J. This case involves breach of contract and negligence claims arising from a title insurance policy issued to the plaintiff by the defendant. . . .

The following facts are undisputed. In 1986, the plaintiff agreed to finance the site acquisition and construction of a seventy-two unit condominium located at 190 North Shore Road in Revere. As security for its financing, the plaintiff became the holder of a note in the amount of $9.5 million, secured by a mortgage on the land and any improvements.[1] The plaintiff hired the law firm of Grant & Artesani P.C. (law firm) to assist in closing the transactions. The law firm was to search the record to assure that the mortgage interest was free from

---

1. The plaintiff gave two loans for the property. The first loan was given for the purchase of the property; the second loan, which was given in May of 1987, was a construction loan for $9.5 million.

defect and to certify to the plaintiff with respect to this matter. The law firm gave a favorable title certification to the plaintiff. The plaintiff also requested that the law firm obtain a title insurance policy. The law firm was an approved agent of the defendant and was authorized to issue policies up to $500,000. With respect to the plaintiff's construction loan, after securing authorization, the law firm issued to the plaintiff a loan policy of the defendant in the face amount of $9.5 million. Pursuant to an agreement between the defendant and the law firm, the law firm was authorized to validate, to countersign, to issue, and to deliver commitments, policies, and endorsements of the defendant on forms provided by the defendant.

In June of 1987, the city of Revere issued a building permit to the owner of 190 North Shore Road to construct the condominium project. On June 3, 1988, the Attorney General requested that Revere order a halt to the construction on the property because the Executive Office of Transportation and Construction (EOTC) had not consented to the issuance of the building permit as required by G.L. c. 40, § 54A (1992 ed.).[2] Therefore, on June 8, 1988, Revere issued a cease and desist order directed to the owner of the property to halt construction.

All or part of the property located at 190 North Shore Road was owned by the Boston and Maine Railroad in 1926. This information was apparent on the record at the registry of deeds.

The title insurance policy issued to the plaintiff . . . provides, in pertinent part:

> SUBJECT TO THE EXCLUSIONS FROM COVERAGE, THE EXCEPTIONS CONTAINED IN SCHEDULE B AND THE PROVISIONS OF THE CONDITIONS AND STIPULATIONS HEREOF, CHICAGO TITLE INSURANCE COMPANY . . . insures . . . against loss or damage . . . sustained or incurred by the insured by reason of:
>
> (1) Title to the estate or interest described in Schedule A being vested otherwise than as stated therein;
>
> (2) Any defect in or lien or encumbrance on such title . . .
>
> (4) Unmarketability of such title. . . .

The policy contained an integration clause which provides:

> This instrument together with all endorsements and other instruments, if any, attached hereto by the Company is the entire policy and contract between the insured and the Company.
>
> Any claim of loss or damage, whether or not based on negligence, and which arises out of the status of the lien of the insured mortgage or of the title to the estate or interest covered hereby or any action asserting such claim, shall be restricted to the provisions and conditions and stipulations of this policy.

---

2. General Laws c. 40, § 54A (1992 ed.), provides in pertinent part: "If a city or town or any other person purchases any lands formerly used as a railroad right-of-way or any property appurtenant thereto formerly used by any railroad company in the commonwealth, no permit to build a structure of any kind on land so purchased shall be issued by any city or town in the commonwealth without first obtaining, after public hearing, the consent in writing to the issuance of such permit from the secretary of the executive office of transportation and construction."

The exclusions from coverage provides in pertinent part as follows:

(1) (a) Governmental police power.

(b) Any law, ordinance or governmental regulation relating to environmental protection.

(c) Any law, ordinance or governmental regulation (including but not limited to building and zoning ordinances) restricting or regulating or prohibiting the occupancy, use or enjoyment of the land, or regulating the character, dimensions or location of any improvement now or hereafter erected on the land, or prohibiting a separation in ownership or a change in the dimensions or area of the land or any parcel of which the land is or was a part.

(d) The effect of any violation of the matters excluded under (a), (b) or (c) above, unless notice of a defect, lien or encumbrance resulting from a violation has been recorded at Date of Policy in those records in which under state statutes, deeds, mortgages, lis pendens, liens or other title encumbrances must be recorded in order to impact constructive notice to purchasers of the land for value and without knowledge; provided, however, that without limitation, such records shall not be construed to include records in any of the offices of federal, state or local environmental protection, zoning, building, health or public safety authorities.

On November 16, 1990, the plaintiff gave the defendant notice of claims under the title insurance policy. The defendant denied coverage on the ground that the effect of G.L. c. 40, § 54A, was not an insured risk under the policy and further denied that it had any obligations or duties to the plaintiff beyond those specified in the policy. The plaintiff commenced this action against the defendant asserting claims for breach of contract (counts I and IV), negligence (counts II and III), and negligent misrepresentation (count V). The defendant moved for summary judgment on all claims. . . .

The judge began her analysis of the contract claims with the observation that, in general, building and zoning laws are not treated as encumbrances. She went on to rule: "Even assuming, however, that the restriction on use created by G.L. c. 40, § 54A is an encumbrance on the property or renders title unmarketable, there is no coverage under the policy because the exclusions clearly apply." The Appeals Court interpreted the judge's action as an expression of doubt on whether coverage existed, and only discussed the applicability of the policy exclusions. We begin our discussion with consideration of the coverage issue.

Contract Claims

Count I. In support of its claim for breach of contract . . . , the plaintiff contends that the provision in G.L. c. 40, § 54A, which requires that EOTC consent to the owner's intended use of the property, constitutes an encumbrance on or defect in the title to the property or that it renders title to the property unmarketable. . . .

It is well established that building or zoning laws are not encumbrances or defects affecting title to property. . . . Such restrictions are concerned with the use of the land. There is a difference between economic lack of marketability, which concerns conditions that affect the use of land, and title marketability, which relates to defects affecting legally recognized rights and incidents of ownership. An individual can hold clear title to a parcel of land, although the same parcel is valueless or considered economically unmarketable because of some restriction or regulation on its use. . . . A title insurance policy provides protection against defects in, or liens or encumbrances on, title. Such coverage affords no protection for governmentally imposed impediments on the use of the land or for impairments in the value of the land.

. . . The requirement of EOTC approval, prior to the issuance of a building permit, is a restriction on the use of the property, but it does not affect the owner's title to the property. It is a restriction that may affect the value of the property and the marketability of the parcel, but it has no bearing on the title to the property. . . . The existence of the statutory restriction, therefore, does not give rise to coverage under the policy.

In light of the unambiguous coverage terms of the policy, we do not look beyond the four corners of the policy concerning whether coverage is customarily available with respect to such right-of-way statutes. We also conclude that, to the extent it is material, there is no evidence the circumstances surrounding issuance of the policy created a reasonable expectation in the plaintiff that it acquired more extensive coverage than that stated in the policy.[3] Summary judgment was appropriately granted for the defendant on count I. . . .

Count IV. The plaintiff also alleges that the defendant failed to examine, review, and analyze the title to the premises and to notify the plaintiff of any facts regarding title. We agree with the judge, as apparently did the Appeals Court, that no such contractual obligation exists. The plaintiff did not request a report from the defendant regarding the status of title to the property. The defendant was not employed to examine the title, rather, the plaintiff purchased a policy to insure against existing defects and encumbrances on the title. The defendant has demonstrated that proof of a contract to examine and analyze the status of the title, an essential element to the plaintiff's claim for breach of contract in count IV, is unlikely to be presented at trial. Therefore, summary judgment was appropriately granted for the defendant on count IV.

Negligence claims. The judge ruled that the defendant had no duty to disclose the prior use of the property as a railroad right-of-way . . . and further ruled that the defendant had not voluntarily assumed such a duty. Therefore, the judge granted summary judgment for the defendant on the plaintiff's negligence claims. The Appeals Court concluded that, whether the defendant had assumed an obligation, not cast on it by the terms of the policy, to disclose matters affecting the property that an examination of the registry would reveal is a matter for further development. We conclude that the granting of summary judgment was not appropriate on these claims because there is a factual dispute whether the defendant voluntarily assumed a duty to inform the plaintiff of these matters.

The plaintiff argues that the issuance of a policy places a duty on a title insurance company to search for, and to disclose to the insured, any reasonably discoverable information that would affect the insured's decision to proceed with the purchase. As a general rule, we decline to impose such a duty. A title insurance company's duty to the insured is governed by the terms of the policy. . . . Its

---

3. The evidence presented by the plaintiff, with respect to its reasonable expectations, focuses on the belief that right-of-way statutes are normally delineated as an exception to coverage. However, even if such a practice was accepted, the failure to include such a statute as an exclusion does not mean that coverage is available, where the express policy terms do not provide for coverage.

liability is limited to the policy, and it will not be liable for negligence in searching the records. However, if the title insurance company agrees to conduct a search and to provide the insured with an abstract of title, it may expose itself to liability for negligence as a title searcher, in addition to any liability under the policy. *See* Focus Inv. Assocs. v. American Title Ins. Co., 992 F.2d 1231 (1st Cir. 1993), and cases cited. A title insurance company thus may be found liable on a negligence claim if the act complained of was a direct result of duties voluntarily assumed by the insurer, in addition to the contract to insure title. Brown's Tie & Lumber Co. v. Chicago Title Co., 115 Idaho 56, 59, 764 P.2d 423 (1988). The plaintiff met its burden in opposition to the allowance of summary judgment on this issue. It offered evidence that the defendant's advertising claimed knowledge of local laws and practices, and might fairly be interpreted as an assurance that all matters recorded at the registry which might influence the decision to buy the property would be called to the insured's attention. This evidence might warrant the finding that the defendant assumed a duty to notify the plaintiff of the applicability of the provisions of § 54A.

We reject the defendant's argument that it cannot be liable for any loss or damage resulting from its negligence because of the language in the policy's integration clause, which limits liability to the provisions and conditions set forth in the policy. In most instances, an insurance contract is not a negotiated agreement, rather its conditions are predominantly dictated by the insurance company to the insured. Darcy v. Hartford Ins. Co., 554 N.E.2d 28 (Mass. 1990). In this context, we must look at whether the clause exculpating the defendant from loss arising from its own negligence is unfair or unconscionable. This analysis requires a balancing of the freedom of contract against possible harm to the public resulting from allowing such exculpation. *See* Jackson v. First Nat'l Bank, 415 Ill. 453, 459-460, 114 N.E.2d 721 (1953). In recognition of the needs and expectations of the purchaser of the policy, his or her lack of bargaining power, and the public policy implications of allowing such a disclaimer of liability, we conclude that a claim based on a breach of duty to exercise due care in notifying an insured of matters discovered in a title search voluntarily assumed outside the policy is not barred by the integration clause.

Summary judgment on the plaintiff's contract claims (counts I and IV) is affirmed. Summary judgment is vacated, with respect to counts II, III and V, and the action is remanded for further proceedings consistent with this opinion.

Notes and Questions

1. Title companies insure the title of buyers and the liens of mortgagees in real estate. The title insurance company is different than most other insurance companies in that the title company is not insuring based on an actuarial estimate of how many defective titles will emerge in a given pool of insured properties. Rather, the title company searches the title of the specific piece of property in the land records, provides a title report to the buyer (or mortgagee) applying for insurance, and then essentially guarantees that its search and report were accurate by promising to pay the insured for her loss if the title turns out to be not as was shown on the title report and policy. So, if it emerges that there was a prior fee title to the property, or an outstanding mortgage or easement not reported by the insurer, the title company must make good for the loss. The insured pays a one-time premium on the issuance of the insurance.

Title insurers do take a few actuarial risks. For example, they insure against loss of title without excepting loss of title due to a forged deed in the chain of title. They do so based on their experience of how often this occurs, and figure this into the premium schedule.

In some jurisdictions, the traditional practice was to provide the buyer with an attorney's opinion as to the quality of title rather than a title insurance policy. Would you recommend that your client insist on a title policy rather than a lawyer's opinion?

For an excellent treatise on title insurance, see D. Barlow Burke, *The Law of Title Insurance* (2d ed. 1992).

2. The American Land Title Association promulgates form title policies that are used by the approximately half-dozen major American title insurance companies. There is an A.L.T.A. Owner's Policy and an A.L.T.A. Loan Policy (for mortgagees) which are very similar.

The A.L.T.A. Owner's Policy insures the buyer against "loss or damage, not exceeding the Amount of Insurance [usually the purchase price—EDS.], sustained or incurred" because title is vested in another, there is a defect or lien or encumbrance on title, or title is unmarketable. The policy also contains Exclusions from coverage. Among others, these include:

1(a). Any law, ordinance, permit, or governmental regulation (including those related to building and zoning) restricting, regulating, prohibiting or relating to

(i) the occupancy, use, or enjoyment of the land;

(ii) the character, dimensions or location of any improvement erected on the land;

(iii) the subdivision of land; or

(iv) environmental protection;

or the effect of any violation of these laws, ordinances or governmental regulations. This exclusion 1(a) does not modify or limit the coverage provided under Covered Risk 5. . . .

3. Defects, liens, encumbrances, adverse claims or other matters:

(a) created, suffered, assumed or agreed to by the Insured Claimant;

(b) not Known to the Company, not recorded in the Public Records at Date of Policy, but Known to the Insured Claimant and not disclosed in writing to the Company by the Insured Claimant prior to the date the Insured Claimant became an Insured under this policy;

(c) resulting in no loss or damage to the Insured Claimant;

(d) attaching or created subsequent to Date of Policy (however, this does not modify or limit the coverage provided uner Covered Risk 9 and 10); or

(e) resulting in loss or damage that would not have been sustained if the Insured Claimant had paid value for the Title.

Schedule B of the policy contains Exceptions from coverage. Some of these exceptions are standard, for example:

1. Parties in Possession

Rights or claims of parties in possession not recorded in the Public Records.

2. Easements

Easements or claims of easements not recorded in the Public Records.

3. Survey Exception

Any encroachment, encumbrance, violation, variation, or adverse circumstance that would be disclosed by an inspection or an accurate and complete land survey of the Land.

4. Statutory Liens for Services, Labor, or Material

Any statutory lien for services, labor, or material arising from construction of an improvement or work related to the Land and not recorded in the Public Records.

5. Tax Liens

Liens for real estate taxes, assessments and other charges imposed by a governmental authority that are not shown as existing liens by its records.

The Conditions and Stipulations of the policy also limit coverage. Definitions are included in this section, such as

1. . . . (f) "Knowledge" or "Known": Actual knowledge, not constructive knowledge or notice that may be imputed to an Insured by reason of the Public Records or any other records that impart constructive notice of matters affecting the Title. . . .

(i) "Public Records": Records established under state statutes at Date of Policy for the purpose of imparting constructive notice of matters relating to real property to purchasers for value and without Knowledge. With respect to Covered Risk 5(d), "Public Records" shall also include environmental protection liens filed in the records of the clerk of the United States District Court for the district where the Land is located. . . .

(k) "Unmarketable Title": Title affected by an alleged or apparent matter that would permit a prospective purchaser or lessee of the Title or lender on the Title to be released from the obligation to purchase, lease, or lend if there is a contractual condition requiring the delivery of marketable title.

Other important Conditions and Stipulations include

2. Continuation of Insurance

The coverage of this policy shall continue in force as of Date of Policy in favor of an Insured but only so long as the Insured retains an estate or interest in the Land, or holds an obligation secured by a purchase money Mortgage given by a purchaser from the Insured, or only so long as the Insured shall have liability by reason of warranties in any transfer or conveyance of Title. This policy shall not continue in force in favor of any purchaser from the Insured of either (i) an estate or interest in the Land; or (ii) an obligation secured by a purchase money Mortgage given to the Insured. . . .

15. Liability Limited to This Policy; Policy Entire Contract.

(a) This policy together with all endorsements, if any, attached to it by the Company is the entire policy and contract between the Insured and the Company. In interpreting any provision of this policy, this policy shall be construed as a whole.

(b) Any claim of loss or damage that arises out of the status of the Title or by any action asserting such claim, shall be restricted to this policy.

(c) Any amendment of or endorsement to this policy must be in writing and authenticated by an authorized person, or expressly incorporated by Schedule A of this policy.

(d) Each endorsement to this policy issued at any time is made a part of this policy and is subject to all of its terms and provisions. Except as the endorsement expressly states, it does not (i) modify any of the terms and provisions of the policy, (ii) modify any prior endorsement, (iii) extend the Date of Policy, or (iv) increase the Amount of Insurance.

Consider whether the purchaser of the property would be covered under the A.L.T.A. provisions if, after taking possession, her possession is challenged based on title issues of the type described in (a) *Conklin v. Davi*; (b) *Seymour v. Evans*; (c) *Ryczkowski v. Chelsea Title*; and (d) *Sanborn v. McLean*.

3. Do you accept the reasoning of the *Somerset Savings Bank* court for finding no liability? Would the result have been different if there had been a recorded restrictive covenant requiring the approval of the Secretary before building? Is subsection (c) of the exclusions from coverage really not relevant to the decision?

Do you agree with the *Somerset Savings Bank* court that the title company should have no independent duty to accurately search and disclose defects to the insured? Consider paragraph 15 of the Conditions and Stipulations set out in Note 2.

Problems: Compare Title Insurance with General Warranty Covenant

1. Compare the advantages and disadvantages to the grantee/insured of a covenant of general warranty and a title insurance policy.

2. A purchased a piece of property bordering B's land, and bought a title policy similar to the one described in Note 2 above. Before buying, A learned that O, A's predecessor in title, had built a fence along the border of the two parcels and B had torn it down. After A moved in, she built a new fence. B tore it down, and then brought an action to quiet title, claiming a 10-foot strip of A's parcel. B prevailed in his action. Can A recover from her title insurer? *See Laabs v. Chicago Title Insurance Co.*, 241 N.W.2d 434 (Wis. 1976).

3. Title Company issued a policy in favor of Buyer of a 10-acre tract of realty. In performing its search, Title Company failed to find a prior recorded deed giving a fee interest to Xavier in a one-acre portion of the property. Xavier had built a small home on his lot by the time of the sale to Buyer. The title policy expressly provided that "nothing in this policy shall be construed as insuring against loss by reason of the right, title, or occupancies of parties in actual possession of any or all of the property at the effective date of this policy." Can Buyer succeed on a claim against Title Company because of Xavier's occupancy? Would the result be the same if the policy contained Schedule B described in the first Note 2 above? *See Horn v. Lawyers Title Insurance Corp.*, 557 P.2d 206 (N.M. 1976); *Pruett v. Mississippi Valley Title Insurance Co.*, 271 So. 2d 920 (Miss. 1973).

CHAPTER 10

Protection Against Discrimination
in Housing

Residential segregation is not a neutral fact; it systematically undermines the social and economic well-being of blacks in the United States.

Douglas S. Massey & Nancy A. Denton, *American Apartheid:*
Segregation and the Making of the Underclass (1993)

The ethnic, religious, and racial diversity in America led to prolonged struggles throughout the 20th century over housing segregation based on race, religion, and national origin.[1] In the later part of the century, concerns about discrimination against families with children and people with handicaps, and discrimination based on gender, marital status, and sexual orientation also came to the fore. In this chapter we can only hope to introduce you to this subject, which you can pursue in more specialized courses on housing and civil rights.

A. PROTECTION UNDER THE FEDERAL CONSTITUTION

FOURTEENTH AMENDMENT TO THE U.S. CONSTITUTION

Section 1. All persons born or naturalized in the United States, and subject to the jurisdiction thereof, are citizens of the United States and of the state wherein they reside. No state shall make or enforce any law which shall abridge the privileges or immunities of citizens of the United States; nor shall any state deprive any person of life, liberty, or property, without due process of law; nor deny to any person within its jurisdiction the equal protection of the laws.

---

1. The history of the creation of black ghettos in America, fostered by the U.S. government through the Home Owners' Loan Corporation program created in 1933, which began the notorious practice of "redlining" black areas, making loans unavailable, and the Federal Housing Administration and Veterans Administration during the 1940s and 1950s, is detailed in Douglas S. Massey & Nancy A. Denton, American Apartheid: Segregation and the Making of the Underclass ch. 2 (1993). *See also* John Yinger, Closed Doors, Opportunities Lost: The Continuing Costs of Housing Discrimination (1995).

SHELLEY v. KRAEMER
Supreme Court of the United States
334 U.S. 1 (1948)

VINSON, C.J. These cases present for our consideration questions relating to the validity of court enforcement of private agreements, generally described as restrictive covenants, which have as their purpose the exclusion of persons of designated race or color from the ownership or occupancy of real property. Basic constitutional issues of obvious importance have been raised.

The first of these cases comes to this Court on *certiorari* to the Supreme Court of Missouri. On February 16, 1911, thirty out of a total of thirty-nine owners of property fronting both sides of Labadie Avenue between Taylor Avenue and Cora Avenue in the city of St. Louis, signed an agreement, which was subsequently recorded, providing in part:

> . . . the said property is hereby restricted to the use and occupancy for the term of Fifty (50) years from this date, so that it shall be a condition all the time and whether recited and referred to as (sic) not in subsequent conveyances and shall attach to the land, as a condition precedent to the sale of the same, that hereafter no part of said property or any portion thereof shall be, for said term of Fifty-years, occupied by any person not of the Caucasian race, it being intended hereby to restrict the use of said property for said period of time against the occupancy as owners or tenants of any portion of said property for resident or other purpose by people of the Negro or Mongolian Race.

The entire district described in the agreement included fifty-seven parcels of land. The thirty owners who signed the agreement held title to forty-seven parcels, including the particular parcel involved in this case. At the time the agreement was signed, five of the parcels in the district were owned by Negroes. One of those had been occupied by Negro families since 1882, nearly thirty years before the restrictive agreement was executed. The trial court found that owners of seven out of nine homes on the south side of Labadie Avenue, within the restricted district and "in the immediate vicinity" of the premises in question, had failed to sign the restrictive agreement in 1911. At the time this action was brought, four of the premises were occupied by Negroes, and had been so occupied for periods ranging from twenty-three to sixty-three years. A fifth parcel had been occupied by Negroes until a year before this suit was instituted.

On August 11, 1945, pursuant to a contract of sale, petitioners Shelley, who are Negroes, for valuable consideration received from one Fitzgerald a warranty deed to the parcel in question.[1] The trial court found that petitioners had no actual knowledge of the restrictive agreement at the time of the purchase.

On October 9, 1945, respondents, as owners of other property subject to the terms of the restrictive covenant, brought suit in Circuit Court of the city of St. Louis praying that petitioners Shelley be restrained from taking possession of the property and that judgment be entered divesting title out of petitioners

---

1.   The trial court found that title to the property which petitioners Shelley sought to purchase was held by one Bishop, a real estate dealer, who placed the property in the name of Josephine Fitzgerald. Bishop, who acted as agent for petitioners in the purchase, concealed the fact of his ownership.

Shelley and revesting title in the immediate grantor or in such other person as the court should direct. The trial court denied the requested relief on the ground that the restrictive agreement, upon which respondents based their action, had never become final and complete because it was the intention of the parties to that agreement that it was not to become effective until signed by all property owners in the district, and signatures of all the owners had never been obtained.

The Supreme Court of Missouri sitting en banc reversed and directed the trial court to grant the relief for which respondents had prayed. That court held the agreement effective and concluded that enforcement of its provisions violated no rights guaranteed to petitioners by the Federal Constitution. At the time the court rendered its decision, petitioners were occupying the property in question.

The second of the cases under consideration comes to this Court from the Supreme Court of Michigan. The circumstances presented do not differ materially from the Missouri case. . . .

Petitioners . . . place . . . primary reliance on their contentions, first raised in the state courts, that judicial enforcement of the . . . agreements in these cases has violated rights guaranteed to petitioners by the Fourteenth Amendment of the Federal Constitution . . . .

Whether the equal protection clause of the Fourteenth Amendment inhibits judicial enforcement by state courts of restrictive covenants based on race or color is a question which this Court has not heretofore been called upon to consider. . . .

. . . In the Missouri case, . . . [n]ot only does the restriction seek to proscribe use and occupancy of the affected properties by members of the excluded class, but as construed by the Missouri courts, the agreement requires that title of any person who uses his property in violation of the restriction shall be divested. The restriction of the covenant in the Michigan case seeks to bar occupancy by persons of the excluded class. . . . The restrictions . . . are directed toward a designated class of persons and seek to determine who may and who may not own or make use of the properties for residential purposes. The excluded class is defined wholly in terms of race or color. . . .

It cannot be doubted that among the civil rights intended to be protected from discriminatory state action by the Fourteenth Amendment are the rights to acquire, enjoy, own and dispose of property. Equality in the enjoyment of property rights was regarded by the framers of that Amendment as an essential pre-condition to the realization of other basic civil rights and liberties which the Amendment was intended to guarantee. Thus, § 1978 of the Revised Statutes, derived from § 1 of the Civil Rights Act of 1866 . . . enacted . . . while the Fourteenth Amendment was also under consideration, provides:

> All citizens of the United States shall have the same right, in every State and Territory, as is enjoyed by white citizens thereof to inherit, purchase, lease, sell, hold, and convey real and personal property.

. . . It is likewise clear that restrictions on the right of occupancy of the sort sought to be created . . . in these cases could not be squared with the requirements of the Fourteenth Amendment if imposed by state statute or local ordinance. . . . In the case of Buchanan v. Warley, [1917, 245 U.S. 60,] a unanimous

Court declared unconstitutional the provisions of a city ordinance which denied to colored persons the right to occupy houses in blocks in which the greater number of houses were occupied by white persons, and imposed similar restrictions on white persons with respect to blocks in which the greater number of houses were occupied by colored persons. . . . [I]n that case, this Court stated: "The Fourteenth Amendment and these statutes enacted in furtherance of its purpose operate to qualify and entitle a colored man to acquire property without state legislation discriminating against him solely because of color."

In Harmon v. Tyler, 1927, 273 U.S. 668, a unanimous court . . . declared invalid an ordinance which forbade any Negro to establish a home on any property in a white community or any white person to establish a home in a Negro community, "except on the written consent of a majority of the persons of the opposite race inhabiting such community or portion of the City to be affected."

The precise question before this Court in both the *Buchanan* and *Harmon* cases, involved the rights of white sellers to dispose of their properties free from restrictions as to potential purchasers based on considerations of race or color. But that such legislation is also offensive to the rights of those desiring to acquire and occupy property and barred on grounds of race or color, is clear, not only from the language of the opinion in Buchanan v. Warley, but from this Court's disposition of the case of City of Richmond v. Deans, 1930, 281 U.S. 704. There, a Negro, barred from the occupancy of certain property by the terms of an ordinance similar to that in the *Buchanan* case, sought injunctive relief in the federal courts to enjoin the enforcement of the ordinance on the grounds that its provisions violated the terms of the Fourteenth Amendment. Such relief was granted, and this Court affirmed. . . .

But the present cases, unlike those just discussed, do not involve action by state legislatures or city councils. Here the particular patterns of discrimination and the areas in which the restrictions are to operate, are determined, in the first instance, by the terms of agreements among private individuals. Participation of the State consists in the enforcement of the restrictions so defined. The crucial issue with which we are here confronted is whether this distinction removes these cases from the operation of the prohibitory provisions of the Fourteenth Amendment.

Since the decision of this Court in the Civil Rights Cases, 1883, 109 U.S. 3, the principle has become firmly embedded in our constitutional law that the action inhibited by the first section of the Fourteenth Amendment is only such action as may fairly be said to be that of the States. That Amendment erects no shield against merely private conduct, however discriminatory or wrongful.

We conclude, therefore, that the restrictive agreements standing alone cannot be regarded as a violation of any rights guaranteed to petitioners by the Fourteenth Amendment. So long as the purposes of those agreements are effectuated by voluntary adherence to their terms, it would appear clear that there has been no action by the State and the provisions of the Amendment have not been violated. . . .

But here there was more. These are cases in which the purposes of the agreements were secured only by judicial enforcement by state courts of the restrictive terms of the agreements. The respondents urge that judicial enforcement of private agreements does not amount to state action; or, in any event, the participation of the State is so attenuated in character as not to amount to state action within the meaning of the Fourteenth Amendment. Finally, it is suggested, even if the States in these cases may be deemed to have acted in the constitutional sense, their action did not deprive petitioners of rights guaranteed by the Fourteenth Amendment. . . .

That the action of state courts and of judicial officers in their official capacities is to be regarded as action of the State within the meaning of the Fourteenth Amendment, is a proposition which has long been established by decisions of this Court. . . .

We have no doubt that there has been state action in these cases in the full and complete sense of the phrase. The undisputed facts disclose that petitioners were willing purchasers of properties upon which they desired to establish homes. The owners of the properties were willing sellers; and contracts of sale were accordingly consummated. It is clear that but for the active intervention of the state courts, supported by the full panoply of state power, petitioners would have been free to occupy the properties in question without restraint.

These are not cases . . . in which the States have merely abstained from action, leaving private individuals free to impose such discriminations as they see fit. Rather, . . . the States have made available . . . the full coercive power of government to deny to petitioners, on the grounds of race or color, the enjoyment of property rights in premises which petitioners are willing and financially able to acquire and which the grantors are willing to sell. The difference between judicial enforcement and nonenforcement of the restrictive covenants is the difference to petitioners between being denied rights of property available to other members of the community and being accorded full enjoyment of those rights on an equal footing.

The enforcement of the restrictive agreements by the state courts in these cases was directed pursuant to the common-law policy of the States. . . . In the Missouri case, enforcement of the covenant was directed in the first instance by the highest court of the State after the trial court had determined the agreement to be invalid for want of the requisite number of signatures. In the Michigan case, the order of enforcement by the trial court was affirmed by the highest state court. The judicial action in each case bears the clear and unmistakable imprimatur of the State. . . . [P]revious decisions of this Court have established the proposition that judicial action is not immunized from the operation of the Fourteenth Amendment simply because it is taken pursuant to the state's common-law policy. Nor is the Amendment ineffective simply because the particular pattern of discrimination, which the State has enforced, was defined initially by the terms of a private agreement. State action, as that phrase is understood for the purposes of the Fourteenth Amendment, refers to exertions of state power in all forms. And when the effect of that action is to deny rights subject to the protection of the Fourteenth Amendment, it is the obligation of this Court to enforce the constitutional commands.

. . . [F]reedom from discrimination by the States in the enjoyment of property rights was among the basic objectives sought to be effectuated by the framers of the Fourteenth Amendment. . . . Because of the race or color of these petitioners they have been denied rights of ownership or occupancy enjoyed as a matter of course by other citizens of different race or color. The Fourteenth Amendment declares "that all persons, whether colored or white, shall stand equal before the laws of the States, and, in regard to the colored race, for whose protection the amendment was primarily designed, that no discrimination shall be made against them by law because of their color." Strauder v. West Virginia, 100 U.S. at

307. Only recently this Court has had occasion to declare that a state law which denied equal enjoyment of property rights to a designated class of citizens of specified race and ancestry, was not a legitimate exercise of the state's police power but violated the guaranty of the equal protection of the laws. Oyama v. California, 1948, 332 U.S. 633. Nor may the discriminations imposed by the state courts in these cases be justified as proper exertions of state police power. . . .

Respondents urge, however, that since the state courts stand ready to enforce restrictive covenants excluding white persons from the ownership or occupancy of property covered by such agreements, enforcement of covenants excluding colored persons may not be deemed a denial of equal protection of the laws to the colored persons who are thereby affected.[28] This contention does not bear scrutiny. The parties have directed our attention to no case in which a court, state or federal, has been called upon to enforce a covenant excluding members of the white majority from ownership or occupancy of real property on grounds of race or color. But there are more fundamental considerations. The rights created by the first section of the Fourteenth Amendment are, by its terms, guaranteed to the individual. The rights established are personal rights. It is, therefore, no answer to these petitioners to say that the courts may also be induced to deny white persons rights of ownership and occupancy on grounds of race or color. Equal protection of the laws is not achieved through indiscriminate imposition of inequalities.

Nor do we find merit in the suggestion that property owners who are parties to these agreements are denied equal protection of the laws if denied access to the courts to enforce the terms of restrictive covenants and to assert property rights which the state courts have held to be created by such agreements. The Constitution confers upon no individual the right to demand action by the State which results in the denial of equal protection of the laws to other individuals. And it would appear beyond question that the power of the State to create and enforce property interests must be exercised within the boundaries defined by the Fourteenth Amendment. . . .

The historical context in which the Fourteenth Amendment became a part of the Constitution should not be forgotten. Whatever else the framers sought to achieve, it is clear that the matter of primary concern was the establishment of equality in the enjoyment of basic civil and political rights and the preservation of those rights from discriminatory action on the part of the States based on considerations of race or color. Seventy-five years ago this Court announced that the provisions of the Amendment are to be construed with this fundamental purpose in mind. Upon full consideration, we have concluded that in these cases the States have acted to deny petitioners the equal protection of the laws guaranteed by the Fourteenth Amendment. Having so decided, we find it unnecessary to consider whether petitioners have also been deprived of property without due process of law or denied privileges and immunities of citizens of the United States.

28.   It should be observed that the restrictions relating to residential occupancy contained in ordinances involved in the *Buchanan, Harmon* and *Deans* cases, cited *supra,* and declared by this Court to be inconsistent with the requirements of the Fourteenth Amendment, applied equally to white persons and Negroes.

For the reasons stated, the judgment of the Supreme Court of Missouri and the judgment of the Supreme Court of Michigan must be reversed.

Notes and Questions

1. The only reported decision involving racial covenants prior to 1915 was *Gandolfo v. Hartman*, 49 F. 181 (C.C.S.D. Cal. 1892), in which the court held a covenant prohibiting use by "Chinamen" invalid because it violated the Fourteenth Amendment and was contrary to a treaty with China. Unfortunately, this decision was ignored in later cases, and most of the states that confronted the validity of racial restrictions before the decision in *Shelley* held them valid, even those that went beyond use restrictions to prohibit sale or transfer to non-Caucasians.

2. Could privately created racial covenants have been outlawed on grounds of public policy rather than by stretching the concept of state action to fit them under the Fourteenth Amendment? In a Canadian decision invalidating a covenant prohibiting sale of land to "Jews or persons of objectionable nationality," *Re Drummond Wren*, [1945] O.R. 778, 4 D.L.R. 674, the court said:

> [T]he consequences of judicial approbation of such a covenant are portentous. . . . [N]othing could be more calculated to create or deepen divisions between existing religions and ethnic groups in this province, or in this country, than the sanction of a method of land transfer which would permit the segregation and confinement of particular groups to particular business or residential areas. . . . Ontario, and Canada, too, may well be termed a province, and a country of minorities in regard to the religious and ethnic groups which live therein. It appears to me to be a moral duty, at least, to lend aid to all forces of cohesion, and similarly to repel all fissiparous tendencies which would imperil national unity.
>
> The common law courts have, by their actions over the years, obviated the need for rigid constitutional guarantees in our policy by their wise use of the doctrine of public policy as an active agent in the promotion of the public weal. While courts and eminent judges have, in view of the powers of our legislatures, warned against inventing new heads of public policy, I do not conceive that I would be breaking new ground were I to hold the restrictive covenant impugned in this proceeding to be void as against public policy. . . . If the common law of treason encompasses the stirring up of hatred between different classes of His Majesty's subjects, the common law of public policy is surely adequate to void the restrictive covenant which is here attacked.

3. In *Hurd v. Hodge*, 334 U.S. 24 (1948), a companion case to *Shelley*, the Court adhered to the position taken in *Corrigan v. Buckley*, 271 U.S. 323 (1926), that private racial covenants were not invalid under federal law, but held that they could not be enforced by federal courts. Instead of basing the decision on the Due Process Clause of the Fifth Amendment, however, the Court drew on the Civil Rights Act of 1866 to hold that enforcement would violate federal public policy. The Court thus reversed the trial court's decision enforcing a covenant by a judgment "declaring null and void the deeds of the Negro petitioners; enjoining . . . the white property owners who had sold the houses to the Negro petitioners, from leasing, selling or conveying the properties to any Negro or colored person; enjoining the Negro petitioners from leasing or conveying the

properties and directing those petitioners to remove themselves and all of their
personal belongings from the premises within sixty days." The Supreme Court
said:

> It is not consistent with the public policy of the United States to permit federal
> courts in the Nation's capital to exercise general equitable powers to compel action
> denied the state courts where such state action has been held to be violative of the
> guaranty of the equal protection of the laws. We cannot presume that the public
> policy of the United States manifests a lesser concern for the protection of such
> basic rights against discriminatory action of federal courts than against such action
> taken by the courts of the States.

4. Two questions left open by *Shelley* were answered in *Barrows v. Jackson*, 346
U.S. 249 (1953): whether awarding damages against a seller who sold to a non-
Caucasian in violation of a covenant would violate the Fourteenth Amendment;
and whether a Caucasian seller has standing to raise the constitutional rights of
a non-Caucasian buyer as a defense to the damages claim. The Court answered
both questions in the affirmative, saying:

> If a state court awards damages for breach of a restrictive covenant, a prospec-
> tive seller of restricted land will either refuse to sell to non-Caucasians or else will
> require non-Caucasians to pay a higher price to meet the damages which the seller
> may incur. Solely because of their race, non-Caucasians will be unable to purchase,
> own, and enjoy property on the same terms as Caucasians. . . .
>
> There is such a close relationship between the restrictive covenant here and the
> sanction of a state court which would punish respondent for not going forward
> with her covenant, and the purpose of the covenant itself, that relaxation of the
> [standing] rule is called for here . . . . The law will permit respondent to resist
> any effort to compel her to observe such a covenant, so widely condemned by the
> courts, since she is the one in whose charge and keeping reposes the power to con-
> tinue to use her property to discriminate or to discontinue such use.

B.   PROTECTION UNDER THE CIVIL RIGHTS
ACT OF 1866 AND THE FEDERAL
FAIR HOUSING ACT

Although courts were forbidden to enforce racial and religious covenants after
the decisions in *Shelley* and *Barrows*, such covenants remained in widespread use
and, coupled with discriminatory lending practices and "racial steering" practices of real estate brokers, led to continued and increasing segregation in the
American housing market. Two major developments took place in 1968: adoption of Title VIII, the Fair Housing provision of the Civil Rights Act of 1968; and
the decision in *Jones v. Alfred H. Mayer Co.*, which breathed new life into the Civil
Rights Act of 1866. We look first at the earlier statute.

THE CIVIL RIGHTS ACT OF 1866, 42 U.S.C. § 1982

All citizens of the United States shall have the same right, in every state and Territory, as is enjoyed by the white citizens thereof to inherit, purchase, lease, sell, hold, and convey real and personal property.

JONES v. ALFRED H. MAYER CO.

Supreme Court of the United States
392 U.S. 409 (1968)

STEWART, J. . . . On September 2, 1965, the petitioners filed a complaint in the District Court for the Eastern District of Missouri, alleging that the respondents had refused to sell them a home in the Paddock Woods community of St. Louis County for the sole reason that petitioner Joseph Lee Jones is a Negro. Relying in part upon [42 U.S.C.] § 1982, the petitioners sought injunctive and other relief. The District Court sustained the respondents' motion to dismiss the complaint, and the Court of Appeals for the Eighth Circuit affirmed, concluding that § 1982 applies only to state action and does not reach private refusals to sell. We granted *certiorari* to consider the questions thus presented. . . . We hold that § 1982 bars all racial discrimination, private as well as public, in the sale or rental of property, and that the statute, thus construed, is a valid exercise of the power of Congress to enforce the Thirteenth Amendment.

At the outset, it is important to make clear precisely what this case does not involve. Whatever else it may be, 42 U.S.C. § 1982 is not a comprehensive open housing law. In sharp contrast to the Fair Housing Title (Title VIII) of the Civil Rights Act of 1968, the statute in this case deals only with racial discrimination and does not address itself to discrimination on grounds of religion or national origin. It does not deal specifically with discrimination in the provision of services or facilities in connection with the sale or rental of a dwelling. It does not prohibit advertising or other representations that indicate discriminatory preferences. It does not refer explicitly to discrimination in financing arrangements or in the provision of brokerage services. It does not empower a federal administrative agency to assist aggrieved parties. It makes no provision for intervention by the Attorney General. And, although it can be enforced by injunction, it contains no provision expressly authorizing a federal court to order the payment of damages.[2]

Hurd v. Hodge did not present the question whether purely private discrimination, unaided by any action on the part of government, would violate § 1982 if its effect were to deny a citizen the right to rent or buy property solely because of his race or color.

The only federal court (other than the Court of Appeals in this case) that has ever squarely confronted that question held that a wholly private conspiracy among white citizens to prevent a Negro from leasing a farm violated § 1982.

---

2.   All of these provisions are included in the Federal Fair Housing Act (Title VIII of the Civil Rights Act of 1968), which we take up next.—EDS.

United States v. Morris, D.C., 125 F. 322. It is true that a dictum in *Hurd* said that § 1982 was directed only toward "governmental action," but neither *Hurd* nor any other case before or since has presented that precise issue for adjudication in this Court. . . .

In plain and unambiguous terms, § 1982 grants to all citizens, without regard to race or color, "the same right" to purchase and lease property "as is enjoyed by white citizens." . . . [T]hat right can be impaired as effectively by "those who place property on the market" as by the State itself. . . . [W]henever property "is placed on the market for whites only, whites have a right denied to Negroes." So long as a Negro citizen who wants to buy or rent a home can be turned away simply because he is not white, he cannot be said to enjoy "the *same* right . . . as is enjoyed by white citizens . . . to . . . purchase [and] lease . . . real and personal property."

On its face, therefore, § 1982 appears to prohibit *all* discrimination against Negroes in the sale or rental of property—discrimination by private as well as discrimination by public authorities. Indeed, even the respondents seem to concede that, if § 1982 "means what it says"—to use the words of the respondents' brief—then it must encompass every racially motivated refusal to sell or rent and cannot be confined to officially sanctioned segregation in housing. Stressing what they consider to be the revolutionary implications of so literal a reading of § 1982, the respondents argue that Congress cannot possibly have intended any such result. Our examination of the relevant history, however, persuades us that Congress meant exactly what it said. . . .

President Andrew Johnson vetoed the Act on March 27, and in the brief congressional debate that followed, his supporters characterized its reach in all embracing terms. One stressed the fact that § 1 would confer "the right . . . to purchase . . . real estate . . . without any qualification and without any restriction whatever . . . ." Another predicted, as a corollary, that the Act would preclude preferential treatment for white persons in the rental of hotel rooms and in the sale of church pews. Those observations elicited no reply. On April 6 the Senate, and on April 9 the House, overrode the President's veto by the requisite majorities, and the Civil Rights Act of 1866 became law. . . .

The remaining question is whether Congress has power under the Constitution . . . to prohibit all racial discrimination, private and public, in the sale and rental of property. Our starting point is the Thirteenth Amendment, for it was pursuant to that constitutional provision that Congress originally enacted what is now § 1982. The Amendment consists of two parts . . . .

> Section 1. Neither slavery nor involuntary servitude, except as a punishment for crime whereby the party shall have been duly convicted, shall exist within the United States, or any place subject to their jurisdiction.

> Section 2. Congress shall have power to enforce this article by appropriate legislation.

. . . [T]he Thirteenth Amendment "is not a mere prohibition of state laws establishing or upholding slavery, but an absolute declaration that slavery or involuntary servitude shall not exist in any part of the United States." Civil Rights Cases, 109 U.S. 3, 20. It has never been doubted, therefore, "that the power vested in Congress to enforce the article by appropriate legislation," includes the power to enact laws "direct and primary, operating upon the acts of individuals, whether sanctioned by state legislation or not."

Thus, the fact that § 1982 operates upon the unofficial acts of private individuals, whether or not sanctioned by state law, presents no constitutional problem. If Congress has power under the Thirteenth Amendment to eradicate conditions that prevent Negroes from buying and renting property because of their race or color, then no federal statute calculated to achieve that objective can be thought to exceed the constitutional power of Congress simply because it reaches beyond state action to regulate the conduct of private individuals. The constitutional question in this case, therefore, comes to this: Does the authority of Congress to enforce the Thirteenth Amendment "by appropriate legislation" include the power to eliminate all racial barriers to the acquisition of real and personal property? We think the answer to that question is plainly yes. . . .

CIVIL RIGHTS ACT OF 1968, TITLE VIII — FAIR HOUSING & TITLE VIII[3]

§ 3601. Declaration of Policy. It is the policy of the United States to provide, within constitutional limitations for fair housing throughout the United States.

As enacted in 1968, the Fair Housing Act prohibited discrimination on the grounds of race, color, religion, and national origin. Its coverage was expanded in 1974 to include sex and again in 1988 to cover familial status and handicap.[4] The basic prohibitions of the Act are contained in § 3604.

§ 3604. Discrimination in the Sale or Rental of Housing and Other Prohibited Practices. . . . . [E]xcept as exempted by § 3603(b) and 3607 of this title, it shall be unlawful—

(a) To refuse to sell or rent after the making of a bona fide offer, or to refuse to negotiate for the sale or rental of, or otherwise make unavailable or deny a dwelling to any person because of race, color, religion, sex, familial status, or national origin.

(b) To discriminate against any person in the terms, conditions, or privileges of sale or rental of a dwelling, or in the provision of services or facilities in connection therewith because of race, color, religion, sex, familial status, or national origin.

(c) To make, print, or publish, or cause to be made, printed, or published any notice, statement, or advertisement, with respect to the sale or rental of a dwelling that indicates any preference, limitation, or discrimination based on race, color, religion, sex, handicap, familial status, or national origin, or an intention to make any such preference, limitation, or discrimination.

(d) To represent to any person because of race, color, religion, sex, handicap, familial status, or national origin that any dwelling is not available for inspection, sale, or rental when such dwelling is in fact so available.

---

3. The Act, known as the Federal Fair Housing Act (FFHA), is codified at 42 U.S.C. §§ 3601-3619. For the sorry history of the federal government's contributions to the creation of segregation in American housing, see Florence Wagman Roisman, *Intentional Racial Discrimination and Segregation by the Federal Government as a Principal Cause of Concentrated Poverty: A Response to Schill and Wachter,* 143 U. Pa. L. Rev. 1351 (1995).

4. *See* Kushner, *The Fair Housing Amendments Act of 1988: The Second Generation of Fair Housing and Urban Development,* 42 Vand. L. Rev. 1049 (1989).

(e) For profit, to induce or attempt to induce any person to sell or rent any dwelling by representations regarding the entry or prospective entry into the neighborhood of a person or persons of a particular race, color, religion, sex, handicap, familial status, or national origin.

Unlike § 1982 of the 1866 Act, the Fair Housing Act contains a number of exemptions. The most important are contained in the following section.

§ 3603(b) Exemptions. Nothing in § 3604 . . . (other than subsection (c)) shall apply to

(1) any single-family house sold or rented by an owner: *Provided,* That such private individual owner does not own more than three such single-family houses at any one time: *Provided further,* That in the case of the sale of any such single-family house by a private individual owner not residing in such house at the time of such sale or who was not the most recent resident of such house prior to such sale, the exemption granted by this subsection shall apply only with respect to one such sale within any 24-month period: . . . *Provided further,* That . . . the sale or rental . . . shall be excepted only if such house is sold or rented (A) without the use in any manner of the sales or rental facilities or . . . the services of any real estate broker, agent, or salesman . . . and (B) without the publication, posting or mailing, after notice, of any advertisement or written notice in violation of § 3604(c) . . . ; but nothing in this proviso shall prohibit the use of attorneys, escrow agents, abstractors, title companies, and other such professional assistance as necessary to perfect or transfer the title, or

(2) rooms or units in dwellings containing living quarters occupied or intended to be occupied by no more than four families living independently of each other, if the owner actually maintains and occupies one of such living quarters as his residence.

Notes and Questions

1. You recently heard your next-door neighbor of several years, whose house has a "for sale by owner" sign out front, tell a Hispanic couple with poor English that the property had already sold and was "in escrow." Two hours later, you heard him tell an Asian couple that the house was available and quote them a price. You know the Hispanic couple and would like to have them for neighbors. Should you call and advise them to seek legal assistance?

2. If real estate advertisements in the largest local newspaper regularly feature Caucasian models and seldom or never include black models, has the newspaper violated § 3604(c)? *See Housing Opportunities Made Equal, Inc. v. Cincinnati Enquirer,* 943 F.2d 644 (6th Cir. 1991); *Ragin v. New York Times Co.,* 923 F.2d 995 (2d Cir. 1990), *cert. denied,* 502 U.S. 821 (1991); Reginald L. Robinson, *White Cultural Matrix and the Language of Nonverbal Advertising in Housing Segregation: Toward an Aggregate Theory of Liability,* 25 Cap. U. L. Rev. 101 (1996); Comment, *When the Medium Becomes the Message: A Proposal for Principal Media Liability for the Publication of Racially Exclusionary Real Estate Advertisements,* 40 UCLA L. Rev. 199 (1992).

3. Does a landlord who advertises only in a Korean language newspaper violate the statute? Does a landlady who rents out rooms in her home to graduate students and freelances as a Russian translator violate the statute by advertising for a native Russian speaker? *See Holmgren v. Little Village Community Reporter,* 342

F. Supp. 512 (N.D. Ill. 1971) (indicating language preference in newspaper ad is national origin discrimination); R. Ian Forrest, Note, *Kàn Bú Tài D ng: The Fair Housing Act, Language Discrimination, and Chinese Classifieds*, 101 Ky. L.J. 839 (2012-2013).

4. What about a landlord who posts notices only on the community bulletin board in the local women's center, or in a gated community that has no minority residents? Or who advertises for a "mature" nonsmoking female? *See Jancik v. Department of Housing & Urban Development*, 44 F.3d 553 (7th Cir. 1995) (advertisement for "mature person" discriminated against families with children). See the HUD.gov website for guidelines on advertising to meet the requirements of the FHA.

5. Does the FHA apply to people advertising for roommates? *Fair Housing Council of San Fernando Valley v. Roommate.Com, LLC*, 666 F.3d 1216 (9th Cir. 2012), held that it does not (holding that the FHA applied inside a home or apartment would be a serious invasion of privacy, autonomy, and security). In a story about the case, Adam Liptak of the New York Times reported that one of the advertisements at issue said: "I am not looking for freaks, geeks, prostitutes (male or female), druggies, pet cobras, drama, black Muslims or mortgage brokers," *Fair Housing, Free Speech and Choosy Roommates*, N.Y. Times, Jan. 22, 2007.

6. If a property owners association blocks purchase of a unit by a member of a minority by exercising a right of first refusal, has it violated § 3604? *See Phillips v. Hunter Trails Community Ass'n*, 685 F.2d 184 (7th Cir. 1982) (trial court properly rejected Neighborhood Association's economic defense that its effort to block proposed sale to black businessman was an honest effort to protect property values rather than intentional racial discrimination in violation of Fair Housing Act).

7. Can a landlord pursue a race-conscious rental policy to maintain "racial balance" or prevent "white flight"? In *United States v. Starrett City Associates*, 840 F.2d 1096 (2d Cir. 1988), the United States Attorney General brought an action under the Fair Housing Act claiming that Starrett City, a housing development consisting of 46 high-rise buildings and 5,881 apartments, violated § 3604 by using racial quotas to limit the racial composition in the project to 64 percent white, 22 percent African-American, and 8 percent Latino residents. As a result, the waiting lists for qualified nonwhite applicants were much longer than for white applicants. Starrett City defended its use of quotas as necessary to maintain a racially integrated community. The court of appeals held the quotas illegal, refusing to treat them as valid affirmative action plans because the use of racial distinctions was not designed as a temporary measure to achieve a defined goal. Did the court properly resolve the tension between the competing goals of eliminating discrimination and achieving integration?

8. Practices that have discriminatory effects, even though they involve no direct discriminatory actions, may violate the Fair Housing Act. *See, e.g., Metropolitan Housing Development Corp. v. Village of Arlington Heights*, 558 F.2d 1283 (7th Cir. 1977), *cert. denied*, 434 U.S. 1025 (1978) (significant discriminatory effect of zoning decisions violates the Fair Housing Act); *Moore v. Townsend*, 525 F.2d 482 (7th Cir. 1975) (if it is established that race played some part in the refusal to deal, there may be a violation of the Act); *United States v. Mitchell*, 580 F.2d 789 (5th Cir. 1986) (steering to a certain group of apartments in a complex based on race violates the Act because it effectively denies access to equal housing opportunities); *United States v. Henshaw Bros.*, 401 F. Supp. 399 (E.D. Va. 1974) (Fair Housing

Act prohibits not only direct discrimination but also practices with racially discouraging effects; steering evidences an intent to influence the choice of the renter on an impermissible racial basis). On the importance of combating discrimination in housing, see Florence Wagman Roisman, *Sustainable Development in Suburbs and Their Cities: The Environmental and Financial Imperatives of Racial, Ethnic, and Economic Inclusion*, 3 Widener L. Symp. J. 87 (1998).

9. The Fair Housing Act also prohibits discrimination in the extension of credit in real estate transactions, § 3605, and in membership in and access to real estate brokers' organizations and multiple listing services, § 3606. Provisions of the Act may be enforced by a complaint to HUD (the Department of Housing and Urban Development), by private suit in state or federal court, and by the Justice Department.

10. For comprehensive coverage of the federal Fair Housing Act and other antidiscrimination statutes, see Robert G. Schwemm, *Housing Discrimination: Law and Litigation* (looseleaf volumes, copyright 2008-2014).

Have Fair Housing Laws Made a Difference?

Housing discrimination has become more subtle since it became illegal, but it persists, particularly in "steering" racial and ethnic minorities to fewer and different rental and purchase opportunities than whites. See U.S. Department of HUD, Housing Discrimination Against Racial and Ethnic Minorities 2012, http://www.huduser.org/portal/Publications/pdf/HUD-514_HDS2012.pdf, which found that racial and ethnic minorities are likely to be shown fewer available rental units or homes for sale than equally qualified whites and the 2008 Symposium issue of the Indiana Law Review, introduced by Florence Wagman Roisman in *Living Together: Ending Racial Discrimination and Segregation in Housing*, 41 Ind. L. Rev. 507 (2008).

In an interesting article, Professor Richard Sander showed that the incidence of discrimination fell sharply from the 1960s to the 1980s, but that blacks are still highly segregated from whites. In *Housing Segregation and Housing Integration: The Diverging Paths of Urban America*, 52 U. Miami L. Rev. 977 (1998), Sander analyzes the result from his study of 60 metropolitan areas in the United States. His analysis suggest that although blacks migrated out of ghettos in very large numbers in the 1970s, the demographic structure of the city determined whether the migration led to long-term integration or resegregation. In cities with long-standing ethnic rivalries, large black populations, and slow general growth, black migration tended to be concentrated in a relatively small number of neighborhoods, and often prompted white flight, leaving blacks segregated, albeit in possession of better housing. In these cities, the durability of segregation, and the fear that blacks "moving in" to a neighborhood would precipitate neighborhood "tipping," became a key cause of continuing discrimination.

By contrast, in cities with relatively small black populations, few white ethnic enclaves, and dynamic population growth, stable integration was much more likely to occur. In Seattle, Minneapolis, and San Antonio, for example, fully one-third of black residents lived in integrated neighborhoods in 1980. Sander concluded that attacks on discrimination alone were not likely to change segregation levels very much: "[S]uccessful desegregation in our most segregated cities will come only through programs aimed at simulating the interrelated conditions that occur spontaneously in the desegregating cities."

C.   DISCRIMINATION AGAINST THE HANDICAPPED

§ 3604. Discrimination in the Sale or Rental of Housing and Other Prohibited Practices. . . .

[I]t shall be unlawful—

(f) (1) To discriminate in the sale or rental, or to otherwise make unavailable or deny, a dwelling to any buyer or renter because of a handicap of—

(A) that buyer or renter,

(B) a person residing in or intending to reside in that dwelling after it is so sold, rented, or made available; or

(C) any person associated with that buyer or renter.

(2) To discriminate against any person in the terms, conditions, or privileges of sale or rental of a dwelling, or in the provision of services or facilities in connection with such dwelling, because of a handicap of—

(A) that person; or

(B) a person residing in or intending to reside in that dwelling after it is so sold, rented, or made available; or

(C) any person associated with that person.

(3) For purposes of this subsection, discrimination includes—

(A) a refusal to permit, at the expense of the handicapped person, reasonable modifications of existing premises occupied or to be occupied by such person if such modifications may be necessary to afford such person full enjoyment of the premises except that, in the case of a rental, the landlord may where it is reasonable to do so condition permission for a modification on the renter agreeing to restore the interior of the premises to the condition that existed before the modification, reasonable wear and tear excepted;

(B) a refusal to make reasonable accommodations in rules, policies, practices, or services, when such accommodations may be necessary to afford such person equal opportunity to use and enjoy a dwelling; or

(C) in connection with the design and construction of covered multifamily dwellings for first occupancy after the date that is 30 months after September 13, 1988, a failure to design and construct those dwellings in such a manner that—

(i) the public use and common use portions of such dwellings are readily accessible to and usable by handicapped persons;

(ii) all the doors designed to allow passage into and within all premises within such dwellings are sufficiently wide to allow passage by handicapped persons in wheelchairs; and

(iii) all premises within such dwellings contain the following features of adaptive design:

(I) an accessible route into and through the dwelling;

(II) light switches, electrical outlets, thermostats, and other environmental controls in accessible locations;

(III) reinforcements in bathroom walls to allow later installation of grab bars; and

(IV) usable kitchens and bathrooms such that an individual in a wheelchair can maneuver about the space. . . .

(9) Nothing in this subsection requires that a dwelling be made available to an individual whose tenancy would constitute a direct threat to the health or safety of other individuals or whose tenancy would result in substantial physical damage to the property of others.

HILL v. COMMUNITY OF DAMIEN OF MOLOKAI

Supreme Court of New Mexico
911 P.2d 861 (N.M. 1996)

FROST, J. . . . Defendant-Appellant Community of Damien of Molokai appeals from the district court's ruling in favor of Plaintiffs-Appellees, enjoining the further use of the property . . . as a group home for individuals with AIDS. Plaintiffs-Appellees argue that the group home violates a restrictive covenant. The Community contends that the group home is a permitted use under the covenant and, alternatively, that enforcing the restrictive covenant against the group home would violate the Federal Fair Housing Act.

. . . The Community is a private, nonprofit corporation which provides homes to people with AIDS as well as other terminal illnesses. In December 1992 the Community leased the residence at 716 Rio Arriba, S.E., Albuquerque, located in a planned subdivision called Four Hills Village, for use as a group home for four individuals with AIDS. The four residents who subsequently moved into the Community's group home were unrelated, and each required some degree of in-home nursing care.

Plaintiffs-Appellees (Neighbors) live in Four Hills Village on the same dead-end street as the group home. . . . The applicable covenant provides in relevant part:

No lot shall ever be used for any purpose other than single family residence purposes. No dwelling house located thereon shall ever be used for other than single family residence purposes, nor shall any outbuildings or structure located thereon be used in a manner other than incidental to such family residence purposes. The erection or maintenance or use of any building, or the use of any lot for other purposes, including, but not restricted to such examples as stores, shops, flats, duplex houses, apartment houses, rooming houses, tourist courts, schools, churches, hospitals, and filling stations is hereby expressly prohibited.

. . . After hearing evidence at two separate hearings, the trial court held that the restrictive covenant prevented the use of the Community's house as a group home for people with AIDS and issued a permanent injunction against the Community. . . . The Community appealed. . . .

. . . In reaching its conclusion . . . the trial court . . . found . . . that the "Community uses of the residence are much closer to the uses commonly associated with health care facilities, apartment houses, and rooming houses than uses which are commonly associated with single family residences." . . .

It is undisputed that the group home is designed to provide the four individuals . . . with a traditional family structure, setting, and atmosphere, and that the individuals who reside there use the home much as would any family with a disabled family member. The four residents share communal meals. They provide support for each other socially, emotionally, and financially. They also receive spiritual guidance together from religious leaders who visit them on Tuesday evenings.

To provide for their health care needs, the residents contract with a private nursing service for health-care workers. These health-care workers do not reside at the home, and they are not affiliated with the Community in any way. . . . [These] services . . . are precisely the same services to which any disabled individual would be entitled regardless of whether he or she lived in a group home or alone in a private residence. . . .

The Community's role . . . is to provide oversight and administrative assistance. It organizes the health-care workers' schedules to ensure that a nurse is present twenty-four hours per day, and it provides oversight to ensure that the workers are doing their jobs properly. It also receives donations of food and furniture on behalf of the residents. . . . A Community worker remains at the house during the afternoon and evening but does not reside at the home. The Community, in turn, collects rent from the residents based on the amount of social security income the residents receive, and it enforces a policy of no drinking or drug use in the home.

The Community's activities . . . do not render the home a nonresidential operation such as a hospice or boarding house. As the South Carolina Supreme Court noted when faced with a similar situation involving a group home for mentally impaired individuals:

> This Court finds persuasive the reasoning of other jurisdictions which have held that the incident necessities of operating a group home such as maintaining records, filing accounting reports, managing, supervising, and providing care for individuals in exchange for monetary compensation are collateral to the prime purpose and function of a family housekeeping unit. Hence, these activities do not, in and of themselves, change the character of a residence from private to commercial. [Rhodes v. Palmetto Pathway Homes, Inc., 400 S.E.2d 484 (S.C. 1991).]

In Jackson v. Williams, 714 P.2d 1017 (Okla. 1985), the Oklahoma Supreme Court similarly concluded:

> The essential purpose of the group home is to create a normal family atmosphere dissimilar from that found in traditional institutional care for the mentally handicapped. The operation of a group home is thus distinguishable from a use that is commercial—i.e., a boarding house that provides food and lodging only—or is institutional in character.

. . . We agree . . . that the purpose of the group home is to provide the residents with a traditional family structure and atmosphere. . . .

The Neighbors also argue on appeal that the four, unrelated residents of the group home do not constitute a "single family" . . . . The Neighbors contend that . . . the term "family" encompasses only individuals related by blood or by law. We disagree.

The word "family" is not defined in the restrictive covenant and nothing in the covenant suggests that it was the intent of the framers to limit the term to a discrete family unit comprised only of individuals related by blood or by law. Accordingly, the use of the term "family" in the covenant is ambiguous. [W]e must resolve any ambiguity in the restrictive covenant in favor of the free enjoyment of the property. This rule of construction therefore militates in favor of a conclusion that the term "family" encompasses a broader group than just related individuals and against restricting the use of the property solely to a traditional nuclear family.

In addition, there are several other factors that lead us to define the term "family" as including unrelated individuals. First, the Albuquerque municipal zoning ordinance . . . includes within the definition of the term "family" "any group of not more than five [unrelated] persons living together in a dwelling." . . .

The Neighbors argue that the zoning code definition is irrelevant to the scope of the covenant. . . . However, we agree with the Colorado Court of Appeals which noted, "While [the zoning] statute has no direct applicability to private covenants, it is some indication of the type of groups that might logically, as a matter of public policy, be included within the concept of a single family." Turner v. United Palsy Ass'n, 772 P.2d 628 (Colo. Ct. App. 1988) (construing term "family" in covenant to include unrelated group home residents).

Second, there is a strong public policy in favor of including small group homes within the definition of the term "family." The federal government has expressed a clear policy in favor of removing barriers preventing individuals with physical and mental disabilities from living in group homes in residential settings and against restrictive definitions of "families" that serve to exclude congregate living arrangements for the disabled. The FHA squarely sets out this important public policy. As the court in United States v. Scott, 788 F. Supp. 1555 (D. Kan. 1992), stated, "The legislative history of the amended Fair Housing Act reflects the national policy of deinstitutionalizing disabled individuals and integrating them into the mainstream of society." The *Scott* court further noted that the Act "is intended to prohibit special restrictive covenants or other terms or conditions, or denials of service because of an individual's handicap and which . . . exclude, for example, congregate living arrangements for persons with handicaps." . . . This policy is applicable to the present case because the FHA's protections for handicapped people extend to individuals with AIDS. . . . The Developmental Disabilities Assistance and Bill of Rights Act, 42 U.S.C. § 6000 and the Rehabilitation Act of 1973, 29 U.S.C. § 701 also identify a national policy favoring persons with disabilities living independently in normal communities and opposing barriers to this goal. In New Mexico, the Developmental Disabilities Act expresses a clear state policy in favor of integrating disabled individuals into communities. . . .

Third, other jurisdictions have consistently held that restrictive covenants mandating single-family residences do not bar group homes in which the occupants live as a family unit. . . .

The individuals living in the Community's group home do operate as a family unit. Much of the activities of the residents are communal in nature. More importantly, the residents provide moral support and guidance for each other and together create an environment that assists them in living with the disease that has afflicted them. We find that the Community's group home "exhibits [the] kind of stability, permanency and functional lifestyle which is equivalent to that of the traditional family unit." We therefore conclude that the Community's use of the property as a group does not violate the Four Hills restrictive covenant.

The Neighbors strenuously argue that the covenant should be interpreted to exclude the group home because the group home's operation has an adverse impact on the neighborhood. In support of this claim, the Neighbors point to the trial court's findings that "the amount of vehicular traffic generated by [the] Community's use of the house . . . greatly exceeds what is expected in an average residential area" and that, as a result, "the character of [the] residential neighborhood relative to traffic and to parked vehicles has been significantly altered to the detriment of this residential neighborhood . . . ." . . .

However, the Neighbors fail to appreciate that the amount of traffic generated by the group home simply is not relevant to determining whether the use of the house as a group home violated the covenant in this case. . . . [T]he restrictive covenants . . . are not directed at either traffic or on-street parking. The . . . covenants . . . merely regulate the structural appearance and use of the homes. . . . [N]ot one of the fifteen provisions and numerous paragraphs . . . attempts to control the number of automobiles that a resident may accommodate on or off the property nor the amount of traffic a resident may generate.

. . . The Neighbors do suggest, however, that the volume of traffic demonstrates that the group home is not functionally equivalent to a traditional single-family residence . . . . There is no evidence that the volume of traffic . . . interferes with the structural appearance of the house in violation of the covenants. Nor does the amount of traffic or parked vehicles alter the residential nature of the group home . . . .

The Community's second contention is that the trial court erred in concluding that the FHA did not apply . . . . Although we have already agreed with the Community . . . that it did not violate the restrictive covenants, given the importance of the issues raised, we review the Community's second claim in order to correct the trial court's erroneous ruling on the legal effect of the FHA. We find that, even if we were to adopt the Neighbors' proposed definition that the term "family" only included individuals related by blood or by law, we would still find for the Community because such a restriction would violate the FHA.

[It is] apparent that the trial court believed that a facially neutral restriction which is equally applicable to both handicapped and nonhandicapped individuals does not implicate the FHA. However, this view of the FHA is incorrect. . . .

Courts have interpreted . . . [§ 3604(f)] as creating three distinct claims for violations . . . discriminatory intent, disparate impact, and reasonable accommodation. . . . The Community has raised each of these claims . . . .[3] . . .

3. The Community also raises a claim under § 3617 of the FHA which provides:

It shall be unlawful to coerce, intimidate, threaten, or interfere with any person in the exercise or enjoyment of, or on account of his having exercised or enjoyed, or on account of his having aided or encouraged any other person in the exercise or enjoyment of, any right granted or protected by section 3603, 3604, 3605, or 3606 of this title.

However, we need not address this claim given our resolution of the Community's § 3604 claims.

A discriminatory-intent claim focuses on whether a defendant has treated handicapped individuals differently from other similarly situated individuals. "To prevail on its claim . . . the plaintiff is not required to show the defendants were motivated by some purposeful, malicious desire to discriminate against HIV-infected persons." "[The] 'plaintiff need only show that the handicap of the potential residents [of a group home], a protected group under the FHA, was in some part the basis for' the policy being challenged." . . .

. . . The Community presented evidence that the Neighbors' traffic complaints began a few days after a newspaper article was published that described the group home and that the Neighbors inquired into the availability of other possible sites for the home outside of their neighborhood. The Community also identified several covenant violations by other landowners in the neighborhood that were not being prosecuted. However, this evidence is equivocal at best. Absent further evidence of an intent to enforce the covenant because of some animus toward the use of the property as a group home because the residents have AIDS, the Community's allegations are insufficient to support a claim for discriminatory enforcement of the covenant.

To demonstrate a violation of the FHA under the disparate-impact analysis, a plaintiff need only prove that the defendant's conduct actually or predictably results in discrimination or has a discriminatory effect. The court in Metropolitan Housing Development Corp. v. Village of Arlington Heights, 558 F.2d 1283, 1290 (7th Cir. 1977), *cert. denied*, 434 U.S. 1025, 54 L. Ed. 2d 772, 98 S. Ct. 752 (1978), set out four factors to be balanced when evaluating a discriminatory-impact claim: 1) how strong is plaintiff's showing of discriminatory impact; 2) is there any evidence of discriminatory intent; 3) what is the defendant's interest in taking the challenged action; 4) is the plaintiff seeking to compel the defendant to affirmatively provide housing to the handicapped or merely to restrain the defendant from interfering with individual landowners who wish to provide this housing. . . .

. . . A covenant that restricts occupancy only to related individuals or that bars group homes has a disparate impact not only on the current residents of the Community's group home who have AIDS but also on all disabled individuals who need congregate living arrangements in order to live in traditional neighborhoods and communities. . . . Of course, one possible consequence of congregate living arrangements is that they have the potential to generate more traffic than a typical nuclear family. In the present case the trial court made a finding that the increased traffic generated by the Community's group home has negatively affected the residential character of the neighborhood. However, we find it significant that the trial court rejected the Neighbors' proposed finding of fact that this additional traffic posed any increased safety hazard to the neighborhood.

Accordingly, we conclude that the negative effects of increased traffic, without any additional harms, are outweighed by the Community's interest in maintaining its congregate home for individuals with AIDS. Because the Community has proved a "disparate impact" under the FHA, the Neighbors cannot enforce the covenant against the Community. . . .

The Community's third claim under the FHA is that the Neighbors failed to make reasonable accommodations under § 3604(f)(3)(B) . . . . "'Reasonable accommodation' has been defined [to include] 'changing some rule that is generally applicable so as to make its burden less onerous on the handicapped individual.' " . . . [S]*ee also* United States v. City of Philadelphia, 838 F. Supp. 223 (E.D. Pa. 1993) (noting that cities must waive, change, or make exceptions in restrictive zoning rules to afford handicapped individuals equal opportunity to use and enjoy housing), *aff'd*, 30 F.3d 1488 (3d Cir. 1994). In *City of Philadelphia*, the court explained that "an accommodation is not reasonable (1) if it would require a fundamental alteration in the nature of a program, or (2) if it would impose undue financial or administrative burdens on the defendant." Although § 3604(f)(3)(B) is more frequently applied to restrictive zoning ordinances, it is equally applicable to restrictive covenants. . . .

The Neighbors do not suggest that allowing the group home to operate would impose any financial or administrative burdens on them. Nonenforcement of the single-family residence requirement against the Community's group home would not fundamentally alter the nature of the restrictions. . . . Accordingly, we conclude that nonenforcement of the Four Hills restrictive covenants against the Community's group home would not impose an undue hardship or burden on the Neighbors and would not interfere with the plain purpose of the covenants. . . . "A reasonable accommodation would have been not to seek enforcement of the covenant." . . .

. . . [T]he trial court's ruling is reversed and the injunction is vacated.

Notes and Questions

1. Suppose that the Neighbors had learned of the proposed sale to the Community of Damien, in time to outbid the Community and purchase it themselves. Would they have violated § 3604(f)? *See Step-By-Step, Inc. v. Lazarus*, 1997 WL 853508 (M.D. Pa. 1997) (the Act applies to a buyer who purchases a property with the intention of preventing the purchase by an entity planning to use the property as a group home for members protected under the Act); *United States v. Wagner*, 940 F. Supp. 972 (N.D. Tex. 1996) (judgment under § 3617 obtained against neighbors who filed suit to intentionally block sale of property for use as a home for mentally retarded children).

2. If the Neighbors had obtained bank financing to complete their purchase, would the bank have violated the Act? See *United States v. Hughes*, 849 F. Supp. 685 (D. Neb. 1994), which held that a bank violated the Act when it financed the purchase of a property with the intention of aiding the purchasers in keeping the home from being purchased by other buyers because the buyers were associated with mentally ill persons.

3. What is a handicap leading to protection under the Act? Section 3602(h) defines handicap as "a physical or mental impairment which substantially limits one or more of [a] person's major life activities." *City of Edmonds v. Oxford House*, 514 U.S. 725 (1995), held that a group home for recovering alcoholics is covered by the Act. Recovering drug addicts are also covered. *United States v. Southern Management Corp.*, 955 F.2d 914 (4th Cir. 1992). What about a home for battered women? Or "at risk" children?

The Parkwood Association sued Lutheran Family Services, lessee of a house in the Parkwood subdivision, claiming it violated the covenant prohibiting maintenance of any reform school, asylum, or similar institution by its operation of a temporary emergency shelter group home for children between the ages of 11 and 17 years. The shelter provided 15 to 30 days of emergency care for up to five children at a time. The target population were undisciplined, delinquent, or at-risk youth who needed emergency placement to determine needed services. The children were monitored 24 hours a day by at least two supervisors, who acted as surrogate parents. In *Parkwood Ass'n v. Capital Health Care Investors*, 514 S.E.2d 542 (N.C. Ct. App. 1999), the court held that enforcing the covenant did not limit the availability of housing on the basis of handicap.

4. Zoning that interferes with location of group homes for the handicapped may violate the FHA. In *City of Edmonds v. Oxford House*, 514 U.S. 725 (1995), the Supreme Court held that zoning provisions limiting the number of unrelated persons who can live together are not exempt from the Act as "reasonable . . . restrictions regarding the maximum number of occupants permitted to occupy a dwelling" under § 3607(b) and discriminate against group homes for the handicapped. *See* Laurie C. Malkin, *Troubles at the Doorstep: The Fair Housing Amendments Act of 1988 and Group Homes for Recovering Substance Abusers*, 144 U. Pa. L. Rev. 757, 804 (1995).

5. Does reasonable accommodation include requiring landlords to waive policies against accepting housing vouchers or cosigners for handicapped persons whose disability limits their ability to earn an income? *See* Brian R. Rosenau, Note, *Gimme Shelter: Does the Fair Housing Amendments Act of 1988 Require Accommodations for the Financial Circumstances of the Disabled?*, 46 Wm. & Mary L. Rev. 787 (2004).

6. Protections beyond those provided by the FHA are extended to disabled persons by the Americans with Disabilities Act of 1990, 42 U.S.C. §§ 12101-12213. That Act requires lessors and lessees to make newly constructed places of "public accommodation," such as restaurants, stores, and offices, accessible to disabled persons and to provide auxiliary aids and services for disabled persons. Lessors of existing places of public accommodation must remove architectural barriers to access if removal is "readily achievable." 42 U.S.C. § 12183(9).

D.   DISCRIMINATION ON THE BASIS OF FAMILIAL STATUS

§ 3602. Definitions . . .

(k) **"Familial status"** means one or more individuals (who have not attained the age of 18 years) being domiciled with—

(1) a parent or another person having legal custody of such individual or individuals;

or

(2) the designee of such parent or other person having such custody, with the written permission of such parent or other person.

The protections afforded against discrimination on the basis of familial status shall apply to any person who is pregnant or is in the process of securing legal custody of any individual who has not attained the age of 18 years.

§ 3607. Exemption . . .

(b) Numbers of occupants; housing for older persons; persons convicted of making or distributing controlled substances; good faith defense.

(1) Nothing in this subchapter limits the applicability of any reasonable local, State, or Federal restrictions regarding the maximum number of occupants permitted to occupy a dwelling. Nor does any provision in this subchapter regarding familial status apply with respect to housing for older persons.

(2) As used in this section, "housing for older persons" means housing—

(A) provided under any State or Federal program that the Secretary determines is specifically designed and operated to assist elderly persons (as defined in the State or Federal program); or

(B) intended for, and solely occupied by, persons 62 years of age or older; or

(C) intended and operated for occupancy by persons 55 years of age or older, and—

(i) at least 80 percent of the occupied units are occupied by at least one person who is 55 years of age or older;

(ii) the housing facility or community publishes and adheres to policies and procedures that demonstrate the intent required under this subparagraph; and

(iii) the housing facility or community complies with rules issued by the Secretary for verification of occupancy, which shall—

(I) provide for verification by reliable surveys and affidavits; and

(II) include examples of the types of policies and procedures relevant to a determination of compliance with the requirement of clause (ii). Such surveys and affidavits shall be admissible in administrative and judicial proceedings for the purposes of such verification. . . .

SIMOVITS v. CHANTICLEER CONDOMINIUM ASS'N

United States District Court, Northern District of Illinois, Eastern Division
933 F. Supp. 1394 (N.D. Ill. 1996)

KEYS, U.S. Magistrate J. . . . The Simovits owned a condominium in the Chanticleer Condominium Complex, an eighty-four unit housing facility located in Hinsdale, Illinois. Since 1985, the Association has had a restrictive covenant in its Declaration of Condominium Ownership, stating that "no minor children under the age of eighteen (18) years may reside in any unit purchased after the effective date of this amendment," without the prior written approval of the Board of Managers. Residents who violate the Covenant are subject to injunctive relief and a $10,000 fine. This provision is construed as barring an owner from selling a unit to anyone with children under the age of eighteen.

A large number of Chanticleer's residents are fifty-five years of age or older. However, there is no requirement that residents must be fifty-five years old or older. According to the president of the Association, Jim Londos, Chanticleer is intended for people who are "any age over 18." In fact, the last two sales of Chanticleer units have been to people under the age of fifty-five.

The Simovits purchased their Chanticleer condominium in June of 1993, for $130,000. Prior to the closing, they appeared before the Association's screening committee. The purpose of this meeting was to explain the Association's rules and regulations, including the Covenant. Mr. Simovits informed the board that he believed the Covenant to be illegal. Nonetheless, the Simovits signed a statement acknowledging the rules and agreeing to abide by them.[3]

Shortly after moving into Chanticleer, Mr. Simovits ran for a position on the Association's board. During his campaign, he published a newsletter to introduce himself to the residents of Chanticleer. In that newsletter, Mr. Simovits stated that "I like Chanticleer as an adult community and would like to keep it that way." He testified that these comments were politically motivated: "by that time, I knew that many of the residents were elderly and they liked the place as it was. I needed some votes." Mr. Simovits lost the election.

The Simovits put their Chanticleer condominium on the market in May of 1995, for $187,500. A prospective buyer . . . expressed an interest in the condominium. However, the Simovits decided not to enter into negotiations with . . . [her] because she had a minor child and they did not wish to cause any problems. After several weeks passed without any interested buyers, the Simovits were forced to lower their asking price . . . to $179,500 in July and again, in August, to $169,900. In early November, another prospective buyer . . . expressed an interest in the Simovits' condominium. . . . At that time, the condominium was on the market for $169,900. The potential buyer had three children, all under the age of eighteen.

When Mr. Simovits informed Mr. Londos that he had a potential buyer with minor children, Mr. Londos replied that the Covenant prohibited such a sale. Mr. Londos also told Ms. Swartz [the buyer's agent] about the Covenant. Ms. Swartz testified that, after she told the prospective buyer about the rule, the prospect was no longer interested . . . .

On the same day he informed Mr. Simovits that he could not sell to this prospective buyer, Mr. Londos contacted the Association's lawyer, who called the Simovits on November 8, 1995, warning them that the Covenant prohibited a sale to a person with minor children. On November 14, 1995, Mr. Londos received a letter from the Association's lawyer regarding the Simovits and the questionable legality of the Covenant. The letter warned Mr. Londos that discriminating against families with children is illegal. The letter stated that the statutory exemptions to the FHA are "strictly construed" and that "unless Chanticleer can produce hard evidence that the community meets these narrowly construed exemptions, the financial liability to Chanticleer could be substantial." Mr. Londos shared the contents of this letter with the Association's board members on the day he received it. Despite the warnings in the letter, the Association decided to continue to prevent the Simovits from selling to a buyer with minor children.

Immediately after contacting the Association's lawyer in early November, Mr. Londos began to compile a list of all the Chanticleer residents' ages to determine the percentage of residents who were fifty-five years of age or older. This

---

3.   Mr. Simovits testified that his lawyer informed him that, despite his belief regarding the illegality of the Covenant, he had to sign this statement in order to finalize the closing on the condominium.

was the first time the Association had conducted a survey of this nature. In compiling the survey, Mr. Londos speculated as to the residents' ages. He testified that he "had a pretty good idea . . . in [his] head who was of what age." He did not take any steps to verify these presumptions. Consequently, the list contained inaccuracies.

In preparation for the hearing . . . , Mr. Londos conducted another similar survey. In this . . . survey, . . . Mr. Londos used signed affidavits to verify the residents' ages. However, he did not obtain affidavits from all of Chanticleer's residents. He resorted to guessing the ages of those residents who did not submit an affidavit.[7]

On April 15, 1996, the Simovits entered into a contract to sell their condominium to . . . a couple without children, for $145,000. However, the buyers were young, and thus wanted the Covenant waived. The Association agreed to waive it, and the deal closed on April 30, 1996.

The Simovits allege that, as a result of the Covenant, they lost numerous opportunities to sell their condominium at a higher price. They enlisted HOPE Fair Housing Center, a not-for-profit agency dedicated to promoting equal opportunity housing, to challenge the legality of the Covenant.

The Simovits brought suit for the economic damages that they suffered as a result of the Covenant. They allege that the Covenant diminished the value of their condominium by $30,000. . . . [T]he Simovits [also] allege that . . . [b]ecause the Covenant delayed the sale of their condominium, . . . they paid an extra $3,560.15 in mortgage payments. Moreover, the Simovits allege that they were emotionally injured as a result of the enforcement of the Covenant. Mr. Simovits testified to a special sensitivity to discrimination due to events in his past. Mrs. Simovits testified that her husband suffered from chest and stomach pains, as well as sleeplessness, as a result of their inability to sell the condominium. Mrs. Simovits testified that she suffered from extreme anxiety, headaches, and abdominal distress due to their inability to sell. Mr. and Mrs. Simovits seek $10,000 each in emotional injury damages.

. . . HOPE is suing for the time and money it devoted to helping the Simovits. HOPE alleges that it diverted its time and resources away from housing counseling in order to help the Simovits pursue this action against the Association. According to . . . HOPE's executive director, HOPE spent $2,806 in out-of-pocket expenses and $4,424 in staff time on the Simovits' case. Additionally, HOPE asks for $35,000 in monitoring and compliance expenses.

The Simovits and HOPE both seek punitive damages in the amount of $10,000 from the Association. In addition, the Simovits and HOPE seek a 5 year injunction against the Association, requiring them to permit residency at Chanticleer regardless of family status.

The following issues are before the Court: (1) whether the Simovits and/ or HOPE have standing to sue under the FHA; (2) whether the Association is liable under the FHA for discrimination based on familial status; (3) whether the Association's defenses to liability are viable; and (4) if the Court finds the

---

7.   Mr. Londos' testimony regarding how he determined the ages of those residents who did not submit an affidavit illustrates the speculative nature of these surveys. When asked how he knew one resident was over the age of fifty-five, Mr. Londos stated that "I have seen her at the meetings. She is definitely over 55."

Association liable and its defenses untenable, what remedies are available to the Simovits and HOPE.

I. STANDING

The Association argues that the Simovits lack standing in this case because they were not the victims of discrimination. However, to have standing to sue under the FHA, the Simovits need not be victims of discrimination. *See* Gladstone Realtors v. Village of Bellwood, 441 U.S. 91 (1979) (Caucasian residents have standing under FHA to challenge racial discrimination . . . in their neighborhood).

The Simovits' pleadings satisfy the FHA's permissive standing requirements. The Simovits allege that they lost opportunities to sell their condominium at a price higher than the $145,000 [they] obtained . . . . Also, the Simovits allege that they suffered financial strain due to the additional mortgage payments they incurred. . . .

The Association alleges that the Simovits are not in the class of people covered by HOPE's mission statement because the Simovits endorsed the Covenant [and] therefore, . . . HOPE lacks standing to sue in this case. However, "the only injury that need be shown to confer standing on a fair-housing agency is deflection of the agency's time and money from counseling to legal efforts directed against discrimination." . . .

II. LIABILITY

The question of the Association's liability under the FHA . . . turns on whether or not Chanticleer meets the exemption for "housing for older persons" in § 3607(b)(2) of the FHA. One category of "housing for older persons" is "housing intended and operated for occupancy by persons 55 years and older."

Prior to December 28, 1995, the FHA required the following to meet the "55 years and older" exemption: (1) the facility has significant facilities and services specifically designed to meet the physical and social needs of older persons; (2) at least eighty percent of the units are occupied by one person age fifty-five or over; and (3) the complex publishes and adheres to policies which demonstrate an intent to provide housing for persons age fifty-five and older.

However, on December 28, 1995, Congress eliminated this "significant facilities and services" requirement. . . . Under the Housing for Older Persons Act of 1995, the following are the requirements to qualify as "age 55 years and older" housing: (1) at least eighty percent of the occupied units are occupied by at least one person who is fifty-five years of age or older; (2) the housing facility publishes and adheres to policies and procedures that demonstrate the intent to provide housing for persons age fifty-five or older; and (3) the housing facility complies with HUD rules and regulations for verification of occupancy. The statute requires that the defendant meet all of the above requirements to qualify for the exemption. In addition, the defendant has the burden of proving that it meets the above requirements. . . .

. . . The Association has failed to provide reliable evidence that, since 1985, eighty percent of the occupied dwellings at Chanticleer have had at least one person fifty-five years of age or older in residence. . . . Mr. Londos merely estimated the ages of the Chanticleer residents, neglecting to verify them by using affidavits or other signed statements. . . . Moreover, the circumstances surrounding the taking of this survey—upon the advice of counsel in response to Mr. Simovits' threat to file a lawsuit—makes it clear that, even if the eighty percent requirement were met, it was merely fortuitous and is not indicative of any intent to provide housing for persons age fifty-five or older. . . .

. . . The Association freely admits that it does not publish and adhere to policies and procedures that demonstrate an intent to provide housing for persons aged fifty-five years or older.[18] Thus, the Association has, in fact, conceded its liability under the FHA, since qualification for the exemption requires that all three of its requirements be met. . . .

III.　DEFENSES

[Discussion of court's rejection of the Association's arguments that the Simovits should be barred from enforcing their rights under the FHA by the equitable defenses of estoppel, laches, unclean hands, and waiver omitted.—Eds.]

IV.　REMEDIES

The FHA provides that, where a defendant has engaged in a discriminatory housing practice, "the court may award to the plaintiff actual and punitive damages . . . and as the court deems appropriate . . . any permanent or temporary injunction." § 3613(c)(1).

A.　*Economic Damages.*

While all three experts are professional real estate appraisers, and all valued the Simovits' condominium the same, with the Covenant, their differences of opinion as to whether and to what extent the Covenant has an impact on the value of the property is inexplicable and irreconcilable and can be attributable only to their alignments with the respective parties. The Defendant's experts' opinion that the Covenant has no impact on the value of the units simply defies logic. On the other hand, Plaintiffs' expert's opinion that the Covenant decreases the value of the property by $30,000 appears excessive. The Court discredits Defendant's experts in this regard and credits plaintiff's expert only to the extent that the Covenant had some adverse impact on the value of the property. The Court, then, is left with the necessity of determining a non-arbitrary figure regarding the diminution in value of the property as a result of the Covenant. . . . [Valuation discussion omitted.]

18.　The Association argues that it is in "effective compliance" with this prong of the statute because Chanticleer has a "longstanding reputation" in the community as a facility for older persons. However, the "exemptions from the Fair Housing Act are to be construed narrowly, in recognition of the important goal of preventing housing discrimination." . . . The Association's argument for "effective compliance" directly conflicts with this principle of narrow construction.

The Simovits are entitled to the difference between the amount at which they sold their property, $145,000, and what they reasonably could have realized but for the Covenant, $157,500. Accordingly, they are awarded $12,500 in damages as compensation for the reduction in value of their condominium.

The Covenant created a delay in selling the condominium . . . , causing the Simovits to incur $3,560.15 in additional mortgage obligations. [B]ut for the Covenant, the Simovits would not have incurred these costs. Thus, the Simovits are entitled to the $3,560.15 . . . .

HOPE seeks recovery of $7,230 in economic losses stemming from the time and resources it devoted to helping the Simovits. The Court awards these damages. The Court, however, declines to award the $35,000 in monitoring and compliance costs sought by HOPE. The goals of monitoring the Association can be achieved through more equitable means, as set forth in the Court's Order below.

B. Emotional Distress Damages.

Mr. and Mrs. Simovits seek $10,000 each in emotional injury damages. In order for the Simovits to recover for emotional injuries, a causal connection must exist between their alleged injuries and the Association's discriminatory conduct. . . . [The Court finds] the Simovits suffered, at most, only indirect effects of the "no children" policy; they were not denied housing on the basis of their familial status. . . . [T]he Record does not support an award for emotional damages . . . .

C. Punitive Damages.

The Simovits and HOPE seek $10,000 each (for a total of $20,000) in punitive damages from the Association. Under § 3613(c)(1) of the FHA, the court may award punitive damages to a prevailing party in a housing discrimination case. . . . The Record in this case contains overwhelming evidence of the Association's reckless disregard for the Simovits' and HOPE's rights. Most significant is the Association's failure to heed the warnings of its lawyer. Despite these warnings, the Association persisted in enforcing the Covenant . . . . The Minutes of the Association's November 14, 1995 Board of Managers' meeting show that this was a calculated gamble. Moreover, the Association republished its resident directory containing the rules and regulations, including the Covenant, to all residents in March, 1996. This callous and reckless disregard for the Simovits' rights entitles them to punitive damages.

Likewise, the Association showed a reckless disregard for HOPE's rights. The Association's continued publication and enforcement of the Covenant, despite warnings of the Covenant's illegality, directly conflicted with HOPE's mission of providing equal housing opportunities to the people of DuPage County. This reckless disregard for HOPE's rights entitles them to punitive damages.

There is no formula for determining the amount of punitive damages; however, the size of the award should be sufficient to "'punish [the defendant] for his outrageous conduct and to deter him and others like him from similar conduct in the future.'" At the end of 1995, the Association had a cash balance of $44,000.[25] A punitive award of $20,000, approximately one-half of its cash reserves, certainly serves the goals of punishment and deterrence. Moreover, a $20,000 punitive award is not excessive; the Seventh Circuit has affirmed even larger punitive awards in past housing discrimination cases.[26] Thus, a $10,000 award to the Simovits and another $10,000 award to HOPE constitute reasonable punitive awards.

D. Injunctive Relief.

Section 3613(c)(1) also authorizes the Court to order injunctive relief. The testimony herein shows that the Association has no intention of discontinuing the enforcement of the Covenant unless enjoined and that an injunction is necessary to redress its "long-standing reputation . . . within the community as a community for older persons." The Court is unaware of the pervasiveness of this reputation; however, it is certain that, since the enactment of the Covenant in 1985, families with children have been wrongfully denied the opportunity to live at Chanticleer. Although this type of harm can not be cured by monetary awards alone, the Court has adequate flexibility in fashioning equitable relief to remedy the effects of the Association's discrimination.

CONCLUSION

The Court finds that the Association is liable for discrimination based on familial status under the FHA. Therefore, the Association shall comply with the following:

ORDER: IT IS HEREBY ORDERED THAT:

1. By the close of business on September 6, 1996, the Association shall pay the Simovits $26,060.15 in damages. . . .

3. From August 1, 1996 through August 1, 1999, the Association is hereby enjoined from attempting to qualify for any of the "housing for older persons" exemptions provided for in § 3607(b)(2) of the FHA.

4. The Association shall, no later than August 15, 1996, remove from its bylaws, rules, regulations and/or Declaration of Condominium Ownership any policies that discriminate against families with children. Written notification of such action shall be sent to all owners and tenants of units at Chanticleer and to HOPE.

5. By the close of business on the first Friday of January, beginning January 3, 1997, and continuing through January 7, 2000, the Association shall submit annual reports to HOPE containing the following information:

a. A copy of every person's application for the Association's approval to purchase at Chanticleer during the prior year, and a statement indicating the

---

25. According to the Association's audited balance sheet as of December 31, 1995, it had $44,180 in its Replacement Fund. The audit report states that this fund is used to accumulate resources for future repairs and replacements.

26. In Phillips v. Hunter Trails Comm. Ass'n, 685 F.2d 184, 191 (7th Cir. 1982), the Seventh Circuit affirmed a punitive award of $100,000 to a married couple.

person's name and familial status, whether that person was rejected or accepted, the date on which the person was notified of acceptance or rejection, and, if rejected, the reason for such rejection; and

b. Current occupancy statistics of Chanticleer, indicating the ages of all residents occupying each of the units at Chanticleer.

6. By the close of business on August 26, 1996, the Association shall send written notice, to all real estate brokerage firms listed in the Hinsdale Yellow Pages, consisting of a statement explaining that the Association's discriminatory policies are no longer in effect and that families with children are welcome to reside at Chanticleer. A copy of each letter shall also be sent to HOPE.

Notes and Questions

1. In an apartment complex, do rules that require children to be supervised by a responsible adult at all times and prohibit children in the pool area at any time unless accompanied by a parent or legal guardian illegally discriminate on the basis of family status? *See Iniestra v. Cliff Warren Investments, Inc.,* 886 F. Supp. 2d 1161 (C.D. Cal. 2012) (yes, even if the underlying safety and noise concerns were compelling business necessities, the rules are not the least restrictive means of achieving the goals).

2. Does an ad like the following violate the statute?

Great bachelor pad . . . Our one bedroom apartments are a great bachelor pad for any single man looking to hook up.

See Miami Valley Fair Housing Center, Inc. v. Connor Group, 725 F.3d 571 (6th Cir. 2013) (no).

E.   DISCRIMINATION ON THE BASIS OF MARITAL STATUS AND SEXUAL ORIENTATION

Since neither marital status nor sexual orientation is a prohibited basis of discrimination under the Federal Fair Housing Act, or § 1982 of the Civil Rights Act, cases in this area arise under state or local laws. Federal law does come into play, however, when a property owner claims that enforcement of the state law deprives her of rights protected by the federal constitution.

SMITH v. FAIR EMPLOYMENT AND HOUSING COMMISSION

Supreme Court of California
913 P.2d 909 (Cal. 1996)

WERDEGAR, J. The California Fair Employment and Housing Act . . . (FEHA) declares it to be "unlawful . . . [f]or the owner of any housing accommodation to discriminate against any person because of the . . . marital status . . . of that person" . . . .

[Evelyn Smith owns and leases four rental units located in two duplexes in Chico, California. She is a Christian who refused to rent to unmarried couples because she believes that sex outside marriage is sinful, and that if she permits people to engage in extramarital sex in her apartments, God will prevent her from meeting her deceased husband in the hereafter. When Gail Randall and Kenneth Phillips inquired about a unit Smith had advertised for rent, she told them she did not rent to unmarried couples and asked whether they were married. They lied, and Randall signed her name as "Gail Phillips" on the lease application and the lease. On the day the lease was signed, Randall called Smith to ask if she doubted that they were married and wanted to see their marriage license. Smith said no. However, later that same day, Phillips called back and told Smith that they weren't married. Smith said she could not rent to them and returned their deposit.]

Randall and Phillips filed separate complaints against Smith with the [Fair Employment and Housing Commission] . . . [which] issued two accusations . . . [alleging that] Smith had violated Government Code section 12955,[1] Civil Code section 51 (the Unruh Civil Rights Act),[2] and Government Code section 12948.[3] . . .

The commission . . . [subsequently] issued its decision in favor of Randall and Phillips. Smith sought review of the commission's decision by petition for writ of mandate. . . . The Court of Appeal reversed. . . . We granted review.

A. Does FEHA Prohibit Housing Discrimination Against Unmarried Couples?

. . . Smith argues "the statutory ban on marital status discrimination does not include [unmarried] cohabiting couples." The argument lacks merit. . . . The usual and ordinary meaning of the words "marital status," as applied to two prospective tenants, is that a landlord may not ask them whether they are married or refuse to rent to them because they are, or are not. Smith asked whether Randall and Phillips were married and refused to rent to them because they were not. . . .

Various *amici curiae* argue that Smith's refusal to rent to Randall and Phillips does not violate FEHA because it was based on Smith's assumptions about their

---

1. . . . It shall be unlawful:

 (a) For the owner of any housing accommodation to discriminate against any person because of the race, color, religion, sex, marital status, national origin, ancestry, familial status, or disability of that person.
 (b) For the owner of any housing accommodation to make or to cause to be made any written or oral inquiry concerning the race, color, religion, sex, marital status, national origin, ancestry, familial status, or disability of any person seeking to purchase, rent or lease any housing accommodation. . . .

2. . . . "All persons within the jurisdiction of this state are free and equal, and no matter what their sex, race, color, religion, ancestry, national origin, or disability are entitled to the full and equal accommodations, advantages, facilities, privileges, or services in all business establishments of every kind whatsoever."

3. "It shall be an unlawful practice . . . to deny or to aid, incite, or conspire in the denial of the rights created by Section 51 or 51.7 of the Civil Code."

sexual conduct rather than their marital status. The high courts of Alaska and Massachusetts recently rejected similar arguments. (Swanner v. Anchorage Equal Rights Com'n (Alaska 1994) 874 P.2d 274; Attorney General v. Desilets (Mass. 1994) 636 N.E.2d 233.) Interpreting a statute analogous to FEHA, the court in *Swanner* explained its conclusion . . . : a landlord "cannot reasonably claim that he does not rent or show property to cohabiting couples based on their conduct (living together outside of marriage) and not their marital status when their marital status (unmarried) is what makes their conduct immoral in his opinion." The opinion of the Supreme Judicial Court of Massachusetts . . . is to the same effect.

Smith argued before the commission, and various *amici curiae* argue here, that Government Code section 12955 can be read as protecting single, married, widowed, and divorced individuals rather than unmarried couples. However, to acknowledge the statute protects the former, as it undoubtedly does, in no way tends to show it does not also protect the latter. The statutory language banning discrimination based on "marital status" naturally carries both meanings.

Our own Legislature's use of the words "marital status" in other statutes confirms this. Where the Legislature has, in some particular context, wished to treat married and unmarried couples identically, it has chosen to convey that idea by requiring equal treatment regardless of "marital status." . . .

The commission has interpreted Government Code section 12955 to protect unmarried couples since 1980, when FEHA was enacted. . . . Final responsibility for interpreting the law rests with the courts rather than with administrative agencies. . . . Still, the commission's interpretation of FEHA is entitled to consideration because the commission is the agency charged with the statute's administration. . . .

The language prohibiting discrimination in housing accommodations "because of . . . marital status" derives from the Rumford Fair Housing Act of 1963 . . . which FEHA superseded. As originally enacted, the Rumford Act did not refer to "marital status." The Legislature added those words in 1975. . . .

While the 1975 amendment was under consideration, representatives of the Attorney General's Office advised the Legislature in hearings that one of its effects would be to override prior law . . . which the Attorney General had interpreted as permitting licensed realtors acting as property managers to select tenants "on the basis of a blood or marital relationship between the prospective occupants or a lack of such relationship . . . ." . . .

That the Legislature understood the 1975 amendment would protect unmarried cohabitants can also be inferred from the text of the amendment. An exception to the amendment, which continues in FEHA . . . , expressly permitted "any postsecondary educational institution" to provide "housing accommodations reserved for either male or female students . . . or . . . married students . . . ." The exception had no apparent purpose unless the amendment, without the exception, would have required educational institutions to permit unmarried male and female students to live together, or prevented discrimination in favor of married students. . . .

. . . Some of the cases Smith cites are of little value for our purposes. The courts in Illinois, Minnesota, and Washington had the burden of reconciling statutes barring discrimination because of "marital status" with other statutes criminalizing private sexual conduct between consenting adults. . . . We do not labor under the same burden.[10] In 1975, a few months before the Legislature amended the Rumford Act to prohibit housing discrimination because of "marital status," the Legislature repealed the laws criminalizing private, sexual conduct between consenting adults. . . .

Smith also cites an opinion by the high court of Wisconsin, in which the court declared a county ordinance similar to FEHA "invalid to the extent that it [sought] to protect 'cohabitants' . . . ." (County of Dane v. Norman (Wis. 1993) 497 N.W.2d 714.) The court reasoned the county had no power to enact statutes "inconsistent with the public policy of [Wisconsin,] which seeks to promote the stability of marriage and family." We have no analogous power to invalidate a state statute . . . on nonconstitutional grounds. The argument is illogical in any event: One can recognize marriage as laudable, or even as favored, while still extending protection against housing discrimination to persons who do not enjoy that status.

A lower court in Maryland (Prince George's County v. Greenbelt Homes, Inc. (1981) 431 A.2d 745) did interpret a statutory ban on "marital status" discrimination as not protecting unmarried couples. The court permitted a housing association to refuse to approve the sale of a house to an unmarried couple. The court reasoned that "neither complainant (each of whom was 'single,' 'unmarried') was denied membership individually because of his or her individual marital status. While each separately had a marital status, collectively they did not." The Maryland court's reasoning cannot easily be applied to California law. . . .

Ultimately, the question must be answered as a matter of California law. In view of Government Code section 12955's language, its uniform and longstanding interpretation by the commission and the courts, and its legislative history, we conclude that FEHA does protect unmarried cohabitants against housing discrimination.[11]

B.   Does Federal or State Law Require the State to Exempt Smith from FEHA to Avoid Burdening Her Religious Exercise?

Having concluded that Smith violated FEHA, we must now determine whether the state is required to exempt her from that law to avoid burdening her exercise of religious freedom. Although the question has arisen in three other states, only the Supreme Court of Alaska has decided it. That court rejected the landlord's claim to an exemption. (Swanner v. Anchorage Equal Rights Com'n, *supra, cert. den.* (1994) 115 S. Ct. 460.) . . .

Smith's claim to an exemption implicates three areas of law: the First Amendment to the United States Constitution, the Religious Freedom

---

10.   Were we to adopt Smith's interpretation of Government Code section 12955, however, we would need to reconcile it, if possible, with the holding that persons in this state have a constitutional right to live with others who are not related by blood, marriage, or adoption, as an aspect of the right to privacy. (City of Santa Barbara v. Adamson (1980) 27 Cal. 3d 123, 130-137, 164 Cal. Rptr. 539, 610 P.2d 436.)

11.   In view of the conclusion that FEHA does prohibit discrimination against unmarried couples, there is a proper basis for the commission's decision. It is, therefore, unnecessary to decide whether the Unruh Civil Rights Act (Civ. Code, § 51) has the same effect. . . .

Restoration Act of 1993 (42 U.S.C. §§ 2000bb *et seq.*), and article I, section 4, of the California Constitution. We consider each in turn.

1.   *The First Amendment*

The First Amendment does not support Smith's claim. Her religion may not permit her to rent to unmarried cohabitants, but "the right of free exercise does not relieve an individual of the obligation to comply with a 'valid and neutral law of general applicability on the ground that the law proscribes (or prescribes) conduct that his religion prescribes (or proscribes).'" (Employment Division v. Smith (1990) 494 U.S. 872, quoting United States v. Lee (1982) 455 U.S. 252.) The statutory prohibition against discrimination because of marital status is a law both generally applicable and neutral towards religion. The law is generally applicable in that it prohibits all discrimination without reference to motivation. The law is neutral in that its object is to prohibit discrimination irrespective of reason, not because it is undertaken for religious reasons. Consequently, section 12955 does not violate the free exercise clause as interpreted in Employment Division v. Smith.

In 1990, in the case of Employment Division v. Smith, the high court abandoned balancing as a way of adjudicating religiously motivated challenges to generally applicable laws. The case was brought by employees of a private drug rehabilitation program, who were fired from their jobs and denied state unemployment benefits because they had used the drug peyote for sacramental purposes at a ceremony of the Native American Church. The employees challenged the denial of benefits as a violation of the free exercise clause. The Oregon Supreme Court ordered the benefits reinstated. The court reasoned the state's interest in preserving the financial integrity of the unemployment compensation fund did not outweigh the burden on the plaintiffs' religious exercise.

The United States Supreme Court reversed. [T]he court explained: "We have never held that an individual's religious beliefs excuse him from compliance with an otherwise valid law prohibiting conduct that the State is free to regulate." . . .

In 1993, Congress restored the "compelling interest" test as a matter of statutory law by enacting the Religious Freedom Restoration Act. . . .

Employment Division v. Smith disposes of Smith's claim under the free exercise clause of the federal Constitution. . . .

The Religious Freedom Restoration Act[5]

The Religious Freedom Restoration Act (RFRA) provides that "[g]overnment shall not substantially burden a person's exercise of religion even if the burden results from a rule of general applicability, except as provided in subdivision (b)." Under subdivision (b), "[g]overnment may substantially burden a person's exercise of religion only if it demonstrates that application of the burden to the

---

5.   Although the Supreme Court subsequently held RFRA's application to the states unconstitutional in Boerne v. Flores, 521 U.S. 507 (1997), finding that Congress exceeded its power under § 5 of the Fourteenth Amendment, this discussion remains relevant because of the court's assumption that the California Constitution imposes the same standard as RFRA.—Eds.

person (1) is in furtherance of a compelling governmental interest; and (2) is the least restrictive means of furthering that compelling governmental interest."

Read together, RFRA, the decisions interpreting RFRA, and the decisions interpreting the free exercise clause prior to *Employment Division v. Smith* prescribe the following analysis for cases in which a neutral, generally applicable law is claimed to burden the exercise of religion: (1) The burden must fall on a religious belief rather than on a philosophy or a way of life. (2) The burdened religious belief must be sincerely held. (3) The plaintiff must prove the burden is substantial or, in other words, legally significant. (4) If all of the foregoing are true, the government must "demonstrate . . . that application of the burden to the person . . . is in furtherance of a compelling governmental interest; and . . . is the least restrictive means of furthering that compelling governmental interest." . . .

Randall, Phillips, and various *amici curiae* urge us to add a preliminary step to this analysis by asking, first, whether the activity subject to the challenged law constitutes the exercise of religion. The renting of apartments does not, they argue, and for that reason is not entitled to protection under RFRA.

We cannot dispose of Smith's claim so easily. The religious practice FEHA is alleged to burden is not the renting of apartments, but Smith's practice of not committing the sin she believes inheres in renting to unmarried cohabitants. That the alleged burden is indirect is irrelevant . . . . While the renting of apartments may not constitute the exercise of religion, if Smith claims the laws regulating that activity indirectly coerce her to violate her religious beliefs, we cannot avoid testing her claim under . . . RFRA. . . .

That Smith's Christian beliefs are religious and that she sincerely holds them is not seriously in question. An effort was made in the hearing before the commission to show that Smith's church, the Presbyterian Church, U.S.A., does not share her view that renting to unmarried couples is a sin. That such testimony might help to evaluate a person's sincerity is not inconceivable. "One can, of course, imagine an asserted claim so bizarre, so clearly nonreligious in motivation, as not to be entitled to protection under the Free Exercise Clause. . . ." (Thomas v. Review Board, [450 U.S. 707 (1981)] . . . .) However, "religious beliefs need not be acceptable, logical, consistent, or comprehensible to others in order to merit First Amendment protection." Instead, all that is necessary to establish the required sincerity is "an honest conviction" that one's religion prohibits the conduct required by law. We therefore continue with the required analysis.

The parties disagree on the question whether Government Code § 12955 . . . substantially burdens the exercise of her religion. The answer to the question is critical. . . . [U]nless the challenged law imposes a substantial burden, the government need not demonstrate a compelling interest justifying the law or show that the law is the least restrictive means to further the interest. . . .

One can imagine an accommodation doctrine, such as that which RFRA embodies, without the threshold requirement of a substantial burden. The resulting law would look something like this: When a person understood his or her religious beliefs as demanding that an activity be conducted in a particular way, and when the state required the activity to be conducted in a different way, the state would in every such instance be obliged to justify its law with a compelling interest and a showing that the law represented the least restrictive means to further the interest. Because religious beliefs can affect all aspects of life, and because each person may define his or her own religious beliefs, even if those beliefs are not "acceptable, logical, consistent, or comprehensible to others"

. . . to abandon the threshold requirement of a substantial burden would considerably alter the nature and efficacy of legal duties in our constitutional system: Each person would unilaterally decide, in each of the multitude of situations affected by state regulation, which laws to obey and which to ignore. This would turn on its head the ordinary assumption that legislation on economic and social matters need only have a rational basis; instead, any declaration of sincerely held religious belief, however "[in]comprehensible" . . . would require the state to justify any conflicting law under the compelling interest standard or forego its uniform enforcement.

. . . While the cases decided before *Smith* do provide guidance on the question of what constitutes a substantial burden, they do not offer a generally applicable definition . . . or a generally applicable test. . . . Instead, the pre-*Smith* cases disclose a case-by-case approach to the problem of deciding whether the government should be obliged to justify a challenged law under the compelling interest test. . . .

The decision in Sherbert v. Verner [374 U.S. 398 (1963)] is the first of a line of cases holding that a state may not refuse to pay unemployment compensation to a claimant who quit a job for religious reasons. . . . The Supreme Court has articulated the rule of these cases as follows: Where the state conditions receipt of an important benefit upon conduct proscribed by a religious faith, or where it denies such a benefit because of conduct mandated by religious belief, thereby putting substantial pressure on an adherent to modify his behavior and to violate his beliefs, a burden upon religion exists. . . .

This case . . . differs from the unemployment-compensation cases in two significant respects. First, the degree of compulsion involved is markedly greater in the unemployment-compensation cases than in the case before us. In the former instance, one can avoid the conflict between the law and one's beliefs about the Sabbath only by quitting work and foregoing compensation. To do so, however, is not a realistic solution for someone who lives on the wages earned through personal labor. In contrast, one who earns a living through the return on capital invested in rental properties can, if she does not wish to comply with an antidiscrimination law that conflicts with her religious beliefs, avoid the conflict, without threatening her livelihood, by selling her units and redeploying the capital in other investments.

Second, the landlord's request for an accommodation in the case before us has a serious impact on the rights and interests of third parties. This factor was not present in the unemployment-compensation cases. Because Smith is involved in a commercial enterprise, the state cannot exempt her from the antidiscrimination provisions of FEHA without affecting the members of the public she encounters in the course of her business. . . . [T]o permit Smith to discriminate would sacrifice the rights of her prospective tenants to have equal access to public accommodations and their legal and dignity interests in freedom from discrimination based on personal characteristics. (*Cf.* Heart of Atlanta Motel, Inc. v. United States (1964) 379 U.S. 241, 250 ["the fundamental object of [federal civil rights legislation] was to vindicate 'the deprivation of personal dignity that surely accompanies denials of equal access to public establishments.'"].) No comparable impairment of the rights of third parties is entailed in requiring the state to pay unemployment compensation to a worker who quits a job that conflicts with his or her religious beliefs. Even if one were to postulate that the rulings in Sherbert v. Verner and its progeny marginally increased the costs to employers of unemployment insurance, the resulting impact on third parties is still far more attenuated than the impact on the prospective tenants in the case before us.

. . . Wisconsin v. Yoder, [406 U.S. 205 (1972)] is also distinguishable. In *Yoder*, a law requiring all children to attend public high school burdened the religious exercise of Amish parents; the parent's beliefs required them to educate their children at home after the eighth grade, a formative period of life, in order to protect their children from worldly influences and teach them the values and skills necessary for integration into the Amish religious community. To find the burden substantial was reasonable since the law was wholly incompatible with the Amish beliefs: Adolescence comes only once; if spent in the public schools, the harm to the Amish way of life is permanent. In contrast, the landlord in this case does not claim that her religious beliefs require her to rent apartments; the religious injunction is simply that she not rent to unmarried couples. No religious exercise is burdened if she follows the alternative course of placing her capital in another investment.

The proposition that a burden on religion is not substantial if one can avoid it without violating one's religious beliefs is not of itself, we emphasize, a generally applicable test for identifying substantial burdens. As a factor to consider, however, the proposition finds support in cases decided before Employment Division v. Smith. Such was the reasoning, for example, in Tony & Susan Alamo Foundation v. Secretary of Labor, [471 U.S. 290 (1985)]. In that case, the employees of a religious foundation, who worked for room and board, objected on religious grounds to receiving the monetary wages required by the Fair Labor Standards Act . . . . The court rejected the claim with this reasoning: "It is virtually self-evident that the Free Exercise Clause does not require an exemption from a governmental program unless, at a minimum, inclusion in the program actually burdens the claimant's freedom to exercise religious rights. . . . Even if the Foundation were to pay wages in cash, or if the associates' beliefs precluded them from accepting the statutory amount, there is nothing in the Act to prevent the associates from returning the amounts to the Foundation, provided that they do so voluntarily. . . .

The decision in Braunfeld v. Brown, [366 U.S. 599 (1961)], is to the same effect. In that case, Orthodox Jewish shopkeepers, who observed Saturday as the Sabbath, challenged a law requiring shops to close on Sunday. The shopkeepers, who thus could open for business only five days a week, argued the law placed them at a serious economic disadvantage as compared to other merchants whose religious beliefs permitted them to conduct business six days a week. In this way, they argued, the law coerced them to violate their beliefs.

The United States Supreme Court rejected the shopkeepers' claim. The court reasoned that the law "d[id] not make unlawful any religious practices of [the shopkeepers]; the Sunday law simply regulates a secular activity and, as applied to appellants, operates so as to make the practice of their religious beliefs more expensive." . . . As the high court recognized, for the shopkeepers . . . to have avoided the conflict between their religious beliefs and the Sunday-closing law by "engaging in some other commercial activity" might well have entailed an economic cost. Likewise, we may assume that for the landlord in this case to avoid the conflict between FEHA and her religious beliefs by shifting her capital from rental units to another investment would also entail a cost. An economic cost, however, does not equate to a substantial burden for purposes of the free exercise clause. . . .

The proposition that an incidental burden on religious exercise is not substantial if it can be described as simply making religious exercise more expensive finds support in several cases in addition to those already cited. This factor, like the ability of a person to avoid a conflict between law and beliefs without violating those beliefs . . . , may not constitute a generally applicable test for identifying substantial burdens. Nevertheless, the factor is one that courts under the relevant case law may properly consider. . . .

One last factor that is relevant here, to which we have already alluded, also properly informs the inquiry into whether an asserted burden on religion is substantial. This is whether the granting of an accommodation would detrimentally affect the rights of third parties. The parties have not brought to our attention a single case in which the Supreme Court exempted a religious objector from the operation of a general law when the court also recognized that the exemption would detrimentally affect the rights of third parties. . . . The exemption from FEHA Smith seeks can be granted only by completely sacrificing the rights of the prospective tenants. . . . To say that the prospective tenants may rent elsewhere is to deny them the full choice of available housing accommodations enjoyed by others in the rental market. . . . [It] is also to deny them the right to be treated equally by commercial enterprises; this dignity interest is impaired by even one landlord's refusal to rent, whether or not the prospective tenants eventually find housing elsewhere. In short, were we to grant the requested accommodation, Smith would have more freedom and greater protection for her own rights and interests, while Phillips and Randall would have less freedom and less protection. . . .

This set of facts does not, under the relevant case law, support Smith's argument that requiring her to comply with FEHA's antidiscrimination provisions substantially burdens her religious exercise. Accordingly, we have no occasion to determine whether application of the statute to her furthers a compelling state interest or is the least restrictive means to further such an interest.[21] In concluding Government Code § 12955 does substantially burden Smith's religious exercise, the Court of Appeal erred.

The California Constitution

The last question we must address is whether the California Constitution exempts Smith from the requirements of FEHA. The pertinent constitutional provision that particularly concerns us is article I, section 4. As relevant here, the section provides: "Free exercise and enjoyment of religion without discrimination or preference are guaranteed. This liberty of conscience does not excuse acts that are licentious or inconsistent with the peace or safety of the State."

California courts have typically construed [this] provision to afford the same protection for religious exercise as the federal Constitution before Employment Division v. Smith. The analysis that disposes of Smith's claim under RFRA also disposes of her claim under article I, section 4, of the state Constitution. . . .

The judgment of the Court of Appeal . . . is reversed.

---

21. Only one court has reached the issue in the present context. The Alaska Supreme Court concluded the state had a compelling interest in protecting unmarried cohabitants against housing discrimination, and that application of the statute was the least restrictive means of furthering the state's interest. (Swanner v. Anchorage Equal Rights Comm'n) . . . .

Notes and Questions

1. If the California statute had included the following definition: "Marital status" means whether a person is single, married, remarried, divorced, separated, or a surviving spouse, would the outcome have been different? *See State by Cooper v. French*, 460 N.W.2d 2 (Minn. 1990) (plain language shows legislature's intent to address status of individual only, and not individual's relationship with spouse, fiancé, or domestic partner).

2. Many state statutes bar discrimination in housing based on "marital status" without defining the term. Courts have split on the issue whether discrimination against unmarried couples is covered by the statute. In interpreting their statutes, courts in different states have apparently been influenced by quite different policies. Compare the California court's view in *Smith* with that of the Supreme Court of Minnesota in *State by Cooper v. French*, 460 N.W.2d 2, 8, 11 (Minn. 1990). The Minnesota court, which placed great reliance on the existence of a state statute barring fornication, said:

> It is simply astonishing . . . that the argument is made that the legislature intended to protect fornication and promote a lifestyle which corrodes the institutions which have sustained our civilization, namely, marriage and family life. If the legislature intended to protect cohabiting couples and other types of domestic partners, it would have said so. . . .

> There are certain moral values and institutions that have served western civilization well for eons. *See* Maynard v. Hill, 125 U.S. 190, 211 (1888)[6] (characterizing marriage as "the foundation of family and society, without which there would be neither civilization nor progress"), *cited with approval in* Zablocki v. Redhail, 434 U.S. 374, 384 (1978). This generation does not have a monopoly on either knowledge or wisdom. Before abandoning fundamental values and institutions, we must pause and take stock of our present social order: millions of drug abusers; rampant child abuse; a rising underclass without marketable job skills; children roaming the streets; children with only one or no parent at all; and children growing up with no one to guide them in developing any set of values. How can we expect anything else when the state itself contributes, by arguments of this kind, to further erosion of fundamental institutions that have formed the foundation of our civilization for centuries?

3. Courts that have tackled the First Amendment issues raised by the religious landlord cases have reached different conclusions, largely based on their differing views as to the strength of the state's policy against discrimination, the extent of the burden imposed on the landlord's free exercise of religion, and the potential problems that would be caused by allowing widespread exemptions to secular laws on the basis of religious beliefs.

In contrast to the California and Alaska Supreme Courts' holdings that protecting unmarried couples from discrimination by landlords does not

---

6. *Maynard v. Hill* involved a couple who left Vermont with their two children to go west in 1850. The man left his wife and children in Ohio and headed for California, promising to send support money and to come back to get them or send for them in two years. Instead, he settled in Washington, and after two years, obtained an act from the territorial legislature purporting to give him a divorce. He then married another woman in 1853. After his death in 1879, a dispute arose as to his property. The Supreme Court upheld the validity of the divorce granted by the legislature even though the wife was not in the territory and was not given notice of the legislation. —EDS.

unconstitutionally burden the landlords' free exercise of religion, a panel of the Ninth Circuit Court of Appeals came to the opposite conclusion in *Thomas v. Anchorage Equal Rights Commission*, 165 F.3d 692 (9th Cir. 1999). The Michigan court reached the same conclusion as the California and Alaska courts in *McCready v. Hoffius*, 586 N.W.2d 723 (Mich. 1998), but changed its mind after the *Thomas* case and remanded to the trial court for further consideration, 593 N.W.2d 545 (Mich. 1999).

4. In *Burwell v. Hobby Lobby Stores, Inc.*, decided in June 2014, the U.S. Supreme Court held that the Affordable Care Act's requirement that businesses provide health insurance coverage that includes contraceptive coverage, or pay a fine, substantially burdened the exercise of religion within the meaning of RFRA of the corporate owners of the businesses. The Court said:

> The Hahns and Greens believe that providing the coverage demanded by the HHS regulations is connected to the destruction of an embryo in a way that is sufficient to make it immoral for them to provide the coverage. This belief implicates a difficult and important question of religion and moral philosophy, namely, the circumstances under which it is wrong for a person to perform an act that is innocent in itself but that has the effect of enabling or facilitating the commission of an immoral act by another.

How might this decision affect the California court's view on whether requiring a landlord like Mrs. Smith to rent to unmarried couples is a substantial burden on her religion? Is California's interest in prohibiting discrimination in housing on the basis of marital status a compelling state interest? Is prohibiting discrimination by landlords the least restrictive way to accomplish it?

5. Protection against discrimination on the basis of gender identity or sexual orientation is not covered by the FHA, but is covered by many state statutes and local ordinances. It has also been extended by HUD, which in 2012 issued its *Equal Access to Housing in HUD Programs Regardless of Sexual Orientation or Gender Identity Rule*, providing for access to all HUD programs for housing assistance and financing. *See* Melissa Klimkiewicz, Kendra C. Kinnaird & Ena P. Koukourinis, *HUD's Equal Access Rule: A New Chapter in Fair Lending Compliance*, 33 No. 5 Banking & Fin. Services Pol'y Rep. 1 (2014).

6. How will courts resolve conflicts between statutes prohibiting discrimination on the basis of sexual orientation and gender identity and claims of religious freedom to discriminate? See Natacha Lam, *Clash of the Titans: Seeking Guidance for Adjudicating the Conflict Between Equality and Religious Liberty in LGBT Litigation*, 23 Tul. J.L. & Sexuality 113 (2014), for a pre-*Hobby Lobby* analysis in light of the marital status cases.

PART IV

LAND USE PLANNING AND REGULATION

Until the 20th century, there was little land use planning or regulation in the United States. Incompatible land uses were legally controlled by nuisance actions, if they were controlled at all. With the industrial revolution, there were increased demands for regulation of incompatible uses, particularly to protect urban residential areas. In the 19th century, land developers began to use covenants and easements to create protected residential areas, and by the end of the 20th century, covenant regimes were in widespread use, governing substantial numbers of residential and commercial properties. Common interest communities, governed by covenant regimes, allow widespread sharing of maintenance costs and amenities, as well as detailed regulation of uses made of the land.

State and local governments began using zoning in the early 20th century to separate incompatible uses and to regulate size, height, and density of structures for safety. By the beginning of the 21st century, governmental land use regulations were pervasive, covering coastal and rural lands, as well as urban and suburban land with intricate arrays of restrictions. Many states required local governments to have comprehensive plans, in addition to zoning, that included elements covering housing, transportation, open space, conservation, safety, noise, and the like. Local governments were also using their eminent domain power to facilitate economic development and redevelopment projects, often controversially.

Despite the widespread use of zoning and covenants, incompatible land uses still provoke private nuisance suits. We return to the study of nuisance, introduced in Chapter 1, in Chapter 11. Chapter 12 covers easements and covenants, the basic tools private land developers use to facilitate shared uses and impose controls on how the land is used. In Chapter 13, we study the fundamental constraints on use of the eminent domain power and land use regulations imposed by the Fifth and Fourteenth Amendments to the U.S. Constitution. We leave further treatment of zoning and public land use planning and environmental regulation to the upper class curriculum.

CHAPTER 11

Nuisance

SIC UTERE TUO UT ALIENUM NON LAEDAS

We begin this chapter with a case that explores the difference between trespass and nuisance.

ADAMS v. CLEVELAND-CLIFFS IRON CO.

Court of Appeals of Michigan
602 N.W.2d 215 (1999)

O'CONNELL, J. Defendants appeal . . . from a jury verdict awarding damages in trespass for invasions of plaintiffs' property by intrusions of dust, noise, and vibrations. . . . [T]his appeal presents the question whether Michigan recognizes a cause of action in trespass stemming from invasions of these intangible agents. . . . We conclude that the law of trespass in Michigan does not cover airborne particulate, noise, or vibrations, and that a complaint alleging damages resulting from these irritants normally sounds instead in nuisance.

I. FACTS

Plaintiffs brought suit seeking damages in both trespass and nuisance, complaining of dust, noise, and vibrations emanating from the Empire Mine, which is operated by defendant Cleveland-Cliffs Iron Company . . . .

The Empire Mine is one of the nation's largest mines, producing eight million tons of iron ore annually. The mine operates twenty-four hours a day, year round. At the time this action was commenced, all but three plaintiffs lived near the mine, in the village of Palmer . . . . Cleveland-Cliffs . . . employs approximately 2,200 persons, making it the area's largest civilian employer.

The Empire Mine was originally dug in the 1870s, then expanded in the 1960s. A second pit was added in 1987, and a third in 1990-91.[2] The mine engages in blasting operations approximately three times a week, year round,

---

2.   With each expansion, surface material, also called "overburden," consisting of soil, subsoil, and rock was blasted loose then stockpiled at the edge of the mine property. As the mine was dug deeper, waste rock was likewise blasted loose and stockpiled. The resulting mass of overburden and waste rock is unsightly and so large that residents of Palmer have nicknamed it "Mt. Palmer" and say that it causes their town to have early sunsets.

and the extraction and processing of the iron ore generates a great deal of airborne dust. Plaintiffs complain that the blasting sends tremors through their property and that defendants' dust constantly accumulates inside and outside plaintiffs' homes. Plaintiffs assert that these emanations aggravate their need to clean and repaint their homes, replace carpets and drapes, repair cracks in all masonry, replace windows, and tend to cause plumbing leaks and broken sewer pipes.

According to the testimony, the dust from the mine is fine, gritty, oily, and difficult to clean. Some plaintiffs complained that they seldom opened their windows because of the dust, and virtually every plaintiff complained that the snow in Palmer tended to be gray or black. Evidence presented at trial indicates that the emissions from the mining operations have consistently remained within applicable air-quality standards and that the amount of particulate matter accumulating over Palmer each month amounts to less than the thickness of a sheet of paper, but that this amount is nonetheless four times greater than what normally settles onto surrounding communities.

In addition to concerns about the dust, many plaintiffs testified that the noise and vibrations from the blasts caused them to suffer shock, nervousness, and sleeplessness. Finally, several plaintiffs asserted that these conditions diminished the value of their homes, in some cases to the point of rendering them unmarketable.

At the close of proofs, the trial court instructed the jury concerning both trespass and nuisance. The jury found that three of the plaintiffs were not entitled to recover under either theory. Concerning the remaining fifty-two plaintiffs, however, the jury was unable to agree on a verdict regarding the nuisance claim, but returned a verdict in favor of these plaintiffs with regard to the trespass claim, awarding damages totaling $599,199. The court denied defendants' posttrial motions for a new trial or judgment notwithstanding the verdict.

The sole issue that defendants raise on appeal is the propriety of the trial court's jury instruction concerning plaintiffs' trespass claim:

> Every unauthorized intrusion onto the lands of another is a trespass upon those lands, and it gives rise to a right to recover damages for the trespass, if any damages were caused by the trespass. So a landowner who causes emissions, dust, vibration, noise from his property onto another [sic] property assumes the risk of trespass, if the dust, vibration, noise affects the neighbor's property, or if he causes by his actions, damages or invasion of his neighbor's land.

. . .

II. TRESPASS AND NUISANCE

The general concept of "property" comprises various rights—a "bundle of sticks" . . . . [T]he right to exclude others . . . and the right to quiet enjoyment of one's land have customarily been regarded as separate sticks in the bundle. . . . [P]ossessory rights to real property include as distinct interests the right to exclude and the right to enjoy, violations of which give rise to the distinct causes of action respectively of trespass and nuisance. Prosser & Keeton, *Torts* (5th ed.), § 87, p. 622.

A. Historical Overview

"At common law, trespass was a form of action brought to recover damages for any injury to one's person or property or relationship with another." Black's Law Dictionary (6th ed.), p. 1502. This broad usage of the term "trespass" then gave way to a narrower usage, referring to intrusions upon a person's "tangible property, real or personal." Prosser & Keeton, *supra* at § 13, p. 67. Today, the general concept of "trespass" has been refined into several specific forms of trespass . . . and related doctrines known by various names. Landowners seeking damages or equitable relief in response to violations of their possessory rights to land now generally proceed under the common-law derivatives of strict liability, negligence, nuisance, or trespass to land.[8] It is the latter two products of this evolution from the general concept of trespass that are at issue in the present case.

. . . Because a trespass violated a landholder's right to exclude others from the premises, the landholder could recover at least nominal damages even in the absence of proof of any other injury. Recovery for nuisance, however, traditionally required proof of actual and substantial injury.[9] Further, the doctrine of nuisance customarily called for balancing the disturbance complained of against the social utility of its cause.[10]

Traditionally, trespass required that the invasion of the land be direct or immediate and in the form of a physical, tangible object. See, e.g., Williams v. Oeder, 103 Ohio App. 3d 333 (1995) (noting then abandoning those traditional requirements); Davis v. Georgia-Pacific Corp., 251 Or. 239 (1968) (abandoning the traditional requirements); Norwood v. Eastern Oregon Land Co., 139 Or. 25 (1931), modified 139 Or. 25 (1932) (wrongful diversion of water onto another's land does not constitute trespass to land). Under these principles, recovery in trespass for dust, smoke, noise, and vibrations was generally unavailable because they were not considered tangible or because they came to the land via some intervening force such as wind or water. Instead, claims concerning these irritants were generally pursued under a nuisance theory.

B. Recent Trends

Plaintiffs urge this Court to hold that they are entitled to recover in trespass for invasions of their premises by intangible things without regard for how these annoyances came to their land. Plaintiffs would have us follow the example of certain courts from other jurisdictions, which have eliminated the traditional requirements for trespass of a direct intrusion by a tangible object, directing

---

8. See generally Keeton, Trespass, Nuisance, and Strict Liability, 59 Columbia L R 457, 459 (1959).

9. To put it another way, "Trespass was liability-producing regardless of the degree of harm the invasion caused, while nuisance required substantial harm as a liability threshold." Halper, Untangling the Nuisance Knot, 26 B C Envt'l Aff L R 89, 121-122 (1998), citing 4 Restatement Torts, 1st, ch. 40, p. 225.

10. See Halper, supra at 122 ("the Restatement (First) expected plaintiffs to bear uncompensated harms that might, for them, be quite severe, if the utility of the defendant's conduct to society at large was great enough").

the inquiry instead toward the nature of the interest harmed. These courts have permitted recovery in trespass for indirect, intangible invasions that nonetheless interfered with exclusive possessory interests in the land. See 75 Am Jur 2d, *Trespass*, § 33, p. 33 and cases cited. See also Mercer v. Rockwell Int'l Corp., 24 F. Supp. 2d 735, 743 (W.D. Ky., 1998) (allowing an action in "negligent trespass" concerning intrusions of invisible polychlorinated biphenyls [PCBs] that actually harm the property); *Williams, supra* (airborne particulate matter from a sand and gravel processing facility, an asphalt plant, and a concrete plant constituted trespass); Martin v. Reynolds Metals Co., 342 P.2d 790 (Or. 1959) (trespass may stem from fluoride compounds in the form of gases and particles). We agree with the characterization of cases of this sort found in Prosser & Keeton as being "in reality, examples of the tort of private nuisance or liability for harm resulting from negligence," not proper trespass cases. . . .

. . . [T]he traditional view of trespass required a direct entry onto the land by a tangible object. However, recent trends have led to an erosion of these requirements. Some courts have eliminated the requirement of a direct entry onto the land. E.g., Bradley v. American Smelting & Refining Co., 104 Wash. 2d 677 (1985); Borland v. Sanders Lead Co., Inc., 369 So.2d 523 (Ala., 1979); *Martin* (observing the trend without deciding whether to join it) . . . . Some courts have likewise eliminated the requirement of a tangible object. . . . See also *Martin* . . . (trespass to land may be accomplished by "a ray of light, by an atomic particle, or by a particulate of fluoride"). In some cases the direct-and-tangible inquiry has been supplanted by an inquiry into the force and energy of the intruding agent.

The courts that have deviated from the traditional requirements of trespass, however, have consequently found troublesome the traditional principle that at least nominal damages are presumed in cases of trespass. . . . [T]o avoid subjecting manufacturing plants to potential liability to every landowner on whose parcel some incidental residue of industrial activity might come to rest, these courts have grafted onto the law of trespass a requirement of actual and substantial damages. . . . Logically following from a requirement of substantial damages is the weighing of those damages against the social utility of the activity causing them. . . .

We do not welcome this redirection of trespass law toward nuisance law. The requirement that real and substantial damages be proved, and balanced against the usefulness of the offending activity, is appropriate where the issue is interference with one's use or enjoyment of one's land; applying it where a landowner has had to endure an unauthorized physical occupation of the landowner's land, however, offends traditional principles of ownership. The law should not require a property owner to justify exercising the right to exclude. To countenance the erosion of presumed damages in cases of trespass is to endanger the right of exclusion itself.

To summarize, the effects of recent trends in the law of trespass have included eliminating the requirements of a direct invasion by a tangible object, requiring proof of actual and substantial damages, and weighing the plaintiff's damages against the social utility of the operation causing them. This so-called "modern view of trespass" appears, with all its nuances and add-ons, merely to replicate traditional nuisance doctrine as recognized in Michigan. Indeed, the trends recognized or advanced by *Bradley, Borland, Martin*, and their kindred spirits have conflated nuisance with trespass to the point of rendering it difficult to delineate the difference between the two theories of recovery. . . .

III. HOLDING

Recovery for trespass to land in Michigan is available only upon proof of an unauthorized direct or immediate intrusion of a physical, tangible object onto land over which the plaintiff has a right of exclusive possession. Once such an intrusion is proved, the tort has been established, and the plaintiff is presumptively entitled to at least nominal damages. Where the possessor of land is menaced by noise, vibrations, or ambient dust, smoke, soot, or fumes, the possessory interest implicated is that of use and enjoyment, not exclusion, and the vehicle through which a plaintiff normally should seek a remedy is the doctrine of nuisance. To prevail in nuisance, a possessor of land must prove *significant harm* resulting from the defendant's *unreasonable interference* with the use or enjoyment of the property. . . . Thus, in nuisance, the plaintiff must prove all damages, which may be awarded only to the extent that the defendant's conduct was "unreasonable" according to a public-policy assessment of its overall value. In the present case, because the intrusions of which plaintiffs complained were intangible things, the trial court erred in allowing the jury to award damages in trespass. Instead, any award of damages would have had to proceed from plaintiffs' alternative but (as yet) unsuccessful theory of nuisance.

. . . We prefer to retain the traditional elements [of trespass], however, because they serve as gatekeepers—safeguarding genuine claims of trespass and keeping the line between the torts of trespass and nuisance from fading into a "wavering and uncertain" ambiguity. Further, retaining the distinction between the two theories of recovery limits the possibilities for dual liability stemming from the same conduct and results. See Reynolds, *Distinguishing Trespass and Nuisance: A Journey Through a Shifting Borderland,* 44 Okla. L.R. 227, 229 (1991).

The trial court's instruction . . . erroneously conflated trespass with nuisance and produced the anomalous result that the jury failed to reach agreement on the nuisance claim while awarding damages for intrusions of intangible things pursuant to the trespass claim.

A. Tangible

Because noise or vibrations are clearly not tangible objects, we hold that they cannot give rise to an action in trespass in this state.[12] We further hold that dust must generally be considered intangible and thus not actionable in trespass. We realize, of course, that dust particles are tangible objects in a strict sense that they can be touched and are comprised of physical elements. However, we agree with those authorities that have recognized, for practical purposes, that dust, along with other forms of airborne particulate, does not normally present itself as a significant physical intrusion. . . . Dust particles do not normally occupy the land on which they settle in any meaningful sense; instead they simply become a

---

12.   This holds even if the noise or vibrations are so intense as to shatter all glass and fell all masonry or otherwise so persistent as to drive all persons from the premises. Although such hazards would indeed infringe on a landowner's possessory interest, it is the interest in use and enjoyment of the premises, not in exclusion from them, and therefore the cause of action lies not in trespass, but in nuisance or the related doctrines of negligence or strict liability.

part of the ambient circumstances of that space. If the quantity and character of the dust are such as to disturb the ambiance in ways that interfere substantially with the plaintiff's use and enjoyment of the land, then recovery in nuisance is possible.

B. Direct

. . . We hold that the direct invasion requirement for an action in trespass to land is still alive in Michigan. The question then becomes, how strong must the connection between cause and effect be in order to satisfy this requirement?[14] We agree with the Restatement view that "[i]t is enough that an act is done with knowledge that it will to a substantial certainty result in the entry of the foreign matter." 1 Restatement Torts, 2d, § 158, comment *i*, p. 279. Thus, a "direct or immediate" invasion . . . is one that is accomplished by any means that the offender knew or reasonably should have known would result in the physical invasion of the plaintiff's land. . . .

C. Damages

. . . The trial court told the jury that "trespass . . . gives rise to a right to recover damages for the trespass, if any damages were caused by the trespass." This instruction would be appropriate for nuisance, or negligence, under which theories the plaintiff must prove all damages, but not for trespass. A jury instruction with respect to the latter should announce that because the violation of the right to exclude causes cognizable injury in and of itself, a plaintiff proving that violation is presumptively entitled to at least nominal damages. The jury should be further instructed that beyond the presumed damages, the plaintiff may recover any additional, actual damages proved.

. . . We hold that recovery in trespass is appropriate for any *appreciable* intrusion onto land in violation of the plaintiff's right to exclude, while recovery in nuisance is appropriate for only *substantial* and *unreasonable* interference with the plaintiff's right to quiet enjoyment.

IV. CONCLUSION

There is no need to reformulate the traditional law of trespass to accommodate the problems of airborne pollution, noise, or vibrations, because the doctrines of nuisance and related causes of action have always stood ready to provide remedies. Trespass in Michigan remains a distinct doctrine providing a remedy for violation of a distinct property right. A possessor of land proving a direct or immediate intrusion of a physical, tangible object onto the land is presumptively entitled to recover at least nominal damages even absent any proof

---

14.   Because we conclude that no trespass existed in the present case because the intrusions at issue were not tangible things, we need not decide whether defendants caused those intrusions to enter plaintiffs' land by direct or immediate means for purposes of trespass law.

of actual injury and may recover additional damages for any injuries actually proved.

Because Michigan does not recognize a cause of action in trespass for airborne particulate, noise, or vibrations, we hereby vacate the jury verdict in this matter and remand this case to the trial court for further proceedings consistent with this opinion. . . .

Notes and Questions

1. What will the plaintiffs have to show to prevail on their nuisance claims? How is this different from what was needed to prevail in trespass?

2. Do you agree with the court that it is important to retain the traditional distinctions between trespass to land and nuisance?

3. In *Johnson v. Paynesville Farmers Union Cooperative Oil Co.*, 817 N.W.2d 693 (Minn. 2012), the plaintiff sued for damages to its organic farm operation from drifting pesticides sprayed on adjacent conventionally farmed fields. The Minnesota Supreme Court took the same position as the court in *Adams v. Cleveland-Cliffs*, holding that invasion by sprayed pesticides is not a trespass, but may be a nuisance if it unreasonably interferes with plaintiff's use and enjoyment of his land as an organic farm.

BOOMER v. ATLANTIC CEMENT COMPANY, INC.

Court of Appeals of New York
257 N.E.2d 870 (1970)

BERGAN, J. Defendant operates a large cement plant near Albany. These are actions for injunction and damages by neighboring land owners alleging injury to property from dirt, smoke and vibration emanating from the plant. A nuisance has been found after trial, temporary damages have been allowed; but an injunction has been denied.

The public concern with air pollution arising from many sources in industry and in transportation is currently accorded ever wider recognition accompanied by a growing sense of responsibility in State and Federal Governments to control it. Cement plants are obvious sources of air pollution in the neighborhoods where they operate. . . .

Effective control of air pollution is a problem presently far from solution even with the full public and financial powers of government. . . . It seems apparent that the amelioration of air pollution will depend on technical research in great depth; on a carefully balanced consideration of the economic impact of close regulation; and of the actual effect on public health. It is likely to require massive public expenditure and to demand more than any local community can accomplish and to depend on regional and interstate controls.

A court should not try to do this on its own as a by-product of private litigation and it seems manifest that the judicial establishment is neither equipped in the limited nature of any judgment it can pronounce nor prepared to lay down and implement an effective policy for the elimination of air pollution. This is an area beyond the circumference of one private lawsuit. It is a direct responsibility for government and should not thus be undertaken as an incident to solving a dispute between property owners and a single cement plant—one of many—in the Hudson River valley.

The cement making operations of defendant have been found by the court of Special Term to have damaged the nearby properties of plaintiffs in these two actions. That court . . . accordingly found defendant maintained a nuisance and this has been affirmed at the Appellate Division. The total damage to plaintiffs' properties is, however, relatively small in comparison with the value of defendant's operation and with the consequences of the injunction which plaintiffs seek.

The ground for the denial of injunction, notwithstanding the finding both that there is a nuisance and that plaintiffs have been damaged substantially, is the large disparity in economic consequences of the nuisance and of the injunction. This theory cannot, however, be sustained without overruling a doctrine which has been consistently reaffirmed in several leading cases in this court and which has never been disavowed here, namely that where a nuisance has been found and where there has been any substantial damage shown by the party complaining an injunction will be granted.

The rule in New York has been that such a nuisance will be enjoined although marked disparity be shown in economic consequence between the effect of the injunction and the effect of the nuisance.

The problem of disparity in economic consequence was sharply in focus in Whalen v. Union Bag & Paper Co., 208 N.Y. 1, 101 N.E. 805. A pulp mill entailing an investment of more than a million dollars polluted a stream in which plaintiff, who owned a farm, was "a lower riparian owner." The economic loss to plaintiff from this pollution was small. This court, reversing the Appellate Division, reinstated the injunction granted by the Special Term against the argument of the mill owner that in view of "the slight advantage to plaintiff and the great loss that will be inflicted on defendant" an injunction should not be granted. "Such a balancing of injuries cannot be justified by the circumstances of this case," Judge Werner noted. He continued: "Although the damage to the plaintiff may be slight as compared with the defendant's expense of abating the condition, that is not a good reason for refusing an injunction."

Thus the unconditional injunction granted at Special Term was reinstated. The rule laid down in that case, then, is that whenever the damage resulting from a nuisance is found not "unsubstantial," viz., $100 a year, injunction would follow. This states a rule that had been followed in this court with marked consistency. . . .

Although the court at Special Term and the Appellate Division held that injunction should be denied, it was found that plaintiffs had been damaged in various specific amounts up to the time of the trial and damages to the respective plaintiffs were awarded for those amounts. The effect of this was, injunction having been denied, plaintiffs could maintain successive actions at law for damages thereafter as further damage was incurred.

The court at Special Term also found the amount of permanent damage attributable to each plaintiff, for the guidance of the parties in the event both sides stipulated to the payment and acceptance of such permanent damage as a settlement of all the controversies among the parties. The total of permanent damages to all plaintiffs thus found was $185,000. . . .

This result at Special Term and at the Appellate Division is a departure from a rule that has become settled; but to follow the rule literally in these cases would be to close down the plant at once. This court is fully agreed to avoid that immediately drastic remedy; the difference in view is how best to avoid it.*

One alternative is to grant the injunction but postpone its effect to a specified future date to give opportunity for technical advances to permit defendant to eliminate the nuisance; another is to grant the injunction conditioned on the payment of permanent damages to plaintiffs which would compensate them for the total economic loss to their property present and future caused by defendant's operations. . . . [T]he court chooses the latter alternative.

If the injunction were to be granted unless within a short period—e.g., 18 months—the nuisance be abated by improved methods, there would be no assurance that any significant technical improvement would occur.

The parties could settle this private litigation at any time if defendant paid enough money and the imminent threat of closing the plant would build up the pressure on defendant. If there were no improved techniques found, there would inevitably be applications to the court at Special Term for extensions of time to perform on showing of good faith efforts to find such techniques.

Moreover, techniques to eliminate dust and other annoying by-products of cement making are unlikely to be developed by any research the defendant can undertake within any short period, but will depend on the total resources of the cement industry nationwide and throughout the world. The problem is universal wherever cement is made. . . . If at the end of 18 months the whole industry has not found a technical solution a court would be hard put to close down this one cement plant if due regard be given to equitable principles.

On the other hand, to grant the injunction unless defendant pays plaintiffs such permanent damages as may be fixed by the court seems to do justice between the contending parties. All of the attributions of economic loss to the properties on which plaintiffs' complaints are based will have been redressed. . . . The limitation of relief granted is a limitation only within the four corners of these actions and does not foreclose public health or other public agencies from seeking proper relief in a proper court.

It seems reasonable to think that the risk of being required to pay permanent damages to injured property owners by cement plant owners would itself be a reasonable effective spur to research for improved techniques to minimize nuisance.

The power of the court to condition on equitable grounds the continuance of an injunction on the payment of permanent damages seems undoubted. . . .

The damage base here suggested is consistent with the general rule in those nuisance cases where damages are allowed. "Where a nuisance is of such a permanent and unabatable character that a single recovery can be had, including the whole damage past and future resulting therefrom, there can be but one recovery." It has been said that permanent damages are allowed where the loss recoverable would obviously be small as compared with the cost of removal of the nuisance. . . .

---

* Respondent's investment in the plant is in excess of $45,000,000. There are over 300 people employed there.

[I]t seems fair to both sides to grant permanent damages to plaintiffs which will terminate this private litigation. The theory of damage is the "servitude on land" of plaintiffs imposed by defendant's nuisance. . . .

The judgment, by allowance of permanent damages imposing a servitude on land, which is the basis of the actions, would preclude future recovery by plaintiffs or their grantees.

This should be placed beyond debate by a provision of the judgment that the payment by defendant and the acceptance by plaintiffs of permanent damages found by the court shall be in compensation for a servitude on the land. . . .

The orders should be reversed, without costs, and the cases remitted to Supreme Court, Albany County to grant an injunction which shall be vacated upon payment by defendant of such amounts of permanent damage to the respective plaintiffs as shall for this purpose be determined by the court.

JASEN, Judge (dissenting). . . . It has long been the rule in this State, as the majority acknowledges, that a nuisance which results in substantial continuing damage to neighbors must be enjoined. To now change the rule to permit the cement company to continue polluting the air indefinitely upon the payment of permanent damages is, in my opinion, compounding the magnitude of a very serious problem in our State and Nation today. . . .

The specific problem faced here is known as particulate contamination because of the fine dust particles emanating from defendant's cement plant. The particular type of nuisance is not new, having appeared in many cases for at least the past 60 years. . . . It is interesting to note that cement production has recently been identified as a significant source of particulate contamination in the Hudson Valley. This type of pollution, wherein very small particles escape and stay in the atmosphere, has been denominated as the type of air pollution which produces the greatest hazard to human health. We have thus a nuisance which not only is damaging to the plaintiffs, but also is decidedly harmful to the general public.

. . . In permitting the injunction to become inoperative upon the payment of permanent damages, the majority is, in effect, licensing a continuing wrong. It is the same as saying to the cement company, you may continue to do harm to your neighbors so long as you pay a fee for it. Furthermore, once such permanent damages are assessed and paid, the incentive to alleviate the wrong would be eliminated, thereby continuing air pollution of an area without abatement.

It is true that some courts have sanctioned the remedy here proposed by the majority in a number of cases, but none of the authorities relied upon by the majority are analogous to the situation before us. In those cases, the courts, in denying an injunction and awarding money damages, grounded their decision on a showing that the use to which the property was intended to be put was primarily for the public benefit. Here, on the other hand, it is clearly established that the cement company is creating a continuing air pollution nuisance primarily for its own private interest with no public benefit. . . .

I would enjoin the defendant cement company from continuing the discharge of dust particles upon its neighbors' properties unless, within 18 months, the cement company abated this nuisance. . . .

It is not my intention to cause the removal of the cement plant from the Albany area, but to recognize the urgency of the problem stemming from this stationary source of air pollution, and to allow the company a specified period of time to develop a means to alleviate this nuisance.

I am aware that the trial court found that the most modern dust control devices available have been installed in defendant's plant, but, I submit, this does not mean that better and more effective dust control devices could not be developed within the time allowed to abate the pollution.

Moreover, I believe it is incumbent upon the defendant to develop such devices, since the cement company, at the time the plant commenced production (1962), was well aware of the plaintiffs' presence in the area, as well as the probable consequences of its contemplated operation. Yet, it still chose to build and operate the plant at this site.

In a day when there is a growing concern for clean air, highly developed industry should not expect acquiescence by the courts, but should, instead, plan its operations to eliminate contamination of our air and damage to its neighbors. . . .

Notes and Questions

1. Until the 19th century, any substantial interference with use and enjoyment of plaintiff's land was actionable in nuisance. During the 19th century, courts began to give increasing weight to the right of defendants to make reasonable uses of their land even though plaintiff's use and enjoyment might be thereby diminished. This led to considerations of the suitability of the locality for the conflicting uses, among other circumstances, in determining whether defendant's activity was a nuisance. Once a nuisance was found, however, courts generally followed the *Whalen v. Union Bag* rule that plaintiff was entitled to an injunction. *See* Jeff L. Lewin, *Compensated Injunctions and the Evolution of Nuisance Law,* 71 Iowa L. Rev. 775 (1985).

2. On what basis might the trial court in *Boomer* have found that the cement plant created a nuisance?

3. Does it make sense to provide monetary compensation instead of injunctive relief in nuisance cases? If the plaintiffs are successful in their nuisance claim against Cleveland-Cliffs Iron Co. in the previous case, what remedy should be granted?

4. The court in *Boomer* effectively forces the plaintiffs to sell the defendant a servitude to continue polluting their lands. Is this fair? Would it have been better for the court to treat the air pollution as a continuing nuisance giving the plaintiffs the right to sue for damages as they accrued? Which remedy would provide a greater incentive to the cement company to reduce its emissions?

5. The dissent objects to the majority's licensing a continuing wrong, but also says that it is not his intention to cause removal of the cement plant. If the court had issued an injunction as the dissent claimed it should, what would have happened if the cement company could not reduce its emissions within the 18-month period?

What Is a Nuisance? The Role of Social Utility

Section 822 of the *Restatement (Second) of Torts* (1979) (hereafter the Restatement) states that an invasion of an interest in the private use and enjoyment of land is a nuisance if it is either intentional and unreasonable, or the result of negligent or reckless conduct, or of abnormally dangerous conditions or activities. Most cases involving conflicts with industrial and agricultural uses, like *Boomer*, involve intentional, rather than negligent conduct (the defendant knows that the invasion is likely to result from its conduct, Rest. § 825(b)). The question then arises: What is unreasonable?

Section 826 of the Restatement provides two criteria for determining that an intentional invasion, like the particulate matter emitted by the cement plant, is unreasonable:

(a) the gravity of the harm outweighs the utility of the actor's conduct, or

(b) the harm caused by the conduct is serious and the financial burden of compensating for this and similar harm to others would not make the continuation of the conduct not feasible.

Although the court in *Boomer* did not cite this provision of the Restatement, the result is the same as that which would be reached under subsection (b). Not all courts, however, accept the idea that an activity may be a nuisance even if its social utility outweighs the harm to the use and enjoyment of plaintiff's land. In *Carpenter v. The Double R Cattle Co., Inc.*, 701 P.2d 222 (Idaho 1985), the majority held that defendant's feedlot for 9,000 cattle was not a nuisance to the neighbors despite the substantial harm to their interests, saying:

The State of Idaho is sparsely populated and its economy depends largely upon the benefits of agriculture, lumber, mining and industrial development. To eliminate the utility of conduct and other factors listed by the trial court from the criteria to be considered in determining whether a nuisance exists, as the appellant has argued throughout this appeal, would place an unreasonable burden upon these industries.

The dissent strongly disagreed:

The majority today continues to adhere to ideas on the law of nuisance that should have gone out with the use of buffalo chips as fuel. We have before us today homeowners complaining of a nearby feedlot—not a small operation, but rather a feedlot which accommodates 9,000 cattle. The homeowners advanced the theory that after the expansion of the feedlot in 1977, the odor, manure, dust, insect infestation and increased concentration of birds which accompanied all of the foregoing, constituted a nuisance. If the odoriferous quagmire created by 9,000 head of cattle is *not* a nuisance, it is difficult for me to imagine what is. However, the real question for us today is the legal basis on which a finding of nuisance can be made.

. . . I . . . agree wholeheartedly that the interests of the community should be considered in determining the existence of a nuisance. However, where this primitive rule of law fails is in recognizing that in our society, while it may be desirable to have a serious nuisance continue because the utility of the operation causing the nuisance is great, at the same time, those directly impacted by the serious nuisance deserve some compensation for the invasion they suffer as a result of the continuation of the nuisance. This is exactly what the more progressive provisions of § 826(b) of the Restatement (Second) of Torts addresses. . . .

The majority's rule today overlooks the option of compensating those who suffer a nuisance because the interests of the community outweigh the interests of those afflicted by the nuisance. This unsophisticated balancing overlooks the possibility that it is not necessary that one interest be ignored when the community interest is strong. We should not be adopting a rule of preference which suggests that if the community interest is preferred any other interest must be disregarded. . . .

The majority's rule today suggests that part of the cost of industry, agriculture or development must be borne by those unfortunate few who have the fortuitous luck to live in the immediate vicinity of a nuisance producing facility. Frankly, I think this naive economic view is ridiculous in both its simplicity and its outdated view of modern economic society. The "cost" of a product includes not only the amount it takes to produce such a product but also includes the external costs: the damage done to the environment through pollution of air or water is an example of an external cost. In the instant case, the nuisance suffered by the homeowners should be considered an external cost of operating a feedlot and producing beef for public consumption. . . . If a feedlot wants to continue, I say fine, providing compensation is paid for the serious invasion (the odors, flies, dust, etc.) of the homeowner's interest. My only qualification is that the financial burden of compensating for this harm should not be such as to force the feedlot (or any other industry) out of business. The true cost can then be shifted to the consumer who rightfully should pay for the *entire* cost of producing the product he desires to obtain. . . .

In cases involving uses that are smelly or dirty, it is relatively easy to view the dirty, smelly user as a wrongdoer, and the neighbor as a victim, even if the activity itself creates social utility. The tort framework of nuisance law makes cases that involve non-offensive but conflicting uses more difficult. Professor R. Lisle Baker in *My Tree Versus Your Solar Collector or Your Well Versus My Septic System?—Exploring Responses to Beneficial But Conflicting Neighboring Uses of Land*, 37 B.C. Envt'l Aff. L. Rev. 1 (2010), analyzes this problem and explains why private nuisance law is fundamentally unsuited to resolving it. "The situation of 'good' neighbors in conflict . . . involves reconciling or preferring one of two apparently equal rights, rather than righting an apparent wrong. . . . [I]t is difficult to imagine in the abstract that growing redwood trees or installing a solar collector, or drilling a well or installing a septic system, would expose either landowner to liability to his neighbor in tort . . . ."

Professor Henry E. Smith in *Exclusion and Property Rules in the Law of Nuisance*, 90 Va. L. Rev. 965, 1016 (2004), suggests that many nuisance cases can be understood in terms of location and directional causation, or who moved what where. If nothing moves from the defendant's parcel to the plaintiff's, courts are less likely to find a nuisance than when smoke, odors, pesticides, and the like move from defendant's land to plaintiff's.

Light and Air

Cases involving claims that interference with the flow of light and air or sunlight to plaintiff's land is a nuisance are generally not successful, but there are some exceptions.

Fontainebleau Hotel Corp. v. Forty-five Twenty-Five, Inc., 114 So. 2d 357 (Fla. Ct. App. 1959), held that construction of an addition to a hotel that blocked the sunshine to plaintiff hotel's pool was not a nuisance. *Prah v. Maretti*, 321 N.W.

182 (Wis. 1982), held that construction of a residence that would interfere with efficacy of solar collectors on plaintiff's residence would be a nuisance, if unreasonable. To determine reasonableness, the court should consider evidence of all the circumstances including "the extent of the harm to the plaintiff, the suitability of solar heat in that neighborhood, the availability of remedies to the plaintiff, and the costs to the defendant of avoiding the harm."

Professor Carol M. Rose criticized the *Prah* case in *Crystals and Mud in Property Law,* 40 Stan. L. Rev. 577, 604-05 (1988):

> [W]hat seemed to be a workable crystalline rule about sunlight rights—that your neighbor has no right to the sunlight that crosses your lot unless your neighbor has gotten an easement from you—has been transformed into a mud doctrine. Now, if you block the light, your neighbor may have a nuisance action against you . . . . Does it matter that you built first? Could you or your neighbor have adjusted your respective buildings to avoid the problem? How valuable was the sunlight to you, and how valuable to your neighbor? . . . You don't know whether your building will be found a nuisance or not and you won't really know until you go through the pain and trouble of getting a court to decide the issue . . . .

Some states have enacted statutory rules governing conflicts over shading solar energy devices, but they may not cover all conflicts that arise. *See Sher v. Lederman,* 226 Cal. Rptr. 698 (Ct. App. 1986), holding that California Solar Shade Control Act protected only solar collectors, not a passive solar house.

Opponents of wind farms have used private nuisance actions to delay and restrict development of projects with varying degrees of success. *See* Stephen Harland Butler, *Headwinds to a Clean Energy Future: Nuisance Suits Against Wind Energy Projects in the United States,* 97 Cal. L. Rev. 1337 (2009). Ryan Kusmin, *Sucking the Air Out of Wind Energy: Nuisance Litigation and Its Effect on Wind Energy Development,* 88 Wash. U. L. Rev. 707 (2011), suggests a statutory solution that would protect neighbors by license and siting requirements and shielding developers from nuisance litigation.

Sensitive Uses

Restatement (Second) of Torts § 821F. Significant Harm

There is liability for a nuisance only to those to whom it causes significant harm, of a kind that would be suffered by a normal person in the community or by property in normal condition and used for a normal purpose.

A classic case illustrating harm that is not deemed significant for nuisance liability is *Amphitheaters, Inc. v. Portland Meadows,* 198 P.2d 847 (Or. 1948). The outdoor theater owner's suit against an adjoining race track operator claiming that its lights interfered with viewing the theater's screen was not successful.

Coming to the Nuisance and Changing Neighborhoods

If someone moves into an area in which industrial or agricultural uses are normal and then claims that the noises, smells, and dirt accompanying those uses are nuisances, that person is likely to lose on the grounds that the person "came to the nuisance" or that the uses are not unreasonable given the location. However, uses that are reasonable at one time or place may become unreasonable over time as an area changes character or technology or community standards change. Normally, what happens is that the older, now offensive, use is forced to clean up its operation or move. However, legislatures in some states have sought to preserve agricultural land from suburbanization by enacting so-called right-to-farm laws that insulate farmers from private nuisance suits. Those laws may not, however, insulate them from nuisance actions brought by other farmers. *See, e.g., TDM Farms, Inc. v. Wilhoite Family Farm LLC*, 969 N.E.2d 97 (Ind. Ct. App. 2012). The court held that the right-to-farm act did not apply to a suit by a hog farm operator against a commercial hog farming operation that intentionally introduced a highly contagious virus to a neighboring farm to immunize the hogs.

Spur Industries, Inc. v. Del E. Webb Development Co., 494 P.2d 700 (Ariz. 1972), is a very famous case in which a large new residential development in a rural area turned a cattle feedlot into a nuisance. The court noted that if only the developer's interests been at stake, it would have denied Del Webb's request for an injunction on the ground that it came to the nuisance. Because of the interests of the residents of the new town, however, the developer was awarded an injunction but required to pay the costs of moving or shutting down the feedlot. The court said:

> It does not seem harsh to require a developer, who has taken advantage of the lesser land values in a rural area as well as the availability of large tracts of land on which to build and develop a new town or city in the area, to indemnify those who are forced to leave as a result.

This compensated injunction is highly unusual, if not unique. *See* Jeff L. Lewin, *Compensated Injunctions and the Evolution of Nuisance Law*, 71 Iowa L. Rev. 775 (1985).

The idea of the compensated injunction was elaborated in a famous article by Guido Calabresi and A. Douglas Melamed, *Property Rules, Liability Rules, and Inalienability: One View of the Cathedral*, 85 Harv. L. Rev. 1089 (1972). They observed that entitlements are protected either by property rules or liability rules. Property rules allow the holder to decide whether or not to sell the entitlement and at what price. Liability rules force the entitlement holder to sell it at a price determined by a court or some other governmental mechanism. They suggested that there are four possible remedies available in nuisance actions between two neighbors: (1) injunction in favor of neighbor A against activity by neighbor B (property rule); (2) damages in favor of neighbor A against neighbor B (liability rule); (3) no injunction or damages to neighbor A, B entitled to continue use (property rule); and (4) injunction against neighbor B but only if A pays B damages (liability rule). Under remedies (1) and (3), the entitlement can be obtained only by a voluntary transaction between the parties. Under (1), B can try to buy the entitlement from A; under (3) A can try to buy the entitlement from B. Under remedies (2) and (4), the entitlement can be obtained by paying a judicially determined price. The authors observed that remedies (1), (2), and (3) had all been used in nuisance cases, but that (4) had not.

CHAPTER 12

Servitudes and Common Interest Communities

A. INTRODUCTION

Servitudes are used to create rights and obligations that "run with the land"—automatically passing to subsequent owners and occupiers whether or not they have been assigned the rights or assumed the obligations. Servitudes are widely used in real estate development for a variety of purposes. Some of the most common uses include:

- Creating permanent rights to use land belonging to others for limited purposes such as driveways, bikeways, utility lines, and railroads;
- Restricting use of land to protect residential neighborhoods, to preserve views, to control the mix of businesses and limit competition in shopping centers, and for historic preservation and conservation;
- Obligating landowners to pay for community facilities and services provided by merchants' or homeowners' associations; and
- Creating rights to remove sand and gravel, timber, and wildlife from land belonging to others.

The rights created by servitudes are called "benefits" and the obligations are called "burdens." If either the benefit or the burden runs with an interest in the land, a servitude has been created. Because both the benefit and burden do not necessarily run with an interest in land, it is important to analyze benefits and burdens separately. Benefits and burdens that run with the land are called "**appurtenant**"; those that do not are called "**in gross**."

Running with the Land and Running with Interests in the Land

Benefits and burdens are sometimes said to run with the land and at other times to run with an interest in land. Technically speaking, a benefit or burden runs with the land when all successor owners and occupiers of the land are entitled to enjoy the benefit or are bound by the burden. When only successors to the interest (usually an estate) owned by one of the original parties are bound or benefited by the servitude, the benefit or burden runs with an interest in the land. Lawyers and judges do not always speak technically, however, and often simply say that a benefit or burden—or simply that a servitude—runs with the land even when it in fact runs only with a particular estate in the land. In this book we generally use the shorter "runs with the land" rather than "runs with the land or an interest in land," but you should remember that the phrase is shorthand.

Generally speaking, the benefits and burdens of easements, profits, and restrictive covenants run with the land while benefits and burdens of affirmative covenants run with an estate in land. To take a familiar example, the burden of a tenant's covenant to pay rent runs to an assignee of the leasehold, but not to a sublessee. The burden of an affirmative covenant runs with the estate, not with the land, and the taker of a lesser estate than that held by the covenantor is not bound. By contrast, however, the tenant's covenant not to use the premises for nonresidential purposes runs to both assignees and sublessees. The burden of a restrictive covenant runs with the land to any subsequent occupier of the land. We take up questions about which benefits and burdens run to whom in more detail later in the chapter.

A basic principle that operates in this area, as it does throughout property law, is that you cannot convey an interest greater than you own. Thus, the owner of a 50-year leasehold can sell and convey an easement to a neighbor, but the easement burdens only the leasehold estate. The holder of the leasehold does not have the power to burden the fee simple. The easement binds all occupiers of the land so long as the leasehold remains in existence, but terminates when the leasehold terminates.

Types of Servitudes and Servitude Categories

There are two basic types of servitudes: easements and covenants. An **easement** creates a right to enter and use land belonging to another and obligates the landowner to refrain from interfering with the authorized use. An easement does not impose affirmative burdens on the servient owner.[1] A **covenant** is a promise by or to a landowner intended to bind or benefit successors to the land that either:

- Obligates the landowner to use or refrain from using the land in a particular way (a restrictive covenant); or
- Obligates the landowner to make payments or provide some other performance to another (an affirmative covenant); or
- Entitles the landowner to receive payments or some other performance from another.

In addition to easements and covenants, there are five subsidiary servitude categories that either build on or combine elements of easements and covenants. A "profit à prendre,"[2] usually called a "profit" for short, adds to an easement the

---

1. The easement to maintain fences was historically recognized as an exception to the general rule that easements could not impose affirmative burdens. Today such an obligation would be imposed by covenant.
2. Profit à prendre comes from law French and means a right to take something.

right to remove a natural resource such as timber, sand, or gravel, or the right to hunt and fish on the land. An "executed parol license" is a **license** (a revocable right to use land) that has become irrevocable by estoppel. It is functionally identical to an easement. A "negative easement" restricts the use that can be made of a particular parcel of land. It serves the same function as a restrictive covenant. An "**equitable servitude**" is a covenant that is enforceable by injunction and historically shared some of the characteristics of an easement. Finally, a "**conservation easement**" is a statutorily recognized servitude[3] that combines elements of easements and covenants to create servitudes for conservation and historic preservation purposes that may be held by charitable organizations and governmental bodies.

Common Interest Communities

In "common interest communities," the owners of individual lots or units also have rights to use common property held by the owners as a group, and are obligated to pay assessments for management and maintenance of the common property. Common interest communities overcome free-rider and tragedy of the commons problems by providing a vehicle for management and financial support of the common property through a property owners' association that has the power to manage the property and levy assessments on the individual lots or units. Much of America's newer housing stock is located in common interest communities, which include condominiums, cooperatives, town-house communities, planned communities, and standard subdivisions with mandatory-membership homeowner associations. The common interest community may also be used for commercial developments that combine common property with individual ownership of parcels or units.

A Bit of History: Disintegration and Integration of Servitudes Law

Roman law recognized servitudes as a body of law that encompassed rights-of-way, rights to remove natural resources from the land of another, and various forms of building restrictions and rights to encroach on the land of another. English law, however, followed a different path. From the earliest days of the common law, what later came to be known as easements and profits were placed in the category of "incorporeal hereditaments," a variety of rights created by grant, rather than by feoffment, that were nonetheless treated as real property. According to Blackstone,[4] these were the incorporeal hereditaments:

- Advowsons: right to appoint the minister of a particular church
- Annuities: right to an annual payment
- Commons: profits for pasturage, fishing (piscary), digging turf (turbary), or cutting wood (estovers)

3. State statutes vary but many of them are modeled on the Uniform Conservation Easement Act of 1981.
4. 2 Blackstone's Commentaries 20-43 (1776) (Special Edition, Legal Classics Library, 1983).

- Corodies: right to receive food and maintenance, or a pension, from a religious house or ecclesiastic
- Franchises: privileges granted by the crown for a wide variety of things including holding a court, fair, or market, taking tolls, or maintaining a "bailiwick" free of the county sheriff's jurisdiction
- Offices and dignities: the right to hold and exercise a public or private employment, such as magistrate, bailiff, receiver, etc.
- Rents: right to services from the tenant, or to payment in kind or in money from produce of the land
- Tithes: right to a tenth of annual crops, offspring, milk, and wool of domestic animals, and of profits from trades and occupations
- Ways: right of going over another's ground

Running covenants developed much later and quite separately from incorporeal hereditaments. As a result, the rules and terminology applied to easements and profits on the one hand, and to covenants on the other, were quite different.

Although its roots are much older, our modern law of servitudes really begins in the 19th century when the effects of the industrial revolution created significant new demand for transportation corridors and new forms of land use arrangements. Canal and railroad rights-of-way were often acquired by purchasing or condemning easements rather than fee simple ownership of the land. Increased competition in the business world led to use of covenants to lock in supplier and transportation contracts and to protect against competition. In addition, increasing urbanization and affluence, as well as increased pollution, noise, and traffic, led to demands for residential neighborhoods with amenities and protection from commercial and industrial uses. The law of covenants, which previously had operated primarily in the landlord-tenant arena, developed significantly to accommodate the new demands for residential neighborhoods.

Throughout the 19th century, easements and covenants inhabited separate worlds for the most part, but in the 20th century American land developers increasingly used them together as they built more complex residential subdivisions. It became increasingly apparent that easements and covenants had many similarities and the first Restatement of Property, published in 1944, returned to the Roman usage, treating them together in a volume titled "Servitudes." Although easements and covenants were now recognized as falling under the larger category of servitudes, the first Restatement viewed them as governed by distinct bodies of law, each with its own rules and terminology. The law of covenants presented by that Restatement was exceedingly complex.

After World War II, land development in the United States went to a whole new level with the growth of mass-produced residential communities, shopping centers, and industrial parks, many of which used combinations of easements and covenants to create shared use rights, restrictions on permissible uses, affirmative obligations to contribute to maintenance, and governance structures to manage common property and enforce restrictions. The advent of condominiums in the 1960s brought a huge increase in the number of common interest communities and further blurring of the old lines between easements and covenants. The law of servitudes also drew increasing attention from scholars intrigued and dismayed by its complexity.

Recognizing that substantial changes in servitudes law had taken place on the ground (if not in judicial rhetoric), and that the law had grown needlessly complex, the American Law Institute undertook a project in 1986 to simplify, clarify, and rationalize the law of servitudes. That project culminated with publication of the *Restatement (Third) of Property, Servitudes* (2000), which integrates the law of easements, profits, and covenants into a substantially simpler modern law of servitudes. The Restatement (Third) reduces the number of servitude categories to three: profits, easements, and covenants. Irrevocable licenses are treated as easements; negative easements and equitable servitudes are treated as covenants. In this chapter we refer frequently to the Restatement (Third). Although we believe that there is—or should be—very little difference in the rules that apply to easements and covenants, we take them up separately for ease of study. Profits and irrevocable licenses are covered in connection with easements in Section B; equitable servitudes, negative easements, conservation easements, and common interest communities are covered in connection with covenants in Section C.

B.   EASEMENTS AND PROFITS

Easements and profits create nonpossessory rights—use rights that amount to something less than rights to possession. Possession remains with the owner of the land burdened by an easement or profit, who is called the "**servient**" or "burdened" owner and retains the right to make all uses of the property that do not interfere with reasonable use of the easement or profit. The owner of land benefited by an easement, who is called the "**dominant**" or "benefited" owner, has the right to use the servient estate in a manner that is reasonably necessary for convenient use of the easement. Easements and profits are interests in land subject to the Statute of Frauds and "property" entitled to constitutional protection. Ordinarily, they are—and are required to be—created by written instruments, but they may also be created by estoppel, implication, and prescription.

English common law, following the Roman model, refused to allow the creation of easements in gross (meaning an easement with the benefit in gross). However, when easements in gross were needed, as for railroads, canals, or pipelines, Parliament readily authorized their creation by special statutes.[5] American courts rejected this limitation on common-law easements, which could have delayed and interfered with development of the country's transportation infrastructure. Early on, they recognized easements in gross, at least for commercial purposes.

The normal method of creating an easement is by deed. Easements should be carefully drafted because they can have a significant impact on the value of the servient estate. However, many are not. One of the questions that frequently arises is whether a given deed was intended to create an easement at all. Sometimes the landowner will claim that the deed conveyed only a license and sometimes the grantee will claim that the deed conveyed a fee simple.

---

5.   Michael F. Sturley, *"The Land Obligation": An English Proposal for Reform*, 55 S. Cal. L. Rev. 1417 (1982).

1. *Creation of Easements and Profits*

a. Intent

(i) Easement or Fee?

BROWN v. THE PENN CENTRAL CORPORATION

Supreme Court of Indiana
510 N.E.2d 641 (1987)

PIVARNIK, J. . . . The facts set out by the Court of Appeals are as follows:

On July 6, 1871 the Detroit, Eel River and Illinois Railroad (railroad) acquired by deed an interest in certain lands in the Town of Churubusco, Indiana. . . . The land described in the deed included both a right-of-way, 100 feet in width, and a strip conveyed for "depot and railroad purposes." This depot ground and railroad property was originally 200 feet in width and extended 1000 feet in length along the south side of the right-of-way. The appellants are the owners of several lots of real estate in Churubusco, which are contiguous to the railroad right-of-way and the ground designated "for depot and railroad purposes." The appellee, Penn Central Corporation (Penn Central) is the successor to the original grantee railroad corporation.

Penn Central ceased operating the railroad through Churubusco and abandoned the right-of-way on November 30, 1973. However, it continued to collect rents from two tenants which were occupying space on the depot and railroad property. Subsequently, the appellants brought an action to quiet title to these lands in themselves. The trial court held that the railroad received nothing more than an easement as to the right-of-way, which was extinguished when it was no longer used for railroad purposes. The court, however, ruled against the appellants as to the depot and railroad property, and held that Penn Central was vested with fee simple title to this strip.

Omitting the formal portions, the deed in question reads as follows:

KNOW ALL MEN BY THESE PRESENTS

That Western Ackley and Caroline Ackley, his wife of Whitley County, Indiana in consideration of the location and construction of the Detroit, Eel River and Illinois Railroad, and three hundred dollars, to them in hand paid . . . , the receipt of which is hereby acknowledged, do give, grant, bargain, sell and convey to said Company, the Right of Way for the use of the Railroad of said Company over and across:

[The North West quarter of the South West quarter of Section Thirteen (13) in Township Thirty-Two (32) North of Range Ten (10) East. Also the East 1/2 of the North half of the South West quarter of said Section Thirteen (13) and the West part of the North half of the South East quarter of said Section Thirteen (13) in said County of Whitley. Also a strip Two hundred feet in width on the South Side of the Right of Way hereby conveyed and adjoining the same and one thousand feet in length extending from the Public Highway on the East line of said road being for Depot and Rail Road purposes.] for the width of fifty feet on each side of the center line of said Road, as located by the Logansport and Northern Indiana Rail

Road Company, and as now located, and for the distance between the limits of said track, to include, also, the right of said Company to take materials, except timber, for the construction and repairs of said Road at any point within fifty feet of said line, together with the Right of Way over said tract of land sufficient to enable said Company to construct and repair its Road, and the right to conduct water by aqua-duces, (sic) and the right of making proper drains.

To Have and to Hold the same Rights and Privileges to the use of said Company, so long as the same shall be required for the use and purposes of said Road, in as full, perfect, and ample a manner as may be required for that purpose.

The portion of the deed contained in our brackets was handwritten. The remaining portion of the deed was pre-printed. It appears that the deed was designed in this manner so that a description of the land acquired could be inserted in hand-written form. This particular deed form was prepared by the railroad for use in acquiring railroad right-of-ways.

. . . [W]hen a railroad prepares a conveyance form, it is responsible for the printed words. . . . Thus, we will construe the form in the light most favorable to the grantors.

A deed that conveys a *right* generally conveys only an easement. . . . The general rule is that a conveyance to a railroad of a strip, piece, or parcel of land, without additional language as to the use or purpose to which the land is to be put or in other ways limiting the estate conveyed, is to be construed as passing an estate in fee, but reference to a right-of-way . . . generally leads to its construction as conveying only an easement. Here, the deed . . . contains additional language which indicates the purpose to which the land was to be put. The deed states the strip of land was to be "for Depot and Rail Road purposes." Further, the granting clause, which was pre-printed above the hand-written portion of the deed, expressly states the grantors were conveying a right-of-way. We find the deed clearly falls within the general rule and must be construed as conveying only an easement in the strip of land in question.

. . . We do not agree with the Court of Appeals that the deed is a hybrid, purporting to convey both a right-of-way, and a separate strip of land. Rather, we read the deed as granting a right-of-way which includes the strip of land. Supporting our construction is the fact that the grant is limited by the hand-written portion which states, "for Depot and Rail Road purposes." . . .

If one were to speculate as to what the parties intended back in 1871, several questions arise. If the railroad purchased the strip of land in fee simple, why was this not expressed in the deed? The fact that the railroad used a pre-printed right-of-way form indicates to us that this is what they were bargaining for with the grantor. Surely the railroad, the more experienced party in this transaction, would have included words to indicate the strip of land was to be conveyed in fee simple if that was the parties' intent. . . .

Further, we are mindful of the public policy in this State . . . [as stated in] Ross, Inc. v. Legler 199 N.E.2d 346 (Ind. 1964) . . . :

Public policy does not favor the conveyance of strips of land by fee simple titles to railroad companies for right-of-way purposes, either by deed or condemnation. This policy is based upon the fact that the alienation of such strips or belts of land from and across the primary or parent bodies of the land from which they are severed, is obviously not necessary to the purpose for which such conveyances are made after abandonment of the intended uses as expressed in the conveyance, and that thereafter such severance generally operates adversely to the normal and best use of the property involved. . . .

We conclude that . . . [t]he railroad's right-of-way was an easement to use the land to carry on the railroad's business. When Penn Central abandoned the right-of-way in 1973, the easement was extinguished. . . .

Notes and Questions

1. *Easement or fee?* As railroads cut back service and abandoned tracks all over the country in the latter half of the 20th century, the question whether they owned easements or fee simple interests assumed great importance. Land they owned in fee simple could be used or disposed of as the railroads pleased. Easements could be used only for purposes within the scope of the easement and, if abandoned, the easements terminated. Substantial litigation has been the result. Although many courts agree with the Indiana court that use of the term *right-of-way* leads to the conclusion that an easement was granted rather than a fee, there are cases that come out the other way. *See, e.g., City of Manhattan Beach v. Superior Court*, 914 P.2d 160 (Cal. 1996) (grant of "right-of-way for steam railroad" conveyed fee simple; railroad had sold the land to city for park and jogging path; heir hunters were behind the suit).

The question whether still-operating railroads own easements or fee simple interests has also become important since communications companies began laying fiber optic cable alongside the tracks in the 1980s and 1990s under rights purchased from the railroads. Class actions were brought on behalf of landowners across the country claiming they, rather than the railroads, were entitled to payments made by the companies laying the cables.

2. In 1983, Congress enacted the Rails-to-Trails Act, 16 U.S.C. § 1247, to preserve discontinued railroad corridors for future rail use and to permit public recreational use of discontinued railroad rights-of-way. It authorized the Interstate Commerce Commission to permit discontinuance of rail service and transfer of the right-of-way to a public or private group willing to maintain it as a public trail. If the railroad had only an easement, and if a court finds that use of the easement for a walking or bike trail exceeds the scope of the easement, transfer of the right-of-way for public recreational use constitutes a taking of the servient owner's land, which is illegal unless just compensation is paid. *See, e.g., Preseault v. United States*, 100 F.3d 1525 (Fed. Cir. 1996).

(ii)   Easement or License?

STRATIS v. DOYLE

New York Supreme Court, Appellate Division
575 N.Y.S.2d 400 (1991)

MAHONEY, P.J. . . . By deed dated March 2, 1979, defendant William J. Doyle granted his neighbor Donald Abbatiello a right-of-way across his property for the purpose of constructing a driveway. The deed also provided that "[Abbatiello] agrees that he will construct and maintain such driveway upon the lands described above in a good, workmanlike manner [and] that the same will be completed by April 1, 1980." . . . Doyle sold some of the property over which the right-of-way was to pass to defendant . . . Dennebaum. Thereafter, Abbatiello's property passed to his mortgagee which ultimately conveyed it to plaintiffs as tenants in common.

Plaintiffs commenced this . . . action alleging that Doyle improperly interfered with their use of the right-of-way. . . . [Defendants] answered . . . alleging that the right-of-way was merely a license, personal to Abbatiello, and not an easement appurtenant and, alternatively, that if the right-of-way was an easement, a condition subsequent requiring construction and maintenance of a driveway had failed, resulting in a forfeiture of the right-of-way.

. . . Supreme Court correctly determined, as a matter of law, that the grant of the right-of-way was an easement. The interest created was by warranty deed, suggesting a transfer of an interest in real property; the word "grant" is used, suggesting that an easement was intended; specific words of inheritance are used; and no rights of revocation are withheld. . . . Hence, we conclude that the grant of a nonexclusive right by Doyle to construct and maintain a right-of-way across his property created an easement rather than a license. . . .

Next, we reject defendants' argument that the deed's language . . . created a condition subsequent, the failure of which results in a forfeiture of any alleged easement. . . . Conditions subsequent are disfavored and are not found to exist unless the intention to create them is clearly expressed. . . . [N]othing in the deed expresses an intent to create such a condition. . . . Considering this and Doyle's failure to retain any expressed or implied reversionary interest or a right of reentry . . . we hold that the deed contains only a covenant . . . and not a condition subsequent.

Notes and Questions

1. *Meaning of "license" and "personal."* Doyle claimed that the right-of-way was "merely a license, personal to Abbatiello." Although the language suggests that the two go together, in fact, they are separate concepts. *License* in this context ordinarily means that the right to use the land is unconditionally revocable by the landowner. *Personal* means that the use right is not transferable. A use right may be revocable but transferable, or it may be transferable but not revocable, or it may be both revocable and not transferable. Unconditionally revocable use rights are not servitudes because they do not bind either the original or any successor owners of the land. Personal rights, however, may be servitudes if they are not revocable. For example, if Doyle had granted Abbatiello a right-of-way that terminated when Abbatiello died or transferred his property, Abbatiello would have had a nontransferable, nonrevocable use right that would be properly classified as an easement. The burden of the easement would run to Doyle's successors if he transferred his property before the easement terminated.

2. *Difference between a covenant and a condition subsequent.* If a covenantor is found to have breached a covenant, the covenantee is generally entitled to damages or injunctive relief—contractual remedies. By contrast, if a property owner is found to have breached a condition subsequent, the property owner generally forfeits the property to the beneficiary of the condition—the person who holds the right of entry or power of termination. Notice that easements can be made subject to conditions that allow termination. When creating easements, people too often fail to think about the conditions under which they should be able to modify or terminate the easement granted. Why did the court construe the language in this instrument to create a covenant rather than a condition?

3. *Easement benefits and burdens run with the land.* Notice that Dennebaum, as well as Doyle, is bound by the easement because he now owns part of the servient estate. Even if his deed said nothing about the easement, Dennebaum is bound, unless the easement was not recorded and he takes free of it under the recording act. Notice, too, that the benefit of the easement passed from Abbatiello to his mortgagee and from the mortgagee to the plaintiffs. Even if the plaintiffs' deed did not mention the easement, the benefit passed to them automatically as an appurtenance to the property (the dominant or benefited estate).

4. *Exclusive and non-exclusive benefits.* The court concluded that Doyle granted Abbatiello a non-exclusive right to construct and maintain a driveway. Non-exclusive in this context means that Abbatiello will not have the right to exclude others from using the driveway. Doyle may not interfere with Abbatiello's use of the driveway, but may use it himself and grant others the right to use it so long as the additional use does not unreasonably interfere with Abbatiello's use (or his successor's use). *See* Restatement (Third) § 4.9, comments *d* and *e* (use of improvements constructed for enjoyment of easement; creation of additional servitudes). In the absence of an agreement to the contrary, all users of an easement may be required to contribute to its maintenance, Restatement (Third) §4.13(3) and (4). If the deed does not specify whether an easement is exclusive or non-exclusive, courts will look at the nature of the easement, the consideration paid, and other available evidence to try to determine the parties' likely intent.

5. *Easement or license?* Restatement (Third) § 2.2, comment *h* states:

> Payment of consideration and use of formality appropriate to a land transaction usually indicate that the parties intended a servitude. Lack of formality or words of conveyance, and lack of consideration, tend to indicate that a license was intended. The existence of a close personal relationship between the parties may buttress the conclusion that a license was intended.

6. *Labels are not determinative.* The label used may be significant, but is not determinative. Irrevocable rights of limited duration are sometimes created by instruments denominated licenses, probably because of statements in some older authorities that easements must be perpetual. If other provisions of the instrument, or the circumstances, make it clear that the "licensor" was not intended to have the power to revoke during the term of the arrangement, the instrument is effective to create a servitude. There is no reason that easements should have to be perpetual.

7. *Who can create an easement?* The owner of any estate in land or easement benefit has the power to create an easement or covenant burdening that estate or easement—but cannot create an easement that would burden an estate that belongs to someone else. So, the owner of a life estate or leasehold can create an easement that will last for the duration of the life estate or leasehold, but cannot burden the reversion or remainder in fee simple with the easement. *See*

Restatement (Third) § 2.5: "A servitude may be created to burden or benefit any estate in land or another servitude." The owner of an easement benefit, likewise, can burden it with a servitude. For example, the owner of a pipeline easement in gross might burden it by covenanting with the servient owner to maintain landscaping over and along the pipeline right-of-way.

8. *Licenses and prescriptive easements.* Licenses are often said to be revoked when the land is transferred, but such statements should be taken with a grain of salt. Absent an enforceable agreement to the contrary, or circumstances producing an estoppel, the landowner is free to revoke the license at any time, but, until the license is revoked, use by the licensee remains permissive. Something more than a change of ownership is required to convert the licensee's use from permissive to hostile. *See* Restatement (Third) § 2.16, comment *f.*

b.   Creation by Estoppel

Servitudes are created by estoppel when a landowner is estoped to deny the existence of a servitude. This typically happens when the landowner represents to someone, usually a prospective purchaser, that the landowner's property is burdened with a servitude benefiting the property the purchaser is interested in, or when the landowner gives someone, usually a neighbor, permission to use the land but doesn't agree to create a servitude. The situations in which the landowner will be estopped to deny that a servitude has been created are described by the Restatement:

Restatement (Third) § 2.10, Servitudes Created by Estoppel

If injustice can be avoided only by establishment of a servitude, the owner or occupier of land is estopped to deny the existence of a servitude burdening the land when:

(1) the owner or occupier permitted another to use that land under circumstances in which it was reasonable to foresee that the user would substantially change position believing that the permission would not be revoked, and the user did substantially change position in reasonable reliance on that belief; or

(2) the owner or occupier represented that the land was burdened by a servitude under circumstances in which it was reasonable to foresee that the person to whom the representation was made would substantially change position on the basis of that representation, and the person did substantially change position. . . .

MUND v. ENGLISH
Court of Appeals of Oregon
684 P.2d 1248 (Or. Ct. App. 1984)

ROSSMAN, J. . . . Plaintiffs are the son and daughter-in-law of defendant. In 1977, plaintiffs and defendant, together with the deceased husband of defendant, purchased adjoining one acre parcels of property . . . . In that year, a water well was drilled on defendant's property. Equipment and pipes were installed so that plaintiffs and defendant received water from the one well. In less than a year after the installation, the parties began to quarrel about their rights to the well and water. The fighting has continued since then, culminating in this suit for declaratory judgment and specific performance.

Plaintiffs contend that, from the beginning, their interest in the well was to have been a permanent and irrevocable interest. Defendant claims that plaintiffs' rights were not permanent and were subject to certain conditions. The trial court found for defendant. On *de novo* review, we agree with the trial court that plaintiffs failed to prove that the parties had agreed that defendant would deed a one-half interest in the well to plaintiffs, as well as a permanent easement over the land for the installation of the water system. There simply was no meeting of the minds. However, the facts clearly show that defendant did grant an irrevocable license to plaintiffs. . . . Accordingly, we reverse. . . .

Defendant argues that an irrevocable license can only be established when there is proof of an agreement for a permanent easement which is taken out of the Statute of Frauds (requiring a writing) by part performance. . . . Although it is true that, in most jurisdictions, an oral license may be revoked, Oregon has consistently held that, when a licensee makes valuable improvements on the basis of a promise, the licensor will not be permitted to assert that the license could be revoked. An irrevocable license does not depend on proof of the agreement of the parties but arises by operation of law to prevent an injustice. . . .

. . . Defendant admits that she and her deceased husband granted plaintiffs the right to use the well and to install a pipeline to plaintiffs' property. The testimony of plaintiffs and defendant as to the permanency of this agreement is in direct dispute, and the testimony of the attorney who was to draft an agreement for the parties was indeterminant. The attorney admitted that he could not find a record of his meeting and that he had only a general recollection of the event. He recalled a lack of agreement as to whether the parties wanted a contract or a deed of easement, but he could not recall any specifics.

However, the circumstances here show a permanent arrangement. Plaintiffs and defendant shared the installation costs of the well and water system. Plaintiff Mr. Mund and defendant's husband worked together installing the system. The parties have continued to share operating expenses. Even more significantly, plaintiffs secured a $40,000 commercial loan in 1977 and constructed a residence on their property. There was, and is, no other source of domestic water for plaintiffs. The improvements made by plaintiffs clearly show their reliance on a permanent agreement. The law will not permit defendant to claim that she can withdraw the license to use the well.

Reversed and remanded for entry of a decree granting plaintiffs a one-half interest in the water well and water system on defendant's property, granting plaintiffs an easement over defendant's property for the purpose of access to the water system and requiring plaintiffs and defendant to share equally the cost of maintaining the system.

Notes and Questions

1. What is the basis for finding that the plaintiffs had acquired a servitude? Express agreement? Implied agreement? Permission given under circumstances that should have led the defendant to realize that the plaintiffs would rely on continued access? Does the situation meet the Restatement standard "if injustice can be avoided only by . . ."?

2. What is an irrevocable license to use land belonging to another, sometimes called an executed parol license? Restatement (Third) § 1.2 says it is an easement.

3. If the Munds' house is destroyed in an earthquake, does their right to use the well terminate? The first Restatement said that an executed parol license would continue "to the extent necessary to realize upon [the licensee's] expenditures." Restatement (Third) rejects any distinction between easements and irrevocable licenses, but provides that a court may modify or terminate either "when a change has taken place since the creation of the servitude that makes it impossible as a practical matter to accomplish the purpose for which the servitude was created." *See* Restatement § 7.10.

4. Should courts be more insistent on complying with the formality of a written instrument to create an interest in land? The court in *Henry v. Dalton*, 151 A.2d 362 (R.I. 1959), held that the defendant was not estopped to revoke permission for use of a common driveway straddling the boundary between their lots despite the plaintiff's construction of a garage and contributions to construction and maintenance of the drive, saying:

> ". . . [A] parol license . . . is revocable at the option of the licensor, and this, although the intention was to confer a continuing right and money had been expended by the licensee upon the faith of the license. This is plainly the rule of the statute. It is also, we believe, the rule required by public policy. It prevents the burdening of lands with restrictions founded upon oral agreements, easily misunderstood. It gives security and certainty to titles, which are most important to be preserved against defects and qualifications not founded upon solemn instruments." . . .
>
> Counsel for the complainants urge that the statute of frauds . . . is designed to protect against fraud and should not be used to assist in the perpetration of fraud. We are in accord with this contention, but are not convinced that in the circumstances of the instant case the respondent's revocation of the complainants' license is fraudulent within any acceptable definition of that term. The right which complainants seek to establish in the land of the respondent is essentially an easement and should be the subject of a grant, expressed in the solemnity of a written instrument. It is no hardship for one in the position of these complainants either to secure an easement in perpetuity in the manner provided by the statute, or, such being refused, to weigh the advantages inuring to them as against the uncertainty implicit in the making of expenditures on the basis of a revocable license.

c. Creation by Implication

Servitudes may arise by implication from a variety of circumstances surrounding conveyance of a parcel of land. For example, if a conveyance landlocks a parcel, an easement for access will be implied across the parcel from which its ownership was severed. This is called an easement by necessity. If a conveyance is made by reference to a map that shows streets, or a park, or other community facility, on land owned by the grantor, an easement to use the facility shown on the map will ordinarily be implied. In subdivisions subject to servitudes designed to implement a general plan of development, reciprocal servitudes binding and benefiting all lots in the subdivision are usually implied. Servitudes may also arise by inference from prior use of one parcel to benefit another.

(i)   Implied on the Basis of Prior Use

VAN SANDT v. ROYSTER
Supreme Court of Kansas
83 P.2d 698 (Kan. 1938)

ALLEN, J. The action was brought to enjoin defendants from using and maintaining an underground lateral sewer drain through and across plaintiff's land. The case was tried by the court, judgment was rendered in favor of defendants, and plaintiff appeals.

In the city of Chanute, Highland Avenue running north and south intersects Tenth Street running east and west. In the early part of 1904 Laura A.J. Bailey was the owner of a plot of ground lying east of Highland Avenue and south of Tenth Street. Running east from Highland Avenue and facing north on Tenth Street the lots are numbered, respectively, 19, 20 and 4. In 1904 the residence of Mrs. Bailey was on lot 4 on the east part of her land.

In the latter part of 1903, or the early part of 1904, the city . . . constructed a public sewer in Highland Avenue, west of lot 19. About the same time a private lateral drain was constructed from the Bailey residence on lot 4 running in a westerly direction through and across lots 20 and 19 to the public sewer.

On January 15, 1904, Laura A. J. Bailey conveyed lot 19 to John J. Jones, by general warranty deed with usual covenants against encumbrances, and containing no exceptions or reservations. Jones erected a dwelling on the north part of the lot. In 1920 Jones conveyed . . . to . . . Reynolds [who] conveyed to the plaintiff, who has owned and occupied the premises since [1924].

In 1904 Laura A. J. Bailey conveyed lot 20 to one Murphy, who built a house thereon, and by mesne conveyances the title passed to the defendant Louise Royster. The deed to Murphy was a general warranty deed without exceptions or reservations. The defendant Gray has succeeded to the title to lot 4 upon which the old Bailey home stood at the time Laura A. J. Bailey sold lots 19 and 20.

In March, 1936, plaintiff discovered his basement flooded with sewage and filth to a depth of six or eight inches, and upon investigation he found for the first time that there existed on and across his property a sewer drain extending in an easterly direction across the property of Royster to the property of Gray. The refusal of defendants to cease draining and discharging their sewage across plaintiff's land resulted in this lawsuit. . . .

The drain pipe in the lateral sewer was several feet under the surface of the ground. There was nothing visible on the ground in the rear of the houses to indicate the existence of the drain or the connection of the drain with the houses.

As a conclusion of law the court found that "an appurtenant easement existed in the said lateral sewer as to all three of the properties involved in the controversy here." Plaintiff's prayer for relief was denied and it was decreed that plaintiff be restrained from interfering in any way with the lateral drain or sewer.

Plaintiff contends that the evidence fails to show that an easement was ever created in his land, and assuming there was an easement created, as alleged, that he took the premises free from the burden of the easement for the reason that he was a bona fide purchaser, without notice actual or constructive.

Defendants contend: (1) That an easement was created by implied reservation on the severance of the servient from the dominant estate by the deed from Mrs. Bailey to Jones; (2) there is a valid easement by prescription.

In finding No. 11, the court found that the lateral sewer "was an appurtenance to the properties belonging to plaintiff and Louise Royster, and the same is necessary to the reasonable use and enjoyment of the said properties of the parties."

. . . [A]n owner cannot have an easement in his own land. However, an owner may make use of one part of his land for the benefit of another part, and this is frequently spoken of as a quasi easement.

> . . . [T]he part of the land which is benefited [is] referred to as the "quasi dominant tenement" and the part which is utilized for the benefit of the other part [is] referred to as the "quasi servient tenement." . . .
>
> If the owner of land, one part of which is subject to a quasi easement in favor of another part, conveys the quasi dominant tenement, an easement corresponding to such quasi easement is ordinarily regarded as thereby vested in the grantee of the land, provided, it is said, the quasi easement is of an apparent, continuous, and necessary character. [2 Tiffany, *Real Property* (2d Ed.) pp. 1272, 1273.]

Following the famous case of Pyer v. Carter, 1 Hurl. & N. 916, some of the English cases, and many early American cases, held that upon the transfer of the quasi servient tenement there was an implied reservation of an easement in favor of the conveyor. [N]o distinction was made between an implied reservation and an implied grant.

The case, however, was overthrown in England by Suffield v. Brown, 4 De G.J. & S. 185 . . . . In [*Suffield*] the court said:

> It seems to me more reasonable and just to hold that if the grantor intends to reserve any right over the property granted, it is his duty to reserve it expressly in the grant, rather than to limit and cut down the operation of a plain grant. . . . I cannot agree that the grantor can derogate from his own absolute grant so as to claim rights over the thing granted, even if they were, at the time of the grant, continuous and apparent easements enjoyed by an adjoining tenement which remains the property of him the grantor.

Many American courts of high standing assert that the rule regarding implied grants and implied reservations is reciprocal and that the rule applies with equal force and in like circumstances to both grants and reservations. . . . On the other hand perhaps a majority of the cases hold that in order to establish an easement by implied reservation in favor of the grantor the easement must be one of strict necessity, even when there was an existing drain or sewer at the time of the severance. . . .

We are inclined to the view that the circumstance that the claimant of the easement is the grantor instead of the grantee, is but one of many factors to be considered in determining whether an easement will arise by implication. An easement created by implication arises as an inference of the intentions of the parties to a conveyance of land. The inference is drawn from the circumstances under which the conveyance was made rather than from the language of the conveyance. The easement may arise in favor of the conveyor or the conveyee. . . .

At the time John J. Jones purchased lot 19 he was aware of the lateral sewer, and knew that it was installed for the benefit of the lots owned by Mrs. Bailey, the common owner. The easement was necessary to the comfortable enjoyment of the grantor's property. If land may be used without an easement, but cannot be used without disproportionate effort and expense, an easement may still be implied in favor of either the grantor or grantee on the basis of necessity alone. This is the situation as found by the trial court.

Neither can it be claimed that plaintiff purchased without notice. At the time plaintiff purchased the property he and his wife made a careful and thorough inspection of the property. They knew the house was equipped with modern plumbing and that the plumbing had to drain into a sewer. Under the facts as found by the court, we think the purchaser was charged with notice of the lateral sewer. It was an apparent easement . . . .

The author of the annotation on easements by implication in 58 A.L.R. at page 832, states the rule as follows:

> While there is some conflict of authority as to whether existing drains, pipes, and sewers may be properly characterized as apparent, within the rule as to apparent or visible easements, the majority of the cases which have considered the question have taken the view that appearance and visibility are not synonymous, and that the fact that the pipe, sewer, or drain may be hidden underground does not negative its character as an apparent condition; at least, where the appliances connected with and leading to it are obvious.

As we are clear that an easement by implication was created under the facts as found by the trial court, it is unnecessary to discuss the question of prescription.

The judgment is affirmed.

Notes and Questions

1. Since *Van Sandt v. Royster* was decided, the weight of authority in the United States has shifted decidedly in favor of the rule that only reasonable necessity is required, whether the implied easement is in favor of the grantor or the grantee. Is this a good move? What do you suppose is the purpose for the requirement that the prior use be reasonably necessary? Why not imply an easement for the continuance of all uses made at the time of severance?

2. Was this decision fair to the plaintiff? If the plaintiff had won, what would have happened next? In a case like this, does the Coase theorem,[6] that location of the legal entitlement will not affect efficiency because the parties will bargain their way to an efficient solution, apply? If true, is it helpful?

3. What is the purpose of the requirement that the prior use be "apparent"? Restatement (Third) § 2.12 states that a servitude to continue a prior use will be

---

6.   The Coase theorem is discussed in Chapter 1.

implied if at the time of the severance "the parties had reasonable grounds to expect that the conveyance would not terminate the right to continue the prior use." The following factors are listed as tending to establish that there are reasonable grounds for the expectation:

(1) the prior use was not merely temporary or casual, and

(2) continuance of the prior use was reasonably necessary to enjoyment of the parcel, estate, or interest previously benefited by the use, and

(3) existence of the prior use was apparent or known to the parties, or

(4) the prior use was for underground utilities serving either parcel.

Comment *g*, addressing underground utilities whose shared use was not known to the parties, says:

> . . . [W]hen the parcels are served by utilities, the parties reasonably expect that the conveyance will not terminate the right to continued utility services. From the standpoint of the purchaser of the parcel served by the utility lines, continued utility service is part of the land package he believes he is buying. From the standpoint of the grantor, whose retained parcel is served by the utility lines, the right to cut off her utility services is not part of the package she is selling.

> The economic factors often buttress the conclusion that a servitude to continue the prior use should be implied. Implying the servitude will normally impose a relatively slight economic burden, while the costs of relocating the utility lines will often be high. Refusal to imply a servitude to continue the prior use puts the party whose land carries the utility lines serving the other parcel in a position to exact a much higher price for granting the servitude than would be warranted by the reduction in value to his land. When the economic factors do not fit this pattern, they may provide the basis for concluding that a servitude should not be implied. . . .

4. Who is responsible for repairing the sewer line on plaintiff's property? All the parties who use it. *See* Restatement (Third) § 4.13.

5. Should subsequent bona fide purchasers take free of unrecorded invisible easements implied on the basis of prior use? Restatement (Third) § 7.14 provides that, unless the applicable recording act requires a different result, an easement for underground utilities implied on the basis of prior use is not subject to extinguishment under the recording act.

(ii) *Implied on the Basis of Necessity*

MORRELL v. RICE

Supreme Judicial Court of Maine
622 A.2d 1156 (Me. 1993)

CLIFFORD, J. . . . The Morrells, owners of a ten-acre parcel of land in Brunswick fronting on Middle Bay, but with no road frontage, sought in the Superior Court a determination that their land is benefitted by an easement by necessity over abutting land owned by the Rices. The Rice land has frontage on the Harpswell

Road. The Morrell and Rice parcels, which are located on a peninsula, originally were in common ownership; severance of the two parcels of land from the common owner occurred in 1810 in an intrafamily transaction. . . .

At trial, Robert Morrell testified that a portion of his land abuts that of the Rices, that his land is bordered by marshes and tidal flats on two sides, and that the only access to his property by land is from the Harpswell Road, across the Rice land. Although a portion of the Morrells' land fronts on tidal marsh, at low tide the water recedes approximately 1000 yards and the flats freeze in the winter months, thereby severely limiting the times when access by boat is possible. Morrell testified that at the time he bought his land in 1971, he understood that access over the Rice property to his land had existed for many years. There is evidence of an old roadway going through the Rice property to the Morrell parcel.

The court determined that the Morrells established the existence of an easement by necessity.[2] The court found the intrafamily land transfers as evidenced by the deeds of 1810 to be "essentially contemporaneous," that the Harpswell Road existed in 1810, and the obvious access from the Harpswell Road to what is now the Morrell parcel was across the Rice land. The court also found that, except for the Rice land, the Morrell land was surrounded by marsh, and although there was tidal frontage, access to the sea was not realistic. The court established the location and condition of the easement, and this appeal followed.

The Rices first contend that the court's conclusion that their land is burdened by an easement by necessity is flawed because of the absence of unity of title and because there is alternative access to the Morrell land.

An easement by necessity, an easement implied in the law, may be created when a grantor conveys a lot of land from a larger parcel and that conveyed lot is "landlocked" by the grantor's surrounding land and cannot be accessed from a road or highway. Because of the strict necessity of having access to the landlocked parcel, an easement over the grantor's remaining land benefitting the landlocked lot is implied as a matter of law irrespective of the true intent of the common grantor. . . .

An easement by necessity also may be created when there are simultaneous conveyances by a common grantor, and one of the conveyed lots is landlocked and inaccessible. In such a case, an easement over the other simultaneously conveyed lot to benefit the inaccessible lot may be implied. . . .

The Rices contend that the 1810 conveyances creating their parcel of land and that of the Morrells were not simultaneous . . . , precluding the creation of an easement by necessity. Although the deeds do have different dates, they are proximate in time. More importantly, the transactions involve several grantors, all members of the Givens family, and are acknowledged on the same date before the same notary public. Certainly it is not unreasonable to infer that some of the grantors may have signed the deeds at different times, but that delivery of the deeds, the essential act of actual conveyance, occurred simultaneously. It is also not unreasonable to conclude that the family would not have intended one of the lots being created to have no access. The court's finding that the deeds were

2.   The Morrells' complaint did not allege the existence of a quasi-easement, and although it was discussed at trial, the Morrells have not pursued the issue on appeal. . . .

conveyed simultaneously is consistent with the public policy that lands should not be unfit for use . . . and is not clearly erroneous.

The Rices next contend that . . . the Morrells' claim of an easement by necessity must fail because there was access to the Harpswell Road over the remaining land of the common grantor. . . . The Morrells' land is located on the peninsula in such a way that, even if the common grantor still owned land at the time when the present Morrell and Rice parcels were originally conveyed, that land was separated from the Morrell parcel by tidal marsh. Therefore, the Morrells' predecessor in title could not have used the grantor's remaining land to access the Harpswell Road.

[margin note: ① argue common land for road/access]

The Rices also contend that the Morrell land is accessible from the sea, making an easement across their land unnecessary and precluding the creation of an easement by necessity. It is true that a showing of access to land across navigable water could in some circumstances defeat a claim of an easement by necessity. . . . Kingsley v. Gouldsborough Land Improvement Co., 29 A. 1074 (Me. 1894).[4] In this case, however, the court's finding that the Morrells' land was not accessible by the sea is not clearly erroneous. . . . There was evidence that to dredge the area to enable boat access at all times, assuming that all environmental and other permits could be obtained,[6] would cost approximately $300,000. Moreover, the flats freeze in the winter months. . . .

[margin note: ② no need for easement by necessity, if necessity, if access by sea.]

[margin note: water access expensive & limited in winter.]

The scope of the easement as determined by the Superior Court is disputed by both parties. The Rices object to the court's inclusion in the easement of the right to install underground utilities across their land. The Morrells, on the other hand, contend that the court erred in restricting the use of the easement to serve only a single-family residence.

Whether an implied easement exists is determined by examining the circumstances existing at the time the landlocked parcel is severed from the parcel with access. The scope of use of the easement, however, is not determined solely in reference to the time of its creation. Rather, the better rule is that the scope should be defined with reference to the reasonable enjoyment of the land and all lawful uses to which it may be put. . . .

[margin note: look for use/enjoyment of the land]

An easement created by necessity can include not only the right of entry and egress, but also the right to make use of the easement for installation of utilities, essential for most uses to which property may reasonably be put in these times. . . . In this case, in the absence of any evidence that underground utilities would present an undue burden to the Rices' land, the court did not err in concluding that the right to install such utilities was included in the easement.

For the same reasons, we are persuaded that the court's decision to limit the easement to serve only a single-family use of the Morrell property is not justified on this record. An easement by strict necessity should benefit the dominant estate for any lawful and reasonable use. There was no evidence that the only lawful use of the Morrell land would be for one single-family home. Nor

[margin note: balance of Dominant & servient land]

---

4.   We have not reexamined in recent years, in light of the changed conditions of transportation based on the ascendancy of the automobile, the extent to which water access would still preclude an easement by necessity. *See, e.g.,* Attaway v. Davis, 707 S.W.2d 302 (Ark. 1986) (not reasonable to require landowner to access property by boat now that travel is almost always by motor vehicle) . . . .

6.   There was evidence that because of environmental laws it would be very unlikely that permits could be obtained.

was there evidence as to the extent of the burden on the Rice land should the Morrell land be used by more than one family, or for other than residential purposes. Whether the use of the easement for a particular purpose in the future will cause an undue burden on the Rice property would have to be determined in the context of that use.

Judgment modified to delete restriction on use of easement to single-family residence, and, as modified, affirmed.

Notes and Questions

1. *Basis for easement by necessity.* In *Hurlocker v. Medina*, 878 P.2d 348 (1994), the New Mexico Court of Appeals explored the question whether easements by necessity are based on public policy or the implied intent of the parties:

> English courts began to develop general principles to deal with the conveyance of landlocked realty as early as the fourteenth century. James W. Simonton, *Ways by Necessity*, 25 Colum. L. Rev. 571, 572 (1925). From an early date it was a recognized legal maxim that "anyone who grants a thing to someone is understood to grant that without which the thing cannot be or exist." *Id.* In the seventeenth century Chief Justice Glyn added, "it is not only a private inconvenience, but it is also to the prejudice of the public weal, that land should lie fresh and unoccupied[.]" *Id.* at 574 (quoting from Packer v. Welsted, 2 Sid. 39, 111 (1658)). Public policy remained the stated basis for the servitude of necessity until the nineteenth century when the focus shifted back to the intent of the parties. Restatement, [Third] § 2.15, cmt. *a*, at 185.
>
> Several factors dictate that the easement by necessity rests more heavily upon the intent of the parties than a public policy in favor of productive land use. First, it may well be questioned whether it is still universally in the public interest to prohibit land from lying "fresh and unoccupied." *See* . . . James D. Griffin, Comment, *Land Use Planning—New Mexico's Green Belt Law*, 8 Nat. Resources J. 190 (1968).
>
> Second, it is clear that if the imposition of easements by necessity were truly required by public policy, those conveyances which clearly negated any access would be void. *See* Edmond H. Bodkin, *Easements of Necessity and Public Policy*, 89 Law Q. Rev. 87, 90 (1973). However, "[t]he public policy favoring the productive use of land does not override the landowner's freedom to give up the right to ingress and egress." Bruce *&* Ely, *supra*, § 4.02[3], at 4-26; *see also* Gerald Korngold, Private Land Use Arrangements § 3.10, at 44 (1990).
>
> Third, the law allows landlocked parcels to remain in that condition where they do not meet the requirements for imposition of an easement by necessity. . . .
>
> Fourth, operational rules by which easements by necessity are construed also indicate that the implied intent of the parties, rather than public policy, is the basic rationale underlying easements by necessity. For example, the required necessity must exist at the time of severance. This requirement is based on the concept that if the estate is readily accessible by other means at the time of severance, there can be little basis to infer intent to preserve access. *See* . . . Stewart E. Sterk, *Neighbors in American Land Law*, 87 Colum. L. Rev. 55, 64 (1987).
>
> Finally, the imposition of an easement for public policy reasons can raise questions of compensation. Korngold, *supra*, § 3.09, at 42. Compensation problems are

avoided by viewing the common grantor of the two estates, rather than governmental policy, as the source of the burden upon the servient tenement.

Therefore, the implied intention of the parties is a more reliable foundation than public policy upon which to build the analytical framework necessary to sustain easements by necessity; it is only when the record provides absolutely no insight from which an inference as to the intent of the parties can be drawn that public policy is employed as a significant factor.

2. *Unity of title.* In the principal case, *Morrell v. Rice*, the court held an easement by necessity may be created when there are simultaneous conveyances by a common grantor that result in landlocking one of the parcels conveyed, as well as when the grantor carves out a parcel from a larger one and the conveyance landlocks one or the other of the parcels. Most courts agree. The *Hurlocker* court rejected an argument, based on a line of Texas cases, that an easement by necessity can arise only when the lack of access was created on division of a single previously undivided parcel, stating:

> [T]o the extent . . . Texas cases have required a previously undivided parcel to support unity of title, we find the *Restatement of the Law Property (Servitudes)* Section 2.15 (Tentative Draft No. 1, 1989) persuasive and decline to adopt the Texas position.

The most recent proposed revisions to the Restatement specifically recognize ownership, not lot divisions, as the key element when considering unity of title. Section 2.15, which covers "Servitudes by Necessity," makes it clear unity of title does not require the dominant and servient estates be severed from a previously undivided single parcel. Comment *c* to proposed Section 2.15 provides in part:

> Servitudes by necessity arise only on severance of rights held in a unity of ownership. This severance can take place when a grantor, who owns several parcels, conveys one or more to others. It can also take place when a grantor divides a single parcel into two or more parcels, and, it can take place when a grantor conveys less than full ownership in a single parcel.

3. *Conveyance of public domain lands.* Does an easement by necessity arise when the federal government conveys to a private party a parcel that is completely surrounded by federally owned land? In 1878, the United States conveyed the Chino Quartz Mine by patent to F. Novella. All the land surrounding the mine was federal land. Sometime after 1991, the owners of the Chino Quartz Mine brought a quiet title action to establish an easement in a private road that ran from the mine to a county road, crossing several parcels that were owned by the United States in 1878, but were now in private ownership. In *Kellogg v. Garcia*, 125 Cal. Rptr. 2d 817, 826 (2002), the California Court of Appeal overturned the trial court's holding that "original ownership by the United States does not constitute the necessary unity of ownership to support an easement by necessity." The appeals court concluded that:

> Since an easement by way of necessity is based on the presumption that a conveyance seeks to transfer "whatever is necessary for the beneficial use of the property" [citation omitted] . . . [t]here is absolutely no reason to impute a different intention to the federal government when conveying western lands. . . . After all, particularly in the 19th century—when the West was being settled—the federal government had no reason to render the land it conveyed unfit for occupancy or cultivation. Quite the opposite.

4. Is it fair to require the Rices to give the Morrells an easement without compensation? If they purchased without actual or constructive notice of the Morrell's claim, are they protected by the recording act? Restatement § 7.14 provides that the benefit of an unwritten, unrecorded servitude is not extinguished if extinguishment "would result in depriving the dominant estate of rights of way for access or utilities necessary to reasonable enjoyment of the land" unless the statute requires a different result.

5. What if the Morrells had not been able to establish common ownership just prior to the severance that landlocked their parcel? In some states, statutes provide a means by which access over neighboring land can be acquired, without regard to prior common ownership, on payment of fair compensation determined by the court. In the absence of such a statute, is there anything they could do to gain land access to their property?

6. When is an easement necessary? The court in *Morrell v. Rice* suggested, although it did not decide, that year-round usable water access would not obviate the necessity of land access, a position that is increasingly taken by courts in the current era, at least for property other than summer fish camps. *See, e.g., Hancock v. Henderson*, 202 A.2d 599 (Md. 1964); *Parker v. Putney*, 492 S.E.2d 159 (Va. 1997). What about access for private planes to get from hangars to an airport runway? *Chandler Flyers, Inc. v. Stellar Development Corp.*, 592 P.2d 387 (Ariz. Ct. App. 1979), said no: "Although transportation by private plane is becoming more common, we cannot say as a matter of law that a property owner is entitled to aircraft access in order to make reasonable use of his property."

7. *Scope of an easement by necessity.* Surprisingly few cases have considered the question whether an easement by necessity includes the right to run utility lines as well as the use of the surface for pedestrian and vehicular access. Can you construct a plausible argument that there is no necessity for power, telephone, or cable television lines on or under the ground? What about water and sewer lines?

8. *Duration of an easement by necessity.* Unlike an easement implied on the basis of prior use, an easement by necessity terminates when other access becomes available to the landlocked parcel. Restatement § 4.3(1). The duration of an easement based on prior use, like an expressly created easement, is indefinite (Restatement § 4.3(5)) and potentially perpetual so long as the easement continues to serve some purpose for which it was created (Restatement § 7.10, Modification and Termination Because of Changed Conditions). Does this distinction make sense?

d. Creation by Prescription

PAXSON v. GLOVITZ

Court of Appeals of Arizona
50 P.3d 420 (2002) (as amended, 2003)

EHRLICH, J. . . . Paxson and Glovitz own adjoining parcels of residential property. . . . [I]n 1979, the Murphys and Baker [then owners of the two parcels] orally agreed to create an easement running east and west straddling the . . . boundary line. . . . Intending to settle the matter "for all time," they agreed that the easement would be twenty feet wide, ten feet on either side of the dividing property line. . . . [T]he easement was never recorded, and no written grant of easement was produced. There is, however, no dispute as to the original intention to create the easement . . . .

In 1984, the Daleidens purchased the Murphys' . . . parcel. . . . The Daleidens owned the property until 1998, when they sold it to Glovitz. When they bought the property, the Murphys and Baker told them that the paved roadway was for garbage collection and other public access, and, during the time the Daleidens owned the property, the roadway was used by members of the public, by visitors to their home and by the residents of the house now owned by Paxson, as well as by utility, postal, and other private and commercial vehicles. The Daleidens believed that this use was as a matter of right; they gave no permission.

Paxson acquired the Baker parcel in 1995. She was shown the paved easement and told that it was for her use and for that of the general public. . . . When Glovitz purchased the property, he . . . was told that . . . [the driveway] had always been used for ingress and egress by neighbors as well as by the public. Glovitz knew that the twenty-foot-wide driveway extended ten feet onto the property he was purchasing. . . .

In September 2000, Glovitz began to construct a block fence along his property line where the driveway ran, and Paxson filed this action to obtain an easement by prescription for the ten-foot portion of the driveway extending onto Glovitz's land. . . .

The superior court . . . granted Glovitz summary judgment. . . . Glovitz then moved for an award of attorneys' fees[2] . . . on the basis that Paxson's claim had no basis in fact or law. The superior court granted the motion . . . quieting title to the property and awarding Glovitz fees of $38,810.50 against Paxson and her counsel, jointly and severally. . . .

While neither the parties nor we have discovered any Arizona case controlling the resolution of this case, there is longstanding Arizona authority on the closely related subject of adverse possession that sets forth applicable principles. These same principles underlie the rule of the RESTATEMENT: SERVITUDES § 2.16 relating to prescriptive easements, and we conclude that the Restatement rule is the one that we should follow in resolving this dispute.[3]

A. Requirements of a Prescriptive Easement

. . . There is no dispute in this case that the easement was created in 1979 and that it has been actually and visibly used since that time, a period of more than ten years [the statutory period]. The only issue is whether the circumstances of the creation of the easement were, in legal effect, adverse or permissive. Glovitz argues that the use was permissive because it began and continued by agreement. Paxson contends that the Murphys and Baker "imperfectly" created the

---

2. [Arizona Civil Procedure] Rule 11 (a) authorizes fee awards for claims that are not well-founded or interposed for improper purpose. . . .

3. In the absence of contrary precedent, Arizona courts look to the Restatement. Campbell v. Westdahl, 148 Ariz. 432, 436, 715 P.2d 288, 292 (App.1985) (applying *Restatement (Second) of Property* § 15.2 (1977)).

easement by not complying with the formalities to place it of record, thus inaugurating a use adverse to the owners' title just as the parol gift of real property served to begin an adverse possession in *Tenney* [v. Luplow, 442 P.2d 107 (Ariz. 1968)]. . . .

Glovitz's argument that the use was permissive runs contrary to the undisputed intent of the parties to relinquish their exclusive rights to their land permanently in favor of adverse rights to use the easement . . . . [T]he Murphys and Baker made an oral grant of easement. It long has been recognized in Arizona that an oral or parol grant of *title* to real property, while unenforceable because of the Statute of Frauds, will, when coupled with possession, give rise to the beginning of an adverse possession. . . . The principles of these adverse possession cases sensibly apply to Paxson's claim of prescriptive easement.

. . . RESTATEMENT: SERVITUDES applies these same principles to easements by prescription. . . . Section 2.16 provides in pertinent part that an easement by prescription may be created by "a use that is made pursuant to the terms of an intended but imperfectly created servitude." Comment *a* to § 2.16 gives the rationale for the rule and adds that it applies when "people try to create a servitude but fail, initially because they do not . . . reduce their agreement to writing, or because they fail to comply with some other formal requirement imposed in the jurisdiction." If the parties then proceed to act as though they were successful for the prescribed time, the servitude is created as long as the other requirements for such servitude are met. As stated in Comment *a*, complying with the terms of the easement for the set period "substitutes for compliance with the required formality because it provides satisfactory proof of the existence and terms of the servitude and resolves any doubts as to the parties' intent that may have been created by their failure to comply with the formality."

As further explained in Comment *a*, the drafters of the Restatement have specifically enunciated this rule to clear confusion that could arise over the words "adverse" or "hostile" when applied to an imperfectly created easement. Indeed, if the requirement of hostility is taken "too literally," it could lead to "the erroneous conclusion that use pursuant to an oral grant cannot give rise to a prescriptive right because it is not adverse," whereas, not only may a prescriptive easement be based upon a continuing adverse use for the period of the statute of limitations, but also, as explained in Comment *b* to § 2.17, the long-continued use may act to "perfect a flawed title." . . .

The predecessors in title to Paxson and Glovitz attempted to create an easement in 1979; this effort was "imperfect" for lack of compliance with the necessary procedures. The property owners who agreed to create the easement and their grantees acted to recognize it thereafter, from 1979 until Glovitz acted in 2000, a period in excess of the prescriptive period of ten years. An easement by prescription had, therefore, been established before Glovitz bought the property in 1998. . . .

B.   Scope of the Easement

As an alternate basis for summary judgment, Glovitz contended that Paxson had improperly expanded the scope of the easement because she was using or intending to use her property in ways allegedly different from its historical uses. . . . The holder of an easement is entitled to use it "in a manner that is reasonably necessary for the convenient enjoyment" of the easement or servitude. RESTATEMENT: SERVITUDES § 4.10. As stated in § 4.10, the "manner, frequency, and intensity of the use may change over time to take advantage of developments in technology and to accommodate normal development of the dominant estate or enterprise benefitted by the servitude." Section 4.10 further explains that permissible uses of an easement are any uses which do not "cause unreasonable damage to the servient estate or interfere unreasonably with its enjoyment."

[handwritten margin note: manner can change over time. any use is fine if no damage or interference w/ enjoyment.]

Although Glovitz complained of the uses Paxson allegedly is making of her *property*, he presented no evidence that her use of the *easement* was causing unreasonable damage or interfering unreasonably with the enjoyment of his property, nor is there evidence that Paxson is using her property in an unlawful manner. Rather, Paxson disputes that she is using the easement for any purpose substantively different from its historical uses. Such a controversy creates an issue of fact that could not be resolved by summary judgment. More importantly, the appropriate remedy for an unreasonable use of an easement is to seek injunctive relief to limit the use, plus damages if warranted. . . .

C. Attorneys' Fees and Costs

The resolution of this matter in favor of Paxson serves to reverse the attorneys' fees awarded to Glovitz. . . . As the prevailing parties on appeal, Paxson and Cox are entitled to recover their costs on appeal. . . .

Comparing Easements by Implication from Prior Use, by Necessity, and by Prescription

In a situation such as that in the *Morrell* case, plausible arguments might have been made for an easement implied on the basis of prior use or an easement acquired by prescription, as well as an easement by necessity. Given the choice, which should they have pursued? Consider first what is required to establish that one has been created. Proof of common ownership of the two parcels in the past is required for an easement by necessity or prior use but not for a prescriptive easement. But non-permissive, open and notorious, and continued use for the prescriptive period must be established for the latter. As between necessity and prior use, the degree of necessity may be less for an easement based on prior use.[7] And, of course, use prior to severance must be established for an easement based on prior use, but no use need be shown for an easement by necessity.

[handwritten margin note: Creation]

Next, consider the scope of the easement that will be acquired. Restatement § 4.1 states that "a servitude should be interpreted to give effect to and be consistent with: . . . (b) the intentions or reasonable expectations of the parties to a

[handwritten margin note: scope]

7. *See* Peter Glenn, *Implied Easements in the North Carolina Courts: An Essay on the Meaning of "Necessary,"* 58 N.C. L. Rev. 223 (1979).

servitude created by implication, necessity, or estoppel; and (c) the reasonable expectations of the party against whom a servitude is created by prescription." Which will allow for greater development of the dominant estate? Probably the easement by necessity since the expectations of the parties will not have been shaped by the use that gave rise to creation of the easement.

Finally, consider the duration of the easement. An easement by necessity lasts only so long as the necessity lasts. When the parcel is no longer landlocked because the dominant owner has acquired other access, either public or private, the easement terminates. By contrast, both the easement based on prior use and the easement acquired by prescription are of unlimited duration and are not affected by the dominant owner's acquisition of other means of access to the property. So which is better? It depends.

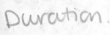

e.   Creation by Dedication, Condemnation, and Other Forced Sales

Servitudes can be acquired by the exercise of eminent domain, by inverse condemnation, and by dedication, in addition to the other methods we have studied in this chapter. Public rights in beaches acquired through implied dedication and customary use are covered in Chapter 3. Eminent domain and inverse condemnation, which can be used to acquire or extinguish servitudes, as well as to acquire other property interests, are covered in Chapter 13. Dedication is like an express grant but is normally used to describe a transfer to a public body or to the public in general. Subdivision plats often contain a dedication of roads to the public, for example. More on the intricacies of transferring interests in land to public bodies can be found in Restatement § 2.18[8] and in courses and treatises on local government. For general treatments of the creation of servitudes, see Gerald Korngold, *Easements, Real Covenants, and Equitable Servitudes* (2d ed. 2004), and Jon W. Bruce & James W. Ely, Jr., *The Law of Easements and Licenses in Land* (looseleaf copyright 2001-2014).

Forced sales of servitudes by unwilling landowners may occur in a variety of circumstances. Statutes in some states provide landlocked property owners with the right to acquire easements by necessity on the payment of compensation determined by appraisal. The government's power to force sales by condemnation has often been extended by statute to public utilities, railroads, and companies that build canals for transportation, irrigation, or drainage purposes.

When a court refuses to order removal of an encroachment, enjoin further use of one person's land by another, or to enjoin a nuisance, the court in effect creates an easement in favor of the wrongdoer. If the court awards damages to the landowner, as in *Boomer v. Atlantic Cement Co.* (in Chapter 11), there has been a forced sale of the easement. Damages are not always awarded, however, particularly for minor, innocent encroachments, which courts refuse to enjoin on the basis of the relative hardships doctrine. If the right to maintain the encroachment or continue another trespass is affirmatively granted, the resulting right is called an "equitable easement" in California. *See, e.g., Linthicum v. Butterfield*, 175 Cal. App. 4th 259 (2009) (equitable easement to continue use of

---

8.   For a thoughtful analysis of problems posed by publicly held servitudes, see Stewart E. Sterk, *Publicly Held Servitudes in the New Restatement*, 27 Conn. L. Rev. 157 (1994).

road over former U.S. Forest Service land granted to landowners whose parcels would be landlocked by grant of injunction against further use; continuance of roadway easement would not prevent building home on servient parcel and grant of injunction would practically amount to enabling extortion). California has gone further and recognized that a landowner seeking an easement may use the equitable easement doctrine affirmatively to acquire an easement over neighboring land. In *Tashakori v. Lakis*, 196 Cal. App. 4th 1003 (2011), the court awarded the owner of a landlocked parcel an equitable easement over a neighboring parcel to use an existing driveway on the grounds that the owner of the landlocked parcel bought it with the good-faith belief it had access rights and there was no actual harm to the servient parcel because the driveway was already subject to easements benefiting two other homes.

GOULDING v. COOK

Supreme Judicial Court of Massachusetts
661 N.E.2d 1322 (Mass. 1996)

FRIED, J. . . . The parties own neighboring residences in Scituate. When installation of another neighbor's swimming pool caused the Cooks's cesspool, which was partly under that neighbor's land, to malfunction, they were forced to find an alternative sewage disposal system. The town required a septic system, and the only suitable site for such a system was on a 2,998 square foot triangle of land that the Cooks claimed belonged to them but which the Gouldings claimed was part of their residential property. While the town was pressing them, the Cooks negotiated with the Gouldings to no avail. The matter came to litigation. The Gouldings sought a preliminary injunction against the Cooks's use of their land as well as a declaration that they were the fee simple owners of the land, free of any claims by the Cooks. The preliminary injunction was denied on August 8, 1991, and thereafter the Cooks entered on the land and installed the septic system. The Land Court entered a final judgment . . . finding ownership in the disputed triangle to be in the Gouldings but granting an easement to the Cooks . . . "at a price to be negotiated by the parties and with provisions for maintenance, repair and replacement as counsel so agree." . . . [T]he Appeals Court affirmed. We granted the plaintiffs' application for further appellate review.

It is commonplace today that property rights are not absolute, and that the law may condition their use and enjoyment so that the interests of the public in general or of some smaller segment of the public, perhaps even just immediate neighbors, are not unduly prejudiced. Restrictions from architectural approvals to zoning regulations are accepted features of the legal landscape. . . . But, except in "exceptional" cases,[3] we draw the line at permanent

---

3. . . . In rare cases, referred to in our decisions as "exceptional" courts of equity have refused to grant a mandatory injunction and have left the plaintiff to his remedy of damages, "where the unlawful encroachment has been made innocently, and the cost of removal by the defendant would be greatly disproportionate to the injury to the plaintiff from its continuation, or where the substantial rights of the owner may be protected without recourse to an injunction, or where an injunction would be oppressive and inequitable. But these are the exceptions. . . . What is just and equitable in cases of this sort depends very much on the particular facts and circumstances disclosed." . . .

physical occupations amounting to a transfer of a traditional estate in land. . . . And certainly that line, because the interests on either side of it are themselves conventional and the creatures of the law, is often hard to draw. But we are committed to maintaining it, because the concept of private property represents a moral and political commitment that a pervasive disposition to balance away would utterly destroy. The commitment is enshrined in our Constitutions. Where the line is crossed and the commitment threatened, even in the interests of the general public, just compensation is required. And by implication, where the encroachment is not for a public use, the taking may not be justified at all. Although we deplore the disposition to turn every dispute into a Federal (constitutional) case and no constitutional claim was—or needed to be—made here, it is to these constitutional commitments that the dissent in the Appeals Court's decision referred when it observed that "[o]ur law simply does not sanction this type of private eminent domain." For an analysis that comes to this same conclusion from another perspective, see Kaplow, *Property Rules Versus Liability Rules: An Economic Analysis*, 109 Harv. L. Rev. 713, 757-773 (1996).

No doubt the Cooks considered themselves in desperate straits, but theirs was not the kind of desperation that justifies self-help with financial adjustments thereafter. . . . *See generally* Keeton, *Conditional Fault in the Law of Torts*, 72 Harv. L. Rev. 401 (1959). It is not cynicism to suppose that some sum of money would suffice to assuage the Goulding's sense of having been imposed on and thus to suggest that one way of looking at this case is to ask who shall set that sum and where will the bargaining advantage lie. . . . The Cooks, threatened with possible destruction of their ability to use their home at all, might have been willing to pay a very large sum . . . . The Appeals Court's disposition may be seen as moved by its revulsion at the thought that the Gouldings should be able to extract so large a rent for so minor an accommodation. The power of eminent domain is granted just to prevent private property owners from extracting such strategic rents from the public. . . . [T]he Land Court, by denying the Gouldings an injunction, assigned to itself the authority to establish the price . . . .

Like most propositions in the law the one we reaffirm now has some play at the margins. Accordingly, the Appeals Court is quite right that the courts will not enjoin truly minimal encroachments, especially when the burden on a defendant would be very great. The classic example is given in *Restatement (Second) of Torts* § 941 comment *c*:

> The defendant has recently completed a twenty-story office building on his lot. The work was done by reputable engineers and builders, and they and the defendant all acted in good faith and with reasonable care. It is, however, found that from the tenth floor upward the wall on the plaintiff's side bulges outward and extends over the line. The extent of the encroachment varies at different points, the maximum being four inches.

Such accommodation recognizes the necessarily approximate nature of all legal lines and principles. To extend the accommodation to this case where the defendants seek to install a potentially permanent, possibly malodorously malfunctioning septic system encroaching on a spatially significant portion of the plaintiffs' lot is not to accommodate the principle but to obliterate it in favor of a general power of equitable adjustment and enforced good neighborliness. That is particularly the case here, where the defendants' "good faith" consists at most in an honest belief supported by objective facts that they were the owners of the land. Although this claim was sharply disputed, they were told that they proceeded at their peril, and the matter was in litigation and awaiting disposition when they went ahead and acted.[4] It changes nothing that what we have here is the Land Court's decision to deny injunctive relief, an equitable power which leaves much to the court's discretion, if that discretion was exercised on a legal criterion that we conclude is incorrect. . . .

[W]e hold that the Cooks must remove the septic system and pay damages. . . .

Notes and Questions

1. Two other cases decided about the same time as *Goulding v. Cook* were more protective of the encroacher. In *Newmark v. Vogelgesang*, 915 S.W.2d 337 (Mo. Ct. App. 1996), the court denied an injunction requiring removal of encroachments from a newly built gas station conditioned on payment of $500 in damages based on a valuation of $1 per square foot for the property taken. The court reasoned that granting an injunction would cause disproportionate hardship to the gas station and provide little benefit to the abutting owner. Similarly, in *Szymczak v. LaFerrara*, 655 A.2d 76 (N.J. Super. Ct. App. Div. 1995), a New Jersey court reversed the issuance of an injunction requiring removal of a 19-foot encroachment of the Szymczaks' house on LaFerrara's vacant lot and remanded for a determination of damages. Although there was no mutual mistake and no grounds for estoppel against LaFerrara, and the LaFerrara lot was made unbuildable by the encroachment, the court held that denial of the injunction was required by the relative hardship doctrine. The Szymczaks had built in good faith in reliance on an erroneous survey, and moving the house would cost at least $88,000. LaFerrara had held his lot for 20 years as an investment and had no immediate plans to build on it or any special personal purpose for developing it. Can these cases be distinguished from *Goulding v. Cook*, or do they simply reflect a different judicial philosophy?

2. Theoretically, how much should the Cooks be willing to pay for an easement for their septic tank? Is there any moral or legal reason why the law should protect them from having to pay that amount? Is there any way they can avoid having to pay that amount?

f. Creating Easements for Third Parties

If a landowner wants to create an easement in favor of one person when transferring ownership of the land to another, an old rule—the "stranger to the deed" rule—may require that the transaction be done in two steps: first a deed conveying the easement, then a deed conveying the fee simple subject to the easement. *See Estate of Thomson v. Wade*, 509 N.E.2d 309 (N.Y. 1987); *Tripp v. Huff*, 606 A.2d 792 (Me. 1992); John E. Lansche, Jr., Note, *Ancient, Antiquated and Archaic: South Carolina Fails to Embrace the Rule That a Grantor May Reserve an*

---

4. Although, as the Appeals Court properly noted, notice of an opposing claim is not decisive on the question of good faith, the instant case presents a situation where there was more than mere notice; the parties were in litigation. . . .

Easement in Favor of a Third Party, 52 S.C. L. Rev. 269 (2000). The only thing to be said for the rule is that the easement may be easier to find in the recording system if created by a separate deed than if created in a deed to someone else of the fee simple.

The stranger to the deed rule, as its name suggests, applies to conveyances, not contracts, and predates the development of the relatively modern third-party beneficiary doctrine in contracts. New York allows enforcement of covenants by third-party beneficiaries. *See Vogeler v. Alwyn Improvement Corp.*, 159 N.E. 886 (N.Y. 1928) (restrictive covenant imposed on grantee to benefit land owned by a neighbor enforceable by the neighbor as an intended third-party beneficiary); *The Nature Conservancy v. Congel*, 689 N.Y.S.2d 317 (App. Div. 1999) (third-party beneficiary doctrine allows neighbors to enforce covenant created for their benefit when a quarry was sold).

Many states have rejected the stranger to the deed rule as an archaic feudal relic that frustrates intent, *see, e.g., Willard v. First Church of Christ, Scientist*, 498 P.2d 987 (Cal. 1972); *Nelson v. Parker*, 687 N.E.2d 187 (Ind. 1997). Restatement (Third) § 2.6 states that "[t]he benefit of a servitude may be granted to a person who is not a party to the transaction that creates the servitude."

2.   *Scope of Easements and Profits*

Restatement (Third) § 4.10, Use Rights Conferred by a Servitude

Except as limited by [its] terms . . . the holder of an easement or profit is entitled to use the servient estate in a manner that is reasonably necessary for the convenient enjoyment of the servitude. The manner, frequency, and intensity of the use may change over time to take advantage of normal developments in technology and to accommodate normal development of the dominant estate or enterprise benefited by the servitude. Unless authorized by the terms of the servitude, the holder is not entitled to cause unreasonable damage to the servient estate or interfere unreasonably with its enjoyment.

Reasonably necessary uses of the servient estate may include so-called secondary easements, which are rights to use other parts of the servient estate to gain access to the easement or subject of a profit and access for maintenance and repairs. Reasonably necessary uses may also include the right to construct improvements for use of the easement or profit. Conceptually, these secondary easements may be viewed as easements by necessity or inherently included within the primary use rights granted.

Except as limited by the easement's terms, the holder of the servient estate is entitled to make any use of the servient estate that does not unreasonably interfere with enjoyment of the easement, Restatement § 4.9. When conflicts arise between the easement holder and the servient estate,[9] courts should apply the

---

9.   Efforts by the easement holder to pave a roadway or line an irrigation ditch sometimes precipitate lawsuits. *See, e.g.,* Hayes v. Aquia Marina, Inc., 414 S.E.2d 820 (Va. 1992) (proposed paving reasonable); Big Cottonwood Tanner Ditch Co. v. Moyle, 174 P.2d 148 (Utah 1946) (lining irrigation ditch to prevent loss of water reasonable in arid climate despite damage to servient estate from loss of riparian foliage). Gates and fences, too, often provoke controversy. For a collection of cases, see Reporter's Note to Restatement § 4.10.

public policy favoring socially productive uses of land, which usually means that a balance should be struck that maximizes utility of the easement while minimizing the impact on the servient estate. Restatement § 4.10, comment *b*.

What are normal developments in technology and normal development of a dominant estate? Can an easement created in the 19th century for a "horse cartway" be used for automobiles in the 20th century? Can a "bridle trail" be used by motorcycles? Can a "walkway" be used by skateboarders or motorized scooters? Can a "railroad" easement be converted to a street or a hiking trail? There is a substantial amount of litigation over the scope of easements. The question is always whether the kind and intensity of use is within what the parties contemplated when the easement was created. Easements created by prescription are generally confined more closely to the original uses than expressly created easements, but do allow some room for adaptation over time. The rule that protects the servient estate from unreasonable damage or interference with its enjoyment gives courts a considerable amount of latitude in deciding these cases.

a. Location, Relocation, and Use of Easements

Restatement (Third) § 4.8 Location, Relocation, and Dimensions of a Servitude

Except where the location and dimensions are determined by the instrument or circumstances surrounding creation of a servitude, they are determined as follows:

(1) The owner of the servient estate has the right within a reasonable time to specify a location that is reasonably suited to carry out the purpose of the servitude.

(2) The dimensions are those reasonably necessary for enjoyment of the servitude.

(3) Unless expressly denied by the terms of an easement, as defined in § 1.2, the owner of the servient estate is entitled to make reasonable changes in the location or dimensions of an easement, at the servient owner's expense, to permit normal use or development of the servient estate, but only if the changes do not

(a) significantly lessen the utility of the easement,

(b) increase the burdens on the owner of the easement in its use and enjoyment, or

(c) frustrate the purpose for which the easement was created.

Section 4.8(3), which allows the servient owner unilaterally to relocate an easement, rejects the traditional common-law rule in favor of the civil-law rule in force in Louisiana and a few other states. The rationale for the change is that the old rule gave the owner of the easement veto power over any development of the servient estate that required moving an existing easement while leaving the owner of the servient estate vulnerable to any changes in use of the easement reasonably necessary for normal development of the dominant estate. The veto power was often used to prevent development of the servient estate for reasons completely unrelated to interference with utility of the easement for the purpose for which it was acquired. *See, e.g., Cottonwood Duplexes, LLC v. Barlow*, 210 Cal. App. 4th 1501 (2012), and Susan F. French, *Making Easements Is Easy, Remaking Them Is Hard: Should the Law Help Out?*, Prob. & Prop., Sept.-Oct. 2013, p.34.

Section 4.8(3) has proved highly controversial. Some courts have embraced it, *see, e.g., MPM Builders LLC v. Dwyer* (Mass. 2004); *Roaring Fork Club v. St. Jude's*

Co., 36 P.3d 1229 (Colo. 2001) (en banc); others have gone out of their way to reject it, *see, e.g.*, *AKG Real Estate, LLC v. Kosterman*, 717 N.W.2d 835 (Wis. 2006).

The Wisconsin court rejected § 4.8(3), saying:

> We agree with . . . the courts that have rejected the *Restatement (Third) of Property: Servitudes* §§ 4.8(3) and 7.10(2) in favor of preventing the owners of servient estates from unilaterally relocating or terminating express easements. . . . These courts have rejected the position advanced by the *Restatement* as a threat to the certainty of property rights and real estate transactions, as a catalyst for increased litigation, and as a means for purchasers of servient estates to reap a windfall at the expense of owners of dominant estates. We agree that these reasons for rejecting the *Restatement*'s position are more compelling than the economic inefficiencies that might result from bilateral monopolies and holdout easement owners.[9] . . .

The Massachusetts court adopted § 4.8(3), saying:

> Section 4.8(3) is a default rule, to apply only in the absence of an express prohibition against relocation in the instrument creating the easement and only to changes made by the servient, not the dominant, estate owner.[4] It "is designed to permit development of the servient estate to the extent it can be accomplished without unduly interfering with the legitimate interests of the easement holder." [Restatement] comment *f*, at 563. Section 4.8(3) maximizes the over-all property utility by increasing the value of the servient estate without diminishing the value of the dominant estate; minimizes the cost associated with an easement by reducing the risk that the easement will prevent future beneficial development of the servient estate; and encourages the use of easements. See . . . Roaring Fork Club, L.P. v. St. Jude's Co., 36 P.3d 1229, 1236 (Colo. 2001). Regardless of what heretofore has been the common law, we conclude that § 4.8(3) of the Restatement is a sensible development in the law and now adopt it as the law of the Commonwealth.
>
> We are persuaded that § 4.8(3) strikes an appropriate balance between the interests of the respective estate owners by permitting the servient owner to develop his land without unreasonably interfering with the easement holder's rights. The rule permits the servient owner to relocate the easement subject to the stated limitations as a "fair tradeoff for the vulnerability of the servient estate to increased use of the

---

9.   As Professor Epstein states:

> Ownership is meant to be a bulwark against the collective preferences of others; it allows one, rich or poor, to stand alone against the world no matter how insistent or intense its collective preferences. To say that ordinary ownership presents a holdout problem is not to identify a defect in the system; it is to identify one of its essential strengths. If a holdout is adamant, no private party can *force* him to sell the land in question at any price. The state may intervene under its eminent domain powers, but only when it acts for "public use," and not for the narrow interests of B (or those whom he wishes to serve).

Richard A. Epstein, *Notice and Freedom of Contract in the Law of Servitudes*, 55 S. Cal. L. Rev. 1353, 1366-67 (1982).

4.   We previously have concluded that the dominant estate owner, that is, the easement holder, may not unilaterally relocate an easement. See Kesseler v. Bowditch, 223 Mass. 265, 269-270, 111 N.E. 887 (1916); Jennison v. Walker, 77 Mass. 423, 11 Gray 423, 426 (1858). According to the Restatement, many jurisdictions have erroneously expanded that sensible restriction into one that prevents the owner of the servient estate from relocating the easement without the consent of the easement holder. Restatement (Third) of Property (Servitudes) § 4.8(3) comment *f*, at 563 (2000).

easement to accommodate changes in technology and development of the dominant estate." Restatement . . . comment *f.* Therefore, under § 4.8(3), the owner of the servient estate is "able to make the fullest use of his or her property allowed by law, subject only to the requirement that he or she not damage other vested rights holders." Roaring Fork Club, L.P. v. St. Jude's Co.

It is a long-established rule in the Commonwealth that the owner of real estate may make any and all beneficial uses of his property consistent with the easement. . . . The . . . cases make clear that the rights of the owner of the easement are protected notwithstanding changes made by the servient estate owner as long as the purpose for which the easement was originally granted is preserved. . . . We conclude that § 4.8(3) is consistent with these principles in its protection of the interests of the easement holder: a change may not significantly lessen the utility of the easement, increase the burden on the use and enjoyment by the owner of the easement, or frustrate the purpose for which the easement was created. The servient owner must bear the entire expense of the changes in the easement. . . .

Dwyer urges us to reject the Restatement approach. He argues that adoption of § 4.8(3) will devalue easements, create uncertainty in property interests, and lead to an increase in litigation over property rights.[5] Our adoption of § 4.8(3) will neither devalue easements nor place property interests in an uncertain status. An easement is by definition a limited, nonpossessory interest in realty. . . . An easement is created to serve a particular objective, not to grant the easement holder the power to veto other uses of the servient estate that do not interfere with that purpose.

The limitations embodied in § 4.8(3) ensure a relocated easement will continue to serve the purpose for which it was created. So long as the easement continues to serve its intended purpose, reasonably altering the location of the easement does not destroy the value of it. For the same reason, a relocated easement is not any less certain as a property interest. The only uncertainty generated by § 4.8(3) is in the easement's location. A rule that permits the easement holder to prevent any reasonable changes in the location of an easement would render an access easement virtually a possessory interest rather than what it is, merely a right of way. . . . Finally, parties retain the freedom to contract for greater certainty as to the easement's location by incorporating consent requirements into their agreement.

"Clearly, the best course is for the [owners] to agree to alterations that would accommodate both parties' use of their respective properties to the fullest extent possible." Roaring Fork Club, L.P. v. St. Jude's Co., *supra* at 1237. . . . In the absence of agreement between the owners of the dominant and servient estates concerning the relocation of an easement, the servient estate owner should seek a declaration from the court that the proposed changes meet the criteria in § 4.8(3). Such an action gives the servient owner an opportunity to demonstrate that relocation com-

---

5.   Dwyer correctly states that the majority of jurisdictions require mutual consent to change the location of an easement. . . . However, most of these decisions were issued prior to the publication of the Restatement (Third) of Property (Servitudes) (2000) . . . . Of the State appellate courts that have addressed the issue since § 4.8(3) was drafted, four have adopted, or referred with approval to, the rule in some form. See Roaring Fork Club, L.P. v. St. Jude's Co., 36 P.3d 1229, 1236, 1238 (Colo. 2001) (adopting rule but requiring declaratory judgment prior to relocation); Lewis v. Young, 92 N.Y.2d 443, 452, 682 N.Y.S.2d 657, 705 N.E.2d 649 (1998) (adopting rule for easements not expressly defined in grant); Goodwin v. Johnson, 357 S.C. 49, 57-58, 591 S.E.2d 34 (Ct. App. 2003) (adopting Restatement position for easements by necessity); Burkhart v. Lillehaug, 664 N.W.2d 41, 43-44 (S.D. 2003) (applying Restatement § 4.8([3]) to changes made to easement). We have found only two State appellate courts that have expressly rejected it. See Herren v. Pettengill, 273 Ga. 122, 124, 538 S.E.2d 735 (2000); MacMeekin v. Low Income Hous. Inst., Inc., 111 Wash. App. 188, 207, 45 P.3d 570 (2002).

ports with the Restatement requirements and the dominant owner an opportunity to demonstrate that the proposed alterations will cause damage. The servient owner may not resort to self-help remedies, . . . and, as M.P.M. did here, should obtain a declaratory judgment before making any alterations.

Although Dwyer may be correct that increased litigation could result . . . , we do not reject desirable developments in the law solely because such developments may result in disputes spurring litigation. Section 4.8(3) "imposes upon the easement holder the burden and risk of bringing suit against an unreasonable relocation," but this "far surpasses in utility and fairness the traditional rule that left the servient land owner remediless against an unreasonable easement holder." Roaring Fork Club, L.P. v. St. Jude's Co., *supra* at 1237, quoting Note, *Balancing the Equities: Is Missouri Adopting a Progressive Rule for Relocation of Easements?*, 61 Mo. L. Rev. 1039, 1060 (1996). We trust that, over time, uncertainties will diminish and litigation will subside as easement holders realize that in some circumstances unilateral changes to an easement, paid for by the servient estate owner, will be enforced by courts. Dominant and servient estate owners will have an incentive to negotiate a result rather than having a court impose one on them.

For an assessment of earlier cases accepting and rejecting § 4.8(3), see Susan F. French, *Relocating Easements: Restatement (Third) § 4.8(3)*, 38 Real Prop. Prob. & Tr. J. 1 (2003). *See also* Jon W. Bruce & James W. Ely, Jr., *The Law of Easements and Licenses in Land* ch. 8, Utilization and Maintenance of Easements (looseleaf edition) (rejecting § 4.8(3).)

b.   Use of Easement for Non-Dominant Land

BROWN v. VOSS

Supreme Court of Washington (en banc)
715 P.2d 514 (Wash. 1986)

BRACHTENBACH, J. In 1952 the predecessors in title of parcel A granted to the predecessor owners of parcel B a private road easement across parcel A for "ingress to and egress from" parcel B. Defendants acquired parcel A in 1973. Plaintiffs bought parcel B on April 1, 1977 and parcel C on July 31, 1977, but from two different owners. Apparently the previous owners of parcel C were not parties to the easement grant. [Parcel A lies immediately south of Parcel B, which, in turn, lies immediately south of Parcel C. The easement runs across Parcel A, and then across additional properties not involved in this litigation to a public highway.]

When plaintiffs acquired parcel B a single family dwelling was situated thereon. They intended to remove that residence and replace it with a single family dwelling which would straddle the boundary line common to parcels B and C.

Plaintiffs began clearing both parcels B and C and moving fill materials in November 1977. Defendants first sought to bar plaintiff's use of the easement in April 1979 by which time plaintiffs had spent more than $11,000 in developing their property for building.

Defendants placed logs, a concrete sump and a chain link fence within the easement. Plaintiffs sued for removal of the obstructions, an injunction against defendant's interference with their use of the easement and damages. Defendants counterclaimed for damages and an injunction against plaintiffs using the easement other than for parcel B.

The trial court awarded each party $1 in damages. The award against the plaintiffs was for a slight inadvertent trespass outside the easement. . . . [In addition,] the court denied defendant's request for an injunction and granted the plaintiffs the right to use the easement for access to parcels B & C "as long as plaintiffs' properties (B and C) are developed and used solely for the purpose of a single family residence." The Court of Appeals reversed . . . .

. . . As a general rule, an easement appurtenant to one parcel of land may not be extended by the owner of the dominant estate to other parcels owned by him, whether adjoining or distinct tracts, to which the easement is not appurtenant. . . .

Plaintiffs, nonetheless, contend that extension of the use of the easement for the benefit of nondominant property does not constitute a misuse of the easement, where as here, there is no evidence of an increase in the burden on the servient estate. We do not agree. If an easement is appurtenant to a particular parcel of land, any extension thereof to other parcels is a misuse of the easement. Wetmore v. Ladies of Loretto, Wheaton, 220 N.E.2d 491 (Ill. Ct. App. 1966). . . . Although, as plaintiffs contend, their planned use of the easement to gain access to a single family residence located partially on parcel B and partially on parcel C is perhaps no more than technical misuse of the easement, we conclude that it is misuse nonetheless.

However, it does not follow . . . that defendants are entitled to injunctive relief. Since the awards of $1 in damages were not appealed, only the denial of an injunction to defendants is in issue. Some fundamental principles applicable to a request for an injunction must be considered. (1) The proceeding is equitable and addressed to the sound discretion of the trial court. (2) The trial court is vested with a broad discretionary power to shape and fashion injunctive relief to fit the particular facts, circumstances, and equities of the case before it. Appellate courts give great weight to the trial court's exercise of that discretion. (3) One of the essential criteria for injunctive relief is actual and substantial injury sustained by the person seeking the injunction. . . .

The trial court found as facts, upon substantial evidence, that plaintiffs have acted reasonably in the development of their property, that there is and was no damage to the defendants from plaintiffs' use of the easement, that there was no increase in the volume of travel on the easement, that there was no increase in the burden on the servient estate, that defendants sat by for more than a year while plaintiffs expended more than $11,000 on their project, and that defendants' counterclaim was an effort to gain "leverage" against plaintiffs' claim. In addition, the court found from the evidence that plaintiffs would suffer considerable hardship if the injunction were granted whereas no appreciable hardship or damages would flow to defendants from its denial. Finally, the court limited plaintiffs' use of the combined parcels solely to the same purpose for which the original parcel was used—i.e., for a single family residence.

. . . [T]he only . . . issue is whether, . . . as a matter of law, the trial court abused its discretion in denying defendants' request for injunctive relief. Based upon the equities of the case, . . . we are persuaded that the trial court acted within its discretion. . . .

no injunctive relief.

DORE, J. (dissenting). . . . Misuse of an easement is a trespass. . . . The Browns' use of the easement to benefit parcel C, especially if they build their home as planned, would involve a continuing trespass for which damages would be difficult to measure. Injunctive relief is the appropriate remedy under these circumstances. In Penn Bowling Rec. Ctr., Inc. v. Hot Shoppes, Inc., 179 F.2d 64 (D.C. Cir. 1949), the court states:

use of easement would benefit parcel C - not allowed.

> It is contended by appellant that since the area of the dominant and nondominant land served by the easement is less than the original area of the dominant tenement, the use made by appellant of the right of way to serve the building located on the lesser area is not materially increased or excessive. It is true that where the nature and extent of the use of an easement is, by its terms, unrestricted, the use by the dominant tenement may be increased or enlarged. . . . But the owner of the dominant tenement may not subject the servient tenement to use or servitude in connection with other premises to which the easement is not appurtenant. . . . And when an easement is being used in such a manner, an injunction will be issued to prevent such use. . . .

Browns created their own problem.

The Browns are responsible for the hardship of creating a landlocked parcel. They knew or should have known from the public records that the easement was not appurtenant to parcel C. . . . In encroachment cases this factor is significant. . . . "The benefit of the doctrine of balancing the equities, or relative hardship, is reserved for the innocent defendant who proceeds without knowledge or warning that his structure encroaches upon another's property or property rights."

In addition, an . . . injunction would merely require the Browns to acquire access to parcel C . . . . One possibility would be to condemn a private way of necessity over their existing easement in an action under RCW 8.24.010.

Notes and Questions

1. What is the rationale for the traditional default rule that the scope of an appurtenant easement is limited to serving the original dominant estate? What kinds of problems might arise if the dominant owner were free to extend the easement to other contiguous properties? Is this rule necessary in light of the rule that, although use of an easement can increase to serve needs created by normal development of the dominant estate, the easement owner is not entitled to cause unreasonable damage to the servient estate or to interfere unreasonably with its enjoyment?

2. Are there grounds for finding that the Browns acquired an easement by estoppel?

3. If the Browns had asked your advice before purchasing parcels B and C, or after the purchase but before starting to build their new house, what advice would you have given? How would you have estimated the relative costs and advantages of (a) seeking permission, (b) attempting to purchase an additional easement, (c) bringing an action to acquire an equitable easement; (d) bringing an action for a statutory easement by necessity, or (e) proceeding with construction without seeking permission? If the Browns had not sought permission and the Vosses had done nothing, would the Browns eventually have acquired the additional easement rights by prescription?

4. If you represent a developer who is negotiating the purchase of an easement to serve a tract the developer now owns, and the developer hopes to acquire additional adjacent properties in the future, how will you draft the easement to ensure it can be used to serve after-acquired properties?

c.   Succession, Exclusivity, Assignability, and Divisibility

An easement or profit is binding on all subsequent owners and occupiers of the servient property (except the holder of a paramount title) until it terminates. Likewise, the benefit of an appurtenant easement passes to all subsequent owners and occupiers of the dominant property, including adverse possessors. If ownership of either servient or dominant land is split into present and future interests, the benefits and burdens remain with the persons in possession. The vertical privity doctrine, which has traditionally been used to allocate some covenant burdens and benefits to the future interest holders, rather than to the present possessors, has never been applied to easements and profits.

Other succession questions arise, however, when the dominant or servient property is subdivided. The default rule applied in such situations is that the parts of the land on which the easement or profit is located remain burdened and that all parts of a dominant parcel are entitled to use easements appurtenant to the parcel. If the increased use due to subdivision of the dominant parcel will unreasonably increase the burden on the servient estate, use rights may be apportioned among the lots to reduce the burden to acceptable levels. *See* Restatement (Third) § 5.7.

After an easement has been created, questions may arise over the right of the servient owner to use the easement or to grant additional easements in the same area. Questions may also arise over the right of the owner of an easement in gross to assign the easement in whole or in part, and over the right of a profit owner to divide the profit among several assignees.

Problem

Liebler owns a unit in the Point Loma Tennis Club condominium development. The declaration provides that every unit owner is a member of the PLTC Association and prohibits severance of an owner's interest in the common areas from ownership of a unit. Common areas include tennis courts. Liebler rents out his unit but regularly plays tennis on the PLTC courts, as do his tenants. After receiving complaints from other unit owners, the Association notified Liebler that he is not entitled to use common area recreational facilities. Liebler has continued to play tennis, and the Association has sued for an injunction. How should the case come out? *See Liebler v. Point Loma Tennis Club*, 40 Cal. App. 4th 1600 (1995).

CITY OF PASADENA v.
CALIFORNIA-MICHIGAN LAND & WATER CO.

Supreme Court of California (en banc)
110 P.2d 983 (Cal. 1941)

[margin note: PP] GIBSON, C.J. This is an action for injunction. . . . [F]rom a judgment entered for the defendant the plaintiff prosecutes this appeal.

[margin note: Facts.] The parties are competing vendors of water service in an unincorporated area situated between the cities of Arcadia and Pasadena. The defendant, under claim of right and with the admitted permission of the servient owners, installed water mains and service connections in certain five-foot easements theretofore granted to the plaintiff and partly occupied by its water mains and connections. *[margin note: TT claims]* This action was commenced by the plaintiff on the theory that the owners of the servient tenements had no power to grant easements similar to plaintiff's in the same five-foot strip of land. . . . Plaintiff's contention was that it had a right to occupy the five-foot strip completely if the necessity arose, and that the defendant's installation substantially interfered both with plaintiff's present partial occupation of the land and with its possible future use . . . .

[margin note: Δ interfered w/ TT future interest.] In this appeal plaintiff contends primarily that the easement granted to the defendant was an unreasonable interference with its prior easement as a matter of law. . . .

The easements . . . are described as follows: . . . "Easements for the purpose of installing and maintaining water mains and connections thereto . . . all of said easements being five feet in width. . . ." This language eliminates at once *[margin note: no exclusive easements.]* the suggestion that appellant's easement was a so-called "exclusive easement." . . . [T]here is no language in this grant which indicates any intention to make the easement held by the City of Pasadena an exclusive one . . . and any such intention would seem clearly contrary to the admitted facts, since prior easements in the same land were in effect at the time when appellant's easements were granted. Furthermore, an "exclusive easement" is an unusual interest in *[margin note: exclusive easement Rule.]* land; it has been said to amount almost to a conveyance of the fee. No intention to convey such a complete interest can be imputed to the owner of the servient tenement in the absence of a clear indication of such an intention. . . .

. . . The general rule is clearly established that, despite the granting of an easement, the owner of the servient tenement may make any use of the land that does not interfere unreasonably with the easement. It is not necessary for him to make any reservation to protect his interests in the land, for what he does not convey, he still retains. . . . [H]e retains also the power to transfer these rights to third persons. . . . [T]he right of the defendant . . . is derived from the owner of the servient tenements, and whether it is a permissible use is to be determined by whether the owner of the servient tenements could have used the land in that manner.

Whether a particular use of the land by the servient owner, or by someone acting with his authorization, is an unreasonable interference is a question of fact. *[margin note: Tct.]* [T]he trial court found that there was no such unreasonable interference . . . . Appellant [argues that] because this is an easement of defined width and location, . . . the easement holder has the right to occupy it to the full width if it ever desires to do so. Therefore, . . . any use of the strip of land for laying other water pipes should be held to be unreasonable interference as a matter of law.

Appellant relies upon cases which hold that a surface right of way of defined width gives the easement holder the absolute right to occupy the surface to that width whenever he chooses. These cases depend upon the theory that the easement granted is completely and clearly defined . . . . They do not necessarily require a similar conclusion where the easement is for the limited purpose of laying underground water pipes. . . . There is a clear distinction in purpose between a right of way over the surface of the land to be used by moving vehicles and an easement for the laying of water mains in a relatively fixed and permanent position. In the case of an easement for laying underground water pipes there are important factors to be considered in addition to the width and location of the easement. These include, for example, the number and size of the pipes, the right to shift the pipes around at will, and the depth at which the pipes are to be laid. . . . [T]he extent of the burden which the parties intend to impose . . . is not definitely fixed merely by a specification of width and location. . . . [E]ven with surface rights of way, a specification of width and location does not always determine the extent of the burden imposed upon the servient land.

. . . It is, of course, possible to draft an instrument which would fully define both the location and the burden of the easement, or which would make the easement exclusive. But . . . the fact that these easements were granted for the limited purpose of securing domestic water service for the individual owners in this real estate subdivision and that no indication appears that the parties intended to protect the city against competition, we are unable to find any intent, either expressed or implied, that the owners were never to grant similar easements to anyone else. Hence, the mere granting of the second easement to the defendant did not interfere with appellant's prior easement as a matter of law. . . .

We do not wish to be understood, however, as limiting the rights granted to the City of Pasadena . . . which were properly found to be prior and paramount to those of the defendant. . . . It is possible that the city may, at some future time, be faced with the necessity of expanding or changing its present system, and on its behalf it is asserted that the presence of defendant's pipes may seriously hamper the reasonable use of the city's prior easement . . . . But if, in the reasonable use of its prior easement, the city requires the space occupied by the pipes of the defendant, its paramount right must prevail. . . .

Under the present facts no basis is shown for the relief sought. Whether a different conclusion may be required by changed circumstances in the future cannot now be determined with certainty, and need not therefore be decided. The judgment is affirmed.

Notes and Questions

1. *Exclusive easements.* Although courts frequently speak of the issue of exclusivity *vel non* as a simple either-or proposition, exclusivity is a bit more complicated. Unless the terms of the easement preclude the servient owner from using the area in which the easement is located, the servient owner is free to use it and to authorize others to do so long as there is no unreasonable interference. Ordinarily, the parties do not intend to exclude the servient owner from noninterfering uses, and an entity that acquires its easement by eminent domain does not want to pay for such an easement because the price would be close to that of a fee simple.

2. What easement rights should a water utility acquire? Should Pasadena have negotiated for exclusive right to use the immediate subsurface area that would be suitable for water pipes but leave the servient owner free to make noninterfering uses of the surface as well as of the subsurface below the area where water pipes would be located? Such an easement would be more expensive than the one the court held they had created but less expensive than a completely exclusive easement. Another variation on the exclusivity theme is raised by the question whether the servient owner can use facilities constructed by the easement owner for use of the easement. If the facilities consist of towers, poles, or pipelines, the usual assumption is that the servient owner was not intended to have such rights. If the facility consists of a roadway, however, a further look at the circumstances would be required to answer the question. The lesson in all of this, of course, is that easements should be carefully drafted to spell out the intended use rights of the parties.

FAIRBROTHER v. ADAMS

Supreme Court of Vermont
378 A.2d 102 (1977)

BILLINGS, J. . . . In September, 1959, the Fairbrothers conveyed a parcel of land of approximately three acres, upon which a camp was situated, to W. B. Adams and Allen C. Adams. The warranty deed contained provisions concerning water rights, woodcutting rights, and hunting and fishing rights.

The relevant language of the deed is as follows:

It being a small parcel of land out of the Fairbrother farm as deeded to Henry E. and Hazel E. Fairbrother by Ernest H. Fairbrother by deed dated July 30, 1954 . . . . There is also conveyed herewith the hunting and fishing rights on the other lands of the Fairbrother farm.

The questions at issue are whether the deed conveyed exclusive hunting and fishing rights; what is the scope of those rights, *i.e.*, whether those rights are personal only or alienable and assignable; [and] if the latter, what parts or all of the unconveyed remainder of the Fairbrother farm was subject to them. . . .

The parties agree that the granting of hunting and fishing rights by a deed conveyance creates a profit à prendre, which is an interest in land. The . . . deed clearly conveys such an interest. The warranty deed expresses the intent that hunting and fishing rights be conveyed for the "other lands of the Fairbrother farm." What constitutes the "Fairbrother farm" will be determined by what land the [1954] deed described . . . .

The hunting and fishing rights are exclusive. The language of the deed used the definite article "the," which implies exclusivity. A grantor may give an exclusive right. . . . This clause will be construed against the grantor whose attorney drew the deed. . . .

The trial court held that the deed in question lacked words of inheritance or assignability in the granting clause, and that because of this, the rights conveyed were purely personal. We disagree.

Profits à prendre being interests in land which may be granted as a separate and distinct property from the freehold of the land imply inheritance and assignability unless expressly reserved. . . . The language of the grant and of the habendum is the language of the printed form common to Vermont deeds well beyond our memory, and is in the customary location that evidences alienability and assignability without repetition in each paragraph of the descriptions as plaintiffs would have us hold.

The deed was clear and unambiguous in these particulars. . . . The judgment below is vacated and the cause is remanded with direction to declare the assignability of the hunting and fishing rights and their exclusive nature . . . .

Notes and Questions

1. On what basis did the court find that the profit granted to the Adamses was exclusive? Does exclusive mean that the Fairbrothers could not hunt on their own farm? Or does it mean something else? What do you think the parties most likely intended?

2. How extensive are the constraints that a hunting and fishing profit imposes on the servient estate? Is it effectively like a conservation easement that may prevent development of the property? Conversely, how extensive are the rights granted to the Adamses? Can they stock the streams with fish? Plant vegetation to attract birds? Build duck blinds? Bring in exotic animals and fence the farm to keep them in? Should the Fairbrothers' lawyer be held liable for malpractice?

3. The court held that the profit is assignable. Can the Adamses sell it to a hunting and fishing club? Can they bring in paying guests?

4. *Central Oregon Fabricators, Inc. v. Hudspeth*, 977 P.2d 416 (Or. Ct. App. 1999), found the hunting and fishing rights granted on a 24,000-acre mountain property more restricted than those in the Fairbrothers' case. A grant to the grantees, "their heirs and assigns, and personal guests" could only be assigned to natural persons, not entities, and personal guests did not include paying customers.

Assignability and Divisibility of Easements and Profits in Gross

Although the English common law did not recognize easements in gross, profits in gross were allowed and were assignable. American courts allowed easements in gross, but early cases held that only commercial easements in gross were assignable. The first Restatement took the position that whether a noncommercial easement in gross was assignable was determined by a number of factors, including the personal relations between the parties, the extent of the probable increase in burden on the servient estate resulting from alienability of the easement due to increased physical use or decreased value, and the consideration paid. Judge Clark, a leading authority on servitudes law, sharply criticized the distinction drawn between commercial and noncommercial easements on the ground that it was confusing, unworkable, and not supported by the case law. *See* Charles Clark, *The American Law Institute's Law of Real Covenants*, 52 Yale L.J. 699, 715 (1943). Restatement (Third) § 4.6 takes the position that a servitude benefit in gross is freely transferable unless it is "personal." It provides that:

A benefit is personal if the relationship of the parties, consideration paid, nature of the servitude, or other circumstances indicate that the parties should not reasonably have expected that the servitude benefit would pass to a successor to the original beneficiary.

Even if benefits in gross are assignable, the further question whether they can be divided sometimes arises. Two cases illustrate the problem. In *Stanton v. T.L. Herbert & Sons, Inc.*, 211 S.W. 353 (Tenn. 1919), Jordan, a building contractor, conveyed an island in the Cumberland River to Stanton in 1911, reserving "an easement or privilege" to remove sand and gravel from the island for a period of 10 years. Jordan later assigned the profit to three of the largest contractors in Nashville who were engaged in building an enormous munitions plant for the government as part of the World War I effort. Observing that the amount of sand and gravel removed far exceeded any quantities imagined at the time of the conveyance, the court adopted the old English rule that if a profit was assigned to more than one person, the assignees had to operate jointly, or "as one stock" in exploiting the resource.[10] It thus held that the profit was not divisible, and awarded damages for the value of the material removed.

In *Orange County, Inc. v. Citgo Pipeline Co.*, 934 S.W.2d 472 (Tex. Ct. App. 1996), a 1952 easement for pipelines specified the amount of compensation to be paid the servient owner for each additional pipeline laid. Two pipelines were constructed in the servient estate. In 1987, Citgo assigned one pipeline to Cities Service, retained ownership of the other, and reserved to itself an undivided one-half interest in the easement. The court held the division valid because it caused no additional burden to the servient estate.

The *Citgo* case represents the modern view that partial assignments of benefits in gross are permissible so long as the resulting use does not burden the estate beyond what was originally contemplated. Restatement (Third) § 5.7 provides:

> Transferable benefits in gross may be divided unless contrary to the terms of the servitude, or unless the division unreasonably increases the burden on the servient estate.

A further issue arises when the assignee makes a new use of an easement. The question is whether the new use is within the scope of the easement, a question posed in the following problem.

Problem

In 1964, the Cooks, owners of a 150-acre farm, granted an easement to the Dayton Power and Light Company, its successors and assigns forever, for the transmission and/or distribution of electric energy. In 1984, the power company entered into a Pole Attachment and Joint Use of Trench Agreement with Centel Cable Company, allowing Centel to attach coaxial cable carrying television signals to the power company's poles. When Centel attempted to enter the property in 1985 to repair a broken cable wire, the Cooks refused to allow

---

10.   Earl of Huntington v. Lord Mountjoy, 4 Leo. 147, 1 And. 307, Godb. 18.

entry, which caused about 300 cable customers to experience a longer period of interrupted service. Entry was finally made over the Cooks' objection. Centel then sued the Cooks, asking for declaratory relief and an injunction against their annoying, obstructing, or otherwise interfering with Centel's maintenance and repair of the cable. The Cooks counterclaimed for $10,000 in damages for trespass and for an injunction against Centel's further entry on their land. What result? *See Centel Cable Television Co. of Ohio, Inc. v. Cook*, 567 N.E.2d 1010 (Ohio 1991).

3. Modification and Termination of Easements and Profits

Servitudes can be terminated by agreement of the parties, by release or abandonment of the benefit, by prescription, by condemnation, and by merger of the burdened and benefited properties into one ownership. They may also be modified or terminated by a court when they no longer serve a useful purpose under the changed conditions, or frustration of purpose, doctrine. Traditionally, the changed conditions doctrine applied only to covenants not easements. Some courts have refused to extend it to easements even though it is substantially similar to the frustration of purpose doctrine, which traditionally has applied to easements. *See, e.g., AKG Real Estate, LLC v. Kosterman*, 717 N.W.2d 835 (Wis. 2006).

Restatement (Third) § 7.10, Modification and Termination of a Servitude Because of Changed Conditions

(1) When a change has taken place since the creation of a servitude that makes it impossible as a practical matter to accomplish the purpose for which the servitude was created, a court may modify the servitude to permit the purpose to be accomplished. If modification is not practicable, or would not be effective, a court may terminate the servitude. Compensation for resulting harm to the beneficiaries may be awarded as a condition of modifying or terminating the servitude.

(2) If the purpose of a servitude can be accomplished, but because of changed conditions the servient estate is no longer suitable for uses permitted by the servitude, a court may modify the servitude to permit other uses under conditions designed to preserve the benefits of the original servitude.

(3) The rules stated in § 7.11 govern modification or termination of conservation servitudes held by public bodies and conservation organizations, which are not subject to this section.

C. COVENANTS

When American courts began to encounter covenant disputes in the 19th century, they borrowed heavily from English law. Although they modified the English rules in significant respects, it is difficult to understand the variety of rules encountered in American case law without some knowledge of the English law that provided their starting point.

1.   The English Background

Covenants that run with the land developed quite slowly in English law. Their origins lie in feudal warranties of title and the feudal incidents and services, in which the courts had worked out the concept that a person may become liable for the obligations of another by taking his place as owner of the land. *See* Oliver Wendell Holmes Jr.'s *Lecture XI, Successions Intervivos,* in *The Common Law* (1881). Milestones in the development of modern covenants law include:

- **1369:** *Pakenham's Case,* Y.B. 42 Ed. III. 3, pl. 14, decided that the current owner of a manor could bring an action to enforce a covenant that a prior and convent would sing every week in the manor chapel even though the covenant had been made with a predecessor in title.
- **1540:** The Statute of Henry VIII, c. 34, provided that the benefits of lease covenants run with the reversion, enabling Henry VIII to enjoy the leases confiscated for the crown on dissolution of the monasteries.
- **1583:** *Spencer's Case,* 77 Eng. Rep. 72 (K.B. 1583), faced with the question whether an assignee of a 21-year lease term was liable on the tenant's covenant to build a wall, announced that the burden of a covenant will run to an assignee if three conditions are met: (1) the covenant was intended to bind assigns;[11] (2) the covenant touched and concerned the land; and (3) there was privity of estate. The judges did not explain what they meant by touch and concern or privity.

Covenant elements.

- **1834:** *Keppell v. Bailey,* 2 My. & K. 517, 39 Eng. Rep. 1042, made it clear that privity[12] means a tenurial (landlord-tenant) relationship between covenantor and covenantee and refused to grant equitable enforcement against the successor to a covenant made between owners in fee. The court refused to enforce a covenant, made by the owner of an ironworks, to buy limestone from a particular quarry and ship it via the Trevil Railroad because:

  > . . . [I]t must not . . . be supposed that incidents of a novel kind can be devised and attached to property at the fancy or caprice of any owner. [G]reat detriment would arise and much confusion of rights if parties were allowed to invent new modes of holding and enjoying real property, and to impress upon their lands and tenements a peculiar character, which should follow them into all hands, however remote.

- **1848:** *Tulk v. Moxhay,* 2 Phil. 774, 41 Eng. Rep. 1143, enforced in equity, against a successor owner of the fee, a covenant requiring the purchaser of

---

11.   The court distinguished between covenants relating to things in existence (in esse) and to things not yet in existence. As to the former, intent to bind successors could be found in evidence surrounding creation of the covenant; as to the latter, the covenant itself must express the intent that assigns be bound. This distinction has disappeared from modern law.

12.   This is what is called *horizontal privity.* It specifies the required relationship between covenantor and covenantee. *Vertical privity,* by contrast, specifies the required relationship between the covenantor and the successor against whom enforcement is sought or between the covenantee and the successors who seeks to enforce the covenant.

Leicester Square garden, and his heirs and assigns, to keep the garden in an open state without any buildings. The court explained:

> That this Court has jurisdiction to enforce a contract between the owner of land and his neighbour purchasing a part of it, that the latter shall either use or abstain from using it in a particular way, is what I never knew disputed. . . . It is said that, the covenant being one which does not run with the land, this court cannot enforce it; but the question is, not whether the covenant runs with the land, but whether a party shall be permitted to use the land in a manner inconsistent with the contract entered into by his vendor, and with notice of which he purchased. Of course, the price would be affected by the covenant, and nothing could be more inequitable than the original purchaser should be able to sell the property the next day for a greater price, in consideration of the assignee being allowed to escape from the liability which he had himself undertaken. . . . [I]f an equity is attached to the property by the owner, no one purchasing with notice of that equity can stand in a different situation from the party from whom he purchased.

- **1881:** *Haywood v. The Brunswick Permanent Benefit Bldg. Soc'y*, 8 Q.B.D. 403, 409, refused to enforce, against a successor, a covenant by a purchaser of the fee to repair the buildings on the property, holding that *Tulk v. Moxhay* was limited to enforcing covenants that restrict use of land. As Cotton, L.J., explained: "The covenant to repair can only be enforced by making the owner put his hand into his pocket, and there is nothing which would justify us in going that length."
- **1914:** *London County Council v. Allen*, 3 K.B. 642, 660, refused to allow enforcement in equity against a successor fee owner because the benefit was in gross. To gain approval for a proposed new street a property owner had executed a deed to the County Council covenanting for himself, his heirs and assigns, not to build on the part of his land lying at the end of the proposed street to allow for future continuation of the street. The court explained:

. . . I am of opinion that the doctrine in *Tulk v. Moxhay* does not extend to the case in which the covenantee has no land capable of enjoying, as against the land of the covenantor, the benefit of the restrictive covenant. The doctrine is either an extension in equity of the doctrine in *Spencer's Case* (in which ownership of land by both covenantor and covenantee is essential) or an extension in equity of the doctrine of negative easements, a doctrine applicable not to the case of easements in gross, but to an easement enjoyed by one land upon another land. Where the covenantee has no land, the derivative owner claiming under the covenantor is bound neither in contract nor by the equitable doctrine which attaches in the case where there is land capable of enjoying the restrictive covenant.

English covenants law thus developed two branches: covenants that could be enforced at law, which were called "real covenants," and covenants that could be enforced in equity, which came to be called "equitable servitudes." The following chart shows what could be enforced by and against successors in law and in equity:

ENGLISH COVENANTS LAW

At Law (Real Covenants) *Damages*	In Equity (Equitable Servitudes) *injunctions.*
At Law **(Real Covenants)** *Burdens:* *Only* lease covenants are enforceable against successors to covenantor's estate, but notice is not necessary *Benefits:* *All* covenants are enforceable by successors to covenantee's estate	**In Equity** **(Equitable Servitudes)** *Burdens:* *Only* negative covenants with appurtenant benefits are enforceable against successors to the covenantor's land *and only* against successors who took with notice *Benefits:* *All* covenants are enforceable by successors to covenantee's land

We can summarize the developed English law of covenants as follows: Covenant benefits run both at law and in equity with the estate or the land owned by the covenantee, if intended to do so by the covenanting parties, and if the benefit touches and concerns that estate or land. The burdens of lease covenants run at law to assignees of the term or of the reversion, if intended to do so and if the burden touches and concerns the leased land. No other covenant burdens run with the land at law, but negative covenants with appurtenant benefits will run in equity against successors with notice. Affirmative covenants between fee owners and covenants with benefits in gross cannot be enforced against successors, either at law or in equity.

Why did English law develop this complicated dual structure? Two deficiencies in English law are largely responsible: England did not have an effective recording act until 1925; and there was no doctrine allowing modification or termination of covenants without consent of all the parties. In addition, as shown by the quotation from *Keppel v. Bailey, supra,* courts were concerned that, given a free hand, landowners would create a proliferation of covenants that would complicate and clog land titles. Allowing unfettered discretion to create running covenants would lead to an impaired real estate market by increasing transaction costs and by imposing long-term obligations that would depress land values. Limiting privity to landlord-tenant relationships responded to the lack of a recording act; limiting equitable enforcement to negative covenants with appurtenant benefits responded to the lack of modification or termination doctrines and to the concern that proliferation of covenants would depress land values.

1. *Horizontal Privity Limited to Landlord-Tenant Relationship.* Until adoption of the 1925 recording act, English law did not protect purchasers without notice against legal interests in land. The bona fide purchaser doctrine, developed in equity, only protected against equitable interests. Allowing enforcement of covenant burdens at law would have made purchasers of land burdened by covenants personally liable to perform them, whether or not they purchased with notice. This was acceptable with respect to lease covenants because purchasers of both the leasehold and the reversion would naturally get notice of the covenants by examining the lease before buying. Holding purchasers without notice liable on covenants made by a prior owner with the owner of a different property or a

notice by examining.

business, or anyone other than a tenant, was not acceptable because purchasers had no sure way to determine the existence of such covenants and assess the risks of purchasing the property. Similar concerns did not arise with respect to running benefits, because the result for a purchaser without notice would be a windfall. Thus, we see that benefits were allowed to run freely from an early date. Allowing covenant burdens to run in equity solved the notice problem because the covenant was regarded as creating only an equitable interest, subject to the bona fide purchaser doctrine. Thus, *Tulk v. Moxhay* allowed enforcement in equity against a successor who took with notice.

2. *Only Negative Burdens Run in Equity.* Limiting equitable enforcement to negative covenant burdens responded to several concerns. First, some of the affirmative covenants courts encountered in the 19th century were essentially anticompetitive, like the supply and transportation covenant involved in *Keppell v. Bailey*, and courts were leery of such arrangements. By contrast, the most common negative covenants prohibited particular uses of the land to protect the quality of life in residential neighborhoods, something courts considered legitimate and useful. Second, prohibitory injunctions were preferable from the standpoint of judicial administration. Issuance of mandatory injunctions requiring performance of affirmative covenants could mire courts down in messy enforcement problems. Third, negative covenants may pose less risk to land values. In the worst case scenario, enforcement of a restrictive covenant prevents the landowner from making any economically viable use of the land. A purchaser of burdened land risks only the value of the investment in the land. An affirmative covenant, by contrast, requires the landowner "to reach into his pocket," which creates a liability that may be more difficult to assess, and potentially might even exceed the value of the land. Refusing to enforce affirmative burdens limits risk for buyers, which helps real estate markets and tends to increase property values. Another factor that undoubtedly came into play as well was the difficulty of terminating covenants. By the end of the 19th century, courts were beginning to develop a changed conditions doctrine that could be used to refuse enforcement to land use restrictions that had lost their utility due to neighborhood change, but development of a doctrine to allow judicial modification or termination of affirmative covenants may have seemed more difficult. Refusing to enforce affirmative burdens against successors avoided all these problems. Similar concerns had much less force with respect to lease covenants because leases are generally of relatively short duration and both landlord and tenant have an interest in the impact of the covenants on the value of the land.

3. *Burdens Can't Run If Benefit Is in Gross.* Two problems may be exacerbated when the benefit of a covenant is in gross rather than appurtenant. Locating the holder of the benefit may be more difficult. The holder of an appurtenant benefit can usually be located by tracing ownership of the benefited parcel through the land and property tax records. Finding the owner of a benefit in gross may be difficult today and certainly was more difficult in the early 20th century before the days of the internet. In addition, it may be more difficult to negotiate modification and termination of a servitude when the benefit is in gross than when the benefit is appurtenant. An appurtenant benefit is generally tied to land in close proximity to the burdened property, which means that the parties are most likely neighbors and they both have a stake in maintaining property values in the community. When this is true, it is likely that they will agree to covenant modifications or termination when the covenant becomes obsolete or unduly

depresses land values in the area. To the extent that owners of benefits in gross are not members of the community or are not affected by any decrease in value of the servient estate due to the covenant, useful modification and termination of the covenant is less likely to occur.[13] Of course, neither of these reasons explains the result in *London County Council v. Allen, supra,* where the holder of the benefit in gross was the local governmental body. The Council would be easy to locate and should have had an interest in the economic health of the community, including the burdened property. The court there did not explore the dangers of benefits in gross or the policy implications of depriving the County Council of the ability to use running covenants for land use regulation. The decision simply applied the easement rule prohibiting benefits in gross on the ground that equitable servitudes are an extension of negative easements.

Negative Easements in English Law

As easement law was crystallizing out from the broader category of incorporeal hereditaments in the early 19th century, four negative easements emerged. These easements differ from positive easements in that they obligate a landowner not to do something on his or her own land that would interfere with the ordinary use and enjoyment of a neighbor's land. The four easements, which are often acquired by prescription (20 years' enjoyment), give a neighbor the right to block development that interferes with (1) the flow of water in an artificial stream; (2) the flow of wind and air through a defined channel; (3) the flow of light to windows; and (4) support for a building from a building on the neighbor's land.

To get an idea how negative easements work in England, consider *Allen v. Greenwood,* [1980] Ch. 119, in which the House of Lords tackled the question whether a prescriptive easement for light and air had been violated when a landowner built a fence that shaded half of his neighbors' greenhouse. The neighbors had used the greenhouse, which was up against the lot line, for more than 20 years to grow tomatoes and flowers for their own use. As a result of the fence, the shaded half of the greenhouse was no longer suitable for its previous uses. The defendant argued that plaintiffs were entitled only to enough light to read or carry out ordinary household tasks, not to enough sunlight to grow tomatoes. The court rejected the argument. In the course of his opinion, Lord Goff said:

> I would hold that in the case of a greenhouse, light required for its normal use is ordinary. . . . It cannot, I think, be right to say that there is no nuisance because one can see to go in and out of a greenhouse and to pot plants which will not flourish, and to pick fruit which cannot properly be developed and ripened, still less because one can see to read a book.

The same forces that led to increasing use of covenants in the early 19th century led to increased demand for negative easements and received the same

----

13.   See Gerald Korngold, *Privately Held Conservation Servitudes: A Policy Analysis in the Context of In Gross Real Covenants and Easements,* 66 Tex. L. Rev. 533 (1988), for further development of this idea.

response from the courts. Just as *Keppell v. Bailey* restricted the use of covenants to leases, the courts restricted negative easements to the four categories. Negative easements were even more dangerous than covenants because they could be acquired by prescription without notice to the servient owner. The decision in *Tulk v. Moxhay* solved the notice problem for restrictive covenants and, since the mid-19th century, has provided the primary private law vehicle for protecting property against unwanted development. English courts continue to recognize the four traditional negative easements, but have remained leery of new ones.

This, then, was the body of English law that American courts borrowed and adapted in fashioning the American law of covenants.

2.   *Covenants and Negative Easements in America*

One very significant difference between England and the United States in the mid-19th century, when demand for servitudes began to rise, was that the American states already had recording acts that protected bona fide purchasers from legal as well as equitable interests. There was thus no need to limit running legal burdens to lease covenants as the English did, and, really, no need for a horizontal privity requirement at all. New York and New Jersey eliminated the horizontal privity requirement and adopted a rule that prohibited enforcement of affirmative burdens against successors, except in lease covenants. Most of the other states retained a horizontal privity requirement, but expanded the relationships that met the requirement to include grantor-grantee and servient owner-easement holder. In these states, the impact of the horizontal privity requirement was to prevent neighbors from entering into covenant arrangements that could be enforced at law and require that covenants enforceable at law be created in deeds conveying either the benefited or burdened estate or an easement. The horizontal privity requirement also prevented businesses from enforcing at law long-term covenants to provide services or products to landowners after the original covenantor had conveyed the land to a successor.

Aside from the horizontal privity requirement, American courts adopted most of the rest of English covenants law, including the dual structure of real covenants and equitable servitudes, pretty much intact. Although there are some exceptions, most states where questions arose expressed doubts that burdens could run if benefits were in gross and doubts that affirmative burdens could be enforced in equity. New York and New Jersey initially refused to enforce affirmative burdens either at law or in equity. In addition to these requirements, American states also adopted the touch or concern and vertical privity requirements. Over the course of the 20th century, American courts continued to adapt covenants law to meet the demand for different types of real estate development that increasingly came to rely on running covenants. American legislatures, too, have helped reshape servitudes law as they have removed common-law barriers that might have impeded development of condominiums and other common interest communities and conservation and historic preservation servitudes.

American courts adopted negative easements, as well as covenants, from English law, but early rejected the idea that they could be acquired by prescription on the ground that prescriptive negative easements would create undesirable barriers to development. Although there was thus no need to limit creation of negative easements, doubts have persisted about using negative easements for new purposes. One case did recognize an easement for view, *Petersen v. Friedman*, 328 P.2d 264 (Cal. Ct. App. 1958), but covenants and statutory easements are used much more frequently than common-law negative easements.

RUNYON v. PALEY
Supreme Court of North Carolina
416 S.E.2d 177 (N.C. 1992)

MEYER, J. This case involves a suit to enjoin defendants from constructing condominium units on their property adjacent to the Pamlico Sound on Ocracoke Island. . . . The sole question presented for our review is whether plaintiffs are entitled to enforce the restrictive covenants.

On 17 May 1937, Ruth Bragg Gaskins acquired a four-acre tract of land located in the Village of Ocracoke bounded on the west by the Pamlico Sound and on the east by Silver Lake.[14] . . . One and one-half acres of the sound-front property, part of which is at issue here, were conveyed by Mrs. Gaskins and her husband to plaintiffs Runyon on 1 May 1954. On 6 January 1960, the Runyons reconveyed the one and one-half acre tract, together with a second tract consisting of one-eighth of an acre, to Mrs. Gaskins. By separate deeds dated 8 January 1960, Mrs. Gaskins, then widowed, conveyed to the Runyons a lake-front lot and a fifteen-foot-wide strip of land that runs to the shore of Pamlico Sound from the roadway separating the lake-front and sound-front lots. This fifteen-foot strip was part of the one and one-half acre parcel that the Runyons had reconveyed to Mrs. Gaskins.

The next day, 9 January 1960, Mrs. Gaskins conveyed the remainder of the one and one-half acre parcel to . . . [the] Brughs [subject to restrictions as follows]:

> BUT this land is being conveyed subject to certain restrictions as to the use thereof, running with said land by whomsoever owned, until removed as herein set out . . . .
>
> (1) Said lot shall be used for residential purposes and not for business, manufacturing, commercial or apartment house purposes; provided, however, this restriction shall not apply to churches or to the office of a professional man which is located in his residence, and
>
> (2) Not more than two residences and such outbuildings as are appurtenant thereto, shall be erected or allowed to remain on said lot. This restriction shall be in full force and effect until such time as adjacent or nearby properties are turned to commercial use, in which case the restrictions herein set out will no longer apply.

---

14. Ocracoke Island is part of the Outer Banks off the coast of North Carolina. Blackbeard, the pirate Edward Teach, was killed in Teach's Hole Channel, just off what is now Ocracoke Village, in 1718. Silver Lake is not a lake at all, but a bay with a narrow entrance to Pamlico Sound. You can find maps of the Village at www.ocracokeislandrealty.com, http://www.insiders.com/outerbanks/map-ocracokevillage.htm, and http://www.ocracokevillage.com/map.htm. The colorful history and names of early families on Ocracoke can be found at www.rootsweb.com/-nchyde/OCRAHIST.HTM. The first Gaskins on the island was a Collector of Customs at Port Ocracoke in 1789. — EDS.

The word "nearby" shall, for all intents and purposes, be construed to mean within 450 feet thereof. . . .

Prior to the conveyance of this land to the Brughs, Mrs. Gaskins had constructed a residential dwelling in which she lived on lake-front property across the road from the property conveyed to the Brughs. Mrs. Gaskins retained this land and continued to live on this property until her death in August 1961. Plaintiff Williams . . . has since acquired the property retained by Mrs. Gaskins.

By mesne conveyances, defendant Warren D. Paley acquired the property conveyed by Mrs. Gaskins to the Brughs. Thereafter, . . . Paley . . . entered into a partnership with defendant Midgett Realty and began constructing condominium units on the property.

. . . [The trial court and Court of Appeals ruled that plaintiffs could not enforce the covenants] concluding that the restrictive covenants were personal to Mrs. Gaskins and became unenforceable at her death. . . .

. . . The significant distinction between . . . [real and personal] covenants is that a personal covenant creates a personal obligation or right enforceable at law only between the original covenanting parties, . . . whereas a real covenant creates a servitude upon the land subject to the covenant . . . for the benefit of another parcel of land . . . .

I. REAL COVENANTS AT LAW

A . . . real covenant . . . runs with the land of the dominant and servient estates only if (1) the subject of the covenant touches and concerns the land, (2) there is privity of estate between the party enforcing the covenant and the party against whom the covenant is being enforced, and (3) the original covenanting parties intended the benefits and the burdens of the covenant to run with the land. . . .

A. Touch and Concern

As noted by several courts and commentators, the touch and concern requirement is not capable of being reduced to an absolute test or precise definition. . . . Focusing on the nature of the burdens and benefits created by a covenant, the court must exercise its best judgment to determine whether the covenant is related to the covenanting parties' ownership interests in their land. . . .

For a covenant to touch and concern the land, it is not necessary that the covenant have a physical effect on the land. It is sufficient that the covenant have some economic impact on the parties' ownership rights by, for example, enhancing the value of the dominant estate and decreasing the value of the servient estate. . . . It is essential, however, that the covenant in some way affect the legal rights of the covenanting parties as landowners. Where the burdens and benefits created by the covenant are of such a nature that they may exist independently from the parties' ownership interests in land, the covenant does not touch and concern the land and will not run with the land. . . .

. . . [T]he nature of the restrictive covenants . . . in this case (building or use restrictions) is strong evidence that the covenants touch and concern the dominant and servient estates. . . . [A] restriction limiting the use of land clearly touches and concerns the estate burdened with the covenant because it restricts the owner's use and enjoyment of the property and thus affects the value of the property. . . . A use restriction does not, however, always touch and concern the dominant estate. *See* Stegall v. Housing Authority, 178 S.E.2d 824 (N.C. 1971) (. . . covenant did not . . . touch and concern . . . where the record failed to disclose the location of the grantor's property "in the area" or the distance from the grantor's property to the restricted property). To . . . touch and concern the dominant estate, it must be shown that the covenant somehow affects the dominant estate by, for example, increasing the value of the dominant estate.

. . . [P]laintiffs have shown that the covenants . . . touch and concern not only the servient estate . . . , but also the properties owned by plaintiffs. The[ir] properties . . . comprise only a portion of what was at one time a four-acre tract. . . . If able to enforce the covenants . . . , plaintiffs would be able to restrict the use of defendants' property to . . . accord with the restrictive covenants. Considering the close proximity of the lands involved . . . and the relatively secluded nature of the area . . . , we conclude that the right to restrict the use of defendants' property would affect plaintiffs' ownership interests in the property owned by them, and therefore the covenants touch and concern their lands.

B.   *Privity of Estate*

. . . [T]he party seeking to enforce the covenant must also show that he is in privity of estate with the party against whom he seeks to enforce the covenant. . . . Although the origin of privity of estate is not certain, the privity requirement has been described as a substitute for privity of contract, which exists between the original covenanting parties and which is ordinarily required to enforce a contractual promise. . . .

For . . . enforcement at law . . . , most states require two types of privity: (1) privity of estate between the covenantor and covenantee at the time the covenant was created ("horizontal privity"), and (2) privity of estate between the covenanting parties and their successors in interest ("vertical privity"). . . . The majority of jurisdictions have held that horizontal privity exists when the original covenanting parties make their covenant in connection with the conveyance of an estate in land from one of the parties to the other. . . . A few courts, on the other hand, have dispensed with the showing of horizontal privity altogether, requiring only a showing of vertical privity. . . .

Vertical privity, which is ordinarily required to enforce a real covenant at law, requires a showing of succession in interest between the original covenanting parties and the current owners of the dominant and servient estates. . . .

We adhere to the rule that a party seeking to enforce a covenant as one running with the land at law must show the presence of both horizontal and vertical privity. To show horizontal privity, it is only necessary that a party seeking to enforce the covenant show that there was some "connection of interest" between the original covenanting parties, such as, here, the conveyance of an estate in land. . . .

[P]laintiffs have shown the existence of horizontal privity. The record shows that the covenants . . . were created in connection with the transfer of an estate in fee. . . . By accepting the deed of conveyance, defendants' predecessors in title, the Brughs, covenanted to use the property for the purposes specified in the deed and thereby granted to Mrs. Gaskins a servitude in their property.

To review the sufficiency of vertical privity in this case, it is necessary to examine three distinct relationships: (1) the relationship between defendants and the Brughs as the covenantors; (2) the relationship between plaintiff Williams and the covenantee, Mrs. Gaskins; and (3) the relationship between plaintiffs Runyon and Mrs. Gaskins. The evidence . . . shows that . . . defendant Warren Paley succeeded to a fee simple estate in the property. Thus, he is in privity of estate with the covenantors. Any legal interests held by the other defendants were acquired by them from defendant Warren Paley. As successors to the interest held by defendant Warren Paley, they too are in privity of estate with the covenantors. Plaintiff Williams has also established a privity of estate between herself and the covenantee. Following the death of Mrs. Gaskins, the property retained by Mrs. Gaskins was conveyed by her heirs to her daughter, . . . [who] conveyed to plaintiff Williams a fee simple absolute in that property. . . . [T]hat defendants and plaintiff Williams did not acquire the property directly from the original covenanting parties is of no moment. . . . [D]efendants and plaintiff Williams have succeeded to the estates then held by the covenantor and covenantee, and thus they are in vertical privity . . . . Such would be true even if the parties had succeeded to only a part of the land burdened and benefitted by the covenants. . . .

Plaintiffs Runyon have not, however, made a sufficient showing of vertical privity. . . . The only interest in land held by the Runyons was acquired by them prior to the creation of the covenant. . . . Because the Runyons were not parties to the covenant and are not in privity with the original parties, they may not enforce the covenant as a real covenant running with the land at law.

C. Intent of the Parties

Defendants argue that . . . the covenanting parties . . . intended that the restrictions be enforceable only by Mrs. Gaskins, the original covenantee. According to defendants, such a conclusion is necessitated where, as here, the instrument creating the covenants does not expressly state that persons other than the covenantee may enforce the covenants. We disagree. Defendants correctly note that our law does not favor restrictions on the use of real property. It is generally stated that "[restrictions in a deed will be regarded as for the personal benefit of the grantor unless a contrary intention appears, and the burden of showing that they constitute covenants running with the land is upon the party claiming the benefit of the restriction." This, however, does not mean that we will always regard a restriction as personal to the covenantee unless the restriction expressly states that persons other than the covenantee may enforce the covenant. . . .

Ordinarily, the parties' intent must be ascertained from the deed or other instrument creating the restriction. . . . However, when the language . . . is ambiguous, the court . . . must look to the language of the instrument, the nature of the restriction, the situation of the parties, and the circumstances surrounding their transaction. . . . [T]he language of the deed creating the restrictions at issue here is ambiguous with regard to the intended enforcement of the restrictions. The deed from Mrs. Gaskins to the Brughs . . . unequivocally expresses the parties' intention that the burden of the restrictions runs with the land conveyed by the deed. . . . [The] habendum clause . . . also included language providing that the estate granted shall be "*subject always* to the restrictions as to use as hereinabove set out." We conclude that the language . . . is such that it can reasonably be interpreted to establish an intent . . . not only to bind successors to the covenantor's interest, but also to benefit the property retained by the covenantee.

Having determined that the instrument creating the restrictions at issue here is ambiguous . . . we must determine whether plaintiff Williams has produced sufficient evidence to show that the covenanting parties intended that the covenants be enforceable by the covenantee's successors in interest. Defendants argue . . . (1) the covenants do not expressly state that the benefit of the covenant was to run with any land retained by the covenantee; and (2) plaintiff Williams has not shown that the property was conveyed as part of a general plan of subdivision . . . subject to uniform restrictions. [S]uch evidence is not the only evidence that may be used to prove the parties' intent.

We find strong evidence . . . to suggest that the covenanting parties intended the restrictive covenants to be real covenants, the benefit of which attached to the land retained by . . . the covenantee. . . . The covenants expressly prohibit the use of the property for "business, manufacturing, commercial or apartment house purposes." . . . As noted by some courts, restrictions limiting the use of property to residential purposes have a significant impact on the value of neighboring land, and thus the very nature of such a restriction suggests that the parties intended that the restriction benefit land rather than the covenantee personally. . . . We need not decide whether the nature of a building or use restriction, in and of itself, is sufficient . . . however. [T]he evidence also shows that the property now owned by defendants was once part of a larger, relatively secluded tract. . . . Prior to conveying the property now owned by defendants, Mrs. Gaskins had erected on a portion of the tract a single-family residence in which she lived. At some point, her property was subdivided into several lots. Mrs. Gaskins conveyed several of these lots, on which residences were thereafter erected. Although none of these deeds of conveyance contained restrictions limiting the use of the property to residential purposes, it is reasonable to assume that Mrs. Gaskins, by later restricting the use of defendants' property, intended to preserve the residential character and value of the relatively secluded area. This evidence is further supported by the fact that Mrs. Gaskins retained land across the road from the property now owned by defendants and continued to reside in her dwelling located on the retained land. . . . [This] evidence . . . strongly supports a finding that the covenanting parties intended that the restrictive covenants inure to the benefit of Mrs. Gaskins' land and not merely to Mrs. Gaskins personally.

Moreover . . . [t]he pertinent language of the deed provides that the property was conveyed subject to certain use restrictions "running with said land by whomsoever owned, until removed," and that the property is "subject always to the restrictions." . . . [T]his language suggests a broad, rather than a limited, scope of enforcement. . . . [T]he trial court erred in concluding that plaintiff Williams . . . was not entitled to enforce the restrictive covenants against defendants.

II. EQUITABLE SERVITUDES

With regard to plaintiffs Runyon, we must go further because, in certain circumstances, a party unable to enforce a restrictive covenant as a real covenant running with the land may nevertheless be able to enforce the covenant as an equitable servitude. Although damages for breach of a restrictive covenant are available only when the covenant is shown to run with the land at law, "*performance* of a covenant will be decreed in favor of persons claiming under the parties to the agreement or by virtue of their relationship thereto, notwithstanding the technical character and form of the covenant." . . . [T]o enforce a restrictive covenant on the theory of equitable servitude, it must be shown (1) that the covenant touches and concerns the land, and (2) that the original covenanting parties intended the covenant to bind the person against whom enforcement is sought and to benefit the person seeking to enforce the covenant. . . .

A. Touch and Concern

Whether a covenant is of such a *character* that it touches and concerns land is determined according to the same principles applicable to real covenants running at law. Unlike with real covenants, however, it is not always necessary to show that both the burden and the benefit touch and concern land. . . . [T]he touch and concern element need only be established where the covenant is sought to be enforced either by or against successors in interest to the original or named parties to the covenant. Where, for example, a covenantee or a named beneficiary seeks to enforce the restriction against the covenantor's successor in interest, the party seeking enforcement need not show that the benefit touches and concerns his land but need show only that the burden touches and concerns the land of the party against whom he seeks to enforce the restriction. . . . Similarly, a successor in interest to the covenantee or to a named beneficiary who seeks to enforce the restriction against the original covenantor must show only that the benefit of the restriction touches and concerns the successor's land. Where, however, the covenant is sought to be enforced by *and* against parties neither of whom were the covenanting parties or named beneficiaries, the party seeking to enforce the restriction must show that the covenant touches and concerns the land of both.

. . . Because a covenant that touches and concerns the land at law will also touch and concern the land in equity, we need not further examine this requirement.

B. Intent of the Parties

A party who seeks to enforce a covenant as an equitable servitude against one who was not an original party to the covenant must show that the original covenanting parties intended that the covenant bind the party against whom enforcement is sought . . . .

If the party seeking enforcement was not an original party to the covenant, he must show that the covenanting parties intended that he be able to enforce the restriction. . . . It is presumed in North Carolina that covenants may be enforced only between the original covenanting parties. However, this presumption may be overcome by evidence that (1) the covenanting parties intended that the covenant personally benefit the party seeking enforcement, or (2) the covenanting parties intended that the covenant benefit property in which the party seeking enforcement holds a present interest. . . . The latter may be shown by evidence of a common scheme of development, . . . of succession of interest to benefitted property retained by the covenantee, . . . or of an express statement of intent to benefit property owned by the party seeking enforcement. . . .

[P]laintiffs Runyon have failed to show that the original covenanting parties intended that they be permitted to enforce the covenants either in a personal capacity or as owners of any land they now own. The Runyons were not parties to the covenants, and neither they nor their property are mentioned, either explicitly or implicitly, as intended beneficiaries in the deed creating the covenants or in any other instrument in the public records pertaining to defendants' property. Although they own property closely situated to defendants', in an area which was primarily residential at the time the restrictive covenants were created, they did not acquire their property as part of a plan or scheme to develop the area as residential property. In fact, they acquired their property free of any restrictions as to the use of their property. Finally, the Runyons purchased their property prior to the creation of the restrictive covenants at issue here, and thus they cannot be said to be successors in interest to any property retained by the covenantee that was intended to be benefitted by the covenants.

An affidavit filed by Mr. Runyon is the only evidence tending to support the Runyons' claim that they were intended beneficiaries of the covenants. This affidavit, filed with plaintiffs' motion for summary judgment, states that the covenants were created as a result of a "three-party land swap" whereby the Runyons conveyed their sound-front property to effectuate two transfers of the property: the transfer of a fifteen-foot-wide strip of land to the Runyons for access to the Pamlico Sound and the transfer of the remainder of the property to the Brughs, defendants' predecessors in interest. Mr. Runyon alleges in his affidavit that the covenants were included in the deed of conveyance to the Brughs "for the benefit of the land retained by [Mrs.] Gaskins and neighboring property owners, specifically including and intending to benefit [the Runyons]."

This affidavit . . . , no matter how informative of the parties' intent, is not competent evidence. . . . Unlike the evidence relied upon to support plaintiff Williams' claim, the allegations contained in this affidavit reference no matters of public record that tend to explain ambiguous deed language by showing the parties' situation or the circumstances surrounding their transaction. . . . [T]his affidavit is an attempt to use inadmissible parol evidence to add to or vary the terms of the instrument to include the Runyons . . . as named beneficiaries to the covenants. Moreover, even if the allegations of the affidavit were admissible to explain some ambiguous language of the instrument, the affidavit would still be incompetent under our well-established rule that declarations and testimony of the parties are not admissible to prove the covenanting parties' intent.

III. NOTICE

. . . [A] restrictive covenant is not enforceable, either at law or in equity, against a subsequent purchaser of property burdened by the covenant unless notice of the covenant is contained in an instrument in his chain of title. N.C.G.S. § 47-18 provides:

> No . . . conveyance of land . . . shall be valid to pass any property interest as against . . . purchasers for a valuable consideration . . . but from the time of registration thereof in the county where the land lies. . . .

Unlike in many states, actual knowledge, no matter how full and formal, is not sufficient to bind a purchaser in our state with notice of the existence of a restrictive covenant. . . .

. . . [D]efendants contend that . . . a restrictive covenant is not enforceable against a subsequent purchaser of the property unless the instruments in the chain of title *expressly* state "*both* an intention to bind succeeding grantees and an intention to permit enforcement by successors of the grantor or named beneficiaries."

While it would be advisable to include an express provision with respect to the rights of enforcement in the conveyance that creates them, we do not agree that such notice . . . is required. . . . [W]e have required the certainty of an express statement in the chain of title only with respect to the *existence* of a restrictive covenant. . . . Where . . . the restriction is contained in the chain of title, we have not hesitated to enforce the restriction . . . when the court may reasonably infer that the covenant was created for the benefit of the party seeking enforcement. . . .

In this case, a proper search of the public records pertaining to defendants' property would have revealed not only the existence of the restrictive covenants, but also that prior to the conveyance the property was part of a larger tract owned by Mrs. Gaskins. Upon conveying the property to defendants' predecessors, Mrs. Gaskins did not part with all of her property but retained adjacent or nearby property that would be benefitted by the restrictive covenants. From this evidence, it reasonably may be inferred that the restrictive covenants were intended to benefit the property retained by Mrs. Gaskins. . . .

. . . While the records in defendants' chain of title unambiguously provide notice of the restrictive covenants, they do not in any way suggest any right of enforcement in favor of the Runyons, either personally or as owners of any land. The day before the restrictive covenant was created, the Runyons did acquire from Mrs. Gaskins a fifteen-foot strip of land adjacent to the restrictive property. Even assuming *arguendo* that recordation of this conveyance would have provided some notice of Mrs. Gaskins' intent to benefit the Runyons, . . . this conveyance . . . was not recorded by them until some fifteen to sixteen years after the Brughs recorded their deed of conveyance from Mrs. Gaskins. . . .

[W]e conclude that the restrictive covenants . . . are real covenants appurtenant to the property retained by Mrs. Gaskins . . . . As a successor in interest to . . . [that] property . . . plaintiff Williams is . . . entitled to seek enforcement of the restrictive covenants against defendants. . . . We further conclude that the Runyons have not proffered sufficient evidence to show that they have standing to enforce the restrictive covenants, either personally or as owners of any land intended to be benefitted by the restrictions. We therefore affirm that part of the Court of Appeals' decision that affirmed the trial court's dismissal of the Runyons' claim.

Notes and Questions

1. *Aftermath.* What difference did it make that only plaintiff Williams was entitled to enforce the covenant? Williams pursued the case and judgments enforcing the covenants against Paley and Midgett Realty were entered in December 1992 and again in May 1995. The land records for Hyde County, North Carolina (www.hyderod.com) show a consent judgment entered June 16, 1995, that modified the earlier judgments to allow defendants to retain two condominium units on the restricted lot without violation of the covenants. It also ordered defendants to remove two other units by July 30, 1995, and the foundations for four additional units from the property by November 30, 1995. Owners of the remaining six Ocracoke Horizon Condominium units (apparently on adjacent property not acquired from Ruth Gaskins) were permitted to retain access rights across the existing driveway and rights to use the existing septic field. Defendants were ordered to pay $50,000 to Mrs. Williams as compensatory damages, costs, and attorneys' fees.

In 1999, plaintiff Williams conveyed the benefitted parcel to Timothy W. Midgett, presumably of Midgett Realty, together with "all her rights, titles and interests in and to the enforcement of any restrictive covenants which run with the land being conveyed or which are personal to the Grantor or any predecessor in title." *See* deed dated Oct. 27, 1999, recorded in Book 173, p. 397. Where did this leave the Runyons and the other neighbors to whom Ruth Gaskins had conveyed lots?

Mary Runyon died in 1996 and her husband, Charles, died in November 1999. On October 13, 2000, the three Runyon children sold the lot acquired from Ruth Gaskins to Brant and Beverly Godfrey. On the same date they donated the 15-foot strip to the Ocracoke Preservation Society, conveying the land subject to the condition that it be used "for the sole purpose of providing free public pedestrian access between Pamlico Sound and Silver Lake Road in perpetuity." In the event the Preservation Society is dissolved or refuses to allow free public access, title "shall then automatically vest in and be owned by the North Carolina Land Trust, to be held by it for the same purposes." *See* Deed Book 177, p. 927.

2. The Runyon children's deed to the Godfreys (Book 177, p. 917) states that the land conveyed shall be subject to restrictions "which shall run with and bind the land" that prohibit subdivision and restrict use to residential purposes only. The deed contains the following provision:

These covenants shall remain in full force and effect for a period of thirty years . . . and shall automatically renew for successive ten-year periods thereafter, until such time as the adjoining property contiguous to subject property (Leonard Meeker, now or formerly as described in Deed Book 129, page 167 and Deed Book 75, page 409, Hyde County Registry, and/or that the remaining parcel across SR 1328 owned by the grantors herein) shall in whole or in part be utilized for purposes other than single family residential.

Is this language sufficient to allow the owner of the Meeker parcel to enforce the restrictions? How would you draft a clause to give enforcement rights to the Meeker parcel?

3. Compare the law of covenants described by the North Carolina Supreme Court in the principal case with the law of England described in the introduction to this section. How does it differ on horizontal privity, benefits in gross, and notice?

4. What is the difference between a real covenant and an equitable servitude in North Carolina?

5. *Benefits in third parties.* The court says that the Runyons would have been entitled to enforce the covenants if they now owned some of the land Ruth Gaskins owned when the covenant was made, or if the intent to make the Runyons beneficiaries appeared in the deed or in another instrument in the public records pertaining to the burdened property. In the first case, the Runyons would have been in vertical privity with Gaskins and entitled to sue as her successor. In the second, they would have been third-party beneficiaries of the covenant and entitled to sue. The North Carolina court follows the modern trend in recognizing that covenant benefits can be created in third parties.

6. Is there any reason why a court should refuse to enforce a servitude created to protect the neighbors? Most courts that have considered the question in the modern era have agreed with the court in the principal case. Justice Musmanno, writing for the Supreme Court of Pennsylvania in *Mariner v. Rohanna*, 92 A.2d 219 (Pa. 1952), a case involving a covenant prohibiting use of a parcel for an automobile junkyard, said:

> [A] property owner, regardless of whether he is conveying an entire tract not a part of a plan of lots, or whether he is conveying one or several lots of a plan of lots, has the right to dispose of his property with a limited restriction on its use, however much the restriction may affect the value or the nature of the estate. The benefits of the restriction need not run to the grantor-promisee alone or to the owners of other lots in a plan of lots deeded by him. As in the case of other covenants, third parties may be made the beneficiaries of a restriction and may enjoin its breach so long as it is clearly shown that the covenant was for their benefit.

But the Supreme Judicial Court of Maine, in *Brown v. Fuller's Heirs*, 347 A.2d 127 (Me. 1975), refused to enforce a covenant to protect the testator's neighbors. The covenant banned commercial and high-rise construction on property she devised to a hospital. The court said:

> It has long been thought contrary to public policy, however, to enforce as an equitable servitude a restriction imposed for the benefit of land in which, at the time of the origin of the restriction, the person creating it lacks a legally cognizable interest.

Instead of identifying the public policy implicated by equitable enforcement of a servitude created to benefit third parties, however, the court rested its decision on *stare decisis*:

> *Stare decisis* must operate with plenary force in the law of real property to maintain the certainty and predictability which Courts, traditionally, have made the

benchmark of this area of jurisprudence and upon which, accordingly, the public
has been induced to place strong reliance.

Is this argument persuasive? Who is likely to rely on the rule prohibiting creation of benefits in gross?

7. In a state like Maine, how can a landowner desiring to sell property protect
her neighbors from unwanted development? Can it be done by her will? What
about a defeasible fee? If the landowner is willing to transfer rights to the neighbors during her lifetime, how would you go about giving them either enforceable covenant benefits or the right to take title to the property if the prohibited
development occurred?

Can you think of any reason why the law should insist on such complication?
Why it should deny protection to neighbors? Should the lawyer who fails to create an enforceable covenant or forfeiture right in the neighbors be liable for
malpractice?

8. Another old doctrine holds that only a party owning land that will benefit from covenant enforcement is entitled to seek enforcement by injunction.
Although this rule tends to prevent abusive use of covenants by persons whose
only interest in enforcement is forcing a buyout by the burdened party, it cuts
too broadly. It is often desirable to create covenants enforceable by conservation and preservation groups, by governmental agencies, and by others whose
interest in covenant enforcement is not tied to ownership of land in the vicinity.
Restatement (Third) § 8.1, substitutes a requirement, applicable to enforcement
using legal as well as equitable remedies, to show either ownership of benefited
land or a legitimate interest in covenant enforcement.

9. Restatement (Third) § 2.6 freely permits creation of benefits in third parties and benefits in gross for all servitudes. Comment *b* explains:

> The underlying rationale . . . is that the intent of the parties to create servitude
> benefits in others should be given effect. The old rules prohibiting creation of ser-
> vitude benefits in gross, and requiring separate conveyances for the creation of a
> servitude and simultaneous transfer of the burdened estate, were designed to serve
> purposes that are now obscure. They have little modern utility and trap the poorly
> represented. They frustrate intent and, to the extent they retain any force, should
> be discarded.

SONOMA DEVELOPMENT, INC. v. MILLER

Supreme Court of Virginia
515 S.E.2d 577 (1999)

KINSER, J. In a decree dated July 29, 1998, the circuit court upheld the validity of a "Declaration of Restriction" and ordered Sonoma Development, Inc.
(Sonoma), to remove all improvements that were within three feet of the north
wall of a residence owned by . . . the Millers. . . . This appeal concerns the circuit
court's finding that horizontal privity existed between the original covenanting
parties. . . .

. . . Alfred E. Schaer and Mary Schaer . . . owned two adjacent lots, numbered
Lot 38 and Lot 39, in . . . "Old Town" in the City of Alexandria. . . . The lots are

long and narrow, and share a common sideline that runs from the front to the back of the lots.

When the Schaers owned both lots, a three-story, brick house was situated on Lot 38, but Lot 39 was vacant. The north wall of the house on Lot 38 physically encroaches upon the southern boundary line of Lot 39 by 0.1 foot at the northeast corner of the dwelling and by 0.2 foot at the northwest corner of the dwelling.

In 1995, the Millers entered into a real estate contract with the Schaers for the purchase of Lot 38. Because the Millers were concerned about future development on Lot 39, the contract included a provision requiring the Schaers to provide a deed restriction on Lot 39 prohibiting the use of a common wall with Lot 38 and requiring a sufficient easement to facilitate maintenance of the portion of the dwelling that encroaches on Lot 39. On June 30, 1995, . . . the Schaers executed a "Declaration of Restriction" requiring "[t]hat no improvement of any kind be constructed upon Lot 39 within three (3) feet of the north wall of the existing dwelling on Lot 38." . . .

On the same day, the Schaers executed a "Declaration of Easement" in which they granted an easement on Lot 39 "for the benefit of lot 38 to permit the house to remain in its present position . . . and to permit ingress and egress unto lot 39 as reasonably necessary to repair and maintain the northern wall of the house." Like the "Declaration of Restriction," the "Declaration of Easement" named the Schaers as the "Grantors" but did not specify anyone as the "Grantee." The "Declaration of Easement" did, however, state that the Schaers had agreed to sell Lot 38 to the Millers. . . . [B]oth documents were recorded in the clerk's office of the circuit court.

Also on June 30, 1995, the Schaers executed a deed conveying Lot 38 to the Millers. The deed states that the "conveyance is made subject to recorded conditions, restrictions and easements affecting the property hereby conveyed."

In February 1997, Sonoma purchased Lot 39 from the Schaers. The deed from the Schaers to Sonoma, dated February 21, 1997, specifies that the conveyance is "subject to easements, restrictive covenants, restrictions and rights-of-way of record."[1]

In the spring of 1997, Sonoma . . . [built] a house on Lot 39. The Millers commenced this action because the house . . . violates the three-foot setback requirement contained in the "Declaration of Restriction." . . .

In Virginia, we recognize two types of restrictive covenants: "the common law doctrine of covenants running with the land and restrictive covenants in equity known as equitable easements and equitable servitudes." . . . [T]he Millers acknowledge that the "Declaration of Restriction" does not fall within the second category of restrictive covenants. Thus, the issue is whether that document creates a valid common law restrictive covenant that runs with the land . . . .

To enforce a real covenant in Virginia, a party must prove the following elements: (1) privity between the original parties to the covenant (horizontal privity);[3] (2) privity between the original parties and their successors in interest

---

1. First American Title Insurance Company issued a title insurance policy to Sonoma on February 26, 1997. The policy lists the "Restrictive Covenants" and "Declaration of Easement" as items that are excluded from coverage under the policy.

3. A number of jurisdictions have abolished the requirement of horizontal privity. . . . The *Restatement (Third) of Property: Servitudes* § 2.4 (Tentative Draft No. 1, 1989), states that horizontal privity between the parties is not required to create a servitude. . . .

(vertical privity); (3) an intent by the original covenanting parties that the benefits and burdens of the covenant will run with the land; (4) that the covenant "touches and concerns" the land; and (5) the covenant must be in writing. . . . Sonoma contends that . . . horizontal privity did not exist between the original covenanting parties, the Schaers and the Millers, because only the Schaers were named as a party in the "Declaration of Restriction." . . . Sonoma posits that horizontal privity must be demonstrated within the four corners of a single document. . . .

With regard to the precise issue presented in this appeal, we conclude that horizontal privity did exist . . . . We are not willing to say that, in every situation, only one document can be examined . . . to determine if horizontal privity existed between the original covenanting parties. . . .

To establish horizontal privity, the party seeking to enforce the real covenant must prove that "the original covenanting parties [made] their covenant in connection with the conveyance of an estate in land from one of the parties to the other." Runyon v. Paley, 416 S.E.2d 177, 184 (N.C. 1992). . . . The *Restatement of Property* § 534(a) (1944), provides that horizontal privity is satisfied when "the transaction of which the promise is a part includes a transfer of an interest either in the land benefited by or in the land burdened by the performance of the promise." In other words, the covenant must be part of a transaction that also includes the transfer of an interest in land that is either benefited or burdened by the covenant. . . .

. . . In the context of the present case, we find that the transaction of which the covenant was a part commenced with the real estate contract between the Schaers and the Millers, and culminated with the deed conveying Lot 38 to the Millers. The "Declaration of Restriction" fulfilled the Schaers' contractual obligation . . . and was executed in conjunction with the deed to the Millers. Thus, it was part of a transaction that included the transfer of an interest in the land benefited by the real covenant.[5] . . .

Sonoma does not dispute that it had notice of the "Declaration of Restriction." . . .

If parties, for valuable consideration, with their eyes open, contract that a particular thing shall not be done, all that a court of equity has to do is to say by way of injunction that which the parties have already said by way of covenant—that the thing shall not be done; and in such case the injunction does nothing more than give the sanction of the process of the court to that which already is the contract between the parties. It is not, then, a question of convenience or inconvenience, or of the amount of damage or injury—it is the specific performance, by the court, of that negative bargain which the parties have made, with their eyes open, between themselves.

. . . We . . . stated in Lindsay v. James, 51 S.E.2d 326 (Va. 1949), that "[r]elief by way of a mandatory injunction will not be denied merely because the loss caused will be disproportionate to the benefits accruing to the opposing party where it appears that the obstruction or the violation of a right was made with full knowledge and understanding of the consequences which result." . . . An

---

5. Sonoma does not dispute the validity of the "Declaration of Easement" even though the Schaers were the only parties named in that document. Yet, it is part of the same transaction as the "Declaration of Restriction."

injunction was the appropriate remedy to enforce the terms of the "Declaration of Restriction."

For the reasons stated, we will affirm the judgment of the circuit court.

Notes and Questions

1. What is the difference between a real covenant and an equitable servitude in Virginia? The Schaers' covenant would have been enforceable as an equitable servitude under the English rules—the burden was negative, the benefit was appurtenant to the adjacent property owned by the plaintiff, and Sonoma Development purchased with notice of the covenant. What is missing? Apparently, Virginia is one of the few states that has limited equitable servitudes to "general plan" covenants—covenants imposed by a subdivider (or other developer) on all the lots in a subdivision to implement a general plan of development, as, for example, by restricting all lots to residential use only. If that is indeed the case, all covenants that qualify as equitable servitudes would also meet the horizontal privity requirement because general plan covenants are imposed by the deeds from the developer to the original purchasers.

Which covenants would not fit into either of the Virginia categories of running covenants? If the Schaers had restricted the height of any building that could be erected on Lot 39 for the benefit of their neighbors, the owners of Lot 40, would the owners of Lot 40 have been able to enforce the covenant against Sonoma Development? Can you think of any policy reason why the Virginia courts should refuse to enforce such a covenant? Can you think of a way for next-door neighbors to create enforceable running covenants?

2. Does it matter whether a covenant is enforced as a real covenant or an equitable servitude? How was the real covenant in this case enforced? Should covenant beneficiaries be able to obtain either damages or an injunction without regard to whether the covenant qualifies as a real covenant or an equitable servitude so long as the covenant meets the requirements for one or the other? Restatement (Third) § 8.3 says that "a servitude may be enforced by any appropriate remedy or combination of remedies which may include declaratory judgment, compensatory damages, punitive damages, nominal damages, injunctions, restitution, and imposition of liens."

3. Does horizontal privity serve a useful function? Comment *b* to Restatement (Third) § 2.4 explains the rationale for eliminating a horizontal privity requirement:

> In American law, the horizontal privity requirement serves no function beyond insuring that most covenants intended to run with the land will be created in conveyances. Formal creation of covenants is desirable because it tends to assure that they will be recorded. However, the horizontal privity requirement is no longer needed for this purpose. In modern law, the Statute of Frauds and recording acts perform that function.
>
> Application of the horizontal privity requirement prevents enforcement at law of covenants entered into between neighbors and between other parties who do not transfer or share some other interest in the land. The rule can easily be circumvented by conveyance to a strawperson who imposes the covenant in the reconveyance. Since the rule serves no necessary purpose and simply acts as a trap for the

poorly represented, it has been abandoned. As a matter of common law, horizontal privity between the covenanting parties is no longer required to create a servitude obligation.

Differences Between Real Covenants and Equitable Servitudes in American Law

As you have seen from the *Runyon v. Paley* and *Sonoma Development v. Miller* cases, American courts continue to recognize both real covenants and equitable servitudes and to apply some different requirements for enforcing the burden of a covenant against a successor to the covenantor. Before going on, it might be helpful to look at the differences and similarities in a bit more detail.

burden v. successor.

TRADITIONAL VIEW OF AMERICAN REQUIREMENTS FOR CREATING RUNNING COVENANTS

Requirement	Real Covenant	Equitable Servitude
• Intent	Required	Required
• Horizontal Privity	Required	Not required
• Existence of General Plan	Not required	Not required, except in Virginia and maybe a few other states
• Writing	Required	Required, but implied servitudes and servitudes by estoppel are allowed
• Benefits in Gross	Probably OK, but first Restatement said no	Not allowed, but many exceptions
• Affirmative Burdens	OK	OK, but a few exceptions
• Touch or Concern	Required	Required
• Vertical Privity	Succession to *same* estate required for burdens	Succession to *some* estate required
• Notice	Required by recording act (actual, inquiry, or constructive notice)	Required (actual, inquiry, or constructive except that North Carolina requires record notice)

If you find this material a bit overwhelming or mystifying, you can find a complete functional analysis of the traditional requirements in Susan F. French, *Toward a Modern Law of Servitudes: Reweaving the Ancient Strands*, 55 S. Cal. L. Rev. 1261 (1982). That article concludes that there are no longer any important differences between real covenants and equitable servitudes and that the law would be more useful if it recognized that the meaningful differences lie not in the relationship between the covenanting parties (horizontal privity) but in the nature of the performance called for. In determining whether a covenant should be enforced against a successor who has a lesser estate than the covenantor, for example, what matters is whether the covenant calls for the payment of money or restricts the use that can be made of the premises. The lessee of a condominium should not be liable for the covenant requiring payment of maintenance assessments (unless the lease so provides), but should be bound by the covenant prohibiting nonresidential uses, for example.

The Restatement (Third) would eliminate any remaining distinctions between equitable servitudes and real covenants. Section 2.4 states that horizontal privity is not required to create a servitude, and § 2.6 provides that benefits in gross may be freely created. To create a servitude under the Restatement (Third), the only requirements are intent and, either a writing that satisfies the Statute of Frauds, or circumstances that create exceptions to the Statute (implication, estoppel, prescription). A servitude created in this manner is valid unless it is illegal or violates public policy. Which successors are bound or benefited by covenants is determined by the nature of the performance called for, and defenses based on notice arise out of the recording acts. Compare the following chart with the previous one to see the simplification effected by Restatement (Third):

RESTATEMENT REQUIREMENTS FOR CREATING RUNNING COVENANTS

Requirement	
• Intent	Required
• Horizontal Privity	Not required
• Existence of General Plan	Not required
• Writing	Required, but creation by estoppel and implication are allowed
• Benefits in Gross	OK
• Affirmative Burdens	OK
• Touch or Concern	Not required; covenant OK unless illegal or against public policy
• Vertical Privity	Required for affirmative burdens only
• Notice	Recording Act

Conservation and Historic Preservation Servitudes

Interest in preserving open space, historic buildings, scenic views, and wild-life habitat, beginning in the late 1950s and early 1960s, led to increased de-mand for servitudes that could serve those purposes. Availability of federal income tax deductions (as charitable contributions) for donation of such servitudes, beginning in 1964, substantially increased interest in finding a vehicle that would allow landowners to retain ownership of their land while committing it to conservation or similar purposes. Easements and covenants were the most likely candidates, but traditional doctrines imposed obstacles to using either. Easements could not be used to impose affirmative burdens (such as requiring the landowner to maintain an historic facade or restore wildlife habitat) and there were doubts whether new types of easements would be recognized. There were also doubts whether noncommercial ease-ments in gross would be assignable. Covenants required either horizontal privity if they were to be enforced at law, or appurtenant benefits if they were to be enforced in equity. Since conservation servitudes typically benefit either conservation organizations or governmental bodies and typically are not accompanied by the transfer of any other interest in the burdened land, they run into problems on both counts. Because of these problems with tra-ditional servitudes doctrine, legislation at both the federal and state levels has been enacted to authorize the creation of servitudes to preserve views, to prevent the erection of billboards along highways, to protect historic build-ings, to preserve open space, and to protect habitat for plants and wildlife. Much of it, like the Uniform Conservation Easement Act of 1981, names the statutorily authorized servitude an "easement" even though it shares many covenant characteristics.

Most recently, interest in developing brownfields (parcels previously contami-nated by industrial or commercial activity) has led to efforts to create a uniform act that would end questions about the enforceability of covenants not to sue on grounds such as lack of horizontal privity, touch or concern, lack of an appur-tenant benefit, or lack of assignability. The statutory servitudes envisioned by the drafters of the Uniform Environmental Covenants Act will take the form of covenants, rather than easements, but, like the servitudes authorized by the Uniform Conservation Easement Act, may combine elements of easements and covenants. The Restatement (Third) eliminates the traditional barriers to cre-ation of common-law conservation and preservation servitudes by eliminating the horizontal privity requirement, recognizing the enforceability of benefits in gross, and allowing assignment of benefits in gross. It also provides special rules making termination by changed circumstances more difficult for conser-vation servitudes held by governmental bodies and conservation organizations. *See* Restatement (Third) §§ 1.6, 7.11.

3. Creation of Running Covenants

Covenants may be created expressly by a written instrument that satisfies the Statute of Frauds, by estoppel, by implication, and by prescription.

a. Express Creation by Written Instrument

Covenants are usually created either by a deed as in *Runyon v. Paley* or by a declaration as in *Sonoma Development v. Miller*. Whether using a deed or a declaration, a carefully drafted instrument will identify the covenantor and covenantee, the property burdened by the covenant, the property benefited by the covenant if the benefit is appurtenant, and the parties intended to have enforcement rights if the benefit is in gross. It will also state that the burdens, or benefits, or both, are intended to run with the land to successors. Although this level of detail is highly desirable, many less carefully drafted instruments have been given effect when the intent to create a running covenant was clear, and the covenantor and the burdened property were identified. Courts are often willing to infer the identity of the intended benefited parcel from the circumstances surrounding creation of the instrument and to infer the intent that the benefits or burdens run with the land from the nature of the covenant. For example, when a developer creates a new subdivision and records a declaration of covenants restricting use of the lots to residential purposes, courts readily infer that each lot in the subdivision is the intended beneficiary of the restrictions placed on every other lot in the subdivision. *See* Restatement (Third) § 2.14(1), Servitudes Implied From General Plan.

Courts can infer intent when not expressly written.

The question sometimes arises whether a landowner can unilaterally impose a covenant or other servitude on his or her land. The answer is generally no—a servitude is not effective unless created as the result of a contract or conveyance, which means there must be another party involved. Developers typically record a declaration of covenants for a new subdivision before selling any lots. Until the first lot is sold subject to the declaration, it has no effect—the developer is free to change the covenants or to withdraw the declaration altogether. Once the first lot has been sold, however, the covenants are effective and the consent of the lot owners is necessary if the developer wants to make changes.

to create a servitude, another party must be involved.

When a declaration of covenants has been unilaterally recorded by a landowner and the land is later sold without mention of the declaration, do they become binding on the purchaser? There are two issues here: What did the parties intend? And if their intent was not expressed in the deed, have they complied with the Statute of Frauds? *Citizens for Covenant Compliance v. Anderson*, 906 P.2d 1314 (Cal. 1995), held that a recorded declaration of covenants (CC&R's) for a subdivision became effective when the developer sold the lots even though the deeds did not refer to the declaration, saying:

> The law may readily conclude that a purchaser who has constructive notice, and therefore knowledge, of the restrictions, takes the property with the understanding that it, as well as all others lots in the tract, is subject to the restrictions, and intends and agrees to accept their burdens and benefits, even if there is no additional documentation evidencing the intent at the time of the conveyance. . . . The necessity of a writing because of the "policy considerations" underlying the statute of frauds . . . is not implicated here. Both the recorded CC&R's and the conveyance that triggered them are in writing.

Local governments often grant approval for a zoning variance or building permit subject to conditions on the use that can be made of the property or *release must be recorded*

a release of liability for the grant of the permit. To make the conditions or release effective, they require the landowner to record a covenant restricting use of the property. These covenants become effective on recordation because they are created pursuant to a contract with the local governmental body. Even if these covenants are effective as between the local governmental body and the landowner, are they enforceable against successors to the burdened property? English law said no (*London County Council v. Allen*), but American courts have generally accepted this form of land use regulation as legitimate. *See, e.g., Middlefield v. Church Mills Knitting Co.*, 35 N.E. 780 (Mass. 1894) (covenant to build replacement bridge as condition for permit to build dam that would flood out old bridge); *1515-1519 Lakeview Boulevard Condominium Ass'n v. Apartment Sales Corporation*, 43 P.3d 1233 (en banc) (Wash. 2000) (covenant not to sue city for granting building permit in area prone to landslides). Restatement (Third) § 2.6 removes the obstacle to enforcing such covenants by providing that landowners may freely create servitudes with benefits in gross.

Note: Relationship Between Covenants and Zoning

Zoning imposes use restrictions designed to segregate land uses to protect residential areas from commercial and industrial uses and to limit, generally, the opportunities for nuisances to arise from incompatible uses. Now that most developed property is covered by zoning, why do developers continue to use privately created restrictive covenants? What happens if the zoning and covenants are different? Taking the second question first: whichever is more restrictive prevails. If the zoning, for example, permits both single-family and duplex residential development, but the covenants permit only single-family detached residences, the covenant prevails, and vice versa. If they are completely incompatible, however, the zoning prevails. For example, if the covenant permits only commercial use and the zoning permits only residential use, the zoning prevails because use for a purpose prohibited by the zoning ordinance is illegal.

Why do developers use covenants? One reason is that covenants give more stability (they are harder to change) and lodge control with the property owners (who have to agree to make any changes). Zoning, by contrast, is a product of the city or county political process and is subject to change by the appropriate public body. Consent of the affected property owners is not necessarily required. Another reason is that covenants often provide more stringent and detailed regulations than the city or county is willing or able to include in a zoning ordinance.

Problem

You have been contacted by a group of property owners in an older central city who would like to turn their neighborhood into a common interest community with restrictive covenants, mandatory membership in a community association, architectural controls, and the power to assess property owners for neighborhood cleanup and beautification, security guards, and the costs of covenant enforcement. Will they be able to do this? What is likely to be the biggest stumbling block?

If the property owners can enlist sufficient political support, can similar benefits be obtained using zoning or other public law mechanisms? Robert C. Ellickson, in *New Institutions for Old Neighborhoods,* 48 Duke L.J. 75 (1998), suggests that the advantages now enjoyed by so many suburban communities could be obtained by enactment of statutes authorizing supermajorities of property owners to create Block Improvement Districts with assessment powers. These districts, modeled after the Business Improvement Districts used in many cities, could overcome the free-rider problems that are likely to prevent the creation of a workable servitudes regime in an existing neighborhood. When you study the materials on eminent domain in Chapter 13, think about whether, as an alternative, the city could condemn the property in a neighborhood for the purpose of reconveying it to the existing owners subject to common interest community servitudes.

b. Creation by Estoppel

SHALIMAR ASSOCIATION v. D.O.C. ENTERPRISES, LTD.

Court of Appeals of Arizona
688 P.2d 682 (Ariz. Ct. App. 1984)

FROEB, J. . . . Shalimar Estates is a residential land development consisting of [a golf course and adjacent residential lots] on 134 acres . . . in Tempe, Arizona. . . . The original developer of the Shalimar property was Karl Guelich and Associates. . . .

. . . Guelich and Associates designed a golf course which was intended as an integral part of the general plan . . . [created] for the purpose of inducing people to buy property in the Shalimar subdivisions and [which] was intended to be for the benefit of those purchasers and their successors in interest. A map showing the proposed development was shown to potential lot buyers and was recorded . . . in August 1960. Guelich and Associates also . . . recorded . . . certain restrictions which contained three paragraphs referring to a golf course:

5. No structure shall be located nearer than thirty feet to any property line abutting on the golf course property; . . .

9. . . . Landscaping shall be planned . . . so as to avoid undue obstruction of the view of the golf course from the lots, and all property lines abutting on the golf course shall be fenced with 3 feet high grape stake fencing or equivalent.

17. It is contemplated that a golf course may be constructed on that certain part designated as Tract "A" in Shalimar Estates, and the terms "golf course property" and "golf course" as used herein shall mean the golf course which may be constructed on those tracts as shown by the recorded plat of Shalimar Estates.

No restrictions were recorded against the golf course property itself. . . . The golf course was constructed in 1960 and 1961 . . . . [B]rochures and sales materials which depict and describe the golf course were placed on file as a public record with the Arizona Department of Real Estate. Residential lot sales began in 1961. The brochures provided to lot purchasers showed a golf course surrounded by numbered home lots.

Sales were made with representations that the golf course would be maintained as such until the year 2000, with provision for an extension of 25 years. The duration of this promise was to be the same as the period of the recorded restrictions . . . . Salesmen for Guelich and Associates promised to develop, maintain, and operate the Shalimar Golf Course. . . . A higher price was charged for lots adjoining the golf course. . . .

The trial court found . . . that the homeowners who purchased lots adjoining the golf course had a right to rely and did in fact rely upon the representations made to them that the use of the golf course was restricted to that purpose for the term of the restrictions. . . .

In 1976, . . . the Hills purchased the subject property from Guelich and Associates. . . . The Hills continued to maintain and operate it as a golf course until July 2, 1979, when they sold it to appellants. [They and Guelich] believed the golf course property was required to be used as a golf course and operated it as such.

. . . [A]ppellants . . . first became interested in the property in July 1978 when one of the individual appellants, Steven Otto, visited Phoenix. Otto is an attorney licensed to practice in Canada and has specialized in real estate matters. The other individual appellants, . . . also Canadians, are experienced real estate agents. All of the individual appellants are experienced in real estate investments.

The golf course was operating during Otto's first visit, but it did not appear to him to be doing well. . . . Appellants' real estate agent later approached L.B. Hill and convinced him to begin negotiations for the sale of the golf course. In November 1978, appellants came to Arizona, and in the period that followed presented several offers. The first offers which appellants made to Hill for the purchase of the golf course contained the following contingency. . . .

> Verification by Phoenix Title and Trust or any qualified successor, that paragraph number 17 does not affect the lands in Tract A [the golf course] and that there is nothing on the title to prevent the development of the land on Tract A in accordance with proper zoning laws. . . .

. . . Hill refused the offers which contained this contingency. Hill told appellants that if the subject property could be used for a purpose other than a golf course, the property would be worth $2,000,000 rather than the $685,000 he was seeking for it. . . .

Prior to purchasing the golf course, appellants saw the recorded plats for Shalimar Estates and Shalimar West which showed Tract A, the golf course property, surrounded by residential lots, . . . the restrictions, which contained numerous references to the golf course, and the plat for Shalimar West, which contains an easement for a golf cart path. Appellants saw and drove on the golf course. . . .

Appellants were informed by City of Tempe officials that any development of the area would be "highly controversial" and would be vigorously opposed by the homeowners. Appellants made no inquiry of and had no discussion with City of Tempe officials as to any legal restrictions on the property other than zoning. Appellants intentionally made no inquiry of the developer, Mr. Guelich, or of any homeowners in the area.

The case was tried to the trial court without a jury and decided in favor of the homeowners. The trial court found that had appellants inquired of Mr. Guelich or the homeowners, they would have been informed that restrictions existed. . . . [A]ppellants paid $685,000, which the trial court found is approximately the value of a golf course like Shalimar. The trial court found that appellants were not bona fide purchasers without notice. The court concluded that appellants were bound to maintain Tract A as a golf course until the year 2025 A.D. . . .

The issue we must decide is whether restrictions upon the use of land may arise other than by deed or written instrument so as to bind a purchaser with notice. . . .

. . . [A]ppellants argue that restrictions upon the use of land are in derogation of the natural right which an owner possesses to use and enjoy his property and are not favored in the law. Consequently, they argue, restrictive covenants are construed strictly against their establishment . . . and liberally in support of the unrestricted use of the land. Although we readily recognize these principles, they are not in conflict with our decision in this case. There is more than sufficient evidence to support the conclusion of the trial court and to overcome the presumption set forth. . . .

. . . We recognize that equitable restrictions are generally considered interests in land which come within the provisions of the Statute of Frauds. Nevertheless, we find that both estoppel and part performance apply to the golf course restriction to take it out of the Statute of Frauds. Here Guelich and Associates orally represented to the homeowners that the golf course property retained by them was subject to restrictions which would ensure the existence of the golf course until the year 2025. "It would not be fair, under such circumstances, to permit the grantor (or the grantor's successors taking with notice) to raise the absence of a writing as a defense." . . . Furthermore, the conduct of the previous owners of the golf course property can only be consistent with the claimed oral representations made by Guelich, and therefore part performance applies to take this matter out of the Statute of Frauds.

Appellants contend that the trial court erred in admitting parol evidence to establish restrictions upon the use of the property . . . . It is, of course, well settled in Arizona that parol evidence cannot be used to vary the terms of a written contract. In view of this basic rule, appellants argue that the homeowners could not vary the terms of the recorded restrictions placed against the Shalimar property.

We hold that the parol evidence rule does not apply in this case. The imposition of an equitable restriction involved here is not dependent upon nor does it purport to vary an integrated written contract for the sale of an interest in real property. To the contrary, the restrictive covenant implied here is consistent with the terms of the deeds and other recorded restrictions. . . .

We return now to the decision of the trial court. It found that an implied covenant restricting the use of the property to a golf course arose from the sale of adjacent lots to the homeowners. The court found that it was enforceable against appellants as subsequent purchasers who took their ownership with notice of the restriction. We find there is ample evidence to uphold this determination. . . .

Appellants argue that their sole duty of inquiry was to check recorded documents and, because they did so and found no restrictions, they should not be bound by an implied restrictive covenant.

A subsequent purchaser of a servient tenement is bound to take notice of rights that may be evident upon an inspection of the premises as well as those of which he may learn by an inspection of the records. . . . [T]he trial court found that appellants did not satisfy their duty of inquiry. . . . There is ample evidence that appellants had actual knowledge of the facts upon which the golf course restriction was based. . . . Consequently, they will not be afforded the protection the law gives to an innocent purchaser. . . .

Appellants next argue that economic frustration renders the golf course restriction unenforceable. They point out that the trial court found that historically the golf course had not been profitable to its owners. They acknowledge that they have never attempted to operate the golf course themselves, but argue that they should not be required to do so and suffer a loss just to show that the golf course is not profitable. Appellants further argue that to require them to actively operate the golf course, even at a loss, amounts to "outright bondage" rather than just a negative restraint on the use of the land.

Although changed circumstances may occur that would justify granting relief from restrictive covenants, such changes must frustrate and defeat the original purpose of the restrictions in order to warrant voiding them. The trial court determined that the purpose of the golf course has not been defeated nor frustrated by any change affecting the golf course and the Shalimar subdivisions.

A mere change in economic conditions rendering it unprofitable to continue the restrictive use is not alone sufficient to justify abrogating the restrictive covenant. . . . In Williams v. Butler, 418 P.2d 856 (N.M. 1966) the Supreme Court of New Mexico held that lack of economic feasibility to develop a tract as a golf course, tennis courts, swimming pool and other athletic facilities was not a ground for relieving landowners of the covenants. The court noted that if the original purpose of the covenant can still be realized, it will be enforced even though unrestricted use of the property would be more profitable to its owner. . . . We conclude that the record supports the trial court's denial of the claim that changed circumstances warrant abrogating the golf course restriction.

Appellants next assert that they cannot constitutionally be required to maintain their property in a certain manner. They also raise many questions regarding the manner of enforcement of the restriction, such as when must the golf course be opened and how often must it be watered and mowed. Appellants cite no authority for the assertion that it would be unconstitutional to require them to maintain their property as a golf course. We recognize that some New York and English cases sustain the contention that affirmative covenants may not run with the land so as to be enforceable against successors in interest of the original covenantor. However, considerable authority in the United States is otherwise. . . . The majority of courts enforce both negative and affirmative covenants which run with the land.

We recognize that problems may arise regarding the operation of the golf course and, if they do, it may be necessary for the trial court to consider further orders relating thereto. The trial court believed that proper management on the part of appellants, together with cooperation from the homeowners, could make the operation of the golf course feasible. We find the judgment of the court to be a reasonable equitable remedy under the difficult circumstances of this case and will not assume that the possibility of future intervention by the court should render the present judgment unenforceable. . . .

Appellants next argue that the duration of the restriction should continue only for a reasonable length of time instead of the period fixed by the court. . . .

Contrary to appellants' contention, the court could find from the testimony that the developer represented to the homeowners that the golf course restriction would exist until the year 2000 and then would be renewed for an additional 25 years unless rejected by the majority of the homeowners. . . . The investigation made by appellants led to an examination of the restrictions recorded against the Shalimar subdivision property. . . . It is reasonable that the golf course use restriction was intended to remain in effect at least as long as the other related restrictions. Reasonable inquiry would have led to the homeowners themselves and their understanding of the restriction assuring the existence of the golf course. We conclude that appellants were placed on inquiry notice and, had they made a reasonable investigation, would have learned of the duration of the implied restriction. . . .

The judgment of the trial court is affirmed.

Notes and Questions

1. The usual consequence of failing to comply with the Statute of Frauds is that the interest created is revocable. On what basis did the court decide to enforce the oral covenants? Does the situation fit within Restatement § 2.9, which provides:

> The consequences of failure to comply with the Statute of Frauds . . . do not apply if the beneficiary of the servitude, in justifiable reliance on the existence of the servitude, has so changed position that injustice can be avoided only by giving effect to the parties' intent to create a servitude.

2. Why did the developer retain ownership of the golf course rather than transferring it to an association comprising all the owners in Shalimar Estates? What would you recommend to a developer who is interested in retaining the potential benefits of golf course ownership but wants to retain the flexibility to change uses if the golf course operation becomes unprofitable?

3. If it becomes economically infeasible to continue operating the golf course, what should be done with the golf course tract? *See Oceanside Community Ass'n v. Oceanside Land Co.*, 195 Cal. Rptr. 14 (Ct. App. 1983) (equitable lien against golf course property imposed in favor of homeowners for each month golf course was not maintained).

4. The covenants in Shalimar Estates, created in 1960, are set to terminate in the year 2025. Developers seldom use "drop-dead" provisions like that anymore. Instead, they provide that the covenants continue automatically unless a specified percentage of the owners decide to modify or terminate them. What will happen to Shalimar Estates in 2025? Restatement § 6.10 provides that owners holding a majority of the voting power in a common interest community[15] have an implied power to amend the covenants to extend their term.

---

15.   In a common interest community, the lot owners are subject to covenants requiring them to contribute to the support of common property or facilities or to pay dues to an owners association that provides services to the lot owners or enforces the covenants. Restatement (Third) § 1.8.

c.   Covenants Created by Implication

Although not restricted to situations involving real estate developers, most implied covenants are found to have been created when a developer sold property in a new development. Before zoning became widespread, and in the era when subdividers inserted covenants in individual deeds to create protected residential neighborhoods, the implied reciprocal servitude doctrine, which held that when a developer sells lots subject to restrictions designed to implement a general plan of development, all the property in the general plan is burdened and benefited by reciprocal servitudes,[16] was quite important. It protected lot buyers' expectations that all lots in the subdivision would be similarly restricted, preventing a developer from changing the nature of the development after some of the lots had been sold. Since the middle of the 20th century, however, the doctrine has become less important because most developers now record a declaration of servitudes for the entire subdivision, or phase of a project, before selling lots, rather than relying on covenants in the individual deeds to create the general plan. Zoning, too, has become widespread and usually protects residential neighborhoods from construction of gas stations or other commercial operations. Today the primary impact of the implied reciprocal servitudes doctrine is reflected in the practice of "phasing" projects so that developers do not get locked in by the doctrine. By specifying phases, they make it clear that their remaining land is not part of the "general plan" covered by the restrictions, which retains flexibility to adapt future phases to changed market conditions.

Implied servitudes remain important in other situations, however. When the maps, advertisements, and sales representations for a new development have led purchasers to believe the developer is obligated to complete and maintain roads, utilities, recreational facilities, and other amenities, or to convey common areas to a property owners' association, courts may find implied servitudes that bind the developer's successors to complete the development in accord with the representations. *Shalimar Association v. D.O.C. Enterprises, Ltd.* is an example of a case in which the court could have found an implied covenant by the developer to maintain the golf course even if it did not find that an express promise had been made.

Another situation in which implied covenants may be found arises when a developer creates a project with common property but fails to provide for ongoing management or maintenance of the property. If the lot owners should reasonably have expected that management and support of the common property would be necessary, a court may find implied covenants to allow an association of owners to manage the property and to pay assessments for maintenance of the property. *See* Restatement (Third) §§ 6.3 and 6.5.

d.   Covenants Created by Prescription and Eminent Domain

Prescription. In the United States, failing to develop your land, or using it in a particular way, for the prescriptive period does not give rise to prescriptive

---

16.   *See Sanborn v. McLean* in Chapter 9.

rights in the neighbors to maintain the status quo. Unlike the uses that give rise to prescriptive easements, uses that might give rise to prescriptive covenants do not involve a trespass or other wrong to the neighbors so there is no statute of limitations to run against the neighbor. Unlike the English courts, American courts rejected the idea that negative easements could be acquired by prescription. There is one situation, however, in which covenants can be created by prescription. If landowners believe that they are bound by covenants and perform the covenants for the prescriptive period, the covenants may become validated by prescription even if there was some defect in their creation. For example, if a statute requires that a declaration of covenants for a development be recorded to be effective, unrecorded covenants, or covenants recorded out of the chain of title, may become effective after the landowners have complied with the covenants for the requisite period.[17] Restatement (Third) § 2.16, Illustration 3, provides:

> The Developer of Green-Acres, a 200-lot subdivision, executed a declaration of servitudes that created a homeowners association, transferred a clubhouse and recreational facilities to the association, automatically made all lot owners members of the association, and imposed obligations on each lot owner to pay assessments to cover the expenses of the association, including maintenance of facilities owned by the homeowners association. Copies of the declaration were provided to all prospective purchasers, but it was not recorded until after 10 lots had been sold and their deeds recorded. The deeds did not refer to the declaration but stated that the property was conveyed subject to easements and restrictions of record. The remaining 190 lots were sold after the declaration was recorded. The homeowners association is levying assessments and receiving payments from owners of the 10 lots. It is enjoying the benefit of an intended but imperfectly created servitude . . . [which will become a servitude if continued without effective interruption for the prescriptive period].

Eminent domain. Although governmental bodies usually exercise eminent domain powers to acquire a fee simple or an easement in land, there is no theoretical barrier to acquiring the benefit of a covenant by eminent domain. If imposing desired restrictions on development cannot be accomplished by zoning or other regulation without violation of the Takings Clause, a governmental body could accomplish the same result by acquiring covenant benefits, which would cost less than acquiring a fee simple in the property.

4.   Validity of Servitudes

In this section we take up the interesting and sometimes difficult question whether there are certain kinds of rights or obligations that people should not be allowed to tie to land ownership or occupancy. Historically, courts have imposed numerous limits on servitudes. Modernly, the view has prevailed that

---

24.   *See* Paxson v. Glovitz, *supra*, for another application of the intended but imperfectly created servitude doctrine under which an agreed-to use is regarded as an adverse use for prescription purposes.

fewer but better limits are needed. The old view struck indiscriminately at benefits in gross, covenants created without horizontal privity, affirmative covenants, covenants to pay money other than rent, covenants against competition, and covenants that did not touch or concern the land, often without identifying the evil threatened by the servitude. At the same time, it failed to invalidate truly evil servitudes such as racial restrictions. The modern view aims directly at servitudes that pose a demonstrable risk of harm to the public good.

Restatement (Third) § 3.1, Validity of Servitudes: General Rule

A servitude created as provided in Chapter 2 is valid unless it is illegal or unconstitutional or violates public policy. Servitudes that are invalid because they violate public policy include, but are not limited to:

(1) a servitude that is arbitrary, spiteful, or capricious;

(2) a servitude that unreasonably burdens a fundamental constitutional right;

(3) a servitude that imposes an unreasonable restraint on alienation under § 3.4 or § 3.5;

(4) a servitude that imposes an unreasonable restraint on trade or competition under § 3.6; and

(5) a servitude that is unconscionable under § 3.7.

The Touch or Concern Doctrine and the Restatement (Third)

In addition to the normal legal constraints imposed on all private contractual arrangements, the traditional law of covenants invalidated servitudes that did not touch or concern the land. Probably designed to prevent reinstitution of feudal services[18] or clogging of titles, or both, the touch or concern doctrine primarily operated to prevent landowners from burdening their property with open-ended financial obligations. It did not, of course, prevent them from incurring mortgages and other liens that bound their property in the hands of successors, but most such liens are for a fixed amount. Covenants, by contrast, are often used to impose obligations that are indefinite in both value and duration. For example, railroads sometimes used to acquire easements in exchange for a covenant to provide free passage to the servient owner (and his heirs and assigns). Pipeline companies did the same thing, promising free natural gas hookups to the servient owner. Covenants have also been used to create obligations to pay perpetual rents and to pay commissions on future sales or leases, and today are routinely used to impose obligations to pay assessments to common interest community associations.

---

18.   A. Dan Tarlock, in *Touch and Concern Is Dead, Long Live the Doctrine*, 77 Neb. L. Rev. 804, 816 (1998), views *Spencer's Case*, the 1583 decision that first held that the burden of a lease covenant could run to an assignee of the tenant, but only if it touched or concerned the land, as "a perfect reflection of the transition from the medieval to the modern world that occurred in the 16th century."

In the 19th and early 20th centuries, the touch or concern doctrine was used to invalidate many of these open-ended affirmative covenants, in opinions that expressed little concern for the loss of expected benefits by the covenantee and the windfall to the covenantor.[19] Courts seldom offered any rationale for the results other than the conclusion that the burden of the covenant failed to touch or concern the land. The touch or concern doctrine was also used in a few states to invalidate covenants against competition on the ground that the benefit touched the covenantee's business rather than the covenantee's land. The touch or concern doctrine began to break down as builders increasingly used party wall covenants to provide for sharing the costs of common walls,[20] and then crumbled as developers created common interest communities — developments with commonly owned streets, parks, and other facilities that needed collective management and financial support — and shopping center owners responded to the demands of important tenants for covenants against competition.

In the Restatement (Third), the touch or concern doctrine has been completely displaced by the rule that a covenant is valid unless it can be shown to be illegal, unconstitutional, or against public policy. This change is intended to complete the process begun by the courts that, faced with a challenge to the validity of a servitude, had increasingly looked to the substance of the rights and obligations and their potential impact if tied to the land, rather than the question whether they touched or concerned. An important purpose in restating the rule in terms of public policy is to encourage courts to focus on the real risks that servitudes can pose to society's interest in the long-range utility of its land resources and to articulate the real reasons for their decisions on servitude validity questions.[21]

Whether the Restatement approach will prove better than the old touch or concern doctrine is the subject of spirited debate among academics. Current defenders of the touch or concern doctrine include Professors Dan Tarlock[22] and Jeffrey Stake.[23] For both of them, the vagueness of the touch or concern doctrine is a virtue, allowing courts more flexibility to achieve the desired ends of fairness (Tarlock) or efficiency (Stake). In Tarlock's view, the core function performed by touch or concern is to ensure fairness to residents in common

19. Tarlock argues that the touch or concern doctrine allowed "judicial screening of remote bargains that impose unreasonable fiscal burdens on landowners," *id.* at 815, suggesting that the doctrine allowed courts to avoid results that would have been unfair. This suggests that in fact courts made a substantive decision that the expectations of benefit were not legitimate and there was no windfall to the landowner freed from the covenant burden.

20. On party wall covenants, generally, see Ralph W. Aigler, *The Running with the Land of Agreements to Pay for a Portion of the Cost of Party Walls*, 10 Mich. L. Rev. 187 (1912); Clark, Real Covenants and Other Interests Which Run with the Land ch. 5, at 144 *et seq.* (2d ed. 1947); American Law of Property § 9.21 (Casner ed. 1952).

21. Restatement § 3.1 cmt. *a*:

The purpose of changing from the touch or concern doctrine to the rule stated in § 3.1 is to allow innovative land development practices using servitudes, but it is not intended to remove courts from their historic role of safeguarding the public interest in maintaining the social utility of land resources. By reformulating the inquiry to ask the question directly — whether the servitude in issue poses such a threat to the public welfare that the rights or obligations it creates should not be allowed to run with land — the law will encourage clearer identification of the issues and clearer explanations of the reasons why servitudes may not be used to implement particular arrangements than was ever possible using the touch or concern doctrine.

22. A. Dan Tarlock, *Touch and Concern Is Dead, Long Live the Doctrine*, 77 Neb. L. Rev. 804 (1998).

23. Jeffrey E. Stake, *Toward an Economic Understanding of Touch and Concern*, 1988 Duke L.J. 925.

interest communities by preserving a nexus between assessment burdens and benefits received, and by preventing diversion of assessment revenue to others. In his view, the Restatement standards will provide less protection because courts will be reluctant to invalidate covenants on the grounds of public policy and unconscionability. In Stake's view, the touch or concern doctrine allows courts to allocate the burden and benefit of a covenant to either the original party or a successor, depending on which outcome is more efficient. His concern is that a rule formulated in terms of efficiency would invite mishandling by judges and lawyers whose understanding of the economic concept of efficiency is often somewhat fuzzy.

Another view is that neither the touch or concern doctrine nor the Restatement approach is adequate to protect property owners from homeowner and condominium association covenants that destroy value by imposing excessive restrictions or requiring payments for facilities not owned by the association that are excessive or provide facilities homeowners do not value. Marcy Allen, Note and Comment, *A Touchy Subject: Has the Restatement Replaced the Touch and Concern Doctrine with an Equally Troublesome Test?*, 65 Baylor L. Rev. 1034 (2013), replacing the touch and concern doctrine with an expanded changed conditions doctrine.

a.   Open-Ended Covenants to Pay Money

NEPONSIT PROPERTY OWNERS' ASS'N, INC. v. EMIGRANT INDUSTRIAL SAVINGS BANK

Court of Appeals of New York
15 N.E.2d 793 (N.Y. 1938)

LEHMAN, J. The plaintiff, as assignee of Neponsit Realty Company, has brought this action to foreclose a lien upon land which the defendant owns. The lien, it is alleged, arises from a covenant, condition or charge contained in a deed . . . from Neponsit Realty Company to a predecessor in title of the defendant. The defendant purchased the land at a judicial sale. The referee's deed to the defendant and every deed in the defendant's chain of title . . . purports to convey the property subject to the covenant, condition or charge . . .

[I]n January, 1911, Neponsit Realty Company, as owner of a tract of land . . . filed in the office of the clerk of the county a map of the land. The tract was developed for a strictly residential community, and Neponsit Realty Company conveyed lots in the tract to purchasers, describing such lots by reference to the filed map and to roads and streets shown thereon. In 1917, Neponsit Realty Company conveyed the land now owned by the defendant to . . . Deyer and his wife by deed which contained the covenant upon which the plaintiff's cause of action is based:

> And the party of the second part for the party of the second part and the heirs, successors and assigns of the party of the second part further covenants that the property conveyed by this deed shall be subject to an annual charge in such an amount as will be fixed by the party of the first part, its successors and assigns, not,

however exceeding in any year the sum of four ($4.00) Dollars per lot 20 x 100 feet. The assigns of the party of the first part may include a Property Owners' Association which may hereafter be organized for the purposes referred to in this paragraph, and in case such association is organized the sums in this paragraph provided for shall be payable to such association.

The party of the second part for the party of the second part and the heirs, successors and assigns of the party of the second part covenants that they will pay this charge to the party of the first part, its successors and assigns on the first day of May in each and every year, and further covenants that said charge shall on said date in each year become a lien on the land and shall continue to be such lien until fully paid.

Such charge shall be payable to the party of the first part or its successors or assigns, and shall be devoted to the maintenance of the roads, paths, parks, beach, sewers and such other public purposes as shall from time to time be determined by the party of the first part, its successors or assigns. And the party of the second part by the acceptance of this deed hereby expressly vests in the party of the first part, its successors and assigns, the right and power to bring all actions against the owner of the premises hereby conveyed or any part thereof for the collection of such charge and to enforce the aforesaid lien therefor.

These covenants shall run with the land and shall be construed as real covenants running with the land until January 31st, 1940, when they shall cease and determine.

. . . Regardless of the intention of the parties, a covenant will run with the land and will be enforceable against a subsequent purchaser of the land . . . only if the covenant complies with certain legal requirements. These requirements rest upon ancient rules and precedents. The age-old essentials of a real covenant, aside from the form of the covenant, may be summarily formulated as follows: (1) It must appear that grantor and grantee intended that the covenant should run with the land; (2) it must appear that the covenant is one "touching" or "concerning" the land with which it runs; (3) it must appear that there is "privity of estate" between the promisee or party claiming the benefit of the covenant and the right to enforce it, and the promisor or party who rests under the burden of the covenant. *Clark on Covenants and Interests Running with Land*, p. 74. Although the deeds of Neponsit Realty Company conveying lots in the tract it developed "contained a provision to the effect that the covenants ran with the land, such provision in the absence of the other legal requirements is insufficient to accomplish such a purpose." . . .

The covenant in this case . . . is an affirmative covenant to pay money for use in connection with, but not upon, the land . . . . Does such a covenant "touch" or "concern" the land? These terms are not part of a statutory definition . . . . Rather they are words used by courts in England in old cases to describe a limitation which the courts themselves created or to formulate a test which the courts have devised and which the courts voluntarily apply. In truth such a description or test so formulated is too vague to be of much assistance and judges and academic scholars alike have struggled, not with entire success, to formulate a test at once more satisfactory and more accurate. "It has been found impossible to state any absolute tests to determine what covenants touch and concern land and what do not. The question is one for the court to determine in the exercise of its best judgment upon the facts of each case." . . .

Pays doesn't concern or touch land.

court had to work way around rule.

It has been often said that a covenant to pay a sum of money is a personal affirmative covenant which usually does not concern or touch the land. Such statements are based upon English decisions which hold in effect that only covenants, which compel the covenanter to submit to some restriction on the use of his property, touch or concern the land, and that the burden of a covenant which requires the covenanter to do an affirmative act, even on his own land, for the benefit of the owner of a "dominant" estate, does not run with his land. . . . [I]n many jurisdictions of this country the narrow English rule has been criticized and a more liberal and flexible rule has been substituted. In this State the courts have not gone so far.[24] We have not abandoned the historic distinction drawn by the English courts. So this court has recently said: "Subject to a few exceptions not important at this time, there is now in this state a settled rule of law that a covenant to do an affirmative act, as distinguished from a covenant merely negative in effect, does not run with the land so as to charge the burden of performance on a subsequent grantee . . . ." . . .

affirmative covenant does not run w/ land.

. . . [There are] some exceptions or limitations in the application of the general rule. . . . It may be difficult to classify these exceptions or to formulate a test of whether a particular covenant to pay money or to perform some other act falls within the general rule. . . . At least it must "touch" or "concern" the land in a substantial degree, and though it may be inexpedient and perhaps impossible to formulate a rigid test or definition which will be entirely satisfactory or which can be applied mechanically in all cases, we should at least be able to state the problem and find a reasonable method of approach to it. It has been suggested that a covenant which runs with the land must affect the legal relations—the advantages and the burdens—of the parties to the covenant, as owners of particular parcels of land and not merely as members of the community in general, such as taxpayers or owners of other land. (Clark, *op. cit.* p. 76. *Cf.* Professor Bigelow's article on *The Contents of Covenants in Leases*, 12 Mich. L. Rev. 639; 30 Law Quarterly Review, 319.) That method of approach has the merit of realism. The test is based on the effect of the covenant rather than on technical distinctions. Does the covenant impose, on the one hand, a burden upon an interest in land, which on the other hand increases the value of a different interest in the same or related land?

if covenant runs w/ land effects property owners

concern interest in land.

Even though we accept that approach and test, it still remains true that whether a particular covenant is sufficiently connected with the use of land to run with the land, must be in many cases a question of degree. A promise to pay for something to be done in connection with the promisor's land does not differ essentially from a promise by the promisor to do the thing himself, and both promises constitute, in a substantial sense, a restriction upon the owner's right to use the land, and a burden upon the legal interest of the owner. On the other hand, a covenant to perform or pay for the performance of an affirmative act disconnected with the use of the land cannot ordinarily touch or concern the land in any substantial degree. Thus, unless we exalt technical form over substance, the distinction between covenants which run with land and covenants which are personal, must depend upon the effect of the covenant on the legal

Question of degree if runs w/ land.

pay concerns the land?

24. New York's rule against affirmative covenants reaches the same result as that produced in England by the combination of the horizontal privity requirement requiring a landlord-tenant relationship for creation of a running covenant enforceable at law and the rule that affirmative covenants could not be enforced in equity.—EDS.

rights which otherwise would flow from ownership of land and which are connected with the land. The problem then is: Does the covenant in purpose and effect *substantially* alter these rights? . . .

. . . [S]tressing the intent and substantial effect of the covenant rather than its form, it seems clear that the covenant may properly be said to touch and concern the land of the defendant and its burden should run with the land. True, it calls for payment of a sum of money to be expended for "public purposes" upon land other than the land conveyed by Neponsit Realty Company to plaintiff's predecessor in title. By that conveyance the grantee, however, obtained not only title to particular lots, but an easement or right of common enjoyment with other property owners in roads, beaches, public parks or spaces and improvements in the same tract. For full enjoyment in common by the defendant and other property owners of these easements or rights, the roads and public places must be maintained. In order that the burden of maintaining public improvements should rest upon the land benefited by the improvements, the grantor exacted from the grantee of the land with its appurtenant easement or right of enjoyment a covenant that the burden of paying the cost should be inseparably attached to the land which enjoys the benefit. It is plain that any distinction or definition which would exclude such a covenant from the classification of covenants which "touch" or "concern" the land would be based on form and not on substance.

Another difficulty remains. Though between the grantor and the grantee there was privity of estate, the covenant provides that its benefit shall run to the assigns of the grantor who "may include a Property Owners' Association which may hereafter be organized for the purposes referred to in this paragraph." The plaintiff has been organized to receive the sums payable by the property owners and to expend them for the benefit of such owners. Various definitions have been formulated of "privity of estate" in connection with covenants that run with the land, but none of such definitions seems to cover the relationship between the plaintiff and the defendant in this case. The plaintiff has not succeeded to the ownership of any property of the grantor. It does not appear that it ever had title to the streets or public places upon which charges which are payable to it must be expended. It does not appear that it owns any other property in the residential tract to which any easement or right of enjoyment in such property is appurtenant. It is created solely to act as the assignee of the benefit of the covenant, and it has no interest of its own in the enforcement of the covenant.

The arguments that under such circumstances the plaintiff has no right of action to enforce a covenant running with the land are all based upon a distinction between the corporate property owners association and the property owners for whose benefit the association has been formed. If that distinction may be ignored, then the basis of the arguments is destroyed. . . .

The corporate plaintiff has been formed as a convenient instrument by which the property owners may advance their common interests. . . . Only blind adherence to an ancient formula devised to meet entirely different conditions could constrain the court to hold that a corporation formed as a medium for the enjoyment of common rights of property owners owns no property which would benefit by enforcement of common rights and has no cause of action in equity to enforce the covenant upon which such common rights depend. . . . In substance if not in form the covenant is a restrictive covenant which touches and concerns the defendant's land, and in substance, if not in form, there is privity of estate between the plaintiff and the defendant. . . .

The order [denying defendant's motion for judgment on the pleadings] should be affirmed, with costs, and the certified questions answered in the affirmative.

Notes and Questions

1. *Neponsit* is the leading case on the validity of assessment covenants in common interest communities. Did the court make the right decision in carving out an exception from the rule that covenants to pay money (other than rent) could not be made to run with the land? What kinds of risks do these covenants pose to homeowners or to the public good?

2. In trying to decide which covenants should be allowed to run with land (or in the Restatement view, which ones *should not* be allowed to run with land), how helpful is the Clark/Bigelow test approved by the court? Can it be said that a covenant affects the legal relations of the parties as owners of the particular parcels without deciding whether it runs or not? How can you tell whether a covenant imposes a burden on land that increases the value of a different interest in the same or related land without knowing whether the covenant runs or not? What concerns should be taken into account in deciding whether a covenant may be made to run?

3. Do you see any risks either to the Neponsit owners or the public generally in the provisions that assessments are capped at $4 per year and the covenants expire in 1940? How should these problems (if they are problems) be handled?

4. What would have happened if courts in the United States had not validated assessment covenants? In England, where affirmative covenants can only be created in leases, modern real estate developments either were structured as very long-term leases, or each deed contained a covenant obligating the grantee to include the covenants in the next conveyance. Charles Harpum, Stuart Bridge & Martin Dixon, *Megarry & Wade, The Law of Real Property* 1384-88 (8th ed. 2012). Do you see how these devices work?

5. The defendant here was the purchaser at a foreclosure sale. Why doesn't the foreclosure extinguish the servitudes? If the mortgage lien had priority over the servitudes, it would; but the declaration of servitudes was no doubt recorded before the mortgage was granted.[25]

6. The court in *Neponsit* wrestles with the question whether the property owners association can be made the beneficiary of the covenant to pay assessments. Why was this a problem? The court discusses the question in terms of "privity," but the problem seems much closer to the question whether benefits can be granted to strangers to the deed. How should the issue be resolved today?

---

25. *See* Restatement § 5.2, Persons to Whom an Appurtenant Benefit or Burden Runs, comment *i*, Acquisition of title by virtue of lien foreclosure proceedings, and § 7.9, Termination by Foreclosure Sale.

7. Do assessments paid to community associations have to provide direct benefits to lot owners? *Workman v. Brighton Properties, Inc.*, 976 P.2d 1209 (Utah 1999), upheld assessments authorized by the CC&R's that created a single association for two subdivisions located about one mile apart, even though some expenditures benefited only the lots in one subdivision or the other. The court noted that the objecting lot owner was fully aware of the obligation to pay assessments at the time of purchase, that requiring lot owners to pay only for services from which they directly benefit would result in complicated bookkeeping and numerous disputes, that it might lead to gerrymandering projects to meet some artificial benefit requirement, and that there was no evidence to indicate that the officers of the association had abused their authority or systematically used the assessment power to disproportionately benefit one group of lot owners over another.

Professor Tarlock suggests that one advantage of the touch or concern doctrine is that it allows courts to avoid abuse of the assessment power. *Touch and Concern Is Dead, Long Live the Doctrine*, 77 Neb. L. Rev. 804, 831 (1998). Restatement § 6.13 provides that an association has the duty to treat its members fairly and exercise its discretionary powers (including its assessment powers) reasonably. If the Brighton officers had systematically preferred one subdivision to the other, what would be the relative advantages and disadvantages of these two approaches to lawyers representing the disadvantaged lots owners or the association? Which would be more useful to the judge required to decide the case?

8. Should a developer be allowed to retain ownership of streets, recreation facilities, or utilities in a subdivision? To provide utility or other services to the development and require lot owners to pay whether or not they use them? To require homeowners to pay for things located outside the development? In *Eagle Enterprises, Inc. v. Gross*, 349 N.E.2d 816 (N.Y. 1976), the Court of Appeals held that a covenant to take and pay for water to be supplied from May to October for an annual fee of $35 did not touch and concern the covenantor's land and thus was not enforceable against a successor who had converted his summer property into a year-round residence and dug his own well. The covenant was imposed by the developer, which had created a water company to supply water to the subdivision. The court concluded that the covenant did not substantially affect the ownership interests of landowners in the subdivision, stating that there was no evidence that other owners would be deprived of water or that the price would become prohibitive.

Most courts that have faced the question, however, have upheld the covenants, at least where the arrangement did not seem grossly unfair. In *Streams Sports Club, Ltd. v. Richmond*, 457 N.E.2d 1226, 39 A.L.R. 4th 119 (1983), the court held that the obligation of condominium covenants to pay dues to a for-profit sports club retained by the developer and later sold to the plaintiff ran with the land. The court reasoned that the right to use the facilities touched and concerned the land because it provided a benefit to unit owners even though they personally had no interest in using the club, and the arrangement was not so one-sided or unfair as to render it unconscionable. *Bennett v. Behring Corp.*, 466 F. Supp. 689 (S.D. Fla. 1979), upheld covenants requiring grantees to pay for use of recreational facilities owned by the developer and leased to the community association against a charge that they were unconscionable. The purchasers had notice of the payment requirements, and the price charged was comparable to prices for similar facilities.

9. In *Cloud v. Association of Owners, Satellite Apartment Building, Inc.*, 857 P.2d 435 (Colo. Ct. App. 1992), a covenant reserving 80 guest rooms located on apartment floors for use as hotel rooms and providing for payment of 10 percent of gross receipts to the developer and 90 percent to the association for the common expense fund was held not unconscionable even though the arrangement did not terminate when the developer stopped providing management services and the arrangement was made while the developer still had total control of the association. The arrangement was unambiguously set forth in the recorded declaration, and, in the court's view, it also benefited the unit owners. How long should an arrangement like this be allowed to continue? On what grounds would a court be justified in terminating it?

10. Providers of public utilities often have been granted monopoly status by state statute or local ordinance but are then subject to regulation by a public utilities commission that has the power to set rates. Should the rates of private utility suppliers who create monopoly positions for themselves using servitudes be subject to judicial review for fairness? Should it make any difference whether the supplier is the community association or an outsider?

What standard should govern the validity of arrangements by which the developer or someone else arranges to receive future or continuing payments from landowners? Restatement (Third) largely abandons the attempt to control open-ended financial obligations through validity constraints, providing only that irrational and unconscionable arrangements are invalid *ab initio*. It places primary reliance, instead, on controlling the long-term effects of such arrangements through the modification and termination provisions of Restatement § 7.12.

Restatement (Third) § 7.12, Modification and Termination of Certain Affirmative Covenants

(1) A covenant to pay money or provide services terminates after a reasonable time if the instrument that created the covenant does not specify the total sum due or a definite termination point. This subsection does not apply to an obligation to pay for services or facilities concurrently provided to the burdened estate.

(2) A covenant to pay money or provide services in exchange for services or facilities provided to the burdened estate may be modified or terminated if the obligation becomes excessive in relation to the cost of providing the services or facilities or to the value received by the burdened estate; provided, however, that modification based on a decrease in value to the burdened estate should take account of any investment made by the covenantee in reasonable reliance on continued validity of the covenant obligation. This subsection does not apply if the servient owner is obliged to pay only for services or facilities actually used and the servient owner may practicably obtain the services or facilities from other sources.

(3) The rules stated in (1) and (2) above do not apply to obligations to a common interest community or to obligations imposed pursuant to a conservation servitude.

Do you see the reason for treating obligations to common interest communities differently from obligations to others?

b. Covenants Not to Sue

1515-1519 LAKE VIEW BOULEVARD CONDOMINIUM ASS'N v. APARTMENT SALES CORP.

Supreme Court of Washington (en banc)
43 P.3d 1233 (2002)

CHAMBERS, J. The 1515-1519 Lakeview Boulevard Condominium Association (homeowners) are the owners of three condominiums that were rendered uninhabitable when the soil underlying the property gave way precipitously during winter storms. The homeowners brought suit against . . . the City of Seattle (city). The homeowners argued the city should not have permitted the condominiums to be built due to the latent risk of soil movement. . . . Before allowing the condominiums to be constructed, the city, concerned about the possibility of landslides, had imposed several conditions on the developer. These conditions included a covenant exculpating the city from liability for damages caused by soil movement. In this case, we are asked to determine whether an exculpatory covenant recorded in a deed runs with the land. . . . [The homeowners did not dispute that the covenant was properly recorded or that they had notice. — EDS.]

1. *Sovereign Immunity*

We must first decide whether the abolition of sovereign immunity, RCW 4.96.010, is violated when a local government requires, as a condition of granting a building permit, an exculpatory covenant tailored to alleviate specific concerns unique to a particular project. We hold that exculpatory covenants do not categorically violate sovereign immunity. However, blanket grants of immunity secured routinely for performance of public functions do not differ meaningfully from ordinances immunizing local governments for their own negligence, and will be invalidated. . . .

The city contends innovative land use instruments, such as exculpatory covenants, should be encouraged because the Growth Management Act, chapter 36.70A RCW, is channeling development onto more and more marginal lots. The city is also concerned that if it denies building permits, it runs the risk of committing regulatory takings or inverse condemnation . . . . The city argues that requiring the release and requiring the developers to have insurance and inform subsequent purchasers of the danger is a fair way to allow development. This argument suggests that property owners of land marginal for development because of the composition, topography, location, or other characteristic of the property should be free to propose creative solutions, and accept the risks of development.

We hold that a local government and a property owner may reach an arm's-length, bargained-for agreement which may include waivers of liability for risks created by the proposed use of property because of the shape, composition, location or other characteristic unique to the property sought to be developed.

Here we find that the exculpatory language of the covenant was tailored to the specific risks presented by the proposed development of the property and appropriately limited in scope to the danger of soil movement. Therefore it does not violate this State's abolition of sovereign immunity by functionally enacting blanket immunity.

2. Enforceability of the Covenant Against Successive Owners

The homeowners argue that this covenant may not be enforced against them on the theory exculpatory waivers do not "run with the land" and therefore cannot bind successors in interest. . . .

Generally, there are five elements required for a covenant to run:

(1) a promise which is enforceable between the original parties; (2) which touches and concerns; (3) which the parties intended to bind successors; and (4) which is sought to be enforced by an original party or a successor, against an original party or a successor in possession; (5) who has notice of the covenant or has not given value.

Four of these elements are not seriously disputed by the parties before this Court. The issue before us is whether an exculpatory covenant touches and concerns the land.[4] Professor Stoebuck noted:

If there ever was a rule that a running covenant had to touch and concern land in a physical sense, it has long since been abandoned in America. The most that can be said concerning American doctrine is that the meaning of touch and concern tends to become less clear as physical contact becomes less direct.[26]

This Court has not adopted a strict test for "touch and concern," instead we have established an analytical approach:

Generally speaking, a covenant touches or concerns the land if it is such as to benefit the grantor or the lessor, or the grantee or lessee, as the case may be. As the term implies, the covenant must concern the occupation or enjoyment of the land granted or demised and the liability to perform it, and the right to take advantage of it must pass to the assignee. Conversely, if the covenant does not touch or concern the occupation or enjoyment of the land, it is the collateral and personal obligation of the grantor or lessor and does not run with the land.

. . . It is an open question whether a covenant warning of risk and exculpating liability for that risk touches and concerns the land. The only court to reach whether such covenant would run held, without analysis of touch and concern,

---

4. The recently published *Restatement (Third) of Property* has abolished "touch and concern" as an element of enforceable covenants. In its stead, the Restatement provides that a servitude is valid unless it is illegal, unconstitutional, or violates public policy. *Restatement (Third) of Property: Servitudes* § 3.1 (2000). Whether this Court should adopt the Restatement was not raised until the motion for reconsideration to the Court of Appeals opinion, and will not be considered for the first time on review of this Court.

26. William B. Stoebuck, *Running Covenants: An Analytical Primer*, 52 Wash. L. Rev. 861 (1977) — EDS.

that it did run. *Phillips v. Altman*, 412 P.2d 199 (Ok. 1966) (covenant not to sue for damages arising from oil and gas pollution ran with the land and was not void as against public policy).

The city relies upon *Hollis* [v. Garwell, 974 P.2d 836 (Wash. 1999),] to support an argument that this Court has abandoned the requirement of "touch and concern." *Hollis* does not extend so far. *Hollis* was limited to mutual covenants in a subdivision. . . . This Court has not relaxed the touch and concern requirement for the enforceability of covenants in settings other than subdivisions and we decline to do so now.

We conclude that this covenant satisfies the touch and concern doctrine as used in this State. Read as a whole, the covenant burdens the use of land, since the covenant is limited to the reasonable enjoyment of the land and limits rights normally associated with ownership. Further, few things touch and concern land more than the soil itself. This is sufficient to meet the requirements. The city is exculpated for losses that are not caused by the city's own negligence arising from soil movement, as reasonably contemplated by the parties to the covenant. Therefore, we hold that this covenant runs with the land. . . .

Notes and Questions

1. The court refused to consider whether it should adopt the Restatement Third's approach to determining the validity of a covenant because the question was not raised early enough in the proceedings (footnote 4). If it had used § 3.1 instead of the touch or concern doctrine, how would you expect the court to have analyzed the issue whether the homeowners were bound by the covenant not to sue?

2. How persuasive is the court's touch or concern analysis? Would you predict that other courts would reach the same conclusion about covenants not to sue? In *El Paso Refinery, L.P. v. TRMI Holdings, Inc.*, 302 F.3d 343 (5th Cir. 2002), the court held that a covenant not to sue a prior owner for environmental cleanup costs did not touch or concern the land because:

> Any burden or benefit created by the . . . Deed affects only TRMI [the prior owner] personally and has no direct impact upon the land itself. The Refinery's owner may, in accordance with the deed's provisions, take remedial action or not take remedial action, pollute or not pollute, as long as contribution is not sought from TRMI. The covenant does not compel nor preclude the promisor or any subsequent owner from doing anything on the land itself. The covenant is not predicated upon an agreement to refrain from taking any action on the land, as in the case of a negative covenant. . . . Nor does it permit TRMI, the promisee to enter or utilize the land for any purpose. . . . Rather, it is a continuing and non-contingent contractual agreement under which the Debtor [El Paso] agrees to refrain from seeking environmental remediation or damages from TRMI. A personal contractual arrangement does not qualify as a covenant. . . .

Can you distinguish these two cases? Are the issues the same? If the Washington court faces the question whether a covenant shifting the costs of environmental cleanup from the grantor to subsequent owners runs to successors, what result would you expect it to reach?

3. For a comparison of the utility of the touch or concern doctrine and Restatement (Third) § 3.1 using these two cases and three others (including *Davidson Bros. v. Katz, infra*), see Susan F. French, *Can Covenants Not to Sue, Covenants Against Competition and Spite Covenants Run with Land? Comparing Results Under the Touch or Concern Doctrine and the Restatement Third, Property (Servitudes),* 38 Real Prop. Prob. & Tr. J. 267 (2003).

4. Problems caused by the touch and concern doctrine and doubts about the validity and transferability of benefits in gross have led the National Council of Commissioners on Uniform States Laws to promulgate a Uniform Environmental Covenants Act. Similar problems previously led to creation of the Uniform Conservation Easement Act, which has been enacted in many states.

c.   Direct and Indirect Restraints on Alienation

Covenants requiring the owner of a fee simple estate to obtain the consent of another before transferring the fee simple are generally invalid restraints on alienation unless justified to protect legitimate interests of the person whose consent is required. Restraints imposed as part of an affordable housing program, for example, are justified, but restraints designed to allow a developer to screen successive purchasers generally are not. *See Kenney v. Morgan*, 325 A.2d 419 (Md. Ct. Spec. App. 1974) (covenant requiring developer's consent to transfer any lot unless a majority of owners of lots adjoining or facing the lot within a distance of five lots had consented in writing held an invalid restraint on alienation). The financial interdependence of owners of cooperative housing is often considered strong enough to justify consent requirements, but that of condominium and other common interest community owners usually is not.

Options and rights of first refusal both have legitimates uses but, if not appropriately limited, can severely interfere with alienability of land. Outstanding options to purchase for a fixed price, rather than market value, have a particularly detrimental effect on both marketability and investment in the property. To avoid invalidity, a fixed-price option must be limited in duration, and ordinarily, to a period considerably shorter than that which the Rule Against Perpetuities would allow.[27] Rights of first refusal to purchase at the same price as a bona fide offer from a third party are less problematic but, to avoid being unreasonable, must provide a relatively short time for the decision to exercise the right and consummate the purchase. *See* Restatement § 3.4, Direct Restraints on Alienation, which provides, "A servitude that imposes a direct restraint on alienation of the burdened estate is invalid if the restraint is unreasonable. Reasonableness is determined by weighing the utility of the restraint against the injurious consequences of enforcing the restraint."

---

27.   *See, e.g.,* Proctor v. Foxmeyer Drug Co., 884 S.W.2d 853 (Tex. App. 1994) (1985 agreement granting option to purchase warehouse at its book value within 30 days after use as warehouse terminated held void in 1992 when book value was $80,000 and market value was $550,000).

Problem

You represent a client who has entered a contract to purchase part of the former Delta Plantation in South Carolina. The title report reveals the following covenant contained in a prior recorded deed to the property:

> The property shall never be leased, sold, bequeathed, devised or otherwise transferred, permanently or temporarily, to any person or entity that may be described as being part of the Yankee race. "Yankee" . . . shall mean any person or entity born or formed north of the Mason-Dixon line, or any person or entity who has lived or been located for a continuous period of one (1) year above said line.

Your client, who was born in Boston, Massachusetts, wants to know if the covenant is enforceable. *See* Alfred L. Brophy & Shubha Ghosh, *Whistling Dixie: The Invalidity and Unconstitutionality of Covenants Against Yankees*, 10 Vill. Envtl. L.J. 57 (1999).

Many covenants may indirectly restrain alienation by limiting the use that can be made of the property, reducing the amount realizable by the owner on sale or transfer, or by otherwise reducing the value of the property. Such restraints are generally not invalid unless they are irrational or the covenant is invalid for some other reason. Restatement (Third) § 3.5. Comment *c* discusses covenants requiring payment of club dues, transfer fees, and "quarter sales" (an arrangement where the buyer of property is required on resale to pay some percentage of the sales price or a fixed sum to the seller or some other party). Although such covenants may be invalid if unconscionable, or modified or terminated under the conditions stated in § 7.12, *supra*, they are not invalid as restraints on alienation.

Caulette v. Stanley Stillwell & Sons, Inc., 170 A.2d 52 (N.J. Super. Ct. App. Div. 1961), held that a covenant reserving to the grantor "the right to build or construct the original dwelling or building" on the one-acre plot conveyed was void and ordered it stricken from the deed. Even if the clause were construed to give the grantor a primary option to build whenever the grantees should decide to construct a building on the premises, the court held that the covenant would be unenforceable because the benefit did not touch or concern. According to the court, it would make no difference if the grantor had sold the land at a relatively low price, expecting to make his profit on construction of the house:

> While there is nothing in the law precluding such an arrangement, as a contract *inter partes*, this form of contract, contemplating a single personal service upon the property, does not affect the title. And the stipulation . . . that this was a covenant running with the land cannot override the inherently personal nature of their arrangement under established legal principles.

Why did the contractor try to make this arrangement—which the court characterizes as for "a single personal service"—run with the land? What other alternatives are available to a developer who wants to make part of her profit through construction of the houses? Should this type of covenant be allowed to run to a successor? If not, how could a court justify the result if it did not use the touch and concern doctrine?

Problems: Validity

1. Your developer client is putting together a project for a large residential development in which land will be set aside for a public elementary school. The development will also include a community clubhouse, swimming pool, ball field, and tennis courts that will be owned and managed by a community association comprising all the lot owners in the project. The developer wants to provide a source of supplemental funds for the school to ensure that it will be attractive to her target market of upscale young professionals. She proposes using a transfer fee of 1 percent of the gross sale price payable on all future sales of property in the development. What advice do you give her?

2. To defuse anticipated objection to a proposed residential housing project on land that includes some environmentally sensitive areas, your developer client proposes to convey the most sensitive acreage to a nonprofit conservation organization that will be created to manage the property and to carry out environmental educational programs. The developer needs to provide an assured source of funding for the nonprofit. What would you recommend?

3. Another developer client recently heard about a statute that gives artists 5 percent of the price on every resale of a work of fine art for more than $1,000 until 20 years after the death of the artist.[28] Reasoning that his creative work also results in substantial gains to the purchasers of his homes over time, he asks that you draft a covenant that he can include in the deeds for all his projects. Instead of 5 percent, he suggests use of .05 percent "to avoid looking greedy." What is your response to this request?

d. Covenants Against Competition

DAVIDSON BROS., INC. v. D. KATZ & SONS, INC.

Superior Court of New Jersey, Appellate Division
643 A.2d 642 (N.J. Super. Ct. App. Div. 1994)

D'ANNUNZIO, J. Plaintiff Davidson Bros., Inc. (Davidson) appeals from a trial court judgment entered . . . on remand from the Supreme Court. Applying the reasonableness test formulated by the Supreme Court, the trial court determined that a covenant prohibiting the use as a supermarket of a property in downtown New Brunswick, New Jersey, was unenforceable. We now affirm.

Davidson operated a number of supermarkets in New Jersey. In 1952, it opened a supermarket of 10,000 square feet on George Street in downtown New Brunswick. In June 1978, Davidson took over an existing supermarket located at Elizabeth Street, also in New Brunswick but approximately two miles from the George Street store (hereinafter George Street). . . . Davidson closed George

---

28. Cal. Civ. Code § 986: "Whenever a work of fine art is sold and the seller resides in California or the sale takes place in California, the seller or the seller's agent shall pay to the artist . . . five percent of the amount of such sale." If the artist cannot be located, the five percent is to be paid to the Arts Council.

Street in February 1979 because its volume had decreased after Davidson acquired Elizabeth Street. It sold George Street in September 1980 to defendant D. Katz & Sons, Inc. (Katz), a rug merchant. The deed to Katz contained the covenant in issue:

> The lands and premises described herein . . . are conveyed subject to the restriction that said lands and premises shall not be used as and for a supermarket or grocery store of a supermarket type, however designated, for a period of forty (40) years from the date of this deed. This restriction shall be a covenant attached to and running with the lands.

The closing of George Street as a supermarket created a hardship for downtown residents, most of whom did not own or have ready access to motor vehicles. In response to their plight, the city government sought to attract another supermarket operator to the downtown area. The city's efforts culminated in the acquisition of George Street from Katz by the defendant New Brunswick Housing Authority, and the leasing of the property, for one dollar a year, to defendant C-Town, on condition that C-Town invest at least $10,000 for improvements and operate George Street as a supermarket.

Davidson commenced this action to enforce the covenant. Davidson appealed from an adverse summary judgment and we affirmed in an unreported opinion, utilizing traditional "touch and concern" analysis applicable to covenants alleged to run with the land.[29] Our Supreme Court granted Davidson's petition for certification and reversed and remanded for a trial. In doing so, the Court determined that "rigid adherence" to the "touch and concern" requirement was no longer warranted. It held that enforceability of a covenant would depend on its reasonableness, and that the principle of "touch and concern" is "but one of the factors." . . .

On remand, Davidson no longer sought injunctive relief . . . [a change in position] caused by Davidson's sale of its Elizabeth Street store to another supermarket operator in 1989 . . . . Davidson limited its claim to damages consisting of lost sales and profits during the two year period it competed with C-Town, and the reduced value of its Elizabeth Street store due to C-Town's competition.

Davidson's accountant testified that sales at Elizabeth Street for 1988 and 1989 were $1,452,000 less than they would have been had the George Street store not reopened. He calculated the lost profit on those sales to be $350,000. He also opined that due to the lower sales volume, Davidson sold the Elizabeth Street for $567,000 less than it should have sold for.

Defendants' accountant disagreed. He testified that although Elizabeth Street may have lost sales due to C-Town's operation of George Street, those lost sales would not have been profitable. Defendants' accountant also testified that the Elizabeth Street store did not lose value as a result of C-Town's competition.

After a lengthy trial, the trial court . . . found that the 40 year term was unreasonably long . . . ; that the covenant imposed an unreasonable restraint of trade . . . ; and that it was contrary to the public interest. . . . [T]he court ruled that the

---

29. New Jersey, like Massachusetts, had refused to enforce a covenant not to compete on the ground that the covenant benefited the business of the covenantee, and thus did not touch or concern the land. New Jersey finally overruled its old decisions in Davidson Bros., Inc. v. D. Katz & Sons, Inc., 579 A.2d 288 (N.J. 1990).—Eds.

covenant adversely impacted the public interest because "there is a substantial public need for the supermarket under the circumstances of this case."

The trial court deemed the damages issue to be moot because of its determination that the covenant was unreasonable and unenforceable. However, the court announced that it was unable to determine from the evidence that Davidson had sustained damages due to C-Town's competition.

We now affirm on the ground that the covenant was so contrary to public policy that it should not be recognized as a valid, enforceable obligation.

The proofs established that New Brunswick is a small city which continues to suffer from many of the maladies affecting the larger cities of New Jersey and the nation, especially in its core downtown area. This area, where George Street is located, has been the focus of a large scale redevelopment and revitalization effort measured in decades. Although this effort's emphasis has been on commercial projects primarily, the downtown area is also the site of many low to moderate income housing projects of the New Brunswick Housing Authority. These were federally funded projects, and many of their residents depended on George Street for their shopping requirements before Davidson closed the store. George Street is within two blocks of four of those housing projects with a total of 726 units.

The testimony of New Brunswick's Director of Policy, Planning and Economic Development . . . provided a demographic profile of the city. There are a total of 3,148 households in the downtown area. Twenty-six percent of those households are below the poverty level, compared with seventeen percent in the balance of the city. Of the "family households" downtown, twenty-eight percent are female householders with children, compared with fourteen percent in the balance of the city. Of the female headed households, fifty-four percent are below the poverty level, which is consistent with the balance of the city. Thirty-seven percent of the downtown housing units have no vehicle, almost twice as many as the balance of the city. Seven hundred and forty-three downtown units are occupied by persons sixty-five years and older; twenty-one percent of those seniors are below the poverty level, almost double the proportion in the rest of the city. The downtown area, therefore, contains the city's greatest concentration of disadvantaged persons.

Davidson's closing of George Street further disadvantaged them. No other supermarket was within walking distance. For those who lacked access to motor vehicles, buses, taxis and dependence on others replaced a walk to the supermarket. The problem was especially difficult for female heads of household who used to send their children to the store or have their children accompany them. With the elimination of George Street, getting to the supermarket was a particularly difficult exercise in logistics and child care.

But inconvenience was not the only cost. Dr. James J. O'Connor testified for defendants as an expert in food marketing and distribution. . . . Shortly before his testimony in this case, Dr. O'Connor had completed a study for the United States Department of Agriculture regarding supermarkets in United States cities. According to Dr. O'Connor, the absence of a supermarket in a low income city neighborhood makes food more expensive[1] and has a negative impact on diet and, therefore, on the inner city population's health.

---

1. According to Dr. O'Connor, "none of us, as well-off as we are, would pay what the poor pay for a bottle of mayonnaise."

Dr. O'Connor also stated that the absence of a supermarket contributes to inner city decay, because a supermarket is a retail anchor that attracts other retail operations. Withdrawal of a supermarket tends to force other merchants to leave the same neighborhood. The resulting vacuum is filled by convenience stores or "ma and pa" groceries. They are more expensive and lack variety. They rarely have produce and, if they do have it, it is of poor quality. Moreover, selection of poultry and fish is very limited and very expensive. Dr. O'Connor opined that there is a general lack of inner city supermarkets in the nation, which poses a significant social policy problem.

Dr. O'Connor's uncontradicted testimony is consistent with the conclusions reached by a congressional committee. House Select Comm. on Hunger, 100th Cong., 1st Sess., Obtaining Food: Shopping Constraints on the Poor (Comm. Print 1987) . . . : "low-income consumers are unable to maximize their limited expendable resources for a basic need—food—because of the barriers of . . . location and transportation. Hence, the grip of hunger and poverty tightens around the low-income consumer." The committee recognized the exacerbating impact of "supermarket migration" on this problem: . . .

New Brunswick's initial efforts to respond to the problem were unsuccessful. It attempted to provide and organize transportation, an option that proved to be ineffective. It also sought to find a downtown property easily adaptable to supermarket use and to attract another supermarket operator to run it. Other than the George Street store, however, there was none available.

Senator John Lynch, the Mayor of New Brunswick during the relevant period, testified that initial approaches to supermarket operators were unsuccessful because too much capital was required to rehabilitate and convert other buildings to supermarket use. According to Senator Lynch the "problem was making the bottom line work because of assembling the property, providing relocation costs, dealing with [environmental] laws, all of those things that add cost to the bottom line." Moreover, many properties that had conversion potential were unavailable or had other problems. On the other hand, George Street, the former supermarket, was capable of being easily reconverted to supermarket use.

New Jersey courts have refused to enforce contracts that violate public policy. *See* Vasquez v. Glassboro Service Ass'n, Inc., 415 A.2d 1156 (N.J. 1980) (contract requiring migrant farmworker to leave barracks immediately upon discharge violates public policy). . . . "The sources of public policy include federal and state legislation and judicial decisions." The rehabilitation of our inner cities is a public policy of this State often expressed in relevant legislation.[30] Other laws, too numerous to describe in detail, reveal how urban rehabilitation is imbedded in public policy and the public interest. . . .

Davidson's withdrawal from George Street caused difficulties and hardships . . . and made the downtown area a less hospitable and desirable place. Davidson had the right to terminate its George Street operation. In doing so, however, it imposed a restriction on the use of its former property designed to impede the relocation of another supermarket operation to the downtown area. . . . Consequently, the covenant, if enforced through injunctive relief or exposure to a judgment for damages, presented a formidable obstacle to remediation

---

30.   The court's discussion of the New Jersey Economic Development Authority Act and the New Jersey Urban Enterprise Zones Act is omitted.—Eds.

of the harm caused by Davidson's withdrawal. By harm, we mean the personal hardship caused by the withdrawal of a supermarket as well as the damage to the ongoing efforts of government and private enterprise to revitalize the city. We are persuaded, therefore, that, in the absence of any equivalent reciprocal benefit to the city, Davidson's scorched earth policy is so contrary to the public interest in these circumstances that the covenant is unreasonable and unenforceable. . . .

Affirmed.

Notes and Questions

1. Public policy is surely an appropriate ground for refusing to enforce a covenant like that in *Davidson Bros.* by injunction, but does it provide sufficient grounds for refusing to enforce it by an award of damages?[31] Would requiring payment of damages be against public policy?

2. If the benefit of a covenant is considered an interest in land, which the city could have acquired for public benefit by exercising its power of eminent domain, should it have been required to do so? Does the court's ruling in effect take Davidson Bros.'s property for public use without payment of just compensation as required by the Fourteenth Amendment?[32] Does the fact that the benefit would previously have been unenforceable under New Jersey's touch or concern doctrine insulate this ruling from a claim that it constitutes an unconstitutional taking of property under *Lucas v. South Carolina Coastal Council*, 505 U.S. 1003 (1992), *infra*, Chapter 13?

3. May a common interest community own and operate businesses and protect them against competition by prohibiting individual landowners from competing with community owned businesses? In *Amana Society v. Colony Inn, Inc.*, 315 N.W.2d 101, 117 (Iowa 1982), the court disapproved of covenants giving the society the right to issue revocable annual permits for all business use of property conveyed into private ownership.[33] Although the board of directors of the Society limited permits to protect its own business operations, the court based its disapproval on the broader ground that:

---

31.   The concurring opinion of Pollock, J., in the New Jersey Supreme Court took the position that the only question on remand should have been whether injunction or damages was the appropriate remedy, saying: "[This] case presents a tension between two worthy objectives: the continued operaton of the supermarket for the benefit of needy citizens, and the enforcement of the covenant. An award of damages . . . rather than . . . an injunction would permit realization of both objectives." Davidson Bros., Inc. v. D. Katz & Sons, Inc., 579 A.2d 288, 300 (N.J. 1990).

32.   Restatement (Third) takes the position that all servitudes are interests in land subject to the Statute of Frauds, *see* § 2.8. It does not address the question whether covenant benefits are "property" within the meaning of the Takings Clause, but its treatment of all servitudes as comparable interests strongly suggests that the answer should be yes. *Accord*, Southern California Edison Co. v. Bourgerie, 507 P.2d 964 (Cal. 1973). States have divided on the question, *see* Am. Jur. 2d *Eminent Domain* § 175. Negative Easements or Restrictive Covenants (online update May 2003).

33.   The Amana Society, which originally owned virtually all the property in the Amana colonies, was forced by a cash crisis during the Depression of the 1930s to transfer some of its land to its members individually. Beginning in 1932, about 600 parcels were conveyed subject to extensive deed restrictions. The case held that the deed restrictions were extinguished by the Society's failure to record notices to preserve them under a "stale uses" statute enacted in 1965, and were not saved from extinction as a general plan of land use restrictions.

The "general plan" in this case is that there shall be no binding plan at all, that land use control will be whatever the board of directors might say it is. This form of control is the antithesis of stability; no one could build a house with any assurance that the board would not permit a rendering plant to be built next door, or start a business with any assurance that the board would allow him to continue operating it. Rather than promoting stability and fairness . . . the Society's version of the general scheme theory here would create instability and foster unfairness.

In response to the Society's arguments that enforcement of the covenants provided the only practical means of preserving the unique character of the Amana colonies, the court pointed out that it could seek county zoning, incorporate as a municipality and enact its own zoning, or establish an historic preservation district.

Greenbelt Homes, Inc. v. Nyman Realty, Inc., 426 A.2d 394 (Md. Ct. Spec. App. 1981). Greenbelt Homes, Inc., is a large (1,600-unit) cooperative housing development built by the federal government during the 1930s and 1940s that was turned over to GHI, a member-owned nonprofit corporation in 1952. As is usual in cooperatives, GHI holds title to the land and buildings, pays the taxes and insurance, and supplies maintenance and various other services to residents. Members sign a mutual ownership contract, similar to the proprietary lease used in other cooperatives, which gives them a right of perpetual use and enjoyment in their houses and obligates them to pay monthly assessments and abide by restrictions contained in the contract, and rules and regulations adopted by GHI. Membership cannot be sold until a member has resided in the co-op for at least two years, and sales are subject to a right of first refusal held by GHI. Until June 1978, GHI offered, but did not require members to use, brokerage services provided by GHI when they sold their houses. All sales were, however, subject to payment to GHI of a $215 administrative fee and inspection fee.

In 1978, GHI expanded its real estate sales staff and adopted a rule replacing the old fees with a 5.5 percent sales commission payable on all sales, whether its services were used or not. Local real estate agents, not part of the GHI staff, sued contending GHI had violated Maryland antitrust laws. The court agreed, holding that GHI had created a tie-in arrangement that constituted an unreasonable restraint on trade. It reasoned that the restraint was unreasonable because GHI had sufficient economic power to force buyers to use its sales services whether they wanted to or not, and the amount of commerce affected was not insubstantial because upwards of 200 houses in Greenbelt Homes sold each year.

Notes and Questions

1. If this arrangement had been challenged by members of the co-op rather than a real estate broker prevented from competing with GHI, would the outcome have been the same? Richard Craswell, *Tying Requirements in Competitive Markets: The Consumer Protection Issues*, 62 B.U. L. Rev. 661 (1982), suggests that tying arrangements in unconcentrated markets like condominiums and subdivision housing are better dealt with as consumer protection issues than as antitrust problems. By focusing on the effect of the arrangement on the consumer who is forced to buy unwanted goods or deprived of the power to select the provider of her choice, courts may more easily come to the conclusion that the obligations imposed are unduly harsh and unconscionable than if forced to find a substantial impact on competition. Craswell points out that tying arrangements often involve potential future costs that are very difficult to estimate accurately at the time the first purchasers buy into a development.

2. What kinds of services should the developer of a common interest community be able to tie into the development and support by assessments? Recreational facilities, street maintenance, garbage service, cable television, and security are widely accepted. What about homeowners insurance, day care, social activities, food service, health care? What kinds of activities should the developer be able to subject to fees to support community activities? Submission of plans for architectural approval? Parking? Transfer of property? Leasing? If the arrangement is included in the recorded CC&R's, validity of such provisions is governed by Restatement § 3.1. If it is adopted later by the board of the association, validity is governed by Restatement § 6.5(2):

> Unless expressly authorized by the declaration, fees for services rendered, or for the use of common property, must be reasonably related to the costs of providing the service, or providing and maintaining the common property, or the value of the use or service.

3. *When may outsiders challenge the validity of the covenants, rules, or practices of a common interest community?* In another case involving anticompetitive practices, the California Supreme Court held that the management of Leisure World, a private, gated community of 20,000 residents, was not entitled to exclude the publisher of a giveaway newspaper that would compete for advertising revenue with the Leisure World house organ. *Laguna Publishing Co. v. Golden Rain Foundation*, 182 Cal. Rptr. 813 (Ct. App. 1982). Closed communities may also be required to provide some access to political organizations. In *Guttenberg Taxpayers & Rentpayers Ass'n v. Galaxy Towers Condominium Ass'n*, 688 A.2d 156 (N.J. Super. Ct. Ch. Div. 1996), the condominium association in a community comprising 1,075 units in three high-rise buildings that actively endorsed political candidates and distributed leaflets door to door and in the common areas was required to provide equal access to other political organizations. As we saw in Chapter 10, outsiders are also able to challenge restrictions or decisions of common interest communities that deny them housing opportunities under the Federal Fair Housing Act.

e.   Design Controls

Design controls are a common feature of modern real estate developments, which usually require submission of plans and approval by the developer or an architectural control committee before construction begins. Although they provide a source of numerous and often rancorous disputes, courts now routinely uphold the validity of the covenants but require that the power to disapprove plans be exercised reasonably. *See, e.g., Rhue v. Cheyenne Homes, Inc.*, 449 P.2d 361 (Colo. 1969) (covenants need not provide specific guidelines to architectural control committee). A few courts, unlike the court in *Rhue*, have held that design covenants are invalid unless they provide sufficient guidelines to enable an owner to determine what is acceptable. *See, e.g., Prestwick Landowners' Ass'n v. Underhill*, 429 N.E.2d 1191 (Ohio Ct. App. 1980).

Are there drawbacks to including specific requirements? In *Davis v. Huey*, 620 S.W.2d 561 (Tex. 1981), the covenants included specific setback requirements of 25 feet from the front lot line, 5 feet from the side lines, and 15 feet from the rear line, and also required submission of plans to the developer or an architectural committee, providing that refusal to approve could be based "on any ground, including purely aesthetic grounds, which in the sole and uncontrolled discretion of the developer . . . shall seem sufficient." The court held the developer's refusal to approve the plans because the house was placed 25 feet from the rear lot line, which created a smaller backyard than other houses in the neighborhood, was void. The developer did not have the power to demand more than that required by the specific restrictions.

What is reasonable?[34] In *Riss v. Angel*, 934 P.2d 669 (Wash. 1997), refusal to approve proposed plans for a house subjected the association, individual board members, and members who ratified the board's decision to liability. Their actions were held unreasonable because the decision was made without a comparison study of other homes in the development and was based on a lobbying campaign by board members that included an inaccurate, misleading photo montage. In addition, the board's conditions for approval included lowering the roofline to a height below that specified in the covenants and reducing the new house to a size smaller than the existing house on the lot. The Riss case is discussed in Casey J. Little, Note, *Riss v. Angel: Washington Remodels the Framework for Interpreting Restrictive Covenants*, 73 Wash. L. Rev. 433 (1998).

Satellite dishes and other antennas. Prior to enactment of the Telecommunications Act of 1996, courts often held that satellite dishes were structures requiring architectural committee approval and allowed disapproval on aesthetic grounds. The scope of design review has been significantly curtailed by the Federal Communications Commission in applying regulations issued pursuant to the Act. *In re Holliday*, CSR 5399-0, adopted Oct. 6, 1999, by the Chief of the Cable Services Bureau, held that the Crooked Creek Villages Homeowners Association violated the Act by filing suit against homeowners who, without seeking approval required by the architectural control covenant, installed six masts secured to the ground by guy wires in the rear of their lot. There were five masts approximately 30 feet in height that were roughly even with the petitioners' roofline, two of which simply provided support to another mast, and one 10-foot mast. The petitioners affixed five television antennas and three satellite dish antennas to these masts. The antennas provided reception for 10 television sets, 9 videocassette recorders, and 7 satellite receivers. The Association's action violated the Act because it had not established that its policy limiting antenna height and limiting each home to one satellite dish and one antenna was justified by legitimate safety or historic preservation considerations. The Association also failed to demonstrate that its restrictions did not impair the installation, maintenance, or use of over-the-air reception antennas.

---

34. For a collection of cases answering the question whether a design control power was exercised reasonably or unreasonably, see the Reporter's Note to Restatement § 6.9, Design Control Powers.

Colors. Paint color provokes lots of controversy, particularly when it's purple. Timothy Egan, *House of a Different Color Is Shunned,* N.Y. Times, June 3, 1993, tells the story of the Jones family in Washington state who were sued by the homeowners association for painting their house purple without approval (which apparently would not have been given). The superior court ordered the Joneses to repaint or face contempt sanctions of $2,000 per day and possible imprisonment.

Novelist Sandra Cisneros, recipient of a MacArthur Foundation genius grant in 1995, and author of *Woman Hollering Creek* and *The House on Mango Street,* got into trouble with the San Antonio Historic and Design Review Commission for painting her house, located in a neighborhood of 19th century stately Victorians, Sherwin Williams' Corsican Purple, trimmed with hyacinth and turquoise. Cisneros, dressed in a ruby red dress with lime green serape and black and aqua cowboy boots etched with prickly pear cactus, told the Commission that color is her heritage: "We don't have beautiful showcase houses to tell the story of the class of people I come from, but our inheritance is in our sense of color—and it's something that has withstood a conquest, plagues, genocide, death, defeat." The Commission, like many homeowner associations, had an approved palette of colors. Approved colors included "Colonial Revival Tan," "Plymouth Green," and "Chelsea Gray."[35]

f.   Covenants Restricting Household Occupants and Personal Freedoms

Covenants that restrict occupancy on the basis of race, religion, national origin, or sex, and covenants that deny children and the handicapped the right to live in a particular dwelling are invalid, as you learned in Chapter 10, because they violate the federal Constitution, or one or more of the various federal and state civil rights acts.

In this chapter we take up the question whether servitudes law imposes additional limits on covenants that discriminate against potential owners and occupants on grounds related to composition of their household and covenants that restrict personal freedoms. Covenants that prohibit pets, signs (including for-sale and political signs), and displays of flags (particularly the American flag) have generated substantial controversy. Typical covenants also raise issues when they restrict a resident's ability to place religious structures or symbols on the exterior of a home. Challenges may be raised to a covenant as a whole, or as applied to a particular situation. Under traditional servitudes law, the issue was framed in terms of reasonableness, or unreasonableness. Under the Restatement (Third) § 3.1, the question is whether the covenant, or application of the covenant, violates public policy because it is arbitrary or because it unreasonably burdens a fundamental constitutional right. Using servitudes law to address these issues avoids the sometimes difficult question whether enforcement of private covenants involves state action.

---

35.   Holiday decorations provide another fertile source of controversy, and overly strict regulations may, of course, raise problems of interference with religious expression.

NAHRSTEDT v. LAKESIDE VILLAGE CONDOMINIUM ASS'N, INC.

Supreme Court of California (en banc)
878 P.2d 1275 (Cal. 1994)

KENNARD, J. . . . Lakeside Village is a large condominium development in Culver City, Los Angeles County. It consists of 530 units spread throughout 12 separate 3-story buildings. The residents share common lobbies and hallways, in addition to laundry and trash facilities.

The Lakeside Village project is subject to . . . covenants, conditions and restrictions (hereafter CC&R's) . . . in the developer's declaration recorded . . . April 17, 1978. . . . Ownership of a unit includes membership in the project's homeowners association, the Lakeside Village Condominium Association (hereafter Association), the body that enforces the project's CC&R's, including the pet restriction, which provides in relevant part: "No animals (which shall mean dogs and cats), livestock, reptiles or poultry shall be kept in any unit."[3]

In January, 1988, plaintiff Natore Nahrstedt purchased a Lakeside Village condominium and moved in with her three cats. When the Association learned of the cats' presence, it demanded their removal and assessed fines against Nahrstedt for each successive month that she remained in violation of the condominium project's pet restriction.

Nahrstedt . . . [sued] the Association, its officers, and two of its employees, asking the trial court to invalidate the assessments, to enjoin future assessments, to award damages for violation of her privacy when the Association "peered" into her condominium unit, to award damages for infliction of emotional distress, and to declare the pet restriction "unreasonable" as applied to indoor cats (such as hers) that are not allowed free run of the project's common areas. Nahrstedt also alleged she did not know of the pet restriction when she bought her condominium.

The Association demurred to the complaint. The Association argued that the pet restriction furthers the collective "health, happiness and peace of mind" of persons living in close proximity within the Lakeside Village condominium development, and therefore is reasonable as a matter of law. The trial court sustained the demurrer as to each cause of action and dismissed Nahrstedt's complaint. Nahrstedt appealed.

A divided Court of Appeal reversed . . . . In the majority's view, the complaint stated a claim for declaratory relief based on its allegations that Nahrstedt's three cats are kept inside her condominium unit and do not bother her neighbors. According to the majority, whether a condominium use restriction is "unreasonable," as that term is used in [Civil Code] section 1354, hinges on the facts of a particular homeowner's case. Thus, the majority reasoned, Nahrstedt would be entitled to declaratory relief if application of the pet restriction in her case would not be reasonable. The Court of Appeal also revived Nahrstedt's causes of action for invasion of privacy, invalidation of the assessments, and injunctive relief, as well as her action for emotional distress based on a theory of negligence.

---

3. The CC&R's permit residents to keep "domestic fish and birds."

issue:

. . . [W]e granted review to decide when a condominium owner can prevent enforcement of a use restriction that the project's developer has included in the recorded declaration of CC&R's.

Today, condominiums, cooperatives, and planned-unit developments with homeowners associations have become a widely accepted form of real property ownership. These ownership arrangements are known as "common interest" developments. The owner not only enjoys many of the traditional advantages associated with individual ownership of real property, but also acquires an interest in common with others in the amenities and facilities included in the project. . . .

The viability of shared ownership of improved real property rests on the existence of extensive reciprocal servitudes, together with the ability of each co-owner to prevent the property's partition. (Natelson, *Law of Property Owners Associations,* (1989) § 1.3.2.1, p. 19 . . . .)

common property interests?

The restrictions on the use of property in any common interest development may limit activities conducted in the common areas as well as in the confines of the home itself. (Reichman, *Residential Private Governments* (1976) 43 U. Chi. L. Rev. 253, 270; Natelson, *Consent, Coercion, and "Reasonableness,"* 51 Ohio St. L.J. [41] at p. 48, fn. 28 [(1990)] [as of 1986, 58 percent of high-rise developments and 39 percent of townhouse projects had some kind of pet restriction] . . . .[5]

Restrictions on property use are not the only characteristic of common interest ownership. Ordinarily, such ownership also entails mandatory membership in an owners association, which, through an elected board of directors, is empowered to enforce any use restrictions contained in the project's declaration or master deed and to enact new rules governing the use and occupancy of property within the project. Because of its considerable power in managing and regulating a common interest development, the governing board of an owners association must guard against the potential for the abuse of that power.[6] As Professor Natelson observes, owners associations "can be a powerful force for good or for ill" in their members' lives. Therefore, anyone who buys a unit in a common interest development with knowledge of its owners association's discretionary power accepts "the risk that the power may be used in a way that benefits the commonality but harms the individual." Generally, courts will uphold decisions made by the governing board of an owners association so long as they represent good faith efforts to further the purposes of the common interest development, are consistent with the development's governing documents, and comply with public policy.

must join board)

but watch for abuse of power.

uphold board's decision when:

Thus, subordination of individual property rights to the collective judgment of the owners association together with restrictions on the use of real property comprise the chief attributes of owning property in a common interest development. As the Florida District Court of Appeal observed in Hidden Harbour Estates, Inc. v. Norman (Fla. Dist. Ct. App. 1975) 309 So. 2d 180 [72 A.L.R.3d 305], . . . : "[I]nherent in the condominium concept is the principle that to

---

5.   Even the dissent recognizes that pet restrictions have a long pedigree . . . [in] citing Crimmins, The Quotable Cat (1992) p. 58 [English nuns living in a nunnery prohibited in 1205 from keeping any pet except a cat].

6.   The power to regulate pertains to a "wide spectrum of activities," such as the volume of playing music, hours of social gatherings, use of patio furniture and barbecues, and rental of units. (Note, . . . [*Community Association Use Restrictions: Applying the Business Judgment Doctrine,* 64 Chi. Kent L. Rev. 653, 669 (1988)].)

promote the health, happiness, and peace of mind of the majority of the unit owners since they are living in such close proximity and using facilities in common, each unit owner must give up a certain degree of freedom of choice which he [or she] might otherwise enjoy in separate, privately owned property. Condominium unit owners comprise a little democratic subsociety of necessity more restrictive as it pertains to use of condominium property than may be existent outside the condominium organization."

Notwithstanding the limitations on personal autonomy . . . , common interest developments have increased in popularity in recent years, in part because they generally provide a more affordable alternative to ownership of a single-family home. (*See* Frances T. v. Village Green Owners Assn. (1986) 42 Cal. 3d 490 [noting that common interest developments at that time accounted for as much as 70 percent of the new housing market in Los Angeles and San Diego Counties]; *see also* McKenzie, *Welcome Home. Do as We Say.*, N.Y. Times (Aug. 18, 1994) p. 23A, col. 1 [stating that 32 million Americans are members of some 150,000 homeowners associations and predicting that between 25 to 30 percent of Americans will live in community association housing by the year 2000].)

One significant factor in the continued popularity of the common interest form of property ownership is the ability of homeowners to enforce restrictive CC&R's against other owners (including future purchasers) of project units. Generally, however, such enforcement is possible only if the restriction that is sought to be enforced meets the requirements of equitable servitudes or of covenants running with the land. . . .

In California, . . . common interest development use restrictions contained in a project's recorded declaration [are] "enforceable . . . unless unreasonable." Civ. Code § 1354 (a).

In states lacking such legislative guidance, some courts have adopted a standard under which a common interest development's recorded use restrictions will be enforced so long as they are "reasonable." (*See* Riley v. Stoves (1974) 22 Ariz. App. 223 [asking whether the challenged restriction provided "a reasonable means to accomplish the private objective"].) Others would limit the "reasonableness" standard only to those restrictions adopted by majority vote of the homeowners or enacted under the rulemaking power of an association's governing board, and would not apply this test to restrictions included in a planned development project's recorded declaration or master deed. Because such restrictions are presumptively valid, these authorities would enforce them regardless of reasonableness. . . .

In Hidden Harbour Estates v. Basso (Fla. Dist. Ct. App. 1981) 393 So. 2d 637, the Florida court distinguished two categories of use restrictions: use restrictions set forth in the declaration or master deed of the condominium project itself, and rules promulgated by the governing board of the condominium owners association or the board's interpretation of a rule. The latter category of use restrictions, the court said, should be subject to a "reasonableness" test, so as to "somewhat fetter the discretion of the board of directors." Such a standard, the court explained, best assures that governing boards will "enact rules and make decisions that are reasonably related to the promotion of the health, happiness and peace of mind" of the project owners, considered collectively.

By contrast, restrictions contained in the declaration or master deed of the condominium complex, the Florida court concluded, . . . are "clothed with a very strong presumption of validity" and should be upheld even if they exhibit some degree of unreasonableness. Nonenforcement would be proper only if such restrictions were arbitrary or in violation of public policy or some fundamental constitutional right. The Florida court's decision was cited with approval recently by a Massachusetts appellate court in Noble v. Murphy, 612 N.E.2d 266 (Mass. Ct. App. 1993).

In *Noble*, . . . [t]he . . . court upheld the validity of [a pet] restriction [contained in the project's master deed]. The court stated that "[a] condominium use restriction appearing in originating documents which predate the purchase of individual units" was entitled to greater judicial deference than restrictions "promulgated after units have been individually acquired." The court reasoned that "properly-enacted and evenly-enforced use restrictions contained in a master deed or original bylaws of a condominium" should be insulated against attack "except on constitutional or public policy grounds." This standard, the court explained, best "serves the interest of the majority of owners [within a project] who may be presumed to have chosen not to alter or rescind such restrictions," and it spares overcrowded courts "the burden and expense of highly particularized and lengthy litigation."

Indeed, giving deference to use restrictions contained in a condominium project's originating documents protects the general expectations of condominium owners "that restrictions in place at the time they purchase their units will be enforceable." (Note, *Judicial Review of Condominium Rulemaking*, . . . [1981], 94 Harv. L. Rev. 647, 653; Ellickson, *Cities and Homeowners' Associations* (1982) 130 U. Pa. L. Rev. 1519, 1526-1527 [stating that association members "unanimously consent to the provisions in the association's original documents" and courts therefore should not scrutinize such documents for "reasonableness"].) This in turn encourages the development of shared ownership housing—generally a less costly alternative to single-dwelling ownership—by attracting buyers who prefer a stable, planned environment. It also protects buyers who have paid a premium for condominium units in reliance on a particular restrictive scheme.

. . . [W]hen enforcing equitable servitudes, courts are generally disinclined to question the wisdom of agreed-to restrictions. This rule does not apply, however, when the restriction does not comport with public policy. Equity will not enforce any restrictive covenant that violates public policy. (*See* Shelley v. Kraemer . . . ; [Cal. Civ. Code] § 53(b) [voiding property use restrictions based on "sex, race, color, religion, ancestry, national origin, or disability"].) Nor will courts enforce as equitable servitudes those restrictions that are arbitrary, that is, bearing no rational relationship to the protection, preservation, operation or purpose of the affected land.

These limitations on the equitable enforcement of restrictive servitudes that are either arbitrary or violate fundamental public policy are specific applications of the general rule that courts will not enforce a restrictive covenant when "the harm caused by the restriction is so disproportionate to the benefit produced" by its enforcement that the restriction "ought not to be enforced." (*Rest., Property*, § 539, com. *f* pp. 3229-3230.) When a use restriction bears no relationship to the land it burdens, or violates a fundamental policy inuring to the public at large, the resulting harm will always be disproportionate to any benefit. . . .

When courts accord a presumption of validity to . . . recorded use restrictions . . . it discourages lawsuits by owners of individual units seeking personal exemptions from the restrictions. This . . . promotes stability and predictability in two ways. It provides substantial assurance to prospective condominium purchasers that they may rely with confidence on the promises embodied in the project's recorded CC&R's. And it protects all owners in the planned development from unanticipated increases in association fees to fund the defense of legal challenges to recorded restrictions.

When courts treat recorded use restrictions as presumptively valid, and place on the challenger the burden of proving the restriction "unreasonable" . . . associations can proceed to enforce reasonable restrictive covenants without fear that their actions will embroil them in costly and prolonged legal proceedings. Of course, when an association determines that a unit owner has violated a use restriction, the association must do so in good faith, not in an arbitrary or capricious manner, and its enforcement procedures must be fair and applied uniformly. . . .

There is an additional beneficiary of legal rules that are protective of recorded use restrictions: the judicial system. Fewer lawsuits challenging such restrictions will be brought, and those that are filed may be disposed of more expeditiously, if the rules courts use in evaluating such restrictions are clear, simple, and not subject to exceptions based on the peculiar circumstance or hardships of individual residents in condominiums and other shared-ownership developments.

Contrary to the dissent's accusations that the majority's decision "fray[s]" the "social fabric," we are of the view that our social fabric is best preserved if courts uphold and enforce solemn written instruments that embody the expectations of the parties rather than treat them as "worthless paper" as the dissent would. Our social fabric is founded on the stability of expectation and obligation that arises from the consistent enforcement of the terms of deeds, contracts, wills, statutes, and other writings. To allow one person to escape obligations under a written instrument upsets the expectations of all the other parties governed by that instrument (here, the owners of the other 529 units) that the instrument will be uniformly and predictably enforced.

Refusing to enforce the CC&R's contained in a recorded declaration, or enforcing them only after protracted litigation that would require justification of their application on a case-by-case basis, would impose great strain on the social fabric of the common interest development. . . . It would put the owners and the homeowners association in the difficult and divisive position of deciding whether particular CC&R's should be applied to a particular owner. Here, for example, deciding whether a particular animal is "confined to an owner's unit and create[s] no noise, odor, or nuisance" is a fact-intensive determination that can only be made by examining in detail the behavior of the particular animal and the behavior of the particular owner. Homeowners associations are ill-equipped to make such investigations, and any decision they might make in a particular case could be divisive or subject to claims of partiality.

Enforcing the CC&R's contained in a recorded declaration only after protracted case-by-case litigation would impose substantial litigation costs on the owners through their homeowners association, which would have to defend not only against owners contesting the application of the CC&R's to them, but also against owners contesting any case-by-case exceptions the homeowners association might make. In short, it is difficult to imagine what could more disrupt the harmony of a common interest development than the course proposed by the dissent. . . .

holding.

Under the holding we adopt today, the reasonableness or unreasonableness of a condominium use restriction . . . is to be determined . . . by reference to the common interest development as a whole. . . . We conclude, as a matter of law, that the recorded pet restriction . . . is not arbitrary, but is rationally related to health, sanitation and noise concerns legitimately held by residents of a high-density condominium project such as Lakeside Village. . . .

Nahrstedt's complaint does contend that the restriction violates her right to privacy under the California Constitution, article I, section 1.[11] Because a land-use restriction in violation of a state constitutional provision presumably would conflict with public policy we construe Nahrstedt's contention as a claim that the Lakeside Village pet restriction violates a fundamental public policy and for that reason cannot be enforced. The pertinent question, therefore, is whether the privacy provision in our state Constitution implicitly guarantees condominium owners or residents the right to keep cats or dogs as household pets. We conclude that California's Constitution confers no such right. . . .

TT argues restriction violates public policy.

We discern no fundamental public policy that would favor the keeping of pets in a condominium project. There is no federal or state constitutional provision or any California statute that confers a general right to keep household pets in condominiums or other common interest developments.[12] Nor does case law offer any support for the position that the recognized scope of autonomy privacy encompasses the right to keep pets: courts that have considered condominium pet restrictions have uniformly upheld them.

no constitutional provision or case law to support TT's contention

. . . For many owners, the pet restriction may have been an important inducement to purchase into the development. Because the homeowners collectively have the power to repeal the pet restriction, its continued existence reflects their desire to retain it.

Plaintiff's allegations, even if true, are insufficient to show that the pet restriction's harmful effects substantially outweigh its benefits to the condominium development as a whole, that it bears no rational relationship to the purpose or function of the development, or that it violates public policy. We reverse the judgment of the Court of Appeal, and remand for further proceedings consistent with the views expressed in this opinion.

ARABIAN, J., dissenting. "There are two means of refuge from the misery of life: music and cats."[1]

I respectfully dissent. While technical merit may commend the majority's analysis, its application to the facts presented reflects a narrow, indeed chary, view of the law that eschews the human spirit in favor of arbitrary efficiency. In my view, the resolution of this case well illustrates the conventional wisdom, and fundamental truth, of the Spanish proverb, "It is better to be a mouse in a cat's mouth than a man in a lawyer's hands."

I find the . . . "pet restriction" . . . patently arbitrary and unreasonable within the meaning of Civil Code section 1354. Beyond dispute, human beings have

---

11.   That provision states: "All people are by nature free and independent and have inalienable rights. Among these are enjoying and defending life and liberty, acquiring, possessing, and protecting property, and pursuing and obtaining safety, happiness, and *privacy*." (Italics added.)

12.   With respect to either disabled individuals living in rented housing or elderly persons living in publicly funded housing, the situation is otherwise. The Legislature has declared its intent that, in specified circumstances, these two classes of Californians be allowed to keep pets. . . .

1.   Albert Schweitzer.

long enjoyed an abiding and cherished association with their household animals. Given the substantial benefits derived from pet ownership, the undue burden on the use of property imposed on condominium owners who can maintain pets within the confines of their units without creating a nuisance or disturbing the quiet enjoyment of others substantially outweighs whatever meager utility the restriction may serve in the abstract. It certainly does not promote "health, happiness [or] peace of mind" commensurate with its tariff on the quality of life for those who value the companionship of animals. Worse, it contributes to the fraying of our social fabric.

[handwritten margin note: benefit of having animal, kept in unit, is more than cost...]

The majority's failure to consider the real burden imposed by the pet restriction unfortunately belittles and trivializes the interest at stake here. Pet ownership substantially enhances the quality of life for those who desire it. When others are not only undisturbed by, but completely unaware of, the presence of pets being enjoyed by their neighbors, the balance of benefit and burden is rendered disproportionate and unreasonable, rebutting any presumption of validity. Their view, shorn of grace and guiding philosophy, is devoid of the humanity that must temper the interpretation and application of all laws, for in a civilized society that is the source of their authority. As judicial architects of the rules of life, we better serve when we construct halls of harmony . . . than walls of wrath. . . .

Notes and Questions

1. If the recorded CC&R's are amended to add a pet restriction, can the restriction be applied to owners who purchased units before the amendment? *See Villa de Las Palmas Homeowners Ass'n v. Terifaj*, 90 P.3d 1223 (Cal. 2004) (yes, deferential *Nahrstedt* standard applies to amendments to recorded declaration the same as to the original declaration).

2. If *Nahrstedt* had involved a guide dog needed by a handicapped person within the meaning of the Federal Fair Housing Act, would the Association have been able to enforce its pet restriction against her? *See Hill v. Community of Damien of Molokai*, 911 P.2d 861 (N.M. 1996), *supra* Chapter 10.

3. If the pet restriction had been adopted by the board of the Association rather than contained in the declaration, would the outcome have been different? A number of courts, following *Hidden Harbor Estates, Inc. v. Basso*, 393 So. 2d 637 (Fla. Dist. Ct. App. 1981),[36] apply a more stringent standard to association rules. Restatement (Third) § 6.7 provides that rules must be reasonable, and, unless expressly authorized by the declaration, an association lacks power to adopt rules that "restrict the use or occupancy of, or behavior within, individually owned lots or units" unless designed to protect other members of the community from unreasonable interference with their rights to enjoy either the common property or their individual properties. How would the pet restriction fare under this standard?

36. This distinction is discussed in Robert C. Ellickson, *Cities and Homeowners Associations*, 130 U. Pa. L. Rev. 1519 (1982). *See also* Gerald E. Frug, *Cities and Homeowners Associations: A Reply*, 130 U. Pa. L. Rev. 1589 (1982); Robert C. Ellickson, *A Reply to Michelman and Frug*, 130 U. Pa. L. Rev. 1602 (1982). *See also* Gregory S. Alexander, *Freedom, Coercion and the Law of Servitudes*, 73 Cornell L. Rev. 883 (1988); Richard A. Epstein, *Covenants and Constitutions*, 73 Cornell L. Rev. 906 (1988); Uriel Reichman, *Residential Private Governments: An Introductory Survey*, 43 U. Chi. L. Rev. 253 (1976).

4. California Civil Code § 1360.5, enacted in 2000, prohibits common interest developments governing documents adopted or amended after January 1, 2001, from prohibiting owners from keeping at least one pet, defined as any domesticated bird, cat, dog, aquatic animal kept in an aquarium, subject to reasonable rules and regulations. The statute also provides that new rules restricting the number of pets an owner may keep, shall not apply to pets currently kept by an owner if the pet conforms to the previous rules.

5. Are pet restrictions a good idea? *See* Zhenguo Lin, Marcus T. Allen & Charles C. Carter, *Pet Policy and Housing Prices: Evidence from the Condominium Market*, 47 J. Real Est. Fin. & Econ. 109 (2013): "Our results suggest that an unrestricted pet policy creates a significant premium in condominium price, along with discounts for condominiums that do not allow pets or have pet restrictions."

6. Justice Arabian, dissenting in *Nahrstedt*, would no doubt have held the pet restriction invalid as against public policy under Restatement § 3.01(2) (as "a servitude that unreasonably burdens a fundamental constitutional right"). Although the right to choose your living companions is regarded by many courts as part of your protected right of association, nonhuman companions are seldom included in the protected circle. Even with human companions, courts vary on the extent of protection afforded. See Gerald Korngold, *Single Family Use Covenants: For Achieving a Balance Between Traditional Family Life and Individual Autonomy*, 22 U.C. Davis L. Rev. 951 (1989), for a thoughtful analysis of the public policy concerns presented by the single-family use covenants so prevalent in suburban America. *Park Redlands Covenant Control Commission v. Simon*, 226 Cal. Rptr. 199 (Ct. App. 1986), held that an attempt to enforce age restrictions to prevent the owners from sharing their home with their children and grandchildren violated the California constitutional right of privacy.

What other kinds of covenants might unreasonably burden fundamental constitutional rights? Likely candidates are restrictions on patriotic displays of the flag and restrictions on political yard signs. *See Gerber v. Longboat Harbour North Condominium, Inc.*, 724 F. Supp. 884 (M.D. Fla. 1989) (enforcement of covenant to prohibit flying American flag violated homeowner's constitutional right of free speech); *City of Ladue v. Gilleo*, 512 U.S. 43 (1994) (city ordinance prohibiting signs held invalid as applied to political yard signs, "a venerable means of communication that is both unique and important"). Some courts have upheld private restrictions on signs that would be invalid if imposed by a governmental body on the ground that private parties are competent to contract away constitutional rights. *See, e.g., Midlake on Big Boulder Lake Condominium Ass'n v. Cappuccio*, 673 A.2d 340 (Pa. Super. Ct. 1996) (for-sale sign; individual's right to contractually restrict or give up constitutional rights is "one of the fundamental precepts which we recognize").

Judicial Review of Association Decision Making

The extent to which courts should defer to private decision making in the common interest community arena has been the subject of a lively debate in both academic circles and judicial decisions.[37] Views range from those who see the servitude package as part of a contract accepted by each purchaser, on which all

---

37. Some of the many interesting articles on the subject include Gregory S. Alexander, *Dilemmas of Group Autonomy: Residential Associations and Community*, 75 Cornell L. Rev. 1 (1989); Clayton

community members are entitled to rely, to those who believe purchasers either are unaware of the ramifications of the servitude package or are coerced into accepting it to get the property they want.[38]

Views as to the extent of the governance power of the association exercised through its rule-making powers,[39] its decisions as to enforcement matters, and its decisions on management of the property similarly vary.[40] Some believe courts should defer to the democratic decision-making processes in the community, intervening only in cases of conflict of interest, bad faith, or arbitrary discrimination—the "business judgment rule" adopted by the New York Court of Appeals in *Levandusky v. One Fifth Avenue Apartment Corp.*, 553 N.E.2d 1317 (N.Y. 1990). Others believe courts should review association decision making using the reasonableness standard articulated in *Hidden Harbour Estates Inc. v. Basso*, 393 So. 2d 637 (Fla. Dist. Ct. App. 1981). The primary difference between the two approaches may lie in the location of the burden of proof. According to the court in *Levandusky*, the reasonableness rule places the burden of proof on the association to justify its action, thus inviting litigation and second-guessing by courts, whereas the business judgment rule places the burden on the property owner challenging the board's action. Robert G. Natelson argues against the business judgment rule's lesser standard of review:[41]

> Good association management can add significant value, both financial and nonfinancial to the units it governs. Unscrupulous or careless management can cause enormous suffering and loss. . . . For most people, their home is the largest investment they will ever make. Beyond its financial value, a dwelling unit has a unique value. Association mismanagement not only can depress market value, it can make living there uncomfortable, sometimes even dangerous.

California has adopted the business judgment rule for ordinary maintenance decisions, but not necessarily for other kinds of board decisions. *See Lamden v. La Jolla Shores Clubdominium Homeowners Ass'n*, 980 P.2d 940 (Cal. 1999):

P. Gillette, *Courts, Covenants, and Communities*, 61 U. Chi. L. Rev. 1375 (1994); Robert G. Natelson, *Consent, Coercion and "Reasonableness" in Private Law: The Special Case of the Property Owners Association*, 51 Ohio St. L.J. 41 (1990); Glen O. Robinson, *Explaining Contingent Rights: The Puzzle of "Obsolete" Covenants*, 91 Colum. L. Rev. 546 (1991).

38. The results of an empirical study of common interest communities may be found in Common Interest Communities: Private Governments and the Public Interest (Stephen E. Barton & Carol J. Silverman eds., 1994).

39. Newspaper stories provide many illustrations of rule making seemingly gone amok. One board adopted a rule setting a 35-pound limit on dogs, which caused a lot of unhappiness to owners and dogs alike. *Residents Barking up a Storm over Paunchy Dogs*, AP, Chi. Trib., June 28, 1992. Another board notified a 51-year-old woman that she had been seen "kissing and doing bad things for over 1 hour" while parked in the driveway and would be fined if it happened again. Although the board later apologized (they had fingered the wrong culprit), the story lives on. Los Angeles Times, June 16, 1991.

40. Stewert E. Sterk, *Minority Protection in Residential Private Governments*, 77 B.U. L. Rev. 273 (1997), reviews the many arguments that can be raised for and against protecting dissenting community members from the majority and concludes that judicial intervention is only necessary to prevent the majority from redistributing wealth; otherwise, courts should allow the democratic process to resolve community disputes. Other articles include James L. Winokur, *The Mixed Blessings of Promissory Servitudes: Toward Optimizing Economic Utility, Individual Liberty, and Personal Identity*, 1989 Wis. L. Rev. 1; Gerald Korngold, *Resolving the Flaws of Residential Servitudes and Owners Associations: For Reformation Not Termination*, 1990 Wis. L. Rev. 513; James L. Winokur, *Reforming Servitude Regimes: Toward Associational Federalism and Community*, 1990 Wis. L. Rev. 537.

41. Robert G. Natelson, Law of Property Owners Associations § 10.3.3 (1989).

Where a duly constituted community association board, upon reasonable investigation, in good faith and with regard for the best interests of the community association and its members, exercises discretion within the scope of its authority under relevant statutes, covenants and restrictions to select among means for discharging an obligation to maintain and repair a development's common areas, courts should defer to the board's authority and presumed expertise. Thus, we adopt today for California courts a rule of judicial deference to community association board decisionmaking that applies . . . when owners in common interest developments seek to litigate ordinary maintenance decisions entrusted to the discretion of their associations' boards of directors.

The Restatement takes a path down the middle, imposing duties to use ordinary care in managing the property and financial affairs of the community, to treat members fairly, and to act reasonably in the exercise of its discretionary powers, including rulemaking, enforcement, and design control powers, but placing the burden of proof on the member who challenges the association's action. *See* Restatement (Third) § 6.13.

5.   *Succession to Covenants: Vertical Privity and Restatement (Third)*

To be entitled to enforce a covenant, anyone other than the original covenantee must show that he or she now owns some land that was intended to be benefited by the covenant, which ordinarily requires showing that the covenantee was a predecessor in title, or that the claimant now owns land held by a third-party beneficiary of the covenant. If the benefit is in gross, an assignment must be shown. People who are not assignees of benefits in gross or owners of land intended to be benefited by the covenant lack standing to sue to enforce the covenant, no matter how much their land might benefit. Although vertical privity is often used to describe this required connection to the original beneficiaries of a covenant, the same connection is needed to enforce easements and profits. In the easement/profit context, this requirement may simply be referred to as a standing requirement.

To enforce a covenant burden against someone, it is also necessary to show that the person is connected to the covenantor, either by current ownership of land intended to be burdened by the covenant, or by express assumption of the obligation. Because covenants grew out of contract rather than grant, courts used the privity concept to justify imposing obligations made by others on subsequent owners of the property. The law of vertical privity in England developed exclusively in the context of lease covenants because fee covenants did not run at law. Privity was not required in equity, and covenant burdens passed to successors in the same way that easements did. The doctrinal picture was more complicated in the United States. Interestingly, however, outside of the landlord-tenant law context, the cases applying the vertical privity doctrine have all involved simple standing issues, where vertical privity really is not needed, rather than the more complicated issues for which it might have been useful.

Succession to burdens. The traditional vertical privity doctrine distinguishes between burdens that run at law, which run only to successors to the *same* estate as that held by the covenantor ("strict" vertical privity), and burdens in equity, which run to successors to *some* estate held by the covenantor ("relaxed" vertical privity). The difference is that lessees and life tenants are bound in equity but not at law. This distinction made sense, at least as to lessees, when only negative covenants were enforceable in equity, but lost its utility when equity began to enforce affirmative covenants. Lessees, for example, should not automatically be bound on the fee owner's covenant to pay assessments to a homeowner association, but should be bound by the restriction limiting use of the property to residential purposes. Arguably, however, a life tenant should be liable to pay the homeowner assessments, as well as to comply with restrictions on the property.

Succession to benefits. According to traditional doctrine, relaxed vertical privity is required for benefits to run at law and in equity. What this means is that, if the benefited property is leased, or carved up into a life estate and remainder, both tenant and landlord, or life estate and remainderman, are entitled to the benefit of the covenant. This makes sense for negative covenants, but presents problems with some affirmative covenants. If the covenant calls for the delivery of services to the premises, there is no problem, but what of covenants to pay money to the landowner for use of an easement, or covenants entitling the owner to vote on special assessments and for elections to the board of directors of the homeowner association? The vertical privity doctrine, which purports to determine these questions by whether enforcement is sought at law or in equity, no longer produces sensible solutions, if it ever did. Because no cases involving these questions seem to have reached appellate courts, it seems doubtful that a modern court would use the vertical privity doctrine to resolve these kinds of problems.

Restatement (Third). Because the traditional vertical privity doctrine fails to recognize that there are differences among lessees, life tenants, and adverse possessors with respect to who should be bound and benefited by covenants and because the law/equity divide fails to separate benefits and burdens that should run from those that should not, the Restatement adopts a different approach. It distinguishes between affirmative and negative covenants. Negative covenants are treated the same as easements—all occupiers of the burdened land are bound not to interfere with the easement, and all occupiers of the benefited land are entitled to use the easement. Thus, occupiers are bound by negative covenants burdening the land and are entitled to enforce those that benefit the land. Restatement (Third) § 5.2. Separate consideration is given to the question of which affirmative covenant burdens and benefits run to lessees, life tenants, and adverse possessors. Section 5.3 provides that the benefit of covenants to repair, maintain, and render services to the property run to lessees, as well as covenant benefits that can be enjoyed by the lessee without diminishing their value to the fee owner and without materially increasing the burden of performance of the covenant. It also provides that the only affirmative covenant burdens that run to lessees are those that can more reasonably be performed by the person in possession of the premises than by the holder of the reversion. Rules for life tenants and adverse possessors who have not yet gained title are set out in §§ 5.4 and 5.5. Persons who acquire title by adverse possession acquire all the appurtenant benefits and take subject to all the servitudes burdening the property when the adverse possession began under § 5.2.

6. *Modification, Amendment, and Termination of Covenants*

Covenants, like easements and profits, may be terminated by expiration, release, abandonment, merger, estoppel, prescription, and condemnation. With

[handwritten margin note: need consent of interested parties.]

the consent of all the interested parties, covenants can be modified as well as terminated. Even without unanimous consent, there are a number of ways in which covenants can be modified or terminated. One of the parties to a covenant (usually the developer) may retain a power of modification. Modern declarations for subdivisions and common interest communities routinely include provisions for amendment by a specified percentage of lot or unit owners, and often provide that at specified intervals, a majority or greater percentage of the owners may terminate the servitudes. Members of common interest communities also often enjoy statutory and implied amendment powers. Although amendment powers are often granted in broad language, courts tend to protect the minority of owners from amendments that unfairly shift burdens to them or benefits to the majority. For example, amendments that change the basis for allocating assessments among units are nearly always held invalid. *See* Steward E. Sterk, *Minority Protection in Residential Private Governments*, 77 B.U. L. Rev. 273 (1997).

[handwritten margin note: One party may have power to maintain.]

In addition to the parties' powers of modification and termination, courts may modify and terminate covenants under the changed conditions doctrine.

a. Changed Conditions

Restatement (Third) § 7.10, Modification and Termination of a Servitude Because of Changed Conditions

(1) When a change has taken place since the creation of a servitude that makes it impossible as a practical matter to accomplish the purpose for which the servitude was created, a court may modify the servitude to permit the purpose to be accomplished. If modification is not practicable, or would not be effective, a court may terminate the servitude. Compensation for resulting harm to the beneficiaries may be awarded as a condition of modifying or terminating the servitude.

(2) If the purpose of a servitude can be accomplished, but because of changed conditions the servient estate is no longer suitable for uses permitted by the servitude, a court may modify the servitude to permit other uses under conditions designed to preserve the benefits of the original servitude.

(3) The rules stated in § 7.11 govern modification or termination of conservation servitudes held by public bodies and conservation organizations, which are not subject to this section.

[handwritten: OG → ½ Δ; 62 Acres; ← Δ]

RICK v. WEST

Supreme Court of New York, Westchester County
228 N.Y.S.2d 195 (Sup. Ct. 1962)

HOYT, J. Plaintiffs, the owners of some 62 acres of vacant land in the Town of Cortland, Westchester County, New York, bring this action against the defendant, the owner of a one family house situated on a ½ acre parcel conveyed to her by plaintiffs' predecessor in title, for a declaratory judgment to permit the sale of 15 acres from the tract for a community hospital in spite of restrictive covenants limiting the land to residential use.

Plaintiffs' predecessor in title, Chester Rick, . . . filed . . . a "Declaration of Covenants, Restrictions, Reservations and Agreements" which voluntarily imposed upon the 62 acres covenants restricting them to exclusive residential use with single family dwellings. . . . In October of 1955 defendant contracted to purchase from Rick a half acre lot for the sum of $2,000.00 and in September of 1956 Rick delivered his deed to the defendant conveying said premises and about a year later defendant built her house upon this lot where she now resides. . . .

These restrictions were in effect when the defendant acquired title and they were referred to in her deed and the proof shows that she discussed these restrictions with Rick when purchasing and relied upon them and was influenced by them in deciding to buy the lot and erect and make her home thereon. . . .

In 1959 Rick conveyed to plaintiffs the 62 acre parcel, being all the original tract less the plot sold to the defendant and a few other plots sold by him. In May of 1961 the plaintiffs contracted to sell to the Peekskill Hospital 15 acres from the plot and defendant's refusal to consent to the same is the basis of this litigation.

The original Declaration and the Revision thereof each contained the identical Paragraph Eighth.

> EIGHTH:—These covenants and conditions are prepared to clearly indicate the character of the Community to be established, but it is understood that special unforeseen conditions may require exceptions in certain cases, which may be permitted by the written consent of the seller providing the spirit and intent of these covenants and restrictions are adhered to.

The plaintiffs contend that the proposed sale to the Peekskill Hospital is a "special unforeseen condition" requiring an exception and the plaintiffs' grantor and the plaintiffs have executed a consent and exception pursuant to said Paragraph Eighth to permit the erection of the hospital.

The plaintiffs further claim that since Rick's acquisition of the property in 1947 the neighborhood . . . has changed, that zoning is now in effect where none existed, that a gas transmission line making portions unusable for residential purposes has bisected the property and that a lumber yard, manufacturing and commercial establishments have come into being adjacent to the property and that because of the changed conditions the Declaration and Amended Declaration imposing these restrictions are no longer enforceable and that the restrictions are of no actual or substantial benefit to the defendant.

A declaratory judgment is sought to permit the sale of the 15 acres for the hospital, to declare the restrictions no longer enforceable or of actual or substantial benefit and to declare the defendant be limited to pecuniary damages, if any, for any violations of the restrictions.

The plaintiffs called two witnesses to testify as to the pecuniary damages, if any, that might be sustained by defendant were the proposed hospital to be erected. One witness indicated there would be no depreciation in value and the other indicated a $5,000.00 depreciation. . . .

Plaintiffs' contention that the written contract of the sellers . . . permits exceptions to the covenants and conditions when required by special unforeseen circumstances is untenable. The exception . . . would permit the erection of a hospital on a 15-acre plot on an elevation close to defendant's property toward which . . . the front of defendant's property faces. To sustain this contention would mean that all the covenants and conditions would be subject to repeal by the simple written consent of the sellers. The character and use of the entire 62 acre parcel could thus be changed by the sellers. . . .

Many provisions in the restrictions could be modified without changing "the character of the Community to be established," such as minimum lot size, angle of lots or plantings. The written consent of the sellers could waive or modify these provisions. It can not, however, unencumber a 15 acre tract in the parcel from the residential restrictions.

Plaintiffs contend that substantial changes have occurred in the neighborhood since the filing of the covenants. . . . This contention is equally untenable. The only changes to be considered are those occurring after . . . the . . . restrictions and covenants were filed. The gas transmission line and certain commercial establishments which it is claimed changed the neighborhood came into being before the filing . . . .

The only changes since the . . . filing were two commercial establishments not visible from defendant's property and on the far side of a highway not abutting defendant's lot and not even abutting plaintiffs' tract. There is no evidence of any substantial change in the general neighborhood . . . and there is no change at all within the parcel owned by the plaintiffs. . . .

The rezoning of a large part of the 62-acre parcel to an industrial use, including the area upon which it is desired to build the hospital, and omitting any consideration of the time and manner in which the rezoning was accomplished, can not be considered as affecting the restrictive covenants. . . .

The parcel in question would doubtless by its topography and proximity to fast growing suburban areas make a desirable location for the hospital. The hospital authorities would like to acquire it and the plaintiffs would like to sell it and it may be asked why should defendant owning a most respectable, but modest, home be permitted to prevent the sale or in any event why should the covenants be not determined nonenforceable and the defendant relegated to pecuniary damages.

Plaintiffs' predecessor owned the tract free and clear of all restrictions. He could do with the parcel as he saw best. He elected to promote a residential development and in the furtherance of his plan and as an inducement to purchasers he imposed the residential restrictions. The defendant relied upon them and has a right to continue to rely thereon. It is not a question of balancing equities or equating the advantages of a hospital on this site with the effect it would have on defendant's property. Nor does the fact that defendant is the only one of the few purchasers from plaintiffs' predecessor in title who has refused to release the covenants make defendant's insistence upon the enforcement of the covenants . . . less deserving of the Court's protection and safeguarding of her rights.

The opinion of Judge Cardozo in Evangelical Lutheran Church of the Ascension of Snyder v. Sahlem, 254 N.Y. 161, is quoted at length since the questions therein presented are so similar to those in the case at bar.

> By the settled doctrine of equity, restrictive covenants in respect of land will be enforced by preventive remedies while the violation is still in prospect, unless the attitude of the complaining owner in standing on his covenant is unconscionable

or oppressive. Relief is not withheld because the money damage is unsubstantial or even none at all. . . .

Here, in the case at hand, no process of balancing the equities can make the plaintiff's the greater when compared with the defendant's, or even place the two in equipoise. The defendant, the owner, has done nothing but insist upon adherence to a covenant which is now as valid and binding as at the hour of its making. His neighbors are willing to modify the restriction and forego a portion of their rights. He refuses to go with them. Rightly or wrongly he believes that the comfort of his dwelling will be imperiled by the change, and so he chooses to abide by the covenant as framed. The choice is for him only. Neither at law nor in equity is it written that a license has been granted to religious corporations, by reason of the high purpose of their being, to set covenants at naught. Indeed, if in such matters there can be degrees of obligation, one would suppose that a more sensitive adherence to the demands of plighted faith might be expected of them than would be looked for of the world at large. Other owners may consent. One owner, the defendant, satisfied with the existing state of things, refuses to disturb it. He will be protected in his refusal by all the power of the law.

[Handwritten margin notes: "Cannot compare what their interests are."; "Just b/c purpose of restriction being lifted is large, does not mean Δ has to agree."; "Δ would be protected."]

For the reasons stated in . . . Judge Cardozo's opinion, and since Section 346 of the Real Property Law provides no basis for awarding pecuniary damages when the restriction is not outmoded and when it affords real benefit to the person seeking its enforcement, no consideration can or should be given to any award of pecuniary damages to the defendant in lieu of the enforcement of the restrictions. The plaintiffs, thus, have not established their proof under either cause of action and are not entitled to the declaratory judgment they seek.

[Handwritten margin note: "Δ gets no damages but π denied declaratory judgment"]

Notes and Questions

1. If building a hospital in this location is important to the community, is there anything that can be done to force West to give up her covenant? Would it be appropriate for the town to exercise its powers of eminent domain to extinguish the covenant?

2. Section 346 of the Real Property Law now codified as McKinney's Real Property Acts Law § 1951, provides:

§ 1951. Extinguishment of non-substantial restrictions on the use of land.

1. No restriction on the use of land . . . shall be enforced by injunction . . . or determined to be enforceable, if . . . it appears that the restriction is of no actual and substantial benefit to the persons seeking its enforcement . . . either because the purpose of the restriction has already been accomplished or, by reason of changed conditions or other cause, its purpose is not capable of accomplishment, or for any other reason.

2. . . . [I]f the court shall find that the restriction is of no actual and substantial benefit . . . it may adjudge that the restriction is not enforceable by injunction . . . and that it shall be completely extinguished upon payment, to the person or persons who would otherwise be entitled to enforce it in the event of a breach at the

time of the action, of such damages, if any, as such person or persons will sustain from the extinguishment of the restriction.

Would you recommend that the New York statute be amended along the lines of Mass. Gen. Laws ch. 184, § 30?[42]

> No restriction shall . . . be enforced . . . unless it is determined that the restriction is . . . of actual and substantial benefit to a person claiming rights of enforcement. . . . No restriction determined to be of such benefit shall be enforced . . . except in appropriate cases by award of money damages, if
>
> (1) changes in the character of the properties affected or their neighborhood, . . . in applicable public controls of land use or construction, or in any other conditions or circumstances, reduce materially the need for the restriction or the likelihood of the restriction accomplishing its original purposes or render it obsolete or inequitable to enforce except by award of money damages, or . . .
>
> (4) continuation of the restriction . . . would impede reasonable use of land for purposes for which it is most suitable, and would tend to impair the growth of the neighborhood or municipality in a manner inconsistent with the public interest . . . or
>
> (5) enforcement, except by award of money damages, is for any other reason inequitable or not in the public interest.

3. When, if ever, is it appropriate to force a buyout of a covenant that still has some value (other than its buyout price) to the beneficiary? Carol M. Rose, *Servitudes, Security, and Assent: Some Comments on Professor French and Reichman,* 55 S. Cal. L. Rev. 1403, 1414 (1982), cautions against using the changed conditions doctrine against holdouts:

> The right to "hold out," for whatever idiotic reasons, is an aspect of the right to hold property. It is normally relaxed only through an eminent domain proceeding for a public purpose, a proceeding which is approved by the elected representatives of the community. The mere fact that some other private individual might put my property to a higher market-value use than I do does not mean that he is serving a public purpose, so that I have to "sell" to him at the "price" of market damages. If we are to take servitudes seriously as property rights, then the neighbors' holdout is perfectly legitimate.
>
> Second, the holdout has too often been treated as a rascal. Sometimes the purported holdout has a genuine interest in his property right, however irrationally inflated that interest may seem to the world at large. To protect such an owner, we have to protect the opportunist as well, except insofar as doctrines such as duress or unconscionability enable us to distinguish between the two. And sometimes the holdout may confer a long term benefit, even though the benefit is not obvious at the time. One has only to read Professor Dunham's charming story about the crotchety Montgomery Ward, who thwarted construction in Chicago's downtown

---

42. This statute was upheld against a claim that it unconstitutionally took property interests without compensation in Blakely v. Gorin, 313 N.E.2d 903, 909 (Mass. 1974).

lakeshore park by insisting on his servitude right to an unobstructed vista to the lake, to realize that today's "holdout" may be tomorrow's culture hero.[38]

Comment *b* to Restatement § 8.3, Availability and Selection of Remedies for Enforcement of a Servitude, provides:

> *b.* An award of damages instead of injunctive relief that would allow the other party to buy out of the servitude obligation will seldom be appropriate so long as the servitude continues to serve the purpose contemplated at its creation. This consideration is even more important for conservation and preservation servitudes than for other types of servitudes.

Note: Developers' Powers to Modify or Release Covenants

At one time, retention by the developer of a power to modify or release subdivision restrictions was thought to negate the idea of a general plan of development. Since the existence of a general plan was normally used as the basis for implying that all lots in the subdivision were subject to reciprocal servitudes enforceable by and against each lot, the consequence was that only the developer could enforce the covenants and the only lots subject to the covenants were those whose deeds expressly subjected them to the covenants. In a modern declaration of servitudes that expressly provides enforcement rights to all lot or unit owners, retention of such a power does not affect the reciprocal enforcement rights, but interpretation questions arise as to the extent of the power.

In *Berger v. Van Sweringen Co.*, 216 N.E.2d 54 (Ohio 1966), homeowners successfully challenged the developer's change of restrictions on 80 acres from residential to commercial use to allow construction of a shopping center. The covenants provided:

> 17. The Van Sweringen Company reserves the right to waive, change or cancel any and all of the restrictions . . . in respect to lots or parcels within the Van Sweringen Company's subdivisions, or elsewhere, if in its judgment, the development warrants the same or if, in its judgment, the ends or purposes of said subdivisions would be better served.

The court held that the change was an abuse of discretion and that the "obvious purpose of paragraph 17 was to provide a means whereby one who bought property in good faith could escape the burden of the restrictions if it was found to be impossible to continue the development as planned, and still provide protection for the property of the surrounding owners who bought on the strength of the restrictions." Would the court be able to reach the same result under Restatement § 6.21? "A developer may not exercise a power to amend or modify the declaration in a way that would materially change the character of the development or the burdens on the existing community members unless the declaration fairly apprises purchasers that the power could be used for the kind of change proposed."

---

38. Dunham, *The Chicago Lake Front and A. Montgomery Ward*, 25 U. Chi. L. Sch. Rec. 11 (Winter 1979) (originally published as an appendix in Welfare Council of Metropolitan Chicago, Open Space Areas (1966)).

b. Amendment

EVERGREEN HIGHLANDS ASSOCIATION v. WEST
Supreme Court of Colorado, en banc
73 P.3d 1 (2003)

Justice RICE delivered the Opinion of the Court. . . . Petitioner . . . is the homeowner association for Evergreen Highlands Subdivision—Unit 4. . . . The subdivision consists of sixty-three lots, associated roads, and a 22.3 acre park area which is open to use by all residents of the subdivision. The Association holds title to and maintains the park area, which contains hiking and equestrian trails, a barn and stables, a ball field, a fishing pond, and tennis courts. The park area is almost completely surrounded by private homeowners' lots, with no fence or other boundary separating the park area from the homes. Respondent Robert A. West owns one of the lots bordering directly on the park area, and has used the facilities there to play tennis, fish, and walk his dog.

Evergreen Highlands Subdivision was created and its plat filed in 1972. The plat indicated that the park area was to be conveyed to the homeowners association. Protective covenants for Evergreen Highlands were also filed in 1972, but did not require lot owners to be members of or pay dues to the Association. The Association, however, was incorporated in 1973 for the purposes of maintaining the common area and facilities, enforcing the covenants, paying taxes on the common area, and determining annual fees. The developer conveyed the park area to the Association in 1976. Between the years of 1976 and 1995, when the modification of the covenants at issue in this case occurred, the Association relied on voluntary assessments from lot owners to pay for maintenance of and improvements to the park area. Such expenses included property taxes, insurance for the park area and its structures, weed spraying, tennis court resurfacing, and barn and stable maintenance.

Article 13 of the original Evergreen Highlands covenants provides that a majority of lot owners may agree to modify the covenants, stating in relevant part as follows:

[T]he owners of seventy-five percent of the lots which are subject to these covenants may release all or part of the land so restricted from any one or more of said restrictions, *or may change or modify any one or more of said restrictions*, by executing and acknowledging an appropriate agreement or agreements in writing for such purposes and filing the same in the Office of the County Clerk and Recorder of Jefferson County, Colorado.

. . . In 1995, . . . at least seventy-five percent of Evergreen Highlands' lot owners voted to add a new Article 16 to the covenants. This article required all lot owners to be members of and pay assessments to the Association, and permitted the Association to impose liens on the property of any owners who failed to pay their assessment. Assessments were set at fifty dollars per year per lot.

Respondent purchased his lot in 1986 when membership in the Association and payment of assessments was voluntary, a fact that Respondent contends positively influenced his decision to purchase in Evergreen Highlands. Respondent was not among the majority of homeowners who approved the 1995 amendment to the covenants, and he subsequently refused to pay his lot assessment. When the Association threatened to record a lien against his property, Respondent filed this lawsuit challenging the validity of the 1995 amendment. The Association counterclaimed for a declaratory judgment that it had the implied power to collect assessments from all lot owners in the subdivision, and accordingly sought damages from West for breach of the implied contract. The district court ruled in favor of the Association on the ground that the amendment was valid and binding; therefore, it never reached the merits of the Association's counterclaims.

The court of appeals reversed, finding that the terms "change or modify" as set forth in the modification clause of the covenants did not allow for the addition of a wholly new covenant, but only for modifications to the existing covenants. . . . We granted certiorari and now reverse and remand. . . .

We begin our analysis by examining the modification clause . . . to determine if its scope is broad enough to allow for the addition of a wholly new covenant by the requisite majority of property owners. . . . [T]his is an issue of first impression in Colorado. . . .

We next examine the question whether the Association has an implied right to levy assessments against lot owners in order to maintain common areas of the subdivision. Although many subdivisions have covenants which mandate the payment of assessments for this purpose, others, such as Evergreen Highlands, do not.[3] Without the implied authority to levy assessments, these latter communities are placed in the untenable position of being obligated to maintain facilities and infrastructure without any viable economic means by which to do so. In order to avoid the grave public policy concerns this outcome would create, we today adopt the approach taken by many other states as well as the Restatement of Property, which provides that "the power to raise funds reasonably necessary to carry out the functions of a common interest community will be implied if not expressly granted by the declaration." *Restatement (Third) of Property: Servitudes* § 6.5 cmt. *b* (2000). We therefore hold that, even in the absence of an express covenant mandating the payment of assessments, the Association has the implied power to levy assessments against lot owners in order to raise the necessary funds to maintain the common areas of the subdivision.

A. Modification Clause of the Evergreen Highlands Covenants . . .

1. The Lakeland Line of Cases

The court of appeals adopted the line of cases following Lakeland Property Owners Association v. Larson, 459 N.E.2d 1164 (Ill. Ct. App. 1984). That case involved a situation . . . in which a majority of lot owners voted to add a new covenant creating mandatory assessments and vesting the homeowner association with the power to impose liens for non-payment. Interpreting very similar covenant modification language allowing a majority of the property owners to "change the said covenants in whole or in part," the court disallowed the

---

3. Amicus Curiae Community Associations Institute, a national nonprofit research and education organization, estimates that approximately 2,000 Colorado communities, housing an estimated 450,000 people, fall into the latter category.

adoption of the new covenant. It held that "[t]he provision—clearly directs itself to changes of existing covenants, not the adding of new covenants which have no relation to existing ones." The *Lakeland* reasoning has been adopted by other states. . . .

2.   The Zito *Line of Cases*

Despite the fact that the *Lakeland* reasoning has been followed by other courts as recently as 2000, the same court that decided *Lakeland* issued a contrary opinion in 1992 with little explanation.[4] In Zito v. Gerken, 587 N.E.2d 1048 (Ill. Ct. App. 1992), existing subdivision covenants granted the homeowners association the authority to modify the covenants, although the exact language of the modification clause is not provided. The homeowners association adopted mandatory assessments and disgruntled homeowners sued. This time, however, the Illinois Appellate Court held in favor of the homeowners association, holding that: "[a] restrictive covenant which has been modified, altered or amended will be enforced if it is clear, unambiguous and reasonable"; "[t]he 1987 amendment does not seek to change the character of [the subdivision] or to impose unreasonable burdens upon any lot owners"; and "the terms and conditions of the 1987 amendment impose a minimal collective burden upon the residents." . . .

3.   Application to the Evergreen Highlands Covenants

. . . Respondent contends that these cases can be distinguished by how narrowly or broadly the particular modification clause is written, and argues that the amendatory language in Evergreen Highlands' covenants is much more akin to the narrow language found in the *Lakeland* line of cases than the more expansive language found in the *Zito* line of cases. . . .

There is little substance to the distinction between the "broad" or "narrow" amendatory language . . . . The covenant modification language in [the] *Lakeland* . . . [line of cases] allowed a majority of lot owners to "change" the covenants, and . . . to "change or alter" the covenants. The amendatory language in . . . [the *Zito* line] however, provided that the covenants could be "waived, abandoned, terminated, modified, altered or changed." . . . The last three words—"modified, altered, or changed"—are the same as those in the *Lakeland* line of cases, with the addition of "altered," which is simply a synonym for "change" and "modify." Thus, distinguishing these cases from one another based on the breadth of the language used is an artificial, and ultimately unpersuasive, distinction. . . .

. . . We instead conclude that the different outcomes in the *Lakeland* and *Zito* lines of cases are based on the differing factual scenarios and severity of consequences that the cases present. In those cases where courts disallowed the amendment of covenants, the impact upon the objecting lot owner was generally far more substantial and unforeseeable than the amendment at issue here. *See, e.g., Caughlin Ranch*, 849 P.2d 310 (Nev. 1993) (covenants previously

---

4.   *Zito* was issued by a different division of the Illinois Appellate Court with only a "*but see*" reference to the earlier ruling in *Lakeland*. . . .

imposing assessments only on private lots amended to assess the sole commercial parcel in the subdivision at a substantially higher rate); Boyles v. Hausmann, 517 N.W.2d 610 (Neb. 1994) (changed setback requirement rendered plaintiff's lot unbuildable); Meresse v. Stelma, 999 P.2d 1267 (Wash. Ct. App. 2000) (increased access road easement deprived plaintiff of a portion of his private lot).

In contrast, *Zito*, [and the cases that followed it], like this case, all specifically considered—and allowed—the amendment of covenants in order to impose mandatory assessments on lot owners for the purpose of maintaining common elements of a subdivision. We accordingly find the *Zito* line of cases more applicable to the situation here. This interpretation also avoids the absurd result that could follow from application of the *Lakeland* reasoning; Evergreen Highlands would be unable to adopt a mandatory-assessment covenant when its original covenants were silent on the subject, yet could adopt such a covenant if its original covenants had expressly prohibited a mandatory-assessment covenant.

. . . [T]he amendment in this case was changed according to the modification clause of the original Evergreen Highlands covenants, and it is undisputed that Respondent was on actual notice of that clause when he purchased his lot in 1986. In addition, we note that, at fifty dollars per year, the mandatory assessment imposed on Respondent is neither unreasonable not burdensome. To the contrary, the existence of a well-maintained park area immediately adjacent to Respondent's lot undoubtedly enhances Respondent's property value. . . .

B. The Implied Power of Homeowners Associations to Impose Mandatory Dues on Lot Owners for the Maintenance of Common Areas

. . . This being a question of first impression in Colorado, we first examine case law from other jurisdictions and find it largely in concurrence with our holding. When faced with this issue, a substantial number of states have arrived at the conclusion that homeowner associations have the implied power to levy dues or assessments even in the absence of express authority. . . .

Reflecting this considerable body of law, the newest version of the *Restatement of Property (Servitudes)* [§ 6.5(1) (a)] provides that "a common-interest community has the power to raise the funds reasonably necessary to carry out its functions by levying assessments against the individually owned property in the community . . . ." In addition, as explained in a comment to that section, the power to levy assessments "will be implied if not expressly granted by the declaration or by statute[,]" *see also* Wayne S. Hyatt, *Condominium and Homeowner Association Practice: Community Association Law* 36 (1981) ("The assessment is not equivalent to membership dues or some other discretionary charge. . . . As long as legitimate expenses are incurred, the individual member must bear his or her share.").

We find the Restatement and case law from other states persuasive . . . . In addition, these authorities are in harmony with the legislative purpose motivating the enactment of CCIOA [Colorado Common Interest Ownership Act]. ("That the continuation of the economic prosperity of Colorado is dependent upon the strengthening of homeowner associations . . . through enhancing the financial stability of associations by increasing the association's powers to collect delinquent assessment"); ("That it is the policy of this state to promote effective and efficient property management through defined operational requirements that preserve flexibility for such homeowner associations").

Respondent, however, argues that the implied power to mandate assessments can only be imputed to "common interest communities," which both CCIOA and the Restatement define as residential communities in which there exists a mandatory obligation or servitude imposed on individual owners to pay for common elements of the community. Respondent therefore contends that because the original covenants did not impose such a servitude, Evergreen Highlands is not a common interest community, and accordingly cannot have the implied power to levy assessments against its members pursuant to these authorities.

Respondent's argument, however, relies on the assumption that the servitude or obligation to pay which would have defined Evergreen Highlands as a common interest community was required to have been made express in the covenants or in his deed. This assumption is incorrect. CCIOA provides only that the obligation must arise from the "declarations," which are defined as "any recorded instruments however denominated, that create a common interest community, including any amendments to those instruments and also including, but not limited to, plats and maps." § 38-33.3-103(13), 10 C.R.S. (2002) . . . .

The declarations in effect for Evergreen Highlands in 1986 incorporated all documents recorded up to that date, and included not only: (1) the covenants, but also; (2) the 1972 plat, which noted that the park area would be conveyed to the homeowners association; (3) the 1973 Articles of Incorporation for the Association stating that the Association's purposes were to "own, acquire, build, operate, and maintain" the common area and facilities, to pay taxes on same, and to "determine annual membership or use fees"; and (4) the 1976 deed whereby the developer quit-claimed his ownership in the park area to the Association.

At the time Respondent purchased his lot in 1986, the Evergreen Highlands' declarations made clear that a homeowners association existed, it owned and maintained the park area, and it had the power to impose annual membership or use fees on lot owners. These declarations were sufficient to create a common interest community by implication. As explained by the Restatement:

> An implied obligation may . . . be found where the declaration expressly creates an association for the purpose of managing common property or enforcing use restrictions and design controls, but fails to include a mechanism for providing the funds necessary to carry out its functions. When such an implied obligation is established, the lots are a common-interest community within the meaning of this Chapter.

Restatement (Third) of Property: Servitudes § 6.2 cmt. *a* (2000); *see also id.* at illus. 2 (citing an example virtually identical to that of Evergreen Highlands and finding it a common interest community by judicial decree).

We accordingly adopt the position taken by the Restatement and many other states, and hold that the declarations for Evergreen Highlands were sufficient to create a common interest community by implication. The Association therefore has the implicit power to levy assessments against lot owners for the purpose of maintaining the common area of the subdivision. . . .

Notes and Questions

1. Do you find the distinction the court draws between the *Lakeland* and *Zito* lines of cases persuasive? Restatement (Third) § 6.10(2) provides that amendments that do not apply uniformly to similar lots and amendments that treat members unfairly are not effective without approval of the members whose interests would be adversely affected.

2. If property owners in a community such as Evergreen Highlands are not allowed to amend their covenants to require all the community members to contribute to maintenance of the common property, what is likely to happen? Are there other ways to overcome the free-rider problems created by people like respondent West?

c. Termination

WESTWOOD HOMEOWNERS ASS'N v. LANE COUNTY

Supreme Court of Oregon (en banc)
864 P.2d 350 (Or. 1993)

UNIS, J. ORS 312.270(1) provides that "[w]hen a county acquires real property by foreclosure for delinquent taxes, the conveyance vests in the county title to the property, free from all liens and encumbrances." The issue in this case is whether, under that statute, servitudes that benefit and burden individual lots in a planned unit development[43] survive a tax foreclosure sale at which a county acquires title. . . .

[Westwood PUD is a planned unit development governed by a recorded declaration (CCRs) that includes a covenant requiring all lot owners to be members of and pay assessments to the Westwood Homeowners Association. Assessments, which are secured by liens against the lots, are to be used, among other things, for maintenance of the roads in Westwood. — EDS.]

On May 27, 1988, Lane County acquired title to 15 lots in Westwood PUD as a result of statutory tax foreclosure proceedings under ORS chapter 312 for nonpayment of real property taxes.[6] After the tax foreclosure sale, the Association made assessments against each of the 15 lots for road and common area maintenance fees that were incurred after Lane County acquired title. . . . Lane County refused to pay those charges.

---

43. The words "planned unit development" and "planned community" are used interchangeably in this opinion. [Planned community is covered by the term *common interest community* used in the Restatement and in this book. — EDS.]

6. In 1986, Lane County initiated the statutory foreclosure proceedings. On January 28, 1987, a judgment and decree of foreclosure was entered, foreclosing the 15 lots for nonpayment of real property taxes. As required by statutes then in effect, those properties were held by the Lane County Assessor, acting as the Lane County Tax Collector, for a redemption period of one year. The current redemption period is two years. ORS 312.120. None of the 15 lots was redeemed. On May 27, 1988, the Lane County Tax Collector deeded title to the 15 lots to Lane County in accordance with the provisions of ORS 312.120 and ORS 312.200.

In 1990, the Association filed an action . . . to foreclose the Association's lien on the 15 lots for the approximately $18,000 in unpaid assessments that had accumulated between January 1988 and August 1990. . . . Lane County filed a counterclaim to quiet title or to foreclose the Association's lien if it had not been extinguished by the tax foreclosure. Both parties moved for summary judgment. . . . Lane County argued that the CCRs and the Association's power under the CCRs to make assessments . . . created "liens" or "encumbrances" within the meaning of [the tax foreclosure statute], with the result that . . . the tax foreclosure had extinguished not only all pre-foreclosure liens resulting from assessments against the 15 lots made under the CCRs, but also the CCRs, including the Association's power under the CCRs to make annual and special assessments against the 15 lots. . . .

The Association's position was that, although its liens for pre-foreclosure assessments on the 15 lots were extinguished by the tax foreclosure sale, the CCRs and the Association's power to make assessments were not themselves extinguished. The Association asserted that lots owned by other Westwood PUD home owners benefit from the CCRs, which it asserted are "servitudes," not "liens" or "encumbrances."

The trial court granted summary judgment for the Association, allowed the Association to foreclose against Lane County, and denied Lane County any relief on its counterclaim. On appeal by Lane County, the Court of Appeals affirmed. . . . We allowed Lane County's petition for review to determine the effect of the statutory tax foreclosure sale on the CCRs and the Association's power under the CCRs to make post-tax-foreclosure annual and special assessments. . . .

Whether the CCRs survive the statutory tax foreclosure sale turns on the meaning of the terms "liens" and "encumbrances" in ORS 312.270 (1).

As a threshold matter, we observe that neither "lien" nor "encumbrance" is defined in ORS chapter 311, which governs the collection of property taxes, or in ORS chapter 312, which sets forth the provisions for foreclosure of property tax liens. . . .

The term "lien" has a common and well-understood meaning. A "lien" is a "claim, encumbrance, or charge on property for payment of some debt, obligation or duty." *Black's Law Dictionary* 922 (6th ed. 1990). "A lien is a security right given to a person to sell or seize the collateral subject to the lien." Natelson, *Law of Property Owner Associations*, at 39, § 2.1. In the absence of some suggestion in the statute's text or context that a different meaning was intended, we can apply the foregoing definition to the facts of this case. When we do, the power to make assessments and a covenant to pay assessments are readily distinguishable from a lien for past-due assessments. From . . . the nature or character of the CCRs and the Association's power to make annual and special assessments against the lots in Westwood PUD, it is clear that the CCRs and the Association's power to make assessments . . . are not "liens."

Further support for the proposition that servitudes are not liens can be found in Crawford et al. v. Senosky et al., 128 Or. 229, 274 P. 306 (1929). In that case, this court stated that "the foreclosure of a tax lien does not cut off easements that have been carved out of one property for the benefit of another." The court added:

> "An easement is a servitude upon, and differs from an interest in, or lien upon, the land. It is not a part of, but is so much carved out of the estate in, the land,

and is as much a thing apart from that estate as a parcel of the land itself conveyed from it." . . .

Until and unless the Association exercises its power to make annual or special assessments against a particular lot in Westwood PUD for the purposes specified in the CCRs, there is no lien against that lot, *i.e.*, there is no claim or charge on the lot for payment of some debt, obligation, or duty. We hold that the servitudes created by the Westwood PUD CCRs are not "liens," as that term is used in ORS 312.270(1).

The more difficult question is whether the CCRs, which include the Association's power to make annual or special assessments against the lots within the Westwood PUD, are "encumbrances". . . . The term "encumbrance" may mean different things in different contexts. In the context of a grantor's covenant in a warranty deed . . . that the premises are "free and clear of all encumbrances," this court in Leach v. Gunnarson, 619 P.2d 263 (Or. 1980), stated that "encumbrance" means "any right to or interest in the land, subsisting in a third person, to the diminution of the value of the land, though consistent with the passing of the fee by conveyance."

The word "encumbrance," as used in ORS 312.270(1), could also mean, as the Court of Appeals held in this case, "only those encumbrances that are [in the nature of] money or security interests in the subject property." *See also Black's Law Dictionary, supra,* at 527 (an "encumbrance" is a "claim, lien, charge, or liability attached to and binding real property"). The meaning attributed to the term "encumbrances" . . . by the Court of Appeals is supported by the terms of a related statute, ORS 311.405(7) (a), which provides:

> ". . . liens for *ad valorem* taxes . . . are superior to, have priority over and shall be fully satisfied before all other liens, judgments, mortgages, security interests *or encumbrances* on the property without regard to date of creation, filing or recording." (Emphasis added.)

The requirement that *ad valorem* taxes be fully satisfied before "encumbrances" suggests that the term "encumbrances" as [there] used . . . relates to a claim for money or a security interest in the subject property.

The foregoing conclusion is bolstered by an examination of the method under which real property is assessed for taxation purposes. . . . In Crawford et al. v. Senosky et al., *supra*, this court held that a restrictive covenant (servitude) was not extinguished by a tax sale under a former statute. The court followed the "tax assessment approach," which focuses on the actual assessed value of property on which the tax lien is based:

> The property assessed and the property conveyed upon the tax sale must be the same. If the assessment is only of the servient estate, only that can be conveyed on a tax sale; and, vice versa, if the conveyance on the tax sale, or on the foreclosure of a tax lien, is of all the estate or interests in the land, freed from servitudes as well as liens thereon, then the assessment must be based upon the land as land, regardless of servitudes as well as liens. . . . [I]n making the assessment a deduction must be made for easements, whereas none is made for liens and the like interests. . . .

Under the tax assessment approach, the only interests transferred by a tax sale are those interests that were assessed in establishing the value of the property for *ad valorem* tax purposes.[11] Any interest not assessed would not be transferred by the tax foreclosure deed and would remain in effect. *See* Crawford et al. v. Senosky et al., *supra,* 128 Or. at 232-34, 274 P. 306 (restrictive covenant survives tax sale because, under the tax assessment approach, the tax sale vendee acquires a purely derivative title, which leaves the servitude untouched).

. . . [I]t is reasonable to assume that the tax payable on a dominant lot is assessed not only on the lot itself, but also on any servitudes beneficial to the dominant lot. Applying the current method of assessing real property . . . to servitudes, the burden of a servitude would tend to lower the assessed value of the servient estate, resulting in a lower tax liability. In effect, the servitude is carved out of the land being taxed. On the other hand, the benefit of the servitude would enhance the value of the dominant estate and result in an increased tax liability. Thus, if the servitude is assessed with the dominant tenement, the servitude should be secure from the effect of a tax foreclosure deed.

. . . [T]here are several reasons that persuade us that the legislature would have intended to exclude servitudes from the meaning of the term "encumbrances" in ORS 312.270(1). The CCRs in a planned community are important land use planning devices. CCRs enhance the value and enjoyment of planned community property and induce purchasers to buy lots in the development. Survival of those servitudes ensures that the planned community maintains its planned character. . . . The purchasers of property in a planned community rely on the stability of the planned community arrangement as an assurance that a particular type of lifestyle is maintained. The enforcement of servitudes is essential to foster planned community development. If the benefits of the servitudes, which the lot owners have enjoyed, are extinguished as a result of a tax foreclosure sale, potentially disastrous consequences could result. We do not believe that the legislature would have intended the planned character of a community . . . and the expectations of the homeowners to be defeated in this way.

Indeed, in enacting . . . the Oregon Planned Community Act, . . . the Legislative Assembly recognized the socio-economic utility of private land controls and the importance of protecting the interests of the owners of lots in a planned community:

> It is a matter of statewide concern that the Legislative Assembly address problems associated with homeowners associations in order to make this kind of home ownership pattern an acceptable choice and in order to assure proper maintenance of the projects so that the investment of the owners and the appearance of Oregon communities are protected. . . .

. . . "If the sale of land for nonpayment of taxes extinguishes the burden of a covenant respecting the use of the land sold, then an entire subdivision can

---

11. The tax assessment approach has been criticized as being unrealistic and artificial because, it is asserted, tax assessors rarely have the time or inclination to concern themselves with nonvisible servitudes. Note, *The Effect of Tax Foreclosure Sales on Servitudes:* Olympia v. Palzer, 11 Puget Sound L. Rev. 193, 200 (1987); Kratovil, *Tax Titles: Extinguishment of Easements, Building Restrictions, and Covenants,* 19 Houston L. Rev. 55, 57-58 (1981). The tax assessment approach is, however, accepted by the Restatement of Property § 509, comment *a* (1944).

have the value of each of its lots seriously impaired by the tax delinquency of a single lot owner." 5 Powell, *The Law of Property* 60-157, § 679[4] (Gruber rev. 1993).

We further note that to hold that the tax foreclosure sale extinguished the CCRs arguably would deprive Lane County of all servitude benefits that are appurtenant to those lots as dominant estates. We do not believe that the legislature would have intended such a result. We believe that the legislature would, instead, have intended to protect the servitude benefits to both the dominant and servient estates. . . .

There is yet another reason to support the conclusion that the legislature would have intended the word "encumbrances" to relate to only claims for money or security interests in the subject property. . . . [I]f the tax assessment is only of the servient estate, . . . a tax foreclosure that extinguishes servitudes of the dominant estate arguably would infringe on the constitutional rights of the owners of the dominant tenements, depriving them of their property without due process of law. . . . We see no reason to assume that the legislature would wish to raise such questions.

In sum, we do not believe that the legislature, in enacting ORS 312.270(1), would have intended to extinguish servitudes in a tax foreclosure sale in which the county acquires title to property. We hold that the word "encumbrances" in ORS 312.270(1) does not include servitudes. Consequently, the tax sale of the 15 lots in Westwood PUD did not extinguish the CCRs or the Association's power to make post-tax-foreclosure assessments. Lane County, therefore, took title . . . subject to the servitudes. The decision of the Court of Appeals and the judgment of the circuit court are affirmed.

Notes and Questions

1. If the county had been successful in quieting its title against the encumbrance of the servitudes, would it have been entitled to continue using the streets of Westwood? If so, how would its obligation to contribute to the costs of street maintenance be measured? Should rights to use the association-owned tennis courts and swimming pool be treated the same way?

2. If the county had been successful, would it retain the ability to enforce the covenants against neighboring lots? On what basis could you argue that the benefit of the covenants appurtenant to the 15 lots had been extinguished or were otherwise unenforceable?

3. The court notes that its decision avoids a potential constitutional problem that would be raised if the tax foreclosure sale extinguished the benefit of the covenants held by other Westwood lot owners. At one time, the theory that covenant benefits were "mere" contractual rights, rather than property rights protected by the takings clauses of state and federal constitutions, enjoyed some currency, but the better and majority view, today, is that covenant benefits are property interests subject to the Statute of Frauds and protected by the constitutional takings clauses. *See Southern California Edison Co. v. Bourgerie*, 507 P.2d 964 (Cal. 1973) (en banc); William Stoebuck, *Condemnation of Rights the Condemnee Holds in Lands of Another*, 56 Iowa L. Rev. 293 (1970).

Restatement (Third) § 7.9, Termination by
Foreclosure Sale or Bankruptcy Proceedings

(1) A servitude is not extinguished by foreclosure of a lien against the estate burdened by the servitude unless the lien has priority over the servitude. If the lien was created later than the servitude, but is given priority ahead of earlier created interests by a statute other than a recording act, the foreclosure sale does not extinguish easements, restrictive covenants, conservation servitudes, or servitudes imposed as part of a general plan of development, unless the statute requires otherwise.

(2) No servitude, other than a covenant to pay money that is not imposed as part of a general plan of development, conservation servitude, or easement arrangement, is extinguishable in a bankruptcy proceeding, unless otherwise required by statute.

CHAPTER 13

The Takings Clause

No person shall be held to answer for a capital, or otherwise infamous crime, unless on a presentment or indictment of a grand jury, except in cases arising in the land or naval forces, or in the militia, when in actual service in time of war or public danger; nor shall any person be subject for the same offense to be twice put in jeopardy of life or limb; nor shall be compelled in any criminal case to be a witness against himself, **nor be deprived of** *life, liberty, or* **property, without due process of law; nor shall private property be taken for public use, without just compensation***.

mark need due process

Fifth Amendment to the United States Constitution (1791)

All persons born or naturalized in the United States, and subject to the jurisdiction thereof, are citizens of the United States and of the state wherein they reside. No state shall make or enforce any law which shall abridge the privileges or immunities of citizens of the United States; **nor shall any state deprive any person of life, liberty, or property, without due process of law;** *nor deny to any person within its jurisdiction the equal protection of the laws.*

Section I, Fourteenth Amendment to the United States Constitution (1868)

The content of due process is "a historical product" that traces all the way back to chapter 39 of Magna Carta, in which King John promised that "[n]o free man shall be taken or imprisoned or disseized or exiled or in any way destroyed, nor will we go upon him nor send upon him, except by the lawful judgment of his peers or by the law of the land." The phrase "due process of law" first appeared in a statutory rendition of this chapter in 1354. "No man of what state or condition he be, shall be put out of his lands or tenements nor taken, nor disinherited, nor put to death, without he be brought to answer by due process of law."

CRS (Congressional Research Service) Annotated Constitution[1]

The government's power to take land for public projects, often called the power of eminent domain or condemnation, has long been regarded as an inherent part of sovereignty, but the legal obligation to pay for what is taken is more recent. The Takings Clause of the Fifth Amendment to the U.S. Constitution, effective in 1791, imposed the obligation to pay just compensation on the federal government, but did not apply to the states until incorporated into the

1. Available online at the Cornell University Law School Legal Information Institute website.

811

Fourteenth Amendment in 1897 (*Chicago, B. & Q.R. Co. v. Chicago*, 166 U.S. 226). State constitutions, many of which predate 1897, impose independent obligations to pay for property taken by eminent domain.

When a governmental body, or other entity, with eminent domain power wishes to acquire property, it normally tries to purchase the property. Only if negotiations fail does it initiate eminent domain proceedings, which require a judicial proceeding and, often, a jury trial on the question of just compensation. If the governmental body takes possession of the property without instituting eminent domain proceedings, the property owner may bring an action in "inverse condemnation" for just compensation. In a famous case, *United States v. Causby*, 328 U.S. 256 (1946), the Court held that the United States had taken an easement over plaintiff's chicken farm by flying military aircraft across it at such a low altitude that the farming operations were severely disrupted.

In another famous case, *Loretto v. Teleprompter Manhattan CATV Corp.*, 458 U.S. 419 (1982), the court held that even a minor but permanent physical invasion of property authorized by the government is a compensable taking. In that case, a New York law required that landlords allow installation of cable TV facilities on their buildings.

The Fifth and Fourteenth Amendments impose three limitations on government's ability to take private property: The person deprived must be afforded due process of law; the property must be taken for public use; and just compensation must be paid. Due process requires that the government have a legitimate purpose for taking the property and that the means used be rationally related to the purpose for which it is taken. Just compensation generally means market value—the amount a willing buyer would pay and the amount a willing seller would accept for the property taken. It does not include factors like sentimental value, or the value of belonging to a particular community, except as they are reflected in the market value.

In this chapter we first take up the question of what is a public use, then turn to the question of what constitutes a taking. The second question involves three issues: What is "property" within the meaning of the Takings Clause; when does a governmental action that regulates, but does not take title to or possession of the property, effect a taking; and can judicial decisions that change property law be takings? Finally, we take up "exactions" —the practice of requiring donations of land, interests in land, or money in exchange for granting a permit to develop land.

A. TAKING PROPERTY FOR PUBLIC USE

Although they may be politically controversial, takings of land for governmental purposes like prisons, garbage dumps, and military installations, and for land that will be used by the public, like airports, schools, parks, and highways, are not legally controversial. Likewise, the delegation of eminent domain powers to railroads, pipeline companies, telecommunications companies, and other utilities that require unbroken corridors for their operations, is common and not ordinarily controversial. However, use of eminent domain to assemble land packages for urban renewal and redevelopment purposes where title to the land is transferred to private developers, has been highly controversial.

KELO v. CITY OF NEW LONDON

Supreme Court of the United States
545 U.S. 469 (2005)

Justice STEVENS delivered the opinion of the Court [joined by Justices BREYER, GINSBURG, KENNEDY, and SOUTER].

In 2000, the city of New London approved a development plan that, in the words of the Supreme Court of Connecticut, was "projected to create in excess of 1,000 jobs, to increase tax and other revenues, and to revitalize an economically distressed city, including its downtown and waterfront areas." In assembling the land needed for this project, the city's development agent has purchased property from willing sellers and proposes to use the power of eminent domain to acquire the remainder of the property from unwilling owners in exchange for just compensation. The question presented is whether the city's proposed disposition of this property qualifies as a "public use" within the meaning of the Takings Clause of the Fifth Amendment to the Constitution.

plan for beneficial development.

Δ looking to compensate those that won't sell.

issue: is this a taking?

I

The City of New London sits at the junction of the Thames River and Long Island Sound in southeastern Connecticut. Decades of economic decline led a state agency in 1990 to designate the City a "distressed municipality." In 1996, the Federal Government closed the Naval Undersea Warfare Center, which had been located in the Fort Trumbull area of the City and had employed over 1,500 people. In 1998, the City's unemployment rate was nearly double that of the State, and its population of just under 24,000 residents was at its lowest since 1920.

City - previous economic decline.

These conditions prompted state and local officials to target New London, and particularly its Fort Trumbull area, for economic revitalization. To this end, respondent New London Development Corporation (NLDC)—a private nonprofit entity established some years earlier to assist the City in planning economic development, was reactivated. In January 1998, the State authorized a $5.35 million bond issue to support the NLDC's planning activities and a $10 million bond issue toward the creation of a Fort Trumbull State Park. In February, the pharmaceutical company Pfizer Inc. announced that it would build a $300 million research facility on a site immediately adjacent to Fort Trumbull; local planners hoped that Pfizer would draw new business to the area, thereby serving as a catalyst to the area's rejuvenation. After receiving initial approval from the city council, the NLDC continued its planning activities and held a series of neighborhood meetings to educate the public about the process. In May, the city council authorized the NLDC to formally submit its plans to the relevant state agencies for review. Upon obtaining state-level approval, the NLDC finalized an integrated development plan focused on 90 acres of the Fort Trumbull area.

Δ called to help economic revitilization.

The Fort Trumbull area is situated on a peninsula that juts into the Thames River. The area comprises approximately 115 privately owned properties, as well as the 32 acres of land formerly occupied by the naval facility (Trumbull State Park now occupies 18 of those 32 acres). The development plan encompasses seven parcels. Parcel 1 is designated for a waterfront conference hotel at the center of a "small urban village" that will include restaurants and shopping. This parcel will also have marinas for both recreational and commercial uses. A pedestrian "riverwalk" will originate here and continue down the coast, connecting the waterfront areas of the development. Parcel 2 will be the site of approximately 80 new residences organized into an urban neighborhood and linked by public walkway to the remainder of the development, including the state park. This parcel also includes space reserved for a new U.S. Coast Guard Museum. Parcel 3, which is located immediately north of the Pfizer facility, will contain at least 90,000 square feet of research and development office space. Parcel 4A is a 2.4-acre site that will be used either to support the adjacent state park, by providing parking or retail services for visitors, or to support the nearby marina. Parcel 4B will include a renovated marina, as well as the final stretch of the riverwalk. Parcels 5, 6, and 7 will provide land for office and retail space, parking, and water-dependent commercial uses.

The NLDC intended the development plan to capitalize on the arrival of the Pfizer facility and the new commerce it was expected to attract. In addition to creating jobs, generating tax revenue, and helping to "build momentum for the revitalization of downtown New London," the plan was also designed to make the City more attractive and to create leisure and recreational opportunities on the waterfront and in the park.

The city council approved the plan in January 2000, and designated the NLDC as its development agent . . . . The city council also authorized the NLDC to purchase property or to acquire property by exercising eminent domain in the City's name. The NLDC successfully negotiated the purchase of most of the real estate in the 90-acre area, but its negotiations with petitioners failed. . . . [I]n November 2000, the NLDC initiated the condemnation proceedings that gave rise to this case.

II

Petitioner Susette Kelo has lived in the Fort Trumbull area since 1997. She has made extensive improvements to her house, which she prizes for its water view. Petitioner Wilhelmina Dery was born in her Fort Trumbull house in 1918 and has lived there her entire life. Her husband Charles (also a petitioner) has lived in the house since they married some 60 years ago. In all, the nine petitioners own 15 properties in Fort Trumbull—4 in parcel 3 of the development plan and 11 in parcel 4A. Ten of the parcels are occupied by the owner or a family member; the other five are held as investment properties. There is no allegation that any of these properties is blighted or otherwise in poor condition; . . . they were condemned only because they happen to be located in the development area.

In December 2000, petitioners brought this action in the New London Superior Court. They claimed, among other things, that the taking of their properties would violate the "public use" restriction in the Fifth Amendment. After a 7-day bench trial, the Superior Court granted a permanent restraining order prohibiting the taking of the properties located in parcel 4A (park or marina support). It, however, denied petitioners relief as to the properties located in parcel 3 (office space).[4]

After the Superior Court ruled, both sides took appeals to the Supreme Court of Connecticut. That court held, over a dissent, that all of the City's proposed takings were valid. . . . [R]elying on cases such as Hawaii Housing Authority v. Midkiff, 467 U.S. 229 (1984), and Berman v. Parker, 348 U.S. 26 (1954), the court held that such economic development qualified as a valid public use under both the Federal and State Constitutions.

The three dissenting justices would have imposed a "heightened" standard of judicial review for takings justified by economic development. Although they agreed that the plan was intended to serve a valid public use, they would have found all the takings unconstitutional because the City had failed to adduce "clear and convincing evidence" that the economic benefits of the plan would in fact come to pass. . . .

We granted certiorari to determine whether a city's decision to take property for the purpose of economic development satisfies the "public use" requirement of the Fifth Amendment.

III

Two polar propositions are perfectly clear. On the one hand, it has long been accepted that the sovereign may not take the property of A for the sole purpose of transferring it to another private party B, even though A is paid just compensation. On the other hand, it is equally clear that a State may transfer property from one private party to another if future "use by the public" is the purpose of the taking; the condemnation of land for a railroad with common-carrier duties is a familiar example. Neither of these propositions, however, determines the disposition of this case.

As for the first proposition, the City would no doubt be forbidden from taking petitioners' land for the purpose of conferring a private benefit on a particular private party. See Midkiff ("A purely private taking could not withstand the scrutiny of the public use requirement; it would serve no legitimate purpose of government and would thus be void"); . . . Nor would the City be allowed to take property under the mere pretext of a public purpose, when its actual purpose was to bestow a private benefit. The takings before us, however, would be executed pursuant to a "carefully considered" development plan. The trial judge and all the members of the Supreme Court of Connecticut agreed that there was no evidence of an illegitimate purpose in this case.[6] Therefore, as was

---

4. While this litigation was pending before the Superior Court, the NLDC announced that it would lease some of the parcels to private developers in exchange for their agreement to develop the land according to the terms of the development plan. Specifically, the NLDC was negotiating a 99-year ground lease with Corcoran Jennison, a developer selected from a group of applicants. The negotiations contemplated a nominal rent of $1 per year, but no agreement had yet been signed.

6. . . . [W]hile the City intends to transfer certain of the parcels to a private developer in a long-term lease—which developer, in turn, is expected to lease the office space and so forth to other private tenants—the identities of those private parties were not known when the plan was adopted. It is, of course, difficult to accuse the government of having taken A's property to benefit the private interests of B when the identity of B was unknown.

true of the statute challenged in *Midkiff*, the City's development plan was not adopted "to benefit a particular class of identifiable individuals."

On the other hand, this is not a case in which the City is planning to open the condemned land—at least not in its entirety—to use by the general public. Nor will the private lessees of the land in any sense be required to operate like common carriers, making their services available to all comers. . . . [T]his "Court long ago rejected any literal requirement that condemned property be put into use for the general public." Indeed, while many state courts in the mid-19th century endorsed "use by the public" as the proper definition of public use, that narrow view steadily eroded over time. Not only was the "use by the public" test difficult to administer (*e.g.*, what proportion of the public need have access to the property? at what price?), but it proved to be impractical given the diverse and always evolving needs of society.[8] Accordingly, when this Court began applying the Fifth Amendment to the States at the close of the 19th century, it embraced the broader and more natural interpretation of public use as "public purpose." Thus, in a case upholding a mining company's use of an aerial bucket line to transport ore over property it did not own, Justice Holmes' opinion for the Court stressed "the inadequacy of use by the general public as a universal test." Strickley v. Highland Boy Gold Mining Co., 200 U.S. 527, 531 (1906).[9] We have repeatedly and consistently rejected that narrow test ever since.

The disposition of this case therefore turns on the question whether the City's development plan serves a "public purpose." Without exception, our cases have defined that concept broadly, reflecting our longstanding policy of deference to legislative judgments in this field.

In Berman v. Parker, this Court upheld a redevelopment plan targeting a blighted area of Washington, D.C., in which most of the housing for the area's 5,000 inhabitants was beyond repair. Under the plan, the area would be condemned and part of it utilized for the construction of streets, schools, and other public facilities. The remainder of the land would be leased or sold to private parties for the purpose of redevelopment, including the construction of low-cost housing.

The owner of a department store located in the area challenged the condemnation, pointing out that his store was not itself blighted and arguing that the

---

8.   From upholding the Mill Acts (which authorized manufacturers dependent on power-producing dams to flood upstream lands in exchange for just compensation), to approving takings necessary for the economic development of the West through mining and irrigation, many state courts either circumvented the "use by the public" test when necessary or abandoned it completely. See Nichols, *The Meaning of Public Use in the Law of Eminent Domain*, 20 B.U.L.Rev. 615, 619-624 (1940). For example, in rejecting the "use by the public" test as overly restrictive, the Nevada Supreme Court stressed that "[m]ining is the greatest of the industrial pursuits in this state. All other interests are subservient to it. Our mountains are almost barren of timber, and our valleys could never be made profitable for agricultural purposes except for the fact of a home market having been created by the mining developments in different sections of the state. The mining and milling interests give employment to many men, and the benefits derived from this business are distributed as much, and sometimes more, among the laboring classes than with the owners of the mines and mills. . . . The present prosperity of the state is entirely due to the mining developments already made, and the entire people of the state are directly interested in having the future developments unobstructed by the obstinate action of any individual or individuals." *Dayton Gold & Silver Mining Co.*, 11 Nev., at 409-410, 1876 WL, at *11.

9.   See also Clark v. Nash, 198 U.S. 361 (1905) (upholding a statute that authorized the owner of arid land to widen a ditch on his neighbor's property so as to permit a nearby stream to irrigate his land).

creation of a "better balanced, more attractive community" was not a valid public use. Writing for a unanimous Court, Justice Douglas refused to evaluate this claim in isolation, deferring instead to the legislative and agency judgment that the area "must be planned as a whole" for the plan to be successful. The Court explained that "community redevelopment programs need not, by force of the Constitution, be on a piecemeal basis—lot by lot, building by building." The public use underlying the taking was unequivocally affirmed:

[handwritten margin note: case law: cannot consider sole house or parcel, but development plan as a whole.]

> "We do not sit to determine whether a particular housing project is or is not desirable. The concept of the public welfare is broad and inclusive . . . . The values it represents are spiritual as well as physical, aesthetic as well as monetary. It is within the power of the legislature to determine that the community should be beautiful as well as healthy, spacious as well as clean, well-balanced as well as carefully patrolled. In the present case, the Congress and its authorized agencies have made determinations that take into account a wide variety of values. It is not for us to reappraise them. If those who govern the District of Columbia decide that the Nation's Capital should be beautiful as well as sanitary, there is nothing in the Fifth Amendment that stands in the way."

In Hawaii Housing Authority v. Midkiff, 467 U.S. 229 (1984), the Court considered a Hawaii statute whereby fee title was taken from lessors and transferred to lessees (for just compensation) in order to reduce the concentration of land ownership. We unanimously upheld the statute and rejected the Ninth Circuit's view that it was "a naked attempt on the part of the state of Hawaii to take the property of A and transfer it to B solely for B's private use and benefit." Reaffirming *Berman*'s deferential approach to legislative judgments in this field, we concluded that the State's purpose of eliminating the "social and economic evils of a land oligopoly" qualified as a valid public use. Our opinion also rejected the contention that the mere fact that the State immediately transferred the properties to private individuals upon condemnation somehow diminished the public character of the taking. "[I]t is only the taking's purpose, and not its mechanics," we explained, that matters in determining public use.

[handwritten margin note: look at purpose for taking, not way it is done.]

In that same Term we decided another public use case that arose in a purely economic context. In Ruckelshaus v. Monsanto Co., 467 U.S. 986 (1984), the Court dealt with provisions of the Federal Insecticide, Fungicide, and Rodenticide Act under which the Environmental Protection Agency could consider the data (including trade secrets) submitted by a prior pesticide applicant in evaluating a subsequent application, so long as the second applicant paid just compensation for the data. We acknowledged that the "most direct beneficiaries" of these provisions were the subsequent applicants, but we nevertheless upheld the statute under *Berman* and *Midkiff*. We found sufficient Congress' belief that sparing applicants the cost of time-consuming research eliminated a significant barrier to entry in the pesticide market and thereby enhanced competition.

Viewed as a whole, our jurisprudence has recognized that the needs of society have varied between different parts of the Nation, just as they have evolved over time in response to changed circumstances. Our earliest cases in particular embodied a strong theme of federalism, emphasizing the "great respect" that we owe to state legislatures and state courts in discerning local public needs. . . . For more than a century, our public use jurisprudence has wisely eschewed rigid formulas and intrusive scrutiny in favor of affording legislatures broad latitude in determining what public needs justify the use of the takings power.

IV

Those who govern the City were not confronted with the need to remove blight in the Fort Trumbull area, but their determination that the area was sufficiently distressed to justify a program of economic rejuvenation is entitled to our deference. The City has carefully formulated an economic development plan that it believes will provide appreciable benefits to the community, including—but by no means limited to—new jobs and increased tax revenue. As with other exercises in urban planning and development, the City is endeavoring to coordinate a variety of commercial, residential, and recreational uses of land, with the hope that they will form a whole greater than the sum of its parts. . . . Given the comprehensive character of the plan, the thorough deliberation that preceded its adoption, and the limited scope of our review, it is appropriate for us, as it was in *Berman,* to resolve the challenges of the individual owners, not on a piecemeal basis, but rather in light of the entire plan. Because that plan unquestionably serves a public purpose, the takings challenged here satisfy the public use requirement of the Fifth Amendment.

To avoid this result, petitioners urge us to adopt a new bright-line rule that economic development does not qualify as a public use. . . . [N]either precedent nor logic supports petitioners' proposal. Promoting economic development is a traditional and long-accepted function of government. There is, moreover, no principled way of distinguishing economic development from the other public purposes that we have recognized. In our cases upholding takings that facilitated agriculture and mining, for example, we emphasized the importance of those industries to the welfare of the States in question, . . . in *Berman,* we endorsed the purpose of transforming a blighted area into a "well-balanced" community through redevelopment,[13] in *Midkiff,* we upheld the interest in breaking up a land oligopoly that "created artificial deterrents to the normal functioning of the State's residential land market," and in *Monsanto,* we accepted Congress' purpose of eliminating a "significant barrier to entry in the pesticide market." It would be incongruous to hold that the City's interest in the economic benefits to be derived from the development of the Fort Trumbull area has less of a public character than any of those other interests. Clearly, there is no basis for exempting economic development from our traditionally broad understanding of public purpose.

Petitioners contend that using eminent domain for economic development impermissibly blurs the boundary between public and private takings. Again, our cases foreclose this objection. Quite simply, the government's pursuit of a public purpose will often benefit individual private parties. For example, in *Midkiff,* the forced transfer of property conferred a direct and significant benefit on those lessees who were previously unable to purchase their homes. In *Monsanto,* we recognized that the "most direct beneficiaries" of the data-sharing provisions were the subsequent pesticide applicants, but benefiting them in

13. It is a misreading of *Berman* to suggest that the only public use upheld in that case was the initial removal of blight. The public use described in *Berman* extended beyond that to encompass the purpose of *developing* that area to create conditions that would prevent a reversion to blight in the future. . . . Had the public use in *Berman* been defined more narrowly, it would have been difficult to justify the taking of the plaintiff's nonblighted department store.

this way was necessary to promoting competition in the pesticide market. The owner of the department store in *Berman* objected to "taking from one businessman for the benefit of another businessman," referring to the fact that under the redevelopment plan land would be leased or sold to private developers for redevelopment.[15] Our rejection of that contention has particular relevance to the instant case: "The public end may be as well or better served through an agency of private enterprise than through a department of government—or so the Congress might conclude. We cannot say that public ownership is the sole method of promoting the public purposes of community redevelopment projects."[16]

It is further argued that without a bright-line rule nothing would stop a city from transferring citizen *A*'s property to citizen *B* for the sole reason that citizen *B* will put the property to a more productive use and thus pay more taxes. Such a one-to-one transfer of property, executed outside the confines of an integrated development plan, is not presented in this case. While such an unusual exercise of government power would certainly raise a suspicion that a private purpose was afoot,[17] the hypothetical cases posited by petitioners can be confronted if and when they arise. They do not warrant the crafting of an artificial restriction on the concept of public use.

Alternatively, petitioners maintain that for takings of this kind we should require a "reasonable certainty" that the expected public benefits will actually accrue. Such a rule, however, would represent an even greater departure from our precedent. "When the legislature's purpose is legitimate and its means are not irrational, our cases make clear that empirical debates over the wisdom of takings—no less than debates over the wisdom of other kinds of socioeconomic legislation—are not to be carried out in the federal courts." *Midkiff*. . . . The disadvantages of a heightened form of review are especially pronounced in this type of case. Orderly implementation of a comprehensive redevelopment plan obviously requires that the legal rights of all interested parties be established before new construction can be commenced. A constitutional rule that required postponement of the judicial approval of every condemnation until the likelihood of success of the plan had been assured would unquestionably impose a significant impediment to the successful consummation of many such plans.

---

15. Notably, as in the instant case, the private developers in *Berman* were required by contract to use the property to carry out the redevelopment plan.

16. Nor do our cases support Justice O'CONNOR's novel theory that the government may only take property and transfer it to private parties when the initial taking eliminates some "harmful property use." There was nothing "harmful" about the nonblighted department store at issue in *Berman*; nothing "harmful" about the lands at issue in the mining and agriculture cases, . . . and certainly nothing "harmful" about the trade secrets owned by the pesticide manufacturers in *Monsanto*. In each case, the public purpose we upheld depended on a private party's future use of the concededly nonharmful property that was taken. By focusing on a property's future use, as opposed to its past use, our cases are faithful to the text of the Takings Clause. . . . Justice O'CONNOR's intimation that a "public purpose" may not be achieved by the action of private parties, confuses the purpose of a taking with its mechanics, a mistake we warned of in *Midkiff*. See also *Berman* ("The public end may be as well or better served through an agency of private enterprise than through a department of government").

17. Courts have viewed such aberrations with a skeptical eye. See, *e.g., 99 Cents Only Stores v. Lancaster Redevelopment Agency*, 237 F. Supp. 2d 1123 (C.D. Cal. 2001); cf. *Cincinnati v. Vester*, 281 U.S. 439, 448 (1930) (taking invalid under state eminent domain statute for lack of a reasoned explanation). . . .

Just as we decline to second-guess the City's considered judgments about the efficacy of its development plan, we also decline to second-guess the City's determinations as to what lands it needs to acquire in order to effectuate the project. "It is not for the courts to oversee the choice of the boundary line nor to sit in review on the size of a particular project area. Once the question of the public purpose has been decided, the amount and character of land to be taken for the project and the need for a particular tract to complete the integrated plan rests in the discretion of the legislative branch." *Berman.*

. . . [W]e do not minimize the hardship that condemnations may entail, notwithstanding the payment of just compensation. We emphasize that nothing in our opinion precludes any State from placing further restrictions on its exercise of the takings power. Indeed, many States already impose "public use" requirements that are stricter than the federal baseline. Some of these requirements have been established as a matter of state constitutional law, while others are expressed in state eminent domain statutes that carefully limit the grounds upon which takings may be exercised. As the submissions of the parties and their *amici* make clear, the necessity and wisdom of using eminent domain to promote economic development are certainly matters of legitimate public debate.[24] This Court's authority, however, extends only to determining whether the City's proposed condemnations are for a "public use" within the meaning of the Fifth Amendment to the Federal Constitution. Because over a century of our case law interpreting that provision dictates an affirmative answer to that question, we may not grant petitioners the relief that they seek.

The judgment of the Supreme Court of Connecticut is affirmed.

Justice KENNEDY, concurring.

. . . This Court has declared that a taking should be upheld as consistent with the Public Use Clause, . . . as long as it is "rationally related to a conceivable public purpose." Hawaii Housing Authority v. Midkiff; see also Berman v. Parker. This deferential standard of review echoes the rational-basis test used to review economic regulation under the Due Process and Equal Protection Clauses. The determination that a rational-basis standard of review is appropriate does not, however, alter the fact that transfers intended to confer benefits on particular, favored private entities, and with only incidental or pretextual public benefits, are forbidden by the Public Use Clause.

A court applying rational-basis review under the Public Use Clause should strike down a taking that, by a clear showing, is intended to favor a particular private party, with only incidental or pretextual public benefits, just as a court applying rational-basis review under the Equal Protection Clause must strike down a government classification that is clearly intended to injure a particular class of private parties, with only incidental or pretextual public justifications. . . .

---

24.   For example, some argue that the need for eminent domain has been greatly exaggerated because private developers can use numerous techniques, including secret negotiations or precommitment strategies, to overcome holdout problems and assemble lands for genuinely profitable projects. See Brief for Jane Jacobs as Amicus Curiae 13-15; see also Brief for John Norquist as Amicus Curiae. Others argue to the contrary, urging that the need for eminent domain is especially great with regard to older, small cities like New London, where centuries of development have created an extreme overdivision of land and thus a real market impediment to land assembly. See Brief for Connecticut Conference of Municipalities et al. as Amici Curiae 13, 21; see also Brief for National League of Cities et al. as Amici Curiae.

As the trial court in this case was correct to observe: "Where the purpose [of a taking] is economic development and that development is to be carried out by private parties or private parties will be benefited, the court must decide if the stated public purpose—economic advantage to a city sorely in need of it—is only incidental to the benefits that will be conferred on private parties of a development plan."

A court confronted with a plausible accusation of impermissible favoritism to private parties should treat the objection as a serious one and review the record to see if it has merit, though with the presumption that the government's actions were reasonable and intended to serve a public purpose. Here, the trial court conducted a careful and extensive inquiry into "whether, in fact, the development plan is of primary benefit to . . . the developer [i.e., Corcoran Jennison], and private businesses which may eventually locate in the plan area [e.g., Pfizer], and in that regard, only of incidental benefit to the city." . . .

The trial court concluded . . . that benefiting Pfizer was not "the primary motivation or effect of this development plan"; instead, "the primary motivation . . . was to take advantage of Pfizer's presence." Likewise, the trial court concluded that "[t]here is nothing in the record to indicate that . . . [respondents] were motivated by a desire to aid [other] particular private entities." Even the dissenting justices on the Connecticut Supreme Court agreed that respondents' development plan was intended to revitalize the local economy, not to serve the interests of Pfizer, Corcoran Jennison, or any other private party. This case, then, survives the meaningful rational-basis review that in my view is required under the Public Use Clause.

Petitioners and their *amici* argue that any taking justified by the promotion of economic development must be treated by the courts as *per se* invalid, or at least presumptively invalid. Petitioners overstate the need for such a rule, however, by making the incorrect assumption that review under *Berman* and *Midkiff* imposes no meaningful judicial limits on the government's power to condemn any property it likes. A broad *per se* rule or a strong presumption of invalidity, furthermore, would prohibit a large number of government takings that have the purpose and expected effect of conferring substantial benefits on the public at large and so do not offend the Public Use Clause.

My agreement with the Court that a presumption of invalidity is not warranted for economic development takings in general, or for the particular takings at issue in this case, does not foreclose the possibility that a more stringent standard of review than that announced in *Berman* and *Midkiff* might be appropriate for a more narrowly drawn category of takings. There may be private transfers in which the risk of undetected impermissible favoritism of private parties is so acute that a presumption (rebuttable or otherwise) of invalidity is warranted under the Public Use Clause. This demanding level of scrutiny, however, is not required simply because the purpose of the taking is economic development.

This is not the occasion for conjecture as to what sort of cases might justify a more demanding standard, but it is appropriate to underscore aspects of the instant case that convince me no departure from *Berman* and *Midkiff* is appropriate here. This taking occurred in the context of a comprehensive development plan meant to address a serious citywide depression, and the projected economic benefits of the project cannot be characterized as *de minimis*. The identities of most of the private beneficiaries were unknown at the time the city formulated its plans. The city complied with elaborate procedural requirements that facilitate review of the record and inquiry into the city's purposes. In sum, while there may be categories of cases in which the transfers are so suspicious, or the procedures employed so prone to abuse, or the purported benefits are so trivial or implausible, that courts should presume an impermissible private purpose, no such circumstances are present in this case. . . .

Justice O'CONNOR, with whom THE CHIEF JUSTICE, Justice SCALIA, and Justice THOMAS join, dissenting.

Over two centuries ago, just after the Bill of Rights was ratified, Justice Chase wrote:

> "An ACT of the Legislature (for I cannot call it a law) contrary to the great first principles of the social compact, cannot be considered a rightful exercise of legislative authority . . . . A few instances will suffice to explain what I mean . . . . [A] law that takes property from A. and gives it to B: It is against all reason and justice, for a people to entrust a Legislature with SUCH powers; and, therefore, it cannot be presumed that they have done it." Calder v. Bull, 1 L. Ed. 648 (1798).

Today the Court abandons this long-held, basic limitation on government power. Under the banner of economic development, all private property is now vulnerable to being taken and transferred to another private owner, so long as it might be upgraded—*i.e.,* given to an owner who will use it in a way that the legislature deems more beneficial to the public—in the process. To reason, as the Court does, that the incidental public benefits resulting from the subsequent ordinary use of private property render economic development takings "for public use" is to wash out any distinction between private and public use of property—and thereby effectively to delete the words "for public use" from the Takings Clause of the Fifth Amendment. . . .

Our cases have generally identified three categories of takings that comply with the public use requirement, though it is in the nature of things that the boundaries between these categories are not always firm. . . . First, the sovereign may transfer private property to public ownership—such as for a road, a hospital, or a military base. Second, the sovereign may transfer private property to private parties, often common carriers, who make the property available for the public's use—such as with a railroad, a public utility, or a stadium. But "public ownership" and "use-by-the-public" are sometimes too constricting and impractical ways to define the scope of the Public Use Clause. Thus we have allowed that, in certain circumstances and to meet certain exigencies, takings that serve a public purpose also satisfy the Constitution even if the property is destined for subsequent private use. . . .

This case returns us for the first time in over 20 years to the hard question of when a purportedly "public purpose" taking meets the public use requirement. It presents an issue of first impression: Are economic development takings constitutional? I would hold that they are not. We are guided by two precedents about the taking of real property by eminent domain. In *Berman,* we upheld takings within a blighted neighborhood of Washington, D.C. The neighborhood had so deteriorated that, for example, 64.3% of its dwellings were beyond repair. It had become burdened with "overcrowding of dwellings," "lack of adequate streets and alleys," and "lack of light and air." Congress had determined that the neighborhood had become "injurious to the public health, safety, morals, and welfare" and that it was necessary to "eliminat[e] all such injurious conditions by employing all means necessary and appropriate for the purpose," including eminent domain. Mr. Berman's department store was not itself blighted. Having approved of Congress' decision to eliminate the harm to the public emanating from the blighted neighborhood, however, we did not second-guess its decision to treat the neighborhood as a whole rather than lot-by-lot. . . .

In *Midkiff*, we upheld a land condemnation scheme in Hawaii whereby title in real property was taken from lessors and transferred to lessees. At that time, the State and Federal Governments owned nearly 49% of the State's land, and another 47% was in the hands of only 72 private landowners. Concentration of land ownership was so dramatic that on the State's most urbanized island, Oahu, 22 landowners owned 72.5% of the fee simple titles. The Hawaii Legislature had concluded that the oligopoly in land ownership was "skewing the State's residential fee simple market, inflating land prices, and injuring the public tranquility and welfare," and therefore enacted a condemnation scheme for redistributing title.

In those decisions, we emphasized the importance of deferring to legislative judgments about public purpose. Because courts are ill equipped to evaluate the efficacy of proposed legislative initiatives, we rejected as unworkable the idea of courts' "deciding on what is and is not a governmental function and . . . invalidating legislation on the basis of their view on that question at the moment of decision . . ."; ("[T]he legislature, not the judiciary, is the main guardian of the public needs to be served by social legislation"). Likewise, we recognized our inability to evaluate whether, in a given case, eminent domain is a necessary means by which to pursue the legislature's ends.

Yet for all the emphasis on deference, *Berman* and *Midkiff* hewed to a bedrock principle without which our public use jurisprudence would collapse: "A purely private taking could not withstand the scrutiny of the public use requirement; it would serve no legitimate purpose of government and would thus be void." . . . To protect that principle, those decisions reserved "a role for courts to play in reviewing a legislature's judgment of what constitutes a public use . . . [though] the Court in *Berman* made clear that it is 'an extremely narrow' one."

. . . In both . . . [*Berman and Midkiff*], the extraordinary, precondemnation use of the targeted property inflicted affirmative harm on society—in *Berman* through blight resulting from extreme poverty and in *Midkiff* through oligopoly resulting from extreme wealth. And in both cases, the relevant legislative body had found that eliminating the existing property use was necessary to remedy the harm. Thus a public purpose was realized when the harmful use was eliminated. Because each taking *directly* achieved a public benefit, it did not matter that the property was turned over to private use. Here, in contrast, New London does not claim that Susette Kelo's and Wilhelmina Dery's well-maintained homes are the source of any social harm. . . .

In moving away from our decisions sanctioning the condemnation of harmful property use, the Court today significantly expands the meaning of public use. It holds that the sovereign may take private property currently put to ordinary private use, and give it over for new, ordinary private use, so long as the new use is predicted to generate some secondary benefit for the public—such as increased tax revenue, more jobs, maybe even esthetic pleasure. But nearly any lawful use of real private property can be said to generate some incidental benefit to the public. Thus, if predicted (or even guaranteed) positive side effects are enough to render transfer from one private party to another constitutional, then the words "for public use" do not realistically exclude *any* takings, and thus do not exert any constraint on the eminent domain power.

There is a sense in which this troubling result follows from errant language in *Berman* and *Midkiff*. In discussing whether takings within a blighted neighborhood were for a public use, *Berman* began by observing: "We deal, in other words, with what traditionally has been known as the police power." From there it declared that "[o]nce the object is within the authority of Congress, the right to realize it through the exercise of eminent domain is clear." Following up, we said in *Midkiff* that "[t]he 'public use' requirement is coterminous with the scope of a sovereign's police powers." This language was unnecessary to the specific holdings of those decisions. *Berman* and *Midkiff* simply did not put such language to the constitutional test, because the takings in those cases were within the police power but also for "public use" for the reasons I have described. The case before us now demonstrates why, when deciding if a taking's purpose is constitutional, the police power and "public use" cannot always be equated.

The Court protests that it does not sanction the bare transfer from A to B for B's benefit. It suggests two limitations on what can be taken after today's decision. First, it maintains a role for courts in ferreting out takings whose sole purpose is to bestow a benefit on the private transferee—without detailing how courts are to conduct that complicated inquiry. For his part, Justice KENNEDY suggests that courts may divine illicit purpose by a careful review of the record and the process by which a legislature arrived at the decision to take—without specifying what courts should look for in a case with different facts, how they will know if they have found it, and what to do if they do not. Whatever the details of Justice KENNEDY's as-yet-undisclosed test, it is difficult to envision anyone but the "stupid staff[er]" failing it. See Lucas v. South Carolina Coastal Council, 505 U.S. 1003, 1025-1026, n. 12 (1992). The trouble with economic development takings is that private benefit and incidental public benefit are, by definition, merged and mutually reinforcing. In this case, for example, any boon for Pfizer or the plan's developer is difficult to disaggregate from the promised public gains in taxes and jobs. . . .

The specter of condemnation hangs over all property. Nothing is to prevent the State from replacing any Motel 6 with a Ritz-Carlton, any home with a shopping mall, or any farm with a factory. Cf. Bugryn v. Bristol, 63 Conn. App. 98, 774 A.2d 1042 (2001) (taking the homes and farm of four owners in their 70's and 80's and giving it to an "industrial park"); 99 Cents Only Stores v. Lancaster Redevelopment Agency, 237 F. Supp. 2d 1123 (C.D. Cal. 2001) (attempted taking of 99 Cents store to replace with a Costco); Poletown Neighborhood Council v. Detroit, 410 Mich. 616, 304 N.W.2d 455 (1981) (taking a working-class, immigrant community in Detroit and giving it to a General Motors assembly plant), overruled by County of Wayne v. Hathcock, 471 Mich. 445, 684 N.W.2d 765 (2004); Brief for Becket Fund for Religious Liberty as Amicus Curiae 4-11 (describing takings of religious institutions' properties); Institute for Justice, D. Berliner, Public Power, Private Gain: A Five-Year, State-by-State Report Examining the Abuse of Eminent Domain (2003) (collecting accounts of economic development takings). . . .

. . . Today nearly all real property is susceptible to condemnation on the Court's theory. . . . Any property may now be taken for the benefit of another private party, but the fallout from this decision will not be random. The beneficiaries are likely to be those citizens with disproportionate influence and power in the political process, including large corporations and development firms. As for the victims, the government now has license to transfer property from those with fewer resources to those with more. . . .

could become tyranny of rich.

Justice THOMAS, dissenting.

. . . Today's decision is simply the latest in a string of our cases construing the Public Use Clause to be a virtual nullity, without the slightest nod to its original meaning. . . . Our cases have strayed from the Clause's original meaning, and I would reconsider them. . . .

IV

The consequences of today's decision are not difficult to predict, and promise to be harmful. So-called "urban renewal" programs provide some compensation for the properties they take, but no compensation is possible for the subjective value of these lands to the individuals displaced and the indignity inflicted by uprooting them from their homes. Allowing the government to take property solely for public purposes is bad enough, but extending the concept of public purpose to encompass any economically beneficial goal guarantees that these losses will fall disproportionately on poor communities. Those communities are not only systematically less likely to put their lands to the highest and best social use, but are also the least politically powerful. If ever there were justification for intrusive judicial review of constitutional provisions that protect "discrete and insular minorities," United States v. Carolene Products Co., 304 U.S. 144, 152, n. 4 (1938), surely that principle would apply with great force to the powerless groups and individuals the Public Use Clause protects. The deferential standard this Court has adopted for the Public Use Clause is therefore deeply perverse. It encourages "those citizens with disproportionate influence and power in the political process, including large corporations and development firms," to victimize the weak.

expanding public use to economic benefits disrupts original purpose of "public use"

Those incentives have made the legacy of this Court's "public purpose" test an unhappy one. In the 1950's, no doubt emboldened in part by the expansive understanding of "public use" this Court adopted in *Berman*, cities "rushed to draw plans" for downtown development. B. Frieden & L. Sagalyn, Downtown, Inc. How America Rebuilds Cities 17 (1989). "Of all the families displaced by urban renewal from 1949 through 1963, 63 percent of those whose race was known were nonwhite, and of these families, 56 percent of nonwhites and 38 percent of whites had incomes low enough to qualify for public housing, which, however, was seldom available to them." Public works projects in the 1950's and 1960's destroyed predominantly minority communities in St. Paul, Minnesota, and Baltimore, Maryland. In 1981, urban planners in Detroit, Michigan, uprooted the largely "lower-income and elderly" Poletown neighborhood for the benefit of the General Motors Corporation. J. Wylie, Poletown: Community Betrayed 58 (1989). Urban renewal projects have long been associated with the displacement of blacks; "[i]n cities across the country, urban renewal came to be known as 'Negro removal.'" Pritchett, *The "Public Menace" of Blight: Urban Renewal and the Private Uses of Eminent Domain*, 21 Yale L. & Pol'y Rev. 1, 47 (2003). Over 97 percent of the individuals forcibly removed from their homes by the "slum-clearance" project upheld by this Court in *Berman* were black. Regrettably, the predictable consequence of the Court's decision will be to exacerbate these effects.

The Court relies almost exclusively on this Court's prior cases to derive today's far-reaching, and dangerous, result. But the principles this Court should employ to dispose of this case are found in the Public Use Clause itself . . . . When faced with a clash of constitutional principle and a line of unreasoned cases wholly divorced from the text, history, and structure of our founding document, we should not hesitate to resolve the tension in favor of the Constitution's original meaning. . . .

Notes and Questions

1. The opinion in *Hawaii Housing Authority v. Midkiff* (1984) was written by Justice O'Connor for a unanimous Court that included Justices Blackmun, Brennan, Burger, Powell, Rehnquist, Stevens, and White. (Justice Marshall did not participate in the case.) The language she describes in *Kelo* as "errant" ("[t]he 'public use' requirement is coterminous with the scope of a sovereign's police powers") and not necessary to the decision, was written during a period when the conservative wing of the Court was more concerned about protecting states' rights than about expanding the reach of the federal Takings Clause. As you read further in this chapter, notice how the emphasis has changed.

2. The *Kelo* decision set off a huge public backlash fueled by Justice O'Connor's statement that "[t]he specter of condemnation hangs over all property. Nothing is to prevent the State from replacing any Motel 6 with a Ritz-Carlton, any home with a shopping mall, or any farm with a factory." Less than a week after the decision, the Institute for Justice, which has helped land-owners wage battles against "abusive" eminent domain since 2002, launched a national campaign called "Hands Off My Home" to "focus the outrage over *Kelo* and turn it into meaningful reform." http://www.ij.org/five-years-after-kelo-the-sweeping-backlash-against-one-of-the-supreme-courts-most-despised-decisions. In response, many states adopted legislation restricting use of the eminent domain power for economic development and some state supreme courts refused to apply *Kelo* in interpreting the restrictions on eminent domain power in their state constitutions. *See, e.g., City of Norwood v. Horney*, 853 N.E.2d 1115 (Ohio 2006).

3. In November 2009, Pfizer announced that it was closing its research and development headquarters in New London. At that point, the houses in the Fort Trumbull area had been razed but no new development had occurred and the development agreement with Corcoran Jennison had been terminated. The Wall Street Journal, echoing the Institute for Justice, concluded:

> The aftermath of *Kelo* is the latest example of the futility of using eminent domain as corporate welfare. While Ms. Kelo and her neighbors lost their homes, the city and the state spent some $78 million to bulldoze private property for high-end condos and other "desirable" elements. Instead, the wrecked and condemned neighborhood still stands vacant, without any of the touted tax benefits or job creation. (Review & Outlook, Nov. 11, 2009).

In October 2010, the city moved ahead and entered a new development agreement for the construction of 75 or more condominium units in one- to three-story townhouses. *See* the city's website under "Projects" http://www. ci.new-london.ct.us/.

4. Are Justices Thomas and O'Connor right in believing that eminent domain is most likely to be used in poor and minority communities? How likely is it that "blight" may be used to justify the projects? Should courts give heightened scrutiny to the findings of blight or public benefit when eminent domain is used in those communities? *See* David A. Dana, *Exclusionary Eminent Domain*, 17 Sup. Ct. Econ. Rev. 7 (2009). Should it make any difference whether the project is for a prison or a shopping center?

KELO, POPULARITY, AND SUBSTANTIVE DUE PROCESS
Justice John Paul Stevens (Ret.), 63 Ala. L. Rev. 941 (2012)

The opinion for the Court in *Kelo* is the most unpopular opinion that I wrote during my thirty-four year tenure on the Supreme Court. Indeed, I think it is the most unpopular opinion that any member of the Court wrote during that period. After it was announced, friends and acquaintances frequently told me that they could not understand how I could have authored such an opinion. Outraged citizens sought to retaliate against Justice Souter for joining my opinion; they rallied and gathered petitions urging the city of Weare, New Hampshire, to condemn his home in order to build the "Lost Liberty Hotel" — apparently assuming that our holding would authorize such retaliatory action. . . .

The *Kelo* majority opinion remains unpopular. Recently a commentator named Damon W. Root described the decision as the "eminent domain debacle." Last month, Justice Scalia . . . stated that the Supreme Court had misjudged how far it could "stretch beyond the text of the Constitution" in the *Kelo* decision without provoking overwhelming public criticism and resistance, much as it had done with respect to its prior decisions in the *Dred Scott* case on slavery and in Roe v. Wade on abortion. In Justice Scalia's view, *Kelo* employed a doomed form of constitutional analysis, through which judges attempt to shape the Constitution to what they believe current society views as right and necessary.

. . . I shall . . . point out that Justice Oliver Wendell Holmes's broad reading of the text of the Constitution — which allows the states the same broad discretion in making takings decisions that they possess when engaging in other forms of economic regulation — had been endorsed by two unanimous Court opinions, the first in 1954 in Berman v. Parker and the second in 1984 in Hawaii Housing Authority v. Midkiff. Finally, I shall suggest that if the *Kelo* majority did commit error, that error had nothing to do with the text of the Constitution. At most, the majority may have failed to engage in judicial activism by expanding the doctrine of substantive due process to create a new rule limiting the power of sovereign states to condemn private homes — a rule which no one asked the Court to create. Instead, *Kelo* adhered to the doctrine of judicial restraint, which allows state legislatures broad latitude in making economic policy decisions in their respective jurisdictions, and creates a strong presumption against a construction of the Fourteenth Amendment's Due Process Clause that would make federal judges the final arbiters of policy questions best answered by the voters' elected representatives. . . .

THE JUDICIAL REACTION TO *KELO*
Ilya Somin, 4 Alb. Gov't L. Rev. 1, 2-3 (2011)

Kelo triggered an unprecedented political backlash. Surveys showed that some eighty percent of the public opposed the decision, which was also denounced by politicians and activists from across the political spectrum. Forty-three states and the federal government enacted legislation intended to curb economic development takings; this is probably the broadest legislative reaction ever generated by any Supreme Court ruling.

In addition to the better-known legislative reaction, *Kelo* was also followed by extensive additional property rights litigation in both federal and state courts. In the aftermath of *Kelo*, several state supreme courts addressed the question whether its deferential approach to economic development takings also applied under their state constitutional public use clauses. Both federal and state courts have sought to interpret *Kelo*'s statement that "pretextual" takings are an exception to the decision's generally ultra-deferential approach. Finally, several important recent state court decisions considered the implications of *Kelo* for condemnations of "blighted" property.

Unlike the legislative reaction, which has now been extensively analyzed by several scholars, there is no comprehensive analysis of the judicial reaction to *Kelo*. This is unfortunate because state and federal judges are likely to continue to play an important role in addressing public use issues. Although all but seven states have enacted post-*Kelo* reform laws, the majority of these are weak, providing little or no meaningful protection for property owners. In many states, the fate of property rights still rests in large part in judicial hands.

This article tries to fill the gap in the literature by analyzing the state and federal judicial aftermath of *Kelo*. With a few important exceptions, I conclude that state courts have not reacted to *Kelo* by adopting similarly permissive approaches to public use issues. To the contrary, three state supreme courts have explicitly repudiated *Kelo* as a guide to their state constitutions. Other recent state supreme court decisions have imposed constraints on takings that go beyond *Kelo* even if they have not completely rejected the *Kelo* approach.

By contrast, federal and state courts have been all over the map in their efforts to apply *Kelo*'s restrictions on "pretextual" takings. There is no consensus in sight on this crucial issue. It may be that none will develop unless and until the Supreme Court decides another case in this field.

OPINION OF THE JUSTICES (PUBLIC USE
OF COASTAL BEACHES)
Supreme Court of New Hampshire
649 A.2d 604 (1994)

. . . To the Honorable House [of Representatives of New Hampshire]: The undersigned justices of the supreme court submit the following reply to your questions of May 5, 1994. Following our receipt of your resolution, we invited interested parties to file memoranda with the court on or before September 1, 1994.

SB 636 (the bill), as amended, proposes to amend RSA chapter 483-B (1992) by inserting a new section, 483-B:9-a, titled "Public Use of Coastal Beaches." The legislature's purpose is set out in the bill as follows:

> It is the purpose of the general court in this section to recognize and confirm the historical practice and common law right of the public to enjoy the existing public easement in the greatest portion of New Hampshire coastal beach land subject to those littoral rights recognized at common law. This easement presently existing over the greater portion of that beachfront property extending from where the "public trust" ends across the commonly used portion of sand and rocks to the intersection of the beach and the high ground, often but not always delineated by a sea wall, or the line of vegetation, or the seaward face of the foredunes, this being that beach where violent sea action occurs at irregular frequent intervals making its use for the usual private constructions uneconomical and physically impractical.

The bill defines "coastal beaches" as "that portion of the beach extending from where the public trust shoreland ends, across the commonly used portion of sand and rocks to the intersection of the beach and high ground, often but not always delineated by a seawall, or the line of vegetation, or the seaward face of the foredunes."

The bill states that "New Hampshire holds in 'public trust' rights in all shorelands subject to the ebb and flow of the tide and subject to those littoral rights recognized at common law" and that the "'public trust' shoreland establishes the extreme seaward boundary extension of all private property rights in New Hampshire except for those 'jus privatum' rights validly conveyed by legislative act without impairment of New Hampshire's 'jus publicum' interests." The bill then provides that:

> For an historical period extending back well over 20 years the public has made recognized, prevalent and uninterrupted use of the vast majority of New Hampshire's coastal beaches above the "public trust" shoreland. The legislature recognizes that some public use of the beach area above the public trust lands is necessary to the full enjoyment of the land. The general court recognizes and confirms a public easement flowing from and demonstrated by this historical practice in the coastal beaches contiguous to the public trust shoreland where the public has traditionally had access and which easement has been created by virtue of such uninterrupted public use.

Further, the bill states that "[a]ny person may use the coastal beaches of New Hampshire where such a public easement exists for recreational purposes subject to the provisions of municipal ordinances," but "[t]he provisions of [the bill] shall in no way be construed as affecting the title of property owners of land contiguous to land subject to a public easement." Finally, the new section provides that "[i]n a suit brought or defended under this section, or whose determination is affected by this section, a showing that the area in dispute is within the area defined as 'coastal beach' shall be prima facie evidence that a public easement exists."

Your first question asks "[w]hether New Hampshire law identifies a particular coastal feature or tidal event as outlining the maximum shoreward extension of the public trust area boundary . . . beyond which the probable existence of private property rights may, without a public easement arising from historical practice, restrict any public access under the provisions of Part 1, Article 12 of the New Hampshire Constitution and the 5th amendment of the United States Constitution." We answer in the affirmative.

[T]he New Hampshire Constitution provides that "no part of a man's property shall be taken from him, or applied to public uses, without his own consent, or that of the representative body of the people." This clause requires just compensation in the event of a taking. "The same principle was embodied in the Fifth Amendment to the Constitution of the United States at the insistence of a majority of the States, including New Hampshire, in ratifying the Constitution." Burrows v. City of Keene, 432 A.2d 15, 18 (N.H. 1981). . . .

The public trust has its origins in the concept of the jus publicum, an English common law doctrine under which the tidelands and navigable waters were held by the king in trust for the general public. *See* Sax, *The Public Trust Doctrine in Natural Resource Law: Effective Judicial Intervention*, 68 Mich. L. Rev. 471, 475-76 (1970). The English common law was based, in turn, upon the ancient Roman concept of "natural law" that held that certain things, including the shores, by their nature are common to all. *See* Comment, *The Public Trust Doctrine in Maine's Submerged Lands: Public Rights, State Obligation and the Role of the Courts*, 37 Me. L. Rev. 105, 107-08 (1985). At common law, the king had "both the title and the dominion of the sea, and of rivers and arms of the sea, where the tide ebbs and flows, and all of the lands below high-water mark, within the jurisdiction of the crown of England." Shively v. Bowlby, 152 U.S. 1 (1894). The king held the title to intertidal lands, or jus privatum, absolutely, and in his role as sovereign he held the public rights, or jus publicum, in trust for the benefit of the public. Although the king could convey the lands below the high water mark, any conveyance to a private individual was subject to the jus publicum. The jus publicum included uses "for highways of navigation and commerce, domestic and foreign, and for the purpose of fishing by all the King's subjects."

Following the American Revolution, "the people of each state became themselves sovereign; and in that character hold the absolute right to all their navigable waters and the soils under them for their own common use, subject only to the rights since surrendered by the Constitution to the general government." Martin v. Wadden, 41 U.S. 367 (1842). Upon entering the union, the original thirteen States and all new States acquired title to lands under waters subject to the ebb and flow of the tide. As sovereigns, the States hold the intertidal lands in trust for the public and "have the authority to define the limits of the lands held in public trust and to recognize private rights in such lands as they see fit."

In 1889, this court rejected a Massachusetts law that adopted the low water mark as the boundary between public and private ownership. Concord Co. v. Robertson, 25 A. 718 (N.H. 1889). The Massachusetts rule, embodied in a 1647 ordinance, extended private titles "to encompass land as far as mean low water line or 100 rods from the mean high water line, whichever was the lesser measure." . . . The purpose of the ordinance was "to encourage littoral owners to build wharves."

. . . The [*Robertson*] court . . . concluded that "[t]he introduction of any line other than high-water mark as the marine boundary would overturn common-law rights that had been established here, by a usage and traditional understanding of two hundred years' duration." *Robertson* still represents the law in New Hampshire. While it is settled, therefore, that the public trust in tidewaters in this State extends landward to the high water mark, the following common law questions are not settled: What is the high water mark; where is it located; and how is it located. We do not purport to determine in this opinion answers to such questions.

Your second question asks "[w]hether the effect of [the bill], which recognizes that the public trust extends to those lands 'subject to ebb and flow of the tide' infringes upon existing private property rights as protected by . . . the New Hampshire Constitution and the 5th amendment of the United States Constitution." We answer in the negative.

. . . New Hampshire has long recognized that lands subject to the ebb and flow of the tide are held in public trust. "Land covered by public water is capable of many uses." Concord Co. v. Robertson. "Rights of navigation and fishery are not the whole estate" but rather the public lands are held "for the use and benefit of all the [public], for all useful purposes"; *see* St. Regis Co. v. Board, 26 A.2d 832 (N.H. 1942) (public trust encompasses "all useful and lawful purposes"); State v. Sunapee Dam Co., 50 A. 108, 110 (N.H. 1900) ("in this state the law of public waters is what justice and reason require"). These uses include recreational uses. See Hartford v. Gilmanton, 146 A.2d 851, 853 (N.H. 1958) (public waters may be used to boat, bathe, fish, fowl, skate, and cut ice).

In addition, we have uniformly held that owners of property adjacent to lands held in public trust have common law rights which are "more extensive than those of the public generally." Sundell v. Town of New London, 409 A.2d 1315 (N.H. 1979):

> These private rights of littoral owners include but are not necessarily limited to the right to use and occupy the waters adjacent to their shore for a variety of recreational purposes, the right to erect boat houses and to wharf out into the water. We have also held that these private littoral rights are incidental property rights which are severable from the shore property itself and may be conveyed separate from the littoral property. . . .

. . . Private shorefront owners are entitled to exercise their property rights in the tidelands so long as they do not unreasonably interfere with the rights of the public.

Therefore, to the extent that the term "lands subject to ebb and flow of the tide" applies to tidelands below the high water mark, the bill simply codifies the common law and does not infringe upon private property rights. . . .

Your third question asks "[w]hether the provisions of [the bill], which recognize a public easement in the 'dry sand area' of historically accessible coastal beaches is a taking of private property for a public purpose without just compensation . . . ." Except for those areas where there is an established and acknowledged public easement and subject to the assumptions contained in the discussion below, we answer in the affirmative.

The bill apparently recognizes two property interests in two distinct areas of shoreland. First, the bill establishes that "New Hampshire holds in 'public trust' rights in all shorelands subject to the ebb and flow of the tide." Second, the bill establishes a public easement in land "extending from where the public trust ends across the commonly used portion of sand and rocks to the intersection of the beach and the high ground, often but not always delineated by a sea wall, or the line of vegetation, or the seaward face of the foredunes." This high ground is generally known as the "dry sand" area. . . .

As noted in our answer to your first question, this court has not defined the term "high water mark." Because, however, the bill states that the dry sand area is not within the public trust we will, for purposes of this opinion, base our analysis on that assumption. We construe the bill, therefore, as recognizing public trust rights below the dry sand area and a prescriptive easement in the dry sand.

"To establish a prescriptive easement, the plaintiff must prove by a balance of probabilities twenty years' adverse, continuous, uninterrupted use of the land [claimed] in such a manner as to give notice to the record owner that an adverse claim was being made to it." . . . Although the general public is capable of acquiring an easement by prescription, Elmer v. Rodgers, 214 A.2d 750, 752 (N.H. 1965),

> [e]vidence of continuous and uninterrupted public use of the premises for the statutory period . . . is insufficient alone to establish prescriptive title as a matter of law. The nature of the use must be such as to show the owner knew or ought to have known that the right was being exercised, not in reliance upon his toleration or permission, but without regard to his consent.

. . . While the fact that the owner was also using the premises for the same purposes would not prevent a finding of adverse use by the general public, . . ." [a] permissive use no matter how long or how often exercised cannot ripen into an easement by prescription." . . . The general public may, therefore, acquire coastal beach land by prescription in New Hampshire.

Problems militate, however, against the use of the prescriptive doctrine. "First, there is the obvious problem of establishing factual evidence of the specialized type of adverse use for the requisite period of time . . . needed to create an easement by prescription." 3 R. Powell, *Powell on Real Property* § 34.11[6], at 34-171 (1994). "Secondly, prescriptive easements, by their nature, can be utilized only on a tract-by-tract basis, and thus cannot be applied to all beaches within a state." In a suit to quiet title, adequate evidence may well exist to prove that on a given piece of property, the area landward of the public trust across the dry sand is subject to a public easement. Such a determination is, however, a judicial one. . . .

Although the bill does not completely deprive private property owners of use of their property, "[t]he interference with private property here involves a wholesale denial of an owner's right to exclude the public." . . . "If a possessory interest in real property has any meaning at all it must include the general right to exclude others." . . .

When the government unilaterally authorizes a permanent, public easement across private lands, this constitutes a taking requiring just compensation. See Nollan v. California Coastal Comm'n, 483 U.S. 825 (1987).

Because the bill provides no compensation for the landowners whose property may be burdened by the general recreational easement established for public use, it violates the prohibition contained in our State and Federal Constitutions against the taking of private property for public use without just compensation. Although the State has the power to permit a comprehensive beach access and use program by using its eminent domain power and compensating private property owners, it may not take property rights without compensation through legislative decree. "[A] strong public desire to improve the public condition is not enough to warrant achieving the desire by a shorter cut than the constitutional way of paying for the change." . . .

We emphasize that this opinion does not amount to a judicial decision. An opinion of the justices on proposed legislation is not binding upon the court in the event the proposed legislation should become law and a case should arise requiring its construction. Opinion of the justices, 25 N.H. 537, 538 (1852).

Notes and Questions

1. On what basis does the court conclude that statutory recognition of a public easement in the dry sand areas of the beach would constitute a taking requiring compensation? Is this a necessary conclusion? Could the legislature have defined the public trust to include dry sand areas reasonably necessary for access to the wet sand areas? Or simply to include all property seaward of the line of vegetation? In *Mathews v. Bay Head Improvement Ass'n*, 471 A.2d 355 (N.J.), *cert. denied*, 469 U.S. 821 (1984), the New Jersey Supreme Court held that the public trust may extend to dry sand beaches as reasonably necessary for recreational purposes, rejecting the idea that the trust doctrine is fixed or static. "Archaic judicial responses are not an answer to a modern social problem. . . . [T]he public trust doctrine . . . [can be] molded and extended to meet changing conditions and needs of the public it was created to benefit." Come back to this question after you have read the *Lucas* and *Stop the Beach Renourishment* cases later in this chapter.

2. The doctrine of customary rights—rights based on use from "time immemorial" —has been used in some other states to provide a basis for public rights to use dry sand areas of the beach. In *State ex rel. Thornton v. Hay*, 780 P.2d 671 (Or. 1969), the Supreme Court of Oregon held that all of the dry sand areas of the state's ocean beaches are subject to customary rights for public use. In using the beaches for clam digging and recreation, European settlers had continued aboriginal customs. The court pointed out that adoption of the doctrine of customary rights avoided the need to litigate public rights on a tract-by-tract basis and provided uniform treatment of Oregon ocean-front lands.

3. What are the theoretical problems in allowing use by the general public to acquire rights by prescription? Some states that view prescription as based solely on the running of the statute of limitations have reached the conclusion that the general public cannot acquire prescriptive easements. Do you see why? Others, viewing a prescriptive easement as based on the fiction of a lost grant, have reached the same conclusion on the theory that the unorganized public lacks capacity to take title to an interest in property. In those states, public rights based on long use can be established using a theory of implied dedication by the landowner. *See, e.g., State ex rel. Haman v. Fox*, 594 P.2d 1093 (Idaho 1979). How can a landowner prevent the general public from acquiring prescriptive rights?

4. What practical problems face New Hampshire in trying to establish that the public has acquired prescriptive rights in beach areas not covered by the public trust?

5. The effect of the public trust doctrine is to limit government's ability to divert the shoreland and navigable waterway resources into private hands. Unless the government acts explicitly to extinguish the public trust when it conveys public lands into private ownership, and does so to further trust purposes,

the transferee takes the property subject to the trust. *See, e.g., City of Berkeley v. Superior Court,* 606 P.2d 362 (Cal. 1980) (tidelands conveyed pursuant to 1870 act were subject to public trust). What are the justifications for this doctrine? Does it rest on the value of maintaining open shipping lanes? Public access to or ability to control fisheries? Does it rest on a sense that certain interests are so important that they should not be subject to private ownership? Or that some resources should be available to all without regard to ability to pay? Is there any reason to treat beaches differently from other "natural" areas?

Carol Rose suggests that roads and navigable waterways should be public because the more people who engage in commerce the wealthier a society becomes. In addition, commerce plays an important socializing function, bringing people into dealings with others, or providing a form of social glue. Does this apply to recreation, too? She suggests that it might, and if so, an extension of the public trust might be warranted to secure public access to the beach. She concludes that our law has always provided public access to some areas, like village greens, in which people engage in socializing activities because "[i]n the absence of the socializing and sociable activities that are performed on 'inherently public property,' the public is a shapeless mob whose members neither trade nor converse nor play but only fight. . . ." *The Comedy of the Commons: Custom, Commerce, and Inherently Public Property,* 53 U. Chi. L. Rev. 711, 781 (1986). Are beaches "inherently public property" in this sense?

6. Sparked by Professor Joseph Sax's article, *The Public Trust Doctrine in Natural Resource Law: Effective Judicial Intervention,* 68 Mich. L. Rev. 471 (1970), the public trust doctrine has generated an enormous literature and significant differences in opinion between those who advocate expanding the doctrine to provide more protection for the environment and public access to beaches, and those who view it as an attempt to circumvent constitutional limits on expropriation of private property for public use. You will have an opportunity to study the doctrine in depth if you take a course in environmental law.

What Can Be Taken Using the Eminent Domain Power?

When the Oakland Raiders announced their intention to move the team to Los Angeles in 1980, the City of Oakland sued to take title to the football franchise by eminent domain. In *City of Oakland v. Oakland Raiders,* 646 P.2d 835 (Cal. 1982), the California Supreme Court held that the franchise was property subject to the eminent domain power:

> No constitutional restriction, federal or state, purports to limit the nature of the property that may be taken by eminent domain. . . . Over 125 years ago, the United States Supreme Court rejected a . . . claim that intangible property could not be condemned. In The West River Bridge Company v. Dix (1848) 47 U.S. 507, the high court carefully explained: "A distinction has been attempted . . . between the power of a government to appropriate for public uses property which is corporeal . . . and the like power in the government to resume or extinguish a franchise. The distinction thus attempted we regard as a refinement which has no foundation in reason . . . . We are aware of nothing peculiar to a franchise which can class it higher, or render it more sacred, than other property. A franchise is property, and nothing more; it is incorporeal property . . . ."

A century later, the high court reaffirmed the principle. Reasoning that "the in-tangible acquires a value . . . no different from the value of the business' physical property," it concluded that such intangibles as trade routes of a laundry were con-demnable, upon payment of just compensation therefor, when properly taken for a public use. (Kimball Laundry Co. v. U.S. [1949] 338 U.S. 1) . . . .

Following the reasoning of *Kimball* numerous other decisions both federal and state have expressly acknowledged that intangible assets are subject to condemna-tion. (See, e.g., Liggett & Myers v. U.S. (1927) 274 U.S. 215 (contract to provide tobacco products); Porter v. United States (5th Cir. 1973) 473 F.2d 1329 (right to exploit "collector's value" of personal effects of Lee Harvey Oswald); *In re* Fifth Av-enue Coach Lines, Inc. (1966) 18 N.Y.2d 212 (bus system, including coach routes, operating schedules, etc.)); . . . Similar consequences occur when a private utility is taken in eminent domain by a municipality or utility district . . . ; the most valuable property acquired by condemnation of a utility may be intangible, namely, its fran-chise or right to do business. . . .

For eminent domain purposes, neither the federal nor the state Constitution distinguishes between property which is real or personal, tangible or intangible.

The California Supreme Court also held that taking the franchise could be for a public use if operation of a sports franchise is shown to be an appropriate municipal function. On remand, however, the Court of Appeal determined that condemnation of the franchise would violate the Commerce Clause of the U.S. Constitution. *City of Oakland v. Oakland Raiders*, 220 Cal. Rptr. 153 (1985). The Raiders were based in Los Angeles from 1982 through 1994, but returned vol-untarily to Oakland in 1995.

B.   REGULATORY TAKINGS

The regulatory takings doctrine begins with Justice Holmes's opinion in *Pennsylvania Coal Co. v. Mahon*, 260 U.S. 393 (1922), where he famously stated: "while property may be regulated to a certain extent, if regulation goes too far it will be recognized as a taking" and: *(to what extent?)*

We are in danger of forgetting that a strong public desire to improve the public condition is not enough to warrant achieving the desire by a shorter cut than the constitutional way of paying for the change. . . . [T]his is a question of degree—and therefore cannot be disposed of by general propositions. *"not general"*

Aside from two cases upholding and establishing limits on zoning, *Village of Euclid v. Ambler Realty Co.*, 272 U.S. 365 (1926) (comprehensive zoning is valid exercise of police power even though it reduces plaintiff's land value by 75 per-cent), and *Nectow v. City of Cambridge*, 277 U.S. 183 (1928) (particular zoning classification invalid because it did not promote health, safety, or welfare), the Supreme Court stayed out of the regulatory takings arena until 1978, leaving it to the states to decide when regulations, particularly land use regulations, went too far. *left to states to decide regulatory taking.*

PENN CENTRAL TRANSPORTATION COMPANY v. NEW YORK

Supreme Court of the United States
438 U.S. 104 (1978)

Mr. Justice BRENNAN delivered the opinion of the Court [joined by Justices BLACKMUN, MARSHALL, POWELL, STEWART, and WHITE].

The question presented is whether a city may, as part of a comprehensive program to preserve historic landmarks and historic districts, place restrictions on the development of individual historic landmarks—in addition to those imposed by applicable zoning ordinances—without effecting a "taking" requiring the payment of "just compensation." Specifically, we must decide whether the application of New York City's Landmarks Preservation Law to the parcel of land occupied by Grand Central Terminal has "taken" its owners' property in violation of the Fifth and Fourteenth Amendments.

I

A

Over the past 50 years, all 50 States and over 500 municipalities have enacted laws to encourage or require the preservation of buildings and areas with historic or aesthetic importance. These nationwide legislative efforts have been precipitated by two concerns. The first is recognition that, in recent years, large numbers of historic structures, landmarks, and areas have been destroyed without adequate consideration of either the values represented therein or the possibility of preserving the destroyed properties for use in economically productive ways. The second is a widely shared belief that structures with special historic, cultural, or architectural significance enhance the quality of life for all. . . .

New York City, . . . acting pursuant to a New York State enabling Act, adopted its Landmarks Preservation Law in 1965. . . . The city acted from the conviction that "the standing of [New York City] as a world-wide tourist center and world capital of business, culture and government" would be threatened if legislation were not enacted to protect historic landmarks and neighborhoods from precipitate decisions to destroy or fundamentally alter their character. . . .

The New York City law is typical of many urban landmark laws in that its primary method of achieving its goals is not by acquisitions of historic properties,[6] but rather by involving public entities in land-use decisions affecting these properties and providing services, standards, controls, and incentives that will encourage preservation by private owners and users. While the law does place special restrictions on landmark properties as a necessary feature to the attainment of its larger objectives, the major theme of the law is to ensure the owners of any such properties both a "reasonable return" on their investments and

---

6.   The consensus is that widespread public ownership of historic properties in urban settings is neither feasible nor wise. Public ownership reduces the tax base, burdens the public budget with costs of acquisitions and maintenance, and results in the preservation of public buildings as museums and similar facilities, rather than as economically productive features of the urban scene. . . .

maximum latitude to use their parcels for purposes not inconsistent with the preservation goals.

The operation of the law can be briefly summarized. The primary responsibility for administering the law is vested in the Landmarks Preservation Commission . . . . If the Commission determines, after giving all interested parties an opportunity to be heard, that a building or area satisfies the ordinance's criteria, it will designate a building to be a "landmark," situated on a particular "landmark site," or will designate an area to be a "historic district." . . . [Then] New York City's Board of Estimate, after considering the relationship of the designated property "to the master plan, the zoning resolution, projected public improvements and any plans for the renewal of the area involved," may modify or disapprove the designation, and the owner may seek judicial review of the final designation decision. Thus far, 31 historic districts and over 400 individual landmarks have been finally designated . . . .

Final designation as a landmark results in restrictions upon the property owner's options . . . . First, the law imposes a duty upon the owner to keep the exterior features of the building "in good repair" to assure that the law's objectives not be defeated by the landmark's falling into a state of irremediable disrepair. Second, the Commission must approve in advance any proposal to alter the exterior architectural features of the landmark or to construct any exterior improvement on the landmark site . . . .

In the event an owner wishes to alter a landmark site, three separate procedures are available through which administrative approval may be obtained. First, the owner may apply to the Commission for a "certificate of no effect on protected architectural features" . . . . Denial of the certificate is subject to judicial review. Second, the owner may apply to the Commission for a certificate of "appropriateness," . . . [which] will be granted if the Commission concludes — focusing upon aesthetic, historical, and architectural values — that the proposed construction on the landmark site would not unduly hinder the protection, enhancement, perpetuation, and use of the landmark. Again, denial of the certificate is subject to judicial review. . . . [T]he owner who is denied either a certificate of no exterior effect or a certificate of appropriateness may submit an alternative or modified plan for approval. The final procedure — seeking a certificate of appropriateness on the ground of "insufficient return," provides special mechanisms . . . to ensure that designation does not cause economic hardship.

. . . [D]esignation also enhances the economic position of the landmark owner in one significant respect. . . . [O]wners of real property who have not developed their property to the full extent permitted by the applicable zoning laws are allowed to transfer development rights to . . . [certain nearby lots].

B

. . . Grand Central Terminal, . . . owned by the Penn Central Transportation Co. and its affiliates, is one of New York City's most famous buildings. Opened in 1913, it is regarded not only as providing an ingenious engineering solution to the problems presented by urban railroad stations, but also as a magnificent example of the French beaux-arts style.

The Terminal is located in midtown Manhattan . . . bounded on the west by Vanderbilt Avenue, on the east by the Commodore Hotel, and on the north by the Pan-American Building. Although a 20-story office tower, to have been located above the Terminal, was part of the original design, the planned tower was never constructed.[15] The Terminal itself is an eight-story structure which Penn Central uses as a railroad station and in which it rents space not needed for railroad purposes to a variety of commercial interests. The Terminal is one of a number of properties owned by appellant Penn Central in this area of midtown Manhattan. The others include the Barclay, Biltmore, Commodore, Roosevelt, and Waldorf-Astoria Hotels, the Pan-American Building and other office buildings along Park Avenue, and the Yale Club. At least eight of these are eligible to be recipients of development rights afforded the Terminal by virtue of landmark designation.

On August 2, 1967, following a public hearing, the Commission designated the Terminal a "landmark" and designated the "city tax block" it occupies a "landmark site." The Board of Estimate confirmed this action . . . . Although appellant Penn Central had opposed the designation before the Commission, it did not seek judicial review of the final designation decision.

On January 22, 1968, appellant Penn Central, to increase its income, entered into a renewable 50-year lease . . . with appellant UGP Properties, Inc. . . . [under which] UGP was to construct a multistory office building above the Terminal. UGP promised to pay Penn Central $1 million annually during construction and at least $3 million annually thereafter. The rentals would be offset in part by a loss of some $700,000 to $1 million in net rentals presently received from concessionaires displaced by the new building.

. . . UGP and Penn Central then applied to the Commission for permission to construct an office building atop the Terminal. Two separate plans, both designed by architect Marcel Breuer and both apparently satisfying the terms of the applicable zoning ordinance, were submitted to the Commission . . . . The first, Breuer I, provided for the construction of a 55-story office building, to be cantilevered above the existing facade and to rest on the roof of the Terminal. The second, Breuer II Revised, called for tearing down a portion of the Terminal that included the 42d Street facade, stripping off some of the remaining features of the Terminal's facade, and constructing a 53-story office building. The Commission denied a certificate of no exterior effect . . . . Appellants then applied for a certificate of "appropriateness" as to both proposals. After four days of hearings at which over 80 witnesses testified, the Commission denied this application as to both proposals.

The Commission's reasons for rejecting certificates respecting Breuer II Revised are summarized in the following statement: "To protect a Landmark, one does not tear it down. To perpetuate its architectural features, one does not strip them off." Breuer I, which would have preserved the existing vertical facades of the present structure, received more sympathetic consideration. The Commission . . . focused on the effect that the proposed tower would have on . . . the dramatic view of the Terminal from Park Avenue South. . . . [T]he

---

15.   The Terminal's present foundation includes columns, which were built into it for the express purpose of supporting the proposed 20-story tower.

Commission . . . found the majestic approach from the south to be still unique in the city . . . . In conclusion, the Commission stated:

> ". . . [T]o balance a 55-story office tower above a flamboyant Beaux-Arts facade seems nothing more than an aesthetic joke. . . . [T]he tower would overwhelm the Terminal by its sheer mass. The 'addition' would be four times as high as the existing structure and would reduce the Landmark itself to the status of a curiosity . . . ."

Why Commission denied both certifications

Appellants did not seek judicial review of the denial of either certificate . . . [and] did not avail themselves of the opportunity to develop and submit other plans for the Commission's consideration . . . . Instead, appellants filed suit . . . claiming, *inter alia*, that the application of the Landmarks Preservation Law had "taken" their property without just compensation in violation of the Fifth and Fourteenth Amendments and arbitrarily deprived them of their property without due process of law in violation of the Fourteenth Amendment. Appellants sought a declaratory judgment, injunctive relief barring the city from using the Landmarks Law to impede the construction of any structure that might otherwise lawfully be constructed on the Terminal site, and damages for the "temporary taking" that occurred between August 2, 1967, the designation date, and the date when the restrictions arising from the Landmarks Law would be lifted. The trial court granted the injunctive and declaratory relief, but severed the question of damages for a "temporary taking."

π filed suit claiming law was taken.

PP

Appellees appealed, and the New York Supreme Court, Appellate Division, reversed . . . . [It] concluded that all appellants had succeeded in showing was that they had been deprived of the property's most profitable use, and that this showing did not establish that appellants had been unconstitutionally deprived of their property. (highest court)

App Div: π not constitutionally deprived

The New York Court of Appeals affirmed. That court summarily rejected any claim that the Landmarks Law had "taken" property without "just compensation," indicating that there could be no "taking" since the law had not transferred control of the property to the city, but only restricted appellants' exploitation of it. In that circumstance, the Court of Appeals held that appellants' attack on the law could prevail only if the law deprived appellants of their property in violation of the Due Process Clause of the Fourteenth Amendment. Whether or not there was a denial of substantive due process turned on whether the restrictions deprived Penn Central of a "reasonable return" on the "privately created and privately managed ingredient" of the Terminal.[23] The Court . . . concluded that the Landmarks Law had not effected a denial of due process because: (1) the landmark regulation permitted the same use as had been made of the Terminal for more than half a century; (2) the appellants had failed to show that they could not earn a reasonable return on their investment in the Terminal itself;

Why not affect Due process.

---

23. The Court of Appeals suggested that in calculating the value of the property upon which appellants were entitled to earn a reasonable return, the "publicly created" components of the value of the property—i.e., those elements of its value attributable to the "efforts of organized society" or to the "social complex" in which the Terminal is located—had to be excluded. However, since the record upon which the Court of Appeals decided the case did not, as that court recognized, contain a basis for segregating the privately created from the publicly created elements of the value of the Terminal site and since the judgment of the Court of Appeals in any event rests upon bases that support our affirmance, we have no occasion to address the question whether it is permissible or feasible to separate out the "social increments" of the value of property. . . .

(3) even if the Terminal proper could never operate at a reasonable profit some of the income from Penn Central's extensive real estate holdings in the area, which include hotels and office buildings, must realistically be imputed to the Terminal; and (4) the development rights above the Terminal, which had been made transferable to numerous sites in the vicinity of the Terminal, one or two of which were suitable for the construction of office buildings, were valuable to appellants and provided "significant, perhaps 'fair,' compensation for the loss of rights above the terminal itself." . . .

II . . .

A

. . . The question of what constitutes a "taking" for purposes of the Fifth Amendment has proved to be a problem of considerable difficulty. While this Court has recognized that the "Fifth Amendment's guarantee . . . [is] designed to bar Government from forcing some people alone to bear public burdens which, in all fairness and justice, should be borne by the public as a whole," *Armstrong v. United States*, 364 U.S. 40 (1960), this Court, quite simply, has been unable to develop any "set formula" for determining when "justice and fairness" require that economic injuries caused by public action be compensated by the government, rather than remain disproportionately concentrated on a few persons. Indeed, we have frequently observed that whether a particular restriction will be rendered invalid by the government's failure to pay for any losses proximately caused by it depends largely "upon the particular circumstances [in that] case."

In engaging in these essentially ad hoc, factual inquiries, the Court's decisions have identified several factors that have particular significance. The economic impact of the regulation on the claimant and, particularly, the extent to which the regulation has interfered with distinct investment-backed expectations are, of course, relevant considerations. So, too, is the character of the governmental action. A "taking" may more readily be found when the interference with property can be characterized as a physical invasion by government, see, *e.g.*, United States v. Causby, 328 U.S. 256 (1946), than when interference arises from some public program adjusting the benefits and burdens of economic life to promote the common good.

"Government hardly could go on if to some extent values incident to property could not be diminished without paying for every such change in the general law," Pennsylvania Coal Co. v. Mahon (1922), and this Court has accordingly recognized, in a wide variety of contexts, that government may execute laws or programs that adversely affect recognized economic values. Exercises of the taxing power are one obvious example. A second are the decisions in which this Court has dismissed "taking" challenges on the ground that, while the challenged government action caused economic harm, it did not interfere with interests that were sufficiently bound up with the reasonable expectations of the claimant to constitute "property" for Fifth Amendment purposes. See, *e.g.*, United States v. Willow River Power Co., 324 U.S. 499 (1945) (interest in high-water level of river for runoff for tailwaters to maintain power head is not property); United States

v. Chandler-Dunbar Water Power Co., 229 U.S. 53 (1913) (no property interest can exist in navigable waters); see also . . . Sax, *Takings and the Police Power*, 74 Yale L.J. 36, 61-62 (1964).

More importantly for the present case, in instances in which a state tribunal reasonably concluded that "the health, safety, morals, or general welfare" would be promoted by prohibiting particular contemplated uses of land, this Court has upheld land-use regulations that destroyed or adversely affected recognized real property interests. Zoning laws are, of course, the classic example, see Euclid v. Ambler Realty Co., 272 U.S. 365 (1926) (prohibition of industrial use); Gorieb v. Fox, 274 U.S. 603, 608 (1927) (requirement that portions of parcels be left unbuilt); Welch v. Swasey, 214 U.S. 91 (1909) (height restriction), which have been viewed as permissible governmental action even when prohibiting the most beneficial use of the property.

Zoning laws generally do not affect existing uses of real property, but "taking" challenges have also been held to be without merit in a wide variety of situations when the challenged governmental actions prohibited a beneficial use to which individual parcels had previously been devoted and thus caused substantial individualized harm. Miller v. Schoene, 276 U.S. 272 (1928), is illustrative. In that case, a state entomologist, acting pursuant to a state statute, ordered the claimants to cut down a large number of ornamental red cedar trees because they produced cedar rust fatal to apple trees cultivated nearby. Although the statute provided for recovery of any expense incurred in removing the cedars, and permitted claimants to use the felled trees, it did not provide compensation for the value of the standing trees or for the resulting decrease in market value of the properties as a whole. A unanimous Court held . . . that the State might properly make "a choice between the preservation of one class of property and that of the other" and since the apple industry was important in the State involved, concluded that the State had not exceeded "its constitutional powers by deciding upon the destruction of one class of property [without compensation] in order to save another which, in the judgment of the legislature, is of greater value to the public."

Again, Hadacheck v. Sebastian, 239 U.S. 394 (1915), upheld a law prohibiting the claimant from continuing his otherwise lawful business of operating a brickyard in a particular physical community on the ground that the legislature had reasonably concluded that the presence of the brickyard was inconsistent with neighboring uses. See also United States v. Central Eureka Mining Co., 357 U.S. 155 (1958) (Government order closing gold mines so that skilled miners would be available for other mining work held not a taking); Atchison, T. & S. F. R. Co. v. Public Utilities Comm'n, 346 U.S. 346 (1953) (railroad may be required to share cost of constructing railroad grade improvement); Walls v. Midland Carbon Co., 254 U.S. 300 (1920) (law prohibiting manufacture of carbon black upheld); Reinman v. Little Rock, 237 U.S. 171 (1915) (law prohibiting livery stable upheld); Mugler v. Kansas, 123 U.S. 623 (1887) (law prohibiting liquor business upheld).

Goldblatt v. Hempstead, 369 U.S. 590 (1962) is a recent example. There, a 1958 city safety ordinance banned any excavations below the water table and effectively prohibited the claimant from continuing a sand and gravel mining business that had been operated on the particular parcel since 1927. The Court upheld the ordinance against a "taking" challenge, although the ordinance prohibited the present and presumably most beneficial use of the property and had, like the regulations in *Miller* and *Hadacheck*, severely affected a particular owner. The Court assumed that the ordinance did not prevent the owner's reasonable use of the property since the owner made no showing of an adverse effect on the value of the land. Because the restriction served a substantial public purpose, the Court thus held no taking had occurred. It is, of course, implicit in *Goldblatt* that a use restriction on real property may constitute a "taking" if not reasonably necessary to the effectuation of a substantial public purpose, or perhaps if it has an unduly harsh impact upon the owner's use of the property.

Pennsylvania Coal Co. v. Mahon is the leading case for the proposition that a state statute that substantially furthers important public policies may so frustrate distinct investment-backed expectations as to amount to a "taking." There the claimant had sold the surface rights to particular parcels of property, but expressly reserved the right to remove the coal thereunder. A Pennsylvania statute, enacted after the transactions, forbade any mining of coal that caused the subsidence of any house, unless the house was the property of the owner of the underlying coal and was more than 150 feet from the improved property of another. Because the statute made it commercially impracticable to mine the coal, and thus had nearly the same effect as the complete destruction of rights claimant had reserved from the owners of the surface land, the Court held that the statute was invalid as effecting a "taking" without just compensation. See also Armstrong v. United States, 364 U.S. 40 (1960) (Government's complete destruction of a materialman's lien in certain property held a "taking"); Hudson Water Co. v. McCarter, 209 U.S. 349, 355 (1908) (if height restriction makes property wholly useless "the rights of property . . . prevail over the other public interest" and compensation is required). See generally Michelman, *Property, Utility, and Fairness: Comments on the Ethical Foundations of "Just Compensation" Law*, 80 Harv. L. Rev. 1165, 1229-1234 (1967).

Finally, government actions that may be characterized as acquisitions of resources to permit or facilitate uniquely public functions have often been held to constitute "takings." United States v. Causby, 328 U.S. 256 (1946), is illustrative. In holding that direct overflights above the claimant's land, that destroyed the present use of the land as a chicken farm, constituted a "taking," *Causby* emphasized that Government had not "merely destroyed property [but was] using a part of it for the flight of its planes." See also Griggs v. Allegheny County, 369 U.S. 84 (1962) (overflights held a taking); Portsmouth Co. v. United States, 260 U.S. 327 (1922) (United States military installations' repeated firing of guns over claimant's land is a taking); United States v. Cress, 243 U.S. 316 (1917) (repeated floodings of land caused by water project is taking); but see YMCA v. United States, 395 U.S. 85 (1969) (damage caused to building when federal officers who were seeking to protect building were attacked by rioters held not a taking).

B

. . . [A]ppellants make a series of arguments, which . . . essentially urge that any substantial restriction imposed pursuant to a landmark law must be accompanied by just compensation if it is to be constitutional. Before considering these, we emphasize what is not in dispute. . . . [A]ppellants do not contest that New York City's objective of preserving structures and areas with special historic, architectural, or cultural significance is an entirely permissible governmental goal. They also do not dispute that the restrictions imposed on its parcel are appropriate means of securing the purposes of the New York City law. Finally, appellants do not challenge any of the specific factual premises of the decision below. They accept for present purposes both that the parcel of land occupied by Grand Central Terminal must, in its present state, be regarded as capable of earning a reasonable return, and that the transferable development rights afforded appellants by virtue of the Terminal's designation as a landmark are valuable, even if not as valuable as the rights to construct above the Terminal. In appellants' view none of these factors derogate from their claim that New York City's law has effected a "taking."

. . . They urge that the Landmarks Law has deprived them of any gainful use of their "air rights" above the Terminal and that, irrespective of the value of the remainder of their parcel, the city has "taken" their right to this superadjacent airspace, thus entitling them to "just compensation" measured by the fair market value of these air rights.

Apart from our own disagreement with appellants' characterization of the effect of the New York City law, the submission that appellants may establish a "taking" simply by showing that they have been denied the ability to exploit a property interest that they heretofore had believed was available for development is quite simply untenable. . . . "Taking" jurisprudence does not divide a single parcel into discrete segments and attempt to determine whether rights in a particular segment have been entirely abrogated. In deciding whether a particular governmental action has effected a taking, this Court focuses rather both on the character of the action and on the nature and extent of the interference with rights in the parcel as a whole—here, the city tax block designated as the "landmark site."

Secondly, appellants, focusing on the character and impact of the New York City law, argue that it effects a "taking" because its operation has significantly diminished the value of the Terminal site. Appellants concede that the decisions sustaining other land-use regulations, which, like the New York City law, are reasonably related to the promotion of the general welfare, uniformly reject the proposition that diminution in property value, standing alone, can establish a "taking," see Euclid v. Ambler Realty Co. (75% diminution in value caused by zoning law); Hadacheck v. Sebastian (87 1/2 % diminution in value); and that the "taking" issue in these contexts is resolved by focusing on the uses the regulations permit. Appellants, moreover, also do not dispute that a showing of diminution in property value would not establish a taking if the restriction had been imposed as a result of historic-district legislation, but appellants argue that New York City's regulation of individual landmarks is fundamentally different . . . because the controls imposed by New York City's law apply only to individuals who own selected properties.

Stated baldly, appellants' position appears to be that the only means of ensuring that selected owners are not singled out to endure financial hardship for no reason is to hold that any restriction imposed on individual landmarks pursuant to the New York City scheme is a "taking" requiring the payment of "just compensation." Agreement with this argument would, of course, invalidate not just New York City's law, but all comparable landmark legislation in the Nation. We find no merit in it.

It is true . . . that both historic-district legislation and zoning laws regulate all properties within given physical communities whereas landmark laws apply only to selected parcels. But, contrary to appellants' suggestions, landmark laws are not like discriminatory, or "reverse spot," zoning; that is, a land-use decision which arbitrarily singles out a particular parcel for different, less favorable treatment than the neighboring ones. In contrast to discriminatory zoning, which is the antithesis of land-use control as part of some comprehensive plan, the New York City law embodies a comprehensive plan to preserve structures of historic or aesthetic interest wherever they might be found in the city . . . .

Equally without merit is the related argument that the decision to designate a structure as a landmark "is inevitably arbitrary or at least subjective, because it is basically a matter of taste," thus unavoidably singling out individual landowners for disparate and unfair treatment. The argument has a particularly hollow ring in this case. For appellants not only did not seek judicial review of either the designation or of the denials of the certificates of appropriateness and of no exterior effect, but do not even now suggest that the Commission's decisions concerning the Terminal were in any sense arbitrary or unprincipled. . . . [A] landmark owner has a right to judicial review of any Commission decision, and . . . there is no basis whatsoever for a conclusion that courts will have any greater difficulty identifying arbitrary or discriminatory action in the context of landmark regulation than in the context of classic zoning or indeed in any other context.

Next, appellants observe that New York City's law differs from zoning laws and historic-district ordinances in that the Landmarks Law does not impose identical or similar restrictions on all structures located in particular physical communities. It follows, they argue, that New York City's law is inherently incapable of producing the fair and equitable distribution of benefits and burdens of governmental action which is characteristic of zoning laws and historic-district legislation and which they maintain is a constitutional requirement if "just compensation" is not to be afforded. It is, of course, true that the Landmarks Law has a more severe impact on some landowners than on others, but that in itself does not mean that the law effects a "taking." Legislation designed to promote the general welfare commonly burdens some more than others. . . .[30] Similarly, zoning laws often affect some property owners more severely than others but have not been held to be invalid on that account. For example, the property owner in *Euclid* who wished to use its property for industrial purposes was affected far more severely by the ordinance than its neighbors who wished to use their land for residences.

30.   Appellants attempt to distinguish . . . [*Hadacheck*, Miller v. Schoene, and *Goldblatt*] on the ground that, in each, government was prohibiting a "noxious" use of land and that in the present case, in contrast, appellants' proposed construction above the Terminal would be beneficial. We observe that the uses in issue in *Hadacheck*, *Miller*, and *Goldblatt* were perfectly lawful in themselves. They involved no "blameworthiness, . . . moral wrongdoing or conscious act of dangerous risk-taking which induce[d society] to shift the cost to a pa[rt]icular individual." Sax, *Takings and the Police Power*, 74 Yale L.J. 36, 50 (1964). These cases are better understood as resting not on any supposed "noxious" quality of the prohibited uses but rather on the ground that the restrictions were reasonably related to the implementation of a policy—not unlike historic preservation—expected to produce a widespread public benefit and applicable to all similarly situated property.

Nor, correlatively, can it be asserted that the destruction or fundamental alteration of a historic landmark is not harmful. The suggestion that the beneficial quality of appellants' proposed construction is established by the fact that the construction would have been consistent with applicable zoning laws ignores the development in sensibilities and ideals reflected in landmark legislation like New York City's.

In any event, appellants' repeated suggestions that they are solely burdened and unbenefited is factually inaccurate. . . . [T]he New York City law applies to vast numbers of structures in the city in addition to the Terminal . . . many of which are close to the Terminal. Unless we are to reject the judgment of the New York City Council that the preservation of landmarks benefits all New York citizens and all structures, both economically and by improving the quality of life in the city as a whole—which we are unwilling to do—we cannot conclude that the owners of the Terminal have in no sense been benefited by the Landmarks Law. Doubtless appellants believe they are more burdened than benefited by the law, but that must have been true, too, of the property owners in *Miller*, *Hadacheck*, *Euclid*, and *Goldblatt*.

Appellants' final broad-based attack would have us treat the law as an instance, like that in United States v. Causby, in which government, acting in an enterprise capacity, has appropriated part of their property for some strictly governmental purpose. Apart from the fact that *Causby* was a case of invasion of airspace that destroyed the use of the farm beneath and this New York City law has in nowise impaired the present use of the Terminal, the Landmarks Law neither exploits appellants' parcel for city purposes nor facilitates nor arises from any entrepreneurial operations of the city. . . . The Landmarks Law's effect is simply to prohibit appellants or anyone else from occupying portions of the airspace above the Terminal, while permitting appellants to use the remainder of the parcel in a gainful fashion. This is no more an appropriation of property by government for its own uses than is a zoning law prohibiting, for "aesthetic" reasons, two or more adult theaters within a specified area, see Young v. American Mini Theatres, Inc., 427 U.S. 50 (1976), or a safety regulation prohibiting excavations below a certain level.

C

Rejection of appellants' broad arguments is not, however, the end of our inquiry . . . . We now must consider whether the interference with appellants' property is of such a magnitude that "there must be an exercise of eminent domain and compensation to sustain [it]." Pennsylvania Coal Co. v. Mahon. That inquiry may be narrowed to the question of the severity of the impact of the law on appellants' parcel, and its resolution in turn requires a careful assessment of the impact of the regulation on the Terminal site.

. . . [T]he New York City law does not interfere in any way with the present uses of the Terminal. . . . [A]ppellants may continue to use the property precisely as it has been used for the past 65 years: as a railroad terminal containing office space and concessions. So the law does not interfere with what must be regarded as Penn Central's primary expectation concerning the use of the parcel. More importantly, on this record, we must regard the New York City law as permitting Penn Central not only to profit from the Terminal but also to obtain a "reasonable return" on its investment.

Appellants . . . exaggerate the effect of the law on their ability to make use of the air rights above the Terminal in two respects. First, it simply cannot be maintained, on this record, that appellants have been prohibited from occupying *any* portion of the airspace above the Terminal. . . . [N]othing the Commission has said or done suggests an intention to prohibit *any* construction above the Terminal. The Commission's report emphasized that whether any construction would be allowed depended upon whether the proposed addition "would harmonize in scale, material and character with [the Terminal]." Since appellants have not sought approval for the construction of a smaller structure, we do not know that appellants will be denied any use of any portion of the airspace above the Terminal.

Second, to the extent appellants have been denied the right to build above the Terminal, it is not literally accurate to say that they have been denied *all* use of even those pre-existing air rights. . . . [T]hey are made transferable to at least eight parcels in the vicinity of the Terminal, one or two of which have been found suitable for the construction of new office buildings. Although appellants and others have argued that New York City's transferable development-rights program is far from ideal, the New York courts here supportably found that, at least in the case of the Terminal, the rights afforded are valuable. While these rights may well not have constituted "just compensation" if a "taking" had occurred, the rights nevertheless undoubtedly mitigate whatever financial burdens the law has imposed on appellants and, for that reason, are to be taken into account in considering the impact of regulation.

On this record, we conclude that the application of New York City's Landmarks Law has not effected a "taking" of appellants' property. The restrictions imposed are substantially related to the promotion of the general welfare and not only permit reasonable beneficial use of the landmark site but also afford appellants opportunities further to enhance not only the Terminal site proper but also other properties.

Affirmed.

Mr. Justice Rehnquist, with whom The Chief Justice [Burger] and Mr. Justice Stevens join, dissenting.

. . . The question in this case is whether the cost associated with the city of New York's desire to preserve a limited number of "landmarks" within its borders must be borne by all of its taxpayers or whether it can instead be imposed entirely on the owners of the individual properties.

Only in the most superficial sense of the word can this case be said to involve "zoning." Typical zoning restrictions may, it is true, so limit the prospective uses of a piece of property as to diminish the value of that property in the abstract because it may not be used for the forbidden purposes. But any such abstract decrease in value will more than likely be at least partially offset by an increase in value which flows from similar restrictions as to use on neighboring properties. . . . In the words of Mr. Justice Holmes, speaking for the Court in Pennsylvania Coal Co. v. Mahon, there is "an average reciprocity of advantage."

Where a relatively few individual buildings, all separated from one another, are singled out and treated differently from surrounding buildings, no such reciprocity exists. The cost to the property owner which results from the imposition of restrictions applicable only to his property and not that of his neighbors may be substantial—in this case, several million dollars—with no comparable reciprocal benefits. . . . [T]he landowner is not simply prohibited from using his property for certain purposes, while allowed to use it for all other purposes. . . . [T]he property owner is under an affirmative duty to *preserve* his property *as a landmark* at his own expense. To suggest that because traditional zoning results in some limitation of use of the property zoned, the New York City landmark preservation scheme should likewise be upheld, represents the ultimate in treating as alike things which are different. . . .

I

... Before the city of New York declared Grand Central Terminal to be a land-mark, Penn Central could have used its "air rights" over the Terminal to build a multistory office building, at an apparent value of several million dollars per year. Today, the Terminal cannot be modified in *any* form, including the erection of additional stories, without the permission of the Landmark Preservation Commission . . . .

Appellees do not dispute that valuable property rights have been destroyed. . . . Penn Central, absent the permission of appellees, must forever maintain its property in its present state. The property has been thus subjected to a nonconsensual servitude not borne by any neighboring or similar properties. . . .

... [A]n examination of the two exceptions where the destruction of property does *not* constitute a taking demonstrates that a compensable taking has occurred here.

1. As early as 1887, the Court recognized that the government can prevent a property owner from using his property to injure others without having to compensate the owner for the value of the forbidden use . . . ." The power which the States have of prohibiting such use by individuals of their property as will be prejudicial to the health, the morals, or the safety of the public, is not—and, consistently with the existence and safety of organized society, cannot be—burdened with the condition that the State must compensate such individual owners for pecuniary losses they may sustain, *by reason of their not being permitted, by a noxious use of their property, to inflict injury upon the community.*" Mugler v. Kansas. . . .[8]

The nuisance exception to the taking guarantee is not coterminous with the police power itself. The question is whether the forbidden use is dangerous to the safety, health, or welfare of others. Thus, in Curtin v. Benson, 222 U.S. 78 (1911), the Court held that the Government, in prohibiting the owner of property within the boundaries of Yosemite National Park from grazing cattle on his property, had taken the owner's property. The Court assumed that the Government could constitutionally require the owner to fence his land or take other action to prevent his cattle from straying onto others' land without compensating him. . . . The prohibition in question, however, was "not a prevention of a misuse or illegal use but the prevention of a legal and essential use, an attribute of its ownership."

Appellees are not prohibiting a nuisance. . . . [T]he proposed addition to the Grand Central Terminal would be in full compliance with zoning, height limitations, and other health and safety requirements. Instead, appellees are seeking to preserve what they believe to be an outstanding example of beaux-arts architecture. Penn Central is prevented from further developing its property basically because *too good* a job was done in designing and building it. . . .

... While Penn Central may continue to use the Terminal as it is presently designed, appellees otherwise "exercise complete dominion and control over the surface of the land," United States v. Causby, and must compensate the

---

8.   Each of the cases cited by the Court for the proposition that legislation which severely affects some landowners but not others does not effect a "taking" involved noxious uses of property. . . .

owner for his loss. "Property is taken in the constitutional sense when inroads are made upon an owner's use of it to an extent that, as between private parties, a servitude has been acquired." United States v. Dickinson, 331 U.S. 745 (1947).

2. . . . Here, . . . a multimillion dollar loss has been imposed on appellants; it is uniquely felt and is not offset by any benefits flowing from the preservation of some 400 other "landmarks" in New York City. Appellees have imposed a substantial cost on less than one one-tenth of one percent of the buildings in New York City for the general benefit of all its people. It is exactly this imposition of general costs on a few individuals at which the "taking" protection is directed. . . .

Appellees . . . argue that a taking only occurs where a property owner is denied *all* reasonable value of his property. The Court has frequently held that, even where a destruction of property rights would not *otherwise* constitute a taking, the inability of the owner to make a reasonable return on his property requires compensation under the Fifth Amendment. But the converse is not true. A taking does not become a noncompensable exercise of police power simply because the government in its grace allows the owner to make some "reasonable" use of his property. "[I]t is the character of the invasion, not the amount of damage resulting from it, so long as the damage is substantial, that determines the question whether it is a taking." . . .

Appellees, apparently recognizing that the constraints imposed on a landmark site constitute a taking for Fifth Amendment purposes, do not leave the property owner empty-handed. As the Court notes, the property owner may theoretically "transfer" his previous right to develop the landmark property to adjacent properties if they are under his control. Appellees have coined this system "Transfer Development Rights," or TDR's.

Of all the terms used in the Taking Clause, "just compensation" has the strictest meaning. The Fifth Amendment does not allow simply an approximate compensation but requires "a full and perfect equivalent for the property taken." . . . [T]he determination of whether a "full and perfect equivalent" has been awarded is a "judicial function." The fact that *appellees* may believe that TDR's provide full compensation is irrelevant.

Appellees contend that, even if they have "taken" appellants' property, TDR's constitute "just compensation." Appellants, of course, argue that TDR's are highly imperfect compensation. Because the lower courts held that there was no "taking," they did not have to reach the question of whether or not just compensation has already been awarded. . . . I would remand to the Court of Appeals for a determination of whether TDR's constitute a "full and perfect equivalent for the property taken."[14]

_____

14.   The Court suggests that if appellees are held to have "taken" property rights of landmark owners, not only the New York City Landmarks Preservation Law, but "all comparable landmark legislation in the Nation" must fall. This assumes, of course, that TDR's are not "just compensation" for the property rights destroyed. It also ignores the fact that many States and cities in the Nation have chosen to preserve landmarks by purchasing or condemning restrictive easements over the facades of the landmarks and are apparently quite satisfied with the results. . . . The British National Trust has effectively used restrictive easements to preserve landmarks since 1937. Other States and cities have found that tax incentives are also an effective means of encouraging the private preservation of landmark sites. . . . The New York City Landmarks Preservation Law departs drastically from these traditional, and constitutional, means of preserving landmarks.

Over 50 years ago, Mr. Justice Holmes, speaking for the Court, warned that the courts were "in danger of forgetting that a strong public desire to improve the public condition is not enough to warrant achieving the desire by a shorter cut than the constitutional way of paying for the change." Pennsylvania Coal Co. v. Mahon. The Court's opinion in this case demonstrates that the danger thus foreseen has not abated. . . .

Notes and Questions

1. How useful is a test that has no "set formula" and requires engaging in "essentially ad hoc, factual inquiries" to planners and other government officials? How much flexibility does the *Penn Central* test give to judges in deciding whether to invalidate legislation?

2. *The "denominator" problem.* How are the economic impact on and the investment-backed expectations in the property determined? What is the relevant property? In *Pennsylvania Coal*, the majority focused on the coal required to be left in place; the dissent on the entire parcel in which the coal was located. The majority found the economic impact severe ("to make it commercially impracticable to mine certain coal has very nearly the same effect for constitutional purposes as appropriating or destroying it"). The dissent found it minor ("for aught that appears, the value of the coal kept in place by the restriction may be negligible as compared with the value of the whole property, or even as compared with that part of it which is represented by the coal remaining in place and which may be extracted despite the statute").

How did the majority and dissenters differ over the relevant property in *Penn Central?*

3. *Penn Central*'s balancing test continues to govern all regulatory takings cases except those carved out by a so-called categorical takings test. One such test was established by the *Loretto* case (1982), which held that a government-authorized, permanent, physical occupation of land is a taking without regard to the economic impact or importance of the governmental purpose. Another was established by the *Lucas* case, which we take up next.

[handwritten margin note: Penn Central Balancing test]

4. *Value of transferable development rights.* The New York Times reported on February 25, 2013 that developers William and Arthur Zeckendorf were paying $40 million for 70,000 square feet, or $600 per square foot, for unused development rights so they could add floors to a planned ultra-luxury tower on 60th Street in the old Silk Stocking District. The air rights are being transferred from Christ Church, at the northwest corner of Park Avenue and 60th Street. The new tower will be 51 stories and contain 30 apartments they expect to sell for $8,000 per square foot.

The Wall Street Journal reported October 17, 2013 that a group called Iconplans is proposing a change in the New York ordinance so that air rights held by the 180 nonprofits owning landmark buildings become transferable to a common air rights bank run by Iconplans, which could then sell them for use anywhere within New York City, taking a 10 percent commission.

The Modern Property Rights Movement

MORE UNFINISHED STORIES: *LUCAS, ATLANTA COALITION,* AND *PALILA/SWEET HOME*

Oliver A. Houck, 75 U. Colo. L. Rev. 331, 343-46 (2004)

In 1971 the United States Chamber of Commerce, reeling from the first waves of environmental litigation, commissioned a study from Lewis Powell, Jr., then in private practice. Powell's conclusions were that American free enterprise was under "frontal assault" from those (naming consumer activist Ralph Nader and Yale historian Charles Reich) "who propagandize against the system, seeking insidiously and constantly to sabotage it." The time had come for business to marshal its forces against those who would destroy it, and Powell followed with recommendations for Chamber-sponsored scholars, speakers, think-tanks, textbook evaluation, media surveillance, and political action and litigation. Within months Lewis Powell would go onto the Supreme Court, and within a year the Chamber of Commerce would be founding the first business-sponsored public interest law firm, the Pacific Legal Foundation, with the mission to "promote the general interest of business in the nation's courts." Backed by the construction and homebuilding industry, and in turn backing the industry's own lawsuits, Pacific Legal made land use and property rights its stock in trade, and the California Coastal Commission, striving to implement the federal and state coastal zone programs, its favorite defendant. By 1996 Pacific Legal was proclaiming "a quarter of a century devoted to defending property rights." Pacific Legal's goal, however, was not compensation. The goal was, in its own words, to "get rid of the regulatory state;" and it had lots of company.

The intellectual push for the property rights movement came from Richard Epstein, a University of Chicago professor who . . . published a book recommending that the takings clause be used as a tool to defeat government regulation. [*Takings: Private Property and the Power of Eminent Domain* (Harvard University Press, 1985)] . . . . A reconstruction of takings could undermine "many of the heralded reforms and institutions of the twentieth century: zoning, rent control, workers' compensation laws, transfer payments, [and] progressive taxation." . . . Epstein's new reading of takings was absolute: if any part of a property interest were diminished, if you lost an inch of space or a dollar in value, you had a takings claim. His corollary, in order to defeat the nuisance exception, was to restate the exception in the narrowest terms, actions that physically invaded neighboring property. To implement the agenda, Epstein called for "a level of judicial intervention far greater than we now have, and indeed far greater than we ever have had." All three of his recommendations would find their way to the Supreme Court, and into the majority decision on David Lucas and the South Carolina Beachfront Management Act.

An intellectual theory in their back pocket and early success in California already on the board, the backers of the property rights movement—primarily land developers, contractors and a wide range of industries with no particular properties at risk but high levels of antipathy to environmental constraints—took their offense nationwide. The Olin Foundation and others formed the Federalist

Society ("the cornerstone of our success on the law school campuses"), annually supported by Olin lectures, featuring conservative members of the federal judiciary and, in turn, the basic recruiting device for the conservative and property rights movements. Out of the Society would come, *inter alia*, Justice Antonin Scalia, author of the majority opinion in *Lucas*. Out of the Society and its business funders would also come a range of other initiatives originally suggested by Lewis Powell, including media monitoring, judicial education projects, cadres of sponsored speakers, think tanks, and university institutes, all with the same message: up with private property rights and down with regulations. It would establish a separate federal court of claims for property takings cases (while "liberals . . . [were] somewhat asleep at the switch"), and staff it with the most intransigent true believers it could find. It would enter the Administration through the Office of the Attorney General, whose Solicitor General, also a loyal soldier in the Reagan revolution, later wrote:

> Attorney General Meese and his young advisers—many drawn from the ranks of the then fledgling Federalist Societies and often devotees of the extreme libertarian views of University of Chicago law professor Richard Epstein—had a specific, aggressive, and, it seemed to me, quite radical project in mind: to use the Takings Clause of the Fifth Amendment as a severe brake upon federal and state regulation of business and property. The grand plan was to make government pay compensation as for a taking of property every time its regulations impinged too severely on a property right—limiting the possible uses for a parcel of land or restricting or tying up a business in regulatory red tape. If the government labored under so severe an obligation, there would be, to say the least, much less regulation. [Charles Fried, *Order and Law: Arguing the Reagan Revolution: A Firsthand Account* 183 (1991).]

In short, by the time Mr. Lucas was taking his case through the courts, the legal landscape was undergoing a seismic shift, funded by business and industry, and seeking not the compensation of individual landowners but rather, and quite overtly, the frustration of all government social and environmental programs through the threat of compensation. . . .

LUCAS v. SOUTH CAROLINA COASTAL COUNCIL

Supreme Court of the United States
505 U.S. 1003 (1992)

Justice SCALIA delivered the opinion of the Court [in which REHNQUIST, C.J., and WHITE, O'CONNOR, and THOMAS, JJ., joined.]

In 1986, petitioner David H. Lucas paid $975,000 for two residential lots on the Isle of Palms in Charleston County, South Carolina, on which he intended to build single-family homes. In 1988, however, the South Carolina Legislature enacted the Beachfront Management Act, which had the direct effect of barring petitioner from erecting any permanent habitable structures on his two parcels. A state trial court found that this prohibition rendered Lucas's parcels "valueless." This case requires us to decide whether the Act's dramatic effect on the economic value of Lucas's lots accomplished a taking of private property under the Fifth and Fourteenth Amendments requiring the payment of "just compensation."

I

A

South Carolina's expressed interest in intensively managing development activities in the so-called "coastal zone" dates from 1977 when, in the aftermath of Congress's passage of the federal Coastal Zone Management Act of 1972, the legislature enacted a Coastal Zone Management Act of its own. In its original form, the South Carolina Act required owners of coastal zone land that qualified as a "critical area" (defined in the legislation to include beaches and immediately adjacent sand dunes, to obtain a permit from the newly created South Carolina Coastal Council (respondent here) prior to committing the land to a "use other than the use the critical area was devoted to on [September 28, 1977]."

In the late 1970's, Lucas and others began extensive residential development of the Isle of Palms, a barrier island situated eastward of the city of Charleston. Toward the close of the development cycle for one residential subdivision known as "Beachwood East," Lucas in 1986 purchased the two lots at issue in this litigation for his own account. No portion of the lots, which were located approximately 300 feet from the beach, qualified as a "critical area" under the 1977 Act; accordingly, at the time Lucas acquired these parcels, he was not legally obliged to obtain a permit from the Council in advance of any development activity. His intention with respect to the lots was to do what the owners of the immediately adjacent parcels had already done: erect single-family residences. He commissioned architectural drawings for this purpose.

The Beachfront Management Act brought Lucas's plans to an abrupt end. Under that 1988 legislation, the Council was directed to establish a "baseline" connecting the landward-most "point[s] of erosion . . . during the past forty years" in the region of the Isle of Palms that includes Lucas's lots. In action not challenged here, the Council fixed this baseline landward of Lucas's parcels. That was significant, for under the Act construction of occupiable improvements[2] was flatly prohibited seaward of a line drawn 20 feet landward of, and parallel to, the baseline. The Act provided no exceptions.

B

Lucas promptly filed suit . . . . Lucas did not take issue with the validity of the [Beachfront Management] Act as a lawful exercise of South Carolina's police power, but contended that the Act's complete extinguishment of his property's value entitled him to compensation regardless of whether the legislature had acted in furtherance of legitimate police power objectives. Following a bench trial, the court agreed. . . . The trial court . . . found that the Beachfront Management Act decreed a permanent ban on construction insofar as Lucas's

---

2. The Act did allow the construction of certain nonhabitable improvements, e.g., "wooden walkways no larger in width than six feet," and "small wooden decks no larger than one hundred forty-four square feet."

lots were concerned, and that this prohibition "deprive[d] Lucas of any reasonable economic use of the lots, . . . eliminated the unrestricted right of use, and render[ed] them valueless." The court . . . ordered respondent to pay "just compensation" in the amount of $1,232,387.50.

The Supreme Court of South Carolina reversed. It found dispositive what it described as Lucas's concession "that the Beachfront Management Act [was] properly and validly designed to preserve . . . South Carolina's beaches." Failing an attack on the validity of the statute as such, the court believed itself bound to accept the "uncontested . . . findings" of the South Carolina Legislature that new construction in the coastal zone . . . threatened this public resource. The court ruled that when a regulation respecting the use of property is designed "to prevent serious public harm," (citing, *inter alia*, Mugler v. Kansas, 123 U.S. 623 (1887)), no compensation is owing under the Takings Clause regardless of the regulation's effect on the property's value.

Two justices dissented. They acknowledged that our *Mugler* line of cases recognizes governmental power to prohibit "noxious" uses of property — *i.e.,* uses of property akin to "public nuisances" — without having to pay compensation. But they would not have characterized the Beachfront Management Act's "*primary* purpose [as] the prevention of a nuisance." To the dissenters, the chief purposes of the legislation, among them the promotion of tourism and the creation of a "habitat for indigenous flora and fauna," could not fairly be compared to nuisance abatement. . . . [T]hey would have affirmed the trial court's conclusion that the Act's obliteration of the value of petitioner's lots accomplished a taking. . . .

II

As a threshold matter, we must briefly address the Council's suggestion that this case is inappropriate for plenary review. After briefing and argument before the South Carolina Supreme Court, but prior to issuance of that court's opinion, the Beachfront Management Act was amended to authorize the Council, in certain circumstances, to issue "special permits" for the construction or reconstruction of habitable structures seaward of the baseline. According to the Council, this amendment renders Lucas's claim of a permanent deprivation unripe, as Lucas may yet be able to secure permission to build on his property. "[The Court's] cases," we are reminded, "uniformly reflect an insistence on knowing the nature and extent of permitted development before adjudicating the constitutionality of the regulations that purport to limit it." MacDonald, Sommer & Frates v. Yolo County, 477 U.S. 340 (1986). Because petitioner "has not yet obtained a final decision regarding how [he] will be allowed to develop [his] property," Williamson County Regional Planning Comm'n v. Hamilton Bank of Johnson City, 473 U.S. 172 (1985), the Council argues that he is not yet entitled to definitive adjudication of his takings claim in this Court.

We think these considerations would preclude review had the South Carolina Supreme Court rested its judgment on ripeness grounds, as it was (essentially) invited to do by the Council. The South Carolina Supreme Court shrugged off the possibility of further administrative and trial proceedings, however, preferring to dispose of Lucas's takings claim on the merits. This unusual disposition does not preclude Lucas from applying for a permit under the 1990 amend-ment for *future* construction, and challenging, on takings grounds, any denial. But it does preclude, both practically and legally, any takings claim with respect to Lucas's *past* deprivation, *i.e.,* for his having been denied construction rights during the period before the 1990 amendment. See generally First English Evangelical Lutheran Church of Glendale v. County of Los Angeles, 482 U.S. 304 (1987) (holding that temporary deprivations of use are compensable under the Takings Clause). . . . Lucas had no reason to proceed on a "temporary tak-ing" theory at trial, or even to seek remand for that purpose prior to submission of the case to the South Carolina Supreme Court, since as the Act then read, the taking was unconditional and permanent. Moreover, given the breadth of the South Carolina Supreme Court's holding and judgment, Lucas would plainly be unable (absent our intervention now) to obtain further state-court adjudication with respect to the 1988-1990 period.

In these circumstances, we think it would not accord with sound process to insist that Lucas pursue the late-created "special permit" procedure before his takings claim can be considered ripe. . . .

III

A

Prior to Justice Holmes's exposition in Pennsylvania Coal Co. v. Mahon, 260 U.S. 393 (1922), it was generally thought that the Takings Clause reached only a "direct appropriation" of property, or the functional equivalent of a "practical ouster of [the owner's] possession," Justice Holmes recognized in *Mahon*, how-ever, that if the protection against physical appropriations of private property was to be meaningfully enforced, the government's power to redefine the range of interests included in the ownership of property was necessarily constrained by constitutional limits. If, instead, the uses of private property were subject to unbridled, uncompensated qualification under the police power, "the natural tendency of human nature [would be] to extend the qualification more and more until at last private property disappear[ed]." These considerations gave birth in that case to the oft-cited maxim that, "while property may be regulated to a certain extent, if regulation goes too far it will be recognized as a taking."

Nevertheless, our decision in *Mahon* offered little insight into when, and under what circumstances, a given regulation would be seen as going "too far" for purposes of the Fifth Amendment. In 70-odd years of succeeding "regula-tory takings" jurisprudence, we have generally eschewed any "'set formula'" for determining how far is too far, preferring to "engag[e] in . . . essentially ad hoc, factual inquiries." Penn Central Transportation Co. v. New York City (1978) (quoting Goldblatt v. Hempstead (1962)). See Epstein, *Takings: Descent and Resurrection*, 1987 S. Ct. Rev. 1, 4. We have, however, described at least two discrete categories of regulatory action as compensable without case-specific inquiry into the public interest advanced in support of the restraint. The first encompasses regulations that compel the property owner to suffer a physi-cal "invasion" of his property. In general (at least with regard to permanent invasions), no matter how minute the intrusion, and no matter how weighty the public purpose behind it, we have required compensation. For example, in Loretto v. Teleprompter Manhattan CATV Corp., 458 U.S. 419 (1982), we determined that New York's law requiring landlords to allow television cable companies to emplace cable facilities in their apartment buildings constituted a taking, even though the facilities occupied at most only 1 1/2 cubic feet of the landlords' property. See also United States v. Causby (1946) (physical invasions of airspace); cf. Kaiser Aetna v. United States, 444 U.S. 164 (1979) (imposition of navigational servitude upon private marina).

The second situation in which we have found categorical treatment appropriate is where regulation denies all economically beneficial or productive use of land.[7]

We have never set forth the justification for this rule. Perhaps it is simply, as Justice Brennan suggested, that total deprivation of beneficial use is, from the landowner's point of view, the equivalent of a physical appropriation. See San Diego Gas & Electric Co. v. San Diego, 450 U.S., at 652 (dissenting opinion). "[F]or what is the land but the profits thereof[?]" 1 E. Coke, Institutes, ch. 1, § 1 (1st Am. ed. 1812). Surely, at least, in the extraordinary circumstance when *no* productive or economically beneficial use of land is permitted, it is less realistic to indulge our usual assumption that the legislature is simply "adjusting the benefits and burdens of economic life," in a manner that secures an "average reciprocity of advantage" to everyone concerned. And the *functional* basis for permitting the government, by regulation, to affect property values without compensation—that "Government hardly could go on if to some extent values incident to property could not be diminished without paying for every such change in the general law"—does not apply to the relatively rare situations where the government has deprived a landowner of all economically beneficial uses.

On the other side of the balance, affirmatively supporting a compensation requirement, is the fact that regulations that leave the owner of land without economically beneficial or productive options for its use—typically, as here,

---

7. Regrettably, the rhetorical force of our "deprivation of all economically feasible use" rule is greater than its precision, since the rule does not make clear the "property interest" against which the loss of value is to be measured. When, for example, a regulation requires a developer to leave 90% of a rural tract in its natural state, it is unclear whether we would analyze the situation as one in which the owner has been deprived of all economically beneficial use of the burdened portion of the tract, or as one in which the owner has suffered a mere diminution in value of the tract as a whole. (For an extreme—and, we think, unsupportable—view of the relevant calculus, see Penn Central Transportation Co. v. New York City, 366 N.E.2d 1271 (N.Y. 1977), where the state court examined the diminution in a particular parcel's value produced by a municipal ordinance in light of total value of the takings claimant's other holdings in the vicinity.) Unsurprisingly, this uncertainty regarding the composition of the denominator in our "deprivation" fraction has produced inconsistent pronouncements by the Court. Compare Pennsylvania Coal Co. v. Mahon (1922) (law restricting subsurface extraction of coal held to effect a taking), with Keystone Bituminous Coal Assn. v. DeBenedictis, 480 U.S. 470 (1987) (nearly identical law held not to effect a taking); see also . . . Rose, *Mahon* Reconstructed: Why the Takings Issue is Still a Muddle, 57 S. Cal. L. Rev. 561, 566–569 (1984). The answer to this difficult question may lie in how the owner's reasonable expectations have been shaped by the State's law of property—*i.e.*, whether and to what degree the State's law has accorded legal recognition and protection to the particular interest in land with respect to which the takings claimant alleges a diminution in (or elimination of) value. In any event, we avoid this difficulty in the present case, since the "interest in land" that Lucas has pleaded (a fee simple interest) is an estate with a rich tradition of protection at common law, and since the South Carolina Court of Common Pleas found that the Beachfront Management Act left each of Lucas's beachfront lots without economic value.

by requiring land to be left substantially in its natural state—carry with them a heightened risk that private property is being pressed into some form of public service under the guise of mitigating serious public harm. . . . The many statutes on the books, both state and federal, that provide for the use of eminent domain to impose servitudes on private scenic lands preventing developmental uses, or to acquire such lands altogether, suggest the practical equivalence in this setting of negative regulation and appropriation. . . .

We think, in short, that there are good reasons for our frequently expressed belief that when the owner of real property has been called upon to sacrifice *all* economically beneficial uses in the name of the common good, that is, to leave his property economically idle, he has suffered a taking.[8]

B

The trial court found Lucas's two beachfront lots to have been rendered valueless by respondent's enforcement of the coastal-zone construction ban.[9] Under Lucas's theory of the case, which rested upon our "no economically viable use" statements, that finding entitled him to compensation. Lucas believed it unnecessary to take issue with either the purposes behind the Beachfront Management Act, or the means chosen by the South Carolina Legislature to effectuate those purposes. The South Carolina Supreme Court, however, thought otherwise. In its view, the Beachfront Management Act was no ordinary enactment, but involved an exercise of South Carolina's "police powers" to mitigate the harm to the public interest that petitioner's use of his land might occasion. By neglecting to dispute the findings enumerated in the Act or otherwise to challenge the legislature's purposes, petitioner "concede[d] that the beach/dune area of South Carolina's shores is an extremely valuable public resource; that the erection of new construction, *inter alia*, contributes to the erosion and destruction of this public resource; and that discouraging new construction in close proximity to the beach/dune area is necessary to prevent a great public harm." In the court's view, these concessions brought petitioner's challenge within a long line of this Court's cases sustaining against Due Process and Takings Clause challenges the State's use of its "police powers" to enjoin a property owner from activities akin to public nuisances.

---

8. Justice STEVENS criticizes the "deprivation of all economically beneficial use" rule as "wholly arbitrary," in that "[the] landowner whose property is diminished in value 95% recovers nothing," while the landowner who suffers a complete elimination of value "recovers the land's full value." This analysis errs in its assumption that the landowner whose deprivation is one step short of complete is not entitled to compensation. Such an owner might not be able to claim the benefit of our categorical formulation, but, as we have acknowledged time and again, "[t]he economic impact of the regulation on the claimant and . . . the extent to which the regulation has interfered with distinct investment-backed expectations" are keenly relevant to takings analysis generally. Penn Central Transportation Co. v. New York City (1978). It is true that in at least some cases the landowner with 95% loss will get nothing, while the landowner with total loss will recover in full. But that occasional result is no more strange than the gross disparity between the landowner whose premises are taken for a highway (who recovers in full) and the landowner whose property is reduced to 5% of its former value by the highway (who recovers nothing). Takings law is full of these "all-or-nothing" situations.

9. This finding was the premise of the petition for certiorari, and since it was not challenged in the brief in opposition we decline to entertain the argument in respondent's brief on the merits that the finding was erroneous. . . .

It is correct that many of our prior opinions have suggested that "harmful or noxious uses" of property may be proscribed by government regulation without the requirement of compensation. For a number of reasons, however, we think the South Carolina Supreme Court was too quick to conclude that that principle decides the present case. The "harmful or noxious uses" principle was the Court's early attempt to describe in theoretical terms why government may, consistent with the Takings Clause, affect property values by regulation without incurring an obligation to compensate — a reality we nowadays acknowledge explicitly with respect to the full scope of the State's police power. . . . We made this very point in *Penn Central Transportation Co.*, where, in the course of sustaining New York City's landmarks preservation program against a takings challenge, we rejected the petitioner's suggestion that *Mugler* and the cases following it were premised on, and thus limited by, some objective conception of "noxiousness" . . . .

"Harmful or noxious use" analysis was, in other words, simply the progenitor of our more contemporary statements that "land-use regulation does not effect a taking if it 'substantially advance[s] legitimate state interests' . . . ." . . . Agins v. Tiburon, 447 U.S. 255 at 260 (1980).

The transition from our early focus on control of "noxious" uses to our contemporary understanding of the broad realm within which government may regulate without compensation was an easy one, since the distinction between "harm-preventing" and "benefit-conferring" regulation is often in the eye of the beholder. It is quite possible, for example, to describe in *either* fashion the ecological, economic, and esthetic concerns that inspired the South Carolina Legislature in the present case. One could say that imposing a servitude on Lucas's land is necessary in order to prevent his use of it from "harming" South Carolina's ecological resources; or, instead, in order to achieve the "benefits" of an ecological preserve.[11] Compare, *e.g.,* Claridge v. New Hampshire Wetlands Board, 485 A.2d 287, 292 (N.H. 1984) (owner may, without compensation, be barred from filling wetlands because landfilling would deprive adjacent coastal habitats and marine fisheries of ecological support), with, *e.g.,* Bartlett v. Zoning Comm'n of Old Lyme, 282 A.2d 907 (Conn. 1971) (owner barred from filling tidal marshland must be compensated, despite municipality's "laudable" goal of "preserv[ing] marshlands from encroachment or destruction"). Whether one or the other of the competing characterizations will come to one's lips in a

---

11. In the present case, in fact, some of the "[South Carolina] legislature's 'findings'" to which the South Carolina Supreme Court purported to defer in characterizing the purpose of the Act as "harm-preventing," seem to us phrased in "benefit-conferring" language instead. For example, they describe the importance of a construction ban in enhancing "South Carolina's annual tourism industry revenue," in "provid[ing] habitat for numerous species of plants and animals, several of which are threatened or endangered," and in "provid[ing] a natural healthy environment for the citizens of South Carolina to spend leisure time which serves their physical and mental well-being." It would be pointless to make the outcome of this case hang upon this terminology, since the same interests could readily be described in "harm-preventing" fashion.

Justice BLACKMUN, however, apparently insists that we *must* make the outcome hinge (exclusively) upon the South Carolina Legislature's other, "harm-preventing" characterizations, focusing on the declaration that "prohibitions on building in front of the setback line are necessary to protect people and property from storms, high tides, and beach erosion." He says "[n]othing in the record undermines [this] assessment," apparently seeing no significance in the fact that the statute permits owners of *existing* structures to remain (and even to rebuild if their structures are not "destroyed beyond repair"), and in the fact that the 1990 amendment authorizes the Council to issue permits for new construction in violation of the uniform prohibition.

particular case depends primarily upon one's evaluation of the worth of competing uses of real estate. . . . A given restraint will be seen as mitigating "harm"
to the adjacent parcels or securing a "benefit" for them, depending upon the
observer's evaluation of the relative importance of the use that the restraint
favors. See Sax, *Takings and the Police Power*, 74 Yale L.J. 36, 49 (1964) ("[T]he
problem [in this area] is not one of noxiousness or harm-creating activity at all;
rather it is a problem of inconsistency between perfectly innocent and independently desirable uses"). Whether Lucas's construction of single-family residences
on his parcels should be described as bringing "harm" to South Carolina's adjacent ecological resources thus depends principally upon whether the describer
believes that the State's use interest in nurturing those resources is so important
that *any* competing adjacent use must yield.[12]

When it is understood that "prevention of harmful use" was merely our early
formulation of the police power justification necessary to sustain (without compensation) *any* regulatory diminution in value; and that the distinction between
regulation that "prevents harmful use" and that which "confers benefits" is difficult, if not impossible, to discern on an objective, value-free basis; it becomes
self-evident that noxious-use logic cannot serve as a touchstone to distinguish
regulatory "takings"—which require compensation—from regulatory deprivations that do not require compensation. *A fortiori* the legislature's recitation of
a noxious-use justification cannot be the basis for departing from our categorical rule that total regulatory takings must be compensated. If it were, departure would virtually always be allowed. The South Carolina Supreme Court's
approach would essentially nullify *Mahon*'s affirmation of limits to the noncompensable exercise of the police power. Our cases provide no support for this:
None of them that employed the logic of "harmful use" prevention to sustain
a regulation involved an allegation that the regulation wholly eliminated the
value of the claimant's land.[13]

Where the State seeks to sustain regulation that deprives land of all economically beneficial use, we think it may resist compensation only if the logically antecedent inquiry into the nature of the owner's estate shows that the proscribed
use interests were not part of his title to begin with. This accords, we think, with
our "takings" jurisprudence, which has traditionally been guided by the understandings of our citizens regarding the content of, and the State's power over, the
"bundle of rights" that they acquire when they obtain title to property. It seems
to us that the property owner necessarily expects the uses of his property to be
restricted, from time to time, by various measures newly enacted by the State
in legitimate exercise of its police powers; "[a]s long recognized, some values

---

12. In Justice BLACKMUN's view, even with respect to regulations that deprive an owner of all
developmental or economically beneficial land uses, the test for required compensation is whether
the legislature has recited a harm-preventing justification for its action. Since such a justification
can be formulated in practically every case, this amounts to a test of whether the legislature has a
stupid staff. We think the Takings Clause requires courts to do more than insist upon artful harm-
preventing characterizations.

13. *E.g.,* Mugler v. Kansas (1887) (prohibition upon use of a building as a brewery; other uses
permitted); Plymouth Coal Co. v. Pennsylvania (1914) (requirement that "pillar" of coal be left
in ground to safeguard mine workers; mineral rights could otherwise be exploited); Reinman v.
Little Rock (1915) (declaration that livery stable constituted a public nuisance; other uses of the
property permitted); Hadacheck v. Sebastian (1915) (prohibition of brick manufacturing in residential area; other uses permitted); Goldblatt v. Hempstead (1962) (prohibition on excavation;
other uses permitted).

are enjoyed under an implied limitation and must yield to the police power." Pennsylvania Coal Co. v. Mahon. And in the case of personal property, by reason of the State's traditionally high degree of control over commercial dealings, he ought to be aware of the possibility that new regulation might even render his property economically worthless (at least if the property's only economically productive use is sale or manufacture for sale). See Andrus v. Allard, 444 U.S. 51 (1979) (prohibition on sale of eagle feathers). In the case of land, however, we think the notion pressed by the Council that title is somehow held subject to the "implied limitation" that the State may subsequently eliminate all economically valuable use is inconsistent with the historical compact recorded in the Takings Clause that has become part of our constitutional culture.[15]

Where "permanent physical occupation" of land is concerned, we have refused to allow the government to decree it anew (without compensation), no matter how weighty the asserted "public interests" involved, Loretto v. Teleprompter Manhattan CATV Corp. — though we assuredly *would* permit the government to assert a permanent easement that was a pre-existing limitation upon the land owner's title. Compare Scranton v. Wheeler, 179 U.S. 141, 163 (1900) (interests of "riparian owner in the submerged lands . . . bordering on a public navigable water" held subject to Government's navigational servitude), with Kaiser Aetna v. United States, 444 U.S., at 178-180 (imposition of navigational servitude on marina created and rendered navigable at private expense held to constitute a taking). We believe similar treatment must be accorded confiscatory regulations, *i.e.,* regulations that prohibit all economically beneficial use of land: Any limitation so severe cannot be newly legislated or decreed (without compensation), but must inhere in the title itself, in the restrictions that background principles of the State's law of property and nuisance already place upon land ownership. A law or decree with such an effect must, in other words, do no more than duplicate the result that could have been achieved in the courts — by adjacent landowners (or other uniquely affected persons) under the State's law of private nuisance, or by the State under its complementary power to abate nuisances that affect the public generally, or otherwise.[16]

15. After accusing us of "launch[ing] a missile to kill a mouse," Justice BLACKMUN expends a good deal of throw-weight of his own upon a noncombatant, arguing that our description of the "understanding" of land ownership that informs the Takings Clause is not supported by early American experience. That is largely true, but entirely irrelevant. The practices of the States *prior* to incorporation of the Takings and Just Compensation Clauses [1897], which, as Justice BLACKMUN acknowledges, occasionally included *outright physical appropriation* of land without compensation, were out of accord with *any* plausible interpretation of those provisions. Justice BLACKMUN is correct that early constitutional theorists did not believe the Takings Clause embraced regulations of property at all, but even he does not suggest (explicitly, at least) that we renounce the Court's contrary conclusion in *Mahon.* Since the text of the Clause can be read to encompass regulatory as well as physical deprivations (in contrast to the text originally proposed by Madison, see Speech Proposing Bill of Rights (June 8, 1789), in 12 J. Madison, The Papers of James Madison 201 (C. Hobson, R. Rutland, W. Rachal, & J. Sisson ed. 1979) ("No person shall be . . . obliged to relinquish his property, where it may be necessary for public use, without a just compensation"), we decline to do so as well.

16. The principal "otherwise" that we have in mind is litigation absolving the State (or private parties) of liability for the destruction of "real and personal property, in cases of actual necessity, to prevent the spreading of a fire" or to forestall other grave threats to the lives and property of others. Bowditch v. Boston, 101 U.S. 16 (1880); see United States v. Pacific R., Co., 120 U.S. 227 (1887).

On this analysis, the owner of a lake-bed, for example, would not be entitled to compensation when he is denied the requisite permit to engage in a land-filling operation that would have the effect of flooding others' land. Nor the corporate owner of a nuclear generating plant, when it is directed to remove all improvements from its land upon discovery that the plant sits astride an earthquake fault. Such regulatory action may well have the effect of eliminating the land's only economically productive use, but it does not proscribe a productive use that was previously permissible under relevant property and nuisance principles. The use of these properties for what are now expressly prohibited purposes was *always* unlawful, and (subject to other constitutional limitations) it was open to the State at any point to make the implication of those background principles of nuisance and property law explicit. See Michelman, *Property, Utility, and Fairness, Comments on the Ethical Foundations of "Just Compensation" Law,* 80 Harv. L. Rev. 1165, 1239-1241 (1967). In light of our traditional resort to "existing rules or understandings that stem from an independent source such as state law" to define the range of interests that qualify for protection as "property" under the Fifth and Fourteenth Amendments, . . . this recognition that the Takings Clause does not require compensation when an owner is barred from putting land to a use that is proscribed by those "existing rules or understandings" is surely unexceptional. When, however, a regulation that declares "off-limits" all economically productive or beneficial uses of land goes beyond what the relevant background principles would dictate, compensation must be paid to sustain it.

The "total taking" inquiry we require today will ordinarily entail (as the application of state nuisance law ordinarily entails) analysis of, among other things, the degree of harm to public lands and resources, or adjacent private property, posed by the claimant's proposed activities, see, *e.g.,* Restatement (Second) of Torts §§ 826, 827, the social value of the claimant's activities and their suitability to the locality in question, see, *e.g., id.,* §§ 828(a) and (b), 831, and the relative ease with which the alleged harm can be avoided through measures taken by the claimant and the government (or adjacent private landowners) alike, see, *e.g., id.,* §§ 827(e), 828(c), 830. The fact that a particular use has long been engaged in by similarly situated owners ordinarily imports a lack of any common-law prohibition (though changed circumstances or new knowledge may make what was previously permissible no longer so, see *id.,* § 827, Comment *g.* So also does the fact that other landowners, similarly situated, are permitted to continue the use denied to the claimant.

It seems unlikely that common-law principles would have prevented the erection of any habitable or productive improvements on petitioner's land . . . . The question, however, is one of state law to be dealt with on remand. We emphasize that to win its case South Carolina must do more than proffer the legislature's declaration that the uses Lucas desires are inconsistent with the public interest, or the conclusory assertion that they violate a common-law maxim such as *sic utere tuo ut alienum non laedas.* As we have said, a "State, by *ipse dixit,* may not transform private property into public property without compensation . . . ." Instead, as it would be required to do if it sought to restrain Lucas in a common-law action for public nuisance, South Carolina must identify background principles of nuisance and property law that prohibit the uses he now intends in the circumstances in which the property is presently found. Only on this showing can the State fairly claim that, in proscribing all such beneficial uses, the Beachfront Management Act is taking nothing.[18] . . .

Justice KENNEDY, concurring in the judgment.

. . . I share the reservations of some of my colleagues about a finding that a beach-front lot loses all value because of a development restriction. While the Supreme Court of South Carolina on remand need not consider the case subject to this constraint, we must accept the finding as entered below. Accepting the finding as entered, it follows that petitioner is entitled to invoke the line of cases discussing regulations that deprive real property of all economic value. See Agins v. City of Tiburon (1980).

. . . The rights conferred by the Takings Clause and the police power of the State may coexist without conflict. Property is bought and sold, investments are made, subject to the State's power to regulate. Where a taking is alleged from regulations which deprive the property of all value, the test must be whether the deprivation is contrary to reasonable, investment-backed expectations.

There is an inherent tendency towards circularity in this synthesis, of course; for if the owner's reasonable expectations are shaped by what courts allow as a proper exercise of governmental authority, property tends to become what courts say it is. Some circularity must be tolerated in these matters, however, as it is in other spheres. The definition, moreover, is not circular in its entirety. The expectations protected by the Constitution are based on objective rules and customs that can be understood as reasonable by all parties involved.

In my view, reasonable expectations must be understood in light of the whole of our legal tradition. The common law of nuisance is too narrow a confine for the exercise of regulatory power in a complex and interdependent society. The State should not be prevented from enacting new regulatory initiatives in response to changing conditions, and courts must consider all reasonable expectations whatever their source. The Takings Clause does not require a static body of state property law; it protects private expectations to ensure private investment. I agree with the Court that nuisance prevention accords with the most common expectations of property owners who face regulation, but I do not believe this can be the sole source of state authority to impose severe restrictions. Coastal property may present such unique concerns for a fragile land system that the State can go further in regulating its development and use than the common law of nuisance might otherwise permit.

The Supreme Court of South Carolina erred, in my view, by reciting the general purposes for which the state regulations were enacted without a determination that they were in accord with the owner's reasonable expectations and therefore sufficient to support a severe restriction on specific parcels of property. The promotion of tourism, for instance, ought not to suffice to deprive specific property of all value without a corresponding duty to compensate.

18. Justice BLACKMUN decries our reliance on background nuisance principles at least in part because he believes those principles to be as manipulable as we find the "harm prevention"/"benefit conferral" dichotomy. There is no doubt some leeway in a court's interpretation of what existing state law permits—but not remotely as much, we think, as in a legislative crafting of the reasons for its confiscatory regulation. We stress that an affirmative decree eliminating all economically beneficial uses may be defended only if an *objectively reasonable application* of relevant precedents would exclude those beneficial uses in the circumstances in which the land is presently found.

Furthermore, the means, as well as the ends, of regulation must accord with the owner's reasonable expectations. Here, the State did not act until after the property had been zoned for individual lot development and most other parcels had been improved, throwing the whole burden of the regulation on the remaining lots. This too must be measured in the balance. . . .

Justice BLACKMUN, dissenting.

Today the Court launches a missile to kill a mouse.

The State of South Carolina prohibited petitioner Lucas from building a permanent structure on his property from 1988 to 1990. Relying on an unreviewed (and implausible) state trial court finding that this restriction left Lucas' property valueless, this Court granted review to determine whether compensation must be paid in cases where the State prohibits all economic use of real estate. According to the Court, such an occasion never has arisen in any of our prior cases, and the Court imagines that it will arise "relatively rarely" or only in "extraordinary circumstances." Almost certainly it did not happen in this case.

Nonetheless, the Court presses on to decide the issue, and as it does, it ignores its jurisdictional limits, remakes its traditional rules of review, and creates simultaneously a new categorical rule and an exception (neither of which is rooted in our prior case law, common law, or common sense). I protest not only the Court's decision, but each step taken to reach it. More fundamentally, I question the Court's wisdom in issuing sweeping new rules to decide such a narrow case. Surely . . . the Court could have reached the result it wanted without inflicting this damage upon our Takings Clause jurisprudence.

My fear is that the Court's new policies will spread beyond the narrow confines of the present case. For that reason, I, like the Court, will give far greater attention to this case than its narrow scope suggests—not because I can intercept the Court's missile, or save the targeted mouse, but because I hope perhaps to limit the collateral damage. . . .

I

A

In 1972 Congress passed the Coastal Zone Management Act. The Act was designed to provide States with money and incentives to carry out Congress' goal of protecting the public from shoreline erosion and coastal hazards. In the 1980 amendments to the Act, Congress directed States to enhance their coastal programs by "[p]reventing or significantly reducing threats to life and the destruction of property by eliminating development and redevelopment in high-hazard areas."[1]

---

1. The country has come to recognize that uncontrolled beachfront development can cause serious damage to life and property. Hurricane Hugo's September 1989 attack upon South Carolina's coastline, for example, caused 29 deaths and approximately $6 billion in property damage, much of it the result of uncontrolled beachfront development. See Zalkin, *Shifting Sands and Shifting Doctrines: The Supreme Court's Changing Takings Doctrine and South Carolina's Coastal Zone Statute,* 79 Calif. L. Rev. 205, 212-213 (1991). The beachfront buildings are not only themselves destroyed in such a storm, "but they are often driven, like battering rams, into adjacent inland homes." Moreover, the development often destroys the natural sand dune barriers that provide storm breaks.

South Carolina began implementing the congressional directive by enacting the South Carolina Coastal Zone Management Act of 1977. . . . This effort did not stop the loss of shoreline. In October 1986, the Council appointed a "Blue Ribbon Committee on Beachfront Management" to investigate beach erosion and propose possible solutions. In March 1987, the Committee found that South Carolina's beaches were "critically eroding," and proposed land-use restrictions. In response, South Carolina enacted the Beachfront Management Act. The 1988 Act did not change the uses permitted within the designated critical areas. Rather, it enlarged those areas to encompass the distance from the mean high watermark to a setback line established on the basis of "the best scientific and historical data" available.

B

Petitioner Lucas is a contractor, manager, and part owner of the Wild Dune development on the Isle of Palms. He has lived there since 1978. In December 1986, he purchased two of the last four pieces of vacant property in the development.[3] The area is notoriously unstable. In roughly half of the last 40 years, all or part of petitioner's property was part of the beach or flooded twice daily by the ebb and flow of the tide. Between 1957 and 1963, petitioner's property was under water. Between 1963 and 1973 the shoreline was 100 to 150 feet onto petitioner's property. In 1973 the first line of stable vegetation was about halfway through the property. Between 1981 and 1983, the Isle of Palms issued 12 emergency orders for sandbagging to protect property in the Wild Dune development. Determining that local habitable structures were in imminent danger of collapse, the Council issued permits for two rock revetments to protect condominium developments near petitioner's property from erosion; one of the revetments extends more than halfway onto one of his lots.

C

The South Carolina Supreme Court['s] . . . decision rested on two premises that until today were unassailable — that the State has the power to prevent any use of property it finds to be harmful to its citizens, and that a state statute is entitled to a presumption of constitutionality.

The Beachfront Management Act includes a finding by the South Carolina General Assembly that the beach/dune system serves the purpose of "protect[ing] life and property by serving as a storm barrier which dissipates wave energy and contributes to shoreline stability in an economical and effective manner." The General Assembly also found that "development unwisely has been sited too close to the [beach/dune] system. This type of development has jeopardized

---

3. The properties were sold frequently at rapidly escalating prices before Lucas purchased them. Lot 22 was first sold in 1979 for $96,660, sold in 1984 for $187,500, then in 1985 for $260,000, and, finally, to Lucas in 1986 for $475,000. He estimated its worth in 1991 at $650,000. Lot 24 had a similar past. The record does not indicate who purchased the properties prior to Lucas, or why none of the purchasers held on to the lots and built on them.

the stability of the beach/dune system, accelerated erosion, and endangered adjacent property."

If the state legislature is correct that the prohibition on building in front of the setback line prevents serious harm, then, under this Court's prior cases, the Act is constitutional. "Long ago it was recognized that all property in this country is held under the implied obligation that the owner's use of it shall not be injurious to the community, and the Takings Clause did not transform that principle to one that requires compensation whenever the State asserts its power to enforce it." Keystone Bituminous Coal Assn. v. DeBenedictis (1987). The Court consistently has upheld regulations imposed to arrest a significant threat to the common welfare, whatever their economic effect on the owner. . . .

Nothing in the record undermines the General Assembly's assessment that prohibitions on building in front of the setback line are necessary to protect people and property from storms, high tides, and beach erosion. Because that legislative determination cannot be disregarded in the absence of . . . evidence . . . and because its determination of harm to life and property from building is sufficient to prohibit that use under this Court's cases, the South Carolina Supreme Court correctly found no taking.

II

My disagreement with the Court begins with its decision to review this case. . . .

Clearly, the Court was eager to decide this case. But eagerness, in the absence of proper jurisdiction, must—and in this case should have been—met with restraint.

III

The Court's willingness to dispense with precedent in its haste to reach a result is not limited to its initial jurisdictional decision. The Court also alters the long-settled rules of review.

The South Carolina Supreme Court's decision to defer to legislative judgments in the absence of a challenge from petitioner comports with one of this Court's oldest maxims: "[T]he existence of facts supporting the legislative judgment is to be presumed." United States v. Carolene Products Co., 304 U.S. 144 (1938). Indeed, we have said the legislature's judgment is "well-nigh conclusive." Berman v. Parker (1954). See also . . . Village of Euclid v. Ambler Realty, 272 U.S., at 388 (1926) ("If the validity of the legislative classification for zoning purposes be fairly debatable, the legislative judgment must be allowed to control").

. . . [T]his Court always has required plaintiffs challenging the constitutionality of an ordinance to provide "some factual foundation of record" that contravenes the legislative findings. In the absence of such proof, "the presumption of constitutionality must prevail." We only recently have reaffirmed that claimants have the burden of showing a state law constitutes a taking. See Keystone Bituminous Coal (1987). . . .

IV

The Court does not reject the South Carolina Supreme Court's decision simply on the basis of its disbelief and distrust of the legislature's findings. It also takes the opportunity to create a new scheme for regulations that eliminate all economic value. From now on, there is a categorical rule finding these regulations to be a taking unless the use they prohibit is a background common-law nuisance or property principle.

A

I first question the Court's rationale in creating a category that obviates a "case-specific inquiry into the public interest advanced," if all economic value has been lost. If one fact about the Court's takings jurisprudence can be stated without contradiction, it is that "the particular circumstances of each case" determine whether a specific restriction will be rendered invalid by the government's failure to pay compensation. . . . When the government regulation prevents the owner from any economically valuable use of his property, the private interest is unquestionably substantial, but we have never before held that no public interest can outweigh it. Instead the Court's prior decisions "uniformly reject the proposition that diminution in property value, standing alone, can establish a 'taking.'" Penn Central Transp. Co. v. New York City (1978). . . .

Mugler was only the beginning in a long line of cases. . . . [Discussion of cases omitted—EDs.] [I]n *Keystone Bituminous Coal*, the Court summarized over 100 years of precedent: "[T]he Court has repeatedly upheld regulations that destroy or adversely affect real property interests."[11]

The Court recognizes that "our prior opinions have suggested that 'harmful or noxious uses' of property may be proscribed by government regulation without the requirement of compensation," but seeks to reconcile them with its categorical rule by claiming that the Court never has upheld a regulation when the owner alleged the loss of all economic value. Even if the Court's factual premise were correct, its understanding of the Court's cases is distorted. In none of the cases did the Court suggest that the right of a State to prohibit certain activities without paying compensation turned on the availability of some residual

---

11. The Court's suggestion that Agins v. City of Tiburon (1980), a unanimous opinion, created a new per se rule, only now discovered, is unpersuasive. In *Agins*, the Court stated that "no precise rule determines when property has been taken" but instead that "the question necessarily requires a weighing of public and private interest." The other cases cited by the Court, repeat the *Agins* sentence, but in no way suggest that the public interest is irrelevant if total value has been taken. The Court has indicated that proof that a regulation does not deny an owner economic use of his property is sufficient to defeat a facial takings challenge. See Hodel v. Virginia Surface Mining & Reclamation Assn., Inc., 452 U.S. 264 (1981). But the conclusion that a regulation is not on its face a taking because it allows the landowner some economic use of property is a far cry from the proposition that denial of such use is sufficient to establish a takings claim regardless of any other consideration. The Court never has accepted the latter proposition.

The Court relies today on dicta in *Agins, Hodel, Nollan,* and *Keystone* for its new categorical rule. I prefer to rely on the directly contrary holdings in cases such as *Mugler* and *Hadacheck,* not to mention contrary statements in the very cases on which the Court relies. . . .

valuable use. Instead, the cases depended on whether the government interest was sufficient to prohibit the activity, given the significant private cost.[13]

These cases rest on the principle that the State has full power to prohibit an owner's use of property if it is harmful to the public. . . . It would make no sense under this theory to suggest that an owner has a constitutionally protected right to harm others, if only he makes the proper showing of economic loss.[14] See Pennsylvania Coal Co. v. Mahon (1922) (Brandeis, J., dissenting) ("Restriction upon [harmful] use does not become inappropriate as a means, merely because it deprives the owner of the only use to which the property can then be profitably put").

B

Ultimately even the Court cannot embrace the full implications of its *per se* rule: It eventually agrees that there cannot be a categorical rule for a taking based on economic value that wholly disregards the public need asserted. Instead, the Court decides that it will permit a State to regulate all economic value only if the State prohibits uses that would not be permitted under "background principles of nuisance and property law."[15]

Until today, the Court explicitly had rejected the contention that the government's power to act without paying compensation turns on whether the prohibited activity is a common-law nuisance.[16] The brewery closed in *Mugler* itself was not a common-law nuisance, and the Court specifically stated that it was the role of the legislature to determine what measures would be appropriate for the protection of public health and safety. In upholding the state action in *Miller*, the Court found it unnecessary to "weigh with nicety the question whether the

---

13.   The Court seeks to disavow the holdings and reasoning of *Mugler* and subsequent cases by explaining that they were the Court's early efforts to define the scope of the police power. There is language in the earliest takings cases suggesting that the police power was considered to be the power simply to prevent harms. Subsequently, the Court expanded its understanding of what were government's legitimate interests. But it does not follow that the holding of those early cases—that harmful and noxious uses of property can be forbidden whatever the harm to the property owner and without the payment of compensation—was repudiated. To the contrary, as the Court consciously expanded the scope of the police power beyond preventing harm, it clarified that there was a core of public interests that overrode any private interest. See *Keystone Bituminous Coal.*

14.   "Indeed, it would be extraordinary to construe the Constitution to require a government to compensate private landowners because it denied them 'the right' to use property which cannot be used without risking injury and death." *First Lutheran Church*, 258 Cal. Rptr., at 901-902.

15.   Although it refers to state nuisance and property law, the Court apparently does not mean just any state nuisance and property law. Public nuisance was first a common-law creation, see Newark, *The Boundaries of Nuisance*, 65 L. Q. Rev. 480, 482 (1949) (attributing development of nuisance to 1535), but by the 1800's in both the United States and England, legislatures had the power to define what is a public nuisance, and particular uses often have been selectively targeted. See Prosser, *Private Action for Public Nuisance*, 52 Va. L. Rev. 997, 999-1000 (1966); J. Stephen, A General View of the Criminal Law of England 105-107 (2d ed. 1890). The Court's references to "common-law" background principles, however, indicate that legislative determinations do not constitute "state nuisance and property law" for the Court.

16.   Also, until today the fact that the regulation prohibited uses that were lawful at the time the owner purchased did not determine the constitutional question. The brewery, the brickyard, the cedar trees, and the gravel pit were all perfectly legitimate uses prior to the passage of the regulation . . . . This Court explicitly acknowledged in *Hadacheck* that "[a] vested interest cannot be asserted against [the police power] because of conditions once obtaining. To so hold would preclude development and fix a city forever in its primitive conditions."

infected cedars constitute a nuisance according to common law; or whether they may be so declared by statute." Instead the Court has relied in the past, as the South Carolina court has done here, on legislative judgments of what constitutes a harm.[17]

The Court rejects the notion that the State always can prohibit uses it deems a harm to the public without granting compensation because "the distinction between 'harm-preventing' and 'benefit-conferring' regulation is often in the eye of the beholder." Since the characterization will depend "primarily upon one's evaluation of the worth of competing uses of real estate," the Court decides a legislative judgment of this kind no longer can provide the desired "objective, value-free basis" for upholding a regulation. The Court, however, fails to explain how its proposed common-law alternative escapes the same trap.

The threshold inquiry for imposition of the Court's new rule, "deprivation of all economically valuable use," itself cannot be determined objectively. As the Court admits, whether the owner has been deprived of all economic value of his property will depend on how "property" is defined. The "composition of the denominator in our 'deprivation' fraction," is the dispositive inquiry. Yet there is no "objective" way to define what that denominator should be. "We have long understood that any land-use regulation can be characterized as the 'total' deprivation of an aptly defined entitlement . . . . Alternatively, the same regulation can always be characterized as a mere 'partial' withdrawal from full, unencumbered ownership of the landholding affected by the regulation . . . ."

The Court's decision in *Keystone Bituminous Coal* illustrates this principle perfectly. In *Keystone*, the Court determined that the "support estate" was "merely a part of the entire bundle of rights possessed by the owner." Thus, the Court concluded that the support estate's destruction merely eliminated one segment of the total property. The dissent, however, characterized the support estate as a distinct property interest that was wholly destroyed. The Court could agree on no "value-free basis" to resolve this dispute.

Even more perplexing, however, is the Court's reliance on common-law principles of nuisance in its quest for a value-free takings jurisprudence. In determining what is a nuisance at common law, state courts make exactly the decision that the Court finds so troubling when made by the South Carolina General Assembly today: They determine whether the use is harmful. . . . There is nothing magical in the reasoning of judges long dead. They determined a harm in the same way as state judges and legislatures do today. If judges in the 18th and 19th centuries can distinguish a harm from a benefit, why not judges in the 20th century, and if judges can, why not legislators? . . .

---

17. The Court argues that finding no taking when the legislature prohibits a harmful use, such as the Court did in *Mugler* and the South Carolina Supreme Court did in the instant case, would nullify *Pennsylvania Coal*. Justice Holmes, the author of Pennsylvania Coal, joined Miller v. Schoene (1928), six years later. In *Miller*, the Court adopted the exact approach of the South Carolina court: It found the cedar trees harmful, and their destruction not a taking, whether or not they were a nuisance. Justice Holmes apparently believed that such an approach did not repudiate his earlier opinion. . . .

C

Finally, the Court justifies its new rule that the legislature may not deprive a property owner of the only economically valuable use of his land, even if the legislature finds it to be a harmful use, because such action is not part of the "'long recognized'" "understandings of our citizens." These "understandings" permit such regulation only if the use is a nuisance under the common law. Any other course is "inconsistent with the historical compact recorded in the Takings Clause." It is not clear from the Court's opinion where our "historical compact" or "citizens' understanding" comes from, but it does not appear to be history. [Blackmun's extensive discussion of the history of regulations and takings in America is omitted.]

. . . I find no clear and accepted "historical compact" or "understanding of our citizens" justifying the Court's new takings doctrine. Instead, the Court seems to treat history as a grab bag of principles, to be adopted where they support the Court's theory, and ignored where they do not. If the Court decided that the early common law provides the background principles for interpreting the Takings Clause, then regulation, as opposed to physical confiscation, would not be compensable. If the Court decided that the law of a later period provides the background principles, then regulation might be compensable, but the Court would have to confront the fact that legislatures regularly determined which uses were prohibited, independent of the common law, and independent of whether the uses were lawful when the owner purchased. What makes the Court's analysis unworkable is its attempt to package the law of two incompatible eras and peddle it as historical fact.[26] . . .

Justice STEVENS, dissenting. . . .

II

. . . [T]he Court starts from the premise that this Court has adopted a "categorical rule that total regulatory takings must be compensated," and then sets itself to the task of identifying the exceptional cases in which a State may be relieved of this categorical obligation. The test the Court announces is that the regulation must do no more than duplicate the result that could have been achieved under a State's nuisance law. Under this test the categorical rule will apply unless the regulation merely makes explicit what was otherwise an implicit limitation on the owner's property rights.

In my opinion, the Court is doubly in error. The categorical rule the Court establishes is an unsound and unwise addition to the law and the Court's formulation of the exception to that rule is too rigid and too narrow.

---

26. The Court asserts that all early American experience, prior to and after passage of the Bill of Rights, and any case law prior to 1897 are "entirely irrelevant" in determining what is "the historical compact recorded in the Takings Clause." Nor apparently are we to find this compact in the early federal takings cases, which clearly permitted prohibition of harmful uses despite the alleged loss of all value, whether or not the prohibition was a common-law nuisance, and whether or not the prohibition occurred subsequent to the purchase. I cannot imagine where the Court finds its "historical compact," if not in history.

. . . [T]he Court suggests that "regulations that leave the owner . . . without economically beneficial . . . use . . . carry with them a heightened risk that private property is being pressed into some form of public service." As discussed more fully below . . . , I agree that the risks of such singling out are of central concern in takings law. However, such risks do not justify a *per se* rule for total regulatory takings. There is no necessary correlation between "singling out" and total takings: A regulation may single out a property owner without depriving him of all of his property, see, *e.g.,* Nollan v. California Coastal Comm'n; and it may deprive him of all of his property without singling him out, see, e.g., Mugler v. Kansas; Hadacheck v. Sebastian. What matters in such cases is not the degree of diminution of value, but rather the specificity of the expropriating act.

In short, the Court's new rule is unsupported by prior decisions, arbitrary and unsound in practice, and theoretically unjustified. In my opinion, a categorical rule as important as the one established by the Court today should be supported by more history or more reason than has yet been provided.

The Nuisance Exception

Like many bright-line rules, the categorical rule established in this case is only "categorical" for a page or two in the U.S. Reports. No sooner does the Court state that "total regulatory takings must be compensated," than it quickly establishes an exception to that rule. . . .

Under our reasoning in *Mugler*, a State's decision to prohibit or to regulate certain uses of property is not a compensable taking just because the particular uses were previously lawful. Under the Court's opinion today, however, if a State should decide to prohibit the manufacture of asbestos, cigarettes, or concealable firearms, for example, it must be prepared to pay for the adverse economic consequences of its decision. One must wonder if government will be able to "go on" effectively if it must risk compensation "for every such change in the general law."

> The Court's holding today effectively freezes the State's common law, denying the legislature much of its traditional power to revise the law governing the rights and uses of property. Until today, I had thought that we had long abandoned this approach to constitutional law. More than a century ago we recognized that "the great office of statutes is to remedy defects in the common law as they are developed, and to adapt it to the changes of time and circumstances." Munn v. Illinois, 94 U.S. 113, 134 (1877). As Justice Marshall observed about a position similar to that adopted by the Court today:

>> "If accepted, that claim would represent a return to the era of Lochner v. New York, 198 U.S. 45 (1905), when common-law rights were also found immune from revision by State or Federal Government. Such an approach would freeze the common law as it has been constructed by the courts, perhaps at its 19th-century state of development. It would allow no room for change in response to changes in circumstance . . . ." (concurring opinion).

Arresting the development of the common law is not only a departure from our prior decisions; it is also profoundly unwise. The human condition is one of constant learning and evolution—both moral and practical. Legislatures implement that new learning; in doing so they must often revise the definition of property and the rights of property owners. Thus, when the Nation came to understand that slavery was morally wrong and mandated the emancipation of all slaves, it, in effect, redefined "property." On a lesser scale, our ongoing self-education produces similar changes in the rights of property owners: New appreciation of the significance of endangered species, the importance of wet-lands, and the vulnerability of coastal lands shapes our evolving understandings of property rights. . . .

In analyzing takings claims, courts have long recognized the difference between a regulation that targets one or two parcels of land and a regulation that enforces a statewide policy. . . . In considering Lucas' claim, the generality of the Beachfront Management Act is significant. The Act does not target par-ticular landowners, but rather regulates the use of the coastline of the entire State. . . . South Carolina's Act is best understood as part of a national effort to protect the coastline, one initiated by the federal Coastal Zone Management Act of 1972. Pursuant to the federal Act, every coastal State has implemented coastline regulations.[9] Moreover, the Act did not single out owners of undevel-oped land. The Act also prohibited owners of developed land from rebuilding if their structures were destroyed, and what is equally significant, from repairing erosion control devices, such as seawalls. In addition, in some situations, owners of developed land were required to "renouris[h] the beach . . . on a yearly basis with an amount . . . of sand . . . not . . . less than one and one-half times the yearly volume of sand lost due to erosion." In short, the South Carolina Act imposed substantial burdens on owners of developed and undeveloped land alike. This generality indicates that the Act is not an effort to expropriate owners of unde-veloped land.

Admittedly, the economic impact of this regulation is dramatic and petition-er's investment-backed expectations are substantial. Yet, if anything, the costs to and expectations of the owners of developed land are even greater: I doubt, however, that the cost to owners of developed land of renourishing the beach and allowing their seawalls to deteriorate effects a taking. The costs imposed on the owners of undeveloped land, such as petitioner, differ from these costs only in degree, not in kind. . . .

In view of all of these factors, even assuming that petitioner's property was rendered valueless, the risk inherent in investments of the sort made by peti-tioner, the generality of the Act, and the compelling purpose motivating the South Carolina Legislature persuade me that the Act did not effect a taking of petitioner's property. . . .

Notes and Questions

1. On remand, the South Carolina Supreme Court held that Lucas's prop-erty had been taken for the period between enactment of the Beachfront Management Act and the 1990 amendment that would allow him to seek a

---

9.   See Zalkin, Shifting Sands and Shifting Doctrines: The Supreme Court's Changing Tak-ings Doctrine and South Carolina's Coastal Zone Statute, 79 Calif. L. Rev. 205, 216-217, nn. 46-47 (1991) (collecting statutes).

special permit: "Coastal Council has not persuaded us that any common law basis exists by which it could restrain Lucas's desired use of his land; nor has our research uncovered any such common law principle." 424 S.E.2d 484 (1992). The case later settled with the state buying Lucas's two lots for $850,000 and paying an additional $725,000 interest, attorneys' fees, and costs. Ultimately, the state sold the lots at auction for $750,000 and houses have been built on both lots.

2. Shortly after the decision in *Lucas*, the South Carolina Coastal Council was placed under the Department of Health and Environmental Control and its director downgraded from deputy status. When the Council denied Isle of Palms property owners permission to build seawalls using 2.5-ton sand bags, on the ground they were hard erosion control devices prohibited by the Beachfront Management Act, it was overruled by the Department of Health and Environmental Control.

3. Was Justice Blackmun correct that the Court had launched a missile to kill a mouse? Ronald H. Rosenberg, *The Non-Impact of the United States Supreme Court Regulatory Takings Cases on the State Courts: Does the Supreme Court Really Matter?*, 6 Fordham Envtl. L.J. 523, 537-41 (1995), found 80 state court cases that referred to the *Lucas* decision. Of those, 57 discussed the *Lucas* case, as opposed to merely citing the case without discussing it. Of the 80 cases, only three relied on *Lucas* in finding a regulatory taking. A later study, Victoria Sutton, *Constitutional Taking Doctrine — Did* Lucas *Really Make a Difference?*, 18 Pace Envtl. L. Rev. 505 (2001), found that one of the three that relied on *Lucas* was reversed by the Colorado Supreme Court. Her search for all state cases citing *Lucas* through June 12, 2000 found 335. She concluded: "Since 1995, the impact of *Lucas* in state courts has increased slightly, being cited 177 times from 1996 through June 12, 2000, with fifty of those cases citing *Lucas* as a distinguishing case or in the dissent." A Westlaw check in the all states database on October 2013 found 690 cases that had cited *Lucas*.

4. Justice Stevens predicted that the Court's categorical rule would "greatly hamper the efforts of local officials and planners who must deal with increasingly complex problems in land-use and environmental regulation." True? *See* Blake Hudson, *The Public and Wildlife Trust Doctrines and the Untold Story of the* Lucas *Remand*, 34 Colum. J. Envtl. L. 99 (2009) ("the ability of government to protect wildlife and the environment without having to pay the owners of regulated land may have been severely limited by the *Lucas* decision—or maybe not"). But see the excerpt from *The Track Record on Takings Legislation: Lessons from Democracy's Laboratories*, set forth below.

5. Does the nuisance exception set forth in *Lucas* apply to *Loretto*'s categorical rule that permanent physical invasions are takings? The question has arisen where the government has entered private property to abate environmental hazards. *See* Miles E. Coleman, *Taking on a Nuisance: Applying* Lucas *to Physical Takings*, 21 Fed. Cir. B.J. 747 (2012).

6. *The denominator problem again.* If the landowner has more than one parcel or divides up a parcel, what is the relevant property for determining whether a taking has occurred? Although the Supreme Court has not established a definitive test for determining the size of the parcel or bundle of rights to use in determining whether the owner's property has been taken, the Court of Appeals for the Federal Circuit has dealt with this question in several cases, most recently in *Lost Tree Village Corp. v. United States*, 707 F.3d 1286 (Fed. Cir. 2013). In that case, a developer that had bought over 2,700 acres pursuant to a 1968 option sued for compensation for denial of a permit to fill 2.13 acres of a 4.9-acre parcel known as Plat 57. Plat 57 consisted of 1.41 acres of submerged lands and 3.58 acres of wetlands. The Court of Appeals reversed a decision of the Court of Federal Claims that the relevant parcel included an adjacent parcel, Plat 55, which the developer was also developing.

The court started with the proposition that the Supreme Court decisions establish that: "First, the property interest taken is not defined in terms of the regulation being challenged; the takings analysis must focus on 'the parcel as a whole.' Second, the 'parcel as a whole' does not extend to all of a landowner's disparate holdings in the vicinity of the regulated property." The court first noted that it (the Federal Circuit Court of Appeals) has taken a "flexible approach, designed to account for factual nuances" when the landowner owns or has held other parcels in the vicinity. It then stated that the "critical issue is the economic expectations of the claimant with regard to the property." If the landowner treats two or more parcels as a single economic unit, they may constitute the relevant property. Or, if two or more parcels are developed at different times and treated as distinct economic units, they may be treated independently.

The Court of Appeals held that Plat 57 alone was the relevant parcel. The developer ignored Plat 57 in the 1980s when it drew up plans for developing the rest of the area, including Plat 55. Only later, when it learned that it would obtain mitigation credits as a result of improvements made by a neighboring landowner, did the developer identify Plat 57 as a potentially profitable development. The court concluded: "Here, Lost Tree did not treat Plat 57 as part of the same economic unit as other land it developed in the John's Island community."

7. Can the owner of a parcel that consists almost entirely of wetlands be denied a fill permit without triggering a compensation requirement? In *Lost Tree Village*, the court said: "While the Government's authority to 'prevent a property owner from filling or otherwise injuring or destroying vital wetlands' is unquestioned, the issue is whether the denial of a fill permit for a particular project imposes a disproportionate loss on the affected landowner." If so, compensation must be paid.

8. Can a developer owning holdings that include wetlands effectively increase the value of its lands by separating the wetlands from the rest of the property and treating them as independent economic units?

9. Is Justice O'Connor's 2005 treatment of noxious use in *Kelo* consistent with Justice Scalia's treatment in *Lucas* (1992)?

10. The *Lucas* case drew a lot of attention. Amicus briefs supporting David Lucas were filed by the United States (by Solicitor General Starr), Senator Steven Symms, the American Farm Bureau Federation, the American Mining Congress, the Chamber of Commerce of the United States, the Defenders of Property Rights, the Institute for Justice (by Richard A. Epstein), the Mountain States Legal Foundation, the National Association of Home Builders, the Northern Virginia Chapter of the National Association of Industrial and Office Parks, the Pacific Legal Foundation, the Fire Island Association, the Long Beach Island Oceanfront Homeowners Association, the South Carolina Policy Council Education Foundation, the National Association of Realtors, and the Washington Legal Foundation. Briefs supporting the Coastal Commission were filed by 26 states, the American Planning Association, the National Growth

Management Leadership Project, the Municipal Art Society of New York, the National Trust for Historic Preservation in the United States, the Sierra Club, and the United States Conference of Mayors.

11. For recent analyses of the problem of determining economic impact, see Daniel L. Siegel, *Evaluating Economic Impact in Regulatory Takings Cases*, 19 Hastings W.-Nw. J. Envtl. L. & Pol'y 373 (2013), and Steven J. Eagle, *Economic Impact in Regulatory Takings Law*, 19 Hastings W.-Nw. J. Envtl. L. & Pol'y 407 (2013).

Government Subsidies and Coastal Development

Hurricane Hugo in September 1989 killed 29 people in South Carolina and caused nearly $6 billion of damage to property, with winds up to 120 miles per hour and 20-foot waves. It passed directly over the Isle of Palms, burying Lucas's two lots under four feet of water, and this was not the first time these lots had been underwater. This raises the question why anyone would pay so much and build such expensive homes in such an unstable area.

One answer is subsidized flood insurance:

> In 1968, Congress established the National Flood Insurance Program, which provides flood insurance coverage in areas where private insurance either was not available or was extremely expensive. It seems no coincidence that five years later, in 1973, a group of investors formed the Isle of Palms Beach and Racquet Club and purchased 1,537 acres on the eastern end of the Isle of Palms for $638,000, or $1,649 per acre.
>
> Shortly thereafter, the Isle of Palms Beach and Racquet Club began the development of Wild Dunes, building a golf course, marina, clubhouse, roads, and sewer and water lines. Over the coming decade, local property prices escalated dramatically.

Dana Beach & Kim Diana Connolly, *A Retrospective on Lucas v. South Carolina Coastal Council: Public Policy Implications for the 21st Century*, 12 Southeastern Envtl. L.J. 1, 10-11 (2003).

Another is more subsidies:

> The United States Army Corps of Engineers has spent billions on hard protections for coastal properties, and now that these have proven ineffective, is running up an even larger tab rebuilding beaches that have washed away once, twice, and will wash away again. The State of Florida has its own multi-hundred-million dollar beach nourishment program, a loss leader among the states. The Federal Highway Administration spends major sums providing fast access to the coasts and bridges to the barrier islands, up to $10 million per mile, projects that are often justified as "hurricane evacuation corridors" without a nod to their obvious effect of moving people directly into the hurricane zone. The Environmental Protection Agency spends hundreds of millions more on fresh water and sewage treatment plants, without which island development could not survive. The acquisition of coastal properties is boosted by federal mortgage guarantees, the second home mortgage deduction, and bargain-rate federal flood insurance. Policies that would cost close to $7,500 on the private market are available for about $950 a year. Meanwhile, following every major hurricane, insured property losses run to half a billion dollars

and more. Lastly, when all else fails, there is federal disaster relief. Twenty years ago, a United States House of Representatives report placed total federal expenditures on coastal barrier development at averages in excess of $25,000 an acre for initial infrastructure, and $53,000 when post disaster assistance is thrown in. That is for each acre, and that was two decades ago. . . .

From 1978 through 2002, the National Flood Insurance Program paid out over $61 million in claims for flood damage on the Isle of Palms. It paid out more than $400 million to the state of South Carolina, and over $11.6 billion to the nation as a whole. More than 70 percent of the program's coverage is on the coast and the barrier islands. Not to be outdone, the Corps of Engineers is prepared to spend an estimated $10 billion pumping sand on the nation's beaches in the years to come, $1 billion alone on a twelve-mile stretch of the New Jersey shore.

Oliver A. Houck, *More Unfinished Stories:* Lucas, Atlanta Coalition, *and* Palila/ Sweet Home, 75 U. Colo. L. Rev. 331, 359-62, 367 (2004).

In 2012, after the program had accumulated $24 billion in losses, Congress moved to rein in the amount of subsidies provided by the flood insurance program, phasing them out for vacation and second homes beginning in 2013. Rates for homes with severe and repeated flooding began to rise on October 1, 2013 and will rise 25 percent annually until they better reflect the risk of flooding. Premiums could go up to as much as $30,000 per year. The increase was enacted just before Hurricane Sandy hit New Jersey and New York and may not survive the political backlash.

THE TRACK RECORD ON TAKINGS LEGISLATION: LESSONS FROM DEMOCRACY'S LABORATORIES

John D. Echeverria & Thekla Hansen-Young,[2]
28 Stan. Envtl. L.J. 439, 441-46 (2009)

For the last several decades there has been a wide-ranging debate in the United States about whether government should be required to pay when it regulates uses of private property. The Supreme Court has long said that in rare and extreme circumstances regulations may rise to the level of compensable "takings" under the Takings Clause of the Fifth Amendment to the U.S. Constitution. Modern "property rights" advocates, however, treat the established reading of the Takings Clause as their point of departure, and argue that regulations should be routinely regarded as takings, with non-compensable regulations reserved for the exceptional cases. Would the nation (or a state or locality) be better off or worse off if the modern property rights argument prevailed?

This question has proven difficult to answer in definitive fashion, with the debate over the property rights agenda mostly proceeding in abstract, hypothetical terms, for the simple reason that the property rights agenda has, generally speaking, gained little traction. On the legal front, the property rights argument, articulated in its most comprehensive fashion by Professor Richard

2. John D. Echeverria is a Professor of Law at Vermont Law School; Thekla Hansen-Young is an Associate with Arnold & Porter LLP and served as a Fellow with the Georgetown Environmental Law & Policy Institute in 2007-08.

Epstein in his 1985 book *Takings: Private Property and the Power of Eminent Domain*, has plainly come a cropper in the Supreme Court. While the thinking of some members of the Supreme Court has been influenced by Epstein's work,[5] not a single justice on the current Court has forthrightly embraced Epstein's reform agenda. Recently, a firm, if narrow, majority of the Court has sworn renewed allegiance to the ad hoc, deferential analytic framework set forth thirty years ago in Penn Central Transportation Co. v. City of New York.[6]

In Congress, the property rights agenda has attracted a good deal of attention but ultimately come to naught. . . .

At the state level, however, property rights advocates have achieved more success. While many states have rejected property rights (or takings) bills altogether, and most of the adopted laws are purely procedural in nature, a half-dozen states have adopted substantive legislation. These laws, popularly called takings "compensation" laws, require the government to pay property owners subject to regulatory restrictions when compensation is not owed under the federal (or state) constitutions. . . .

The arguments for and against the property rights agenda are now familiar. Property rights advocates have argued that requiring the public to pay to enforce regulatory requirements, even when the Constitution does not require it, would improve the fairness of regulatory programs and force public officials to make more judicious and discriminating choices about the rules they adopt and enforce. Opponents have generally argued that takings legislation would impose "budget-busting" financial burdens on taxpayers, confer windfalls on undeserving claimants, and unjustly enrich the legal profession. In addition, opponents have argued, though sometimes with hesitation, that takings legislation would undermine environmental and land use protections.

To attempt to resolve which, if either, side has been closest to the mark, this Article examines in detail the experiences in Florida and Oregon with their takings laws. In 1995, Florida adopted the Bert J. Harris Private Property Rights Act and the related Florida Land Use and Environmental Dispute Resolution Act. In 2004, Oregon voters adopted Measure 37, and three years later adopted Measure 49, which revised and limited Measure 37. This Article also discusses in far more cursory fashion the laws of the four other states that have adopted legislation that goes beyond the constitutional takings standard: Louisiana, Mississippi, Texas, and Arizona. In the case of Arizona, the legislation was adopted in November 2006, and though this law appears to be having impacts similar to those in Florida, it is simply too early to accurately assess the law's likely impacts. In the other three states, the takings laws have largely proven to be dead letters, having no significant impact from any perspective. The failure of these laws to launch, so to speak, may be attributable to the fact that all of them include numeric thresholds for

---

5. In Lucas v. South Carolina Coastal Council, 505 U.S. 1003 (1992), Justice Antonin Scalia wrote an opinion for a narrow majority of the Court embracing Epstein's analytic framework in the circumstance where a regulation renders property valueless. However, Epstein himself criticized the decision because *Lucas* plainly did not adopt Epstein's view that the Takings Clause should apply to virtually all regulations. See Steve Chapman, Takings Exception, Reasononline, Apr. 2005, available at https://www.reason.com/news/show/29662.html (quoting Epstein as saying, "[b]ut what Scalia did in *Lucas*—and what was so terrible about the opinion—was to say essentially that the whole area of partial land-use restrictions is now beyond constitutional scrutiny").

6. See, e.g., Lingle v. Chevron U.S.A. Inc., 544 U.S. 528 (2005); Tahoe-Sierra Pres. Council, Inc. v. Tahoe Reg'l Planning Agency, 535 U.S. 302 (2002).

establishing takings liability, they are either relatively narrow in scope or contain numerous exceptions, and they were adopted in states that lack a strong tradition of using regulations to protect the environment or manage land use. . . .

While the experiences with the property rights agenda in Florida, Oregon, and the other states vary in important respects, . . . our analysis leads to five overarching conclusions:

Eviscerates Regulatory Authority

The virtually invariable effect of successful state takings legislation has been to force state and local governments to not adopt laws and regulations they otherwise would have adopted and to not enforce restrictions already on the books. . . . [T]hese measures have very, very rarely resulted in actual financial payments to property owners . . . . Nor has takings legislation resulted in more discriminating or judicious use of regulatory authorities or legislative powers. At the advent of the modern property rights movement, Professor Charles Fried, who served as Solicitor General in the Reagan administration, made the observation that the outcome of this agenda, if successful, "would be, to say the least, much less regulation." . . . If anything, he underestimated the likely effects of the property rights agenda on regulatory authority.

Primarily Benefits Well-Heeled Special Interests

. . . In Oregon, the primary beneficiaries of Measure 37 were timber companies seeking to subdivide and sell off their resource lands and/or to avoid new restrictions on timber harvesting practices. In Florida, the primary beneficiaries of property rights legislation have been real estate developers and owners of large land holdings.

Increases Land Use Conflicts

. . . In Florida, the property rights legislation has undermined the public's ability to meaningfully influence local legislative and administrative land use decision-making, helping spawn a popular grassroots effort, called Florida Hometown Democracy, dedicated to sharply restricting the ability of local officials to approve any new development. In Oregon, Measure 37, dubbed the "Hate Your Neighbor Act" by some critics, pitted neighbor against neighbor by granting special exemptions from the state's relatively strict land use regulations to a subset of the state's property owners, conferring economic windfalls on those receiving the exemptions while burdening others with new threats of sometimes harmful development on nearby properties.

Promotes Flawed Economics

. . . Both anecdotal evidence and systematic economic research inspired by state takings measures undermine the common assumption that regulatory restrictions invariably have significant adverse effects on property values. . . . [T]he evidence suggests that takings "compensation" awards, far from providing a remedy for significant regulatory losses, generally represent windfalls that reflect the inflated value of special exemptions from restrictions that apply to most of the community.

Undermines Local Land Use Democracy

. . . The Florida and Oregon property rights laws have made it essentially impossible for government to regulate land uses unless it is willing to pay regulated owners. Because government officials have proven unable or unwilling to make such payments, the takings laws have effectively neutered the law-making process in relation to land use. This in turn has limited the practical ability of members of the public to advocate for and defend their communities through the democratic process.

C. JUDICIAL TAKINGS

Until 2010, it was widely assumed that a change in state property law made by a state court was not a taking subject to the just compensation requirement, despite some indications that it might be. Justice Stewart, in a concurring opinion in *Hughes v. Washington*, 389 U.S. 290, 296-97 (1967), wrote:

> To the extent that the decision of the Supreme Court of Washington . . . arguably conforms to reasonable expectations, we must of course accept it as conclusive. But to the extent that it constitutes a sudden change in state law, unpredictable in terms of the relevant precedents, no such deference would be appropriate. For a State cannot be permitted to defeat the constitutional prohibition against taking property without due process of law by the simple device of asserting retroactively that the property it has taken never existed at all. Whether the decision here worked an unpredictable change in state law thus inevitably presents a federal question for the determination of this Court. The Washington court insisted that its decision was "not startling." What is at issue here is the accuracy of that characterization.

JUDICIAL TAKINGS
Barton H. Thompson, Jr.,
76 Va. L. Rev. 1449, 1451-52 (1990)

Whether the takings protections constrain the judiciary in the same manner that they restrict the other branches of government is a crucial question today. Courts have the doctrinal tools to undertake many of the actions that legislatures and executive agencies are constitutionally barred from pursuing under the takings protections—and pressure is mounting for courts to use those tools.[7] Indeed, while paying lip service to stare decisis, the courts on numerous occasions have reshaped property law in ways that sharply constrict previously recognized private interests.[8] Faced by growing environmental, conservationist, and recreational demands, for example, state courts have recently begun redefining a variety of property interests to increase public or governmental rights, concomitantly shrinking the sphere of private dominion. Beaches and waterways previously considered private property have been opened to public use or held to be state property. Private rights to develop tidelands, water, and other unique or valuable resources have been sharply constrained for preservation and other purposes. In other contexts, courts have led the way in requiring privately owned shopping centers to open their premises to unwanted political petitioning, and taken a major role in reordering marital property rights and rights of unmarried cohabitants.

Whether any of these actions would be a taking if attempted by the legislative or executive branch is open to debate; many such legislative and executive actions have, in fact, been held unconstitutional. Whatever one's views of the basic takings issue, however, the question remains: Should the constitutionality of the actions differ merely because the courts, rather than the other branches of government, are reordering property rights? If the legislature or executive may not constitutionally reorder property rights in a particular fashion, should the courts be permitted to do so?

STOP THE BEACH RENOURISHMENT, INC. v. FLORIDA DEP'T OF ENVIRONMENTAL PROTECTION

Supreme Court of the United States
560 U.S. 702 (2010)

SCALIA, J., announced the judgment of the Court and delivered the opinion of the Court with respect to Parts I, IV, and V, in which ROBERTS, C.J., and KENNEDY, THOMAS, GINSBURG, BREYER, ALITO, and SOTOMAYOR, JJ., joined, and an opinion with respect to Parts II and III, in which ROBERTS, C.J., and THOMAS and ALITO, JJ., joined. KENNEDY, J., filed an opinion concurring in part and concurring in the judgment, in which SOTOMAYOR, J., joined. BREYER, J., filed an opinion concurring in part and concurring in the judgment, in which GINSBURG, J., joined. STEVENS, J., took no part in the decision of the case.

---

7. . . . [T]he courts have a wealth of doctrines they may use to reallocate rights of access and use between private owners and the public at large. Through nuisance and contract doctrines, the courts may also reallocate rights of access and use between neighboring landowners and between owners of different estates in the same land. The one major area in which courts have not attempted to "regulate" property rights is in the pricing of property. At least under our current jurisprudence, it is difficult to imagine courts effectively controlling rents. Otherwise, however, the judicial power is a surprisingly flexible substitute for legislative and executive powers.

8. Judicial reshaping of property rights is nothing new. Legal historians have written extensively of the degree to which early American courts reformulated property law for instrumental purposes. See, e.g., M. Horwitz, The Transformation of American Law 31-66, 101-08 (1977). Today, however, courts appear to be overriding common law precedents at a greater pace than ever before (although this may simply be because modern courts more willingly admit to changing the law). See M. Eisenberg, The Nature of the Common Law 135-36 (1988).

Justice SCALIA . . . We consider a claim that the decision of a State's court of last resort took property without just compensation in violation of the Takings Clause . . . .

I

A

Generally speaking, state law defines property interests, . . . including property rights in navigable waters and the lands underneath them . . . . In Florida, the State owns in trust for the public the land permanently submerged beneath navigable waters and the foreshore (the land between the low-tide line and the mean high-water line). Thus, the mean high-water line (the average reach of high tide over the preceding 19 years) is the ordinary boundary between private beachfront, or littoral[2] property, and state-owned land. . . .

Littoral owners have, in addition to the rights of the public, certain "special rights" with regard to the water and the foreshore, . . . rights which Florida considers to be property, generally akin to easements . . . . These include the right of access to the water, the right to use the water for certain purposes, the right to an unobstructed view of the water, and the right to receive accretions and relictions to the littoral property. . . . This is generally in accord with well-established common law, although the precise property rights vary among jurisdictions. . . .

At the center of this case is the right to accretions and relictions. Accretions are additions of alluvion (sand, sediment, or other deposits) to waterfront land; relictions are lands once covered by water that become dry when the water recedes. . . . (For simplicity's sake, we shall refer to accretions and relictions collectively as accretions, and the process whereby they occur as accretion.) In order for an addition to dry land to qualify as an accretion, it must have occurred gradually and imperceptibly—that is, so slowly that one could not see the change occurring, though over time the difference became apparent. . . . When, on the other hand, there is a "sudden or perceptible loss of or addition to land by the action of the water or a sudden change in the bed of a lake or the course of a stream," the change is called an avulsion. . . .

In Florida, as at common law, the littoral owner automatically takes title to dry land added to his property by accretion; but formerly submerged land that has become dry land by avulsion continues to belong to the owner of the seabed (usually the State). . . . Thus, regardless of whether an avulsive event exposes land previously submerged or submerges land previously exposed, the boundary between littoral property and sovereign land does not change; it remains (ordinarily) what was the mean high-water line before the event. . . . It follows from this that, when a new strip of land has been added to the shore by avulsion, the littoral owner has no right to subsequent accretions. . . .

---

2. Many cases and statutes use "riparian" to mean abutting any body of water. The Florida Supreme Court, however, has adopted a more precise usage whereby "riparian" means abutting a river or stream and "littoral" means abutting an ocean, sea, or lake. . . . When speaking of the Florida law applicable to this case, we follow the Florida Supreme Court's terminology.

B

In 1961, Florida's Legislature passed the Beach and Shore Preservation Act. . . . The Act establishes procedures for "beach restoration and nourishment projects," . . . designed to deposit sand on eroded beaches (restoration) and to maintain the deposited sand (nourishment). . . . A local government may apply to the Department of Environmental Protection for the funds and the necessary permits to restore a beach . . . . When the project involves placing fill on the State's submerged lands, authorization is required from the Board of Trustees of the Internal Improvement Trust Fund, . . . which holds title to those lands . . . .

Once a beach restoration "is determined to be undertaken," the Board sets what is called "an erosion control line." . . . It must be set by reference to the existing mean high-water line, though in theory it can be located seaward or landward of that.[2] . . . Much of the project work occurs seaward of the erosion-control line, as sand is dumped on what was once submerged land. . . . The fixed erosion-control line replaces the fluctuating mean high-water line as the boundary between privately owned littoral property and state property. . . . Once the erosion-control line is recorded, the common law ceases to increase upland property by accretion (or decrease it by erosion). . . . Thus, when accretion to the shore moves the mean high-water line seaward, the property of beachfront landowners is not extended to that line (as the prior law provided), but remains bounded by the permanent erosion-control line. Those landowners "continue to be entitled," however, "to all common-law riparian rights" other than the right to accretions. . . . If the beach erodes back landward of the erosion-control line over a substantial portion of the shoreline covered by the project, the Board may, on its own initiative, or must, if asked by the owners or lessees of a majority of the property affected, direct the agency responsible for maintaining the beach to return the beach to the condition contemplated by the project. If that is not done within a year, the project is canceled and the erosion-control line is null and void. . . . Finally, by regulation, if the use of submerged land would "unreasonably infringe on riparian rights," the project cannot proceed unless the local governments show that they own or have a property interest in the upland property adjacent to the project site. . . .

C

In 2003, the city of Destin and Walton County applied for the necessary permits to restore 6.9 miles of beach within their jurisdictions that had been eroded by several hurricanes. The project envisioned depositing along that shore sand dredged from further out. It would add about 75 feet of dry sand seaward of the mean high-water line (to be denominated the erosion-control line). The Department issued a notice of intent to award the permits, . . . and the Board approved the erosion-control line . . . .

The petitioner here, Stop the Beach Renourishment, Inc., is a nonprofit corporation formed by people who own beachfront property bordering the project

---

2. We assume, as the parties agree we should, that in this case the erosion-control line is the pre-existing mean high-water line . . . . Respondents concede that, if the erosion-control line were established landward of that, the State would have taken property . . . .

area (. . . the Members). It brought an administrative challenge to the proposed project, . . . which was unsuccessful; the Department approved the permits. Petitioner then challenged that action in state court . . . . The District Court of Appeal . . . concluded that, contrary to the Act's preservation of "all common-law riparian rights," the order had eliminated two of the Members' littoral rights: (1) the right to receive accretions to their property; and (2) the right to have the contact of their property with the water remain intact. . . . This, it believed, would be an unconstitutional taking . . . . It set aside the Department's final order approving the permits . . . . It also certified to the Florida Supreme Court the following question (as rephrased by the latter court):

"On its face, does the Beach and Shore Preservation Act unconstitutionally deprive upland owners of littoral rights without just compensation?" . . .

The Florida Supreme Court answered the certified question in the negative. . . . It faulted the Court of Appeal for not considering the doctrine of avulsion, which it concluded permitted the State to reclaim the restored beach on behalf of the public. . . . It described the right to accretions as a future contingent interest, not a vested property right, and held that there is no littoral right to contact with the water independent of the littoral right of access, which the Act does not infringe. . . . Petitioner sought rehearing on the ground that the Florida Supreme Court's decision itself effected a taking . . . .[4] The request for rehearing was denied. We granted certiorari . . . .

II

A

Before coming to the parties' arguments in the present case, we discuss some general principles of our takings jurisprudence. The Takings Clause . . . applies as fully to the taking of a landowner's riparian rights as it does to the taking of an estate in land.[5] . . . Moreover, though the classic taking is a transfer of property to the State or to another private party by eminent domain, the Takings Clause applies to other state actions that achieve the same thing. . . . States effect a taking if they recharacterize as public property what was previously private property. See Webb's Fabulous Pharmacies, Inc. v. Beckwith, 449 U.S. 155 (1980).

The Takings Clause . . . is not addressed to the action of a specific branch or branches. It is concerned simply with the act, and not with the governmental actor ("nor shall private property *be taken*" (emphasis added)). There is no textual justification for saying that the existence or the scope of a State's power to expropriate private property without just compensation varies according to the branch of government effecting the expropriation. Nor does common sense recommend such a principle. It would be absurd to allow a State to do by judicial decree what the Takings Clause forbids it to do by legislative fiat. . . .

4. We ordinarily do not consider an issue first presented to a state court in a petition for rehearing if the state court did not address it. But where the state-court decision itself is claimed to constitute a violation of federal law, the state court's refusal to address that claim put forward in a petition for rehearing will not bar our review.

5. We thus need not resolve whether the right of accretion is an easement, as petitioner claims, or, as Florida claims, a contingent future interest.

Our precedents provide no support for the proposition that takings effected by the judicial branch are entitled to special treatment, and in fact suggest the contrary. . . .

IV

We come at last to petitioner's takings attack on the decision below. . . .

. . . Under petitioner's theory, because no prior Florida decision had said that the State's filling of submerged tidal lands could have the effect of depriving a littoral owner of contact with the water and denying him future accretions, the Florida Supreme Court's judgment in the present case abolished those two easements to which littoral property owners had been entitled. This puts the burden on the wrong party. There is no taking unless petitioner can show that, before the Florida Supreme Court's decision, littoral-property owners had rights to future accretions and contact with the water superior to the State's right to fill in its submerged land. Though some may think the question close, in our view the showing cannot be made.

Two core principles of Florida property law intersect in this case. First, the State as owner of the submerged land adjacent to littoral property has the right to fill that land, so long as it does not interfere with the rights of the public and the rights of littoral landowners. . . . Second, . . . if an avulsion exposes land seaward of littoral property that had previously been submerged, that land belongs to the State even if it interrupts the littoral owner's contact with the water. . . . The issue here is whether there is an exception to this rule when the State is the cause of the avulsion. Prior law suggests there is not. In Martin v. Busch, 112 So. 274 (Fla. 1927), the Florida Supreme Court held that when the State drained water from a lakebed belonging to the State, causing land that was formerly below the mean high-water line to become dry land, that land continued to belong to the State. . . . "The riparian rights doctrine of accretion and reliction," the Florida Supreme Court later explained, "does not apply to such lands." . . . This is not surprising, as there can be no accretions to land that no longer abuts the water.

Thus, Florida law as it stood before the decision below allowed the State to fill in its own seabed, and the resulting sudden exposure of previously submerged land was treated like an avulsion for purposes of ownership. The right to accretions was therefore subordinate to the State's right to fill. . . .

The Florida Supreme Court decision before us is consistent with these background principles of state property law. . . . Although the opinion does not cite *Martin* and is not always clear on this point, it suffices that its characterization of the littoral right to accretion is consistent with *Martin* and the other relevant principles of Florida law we have discussed. . . .

The result under Florida law may seem counter-intuitive. After all, the Members' property has been deprived of its character (and value) as oceanfront property by the State's artificial creation of an avulsion. Perhaps state-created avulsions ought to be treated differently from other avulsions insofar as the property right to accretion is concerned. But nothing in prior Florida law makes such a distinction, and *Martin* suggests, if it does not indeed hold, the contrary. Even if there might be different interpretations of *Martin* and other Florida property-law cases that would prevent this arguably odd result, we are not free to adopt them. The Takings Clause only protects property rights as they are established under state law, not as they might have been established or ought to have been established. We cannot say that the Florida Supreme Court's decision eliminated a right of accretion established under Florida law. . . .

V

Because the Florida Supreme Court's decision did not contravene the established property rights of petitioner's Members, Florida has not violated the Fifth and Fourteenth Amendments. The judgment of the Florida Supreme Court is therefore affirmed.

*Syllabus**

. . . Justice SCALIA, joined by THE CHIEF JUSTICE, Justice THOMAS, and Justice ALITO, concluded in Parts II and III that if a court declares that what was once an established right of private property no longer exists, it has taken that property in violation of the Takings Clause. . . .

Justice KENNEDY, joined by Justice SOTOMAYOR, agreed that the Florida Supreme Court did not take property without just compensation, but concluded that this case does not require the Court to determine whether, or when, a judicial decision determining property owners' rights can violate the Takings Clause. If and when future cases show that the usual principles, including constitutional ones that constrain the judiciary like due process, are inadequate to protect property owners, then the question whether a judicial decision can effect a taking would be properly presented. . . .

Justice BREYER, joined by Justice GINSBURG, agreed that no unconstitutional taking occurred here, but concluded that it is unnecessary to decide more than that to resolve this case. Difficult questions of constitutional law—e.g., whether federal courts may review a state court's decision to determine if it unconstitutionally takes private property without compensation, and what the proper test is for evaluating whether a state-court property decision enacts an unconstitutional taking—need not be addressed in order to dispose "of the immediate case." Such questions are better left for another day.

Notes and Questions

1. To what extent will this decision constrain state courts from changing state common law or interpretations of state statutes? Justice Stewart said in the *Hughes* case, "Surely, it must be conceded as a general proposition that the law of real property is, under our Constitution, left to the individual states to develop and administer. And surely Washington or any other state is free to make changes, either legislative or judicial, in its general rules of real property law . . . ." 389 U.S. at 295.

2. Has the Court returned to the position it took in *Shelley v. Kraemer* (1948) that a judicial decision is state action? *See* Nestor M. Davidson, *Judicial Takings*

---

* The syllabus constitutes no part of the opinion of the Court but has been prepared by the Reporter of Decisions for the convenience of the reader.

and State Action: Rereading Shelley *After* Stop the Beach Renourishment, 6 Duke J. Const. L. & Pub. Pol'y 75 (2011) ("it is striking . . . how closely the *Stop the Beach Renourishment* plurality's reasoning seems to echo *Shelley*'s logic").

3. Would the judicial takings doctrine apply to state court decisions that change common-law doctrines in the course of resolving disputes between two private parties or is it limited to decisions that result in private-to-public reassignments of property rights? *See* Timothy M. Mulvaney, *The New Judicial Takings Construct*, 120 Yale L.J. Online 247 (2011).

4. For a discussion of the threat to traditional common-law evolution and federalism problems raised by a judicial takings doctrine, see Stacey L. Dogan & Ernest A. Young, *Judicial Takings and Collateral Attack on State Court Property Decisions*, 6 Duke J. Const. L. & Pub. Pol'y 107 (2011).

JUDICIAL TAKINGS: A MEDLEY OF MISCONCEPTIONS
Laura S. Underkuffler, 61 Syracuse L. Rev. 203, 206-08 (2011)

There is a superficial appeal to the idea of judicial takings. If the goal of the Takings Clause is to protect the individual from unfair government action, isn't the effect on the individual the same, whether that action is by a legislature, an administrator, or a judge? In each case, the individual has lost something she previously had. And if the effect is the same, shouldn't the legal treatment of these actors be the same?

The logic seems unassailable. . . . I will discuss why it is not.

I.   The Misconceptions

The misconceptions that are inherent in the Stop the Beach Renourishment's plurality opinion fall into two general categories. First, the idea of state court judicial takings contradicts the very definition of property on which the plurality insists. Second, the idea of state court judicial takings is fatally at odds with the nature of the judicial function.

A.   The Problem of the Definition of Property

In the *Stop the Beach Renourishment* plurality's view, the idea of a judicial taking proceeds in the following logical sequence:

- An individual has protected property interests.
- A state court eliminates those interests.
- Therefore, a Fifth Amendment taking has (potentially) occurred.

The curious question is this: is this sequence, in favor of state-court judicial takings, compatible with the plurality's parallel assertion that property interests are (of course) defined by state law?

In fact, these two ideas are completely at odds. If "property" for Fifth Amendment purposes is a creature of state law, created with complete authority by the organs of state government, why can't states interpret it, change it, or eliminate it—by judicial, legislative, or executive means—as they see fit? In the particular context presented in this case, if states have the power to define property, it is difficult to see how a judge who is lawfully exercising that power (under state law) has "taken" it. If property is a creature of state law, it is not something that exists apart from the state definitional process; it is what that process declares.

In other words, the idea that states define property rights is completely incompatible with the idea that states, when exercising that definitional power, destroy them. Either they can define them, or they cannot define them; it cannot be both.

This conflict is particularly apparent in the "judicial taking" context, because we are accustomed to thinking of judges as considering, defining, and redefining law. However, the problem is not limited to this context. Whether a state changes previous legal understandings through legislative, executive, or judicial means, the problem is the same: we are trying, through the Takings Clause, to stop the state from doing exactly what it is, under our understanding of the nature of property interests, specifically empowered to do.

It is because of this often unacknowledged conundrum that property as a creature of state law has always been a troubled concept, honored more in the breach than in the practice. Pruneyard Shopping Center v. Robins, [447 U.S. 74 (1980),] in which this doctrine was announced, proceeded—in the understandings of property actually used—to cite (contrarily) those established in federal cases. After *Pruneyard*, the Court has departed from this idea as often as it has adhered to it. Property, with no citations to state law, has been described by the Court as the "bundle" of "traditionally" or "commonly" recognized rights to possess, use, sell, transfer, and exclude; the "fundamental attribute[s] of ownership"; the "ordinary meaning" of "property interest"; the protection of one's "reasonable," "investment-backed," or "historical" expectations; and so on. In fact, in the fifteen important takings cases decided by the Court between 1987 and 2010, only three of the Court's opinions contained anything resembling an interpretation of core property concepts and rights in terms of state law.

The reasons for this reluctance are undoubtedly rooted in the logical conundrum discussed above. If the "property" that the Clause protects is something that—through definitional powers—can be changed or eliminated by a subordinate government, whether through judicial (or other) means, the Takings Clause means nothing. It is an empty shell. Yet, that is the difficulty that "constitutionally cognizable property" as a "creature of state law" has always implied.

D. TEMPORARY TAKINGS

ARKANSAS GAME AND FISH COMMISSION v. UNITED STATES

Supreme Court of the United States
133 S. Ct. 511 (2012)

GINSBURG, J., delivered the opinion of the Court, in which all other Members [ALITO, BREYER, KENNEDY, ROBERTS, SCALIA, SOTOMAYOR, and THOMAS] joined, except KAGAN, J., who took no part.

Periodically from 1993 until 2000, the U.S. Army Corps of Engineers authorized flooding that extended into the peak growing season for timber on forest land owned and managed by petitioner, Arkansas Game and Fish Commission. Cumulative in effect, the repeated flooding damaged or destroyed more than 18 million board feet of timber and disrupted the ordinary use and enjoyment of the Commission's property. The Commission sought compensation from the United States pursuant to the Fifth Amendment . . . . The question presented is whether a taking may occur, within the meaning of the Takings Clause, when government-induced flood invasions, although repetitive, are temporary.

Ordinarily, this Court's decisions confirm, if government action would qualify as a taking when permanently continued, temporary actions of the same character may also qualify as a taking. In the instant case, the parties and the courts below divided on the appropriate classification of temporary flooding. Reversing the judgment of the Court of Federal Claims, which awarded compensation to the Commission, the Federal Circuit held, 2 to 1, that compensation may be sought only when flooding is "a permanent or inevitably recurring condition, rather than an inherently temporary situation." We disagree and conclude that recurrent floodings, even if of finite duration, are not categorically exempt from Takings Clause liability.

I

A

The Commission owns the Dave Donaldson Black River Wildlife Management Area (Management Area or Area), which comprises 23,000 acres along both banks of the Black River in northeast Arkansas. The Management Area is forested with multiple hardwood timber species that support a variety of wildlife habitats. The Commission operates the Management Area as a wildlife and hunting preserve, and also uses it as a timber resource, conducting regular harvests of timber as part of its forest-management efforts. Three types of hardwood oak species—nuttall, overcup, and willow—account for 80 percent of the trees in the Management Area. The presence of these hardwood oaks is essential to the Area's character as a habitat for migratory birds and as a venue for recreation and hunting.

The Clearwater Dam (Dam) is located 115 miles upstream from the Management Area. The Corps constructed the Dam in 1948, and shortly thereafter adopted a plan known as the Water Control Manual (Manual) to determine the rates at which water would be released from the Dam. The Manual sets seasonally varying release rates, but permits planned deviations from the prescribed rates for agricultural, recreational, and other purposes.

In 1993, the Corps approved a planned deviation in response to requests from farmers. From September to December 1993, the Corps released water from the Dam at a slower rate than usual, providing downstream farmers with a longer harvest time. As a result, more water than usual accumulated in Clearwater Lake behind the Dam. To reduce the accumulation, the Corps extended the period in which a high amount of water would be released. . . . [T]his extension yielded downstream flooding in the Management Area, above historical norms, during the tree-growing season, which runs from April to October. If the Corps had released the water more rapidly in the fall of 1993, in accordance with the Manual and with past practice, there would have been short-term waves of flooding which would have receded quickly. The lower rate of release in the fall, however, extended the period of flooding well into the following spring and summer. While the deviation benefited farmers, it interfered with the Management Area's tree-growing season.

The Corps adopted similar deviations each year from 1994 through 2000. . . . During this span of years the Corps proposed Manual revisions that would have made its temporary deviations part of the permanent water-release plan. On multiple occasions between 1993 and 2000, the Commission objected to the temporary deviations and opposed any permanent revision to the Manual . . . . Ultimately, the Corps tested the effect of the deviations on the Management Area. It thereupon abandoned the proposal to permanently revise the Manual and, in 2001, ceased its temporary deviations.

B

In 2005, the Commission filed the instant lawsuit against the United States . . . . Following a trial, the Court of Federal Claims ruled in favor of the Commission . . . .

The Court of Federal Claims found that the forests in the Management Area were healthy and flourishing before the flooding that occurred in the 1990's, and that the forests had been sustainably managed for decades under the water-release plan contained in the Manual. It further found that the Commission repeatedly objected to the deviations from the Manual and alerted the Corps to the detrimental effect the longer period of flooding would have on the hardwood timber in the Management Area.

As found by the Court of Federal Claims, the flooding caused by the deviations contrasted markedly with historical flooding patterns. . . . Although the Management Area lies in a floodplain, in no previously recorded time span did comparable flooding patterns occur. . . .

The court concluded that the Corps' deviations caused six consecutive years of substantially increased flooding, which constituted an appropriation of the Commission's property, albeit a temporary rather than a permanent one. Important to this conclusion, the court emphasized the deviations' cumulative effect. The trees were subject to prolonged periods of flooding year after year, which reduced the oxygen level in the soil and considerably weakened the trees' root systems. The repeated annual flooding for six years altered the character of the property to a much greater extent than would have been shown if the harm caused by one year of flooding were simply multiplied by six. When a moderate drought occurred in 1999 and 2000, the trees did not have the root systems necessary to sustain themselves; the result, in the court's words, was "catastrophic mortality." . . .

This damage altered the character of the Management Area. The destruction of the trees led to the invasion of undesirable plant species, making natural regeneration of the forests improbable in the absence of reclamation efforts. To determine the measure of just compensation, the Court of Federal Claims calculated the value of the lost timber and the projected cost of the reclamation and awarded the Commission $5.7 million.

The Federal Circuit reversed. It acknowledged that in general, temporary government action may give rise to a takings claim if permanent action of the same character would constitute a taking. But it held that "cases involving flooding and [flowage] easements are different." Government-induced flooding can give rise to a taking claim, the Federal Circuit concluded, only if the flooding is "permanent or inevitably recurring." The Court of Appeals understood this conclusion to be dictated by this Court's decisions in Sanguinetti v. United States, 264 U.S. 146 1924), and United States v. Cress, 243 U.S. 316 (1917). We granted certiorari to resolve the question whether government actions that cause repeated floodings must be permanent or inevitably recurring to constitute a taking of property.

II

The Takings Clause is "designed to bar Government from forcing some people alone to bear public burdens which, in all fairness and justice, should be borne by the public as a whole." And "[w]hen the government physically takes possession of an interest in property for some public purpose, it has a categorical duty to compensate the former owner." Tahoe-Sierra Preservation Council, Inc. v. Tahoe Regional Planning Agency, 535 U.S. 302 (2002) (citing United States v. Pewee Coal Co., 341 U.S. 114 (1951)). These guides are fundamental in our Takings Clause jurisprudence. We have recognized, however, that no magic formula enables a court to judge, in every case, whether a given government interference with property is a taking. In view of the nearly infinite variety of ways in which government actions or regulations can affect property interests, the Court has recognized few invariable rules in this area.

True, we have drawn some bright lines, notably, the rule that a permanent physical occupation of property authorized by government is a taking. *Loretto* (1982). So, too, is a regulation that permanently requires a property owner to sacrifice all economically beneficial uses of his or her land. *Lucas* (1992). But aside from the cases attended by rules of this order, most takings claims turn on situation-specific factual inquiries. See *Penn Central* (1978). With this in mind, we turn to the question presented here—whether temporary flooding can ever give rise to a takings claim.

The Court first ruled that government-induced flooding can constitute a taking in Pumpelly v. Green Bay Co. (1872). The Wisconsin Legislature had authorized the defendant to build a dam which led to the creation of a lake, permanently submerging the plaintiff's land. The defendant argued that the land had not been taken because the government did not exercise the right of eminent domain to acquire title to the affected property. Moreover, the defendant urged, the damage was merely "a consequential result" of the dam's construction near the plaintiff's property. Rejecting that crabbed reading of the Takings Clause, the Court held that "where real estate is actually invaded by superinduced additions of water, earth, sand, or other material . . . so as to effectually destroy or impair its usefulness, it is a taking, within the meaning of the Constitution."

Following *Pumpelly*, the Court recognized that seasonally recurring flooding could constitute a taking. United States v. Cress, 243 U.S. 316 (1917), involved the Government's construction of a lock and dam, which subjected the plaintiff's land to "intermittent but inevitably recurring overflows." The Court held that the regularly recurring flooding gave rise to a takings claim no less valid than the claim of an owner whose land was continuously kept under water.

Furthermore, our decisions confirm that takings temporary in duration can be compensable. This principle was solidly established in the World War II era, when "[c]ondemnation for indefinite periods of occupancy [took hold as] a practical response to the uncertainties of the Government's needs in wartime." United States v. Westinghouse Elec. & Mfg. Co., 339 U.S. 261 (1950). In support of the war effort, the Government took temporary possession of many properties. These exercises of government authority, the Court recognized, qualified as compensable temporary takings. See *Pewee Coal Co.*; Kimball Laundry Co. v. United States, 338 U.S. 1 (1949); United States v. General Motors Corp., 323 U.S. 373 (1945). Notably in relation to the question before us, the takings claims approved in these cases were not confined to instances in which the Government took outright physical possession of the property involved. A temporary takings claim could be maintained as well when government action occurring outside the property gave rise to "a direct and immediate interference with the enjoyment and use of the land." United States v. Causby (1946).

Ever since, we have rejected the argument that government action must be permanent to qualify as a taking. Once the government's actions have worked a taking of property, "no subsequent action by the government can relieve it of the duty to provide compensation for the period during which the taking was effective." *First English* (1987). See also *Tahoe-Sierra* ("[W]e do not hold that the temporary nature of a land-use restriction precludes finding that it effects a taking; we simply recognize that it should not be given exclusive significance one way or the other.").

Because government-induced flooding can constitute a taking of property, and because a taking need not be permanent to be compensable, our precedent indicates that government-induced flooding of limited duration may be compensable. No decision of this Court authorizes a blanket temporary-flooding exception to our Takings Clause jurisprudence, and we decline to create such an exception in this case.

III

In advocating a temporary-flooding exception, the Government relies primarily on Sanguinetti v. United States, 264 U.S. 146 (1924). That case involved a canal constructed by the Government . . . . The year after the canal's construction, a "flood of unprecedented severity" caused the canal to overflow onto the claimant's land; less severe flooding and overflow occurred in later years. The Court held there was no taking . . . [based] on settled principles of foreseeability and causation. The . . . Government did not intend to flood the land or have "any reason to expect that such [a] result would follow" from construction of the canal. Moreover, . . . the landowner failed to show a causal connection between the canal and the increased flooding, which may well have been occasioned by changes in weather patterns. . . . In the course of the *Sanguinetti* decision, however, the Court summarized prior flooding cases as standing for the proposition that "in order to create an enforceable liability against the Government, it is, at least, necessary that the overflow be the direct result of the structure, and constitute an actual, permanent invasion of the land." The Government would have us extract from this statement a definitive rule that there can be no temporary taking caused by floods.

We do not read so much into the word "permanent" as it appears in a non-dispositive sentence in *Sanguinetti*. That case, we note, was decided in 1924, well before the World War II-era cases and *First English*, in which the Court first homed in on the matter of compensation for temporary takings. That time factor, we think, renders understandable the Court's passing reference to permanence. If the Court indeed meant to express a general limitation on the Takings Clause, that limitation has been superseded by subsequent developments in our jurisprudence.

. . . The Government also asserts that the Court in *Loretto* interpreted *Sanguinetti* the same way the Federal Circuit did in this case. That assertion bears careful inspection. A section of the Court's opinion in *Loretto* discussing permanent physical occupations parenthetically quotes *Sanguinetti*'s statement that flooding is a taking if it constitutes an "actual, permanent invasion of the land." But the first rule of case law as well as statutory interpretation is: Read on. Later in the *Loretto* opinion, the Court clarified that it scarcely intended to adopt a "flooding-is-different" rule by the obscure means of quoting parenthetically a fragment from a 1924 opinion. The Court distinguished permanent physical occupations from temporary invasions of property, expressly including flooding cases, and said that "temporary limitations are subject to a more complex balancing process to determine whether they are a taking."

There is thus no solid grounding in precedent for setting flooding apart from all other government intrusions on property. And the Government has presented no other persuasive reason to do so. Its primary argument is of the in for a penny, in for a pound genre: reversing the decision below, the Government worries, risks disruption of public works dedicated to flood control. "[E]very passing flood attributable to the government's operation of a flood-control project, no matter how brief," the Government hypothesizes, might qualify as a compensable taking. To reject a categorical bar to temporary-flooding takings claims, however, is scarcely to credit all, or even many, such claims. It is of course incumbent on courts to weigh carefully the relevant factors and circumstances in each case, as instructed by our decisions.

The slippery slope argument, we note, is hardly novel or unique to flooding cases. Time and again in Takings Clause cases, the Court has heard the prophecy that recognizing a just compensation claim would unduly impede the government's ability to act in the public interest. We have rejected this argument when deployed to urge blanket exemptions from the Fifth Amendment's instruction. While we recognize the importance of the public interests the Government advances in this case, we do not see them as categorically different from the interests at stake in myriad other Takings Clause cases. The sky did not fall after *Causby*, and today's modest decision augurs no deluge of takings liability. . . .

At oral argument, the Government tendered a different justification for the Federal Circuit's judgment, one not aired in the courts below, and barely hinted at in the brief the Government filed in this Court: Whether the damage is permanent or temporary, damage to downstream property, however foresee-able, is collateral or incidental; it is not aimed at any particular landowner and therefore does not qualify as an occupation compensable under the Takings Clause. "[M]indful that we are a court of review, not of first view," we express no opinion on the proposed upstream/downstream distinction and confine our opinion to the issue explored and decided by the Federal Circuit.

For the same reason, we are not equipped to address the bearing, if any, of Arkansas water-rights law on this case. The determination whether a taking has occurred includes consideration of the property owner's distinct investment-backed expectations, a matter often informed by the law in force in the State in which the property is located. But Arkansas law was not examined by the Federal Circuit, and therefore is not properly pursued in this Court. Whether arguments for an upstream/downstream distinction and on the relevance of Arkansas law have been preserved and, if so, whether they have merit, are questions appropriately addressed to the Court of Appeals on remand.

IV

We rule today, simply and only, that government-induced flooding tempo-rary in duration gains no automatic exemption from Takings Clause inspection. When regulation or temporary physical invasion by government interferes with private property, our decisions recognize, time is indeed a factor in determining the existence *vel non* of a compensable taking. See *Loretto* (temporary physical invasions should be assessed by case-specific factual inquiry); *Tahoe-Sierra* (dura-tion of regulatory restriction is a factor for court to consider); National Bd. of YMCA v. United States (1969) ("temporary, unplanned occupation" of building by troops under exigent circumstances is not a taking).

Also relevant to the takings inquiry is the degree to which the invasion is intended or is the foreseeable result of authorized government action. So, too, are the character of the land at issue and the owner's "reasonable investment-backed expectations" regarding the land's use. Palazzolo v. Rhode Island, 533 U.S. 606 (2001). Severity of the interference figures in the calculus as well. See Portsmouth Harbor Land & Hotel Co. v. United States, 260 U.S. 327 (1922) ("[W]hile a single act may not be enough, a continuance of them in sufficient number and for a sufficient time may prove [a taking]. Every successive trespass adds to the force of the evidence."). . . .

. . . [T]he judgment of the Court of Appeals for the Federal Circuit is reversed, and the case is remanded for further proceedings consistent with this opinion.

Notes and Questions

1. Why should the temporary character of a physical invasion be a factor in determining whether a taking has occurred, rather than simply a factor in deter-mining the amount of just compensation? Is there a difference between a tres-pass by the government and a taking? If so, where and how should the line be drawn? Should the government's intention matter?

2. If the Corps of Engineers has indeed taken property from the Fish and Game Commission, was it taken for a public use?

3. What is the difference between this case and *Miller v. Schoene* where the court held that the state could choose between two conflicting uses (cedar trees and apple trees) without having to pay compensation to the landowner whose property was destroyed?

ARKANSAS GAME AND FISH COMMISSION v. UNITED STATES: TAKINGS LAW, WITHOUT A THEORY

Richard A. Epstein,
http://PointofLaw.com/columns, December 2012

The losses that were suffered by the AGFC were not done for the benefit of the public as a whole, but for a discrete group of Missouri farmers who benefited from the water supply in question. The ideal solution therefore is to impose some kind of special assessment on the winners to force them to compensate the downstream losers. Chances are they would not be prepared to pay the freight, at which point the correct result is for the Corps to discontinue the flooding, which would minimize the social losses to all parties, resulting from various government activities.

Balancing Forever

In this instance, the government hasn't shown any willingness to seek compensation from the special beneficiaries, which means that special groups have yet a stronger incentive to lobby for particular programs that will give them localized benefits financed by the property losses sustained by others. But Justice Ginsburg's opinion shows no interest whatsoever in either the incentive effects of the compensation rules or in the public-choice dynamics that are unleashed by a narrow application of the Takings Clause. Nor does she worry how future water-management groups might seek to time their releases to minimize their liability to downstream owners. These major omissions come at a high intellectual cost. The only way to get to the right result is to reinstate the District Court's compensation award, without going through the costly and pointless relitigation on remand.

The Supreme Court, however, went into balancing tests with a vengeance. Justice Ginsburg's initial ploy was to explain at great length why its earlier decision in Sanguinetti v. United States did not commit the Court to the position that only permanent takings were compensable. . . . From that conclusion it noted that its increased willingness to allow for compensation cases of temporary total takings, governed by its 1987 decision in First English Evangelical Lutheran Church of Glendale v. County of Los Angeles, indicated a more receptive attitude toward temporary takings. But at this point it just fails to seal the deal. Instead of staying with the *per se* takings cases, the Court embraces in the context of a direct and immediate physical invasion the useless balancing tests developed under its misguided decision in Penn Central Transportation Co. v. City of New York, which, ironically, did say that physical invasion warrant greater scrutiny than regulatory takings. By citing *Penn Central*, the Supreme Court reinforced its unwillingness to back off the extraordinary deference that it shows to government regulators in cases of zoning and other land use restrictions. But the Court was willing to remand this decision on for further consideration on the unpersuasive technical ground that the Federal Circuit looked solely at the temporary nature of the taking, thereby ignoring other factors that could bear on the ultimate decision on compensation.

At this point, the factors came thick and fast, but without rhyme or reason. The Court insisted that some attention should be paid to "the property owner's distinct investment-backed expectations, a matter often informed by the law in force in the States in which the property is located." Why . . . [state] law might be ignored is not explained. It also found relevant "the degree to which the invasion is intended or is the foreseeable result of authorized government action." And the Court thought it was also fair game for the government to challenge the findings of the trial court as they related "to causation, foreseeability, substantiality, and the amount of damages." And the Court then stressed that it was worth considering, as the government urged only on its appeal to the Supreme Court, that "[w]hether the damage is permanent or temporary, damage to downstream property, however foreseeable, is collateral or incidental; it is not aimed at any particular landowner and therefore does not qualify as an occupation compensable."

The use of these multiple criteria reaches its climax in the proposition that what really matters is "the particular circumstances of each case." What is so sad about this unanimous opinion is that it seems to assume that the use of *ad hoc* balancing tests somehow counts as a sign of the Court's own intellectual sophistication. But the exact opposite is true. To mention everything is to understand nothing. There is no evidence as to why these factors are relevant or how they should be taken into account. We thus get complexity without clarity, which is of course a hallmark of many of the balancing tests that are adopted under state tort law. The upshot is the losing combination of high administrative costs and high levels of error. The welter of factors, each with an indeterminate weight, thus cuts off any meaningful prospect of judicial review.

It is all so unnecessary. This case should have been decided on two propositions. The first is whether the water the Corps released caused damage to the plaintiff's land, which the Court of Federal Claims' findings amply demonstrated. The second was that just compensation should be set at the value of the timber lost. The remainder of the factors listed in Justice Ginsburg's opinion have nothing to do with the merits of this case. . . .

E.   RELATION BETWEEN DUE PROCESS AND TAKINGS CLAUSES

LINGLE v. CHEVRON U.S.A., INC.

Supreme Court of the United States
544 U.S. 528 (2005)

Justice O'CONNOR delivered the unanimous opinion of the Court [joined by Justices BREYER, GINSBURG, KENNEDY, REHNQUIST, SCALIA, SOUTER, STEVENS, and THOMAS].

On occasion, a would-be doctrinal rule or test finds its way into our case law through simple repetition of a phrase—however fortuitously coined. A quarter century ago, in Agins v. City of Tiburon, 447 U.S. 255 (1980), the Court declared that government regulation of private property "effects a taking if [such regulation] does not substantially advance legitimate state interests . . . ." Through reiteration in a half dozen or so decisions since *Agins*, this language has been ensconced in our Fifth Amendment takings jurisprudence. . . .

In the case before us, the lower courts applied *Agins*' "substantially advances" formula to strike down a Hawaii statute that limits the rent that oil companies may charge to dealers who lease service stations owned by the companies. The lower courts held that the rent cap effects an uncompensated taking of private property in violation of the Fifth and Fourteenth Amendments because it does not substantially advance Hawaii's asserted interest in controlling retail gasoline prices. This case requires us to decide whether the "substantially advances" formula announced in *Agins* is an appropriate test for determining whether a regulation effects a Fifth Amendment taking. We conclude that it is not. . . .

II

A

The Takings Clause of the Fifth Amendment . . . "does not prohibit the taking of private property, but instead places a condition on the exercise of that power." [I]t "is designed not to limit the governmental interference with property rights *per se*, but rather to secure *compensation* in the event of otherwise proper interference amounting to a taking." . . .

Our precedents stake out two categories of regulatory action that generally will be deemed *per se* takings for Fifth Amendment purposes. . . . Outside these two relatively narrow categories (and the special context of land-use exactions . . .) regulatory takings challenges are governed by the standards set forth in Penn Central Transp. Co. v. New York City. . . .

Although our regulatory takings jurisprudence cannot be characterized as unified, these three inquiries (reflected in *Loretto*, *Lucas*, and *Penn Central*) share a common touchstone. Each aims to identify regulatory actions that are functionally equivalent to the classic taking in which government directly appropriates private property or ousts the owner from his domain. Accordingly, each of these tests focuses directly upon the severity of the burden that government imposes upon private property rights. The Court has held that physical takings require compensation because of the unique burden they impose: A permanent physical invasion, however minimal the economic cost it entails, eviscerates the owner's right to exclude others from entering and using her property—perhaps the most fundamental of all property interests. . . . In the *Lucas* context, of course, the complete elimination of a property's value is the determinative factor. . . . And the *Penn Central* inquiry turns in large part, albeit not exclusively, upon the magnitude of a regulation's economic impact and the degree to which it interferes with legitimate property interests.

B

In Agins v. City of Tiburon, a case involving a facial takings challenge to certain municipal zoning ordinances, the Court declared that "[t]he application of a general zoning law to particular property effects a taking if the ordinance does not substantially advance legitimate state interests, see Nectow v. Cambridge, 277 U.S. 183 (1928), or denies an owner economically viable use of his land, see Penn Central Transp. Co. v. New York City . . . ." Because this statement is phrased in the disjunctive, *Agins'* "substantially advances" language has been read to announce a stand-alone regulatory takings test that is wholly independent of *Penn Central* or any other test. . . . Although a number of our takings precedents have recited the "substantially advances" formula minted in *Agins,* this is our first opportunity to consider its validity as a freestanding takings test. We conclude that this formula prescribes an inquiry in the nature of a due process, not a takings, test, and that it has no proper place in our takings jurisprudence.

There is no question that the "substantially advances" formula was derived from due process, not takings, precedents. In support of this new language, *Agins* cited Nectow v. Cambridge, a 1928 case in which the plaintiff claimed that a city zoning ordinance "deprived him of his property without due process of law in contravention of the Fourteenth Amendment." *Agins* then went on to discuss Village of Euclid v. Ambler Realty Co., 272 U.S. 365 (1926), a historic decision holding that a municipal zoning ordinance would survive a substantive due process challenge so long as it was not "clearly arbitrary and unreasonable, having no *substantial relation to the public health, safety, morals, or general welfare.*" (emphasis added) . . . .

When viewed in historical context, the Court's reliance on *Nectow* and *Euclid* is understandable. *Agins* was the Court's first case involving a challenge to zoning regulations in many decades, so it was natural to turn to these seminal zoning precedents for guidance. . . . Moreover, *Agins'* apparent commingling of due process and takings inquiries had some precedent in the Court's then-recent decision in *Penn Central.* . . . Finally, when *Agins* was decided, there had been some history of referring to deprivations of property without due process of law as "takings," . . . and the Court had yet to clarify whether "regulatory takings" claims were properly cognizable under the Takings Clause or the Due Process Clause . . . .

Although *Agins'* reliance on due process precedents is understandable, the language the Court selected was regrettably imprecise. The "substantially advances" formula suggests a means-ends test: It asks, in essence, whether a regulation of private property is *effective* in achieving some legitimate public purpose. An inquiry of this nature has some logic in the context of a due process challenge, for a regulation that fails to serve any legitimate governmental objective may be so arbitrary or irrational that it runs afoul of the Due Process Clause. . . . But such a test is not a valid method of discerning whether private property has been "taken" for purposes of the Fifth Amendment.

In stark contrast to the three regulatory takings tests discussed above, the "substantially advances" inquiry reveals nothing about the *magnitude or character of the burden* a particular regulation imposes upon private property rights. Nor does it provide any information about how any regulatory burden is *distributed* among property owners. In consequence, this test does not help to identify those regulations whose effects are functionally comparable to government appropriation or invasion of private property; it is tethered neither to the text of the Takings Clause nor to the basic justification for allowing regulatory actions to be challenged under the Clause. . . .

Instead of addressing a challenged regulation's effect on private property, the "substantially advances" inquiry probes the regulation's underlying validity. But such an inquiry is logically prior to and distinct from the question whether a regulation effects a taking, for the Takings Clause presupposes that the government has acted in pursuit of a valid public purpose. The Clause expressly requires compensation where government takes private property "*for public use.*" It does not bar government from interfering with property rights, but rather requires compensation "in the event of *otherwise proper interference* amounting to a taking." . . . Conversely, if a government action is found to be impermissible—for instance because it fails to meet the "public use" requirement or is so arbitrary as to violate due process—that is the end of the inquiry. No amount of compensation can authorize such action. . . .

Finally, the "substantially advances" formula is not only *doctrinally* untenable . . .—its application as such would also present serious practical difficulties. The *Agins* formula can be read to demand heightened means-ends review of virtually any regulation of private property. If so interpreted, it would require courts to scrutinize the efficacy of a vast array of state and federal regulations—a task for which courts are not well suited. Moreover, it would empower—and might often require—courts to substitute their predictive judgments for those of elected legislatures and expert agencies.

. . . [T]he instant case . . . foreshadows the hazards of placing courts in this role. To resolve Chevron's takings claim, the District Court was required to choose between the views of two opposing economists as to whether Hawaii's rent control statute would help to prevent concentration and supracompetitive prices in the State's retail gasoline market. Finding one expert to be "more persuasive" than the other, the court concluded that the Hawaii Legislature's chosen regulatory strategy would not actually achieve its objectives. . . . Based on this and other findings, the District Court enjoined further enforcement of . . . [the] rent cap provision against Chevron. We find the proceedings below remarkable, to say the least, given that we have long eschewed such heightened scrutiny when addressing substantive due process challenges to government regulation. The reasons for deference to legislative judgments about the need for, and likely effectiveness of, regulatory actions are by now well established, and we think they are no less applicable here. . . .

III

. . . [O]ur holding today . . . does not require us to disturb any of our prior holdings. To be sure, we applied a "substantially advances" inquiry in *Agins* itself (finding that the challenged zoning ordinances "substantially advance[d] legitimate governmental goals"), and arguably also in Keystone Bituminous Coal Assn. v. DeBenedictis, 480 U.S. 470 (1987) (quoting " 'substantially advance[s]' " language and then finding that the challenged statute was intended to further a substantial public interest). But in no case have we found a compensable taking based on such an inquiry. . . .

It might be argued that this formula played a role in our decisions in Nollan v. California Coastal Comm'n, 483 U.S. 825 (1987), and Dolan v. City of Tigard, 512 U.S. 374 (1994). . . . But while the Court drew upon the language of *Agins* in these cases, it did not apply the "substantially advances" test that is the subject of today's decision. Both *Nollan* and *Dolan* involved Fifth Amendment takings challenges to adjudicative land-use exactions—specifically, government demands that a landowner dedicate an easement allowing public access to her property as a condition of obtaining a development permit. . . .

In each case, the Court began with the premise that, had the government simply appropriated the easement in question, this would have been a *per se* physical taking. The question was whether the government could, without paying the compensation that would otherwise be required upon effecting such a taking, demand the easement as a condition for granting a development permit the government was entitled to deny. The Court in *Nollan* answered in the affirmative, provided that the exaction would substantially advance the same government interest that would furnish a valid ground for denial of the permit. The Court further refined this requirement in *Dolan*, holding that an adjudicative exaction requiring dedication of private property must also be " 'rough[ly] proportiona[l]' . . . both in nature and extent to the impact of the proposed development." . . .

Although *Nollan* and *Dolan* quoted *Agins*' language, the rule those decisions established is entirely distinct from the "substantially advances" test we address today. Whereas the "substantially advances" inquiry before us now is unconcerned with the degree or type of burden a regulation places upon property, *Nollan* and *Dolan* both involved dedications of property so onerous that, outside the exactions context, they would be deemed *per se* physical takings. In neither case did the Court question whether the exaction would substantially advance *some* legitimate state interest. Rather, the issue was whether the exactions substantially advanced the *same* interests that land-use authorities asserted would allow them to deny the permit altogether. . . .

Twenty-five years ago, the Court posited that a regulation of private property "effects a taking if [it] does not substantially advance [a] legitimate state interes[t]." *Agins*. The lower courts in this case took that statement to its logical conclusion, and in so doing, revealed its imprecision. Today we correct course. We hold that the "substantially advances" formula is not a valid takings test, and indeed conclude that it has no proper place in our takings jurisprudence. . . .

Justice KENNEDY, concurring.

This separate writing is to note that today's decision does not foreclose the possibility that a regulation might be so arbitrary or irrational as to violate due process. Eastern Enterprises v. Apfel, 524 U.S. 498, 539 (1998) (KENNEDY, J., concurring in judgment and dissenting in part). . . .

Notes and Questions

1. How unusual is it for the Supreme Court to disavow one of its precedents, or, as Justice Scalia put it during oral argument in *Lingle*, for it to "eat crow"?

See Daniel A. Jacobs, *Indigestion from Eating Crow: The Impact of Lingle v. Chevron, U.S.A., Inc. on the Future of Regulatory Takings Doctrine*, 38 Urb. Law. 451 (2006).

2. How important is the *Lingle* decision? It certainly gets rid of the confusion that resulted from conflating due process and takings doctrine, but does it do more? *See* Benjamin D. Barros, *At Last, Some Clarity: The Potential Long-Term Impact of Lingle v. Chevron and the Separation of Takings and Substantive Due Process*, 69 Alb. L. Rev. 343, 345 (2005).

F.   EXACTIONS

KOONTZ v. ST. JOHNS RIVER WATER MANAGEMENT DISTRICT
Supreme Court of the United States
133 S. Ct. 2586 (2013)

Syllabus[*]

Coy Koontz, Sr., whose estate is represented here by petitioner, sought permits to develop a section of his property from respondent St. Johns River Water Management District (District), which, consistent with Florida law, requires permit applicants wishing to build on wetlands to offset the resulting environmental damage. Koontz offered to mitigate the environmental effects of his development proposal by deeding to the District a conservation easement on nearly three-quarters of his property. The District rejected Koontz's proposal and informed him that it would approve construction only if he (1) reduced the size of his development and, *inter alia*, deeded to the District a conservation easement on the resulting larger remainder of his property or (2) hired contractors to make improvements to District-owned wetlands several miles away. Believing the District's demands to be excessive in light of the environmental effects his proposal would have caused, Koontz filed suit under a state law that provides money damages for agency action that is an "unreasonable exercise of the state's police power constituting a taking without just compensation."

The trial court found the District's actions unlawful because they failed the requirements of Nollan v. California Coastal Comm'n, 483 U.S. 825 (1987), and Dolan v. City of Tigard, 512 U.S. 374 (1994). Those cases held that the government may not condition the approval of a land-use permit on the owner's relinquishment of a portion of his property unless there is a nexus and rough proportionality between the government's demand and the effects of the proposed land use. The District Court of Appeal affirmed, but the State Supreme Court reversed on two grounds. First, it held that petitioner's claim failed because, unlike in *Nollan* or *Dolan*, the District *denied* the application. Second, the State Supreme Court held that a demand for money cannot give rise to a claim under *Nollan* and *Dolan*.

---

[*] The syllabus constitutes no part of the opinion of the Court but has been prepared by the Reporter of Decisions for the convenience of the reader.

Justice ALITO delivered the opinion of the Court [joined by ROBERTS, C.J., and SCALIA, KENNEDY, and THOMAS, JJ.]

Our decisions in Nollan v. California Coastal Comm'n, and Dolan v. City of Tigard provide important protection against the misuse of the power of land-use regulation. In those cases, we held that a unit of government may not condition the approval of a land-use permit on the owner's relinquishment of a portion of his property unless there is a "nexus" and "rough proportionality" between the government's demand and the effects of the proposed land use. In this case, the St. Johns River Water Management District (District) believes that it circumvented Nollan and Dolan because of the way in which it structured its handling of a permit application submitted by Coy Koontz . . . . The District did not approve his application on the condition that he surrender an interest in his land. Instead, the District, after suggesting that he could obtain approval by signing over such an interest, denied his application because he refused to yield. The Florida Supreme Court blessed this maneuver and thus effectively interred those important decisions. Because we conclude that Nollan and Dolan cannot be evaded in this way, the Florida Supreme Court's decision must be reversed.

Justice KAGAN, with whom Justice GINSBURG, Justice BREYER, and Justice SOTOMAYOR join, dissenting.

In the paradigmatic case triggering review under Nollan v. California Coastal Comm'n and Dolan v. City of Tigard, the government approves a building permit on the condition that the landowner relinquish an interest in real property, like an easement. The significant legal questions that the Court resolves today are whether Nollan and Dolan also apply when that case is varied in two ways. First, what if the government does not approve the permit, but instead demands that the condition be fulfilled before it will do so? Second, what if the condition entails not transferring real property, but simply paying money? . . .

I think the Court gets the first question it addresses right. The Nollan-Dolan standard applies not only when the government approves a development permit conditioned on the owner's conveyance of a property interest (i.e., imposes a condition subsequent), but also when the government denies a permit until the owner meets the condition (i.e., imposes a condition precedent). That means an owner may challenge the denial of a permit on the ground that the government's condition lacks the "nexus" and "rough proportionality" to the development's social costs that Nollan and Dolan require. Still, the condition-subsequent and condition-precedent situations differ in an important way. When the government grants a permit subject to the relinquishment of real property, and that condition does not satisfy Nollan and Dolan, then the government has taken the property and must pay just compensation under the Fifth Amendment. But when the government denies a permit because an owner has refused to accede to that same demand, nothing has actually been taken. The owner is entitled to have the improper condition removed; and he may be entitled to a monetary remedy created by state law for imposing such a condition; but he cannot be entitled to constitutional compensation for a taking of property. So far, we all agree.

Our core disagreement concerns the second question the Court addresses. The majority extends Nollan and Dolan to cases in which the government conditions a permit not on the transfer of real property, but instead on the payment or expenditure of money. That runs roughshod over Eastern Enterprises v. Apfel, 524 U.S. 498 (1998), which held that the government may impose ordinary financial obligations without triggering the Takings Clause's protections. The boundaries of the majority's new rule are uncertain. But it threatens to subject a vast array of land-use regulations, applied daily in States and localities throughout the country, to heightened constitutional scrutiny. I would not embark on so unwise an adventure, and would affirm the Florida Supreme Court's decision. . . .

I

Claims that government regulations violate the Takings Clause by unduly restricting the use of property are generally "governed by the standards set forth in Penn Central Transp. Co. v. New York City . . . ."

Our decisions in *Nollan* and *Dolan* are different: They provide an independent layer of protection in "the special context of land-use exactions." In that situation, the "government demands that a landowner dedicate an easement" or surrender a piece of real property "as a condition of obtaining a development permit." If the government appropriated such a property interest outside the permitting process, its action would constitute a taking, necessitating just compensation. *Nollan* and *Dolan* prevent the government from exploiting the landowner's permit application to evade the constitutional obligation to pay for the property. They do so, as the majority explains, by subjecting the government's demand to heightened scrutiny: The government may condition a land-use permit on the relinquishment of real property only if it shows a "nexus" and "rough proportionality" between the demand made and "the impact of the proposed development." *Nollan* and *Dolan* thus serve not to address excessive regulatory burdens on land use (the function of *Penn Central*), but instead to stop the government from imposing an "unconstitutional condition"—a requirement that a person give up his constitutional right to receive just compensation "in exchange for a discretionary benefit" having "little or no relationship" to the property taken.

Accordingly, the *Nollan-Dolan* test applies only when the property the government demands during the permitting process is the kind it otherwise would have to pay for—or, put differently, when the appropriation of that property, outside the permitting process, would constitute a taking. That is why *Nollan* began by stating that "[h]ad California simply required the Nollans to make an easement across their beachfront available to the public . . . , rather than conditioning their permit to rebuild their house on their agreeing to do so, we have no doubt there would have been a taking" requiring just compensation. And it is why *Dolan* started by maintaining that "had the city simply required petitioner to dedicate a strip of land . . . for public use, rather than conditioning the grant of her permit to [d]evelop her property on such a dedication, a taking would have occurred." Even the majority acknowledges this basic point . . . .

Here, Koontz claims that the District demanded that he spend money to improve public wetlands, not that he hand over a real property interest. . . . The key question then is: Independent of the permitting process, does requiring a person to pay money to the government, or spend money on its behalf, constitute a taking requiring just compensation? Only if the answer is yes does the *Nollan-Dolan* test apply.

But we have already answered that question no. Eastern Enterprises v. Apfel . . . involved a federal statute requiring a former mining company to pay a large sum of money for the health benefits of retired employees. Five Members of the Court determined that the law did not effect a taking, distinguishing between the appropriation of a specific property interest and the imposition of an order to pay money. Justice KENNEDY acknowledged in his controlling opinion that the statute "impose[d] a staggering financial burden" (which influenced his conclusion that it violated due process). Still, Justice KENNEDY explained, the law did not effect a taking because it did not "operate upon or alter" a "specific and identified propert[y] or property right[ ]." Instead, "[t]he law simply imposes an obligation to perform an act, the payment of benefits. The statute is indifferent as to how the regulated entity elects to comply or the property it uses to do so." Justice BREYER, writing for four more Justices, agreed. He stated that the Takings Clause applies only when the government appropriates a "specific interest in physical or intellectual property" or "a specific, separately identifiable fund of money"; by contrast, the Clause has no bearing when the government imposes "an ordinary liability to pay money."

Thus, a requirement that a person pay money to repair public wetlands is not a taking. Such an order does not affect a "specific and identified propert[y] or property right[ ]"; it simply "imposes an obligation to perform an act" (the improvement of wetlands) that costs money. . . . [T]he order to repair wetlands, viewed independent of the permitting process, does not constitute a taking. And that means the order does not trigger the *Nollan-Dolan* test, because it does not force Koontz to relinquish a constitutional right.

The majority tries to distinguish *Apfel* by asserting that the District's demand here was "closely analogous" (and "bears resemblance") to the seizure of a lien on property or an income stream from a parcel of land. The majority thus seeks support from decisions like Armstrong v. United States, 364 U.S. 40 (1960), where this Court held that the government effected a taking when it extinguished a lien on several ships, and Palm Beach Cty. v. Cove Club Investors Ltd., 734 So. 2d 379 (Fla. 1999), where the Florida Supreme Court held that the government committed a taking when it terminated a covenant entitling the beneficiary to an income stream from a piece of land.

But the majority's citations succeed only in showing what this case is *not*. When the government dissolves a lien, or appropriates a determinate income stream from a piece of property—or, for that matter, seizes a particular "bank account or [the] accrued interest" on it—the government indeed takes a "specific" and "identified property interest." But nothing like that occurred here. . . . Koontz could meet [the] obligation from whatever source he chose—a checking account, shares of stock, a wealthy uncle; the District was "indifferent as to how [he] elect[ed] to [pay] or the property [he] use[d] to do so." . . .

The majority thus falls back on the sole way the District's alleged demand related to a property interest: The demand arose out of the permitting process for Koontz's land. But under the analytic framework that *Nollan* and *Dolan* established, that connection alone is insufficient to trigger heightened scrutiny. . . . [T]he heightened standard of *Nollan* and *Dolan* is not a freestanding protection for land-use permit applicants; rather, it is "a special application of the doctrine of unconstitutional conditions, which provides that the government may not require a person to give up a constitutional right—here the right to receive just compensation when property is taken"—in exchange for a land-use permit. As such, *Nollan* and *Dolan* apply only if the demand at issue would have violated the Constitution independent of that proposed exchange. Or put otherwise, those cases apply only if the demand would have constituted a taking when executed *outside* the permitting process. And here, under *Apfel*, it would not.[1]

The majority's approach, on top of its analytic flaws, threatens significant practical harm. By applying *Nollan* and *Dolan* to permit conditions requiring monetary payments—with no express limitation except as to taxes—the majority extends the Takings Clause, with its notoriously "difficult" and "perplexing" standards, into the very heart of local land-use regulation and service delivery. Cities and towns across the nation impose many kinds of permitting fees every day. Some enable a government to mitigate a new development's impact on the community, like increased traffic or pollution—or destruction of wetlands. Others cover the direct costs of providing services like sewage or water to the development. Still others are meant to limit the number of landowners who engage in a certain activity, as fees for liquor licenses do. All now must meet *Nollan* and *Dolan*'s nexus and proportionality tests. The Federal Constitution thus will decide whether one town is overcharging for sewage, or another is setting the price to sell liquor too high. And the flexibility of state and local governments to take the most routine actions to enhance their communities will diminish accordingly.

That problem becomes still worse because the majority's distinction between monetary "exactions" and taxes is so hard to apply. The majority acknowledges, as it must, that taxes are not takings. But once the majority decides that a simple demand to pay money—the sort of thing often viewed as a tax—can count as an impermissible "exaction," how is anyone to tell the two apart? . . . How to separate orders to pay money from . . . well, orders to pay money, so that a locality knows what it can (and cannot) do. State courts sometimes must confront the same question, as they enforce restrictions on localities' taxing power. And their decisions—contrary to the majority's blithe assertion—struggle to draw a coherent boundary. Because "[t]here is no set rule" by which to determine "in which category a particular" action belongs, courts often reach opposite conclusions about classifying nearly identical fees. . . .

Perhaps the Court means in the future to curb the intrusion into local affairs that its holding will accomplish; the Court claims, after all, that its opinion is intended to have only limited impact on localities' land-use authority. The majority might, for example, approve the rule, adopted in several States, that *Nollan* and *Dolan* apply only to permitting fees that are imposed ad hoc, and not to fees that are generally applicable. See, *e.g.,* Ehrlich v. Culver City, 911 P.2d 429 (Cal. 1996). *Dolan* itself suggested that limitation by underscoring that there

---

1.   The majority's sole response is that "the unconstitutional conditions analysis requires us to set aside petitioner's *permit application*, not his ownership of a particular parcel of real property." That mysterious sentence fails to make the majority's opinion cohere with the unconstitutional conditions doctrine, as anyone has ever known it. That doctrine applies only if imposing a condition directly—*i.e.,* independent of an exchange for a government benefit—would violate the Constitution. Here, *Apfel* makes clear that the District's condition would not do so: The government may (separate and apart from permitting) require a person—whether Koontz or anyone else—to pay or spend money without effecting a taking. The majority offers no theory to the contrary: It does not explain, as it must, why the District's condition was "unconstitutional."

"the city made an adjudicative decision to condition petitioner's application for a building permit on an individual parcel," instead of imposing an "essentially legislative determination[ ] classifying entire areas of the city." Maybe today's majority accepts that distinction; or then again, maybe not. At the least, the majority's refusal "to say more" about the scope of its new rule now casts a cloud on every decision by every local government to require a person seeking a permit to pay or spend money.

At bottom, the majority's analysis seems to grow out of a yen for a prophylactic rule: Unless *Nollan* and *Dolan* apply to monetary demands, the majority worries, "land-use permitting officials" could easily "evade the limitations" on exaction of real property interests that those decisions impose. But that is a prophylaxis in search of a problem. No one has presented evidence that in the many States declining to apply heightened scrutiny to permitting fees, local officials routinely short-circuit *Nollan* and *Dolan* to extort the surrender of real property interests having no relation to a development's costs. And if officials were to impose a fee as a contrivance to take an easement (or other real property right), then a court could indeed apply *Nollan* and *Dolan*. See, *e.g.*, Norwood v. Baker, 172 U.S. 269 (1898) (preventing circumvention of the Takings Clause by prohibiting the government from imposing a special assessment for the full value of a property in advance of condemning it). That situation does not call for a rule extending, as the majority's does, to *all* monetary exactions. Finally, a court can use the *Penn Central* framework, the Due Process Clause, and (in many places) state law to protect against monetary demands . . . that simply "go[ ] too far.[3] . . .

[Back to the majority opinion. — EDS.]

Justice ALITO delivered the opinion of the Court [joined by ROBERTS, C.J., and SCALIA, KENNEDY, and THOMAS, JJ.]

III

We turn to the Florida Supreme Court's alternative holding that petitioner's claim fails because respondent asked him to spend money rather than give up an easement on his land. . . . Respondent and the dissent take the same position, citing the concurring and dissenting opinions in Eastern Enterprises v. Apfel, 524 U.S. 498 (1998), for the proposition that an obligation to spend money can never provide the basis for a takings claim.

---

3.   Our *Penn Central* test protects against regulations that unduly burden an owner's use of his property: Unlike the *Nollan-Dolan* standard, that framework fits to a T a complaint (like Koontz's) that a permitting condition makes it inordinately expensive to develop land. And the Due Process Clause provides an additional backstop against excessive permitting fees by preventing a government from conditioning a land-use permit on a monetary requirement that is "basically arbitrary." *Eastern Enterprises v. Apfel*, 524 U.S. 498 (1998) (BREYER, J., dissenting). My point is not, as the majority suggests, that these constraints do the same thing as *Nollan* and *Dolan*, and so make those decisions unnecessary. To the contrary, *Nollan* and *Dolan* provide developers with enhanced protection (and localities with correspondingly reduced flexibility). The question here has to do not with "overruling" those cases, but with extending them. My argument is that our prior caselaw struck the right balance: heightened scrutiny when the government uses the permitting process to demand property that the Takings Clause protects, and lesser scrutiny, but a continuing safeguard against abuse, when the government's demand is for something falling outside that Clause's scope.

. . . [I]f we accepted this argument it would be very easy for land-use permitting officials to evade the limitations of *Nollan* and *Dolan*. Because the government need only provide a permit applicant with one alternative that satisfies the nexus and rough proportionality standards, a permitting authority wishing to exact an easement could simply give the owner a choice of either surrendering an easement or making a payment equal to the easement's value. Such so-called "in lieu of" fees are utterly commonplace, and they are functionally equivalent to other types of land use exactions. For that reason and those that follow, we reject respondent's argument and hold that so-called "monetary exactions" must satisfy the nexus and rough proportionality requirements of *Nollan* and *Dolan*.

Respondent's argument rests on a mistaken premise. Unlike the financial obligation in *Eastern Enterprises*, the demand for money at issue here did "operate upon . . . an identified property interest" by directing the owner of a particular piece of property to make a monetary payment. (opinion of KENNEDY, J.). . . . [T]he monetary obligation burdened petitioner's ownership of a specific parcel of land. In that sense, this case bears resemblance to our cases holding that the government must pay just compensation when it takes a lien—a right to receive money that is secured by a particular piece of property. . . . The fulcrum this case turns on is the direct link between the government's demand and a specific parcel of real property.[2] Because of that direct link, this case implicates the central concern of *Nollan* and *Dolan*: the risk that the government may use its substantial power and discretion in land-use permitting to pursue governmental ends that lack an essential nexus and rough proportionality to the effects of the proposed new use of the specific property at issue . . . .

. . . [P]etitioner does not ask us to hold that the government can commit a *regulatory* taking by directing someone to spend money. . . . Instead, petitioner's claim rests on the more limited proposition that when the government commands the relinquishment of funds linked to a specific, identifiable property interest such as a bank account or parcel of real property, a "*per se* [takings] approach" is the proper mode of analysis under the Court's precedent. Brown v. Legal Foundation of Wash., 538 U.S. 216, 235 (2003). . . .

B

Respondent and the dissent argue that if monetary exactions are made subject to scrutiny under *Nollan* and *Dolan*, then there will be no principled way of distinguishing impermissible land-use exactions from property taxes. We think they exaggerate both the extent to which that problem is unique to the land-use permitting context and the practical difficulty of distinguishing between the power to tax and the power to take by eminent domain. . . .

---

2. Thus, because the proposed offsite mitigation obligation in this case was tied to a particular parcel of land, this case does not implicate the question whether monetary exactions must be tied to a particular parcel of land in order to constitute a taking. That is so even when the demand is considered "*outside* the permitting process." *Post* (KAGAN, J., dissenting). The unconstitutional conditions analysis requires us to set aside petitioner's *permit application*, not his ownership of a particular parcel of real property.

. . . [T]he need to distinguish taxes from takings is not a creature of our holding today that monetary exactions are subject to scrutiny under *Nollan* and *Dolan*. Rather, the problem is inherent in this Court's long-settled view that property the government could constitutionally demand through its taxing power can also be taken by eminent domain.

. . . [O]ur cases show that teasing out the difference between taxes and takings is more difficult in theory than in practice. Brown v. Legal Foundation of Wash., 538 U.S. 216 (2003), is illustrative. . . . [T]he respondents in *Brown* argued that extending the protections of the Takings Clause to a bank account would open a Pandora's Box of constitutional challenges to taxes. . . . But like respondent here, the *Brown* respondents never claimed that they were exercising their power to levy taxes when they took the petitioners' property. Any such argument would have been implausible under state law; in Washington, taxes are levied by the legislature, not the courts. . . .

The same dynamic is at work in this case because Florida law greatly circumscribes respondent's power to tax. . . . If respondent had argued that its demand for money was a tax, it would have effectively conceded that its denial of petitioner's permit was improper under Florida law. Far from making that concession, respondent has maintained throughout this litigation that it considered petitioner's money to be a substitute for his deeding to the public a conservation easement on a larger parcel of undeveloped land.[3]

This case does not require us to say more. We need not decide at precisely what point a land-use permitting charge denominated by the government as a "tax" becomes "so arbitrary . . . that it was not the exertion of taxation but a confiscation of property." For present purposes, it suffices to say that despite having long recognized that "the power of taxation should not be confused with the power of eminent domain," we have had little trouble distinguishing between the two.

C

Finally, we disagree with the dissent's forecast that our decision will work a revolution in land use law by depriving local governments of the ability to charge reasonable permitting fees. Numerous courts—including courts in many of our Nation's most populous States—have confronted constitutional challenges to monetary exactions over the last two decades and applied the standard from *Nollan* and *Dolan* or something like it. . . . Yet the "significant practical harm" the dissent predicts has not come to pass. That is hardly surprising, for the dissent is correct that state law normally provides an independent check on excessive land use permitting fees. . . .

---

3. Citing cases in which state courts have treated similar governmental demands for money differently, the dissent predicts that courts will "struggle to draw a coherent boundary" between taxes and excessive demands for money that violate *Nollan* and *Dolan*. But the cases the dissent cites illustrate how the frequent need to decide whether a particular demand for money qualifies as a tax under state law, and the resulting state statutes and judicial precedents on point, greatly reduce the practical difficulty of resolving the same issue in federal constitutional cases like this one.

We hold that the government's demand for property from a land-use permit applicant must satisfy the requirements of *Nollan* and *Dolan* even when the government denies the permit and even when its demand is for money. . . .

Notes and Questions

1. Would it make sense to limit the heightened scrutiny given exactions to monetary sums that are individually decided by permitting authorities, leaving non-discretionary across-the-board fees to the standard due process, minimal scrutiny, applied to other economic regulations, as suggested by Justice Kagan?

2. Note that Justice Kennedy, author of the concurring opinion in *Eastern Enterprises v. Apfel*, relied on by the respondent and the dissent, joined the majority opinion.

3. In July 2013, Mayor Bloomberg of New York proposed rezoning for Midtown that would allow construction of taller buildings to encourage replacement of older buildings with modern office towers. The proposal includes allowing developers to purchase development rights from the city to build higher than the zoning rules allow at a price of $250 per square foot. The funds raised would be used for pedestrian and transit improvements. The City Club of New York, a good government group headed by Michael Gruen (of *Gruen v. Gruen*), claims that the plan is illegal because the amount of the fee is not calculated based on the impacts caused by the particular project, and the price was based on the value of commercial development rights in the area, rather than on the amount required for needed improvements. A representative of the City Planning Department said that "there is no requirement that the amount of those voluntary payments by owners and developers be calculated based on the 'impacts' caused by the development."[3] Which one is right?

4. *Inclusionary zoning.* The City of San Jose requires developers of residential developments of 20 or more units to set aside 15 percent of the units for affordable housing, 9 percent available for rent by moderate-income households, and 6 percent by very-low-income households. Alternatively, developers can pay an in lieu fee determined by the difference between the median sale price of a market-rate unit in the prior 36 months and the cost of an "affordable housing" unit for a household earning no more than 110 percent of the area median income. A developer can obtain a waiver of the requirement by showing, based on substantial evidence, that there is no reasonable relationship between the impact of a proposed residential development and the requirements. In lieu fees go to the Affordable Housing Fee Fund used exclusively to provide affordable housing.

The California Building Industry Association challenged the ordinance. The trial court held it invalid and enjoined its implementation "unless and until the City . . . provides a legally sufficient evidentiary showing to demonstrate justification and reasonable relationships between such Inclusionary Housing Ordinance exactions and impacts caused by new residential development."

---

3.   David W. Dunlap, *Bloomberg's Plan for Bigger East Midtown Towers Is "Zoning for Dollars," Group Says*, N.Y. Times, Aug. 27, 2013.

The Court of Appeal reversed on June 6, 2013, holding that the ordinance was an exercise of the city's police power, not an exaction, and remanded to allow the plaintiff to attempt to overcome the presumption that the requirements are reasonably related to the city's legitimate purpose of ensuring an adequate supply of affordable housing in the community. *California Bldg. Indus. Ass'n v. City of San Jose*, 157 Cal. Rptr. 3d 813 (Cal. App. 2013). The California Supreme Court granted review on September 11, 2013, 307 P.3d 878. *Koontz* was decided June 25, 2013. Should inclusionary zoning for affordable housing requirements be subject to *Nollan-Dolan*?

TABLE OF CASES

TABLE OF STATUTES

STATE

INDEX

921

Title examination
    costs, 542
    determining status of title,
        536-537
    marketable title acts, 612-613
Title insurance, 543, 618-626
    A.L.T.A. Owner's Policy, 623-625
    American Land Title Association (ALTA),
        623-625
    exclusions from coverage, 623-625
    general warranty covenant compared,
        625-626
    obtaining, 538
Title protection
    title insurance. *See* Title insurance
Torrens system, 613-618
Title registration, 613
Title theory vs. lien theory, 591-592
Torrens system, 613-618
Tort liability, of landlord. *See* Landlord's tort
    liability
Touch or concern doctrine, 735-736, 739,
    771, 772, 773, 778
    assignment of lease, 454
    open-ended covenants, 762-768
    validity of servitudes, 760-762
Townships, 575-576
Tract index, 597, 598-599
Trade dress, 257, 260-264
    defined, 257
Trademark Act of 1946 (Lanham Act), 253,
    260
Trademark law, 252, 253-259
    classic fair use, 268
    confusion, likelihood of, 264, 265, 267
    cyberpiracy, 265-269
    defined, 258
    descriptive marks, 258
    designs, 263
    dilution, 264-265
        by blurring, 264, 265
        exemptions, 264
        by tarnishment, 264, 265
    duration of trademarks, 259
    "famous" trademarks, 264, 265
    federal registration, 259
    functionality doctrine, 255, 256
    generic marks, 263
    nominative fair use, 266-269
    registration, advantages of, 259, 264
    registration, certificate of, 259
    secondary meaning, 254, 264
    trade dress protection. *See* Trade dress
Trademarks
    categories of marks, 258
    celebrity names and images, 259
    color as trademark, 253-258
    disparaging marks, 258
    distinctive mark, 259
    fanciful, arbitrary, or suggestive words or
        designs, 254
    fashion industry, 258
    immoral marks, 258
    parodies, 265
    scandalous marks, 258
"Trail of Tears," 150

Treasure
    sunken. *See* Sunken treasure
    treasure trove. *See* Treasure trove
Treasure Act of 1996 (England), 131, 132
Treasure trove, 124, 130-132
        Treaty of Friendship and General
            Relations, 141
Trees, nuisance law, 28
Trespass, 5, 6-21. *See also* Right to exclude other
    ad coelum doctrine, 18
    aggressive trespasser standard, 152, 170,
        171
    to animals, 33-36
    bad-faith trespasser, 152
    caves, 97
    to chattels, 33-36, 36-45, 88-89
    cyberspace and, 36-45
    first in time, 81-82
    good-faith trespasser, 152
    hunters on private land, 81-82
    nuisance law vs., 669-675
    to personal property, 33-36
Trespass on the case, 76
Tribal claims, 144-151
Trolls, 290-291
Trover, 53, 57, 112
Trusts, 298, 299, 321
    alienability of, 333
    constructive, 52
    dynastic, 333
    equitable title, 332
    legal title, 332
    revocable inter vivos trust, 326
    revocable inter vivos trust. *See* Revocable
        inter vivos trust
    spendthrift clause, 333

U

Underground water, 100-105
    absolute ownership doctrine, 101, 102
    correlative rights doctrine, 104
    damage caused by quarrying operations,
        100-103
    English Rule, 100
    liability for damage, 103
    reasonable use doctrine, 100, 102, 103,
        104
Unenforceable conditions, 313-315
UNESCO Convention on Protection of the
    Underwater Cultural Heritage, 142
Unfair competition, 52, 199, 251-252, 259.
    See also Trademark law
Uniform Anatomical Gift Act, 58
Uniform Commercial Code, 519
Uniform Conservation Easement Act of
    1981, 687, 750, 772
Uniform Environmental Covenants Act, 750,
    772
Uniform Marital Property Act, 500
Uniform Marketable Title Act, 612
Uniform Probate Code, 502, 531
Uniform Residential Landlord and Tenant
    Act (URLTA), 393, 398
    acceptance of rent with knowledge of
        default, 416